SECOND EDITION

Handbook of
MULTICULTURAL
COUNSELING

The editors and contributing authors of this *Handbook* dedicate their efforts to the 12 pioneers in multicultural counseling whose respective life stories appear in Part I of this volume.

Joseph E. Trimble
Teresa D. LaFromboise
Janet E. Helms
William E. Cross, Jr.
Derald Wing Sue
Nadya A. Fouad
Melba J. T. Vasquez
J. Manuel Casas
Paul Bodholdt Pedersen
Amy L. Reynolds
Maria P. P. Root
Daya Singh Sandhu

For your courage, vision, and brilliance; pioneers who have opened our minds and touched our hearts, to you we dedicate this second edition of *Handbook of Multicultural Counseling*

SECOND EDITION

Handbook of
MULTICULTURAL
COUNSELING

Editors

Joseph G. Ponterotto
J. Manuel Casas
Lisa A. Suzuki
Charlene M. Alexander

Sage Publications
International Educational and Professional Publisher
Thousand Oaks ■ London ■ New Delhi

For Information:

Sage Publications, Inc.
2455 Teller Road
Thousand Oaks, California 91320
E-mail: order@sagepub.com

Sage Publications Ltd.
6 Bonhill Street
London EC2A 4PU
United Kingdom

Sage Publications India Pvt. Ltd.
M-32 Market
Greater Kailash I
New Delhi 110 048 India

Printed in the United States of America

Library of Congress Cataloging-in-Publication Data

Handbook of multicultural counseling / [edited] by Joseph G. Ponterotto . . .
 [et al.]. — 2nd ed.
  p. cm.
 Includes bibliographical references and indexes.
 ISBN 0-7619-1983-X (hardcover: acid-free paper) — ISBN 0-7619-1984-8
(pbk.: acid-free paper)
  1. Cross-cultural counseling. 2. Multiculturalism—United States. 3.
Minorities—Counseling of—United States. I. Ponterotto, Joseph G.
 BF637.C6 H3174 2000
 158'.3—dc21   00-012408

01 02 03 04 05 06 07 7 6 5 4 3 2 1

Acquiring Editor:	Nancy Hale
Editorial Assistants:	Heidi Van Middlesworth and Candice Crosetti
Production Editor:	Claudia A. Hoffman
Copy Editor:	Joyce Kuhn
Typesetter:	Tina Hill
Indexer:	Will Ragsdale
Cover Designer:	Michelle Lee

CONTENTS

FOREWORD

THE MEANING OF CULTURE can be elusive. For as we change, the meaning we attribute to our cultural experiences evolves. But, it is our core, our cultural identity, that determines who and what we are, and what we will become, as we are transformed by our relationships with those who are culturally different.

In this day and age, it is difficult to attend any major counseling or psychological conference without having a variety of presentations address such topics as cultural identity development, acculturation, worldviews, or cultural competencies. Although it would be inappropriate to assume that because of its national visibility multicultural counseling has made it into the mainstream of our profession, it is, nevertheless, an important historical benchmark.

While this is a cause for some celebration, it is important to remember that this effort was, and continues to be, the result of persistence and determination on the part of many who continue to this day to be pioneers in the field.

This second edition of *Handbook of Multicultural Counseling* marks an important turning point. It brings together the voices of some pioneers who have paved the way and introduces us to new voices, who, while influenced by the pioneers, have taken different paths. Because the multicultural community is well represented in content and scholarship in this second edition, the reader can be assured that the viewpoints represented in this book speak to the core issues of the field.

I am excited about this *Handbook* because the authors answer the question often posed at many a conference: "Where is the research to support multicultural counseling?" I am equally excited about this *Handbook* because it breaks new ground by using as its anchor oral histories, which demonstrates that for many of us multicultural counseling is not simply a research agenda but a lifelong journey that cannot always be measured. The underlying theme of social justice only reinforces our commitment to this journey.

Those in our profession who are still looking for specific strategies to follow in order to work with minority populations will be disappointed. This *Handbook,* through its extensive review and discussion of multicultural theory, research, assessment, and practice, reminds us that the issues of culture and individual differences are complex and cannot be reduced to mere guidelines.

Editors Ponterotto, Casas, Suzuki, and Alexander have once again helped shape the multicultural conversation by not only presenting the important issues of the day but also by broadening the areas of multicultural counseling to include such topics as family and schools, which are often overlooked.

To those who have often asked "Where is the research?", look no further.

DONALD B. POPE-DAVIS
Editor, *Journal of Multicultural
Counseling and Development*
Associate Editor, *Cultural Diversity &
Ethnic Minority Psychology*
Professor, Department of Psychology
University of Notre Dame
Notre Dame, Indiana

PREFACE

WE ARE BOTH PLEASED and proud to present this second edition of the *Handbook of Multicultural Counseling*. The first edition of the *Handbook*, released in June 1995, was received very favorably by counseling professionals, as measured by both independent scholarly reviews and sales. In fact, the first edition was a best-seller for Sage and, we believe, one of the top selling multicultural counseling texts of the past half-decade.

Since the first edition was published, the field of multicultural counseling has grown significantly. The sheer amount of multicultural literature published in journals and books seems to grow exponentially. Whereas a decade ago or so it was not too difficult to track and catalogue most of the published multicultural counseling literature, now such a task is virtually impossible. Furthermore, whereas multicultural counseling a decade ago was considered a topical area or specialty within counseling, now it is seen as a central core of all counseling and psychotherapy.

The goal of this second edition parallels that of the first edition: "to provide, in one comprehensive treatise, a concise summary of the field's latest developments" (1st ed., p. xi). However, to reach this same goal, the organization and contents of the book has been altered substantially. This radical revision was necessary given the field's rapid evolution.

This second edition presents a new vision for the field. The book is replete with new chapters and new contributing authors. Examples of major changes from the first to the second edition are as follows:

1. Whereas the first edition presented a single-chapter written history of the multicultural counseling field, the second edition addresses historical perspectives through first-person life stories of 12 pioneers in multicultural counseling.
2. Whereas the first edition presented conceptual models of racial and ethnic identity development, this edition concentrates on recent advances and developments in the empirical operationalization of these models in instrument form.
3. Whereas the first edition provided reviews of research in the field, this second edition extends this focus by also covering the "how to" of culturally

sensitive and relevant qualitative and quantitative research. This new edition also reviews and critiques emerging comprehensive theories of multicultural counseling.

As with the first edition, the contributing authors to the second edition represent a broad spectrum of the profession in terms of race, gender, ethnicity, religion, sexual orientation, geographic locale, and employment emphasis. Furthermore, as with the first edition, all royalties from the sale of the book will be donated to multicultural conference organizers to help support student participation. Initial years' royalties will be rotated between the biannual American Psychological Association's (APA) Multicultural Conference and Summit, and the annual Winter Roundtable on Cross-Cultural Counseling hosted by Teachers College, Columbia University.

BOOK CONTENTS

This book is organized along eight major parts or sections. Each part begins with a brief introduction prepared by the editing team. The introductions provide the reader with a "cognitive map" of sorts to help negotiate and maximize utility of the individual chapters. Part I, "Historical Perspectives," presents first-person life stories of 12 "pioneers" in multicultural counseling. These individuals are world-renowned scholars who have been instrumental in the development of the multicultural emphasis within counseling and psychology. Through these poignant and revealing life stories, the reader experiences the history of the field through the eyes of people who helped make history. Importantly, the reader enters into the very private worlds of the pioneers, who, through the courage of their self-disclosure, serve as role models and mentors to us all.

Part II contains three chapters on "Ethics and Professional Issues." In this section, we see that a new conceptualization of ethical practice and decision making in counseling is called for. Simply tinkering with and updating ethical guidelines from multicultural perspectives is not enough; counselors need to have a coherent and reliable strategy for making ethical decisions in multicultural counseling. In this section the reader is also exposed to the evolving challenge of practicing multicultural counseling within complex, interdisciplinary systems of care. Finally, the broader impact of the multicultural counseling movement, and the counselor's critical role in this movement, is discussed.

A basic thesis of this *Handbook* is that counseling functions within a societal context and historical legacy of human relations in the United States. Central to this legacy is a history of inequitable power, oppression, and racism. Part III offers three chapters that define and explore White racism, White and male privilege, and the necessity of new clinical conceptualizations for helping targets of racism. This section presents convincing evidence that issues of power, oppression, racism, and sexism need to be addressed in counseling training and practice.

Part IV presents seven chapters on the "Psychological Measurement of Multicultural Constructs." The reader is provided with the latest information on quantitative instruments designed to operationalize core constructs of acculturation, racial identity, prejudice, and multicultural counseling competence. We are also deeply honored that scholars William E. Cross, Jr., and Beverly J. Vandiver have "gifted" us with the first comprehensive and detailed presentation of the Cross Racial Identity Scale (CRIS). We believe the CRIS will elevate the study of psychological Nigrescence to a new plateau of sophistication and insight.

In Part V, "Theory and Research Design," emerging comprehensive theories of multicultural counseling are summarized and evaluated. Importantly, the recent emphasis in psychology on the establishment of "empirically supported treatments" (ESTs) is critiqued through a multicultural lens. Finally, detailed coverage of both qualitative and quantitative research designs and methods for multicultural research is presented.

Counseling issues relevant to career development, the family, schools, and recent refugees are discussed in Part VI. This section has a strong applied and clinical focus and will be of particular value to the counseling practitioner and supervisor.

Part VII looks at the "Intersection of Identities." As recent theory development and research has emphasized the complexity of multicultural counseling, the salience of an individual's multiple identities has been highlighted. Chief among intersecting identities are those of sexual orientation and feminism. The two chapters comprising this section present in-depth, personally filtered looks at the intersection of multiculturalism with sexual orientation and feminism.

Part VIII, the concluding section of the *Handbook*, has three substantive chapters on multicultural counseling supervision and on multicultural issues salient to both predominantly White and historically Black colleges and universities. The closing "Afterword" is provided by the legendary scholar and activist Thomas A. Parham.

The reader will note that contributing authors have their preferred terms for describing racial/ethnic groups. For example, in referring to Hispanic-origin persons, authors use the terms "Latino," "Hispanic," and "Hispanic American." In describing European Americans, the terms "Euro-American," "Anglo American," and "White American" are used; persons of African ancestry are referred to by various authors as "African American," "Black," and "Black American"; and the terms "Asian American" and "Pacific Islander" are preferred by authors describing Asian and Pacific Island ancestry groups. "Hawaiian Native" is the term applied to persons indigenous to the Hawaiian Islands. In most cases, authors use the term "Native American Indian" and "Alaska Native," respectively, to describe persons indigenous to the lower 48 states and those indigenous to Alaska (see Herring, 1999).

This second edition of *Handbook of Multicultural Counseling* offers the perspectives of 85 scholars in the field of multicultural counseling. It provides both breadth and depth, presents new visions, motivates us to excellence in multicultural research and practice, and incites us to activism on human rights issues. It has been a great honor to gather and organize the many voices presented in the *Handbook.* We hope that readers will be enlightened by the contents of this book and energized by the commitment and passion that characterize its contributing authors.

JOSEPH G. PONTEROTTO
J. MANUEL CASAS
LISA A. SUZUKI
CHARLENE M. ALEXANDER

REFERENCE

Herring, R. D. (1999). *Counseling with Native American Indians and Alaska Natives: Strategies for helping professionals.* Thousand Oaks, CA: Sage.

ACKNOWLEDGMENTS

THE SECOND EDITION of the *Handbook of Multicultural Counseling* represents the culmination of three years of collaborative work among 85 scholars dispersed throughout the United States. The editors acknowledge and thank these contributing authors who worked diligently to produce 40 state-of-the-art chapters that we believe capture the essence of multicultural counseling scholarship. These authors contributed their efforts and donated their valuable time without financial remuneration; they contributed because of their unwavering commitment to social justice and to the development of a mental health care system that works for all people.

We want to thank a marvelous Sage Publications team that, we believe, sets the standard for excellence in professional publishing. Among the Sage staff who assisted us at various points in the *Handbook's* development were senior editors Marquita Flemming (1993–1995), Jim Nageotte (1995–1999), and Nancy Hale (1999–2001). Additional critical contributions by Sage professionals were provided by Claudia Hoffman, Joyce Kuhn, Heather Gotlieb, Heidi Van Middlesworth, Candice Crosetti, and Anna Howland, among others.

With gratitude, we acknowledge the collegial and emotional support of our home institutions: Fordham University, University of California at Santa Barbara, New York University, and Ball State University. Faculty colleagues, students, administrators, and support staff all knew of our commitment to and work on the *Handbook* and offered us constant encouragement during the editing process. Special thanks are extended to Fordham graduate assistants Christian Nutini and Jaclyn Mendelsohn, who provided valuable administrative support.

Finally, the Handbook editors gratefully acknowledge permission to quote or reprint material from the following sources:

American Counseling Association
American Psychological Association
Arte Público Press, University of Houston
Brookings Institution

Chevron Publishing Corporation
Integrated Research Services
Random House, Inc.

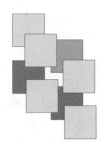

Part I

HISTORICAL PERSPECTIVES: LIFE STORIES OF SOME PIONEERS IN MULTICULTURAL COUNSELING

Part I of this second edition of the *Handbook of Multicultural Counseling* presents 12 life stories of pioneers in the field of multicultural counseling. These individuals, in their own, unedited voice, share their personal histories with the reader. We believe it is interesting to examine the history of the field through the personal stories of individuals who were instrumental in the field's development. The 12 scholars contributing to Part I have all made, and continue to make, significant and lasting contributions to the multicultural emphasis in counseling and psychology. They are clearly pioneers in their efforts to establish cultural pluralism as a central component of all counseling research and practice.

Understandably, there are other pioneers not sharing their personal stories in Part I. In fact, a good number of authors of chapters in other sections of this *Handbook* would clearly be considered pioneers in the multicultural counseling field. Space and planned symmetry of *Handbook* sections limited the number of pioneers we could include in Part I. The 12 chosen pioneers were selected based on the editors' sense of their professional stature and eminence in the field and on their willingness to share very personal information at this point in their careers and lives. Furthermore, in inviting these pioneers we attended to group diversity in terms of race, ethnicity, sexual orientation, religion, geographic region, and immigration status.

Different terms have been used to define the telling of one's personal story: oral history, autobiography, life history, and life story. We have chosen the term "life story" for this section, as we believe this term captures well the essence of the contributions presented here. Atkinson (1998) defines life story as "the story a person chooses to tell about the life he or she has lived, told as completely and honestly as possible, what is remembered of it, and what the teller wants others to know of it" (p. 8). We asked the pioneers to present their life stories with a particular focus on events, experiences, and people that were instrumental to their work and commitment to multiculturalism in counseling. We provided few guidelines to the authors, as we wanted each narrative to take the shape and form most comfortable to the individual pioneer.

The reader will note that the life stories are diverse in terms of format, style, depth of self-disclosure, and length. Many are organized in a chronological sequence; others are presented as a series of critical incidents or as an examination of important life and career questions. By and large, the authors told us in debriefings that writing their personal stories was very challenging. Accustomed to scholarly writing, the focus on one's personal life, family, relationships, struggles, challenges, losses, rewards, and so forth represented a new avenue of public expression, a route understandably accompanied by a sense of uncertainty about one's depth of sharing.

We are honored now to present the life stories of, respectively, Joseph E. Trimble, Teresa D. LaFromboise, Janet E. Helms, William E. Cross, Jr., Derald Wing Sue, Nadya A. Fouad, Melba J. T. Vasquez, J. Manuel Casas, Paul Bodholdt Pedersen, Amy L. Reynolds, Maria P. P. Root, and Daya Singh Sandhu.

REFERENCE

Atkinson, R. (1998). *The life story interview*. Thousand Oaks, CA: Sage.

Chapter 1

A Quest for Discovering Ethnocultural Themes in Psychology

JOSEPH E. TRIMBLE

A deep distress hath humanized my soul.

—William Wordsworth,
"Elegiac Stanza Suggested by a
Picture of Peele Castle in a Storm"

RIGHT NOW, I am sitting in front of the bay window that looks out over the plush green grass that gently slopes down and meets the shores of a small lake. A misty rain falls as it mostly does in the early morning in the months when flowers spread their colors and fragrances. Across the lake to the east a wispy fog sits on Lookout Mountain, and over near Chuckanut Mountain on the west side, streaks of blue sky peek out through the puffy rain clouds. Gaggles of geese are grazing in the grass, and ganders are watching closely for intruders that might pose a threat to young goslings pecking away at some tasty, dainty delicacy. Two bald eagles perch high up in nearby cedar trees scanning the water for their breakfast. Not far away sit a covey of banded doves cooing and flapping about as they guard their nests from scavengers. Lurking in the tall reeds is a small coyote waiting patiently for the moment when he can single out his next meal. Three small otters frolic and gambol near the dock, all the while keeping a sharp eye on the lurking coyote. There is a good deal of commotion this morning as many birds are squawking and shrilling, alerting all others to the early morning drama. For the past 20 years, I have witnessed similar early morning scenes from the same seat where I usually start out my day. Paying attention to all that occurs around me is a lifeway orientation that has its origins in the wisdom of the elders and provided me with direction.

A MODEST AND
HUMBLE LIFEWAY ORIENTATION

Grandfather Sage told us that we should pay attention to all that nature presented us no matter where we were or what we were doing. "Stop and look closely at what's going on around you. Listen carefully to the sounds of birds, the wind, the noise in the air, and take in all of the aromas and fragrances of the life that surrounds you," he would often say in his quiet and gentle manner. During the summer months when we visited him more frequently than other times, we would take long walks through the tall grass in the nearby fields and wander through the narrow trails in the wooded area behind his small farm. Sometimes, he would stop, look around, and occasionally point to something of interest by gently jutting his chin in the general area. "Shush," he would whisper in his soft voice. Then he would add, "Pay real close attention because you're going to see something wonderful happen right about now." We knew that he was sensing much then, so we paid close attention to his admonitions. Each walk through the tall grass and the narrow trails brought us new experiences and filled our lives with wonder and respect for all that Mother Earth and Father Sky had to offer.

Grandfather Sage was a mere 6 years old when he left school. He never returned and never complained to us about his lack of formal education. He loved to read, and whenever he had a spare moment he would pull out a book, newspaper, or magazine from the depths of his overalls pockets and spend the time picking through the printed words. Sometimes, he would look at us and say something like "Did you know that . . ." Then he would fill in the sentence stem with a little bit of trivia gleaned from something he was reading. All of us remember that he was full of wisdom, humor, and inquisitiveness and that he was reflective, generous, and kind. I sure do, and Grandfather Sage's characteristics made an indelible imprint on my life's philosophy and worldview.

Grandpa's advice not only influenced my values and beliefs, but his words influenced the way I scan the world around me no matter where I am or what I am doing. I remember him saying to us repeatedly that we must "look and then think about what you're looking at. Ask questions when you can, but don't be too pushy and nosy. Make sure you run all the things before your eyes and heart before you jump to conclusions because you may hurt some soul with your choices. And remember that all things have souls and spirits, even though you can't see them." As a youngster, I am not too sure I fully understood Grandpa's wisdom and pointers; nonetheless, I accepted his words without hesitation and question. Inquiry, doubt, hesitancy, and skepticism would come later as I ventured away from the security and stability of nature's way and the loving care and attention of kinship.

SUSPENDING NATURE'S
WAY FOR FORMAL EDUCATION

Like most all of my brothers, sisters, and relatives, I graduated high school, but unlike any of my 100 or more close kin, I was the first one to head off to college. I was not supposed to go to college, as my parents and just about everyone else expected me to hit the workforce right after I received my diploma. All of my ancestors did, and so it was expected of all of us. For some unexplained reason, I decided to apply for college. My parents did not approve at first and tried to talk me out of it. When I told Grandfather he nodded approvingly but did not say much else. My first and only acceptance letter arrived soon after my decision, accompanied by a small athletic scholarship.

My parents and Grandfather were not certain what psychology was after I told them that it was to be my area of inquiry and study. My parents wanted to know what I could do with a "psychology education," whereas Grandfather asked me to tell him about psychology when I learned more about the field. Mixed emotions tied in with apprehension, a state of brooding disquietude, and an uneasy sense of responsibility traveled with me when I left home for the beginning of my long journey to a career in psychology.

During my first year and soon after my first psychology course, I quickly learned that to be a psychologist I had to put aside any interpretive tendencies based in presumptions and inferences. Subjective and impressionistic interpretations of human conduct were not acceptable. My professors insisted that the human was a "black box" and that observable behavior was the sole unit of analysis. A few argued forcefully that the study of lower-order species was the true path to understanding human behavior. I struggled constantly with the uncharted and new orientation, especially in courses where the nature-nurture controversy was the prevailing theme. The content and argument presented in several philosophy courses also roused my confusion about the tenets of mind and behavior. More than anything, though, the idea that the human was a hodgepodge of behavioral units ran counter to many folktales and legends I'd heard as a child—tales and legends that dealt with the human's beginnings and one's character development. My overwhelming desire to earn a degree in good fashion eventually compromised my confusion as I gradually accepted the psychological orientation opined by my first round of professors.

The effects of one's enculturation run deep though, so my confusion and accompanying thoughts were never far away. Grandfather told us that most of the time our fate was in the hands of the Creator; however, sometimes we have to be self-reliant. He also would point out that every now and then chance and curiosity could change our life's course, so we must be sensitive to the occasions and circumstances when they are presented to us. In the course of my career, Grandfather's prophecy was fitting, as on several occasions circumstances challenged and eventually reformed my life's course. The first instance occurred when I was a graduate student in 1964 enrolled in an advanced course in personality theory at a reputable New England university. In the early beginnings of the semester, the professor and my colleagues constantly emphasized the importance of mental processes, early childhood experiences, and the universality of personality theories. Without giving it much reflection, one evening I asked a question that would dramatically alter my career path. The question was "Where are the group and cultural influences in the science of the individual?" The professor's reply was gentle, direct, and firm: "Well, the way we divide up the situation is a function of the understanding we bring to the situation." "So," I replied rather meekly, "if we have no understanding about culture's effects on individual behavior, then one is not likely to raise the question. And if psychology's unit of analysis is solely the individual, then one also is not likely to seek answers about group influences." For once, my colleagues were silent. The professor, on the other hand, dismissed the class early and invited me to walk him home on that memorable snowy New England evening. The subject of culture never made its way into the seminar discussion; however, the professor and I continued to discuss the subject in the weeks that followed. During those long walks, we often talked about the lifeways and thoughtways of certain American Indians and how that tied in with understanding personality from a conventional psychological perspective. None of that information ever made it into any of his classes, and that saddened me and indeed caused me a little distress.

The notion that the study of culture belonged in the study of personality and the individual was an epiphany. The insight revitalized my then rapidly waning interest in the field and led me to read the works of the culture and personality field of anthropology. I must confess, though, that I never took a formal course in anthropology. If I had it to do over again I would have. Nonetheless, as I pored over the works of anthropologists such as Margaret Mead, John Honigmann, and Ruth Benedict, I came to the conclusion that psychology was rather exclusive, myopic, prejudiced, and presumptuous to believe and profess that psychological findings applied to all humans regardless of their cultural and ethnic background. Anthropological writings told a different story. I discovered, too, that the words *culture* and *ethnicity* could not be found in psychology textbooks, and it certainly was not the topic of conversation at psychological conventions. Although I was rather distressed by my findings, they provided me with a renewed interest in the field of psychology. I did not know where to take that interest as I knew the choices around me in New England were very limited.

Choice and chance played their hand again. A colleague and I walked into a Boston restaurant one hot and humid spring evening after spending the day attending boring sessions associated with a psychological convention. There my colleague introduced me to one of his friends, a graduate school colleague of years gone by. Our interesting and lively dinner conversation eventually focused on my disillusion with psychology. After listening to my interests, my newly found acquaintance invited me to transfer and enroll in the social psychology program at the University of Oklahoma's Institute of Group Relations. Additionally, he reminded me that Oklahoma was at one time "Indian Territory" and that there were numerous opportunities to work with various tribes through programs at the university.

After a few weeks of deep reflection and contemplation about my future and emerging interests in culture and psychology, I decided to head to the southwestern part of the United States and enroll at the University of Oklahoma. The drive from New England to the southern plains was a long one and thus provided me with the opportunity to assess where I had been and where I was headed. Grandfather Sage's words and witticisms floated in and out of my mind. His words provided me with inspiration that my choice to move on would bring closure to some sour, distressful, and painful past experiences and open up new opportunities that could expand my intellectual curiosity and a new way of living. In retrospect, the decision to move on set a course that far exceeded my expectations and visions. My distress over the past indeed humanized my soul as my emptiness was replaced with excitement and spiritual renewal.

CULTURE, PSYCHOLOGY, AND DISCOVERY

Social psychology at the University of Oklahoma was housed in the Institute of Group Relations located in an old wooden barracks-type building on the edge of the south campus. The program, founded and molded by the eminent social psychologist Muzafer Sherif and his colleagues, emphasized that social psychology was interstitial to all other academic disciplines that in some form or another involved the study of the human condition. Sherif defined social psychology as the scientific study of the experience and behavior of individuals in relation to social stimulus situations. As students we were thoroughly grounded in Sherif's firmly held notion that all behavior and experiences were situational and contextual. Culture and ethnic influences therefore were considered worthy units of study.

To ensure that one's academic experiences reflected the interdisciplinary orientation, students were encouraged to pursue studies outside the field of psychology and include nonpsychologists on their advisory committees. In fact, psychologists often were in the minority on one's committee, and that was not fully respected by several conservative and traditional faculty in the psychology department. My committee consisted of a social psychologist, an ethologist (he was in the psychology department), a sociologist, a philosopher, and a faculty member from social relations, all of whom strongly encouraged my cross-cultural studies especially with and among American Indians.

In the late 1960s, there was little or no information about ethnic and cultural groups in the psychological literature—almost none concerning American Indians. I was puzzled why anthropologists representing the culture and personality school devoted considerable attention to psychological constructs yet psychologists almost completely ignored cultural and ethnic influences on behavior and experiences. Psychology's blithe and myopic view of cultural influences fueled my seemingly insatiable curiosity and interest. My weekend excursions to the communities and homes of my numerous American Indian friends in almost every region of Oklahoma also spurred the interest along more so because I was awakened to and reminded of the extreme prejudice, economic disparity, and alcoholism that surrounded life in the Indian communities. The visits also reminded me that I should not become too absorbed in social psychological abstractions. The application of social psychological knowledge to solving fundamental social problems rapidly became a concern. However, I realized then and still do to this day that I must strive to achieve a balance between theory and real-life problems. Sometimes, that is difficult, as I tend to get totally absorbed in working on the problems and forget the value of research. A pinch or two from my friends and colleagues often helps to joggle my senses and nudges me back to that balance I strive to maintain.

My Oklahoma graduate school classroom experiences were not much different from those I experienced in New England. Students and some faculty viewed my interest in culture, ethnicity, and American Indians with suspicion and contempt. I also had the feeling, a deep and profound one, that a few of my colleagues were quietly racist toward Oklahoma Indians; however, no one ever confronted me on the topic. Occasionally, someone would ask me why I was not majoring in anthropology, with the comment that "anthropology is where one should be to study culture and American Indians." In one late afternoon graduate seminar, I talked openly about my experiences with different Native healers and provided examples of the way each of them worked with those who were in need of assistance. To a person, the students became openly derisive and peppered me with questions concerning the scientific nature of my observations. Challenges were launched at me from all corners of the seminar table directing me to justify the study of traditional Native healing in the context of contemporary social psychology and the rigors of the scientific method. The next morning I found a copy of William James's wonderful and insightful book *Varieties of Religious Experiences* in my mailbox with a note attached that simply said "I want you to know that I share your convictions and so does one of the most prominent American figures in psychology." It was unsigned. I learned many years later that the book and note were provided by the seminar's instructor. Sadly and unfortunately, I was never able to discuss the event with him as he passed away after I made my discovery.

The seminar experience and my interactions with certain faculty and students taught me several valuable lessons. I had to choose my audience prudently when I discussed spiritual matters and the lifeways and thought-ways of indigenous cultures—some psychologists can be unsympathetic and merciless in their criticisms of topics that depart from conventional practices. I also learned that one does not attempt to change deeply held convictions fueled by a lifetime of dedication to one small slice of human behavior as the conversation goes nowhere.

I completed my doctoral degree in 1969, and as promised I discussed my experiences with Grandfather Sage. After spending many hours on the old wooden porch, I believe he grasped what psychology was all about. He summed it up this way: "Well, Joey, so there are really three kinds of people in this world of ours—yesterday people, today people, and tomorrow people—and psychology tries to explain who they are and why they do things." "Indeed, an insightful summative comment," I mused. Maybe more of us should spend some time with our elders, as they may understand our seemingly complex world in the academy more acutely than we do. At that time some 30 years ago, Grandfather provided me with additional advice: (a) Never forget where you came from and the lessons you learned in your childhood; (b) you now have a responsibility to pass along your knowledge, experiences, and skills in ways that are nonthreatening yet informative; and (c) always remember that no one has ever accomplished greatness by themselves.

Soon thereafter, I received additional advice from an Arapaho elder from western Oklahoma who gently reminded me that "the American Indian is a frozen image in the minds of many. You can draw attention to the way we live and the many things that affect our daily lives, particularly the bad ones." I made a commitment to both elders that I would honor their advice and strive to realize their pronouncements. Despite many criticisms, frustrations, and self-doubt, I have faithfully struggled to honor and abide by their wishes.

ON TO A CAREER AND THE
PERSEVERING SEARCH FOR CULTURE IN PSYCHOLOGY

After the defense of my dissertation, I interviewed at several universities and colleges and eventually decided to stay in Oklahoma to begin my long anticipated career in higher education. Upon accepting the appointment, I was carefully reminded by the then department chair and several academic colleagues to set aside my interests in culture and psychology and focus on conventional social psychological research. Although most respected my interests in working with and for American Indian groups, they were really saying that for me to advance up and through the professorial ranks, attention had to be devoted to "acceptable psychological research topics." With some reluctance I designed and conducted several attitude and attitude change studies following Muzafer Sherif's social judgment model and presented the findings at psychological conventions. Interest in the model remains with me, yet a few unintentional and heartening events occurred that would define my research and scholarship for the next 25 years.

In 1971, a well-known social psychologist and I submitted a symposium proposal for consideration at the annual meeting of a regional psychological association. The topic focused on American Indian developmental issues. A proposed multidisciplinary panel consisted of a sociologist, an anthropologist, a psychiatrist, and two social psychologists. The proposal was well written, tightly conceptualized, and emphasized the topic from an interdisciplinary perspective. The proposal was politely rejected. The rationale for the decision essentially stated that (a) psychologists generally are not interested in American Indians; (b) the panel was too interdisciplinary and should have more psychologists represented; and (c) the American Indian population in the region was small, hence there was the likelihood that there would be little interest in the topic. We challenged the Program Chair's decision with a carefully crafted rebuttal and followed it up with a few telephone calls—our letter and telephone calls were never acknowledged. The unpleasant and wrenching experience was a pivotal point in my career and served to solidify my belief that I must bring the experiences of contemporary American Indians into the realm of psychological theory. The experience also reminded me of the ethnocentric bias, provincialism, bigotry, and ignorance of my chosen profession. If psychology professed to increase one's understanding of the human condition, how was it that the credo seemed to apply only to laboratory animals and university-based research participants who, in the main, represented a Euro-American ethnocultural orientation? In discussions with a few other ethnic psychologists, I also discovered that other ethnic groups were excluded from psychological conversations and studies, so that furthered my resolve to bring the subject of culture and ethnicity to the attention of the discipline.

Little twists of fate and chance occurrences have been a major part of my life and indeed have influenced my professional development. In 1972, a prominent social psychologist stopped me in the hallway of a hotel in Tulsa, Oklahoma, and inquired about my interest in American Indians and ethncocultural topics in psychology. We discussed our mutual interests for the better part of the afternoon. The discussion soon led to my contacting the Executive Secretary of the Society for the Psychological Study of Social Issues (SPSSI), Division 9 of the American Psychological Association (APA), for assistance in bringing my concerns to the forefront of discussions within the community of psychology. Assistance was provided in grant form, and my involvement in SPSSI activities rapidly accelerated to the point where I served on the SPSSI Council for two terms, chaired the 1976 American Psychological Association SPSSI convention program, and served a term as SPSSI's representative to the APA Council of Representatives. My involvement in SPSSI and the fervent commitment and support of many of its members bolstered and validated my enthusiasm and commitment for the psychological study of culture and ethnicity and "putting the emic to work." SPSSI has been an advocate and champion for social issues for a long time, and in the early 1970s it was the only division within the APA that supported ethnic minority psychological concerns.

Instead of continuing to conduct conventional and uninspiring social psychological research, I shifted my direction and thus my professional journey toward bringing American Indian social and psychological topics to the attention of the psychological community. Again, another chance event influenced the direction of my scholarship. While attending a meeting of the APA in Honolulu, Hawaii, in the early 1970s, I met Paul Pedersen and spent an afternoon discussing his emerging and newfound interest in culture and counseling. Paul asked me what, if anything, had been written on the effectiveness of counseling and psychotherapy with American Indian populations. "Maybe one or two articles," I answered and added that I thought that conventional counseling and therapy approaches probably were incompatible with most traditional American Indians. I had a little graduate-level training in clinical psychology, so I knew I was on safe ground with my comments. Paul then asked me to write a chapter on the subject for a book he and a few others were editing entitled *Counseling Across Cultures*. I accepted the challenge and a few years later joined Paul, Walter Lonner, and Juris Draguns as the fourth editor—the book now is in its fifth edition and has been awarded several citations. Since I knew little about how effective clinical and counseling approaches might be with various Indian and Native populations, I decided to conduct a little ethnographic research on the topic with Indians from different states largely in the central and south-central plains of the United States. I eventually wrote that chapter and several others like it, although I must confess that each time I did write something I felt very uncomfortable and uneasy mainly because I was fearful that I was creating unnecessary stereotypes and recommending broad generalized counseling considerations. Fortunately, many others have written about counseling American Indians since then, even to the extent of applying the concept to specific tribal groups. My initial and only hope was to bring the subject to the profession's attention and to spur others on to explore and write about the topic.

After a four-year stint as a scientist at a research institute in Seattle, an experience that I wish to forget for many unseemly reasons, in 1978 I accepted an academic position at Western Washington University. Western, as it is affectionately known in local parlance, had a solid and growing reputation for its interest in supporting and advancing cross-cultural psychology through the Center for Cross-Cultural Research located in the Department of Psychology. Walter J. Lonner, founding editor of the well-known *Journal of Cross-Cultural Psychology*, directed the Center's operations and taught several courses in the department dealing with culture and psychology. At that time, it was the only academic institution anywhere that gave credence to the study of culture within a psychological framework, and I was thrilled beyond belief to become a part of the venture. I no longer had to apologize to my colleagues for my interests, research, and scholarship, for the study of culture and ethnicity was openly accepted and promoted in the department and the university. My quest for finding ethnocultural themes in psychology had ended, but with that discovery I began a new journey to focus my energies more directly on fundamental American Indian problems that could be dealt with with solid and practical psychological theory.

My appointment at Western was an entreaty for adventure to explore undertakings that were embedded in the voices of my elders, community members from various reservations, trusted colleagues and friends, and students. My research and scholarship accelerated to the point where over the past 22 years I have published numerous articles and book chapters on stereotypes, intergroup conflict, self-image, alienation, mental health models, adolescent socialization, life-threatening events and the elderly, prevention of substance use and abuse, ethnic identification, cross-cultural counseling and psychotherapy, and research methodology and measurement. In almost all my work, I emphasize the significance of the topic for ethnic minority groups in general and American Indians and Alaska Natives specifically.

Grandfather Sage often reminded us that we should value our relationships with our family, friends, and colleagues and, where possible, invite them to participate in our work. I have always valued collaboration and find that most of the time we benefit intellectually, emotionally, and, dare I say it, spiritually from the ventures. Sometimes, when I am working alone late into the night or very early in the morning I feel the presence of others sitting next to me guiding my thoughts and my fingers as they move about the keyboard. During those moments, I feel a oneness with the world and the life force that flows in and through all things. Once in a while I am reminded of the words of Lone Man, a late-19th-century Lakota, who reportedly said, "I have seen that in any great undertaking it is not enough for a man to depend simply upon himself." I live and work in a world that places a high premium on individual invention and scholarship; yet while I may be the sole author of a written piece, I am continually conscious of the fact that I have never done anything solely and totally by myself—someone or something influenced my thinking and acting that led me to another level or to another idea. If we really reflect on the point, I suspect most would agree that our individual success is built on the encouragement, teachings, advice, and the wisdom of others and that we all really depend on one another for what we are all about in our fields of inquiry and endeavor. We are all connected and related to one another in some form or another, and thus we influence and are influenced by all things in ways we may never know.

My quest for finding ethnocultural influences in psychology is far from over. Indeed, our discipline is now alive with discussions, research, and teaching about ethnic and cultural topics, and the interest is increasing at levels that exceeded my expectations. The interest is changing the field of psychology as more and more people from different ethnocultural groups introduce lifeways and thoughtways that challenge conventional psychological tenets and principles. A knowledge revolution is occurring in the discipline—an ideological revolution of ideas based in cultural-specific perspectives. The field of psychology and its subject matter is becoming more inclusive of the lifeways and thoughtways of all ethnocultural groups. The field is not there yet and has a long journey ahead before no one is truly excluded. In the meantime, all of us deeply devoted and committed to ethnocultural studies should be watching closely just as Grandfather Sage advised.

RELEVANT PUBLICATIONS

Pedersen, P., Draguns, J., Lonner, W., & Trimble, J. (Eds.). (1996). *Counseling across cultures* (4th ed.). Thousand Oaks, CA: Sage. (Selected as one of the Best Health Sciences Books of 1996 by Doody's Health Service Rating)

Trimble, J. E. (1988). Stereotypic images, American Indians and prejudice. In P. Katz & D. Taylor (Eds.), *Toward the elimination of racism: Profiles in controversy* (pp. 181-202). New York: Pergamon.

Trimble, J. E. (1992). Drug abuse preventive intervention perspectives for American Indian adolescents. In L. A. Vargas & J. D. Koss (Eds.), *Working with culture: Psychotherapeutic interventions with ethnic minority children and adolescents* (pp. 246-275). San Francisco: Jossey-Bass.

Trimble, J. E. (1997). Bridging spiritual sojourns and social science research in native communities. In M. H. Bond (Ed.), *Working at the interface of cultures: Eighteen lives in social science* (pp. 166-178). New York: Routledge.

Trimble, J. E. (2000). Social psychological perspectives on changing self-identification among American Indians and Alaska Natives. In R. H. Dana (Ed.), *Handbook of cross-cultural and multicultural personality assessment* (pp. 197-222). Mahwah, NJ: Lawrence Erlbaum.

Correspondence regarding this chapter may be sent to Joseph E. Trimble, Radcliffe Institute for Advanced Study, Harvard University, 10 Garden Street, Cambridge, MA 02138 (e-mail address: trimble@radcliffe.edu).

Chapter 2

WALKING THROUGH COLLAGES

TERESA D. LAFROMBOISE

MY INTEREST IN American Indian psychology literally began as a child listening to stories my great-grandmother used to tell. Each time she came to stay in our home she would share memories of her own childhood in entertaining and instructional stories. For me, those visits with my maternal great-grandmother, who was descended from the Miami tribe of Indiana, were windows into another world. Although the stories I remember her telling were not only about various customs and traditions, they were the reminders of part of my heritage that were necessary given my acculturated upbringing in an unsympathetic southern Indiana town. I found myself wondering what it would have been like to grow up around Indian people.

I don't think my great-grandmother could have anticipated the result of her influence. She not only imparted pride in me being of Miami descent, she also sparked my desire to contribute something meaningful to the American Indian community. This desire crystallized during my college days in the late 1960s when I came upon American Indian scholarship on historical and contemporary Indian issues and witnessed media accounts of Indian protests that accompanied the Civil Rights Movement (such as the occupation of Mt. Rushmore in the sacred Black Hills by Lakota and Ojibwa militants and the invasion of Alcatraz Island by an intertribal group of Bay Area Indian community organizers and college students). I was intrigued by the deep double meaning of the governmental and historical targets of Indian protest and the patient manner of the people who were making the plight of native people known. I was idealistic and naïve. I wanted to be a part of efforts aimed at rectifying genocidal injustices and improving Indian life.

My professional work with American Indian people began the week after I graduated from college in 1971. I knew that one of the greatest areas of need and possibly easiest means of entry into Indian communities was teaching. I first inquired about jobs teaching language arts in reservation schools through the Bureau of Indian Affairs and received no response. I then contacted my first-grade teacher in Catholic school who was Mother Superior of St. Ann's Mission on the Turtle Mountain Ojibwa reservation in Belcourt, North Dakota. She invited me to interview for one of the many vacant slots in either the mission or government school. So I boarded a plane from Indianapolis, Indiana, headed to Grand Forks, North Dakota, the morning after receiving my bachelor's degree from Butler University. For two years I taught junior high, adhering to an open classroom approach and involving most of my students' parents in daily classroom projects and activities. I also married a man from there and enjoyed not only teaching but also being a part of the community. In the spring of the second year, he decided that it was time for us to leave the reservation in order that he complete his undergraduate education.

I quickly became disillusioned about how effective an agent of change a teacher could be when, in my next job, I worked as an Indian culture teacher with Saginaw Chippewa students at Mt. Pleasant High School in central Michigan. The dropout rate of students from this reservation was 80%—a figure not unlike that of many tribes at the time. I found myself focusing more on student retention than on pedagogy. I was on the reservation in committee meetings or home visits after school almost daily, spent a lot of time with students in extracurricular activities, and frequented the school counselor's office with both parents and students in efforts to act as a liaison between the tribal community and the conservative and often racist school administration. Many tribal members felt overwhelmed by the extent and impact of poverty and substance abuse in the community, but most wanted their students to graduate from high school. In their homes I heard the hopes and dreams of parents for their children as they nourished all at the table with beans and fry bread and stories. I repeatedly heard accounts of the many years that had passed when not one Ojibwa student walked across the stage at graduation to receive a diploma.

I also grew increasingly disgruntled about the negative attitudes of the townspeople toward tribal members, so I established an alternative classroom for Indian students within the public high school and worked with the tribe to find funding for a position for a middle school counselor. I knew that these students needed more than a sympathetic teacher's concern. I also knew that I needed to learn to do more than just listen to students' worries and complaints if I were to help them. Once the position was funded, members of the community asked me to apply for the job. I did apply and was rejected due to my lack of formal counseling training and my supposed enmeshment with the community. I made a commitment to myself at that point to pursue a Ph.D. in counseling psychology so that the next time I was turned down for such a position it wouldn't be because of my lack of educational qualifications.

How American Indians listen and how they are listened to became an important part of my research while undertaking my doctorate in counseling psychology, which I received from the University of Oklahoma in 1979. I spent a good deal of energy in courses searching for the relevance between Western psychological approaches and effective clinical work with people raised in traditional cultures. I knew from living with the Ojibwa people that they held negative attitudes toward non-Indian psychologists who were presumably insensitive to the hardships of Indian life. As I listened to lectures on various counseling theories and interventions I would recall conversations with women friends about the grief and anger that accompanied experiences with governmental agencies, such as their last childbirth when they discovered that they had been involuntarily sterilized during the procedure. I remembered the near-tragic delivery of my daughter when the Indian Health Service doctor on duty was too busy at a party upstairs to examine me or tend to the birth but, instead, issued orders to ship me across the state to another Indian Health Service hospital where a willing obstetrician was on duty. Even more sadly, I recalled an elder relative's account of her sister's return to the reservation from boarding school in a coffin after a bout of pneumonia and her brother's untimely and tragic death due to an encounter with a drunk driver just a quarter-mile from her home. For many Indian people to talk about these issues with a professional counselor was often considered treasonous if not pathetic for exposing personal pain to an outsider.

Nevertheless, I plowed through the counseling psychology program and was fortunate to work with urban adults in a counseling practicum at the Oklahoma City Indian Center. I was eventually hired by the Center to establish a counseling service for Indian youths who had been recommended for treatment by school counselors and judges within the juvenile justice system but who refused to enter therapy. This program, christened Oklahoma Indian Youth Services, was originally designed to be an agency to refer youths to clinical services while also advising professional service providers throughout the city in ways of being more culturally sensitive. However, despite numerous attempts at referral, our targeted clients refused to enter into conventional therapy. Instead, they joined groups run by paraprofessional Indian leaders who emphasized group conversations along with participation in cultural and athletic events.

I eventually came to terms with the contrasts in clinical procedures between the university counseling center and the Indian Center and came to believe in the potential for new models in counseling with American Indians. I thought the disconnection resided in the process. I felt that if the counseling process could be made more effective with American Indian clients, they would increasingly seek services to deal with their problems. I worked with psychologists Wayne Rowe and Paul Dauphinais on a number of counseling process studies to identify aspects of relationship-building techniques that could be seen as noninterfering and helpful. Despite our findings of the efficacy of certain social influence variables and styles of counseling with Indian clients, I often sensed that the differences between a counselor's ethnicity and upbringing and those of American Indian clients overpowered the effectiveness of most clinical interventions.

For my dissertation, I adapted culturally appropriate assertion-training procedures with American Indian adults. To do so, I traveled around the country conducting workshops with staff from Indian community agencies. The work on bidialectic communication or message matching by Donald Cheek in *Assertive Black . . . Puzzled White* served as a guide for a kind of assertive code switching, depending on when, where, and with whom one was speaking. In these workshops I began to appreciate the skills of many participants who easily alternated between being quite assertive in advocacy efforts for Indian clients to being rather demure when stating their wants or needs with another Indian person, especially while addressing an elder. Through the assertion training and related consultation with numerous intertribal and tribal groups like the Michigan Indian Homemaker Aide Program, the Indian Child Welfare Act Program, and the Seneca Social Services Program I learned a lot about the therapeutic aspects of humor and self-effacement and the additive effects of biculturalism. It was at this time that I became more intimately aware of my own personal process regarding my ethnic identity as a mixed-race person. People both outside and inside the Indian world challenged me as they sought to understand my mixed background. This reality moved me to a deeper level of self-reflection and became a part of the foundation from which I would work as time moved on.

In 1979, I began my first academic position at the University of Nebraska, worried about how I might teach counselor trainees empathy and interviewing skills for competent work with clients from other cultures. I had accepted a faculty position that called for a specialization in cross-cultural counseling, yet I had no formal training in the subject matter. I had come upon only one book on the subject—*Counseling Across Cultures* edited by Paul Pedersen, Walt Lonner, and Juris Draguns—while reviewing the literature in cross-cultural communication for my dissertation. That year I witnessed Derald Sue reporting on the Cross-Cultural Competencies to Division 17 at the very first APA convention I attended. I remember being quite surprised at the lukewarm reception by counseling psychology academics to his report, despite its clear challenge to the field. Luckily, I secured a grant to attend a summer cross-cultural workshop at Stanford University where I was exposed to the emerging literatures on racial identity development and social policies of community empowerment. The instructor in that workshop was Chalsa Loo. I was impressed by her warmth, teaching style, and clinical acumen, not to mention her manner of leading class critiques of videotaped cross-cultural counseling interviews. My excitement for teaching in this area was invigorated. I returned home eager to make a difference in the field. I pursued further mentoring from Paul Pedersen by arranging for him to come out to Nebraska to co-teach the cross-cultural counseling course with me the following summer.

In the course of my work in Nebraska with Omaha and Winnebago people, I experienced numerous contrasts between conventional approaches to mental health and traditional community-based practices. Shortly after my mother passed away, I was asked to chair the board of directors of Lincoln Indian Center, and I accepted the position in her honor. During that time, an Indian women's inpatient substance abuse treatment center was established. Administrative work with this model program allowed me to see, firsthand, the transforming influence that traditional ceremonies have on community responsiveness and mobilization for change. I witnessed extensive informal caregiving and the psychological support that extended families provide one another. This familial closeness was so special to me, as it reminded me of the days when my own large family on my father's side would fill up our grandparents' home for card games and meals. It was during this time, too, that I learned that an event's success depended on whether proper procedures were followed in extending invitations to elders for their involvement. I was impressed with how naturally the traditional values of kindness, patience, generosity, humility, respect, caring, and honesty were incorporated into treatment by culturally grounded staff.

As I continued to move between the worlds of the Indian center and the university, I continued to struggle with how to contribute to what is now called the multicultural counseling movement, yet make an impact in American Indian psychology. I became troubled by the definition of cross-cultural counseling as a counseling encounter where there are differences between counselor and client based on race, ethnicity, socioeconomic status, age, gender, sexual orientation, religion, and physical disabilities. It seemed to me that students often opted for simulation experiences, interviews, and research papers focusing on clients representing person variables and avoided race or ethnicity when given license to do so through such a broad definition. I continued teaching counseling courses at the university but whenever possible taught cross-cultural counseling courses to American Indian and European American professionals at tribal colleges and universities in Indian country. In these courses, I could incorporate my research and the growing literature on American Indian psychology with experimentation on natural Indian helping styles and cross-cultural counseling techniques. I also required that there be an equal number of students representing American Indian and European American perspectives in these courses to maintain a cross-cultural rather than an ethnic-specific focus. Had material on critical White studies been available, it would have been included.

When I moved to Stanford University in 1983 I had the privilege of working with students like Roberto Gonzales, Don Pope-Davis, Sandy Foster, and Hardin Coleman, individuals who had considerable national and international diversity experiences. I found that my research in the area of American Indian counseling was readily received as a model for applied counseling research with special populations. Fortunately, these students did not wish to wander away from matters of influence on racism but were willing to take counseling diversity to another level. Their subsequent contributions to the field in theory development and research attests to their strong commitment to social justice.

I also tried to keep up the ongoing community service by establishing a Saturday drop-in mental health clinic at the Indian Health Clinic in the tenderloin area of San Francisco. My caseload filled within two weeks, proving to mental health professionals in the city that American Indian people would avail themselves of services when they occurred in an Indian community agency and that the need was great. I also worked as a therapist at the Stanford Student Health Center. As part of my duties I ran an Indian women's support group consisting of some of my individual clients and other Indian female students. Again I was struck by the spontaneous disclosures of women in the group setting compared to their labored revelations in individual work with me. However, as a single parent trying to get tenure, I soon felt I couldn't keep up with the clinical demand and be effective in my position at the university. I had to resign from the position in San Francisco.

Eventually I was asked by community leaders of the Zuni pueblo to assist them in addressing the problem of youth suicide. Along with Stanford students Mary Jiron Belgarde, Benadette September, and Gary Lichtenstein and Zuni teacher Stephanie Antone I developed a school-based suicide prevention curriculum titled *American Indian Life Skills Development*. I truly believe that this intervention study would not have survived if not for the backing of religious and political leaders there. We were alternately challenged and supported by tribal members throughout the implementation and evaluation of the curriculum.

Our first hurdle came as we traveled into Gallup, New Mexico, en route to Zuni from Stanford to introduce the curriculum and begin teacher training. We were greeted with a newspaper article in the *Gallup Independent* that covered a quarter of the front page featuring a posed picture of a young American Indian girl sitting on her bed with a rope by her side with the following caption above it: "Stanford Researchers to Solve the Zuni Suicide Problem." Needless to say, the teachers, all of whom were non-Zuni, were very afraid to be involved in light of this yellow journalism and the cultural taboo that prohibited any Zuni person from thinking about, much less mentioning, the word suicide. To offset teachers' fears and also strengthen community resources, Zuni pueblo council members and school administrators participated in the teacher training on suicide prevention and use of the curriculum. Soon afterward, the on-site coordinator for this project, a non-Indian school counselor, left as a result of buying and selling a Zuni ceremonial mask. To make matters worse, the only other school counselor, a non-Indian woman, immediately resigned from her job, leaving an empty counseling office at the beginning of the crisis intervention section of the curriculum that relied on immediate referral of suicidal youths to help givers. Again the community responded by setting aside agency rivalries to allow Zuni mental health technicians to team-teach the curriculum with the teachers. The way the community coalesced to offset complications that occurred in the implementation of the curriculum reaffirmed my faith that the intervention was on the right path.

Between 1990 and 1994 I worked in the Department of Counseling Psychology at the University of Wisconsin. Just as I was leaving for Madison and terminating with the clients I had seen in the Stanford Counseling Institute, I invited one of my clients, an Apache woman in her late 40s, to attend an acorn festival hosted by Me-Wuk people. My client and her sister joined me in Yosemite Valley where the feasts and dances were held. I had been seeing this client for one year for major recurrent depression and prolonged grief reaction due to her mother's death. I chose to invite her to this particular ceremony because it occurred near the first anniversary of her mother's passing. The first evening that we were in the night dances, shortly after the closing intertribal dance, a woman came up to my client and began praying over her and smudging her with her eagle feather fan. People that gathered around them eventually started crying. Not knowing my client and never having spoken to her before, the medicine woman told my client to "let her go." She repeatedly told her, "It is time to let her go." Shortly thereafter, my client and her sister came to peace with their mother's death and my client's depression lifted. Here again I saw proof in the transformational power of collective support that is often found in ceremonial ways.

My continued encounters with healing experiences and community-based intervention development has strengthened my faith in the tenets of community empowerment. As we find unique applications for the *American Indian Life Skills Development Curriculum* like teen pregnancy, violence, and AIDS prevention or substance abuse prevention, I encounter more and more helping professionals who espouse multicultural competence ideals but still become impatient with the notion of intervening in a manner respectful of community mores and time frames. My experiences in ongoing relationships with spiritual leaders and community advocates has provided me with invaluable assistance in finding ways to intervene yet develop choice. I believe that by waiting for individuals and communities to seek one out rather than actively market to their needs shows respect for tribal sovereignty and self-determination. I feel strongly that psychologists can be seen as helpful in treating symptoms when they work in tandem with traditional support systems to provide adequate resources and manage the central issues needed for change.

I have received great satisfaction and hope from the success of the life skills intervention work and am pleased to know that the curriculum is now being implemented with indigenous people in Australia and New Zealand. My experiences in the field thus far leave me with the desire to continue to strive for balance in my research, practice, and service—balance between attention to developmental processes leading to resilience and the cultural adaptation of treatment modalities. My journey has been composed of a series of collages. Each picture reflects an experience and no experience tells the whole story.

RELEVANT PUBLICATIONS

LaFromboise, T. (1996). *American Indian Life Skills Development Curriculum.* Madison: University of Wisconsin Press.

LaFromboise, T. (1998). American Indian mental health policy. In D. R. Atkinson, G. Morton, & D. W. Sue (Eds.), *Counseling American minorities* (5th ed., pp. 137-158). Boston: McGraw-Hill.

LaFromboise, T., Choney, S., James, A., & Running Wolf, P. (1995). American Indian women and psychology. In H. Landrine (Ed.), *Bringing cultural diversity to feminist psychology* (pp. 197-239). Washington, DC: American Psychological Association.

LaFromboise, T., & Howard-Pitney, B. (1995). The Zuni Life Skills Development Curriculum: Description and evaluation of a suicide prevention program. *Journal of Counseling Psychology, 42,* 479-486.

LaFromboise, T., Trimble, J., & Mohatt, G. (1990). Counseling intervention and American Indian tradition: An integrative approach. *The Counseling Psychologist, 18,* 628-654.

Correspondence regarding this chapter may be sent to Teresa LaFromboise, School of Education, 485 Lausen Mall, Stanford University, Stanford, CA 94305 (e-mail address: Lafrom@leland.stanford.edu).

Chapter 3

LIFE QUESTIONS

JANET E. HELMS

I SUSPECT THAT MY life has been much like everyone else's life in that it began much beyond my recall and continues in its own direction in spite of my best efforts to move it in the direction of fame, fortune, excitement, and/or adventure. To me it is an unremarkable life, a condition for which I am grateful. However, a normally eventful life such as mine does not contribute to very exciting or suspenseful story telling. Story telling is a tradition in my family. Both my father and paternal grandmother were excellent story tellers and my mother wanted to grow up to be Brenda Starr (a cartoon investigative reporter). From them all I learned that if the story isn't interesting enough to tell, then one probably shouldn't tell it. Nevertheless, the editors of the *Handbook* invited me to contribute a chapter, even though I warned them that it would be a sleep-inducing experience for the reader. I suppose they anticipate that many readers of the *Handbook* will be people with insomnia in need of a nonchemical cure.

In an effort to overcome my writer's block, I shared my dilemma with my colleague at Boston College, Susana Lowe, and she and her graduate assistants graciously volunteered to generate some questions about my life whose answers they thought would be of interest to readers. They generated 37 questions, many of which had several parts. I could not address all of them because of space limitations. Some of the questions I have already answered in an interview that I did for Robert Carter. However, there were several that I could not answer and so I have decided to use them as the focus of this chapter because the process of discovering answers to unanswered questions is generally what inspires me to live the life I do. I put the questions into four categories (identity, systemic barriers, professional concerns, and future plans) and chose at least one of the questions from each category as my focus.

IDENTITY

How do you think colleagues or students see you? Are you loved, feared, re-spected, elusive . . . ? Do you feel people's perceptions are accurate? In what ways are you stereotyped at work? What would be an accurate way to de-scribe who you are?

Sometimes, I think it would be fun if a genie granted me three wishes. I would use one of them to see myself through someone else's eyes since on the far too frequent occasions when someone feels obliged to share her or his perceptions of me with me, I am genuinely surprised and sometimes of-fended. I know that invariably my friends give me the nickname "Lady," and I don't know why. My niece says that I will never perfect the "grunge look," even though I keep trying. I guess I'll have to try harder. My graduate students are continually surprised by my interests in basketball, track, fig-ure skating, gymnastics, soap operas and romance novels, Buffy the Vam-pire Slayer (I prefer the TV version), and my artistic nature. What's so unusual? I seem to inspire Whoopi Goldberg dreams for some of my male colleagues and they and Whoopi reportedly have some hot times dealing with their unresolved Oedipal complexes. Need I say that I am offended by this? I don't look anything like Whoopi!

I am convinced that I am a mirror in which people see whatever char-acteristics they need me to have. However, I don't spend much time or psy-chic energy worrying about the contents of their projections. There is not much that I could do to change or control their perceptions anyway, and I wouldn't be able to move if I tried to live up or down to everyone's stereo-types or expectations of me. My general rule with respect to this aspect of me is "if the person doesn't feed, clothe, or love me, then I won't worry about how he or she sees me." My general rule for me is "do what feels right to me and if it works, great! If not, oh well."

If while you were growing up there were African American role models in every profession you could imagine, what do you think you would have be-come? What career?

I think that I am more collectivistic than not. However, this question makes me think that I am perhaps more individualistic than I think of my-self as being. Insofar as I can recall, I have not made any important life deci-sions on the basis of the characteristics of the other people doing whatever it was. My family raised me to believe that I could do anything I wanted to do if I had the appropriate talent and money and could find ways around rac-ism. So, I don't think that the presence of African American women role models in particular professions would have influenced my career decision making. On the other hand, if these women had been philanthropists who contributed money to my education and life support, then I might have pur-sued some of my other interests. For instance, if I had had access to more money at the time, then I might have become a pediatrician. I like children and helping to relieve their pain. I also am fascinated by American history. So, if as an undergraduate I had thought I would be able to feed myself in the future, then I might have become a historical novelist. In any case, I did not have enough money to follow either of these paths, and so I assume that I have become what I was meant to become.

What saddens you most when you reflect back on your formal education? Have things changed? If not, what do you want to see happen in education (K-12, college, graduate school)?

With perhaps the exception that it started too early in the morning, I have always loved school. Maybe that's why I am a professor. It's one of the few careers that allows one to get paid for staying in school. I am a product of state schools from kindergarten through graduate school. So, what I know that qualifies as formal education I learned primarily in these settings. Consequently, I am an advocate for strong support of public educational institutions. At the risk of sounding trite, I think they offer the best chance of equalizing opportunity for people regardless of demographic characteristics.

If anything saddens me, it is that the Rockefellers, Fords, or Kennedys didn't send their children to public schools in the Midwest. I might have acquired more connections. Also, there were no ALANA (African, Latino, Asian, or Native American) men in the colleges or grad schools that I attended. This saddened me a lot! Other than me, there were no ALANA women either, but my goals at the time would have been better satisfied by men.

Some things have changed in the educational system, not necessarily for the better, but other things have not changed. At the pre-college level in urban areas, I think the educational process has become less inspired and inspiring than it was in my day. I am troubled that standardized test scores have become the primary criteria by which children's acquired learning and the quality of the instruction they receive are evaluated. Consequently, teachers are forced to teach the test material. Learning how to take (primarily) multiple-choice tests is boring and should not be the primary focus of pre-college education. By the time they reach college, students (regardless of race) educated under this teach-the-test system cannot write or think in sentences. If this had been my educational experience, then I do not think that I would have acquired my love for learning new things.

Unfortunately, the demographics of future psychologists in colleges and graduate schools also have not changed. There tend to be few ALANA women and even fewer ALANA men in such settings. Even so, women are much less likely to enter academic positions than their male counterparts. I suspect that this is because ALANA women do not receive much encouragement or mentoring toward pursuing academic careers. I know I didn't.

SYSTEMIC BARRIERS

Are students sometimes disrespectful toward you because of your socioracial status and because you're a woman? If so, how does it feel?

I imagine. Students grow up in the same racist and sexist environments as everyone else. So, it would be unusual for them to have escaped that socialization unscathed. It depends on what role I'm in and how the disrespect is manifested. There is everyday disrespect, such as questioning my credentials for doing whatever I happen to be doing at the time, or referring to me as "Mrs. Helms" or "Janet" instead of "Dr. Helms" in formal settings, or letting me know that someone else they know teaches whatever I might be teaching much better than I can. By now, these are ho-hum experiences and I am bored by them. Depending on what mood and role I am in, I may either ignore it or correct the person. I am more likely to correct the person if I anticipate that we will have ongoing interactions.

I hear that the most creative student-generated racism and sexism happens behind my back, which, of course, suits me fine. I suppose that if it happened face-to-face it would make me angry, since the secondhand accounts do. However, I do not respect cowards very much, and my task now is to persuade "friendly" students or colleagues not to share with me racism that their colleagues were too cowardly to share themselves. I would much rather hear about what they have done to cure the racism.

Could you tell a story about a time when you encountered discrimination at the workplace or in your personal life? How did it affect you? Did it influence or inform the work that you do?

Most incidences of discrimination are micro-inequities—that is, little things that people do that in and of themselves are not very meaningful but gradually build up to a point where I want to get away from people. The problem with micro-inequities is that they pass quickly and, even if they didn't, there is often not much I could do about them. There are, of course, the all-too-familiar inequities such as White women grabbing their purses when they enter an elevator that I am in or cab drivers refusing to stop for me. Then there are the inequities that probably occur because I am a Black woman rather than a man and, consequently, am not perceived as being very physically intimidating. I will share with you a couple of these, but then I will share with you a larger event that I thought I handled quite well, if I do say so myself.

I think that I am invisible to White strangers (unless they need help). I have a lot of travel micro-inequities that I could share, but I will just give you one example to illustrate my point. Flight attendants do not assist with carry-on luggage anymore, regardless of the race, age, or gender of the person. Like everyone else, I have to make room for my own bag when I travel. I was returning home from a lecture tour on a jam-packed flight, and there was no obvious room for my carry-on in the overhead compartment above my seat. So, I rearranged and moved several heavy bags so that there would be room for my bag. I turned around to pick up my bag, and while my back was turned a White man put his bag in my space and went back to his seat. He did not say anything to me or even acknowledge that he had seen me with my bag in midair enroute to the space that his bag now occupied. As I was trying to decide whether there was a law against accidentally dropping one's bag on someone's head four rows up, the flight attendant rescued the man's head by finding another space in the back of the plane where I could store my bag.

Not only am I invisible, but White people in service positions also cannot hear me, especially if I am in the midst of other (perceived) White people. This story illustrates this condition. After one of her theatrical performances, I was having a second lunch with my actress niece, her brother, sister, and father, and one of her White college friends and her mother. Her father is White and she attends a predominantly White college in a predominantly White town. So, I suppose it appeared to an outside observer that I was the only person of color at the table. Since I had already eaten once, I only wanted dessert. The waitress took everyone's order in sequence and when she got to me I ordered a dessert and hot tea and requested that she bring my order when she brought everyone else's meal. Needless to say, she brought everyone's meal but nothing for me. My brother-in-law, who is oblivious to racism, and I engaged in a conversation that went something like this:

> Him: She didn't bring your order.
> Me: She didn't hear me because I'm the Black person at the table.
> Him: You're just being too sensitive. She probably thought that you wanted to wait until we were ready for dessert, too.
> Me: Bet?
> Him: Sure. What's the bet?
> Me: You ask her about my order and if she says something that indicates that she didn't hear my order, then you pay for my meals for the rest of this trip. If she says she was waiting until later, then I'll pay for your meals.
> Him: It's a bet. Waitress? My sister-in-law (pointing to me) didn't get her order.
> Waitress: What order? She wasn't here when I took the orders.

I have experienced many variants of this example. Consequently, I will often cue that I am speaking by placing a finger near my lips and waiting for the intended listener to focus on me. I learned the cued-speech skill while working with children with autism in graduate school. I never know when something I learned earlier will come in handy in a new situation.

My favorite example involves something that happened at work. The department chair at an institution where I was a faculty member announced that I was planning to develop a center to study race and culture.

Over the weekend, someone placed an anonymous unstamped postcard in my mailbox. On one side of the card was a picture of African hunters in (presumably) traditional tribal garb (e.g., animal skins, bones through their noses and ears, and white face paint streaks on their dark skins). On the other side of the card, in very poor handwriting, the anonymous writer had written "You must have dropped this when you were looking through your family album."

I wanted to express my gratitude to the gift-giver, but I obviously had no way of identifying him or her. So, I made a poster consisting of both sides of the postcard and my own expression of gratitude: "To my anonymous benefactor, thank you for sending me the beautiful postcard. I hope that our mutual ancestors are as proud of you as you obviously are of them." I hung the poster in the mail room so that the anonymous faculty member or graduate student who placed it in my mailbox would have an opportunity to see it. In retrospect, I suspect that my intervention may have been too intellectually advanced for the intended recipient, but fighting back made me feel good at the time.

There is a reciprocal relationship between my life and my work. My life sometimes reveals to me fights that still need to be won, and my work helps me understand people sufficiently enough to allow me to remain in the battle.

PROFESSIONAL ISSUES

How did you know you wanted to be a professor?
I didn't. I still don't. Being a professor is something that I am trying out until I decide what I really want to do when I grow up.

How would you characterize the state of counseling psychology with regard to multiculturalism? Are multiculturalists taken seriously or tokenized? Any thoughts?
As I say as often as possible, I do not really know what counseling psychologists (or anyone else) mean by "multiculturalism." If it were up to me, I would discard the term because it is essentially meaningless. I do not think that it is particularly useful for guiding research, theory, practice, or conversation because everyone seems to mean something or someone different when they are using the term. I believe that counseling psychology was and continues to be a major force with respect to focusing attention on practical issues of race, culture, gender, sexual orientation, and physical ability status. However, there is still much to be done in each of these domains at both the individual and the systemic level.

Whether "multiculturalists" are taken seriously seems to depend on their area of focus. Based on my experience, I think the field and society generally are much more receptive to the domains of gender, physical ability status, and (sometimes) sexual orientation than they are to race and culture. At the last Multi-Cultural Summit, I was aware, for instance, of how much easier it was for participants to assail a participant for his regressive viewpoints on sexual orientation than they are for them to talk about race and racism at all.

What do you find most significant about the work you do?

I don't really know how to define "significant" in this context. I enjoy much of what I do, particularly if I discover that it has had a positive impact on someone. Enjoyment is significant to me. However, if "significant" means whether my work has promoted world peace or solved a major societal mental health problem, probably not. But I am still working on it.

FUTURE PLANS

If you were to write a pop psychology book, what would it be called, for whom would it be written (i.e., what audience), and what would it accomplish?

I would call it "A Race Is a Nice Thing to Have: A Guide to Being a White Person or Understanding the White Persons in Your Life." It would be a self-help book intended primarily to help White people think about how racist socialization has influenced their mental health and to offer them strategies for overcoming that socialization, if they so desire. It would be for ALANAs (i.e., African, Latino and Latina, Asian and Pacific Islander, and Native Americans). Often, ALANAs are called on to explain to White people how racism affects them, as though it is a foreign concept to Whites. Moreover, such requests often occur under circumstances in which the ALANA person has little power. The book, if it existed, would be the way for them to communicate the message without being the messenger. They could give the White requestor a copy of the book. It would become a bestseller, and I would be extolled far and wide as being the greatest race psychologist since Malcolm X.

RELEVANT PUBLICATIONS

Helms, J. E. (1992). *A race is a nice thing to have: A guide to being a White person or understanding the White persons in your life.* Topeka, KS: Content Communications.

Helms, J. E. (1992). Why is there no study of cultural equivalence in cognitive ability testing? *American Psychologist, 47,* 1083-1101.

Helms, J. E. (1996). Toward a methodology for measuring and assessing racial identity as distinguished from ethnic identity. In G. R. Sodowsky & J. C. Impara (Eds.), *Multicultural assessment in counseling and clinical psychology* (pp. 143-192). Lincoln, NE: Buros Institute.

Helms, J. E. (1999). Another meta-analysis of the White Racial Identity Attitude Scale. *Measurement and Evaluation in Counseling and Development, 32,* 122-137.

Helms, J. E., & Cook, D. A. (1999). *Using race and culture in counseling and psychotherapy*. Needham Heights, MA: Allyn & Bacon.

Correspondence regarding this chapter may be sent to Janet E. Helms, Department of Counseling, Developmental, and Educational Psychology, Boston College, Chestnut Hill, MA 20467 (e-mail address: helmsja@bc.edu).

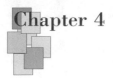

Chapter 4

ENCOUNTERING NIGRESCENCE

WILLIAM E. CROSS, JR.

LET'S SEE, "how did I discover Nigrescence?" The truth of the matter is, it was the other way around. Nigrescence first discovered and transformed me, and then, upon reflection, I found the words to describe the boundaries or stages for my racial epiphany. For a while, I kept my encounter a "secret," thinking it peculiar to my personal history and psychological development. Even after realizing I was hardly unique or alone in my transformative sojourn, it became a struggle to put pen to paper, for I was very insecure as a writer. At the time of my social identity change, I had never published anything! A curious combination of being pushed and hassled by my friends and the unlikely consequences of a wonderful romantic interlude finally led to the writing of my 1971 essay on black identity change. Here is my story.

It was the beginning of my sophomore year at Denver University, and, as I moved from one course registration line to another, I noticed a young man whose physical features suggested he might be part Negro (this was Fall 1960, and "black" was hardly a term we applied to each other). As the recently elected president of the Alpha Chapter of Pi Lambda Phi Fraternity, I was keen to spot new pledges. Pi Lam is a traditionally Jewish fraternity and the Alpha Chapter had been defunct for years. During my freshmen year, Graham Susman, an elderly Jewish progressive and Pi Lam alumnus, approached a group of Negro, white-Protestant, and Jewish DU students, including myself, concerning our interest in reactivating the Alpha Chapter as an "integrated" rather than predominantly Jewish House. We agreed, and I was elected president. I'm not certain what the group saw in me, but they certainly had fun with my sexual naïveté and especially my enthusiasm for "snipes." When they realized I had never been a Boy Scout and "truly" did not know about snipes, they immediately planned a grand snipe hunt. Once captured, we would sell each pelt for $25 and use the money to enhance the chapter treasury. One evening, we set off for the

foothills of the Rockies, where I led the charge down a hillside, thought to
be ideal for chasing snipes toward the river's edge (snipes cannot swim) and
easy capture. Of course, I was equipped with a whistle, a potato sack, and a
flashlight. One by one the brothers peeled off into the hinterland until I was
the lone snipe enthusiast. Yes, right up to the last second I remained naïve
to the snipe's mythology. To this day I cannot recall how I made my way
back to campus, but, when I did, we must have laughed for a year. Actually, I
was a bit disappointed, for I had given much thought to the sale of the pelts.

I made my way toward the tall, brown-skinned young man and extended my hand. When he said his name, I surmised that I was in error about
his being Negro, for with a noticeable accent he introduced himself as Badi
Foster. He repeated his first name several times, as if to anticipate my need
to rehearse it. To further help me through my embarrassment, he stated he
was a Bahai, and his first name in Arabic means "wonderfulness," one of
the 99 qualities of God. His parents named him after one of the martyrs of
the Bahai faith. Upon recovering from the intrigue of his name and religion,
I launched into my Pi Lam appeal, but this all fell to the wayside when we
started to go through that perfunctory aspect of new introductions: "Hey,
where are you from?" Bill Foster, Badi's father, who was Negro, met Ruth
Alexander, a self-described Bohemian white woman from Ohio, in the context of radical activities during the Depression. As often happens with dis-
enchanted radicals, they turned to religion, and in this case to a faith that
not only tolerated their interracial relationship but advocated racial inter-
marriage. They became profound adherents, some would say zealots, and
moved their family from Chicago's South Side to Northern Africa, where
they worked to spread and solidify the Bahai movement and faith. Badi, although an American Negro by birth, spent his adolescence in Morocco and
now spoke Arabic, French, and English. In light of my provincial, midwestern upbringing, meeting Badi was like encountering a Negro from Mars.
Most amazing of all, however, was our next discovery.

Before moving to North Africa, Badi's family lived at 738 East 69th
Street and he attended McCosh Elementary School. Jesus! We were born
within a few blocks of each other, because, although my family now lived in
Evanston, a suburb just north of Chicago, our former Chicago address was
6601 South St. Lawrence, a short walk to Badi's address. And, I also attended
McCosh Elementary. Except for my sister Judy, who was born in Virginia,
all the Cross offspring marked the St. Lawrence address as our birthplace
residence. Badi and I chuckled at the thought of having unknowingly passed
each other in the hallways of McCosh or on a neighborhood street or playground. Years later, my father, a Pullman porter, recalled his association
with several of Badi's older relatives, who were, themselves, dining car
stewards and Pullman porters. Otherwise, no one from either family clan
recalls encountering the other. Yet now, a thousand miles from Chicago,
two Negro strangers from the same neighborhood stood face to face, grin-
ning as if each had just discovered a pot of gold. Thus began a life-long

friendship with a person who would eventually be the best man at my wedding, my mentor when I first became active as a consultant to industry on organizational development and diversity issues, and more to the point of this chapter, the person who recruited me to Princeton University, where, in 1971, I penned an essay on the Negro identity development. Badi even came to play a pivotal role in the actual production of the essay.

In 1963, after receiving a BA in psychology from Denver University, I entered the master's program in clinical psychology at Roosevelt University in Chicago. As I have noted elsewhere (Cross, 1991), almost all Nigrescence theorists were trained in applied psychology, and our "process perspective and training" helped us "see" stages in the stream of consciousness exhibited by African Americans when they experienced identity change. I was initiated into a process perspective at Roosevelt, where, as part of my clinical training, I became familiar with the stages of therapy. We saw that clients progressed through a series of steps in the deconstruction and analysis of their "old" and troublesome sense of self, and worked toward the construction of a new self-concept that typically reconfigured elements of the old self with fresh insights and a modest infusion of new elements. This therapy-process perspective became embedded in my subconscious and, along with another model of identity change that I will discuss shortly, was reactivated a few years later when I tried to decipher the psychological dynamics of the Black Movement. At the time I wrote the model, I was not consciously aware of the role my previous training played in framing my conception of the "stages," although in hindsight, it clearly was operating at the subconscious level.

The other "frame" that eventually guided my observations on change was a religious de-conversion I experienced in college. Entering DU, I was profoundly, if not obsessively, religious, but in trying to make sense of American slavery and the "meaning" of the destruction of the Jews during World War II, I intellectually concluded, in accord with existential philosophy, that there was no god, religion was an illusion, and all belief systems were social inventions. Having begun each day of my youth conversing with the Lord, the discovery that god was dead caused a hailstorm in my soul. I briefly became suicidal in the face of life's meaninglessness, and in pulling myself together, I systematically crushed any inclination toward "belief" and religion. Having prayed every night of my life, it first became surreal not to pray, and my whole body would shake, as I fought the urge to fall to my knees. My memory of this emotional "unlearning" or religious de-conversion was also operating, subconsciously, when I eventually tried to outline the shifts, pulls, and conflicts of the Negro-to-Black conversion experience, especially with regard to the Immersion-Emersion, or transition, stage.

With these two analytic and process-oriented guides packed away in my mind, I had only to be "exposed" to the Black Movement itself, which, in turn, triggered these interpretive frames, resulting in the codification of the stages. My exposure took place in Chicago and Evanston, Illinois, and, although my involvement in the movement would last for years, the experiences that proved crucial to the writing of the model occurred between 1965 and early Fall 1969.

The Vietnam War was in full swing, and I had used a string of deferments to avoid the draft. My only brother, Charles Frank Cross, was in the armed services, stationed in Europe, and I began to feel cowardly and guilty about my status. I was in Jacksonville, Illinois, at Jacksonville State Mental Hospital, where I first completed a one-year clinical internship followed by a one-year staff assignment. My Illinois State educational grant required a time-payback in that for every year of graduate study support I had to work at a state psychiatric institution an equal length of time, and I owed the State two years, inclusive of the internship. The rural city of Jacksonville was in the southern part of the state, and its atmosphere was akin to a small Mississippi hamlet. I hit the mental health system as it was shifting from the warehouse model to the dispersal model, which involved releasing as many clients as possible back into the community. Watching patients, doctors, nurses, and attendants react to the radical shift in patient care eventually added to my ability to understand the identity change processes, only in this case, from a system-change perspective.

I decided that, while it was out of the question to volunteer for the armed services and fight in America's dirty war, I also would no longer seek a deferment. In addition, I felt isolated and estranged from the war protest and Black Power movements, both of which were accorded only limited authentication in southern, rural Illinois. Back up "north" the riots ushered in a sense of urgency for many white corporations, and a large Chicago-based insurance company recruited and hired me at twice my state salary. It sounds somewhat corny now, but at the time I felt I was making history, given the miniscule number of blacks in corporate America. I took the position, and that became my ticket back to Evanston and Chicago. I was employed as a Human Resources management trainee and given the assignment to research, design, and implement an after-school community project as part of the company's response to the recent riots. In researching the topic, I conducted interviews with numerous community leaders, who provided a panoramic view of the history, culture, and problems facing blacks in Chicago and America. I brushed shoulders with some of the best informed observers from the black community, such as the late Clotee Best of the Chicago Urban League, and each interview was like an intense seminar on either black culture or white racism. At the end of most interviews, I was directed to certain articles or books, which I subsequently devoured in short order. In a manner of speaking, I completed a self-directed master's degree in black studies within 12 months. I did not know it at the time, but my conversion to Blackness was in full swing. The death of Martin Luther King, Jr. was my trigger, my encounter. My rage and anger made it impossible to be functional in the all-white world of the insurance company, and after one too many eruptions, I was terminated. By now, I was obsessed with finding ways to "rejoin and pay back my community." On a personal level, I was rolling out of Encounter and dropping head first—body twisting, arms flailing, both fists clinched, Afro growing an inch a day—into Immersion-Emersion.

As fate would have it, I became Director of West Side Service Center (WSSC) of Evanston, a community-action center created by the city of Evanston in conjunction with a cluster of "responsible" black community leaders. The Black Power Movement was omnipresent, and leaders from cities, corporations, and the federal and state governments were beside themselves to find ways to channel black rage into constructive actions. WSSC was charged with creating proactive programs that would engage the youth of Evanston. By now, I was totally consumed by Blackness and relished the thought of leading the group to a higher plane. My presentation to the WSSC board members was grandiose but convincing. I asked them to stop thinking about stopgap or "cooling-off" projects and support, instead, projects designed to increase the involvement of multiple segments of the community (youths, black businessmen, teachers, and black professionals). My "vision" was to engage people "where they were at" and then gently move them to a higher level of consciousness. In addition to organizing different segments of the community, we opened "The House of Blackness," just across the street from the high school, where books on black culture and artwork from Africa could be purchased. On paper, at least, each activity, organization, and sponsored event would overlap with the other, pressing forward the evolution of black consciousness, resulting in a crescendo of unity, and thus, power—or so we, the WSSC board of directors and I, believed.

If during the workweek I was a community leader, the weekends saw me rushing down to Chicago's South Side to attend an OBAC meeting to "confess" and gain new insights that would keep me a few steps "ahead" of the very folks I was "leading." Black artists and cultural nationalists organized the Organization of Black American Culture (OBAC) as an artistic forum, but on Sundays, open meetings were held in which people, ordinary people, stepped forward to confess to their previous cultural backwardness, miseducation, and self-hatred and proclaim the healing power and rejuvenation of their new-found Blackness. In a typical session, Phil Cohran's nimble fingers produced mesmerizing chords from an African thumb piano, as Jeff Donaldson, who would later go on to a distinguished career in the Department of Art at Howard University, held us in utter rapture. Donaldson stood 6-foot 3 or 4 inches, had chiseled features and piercing but warm eyes, a voice that was inherited from Moses, and a general physical and spiritual "presence" that made him ethereal. Part of the meeting was always devoted to a reconnection to our bodies, our hair, our lips, and our total physical images. We, or rather Jeff or an invited speaker, addressed our souls, our music, our art, and our communities. In a manner of speaking, we were being urged to be openly "cultural" as well as "racial."

To this day, I do not consider my model to be one of "race consciousness" but, rather, one of race and culture consciousness because people like Jeff, author Lerone Bennett, editor of *Negro Digest* Hoyt Fuller, and poet Don L. Lee pounded into our heads that "race" was only part of the issue. More important was a black person's consciousness of black culture. Whether light-skinned or ebony, we were charged to go "deep" into our blackness to find meaning and value in our thoughts, actions, values, and deeds. From my vantage point, I "heard" the OBAC spokespersons saying that race was as much an existential as a physical reality and that being identifiably black was both a racial predicament and a cultural opportunity: a predicament in that "others" view our black features as a mark of inferiority, and we are forced to learn how to negotiate this imposed race identity; and an opportunity in that African American history and culture is pregnant with traditions, values, and aesthetic frames, along with rich examples on how to live the good life, *given* one takes advantage of the opportunity to engage, embrace, and help sustain this "cultural identity." The model I eventually produced would not be a race identity analysis, it would be a race and ethnicity or race and cultural identity conception, which simultaneously combined elements of "how one can learn to live and negotiate imposed notions of race" and "how one can learn to embrace blackness as ethnicity or culture." Because I believe so strongly that blackness is far more ethnic-cultural and existential than "racial," it may come as a surprise to the reader that I experience a certain degree of discomfort when one refers to my work solely as "racial." Given my physiognomy (I am very light and have white facial features), the OBAC exchanges freed me from guilt about being too "white-looking," and shifted the focus to my own, and *every* black person's, adventuresome struggle to become existentially black (e.g., the stages of "black" identity development). From that period forward, the expression *shades of black* had a double meaning for me: We, black people, reflect a wide range of skin colors; and we, black people, express an equally wide range of opinions on what it means, existentially speaking, to be black.

At the end of each OBAC meeting, I rushed back to Evanston with a renewed vision and greater confidence that somehow I had become connected to the right cause, the right philosophy of life, and the answer to my personal as well as my group's social problems and cultural challenges. I was totally immersed in the romance and positivity of blackness. Romantic as it might be, my exposure to this emergent new blackness was quite multidimensional. OBAC sessions on Sunday, Peace and Freedom meetings on Tuesday (the integrated political wing of the Black Panther Movement), and Jimmy Reid and his gang for the remainder of the week. Jimmy who? Jimmy Reid was a small-town street hustler, who, in response to the

Movement, organized a group of marginal young men into a wanna-be Black Panther organization. For reasons never completely clear, Jimmy was unable to obtain sanctioning by the real Black Panther Party, whose main office for the region was in Chicago, headed up by a dynamic young man named Mark Hampton. Jimmy's group literally "shared office space" with me and the WSSC staff, and there were times when it was unclear whether Jimmy or I was the "real" director.

I learned so much about the conversion process by observing Jimmy and his crew. At the OBAC meetings and on the campus of nearby Northwestern University, I had already made note of the conversion thrust among the black middle class and upwardly mobile black working class. Now, with Jimmy and company, I watched men of the street, who, seemingly destined for prison, found themselves being transformed by their blackness, if only for a fleeting moment, into focused, dedicated, and totally committed persons. Through their actions I saw that black identity conversion transcended social class. Here were scores of Malcolm Littles, who only yesterday were caught up in hustles and crimes that victimized other blacks, finding rejuvenation through blackness. Yes, much of their paramilitary routine had an unintended Keystone Cops quality to it, in that how on earth could a rag-tag group of men, untrained in warfare, "protect" the black community? WSSC was situated on Church Street, and it would probably take the police two seconds to blow us all away. But it was deeply moving to see these young men in their finest hour, positioned at different points in and around the building, guns loaded and drawn, stationed at windows and a few perched on the roof, waiting in silence to die. The infamous raid on the Chicago headquarters of the Panther Party was in progress, and as soon as the news hit the street, Jimmy and his men became convinced that they would soon be target practice for the Evanston police. It never happened, and within months, Jimmy's group disbanded and all returned to their old ways. For me, it was another lesson learned. Identity must be complemented by material change or else one is forced to fall back on a survival mode. Jimmy himself was found shot to death, assassination style, near the railroad tracks in Evanston. There were so many rumors floating around about his identity, including one that said he was an informant. Be that as it may, I don't think I was totally fooled by Jimmy, for I saw him when he was authentic and had meaning.

My stint as Director of West Side Service Center paralleled my Immersion-Emersion experience. It became clear that I did not have the competencies to become a long-term, street-level community activist and organizer. Although I was a misfit as a community leader, everyone, including Jimmy Reid and a cluster of black college students from Northwestern University, encouraged me to find my calling and stay connected to the Movement. Everyone said I seemed to have a handle on community planning and that drew me to a program in urban planning at an upstate university near Albany, New York. I was admitted and ready to go when I got a call from Badi. By now he was a Fulbright Scholar at Princeton University, and Princeton was about to launch a program in Afro-American Studies. A new program Chair was soon to arrive on campus, but there was also need for an assistant to the Chair, and Badi practically demanded that I accept the position. I left for Princeton in late Summer 1969.

By now the media were constantly presenting negative and grotesque images of black militants that suggested they were angry to the point of mental illness. There was the frequent juxtaposition of "good and responsible" Negroes with "angry and irrational" militants. I began to play back my Nigrescence interpretation of conversion to Badi and my new Princeton associates and countered that the media and community were getting it all wrong. We, black people, were going through a process, and it involved stages, and yes, anger was an important part of it all, but militancy was but a passing stage, not an identity unto itself. This rites-of-passage process seemed to apply to black women as well as black men. It was inevitable that Badi and the folks at Princeton would both encourage and challenge me to write about my ideas, and in the face of such a charge, I was petrified. The thought of actually writing something, for public consumption, was intimidating. True, Hoyt Fuller at *Negro Digest* had encouraged me to think of his journal should I find written expression for my ideas, but no one in my family and none of my close kin or friends had ever published anything! And then something happened to make it all possible.

Joe and Daphne Moore said there was someone I had to meet because we would make a perfect match. I would eventually marry the person they had in mind, but perfect match is not how we would describe ourselves. In fact, for the first 15 years, our stormy marriage was often dysfunctional, and we nearly destroyed ourselves and the spirit of our only child. We separated for 5 years, and at the point of filing for a divorce we reversed course and began to court each other. We remain husband and wife (28 years of marriage), but it seems like a new relationship, a second marriage. We feel most fortunate, because in the best turn of events we have also been reunited with our daughter. Most of this family chaos and reintegration took place long after my partner and I achieved what could only be called advanced states of black consciousness. The difficulties in reaching marital bliss, like the suicide of my dear friend Phillip White, or the drug addiction of a former Movement associate, brought me face to face with the reality that, as important as black consciousness is, it does not address or predict all that must be accomplished by blacks or, for that matter, any group of human beings over the course of a lifetime. At another point in my career, I would parlay such insights into the distinction between "PI" and "RGO," or the personal identity domain of the self-concept as differentiated from the social identity, group identity, or reference group orientation domain. There were many positive human encounters that drove home the same understanding, but, as is often the case, it remains for the horrific and tragic to finally capture one's attention.

Joe and Daphne arranged for me to meet one Dawn Monique Jackson, Princeton's new Assistant Director of Admissions, during a lunch period on the Princeton campus. Joe spotted her from across the room, giving me a full 45 seconds to watch Dawn wind her way toward our table. She was the Second Coming of Angela Davis, only four times as beautiful. Her gigantic Afro slightly bounced as she walked, and her long, unblemished brown neck supported a picturesque face formed by both her Potawatomi and African roots. It was the early 1970s and short dresses were the rage, and this nearly 6-foot-tall creature wore a green-turquoise, polished cotton dress from which glided the most heavenly legs. This was not going to be easy, for I was a virgin until my mid-20s, and though I often could think about nothing else but women and sex, the Movement and blackness improved none of my awkward social skills. Much to my relief, we somehow talked and talked and talked, and I do not recall when the lunch date came to an end.

Soon thereafter, Dawn was with me on another occasion when Badi and his friends challenged me to "put in writing" my stages concept. Dawn could sense my insecurity and, whispering in my ear, offered to help. On our next date, we went to her office in the basement of Nassau Hall, and she typed as I talked through my ideas. The image of people "confessing" at OBAC helped shape the Pre-Encounter Stage, the rage and activism of Jimmy Reid and the students at Northwestern informed the dynamics of the Immersion-Emersion Stage, the rock steadiness, relaxed confidence, and insightfulness of Hoyt Fuller's image (recall, he was the editor of *Negro Digest*) gave hint of the Internalization Stage, and the men and women who authored the books I was, by now, devouring at an amazing pace, such as Carter G. Woodson, W. E. B. Dubois, and Margaret Just Butcher, shed light on the meaning of sustained identity commitment (Internalization-Commitment Stage). My experiences as a clinical psychologist, my observation of the system changes that rocked the hospital where I completed my internship, my struggle with religious de-conversion, and, of course, the mapping of my own personal conversion into blackness all came together to help frame a little essay that has brought me countless blessings and a certain degree of fame. On paper, it was no longer just an autobiographical commentary, it was an attempt to summarize my mental notes on all the women and men I had observed, the actions I had witnessed, and the commentaries I had absorbed from the media, articles, and countless books on the black experience.

Around this time, Badi Foster and fellow Princeton graduate student Vernon Dixon landed a contract with Little, Brown for a book titled *Beyond Black or White*. As the book was in process, I began to interact with William S. Hall. Hall, who is one of America's most accomplished black psychologists, was in the early stages of his career. When I discussed my ideas with him, Hall immediately brainstormed about empirical strategies for testing the model. It is not necessary to go into all the details, but we created a list of short statements that captured various aspects of each stage, for use in a

Q-sort experiment. The items for this Q-sort would eventually be used by Thomas Parham and Janet Helms to fashion the early version of the RIAS (Racial Identity Attitude Scale), the most important and heavily used scale in the study of Nigrescence. As Bill was working on his experiments, I became fearful that somehow my contribution would be lost, even though the plans called for me to be the second author for one publication and the third author for another. Consequently, I wrote a second version of the model and submitted it to my acquaintance, Hoyt Fuller. His journal had recently gone through an identity change of sorts and was now called *Black World* rather than *Negro Digest*. Fuller is one of the unsung heroic figures from the 1960s. He was an exemplar of Stage 4 and 5 behavior, and he worked tirelessly to publish new black poets, essayists, and visionaries. Any number of future giants in the emerging field of black studies found their initial acceptance in Fuller's journal. John Johnson, the owner and publisher of *Ebony*, *Tan* and *Black World*, wanted the journal to remain a sorry imitation of *Reader's Digest*, but Hoyt pushed for a more aggressive, timely publication that gave voice to the new black radicals. As the heat of the Black Movement intensified, Johnson came under increasing pressure to shut *Black World* down, and eventually he did. Hoyt tried to resurrect the journal from his new base in Atlanta, but due to undercapitalization only a few issues of *First World* were produced. Then, suddenly, at the relatively tender age of 55, Fuller died of a massive stroke. At the memorial held for him in Atlanta on May 16, 1981, the witnesses included James Baldwin, Toni Cade Bambara, Gwendolyn Brooks, Howard Dodson, Jeff Donaldson, Mari Evans, George Kent, Richard Long, Haki Madhubuti, Sonia Sanchez, James Turner, and others.

Fuller accepted the piece, and it was published in the July 1971 issue of *Black World*. When I received my copy, I went into a room, closed the door, and sat down. It was a little journal, measuring only 5½ by 7½ inches. At the top of the cover were 2-inch-high bold letters hawking the journal's name. In small print just below the title was the date (July 1971), signification that it was a Johnson Publication, and the price (50 cents). The cover showed the drawing of a baritone saxophone with a huge, translucent red "x" drawn across it, symbolic of the title of the lead article, "The Ban on Black Music," by Imamau Amiri Baraka. Small print in the right lower quadrant called attention to three additional bylines, the first of which stated "Perspective on History," followed by the title of my article. Baraka's article began on page 4, and then as I flipped the pages I came to the opening page of my work. It read "The Negro-to-Black Conversion Experience: Toward a Psychology of Black Liberation," followed by my name. The article ended with my preferred salutation: Harambee and Love. At the very bottom of the last page, my status as a Princeton graduate student was recorded along with this note: "This is Mr. Cross' first published work." In my mind's eye, I read this note differently: "Mr. Cross is the only child of Bill and Margaret Cross to attend college, and this is the first work ever published by any member of their family." I celebrated the moment as much from a family perspective as from a personal one.

What should have been my first publication, the version for the Dixon-Foster text, appeared in late December 1971, but it is seldom referenced. Dr. Hall's empirical study involving the administration of his Q-sort items was published in 1972, and sure enough, a few publications referencing this work refer to the model as the Hall-Cross Model. As the *Black World* version took hold, I ceased to worry about intellectual ownership of the model, with one exception. I was once accused by a key figure in the Black Psychology Movement of having stolen his ideas, but nothing ever came of his ramblings. Had we gone to court, I still had the crude typed version that Dawn had produced years ago in the basement of Nassau Hall; I originally cherished it for romantic reasons, but after the accusation, I filed it for historical and possible litigious purposes.

The original 1971 essay was akin to a report from the field on the black identity dynamics associated with the black power phase of the overall black movement, as gleaned from the perspective of a participant observer. No references were listed because there were none, although I do mention Joseph White's name in the first paragraph and that of Frantz Fanon in the second. I wrote the model before the end of my first term at Princeton and had not undertaken a literature search to discover the connectedness of my ideas with those to be found in the extant literature. This soon changed as Bill Hall asked that I complete the literature review section for his Q-sort study, which we published jointly in 1972. My report to Dr. Hall was almost 50 pages, and he used but a fraction of the material. This was just as well, for I was then free to incorporate the greater portion of the review in the first section of my dissertation. Thereafter, all my publications have been heavily referenced.

THE AFRICANA EXPERIENCE AND *SHADES OF BLACK*

While employed as Director of West Side Service Center, the period of my Immersion-Emersion phase, I was befriended by a number of people, including a handful of black graduate students from Northwestern University. Eric Perkins has since become an accomplished administrator in education, John Higginson is a Professor of African History at U Mass, and the person who took the most interest in my development, James Turner, became one of the pioneers of the Black Studies Movement. Turner's vision led to the establishment of the Africana Studies and Research Center at Cornell University in upstate New York (Ithaca). Turner kept track of my progress at Princeton and hired me on a part-time basis to see how I might fit in the Center. Portions of the data for both my master's and dissertation research were collected at Cornell, and in Summer 1973, I joined the faculty on a full-time basis as an Assistant Professor. So motivated was I to participate in the Black Studies Movement that I never interviewed at another institution. Besides Turner and my newfound colleagues at the Center, Cornell was also home to A. Wade Boykin, who, at the time of this writing, is Chair of the Department of Psychology at Howard University. Over the long hall, the Center provided a place to grow conceptually and theoretically, while my emergent close relationship with Boykin linked me to the empirical wing of the Association of Black Psychologists. In point of fact, I have produced few empirical studies, but my theoretical and interpretive works have been the basis of countless experiments. I have always presented my ideas in conceptual terms that are readily subject to experimental operationalization. This quality of my writing began at Princeton, but it was reinforced through my association with Boykin and the cluster of black scholars who established and ran a series of conferences known as "The Empirical Conference on Black Psychology." The scholars linked to the Conference read like a list of who's who in Black Psychology: Harriette and John McAdoo, A. J. Franklin, James Jackson, Leahcim Semaj, Reginal Jones, Charles Thomas, Hector Jones, Philip Bowman, Katherine Berlew, Vonnie McLoyd, Robert Guthrie, and many others.

I began the Cornell experience as a "social experimental psychologist" and left the Africana Center, some 21 years later, having been transformed into a cultural psychologist. As a cultural psychologist, my work examines the cultural, historical, and economic forces shaping human development and everyday psychological functioning in general, and black identity development and functioning in particular. This shift from traditional to cultural was traversed by nearly anyone with a long-term association at the Africana Center. At Cornell, James Turner gathered together two cohorts of scholars. The first included young Turks, fresh out of graduate school, who, while trained in a particular discipline, showed promise, at least in Turner's eyes, for becoming more interdisciplinary inclined. To nudge us along, Turner also hired established role models such as dramatist Bill Branch, literary scholar Eleanor Traylor, John H. Clark, and "Dr. Ben" (e.g., Y. Ben-Jochannan). The combinations were explosive, and life at the Center was not always easy, but in the long run, the Center's climate pressed each of us to transcend our narrow disciplinary perspectives and grasp the bigger picture. For example, as a psychologist, I was expected not simply to expose students to the traditional psychological literature but to show the links between black psychological functioning and economic trends, historical dynamics, and cultural patterns. As a faculty, we shared each other's papers and challenged our respective disciplinary assumptions. It was not enough for me to explicate black performance on such-and-such psychological measures, I also had to address how, in the aftermath of the Civil War, former slaves moved quickly to establish schools, churches, and a broader, organized community. What psychological forces, in part, made such actions and achievements possible for a people only recently jettisoned from the ravages of slavery?

Shades of Black is, in many ways, a tribute to my experiences at the Center, for it is as much a sociological, historical, and cultural treatise on black identity development and change as it is a psychological one. After 15 years at the Center, I was prepared to argue a radical reinterpretation of black identity. While playing pool with Henry Louis Gates, Jr., I reviewed some of my ideas and he startled me by saying "Well, why don't you write a book?" I glibly stated that was my plan, but Gates sensed both my passion for my ideas and my insecurity about writing a text. He told me he had access to a publisher and that if I was "really" serious he could help make it happen. With that, I no longer had an excuse because in short order Gates produced a book contract. Gates was at Cornell and the Africana Center for only a brief period, but he was like a firestorm, and everywhere he went, he made things happen. By the time I nearly completed the work, my confidence had expanded considerably, and through the assistance of Robert L. Harris, a historian at the Center, I was introduced to a senior editor, Janet M. Francendese, at Temple University Press (TUP). Gates was very gracious and helped cancel the other contract, clearing the way for my work to be published by TUP in 1991.

Shades of Black was my attempt to recenter the discourse on black psychological functioning from that of negativity, self-hatred, and pathology onto a new nexus of identity variability and transformation. In the new scheme, self-hatred would be given its due, but primarily as a fractional component. I wanted to demonstrate a more "normative and positive" black psychology through logical, rational, and well-documented arguments, readily subject to empirical exploration. This meant showing that, aside from the unique psychology of the so-called underclass (working-age blacks out of the workforce for a protracted period of time), blacks have more often than not been able to achieve adequate levels of psychological functioning and identity development. As an important corollary of the first point, it was also necessary to show that only a fraction of black people has ever succumbed to outright self-hatred, despite segregation, racism, and oppression. That is to say, with the exception of underclass dynamics, self-hatred is a minor, not central, theme in the everyday life of most black people. I argued that personality and self-concept variability is easily found in the black community, as are ideological differences; consequently, it is impossible to discuss black identity "as if" it represented but one profile, one identity "type," or a singular personality configuration. I further reasoned that black variability on self-concept and personality measures reflect the multiple pathways blacks have come to chart in the achievement of personal psychological happiness and well-being. From this perspective, ideological and identity variability shows that blacks do not share a single definition of what it means to be black, nor are they in agreement on what it means to live the good black life. I even suggested that for some blacks, having a racial-cultural identity is not important to their everyday existence, despite its significance for the vast majority of blacks. In grafting this new perspective, I discovered major shortcomings in my original Nigrescence Model; consequently, the second part of *Shades of Black* presents a revision of my original 1971 Negro-to-Black Conversion Model.

A FINAL NOTE OF THANKS

By the time this volume comes to print, I will have celebrated my 61st birthday, and the end of my career is just above the horizon. It has been 29 years since the publication of the Negro-to-Black Model, yet scholars and students continue to find value and interest in the Nigrescence concept. If every person has 15 seconds of fame, I am very grateful for what has extended to perhaps a minute or two. It is little known that by the mid-1970s I felt pressure from some peers to "move" on to fresher intellectual terrain. In my moment of doubt, others stepped in to show that Nigrescence is an omnipresent theme in everyday black life. Today, it is a daunting task to conduct a thorough literature review of the Nigrescence literature, as so many have made it the focus of their work. As others extend the concept beyond the reach of my competencies, I nevertheless have benefited by being prominently referenced in their work. For good or bad, the academic world rewards persons who are repeatedly referenced by other scholars; thus, many of you may not be aware of the number of good things your work has helped put on my plate. I, however, am keenly aware and I feel the need to say thank-you. I want to thank the following people for taking Nigrescence Theory seriously—for critiquing it, embracing it, testing it, and in more instances than not, expanding it beyond my expectations and capabilities: Beverly Vandiver, Frank Worrell, Thomas Parham, Janet Helms, Jerome Taylor, the late Jake Milliones, Margaret Spencer, Robert Carter, Janet Swim, Joseph Ponterotto, Allen Ivey, Beverly Tatum, Gerald Jackson, Lee Stokes, Bailey Jackson, Rita Hardiman, Urie Bronfenbrenner, Mon Cochran, James Turner, Emily Smith, Robert Sellers, Linda Clark-Strauss, Peony Fhagen-Smith, Leon Caldwell, Paul Pedersen, Donald B. Pope-Davis, William S. Hall, Milton and Janet Bennett, Lee Knefelkamp, Bobbi Schaetti, Lauri Hyers, James Jones, Robert Sellers, Tuere Binta Cross, Terrell Jones, Randy Weston, Maurianne Adams, Leon Caldwell, James A. Banks, Joe White, A. J. Franklin & Nancy Boyd-Franklin, Allyson Pimentel, Kevin Cokley, and Howard Stevenson. This list is incomplete, and it seems to grow a little each month.

Harambee and Love.

RELEVANT PUBLICATIONS

Cross, W. E., Jr. (1971, July). The Negro-to-Black conversion experience. *Black World*, pp. 13-27.

Cross, W. E., Jr. (1991). *Shades of Black: Diversity in African-American identity*. Philadelphia: Temple University Press.

Cross, W. E., Jr. (1995). The psychology of Nigrescence: Revising the Cross model. In J. G. Ponterotto, J. M. Casas, L. A. Suzuki, & C. M. Alexander (Eds.), *Handbook of multicultural counseling* (pp. 93-122). Thousand Oaks, CA: Sage.

Cross, W. E., Jr., & Strauss, L. (1998). The everyday function of black identity. In J. K. Swim & C. Stangor (Eds.), *Prejudice: The target's perspective* (pp. 268-279). New York: Academic Press.

Cross, W. E., Jr., Strauss, L., & Fhagen-Smith, P. E. (1999). African American identity development across the lifespan: Educational implications. In R. H. Sheets & E. R. Hollins (Eds.), *Racial and ethnic identity in school practices: Aspects of human development* (pp. 29-47). Mahwah, NJ: Lawrence Erlbaum.

Correspondence regarding this chapter may be sent to William E. Cross, Jr., Department of Psychology: Social-Personality Program, Graduate Center, City University of New York, 6th Floor, Office 6301.11, 365 Fifth Avenue, New York, NY 10016-4309 (e-mail address: wcross@gc.cuny.edu).

Chapter 5

SURVIVING
MONOCULTURALISM AND RACISM

A Personal and Professional Journey

DERALD WING SUE

THROUGHOUT MY LIFE, I have been constantly reminded that my racial and cultural heritage are quite different from many in this society. Some of these reminders have been quite pleasant and validating; many, however, serve to invalidate, diminish, and strike at the core of my racial identity. As a person of color, I have been exposed to prejudice, stereotyping, and discrimination. Surviving monoculturalism and racism has helped shape not only my personal identity but my professional one as well. In this chapter, I would like to share with you some of the lessons I have learned about prejudice and discrimination, especially as it relates to growing up culturally different in a predominantly monocultural society.

BEING DIFFERENT
IN A MONOCULTURAL SOCIETY

- My first recollections of racial taunting occurred to me when our family moved to the southeast district of Portland, Oregon, a predominantly White community. Prior to moving, we lived in Chinatown where my brothers and I attended Chinese schools. I recall my first day at the new school.

AUTHOR'S NOTE: This chapter is based on the 1999 Presidential Address given to the Society for the Psychological Study of Ethnic Minority Issues (Division 45 of The American Psychological Association) in Boston, Massachusetts, August 1999.

During the recess and lunch hours, groups of White students would encircle me, calling me a "Chink" or "Chinaman," pull the edges of their eyes back to make them slanted, and make strange sounds (OOAAH YEEEEE) which they thought was how we spoke. Although this experience was most painful and humiliating, I was soon to experience a more devastating one.

• I was standing in front of my third-grade classroom speaking to my brother Stan in Chinese. The teacher stepped out to close the classroom door when she overheard our conversation. Giving me a disapproving look, she turned to me and stated, "Derald, you're in America! When you're in America you speak English. Get into the room now." Words cannot describe the shame and humiliation I felt. What had I done wrong? Why was speaking Chinese bad? The feeling of shame was magnified because it came from a teacher, a role viewed with considerable respect by Chinese culture. When I returned home that afternoon, my mother spoke to me in Cantonese. I remember being curt with her and stating angrily that I never wanted to speak Chinese again because that was the reason why people wouldn't accept us.

At the time of the incidents, I could not fully understand the meaning and impact they had on me. All I discerned was that being different was undesirable. It led me to conclude that these differences were seen as "bad," "deficits," and something to be avoided. As a result, I tried my best to become invisible and/or to blend in with everyone else. Further, when you realize that language is the carrier of one's culture and when one is made to feel ashamed of his/her own language, it is little wonder that many persons of color grow up feeling there is something wrong with them. These early experiences, however, have taught me two valuable lessons that now form the basis of my work.

Lesson 1

Monolingualism and monoculturalism are valued in this society. People who differ in race, culture, and ethnicity are constantly given messages that they are "deviant" and "abnormal." Later in life as I began to study psychology and human behavior, I came to realize that "ethnocentric monoculturalism" was an extremely powerful, insidious, and pervasive force that was institutionalized in all aspects of U.S. society. In our profession of psychology, for example, I have found that the standards of practice and codes of ethics for psychologists are culture-bound and that they unjustly portray racial/ethnic minority cultural values as unhealthy and potentially abnormal. Take, for example, Asian American culture, which values collectivism and the notion of interdependence, where the psychosocial unit of identity resides with the family, group, or collective society. At the other extreme are Western values of individualism, independence, and the separation of the self. Most persons of color, because of their collectivistic orientation, may be perceived by Western standards as dependent, immature, and unhealthily enmeshed in the family.

Lesson 2

Societal pressures for conformance, assimilation, and acculturation (melting pot myth) can do great harm to the culturally different in our society. It may lead to seeing one's physical, behavioral, social, and cultural characteristics as a handicap to be overcome, something to be ashamed of, or something to be denied, and it may lead to negative racial/cultural attitudes, feelings, and behaviors. This was certainly true for me during my early years where I yearned to be either invisible or tried to behave "White" in order to gain acceptance from my schoolmates or peers. I tried to dissociate myself from the Chinese community, prided myself in "speaking good English," and worked out with weights constantly to combat the image of the "weak and frail" Chinese characters portrayed on television.

STEREOTYPES AND PSYCHOLOGICAL HARM

- As a freshman entering Washington High School, I was assigned a counselor, Mr. Knutsen, a well-respected math-science teacher. During the second week of class, he called me into his office and advised me to take a sophomore honors course in physics. Mr. Knutsen stated that he had looked at my past school records and was going to make an exception in having the first freshman ever to take the experimental science course. While I felt flattered, I was also very apprehensive about my ability to compete against advanced sophomore students. Noticing my hesitation, Mr. Knutsen turned to me and said, "Derald, I know you're worried about whether you can handle the course. I want you to know that I have faith in you. You won't have any trouble because *you people are good at that!"*

  I remember my conflicted feelings: grateful to the counselor for his desire to help me and yet strangely uncomfortable. For some reason, I felt trapped. It was only years later that I realized the basis of these feelings. Mr. Knutsen harbored strong stereotypes of Asian Americans: He perceived us as good with numbers and good in the sciences and technology; I was later to discover that he also believed Asians to be "poor in people relationships," "inarticulate," and to "make poor managers." For many years I believed these stereotypes about myself. Were it not for an opposing experience in college, I might today be an unhappy physicist or chemist.

Lesson 3

The power of preconceived notions, images, and stereotypes may trap and track individuals into directions not of their own choosing. Furthermore, victims of pervasive stereotyping may come to believe in them. Throughout high school and most of my college years, I avoided classes in humanities and social sciences because I truly believed I could not handle "people oriented" courses. It was only late in my junior year of college that graduation requirements forced me to take several psychology and anthropology courses. To my surprise, I found them not only fascinating but received excellent grades and encouragement from my psychology professor. As a result, the image I possessed as being socially inept, withdrawn, and unable to understand people began to crumble. I changed my major to psychology and have never regretted that decision. Even though my own personal outcome was a positive one, I often wonder how many youngsters of color are bombarded with false images of themselves, tracked into dead-end career paths, or drop out of the system altogether because they are not given a fair chance or have been victimized by a self-fulfilling prophesy.

GOOD INTENTIONS AND THE INVISIBILITY OF RACISM

Lesson 4

Even the most well-intentioned teacher, counselor, or person inherits racial biases. No one is immune from inheriting the racial prejudices of his or her forebears. Since Euro-Americans are products of their cultural conditioning, they are often socialized into oppressor roles. In many ways, they are also victims. My many experiences with White folks make me realize that they were not born into this society with a conscious desire to be bigoted or racist. My counselor, Mr. Knutsen, was not a mean and evil person intent upon harming me or any other person of color. He was not consciously aware of the stereotypes he harbored, nor was he aware of the negative consequences it might have had on me. Indeed, what makes this situation so problematic was that Mr. Knutsen meant well, his intention to help me was honorable, and he spent extra time and effort to bend the rules to "benefit me." This is precisely why it is difficult getting White folks to realize that their attitudes, beliefs, and behaviors may oppress and hurt others. Because they experience themselves as moral, decent, and fair-minded individuals, they find it intolerable to view themselves as oppressors.

MICRO-INVALIDATIONS AND MICRO-ASSAULTS

- Arriving in Washington to keynote a conference, I hailed a taxi at the airport. The driver started an analysis of the controversial outcome of the Holyfield-Tyson heavyweight fight the day before. We were engaged in a very interesting discussion when he made an offhand comment: "You know, you speak excellent English."

   Later that day, after finishing my keynote address before a large primarily White audience, several attendees approached me to ask questions and make comments. One White women asked me, "Where were you born?" I replied, "Portland, Oregon." She smiled and restated her question. "No, no, I mean, where were you really born . . . what country?" I answered, "The United States." She looked embarrassed and quickly left the podium.

   That evening, I went to dinner with a White colleague, Dave, whom I considered an enlightened friend. As we entered the restaurant, the hostess seemed to stare past me, despite the fact that I was at the front of the line. She chose to ask Dave, who was behind me, "How many for dinner?" I tried to tell myself that she might have mistaken me as part of the party who had entered the restaurant just ahead of us. As we were seated, the waiter brought our menus to the table and placed the wine list on the plate of my companion. Dave was asked to select the wine and allowed the honor of tasting it first. All this was done in a very matter-of-fact manner, but it was clear the waiter considered Dave the person in charge. Later that evening, I leaned over to Dave and commented about what had happened. To my chagrin, Dave, in a chiding tone, said, "Derald, don't be so oversensitive."

Lesson 5

People of color grow up in a society that constantly invalidates them. The overt and intentional acts of bias and discrimination can greatly damage both the psyche and the physical health of minorities, but it is the daily slights, invalidations, and assaults that may in the long run prove much more harmful. As an Asian American, I continue to be viewed as an alien in my own land. Both the taxi driver and the conference attendee were probably "good people" who either meant to compliment me and/or were curious about me, but their comments and questions reveal a biased mind-set: Only White, blue-eyed people and/or those who fit a certain image are considered "real Americans." All others who are of a different color are perceived as not "real citizens" of this country. Admonitions such as "if you don't like it here, go back to _____ [China, Mexico, Africa, etc.]" reveal ethnocentrism of the most damaging kind. These slights represent what is called "micro-assaults." Such assaults occur when people of color are perceived as aliens in their own land, when their physical, linguistic, racial, or cultural differences are considered undesirable or deviant, when their experiential reality is invalidated, or when persons of color are accused of being overly sensitive and paranoid for raising issues of potential bias. Most racial/ethnic minority groups have been exposed to many forms of prejudice, stereotyping, and discrimination; some are overt and deliberate, but most are unintentional "micro-assaults." This term refers to individual acts that alone may appear quite benign or of low impact, but collectively, over an extended period of time, can do much psychological harm to marginalized groups in our society.

OVERT RACISM AND MACRO-ASSAULTS

- On December 15, 1995, my family and I were subjected to one of the most horrendous experiences of our lives. The police in our city obtained a search warrant for our home, broke down the front door, and claimed to have recovered stolen city equipment. They accused my 19-year-old son, who was attending USC at the time of the incident, of taking the equipment without their knowledge or permission. Upon his return from college, he was

arrested on two felony counts and jailed until bail could be arranged. From
the time of his arrest until the dismissal of the charges, we were subjected to
continual delays in setting a trial date and forced to appear in court no less
than nine times. Hoping that my son would plead guilty, the DA's office reduced the charges to misdemeanors. When this did not work, they offered to
drop the charges in return for financial compensation. They finally offered
to dismiss the charges in return for only 10 days of community service. We
refused all offers.

I am not a naive person and certainly not a newcomer to prejudice and
racism. Yet when this incident occurred, I hoped that the charges were the
result of a monumental misunderstanding that could be quickly clarified.
However, the severity of the police actions in breaking down our door and
the many contradictory facts that were uncovered made such a belief difficult to entertain. After eliminating every possible reason for their actions,
we concluded that it smacked of racism and anti-Asian sentiment.

Lesson 6

Racism is most likely expressed against individuals who violate the
normative structures of society and who challenge the system. Let me
briefly outline the basis of this lesson.

My family and I reside in a city that is predominantly White; Asian
Americans are the largest racial/ethnic minority group, comprising 15% of
the general population and 20% of the public schools' enrollment. The
community is very affluent and conservative, with minimal knowledge or
awareness of diversity and multicultural issues. My wife and I have been
very active in the community, helped form the City Asian American Club,
did pro bono work for the schools on multicultural education, sponsored
community forums on racism, voiced our concerns in the past about police
harassment of Asian and African American youths in the community, and
spoke against the failed formation of the Caucasian Students Union at the
high school. As a result, these activities made us highly visible in the community and potential targets of a backlash.

It became evident that my son had been set up for the sequence of
events that followed. Prior to his attending college, he was the volunteer
emergency coordinator for the city and worked closely with the fire and police departments. His technical knowledge was very high and he often re-
paired and serviced ham radios and other communication equipment
owned by the city. This equipment was frequently brought over by the fire
department; they knew we possessed them. When the break-in and arrest
occurred, we were left with many questions.

First, why didn't representatives of the fire or police departments simply pick up the phone and ask for the return of the equipment? Why did the
police choose such extreme measures to intrude into the home of a family
known in the community and certainly known by both departments? According to a judge-neighbor, the forced entry into someone's home is only
done when drugs are involved (which can be flushed down the toilet or

destroyed easily) or if there is clear and imminent danger to someone. Did the police believe we would flush ham radio equipment down the toilet? When the police found that no one was at home, why did they choose to break down our door? Couldn't they have waited for us to return or call us before coming to our home? Do the police always break down doors when they have a search warrant?

Second, we later discovered that false statements had been made. For example, fire department personnel stated that policy forbids the possession of emergency equipment by a private citizen. If it was against department policy, why did the firemen violate their own rules? Additionally, some of our neighbors were willing to testify that they witnessed fire trucks carrying the equipment over. Why did the fire department personnel misrepresent the situation?

The possible answers to these questions are quite disturbing. For example, many of our friends have asked whether such intrusive police actions would have been carried out against a White family. Were we being targeted because of our work in the community? Was this a not-too-subtle message being sent to the Asian American community? While I would never wish such an experience on any family, we have come away from this incident with new insights.

First, my family has always known that our minority status in this society subjects us to various forms of prejudicial actions and stereotypes. Yet to work for social justice and equity and to challenge the prevailing biased practices of a community can invite retaliation of the most extreme kind. It is important for all of us to be prepared and to realize that working for social justice is not an easy task and can take an awesome toll.

Second, fighting racism requires the help and support of many. We could never have survived this terrible ordeal without neighbors, relatives, friends, and colleagues stepping forward. Within weeks of the incident, letters and calls on our behalf from our pastor, the superintendent of public schools, the city Asian American Club, and other neighbors went to both the mayor's and the district attorney's office. Especially effective were letters from my colleagues representing the Asian American Psychological Association, the Association of Black Psychologists, the Rainbow Coalition, and the Society for the Psychological Study of Ethnic Minority Issues. I am especially grateful not only for their moral support but also the strong letters denouncing the police actions and questioning whether racism was involved.

Third, unfortunately, fighting racism also requires the financial resources to hire the best help possible. Directly after the breaking down of our door and prior to my son's arrest, we were fortunate to hire a nationally prominent African American civil rights attorney who had represented Rodney King. He, in turn, quickly placed one of his private investigators on the case and was able to obtain statements from potential witnesses. With these actions, we communicated strongly to the city that we had the financial resources to push forward and were willing to risk going to court. In addition, the reputation of our attorney on matters of civil rights was obviously unsettling to the city.

Fourth, Asian Americans face a peculiar situation not often shared by their African American counterparts. The perception that many have of our group is that we are "quiet," "passive," "won't rock the boat," and "avoid the limelight." While many of our cultural values related to subtlety, indirectness, and working toward consensus are extremely valuable attributes in many situations, it may invite retaliation in a strange sort of way. I cannot prove it, but I believe that when the police officers arrived at our home they were consciously or unconsciously influenced by this stereotype and took personal liberties in breaking down our door.

Finally, fighting racism requires *not taking* the easy way out. It would have been much simpler to have my son accept the 10 days of community service in exchange for dismissal of the charges. We would have avoided the large expenditure of financial resources and the many months of worry and anguish. We chose to fight because our son was innocent, because these actions had larger racial implications, and because we had the support of many.

COMBATING RACISM AND MONOCULTURALISM: DOING THE RIGHT THING

Because of these experiences, I have become keenly aware of the damaging consequences of racism, the widespread stereotypes about Asian Americans (good in math/sciences but poor in people relationships), how physical differences could be objects of scorn, how our culture and lifestyles are often equated with being non-normative, how minorities are often perceived as aliens in their own country, and how the system can be used to "hurt" or "intimidate" those who fight for social justice. Coping with monoculturalism and racism has helped shape not only my personal identity but has played a large part in my desire to study the causes, effects, and methods to ameliorate overt and covert forms of prejudice and discrimination. These experiences have made me aware of the great psychological toll that racism takes on persons of color. It can result in low self-esteem, feelings of rage, depression or hopelessness, anxiety, lowered school performance, health problems, and countless other negative life consequences. I often wondered what caused racism, why people were so intolerant of others, and what we could do to combat bigotry. These questions have been the focus of my research in the field of multicultural education and psychology.

When I was invited to testify before President Clinton's Race Advisory Board in 1998, I shared with them the results of my work on multicultural psychology and race relations. Among many of the points I made were the following:

- Bigotry and racism continue to be two of the most divisive forces in our society.

- The need to address issues of race, culture, and ethnicity has never been more urgent.

- Most citizens of this nation seem ill-equipped to deal with these topics.

- Racial legacies of the past continue to affect current policies and practices of the present, creating unfair disparities between racial/ethnic minority and Euro-American groups.

- Such inequities are often so deeply ingrained in American society that they are nearly invisible.

- The greatest challenge this nation faces is how we can become a multicultural society that values equal access and opportunity.

- Our greatest hope toward solving the problems of prejudice and discrimination lies in the field of *multicultural education.*

The challenge confronting our profession and the nation is not an easy one. It means major changes at the individual level where each and everyone of us (educator, student, employer, employee, law enforcement officer, etc.) needs to confront our biases and prejudices. It means major changes in our institutions and organizations (educational systems, business and industry, judicial system, law enforcement agencies, health care, etc.), where the current policies, practices, programs, and structures serve to deny equal access and opportunity to one group while unfairly benefitting another. It means major changes in our society where public policies that promote multiculturalism are instituted (affirmative action, bilingual education, legislation banning racial profiling, etc.) and those that block multiculturalism are eliminated.

I have also learned that our lives must become a "have to" in being constantly vigilant to manifestations of bias in ourselves and in people around us. While attending workshops and receiving continuing education on multiculturalism are helpful, we must take responsibility to initiate personal growth experiences in the real world. I am convinced that education and training programs must somehow build learning experiences for students that require personal growth through lived reality and experience. Eliminating bias and prejudice cannot be just an intellectual exercise.

In closing I would only remind all of us that race, culture, and ethnicity are functions of every person's development and not limited to "just minorities." As psychologists and educators, we need to recognize that culture is central to everything we do and that we are all representatives of our own cultures. Producing a multicultural society that values diversity is our greatest challenge. How we meet the challenge professionally will determine the viability and relevance of the educational field. How we meet the challenge as individual citizens will also foretell the legacy we leave our sons and daughters. Continuing to deny the importance of multiculturalism is to deny social reality itself. Let us meet the challenge honestly not only because it is good for our profession and our society but because *it is the right thing to do.*

RELEVANT PUBLICATIONS

Atkinson, D. R., Morten, G., & Sue, D. W. (1998). *Counseling American minorities.* Boston: McGraw-Hill.

Sue, D. W., Bingham, R. P., Porche-Burke, L., & Vasquez, M. (1999). The diversification of psychology: A multicultural revolution. *The American Psychologist, 54,* 1061-1069.

Sue, D. W., Carter, R. T., Casas, J. M., Fouad, N. A., Ivey, A. E., Jensen, M., LaFromboise, T., Manese, J. E., Ponterotto, J. G., & Vazquez-Nutall, E. (1998). *Multicultural counseling competencies: Individual and organizational development.* Thousand Oaks, CA: Sage.

Sue, D. W., Ivey, A. E., & Pedersen, P. B. (1996). *A theory of multicultural counseling and therapy.* Pacific Grove, CA: Brooks/Cole.

Sue, D. W., & Sue, D. (1999). *Counseling the culturally different: Theory and practice.* New York: John Wiley.

Correspondence regarding this chapter may be sent to Derald Wing Sue, California School of Professional Psychology, 1005 Atlantic Avenue, Alameda, CA 94501 (e-mail address: dwingsue@aol.com).

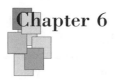

Chapter 6

REFLECTIONS OF A NONVISIBLE RACIAL/ETHNIC MINORITY

NADYA A. FOUAD

ROSIE PHILLIPS BINGHAM was elected Division 17's (Counseling Psychology) first African American president in 1998. Her presidential address was a wonderful call to the Division to strive to embrace diversity; she asserted that while exclusion may be easier, inclusion was better. At the end of her address, noting the changes she had witnessed in the Division, she mentioned that Division 17 had just elected its second woman of color. There was audible speculation in the audience: "Who is she talking about? I don't remember anyone of color running for president this year." Then, when it became clear that I had just been elected president-elect, I heard "But Nadya is White!" I received a number of questions about my ethnicity: What do I call myself? Am I a minority group member? Am I a woman of color, or am I a member of the majority culture? When do I decide to be "out" as a minority? I also received the challenge that because I can "pass" for White, I need to prove my commitment to cultural diversity much more explicitly than do more visible racial/ethnic minority group members.

The audience's reaction and my colleagues' subsequent questions and challenges captured for me the essential struggle that I have faced all my life: the incongruence between how others perceive me and how I perceive myself. I see myself as a racial/ethnic individual, but others view me as a member of the majority culture. I see myself as different from those around me, which informs everything I do. Others view me as a prototypic successful White woman, juggling work and family. I identify very strongly with my mother's Brazilian culture and call myself Hispanic but have been asked to justify why a White woman with an Arab surname can speak knowledgeably about Hispanics.

When Robert Carter began writing about visible racial/ethnic group members (VREGs) in the late 1980s, I wondered about the issues for *non*visible racial/ethnic group members. Clearly, I perceive myself as different from European American native-born individuals, but others perceive me as a member of a privileged majority culture. The incongruence has benefits and liabilities; it has also very much influenced my development both personally and professionally. At times, I have valued the incongruence; at other times, I have tried hard to reduce the perception that I am different from the norm. On the whole, though, my struggles with fitting in and being different have led me to be a counseling psychologist committed to studying culture. I am honored to have been asked to contribute to this section of the *Handbook* and have benefited from reflecting on this struggle. This chapter focuses on four themes that have led to that development: (a) when different is positive, (b) when different is negative, (c) the influence of multiple cultures, and (d) being a nonvisible minority.

WHEN DIFFERENT IS POSITIVE

I was born in a small town in Iowa (Ames). My mother came from Brazil and my father from Egypt to seek graduate degrees at the University of Iowa. They met, courted, and secretly married in 1953. They moved to Iowa State University in Ames for my father to pursue his doctorate in electrical engineering. My mother left her master's program when she discovered she was pregnant with me. I was born in 1955, a natural-born U.S. citizen with foreign parents.

Upon graduation, my father was obligated to return to Egypt and teach as a condition of his grant to study in the United States. I was 6 months old when we left Iowa and moved to Cairo. My earliest recollections are of a strong sense of connection to my father's extended family. I remember being treated as a special grandchild, and that different was good. In part, this difference was due to age; I was an affectionate little girl when my cousins were all difficult teenagers. But it was also due, I believed, to my father's special place in my grandmother's heart. He was the only one of her children to leave, and although he returned, he was living an altered life than she had expected for him. He had chosen his own wife, one who was not Egyptian or Moslem, and was following an occupational path that was not very lucrative in Egypt. Doting on me was a way for her to connect to him, and I loved it.

My grandmother had been raised at a time when the French occupied Egypt and the upper class went to French-speaking schools. She taught me French, and this was the beginning of a multilingual life. I spoke English at home with my parents, French with my grandmother, and Arabic with everyone else. I enjoyed having a language I shared just with my grandmother, and at that point in my life, being multilingual was good. My brother was born during this time, an Egyptian citizen.

My parents left Egypt in 1959 to spend a year in Brazil to be close to my mother's large extended family. While in Rio, my father received an offer to join the faculty at Iowa State in the Department of Electrical Engineering. We moved back to Ames, Iowa, in 1960. I would spend most of the next 15 years there, graduating from Ames High School and receiving my bachelor's degree from Iowa State.

In Ames, I was often uncomfortable about being different from everyone else. I spent lots of time wanting *not* to be different during my elementary grade years, but I was proud of having traveled and lived all over the world, even if I did not have strong memories of those times. I had such a strong sense of linkage with the families in Brazil and Egypt that at times I imagined strings running from Ames to Cairo and Rio connecting us. My parents, and especially my mother, strongly reinforced the notion that I was very special because of my unique background.

In 1969, when I was 13, we went for a two-year visit to the Philippine Islands, and in many ways this was a paradigm shift for my entire family. We were distinct from our friends in Ames because we were going to live overseas, and then when we got to the Philippines, we were unusual because we had come from Iowa. My father was working for the Ford Foundation at the University of the Philippines, and the other Ford Foundation families had set routines and ways of living that my parents chose not to follow, and that made us unique in a good way. Their convictions included a choice that we would not join a particular club because of its racist policies, so we joined a different club. Clearly, in this case, being different was associated with following principles of equity.

Two years later, in 1971, we returned to Ames. While my friends had been navigating middle school, I had traveled and had learned how to adapt to a different school system as well as an entirely new culture. I had learned that my language skills were valued and that my parents' background was an asset. Their international backgrounds attracted interesting people, and we had a wide range of friends and acquaintances. I no longer wanted to define my world by the boundaries drawn around Ames.

During high school, I knew I wanted to be a psychologist and knew graduate school would be competitive. I decided it would be good if I had a number of additional volunteer experiences and so volunteered for "Open Line," a crisis telephone program, as a junior. I tried hard to create a life for myself outside high school so that I would not simply be defined by those boundaries.

WHEN DIFFERENT IS NEGATIVE

Although I sometimes reveled in feeling special because of my unique background, there were many more times that I was uncomfortable when I did not fit in. I learned to speak Portuguese when we moved to Brazil from Egypt but refused to speak Arabic or French. When we moved back to the States and I entered kindergarten, I spoke English, refusing to speak Portuguese. I was intensely interested in "being American" and assimilated into mainstream small-town U.S. life. Being like everyone else was critical even when it meant trying to be—or act like—someone I was not.

There were painful memories, too, of times kids made fun of my name and called my brother names for his darker skin color and of inexplicable hurts that U.S. girls seem to inflict on each other for real or imagined reasons. For example, my third-grade year was several dark months characterized by events such as coming into the classroom and tripping over string put between my desk and the next one. Some girls had decided I was too foreign and so decided not to speak to me for most of the year. Just as suddenly, though, this meanness was over, with no explanation. From that, I took that being foreign was bad and also learned how quickly people could turn on you if they have reason to believe you are different. I was even more determined to try not to be different. I was ashamed of my mother's accent. In second grade, I tried to make her change her speech, even though I identified so closely with my mother that I told people I was Brazilian. Sometimes, my brother and I were like people in a zoo, when people would exclaim, "I've never met a real Brazilian-Egyptian before!" I saw my family through the eyes of the people around us and was not always proud of what they were seeing.

I was field dependent, with an inability to see beyond my immediate world. If we had not moved to the Philippines, I would have defined myself by my perceptions of "popular" and "normal." I was too concerned with fitting in and was more than willing to shape my aspirations by the relatively narrow, concrete things I could see in Ames. I wanted to be a waitress with a name tag on my blouse that said "Marilyn," and more than anything I wanted the black flat slip-on shoes sold at Woolworth's. This was the essence of "American" to me and, as it turned out, was the essence of lower-class aspirations to my mother, who was horrified. I never did get those shoes.

The most intense time for me of trying to fit in was when I went to college. I majored in psychology at Iowa State University. I was very much taken aback by the narrow perspective of many of the other students I met my first year there. This was perhaps the first time in my life that I encountered such parochial views of the world and had to answer questions about my "odd" background without the active support of my family. I met boys who said their parents would not let them date "one of you," which I did not entirely understand but knew it was not good. I struggled to fit in by acting a lot like the other students and denying parts of who I was. I cut classes, played down my academic accomplishments, and socialized with other students. I concluded that assuming leadership roles was the best way to fit in and be like everyone else, so I became a resident assistant my third year of college.

Perhaps the most extreme example of subverting myself to "fit in" occurred during my sophomore year when I began dating a boy I met in the dorm. We became fairly serious, even though we were mismatched in almost every respect. This relationship distressed nearly everyone who knew me. My boyfriend flunked out the fall of my junior year and decided to join the Navy. By this point, I realized I had enough credits to graduate from college. It made sense to graduate and apply to graduate schools so that I could be in school while he was in boot camp. I applied to only master's programs because he did not want to be "Mr. and Dr." My decision was an apology for being more successful than he was and for violating "my role" as a woman.

INFLUENCE OF MULTIPLE CULTURES

Looking back, it appalls me to think of anyone circumscribing another person's aspirations for such stereotypically gendered reasons. It is even more appalling that I agreed it was a reasonable request. I grew increasingly angry at the sexist expectations of my relationship when I went to graduate school and so ended it. I was accepted into the counseling psychology master's program at the University of Minnesota. It turned out that this decision was a major step in defining my professional and personal life. A year into the program I knew I did not have enough knowledge to be a competent therapist and wanted to go on for my doctorate. There are two programs in counseling psychology at the University of Minnesota, both of them with long and illustrious histories and legions of pioneering graduates. A strong identity as a counseling psychologist was formed and fostered there, with friendships that are still among my closest personal and professional relationships.

I began to study culture in graduate school and to understand the multiple cultures in which I had lived. I was a product of my father's Egyptian culture, my mother's Brazilian culture, and the third culture they created in our home. If both had been from the same culture, I am sure that my life would have more focused on their country of origin than it was. Although, for example, we have many rituals around Egyptian food, we celebrated U.S. holidays and traditions rather than those unique to Egypt or Brazil. My parents explicitly lived a life assimilated into the majority culture. They spoke English at home and became American citizens shortly after coming back to the States in 1960. They raised their children with traditional majority culture values to achieve high academic and occupational goals. My parents also instilled in us a passion for equity and a strong interest in intellectual and cross-cultural pursuits. Both my brother and I ended up applying our work in cross-cultural areas. He is an international tax lawyer, travels all over the world, and is multilingual. I have spent my career focusing on culture as a variable in counseling and particularly in vocational counseling and assessment.

I also lived much of my life in a fourth culture, that of a small college town in Iowa. In many ways, this was an idyllic childhood. I was loved, safe and secure. There are many aspects of this culture that are still with me, particularly an appreciation for small-town relationships and obligations. My husband and I are raising our three sons in a small town that is a suburb of Milwaukee, where the circles of their lives overlap and they see their friends at soccer and baseball games, at school, and at the grocery store. I also laugh a bit at myself, realizing that my impulse to bring a covered casserole to a new neighbor or a sick friend comes from my Iowa childhood.

I also was a girl in a sexist world, which constituted a very powerful culture. I was shaped by the messages I received about appropriate behavior for a girl. I was also shaped by my struggles against those messages, for most of them contradicted. I received strong messages about doing my best, about using my brains, about achieving. But it was not always clear how to go about achieving, for I learned very early to be ashamed when I was called ambitious, bossy, or strong. Then, too, I received strong messages about the importance of being a good mother, having a family, and taking care of others rather than myself.

My father is, of course, a product of his own culture, which is not particularly known for an egalitarian ethic. For example, he said, "Girls don't need science" when I was in the ninth grade, but he also was disappointed that I did not become an engineer. He is still my strongest role model of the ideal professor. He won many distinguished awards in his field both as a researcher and as an educator and was inducted into the National Academy of Engineering in 1996. He is proud of what I have accomplished in my career. However, the balance between my husband's career and mine troubles him, as does the amount that I travel and the amount of time I am not with my children.

My mother was also a strong role model as a Brazilian woman who left home in the 1950s to travel to a distant country to study. But I spent many years chastising her for putting her career on hold while she followed my father around the world. It is only as an adult that I realize she was accomplishing her goals of raising a family. Her gift to my brother and me is absolutely unconditional love and the steadfast belief that we can do or be anything we want to. Even though my mother wanted me to have a career, I think she would say her career was being a wonderful mother, and she succeeded beautifully at it. I only hope I can give my children 1/10th of the belief in themselves that my mother has given me.

Thus, I have somehow tried to blend the multiple, sometimes conflicting, cultures of my background. I have strongly identified with my mother's culture, but I also have grown to realize how much all my cultures have contributed to my worldview. This results in my balancing my own cultural perspective in my work, yet my husband and I are raising our three sons largely immersed in the majority culture.

My husband, Bob, and I met in graduate school and married in 1981. He is of German, French, and Irish descent and is now Professor of Management Information Systems. Our families were very similar in educational level (both of our fathers have Ph.D.s), social class, and expectations of their children. Our extended families are very different, though; his has a rich pioneer tradition and they still tell wonderful stories about the early days of settlers in South Dakota. I probably have romanticized this, for it must have been a hard life, but when our first child was born in 1982 I was a bit in awe that my child would belong to that heritage and history. My children view themselves as lucky to have a rich cultural heritage that spans three continents.

NONVISIBLE MINORITY

One of my central struggles has been to negotiate the conflicting expectations of the multiple cultures in which I have lived and others' conflicting attributions of those cultures. As I noted earlier, how I see myself and how others view me differ. At times, I openly counter others' perceptions; at other times, I choose not to do so. This, of course, is the central privilege of nonvisible minorities, for visible racial/ethnic minority group members cannot make the same choice. My visible racial/ethnic friends and family are always aware that others may react to the color of their skin or their facial features and that those reactions may literally be life-threatening. Although I have been the target of anti-Arab discrimination and have dealt with my share of sexism, being a nonvisible minority member means that I do not personally deal with racism.

Thus, my struggles are primarily internal—how I react to the world around me and how at times I struggle against it. I do not fit typical conceptions that others ascribe to me. I am a woman in a traditionally male environment. I look Arab and have an Arab name but identify as Hispanic. I am a mother of three children, two still in elementary school when most highly achieving professional women either do not have children, have only one child, or wait to commit to their career after their children are grown. I am a professional woman in extended families where the women are educated but not career committed. And I view myself as a woman of color married to a White man, living in a predominantly White culture. There are few role models for how to put all of this together.

My multiple cultures come together in my worldview, in our commitment to give our children a passion for equity and an appreciation for diversity, and in my work. I have spent most of my career joining others such as

Fred Leong, Michael Brown, Rosie Bingham, Sharon Bowman, and Consuelo Arbona in pushing vocational psychology as a field to pay greater attention to cultural variables. We have been fairly successful. This is evidenced by a conference on contextual factors in vocational psychology in 1999 and chapters in this and other books devoted to the research in the area. Of course, there is a great deal more we need to know about how class and culture influence the career concerns of clients. But we have begun to influence scholars to address cultural variables, and I am excited about our ability to apply that knowledge to help individuals make culturally appropriate choices.

My multiple cultures come together in my professional service as well. I serve on a number of editorial boards because I feel strongly that a focus on cultural variables must be addressed in published articles. My positions of leadership within Division 17 have been avenues to focus on cultural competence and a way for me to demonstrate a commitment to diversity. I have had the great good fortune to work with some of my heroes in the field— Allen Ivey, Derald Sue, Patricia Arredondo, and Michael D'Andrea. We have formed a team to pull together guidelines for culturally competent practice, education and training, and research, and we hope the American Psychological Association will adopt these. As I write this, Division 17 and the Council of Counseling Psychology Training Programs are planning a national conference for March 2001, focusing on ways that counseling psychology can make a difference.

Writing this chapter has helped me reflect on what being a nonvisible minority means. For me, it has at times meant choosing to not fully explain exactly what my backgrounds are. This translates into not answering the question "That's an unusual name, where do you come from?" or merely saying "Iowa." But at other times, it has meant that I have to go further to help people understand why I am so committed to cultural issues and diversity. I do not have the instant credibility that a person with darker skin color or differently shaped eyes has. However, living a life defined by being a visible racial/ethnic minority is not the only way to foster a commitment to cultural diversity. We need to acknowledge that there are a lot of people like me, who are products of multiple cultures and worlds. We also need to acknowledge that people like me may feel like nonvisible minorities and that our voices need to be heard to truly understand the complex issues of diversity.

RELEVANT PUBLICATIONS

Fouad, N. A. (1999). Validity evidence for interest inventories. In A. Spokane & M. L. Savickas (Eds.), *Vocational interests* (pp. 193-210). Palo Alto, CA: Davies-Black.

Fouad, N. A., & Bingham, R. (1995). Career counseling with racial/ethnic minorities. In B. Walsh & S. Osipow (Eds.), *Handbook of vocational psychology* (2nd ed., pp. 331-366). Hillsdale, NJ: Lawrence Erlbaum.

Fouad, N. A., & Brown, M. (2000). Race, ethnicity, culture, class and human development. In S. D. Brown & R. W. Lent (Eds.), *Handbook of counseling psychology* (3rd ed., pp. 379-410). New York: John Wiley.

Fouad, N. A., Harmon, L. W., & Borgen, F. H. (1997). The structure of interests of employed male and female members of U.S. racial/ethnic minority and nonminority groups. *Journal of Counseling Psychology, 44*, 339-345.

Fouad, N. A., & Smith, P. L. (1996). A test of social cognitive model with middle school students. *Journal of Counseling Psychology, 43*, 338-346.

Correspondence regarding this chapter may be sent to Nadya A. Fouad, Department of Psychology, University of Wisconsin–Milwaukee, P.O. Box 413, Milwaukee, WI 53201 (e-mail address: nadya@uwm.edu).

Chapter 7

REFLECTIONS ON UNEARNED ADVANTAGES, UNEARNED DISADVANTAGES, AND EMPOWERING EXPERIENCES

MELBA J. T. VASQUEZ

IT HAS BEEN AN interesting experience to take time to reflect inwardly and examine the life experiences which I believe have influenced my worldview and commitment to multicultural psychology and social justice.

First, it is with mixed feelings that I am recognized as a "pioneer." I am honored, of course, to be considered in this category. However, the old familiar nagging feeling of doubt threatens; vestiges of the imposter syndrome surface. The old fears, mostly quieted at this stage of my life suggest, "They don't really know me, or they wouldn't have asked. . . . " Nonetheless, I will proceed *as if* I belong. It is what I have usually done, even when those around me didn't think I belonged. Typically, what happens is that before I or those around me know it, I do belong, even if grudgingly (on my part and/or theirs)!

The *American Heritage Dictionary* defines a pioneer in part as "one who ventures into unknown or unclaimed territory . . . An innovator in any field." It was distressing to have entered the field in the late 1970s when so little had been done in the field of ethnic minority and multicultural psychology. Much progress has been made by many in the past three decades, but we still have so much to accomplish. I am amazed that there are still so few of us in this category of "pioneers."

We are asked to describe child and adolescent experiences that were influential in shaping our life experiences from a social, cultural, developmental, economic, and/or environmental perspective. Those do indeed shape our personal lives and professional identities. I have had the opportunity to reflect on those key experiences for the past few months and have

64

some thoughts to share. I would like to frame discussion of those in the context of those experiences I categorize as privileges and "unearned advantages," as well as those that contributed to challenges, oppression, and "unearned disadvantages." I then discuss "empowering experiences" and end with suggestions and recommendations for graduate students and young professionals.

PRIVILEGES AND UNEARNED ADVANTAGES

"Privilege" was defined by Cactus Pryor, a Texas humorist, as the belief, feeling, and attitude that an individual has who was "born on third base" and thinks that they "hit a triple!" This sports metaphor does indeed capture the privilege we observe in White males born with the kinds of opportunities and advantages that lead to feelings of confidence and entitlement. There are many forms of privilege. It was only in the past decade of my life that I realized that I too have had many privileges throughout my life! The notion of "unearned advantages" also speaks to the notion of privilege in society.

I grew up in a small central Texas town during the 1950s. I was the first of seven children born to two firstborn parents. I was the oldest grandchild on my mother's side of the family and the third child (but firstborn of the oldest son) on my father's side. In other words, I had the privilege of a considerable amount of attention, adoration, and regard from my parents, large extended family (including 16 aunts and uncles and all 4 grandparents plus great uncles and aunts, second cousins, and so on!). I enjoyed what I wish every child had. When I walked into a room, faces lit up (most of the time)! I also grew up in a loving small community. The first 5 or 6 years of my life were relatively safe; in retrospect, I grew up in a small college community that was socially segregated. What an incredible experience of "unearned advantages." I had no substantive contact with the White European community until I entered first grade in the public school system.

Another instance of "unearned advantage" is that our parents, although relatively poor, scraped money together to send me and my siblings to the local Catholic parochial school for part of our elementary education. That meant that I attended St. John's Catholic School from fourth through seventh grade. Although the adjustments from public school to Catholic school and then back again were challenging, several of my siblings and I had the advantages of a small private school for a brief time. We had the opportunity to develop good study skills, to develop the capacity to adjust to different environments, and to know the special feeling that came from attending a private school.

I consider myself very lucky to be born into a family where parents were politically active in their local community. There was a unique empowerment that came from being a participant of political rallies, voter registration projects, and related activities. I have no doubt that this role modeling and orientation, including the fact that my mother in particular served as a leader in all activities in which she became involved, have influenced my very strong belief that active involvement can lead to positive change. I saw firsthand as a child that one vocal person can make a difference. Although there were struggles and painful events along the way, the overall effect of my parents' activism was that proactive involvement was the way to direct the pain and anger of disenfranchisement. The privilege of being oriented to activism was a gift handed to me by my parents.

The attitudes on the part of my parents and their Chicano peers in our community was that education was important. The organizations in which my parents and their friends were involved were geared to fund-raise for scholarships for Hispanic students and to further the education of Latino children in the community. As a result of this influence, four of us in my family have at least college bachelor's degrees, and three have technical associate's degrees. Although we fought as children, we are very close as adult siblings. Family is very important to all of us. What an incredible privilege to have siblings who are all productive contributors to their respective communities and with whom we all provide support for one another.

Expectations to achieve were not conveyed in a pressured manner; while I was growing up, very few people in my community, including my parents, had completed high school. We were poor, and the notion of traveling far to go to school was not even a consideration. Yet the messages were clear that it was a time and period when change was happening and that we could take on the identity of those who could take risks to try opportunities. Perhaps the combination of having a paternal grandfather, who immigrated and established a small grocery store business, and a maternal grandfather, whose family was in Texas when Texas was still Mexico and who served as a ranch foreman since way before I was born, influenced the notion that leadership and proactivity were part of who we were. Both grandmothers were kind but strong matriarchs in their own right. Whatever the combination of experiences, I am grateful to have the transgenerational expectation (however subtle) and attitude that we could accomplish what opportunities led us to.

I thus experienced many privileges and "unearned advantages" in the development of motivation and attitudes of persistence and entitlement. Yet these were mixed with feelings of doubt, anxiety, and fear as a result of many challenges and "unearned disadvantages" that mostly came in the form of oppressive and discriminatory experiences.

CHALLENGES, OPPRESSION, AND UNEARNED DISADVANTAGES

When I first entered elementary school in the first grade, I cried daily for weeks and weeks. My mother was very distressed, assuming separation anxiety. She had not expected this, since during the first 6 years of my life I had been versatile in staying with any number of extended relatives; my parents had assumed that entering school would be an easy adjustment. Although what I felt may have been partly "separation anxiety," the experience of entering a White majority school, with not a single teacher or administrator of color, led to my world feeling suddenly unsafe. It was not the color difference but the attitudes of those with power toward those of us of color (primarily Hispanic, since there were very few Asian students, and Black students attended a segregated school). The subtle and not-so-subtle negative attitudes were clear. We were ignored, spoken to more curtly and harshly than the White children, and some of the children of color (mostly boys, as I recall) were treated harshly (e.g., knocked down on the playground) and called racial epithets. I remember feeling incredible empathy for Latino children who were abused on the playground and felt an immediate identification with and protection of those like me. I remember feeling the pain of loss of positive regard at both a personal and a group level but had no words to describe the loss and sadness and lack of safety and resulting anxiety that emerged.

What I learned in that year was that the world was unsafe, after all. When parents hand their children to the school system, they hope that those in charge will take as good care of their children as they did. When the system fails to do so, disadvantage to the children is one of the consequences.

Sometime in those early months, I learned that being a good student was what got some semblance of positive attention and regaining of safety. Fortunately, our parents had shown us the library early in our childhood and taught us to read before entering school.

Although my parents spoke Spanish to each other, they spoke English to us so that we could speak English when we entered school (both parents were "flunked" in the first grade for not speaking English). Ironically, although we technically spoke English better than Spanish, we had accents. I remember one very shaming experience where the teacher forced me to try to say "choo-choo" rather than "shoo-shoo." When I was not able to, I dissolved into tears, fearing being banished from the top reading group where stories were so much more interesting! I remember the quiet and tension from the rest of the students. It was very difficult to not know how to articulate the pain of those kinds of shaming experiences.

Sometime in those early years in elementary school, I had a boyfriend who was White. I do not recall whether we shared the status of "boyfriend/girlfriend" for one week or three months, but he came to school one day and told me that he could no longer be my boyfriend. His mother (who worked at the school) told him that I could not be his girlfriend because I was Mexican. I remember feeling confused and was frightened when my mother expressed outrage when I went home and asked, "Mom, what's wrong with being Mexican?" During those early years, I was confused by the apparent fact that White people had better cars, clothes, and houses; I wondered if that was why they were treated better. I noticed that White people who were also poor were treated like we were treated. Yet I struggled with "internalized racism" and wondered why Whites as a group were more successful until I reached college and began to read about the effects of oppression and the histories of peoples of color as well as about class issues.

I was in college when my feminism began in earnest. It came out of a very mixed experience when I represented one of my organizations in one of the beauty contests held at the university. I was chosen as a semifinalist but very much disliked having to parade in bathing suits, gowns and to perform dance routines in shorts in front of an auditorium full of people. When I was nominated for another similar event, I declined, and my peers and advisers could not understand why. I did not yet have the ability to articulate how much I disliked that patriarchy objectified women by focusing on bodies and looks; all I could say at the time was that I felt too much like a cow being paraded about before the auction.

I experienced various other discriminatory and sexist experiences (and still do to this day), and more of those are described in the context of how they became empowering experiences.

EMPOWERING EXPERIENCES

Parental Role Modeling

I learned quite a bit about social justice from the actions of those around me during my developmental years. My parents each contributed to my positive development in different ways. My father was loving, kind, and socially popular among the Latino community, but he had little contact with the "White world," except in his work first as a farm worker (I suppose we were "sharecroppers" when we lived on that farm, although that was not a term we used) and then as a factory machine operator. My mother was also loving but also assertive in her anger about discriminatory events. My first memory of her advocacy took place in a J. C. Penny store. My mother observed an elderly Mexican American woman attempting to be waited on, holding a bolt of cotton material from which to purchase. The White clerk continued to chat and serve all other White customers who came up after the Latina woman. My mother interrupted the clerk, asked why she hadn't waited on the Latina woman. When the clerk attempted to ignore my mother, my mother loudly asked for the name of the manager and asked to see him immediately. The clerk quickly waited on the elderly Latina. I remember being very little (probably 3 or 4 years old) and very embarrassed at the event. I wished I could disappear into the cracks of the wooden floor of the store. In retrospect, I am, of course, very proud of my mother's willingness to confront cruel and disrespectful treatment of others. She did so often.

Although my mother worked throughout my elementary and high school years as a housekeeper, cook, and child-care person who ironed other people's clothes, she was very clear about the importance of justice, of education, and of the importance of behaving as if we were deserving, even when those around us did not convey that same message. She got her GED (high school equivalency diploma) and then a bachelor's degree at about the time I entered graduate school. By the time she retired a few years ago, she was the executive director of a community action program with a multi-million-dollar budget, had served on the local school board, and served as a consultant and traveled internationally. She still serves as an active leader in her community and has received multiple awards for her contributions. Yesterday, for example, when I called to speak to her at 8 a.m., she did not return my call until 10 p.m. because she'd been a polling judge for local elections all day long and then attended the party for the mayoral candidate who was successful in his campaign to become the community's first Asian mayor. How lucky I am to have such an active, high-energy mother who continues to live what she believes.

Women of Color Allies

I'd like to share a story that illustrates my early formative experiences with women of color as allies. When I was in the second grade and my younger sister was in kindergarten, we rode on a bus to and from school. In 1957, although our school system had not integrated African American students into the schools (*Brown vs. Board of Topeka*, 1954), our bus system was integrated. Therefore, after school, our bus stopped at Bonham Elementary, where the African American children got on the bus after school.

One day, a large White boy, about 2 or 3 years older, who often bullied us all, came and roughly pushed my sister and me into a corner of our seat because he wanted to sit in that space across from his friends. I remember the fear and humiliation I felt for myself and for my sister. Yet we did nothing but sit silently, squashed by his large size. An African American young girl, about his size, saw what happened and came up, pushed his shoulder, and said in a very loud, assertive voice, "What are you doing? You can't do that to them. They're sitting there, can't you see, and you're crowding them. Move. Now!" He looked at her defiantly and said, "This ain't your business." She glared back and said, "It is now." The whole bus got quiet. She repeated in a low voice, "Move. Now." He got up and moved. The young Black girl went to her seat, came back, gave us each a piece of hard candy, and watched over us and others like us for the rest of the year.

I did not at that time know the words *oppression, White male privilege,* and *bullying* as they are used now, but that is some of what my sister and I experienced as a result of that young boy's behavior that day. And I did not know the words *ally, sisterhood,* and *creation of warm women of color spaces,* but I experienced those in my heart that day. And I know that the experience formed a significant set of expectations in my heart and mind. The learning was that girls and women of color stood up for each other against oppression. My assumptions from that day forward included that women of color were very much in the same boat and that we should always stand together. I have wished many times that I could personally thank that person whose name I don't think I ever knew. All I can do is continue to help others when I can.

I learned from this and various other experiences that it was not the end of the world when someone treated you unfairly. Others—or oneself—can stand up to fight it! But it is so nice when an ally with power—and there are many forms of power—stands up to help or even initiates intervention. Building alliances and making connections is clearly a strategy for all of us to be more visible and powerful and is a major strategy for survival in this world in which we live. When we have the power and opportunity to be allies for others who are oppressed, we must all "give back."

1960s Activism

Another very important period of formation was in high school, which I attended in the mid and late 1960s. During my sophomore year in high school, the Blacks and Mexican Americans joined together to begin electing representatives to positions of leadership. I was one of about two dozen students elected as representatives on the Student Council, class officers, cheerleaders, and so forth. Although we were exhilarated by our successes, all of this was not without pain, struggle, and conflict. At one time, I was elected part of the "Homecoming Royalty." I was the only person of color among five young women and five young men. Assuming that I knew what was happening, my favorite English teacher pulled me out of class and told me that she had told her son, who had also been elected a favorite, that if no one else was willing to serve as my escort at the presentation he must do so. She meant to be reassuring and did not realize that I had not yet heard that none of the White boys wanted to walk in with me. I remember feeling shame, humiliation, and confusion. Likewise, when I went to cheerleader camp with the other six cheerleaders (again, the only cheerleader of color that year), no one was my roommate, and I discovered that I had been left out of many slumber parties and events held by the other elected cheerleaders. Loneliness and exclusion were some of the prices to pay during that period. However, the support of my family, friends, and community helped carry me through those periods, even though I did not always share the pain of those experiences with others. Since then, at high school reunions (which I did not attend for the first 15 years), a couple of the "White women" have reached out, expressing regret for the social segregation and treatment of those days. I have been amazed and gratified at the willingness of a couple of the women who wished to "make amends."

White European Allies

I did not trust "Anglo" or "White people" as I thought of them until I was in college. One of my mentors, Dr. Colleen Conoley, went out of her way to ensure that I availed myself of many opportunities as an undergraduate and is responsible for encouraging me to enter graduate school in counseling psychology (I partly trusted her perception that I might do well in graduate school only after also being encouraged to enter a graduate program in sociology by a sociology professor and law school by a constitutional law professor during undergraduate school). Colleen Conoley was herself an alumna of University of Texas at Austin's counseling psychology program, and her son Collie entered the program a year ahead of me. She and her family were my first real White friends, and then I was open to developing other "White friends" during my first two years as a school teacher.

After my first marriage failed, I unintentionally became involved with and married my current partner, Jim Miller. Although it was an adjustment for my parents and community (very few of us had become involved in "mixed marriages"), this experience taught me firsthand that some White men really can "get it" and that many other factors are important in various forms of connection and bonding at personal and professional levels. Many other European Americans evolved as "allies" and good friends. My world expanded during the two years that I taught middle school. I very much enjoyed that experience. It was while simultaneously working on a counselor education master's degree during those two years that I was encouraged to apply to a doctoral program.

In graduate school, several professors made discouraging comments, probably unintentionally at times. But many more were encouraging. My dissertation co-chairs, Gary Hanson and Earl Koile, were brilliant in their capacity to ensure that I maintained my motivation. Other members of the committee, Ira Iscoe, June Gallessich, and Gus Baron, added varied support. They are now colleagues, and we maintain some contact to this day. My former "bosses" Donna McKinley and David Drum (who were Directors at Colorado State University's Counseling Center and University of Texas at Austin Counseling and Mental Health Center, respectively, when I was at each place) are now good friends, and both are responsible for ensuring that I seek the Diplomate from the American Board of Professional Psychology. I engage in a variety of professional projects with two of my colleagues, and close friends, Sally Grenard Moore and Alice Lawler.

Upon joining the American Psychological Association, its Division 17, Counseling Psychology, was my "first home" division. Several of those among the leadership of Division 17, such as Ursula Delworth, John Alcorn, Donna McKinley, Jo-Ida Hansen, Jim Hurst, Al Ivey, Naomi Meara, Linda Forrest, and John Westefeld, encouraged my involvement. Manny Casas asked me to co-chair the Ethnic Minority Committee, which was my first leadership position in Division 17. I was voted president-elect of the division for the year 2000–2001, and will serve as president in 2001–2002.

Many other "White allies" have been influential as well. Laura Brown convinced me to run for president of Division 35, Society for the Psychology of Women, my first division presidency, and Ken Pope invited me to co-author an ethics book with him after having served together on the APA Ethics Committee. Many other colleagues have also become good friends over the years. Many, many others have been supporters in both short- and long-term ways. In fact, more people than I can list have extended kindness in all kinds of ways.

American Psychological Association Minority Fellowship Program and the Public Interest Directorate

During my first year in graduate school, I was awarded one of the first APA Minority Fellowships. The program was directed first by Dalmas Taylor and then by James Jones, both of whom also served as mentors from afar and, in particular, encouraged involvement of Fellows in professional activities, especially in the APA. The program afforded financial support but also another reason to continue to work hard to achieve the goal of completing the doctoral program. Currently, the APA Public Interest Directorate, with Executive Director Henry Tomes, with Offices of Minority Affairs (Bertha Holliday), Women's Programs (Gwen Keita), and other key offices provide valuable staff support to the various projects initiated within APA. The Fellowship program has served as a very important part of my graduate training and professional life.

Other Ethnic Minority Allies

My first introduction to Latino psychologists was at the first Symposium on Chicano Psychology held in 1976 in California toward the end of my second year of graduate school. My peer and close friend to this day, Anna Gonzalez Sorensen, and I were partly supported by Ira Iscoe, then Director of University of Texas Counseling Center and one of the founders of Community Psychology, to attend the conference, where we met several of our future mentors, such as Martha Bernal, Manuel Ramirez, Amado Padilla, Art Ruiz, Manny Casas, and other salient "mentors from afar." It was also with some of those pioneers that I was able to participate in the founding of the National Hispanic Psychological Association just a couple of years after that symposium. It was an exhilarating experience to "immerse" ourselves with other Hispanic psychologists, and even now, that opportunity continues to be an important experience in my professional and personal life.

Other mentors, peers, and students/former students have been supporters, and I have established strong bonds from working on various projects with a wide variety of people, such as Carolyn Payton and Reiko True, women long active in the APA, who encouraged my participation as well. I have coauthored chapters and articles with former students Ay Ling Han, Cynthia de las Fuentes, and Natalie Eldridge. Staff members at the American Psychological Association have become life-long friends, including Gwen Keita and Lillian Comas Diaz, among so many others! John Moritsugu and many others helped found Division 45, Society for the Psychological Study of Ethnic Minority Issues. Pam Reid, first woman of color president of Division 35, invited my active involvement in that Division when she asked me to serve as her program chair. Jessica Henderson Daniel, Janis Sanchez-Hucles, and others have been active supporters in Division 35. Derald Wing Sue, Rosie Phillips Bingham, Lisa Porsche Burke, and Steven James, cofounders and planners of the first and second National Multicultural Conference and Summit, feel as close to me as siblings. It was a privilege to serve as a Division President the same year that Dick Suinn served as APA President.

Affirmative Action

Were it not for Affirmative Action I would not be a psychologist. I was one of the first of several graduate students of color admitted into the doctoral program at the University of Texas in the 1970s in an attempt to diversify the profession of psychology. The admissions program expanded the usual number of students accepted into the program. Although my GRE scores were in the acceptable range, they were not as high as many of the students'. I stubbornly set out to prove that I could achieve despite others' superior scores. That determination, and my mother's internalized belief that I would belong even when others thought I didn't, and the organization of a support system of graduate students of color and of women's groups helped me through the challenges of those years. Although there were no Latino faculty members, there were White faculty members who provided occasional encouragement of the work of interest, and I am grateful to those individuals.

Affirmative Action is indeed an important strategy to promote social justice. Despite the fact that Americans value equality and fairness, it is clear that women and ethnic minorities have historically not benefited from the valuing of those principles. Psychological knowledge can inform the debate, and I'd like to suggest that we all commit to continue supporting these very important strategies.

Affirmative Action most likely contributed to my job acquisitions at Colorado State University and then at the University of Texas at Austin. I am grateful to the director of the CSU Counseling Center at the time, Donna McKinley, and to the head of the department, Dick Suinn, for the support and mentoring they provided. David Drum, director of the University of Texas Counseling Center, also supported my involvement in professional activities. Do I mind that Affirmative Action may have been a consideration in my hirings? On the contrary, I am grateful for the opportunities created by the increased conscientiousness that may have contributed to my consideration.

Were my peers with higher GRE scores superior to me? I remember expressing my vulnerability about my GRE scores to the head of the counseling psychology program, Royal Embree, who told me that a study he had done over several years showed an inverse relationship between the highest scores on GREs with ability to complete the program! He was very kind and encouraging when he shared that information with me.

Did my awareness of being an Affirmative Action designee harm my self-esteem? Although I struggled with the feeling of belonging, that feeling did not come as a result of having been admitted via Affirmative Action strategies. There is some evidence that Affirmative Action may actually raise the self-esteem of women and minorities by providing them with employment and opportunities for advancement. Retired General Colin Powell, after reviewing the results of a major study that challenged much of the conservative thinking about Affirmative Action, dismissed concerns about the alleged stigma that opponents say the program imposes. An article in the September 9, 1998 edition of the *New York Times* reported Powell as saying, "I would tell black youngsters to graduate from the (prestigious) schools magna cum laude and get one of those well-paying jobs to pay for all the therapy they'll need to remove that stigma."

After obtaining my Ph.D., I spent the next 13 years at two different university counseling centers, part of the time serving as training director at each setting (Colorado State University and University of Texas at Austin). Both experiences provided me with the opportunities to develop my interests in ethnic minority psychology, psychology of women, and training and supervision both in my provision of services and in my writings. I also developed my interest in professional activities, becoming involved in a variety of APA divisions, boards and committees, and state and regional associations related to psychology. I have been in full-time private practice for the past 10 years and have continued those professional leadership and volunteer activities as well as my writing. I am driven and motivated by my very strong belief that many pioneers before me contributed to increasing opportunities for many such as myself. I believe that it is partly my responsibility to expand those opportunities for others. It is also important for us to increase the competency of those who deliver services, conduct research, and provide training in areas of diversity, as for populations such as ethnic minorities, women, lesbian, gay, bisexual, and transgendered persons, disabled persons, and others.

STRATEGIES AND RECOMMENDATIONS

The following strategies and recommendations are for those of you who are graduate students or young professionals. They are based on my experiences and on my observations of those of my students of color and clients of color.

- *Take risks.* Allow curiosity and energy to give direction to areas in which you wish to explore your power and salience. Phoebe Eng, in her book *Warrior Lessons* (1999), states that "sometimes we've got to force ourselves into battle—for beliefs, for our boundaries, and to defend big pictures. Becoming a wise fighter, after all, is less about shouting and more about strategy" (p. 197). She also suggests that learning to fight the good fight means understanding that our successes do not imply the failure of others. We must believe that there is plenty to go around. Risk takers often find that true fearlessness is not the elimination of fear, but the transcendence of fear, the movement through it and not against it. Fearlessness means the willingness to "lean into the anxiety and fear."

- *Allow for imperfections and mistakes.* Mistakes are part of life. Acknowledge them to yourself (and to others, if necessary), learn from them, fix them as much as possible, and move on. Do not let them define you. They are a part of every human's experience. Men tend to attribute success to themselves and failures to others. Women tend to attribute success to luck, support of others, and failures to themselves. We must let go of shame and learn the philosophy of "Bummer, oh well!" We must transcend the fear of failure, cast it aside, and listen to our kinder selves.

- *Engage in self-care.* You are the only one who can ensure that you exercise, eat healthily, have a good balance of work, rest, play, and relationships, set appropriate boundaries, and so on. We have to be able to treat ourselves as preciously as we do anyone else.

- *Develop self-confidence.* We must constantly practice how to hold ourselves out with confidence, how to articulate our ideas, and how to face creative conflict in order to reach resolutions. These are simply skills that can be developed through practice. Continue to articulate the value of diversity and inclusion in decision making and power. We need individuals who are able and willing to articulate commitment to diversity issues. Phoebe Eng talks about modern-day warrior women of color. She believes that "power from within" (confidence) is based on the inherent value in each of us, separate from that which represents us to others. Power from within recognizes that groups and alliances are strong and balanced only when each of the members is strong and balanced. If we have power from within, we are relatively freed from the weight of outside expectations, downward pressure, and confining stereotypes. We can be released to act genuinely and freely. Otherwise, "our lives begin to end the day we are silent about things that matter," according to Martin Luther King, Jr.

- *Observe role models and mentors.* Mentors are scarce. Use them situationally—and at a distance. I have received much mentoring and guidance from my peers and, sometimes, have learned lots from watching younger students and professionals. I have also been fortunate to learn from various senior people: of color, White, male, and female. Observe the skills and strengths of others and decide whether you wish to cultivate those as well.

- *Use your anger to empower your lives.* Our upbringing and social codes can make it difficult to allow us to experience anger, and many of us haven't learned how to translate those feelings to create change in the situations around us. We may assume that if we are good and respectful to others, those behaviors will be reciprocated. This expectation can interfere with our right to rage and anger, which can be transformed into healthy, assertive expressions that say "We count," "I am to be respected," "You may not mistreat me," and "I am deserving." Or it may be unbridled and destructive in its expression. Anger is a healthy signal that tells us and those around us where our boundaries are, what we instinctively feel is tolerable or intolerable, and can signal when those limits have been trespassed. Conflict is necessary because difference is inherent in every endeavor. Channeling anger through constructive acts can be empowering.

- *Engage in activism.* We can depend on ourselves as individuals and groups to make a difference. We must also develop alliances with power structures and set up policies and structures to make a difference. Affirmative Action types of strategies are absolutely necessary for continued change.

- *Engage in support systems and provide support to others.* Empowering others can be the same as empowering ourselves. The precious and powerful standing up for each other is one of the most exquisite gifts to give and to receive.

This quote by Nelson Mandela in his inauguration speech is from Lillian Comas-Diaz's editorial in the journal *Cultural Diversity and Mental Health* (1998, Vol. 4, p. 151):

Our deepest fear is not that we are inadequate. Our deepest fear is that we are powerful beyond measure. It is our light, not our darkness, that frightens us. We ask ourselves, who am I to be brilliant, gorgeous, talented, fabulous? Actually, who are you not to be? You are a child of the universe. There is nothing enlightened about shrinking so that other people won't feel insecure around you. We were born to make manifest the glory of creation. It is not just in some of us; it is in everyone. And as we let our own light shine, we unconsciously give other people permission to do the same. As we are liberated from our own fear, our presence automatically liberates others.

RELEVANT PUBLICATIONS

Han, A. L., & Vasquez, M. J. T. (1997). Group interventions and treatment with ethnic minorities. In J. F. Aponte, R. Y. Rivers, & J. Wohl (Eds.), *Psychological interventions and cultural diversity* (2nd ed.). Boston: Allyn & Bacon.

Pope, K., & Vasquez, M. J. T. (1998). *Ethics in psychotherapy and counseling: A practical guide* (2nd ed.). San Francisco: Jossey-Bass.

Vasquez, M. J. T. (1998). Latinos and violence: Mental health implications and strategies for clinicians. *Cultural Diversity and Mental Health, 4,* 319-334.

Vasquez, M. J. T., & de las Fuentes, C. (1999). American-born Asian, African, Latina and Native American adolescent girls: Challenges and strengths. In N. G. Johnson, M. Roberts, & J. Worell (Eds.). *Beyond appearance: A new look at adolescent girls.* Washington, DC: American Psychological Association.

Vasquez, M. J. T., & de las Fuentes, C. (1999). Hate speech or freedom of expression? Balancing autonomy and feminist ethics in a pluralistic society. In M. Brabeck (Ed.), *Practicing feminist ethics in psychology.* Washington, DC: American Psychological Association.

Correspondence regarding this chapter may be sent to Melba J. T. Vasquez, Anderson House at Heritage Square, 2901 Bee Cave Road, Box N, Austin, TX 78746 (e-mail address: MelVasquez@aol.com).

Chapter 8

I DIDN'T KNOW WHERE I WAS GOING BUT I GOT HERE ANYWAY

My Life's Journey Through the Labyrinth of Solitude

J. MANUEL CASAS

Solitude—the feeling and knowledge that one is alone, alienated from the world and oneself. . . . All men, at some moment in their lives, feel themselves to be alone. And they are. To live is to be separated from what we were in order to approach what we are going to be in the mysterious future. Solitude is the profoundest fact of the human condition. Man [sic] is the only being who knows he is alone, and the only one who seeks out another. His nature—if that word can be used in reference to man, who has "invented" himself by saying "No" to nature—consists in his longing to realize himself in another. Man is nostalgia and a search for communion. Therefore, when he is aware of himself he is aware of his lack of another, that is, of his solitude.

—Octavio Paz (1961, p. 195)

WRITING THIS CHAPTER has been one of the most difficult tasks that I have undertaken in my career. I managed to finish two other chapters and an article before I forced myself to sit down and write this one. Except for short "biobibs," I have never written about myself for the purpose of publication and, for that matter, any purpose. While I'm not a shy person, I highly value my privacy, and so sharing my life experiences, and in particular those that relate to my family, is not something I easily do; furthermore, my cultural upbringing underscored the fact that one should not go around "bragging" about one's personal achievements. These reasons aside, I think that the major reason for my seeking to avoid writing this chapter was having to face the emotions, especially the negative ones, that are an inherent part of one's solitary journey through the labyrinth of life.

Having undertaken the task to write this chapter I have opted to examine different pathways in my life's journey that, directly or indirectly, brought me to the place in which I presently find myself. I believe that the journey that I have undertaken has been extremely challenging in more ways than one. The paths that I have followed have been bilingual and bicultural, if not tricultural, in nature; they have richly encompassed racial, ethnic, and sexual orientation perspectives. It is my hope that as you read this chapter you will interpret my journey through life from the perspective of such challenges and experiences.

As I begin writing, I am faced with the reality that it is too easy to ramble when one is reminiscing about, remembering, and/or reconstructing the past in relationship to one's self. Given the limitations of length, in this chapter, I selectively present memories and recollections of my life in chronological progression. The ones that I have chosen to present are those that I believe have had the most significant impact in getting me here to this place in life in which I presently find myself. From a reflective perspective, as I pondered my choice of memories and tried to understand the rationale for my choices, I was reminded of Paz's (1961) cautionary remarks regarding one's historical assessment of self:

> History helps us to understand certain traits of our character, provided we are capable of isolating and defining them beforehand. We are the only persons who can answer the questions asked us by reality and our own being. (p. 73)

Before sharing my life's journey, it should be noted that many of the early descriptions of my life are based on memories provided by my mother in an interview conducted by my niece for a writing project that she was required to conduct for a graduate-level class two years before my mother's death in 1996.

INFANCY AND CHILDHOOD

I was born in Mexico and, if I were to simplistically describe myself from a racial/ethnic perspective, the easy way out would be to say that I am a mestizo. But to do so is to put myself in a melting-pot blender that would result in a destruction of all the unique cultural, social, racial, and ethnic parts that represent my essence. Given the lack of historical/family facts and the physical features that are shared by both my immediate and extended family, I can only surmise that upon arrival of the racially and ethnically diverse Spaniards, my ancestry came to proudly reflect a racial and cultural mixture of the "old" European world, the North African world, and the "new" indigenous one. From a romanticized perspective I have often wondered whether my ancestors were part of the ingenious yet vanquished peoples of Mexico, like the Toltecs, Aztecs, and/or Mayans. While I continue to wonder, what I do know in reference to my more recent indigenous ancestors is that my maternal great-grandparents came from the heartland of the state of Jalisco, where a good number of the people share ancestry with the Huicholes. My paternal great-grandmother was Apache, having been saved by Mexican wagon masters from U.S. cavalry raids on her village and subsequently taken to Mexico where she was raised by my great-grandfather's family. As an aside, something that ties me historically to California, the state in which I have lived, for what I would consider, all of my life, is the fact that in the 1800s my paternal great-grandfather spent a major portion of his life driving a wagon train from the central northern part of Mexico to Sacramento and back again.

Having provided you with a glimpse of my ancestry, I now direct attention to myself. Working from the perspective of mythological time (Paz, 1961), I take the position *that once upon a time* I was born into a family of three (my mother, Elvira, my father, Cruz, and my sister, Carmen, who was 6 at the time) in a small town named La Fundición de Avalos located about eight miles south of the city of Chihuahua in the state of Chihuahua, Mexico. This city is located approximately 350 miles south of El Paso, Texas. My maternal and paternal grandparents and my aunts and uncles (15 on my mother's side and 12 on my father's side) also spent a good portion of their lives in Avalos. Their love and identification with this town is such that to this day, even though the town no longer stands, my few remaining aunts and uncles still reminisce and talk about Avalos as *their* town, the town in which my paternal grandfather was the sheriff.

Avalos was a company-built town owned by the American Smelting and Refining Company (ASARCO), a U.S.-owned company that refined ores like silver, copper, and lead. From the time of my birth onward, I was exposed to the reality of racism and segregation between so-called Americans and Mexicans. The town of Avalos comprised two separate and unequal communities. There was the open community where the Mexicans lived and the secluded, walled-off community where the American "bosses" lived. To enter "their" community one had to be admitted through a guarded gateway. Their homes were to be envied, for they all had running water and bathrooms. The Mexican part of town was composed of rows of small apartment units, 10 per row, some with bathrooms but most without (public showers and toilets were located on alternate rows of the town). Because my father had a trade (i.e., welder), the apartment house that

I was born in was one of the better units in the town. It had two bedrooms, a living room, a dining room, a small kitchen, and, most important of all, a toilet and shower.

For the first 3 years of my life I lived in that apartment along with my mother, father, and older sister, surrounded by aunts, uncles, and cousins. My life with my extended family was so positively enmeshed during those first years of my life that to this day, regardless of the paths that each of us took individually in the labyrinth of our lives, we continue to stay in touch and to help one another in whatever manner possible.

IMMIGRATION FROM
MEXICO TO THE UNITED STATES

Although, in general, my family was economically stable, the advent of World War II and its impact on Mexico as well as the tumultuous nature of Mexican sociopolitical conditions convinced my father that in order to give me and my sister the opportunity to become "all that we could be," it would be necessary to immigrate to the United States, where many of our relatives were already living. Another extremely important fact that convinced my father that leaving Mexico was the right thing to do was the reality that the early 1940s was one of those historical periods when labor shortage in the United States was such that Mexican blue-collar workers and laborers, while not actually welcomed in America, were needed to fuel the wartime economy.

Since I was only 3 when we left Mexico in 1945, I do not remember the emotionality of leaving my homeland and my extended family that had pampered me from the day of my birth and who continue to do so to this day. Years later, I was able to capture some of the feelings involved from my mother's perspective:

> Your father, who was very well-read and could speak a little English, thought it was a good time to leave Mexico and go to another place that offered more opportunities and a better way of life, without the worry of revolution, uprisings, etc. It was extremely difficult for me to buy into this 100%; however, he had always taken good care of all of us and so we started to make our plans. It was hard to sell all our furniture and say goodbye to family and friends, never knowing if we would see them again. We packed several suitcases and came to the United States. We crossed the border at El Paso and continued on the train across New Mexico, Arizona, and then we found ourselves going through grove after grove of orange trees. The train went past San Bernardino and, while it did not stop there, your Aunt Luz and your cousin Teresa were standing alongside the track to wave us through as we made our way north to Los Angeles. We stayed overnight in Los Angeles in a hotel that was not in the best part of town, thus we did not venture far from our room. The next day we continued to Crockett, California, where we were met by your Aunt Maria and your

Uncle Jesús. Your father got a job the following day with ASARCO, the same company that he had worked for in Mexico.

One aspect of our journey from Mexico that I recall, or about which I have heard over the years, and which has had a tremendous impact on me throughout my life, was the fact that in El Paso, Texas, we could not use the bathrooms and drinking fountains that were designated for "White" persons only. We had to search for those services that were relegated to persons of "color" or, to be more specific with the term used during that time, Negroes. This was my introduction to discrimination in the land that was destined to be my home. Numerous subsequent experiences came soon thereafter, and since then, they have not stopped coming in one form or another. To this point, although my father had a job, finding suitable housing became quite a challenge. Once more I turn to my mother who provided a good description of our early experiences in this country:

> Your aunt and uncle lived in Tormey, a small town adjacent to Crockett, and had three rooms in their basement. These rooms became our home. As when I was a child, I was back to having nothing of a material nature, no furniture, no linens, no dishes, etc. Since the U.S. was at war, many things were scarce. As we did not have a car, we would trade our gasoline stamp rations for other things we needed. Tormey was also a company town, but much smaller and with less commodities than Avalos. Your sister started school in a two-room school house. One room was for Grades 1 to 3, the other for 4 to 6. We started looking for a house to live in. There were very few available because the influx of people to California had been tremendous, as men were being shipped overseas from this coast, ships were being built, and many of their families had come west with them. Not only was this a problem, we were Mexicans. No one wanted to rent to Mexicans because they said we were dirty people and did not know how to take care of homes. Eventually we found a landlord that took a chance on us.

We moved to Rodeo, a small blue-collar working town on San Pablo Bay that was adjacent to Tormey. Most of the residents of this town were either Portuguese or Italian and not immune to the prevailing prejudices and discriminatory practices directed at Mexicans and Blacks. To this point, most of the Mexicans lived in one large square town block while the Blacks were relegated to the "projects" that were located on the outskirts of town. During the 1940s and early 1950s social contact between the groups was, for all intents and purposes, nonexistent. This separation of racial/ethnic groups was my introduction to what I now would define as living in a ghetto. But so as not to mislead you, I must admit that in general when contact between persons of the varied groups was made, the process and outcome tended to be positive. I have very fond memories of living in my "ghetto." Very strong friendships among families were formed, friendships that have lasted to this day. In the mid-1950s, my sister, after finishing secretarial school (though an outstanding student, family finances did not enable her to go to college), began to work full-time and helped my parents buy a small house in a more integrated neighborhood. Her willingness to help the family in such a way, as well as helping me in any way possible to prepare for college, further implanted in me the importance of family, the importance and responsibility of caring for and loving one another, and the importance of demonstrating such caring and loving not solely through words but through actions.

MY EARLY EDUCATIONAL EXPERIENCES

My earliest educational experiences were not very positive; in fact, they were quite aversive. At home, we spoke only Spanish. This was a decision made by my parents to ensure that we would not lose our Mexican culture as conveyed through the richness of our language. In addition, my parents did not want us to lose the ability to communicate with our grandparents and the numerous other family members who continued to live in Mexico. In retrospect and in the long run, my sister and I are grateful for this decision; we are both fluently bilingual and can more easily identify and interact with those persons with whom we share a common heritage, whether in the United States, in Mexico, or in any of the major Spanish-speaking countries of the world. In the short run, people's reactions to our being monolingual Spanish-speaking took their toll on us as children in a variety of ways (e.g., self-esteem, self-efficacy, expectations, aspirations, etc.) just as they continue to do so on a large number of Spanish-speaking children. I should add that all was not negative. With our parents' support and encouragement, we developed an "I'll show you" and "do you one better" attitude. Which in retrospect, we did.

Because I was monolingual Spanish-speaking, I was not allowed to attend kindergarten. The explanation provided by school administrators regarding this decision was that I should stay home and learn English before entering grammar school. DUH! The problem was that my mother, with whom I would spend the major portion of the day, did not speak English. There was no TV that I might have used as a vehicle to pick up English words and phrases. Most of the neighbors also spoke Spanish. My parents, not familiar with the U.S. educational system and their rights relative to this system, did not challenge the decision. Unfortunately, decisions such as the one described herein continue to be made on a daily basis, and too many Spanish-speaking parents continue to be kept ignorant and/or deprived of their rights as they relate to the education of their children.

Well, I finally entered first grade, the law saying I had to be admitted into the first grade regardless of the language I spoke. My parents, despite the fact that they only had a sixth-grade education, had a great respect and enthusiasm for learning and began priming me with their enthusiasm very early on. My sister also pitched in. She was in the fifth grade and after dinner would teach me English words that she had learned during the day. On the first day of school, my mother, along with a limited-English-speaking friend, walked me and a friend to school, got me to my classroom, and left. As I entered the classroom, I experienced the kind of aloneness, fear, and alienation that if it were in my power to fix, no other child would ever have to experience. No one looked like me. No one spoke my language. I couldn't communicate with anyone, including the teacher. To solve this communication problem, the teacher came up with a unique and intellectually challenged strategy. I would be seated in the back of the room—not the bus, the room—where I could listen and, with time, eventually pick up the English language.

While not being fully and actively involved in all the learning activities that went on during the day during the first and second grade, I was still required to complete the workbook assignments that were the focus of the day's learning activities. However, for me to complete such assignments required help from someone who was more knowledgeable in English than I was. Such help was not forthcoming from the school. The cooperative learning solution that my family came up with was that my sister and father would tutor me in the evenings. More specifically, my sister would help me through the workbook exercises by lightly writing in the answers, explaining them to me, and then I would erase her writing and copy the answers in my own "handwriting," a process that today would be called learning by imitation and modeling. I was learning slowly but surely. However, one day I forgot to fully erase my sister's writing, and the teacher figured out what we were doing and labeled it "cheating." While I was learning through a family cooperative venue, she was set on my learning through the traditional individualistic and "mission impossible" approach. My parents were called and had to come to the school to deal with this accusation of cheating. Embarrassingly, they responded to the accusation by providing, as well as they could, the rationale for what we were doing as a family to educate ourselves. In spite of, or maybe because of these early educational experiences, with the help of my family, my sister and I developed the tenacity, the determination, and the perseverance to succeed in whatever path we chose to follow.

ADOLESCENCE AND SECONDARY SCHOOL

With advice and direction from my teachers and my family, I took both vocational and college prep courses in high school and did quite well in both areas. The rationale for taking vocational courses was to increase the probability of my finding a job in the blue-collar community in which I lived should I not go on to college. My taking college-oriented courses was to leave the door open for me to go on to higher education to get a professional degree, family and economic conditions permitting.

While attending college to further my education seemed a possibility, I had no clear direction with respect to career goals. Career counseling, for all intents and purposes, did not exist in my school. You could take the Strong Interest Inventory and have it interpreted for you, and that was it. In retrospect, I marvel at the wide array of career options I considered and explored on my own initiative. From the onset, for whatever reason, I never wanted to be a "scientist," but at one time or another I did entertain the notion of being an artist (I was and continue to be a fairly good sketch artist), a high-level dress designer, an architect, a lawyer, a foreign diplomat, or a priest. Being a teacher, a professor, or a psychologist never entered my mind.

During my four years in a high school with a population of approximately 400 students, I was quite involved in extracurricular activities (i.e., the drama club, the school newspaper, the tennis team, class president, editor of the school yearbook, and, most important of all, cheerleader). I have very fond memories of my high school years. I had come to understand and appreciate who I was as a multicultural person, and I had a very ethnically and racially diverse group of friends. Mirroring what I had learned from my parents that friends are developed for life, I still maintain contact with a good number of thesc friends.

GOING ON TO COLLEGE?

I graduated at the top of my class. Unlike most, if not all, of my friends with whom I grew up from childhood, I took all the required college entrance exams and filled out all the admissions materials. At this time, I still wasn't sure whether or not I should go to college (the short-term rcwards of getting a job in one of the surrounding industries were quite enticing). Furthermore, I was well aware of the fact that because of economic conditions and concomitant family responsibilities I might not be able to enroll in just any college, at least not full-time. Two events and one circumstance were quite influential in my deciding to take the path of pursuing a degree in higher education. The first event was the fact that in order for me to go to college I had to work during the summer months in whatever local industry might hire me. Upon graduation, I lucked out and got a job at the local brickyard. Enough said, after working eight hours, day after day, unloading bricks taken out of the kilns and loading them onto railroad cars, I knew that I was not physically able nor did I have any desire to assume the role of Prometheus: While he perpetually pushed a rock up a hill, I perpetually unloaded and loaded rocks. This work experience helped consolidate my respect and support for the hard-working laborers of this country that make the world we take for granted possible, the majority of whom are men and women from racial/ethnic minority groups. Throughout my tenure in college, I continued to work in the summers; however, I was fortunate to move from the brickyard to the local sugar refinery . . . not great but better. The other important event that made it possible for me to go to college was my being admitted to the University of California at Berkeley, which was only approximately 35 miles from where I lived (distance and being close to my family and not prestige were the important variables here in my decision-making process). My going to this university meant that, for economical and family needs, I could live at home and, since neither myself or my family had a car, commute by Greyhound and leave the driving to them. The circumstance that made my attending UC more feasible was the fact that my sister was working in Oakland, a city adjacent to Berkeley. She was part of a driving pool and so, at no cost, every morning I was dropped off just off the Berkeley freeway offramp where I caught a city bus and made my way to the university. In the evening, I would take the city bus into Oakland and meet my sister at her office. Talk about determination.

My stint at UC Berkeley comprised both positive and negative experiences and feelings. Given my need to commute as well as help out at home, I was unable to partake in any extracurricular activities on campus. I did not see the university as a place for me to go and have a "good time." Instead, I saw it as a place to go to learn, study, and prepare myself for my chosen career. I attended UC prior to the establishment of Affirmative Action and concomitant financial aid. Consequently, there were very few racial/ethnic minority students on the campus. Given this situation, I often found myself feeling pretty much alone and estranged from the majority of students who were non-Hispanic White. During my four years at Berkeley, I met very few Hispanic students with whom I shared similar life experiences. Interestingly enough, the place on campus in which I felt most comfortable was International House where many of the foreign students lived and/or hung out.

THE UNIVERSITY:
CHOOSING A MAJOR AND DECIDING ON A CAREER

I enrolled in one of the leading public universities in the world knowing that I wanted to get a college degree but having no idea what I would major in or what career paths I should pursue. While I did take advantage of the limited career counseling that was available, I never really felt that the counseling I received was very helpful. So through the process of elimination I eventually decided to major in political science with a specialization in international affairs and minor in Spanish. I believed that both the major and the minor would allow me to pursue a career in the foreign service, a career that would draw on my cultural and linguistic strengths, my interests in studying and understanding other cultures, as well as my desire to travel and live throughout Latin America.

In the short run, I felt that my decision was the right one. I took classes that I enjoyed very much and studied under some of the best political scientists and philosophers in the nation. In the long run, my decision as it related to the career I wanted to pursue was not on target. In my senior year when I started to fill out the forms to take the exam for entrance into the foreign service, I was brought to the rude awakening that my decision had taken me down a dead-end career path. To be considered for a position in the foreign service, one had to be a citizen of the United States for at least 10 years. I was a permanent resident of this country with a green card. The advice I got from the career counselor was that I become a citizen, wait 10 years, and then take the exam. Did someone forget to give me the right directions for my journey, or did I forget to ask for them? A lesson learned. In future I would not make important decisions on my own without first getting all necessary information from all available resources, a lesson I now persistently pass on to my students.

ALTERNATIVE PATHS

Finding myself at this point on my life's path, I felt somewhat betrayed by the educational/advising system at Berkeley and quite alone in deciding what I would or could do with my B.A. (i.e., I had no mentors, and given my need to commute as well as the size of the classes at Berkeley and the concomitant impersonal teaching/advising approaches used in such classes, I had not developed any close working relationship with any faculty member). Again, making a personal assessment of my interests, needs, and resources, I directed myself toward two possible careers: law or teaching. My choice of law as a career was based on my background in the field of political science/philosophy and my interest in working through the legal system to protect and/or expand the rights of low-income, disenfranchised Hispanic families. My choice of teaching as a career was based on my strong interest in working with children and adolescents who might share similar sociocultural backgrounds like my own as well as the very positive educational experiences that I had had during my middle- and high school years. Again, given my family needs and limited resources, I applied to only three "local" schools: Hastings Law School in San Francisco, Boalt Law School at UC Berkeley, and the Graduate School of Education also at UC Berkeley. I did not score high enough on the law entrance exam to be admitted into either law school but was welcomed with open arms into the School of Education's one-year secondary school credential program. Putting this welcome into a sociohistorical perspective, one must remember that the Vietnam War was at its initial stages during the mid 1960s, the United States was strongly competing with the Soviet Union for world dominance, and, for varied reasons, some tied to the war and others to the competition with the Soviet Union, there was a shortage of teachers, especially so in the sciences and foreign languages (at that time, students in middle schools in California had to take a foreign language). Whereas my being monolingual

Spanish-speaking was held against me as a child, now my ability to speak and teach Spanish was considered an asset. After getting my credential, I had no difficulty finding a job anywhere in the state but opted to take a position that would allow me to continue living at home and, in turn, help my parents financially and otherwise.

I taught middle school (English, social studies, reading, and Spanish) for three years and high school (Spanish) for two years. While I had some very good colleagues and friends in the middle school, I was somewhat isolated. Aside from the janitor, I was the only Hispanic working in a school setting that was, at the least, 97% non-Hispanic White. At the high school level, there was another Hispanic Spanish teacher. We immediately bonded and became the best of friends.

At either level, I was not your traditional teacher who taught by the book. I knew the goals and objectives that my students had to attain within each of my respective classes and would develop creative lesson plans and activities to complement, as much as possible, the learning styles of the students. For instance, I once had to teach a "beginning" Spanish class to a group of educationally and behaviorally challenged boys. Needless to say, I soon learned that teaching by the book was not going to work for any one of us, so I turned the class into "pseudo" gym class, in which we could all participate, and used a variety of sports activities to teach basic words, concepts, and phrases: "corre, corre"—run, run.

The five years that I worked as a teacher were a very rewarding part of my life. To this day, I still maintain contact with some of my students. However, during this period I also came to the realization that teaching subject matter was not what I found to be most rewarding about my job. I came to discover that what I truly enjoyed was working in the capacity of counselor/adviser with high-risk kids and families that were confronted with a variety of social/educational challenges. Consequently, when I took the opportunity to move into high school, in addition to teaching I began working two periods as a counselor while taking night courses in counseling at California State University, San Francisco. I soon realized that for me to move quicker toward the end of my counseling path, I would need to get into a full-time counseling program. But to do this, I would be faced with a lot of financial challenges.

A NEW DIRECTION

Quite serendipitously, I took the right turn at the right time in the labyrinth of my life—a turn that played a most significant role in helping me get to the place in which I presently find myself. Driving home from work one day in early Spring 1970, I was listening to a radio talk show on which Luis Nogales was being interviewed. If my memory serves me right, Luis at that time was Assistant to the President of Stanford University, specializing in

Hispanic issues and students. (Today he is President of Nogales Partners, a major national consulting firm.) In his interview, Luis emphasized how Stanford had a commitment to increasing the number of Hispanic students admitted to the university. He also stated that to this end Stanford had specific resources that could facilitate such admissions and subsequent attendance. He ended his interview by inviting those Hispanics who wanted to attend Stanford and who believed they had the qualifications to give him a call. Enough said. From my past experiences in life I had learned that if I were going to get to where I wanted to go, I had to take the initiative, get all the information necessary to plan out the most expeditious path to reach my destination(s), and take advantage of all the resources available to facilitate my journey. GO FOR IT. So, the next morning I picked up the phone and called Luis. For those of you who know me, the rest is history.

I made an appointment to meet with Luis and, with his help and guidance, applied for admission to the one-year M.A. counseling program in the Graduate School of Education, which was earmarked for practitioners. I also applied to the counseling program at UC Berkeley. I was admitted to both programs; however, Stanford offered me the better deal by guaranteeing full payment of tuition. It should be noted, from a historical perspective, that my admission and the funds offered me were made possible because of money provided by the federal government for increasing the number of counselors working in schools located in low-income, high-risk communities. Again, the impetus for providing such money was to maintain our educational competitiveness with the Soviet Union as well as addressing the needs that were becoming more evident as a result of the Civil Rights Movement. I enrolled at Stanford and for the first time in my life moved away from home and into a small apartment adjacent to the campus. I was introduced to my advisers, John Krumboltz and Carl Thoresen, two individuals who came to play a very important part in my life and for whom I came to develop great respect. Although I was the only Hispanic in the entering class, I did not feel isolated, the faculty was extremely supportive, and my fellow students from across the nation were a joy to work with. To this day, I still maintain contact with some of them. By living near campus I was able to be a part of "college" life, an experience that, as noted above, had been denied me as an undergraduate. The experience was so enjoyable and fulfilling that, at the end of the one-year program, I did not want to leave Stanford to reenter the "real" world of work. An offshoot of this experience was a vow I made to myself to do whatever I could to help students from a background like my own have the opportunity to attend college and experience, if they so desired, college life not as an outsider, a visitor, but as an insider, a resident. I conferred with John and discussed the possibility of my being admitted into the Ph.D. program. He reminded me that I had come into the M.A. program because of a strong desire to work directly with at-risk students and that the Ph.D. program was earmarked not for practitioners per se but for researchers and future academicians. Through our discussions we came to the mutually acceptable agreement that I would go out and work as a full-time counselor for one year (a side path in my life's journey), and if at the end of that year I still wanted to enter the Ph.D. program and direct my energies toward research, I would be welcome to do so.

During the M.A. program, one of my practicums was at a community college. I found that practicum to be quite challenging. So when I started my job search, I concentrated on community colleges. Again, I had no trouble finding jobs. I took a rather challenging one at Laney Community College in Oakland, California. This college was, and I believe still is, composed predominantly of Black and Hispanic students. While seeking to prepare some of the students to go on to a 4-year college, Laney also had some very outstanding vocational programs. The challenges I encountered during my one-year tenure at Laney were not only tied to the job and the extensive needs of the students but also came from the sociopolitical environment in which I was working. The early 1970s in Oakland was a period in which the Black Panther Movement was at its peak. To refresh your memory, this movement included such well-known participants as Angela Davis, Eldridge Cleaver, and Huey Newton. The political scene at Laney was very turbulent. There were times when the administrative building in which I worked was surrounded and closed off from the rest of the campus by the Black Panthers until their demands for social and educational justice were met. My experiences at Laney were eye-opening. They forced me to come to terms with, and more often than not accept, the measures, sometimes a bit extreme, that disenfranchised people (e.g., racial/ethnic minorities, gays, and lesbians) feel necessary to take in order to attain all the rights and privileges to which they are entitled.

In Spring of my year at Laney I met with John Krumboltz, we revisited our agreement, and I was given the go-ahead to proceed to take the necessary steps to be admitted into the doctoral program in counseling psychology at Stanford University. While I was determined to go on and get a Ph.D. (the first ever in my entire extended family—to this day, I'm still the only one), I had to face the very real economic obstacle that was in my path. I had to come up with a financial aid package that would enable me to return to the university. To this end, I made use of all my counseling skills, those decision-making and exploratory skills that I had taught my counselees to use in identifying all the resources that would enable them to move along their respective educational paths. In my search for financial aid, I fortuitously came across information regarding the fact that the Ford Foundation, addressing the dearth of Hispanic professionals in all fields, was launching an initiative to provide fellowships to Hispanic persons interested in and qualified for pursuing a Ph.D. in education and related fields. That was me. Filled with hope and with the glow of religious candles that were lit by my mother to help light my way, I requested all the necessary application information and forms and applied. I was quite fortunate in receiving a three- to four-year Ford Fellowship that not only covered my tuition but also provided me with a monthly living stipend and a budget for buying my books and educational supplies. With such support, I enrolled in the program, becoming the first Hispanic to do so and eventually would become the first Hispanic to graduate from the program.

In retrospect, given the availability of the Ford Fellowships, I and others look back at this time (i.e., the 1970s) as the "golden age" for producing Hispanic educators. While I was at Stanford, there were at least 10 to 11 other Hispanic students in education supported by the Ford Foundation. Most of these students finished their Ph.D.s and went on to successful academic positions (e.g., including myself, at least four are full professors at major universities in the Southwest). Having such a camaraderie of Hispanic peers as well as the outstanding peers whom I worked with directly in the counseling program made my second stint at Stanford even more enjoyable than the first.

From an academic perspective, I was quite fortunate to work with some outstanding professors who helped ground me both academically and professionally. John Krumboltz and Carl Thoresen provided me with a strong basis in a variety of applied and research areas encompassed within the field of counseling psychology (e.g., career counseling, stress management, and self-management). The pioneer Alfredo Castañeda, the first Hispanic professor I had ever met, introduced me to the field of multicultural research when such research was in its embryonic stage. Richard Snow went out of his way to help a non-quantitative-oriented mind learn statistics and, in particular, regression analysis and also introduced me to the area of research relative to aptitude treatment interaction. Albert Bandura, in a very amicable way while walking together in the mornings from the parking lot to our respective offices, introduced me to social learning theory and, more important, its practical uses with at-risk families and children. Richard Gross engendered in me through his dynamic teaching style an interest in the interrelated histories of education and psychology (histories I thought I would never teach but have actually been teaching for the past 20 years). I learned a lot of academic material from each of these professors, but most important of all, through their interactions with me, I learned what it means to be a good teacher and a caring, thoughtful person, attributes that I try to emulate today with the persons with whom I interact in the variety of roles I play.

While enjoying my academic pursuits at Stanford, I also had to deal with the facts that I had begun my Ph.D. in my early 30s and felt the need to move as quickly as possible toward my chosen career, more specifically to do something with my life. With this in mind, I made a contract with my adviser, John Krumboltz, that I would go to school year-round so that I could finish my degree within 3 years. Being able to set such a contract helps me to empathize with my students who, given all of the present APA requirements, are not able to finish in such a short time span. While I may not have taken all the courses they are required to take, I'm not sure that my career accomplishments have been negatively impacted by my not having taken them. Food for thought.

In the early 1970s there was no such thing as multicultural counseling courses or specializations, so with the support of my advisers I developed my own program that, while meeting general requirements, allowed me to study and do research in areas that focused on Mexican American families and children. This arrangement was fine until I had to decide on a dissertation topic. I originally wanted to do a study that was very focused on Mexican American children and families. However, after agonizing discussions with my advisers, I was convinced that I would be more "marketable" if I did a more "traditional" study that was based on the counseling application of some of the emerging cognitive behavioral therapies. Given the times, I now look back and think that the advice I was given was quite appropriate. So I opted to do a very sterile study comparing two mediational self-control techniques for the treatment of speech anxiety. This study was based on a model proposed by Goldfried, Decenteceo, and Weinberg (1974). Again, given my past learning experiences, my work was facilitated because I took the initiative to contact Dr. Goldfried by telephone to get his support and, most important, his therapeutic training manual.

Before completing my doctorate, I began what I considered my final job search. I was on top of the world: a Hispanic male with a Ph.D. in counseling psychology from Stanford University. Because of my need to be close to my family, I sought jobs solely in the Southwest, California in particular. I had made it, or so I thought. I did get quite a few job offers. I won't go into detail relative to these offers, but I want to share with you one that is imprinted in my mind because it once more put me in my place: I was a Mexican American with a degree, not a so-called American with a degree. To this point, I went to the University of Texas at Austin for an interview for a counseling psychology faculty position. After two days of interviews, I was taken by the interviewing faculty to a quite informal farewell dinner. At this rather relaxed event, I was able to ask questions I had not asked previously. Foremost in my mind was why during my two days in Austin I had not had any exposure to the Hispanic population of the community. I wanted to know where they lived. I wanted to have a sense of their living conditions. The response I got sent me running back to California. Relative to my question regarding where Hispanics lived, I was told by a non-Hispanic White male that I would have no problems finding living accommodations in Austin because I did not look like one of them (i.e., Mexicans). Enough said. I took a job at the Counseling and Psychological Services Center at the University of California at Los Angeles (UCLA).

I was the first racial/ethnic minority psychologist hired at this Center. While there was a psychologist from China and one from Chile, they concentrated their work on foreign students—first things first. When I was hired, I was given the charge of being responsible for working with students from diverse backgrounds (i.e., race and ethnicity) and lifestyles (i.e., gays and lesbians). Within a couple of days of my being employed, I once more blatantly faced the reality of society's perspective of me. A senior social worker employed at the Center, the wife of a former chair of the Department of Social Welfare at UCLA, came into my office and directly asked me "What are you?" Being a "smart ass," I decided to milk that question to the fullest. I responded by stating the obvious: "I'm a human being. I'm a male." That was not the answer she was seeking, so she must have felt the need to be more specific: "No, what ethnic group do you belong to?" "You don't look or talk like one of them (i.e., Mexicans) and you have a Ph.D." This was my welcome to the working world of intellectuals and professionals in higher education.

Given my lack of tolerance for any kind of discrimination, I soon took steps to end my being designated as the principal psychologist to work with persons from racial/ethnic and cultural minority groups. As persons from such groups became aware of my existence on campus, I came to have an endless list of appointments. In contrast, some of my non-Hispanic White counterparts, having less appointments, had the luxury during the workday to read the newspaper and/or journal articles. Needless to say, this situation did not last long. I went to the director of the Center and took a strong position regarding the fact that I was carrying a bigger workload than many of my colleagues and, more important, that the reason for this was that they did not feel competent to work with racial/ethnic minority persons and as such these persons were shuffled over to me, even if it meant putting them on a waiting list. My position was that this was a discriminatory practice that had to be addressed or else I would make a public issue of the matter in the process of resigning my position. Things changed. Multicultural-cultural training for the staff was instituted shortly thereafter.

I never really wanted to be a full-time researcher, but I had spent so much time learning to be one I could not let my research skills fall by the wayside, so I negotiated with the Counseling Center director to allow me to spend one day a week working as a consultant/researcher at the Spanish-Speaking Mental Health Research Center, which, at the time, was the place where most of the social/behavioral research on Hispanics was being conducted and/or gathered. It was at this Center where I had the opportunity and privilege to meet and work with some of the principal founding persons of Chicano psychology: Amado Padilla, Rene Ruiz, and Marta Bernal. While at UCLA I also had the great privilege and honor to meet and work with Evelyn Hooker, a person who helped me broaden my perspectives of who I was and what I could do for persons like myself.

My stint at UCLA was short-lived. As previously mentioned, one of my primary purposes for pursuing a Ph.D. was to provide me with the means for getting into positions that might help me work more effectively and efficiently with at-risk Hispanic children and more specifically to do whatever I could to increase the opportunities for Hispanic children to pursue their dreams via higher education. At UCLA, I soon discovered that a "staff" person has little or no power to impact or bring about change in the institution, especially as it relates to students in general and to racial/ethnic minority students in particular. The power lies in the academic faculty. So after two years, I once more initiated a job search for a faculty position. Because of my attachment to my family, I concentrated on jobs in California and was fortunate to land a position as Assistant Professor at the University of California at Santa Barbara—which has been my home base since 1977.

When I started at Santa Barbara, the counseling program consisted of three professors, Don Atkinson, Ray Hosford, and me. We offered both M.A. and Ph.D. degrees. The program that we offered, though quite solid, was generic in nature and did not have a unique emphasis. Over the years, our program became an APA accredited counseling psychology program, grew in size, increased its visibility, established a very strong academic reputation, developed a strong multicultural emphasis, and graduated some very distinguished scholars who are found in institutions across the nation, including but not limited to Joe Ponterotto, Fordham University; Bruce Wampold, University of Wisconsin at Madison; Mike Furlong, University of California at Santa Barbara; Cindy Juntunen, University of North Dakota at Grand Forks; José Abreu, University of Southern California; and Bryan Kim, University of Maryland. With help and direction from colleagues, I pursued my own, rather erratic multicultural research path, giving special attention to Chicano families and children. My pursuits resulted in numerous publications that I hope have been of help to young scholars. My research, publication, and editorial interests enabled me to work with some very notable colleagues, including but not limited to Amado Padilla, Rene Ruiz, Marta Bernal, Melba Vasquez, Paul Pedersen, Joe Ponterotto, Joe Trimble, Esteban Olmedo, Derald Sue, Lillian Comas-Díaz, Puncky Heppner, and Christine Iijima Hall. My efforts were well rewarded in 1998 when, along with Amado Padilla, Marta Bernal, and Manuel Ramirez, I was honored by the Julian Samora Research Institute, Michigan State University, as one of the founding persons of Chicano psychology.

WHERE TO GO FROM HERE

I didn't know where I was going, but I got here anyway. As you can tell from the paths that I have followed in the labyrinth of my life, I did not have a set blueprint that would tell me how and where to go in order to get to this point. I knew that I wanted to get to that position where I worked with and for those persons with whom I most identified: the disenfranchised, immigrants, racial/ethnic minorities, and gays and lesbians. While I hope that I have not reached the end of my life's journey, I gratifyingly state that I am quite satisfied traveling down the path on which I presently find myself. I continue to be quite productive in my academic pursuits: Along with my colleague, Mike Furlong, we have managed to help bring a significant amount of grant money close to the County of Santa Barbara for the development of therapeutic and educational interventions for high-risk children, I co-chair the Chancellor's Outreach Advisory Board that annually oversees the distribution of $2.3 million earmarked for increasing the diversity of students eligible for applying to the University of California, and, most important of all, I have the time to stop and help serve breakfast to children at my local Head Start preschool, the majority of whom are monolingual Spanish-speaking. Looking to the future, I once more turn to Octavio Paz (1961), who strongly asserts that "at the exit from the labyrinth of solitude we will find reunion (which is repose and happiness), and plenitude, and harmony with the world" (p. 196). I look forward to moving from here and following the path that gets me to that future place in my life.

RELEVANT PUBLICATIONS

Heppner, P. P., Casas, J. M., Carter, J., & Stone, G. L. (2000). The maturation of counseling psychology: Multifaceted perspectives, 1978–1998. In S. D. Brown & R. W. Lent (Eds.), *Handbook of counseling psychology* (3rd ed., pp. 3-49). New York: John Wiley.

Ponterotto, J. G., & Casas, J. M. (1991). *Handbook of racial/ethnic minority counseling research.* Springfield, IL: Charles C Thomas.

Ponterotto, J. G., Casas, J. M., Suzuki, L. A., & Alexander, C. M. (1995). *Handbook of multicultural counseling.* Thousand Oaks, CA: Sage.

CITED REFERENCES

Goldfried, M. R., Decenteceo, E. T., & Weinberg, L. (1974). Systematic rationale restructuring as a self control technique. *Behavior Therapy, 5,* 247-254.

Paz, O. (1961). *The labyrinth of solitude: Life and thought in Mexico.* New York: Grove Press.

Correspondence regarding this chapter may be sent to J. Manuel Casas, Counseling/Clinical/School Psychology Program, Graduate School of Education, University of California at Santa Barbara, Santa Barbara, CA 93106 (e-mail address: casas@education.ucsb.edu).

Chapter 9

THE SEAMLESS CULTURAL CONNECTIONS IN MY LIFE

No Beginning . . . No Ending

PAUL BODHOLDT PEDERSEN

IN RETROSPECT, the cultural connections in my life always appear seamless, as they unfold from one salience to the next. I spoke Danish before speaking English, so when I flunked out of kindergarten all I remember are two days of loud noise and everyone being angry at me, making me think I had done something terribly wrong! My parents had never been to Denmark but, in our small farm in Iowa, preferred the Danish language of my grandparents to English. I remember being about 5 years old sitting in the ditch beside the road in front of our "Lilac Hill Farm" thinking that our road was connected to every other road in the world, and then I reached up to touch the road in amazement. I remember our family reading out loud about two or three books a week during cold winter nights, and the whole living room was lined with books, including the "Harvard Classics." I remember people in trouble frequently driving 30 to 40 miles to come and talk about their trouble with my father, who was an unintentional counselor with considerable skill. I remember once-a-month gatherings inside in the winter and outside around a huge bonfire in the summer, eating, talking, and singing both hymns and rowdy drinking songs with much laughing.

Our family was among the "Happy Danes" led by the Danish Bishop N. F. S. Grundtvig who began the Folk School movement in Denmark and believed in bringing cultural enlightenment to all people through the "Living Word." This all happened during the Great Depression when my parents barely paid the mortgage for the farm each month and there was absolutely no extra money, although I never felt "poor." Even when a tornado destroyed all the farm buildings except the house when I was about 8, I viewed our possible relocation to the Emmet County Poor Farm as an exciting new adventure. I learned early the importance of optimism. As my 98-year-old Aunt Agneta put it, "If you are grateful, people will love you, and if you are thankful, God will love you."

As a sophomore at Grand View Junior College in Des Moines, Iowa, my roommate and I found the European History course so exciting that we decided to spend the next summer hitchhiking through Europe. We budgeted the trip at $5 a day each, including the ship passage over and back. We never knew where we would spend the next night, and every day was full of exciting new uncertainties, adventures, and opportunities to learn. My journal from that summer typed out to 120 pages single spaced. We slept in German haystacks, Venetian gondolas, and Swiss police stations and on Italian beaches, but usually we slept in youth hostels with other "sophomores" hitching around on the cheap. That summer was the least expensive tuition and most powerful multicultural education I ever experienced.

When I next moved to the University of Minnesota, I paid for my education by washing dishes at a food co-op and working as a hospital orderly in the psychiatric wards of U of M Hospital. We orderlies were often consulted by the psychiatrists to learn more about what patients were doing in their daily lives, and that is probably where my interest in psychological issues began. I was able to see, through the eyes of the patients and doctors, the mysteries of how we think and glimpse the inner world. I remember being shocked by how "normal" the patients were in the locked wards. I also remember assisting in electric current therapy (ECT) and helping patients "find their way back to reality" afterward. Every day was filled with learning opportunities.

After receiving my B.A. from the U of M in history and philosophy, I decided I needed to stay on for an M.A. in American Studies to better learn my own roots. I focused on American jazz music, the "Akron Plan" of church architecture, and Henry David Thoreau, all of which harmonized wonderfully. Then I went to the Lutheran School of Theology, now located on the University of Chicago campus, for a master's degree in theology. I wanted to find out the answers to "ultimate" questions about who we are and why people do what they do. I was ordained a minister in the Lutheran Church in America, although I never had a congregation.

The Lutheran World Federation in 1962 offered me a chance to teach philosophy and ethics and be Chaplain at Nommensen University in North Sumatra to about 2,500 students for 3 years. There were many anti-American demonstrations during this time. I remember bicycling to teach my ethics class one day and seeing thousands of students in a mob coming toward me. I recognized some of my students from the ethics class who greeted me and said they would try to make it back to class as soon as possible after sacking the British Consulate. On another occasion, a student burst into the ethics class to say they had wrongly arrested the Vice Rector and what were we going to do about it? I led the march on the police station with my students and was later scolded by the Consulate. The head of the Youth Communist Party and the head of the Anti-Communist Secret Youth Underground were both seeing me for counseling on their personal problems. During that time, I translated into the Indonesian language the 400-item, multiscaled Lutheran Youth Research Inventory developed by Merton Strommen in Minneapolis and modeled on the MMPI. I gathered data from hundreds of students in North Sumatra and in Central Java to look at "the role of religion in social change." I learned how psychological processes are alive and healthy in Asia but are usually expressed through philosophy, history, politics, religion, or other fields of study. It was at this point that I became vividly aware of how culturally encapsulated the field of psychological counseling was at that time.

I determined to go back to the University of Minnesota for a Ph.D. in counseling. Clyde Parker was my adviser there. He met with all his advisees in a T-group once a week and his definition of education was "something that happens by accident when you are trying to do something else." One particularly important graduate seminar at the U of M involved no tests or papers but only one original idea written on one side of a single blank page. I wrote about the "problem" as a third member of the counseling dyad and came up with the Triad Training Model from that seminar.

After receiving the M.A. in counseling from the University of Minnesota I decided to transfer to Claremont Graduate School in California to attempt a multidisciplinary Ph.D. in Asian psychological counseling, studying in the fields of religion, cultural history, counseling, and political theory. I expected to spend the rest of my life working in Asia as a counselor. In my dissertation titled "The Role of Religion in Social Change Among the Bataks of North Sumatra," I defined religion as "those principles or ideas which do not change when everything around them changes," like "hinges" making it possible for the door of change to swing open. I have never enjoyed writing anything as much as I enjoyed writing my dissertation. I finished the first draft in a week and could hardly take time to eat or sleep from the excitement. The first chapter alone was nearly 100 pages long and was later expanded to become my first book, *Batak Blood and Protestant Soul.*

I do not regret getting a multidisciplinary Ph.D., but neither do I recommend it to others. You can imagine my trying to explain my doctorate in Asian studies so as to gain membership and later Fellow status in the American Psychological Association. While I consider myself professionally most comfortable with the fields of psychology and counseling, I do not provide a typical background profile. I have become accustomed to looking at the professional field of counseling psychology from the "outside" as an uninvited guest, even though many of my students have become leading insiders.

In 1968, I went back to Taiwan for a year of full-time Mandarin language study and to translate the LYR inventory into Chinese for use in Malaysia, where I spent the next two years with my wife and three children. During the race riots in 1969, the only persons not under attack were foreigners, so I drove ambulances around the otherwise deserted Kuala Lumpur and organized discussion groups to keep students off the streets. My task in Malaysia was to gather data from youths and students throughout Malaysia and Singapore and to teach classes at the University of Malaya in education and society. I learned a lot from my students there and was particularly disturbed by the "acculturation" of those students who went to the United States to study and now found it impossible to fit in back home. I decided then to focus on working with international students in the United States. The U of Minnesota offered me a faculty appointment in Psychoeducational Studies and the International Student Advisors Office. From 1971 to 1978 I worked with international students and taught the cross-cultural counseling course in Psychoeducational Studies. I was also actively involved in teach-ins about why the Vietnam War was misguided and likely to do much more harm than good for both the United States and Southeast Asia.

The book *Counseling Across Cultures*, which is soon coming out in its fifth edition through Sage, was put together at that time for my course. Walt Lonner, Juris Draguns, Joe Trimble, and myself organized a symposium on "Counseling Across Cultures" at the Montreal APA meeting that was so successful we decided to edit a book on the topic. All the publishers I approached turned the proposal down. Finally, the East-West Center in Hawaii agreed to publish the book, since I was a Senior Fellow there in 1975–1976, provided we waive all royalties. The first edition of *Counseling Across Cultures* went through several printings in the first year alone and has done extremely well in the subsequent four editions. Many colleagues in the age 30 to 35 range tell me that *CAC* was the first book they read on multicultural counseling and led to their continuing interest in the topic.

Friends at NIMH encouraged me to write a proposal on cross-cultural training of counselors, which I did in 1978, to be housed at the University of Hawaii and the East-West Center in Honolulu. Derald Sue agreed to be External Evaluator for the Developing Interculturally Skilled Counselors (DISC) project in Hawaii, and Tony Marsella at the U of H agreed to be Director of Training. Our "annual conference" resulted in one book a year plus many other publications and consultations. We offered five or six predoctoral trainee positions a year, which included tuition expenses plus a living stipend. We taught two courses a term in cross-cultural counseling through the Psychology Department and the School of Social Work. We also took teams of trainees to do training at Clark Air Force Base in the Philippines, Yong Son in Korea, the U.S. Army base in Okinawa, Saipan in Micronesia to train local mental health workers, Vancouver (Canada), and elsewhere around the United States and Hawaii. Each team would collectively do a needs assessment, write a training plan, design educational activities, deliver the training and evaluate the training experience. Derald, Tony, and I came up with the competencies in cultural awareness, knowledge, and skill as the criteria for evaluating each class session and training activity in the four-year DISC project. Most if not all the writing I have done since that time originated in what I learned from the students, trainees, faculty, and participants in the DISC project activities.

When the NIMH grant was completed, I moved to Syracuse University to teach in the Counseling and Human Services Department in the School of Education. I worked with my wife, Anne, who was a New Zealand trained organizational psychologist, in the Pacific Science Association, where she was Chair of the Science Communication and Education Committee. The National Science Foundation along with the National Science Council in Taiwan provided eight years of funding to study the reentry of scientists and engineers from Taiwan after completion of their study abroad. Our research indicated that the reentry decision was more profoundly influenced by family and national loyalties than by financial incentives. We both taught at Harvard Summer School every year from 1985 to 1989 and had a chance to spend time with leaders like B. F. Skinner in his home and in ours. It seems ironic to me that Skinner was even more empathic, warm, and genuine than Carl Rogers in spite of their APA debates against one another. In 1987, Anne's brain tumor was diagnosed but, despite all predictions, she continued being productive in her research, writings, and leadership of the PSA until 1996 when she died.

Anne and I both taught in the University of Pittsburgh "Semester at Sea" program, sailing around the world in 1992 teaching courses and working with the 400 mostly undergraduate students aboard ship. I asked my students to write on eight critical incidents they experienced, witnessed, or heard about from their time in each port to illustrate psychological constructs in the "Small Groups," "Cross-Cultural," and "Personality" classes I was teaching. I gathered 300 of the best stories the students submitted in a book I titled *The Five Stages of Culture Shock*. The Greenwood Press copy editor told me this was the only book in her whole career where she would break out laughing while she was copyediting. The opportunities for learning from these experiences were almost unlimited.

In 1995, I moved from Syracuse University to the University of Alabama at Birmingham. I had never expected to live in the South and, if so, certainly not in Birmingham! Much to my surprise, I found the faculty and community at UAB to be perhaps the friendliest and most collegial of any in my professional career. I actually looked forward to faculty meetings! The UAB School of Education has a counseling program in Orot, Israel, and I taught there for a term, learning about the Middle East crisis from the wrong side of the "Green Line." Fred Jandt and I had just organized a conference on "Constructive Conflict Management in a Cultural Context" through The Asia Foundation in Penang, Malaysia, resulting in a book we coedited titled *Constructive Conflict Management: Asia-Pacific Cases.* The experience at Orot further underlined how culturally encapsulated our perspective of conflict and conflict management is by our narrowly defined Euro-American assumptions.

These international experiences also led to another symposium at the International Congress of Psychology in Montreal, which resulted in the book *Multiculturalism as a Fourth Force.* It is increasingly clear that psychology in general, and counseling in particular, is rapidly changing in response to pressure by broadly defined cultural groups for recognition. Culture provides a "best fit" metaphor for understanding these dynamic and complex changes in psychology and counseling. Multiculturalism is not competing with a behavioral, psychodynamic, or humanistic perspective but complements these theories much as the fourth dimension of time complements three-dimensional space. By making culture central rather than marginal to counseling theory, the potency of that theory is increased, not decreased.

When my colleagues ask me why I am wasting my time on cultural things, I respond by asking them if they value accuracy. They almost always say "yes." Then I smile and tell them that we are on the same side. If every behavior is learned and displayed in a separate cultural context, then accurate assessment, meaningful understanding, and appropriate intervention require attention to that cultural context. The cultural perspective is uniquely useful. By reframing all our relationships (parent/child, husband/wife, sister/brother) into a cultural perspective, it becomes possible for two persons or groups to disagree in their behaviors even while sharing the same "common ground" expectations and core values. Not everyone who smiles is your friend, nor is everyone who shouts at you your enemy. I am less interested in training "multicultural" counselors and more interested in training "competent" counselors.

These insights led to my finally publishing *Hidden Messages in Culture-Centered Counseling,* a book I began in 1968, on the Triad Training Model. The more cultural differences in counseling, the more messages will be "hidden." In TTM training, each client is matched with a pro-counselor and an anti-counselor to articulate the positive and negative "hidden" messages to the culturally different counselor or client. I have become convinced that all communication is fundamentally intrapersonal and multicultural as we encode and decode messages, each according to our own culturally learned rules. Each of us has more than 1,000 "culture teachers" sitting in our chair with us whom we have accumulated over a lifetime from friends, enemies, family, fantasies, and elsewhere. Competence begins with the ability to hear those internalized voices in ourselves and in our clients.

All of my professional life I have focused on Asia. Many of the changes occurring in psychology and in counseling are moving in the direction of non-Western and particularly Asian cultures where the "self" is a relational entity, where subjective as well as objective data are respected, and where health is best defined as a "balance" of positive and negative forces in our life. In this "two-directional" perspective, pain is as important as pleasure to finding meaning in life. I accepted a Senior Fulbright Grant to teach at National Taiwan University for the 1999–2000 academic year to learn more about these Asian perspectives and the "Easternization" of psychology. The indigenization of psychology is a popular theme among Asian counselors and psychologists, where talk therapy is less popular among the people than going to a local priest to have your "soul called back" after a traumatic experience.

What have I learned from all these seamlessly connected experiences? First, I have learned about myself and increased my own multicultural awareness. Second, I have learned that behavior is meaningless until and unless that behavior is interpreted in the cultural context where it was learned and is displayed. Third, I have learned that a multicultural perspective complicates one's life but that complexity is my friend, not my enemy. Fourth, I have learned to watch for the "surprises" that indicate learning has just occurred and to articulate that learning quickly before it fades away. Fifth, I have learned the importance of working with a mentor. When students ask where to go for graduate study, I suggest they budget 2 hours a day for one week going through periodicals in the library, searching for a mentor who is doing what they would like to do. Then read everything that mentor wrote and finally write the mentor indicating an interest in working with him or her. Sixth, I have learned the importance of working on multiple related topics at the same time so that working on one project contributes to work on all the other ongoing projects. Finally, I have learned to appreciate the wonderful privilege of meaningful work that gives life its greatest pleasure.

RELEVANT PUBLICATIONS

Pedersen, P. (1995). *Five stages of culture shock: Critical incidents around the world.* Westport, CT: Greenwood.

Pedersen, P. (1999). *Multiculturalism as a fourth force.* Philadelphia: Brunner/Mazel–Taylor & Francis.

Pedersen, P. (2000). *A handbook for developing multicultural awareness* (3rd ed.). Alexandria, VA: American Counseling Association.

Pedersen, P. (2000). *Hidden messages in culture-centered counseling: A triad training model.* Thousand Oaks, CA: Sage.

Pedersen, P., Draguns, J., Lonner, W., & Trimble, J. (in press). *Counseling across cultures* (5th ed.). Thousand Oaks, CA: Sage

Correspondence regarding this chapter may be sent to Paul Bodholdt Pedersen, 1777 Ala Moana Blvd. #726, Honolulu, HI 96815 (e-mail address: pedersen_us@yahoo.com).

Chapter 10

EMBRACING MULTICULTURALISM

A Journey of Self-Discovery

AMY L. REYNOLDS

I have come to believe over and over again that what is most important to me must be spoken, made verbal and shared, even at the risk of having it bruised or misunderstood.

—Audre Lorde (1984, p. 40)

WRITING THIS CHAPTER has been a process, a journey of self-discovery from the moment I received the request. I have thought and reflected for months and have spoken with those who are dear to me about my feelings, my ideas, and especially about my questions. Never before have I written something that was so introspective and personal yet designed to be so public. This process of self-exploration has brought me to a new understanding of my personal history, my racial identity, as well as my personal and professional hopes and dreams.

I begin my story by talking about who I am and what I believe. From that context I can weave the different life experiences and realizations that have shaped who I am and who I will become. I began with the quote by Audre Lorde, who, although I never met her, has been a challenge and inspiration to me for the past 15 years. In my life I have strived to understand and appreciate myself and others. Sometimes, that process has demanded that I accept aspects of myself that I find uncomfortable and tell truths that I have wanted to avoid. Without such truth-telling, none of us can move forward toward valuing each other. I firmly believe that our lives and our futures are forever interconnected. True progress within our profession, our academic communities, or the political system is not possible unless we believe and act as if our survivals are mutual.

To that end, I think it is important that I offer my personal definition of multiculturalism, for it is the basis of the work that I do. I believe multiculturalism is about creating a new world where all people, *because* of who they are (as differentiated from regardless of who they are), are welcomed, appreciated, and celebrated. It moves far beyond a simple "We Are the World" mentality to the challenges of difficult dialogues across differences. It means acknowledging our biases and striving to overcome our limitations. It focuses on raising our awareness of our cultural assumptions about ourselves and the world. Multiculturalism cannot exist if we are not willing to change our minds, our hearts, and our lives. We must build alliances with those who are different from us and not be tempted to surround ourselves in sameness. And finally, we must transform our worldview in order to move beyond our very real human and spiritual limitations.

In concrete terms, I view multiculturalism from both universal and race-based perspectives. I firmly believe that the full range of social identities that influence who we are (race, class, gender, sexual/affectional orientation, religion, language, abilities, and age) must be understood and incorporated into our understanding of multiculturalism. Because of the complexity of diversity, we all experience life from the perspective of those social identities (from either the dominant or target group point of view) whether we realize it or not. And those life experiences shape who we are and how we relate to others. The dominant worldview in this country is dualistic and reductionistic, so most of us primarily think of ourselves in terms of one or two identities; yet those self-perceptions do not take away the complexity of all that we are. However, in addition to these beliefs, I know in my heart that our country and all of us in it are in the midst of a long journey in which race, racial identity, and racism are central to how we view ourselves, each other, and the relationships and community that we are able to create. No matter how hard we try to believe otherwise, we have all internalized racial assumptions that create barriers in our relationships. And these barriers will not be overcome without deliberate self-evaluation and a personal commitment to building relationships with people who are different from us. We must face these challenges if we are to move forward individually and collectively. While some may find the universal and race-based definitions of multiculturalism contradictory, I see them naturally coexisting side by side as a symbol of the diunital (i.e., both/and) thinking that I believe is necessary to the creation of a psychology and a world that fully embrace multiculturalism.

So, how is it that I have come to believe these things? When I look back at my childhood and upbringing, in many ways I have often wondered how it is that I ended up here. I grew up in an all-White environment in a middle-class family of economic and educational privilege in which I never had a personal relationship with a person who was racially different from me until I was 17 years old and involved in high school athletics. And even then, I was merely curious about their racial background and probably didn't give it much more thought than that. My parents rarely, if ever, mentioned or acknowledged race, much less any other kind of difference. When I look back at my childhood, I can probably count on two hands the number of times when I contemplated racial or any other differences. Yet despite little or no encouragement to explore multicultural issues for over half of my life, I now view myself as a professional who is focusing her life's work on multiculturalism and is committed to training others to work more effectively across all types of differences. Now I must be clear here. This is less of a professional choice and more of a personal commitment. You see, I also am a White woman who has been partnered for 12 years with an African American woman with whom I am raising two young biracial children. What I do professionally is merely an extension of what I struggle with on a daily basis. What really matters to me in both my personal and professional life is to being part of creating environments that are inclusive and affirming. I want to help build a world where my two biracial children who are growing up with two moms of different racial backgrounds consistently feel their family is fully accepted and valued.

How my own personal evolution has occurred is somewhat related to how I view multiculturalism. That is what I want to share with you. Not because I think it is the "right" way to do it or the only way to do it but, rather, because it is the process and journey itself (more than the results or outcome) that has mattered to me. This is my story as best as I can articulate it, and even as I write it I know it is probably inaccurate in some ways and definitely incomplete and unfinished. I will try my best to articulate my worldview, although I realize I am not always able to fully step outside myself and appreciate all that influences who I am.

When I look back, I now see that my journey toward multiculturalism began with my faith development. This is a new insight for me and is probably a reflection of where I am in my own spiritual journey. I was raised Catholic, and when I was young and attending catechism class, I believed with all my heart what I was taught: that we should all treat each other fairly and justly and look for godliness in everyone. In many ways, my belief in racial equality, feminism, and multiculturalism grew out of my belief in peace and justice. And those beliefs grew from my faith and convenant with God. My own sense of spirituality and faith has grown in so many directions and ways since I was a child. There have been many times in my life when I really did not participate in any type of faith community and other times, like when I was in graduate school, where I spent many waking hours exploring my spirituality. No matter where I was in that struggle, I always had an unwavering belief in the generosity of God and the capacity of the human spirit. As a lesbian I have had to redefine my faith and my own relationship with God over the years, and while that has been a long journey, I have returned to where I began: a social-justice-based Catholicism that shapes my perceptions of the world, my view of others, and the core values in my life.

While my journey may have begun with my faith, it became politicized as I experienced feminism in the 1970s. I was a girl who wanted to be treated fairly, and my identity as a feminist began with my personal outrage at how differently male and female athletes were treated. Those beliefs were further strengthened in my 20s when I came out as a lesbian to myself and my family. I went through a period of lesbian and feminist immersion while in graduate school that allowed me to redefine myself and feel confident about who I was, despite what society and my parents thought. Living in that lesbian feminist world was crucial to my own sense of self and my ability to understand oppression, especially internalized oppression. It gave me an understanding as to why I had always felt different, like I didn't belong. When I came out and found a community, I thought I'd found an antidote to that feeling of not belonging. I was wrong.

At some point, I began to realize, quietly, inwardly that this lesbian world I was living in was almost completely White. And while many of us spoke out against racism passionately, there was limited racial diversity among us. I slowly began to reflect on earlier life events that had influenced my White identity. I remember how during my training as an undergraduate peer counselor I was told by a Black staff member that I would never understand what it meant to be Black and that would probably always affect my relationships with Blacks and other people of color. That upset me tremendously, and at the age of 20 I experienced the first major event that would forever alter my White racial identity and begin my journey to where I am today. I was determined to prove that person wrong and be a "good" White person. In terms of my racial identity at that point in my life, how I felt about my own race was partially determined by how people of color viewed me. Like many Whites, I operated from a liberal desire to do "right" and not perpetuate racism at any level. I didn't realize at the time that I was operating out of guilt, which made it difficult for me to form genuine relationships with people of color. However, that experience and the insight it gave me, along with several other important life events, forever imprinted on me the centrality of racism in understanding discrimination and oppression.

Fighting racism and understanding my own racial identity (even before I had the words or theory to understand what that meant) have been at the center of my multiculturalism since that significant life event. Initially, it was a cognitive and political understanding. I believed and tried to say all the right things. As a doctoral student I became involved politically in the anti-apartheid struggle on my campus. I passionately cared about the issue and committed my time and energy to the cause. For the first time, I became an activist and really believed that fighting racism was my struggle too.

Then one day in the midst of a conversation about race, a friend of mine who was Black asked me if I had ever spent significant time at an African American friend's home. As I answered no, I slowly realized the significance of my response. If I truly cared about these issues, why were my closest friends almost exclusively White? Why did I not have any deep friendships with people of color? That was a difficult self-realization, and it was in that moment that my entire journey changed as I realized I had the belief and the passion but I never had really changed my life. Despite what I said I believed and what I wanted in the world, I was still living in a predominantly White world with people who were mostly like me. And since that time, I have not been the same. I realized that I needed to learn to be authentic and take the interpersonal risks that were necessary to build deeper relationships with my friends who were people of color. Ever since that time I have continually chosen to put myself in professional and personal situations where I was challenged to grow in my understanding and commitment toward multiculturalism.

Another indelible life experience occurred while I was in graduate school at Ohio State University. I, along with several other doctoral students plus two faculty members, created a multicultural research team that changed the way I viewed myself and the world around me. We were a multiracial group of women who also encompassed differences of age, sexual orientation, class, and spirituality. What began as a research team quickly grew into a multicultural laboratory where we openly examined our beliefs, challenged each other, and tried to develop a new way of looking at psychology and identity development. There were both emotional and mind-bending conversations as well as individual and group conflict. This intense experience showed me how rich my life was when I was immersed in relationships and work where diversity was at the core and how few times in my life I had actually encountered such diversity.

Realizing my desire for more opportunities for immersion in culturally diverse environments caused me to reprioritize my life, which is why I chose to do my internship in Southern California where I knew even more multiracial experiences would be available. I brought with me an enthusiasm for multiculturalism and a willingness to fully examine myself, my beliefs, and my behaviors. As someone who grew up in Midwest suburbia, I had little personal understanding of Latino, Native American, or Asian experiences of the world. I chose to do my internship at UC Irvine because I knew it would take me to a place unlike any I had known. We had a diverse group of interns and staff, and there was much tension and conflict about diversity issues, especially race. I had to face conflict, often based in cultural differences, that made me uncomfortable and unsure of myself. I began to get comfortable with chaos and conflict (mine and others) being at the center of my own multicultural struggle. Like many Whites, speaking my mind felt risky. I learned to say what I felt and challenge others who viewed the world differently. I began to realize that cultural knowledge was far less important than my way of being in the world. So, I began to focus less on content and more on my relationships. A fellow intern adopted me into her family, which was racially and culturally very different from me, and through that friendship I began to see what was in front of me all of the time. With her quiet words and examples, my friend showed me that all I had to do was be myself and be open to hearing the stories of others. Through those stories and relationships, she told me that I would learn all that I needed to know. When I look back now, some of these realizations seem so simple, and I wonder why it sometimes takes me a while to discover them. I already had important and genuine relationships with people of color that developed out of common values and respect for differences. Why did I continue to think that there was some answer out there that could give me more than that?

I left California and drove my car to the Midwest where I worked at the University of Iowa Counseling Center for four years. Despite the fact that I have lived in the Los Angeles area and then later New York City, the great irony is that I probably learned the most about race, racism, and oppression in Iowa City, Iowa. While there, I had the opportunity to affiliate with the Women's Resource and Advocacy Center and the most powerful group of women I have ever known. I joined a group called Women Against Racism. It was a multiracial group of women who were different across as many variables as you could imagine: class, sexual orientation, religion, language, ability, age, and, of course, race, ethnicity, and nationality. We met weekly for the purpose of "personal work," which was to challenge ourselves and each other about issues of difference and sameness. We also focused on educating others, offering local and national workshops. I arrived there a committed White lesbian who was still making sense of what it meant to be a White woman. I left there four years later more humble, more courageous, and more self-aware than I had ever been. I learned to take risks, to admit what I didn't know, and to form genuine and meaningful relationships with women who were different from me. I really learned how to be comfortable with the process of exploring, defining, and redefining who I am. That process has become quite familiar to me, and I have realized that the process is more important than what or who I know.

I also had the opportunity to put my multicultural values and knowledge into my professional life at a completely new level. For the first time, I really began to acknowledge that I had some expertise in the area of multiculturalism and was eager to share it with my colleagues. What is significant here is not that all of a sudden I became an expert, but I suddenly believed and valued my own insight, knowledge, and skills. So, I helped lead an organizational effort to infuse multiculturalism in a counseling center in a predominantly White institution. I believe that we were very successful in our efforts. And not necessarily by the standard outcome data like how many psychologists of color were there, or how many students of color we served. We were effective because everyone who worked there fully engaged in the process of self-examination and organizational exploration to see how we could all more fully embrace multiculturalism. Our collaboration showed me how important and powerful the organizational and systemic aspects are in the struggle to create a multicultural world.

I left Iowa and moved to New York City where I lived for seven wonderful years surrounded by the full richness of diversity. I truly loved the vitality and humanness of that place. It was a place where I couldn't hide from the reality of poverty, racism, mistrust, and despair. I felt so alive and at times so overwhelmed by its enormity. And because I was so frequently surrounded by diversity, whether it be on the subway or on the streets, I came to realize a lot about myself and my own biases and assumptions, especially concerning race and social class. I learned that no matter how hard I had worked to eradicate racism within me I continued to be bombarded at times by my own stereotypes and assumptions about people.

I spent most of my 30s in New York City, and I became fully aware of my limits and grew into a fuller understanding of how I needed and wanted to live my life. I feel such fondness for New York City for very personal reasons. It was in that city that I made a public commitment to love and cherish my life partner. It was there that our two beautiful children were born full of promise and hope. And it was in the early mornings of sitting with my children watching the sun gloriously rise over the city outside my window that I redefined my passion about multiculturalism as being centered in my children and the future. At that moment, multiculturalism became even more personal because it was about my family and how I wanted to live my life.

When I think about it, my family is an illustration of who I am and how multiculturalism fits into my life. Twelve years ago when I met and fell in love with Raechele, my life partner, I had no idea how much our relationship would change my life. Since we first met, we have been aware of and often discussed our differences in terms of race, class, and family experiences. We have challenged each other through the questions we ask ourselves and each other. Despite our apparent differences, it is our similarities in values and dreams that drew us to each other and cement the bond between us. From the beginning, we knew we wanted children and we knew those children would be biracial so that they would look like and represent both of us. Our creation of family and community has been very deliberate and has only strengthened my belief that we are so blessed in our ability to redefine what family means. We had already broken all the rules, so why not start from scratch and create the type of family and community that we believe will most benefit and strengthen us and our children?

When we decided to have children, we chose a family name that was meaningful to us. Raechele and I hyphenate our birth names with our family name in all nonprofessional settings and have given that family name to our children. When we chose names for our children, we decided that one of their names would be one of our core values and their other name would be after a person of color who embodied many of our beliefs. We had naming ceremonies for our children within the first 2 months of their lives to which we invited our community of family and friends to welcome our children into the world and to pledge support for their development as human beings. In everything we do, we try to center our values in faith, culture and community and live our life that way.

Yet those choices have not come without conflict with the outside world or between us. Initially, there were tensions with some of my family members, especially my parents, as they struggled to adjust to our family and the choices we made. And as we have made decisions about our future and how we want to live our lives, Raechele and I have had to struggle with our sometimes differing points of view or suggested solutions to a given problem or concern. When we decided to leave New York City for a simpler, more affordable life in upstate New York, we had to struggle with some of the compromises such a move created. We have moved to a predominantly White community where it has been challenging to immerse our children in culturally diverse environments. While we have very similar values, we often approach the situations or dilemmas from different vantage points. I have come to realize very recently that much of my own racial identity is caught up in how I, as a White woman, parent my children of color and my ability to prepare them for living in a diverse world. This awareness is still unfolding for me and lately I've realized that my struggle is even more personal. It wasn't just about my children. I am also struggling with my own feelings about being back in a predominantly White environment and what I feel I am losing. I have found that I thrive when I can immerse myself in multicultural settings. I feel more in touch with myself, more alive. So many life choices are so complicated and conflicted with sometimes competing strengths and weaknesses. Every day, I strive to understand myself and the choices I make.

As I write all of this, it feels so personal, and yet I realize that it is important to me that I be comfortable with my struggle, regardless of how it looks from the outside. There is so much that I have come to believe that guides this journey for me. Multiculturalism is not who I am or what I believe. My multiculturalism is about how I live my life. Part of that is inevitable because I am involved in an interracial relationship and am coparenting two children of color. Yet it is so much more than that. It is how I spend my money, what food I eat, what types of music I listen to and entertainment I participate in, who my friends are, and how I spend my time. In some of those areas of my life, I am doing well. In other areas, I am not doing so great. So I am constantly struggling to understand myself and my choices. I am striving to live my life as I believe.

In some ways, that is why my view about multiculturalism in general and in my life has come full circle. For me, multiculturalism is about faith and humanity and community and family. If I can strive to evolve in my understanding of myself as a cultural being, a racial being, and all of the other parts of who I am, and if I can be successful in living my life as a congruent and genuine human being where my actions and choices match my values, then I believe I can help make a difference in the world. I can be part of the solution and not part of the problem. While much of what I have written here highlights the challenges of multiculturalism, in some ways it seems so simple. Multiculturalism is about understanding ourselves and others who are different from us. To me, multiculturalism is, at its core, about people and relationships. And all relationships are about discovering our commonalities, our cultural differences, and our personal uniquenesses. Balancing those three aspects of all human interactions is often confusing, frustrating, and scary. It is sort of like this marvelous Pat Parker poem titled "For the White person who wants to be my friend." She said, "The first thing you must do is forget that I am Black. The second thing you must do is never forget I am Black." It is like rubbing your head and patting your stomach at the same time. You think you cannot do both at the same time, so you end up focusing on one instead. I think it is like those figure-ground optical illusions where you know there are two ways to look at the picture and until you free your mind to see both ways you are stuck. But once you realize and remember that both exist simultaneously, you have achieved a new way of viewing the world and hopefully yourself.

As I bring this oral history to a close, I can't help but wonder if I told the story I wanted to tell. Looking back I know I didn't talk enough about racism and oppression and how fighting it daily in ourselves, others, and society as a whole must be at the center of multiculturalism. But somehow that seemed more political and less personal and I was striving to reveal my personal struggle. I also know that multiculturalism is so much more than trying to be a good person or figuring out how we can all get along; yet without those important foundations, how can we take on the structural oppression that threatens to overwhelm us?

Simply put, multiculturalism is about people, especially the many friends, mentors, and teachers in my own journey. So many are personal friends, some have been teachers or supervisors, and some I have never met but found their written words to have great personal significance. Each has taught me so much about myself, other people, and the world around us. In telling my story, I honor each of them for the many gifts they have given me.

Combating racism and oppression and working to build a psychology profession that embraces multiculturalism is not a choice for me. It is as natural and as important as breathing. I think writing this chapter has helped me realize that, given who I am, it is inevitable that this is where I am in my life. This chapter has shown me that I no longer need to wonder why I ended up in the midst of this important issue. I am home, and this is where I belong. As Malcolm X said in his *Autobiography* (1964/1966), "I'm for truth no matter who tells it. I'm for justice, no matter who is for or against it. I'm for whoever and whatever benefits humanity as a whole."

RELEVANT PUBLICATIONS

Myers, L. J., Speight, S. L., Highlen, P. S., Cox, C. I., Reynolds, A. L., Adams, E. M., & Hanley, C. P. (1991). Identity development and world view: An optimal conceptualization. *Journal of Counseling and Development, 70,* 54-63.

Reynolds, A. L. (1995). Challenges and strategies for teaching multicultural counseling courses. In J. Ponterotto, M. Casas, L. Suzuki, & C. Alexander (Eds.), *Handbook of multicultural counseling* (pp. 312-330). Thousand Oaks, CA: Sage.

Reynolds, A. L. (1995). Multicultural counseling and advising as a learning process. In J. Fried (Ed.), *Shifting paradigms in student affairs: A cultural perspective* (pp. 155-170). Washington, DC: ACPA Media.

Reynolds, A. L., & Hanjorgiris, W. F. (2000). Coming out: Lesbian, gay, and bisexual identity development. In R. M. Perez, K. A. DeBord, & K. J. Bieschke (Eds.), *Handbook of counseling and therapy with lesbians, gays, and bisexuals* (pp. 35-56). Washington, DC: American Psychological Association.

Reynolds, A. L., & Pope, R. L. (1991). The complexities of diversity: Exploring multiple oppressions. *Journal of Counseling and Development, 70,* 171-180.

SUGGESTED READINGS

Autobiography of Malcolm X. (1966). New York: Grove Press. (Original work published 1964)

Clark, C., & O'Donnell, J. (Eds.). (1999). *Becoming and unbecoming White: Owning and disowning a racial identity.* Westport, CT: Bergin & Garvey.

hooks, b. (1994). *Teaching to transgress: Education as the practice of freedom.* New York: Routledge.

Lorde, A. (1984). *Sister outsider.* Freedom, CA: Crossing Press.

Pharr, S. (1988). *Homophobia: A weapon of sexism.* Little Rock, AZ: Chardon.

Reagon, B. (1983). Building coalitions. In B. Smith (Ed.), *Home girls: A Black feminist anthology* (pp. 356-369). Rockefeller Center Station, NY: Kitchen Table: Women of Color Press.

Correspondence regarding this chapter may be addressed to Amy L. Reynolds, Staff Psychologist in the Counseling Center, Buffalo State College of New York, 1300 Elmwood Avenue, Buffalo, NY 14222-1095 (e-mail address: reynolal@buffalostate.edu).

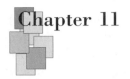

Chapter 11

NEGOTIATING THE MARGINS

MARIA P. P. ROOT

I NEVER WANTED to be White growing up. It is a good thing because I was not. But now, I am almost White in some people's eyes. How this happened tells not only a piece of some of my life story but, in hindsight, has allowed some of my critical thinking around racial and ethnic identity formation.

CHILDHOOD CONTEXT

My transformation of color has not been my own doing but a reflection of a larger racial project in this country. Reflections on my racial transformation, raised by one parent not familiar with the racial system of the United States and the other having internalized the system so well, figured critically into how I have been able to think about identity formation. I had to for survival's sake—both in the world and to make sense out of the subtleties of human interaction.

When I came to the United States with my mother as a small child, we were not White. My mother is a Filipina, not Filipina American, as she always reminds me even after 40-plus years. Whereas my father is a White American, he sustained some subtle and not so subtle demotions in status as a result of marrying a non-White person. Certain neighborhoods, while not closed to him as an individual, became closed to him as part of our family. (In the 1950s up until recently, mixed marriages always resulted in a demotion of status of the White partner.) However, I also think that gender figured in. My father always retained a significant aspect of his Whiteness because he was male and this was his country. Because of this, there was always a gap in his understanding, that although I was his daughter, there were certain barriers I encountered because of the construction of my gender, my race, my ethnicity, and stereotypes of interracial marriage and the children of these marriages.

113

Growing up, people queried me in ways that exposed their own confusion over ethnicity, race, and nationality. As a young child, insistent queries about "where I was from" yielded typical answers. I would give my school or my address, but I would be perplexed by not getting the answer right, cued by the continued questions that basically demanded an explanation for the way I looked. By some time in first grade if I answered the Philippines, a place I hardly remembered, people's questioning would relent. Of course, the variation most mixed-race people or persons with ambiguous phenotypes are asked is "What are you?" as I got older. I had to also learn to answer this question with all the history of race relations, global relations, and war that formed it. My early answers, followed by more questioning, implied that I lacked the intelligence to comprehend the question's simplicity. My lack of comprehension, and later my refusal to make it easy for people, would bring it back to the question "Where are you from?" I became aware at a young age that this line of questioning told me I was different, and it bred a certain level of self-consciousness. To have answered Filipino American was not a viable answer in the 1960s or even early 1970s; further, raised by a mother who only gave up her Philippine citizenship a decade ago, Filipino American did not really exist for her. At the time I was growing up, people hardly knew where the Philippines was or where the origin of such people was geographically located. Arriving in this country at a young age, I belonged to a small age cohort of Philippine-born Americans with Filipinas for mothers, Americans for fathers, negotiating the cultures, customs, foods, and ethnic identity.

Two of my maternal uncles were living in the United States by the time my mother and I arrived, followed shortly thereafter by my aunt, a first cousin of my mother. (The Filipino system of relations is generationally derived so that the cohort of relatives of my mother's age or her cousins and brothers and sister are all considered aunts and uncles.) We always lived within about an hour's drive of each other's families. We celebrated birthdays and holidays together. Because my father had been disowned by his father and my father was an only child, we had only his mother and her sister and her sister's husband as family. Thanksgiving was a holiday reserved for gathering with the "American" side of the family, who also lived fairly close. Meanwhile, I corresponded with one of my aunts in the Philippines and several cousins all throughout my childhood. Filipino culture was reinforced by our isolation from the American and White side of the family, continued correspondence with the Philippines, and the prolonged visits by family and friends (fictive kin). As with other cultures, a visit was always open-ended, and relatives and friends could stay for what might otherwise be seen as rude or too long. I benefited greatly from this contact. I started out multilingual; I regularly received international mail; I had three communion dresses. Some of the Filipino style was also more difficult as I grew older and inevitably wanted to be more like the other kids. The food at our house was different; the food in my lunches was different; my clothes and hairstyles were different until I had more say in style. The physical cutoff from part of my father's family had seemingly little, if any, negative impact on my developmental years. However, in retrospect, its absence and the minimal contact with my paternal grandmother and great-aunt and uncle left us being raised in so many ways Filipino style. Because I was the first child, much of my mother's acculturation was more evident on me than on my brothers, and in part this was a gender issue, too.

In essence, from the beginnings of my conscious memory, I learned to negotiate the margins and became quite comfortable there. We were one of the only two non-White families on the block on which we resided from third grade to my graduation from high school. The neighborhood had a covenant that the family would laugh about forbidding Filipinos in the neighborhood except as gardeners and maids. What was laughable was that it was a working-class neighborhood in which people could not afford to hire gardeners or maids. At family gatherings, amidst the occasional joking about the convenants, overt discussions analyzing the juxtaposition of class and race took place that enabled me to understand the pretense associated with White privilege during those times.

We were watched closely by our neighbors and other people as we grew up. Hindsight has attributed this watchfulness to expecting the worst from us children and the friends we brought home because we were not White. We also experienced this in varying degrees with different teachers at school—surprised that I could perform well or not believing I had completed certain assignments without parental assistance.

There were many subtle ways in which I learned about White privilege. Whereas I can think of many experiences so commonly shared by people of color (e.g., parents disapproving of my dating their sons, expectations that my relatives would be uneducated, or that I would be grateful to receive certain recognition or opportunities), the truth was that on my father's side my relatives were uneducated, not having finished high school. He was the first to go to college and graduate. My Filipino family was educated with advanced degrees and distinguished accomplishments. I remember a not-so-subtle interview with my mother-in-law-to-be over 20 years ago when I was engaged to her son. In a manner of attempting to be sensitive, she asked if my uncle who was going to play the piano at our wedding spoke English. In the context in which the question was asked, one learns early that certain assumptions belie such a question. And being less mature than I am now, I laid the snare and simply answered "Yes." And then she went on to ask about his occupation and offered me some options, janitor being among them. At this point, I gave her information about the family, which not only addressed her assumptions about race and ethnicity but inherently addressed class issues. I explained that he was a Ph.D. chemist as was my other uncle, that both were multilingual, and that this was a well-educated family. It was so interesting that there was never any question about my father's White family and their class standing. Repeated experiences like these over time with well-meaning people, usually people who liked me, were instructive about the juxtaposition of race, class, and ethnicity.

In high school, I remember my debate coach pulling me aside to counsel me that I could do better than the boy I was dating. Because I was going through a phase, if his intentions had been purely about the fact that I was dating some bad characters, his counsel would have been appropriate as a concerned adult. But the counsel included pointing out that I was not like the other non-White kids and that I was jeopardizing my reputation (the possibility of becoming more acceptable to Whites) if I continued to date Black and Chicano kids. The reality is that whereas White boys were interested in me, their parents were not.

The experience of my ambiguity through others' eyes, and the advantage of living in the margins, played out throughout my lifetime in many significant ways that ultimately shaped some of my understanding of what experience is possible by not being clearly recognized or labeled. I grew up in the Los Angeles area during the Watts riots and then significant rioting in the greater Los Angeles schools in my high school years. We would go through lockdowns at school and the call for law enforcement from surrounding cities to bring the high school under control. The conditions surrounding me sound still like what is posed as extreme at some high schools now. Kids were carrying knives and using them; some kids carried guns, but this was less frequent than today. Murders and suicides occurred that were race related. Even though I attended an integrated school, the attitudes were not integrated, and come riot time, there were the Whites and the Blacks. The Chicanos and the few Asians became virtually invisible. This was an instructive experience. Ironically, I was relatively safe being seen as neither Black nor White. The margins was a place of observance of how hostilities and tensions worked, how loyalties were formed, and how group belonging was enacted.

It is interesting how the race of Asians, and particularly mixed-race Asians, has been transformed in the past 25 to 30 years. Whereas some aspects of race seem more fluid, some aspects seem more apparently rigid. I need to remind myself that something has changed about race rules such that, in some contexts, if I am not Black, then I am considered White. With the change in some Asian Americans' status in America's eyes, many of us have been allowed to be honorary Whites ironically during a time where many of us have fought and want to hold on to our ethnic identity.

Whereas in my most recent work I articulate more clearly the co-construction of gender and race, I have multiple experiences upon which to reflect that make the pages of textbook analysis of gender and race very real. Perhaps because I was an observant child, I noticed how I was being genderized. My father came from a fairly traditional and conservative background, and there were definite ideas about how a "young lady" acted, and these would be passed on to me by my grandmother and great-aunt and great-uncle and my father. These comments would include my paternal great-uncle asking how I kept my figure so trim (when I was only 11 and quite a skinny kid) and never on my brothers' physical appearance. My paternal grandmother and great-aunt were likely anorexic as they were so artificially thin-looking and obsessed with staying thin. So being a woman was about looking thin, attending to my figure, and being quiet. And at some level was the message that if this was kept utmost in priorities, despite my difference, I could be an attractive girl and ultimately woman. On my mother's side of the family, an aunt by marriage to one of my uncles, would also struggle with her body, her hair, and manners to model appropriate ways of being a female. On the other hand, my mother's behavior was labeled heathen, pagan, and unfeminine by some relatives; she was not considered fit to instruct a daughter in the rules of womanhood. My mother not only allowed me to be a "tomboy," she encouraged my athleticism and discouraged some very manipulative behaviors associated with femininity. She was questioned and reprimanded by the relatives on both sides for allowing me to be this way lest it influence my sexual orientation. My mother was outspoken, never apologized for her intellectual brightness, and would point out flaws in data or logic in her brothers' or my father's discussions. Her brothers did listen to her. The family stories included recognizing the role of my maternal grandmother as a strong woman basically utilizing her cleverness, entrepreneurial skills, and intellectual brightness to get the family through World War II in the Philippines. My maternal grandfather, though loved and appreciated, was a background figure. There seemed to be no question or reason to hide the fact that my maternal grandmother's line carried the gene for multiple intelligence and that all her children (my mother, aunt, and uncles) had it and were expected to use it.

INFLUENCES

Although I never set out to study myself, and in many ways have not directly, my experiences have undoubtedly informed some of the basis for my work. However, I must say that I never felt tortured about being mixed-race, perhaps because I was raised primarily in a Filipino family and Filipinos are very mixed. It is also possible that individual personality played a part. Whereas I am quite sensitive, there are ways in which I am quite thick-skinned; thus comments have not had as much impact on me as they might have on someone else. I grew up with overt discussions of gender socialization, class structures, colorism, ethnic and racial oppression, and the fact that these were all constructions that subsequently privileged some and disenfranchised others. My father was seldom an active participant in these discussions when he was present; he often left the room. Interpretations of the timing of his leaving were sometimes offered to me privately. My mother was significant to my development as a strong female who never felt the need to apologize or hide her or my intelligence. At the same time, she accepted intelligence as normative and made sure that I never based a significant aspect of my self-worth on this fact. Her belief in herself, her pride in being Filipino to the point at times of being Filipinocentric, her kinship with many American Indian beliefs and spirituality and with people of color, and her disbelief that White persons were superior to anyone, allowed her to pass on tools to challenge subsequent messages I would encounter.

I also have been fortunate to have teachers who encouraged me and were patient in different ways, despite some of their stereotyping of me. These experiences have also allowed me to recognize that people can have their prejudices and may still offer something positive in skills building.

My undergraduate experience at the University of California at Riverside yielded several wonderful professors who inspired me and mentored me. I graduated with a double major in psychology and sociology. This double major was evidence that I was trying to contextualize individual process as well as understand some of the individual differences that might influence group process and even social stratification. Both majors had very strong influences on me. My ultimate decision to pursue a graduate degree in psychology boiled down to my understanding of the variety of jobs I might be able to pursue with an advanced psychology degree in comparison to a sociology degree—whether or not this was factual at the time. My psychology professors who were influential in my interest in psychology were Ovid Tseng (cognitive psychology), Austin Riesen (animal behavior), and Sally Sperling (learning). Their influences show how small acts of kindness and a little bit of individual time can have significant impact on a person. I worked as an undergraduate research assistant with Professors Tseng and Riesen. Both would discuss their work and talk to me as a person capable of following what they were saying or thinking despite the incredible knowledge and experience gap between us. Professor Sperling was one of the few female role models in the psychology department and a great believer in contextual learning and learning from feedback. I remember failing an exam and her enacting a policy with those of us who did fail to take the same exact test with notice so that we could learn from our mistakes.

In sociology, I was very fortunate to take several classes from Jane Mercer (educational assessment) and Edna Bonacich (economic theory of groups and group oppression). Group process was something not discussed in psychology and it made so much sense. Professor Mercer had just developed an alternative intelligence and educational assessment tool in an attempt to remedy the negative evaluation and bias operating against Chicano children in the Riverside County area. She made students think about biases and what we assume is fair. Professor Bonacich introduced me to the literature on slavery of kidnapped Africans and imported Asians and Mexicans, the internment of Japanese Americans, and the genocide of Jews. Class discussions were powerful and encouraged critical thinking. Other than my friends on campus, hers were the only classes in which I was in the company of significant numbers of minority students. The work that some of my other professors taught seemed cutting edge in that path-analytic models were being used to explain the fact that the world is not simple and multiple influences impinge upon a person's experiences at different times. Symbolic Interactionist Theory has left an indelible mark on my theoretical thinking and model building. This sociological influence is apparent in my Ecological Model of Racial and Ethnic Identity Development.

I initially pursued a doctoral degree in experimental psychology, completing the course requirements and a master's degree under William Banks at Pomona College (one of the Claremont Colleges) while I was at Claremont Graduate School. I was very fortunate to work with Professor Banks, who was very patient and kind to me even though he could see that my talent did not rest in this area. I simultaneously worked with Richard Tsujimoto at Pitzer College. I was captivated by his course work on moral development. He was another very kind person who extended himself and made time for simple discussions as I attempted to develop a research project on the codevelopment of moral, social, and cognitive development in children. As I did, my interest in experimental psychology became almost nonexistent. My awareness that I lacked the passion and creativity to overcome the frustrations of experimental psychology led me to terminate my studies. I knew that if I finished the degree I would feel compelled to work as an experimental psychologist, and I knew I would be unhappy and fairly uncreative. I reapplied to graduate school in clinical psychology and was fortunate to have the opportunity to work with Stanley Sue at the University of Washington for two years. He offered course work and discussions that picked up where my undergraduate interest in sociology had ended. Professor Sue's guidance for my first two years of graduate training was critical. He helped students, particularly minority students, develop a network and bonds that have endured through moves and life changes. He also provided the foundation for making the link between psychology and sociology through community psychology. Also critical in my graduate training were Shirley Feldman-Summers for encouraging me to explore the role of gender in mental health and William Friedrich for introducing me to another way of thinking systemically about small systems, particularly families. Although psychology still was not overtly providing me the bridge between cultural information, gender, and group process, family systems work in light of my previous sociology course work provided another layer of conceptualizing group process.

When I completed the internship necessary for the clinical psychology degree, I was exhausted. I carried out my dissertation research during that year and lived an hour's bus commute from campus. Ironically, my goal to complete the degree, even if I was too tired to contemplate the next step, opened the door to considering a clinical career, even though I had explicitly trained to be an academic psychologist. In doing this for what I thought might be an interim year or two, I found that I really enjoyed it and was still able to write and publish. Another influence on staying in clinical work was that I valued lifestyle greatly, which included climate, people, and culture. Seattle provided a definite cohort of Asian Americans, a temperate climate, and friendly people.

In hindsight, I realize that I would not have been able to produce the body of work I have if I had been at a major research university. Conceptual work, which is my forte, is not encouraged nor highly valued in psychology, particularly in the early stages of one's career. My first conceptual work came from my dissertation and centered on the conceptualization of family functioning and gender roles in families in the mid 1980s. Subsequently, my work of the past decade has focused primarily on identity development. One last academic experience informed this work.

I took a visiting professor position at the University of Hawaii in 1990. I had already planned that during this year I would explore the possibility of pulling together a group of researchers and writers who had taken up the theme of racial and ethnic identity in contemporary time but from the perspective of mixed-heritage people and edit a book. However, after several months in Honolulu, the passion to pursue this volume waned. This was the perfect setting to reinforce the notion of how contextualized racial and ethnic experiences are. I even questioned if I had somehow exaggerated the importance of racial and ethnic identity (along with some of my colleagues). However, with several trips back to the mainland, it was clear that this was an issue that needed to be tackled.

My work has benefited from odd juxtapositions of experiences and friends and colleagues who often see things differently from each other. Rather than taking sides, my experience of making sense of the margins has been to take whatever gifts each person offers and come to my own conclusions, which are undoubtedly a synthesis of all the thinking to which I have been exposed. Truly, one's work never develops in a vacuum. Conversations with and the work of several contemporary colleagues across disciplines have influenced my work. Those who have been most salient in both ways include psychologists Laura Brown, William Cross, Jr., Dorsey Green, Christine I. I. Hall, Janet Helms, Ronald C. Johnson, George Kitahara Kich, Robin LaDue, Manuel Ramirez, Derald Sue, Michael Thornton, and Joseph Trimble; sociologists Edna Bonacich, G. Reginald Daniel, Abby Ferber, Cookie White Stephan, and Teresa Kay Williams; philosopher Naomi Zack; historian Paul Spickard; and feminist scholars Gloria Anzaldua, Patricia Hill Collins, and Aida Hurtado. I am indebted to the challenges to which my colleagues before me rose, laying the foundation so that I could do the work I do at this point in time. I am forever indebted to my ancestors who still continue to guide me. Last, I am indebted to my mother who paid the price of being an unconventional woman, which ultimately allowed me to develop into who I am and the work I produce.

RELEVANT PUBLICATIONS

Root, M. P. P. (1992). The impact of trauma on personality: The second reconstruction. In L. Brown & M. Ballou (Eds.), *Theories of personality and psychopathology: Feminist reappraisal.* New York: Guilford.

Root, M. P. P. (1994). Mixed race women. In L. Comas Diaz & B. Green (Eds.), *Women of color and mental health: The healing tapestry.* New York: Guilford.

Root, M. P. P. (1998). Preliminary findings from the Biracial Sibling Project. *Cultural Diversity and Mental Health, 4,* 237-247.

Root, M. P. P. (1999). The biracial baby boom: Understanding ecological constructions of racial identity in the twenty-first century. In R. H. Sheets & E. R. Hollins (Eds.), *Aspects of human development: Racial and ethnic identity in school practices.* Mahwah, NJ: Lawrence Erlbaum.

Root, M. P. P. (2001). *Love's revolution: Interracial marriage.* Philadelphia: Temple University Press.

Correspondence regarding this chapter may be sent to Maria P. P. Root, in private practice, 2457 26th Avenue East, Seattle, WA 98112 (e-mail address: Mariaroot@aol.com).

Chapter 12

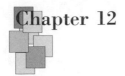

AN ECOCULTURAL ANALYSIS OF AGONIES AND ECSTASIES OF MY LIFE

DAYA SINGH SANDHU

Life's but a walking shadow, a poor player
That struts and frets his hour upon the stage,
And then is heard no more. It is a tale
Told by an idiot, full of sound and fury,
Signifying nothing.

—*The Tragedy of MacBeth*
(Act V, Scene 5, lines 24-28)
by William Shakespeare
(from Mowat & Werstine, 1992)

SOME PEOPLE CALL life difficult. Others describe it as having no significance, calling it an idiot's tale. Despite all the ifs (the middle two letters in spelling life comprise *if*) and buts, I find l*if*e a precious gift from God. In the ocean of eternity, my existence as a human being does not even amount to a drop of water. However, on a personal level, my life story, studded with agonies and ecstasies, is my most cherished treasure. My life is full of memories and recollections; some of them are riveting and cherished, others are painful and avoided. However, good or bad memories are memories that become the prime legacy of one's life.

With thanks to Joseph Ponterotto from the core of my heart for this great opportunity, it is here that I venture to reflect upon my life. As an autobiography, it is a transparent recount of my life experiences through which I perceive it, unmediated and undistorted. I challenge the readers of this chapter to find in it many embedded messages that are culturally diverse from their own.

122

BIRTH AND PARTITION OF INDIA

I was born in 1943 in a small village called Sarhali which is now in District Faislabad in Pakistan. My father, Gurmej Singh, and mother, Gurbachan Kaur, both belonged to Sikh families. It is hard to tell the exact day and month, since no official records are found after the partition in 1947. My parents knew days and months only by way of an indigenous calendar called Bikrami era, which is 57 years ahead of the Christian calendar. My elementary teachers made things easier, tentatively assigning my birth date as March 3, 1943. In the past, parents did not celebrate the birthdays of their children. It is a recent phenomenon in high- and middle-class families to celebrate birthdays of their children. Generally, people celebrate birthdays of some great persons.

My memory dates back when I was 3 and a half years old. Two major events flash in my mind which are authentic, verified by my parents. Unfortunately, these are very troubling and unpleasant memories. I still remember lying in a doctor's office; he was treating me for a high fever. I recall a tall, long-bearded, Moslem doctor, Dr. Fazal Ilahi, saving my life. I admire his broadmindedness treating a Sikh boy during the religious riots.

After winning independence from the British in 1947, India was partitioned into two countries on the basis of two major religions. The majority of Hindus were to remain in India and a new country called Pakistan (*a place for the pious people*) was carved for the Moslems. Hindus or Sikhs living in the newly created country were forced to leave. Similarly, the Moslems living in Hindustan (*a place for the Hindus*) were also made to leave.

During this partition, cultural conflicts and religious riots arose everywhere. Sentiments against Hindus and Sikhs became very high in Pakistan. Unfortunately, my parents had no choice but to leave their home, land, and all their belongings. They hurried to leave everything to save me and my younger brother who was only 2 years old. There was no other transportation but carts pulled by oxen. There was no other food but hastily prepared popcorn. There was no milk for babies, and even water was nowhere to be found. It was the hot month of August, with scorching heat over 100°F. We were not even lucky enough to drink muddy water from ponds because these ponds were filled with dead bodies.

I still can see myself on that ill-fated cart and my younger brother Dilbagh in my mother's lap crying for food and water. His cries and wails still pierce my heart. After several days of hunger and thirst, we reached our native town in Punjab (Punjab literally means five rivers), from which our ancestors had gone to search for more land. Within two weeks, my parents, who were born to rich families, became penniless refugees. The stay in the native village was temporary in the house of some ancestral relatives.

Unfortunately, my brother could never accompany us to the free land. He died of dehydration. Sadly, it was not even possible to cremate his dead body. Politics, power, and prejudice became a deadly combination that turns decent humans into devastating demons.

After two years, the Government of India resettled my parents permanently in a small village, Gahndran, in Jalandhar District, with a population of 5,000. About 10 acres of land was allotted along with a mud house that one of the Moslem families had deserted before leaving for Pakistan.

INDIA WINS INDEPENDENCE

I respect Mahatma Gandhi and Jawahar Lal Nehru for their leadership and sacrifices to gain independence from the British. However, it is sad that many other unsung heroes who laid down their lives to free India from the shackles and atrocities of the British Government are not so well known in the West. I adore and respect Baba Gurdit Singh Sarhali, Shahid (martyr) Bhagat Singh, Shahid (martyr) Udham Singh, Lala Laj Pat Rai, and Subash Chandar Bose. I tend to agree with those who believe that the British left India not solely because of the nonviolent movement of Gandhi but also because British lives were made difficult by the so-called hot group. "When all pleas fail to get justice, it is cowardice not to use the sword" seemed to be the philosophy of this hot group. The Sikh martyrs, as saint-soldiers, already knew this advice of Guru Gobind Singh, who preached it to his followers in the late 17th century.

CHILDHOOD DAYS

I was raised as a lonely, sickly, and only child in a grieving parents' home. My mother's heart was and still is deeper than the ocean. She treasured all the sad feelings and never expressed them in my presence. She taught me how to read and write at home. I did not need any paper or an ink pen. My index finger became my pen, and the dirt on the floor was my never-ending paper. I could read and write in Punjabi before I went to school at age 7. Luckily, I was admitted to the second grade.

My childhood was not all that pleasant. There was deep parental affection from both parents, but there was crippling poverty at home. The mud house we lived in was without electricity and running water. During the heavy monsoon rains, it was very dangerous to live in the mud houses. Once during heavy floods in our area, we had to spend a night in a wooden box. Poverty is cruel and violently painful. I felt utterly empty and lonely as a child. It made me envious of others who had so many brothers and sisters, for I had neither. However, I made a friend with classmate Amar Chand, who belonged to an untouchable family.

When in high school I started writing plays in Punjabi, he would play the role of the comedian on stage. I used to be the stage secretary or the master of ceremonies, since I could never sing or play any musical instrument. It hurt me deeply when Amar Chand died of tuberculosis in the prime of his youth at age 19. Mostly, my friends belonged to low-caste or poverty-stricken families. But all these friends were caring and full of compassion. I could never dare to reach out and make friends with peers from well-to-do families because I felt a sense of rejection from them. I still believe that there is an intense prejudice between the rich and the poor, regardless of race, color, and gender.

Primary school in our village was enjoyable. My teacher, Mr. Vazir Chand, was very challenging but kind and encouraging. His personal interest and encouragement meant a lot to me. I still believe that appreciation and encouragement at the lower level go a long way toward meeting the challenges in later life. I read Shakespeare's plays translated into Punjabi when I was in the fourth grade. I also read the life story of the great American president Abraham Lincoln in the same grade. They both became my life-long heroes.

During the elementary years, I started reading scriptures and learning more about our spiritual ten masters in Sikhism. At the inspiration of my mother, I recited Japji Sikh morning prayer and Rahras, a Sikh evening prayer, on a daily basis. I started building a strong faith in God and His Grace. I learned from the scriptures that if we pray to Him with sincerity, He answers our prayers. It may sound silly, but I wrote my prayer in a letter to Him that I am an only child and asked that He bless me with a sister or a brother. He was kind to listen. My little brother, Gurdial, 12 years younger than me, was born after a year. It was a miracle, considering my mother's age at that time. My parents believe that God gave us back our Dilbagh.

HIGH SCHOOL YEARS

The primary school in our village extended only to the fourth grade. The nearest high school in Nakodar City was three and a half miles away. It was a challenge to walk seven miles as an 11-year-old. In addition to walking, the weather proved to be a problem. It was most difficult when it rained. As a result, my clothes were drenched and my shoes were wet. However, I never worried about my clothes. Mom always hand sewed them.

School and home were both fun places. At school, I had several classmates and teachers to converse with. I made close friendships with many peers. Tarlok Singh Purewal became my fast friend and proved to be a lifelong friend. Also, I had a baby brother to play with at home. On the weekends and during summer vacations, I helped my Dad with the farm work. It was very hard work, and I never thought any work could be harder than hoeing in a sugarcane field in the brutal hot and humid temperatures of 110-115° F. Due to the heat, it was unbearable to wear a shirt, and the sharp blades of the sugarcane plants cut the naked body like a dagger. With sweat dripping into the fresh wounds, the pain was extreme. It made me determined to study harder, as I was convinced that I was unfit to work on the farm. The only part of the farm work I enjoyed was grazing the cattle with other boys of my age. But I always had a book in my hand to study.

During high school, I was deeply influenced by my English teacher, Mr. Baxish Singh. With his encouragement and that of school headmaster Faquir Chand Kirpal, I graduated from high school with highest honors. On the final examination, externally administered by Punjab University, I not only stood first in our school but also received the highest score among surrounding area high schools. It pleased me that my fast friend Tarlok stood beside me as one of the top two scorers on the examination. He was not only my friend, he was also a guide.

I was the first one to graduate from our village, and by placing first, it made me a hero in my village. It also won me a merit scholarship, enabling me to attend the college in Jalandhar City, about 20 miles away from home.

My interest in women also developed in those days when I was 16. In our culture, there is no dating system. If one even made an attempt to approach a girl, it meant trouble. Most likely, one would be humiliated or even murdered. Strong feelings like love and romance are not expressed. You are not allowed to marry someone from your village. This tradition is quite different from large cities. However, whenever possible, I managed to see this *unique she* passing through our fields on the way to her parents' fields. In my whole life, I might have spoken with her two or three times. I learned later on that this type of attraction is called platonic love. Undoubtedly, I felt that it was one-sided platonic love. I started writing short stories, poems, and even novels in Punjabi inspired by this one-sided love. My first poetry book, *Satranghi Pingh (The Rainbow),* contained several poems addressed to her. I spent many sleepless nights troubled by thoughts about her and being love-sick.

COLLEGE DAYS

College days were extremely painful. It was not possible for me to stay in the dormitory. I had neither the money nor the desire to stand being separated from my parents. I decided to attend college by train. Unfortunately, the morning train left at 5:25 a.m. from Nakodar, which necessitated arising at 3:30 a.m. and getting ready to walk three and a half miles by myself to catch this train. The way was like a jungle. Thorny bushes and fear of deadly snakes made this journey hellish during the early-morning darkness. The rainy and chilly days during winter made life unbearable.

These living atrocities made me turn to God more and more for help. Out of fear, I prayed all the way going and returning from college for five years. Leaving home at 3:30 a.m. and returning at 8:30 p.m. was the daily schedule. I managed to find the time to study while at railway platforms waiting for the train or while journeying in the train. At home, I burned the midnight oil. It was a kerosene oil lamp, which made my eyes watery and face quite dark with smoke. Mr. Ram Singh Sachdev, the principal of Lyallpur Khalsa, the college that I attended, was an extremely generous and compassionate person. He exempted me from paying the tuition and asked the librarian to purchase books for me through library funds.

CAREER CHOICE

I wanted to become a medical doctor, and therefore I studied required courses such as physics, chemistry, and biology. However, it was not meant to be. My parents did not have any money to pay the costly expenses at a medical college. Helplessly, I changed my major to English literature. At the time, to become an English professor was the second best thing. I was also influenced by the college's Vice Principal Harbhajan Singh, who taught undergraduate English poetry. A graduate of Oxford University, England, he became my role model. From him I learned about English romantic writers such as Percy Bysshe Shelley, John Keats, and William Wordsworth. Shelley and Keats impressed me the most; their poetry had a lasting impact on my own Punjabi poems written in love for the *unique one*. In 1963, I received my bachelor of arts degree. Again, I stood first in the college. Despite all the financial hardships, I not only survived but I also prevailed.

At the prize distribution ceremony, Sardar Partap Singh Kairon, then Chief Minister of Punjab, encouraged me to continue my studies. He also pledged to help me financially. I joined the teacher training college in Jalandhar. Being so gracious, he sent me scholarship money from his personal funds on a monthly basis until I passed my bachelor of teaching degree. This degree was a requirement for teaching in public schools.

INTEREST IN RELIGION AND SPIRITUALITY

During my college days, I also developed a keen interest in religion and spirituality. As I was born in a Sikh family, naturally I became deeply interested in Sikh gurus and the Sikh Scripture *Shri Guru Granth Sahib*. Unfortunately, the word "guru" appears corrupted in the Western world and is not held in high esteem. The word *gu* in Sanskrit means darkness or ignorance and *ru* means illuminator. So the word guru means the one who removes spiritual darkness or spiritual ignorance.

Sikhism is one of the youngest religions in the world. However, it is the fifth largest in the world based on the number of adherents. It has more than 20 million followers worldwide who reside in more than 21 countries. Guru Nanak, the founder of Sikhism more than five centuries ago, preached the message of universalism. The very gist of tolerance for diversity is expressed in the following *shaloka* (psalm) of *Sri Guru Granth Sahib, Holy Book of the Sikhs* (translated and annotated by Gopal Singh, 1978):

> *Aval Allah noor upaya kudra ke sabh bande.*
> *Ek noor te sabh jag upjiya, kaun bhale ko mande.*
>> God is the Father of us all; His reflection is in everyone of us,
>> Hence do not grade any person as inferior or superior. (p. 1349)

Also,

> *Sabhe ghat Ram bole, Rama bole, Ram bina ko bole re*
>> In every heart there is God, none else than He speaks from there.
>> (Sri Guru Granth Sahib, p. 988)

I sincerely believe that the teachings of Guru Nanak are really the foundation of the present-day movement we call multiculturalism. In support of women, he writes,

> *So kiun manda akhye, jit jaman rajan!*
>> Why demean them who gave birth to kings and prophets!
>> (Sri Guru Granth Sahib, p. 473)

Guru Nanak writes about God in his prologue to *Japji*, the path of devotional meditation. Translated from Punjabi into English, it reads,

> *In the name of the One True Supreme Being,*
> *Who is the Creator of all other beings,*
> *Without fear and hatred;*
> *of timeless form,*
> *unborn, self-existent;*
> *attainable*
> *only through divine grace.* (Sri Guru Granth Sahib, p. 1)

Guru Nanak's following line became an ideal for my life:

> *The truth is high, but higher still is truthful living.*
> (Sri Guru Granth Sahib, p. 62)

But, I hate to admit, it has been very difficult to practice truth.

Guru Nanak also preached three major commandments, *Naam Japna* (worship God), *Kirat Karni* (earn livelihood through hard work), and *Vand Shakna* (share with the needy). Presently, I am fascinated with Guru Nanak's five stages of spiritual journey as described in *Japji*. These stages are *dharma khand* (moral living and rightful action), *jnan khand* (divine knowledge), *saram khand* (spiritual beauty and effort to unfold), *karam khand* (divine grace), and *sach khand* (eternal truth) (Deol & Deol, 1998).

I was also deeply touched with the greatness of the 10th and last guru, Sri Guru Gobind Singh. He was the epitome of sacrifice. He, his father, mother, 4 children, and 15 close relatives laid down their lives for social justice and religious freedom. He is matchless in human history. I consider Guru Gobind Singh a true architect of democratic ideology, human rights, and multiculturalism. He fiercely rebelled against the cruelty and excesses of the oppressive regime of the Mogul emperor Aurangzeb. He instilled courage, gallantry, and ideals of principled living in his followers. He brought about a psychic conversion among the downtrodden and the oppressed. He also uplifted women to equal status and named them Kaurs or "princesses."

As an undergraduate student of English literature, I was influenced by Thomas Carlyle, whose 1937 book *Heroes and Hero Worship* guided difficult paths of my life. In religion and spirituality, it made a lot of sense to me when Carlyle (1937) wrote that a man lives by believing something, not by debating many things. I developed a strong belief in Guru Nanak's teachings. I am amazed how one line from literature could become a source of inspiration. Carlyle's (1937) advice that if a man says his time is not good he is there to make it better became my lifelong guiding principle.

GLORIOUS DAYS
AT THE TEACHER TRAINING COLLEGE

I graduated from the government's Teacher Training College in Jalandhar with a bachelor of teaching degree, which was required to practice teaching. Despite all the traveling afflictions, I had a wonderful time at this college. I loved courses in philosophy of education, educational psychology, and teaching methods. Philosophy Professor Agnihotri and Psychology Professor S. B. Kakkar became my role models. Also, I developed a strong interest in aesthetics. At the encouragement of Professor Kakkar, I published my first paper in English, *Gleams of Aesthetics*, in the college's magazine. I also actively participated in declamation contests, poetry writing, and leadership activities. These were the glorious days of my education and youth in India.

MY FIRST TEACHING JOB

It was a big step down from a medical doctor to become a school teacher when I took my first job as a secondary school teacher at a private school. The pay and my morale were both very low. However, it was exciting to teach high school algebra, geometry, English, and chemistry. These students were barely five or six years younger than me as I started teaching at the age of 21. More than students, they became my friends. On the faculty, I had my former teacher as the headmaster, and five former classmates were now my colleagues. I was also relieved from travel problems. The train would leave from my village directly to this village, and the time traveled was less than half an hour. With the little money that I made as a teacher, I started making my home situation better. Soon we had a better house, but it still was a mud house. It made me realize that more needed to be done to better our situation. When I got another job as a science teacher at the government's high school in Shankar, financially things began getting better. Not only did the job pay better, it was also a permanent job. It was my first time teaching women students who were preparing to become elementary school teachers. As a male teacher, I had the rare privilege to teach these young women, for there was a shortage of female science teachers. There were few coed classes at that time.

MY FIRST MARRIAGE

Most of the marriages at that time were arranged by parents, and mine was no exception. At age 23, I was married to Kuldip. My mother was the only one who saw her before the marriage. There is a belief that marriage is a matter of conditioning of two individuals to each other that requires several sacrifices. Based on life experiences and their wisdom, parents believe that they know better how to join together two people who are compatible. The young people are considered too emotional to make a good decision. Most Hindustani parents will agree with Arnold Lazarus's (1985) observation that "marriage is usually due to lack of judgment, divorce to lack of patience, and remarriage to lack of memory" (p. 33).

Kuldip brought many positive changes in the family in general and in my personal life in particular. We were married in December 1966 and were blessed with a daughter, Jaswinder, in October 1967. Generally, Indian parents prefer boys to girls, but Jaswinder came as a special gift from God as she was the first child born in our family. Also, the first daughter is considered *Lakshmi*, a prototype of the Hindu Goddess Lakshmi, a harbinger of prosperity.

Now as a family man, I continued my studies and earned my master's degree in English from Punjab University to become a college professor. However, on the encouragement of Kuldip's brother, Professor Baxish Singh Balam, we migrated to the United States for my higher studies. He became our prime source of financial help as the Indian government would not allow me to bring more than $8 to the United States because of foreign exchange restrictions.

ACCULTURATIVE EXPERIENCES

We had a great family celebration when I was granted a visa to study for a master's degree in education in the United States. Every one was very excited. Going to America was hailed as a great accomplishment, and I was congratulated by all near and dear. Even my travel agent remarked, "Sir, your life is made." On the day I departed for the United States, I felt very strong and mixed emotions. On one side, I felt exalted and ecstatic that I was going to the promised land, a land of great opportunities. On the other side, it was a day of severe sadness leaving my parents and my brother behind.

Several guests and relatives and people from my village arranged a hero's good-bye at the railway station. Even the train was delayed for 15 minutes to complete the seeing-off festivities. I was heavily garlanded. When the train was ready to leave, the whole scene became very melancholic. It was so difficult to separate from my family, especially from Mom. She kept crying, sobbing, and wailing. One relative, Piara Singh, remarked that leaving home for abroad is like living dead. When the train started, I became extremely sad. It felt as if Heaven had fallen or the whole earth had collapsed beneath my feet. Separation was so intense and unbearable. A line of separation was drawn forever. I kept looking back at my parents and relatives as far as I could see. I wanted to go back so bad that words cannot describe the feeling, but that was not possible now.

I landed in the United States on September 2, 1969. It felt like I arrived in a fairyland. Looking at beautiful sceneries, forests, parks, and long, clean highways with hundreds of cars, I was impressed. I had never seen such cleanliness anywhere. Meeting warm-hearted beautiful people, I became convinced that I was already in paradise. Kuldip, Jaswinder, and I became new members of Professor Balam's house. At that time, he lived in an apartment on the university campus where he taught chemistry.

After a week, this place started looking too lonely. Surroundings were so different from Punjab. There was no hustle and bustle. People never seemed to get out and mingle openly. There were no familiar songs, birds, fields, ponds, or lakes. Everything looked so different. Everything in America looked much bigger: people, cars, fields, bananas, spoons—you name it. I became impressed with the richness and vastness of the country.

But I still missed home, relatives, and parents. At age 26, in the bathroom, I cried many times like a baby. I was very lonely. All of a sudden, I had lost all my friends, parents, and other relatives. I also felt the guilt of leaving my parents behind in India. Arriving in America required my starting over to develop a new sense of myself. A multitude of life changes arose, resulting in a lot of psychological pain.

EDUCATION IN THE UNITED STATES

My classes started on September 6. On the first day my brother-in-law took me to the college about 50 miles away from home. Despite having an M.A. in English, I felt embarrassed over not being able to communicate in English. My major professor admonished me to speak slowly. After more than 30 years, I still remember his remark, "Sandhu, you speak English like Yankees." Sadly, I did not understand what he meant by Yankees at that time. Another professor asked, "Do you commute?" I did not understand what she meant. We never had a car in India, we just used bikes or traveled by train or bus. Communication became a problem for several years. I had to get used to the so-called Southern drawl. Sometimes, even simple greetings were difficult to understand. As I had studied British English, I was more accustomed to greeting someone with "Sir, how do you do?" Not too many people responded to this greeting. Similarly, I had to get acquainted with new spellings of colour, labour, programme, and so on.

Due to language difficulties, I neither fully understood professors' instructions, nor did I dare to meet with them after classes to ask them any questions. It was my fault that I studied diligently all 1,174 pages of a book on 17th-century English literature. Surprisingly, my professor administered her final examination on whatever she taught in the class, which was barely 200 pages of the book. I experienced more problems with spoken English than with written English. I started watching television shows such as *That Girl, The Price is Right, Family Feud, Sonny and Cher,* and *Gunsmoke* not only for fun but to improve my spoken English.

FOOD AND BEVERAGES

Food became a problem. I was not habituated to eating meat in India. Generally, meat is a special dish served on some festival days such as *Diwali* (festival of lamps) or *Holi* (festival of colors). My mother never ate nor cooked meat at home. If my father wanted to eat meat, he had to cook and eat it outside the home. Also, beef is forbidden in Hinduism and Sikhism. Since not many vegetarian foods were available in those days, I just ate french fries. Later on, I started eating eggs, fish, and chicken. However, I also started drinking occasionally with my new friend, Robert Lawson, a classmate at Delta State. I started getting Americanized.

GETTING CLEAN SHAVEN

After migrating to the United States, for almost 6 months I kept my beard, moustache, and long hair and wore a turban as a Sikh. Unfortunately, I experienced people's constant gaze, some out of curiosity and some out of hate. Because many Sikhs become victims of prejudice due to their religious identity and are denied jobs and other opportunities in the Western world, I decided to get clean shaven and remove my turban. It was a very troubling decision indeed. My identity was totally changed from outside and inside. It hurt more inside. The conflict was between my allegiance to the Sikh religion and my desire to benefit from the American dream. Actually, it was a conflict between spiritualism and materialism. Even after more than 30 years, I have not been able to resolve it. I feel a big lump of guilt in my chest that I betrayed Sikh heroes like Bhai Taru Singh, who was beheaded by Moslem oppressors because they could not make him cut his hair and remove his turban to change his Sikh identity.

BECOMING A CITIZEN OF THE UNITED STATES

It was a difficult decision to relinquish my Indian citizenship. I was very excited to become a citizen of the United States, but I was much troubled to say good-bye to my motherland. An inner voice kept torturing me, *"Nobody gives up on one's mother if she is poor."* I cried a lot. My tears were mingled with joy and sadness. Finally, I reconciled the conflict so as to obtain inner peace. I have two Moms: a real one, India, and an adopted one, America.

I was finally getting acclimated to American culture. Now I had a car, a teaching job, and a green card. We were also blessed with our son, Sukhwinder (Johnny). Then tragedy befell. Kuldip and her sister, Harkishan, went to buy groceries in a nearby town. They had a car accident in which both were killed instantly, leaving me a widower with two children and my brother-in-law with five children. It was the most depressing event in my life. I sustained the most excruciating psychological pain when I had to take Kuldip's remains after cremation in a box to India to put them in a pious river. How frail we are as humans who eventually are reduced to ashes!

I was engulfed by all kinds of problems. Without any social support system, I had to stay awake all night to take care of my children. Jaswinder was 5 and Sukhwinder not even 2 years old. It broke my heart when I had to leave Sukhwinder (Johnny) with the baby-sitter in order to teach in the morning.

The loss was also immensely painful. I became extremely depressed. I had only two choices: either return to India with two children or pick up the pieces again and accept God's will and move on with my life. Thinking of India's problems, I decided not to take my children back home. I knew that India's many problems—poverty, politicians, preachers, prejudice, police, population, and pollution—were not going to be easily solved. A common saying that India is a rich country lived in by the poor always haunted me. My flight from India was to give my children new opportunities. I decided to remain in the United States and face the adversities.

Persuaded by my ex in-laws, I returned to India to get remarried. Luckily, this time it was my choice. My parents did not like to impose any restrictions. I met Usha through a matrimonial ad in the local newspaper. It was our great fortune that Usha and I could see each other and talk before deciding to get married. But we only had a couple of hours in the presence of her sister and brothers. She prepared tea and brought Indian sweets. Looking at her stunning beauty, I fell for her at first sight. She hesitated, but we were destined to be together. Usha's sister, Santosh, and her husband, Mr. A. R. Bharti, played a major role in facilitating our matrimonial bond. With the blessings of our parents, we married on July 22, 1974. I became an iconoclast again, for I broke the barriers of the caste system. We belong to different castes and religions. She is Hindu; I am a Sikh. She belongs to *Ksatriya* (warrior) caste; I belong to *Vaisya* (ordinary people) caste. Our marriage of more than 25 years now has taught us that *love* conquers all.

Usha brought new light (her name means morning light) in my life again. My dark melancholic life became worth living again, for Usha brought sunshine with her. Not only was I blessed with her deep love and caring, but God also blessed us with two more sons, Varrinder and Ravinder.

MY JOBS IN THE UNITED STATES

After getting my master's degree in education, I started to look for teaching jobs. I was offered an instructor's position at a predominantly Black college. I was recommended by the chair of the department and members of the selection committee. Unfortunately, the dean decided not to hire me because of my different accent. Sadly, after 30 years, I still cannot change my accent. I felt the pain of prejudice. I believe that skin color, accent, and facial features are some of the high indicators and inviters of prejudice. Unfortunately, they are very hard to change.

Consequently, I ended up teaching in public schools for more than 10 years. It was one of my most frustrating experiences to teach ninth-grade English classes. There were generally six classes everyday and more than 35 students in each. I was not happy. I was getting money to pay my bills, but there was little gratification. I was feeling guilty being paid when I believed that not many students were learning much from me. Also, due to daily discipline problems, I started having splitting headaches.

Luckily, I got a job offer from the Bureau of Indian Affairs to teach remedial English classes. The situation was better than that of the public schools, but I still was not happy. I believe that God does listen if you pray sincerely. My prayers were answered when Choctaw Central School decided to hire me as a guidance counselor. However, I had no training in counseling. I was provisionally hired as long as I became certified within three years. Because I was close to Mississippi State University, approximately 60 miles away, it was only an hour's drive to get this training. While completing certification hours, I became interested in earning a doctoral degree in counseling. I loved the counseling field. It was a welcome relief to study Carl Rogers and Albert Ellis instead of Beowulf and Chaucer. Also, I enjoyed counseling at Choctaw Central School. It is interesting how I was exposed to many cultures and religions such as Hindus, Sikhs, and Moslems in India and African Americans, Native Americans, and European Americans in the United States.

Again, it was with mixed feelings that I left Choctaw Central to join Nichols State University in Louisiana. It was a long awaited dream to teach at the university level. I now became familiar with the French Acadian Americans. Coming to the University also spurred my interest in research and writings. It also gave me the opportunities to attend conventions and conferences. A new vista was opened.

INTEREST IN MULTICULTURALISM

With my personal experiences living in many cultures, speaking many languages (Punjabi, Hindi, English, and some Sanskrit and Urdu), and having familiarity with the many religions of India (Hinduism, Sikhism, Jainism, and Buddhism), my worldview had broadened, and my interest in multicultural issues had soared. To teach a multicultural counseling class, I became familiar with the works of several authors such as Paul Pedersen, Joseph Ponterotto, Derald Wing Sue, Clemmont Vontress, Fredrick Harper, and John McFadden. I loved their writings because the issues they discussed were also very close to my heart. Coming to the University of Louisville in 1991 provided me with many more opportunities to travel and make presentations nationally and internationally. I went to and spoke in Athens, Greece; Banaras and New Delhi, India; Beijing, China; Bratislava, Slovakia; London, England; Paris, France; and Vancouver, Canada. I also enjoyed meeting persons from different countries and cultures. I developed a cosmopolitan outlook on life.

Because universities still have the slogan "publish or perish," I had no choice but to write. Actually, it has become my passion. I am impressed with Paul Pedersen and Joseph Ponterotto both personally and professionally. Their book *Preventing Prejudice: A Guide for Counselors and Educators* stimulated my interested in the topic of prejudice. My first coauthored book with Cheryl Aspy, *Counseling for Prejudice Prevention and Reduction*, was the direct result of their inspiration. I would also like to acknowledge the encouragement and support of Frederick Harper, presently Editor of *International Journal for the Advancement of Counselling*.

PHILOSOPHY BEHIND MY WORKS

Over the past century in psychology and for the past four decades in counseling, the focus has largely been on the individual and on personal development. I believe that now it is time for a paradigm shift. I would like to employ counseling skills to address social ills. For this reason, most of my writings focus on such issues as prejudice, gender equity, and violence. I have already authored or coauthored *Counseling for Prejudice Prevention and Reduction; Empowering Women for Equity: A Counseling Approach; Violence in American Schools: A Practical Guide for Counselors* and *Faces of Violence: Psychological Correlates, Concepts, and Intervention Strategies.*

Of course, some writings are born from my own personal experiences. Such publications include *Acculturative Stress Scale for International Students; Asian and Pacific Islander Americans: Issues and Concerns for Counseling and Psychotherapy; Culturally Responsive Teaching in Multicultural Classrooms; Ethnocultural Background of Asian and Indian Americans and Substance Abuse Treatment;* and my forthcoming book *Spirituality: A Multicultural Perspective.* Finally, I believe that issues relating to diversity, multiculturalism, and interculturalism are going to remain salient issues in the new millennium. I hope that authors like Casas, Courtland Lee, Harper, Ibrahim, Parham, Pederson, Ponterotto, Sue, Vontress, and many more continue to show us the way. They are really my heroes and beacons in the field of multiculturalism.

The United States is truly a land of opportunities. It has always been the land of milk and honey, and I am sure that it will continue to be so for many centuries to come. It is a country where hard work does pay off. Both my brother Gurdial and son Sukhwinder earned their M.D. degrees. Varrinder is preparing for one. Jaswinder became a chemical engineer. The youngest, Ravinder, plans to enter broadcasting or become a movie star. I tell them that the sky is the limit in this beautiful country if one works hard.

I still miss India, its culture, and of course my parents and my wife's family. Somehow, we have managed to visit India every year for the past 10 years. I like the physical comforts in the United States and the peace of mind in India.

I am very concerned about the cultural erosion of my children. It pains me to see this happening before my eyes through the loss of our Sikh religion, Punjabi language, interracial marriage, and other native cultural practices. In this case, I agree with those who feel that due to migration they have gained a lot but have lost a lot more. I agree with Kuldip Kumar of the National Council for Research and Training Center in New Delhi, who, when introducing me to an audience before a presentation, said, "Dr. Sandhu's head is in America, but his heart is in India."

These were prophetic words, for I recently was awarded a one-year Fulbright Scholarship to complete a study during the 2001–2002 period on depression in India and its implications for counseling, training, and research.

RELEVANT PUBLICATIONS

Aspy, C. B., & Sandhu, D. S. (1999). *Empowering women for equity: A counseling approach.* Alexandria, VA: American Counseling Association.

Sandhu, D. S. (Ed.). (1999). *Asian and Pacific Islander Americans: Issues and concerns for counseling and psychotherapy.* Commack, NY: Nova Science.

Sandhu, D. S., & Aspy, C. B. (1997). *Counseling for prejudice prevention and reduction.* Alexandria, VA: American Counseling Association.

Sandhu, D. S., & Aspy, C. B. (Eds.). (2000). *Violence in American schools: A practical guide for counselors.* Alexandria, VA: American Counseling Association.

Sandhu, D. S., & Asrabadi, B. R. (1998). An acculturative stress scale for international students: A practical approach to stress measurement. In C. P. Zalaquett & R. J. Wood (Eds.), *Evaluating stress: A book of resources* (Vol. 2). Lanham, MD/London: Scarecrow.

CITED REFERENCES

Carlyle, T. (1937). *Heroes and hero worship.* London: Thomas Nelson.

Deol, S., & Deol, D. (1998). *Japji: The path of devotional meditation.* Washington, DC: Mount Meru Books.

Lazarus, A. A. (1985). *Marital myths: Two dozen mistaken beliefs that can ruin a marriage or make a bad one worse.* San Luis Obispo, CA: Impact.

Mowat, B. A., & Werstine, P. (Eds.). (1992). *The tragedy of Macbeth/Shakespeare.* New York: Washington Square Press/Pocket Books.

Singh, G. (Trans.). (1978). *Sri Guru Granth Sahib* [English trans.]. Chandigarh, India: World Sikh University Press.

Correspondence regarding this chapter may be addressed to Daya Singh Sandhu, Department of Educational and Counseling Psychology, 320 Education Building, University of Louisville, Louisville, KY 40292 (e-mail address: daya.sandhu@louisville.edu).

Chapter 13

REFLECTIONS ON THE LIFE STORIES OF PIONEERS IN MULTICULTURAL COUNSELING

JOSEPH G. PONTEROTTO

MARGO A. JACKSON

CHRISTIAN D. NUTINI

WE FEEL PRIVILEGED to respond to the collective group of life stories comprising Part I of this second edition of *Handbook of Multicultural Counseling.* We admire the courage of these pioneers in sharing their personal lives with us. Through their self-disclosure, we now see the "person" behind the profound scholarship and pioneering work. The life stories are highly revealing and quite poignant, with both deeply painful and empowering life events described.

From our contacts with the pioneers throughout the writing process, we have come to understand how difficult it can be to expose one's private self to the world public. Pioneer Manuel Casas (Chapter 8) expresses this sentiment well when he shares the challenge of "having to face the emotions, especially the negative ones, that are an inherent part of one's solitary journey through the labyrinth of life" (p. 79).

Contemplating and revealing one's story can also be a very rewarding and meaningful experience. This is highlighted by Robert Atkinson, director of the Center for the Study of Lives at the University of Southern Maine and author of a valuable book on life stories (Atkinson, 1998):

> We become fully aware, fully conscious, of our own lives through the process of putting them together in story form. It is through story that we gain context and recognize meaning. Reclaiming story is part of our birthright. Telling our story enables us to be heard, recognized, and acknowledged by

others. Story makes the implicit explicit, the hidden seen, the unformed formed, and the confusing clear. (Atkinson, 1998, p. 7)

Pioneer Amy Reynolds (Chapter 10) captures the essence of Atkinson's points well in the opening to her life story as follows:

> Writing this chapter has been a process, a journey of self-discovery from the moment I received the request. I have thought and reflected for months and have spoken with those who are dear to me about my feelings, my ideas, and especially about my questions. Never before have I written something that was so introspective and personal yet designed to be so public. This process of self-exploration has brought me to a new understanding of my personal history, my racial identity, as well as my personal and professional hopes and dreams. (p. 103).

The goal of this chapter is threefold: We first provide a context for the value of life stories in counseling generally and in multicultural counseling specifically. Second, we briefly summarize main themes from each of the life stories represented in Chapters 1 through 12. Third, we provide an integration of the life stories by identifying transcendent themes across the pioneers' accounts.

LIFE STORIES IN
COUNSELING PRACTICE AND RESEARCH

The use of life stories as a means to understanding and studying human behavior has a long history in psychology. Early influential work on life stories and personal narratives include Freud's (1910/1957) treatise on Leonardo DaVinci, Allport's (1942) personal document analysis, Murray's (1938) study of individual lives to understand personality development, and Erikson's (1958, 1969) studies of Luther and Gandhi, respectively.

In addition to its use in the early academic study of lives, sharing one's life story has always been an essential component of many forms of counseling and psychotherapy. Atkinson (1998) captures well the impact of the personal narrative on the storyteller:

> What generally happens when we tell a story from our own life is that we increase our working knowledge of ourselves because we discover deeper meaning in our lives through the process of reflecting and putting the events, experiences, and feelings that we have lived into oral expression. (p. 1)

Although life stories have been an accepted component of clinical practice, they have not been utilized extensively in counseling research. It is only in recent years, as the counseling profession has become more embracing of constructivist research paradigms and qualitative research methods, that counseling journals and books have highlighted biographical research (see Morrow & Smith, 2000; Morrow, Rakhsha, & Castañeda, Chapter 29, this volume).

Helping bring credibility to narrative forms of counseling research has been the recent innovative work of numerous counseling psychologists and related professionals. Particularly impressive and enlightening for us in understanding the value and validity of life story research has been the work of Howard (1989, 1991) and colleagues (Howard, Maerlender, Myers, & Curtin, 1992), Polkinghorne (1988), and Atkinson (1998), among others. Interesting collections of life stories can be found in edited volumes by Hoshmand (1998), Josselson and Lieblich (1993, 1995), Heppner (1990), and Bond (1997). An important resource for qualitative researchers, particularly those interested in biographical forms, is Atkinson's Center for the Study of Lives housed at the University of Southern Maine; the collection currently numbers over 300 life stories (see Atkinson, 1998, for a description).

It is beyond doubt that biographical tools, whether they be labeled life stories, life histories, oral histories, personal narratives, or mini-autobiographies (terms sometimes used interchangeably depending on the orienting discipline), are invaluable to counseling students, practitioners, and researchers. Besides serving as important historical documents in the development of the counseling profession (see Heppner, 1990), life stories serve as valuable teaching and mentoring tools for students and newer professionals.

Life stories can be particularly valuable in the study of multicultural lives; in fact a number of the references cited earlier (e.g., Hoshmand, 1998) focus on the life stories of individuals diverse in racial and ethnic background. In a multicultural society such as the United States, where people live in the legacy and context of oppression based on race, religion, income, gender, and sexual orientation, it is essential to hear the stories of diverse people in their own voice.

To this end, we now comment on the life stories of select individuals who have been leaders in the counseling profession's efforts to become more responsive to culturally diverse populations. It is hoped that our review and integration of the life stories will assist readers in understanding the history of the multicultural emphasis in counseling and will facilitate the life stories' teaching and mentoring functions noted earlier.

REFLECTIONS ON INDIVIDUAL PIONEERS

Understandably, each pioneer's life story is quite unique. The 12 pioneers represent a broad spectrum of society, and each scholar has lived through differing life experiences. The pioneers also have much in common, typified by their life's dedication to social justice, to teaching and service delivery, and to promoting multiculturalism in their profession and in society. Later in this chapter we examine some transcendent themes among the pioneers' life stories that give us a glimpse into factors that led to their status as international role models and professional pioneers. First, however, we note some key points that emerged for us specific to each life story. We rely extensively on the pioneers' own words in highlighting points that particularly caught our attention.

Thanks to the modeling of his Grandfather Sage, *Joseph E. Trimble* has always attended to sights, sounds, and smells around him. Early in his life story (Chapter 1) he notes that "paying attention to all that occurs around me is a lifeway orientation that has its origins in the wisdom of the elders and provided me with direction" (p. 3). Professor Trimble's keen senses have provided us with a window to the history of the multicultural movement in psychology.

In his story, we took a number of important messages to heart. Dr. Trimble highlights the importance of the psychology profession not acting as a discipline in isolation. He notes that

> as I pored over the works of anthropologists such as Margaret Mead, John Honigmann, and Ruth Benedict, I came to the conclusion that psychology was rather exclusive, myopic, prejudiced, and presumptuous to believe and profess that psychological findings applied to all humans regardless of their cultural and ethnic background. (p. 6)

As for other multicultural scholars of his generation, there was not much academic support for the study of culture in psychology. He notes that in the 1960s "there was little or no information about ethnic and cultural groups in the psychological literature—almost none concerning American Indians" (p. 8). For this reason, Dr. Trimble was particularly excited about finding a program at the University of Oklahoma's Institute of Group Relations that supported and encouraged his cultural interests. In reflecting on his decision to move to Oklahoma for study, he notes, "In retrospect, the decision to move on set a course that far exceeded my expectations and visions. My distress over the past indeed humanized my soul as my emptiness was replaced with excitement and spiritual renewal" (p. 7).

Like other pioneers in racial/ethnic psychology, Dr. Trimble was motivated by professional rejection. In commenting on a conference committee's rejection of a panel presentation proposal on American Indian psychology, he comments that "the unpleasant and wrenching experience was a pivotal point in my career and served to solidify my belief that I must bring the experiences of contemporary American Indians into the realm of psychological theory" (p. 10).

An important theme throughout Dr. Trimble's life story is his focus on the importance of elders to all people. His profound respect and admiration of elders such as Grandfather Sage is readily apparent, and he continues in

life to be inspired, guided, and comforted by these elders. He admonishes us
to attend to our elders, as he notes that

> Maybe more of us should spend some time with our elders, as they may
> understand our seemingly complex world in the academy more acutely
> than we do. . . . Grandfather provided me with additional advice: (a) never
> forget where you came from and the lessons you learned in your child-
> hood; (b) you now have a responsibility to pass along your knowledge,
> experiences, and skills in ways that are nonthreatening yet informative;
> (c) and always remember that no one has ever accomplished greatness by
> themselves. (p. 9)

Another theme in Professor Trimble's story that resonated with us is
his emphasis on the interconnectedness of life and of all people. Again,
thinking back to the wisdom of his Grandfather Sage, he reflects,

> Sometimes when I am working alone late into the night or very early in
> the morning I feel the presence of others sitting next to me guiding my
> thoughts and my fingers as they move about the keyboard. During these
> moments, I feel a oneness with the world and the life force that flows in
> and through all things. . . . If we really reflect on the point, I suspect most
> would agree that our individual success is built on the encouragement,
> teachings, advice, and the wisdom of others and that we all really depend
> on one another for what we are all about in our fields of inquiry and en-
> deavor. We are all connected and related to one another in some form or
> another and thus we influence and are influenced by all things in ways we
> may never know. (p. 12)

Professor Trimble has spent his career fulfilling a promise made to
Grandfather Sage and an Arapaho elder, a promise he has kept and continues to strive for: "to draw attention to the way we [American Indian peo-
ples] live and the many things that affect our daily lives, particularly the bad
ones" (p. 9). Professor Trimble's writings and speaking engagements have
stimulated and guided a new generation of multicultural scholars, particularly in the area of Native American Indian and Alaska Native psychology.
He is our elder, let us be guided by his wisdom and vision.

   Teresa D. LaFromboise's pride in and commitment to Native American
Indian culture was instilled as a young child while listening to stories told
by her great-grandmother. Growing up acculturated to non-Indian society,
these stories were important to maintaining a strong bond to her Miami
tribal heritage. She reflects back on this period and notes, "I found myself
wondering what it would have been like to grow up around Indian people"
(p. 14). Her desire to contribute to the lives of American Indian people crystallized during her college years when she was exposed to American Indian
scholarship and witnessed civil rights activism on the part of Native American Indians.

Dr. LaFromboise's professional service to Native American Indian people began right after college when she began teaching junior high school in North Dakota. She soon realized that she could be of greater service to her students, their families, and the Indian communities by obtaining a Ph.D. in counseling psychology. Throughout her professional career, Dr. LaFromboise has been in tune with the contradictions between European-based psychological counseling and the culture and needs of Native American Indian people. Much of her professional work has focused on increasing the relevance of "counseling" to American Indian peoples by incorporating Native culture into the process. As she notes,

> I eventually came to terms with the contrasts in clinical procedures between the university counseling center and the Indian center and came to believe in the potential for new models in counseling with American Indians. I thought the disconnection resided in the process. I felt that if the counseling process could be made more effective with American Indian clients, they would increasingly seek services to deal with their problems. (p. 16)

As with other pioneers profiled in this part of the *Handbook*, Dr. LaFromboise describes how her professional work and vision was in part a parallel process to her own identity development. Through her continual contact with American Indian communities and various intervention programs she

> became more intimately aware of my own personal process regarding my ethnic identity as a mixed race person. People both outside and inside the Indian world challenged me as they sought to understand my mixed background. This reality moved me to a deeper level of self-reflection and became a part of the foundation from which I would work as time moved on. (p. 17)

Dr. LaFromboise's ongoing work off university campuses with American Indian organizations and people sensitized her to how counseling intervention would need to be modified to be culturally salient and effective with American Indian people. For example, her administrative work with the Lincoln Indian Center in Lincoln, Nebraska,

> allowed me to see, firsthand, the transforming influence that traditional ceremonies have on community responsiveness and mobilization for change. I witnessed extensive informal caregiving and the psychological support that extended families provide one another. This familial closeness was so special to me, because it reminded me of the days when my own large family on my father's side would fill up our grandparents' home for card games and meals. It was during this time, too, that I learned an event's success depended upon whether proper procedures were followed in extending invitations to elders for their involvement. I was impressed with how naturally the traditional values of kindness, patience,

generosity, humility, respect, caring, and honesty were incorporated into
treatment by culturally grounded staff. (p. 18)

A strong message we receive from the life story of Dr. LaFromboise is
the need to be among the people you hope to serve. So much of her work is
informed by her constant interaction with Native American Indian communities and programs. It is through this community participation where
one sees cultural meaning, where one witnesses healing methods consonant with the beliefs, lifestyles, hopes, and traditions of the people. We end
our comments on pioneer LaFromboise's story with an excerpt that captures this sentiment:

> I invited one of my clients, an Apache woman in her late 40s, to attend an
> acorn festival hosted by Me-Wuk people. My client and her sister joined
> me in Yosemite Valley where the feasts and dances were held. I had been
> seeing this client for one year for major recurrent depression and pro-
> longed grief reaction due to her mother's death. I chose to invite her to this
> particular ceremony because it occurred near the first anniversary of her
> mother's passing. The first evening that we were in the night dances,
> shortly after the closing intertribal dance, a woman came up to my client
> and began praying over her and smudging her with her eagle feather fan.
> People that gathered around them eventually started crying. Not knowing
> my client and never having spoken to her before, the medicine woman
> told my client to "let her go." She repeatedly told her, "It is time to let her
> go." Shortly thereafter my client and her sister came to peace with their
> mother's death and my client's depression lifted. Here again I saw proof in
> the transformational power of collective support that is often found in cer-
> emonial ways. (p. 20)

Janet E. Helms organized her life story around poignant questions
asked her by colleague Susana Lowe and a few graduate students. Professor Helms is frank and candid in her responses and is at times quite funny.
For example, she begins her chapter with the following caution to the editors: "I warned them that it [my story] would be a sleep-inducing experience
for the reader. I suppose they anticipate that many readers of the *Handbook*
will be people with insomnia in need of a nonchemical cure" (p. 22). Dr.
Helms expresses a zest for life and an ongoing need for growth and understanding, as typified in the following statement made in reference to questions posed to her by the interview team: "There were several [questions]
that I could not answer and so I have decided to use them as the focus of this
chapter because the process of discovering answers to unanswered questions is generally what inspires me to live the life I do" (p. 22).

We note in her story a determination and courage to grasp life and project herself into the future. With Dr. Helms, as with many of the other pioneers, the theme of a constant battling with, and negotiating through,
discrimination is apparent. She notes that "most incidences of discrimination are micro-inequities, that is, little things that people do that in and of

themselves are not very meaningful but gradually build up to a point where I want to get away from people" (p. 25). She vividly describes experiences with blatant racism (the unstamped postcard placed in her mailbox) and with a more subtle version (airplane and restaurant invisibility scenes) where she also explains her cued speech coping strategy to facilitate being listened to.

A salient theme throughout Dr. Helms's story is her strength and courage with dealing with macro- and micro-inequities. She confronts these inequities when she believes it meaningful and useful, while choosing not to at other times—thus, in a sense, picking her battles. Furthermore, despite the omnipresence of oppressive forces, Dr. Helms maintains and activates a zest for life, a constant intellectual curiosity, a vibrant sense of humor, and desire to nurture others though mentoring, teaching, research, and service.

We found the life story of pioneer *William E. Cross, Jr.* to be riveting and poignant. His depth of self-disclosure regarding existential struggles, religion, and marriage touched us deeply. With regard to a religious deconversion, he notes that upon entering college

> I was profoundly, if not obsessively, religious, but in trying to make sense of American slavery and the "meaning" of the destruction of the Jews during WWII, I intellectually concluded, in accord with existential philosophy, that there was no god, religion was an illusion, and all belief systems were social inventions. Having begun each day of my youth conversing with the Lord, the discovery that god was dead caused a hailstorm in my soul. I briefly became suicidal in the face of life's meaninglessness. (p. 32)

Professor Cross's chapter is replete with such open and honest reflections. Seldom in the professional literature does an author so intimately allow the reader into one's life, one's struggles, one's epiphanies; by so doing, Dr. Cross provides the reader with the gift of an accessible and demystified role model and mentor.

Professor Cross traces his development and presentation of a Nigrescence model in the contexts of his own personal development and the evolving Black (and other) movement of the 1960s. His personal rollercoaster journey of identity development both informed and was informed by his evolving Nigrescence model. Cross's breadth of knowledge is astounding—besides getting to know him intimately, his life story served for us as a fascinating interdisciplinary course on history, philosophy, sociology, political movements, and the arts.

Interestingly, his account is punctuated with personal and revealing glances into the lives of those who helped and pushed him to develop. These brief snippets show the support that he received and the gratitude that he feels for those who helped mold his personal and professional life.

Derald Wing Sue reminds us of what it is like to feel different and be treated differently. He opens his story directly:

> Throughout my life, I have been constantly reminded that my racial and cultural heritage are quite different from many in this society. Some of these reminders have been quite pleasant and validating; many, however, serve to invalidate, diminish, and strike at the core of my racial identity. As a person of color, I have been exposed to prejudice, stereotyping, and discrimination. Surviving monoculturalism and racism has helped shape not only my personal identity but my professional one as well. (p. 45)

Professor Sue is candid and specific as he comments on the inequities of U.S. society, their effects on minorities, and the duty of individuals to help change the situation. He openly shares painful experiences to highlight the power and extent of everyday racism. While some of these experiences were overt and deliberate, many more were unintentional yet just as invalidating and hurtful. He coins the terms micro-invalidations and micro-assaults to capture the power and negative impact of the unintentional hurts. He uses the term macro-assaults to describe blatant racist attacks, and he poignantly shares the personal and family trauma endured when his son was wrongly arrested and accused of stealing. Dr. Sue reminds us that (a) those who fight inequity may become targets themselves, (b) to fight successfully, one needs the support of many, and (c) financial resources are sometimes needed to pursue justice.

Dr. Sue is candid in sharing "lessons learned" from his life as an Asian American in a monocultural society. Above all, he has learned that "our lives must become a 'have to' in being constantly vigilant to manifestations of bias in ourselves and in people around us" (p. 53).

Nadya A. Fouad eloquently describes her life as a woman of multiple cultures. Having been born in Ames, Iowa, Dr. Fouad spent critical periods of life in Cairo, Egypt, surrounded by her father's extended family; in Rio, Brazil, where her mother's family resided; and in the Philippines when her father was working for the Ford Foundation. She highlights well her strong bond to both extended families when she notes,

> I had such a strong sense of linkage with the families in Brazil and Egypt that at times I imagined strings running from Ames to Cairo and Rio connecting us. My parents, and especially my mother, strongly reinforced the notion that I was very special because of my unique background. (p. 57)

Professor Fouad shares many personal experiences and anecdotes that demonstrate when being culturally different is an empowering positive experience and when it is a frustrating, confusing, and negative experience. She highlights well the pressure many who are culturally diverse (from the Euro-American mainstream) face in trying to fit it, and be more "American." For example, she notes at various points in the story the following:

When we moved back to the States and I entered kindergarten, I spoke English, refusing to speak Portuguese. I was intensely interested in "being American" and assimilated into mainstream small town U.S. life. Being like everyone else was critical even when it meant trying to be—or act like—someone I was not. . . . I was too concerned with fitting in and was more than willing to shape my aspirations by the relatively narrow, concrete things I could see in Ames. I wanted to be a waitress with a nametag on my blouse that said "Marilyn," and more than anything I wanted the black flat slip-on shoes sold at Woolworth's. This was the essence of "American" to me and, as it turned out, was the essence of the lower class aspirations to my mother, who was horrified. I never did get those shoes. (p. 58)

Particularly salient in Dr. Fouad's story are her experiences as a non-visible minority. She discusses her internal struggles in negotiating expectations of multiple cultures while at the same time reacting to others' attributions of those cultures. On one hand, as a light-skinned woman who can "pass" for White, she does not have to deal with everyday racism as experienced by more visible persons of color. On the other hand, as a light skinned person and scholar, "I need to prove my commitment to cultural diversity much more explicitly than do more visible racial/ethnic minority group members" (p. 55).

Eloquently presented in Professor Fouad's life story is the intersection between culture and gender. She shares with us her parents' pride in her professional accomplishments and personal life, while also noting her father's concern that her career success and responsibilities may detract from family life and the mother's role. Dr. Fouad also highlights the oppressive forces that sexism can play in circumscribing one's career aspirations. This rich array of personal experiences has been a central influence in Professor Fouad's successful efforts to move the field of vocational psychology to pay greater attention to cultural and gender variables in research and practice.

Melba J. T. Vasquez frames her life story in the context of privileges or "unearned advantages" and challenges or "unearned disadvantages." She quotes Texas humorist Cactus Pryor in defining "privilege": "the belief, feeling, and attitude that an individual has, who was 'born on third base,' and thinks they hit a triple!" (p. 65). It was in the past decade of her life thus far that Dr. Vasquez realized some of her own unearned advantages, many of which revolved around a loving and supportive family and community. Upon reflection of this childhood she notes,

I had the privilege of a considerable amount of attention, adoration, and regard from my parents, large extended family (including 16 aunts and uncles and all four of my grandparents, and great uncles and aunts, second cousins, and so on!). I enjoyed what I wish every child had. When I walked into a room, faces lit up (most of the time)! I also grew up in a loving small community. (p. 65)

Other privileges for Dr. Vasquez included family resources that allowed attendance in a small private school from 4th through 7th grade, a Chicano community that valued education, and the gift of parents who were empowering and courageous role models through their political activism.

Dr. Vasquez is revealing in sharing the challenges, oppression, and unearned disadvantages of her life. The trauma of beginning first grade in a predominantly Anglo school "with not a single teacher or administrator of color," led to feeling unsafe, an affective state so different from that experienced in her extended family and community. This early childhood oppression and pain is captured well in Dr. Vasquez's voice:

> We were ignored, spoken to more curtly and harshly than the White children, and some of the children of color (mostly boys, as I recall) were treated harshly (e.g., knocked down on the playground), and called racial epithets. I remember feeling incredible empathy for Latino children who were abused on the playground and felt an immediate identification with and protection of those like me. I remember feeling the pain of loss of positive regard at both the personal and group level but had no words to describe the loss and sadness and lack of safety and resulting anxiety that emerged. (p. 67)

Dr. Vasquez's story is replete with other challenges, including the hurt when a White boyfriend's mother put a racist end to their dating; and her own feminist identity "encounter" after the unpleasant experiences of peer pressure to participate in beauty contests.

In her life story, Dr. Vasquez reveals many empowering experiences that helped to shape her worldview and commitment to social justice, from her mother's advocacy in a J. C. Penny store to support the rights of an elderly Mexican American woman to strong alliances with other women of color. Poignant in this regard is Dr. Vasquez's vivid retelling of the school bus incident:

> One day, a large White boy, about two or three years older, who often bullied us all, came and roughly pushed my sister and me into a corner of our seat because he wanted to sit in that space, across from his friends. I remember the fear and humiliation I felt for myself and for my sister. Yet, we did nothing but sit silently, squashed by his large size. An African American young girl, about his size, saw what happened, and came up, pushed his shoulder and said in a very loud assertive voice. "What are you doing? You can't do that to them. They're sitting there, can't you see, and you're crowding them. Move. Now!" He looked at her defiantly, and said, "This ain't your business." She glared back, and said, "It is now." The whole bus got quiet. She repeated in a low voice, "Move. Now." He got up and moved. The young Black girl went to her seat, came back, gave us each a piece of hard candy, and watched over us and others like us for the rest of the year. (p. 69)

Throughout her story, Dr. Vasquez highlights the importance of ethnic minority and White European allies in her work and life. Furthermore, she is gracious in acknowledging her many mentors and role models. Finally, Dr. Vasquez, drawing on her varied personal and professional life experiences, ends her story with a valuable gift to the reader—words of wisdom from a teacher, a healer, an "elder." Chief among these is to take risks, allow for mistakes, take care of yourself, be confident, observe role models, channel your anger for life empowerment, engage in activism, and involve yourself in support systems.

J. Manuel Casas invites the reader to consider his life's journey through the perspective of multiple identities. He frames his story in the stirring prose of renowned Mexican poet Octavio Paz, whose classic *Labyrinth of Solitude* provides the words to help capture the essence of Professor Casas's reflections. Quoting Paz, Dr. Casas notes, "All men [sic], at some point in their lives, feel themselves to be alone. And they are" (p. 78).

Revisiting one's entire past and penning a life story is both a solitary and challenging activity. Dr. Casas is quite candid about this as he expresses,

> Writing this chapter has been one of the most difficult tasks that I have undertaken in my career. . . . While I'm not a shy person, I highly value my privacy and sharing my life experiences, and in particular those that relate to my family, is not something I do easily; furthermore, my cultural upbringing underscored the fact that one should not go around "bragging" about one's personal achievements. (pp. 78-79)

Dr. Casas uses somewhat of a chronological progression to trace his life story. Born in Fundicion de Avalos, a small Mexican town, his ancestry reflects Spanish, North African, and indigenous roots. His paternal great-grandmother, who was Apache, was saved from U.S. cavalry raids on her village by Mexican wagon masters.

Professor Casas was exposed to racism and segregation very early in life. As he notes,

> The town of Avalos, built by a U.S. metal refining company, was comprised of two separate and unequal communities. There was the open community where the Mexicans lived and the secluded, walled-off community where the American "bosses" lived. To enter "their" community one had to be admitted through a guarded gateway. (p. 80)

Because Dr. Casas's father had a trade, their family apartment was one of the better units in the Mexican community: "It had two bedrooms, a living room, a dining room, a small kitchen, and, most important of all, a toilet and shower" (p. 81).

Unstable conditions resulting from the advent of World War II and the Mexican socio-political scene convinced the Casas family to immigrate to the U.S., where some family relatives were already established. En route to Northern California, the family crossed the border in El Paso, Texas, where

> we could not use the bathrooms and drinking fountains that were desig-nated for "White" persons only. We had to search for those services that were relegated to persons of "color" or, to be more specific with the term used during that time, Negroes. This was my first introduction to the ex-perience of discrimination in the land that was destined to be my home. Numerous subsequent experiences came soon thereafter; and, since then they have not stopped coming, in one form or another. (p. 82)

Dr. Casas expressed well the frustrations and challenges he and his sis-ter, as linguistic minorities, faced upon entering American schools:

> On the first day of school, my mother, along with a limited-English-speaking friend, walked me and a friend to school, got me to my classroom and left. As I entered the classroom, I experienced the kind of aloneness, fear, and alienation that, if it were in my power, no other child would ever have to experience. No one looked like me. No one spoke my language. I couldn't communicate with anyone, including the teacher. To solve this communication problem, the teacher came up with a unique and intellec-tually challenged strategy. I would be seated in the back of the room—not the bus—the room, where I could listen and with time eventually pick up the English language. (p. 84)

We are left with many other strong impressions in Dr. Casas's life story. For one, the love and support emanating from his nuclear and extended families served as a significant source of support and strength in his life journey. His respect and admiration for elders, ancestors, teachers, col-leagues, and friends presents itself as a strong theme throughout the story. A second impression is that Professor Casas had little professional mentoring early on, yet he and his sister developed an "I'll show you" atti-tude, and they developed "the tenacity, the determination and the persever-ance to succeed in whatever path we chose to follow" (p. 84). In a situation where opportunities were scarce, it seems as though he created his own through persistence, thoroughness, and creativity.

Finally, his commitment to helping Hispanics, gays and lesbians, and other minorities is obvious. Although at some points he did not know what road to take, and having walked down several career paths, it seems as if the core "reasoning" or "meaning" underlying his choices was always clear: a strong empathy for and link with Hispanics and other disadvantaged mi-nority groups and a desire to be of service to them and make a difference.

In the life story of *Paul Bodholdt Pedersen* we are struck by his im-mense intellectual curiosity and thirst for new and different experiences. Professor Pedersen frames his story in the context of "seamless cultural connections," and even as a child living on a small Iowa farm, he notes,

> I remember being about 5 years old sitting in the ditch beside the road in front of our "Lilac Hill Farm" thinking that our road was connected to every other road in the world, and then I reached up to touch the road in amazement. (p. 96)

Little could Dr. Pedersen know at the time, that indeed he would walk down many of the world's roads in a life and career that has been replete with abundant cultural experiences and prolific written descriptions of psychological life around the world.

Like other pioneers, Dr. Pedersen's early schooling was complicated with English being a second language. As he notes, "I spoke Danish before speaking English, so when I flunked out of kindergarten all I remember are two days of loud noise and everyone being angry at me, making me think I had done something terribly wrong" (p. 96).

Dr. Pedersen sensed at a young age that observing other cultures and traveling constituted invaluable growth experiences. After his sophomore year of college, Dr. Pedersen and his roommate spent the summer hitchhiking through Europe. He notes,

> My journal from that summer typed out to 120 pages single spaced. We slept in German haystacks, Venetian gondolas, Swiss police stations, and on Italian beaches, but usually in Youth Hostels with other "sophomores" hitching around on the cheap. That summer was the least expensive tuition and the most powerful multicultural education I ever experienced. (p. 97)

Another theme throughout Professor Pedersen's story is his lifelong commitment to human service, social justice and political activism. While teaching in North Sumatra, "a student burst into the Ethics class to say they had wrongly arrested the Vice Rector and what were we going to do about it. I led the march on the police station with my students, and was later scolded by the Consulate" (pp. 97-98).

Roughly seven years later, while teaching and conducting research in Malaysia, he shares, "During the race riots in 1969, the only persons not under attack were foreigners, so I drove ambulances around the otherwise deserted Kuala Lumpur and organized discussion groups to keep students off the streets" (p. 99).

It was Professor Pedersen's extensive travels and long-term stays in many countries, particularly in Asia, that broadened his worldview and helped him realize the cultural encapsulation of American psychological counseling. He notes that he "learned how psychological processes are alive and healthy in Asia but are usually expressed through philosophy, history, politics, religion, or other fields of study" (p. 98). Professor Pedersen is clearly one of the most prolific and influential scholars in American and World psychology. He has trained thousands of mental health professionals, and he has left us a legacy through his core message: "If every behavior is learned and displayed in a separate cultural context, then accurate assessment, meaningful understanding, and appropriate intervention requires attention to that cultural context" (p. 101).

Amy L. Reynolds highlights poignantly how her personal and professional life journeys are inextricably intertwined. She states that "multiculturalism is not who I am or what I believe. My multiculturalism is about how I live my life" (p. 110). Early in her life story she notes,

> I now view myself as a professional who is focusing her life's work on multiculturalism and is committed to training others to work more effectively across all types of differences. Now I must be clear here. This is less of a professional choice and more of a personal commitment. You see, I also am a White woman who has been partnered for 11 years with an African American woman with whom I am raising two young biracial children. What I do professionally is merely an extension of what I struggle with on a daily basis. What really matters to me in both my personal and professional life is being part of creating environments that are inclusive and affirming. I want to help build a world where my two biracial children who are growing up with two moms of different racial backgrounds consistently feel their family is fully accepted and valued. (p. 105)

Dr. Reynolds's life story is very revealing as she openly shares with us many personal experiences and identity struggles. She also highlights with great eloquence the intersection of her many identities, particularly racial, gender, sexual orientation, and religious identities. She states the following:

> When I look back, I now see that my journey toward multiculturalism began with my faith development. This is a new insight for me and is probably a reflection of where I am in my own spiritual journey. . . . In many ways, my belief in racial equality, feminism, and multiculturalism grew out of my belief in peace and justice. And those beliefs grew from my faith and covenant with God. . . . While my journey may have begun with my faith, it became politicized as I experienced feminism in the 1970s. I was a girl who wanted to be treated fairly, and my identity as a feminist began with my personal outrage at how differently male and female athletes were treated. Those beliefs were further strengthened in my 20s when I came out as a lesbian to myself and my family. I went through a period of lesbian and feminist immersion while in graduate school that allowed me to redefine myself and feel confident about who I was despite what society and my parents thought. Living in that lesbian feminist world was crucial to my own sense of self and my ability to understand oppression, especially internalized oppression. It gave me an understanding as to why I had always felt different, like I didn't belong. (pp. 105-106)

Dr. Reynolds highlights that multicultural growth and true humanism is a lifelong pursuit. The reader can glean from her story the thousands of hours she has spent contemplating these issues, discussing them with friends, peers, colleagues, and, of course, her life partner, Raechele. Absorbing Dr. Reynolds's and other pioneers' life journeys of personal growth and awareness, we are left with the realization that personal and multicultural competence is not easily achieved. Even as she closes her life story, Professor Reynolds is evaluating her awareness level as she states, "Looking back I know I didn't talk enough about racism and oppression and how fighting it daily in ourselves, others, and society as a whole must be at the center of multiculturalism" (p. 111). One thing is certain, however, with regard to Dr. Reynolds's commitment to social justice; as she exclaims: "Combating racism and oppression and working to build a psychology profession that embraces multiculturalism is not a choice for me. It is as natural and as important as breathing" (p. 111).

Maria P. P. Root describes with poignant clarity the multiple influences shaping her personal and professional identity. Her development has been characterized by an ongoing negotiation of margins vis-à-vis her identity as a Filipina American, a woman, and a scholar, all in the context of a racist and sexist environment. Dr. Root opens her life story with the following words:

> I never wanted to be White growing up. It is a good thing because I was not. But now, I am almost White in some people's eyes. How this happened tells not only a piece of some of my life story but, in hindsight, has allowed some of my critical thinking around racial and ethnic identity formation. (p. 113)

Professor Root's scholarly work reflects, in part, her formative development and her learning to negotiate the margins of multiple cultures and oppressions. She highlights well some of the challenges of interethnic, interracial families during recent decades:

> When I came to the United States with my mother as a small child, we were not White. My mother is a Filipina, not Filipina American, as she always reminds me even after 40-plus years. Whereas my father is a White American, he sustained some subtle and not so subtle demotions in status as a result of marrying a non-White person. Certain neighborhoods, while not closed to him as an individual, became closed to him as part of our family. (p. 113)

In revisiting her early years, Dr. Root highlights the bond she experienced with her Filipino side of the family as her father's family was more distant. She notes that

> Filipino culture was reinforced by our isolation from the American and White side of the family, continued correspondence with the Philippines, and the prolonged visits by family and friends (fictive kin). As with other cultures, a visit was always open-ended, and relatives and friends could

stay for what might otherwise be seen as rude or too long. I benefited greatly from this contact. I started out multilingual; I regularly received international mail; I had three communion dresses. (p. 114)

Quite salient to Dr. Root's story is the strong influence of her mother and maternal grandmother. Discussing her mother's influence, she notes,

My mother was significant to my development as a strong female who never felt the need to apologize or hide her or my intelligence. At the same time, she accepted intelligence as normative and made sure that I never based a significant aspect of my self-worth on this fact. Her belief in herself, her pride in being Filipino to the point at times of being Filipino-centric, her kinship with many American Indian beliefs and spirituality and with people of color, and her disbelief that White persons were superior to anyone, allowed her to pass on tools to challenge subsequent messages I would encounter. (pp. 117-118)

The strength of identity gathered from her relationship with her mother and her mother's side of the family, enabled Dr. Root to negotiate mixed and negative messages. Some of these concerned gender socialization as reflected in the following:

Perhaps because I was an observant child, I noticed how I was being genderized. My father came from a fairly traditional and conservative background, and there were definite ideas about how a "young lady" acted and these would be passed on to me by my grandmother and great-aunt and great-uncle and my father. These comments would include my paternal great-uncle asking how I kept my figure so trim (when I was 11 and quite a skinny kid) and never on my brothers' physical appearances. My paternal grandmother and great-aunt were likely anorexic as they were so artificially thin-looking and obsessed with staying thin. So being a woman was about looking thin, attending to my figure, and being quiet. (pp. 116-117)

Dr. Root's skills in observation and questioning, modeled by her mother, helped her to make sense of life in the margins in multiple contexts, such as race, noted in the following excerpt:

I grew up in the Los Angeles area during the Watts riots and then significant rioting in the greater Los Angeles schools in my high school years. We would go through lockdowns at school and the call of law enforcement from surrounding cities to bring the high school under control. The conditions surrounding me sound still like what is posed as extreme at some high schools now. Kids were carrying knives and using them; some kids carried guns but this was less frequent than today. Murders and suicides occurred that were race related. Even though I attended an integrated school, the attitudes were not integrated and come riot time, there were the Whites and the Blacks. The Chicanos and the few Asians became virtually invisible. This was an instructive experience. Ironically, I was relatively safe being seen as neither Black nor White. The margins was a place of observance of how hostilities and tensions worked, how loyalties were formed, and how group belonging was enacted. (p. 116)

In sharing her life story, Dr. Root pays homage to the many people who influenced her and served as mentors and role models. Beginning with her mother, she goes on to share her undergraduate and graduate experiences and specify the teachers in both psychology and sociology who provided her with contexts to synthesize her life experiences. Dr. Root notes that she grew up with overt family discussions of racism, oppression, and gender socialization. Clearly her social and intellectual curiosity continues to this day as she closes her personal story by thanking the many colleagues with whom she continues those early family discussions and debates. We close our commentary with the words of pioneer Maria Root, who best captures the intersection of her personal and professional lives:

> My work has benefited from odd juxtapositions of experiences and friends and colleagues who often see things differently from each other. Rather than taking sides, my experience of making sense of the margins has been to take whatever gifts each person offers and come to my own conclusions which are undoubtedly a synthesis of all the thinking to which I have been exposed. (p. 120)

Of all the pioneers honored in this section of the *Handbook*, perhaps none presents more of a cross-cultural, intercultural experience than *Daya Singh Sandhu*. Dr. Sandhu immigrated to the United States at the age of 26, having spent his entire childhood, adolescence, and early adulthood in the country of India. Dr. Sandhu's story, poignant, reflective, and deeply personal, provides us with a vivid glimpse of life in India in the 1940s and 1950s, a time full of traumatic cultural, political, and religious conflict. His early life trauma is vividly captured in the following excerpt wherein he describes the period after India's partition into India and Pakistan:

> During this partition, cultural conflicts and religious riots arose everywhere. Sentiment against Hindus and Sikhs became very high in Pakistan. Unfortunately, my parents had no choice but to leave their homeland and all their belongings. They hurried to leave everything to save my younger brother who was only 2 years old. There was no other transportation but carts pulled by oxen. There was no other food but hastily prepared popcorns. There was no milk for babies, and even water was nowhere to be found. It was the hot month of August with scorching heat over 100°F. We were not even lucky enough to drink muddy water from ponds because these ponds were also filled with dead bodies. . . . I can still see myself on that ill-fated cart and my younger brother Dilbagh in my mother's lap crying for food and water. His cries and wails still pierce my heart. After several days of hunger and thirst, we reached our native town in Punjab. . . . Within two weeks, my parents, who were born to rich families, became

> penniless refugees. . . . Unfortunately, my brother could never accompany us to the free land. He died of dehydration. (p. 123)

Dr. Sandhu's early life was characterized by deep love and affection from his parents, but also by deep poverty and a household grieving deeply the loss of a child. Let us again turn to Dr. Sandhu's reflections:

> There was deep parental affection from both parents, but there was crippling poverty at home. The mud house we lived in was without electricity and running water. During the heavy monsoon rains it was very dangerous to live in the mud houses. Once during heavy floods in our area, we had to spend a night in a wooden box. Poverty is cruel and violently painful. I felt utterly empty and lonely as a child. It made me envious of others who had so many brothers and sisters, for I had neither. (p. 124)

A gifted student throughout his life, Dr. Sandhu was offered the opportunity to attend college; but reaching classes each day posed its own challenges, as he recalls,

> College days were extremely stressful. It was not possible for me to stay in the dormitory. I had neither the money nor the guts to stand separated from my parents. I decided to attend college by train. Unfortunately, the morning train left at 5:25 a.m. from Nakodar, which necessitated arising in the morning at 3:30 a.m. and getting ready to walk three and a half miles by myself to catch this train. The way was like a jungle. Thorny bushes and fear of deadly snakes, made this journey hellish during the early morning darkness. The rainy and chilly days during winter made life unbearable. (p. 126)

Dr. Sandhu's academic success throughout life provided him an opportunity to attend graduate school in the United States. Though an exciting opportunity, leaving one's homeland and family is naturally traumatic. We believe Dr. Sandhu captures poignantly the experience of immigrants who travel to the United States in search of life opportunities:

> On the day I departed for the United States, I felt very strong and mixed emotions. On one side, I felt exalted and ecstatic that I was going to the promised land, a land of great opportunities. On the other side, it was a day of severe sadness leaving my parents and my brother behind. . . . Several guests and relatives, and people from my village arranged a hero's good bye at the railway station. Even the train was delayed for 15 minutes to complete the seeing-off festivities. I was heavily garlanded. When the train was ready to leave, the whole scene became very melancholic. It was so difficult to separate from my family, especially from Mom. She kept crying, sobbing, and wailing. One relative, Piara Singh, remarked that leaving home for abroad is like living dead. When the train started, I became extremely sad. It felt as if Heaven had fallen or the whole earth had collapsed beneath my feet. Separation was so intense and unbearable. A line of separation was drawn forever. I kept looking back at my parents and relatives

as far as I could see. I wanted to go back so bad that words can not describe the feeling, but that was not possible now. (p. 131)

Dr. Daya Sandhu speaks vividly of his excitement upon arriving in the United States; he also notes the subsequent challenges of adjusting and acculturating to a very different life in America. In time, he and his family adjusted well to life in the United States, but then another major life challenge arrived:

> I was finally getting acclimated to American culture. Now I had a car, a teaching job, and a green card. We were also blessed with our son, Sukhwinder (Johnny). Then tragedy befell. Kuldip [his wife] and her sister, Harkishan, went to buy groceries in a nearby town. They had a car accident in which both were killed instantly, leaving me a widower with two children and my brother-in-law with five children. It was the most depressing event in my life. I sustained the most excruciating psychological pain when I had to take Kuldip's remains after cremation in a box to India to put them in a pious river. How frail we are as humans who eventually are reduced to ashes! (p. 133)

Impressively, despite challenges and traumas experienced throughout his life, we note in Dr. Sandhu's story a deep sustaining spiritual connection that has assisted him in maintaining a love of life and work. He appears to have found deep meaning in his life experiences that inform and guide his ground-breaking professional work, which includes classic books and journal articles on fighting racial prejudice, gender inequity, and youth violence. He has a deep love and emotional connection to his native India, while also appreciating and cherishing his adopted America. He is clearly a renaissance person, a "multicultural" person.

INTEGRATION OF LIFE STORIES

Certainly, the life stories of the individual pioneers featured in Part I of the *Handbook* are unique. Hopefully, through the reading of the individual chapters and our summary of them, the reader can reflect on the life experiences and personal and professional development of each scholar. Though unique in collective life experiences, the pioneers also share some similarities and common traits. The goal of this final section of the chapter is to explore some themes that transcend the individual lives of the featured scholars. Below, we present 12 themes that we believe transcend many if not all of the pioneers. These themes represent a consensus of the three authors of the present chapter, though, understandably, other readers may note additional or different commonalities.

1. The pioneers believe in and practice "multiculturalism" at the core of their being. Being multicultural, fighting oppression, and seeing strength in diversity are not attitudes or orientations limited to 9:00 a.m. to 5 p.m. hours; the pioneers live out their multicultural orientations in their professional and personal lives. Their professional commitment to multiculturalism and social justice is a reflection of their personal experiences and evolving worldview.

2. All of the pioneers have experienced oppression first-hand. Whether these injustices have been based on race, gender, sexual orientation, language dominance, accent, religion, social class, or a combination of factors, all have experienced the pain, hurt, and frustration of being prejudged, falsely judged, discounted, and disrespected.

3. A strong theme that emerged for us in reading the life stories is that multicultural awareness, comfort, and skill comes from "real world" interactions with cultural diversity. Whether through one's own life experiences that may be culturally different from an imposed Euro-American standard, or from living among diverse people even if one is Euro-American, a great depth of cultural awareness, personal awareness, stereotype reduction, and cultural comfort is achieved. Reading the life stories reinforced for us the need to move multicultural training off campuses and into communities and countries of cultural variance.

4. All of the pioneers are deeply committed to mentoring others, and all serve society in multiple ways. Though all are internationally renowned for the quality and electrifying impact of their published work, they also speak frequently to community groups, teach, mentor, serve individual clients, consult with state and federal agencies, and so on. All the pioneers have deeply touched and helped many students, clients, and colleagues, partial growth through their caring personal interactions with many people.

5. We were also struck by the deep sense of respect that the pioneers displayed for both personal ancestors and professional mentors. Many of the pioneers pay deep tribute to great-grandparents, grandparents, parents, and extended family. Additionally, many of the pioneers thank professional mentors and role models who were instrumental in their own professional and personal development.

6. The collective group of pioneers is very modest. Despite what we and countless other professionals consider to be visionary and groundbreaking contributions to both our profession and society, the pioneers are modest and humble about their work and status in the field. Reading the life stories we asked ourselves, "How can such renowned scholars and famous people be so humble and modest?" On reflection, perhaps that is a trait that contributes to their status as pioneers.

7. Also quite evident in the life stories are the individual acts of courage exhibited by the pioneers. Many of these pioneers represent the first generation of spokespersons for the multicultural counseling movement.

They have had many battles to fight—in their universities, mental health clinics, and professional associations—to ensure cultural inclusion in member representation and daily operations. They have also fought social injustice in their personal and family lives, in some cases risking physical safety in support of human rights for all people. The levels of emotional and physical energy these pioneers have devoted to dealing with and fighting prejudice and injustices seems immeasurable.

8. The pioneers highlight the levels of family and friendship support that have empowered them to fight prejudice and work toward building a multicultural profession and community. The support of parents and grandparents, siblings, life partners and children, and community friends and allies, seems to have boosted the strength of the pioneers to consistently fight prejudice and promote multicultural communities. The pioneers also attribute much of their educational success to this support network, and they all believed that through receipt of the doctoral degree they would have a greater impact on the profession and society.

9. We were moved by the level of spiritualism common to some of the pioneers. Though the group represented many belief systems, some indigenous to this land, others imported, there was a common thread of life's interconnectedness. Some pioneers highlighted people's (and nature's) mutual dependence for life fulfillment. There was an emphasis on peoples' collectivism rather than individualism; that we are all connected in an evolutionary and spiritual way.

10. All of the pioneers see themselves as part of a network of "multiculturalists" who support and rely on one another. Their success in fighting prejudice and coping with a monoculturally oriented profession (and society) rests, in part, on the supportive strength of this multicultural coalition and alliance.

11. The pioneers have developed life and coping skills that emanate from their extensive personal (and professional) multicultural experiences. In a sense, the group members have "multicultural personalities," that are reflected in the ability to negotiate and appreciate multiple cultures; the ability to live and work effectively among different groups and types of people; the ability to see strength and richness in diversity; and the strength and courage to fight human rights injustices in its many virulent forms. Importantly, this multicultural personality and its consequent life skills are modeled and passed on to mentees, students, and clients.

12. A final theme we would like to comment on is that the pioneers have channeled hurtful, painful, and frustrating experiences into positive, humanistic, educational action in support of others, particularly oppressed others. Though outraged by human rights injustices, the pioneers appear to have an inner tranquility, peace, and a secure self- and group-actualized identity. Notwithstanding this inner security and esteem, the pioneers also seem to be involved in an ongoing process of further personal and professional growth and challenges.

CONCLUSION

In this chapter we have shared our impressions of the life stories presented by 12 pioneers in multicultural counseling. We have highlighted themes and quotes that we found particularly impactful in each of the life stories. We were impressed and humbled by the depth of self-disclosure of these scholars, teachers, and healers. We are aware that for many of them, these writings constituted the first deep personal self-disclosures presented for public viewing. Writing their life stories was a challenging and emotionally draining process. We thank them for this window into their lives, and we are certain the stories will mentor thousands of students and professionals who are searching for the link between their own personal and professional identity.

At the close of this chapter, we generated themes that we thought transcended many, and in some cases all, of the pioneers' lives. Certainly, there are other important themes that we missed or did not represent adequately. We invite readers to generate their own transcendent (and pioneer-specific) themes, and we suggest they write down and reflect upon their own life stories in concert with those presented here.

REFERENCES

Allport, G. W. (1942). *The use of personal documents in psychological science.* New York: Social Science Research Council.

Atkinson, R. (1998). *The life story interview.* Thousand Oaks, CA: Sage.

Bond, M. H. (Ed.). (1997). *Working at the interface of cultures: Eighteen lives in social science.* London: Routledge.

Erikson, E. (1958). *Young man Luther: A study in psychoanalysis and history.* New York: Norton.

Erikson, E. (1969). *Gandhi's truth: On the origins of militant nonviolence.* New York: Norton.

Freud, S. (1910/1957). Leonardo da Vinci and a memory of his childhood. In J. Strachey (Ed.), *The standard edition of the complete psychological works of Sigmund Freud* (Vol. 12, pp. 3-82). London: Hogarth. (Original work published 1910)

Heppner, P. P. (Ed.). (1990). *Pioneers in counseling and development: Personal and professional perspectives.* Alexandria, VA: American Counseling Association.

Hoshmand, L. T. (Ed.). (1998). *Creativity and moral vision in psychology: Narratives on identity and commitment in a postmodern age.* Thousand Oaks, CA: Sage.

Howard, G. S. (1989). *A tale of two stories: Excursions into a narrative approach to psychology.* Notre Dame, IN: Academic Publications.

Howard, G. S. (1991). Culture tales: A narrative approach to thinking, cross-cultural psychology and psychotherapy. *American Psychologist, 46,* 188-197.

Howard, G. S., Maerlender, A. C., Myers, P. R., & Curtin, T. D. (1992). In stories we trust: Studies of the validity of autobiographies. *Journal of Counseling Psychology, 39,* 398-405.

Josselson, R., & Lieblich, A. (Eds.). (1993). *The narrative study of lives* (Vol. 1). Thousand Oaks, CA: Sage.

Josselson, R., & Lieblich, A. (Eds.). (1995). *The narrative study of lives: Interpreting experience* (Vol. 3). Thousand Oaks, CA: Sage.

Morrow, S. L., Rakhsha, G., & Castañeda, C. L. (2001). Qualitative research methods for multicultural counseling. In J. G. Ponterotto, J. M. Casas, L. A. Suzuki, & C. M. Alexander (Eds.), *Handbook of multicultural counseling* (2nd ed., pp. 575-603). Thousand Oaks, CA: Sage.

Morrow, S. L., & Smith, M. L. (2000). Qualitative research for counseling psychology. In S. D. Brown & R. W. Lent (Eds.), *Handbook of counseling psychology* (3rd ed., pp. 199-230). New York: John Wiley.

Murray, H. A. (1938). *Explorations in personality.* New York: Oxford University Press.

Polkinghorne, D. E. (1988). *Narrative knowing and the human sciences.* Albany: State University of New York Press.

Part II

ETHICS AND
PROFESSIONAL ISSUES

Part II of the *Handbook* presents three chapters that focus on ethics and professional issues in multicultural counseling. Ridley, Liddle, Hill, and Li open the section (Chapter 14) with a state-of-the-art presentation on ethical practice in multicultural counseling. The limitations of traditional ethical "codes" are highlighted, and the authors introduce a comprehensive and fluid model for ethical decision making. Central to the new model is a focus on critical reflection, creative problem solving, and higher order reasoning skills.

In Chapter 15, Casas, Pavelski, Furlong, and Zanglis tackle two often neglected topics in the multicultural literature: (a) a focus on youths and their families and (b) organized "systems of care." Basing their writing on extensive experience with the Santa Barbara County (California) Multi-agency Integrated System of Care program, the authors highlight a general societal neglect of mental health needs of minority youths, and they describe a model multiservice collaborative program that more effectively meets the needs of minority youths and their families. Integrated throughout the chapter are important policy and research suggestions for practitioners, researchers, and administrators.

Part II closes with Chapter 16, collaboratively written by founders and leaders of the National Institute for Multicultural Competence (NIMC). The primary mission of the NIMC is to promote multiculturalism and confront racism. The authors trace the activities, challenges, and successes of the NIMC since its founding in 1993. Highlighted in the chapter is the "revolutionary" potential that a multicultural perspective brings to American society. The central and critical role of the counseling profession in this revolution is highlighted.

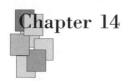

Chapter 14

ETHICAL DECISION MAKING IN MULTICULTURAL COUNSELING

CHARLES R. RIDLEY
MONIQUE C. LIDDLE
CARRIE L. HILL
LISA C. LI

THE CODES OF ETHICS of the various mental health professions, such as those of the American Counseling Association (ACA, 1995) and American Psychological Association (APA, 1992), provide principles and standards of professional conduct. These codes are intended to hold mental health practitioners accountable for their actions (Cottone & Tarvydas, 1998). Underlying these codes is the premise that practitioners, not their clients, are ultimately responsible for conducting themselves in an ethically appropriate manner. However, ethically appropriate conduct is often a difficult responsibility and one marked by considerable ambiguity (Dinger & Coupland, 1999).

Blasi (1980) reported that practitioners' knowledge of ethical codes does not necessarily lead them to appropriate ethical conduct. Some scholars have argued that ethical guidelines are necessary but not sufficient for promoting ethically appropriate behavior (Dinger & Coupland, 1999; Mabe & Rollin, 1986; Pedersen, 1997). In fact, the nature of ethical problems often requires action that is not clearly prescribed by the codes of ethics (Corey, Corey, & Callanan, 1998). For all their merits, the codes do not provide the "thinking tools" to analyze and resolve many ethical problems (Dinger & Coupland, 1999; Drane, 1982; Kitchener, 1984, 1986; Mabe & Rollin, 1986). To bolster this argument, Mabe and Rollin (1986, pp. 294-295) identified some prominent limitations of ethical codes:

1. There are some issues that cannot be handled in the context of a code.

2. There are some difficulties with enforcing the code, or at least the public may believe that enforcement committees are not tough enough on their peers.

3. There is often no way to systematically bring the interests of the client, patient, or research participant into the code construction process.

4. There are parallel forums in which the issues in the code may be addressed, with the results sometimes at odds with the findings of the code (e.g., in the courts).

5. There are possible conflicts associated with codes: between two codes, between the practitioner's values and code requirements, between the code and ordinary morality, between the code and institutional practice, and between requirements within a single code.

6. There is a limited range of topics covered in the code, and because a code approach is usually reactive to issues already developed elsewhere, the requirement of consensus prevents the code from addressing new issues and problems at the "cutting edge."

In addition, Pedersen (1995, 1997) argued that the ACA and APA codes of ethics favor a dominant culture perspective, and these codes minimize or trivialize the role of culture in ethical decision making.

Because of these limitations, practitioners who rigidly apply ethical directives are prone to oversimplify the complexity inherent in ethical problems. Complexity refers to the number and informational depth of conflicting perspectives—all of which are relevant to making decisions and taking action (Schroder, 1977). Oversimplifying complex issues is serious. Practitioners are the final authority for determining what is right in an ethical problem (Tennyson & Strom, 1986) and, as previously noted, are the ones ultimately responsible for taking ethically appropriate action. Paradoxically, the complexity of ethical problems may lead to uncertainty about what action they should take (Tennyson & Strom, 1986). Nowhere is oversimplification more problematic or likely to occur than in multicultural counseling, for here practitioners often encounter conflicting cultural values, unfamiliar behaviors and idioms, and role expectations that differ between themselves and their clients. An unfortunate consequence of oversimplification and its ensuing paradox is that many practitioners engage in unintentional racism (Ridley, 1995).

Therefore, the complexity inherent in many ethical problems requires more critical reflection and creative problem solving than is facilitated by ethical codes. To master the use of these "thinking tools," practitioners need better guidance than is currently available. The purpose of this chapter is to explicate a model of ethical decision making in multicultural counseling.

The model guides practitioners in the use of higher reasoning skills. In offering this model, we make several assumptions: (a) that practitioners are familiar with the ethical codes of their respective mental health professions, (b) that practitioners are motivated to conduct themselves in an ethically appropriate manner, and (c) that the model enables practitioners to transcend oversimplification of complex ethical problems.

To achieve our objective, we organize the chapter into six major sections. First, we discuss some of the prerequisites for responsible ethical decision making. Second, we explain various influences on ethical decision making. Third, we describe the practitioner's multicultural responsibility, laying the foundation for ethical decision making. Fourth, we present our model, which serves as a pragmatic tool for practitioners. Fifth, we describe two entry points of ethical decision making. Sixth, we provide a case example that demonstrates the use of our model.

PREREQUISITES FOR
RESPONSIBLE ETHICAL DECISION MAKING

Making ethically appropriate decisions does not occur automatically. It requires assistance. Three prerequisites enable practitioners to responsibly carry out this process: operationalizing terminology, making the practitioner's ethical perspectives explicit, and having a sound decision-making process.

Operationalizing Terminology

Ethics

The nouns "ethics" and "morality" (and their corresponding adjectives "ethical" and "moral") often are used interchangeably. This leads to confusion. Many authors use the phrase "moral concepts" when discussing ethical principles; however, they ought to use the phrase "ethical concepts." Tennyson and Strom (1986), for example, mistakenly referred to "the complexity of moral dilemmas faced in counseling" (p. 298). Ethical concepts are relevant to professional codes, whereas moral concepts refer to universal principles. Corey and colleagues (1998) probably came closest to distinguishing between ethics and morality: "Ethics are moral principles adopted by an individual or group to provide rules for right conduct. Morality is concerned with perspectives of right and proper conduct and involves an evaluation of actions on the basis of some broader cultural context or religious standard" (p. 3). Kitchener (1984) further identified some basic moral principles that are adopted into ethical codes of practitioners: autonomy, beneficence, nonmaleficence, and fairness. These definitions are helpful, but they are still hampered by ambiguity. Therefore, more clarification is needed.

Morality, or morals, can be understood as general and universal principles of human behavior—core values that exist across cultures. Examples are care for an individual or relationships, human dignity, solidarity, or justice. But these principles are difficult to put into practice without a context that gives them operational meaning. Ethics, on the other hand, refers to the specific and contextual interpretation of general principles of morality. Professional organizations interpret these principles in their ethical codes. Interpretations, however, can change over time as groups and organizations reevaluate their ethical codes and apply them to the myriad of ethical problems that arise. This reevaluation process is demonstrated by the nine revisions of the APA Ethics Code since its initial publication in 1953 (Canter, Bennett, Jones, & Nagy, 1994). With regard to standards of professional conduct then, the issue at hand is one of *ethics*—the interpretation of general moral principles—and not *morality*—the universal principles of human behavior.

Ethical

Based on the distinction between "ethics" and "morality," it follows that the adjective "ethical" should be used instead of "moral" when discussing standards of professional conduct. Therefore, we focus on the use of the adjective "ethical." In the literature, further confusion is created because the adjective "ethical" is variously used. We identify some of these uses, pointing out several problems with them. We also recommend an alternative and lucid use of the term.

Problems with current uses of the adjective "ethical." In the mental health field, there are multiple uses of the adjective "ethical." Four prominent uses are to describe situations, problems, dilemmas, and behaviors. There are several problems with the current uses. First, the field lacks a consensus on definitions. For instance, there is no agreement on what is meant by an ethical situation. Some professionals imply it is a problem that already exists, whereas others imply it is a potential problem. Second, the various terms often are used interchangeably. For instance, the phrases ethical situation, ethical problem, and ethical dilemma sometimes are used as though they have the same meaning. Do these phrases really refer to the same phenomenon, or are they different from each other? The literature provides no clear answers.

In addition, the word "ethical" has a dual connotation. When used to describe a situation, ethical connotes something negative. For example, a practitioner presented an "ethical situation" to his supervisor. He questioned whether acceptance of a client's invitation to a social event constituted a dual relationship. When used to describe a behavior, however, "ethical" typically connotes something positive. An example is this: "The psychologist was ethical to not falsify statistical results even though they contradicted his popular theory." In the context of describing a behavior, the antonym "unethical" connotes something negative. An example is this: "The psychologist was unethical to falsify statistical results because they contradicted his popular theory." Therefore, both the words "ethical" and "unethical" in their current uses can have a negative connotation.

Fourth, the term "dilemma," which appears extensively in the literature, is frequently misused. Examples of its misuse are as follows: when identifying "cultural dilemmas;" "the universal application of [ACA] rules, checklists, and principles create a dilemma for conscientious minorities" (Pedersen, 1997, p. 24); "ethical reasoning of multicultural dilemmas is underscored" (LaFromboise, Foster, & James, 1996, p. 49); and "the ethical dilemma in the treatment-control model pits 'good science' against 'participant welfare'" (Gil & Bob, 1999, p. 48). Professionals routinely use the term dilemma to connote an ethical problem. However, the denotation of dilemma is from the Latin *dilēmma* with the prefix *di* meaning "two" and indicating a choice between two equally unfavorable alternatives.

Collectively, these problems perpetuate unclear thinking and hamper meaningful dialogue in the field. Perhaps, the most serious consequence is the slowing down of progress, and this has immeasurable ramifications.

Proposed use of the adjective "ethical." We propose the following elaboration of the word "ethical." Ethical should be used to modify (give important information about) a concern or problem. An ethical concern is one in which questionable professional conduct or possible conflicts of ethics should be under consideration to establish the seriousness of the concern. The definition has several features that help elucidate the meaning of an ethical concern. First, the definition includes the words "questionable" and "possible" because not all professional conduct in question or possible conflicts are actual ethical problems. Legitimate questions may be raised about them, but the problematic nature of these concerns must be established before they can be deemed an ethical problem. Therefore, once an ethical concern is examined, no real ethical problem may exist. Second, the definition includes the word "should" because not all professional conduct in question or possible conflicts of ethics actually are taken under consideration. Sometimes, these concerns simply are not recognized. Sometimes, they are recognized, but there is no determination of whether or not an ethical problem exists. Obviously, great care must be taken to determine whether or not an ethical concern is an actual ethical problem. Finally, the definition includes the phrase "under consideration." To be under consideration means that the professional conduct in question or possible conflict in ethics is subjected to a discernment process. The purpose of discernment is to determine the veracity of the concern.

An ethical problem is more serious than an ethical concern. We construe an ethical problem as a concern that compromises the integrity of treatment. Integrity is from the Latin *integritās* meaning wholeness. Therefore, integrity of treatment means unimpaired or uncorrupted pursuit of therapeutic outcomes. Inappropriate conduct and unaddressed or mishandled conflicts fit our definition of an ethical problem; they impair or corrupt treatments.

A clinician who discriminates by only providing custodial care to minority clients instead of in-depth psychotherapy is an example of ethically inappropriate conduct. A clinician, who believes a client should receive 12 sessions of therapy but the managed care corporation only authorizes 6 sessions, is caught up in a conflict of ethics. Practitioners should note that both types of ethical problems can coexist in the same counseling case.

In using the phrase "ethical problem," we make two assumptions. We assume that not all inappropriate conduct or unaddressed or mishandled conflicts are ethical problems. A concern must meet the criteria of compromising the integrity of treatment before it can be categorized as an ethical problem. We also assume that dilemmas exist, but rarely are there only two solutions for an ethical problem. Using the word "dilemma" is problematic because it perpetuates dualistic thinking and hinders creative problem solving. We prefer the phrase "ethical problem" over "ethical dilemma" because a problem has many possible solutions—an advantage to practitioners who solve problems creatively.

As indicated in Figure 14.1, First Use, ethical concerns are subject to two possible levels of decision making: discernment and creative problem solving. First, there is a discernment process to determine whether an ethical problem actually exists. The discernment process is facilitated by the use of ethical codes, and in many cases, the process is straightforward. If the discernment process indicates the existence of an ethical problem, subsequent problem solving is needed to determine an appropriate course of action. If the problem is inappropriate conduct, the professional ideally should initiate the course of action. Failure to do so may result in some sort of remediation or sanctioning. If the problem is a conflict of ethics, the course of action may involve some sort of resolution between the various parties. Due to the inherent complexity of ethical problems, creative problem solving is often more complicated than the discernment process. It typically necessitates the use of higher reasoning skills, in addition to the use of ethical codes. Therefore, the phrase "ethical concern" implies that discernment is necessary, and, if an ethical problem is found to exist, creative problem solving should follow.

For instance, a puzzled intern presented an ethical concern to her supervisor. Her Taiwanese client wanted to show respect by engaging in the cultural practice of "gift giving." But the intern questioned whether her acceptance of the client's invitation to the opera would constitute a dual relationship and hence a possible ethical problem. The intern and her supervisor discerned that an ethical problem would exist if she accepted. Of course, the intern did not accept the invitation, and no dual relationship unfolded. Had she accepted, however, she would have had to engage in creative problem solving to produce an ethically appropriate outcome.

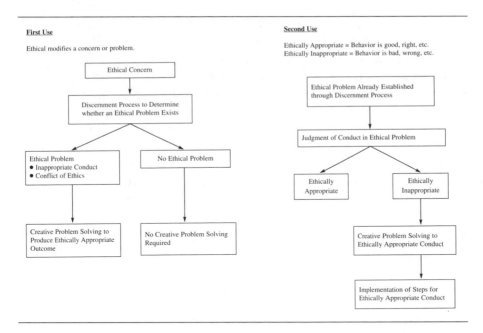

First Use

Ethical modifies a concern or problem.

Second Use

Ethically Appropriate = Behavior is good, right, etc.
Ethically Inappropriate = Behavior is bad, wrong, etc.

Figure 14.1. Proposed Use of the Adjective "Ethical" and Phrases "Ethically Appropriate/Ethically Inappropriate"

Unfortunately, by not accepting the invitation, a conflict of ethics arose. The client was offended because he felt the intern was belittling his culture. Consequently, the intern had to engage in creative problem solving to resolve the conflict.

We argue that defining "ethical concerns" as involving two possible levels of decision making is beneficial. This use includes all the essential subprocesses of ethical decision making, places them in proper sequence, and assists practitioners in discerning when an ethical concern is really an ethical problem. For instance, ethical codes do not indicate whether practitioners should wear formal business suits or casual attire during counseling sessions. Neither style of dress may be discerned as constituting an ethical problem; hence, no creative problem solving is required. On the other hand, ethical codes give indication that an ethical problem may arise if practitioners dress provocatively. If this style of dress is discerned as constituting an ethical problem, creative problem solving is needed to determine an appropriate course of action.

Proposed use of the phrases "ethically appropriate/ethically inappropriate." The most beneficial way to describe judged professional conduct, we argue, is *not* by using the words "ethical" or "unethical." As proposed above and illustrated in Figure 14.1, First Use, the word "ethical" should be used to describe a concern or problem. We propose that judged behavior can be described as "ethically appropriate" (i.e., good, right, etc.) or "ethically

inappropriate" (i.e., bad, wrong, etc.; see Figure 14.1, Second Use). We believe it would be clearer in our earlier illustration to state "The psychologist acted ethically appropriate by not falsifying statistical results even
though they contradicted his popular theory" and "The psychologist acted
ethically inappropriate by falsifying statistical results because they contradicted his popular theory." In these examples, the phrases "ethically
appropriate/ethically inappropriate" refer to behaviors that precede the discernment process. The phrases also can be used to describe behaviors that
follow discernment and creative problem solving. For example, "The psychologist acted ethically appropriate by retracting his conclusions, revising
his data analysis, and submitting his revision."

Making the Practitioner's Ethical Perspectives Explicit

Practitioners make their ethical perspectives explicit by clearly stating
them. Clarification helps practitioners communicate their ideas unambig-
uously, leaving little room for misinterpretation. Three tasks are involved
in making ethical perspectives explicit. The first task is knowing about the
variety of ethical perspectives held by practitioners. In the next major section, we discuss these ethical perspectives. The second task is identifying
one's own ethical perspectives. This requires practitioners to examine their
beliefs about ethics so they can better understand how they view and interpret ethical problems. The third task is to become proficient at articulating
one's ethical perspectives in a professional context (e.g., when speaking
with colleagues, supervisors, or clients). Making ethical perspectives explicit is always crucial, especially during multicultural counseling,
since practitioners' ethical beliefs often are entwined with their cultural
assumptions.

Having a Sound Decision-Making Process

A sound decision-making process enables practitioners to analyze and
resolve complex ethical problems. Without such a process, the possibility
of making flawed, ethically inappropriate decisions increases. A sound process of ethical decision making has several distinguishing characteristics.
First, the process is comprehensive. It contains the critical elements and
subprocesses necessary for arriving at ethically appropriate decisions. Practitioners are guided in piecing together all relevant data in an ethical problem. Second, the process is logical and coherent. It is based on accepted
presuppositions, and it leads to conclusions that are ethically appropriate.
Moreover, there are no gaps or leaps in the process that render decisions unexplainable. Third, the process is practitioner-friendly. It is clear and
directly applicable to the actual ethical problems practitioners encounter.
Finally, the process is collaborative. It engages practitioners, clients, and

other relevant parties in the resolution of ethical problems. All four characteristics are necessary for a decision-making process to be sound. If the process is incomprehensive, illogical and incoherent, not practitioner-friendly, or noncollaborative, the decision-making process is unsound and is more likely to yield ethically inappropriate decisions.

INFLUENCES ON ETHICAL DECISION MAKING

There are many influences on ethical decision making. Two of the more prominent influences are general ethical perspectives and specific ethical perspectives. Both contain subset perspectives, and each subset is grounded in philosophical assumptions about the world and actions judged as right or wrong. Decisions made on the basis of these perspectives are contextualized in various situations. In contextualizing their decision making, individuals can view ethical problems from more than one perspective, and they can alternate between them (Gilligan, 1982). In fact, LaFramboise and her colleagues (1996) claimed that multiculturally competent counselors consider their general and specific ethical perspectives, as well as those of their clients, before making an intervention.

General Ethical Perspectives

Absolutism minimizes the importance of a cultural context and assumes that the same evaluative criteria can be applied across communities. The assumption underlying absolutism leads to the practice of applying a single correct solution to any given ethical problem, regardless of its content (Tjeltveit, 1999). The absolutist position avoids giving credence to the unique meanings and ethical perspectives created among cultural groups. Between-group comparisons are encouraged using standard criteria that usually are derived from the ethical values of the dominant group. Ethical decision making is applied systematically regardless of cultural differences (Berry, Poortinga, Segall, & Dasen, 1992). Casas and Thompson (1991) noted that the philosophical premises of many ethical guidelines for practitioners are absolutist in nature, primarily favoring the values of White, middle-class men.

Relativism assumes that ethical rules and norms emanate within and are limited to distinct communities. What is considered ethically right or wrong is unique to a particular cultural context (Tjeltveit, 1999). This perspective is usually referred to as *cultural relativism.* The relativist position avoids making judgments based on criteria that are external to the community and meanings created among its members. Between-group comparisons are not considered valid because no standard criteria can be used across communities. Ethical decision making ought to be tailored to the beliefs and practices of each particular cultural context (Berry et al., 1992). The key element to relativism is that there are no absolute values that exist outside of a context. Rather values are defined in context: time, place, culture, and in relation to other values. Values have been constructed as a result of human experience and thus cannot be known outside of human experience, and values cannot be known outside of their relation to other values. Relativism is based on the philosophical notion of subjectivity, which claims that there are no objective or universal truths or values. To know is only to know subjectively because human beings by their nature are subjective.

Universalism assumes that some phenomena, such as pleasure or pain, are universal, but the expression of such phenomena may vary across and within cultures. The universalist position encourages between-group and within-group comparisons as long as fundamental phenomena of human life are held constant, and manifestations of those phenomena are the objects of comparison (Berry et al., 1992). Ethical decision making is more complex from a universalist perspective. It requires the acknowledgment of ethical common ground while simultaneously understanding and considering the cultural differences of ethical interpretation (Pedersen, 1995, 1997). Universalism also can be understood as moral realism, a general philosophical concept rejecting skepticism, relativism, and absolutism. Moral realism embraces ethical convictions that transcend context and deny that reality is constructed by members of a particular cultural community. Tjeltveit (1999) stated that "all moral realists would hold, for instance, that the wrongness of rape is real, or genuine, wrongness, whatever any particular individual may choose to believe, or any culture holds" (p. 61). Universalism, as a specific concept of moral realism, agrees with the moral realist that reality is not socially constructed. In addition, "universalists combine the search for culture-specific manifestations of difference with a search for fundamental similarities that link each cultural context with every other context" (Pedersen, 1995, p. 36). Universalism is inherently complex because of this twofold commitment to acknowledging and working with both differences and similarities across cultures.

Specific Ethical Perspectives

There are two specific ethical perspectives—principle or justice ethics and virtue ethics. *Principle ethics* focus on rational, objective, universal, and impartial principles that mandate choices and actions (Jordan & Meara, 1990; Pedersen, 1997). The focus is on identifying and implementing various universal prescriptions (i.e., rules and principles) in order to know the right action to take. This perspective is a hierarchical ordering of universal values in which individual rights are central. LaFramboise and associates (1996) claimed that the justice perspective is "committed to personal liberty, the ideal of autonomy, and the use of a social contract model in which a group of people consent to a set of mutually acceptable principles to justify a social role" (p. 64). A person desires to know what universal laws are applicable to a particular ethical problem so that an individual knows what action ought to be implemented. The justice perspective has its philosophical roots in the writings of Locke, Kant, Rawls, Mill, and Kohlberg.

Virtue ethics focuses on an individual's "motives, intentions, character, and ethical consciousness" which can result in interpreting general principles differently for each cultural context (Pedersen, 1997, p. 24). General rules and principles are used, but they are secondary to virtues. Rules and principles are used when supported or derived from virtues. This is in contrast to principle ethics that focuses on actions alone and does not primarily investigate a person's intention or character. Virtue ethics is similar to the "ethic of care," which has been described as a function of case-based reasoning as opposed to reasoning solely on the basis of rules (Morphis & Riesbeck, 1990). Because the focal point primarily is not on general rules and actions, the virtue perspective focuses on a concern for establishing and preserving good relationships, helping others, and promoting mutual well-being. Virtue ethics has its philosophical roots in the writings of Aristotle, Hume, McIntyre, Williams, and Gilligan.

Context of Ethical Decision Making

Each ethical problem is unique. Although there are similarities across ethical problems, differences always exist. These differences, however slight, must be considered in ethical decision making. One practitioner, for instance, may have sexual intimacy with a minor, and another practitioner with an adult. Both problems involve a dual relationship, but each has its own intricacies. Therefore, despite the similarities, the ultimate resolution of ethical issues depends on the particular issues at play as well as how the practitioner conducts the decision-making process.

To understand how context affects decision making, practitioners should consider (a) the client's psychological and cultural phenomena and (b) the ethical problem itself. Psychological and cultural phenomena inform practitioners about how a client's cultural values and identity, diagnosis, prognosis, strengths, and resources add meaning to the ethical problem. Practitioners should use their understanding of a client's psychological and cultural phenomena to analyze the ethical problem in more detail and formulate more creative solutions. Psychological and cultural phenomena are not discrete categories. For instance, cultural variations exist among experiences of anxiety and depression, perceptions of normalcy and pathology, communication patterns, and motivations for behaviors and manifestations of behaviors.

The ethical problem is also part of the context of ethical decision making. The problem can originate in the client, such as a disclosure of suicidal or homicidal intent. The problem's origin can be external to the client, such as managed care restrictions that jeopardize treatment effectiveness. The problem also can originate in the practitioner, such as a practitioner who reacts negatively toward her gay clients but does not seek supervision or address possible homophobic concerns. Of course, the ethical problem may have several origins. Although the origin of the problem may not be easily identified, practitioners must attempt to identify the origin in order to consider as many factors as possible that are relevant to decision making.

MULTICULTURAL RESPONSIBILITY

Making ethical decisions in multicultural counseling and therapy is a professional's *multicultural responsibility*. By multicultural responsibility, we mean a fusion of personal and professional commitments to consider culture during all ethical encounters. The personal domain of multicultural responsibility encompasses the committed intention to consider culture, moral intuition about what is right and wrong, and deeply ingrained moral traditions (Kitchener, 1984; Tjeltveit, 1999). The professional domain of multicultural responsibility involves the interpretation of ethical principles and standards to one's professional life. It also includes adherence to applicable state laws and federal regulations (Canter et al., 1994).

Our conceptualization of multicultural responsibility does not suggest that either the personal or professional domain is more or less important. The fusion of the personal with the professional is important because practitioners should not act out of duty alone. They should also behave out of a "commitment to rational thinking and an orientation to moral principles" (Tennyson & Strom, 1986, p. 299). We suggest five ways to achieve this fusion.

First, practitioners can examine their philosophical assumptions about culture and ethics and make them explicit. This is accomplished by educating themselves about general and specific ethical perspectives described earlier in this chapter, and exploring their possible prejudices. For example, practitioners can identify racial stereotypes they hold and consider how these perceptions influence their interactions with clients from these cultures. Second, practitioners can examine alternative philosophical assumptions about culture and ethics. The examination could lead them to a more inclusive philosophical approach, as in considering feminist theories and racial theories. Third, practitioners can strive to understand how culture is always relevant in counseling and therapy (Ridley, Li, & Hill, 1998). This could lead them to mindfulness of *when* cultural issues come into play rather than wondering *if* cultural issues affect the client-practitioner relationship. Fourth, practitioners can develop complex thinking skills and creativity (Pope & Vasquez, 1998). This is advantageous over rigid attempts to resolve ethical problems. Fifth, practitioners can make an emotional investment in multicultural responsibility. This investment supersedes an

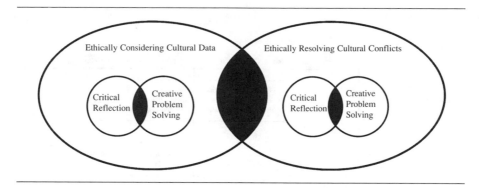

Figure 14.2. Model of Ethical Decision Making: Descriptive Version

intellectual or professional one. Similarly, recommendations have been made to adopt a principle of caring in multicultural counseling and psychotherapy (Casas & Thompson, 1991; Noddings, 1984; Pedersen, 1997).

A MODEL OF ETHICAL DECISION MAKING

Once practitioners operationalize ethical constructs, become aware of influences on their ethical decision making, and commit themselves to being multiculturally responsible, they can engage deliberately and purposefully in decision making to achieve an ethically appropriate outcome. To assist practitioners in this endeavor, we propose a two-dimensional model. One dimension involves the stages of ethical decision making. The two stages are critical reflection and creative problem solving. The other dimension involves the processes of ethical decision making, which are the ethical consideration of cultural data and the ethical resolution of cultural conflicts. There are two versions of the model—one is descriptive and the other prescriptive. Figure 14.2 illustrates the descriptive version.

Stages and processes are different but related dimensions of the model. A stage is "a period, level, or degree in a process of development, growth, or change" (Guralnik, 1986, p. 1385). A process is "a particular method of doing something, generally involving a number of steps or operations" (Guralnik, 1986, p. 1133). Therefore, critical reflection and creative problem solving are stages within the processes of the ethical consideration of cultural data and ethical resolution of cultural conflicts. Figure 14.2 displays the two stages within each of the processes. The two stages partially overlap, suggesting they are separate but sometimes occur simultaneously in an integrative fashion. The two processes partially overlap, also, suggesting they are separate but sometimes occur simultaneously in an integrative fashion. The descriptive version is a broad representation of the complexity

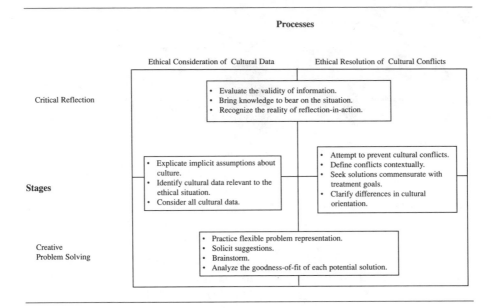

Figure 14.3. Model of Ethical Decision Making: Prescriptive Version

of ethical decision making. It portrays the dimensions of the model, but this version does not demonstrate how these dimensions operate. Therefore, it is difficult to extract from it clear guidelines about how to execute the decision-making process. To compensate for this limitation, we provide a prescriptive version of the model, as shown in Figure 14.3. This version of the model is really the descriptive version seen under a magnifying glass, figuratively speaking, so practitioners can see exactly how to apply each stage within each process.

Stages

Critical Reflection

Critical reflection means that practitioners think about their professional behavior and the implicit meanings of their behavior (Schon, 1983; Tennyson & Strom, 1986). Critical reflection enables an individual to construct or deconstruct arguments, evaluate data, read more carefully, articulate one's ideas more clearly and defensibly, and make better decisions. We offer three suggestions for critical reflection. First, carefully evaluate the validity of information acquired about the ethical problem (Moore & Parker, 1995). This entails deciding when it is reasonable to accept others' claims. Moore and Parker (1995) purported that, "generally speaking, it is reasonable to accept an unsupported claim (1) if it does not conflict with our own observations, with our background knowledge, or with other credible claims; and (2) if it comes from a credible source about which we have no reason to suspect bias" (p. 69). The second suggestion is related to the first; bring knowledge to bear on the problem (Gambrill, 1990). This knowledge includes counseling theories, ethical codes, and an understanding of multicultural issues. Third, recognize that reflection occurs when the counselor is engaged with the client during a session as well as when the clinician is thinking about the problem in private. Not only, then, do practitioners reflect on their behavior before and after they behave—they also reflect on what they do while doing it. Schon (1983) called this *reflection-in-action*.

Creative Problem Solving

A variety of options to solve an ethical problem usually is available. Here is how one counseling psychologist creatively solved an ethical problem. The psychologist had a private practice in addition to teaching at a university. A client told the psychologist that he registered for one of her continuing education courses. The client was very excited. The psychologist immediately recognized that this situation would constitute a dual relationship, and the ethical codes identify this as inappropriate. The psychologist went to great lengths to persuade the client that a dual relationship could bias her clinical judgment and compromise therapy. However, the client was unwilling to be referred to another practitioner, enroll in another section with another professor, or drop the course. In addition, the professor found out that the university did not have a policy that addressed this kind of problem. By making welfare of the client the primary concern and exploring a variety of options with the client and colleagues, the psychologist and client agreed to suspend treatment until the course was over. The psychologist then was able to identify an ethically appropriate alternative that satisfied both parties. A key element to this success was that the psychologist did not fall into dualistic thinking or assume her situation was a false dilemma.

We propose four strategies for creative problem solving. First, be flexible in the representation of the concern or problem (Gellatly, 1986). Concerns and problems often are framed in a singular way (e.g., visually). This can limit the range of potential conceptualizations and solutions. Flexible representation can be achieved by challenging habitual ways of conceptualizing (Weston, 1997). Second, solicit suggestions from others about what to do. This might take place in supervision or in consultation with colleagues. Third, brainstorm with those involved in the situation about how the conflict arose and possible solutions (Weston, 1997). An important rule to brainstorming is not to criticize the ideas generated. Fourth, analyze the goodness-of-fit of each potential solution to the ethical problem (Gellatly, 1986; Weston, 1997). Two criteria used are the ethical validity and pragmatic feasibility of the various options.

Processes

Ethical Consideration of Cultural Data

The *ethical consideration of cultural data* involves the collection and interpretation of cultural information relevant to the ethical problem. We provide three suggestions for considering cultural data. First, explicate implicit assumptions about culture and how these assumptions might influence the therapeutic relationship and ethical problem. For example, practitioners may identify their assumptions as reflecting an individualistic orientation to culture. By identifying the assumptions underlying this orientation, practitioners begin to see more clearly their implicit theory of therapeutic change and how this might undermine a client who has a collectivistic orientation.

Second, identify cultural data relevant to the ethical problem. This entails asking about culture and observing culture (Ridley, Li, & Hill, 1998). Examples of cultural data are signs of cultural transference and cultural countertransference (Ridley, 1995). Consider a White therapist who is counseling an Asian client. The client becomes angry with his therapist because he feels the therapist is being culturally insensitive. The therapist should observe the client's anger in a nonjudgmental way and ask the client about his feelings and perceptions of cultural insensitivity. The therapist should also observe her own reactions to the client. By taking this approach, the therapist can use the anger and her reaction to the client constructively. The therapist can use creative problem solving to determine the best way to incorporate emotional responses evoked by cultural differences into the therapeutic process.

Third, consider all cultural data as potentially relevant to the ethical problem. Each piece of data should be evaluated as to its pertinence to the problem and its potential for contributing to an appropriate solution. Otherwise, important information may be overlooked, which may result in cultural misunderstandings.

Ethical Resolution of Cultural Conflicts

When an ethical problem occurs because of differing cultural values or perspectives, we refer to it as a cultural conflict. This is a case in point of a conflict of ethics, and, as in any ethical problem, cultural conflicts require creative problem solving. We offer four suggestions in regard to the *ethical resolution of cultural conflicts*. First, practitioners should try to prevent cultural conflicts. The ethical consideration of cultural data may help prevent cultural conflicts. Yet while some cultural conflicts are preventable, others are not. Sometimes, cultural conflicts are not initially apparent even to seasoned practitioners. They may reach an impasse in treatment before they realize how subtle cultural differences create conflict. Sometimes, practitioners are simply impervious to cultural differences that should be obvious to them. In either case, the ethical resolution of cultural conflicts is necessary.

Second, practitioners should define cultural conflicts contextually instead of blaming individuals. Cultural conflicts may exist between the practitioner and the client, between the client and the service delivery system, or between the practitioner and the service delivery system. In many cases, practitioners find themselves caught in the middle, especially when they realize that the sources of the conflict are two parties to whom they have an ethical obligation. By defining the problem contextually, more solutions can be generated, and all parties can contribute to the problem solving.

Third, practitioners should seek solutions that are commensurate with treatment goals. Although a variety of solutions are possible, some solutions more than others are likely to facilitate therapeutic change. Fourth, practitioners should clarify through open discussion important differences between their cultural orientations and those of their clients. If these differences are not brought to the surface, the decision-making process will be impeded and the cultural conflict perpetuated.

TWO ENTRY POINTS
OF ETHICAL DECISION MAKING

There are two points at which practitioners can enter into the ethical decision-making process. The point of entrance depends on whether an ethical problem has the *potential to occur* or if an ethical problem *has already occurred*. Understanding these two entry points enables practitioners to make optimal use of our model (see Figure 14.4).

A Potential Ethical Problem

The first point of entry to ethical decision making is before an ethical problem has occurred (see Figure 14.4, First Entry Point). Earlier in the chapter, we used the example of a puzzled intern presenting a concern about her Taiwanese client to her supervisor in which "the intern questioned whether her acceptance of the client's invitation to the opera would constitute a dual relationship and hence a possible ethical problem." A key consideration is that the concern posed a *potential ethical problem* (i.e., the intern had not yet acted upon the concern). We stated that if the intern had acted upon her client's invitation, an ethical problem—specifically a dual relationship—would have ensued. However, it is important to understand how this conclusion was reached.

When confronted with an ethical concern, the first step at this entry point is to discern whether an ethical problem would occur. This depends

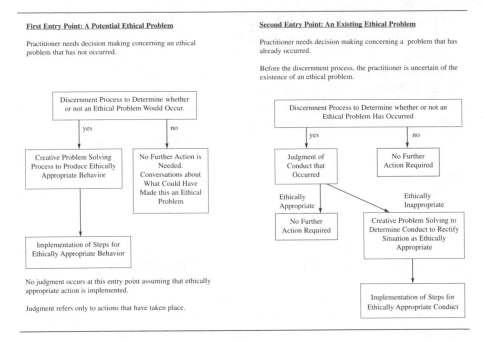

Figure 14.4. Two Entry Points of Ethical Decision Making

on the ensuing conduct of the practitioner. If the conduct would result in an ethical problem, creative problem solving would be necessary. The purpose of the creative problem solving would be to generate behaviors that would prevent the ethical problem. If the ensuing conduct would not result in an ethical problem, creative problem solving would not be necessary.

An Existing Ethical Problem

The second point of entry in ethical decision making is after an ethical problem already has occurred (see Figure 14.4, Second Entry Point). Assuming in the previous example that the intern had gone to the opera with her client, the next day she solicits advice from her supervisor. The first step would still be to discern whether or not an *ethical problem exists.* As stated earlier, practitioners too often skip this step and assume that an ethical problem does exist. Also, as stated earlier, careful critical reflection at this point can identify one's assumptions that may be used mistakenly to identify a concern that is a problem, when in fact it is not. Without proper discernment, practitioners make poor judgments. The discernment process is a prerequisite that informs one's judgment. In contrast to the other entry point in which judgment did not occur, if an ethical problem is identified, judgment of the practitioner's action needs to take place. If the action is judged ethically appropriate, no further action is required. However, if the action is judged ethically inappropriate, critical reflection and creative problem solving are used to determine corrective actions to rectify the problem.

Case Example

A 12-year old boy who is biracial is referred to a community mental health center. The boy's father is African American, and his mother is White. The school counselor, who referred the boy, claims that he acts out in school. She believes he has a conduct disorder. In addition, the boy is doing poorly in his schoolwork. The boy is assigned to a psychology intern who is a White female. During the intake, the boy reveals that he is the object of harassment and racial slurs. For example, he has been teased for being a "half-breed." Unfortunately, most of the harassment occurs on the playground and out of the view of the professional staff. The intern formulates a tentative clinical hypothesis that the boy's reaction to racism reveals some ego strength. Over the course of several appointments, the intern begins to piece together several conflicting facts. First, the intern observes that a disproportionate number of minority clients at the center were diagnosed as having a conduct disorder or antisocial personality disorder. When she inquires about this with her supervisor, a senior psychologist, he states they use the same *DSM-IV* criteria to assess all of their clients. She raised the topic of multicultural issues in assessment, but the supervisor states that multicultural theories lack scientific support, and therefore, they should not be used. Second, the intern cannot gain cooperation from the school. In fact, the school counselor denies that there is a racial problem in the school, insisting only that the boy was a troublemaker. Third, she notices that the boy seems to be attracted to her. It dawns on her that he might be displaying an affectionate transference because her physical features are similar to the boy's mother. Finally, she finds the boy's parents to be religious fundamentalists. The parents believe that as a family they need to pray more, and the boy needs to sincerely repent and confess his hidden sins. If this happens, the parents believe God would work things out.

1. Practice flexible representation of the concerns. Several ethical principles and standards help the intern frame her ethical concerns. If an ethical problem is found to exist, the principles and standards also will help define the cultural conflict contextually. For instance, the mental health center does not consider multicultural issues when formulating case conceptualizations, and the boy's school denies having a racial problem. Furthermore, both the intern's supervisor and the school counselor suggest that the intern make a diagnosis of conduct disorder, but the intern questions the validity of this recommendation. If she complies, she may engage in unfair discrimination (Standard 1.10, APA, 1992). A related issue is whether the intern should confront on a systemic level the mental health center and the school about their possible discriminatory practices. This relates to the principle of social responsibility (Principle F, APA, 1992) as well as Standard 8.03, which addresses ethical conflicts between practitioners and affiliated organizations (APA, 1992). A third concern pertains to how the intern handles the family's religious beliefs in relation to treatment. According to Standard 1.06 (APA, 1992), the intern should choose interventions based on scientifically and professionally derived knowledge. Bringing her knowledge to bear on the problem, the intern questions whether the family's religious persuasions are compatible with scientifically based interventions.

2. *Discern whether an ethical problem exists.* The ethical concerns involve both questionable professional conduct and cultural conflicts, both of which are subject to being unaddressed or mishandled. Based on the relevance of the above principles and standards, a complex ethical problem exists. The complexity of this problem suggests that some of the issues have already occurred, and others have the potential to occur. On the one hand, some degree of unfair discrimination in the delivery systems (i.e., school and mental health center) may have already occurred. On the other hand, the mishandling of transference and the family's religious beliefs may not have occurred and, therefore, are preventable.

3. *Make ethical perspectives explicit.* In this case, the intern needs to be familiar with various ethical perspectives and investigate whether she assumes absolutist, relativist, universalist, and/or other perspectives. The intern discovers that her perspective is characterized by univeralist assumptions and is rooted in virtue ethics. She needs to be able to articulate her perspective to others during the creative problem solving, realizing that this is a process of reflection-in-action.

4. *Solicit suggestions from others about what to do.* The intern had to consult with professionals other than her supervisor because he is participating in the problem. She calls a professor in her doctoral program, who is a leading scholar in multicultural counseling. The professor recommends a recently published article that the intern could share with the supervisor. The article provides helpful guidelines for incorporating multicultural issues in assessment and treatment.

5. *Explicate implicit assumptions about culture.* The intern realizes that she is quick to assume that most cases of discrimination are intentional and malicious, fueling her anger about the problem. She challenges her own assumptions. The intern reminds herself that many instances of discrimination are unintentional and rooted in ignorance as opposed to malicious intent. She makes a cognitive commitment to remember this during the creative problem solving. Also, the intern identifies herself as an agnostic. She knows that her beliefs might impact her decision making, but she is committed to respecting the religious beliefs of her client and his family.

6. *Brainstorm with the client and associated professionals about how concern about the ethical problem arose.* Explore the development of the

cultural conflict and how it might have been avoided. Do not censor any ideas and offer thoughts that initially may not seem relevant. For our example, the intern tried to involve in the brainstorming the supervisor, school counselor, client, and parents. She was not able to arrange a group meeting, but she met separately with each party. The intern expressed her ethical perspectives and how they related to her interpretation of the problem. She also listened to the perspectives of the other participants in order to identify and consider all cultural data.

7. *Once the genesis of the cultural conflict has been explored, brainstorm about possible solutions.* Delay judgments about any potential solution—all are potentially valid at this point. In this case, solutions were generated in regard to the case conceptualization, systemic issues at the mental health center and school, and the family's religious beliefs in relation to treatment. Potential solutions include (a) diagnosing the boy with a conduct disorder regardless of the intern's true opinion, (b) diagnosing the boy according to the intern's true opinion, which is based on cultural considerations as well as other professional and scientific knowledge, (c) not confronting the mental health center and/or the school about their discriminatory practices, (d) confronting the mental health center and/or the school about their discriminatory practices, (e) developing treatment interventions without regard for the family's religious beliefs, (f) relying solely on the family's religious beliefs to design the treatment plan, and (g) collaborating with the family and striking a balance in treatment planning.

8. *Analyze the goodness-of-fit of each potential solution based on whether it is ethically valid, pragmatically feasible, and commensurate with treatment goals.* In this example, solution (a) (i.e., diagnosing the boy with a conduct disorder regardless of the intern's true opinion) is not ethically valid. It does not support the welfare of the boy, and it may perpetuate unfair discrimination. The intern decides to implement solution (b) (i.e., diagnosing the boy according to the intern's true opinion based on cultural considerations), which is ethically valid and pragmatically feasible. Still, this may put the intern in a precarious position with her supervisor and the school counselor. The intern decides that she cannot exercise solution (b) without also executing solution (d) (i.e., confronting the mental health center and/or the school about their discriminatory practices). In addition, opting for solution (c) (i.e., not confronting the mental health center and/or the school about their discriminatory practices) would be condoning unfair discrimination. Although the intern decides to combine solutions (b) and (d), she does not believe she can exercise too many degrees of freedom because of her status as an intern. She decides to explain to her supervisor and the school counselor why she might not give the boy a diagnosis of conduct disorder. She also decides to express her concerns about unfair discrimination in a nonthreatening way and encourage each of them to explore the possibility that their institution engages in unfair discrimination. To corroborate her position, she provides her supervisor with the article

recommended by her professor. Solution (e) (i.e., develop treatment interventions without regard for the family's religious beliefs) is not ethically
valid because it fails to respect the client. Solution (f) (i.e., rely solely on the
family's religious beliefs to design the treatment plan) is not ethically valid
because it fails to rely on science. The intern chooses solution (g) (i.e., collaborate with the family and strike a balance in treatment planning). The
intern encourages the family to discuss the situation with their pastor but
also educates the family about the benefits of scientifically based interventions. The family questions the intern about her religious beliefs. The intern is open and honest about her agnosticism, and she and the family
clarify their differences in religious orientation. However, she clearly expresses her respect for the family's religious beliefs.

In the event that a resolution is not reached, the process should be repeated. Perhaps, an error was made during the discernment process, such as
inaccurately defining the cultural conflict. Perhaps, an error was made during the creative problem solving, such as devising a solution that was not
commensurate with treatment goals. Critical reflection and creative problem solving are progressive stages within the processes of considering cultural data and resolving cultural conflicts. However, the stages and
processes are integrative and cyclical. This allows for multiple decision-
making trials until an ethically appropriate solution is found and successfully implemented.

CONCLUSION

Ethical codes are not a panacea in assisting practitioners in ethical decision making. In fact, ethical codes have many limitations, the most serious
perhaps being that they tend to reflect the dominant culture's values at
the expense of minority values. Singular reliance on ethical codes may
lead to oversimplification of ethical problems in multicultural counseling.
Assistance is needed for practitioners to navigate decision making when
professional codes are inadequate or fail to gauge the intricacies of actual
professional practice. With ethical codes as a foundation, practitioners
must also possess cognitive complexity and awareness that culture in some
way influences all ethical problems.
There are several prerequisites for responsible ethical decision making. A basic tenet is that practitioners make explicit what is implicit. By
making their ethical perspectives explicit, practitioners are better able to
understand the ethical perspectives of their clients. This sets the stage for
practitioners to collaborate. We operationalized several terms to assist
practitioners in making their particular ethical viewpoints explicit. We distinguished between the terms "ethics" and "morality" and also the phrases
"ethical concern" and "ethical problem." We also discouraged the use of

the phrase "ethical dilemma" and encouraged the use of the phrases "ethically appropriate/ethically inappropriate."

Practitioners must develop awareness of the influences on ethical decision making. These include the degree of absolutism, relativism, and universalism reflected in practitioner ethical viewpoints as well as the degree to which principle/justice or virtue ethics impact their decision making. Practitioners also must understand the degree to which these domains are reflected in their clients' ethical viewpoints. Then they must recognize how the context of decision making itself can fuel ethical problems and sway ethical decisions.

Making ethical decisions is a *multicultural responsibility*, a fusion of the practitioner's personal and professional commitments to consider culture in all ethical concerns. In response to this need, we presented a two-dimensional model. The model consists of two stages—critical reflection and creative problem solving—and two processes—ethical consideration of cultural data and ethical resolution of cultural conflicts. The model allows for two entry points into ethical decision making and accounts for numerous possibilities and choices. Additionally, the model facilitates the use of higher reasoning skills. Equipped with these skills, practitioners can move beyond rigid application of ethical codes and better face the complex reality of ethical decision making in multicultural counseling.

REFERENCES

American Counseling Association. (1995). *Code of ethics and standards of practice.* Alexandria, VA: Author.

American Psychological Association. (1992). Ethical principles of psychologists and code of conduct. *American Psychologist, 47,* 1597-1611.

Berry, J. W., Poortinga, Y. H. Y., Segall, M. H., & Dasen, P. J. (1992). *Cross cultural psychology: Research and applications.* Cambridge, UK: Cambridge University Press.

Blasi, A. (1980). Bridging moral cognition and moral action: A critical review of the literature. *Psychological Bulletin, 88,* 1-45.

Canter, M. B., Bennett, B. E., Jones, S. E., & Nagy, T. F. (1994). *Ethics for psychologists: A commentary on the APA ethics code.* Washington, DC: American Psychological Association.

Casas, J. M., & Thompson, C. E. (1991). Ethical principles and standards: A racial-ethnic minority research perspective. *Counseling and Values, 35,* 186-195.

Corey, G., Corey, M. S., & Callanan, P. (1998). *Issues and ethics in the helping professions* (5th ed.). Pacific Grove, CA: Brooks/Cole.

Cottone, R. R., & Tarvydas, V. M. (1998). *Ethical and professional issues in counseling.* Upper Saddle River, NJ: Prentice Hall.

Dinger, T. J., & Coupland, S. (1999). Ethical codes, decision-making and Christian faith. *Journal of Psychology and Christianity, 18*(3), 270-274.

Drane, J. F. (1982). Ethics and psychotherapy: A philosophical perspective. In M. Rosenbaum (Ed.), *Ethics and values in psychotherapy* (pp. 15-50). New York: Free Press.

Gambrill, E. (1990). *Critical thinking in clinical practice.* San Francisco: Jossey-Bass.

Gellatly, A. (1986). *The skilful mind: An introduction to cognitive psychology.* Milton Keynes, UK: Open University Press.

Gil, E. F., & Bob, S. (1999). Culturally competent research: An ethical perspective. *Clinical Psychology Review, 19*, 45-55.

Gilligan, C. (1982). *In a different voice.* Cambridge, MA: Harvard University Press.

Guralnik, D. B. (Ed.). (1986). *Webster's New World dictionary of the American language* (2nd ed.). New York: Prentice Hall.

Jordan, A. E., & Meara, N. M. (1990). Ethics and the professional practice of psychologists: The role of virtues and principles. *Professional Psychology: Research and Practice, 21*, 107-114.

Kitchener, K. S. (1984). Intuition, critical evaluation and ethical principles: The foundation of ethical decisions in counseling psychology. *The Counseling Psychologist, 24*, 4-77.

Kitchener, K. S. (1986). Teaching applied ethics in counselor education: An integration of psychological processes and philosophical analysis. *Journal of Counseling and Development, 64*, 306-310.

LaFromboise, T. D., Foster, S., & James, A. (1996). Ethics in multicultural counseling. In P. B. Pedersen, J. G. Draguns, W. J. Lonner, & J. E. Trimble (Eds.), *Counseling across cultures* (4th ed., pp. 47-72). Thousand Oaks, CA: Sage.

Mabe, A. R., & Rollin, S. A. (1986). The role of a code of ethical standards in counseling. *Journal of Counseling and Development, 64*, 294-297.

Moore, B. N., & Parker, R. (1995). *Critical thinking* (4th ed.). Mountain View, CA: Mayfield.

Morphis, M., & Riesbeck, C. K. (1990). Feminist ethics and case-based reasoning: A marriage of purpose. *International Journal of Applied Philosophy, 5*(2), 15-28.

Noddings, N. (1984). *Caring: A feminine approach to ethics and moral education.* Berkeley: University of California Press.

Pedersen, P. B. (1995). Culture-centered ethical guidelines for counselors. In J. G. Ponterotto, J. M. Casas, L. A. Suzuki, & C. M. Alexander (Eds.), *Handbook of multicultural counseling* (pp. 34-49). Thousand Oaks, CA: Sage.

Pedersen, P. B. (1997). The cultural context of American Counseling Association Code of Ethics. *Journal of Counseling and Development, 76*, 23-28.

Pope, K. S., & Vasquez, M. J. T. (1998). *Ethics in psychotherapy and counseling: A practical guide* (2nd ed.). San Francisco: Jossey-Bass.

Ridley, C. R. (1995). *Overcoming unintentional racism in counseling and therapy: A practitioner's guide to intentional intervention.* Thousand Oaks, CA: Sage.

Ridley, C. R., Li, L. C., & Hill, C. L. (1998). Multicultural assessment: Reexamination, reconceptualization, and practical application. *The Counseling Psychologist, 26*, 827-910.

Schon, D. A. (1983). *The reflective practitioner: How professionals think in action.* New York: Basic Books.

Schroder, H. M. (1977, April). *Developing adaptability to complexity.* Paper presented at the conference on Developing Cognitive Complexity, University of Augsburg, Augsburg, West Germany.

Tennyson, W. W., & Strom, S. M. (1986). Beyond professional standards: Developing responsibleness. *Journal of Counseling and Development, 64*, 298-302.

Tjeltveit, A. C. (1999). *Ethics and values in psychotherapy.* London: Routledge.

Weston, A. (1997). *Practical companion to ethics.* New York: Oxford University Press.

Correspondence regarding this chapter may be sent to Charles R. Ridley, Professor, Department of Counseling and Educational Psychology, Wright Education Building, Indiana University, 201 N. Rose Avenue, Bloomington, IN 47405-1006 (e-mail address: cridley@indiana.edu).

Chapter 15

ADVENT OF SYSTEMS OF CARE

Practice and Research Perspectives and Policy Implications

J. MANUEL CASAS
RENEE PAVELSKI
MICHAEL J. FURLONG
IRIS ZANGLIS

All children will grow up in safe, healthy and nurturing homes, schools, and communities. Their resultant sense of self-worth, along with equal access to resources, will empower them to develop their unique potential, with a strong sense of responsibility to self, culture, and society.

—Vision Statement,
Santa Barbara County KIDS Network

AN APPRECIATION OF how race, ethnicity, and associated constructs such as nativity and acculturation levels and socioeconomic and demographic environments (Aneshensel & Sucoff, 1996) influence mental health outcomes is becoming increasingly important as the United States becomes increasingly diverse. Among minority youths, these factors all influence the development of emotional and behavioral disorders, how and

AUTHORS' NOTE: Support for this chapter, which is based on an article published in *Harvard Journal of Hispanic Policy*, was provided in part by the Santa Barbara County Multiagency Integrated System of Care (MISC). Its contents are solely the responsibility of the authors and do not necessarily represent the official views of Santa Barbara County, California.

where they are diagnosed and treated, and the effectiveness of interventions in improving the quality of their life (Abe-Kim & Takeuchi, 1996; Ruiz, 1993; Takeuchi, Bui, & Kim, 1993; Takeuchi, Sue, & Yeh, 1995). Attending to the mental health needs of racial/ethnic minority youths is a critical aspect in nurturing their general growth and development (Nuttal, Sanchez, Osorio, Nuttal, & Varvogli, 1996).

An issue for children and adolescents of color is that they often do not have access to appropriate mental health services (Bui & Takeuchi, 1992; Hough, Landsverk, Karno, & Burnam, 1987). Furthermore, when services are provided, individuals from diverse cultures are more likely to be misdiagnosed than are White Americans (Hoernicke, Kallam, & Tablada, 1994), in part due to communication problems related to language differences, cultural nuances, and, at times, clinician bias (Pumariega & Cross, 1997; Singh, 1998). Until the publication of *DSM-IV* (American Psychiatric Association, 1994), clinicians did not have the benefit of cultural formulation guidelines for psychiatric diagnosis. Previously, the focus was on treating mental disorders rather than the people who have these disorders within a broader ecological context (Sue, Bingham, Posché-Burke, & Vasquez, 1999).

It is important to emphasize that underutilization of the mental health system by minority populations is *not* a function of fewer or less severe presenting needs (Hough et al., 1987; Pumariega & Vance, 1999). The source of this underutilization is related to practical concerns such as economic difficulties (lack of or inadequate insurance), lack of child care, time conflicts, and language barriers (Marín, Marín, Padilla, & De la Rocha, 1983). Minority individuals recognize the need for mental health services, but contextual factors often act as barriers to their reaching services. For many of these individuals, language, communication difficulties, and cultural beliefs can discourage individuals from seeking mental health services. A Latino youth, for example, with a serious emotional disturbance is more likely to be assessed in a language not his or her own even though this circumstance requires staff with high levels of cultural sensitivity and the ability to communicate effectively in highly emotional situations (Isaacs-Shockley, Cross, Bazron, Dennis, & Benjamin, 1996).

TRENDS AND THEMES IN PREVIOUS RESEARCH

The importance of addressing the influence of culture on mental health was emphasized in the U.S. Surgeon General's (1999) *Report on Mental Health:*

A number of central concepts and guiding assumptions underpin our current understanding of children's mental health and illness. These have variously been defined by different investigators, but by and large these tenets are based on the premise that psychopathology in childhood arises from the complex multilayered interactions of specific characteristics of the child (including biological, psychological, and genetic factors), his or her environment (including parent, sibling, and family relations, peer and neighborhood factors, school *and* community factors, and the larger socio-cultural context), and the specific manner in which these factors interact with and shape each other over the course of development. (p. 127, emphasis added)

Research relative to the provision of mental health services to racial or ethnic minority children and their families has emphasized the importance of these sociocultural factors:

- Descriptions of psychosocial and environmental factors that put racial or ethnic minority persons at risk for experiencing mental health problems (e.g., Rogler, Malgady, Constantino, & Blumenthal, 1987)
- Epidemiological perspectives of the prevalence of specific psychologically based problems in ethnic minority populations (e.g., Casas, 1985)
- Documentation of the types of interventions and service provider characteristics more complementary to culturally rooted expectations (e.g., Atkinson & Lowe, 1995)
- Examination of the effectiveness of traditional mental health interventions and approaches (e.g., Keefe & Casas, 1980)
- Identification of factors that impact the provision and utilization of services: (a) *predisposing factors*—cultural values inherent in ethnic minority individuals that predispose them to seek out alternative sources of help; (b) *enabling factors*—financial resources, availability of ethnic specific mental health services; and (c) *disenabling factors*—inattention to sociocultural variables that are relevant to or impact the client, lack of bilingual counselors, lack of ethnically similar counselors, reliance on western-oriented counseling theories and strategies, lack of culturally sensitive/knowledgeable counselors (e.g., Knitzer, 1982; Ponterotto & Casas, 1991; Ponterotto, Casas, Suzuki, & Alexander, 1995)

Abe-Kim and Takeuchi (1996) identified themes and issues that ethnic minorities face in the mental health system. They reported that ethnic minorities in the United States may (a) experience a disproportionate burden of health illnesses and disease compared to White Americans, (b) encounter the greatest number of barriers to accessing health and mental health services, (c) have the fewest financial resources to obtain appropriate services and are subsequently overrepresented in the numbers of Americans who are uninsured or underinsured, and (d) experience lower quality of care when they do receive health and mental health services. Furthermore, other research has found that in addition to the underutilization of service problem, minority youths, when provided mental health treatment, are often served in more restrictive out-of-home centers or juvenile probation settings (Pumariega & Vance, 1999). In one investigation, African Americans and White Americans in these facilities were referred for mental health evaluations in a juvenile justice system at a higher rate than Latino youths, even though Latinos constituted over 50% of the detained population (Wordes, Bynum, & Corley, 1994). This points to the misperception of fewer mental health symptoms among Latino youths, a situation that has also been found in teachers' rating of Latino students' behaviors related to attention deficit disorders (Dominquez de Ramirez & Shapiro, 1998; McDermott & Spencer, 1997).

ADDRESSING SERVICE INEQUITIES

Given the shortcomings of traditional mental health services for minority youths, various policy-oriented task forces have been initiated to promote possible solutions. For example, the Council for Children With Behavior Disorders (CCBD) established the Committee on Ethnic and Multicultural Concerns in 1982 (Bullock, 1999), which urged professionals to undertake efforts to ensure that the following goals are achieved:

- Removal from special programs of all culturally different students who are not truly exhibiting emotional or behavioral disorders but, rather, are displaying culturally based behavior (e.g., withdrawing from certain social interactions)
- Provision of respectful and culturally appropriate educational and treatment services to culturally different students *who do not have* emotional or behavioral disorders
- Implementation of culturally and linguistically competent assessment procedures
- Recruitment of culturally diverse professionals
- Provision of pre-service and in-service training in modifications of practice that better address the characteristics of culturally different students with emotional or behavioral disorders
- Creation of welcoming institutional atmospheres in which culturally different students with emotional and behavioral disorders feel valued and respected as well as physically and psychologically safe
- Enhancement of the cultural knowledge base of professionals, clients/students, and the public at large

A growing body of research provides evidence that addressing and attaining the policy objectives established by the CCBD Committee on Ethnic and Multicultural Concerns can result in positive developmental and mental health outcomes for minority youths. For example, it has been found that ethnic and language matching between client and mental health professional are associated with a decrease in dropout rate and an increase in the use of services by ethnic minorities (Takeuchi, Uehara, & Maramba, 1999). Although more is known about how to better serve ethnic minorities, extant culturally sensitive models have focused almost exclusively on adult populations and research of the microcounseling process (e.g., counselor characteristics and acculturation).

The importance of addressing cultural competence in mental health services was emphasized at the first Multicultural Conference coordinated in January 1999 by the American Psychological Association. Among the notable topics that were broadly addressed and discussed by the participants were (a) the impact of biases on scientific pursuits as they relate to ethnic minority groups; (b) issues and challenges inherent in the teaching of multiculturalism and diversity; (c) the implications of multiracial/biracial identity relative to education, training, and practice; (d) the development of strategies for multicultural organizational change, political action and advocacy for multicultural changes; and (e) the implications of individual, professional, and organizational multicultural competence on research, education training, and practice. Of particular importance to the thrust of this chapter is that the topic of the unique needs of minority youths in general and those with serious emotional and behavioral disorders in particular was all but ignored (Sue et al., 1999) by the APA conference participants. What is lacking, at times even among professionals interested in multicultural issues, is the specific implementation of research programs, policy initiatives, and service programs that tackle the issues and diverse needs of culturally diverse youths and in particular those with serious emotional and behavioral disorders.

PURPOSE OF THE CHAPTER

Given the need to better understand and serve racial/ethnic minority youths with serious emotional and behavioral disorders, the basic guiding philosophy, values, and principles inherent in a system of care are first presented. This discussion underscores the reasons why a system of care may be an effective means to address the needs of these youths. The system of care values and principles that cut across racial-ethnic and cultural boundaries and are relevant to *all* children are then identified. Close attention is directed to those key elements of a system of care that are most important and relevant to these youths and families. In addition, discussion is focused on research and policy implications that must be addressed in order to enhance the ability of these system of care elements to increase the probability of realizing positive mental health outcomes for racial/ethnic minority youths with serious emotional disturbance and their families. In this discussion, we draw extensively on the experiences of staff and researchers working since 1994 on the Santa Barbara County system of care initiative, Multiagency Integrated System of Care (MISC). It should be noted that a briefer and less research-focused article on this topic was published in the

Harvard Journal of Hispanic Policy (Casas, Pavelski, Furlong, & Zanglis, 2001). Parts of that article are contained in this chapter with permission from the publishers.

SYSTEMS OF CARE: PROMISING MENTAL HEALTH SERVICE MODEL FOR RACIAL/ETHNIC MINORITY YOUTHS

Systems of Care Philosophy

The systems of care mental health service model has received much attention at both state and federal levels, in part because it promotes the delivery of culturally sensitive and effective services for minority youths and their families. Public policy has supported the development of systems of care by distributing grants nationally through the Center for Mental Health Services (CMHS) and private foundations (Pumariega & Vance, 1999). These grant initiatives have envisioned systems of care as emphasizing comprehensive and individualized services provided within the least restrictive environment, full participation of the families involved, and coordination among all agencies and programs serving children and adolescents. The systems of care concept, therefore, represents not just a network of coordinated services but, rather, encompasses a philosophy about how services should be delivered to youths and their families.

The philosophy upon which the broader systems of care movement was developed is predicated on specific core values, which call for developing service systems that are child centered, family focused, community based, and culturally competent. In addition, the concept of systems of care extends beyond the concept of a continuum of services (Stroul, 1993). It also includes specific mechanisms, structures, and processes necessary to ensure that services for youths are provided in a coordinated, cohesive, comprehensive manner, such as through interagency case review, case management, and system-level coordination of services. In particular, the system of care's guiding principles (see Table 15.1) state that "children with emotional disturbance should receive services without regard to race, religion, national origin, sex, physical disability, or other characteristics, and services should be sensitive and responsive to cultural differences and special needs" (Stroul, 1996, p. 6).

Santa Barbara County Multiagency Integrated System of Care (MISC)

The Santa Barbara County MISC, for example, is one of more than 40 sites nationwide that received federal grants from the CMHS to develop and

TABLE 15.1 System of Care Core Values and Guiding Principles

Core values

- The system of care should be child-centered.
- The system of care should be community-based.
- The system of care should be culturally competent.

Guiding principles

- Children with emotional disturbance should have access to a comprehensive array of services.
- Children with emotional disturbance should receive individualized services.
- Children with emotional disturbance should receive services within the least restrictive environment.
- The families and surrogate families of children with emotional disturbance should be full participants in all aspects of service delivery.
- Children with emotional disturbance should receive services that are integrated.
- Children with emotional disturbance should be provided with case management.
- Early identification and intervention for children with emotional problems should be promoted.
- Children with emotional disturbance should be ensured smooth transition to services across the life span.
- The rights of children with emotional disturbance should be protected.
- Children with emotional disturbance should receive services without regard to race, religion, national origin, sex, physical disability, or other characteristics.

NOTE: Adapted from Stroul and Friedman (1986, 1996).

evaluate a system of care for youths with serious emotional and behavioral disorders and their families. The MISC coordinates services among family members and these child-serving agencies: mental health, probation, child welfare services, public health, nonprofit organizations, and public schools. The objective of this coordination effort is to provide a research-driven, family-focused, comprehensive continuum of community-based services, which is consistent with Stroul and Friedman's (1986, 1996) system of care principles. Staff from each of these partner agencies is co-located at one of three sites that offer one-stop services to families. The continuum of services includes (a) assessment, (b) intensive case management, (c) home- and school-based services, (d) after-hours and weekend crisis response, (e) individual/group/family therapy, and (f) medication treatment. The MISC provides services with the goals of helping youths reside with families, live in safety, achieve success in school, abide by the law, develop supportive relationships with others, and maintain physical health. The MISC specifically includes a training initiative to increase the cultural competence of all staff. The need for culturally competent services in Santa Barbara's MISC is clearly shown by the fact that more than 50% of all youths are from racial or ethnic minority backgrounds, which reflects the demographics of the county.

How Does the System of Care Model Offer a Viable Mechanism for Serving Racial/Ethnic Minority Youths and Their Families?

The recent U. S. Surgeon General's (1999) report on mental health recognizes the need for children's services to draw on natural support systems: "A key to the success of mental health programs is how well they use and are connected with established accepted, credible community supports. The more this is the case, the less likely families view such help as threatening and as carrying stigma; this is particularly true for families who are members of racial and ethnicity minority groups" (p. 186). The elements that give the system of care model the potential to address the needs of racial/ethnic minority youths and their families is its (a) attention to comprehensive and coordinated treatment approaches, (b) focus on intensive case management, and (c) commitment to cultural competency in the provision of services (Boles & Curtis-Boles, 1996). The system of care model's emphasis on working with family members as partners and experts in the provision of care is in concert with the family-based support mechanisms characterizing many racial/ethnic minority families. More specifically, this model is based on the premise that it can help all clients, and in particular racial or ethnic minority clients, and maintain the necessary balance between managing external stressors, including racism and oppression, and the intrapsychic reactions they face due to the nature of their illness, difficult socioeconomic conditions, and, at times, unresponsive or inadequate mental health or educational system services.

SYSTEMS OF CARE CORE VALUES AND GUIDING PRINCIPLES AND POLICY IMPLICATIONS

As shown in Table 15.1, systems of care programs share a set of core values and guiding principles that distinguish them from traditional mental health service systems. As will be made evident, these core values and principles also have the potential to provide more appropriate and effective mental health services to racial/ethnic minority children with serious emotional disturbances and their families in a way that draws naturally on their cultural strengths. As noted above, certain values and principles cut across racial/ethnic and cultural boundaries and are subsequently relevant to all children. These include the following system of care elements: (a) Services should be child centered; (b) services should be integrated; (c) services should be coordinated by a case manager; (d) the rights of children should be protected; and (e) services should be provided without regard to race, religion, national origin, sex, physical disability, or other characteristics. Given their generic nature, these elements are not addressed in this section;

instead, attention is directed to those key elements of a system of care that
we believe are most important and relevant to racial/ethnic minority
youths and families, which include the following:

- Services should be community based.
- Services should be culturally competent.
- Children should have access to a comprehensive array of services.
- Children should receive individualized services.
- Services should be provided within the least restrictive environment.
- The families and surrogate families of children should be full participants in
  all aspects of service delivery.
- Early identification and intervention for children should be promoted.
- Children should be ensured smooth transition to services across the life
  span.

To this end, we provide a brief summary of each element (for the sake of
brevity, when possible, elements that share common attributes are combined), present research supporting the inclusion of the elements within a
system of care, and then selectively highlight key policy issues that need to
be addressed by communities seeking to successfully implement systems
of care with racial/ethnic minority families. Specific attention is given to
research based on the fact that there is unanimous support in the field of
mental health that psychologists should have access to and use all available
data to reduce the uncertainty about best practice and cost that underlies
systems of care (Kiesler, 2000).

Systems of Care Should Be
Community Based and Culturally Competent

Summary

The element relative to the community-based aspect of a system of care
can be interpreted in either of these two ways: (a) The system should be
based on community/cultural beliefs/values, or (b) actual services should
be provided within the community itself and with appropriate community
participation in all aspects of the system. In this section, we address the first
interpretation, with special attention given to the importance of cultural
sensitivity and competence. The second interpretation is addressed later in
this chapter in the section on children with emotional disturbances having
access to an individualized and comprehensive service plan within a least
restrictive community-based environment. It should be noted that while
this chapter mainly addresses racial/ethnic minority cultures, for the purpose of the discussion in this section, culture is considered to be "the shared
values, traditions, arts, history, folklore, and institutions of a group of

people unified by race, ethnicity, nationality, language, religious beliefs, spirituality, socioeconomic status, social class, sexual preference, politics, gender, age, disability, or any other cohesive group variable" (Singh, 1998, p. 425).

One of the three core values of systems of care is concerned with "the system of care [being] culturally competent, with agencies, programs, and services [being] responsive to the cultural, racial, and ethnic differences of the population they serve" (Stroul & Friedman, 1996, p. 6). To this point, cultural competence is a concept that should drive changes in the way systems of care are designed and implemented. To make appropriate changes, systems first need to assess cultural attitudes, professional attitudes, values, and beliefs that underscore the services they presently provide, and then take appropriate steps to ensure that such values and beliefs are compatible with the populations that they are seeking to serve (Ponterotto & Casas, 1991). These efforts may require fundamental changes in existing structures, policies, and priorities (Casas, 1985).

Unfortunately, mental health professionals' training has traditionally been based solely on European American, middle-class culture. Furthermore, as noted in other chapters in this volume, problems are frequently encountered when this framework is applied to a client whose cultural experiences are not European American and/or middle class. Underscoring this fact, Isaacs-Shockley, Cross, Bazron, Dennis, and Benjamin (1996) state, "In short, children and adolescents of color often do not get their needs met in the present system . . . [and] the data are clear: current systems of care provide differential [i.e., worse] treatment to children of color" (p. 24). The process of recognizing and respecting other cultures and providing services in a way congruent with those cultures is the basis of cultural awareness, sensitivity, and competency.

Given the demographic trends of Santa Barbara County (e.g., 49% of youths between the ages of 0 and 17 are now Latinos), the County's system of care, MISC, which includes professionals outside the mental health system, has heightened concern for issues of culture. Such issues have given impetus to addressing questions such as the following: What does being culturally competent mean at both an agency or system level and the individual level? What would this look like? What are the standards to which the staff should be held, and how can such standards be measured? What is the impetus for valuing culture and delivering services in a manner congruent with the client's own cultural values?

In addressing such questions, some conclusions have been reached by the MISC staff. *Cultural awareness* has been defined as the understanding of differences within and between cultures. *Cultural sensitivity* is considered to represent a step beyond awareness—not attributing positive or negative values to the differences within and between cultures. These nonjudgmental perspectives set the stage for *cultural competence,* or the possession of skills and knowledge necessary to work with individuals from different cultures in a manner congruent with their values. Stated differently, a culturally competent counselor or case manager does not force an Anglo, middle-class framework on racial/ethnic minority clients.

Research

It should be noted that the importance given to cultural sensitivity and competency in counseling and concomitantly in a system of care is reflective not only of the changing demographic reality but also in a growing body of research previously identified in this chapter and amply addressed throughout the *Handbook*; hence, it is not repeated here.

Policy Considerations

To ensure that the community is amply represented in making decisions and setting policy, the written goals and objectives of the respective boards, commissions, and so forth that oversee or fund a system of care must clearly stipulate the inclusion of community persons. Whenever possible, the process by which such persons are appointed or elected should be addressed with some detail. Because elected officials make many relevant appointments, it behooves racial/ethnic minority communities to ensure that they have a voice in the care of their children by exerting their right to vote. In making appointments, every effort should be made to get "new faces" on the advisory boards that represent a good cross section of the community (e.g., socioeconomic level, diversity with respect to length of residency in the United States, acculturation level, and varying levels of education). In particular, efforts should support getting grassroot community members (including parents whose children are receiving services) involved in decision-making and policy-setting activities of a system of care.

To ensure ongoing active participation, boards and commissions should meet at times when the greatest number of community partners can attend and in locations that are within easy reach of the community. In many low-income Latino communities, a history of participation in governing bodies is nonexistent. Should this be the case, efforts should be directed by the system of care toward developing a concerted outreach process to identify potential participants. Such efforts should include the training of participants to help them understand the role that they are being asked to assume. A mentoring process of pairing "old-timers" with "new faces" might help expedite this training process. The concept of cultural competence is often addressed in broad and generic terms that are difficult to assess and measure, if and when attained. Cognizant of this fact, the comments contained herein, while reflective of the literature on systems of care, are largely based on six years of experience implementing a system of care that serves more Latino youths than any other racial/ethnic group. Consequently, attention is directed to specific and pragmatic issues and recommendations that need to be addressed from the perspective of planning, training, and implementation.

Issues related to working in a culturally competent manner with Latinos are exemplified in discussions we had with clinicians providing services in Head Start centers. One clinician noted that having MediCal pay for counseling services, utilizing bilingual counselors and care coordinators, and providing transportation are all ways to more competently serve this population. However, there are some service delivery problems. Specifically, there is an alarmingly low number of Latino counselors and physicians (Bui & Takeuchi, 1992), and many mental health care professionals are not familiar with certain sociocultural issues that are pertinent when working with Latino families. For example, it is erroneous to assume that English-speaking Latino families have Euro-American values or that what some may see as "racial/ethnic cultural" issues are really a reflection of socioeconomic conditions (i.e., what Oscar Lewis, 1966, referred to as the "culture of poverty"). These Head Start clinicians also outlined practical policy suggestions for developing a culturally competent system of care. They stated that bicultural (not just bilingual) individuals should be represented to a greater degree in the direct service staff.

For a system of care to deliver culturally competent services, it is necessary that the issues and recommendations identified above be accepted and implemented at all levels (e.g., clerical staff, administrative staff, service providers, and clinicians). To ensure such implementation, it behooves policymakers to make it blatantly clear that cultural competency is a vital and integral part of a system of care. To this end, the importance of cultural competency must be embedded throughout all the documents that establish the values and principles that guide a system of care (e.g., vision and mission statement, goals, objectives, strategies, and standards). Suffice it to say that if cultural competency is to become synonymous with systems of care, attention to such competency cannot be an "afterthought" paragraph contained in such documents. Finally, to ensure that *all* employees are adept at implementing and maintaining culturally competent services on an ongoing basis, it is necessary for systems of care to establish periodic, required training activities that focus on cultural competency. Emphasis is placed on the term "ongoing" to differentiate from the proliferation of one-time, cure-all approaches that have characterized previous efforts. Activities that focus on cultural competency should be given at regular intervals and consistently updated to ensure that the most recent information and effective approaches are presented. From a policy perspective and also to ensure such consistency, systems of care should establish a regular staff position devoted to cultural competency matters.

Children With Emotional Disturbances Should Have Access to an Individualized and Comprehensive Service Plan Within a Least Restrictive Community-Based Environment

Summary

These elements of a system of care share common attributes and are usually applied comprehensively; therefore, for the sake of brevity, all are interactively addressed in this section. These elements are based on the core value of a system of care that holds that children with emotional disturbances should have access to an individualized and comprehensive service plan that addresses the child's physical, emotional, social, and educational needs in a least restrictive, community-based environment. A major principle that underscores these elements is the strong emphasis placed on unconditional care and *wrapping services* around the youths and their families (Katz-Leavy, Lourie, Stroul, & Zeigler-Dendy, 1992). It should be noted that a commitment to unconditional care often breaks the cycle of rejection that many of these troubled youths and families have previously experienced (Burchard, 1988).

Comprehensive and individualized wraparound services draw on all available treatment resources for youths and their families: formal and informal or traditional and nontraditional (e.g., enlisting family members or friends as "service providers"). This broad range of treatments has been termed a "continuum of care" (Stroul & Friedman, 1986) and is considered an essential aspect of a system of care. The continuum of care is intended to deliver needed services on an individualized basis and in a coordinated manner, using case management and interdisciplinary teams to integrate treatment programs and to facilitate transition between services (Bickman, 1996). Burchard (1988) states that the underlying foundation of wraparound services is to identify those children who are the most severely emotionally disturbed and "wrap" services around them to facilitate their adjustment in the mainstream. The process of individualizing services entails a thorough, ecological assessment, completed by the case manager and interagency team (e.g., psychologist, social worker, probation officer, public health nurse, school personnel, and family members) that identifies strengths and needs of the youths and families in all life domains. This precedes and facilitates the development of a comprehensive individualized service plan, or wraparound plan, which reflects the specific needs and strengths of the youths and families (Clarke, Schaefer, Burchard, & Welkowitz, 1992). The implementation of wraparound plans, if properly done, has the potential to help many racial/ethnic minority families that find themselves with a multiplicity of problems and challenges.

Determining the proper placement of a child with a disability is a vital concern of all service delivery systems, including those in education, mental health, social service, and juvenile justice. Placement dictates not only the physical location of where a child learns but may also impact a youth's social status, ability to fulfill roles, and responsiveness to services (Kauffman & Lloyd, 1995). Under the Individuals With Disabilities Education Act (IDEA, 1990, the amendments to PL94-142: the Education for All Handicapped Children Act of 1975, amended again in 1998), multiple placement options should be available to children with disabilities to ensure an appropriate education in the least restrictive environment. Yet youths with emotional and behavioral disturbances (EBD) present service delivery systems with some of the most complex needs of any disability group. In addition, what constitutes an "appropriate" placement for them may be operationalized differently across the spectrum of systems and between professionals and family members. Sensitive to this fact, a major structural component of systems of care is the development of broad continuums of community-based services for youths with emotional disturbances and their families. Recent research in children's mental health has increased awareness of the need to move beyond a client-versus-system focus and to look at the roles that communities can play in their responses to systems of care (Gutierrez-Mayka & Contreras-Neira, 1998). Many communities have designed innovative services such as intensive nonresidential and residential components that better address in a less restrictive manner the needs of the youths and families they serve (Stroul, 1993). In this respect, such systems of care have been able to serve the needs of the youths and families within their home communities rather than sending the youths to out-of-home (e.g., juvenile detention centers, foster care homes, or hospitals) or out-of-community placements.

As indicated above, reducing the use of restrictive treatment environments and out-of-home placements is a critical goal of a system of care development (Stroul & Friedman, 1996). There has been a clear historical pattern of overutilization of costly and restrictive inpatient and residential treatment settings for youths with EBD (Sondheimer, Schoenwald, & Rowland, 1994). Creating a wide array of services that are intensive and community based allows communities to divert many youths from more expensive and restrictive environments to services within their own communities, or better yet, within their own homes. From another perspective, not only does serving youths within the home, the community, or county work to contain costs, it also respects the value of family within the context of providing treatment. Addressing this fact, Gutierrez-Mayka and Contreras-Neira (1998) suggest three culturally competent strategies for engaging minority communities in reform efforts that seek to serve youths in less restrictive environments:

- Using an ethnographic and ecological approach to learning about the community and the cultural norms by which its members behave

- Developing and/or nurturing an attitude that is open, receptive, respectful, and unbiased toward engaging in partnerships with the community
- Facilitating an environment that encourages the willingness of professional outsiders to come into the community as learners and facilitators rather than as teachers and overseers

Research

Unlike other elements of a system of care, the ones addressed here have received a good share of research attention from a variety of perspectives. Advocates of systems of care for youths with SED posit that wraparound service systems provide higher quality, more appropriate, and more cost-effective care (Clarke et al., 1992; Stroul, 1993). Some of these claims are beginning to be substantiated by outcomes from operational systems of care serving this target population and by research examining wraparound service approaches. Most of the research literature contains case descriptions, single project assessments (e.g., Burchard & Clarke, 1990), formal attempts to study statewide initiatives (e.g., Bruns, Burchard, & Yoe, 1995), cost studies establishing the fiscal soundness of wraparound planning, repeated measures designs (e.g., Clarke, Schaefer, Burchard, & Welkowitz, 1992), and descriptions of demonstration projects and wraparound principles. Nonetheless, in all fairness, other data (e.g., Bickman, 1996) suggest that outcomes may not be different from traditional service delivery systems, although clients report greater satisfaction with systems of care services— a potential benefit when working with racial/ethnic minority families.

Having practiced system of care service delivery for almost two decades and enacted coordinated service planning into state law, Vermont is a leader in producing literature about results of the wraparound process. For Vermont's "Project Wraparound," a community-based, individualized program that served youths with severely maladjusted behavior and their families by providing intensive home- and school-based wraparound services, Clarke and his colleagues (1992) examined longitudinal data for 19 youths concerning their adjustment in the home and in school. The authors found evidence that the functioning of families and the quality of the emotional care provided to their children had improved after one year. Another demonstration project study conducted by Bruns, Burchard, and Yoe (1995) found that after one year of wraparound services the incidence of 27 children's negative behaviors decreased while their positive behaviors increased. In addition, although 70% of the youths previously had been in inpatient or residential treatment settings, 89% were maintained in the community after one year, reflecting a movement toward less restrictive placements. Furthermore, other studies in Vermont have suggested that youths receiving wraparound programs are more satisfied with their services and that this satisfaction is correlated with a reduction in problem behaviors (Rosen, Heckman, Carro, & Burchard, 1994).

A Wisconsin countywide program called "Wraparound Milwaukee"—serving youths identified by juvenile justice or child welfare agents with community-based services—has also published compelling data supporting the efficacy of the wraparound process. Currently serving about 650 clients via 170 agencies and providers, Wraparound Milwaukee's reduction in residential treatment has freed about $9 million since 1996—funds now redirected to community-based services. In addition to this 60% drop in restrictive placements and significant cost savings, the wraparound services have also demonstrated improved clinical outcomes and community safety. According to Kiesler (2000), "the most cost-effective treatment of the seriously mentally ill involves treatment outside an inpatient unit and in the community" (p. 486).

Finally, the effectiveness of the Alaska Youth Initiative (Burchard, 1988), a project in which individualized care was used to return children from out-of-state residential programs, further illustrates the potential success of using these individualized wraparound strategies. After approximately two years of individualized care, the majority of the children and adolescents initially in out-of-state residential treatment programs were placed successfully in less restrictive programs within their home state of Alaska (Burchard & Clarke, 1990). Such positive placement-related outcomes for youths and families are one of the foundation goals of systems of care.

Complementing efforts that focus on the provision of least restrictive mental health services is work that directs attention to the provision of least restrictive educational services. Since all children spend a significant amount of time in educational settings, such attention is warranted. When examining the characteristics of youths with emotional behavioral disorders in various educational placements, past studies sought to predict placements or show systematic differences in youths by their behavioral characteristics. In studies examining perceptions of students' behavior in various settings, more severe disorders were generally associated with more restrictive placements. Teachers rated hyperactivity and emotional disorders as more prevalent and severe in youths placed in psychiatric hospitals or segregated classrooms, respectively (Mattison, Humphrey, Kales, & Wallace, 1986; McClure, Ferguson, Boodoosingh, Turgay, & Stavrakaki, 1989). Students in self-contained classrooms were also found to exhibit more anxious and fearful behaviors and conduct disorders than peers placed in resource rooms (Sinclair & Alexson, 1992; Sindelar, King, Cartland, Wilson, & Meisel, 1985). Additionally, Kauffman, Cullinan, and Epstein (1987) found that students with higher IQs, higher academic performance, and lower anxious/withdrawn ratings tended to be placed in less restrictive settings. In a series of studies by Mattison, Morales, and Bauer (1991, 1992), boys in segregated classes were shown to have more externalizing disorders (specifically conduct disorder and oppositional defiant disorder) and multiple diagnoses (attention deficit disorder with conduct disorder or oppositional defiant disorder), and girls placed in the various settings could not be differentiated by past educational interventions, psychiatric disorder, or IQ scores. Although some unique differences were found between groups on diagnostic categories in these studies, regression analyses revealed that these variables were not significant predictors of educational placement. Finally, Silver et al. (1992) documented that youths in residential settings exhibited more severe behavior problems, had greater risk factors in their lives, and had more experiences with agencies and treatment modalities than peers served in the special education system.

Based on compelling evidence of ambiguous and nonsignificant findings, some researchers speculated that placement decisions may be based more on subjective data and availability of placement options instead of objective psychoeducational characteristics of achievement, diagnoses, and behavior (Kauffman, Cullinan, & Epstein, 1987). Youths with EBD placed in mental health or juvenile justice systems were found to differ solely on demographic and historical factors. Westendorp, Brink, Roberson, and Ortiz (1986) found that ethnicity was the most powerful discriminating variable that differentiated youths in corrections from youths in psychiatric hospitals. The results of these studies indicated that African American youths were more likely than Caucasian youths to be placed within the juvenile justice system. In addition, other demographic and historical variables such as SES, parental marital history, gender, and previous mental health and drug use histories were found to significantly differentiate youths in mental health settings from youths in correctional settings. Yet these variables accounted for only 35% of the variance in placements. Furthermore, psychological and academic measures did not contribute to the variance at all (Westendorp et al., 1989). From this quantitative evidence and after subsequent qualitative review of placement meetings, Hallenbeck, Kauffman, and Lloyd (1993) asserted that much of the costly and time-consuming information gathered through psychoeducational evaluations may not influence placement decisions as significantly as demographic and historical factors.

Along these lines, a review of available studies brings to attention the lack of consistency among variables that distinguish groups of students with EBD in various educational placements. While significant differences in behavior may have been expected when extreme groups of students were compared, numerous results have demonstrated that factors such as ethnicity (e.g., Cohen et al., 1990), gender (e.g., Caseau, Luckasson, & Kroth, 1994), or family history (e.g., Westendorp et al., 1989) are more predictive of placement than psychiatric diagnoses or academic performance. Two potential weaknesses of this field of research are that previous studies failed to consider a full continuum of placements within the educational, mental health, and juvenile justice systems and did not include important demographic, child, family, and educational factors of a diverse population of students with EBD.

In addition to achieving better behavioral outcomes, systems of care are intended to be designed to achieve desired outcomes in a cost-effective manner. Containing and reducing costs for services have been demonstrated by such strategies as reallocating existing funds from expensive out-of-home care to in-home and prevention-oriented services (Meyers, 1994). In 1987, three California counties were legislatively enabled via Assembly Bill 377 (AB377) to replicate an innovative system of care model implemented in Ventura County, California. These three California counties (San Mateo, Santa Cruz, and Riverside) are collectively referred to as the "AB377 counties." In a preliminary evaluation of the AB377 counties systems of care, Rosenblatt and Attkisson (1993) found that foster home and state hospital utilization and overall expenditures were lower for the counties replicating the innovative system of care than for California as a whole. However, only one county, Santa Cruz, actually reduced its overall expenditures, whereas the other two counties' expenditures remained approximately the same. This may, however, be a result of communities identifying and serving more youths with EBD. Other systems of care sites have shown distinct reductions in costs by providing individualized and less restrictive services. For example, the services for 40 youths served in Vermont's "New Directions" system of individualized care cost an average of $48,000 per year, as compared to 26 youths with similar problematic behaviors who were redirected to residential treatment placements in other states, costing $59,000 per child annually (see Bruns et al., 1995). Furthermore, a preliminary cost study of the system of care in Santa Barbara County found reductions in projected group home expenditures of approximately $3.4 million over a two-year period (Santa Barbara County MISC, 2000).

Policy

Wraparound service plans entail an ecological assessment that takes into consideration the strengths and needs of the youths and families in all life domains; therefore, it is necessary to consider how presenting problems are associated with sociocultural variables including, but not limited to, race, ethnicity, culture, language, socioeconomic level, and living conditions. Giving consideration to such variables may require that universities and service providing institutions reconceptualize the type of training being provided to mental health professionals. The reason for this is that dealing solely with intrapsychic or externalizing issues is not enough to help children with emotional and behavioral disorders. They and their families need to be provided with services that expediently address all needs that impact the prevailing disorder(s) within the family's personal sociocultural context. To this end, counselors may need to expand their skills, roles, and responsibilities (see Atkinson & Lowe, 1995).

If a wraparound plan is to be appropriately and successfully implemented, it is important that the family be treated as an equal partner in the formulation of interventions. Here again, there is a need to establish policy that clearly stipulates the equitable involvement of families. Professionals need to be reminded, especially in reference to racial/ethnic minority families, that the real experts on the presenting problems are the families and that the most successful outcomes for targeted children are those in which the family is involved in the context of the community. To ensure consistency, the development and implementation of wraparound plans may require ongoing training. This is especially important if there is regular staff turnover. From past experience, it appears that the implementation of wraparound meetings can be greatly facilitated if the interagency teams are co-located in one place. This also helps families in need to receive help from one place at one time rather than having to go from agency to agency to get their diverse needs met—promoting action-oriented as opposed to appointment-oriented service delivery. To accomplish co-location of agencies requires that the respective service agencies come to the table and reformulate service policies. Unfortunately, many agencies are very much entrenched in doing "business as usual." Consequently, if reformulation is to become a reality it requires that racial/ethnic minority communities, through their leaders, take the initiative to make co-location a reality.

Given the positive outcomes that are associated with treating children in their communities using less restrictive approaches, it behooves mental health and social service administrators to collect and provide substantive data to relevant commissions, county boards of supervisors, and state departments of health that underscore the cost-effectiveness that can be realized as a result of using such approaches. These governing bodies could in turn develop policies and procedures and associated resources to facilitate the implementation of such approaches. While it is expected that most families would want to keep their children close to home, if not in the home itself, the incentives for wanting this may differ for racial/ethnic minority families. Policymakers should take these differences into consideration. For one thing, if the children are monolingual Spanish-speaking and are placed outside the home and community, there is a high probability that the setting into which they are sent may not have Spanish-speaking professionals and/or support staff. Finding themselves linguistically isolated could very likely create stressful situations that impede their treatment progress. The same could be said for those children who identify strongly with their respective culture. Would the setting to which they are sent be sensitive to and respectful of their ethnic-cultural identity? For many racial/ethnic minority children, the existence of an extended family (e.g., uncles, aunts, grandparents, cousins, *padrinos*, or *madrinas*) is an important and viable resiliency resource for maintaining or improving their well-being. Again, depriving these children of such a resource could negatively impact their well-being.

Families Are Full Participants
in All Aspects of Service Delivery

Summary

Research has demonstrated that family empowerment and involvement are critical to successful outcomes for children, and systems of care
efforts recognize the valuable resources that families can bring to service
delivery (Ronnau, 1995). The principle of family participation focuses on
the system's responsiveness to families and family members' authentic involvement in service delivery and planning demonstrated by (a) respect for
families, (b) recognition of family strengths, (c) involvement of families in
setting priorities, and (d) centering service delivery on the holistic needs of
families. Along these lines, there is growing sentiment in the mental health
field that services provided to families and children with disabilities should
be designed to empower their recipients (Freund, 1993; Parsons, 1991;
Sluyter, 1994). In particular, it is now generally accepted that families of
children with serious emotional disorders must be full participants in all
aspects of the planning and delivery of services (Stroul & Friedman, 1986). It
is the professionals' responsibility to restructure the service delivery system so that families may increase their social power and be able to access
the full spectrum of services and resources that they need.

Consumer satisfaction and family empowerment are emerging values
in system reform efforts to serve youths with EBD and their families. Increasingly, the focus on family participation, family strengths, family priorities, and self-efficacy has become a central goal of efforts to improve and
integrate services for families and their children (Dunst & Paget, 1991;
Koren, DeChillo, & Friesen, 1992; Stroul & Friedman, 1986).

Research

As public health and safety agencies move away from heavy reliance on
traditional models of service delivery to an ecological and more flexible
array of tailored supports, it is imperative that they pause to examine the
basic values and principles that underlie their efforts (Sluyter, 1994). It is
one thing to prescribe techniques for ideal parent-professional collaboration and family empowerment; it is quite another to promote a pervasive
quality of partnership such that family values, priorities, and efforts are sincerely utilized as integral parts of the service delivery process (DeChillo,
Koren, & Schultze, 1994). To this end, while empowerment has had broad
appeal as a general ideal, it has proved to be somewhat obscure as a research
construct due to disagreement about its specific dimensions and definition
(Koren, DeChillo, & Frieson, 1992). Koren et al. (1992) asserted, "Empowerment has been variously described as both a process and a state, as both an
individual and collective characteristic, as an attitude, perception, ability,

knowledge and action, and as a phenomenon that can be manifested in a range of circumstances and environments" (p. 306). But the need for valid and reliable measures of empowerment is especially important in view of the increasing number of service delivery models that feature empowerment as a major goal.

To date, efforts to quantitatively measure empowerment have been limited. Gutierrez and Ortega (1991) discussed three levels of empowerment: (a) the *personal level*, which is concerned with the individual's feelings of self-efficacy and personal power; (b) the *interpersonal level*, which is concerned with an individual's ability to influence others; and (c) the *political level*, which is concerned with social action and social change. These researchers developed three measures to assess different aspects of empowerment: Two of their measures focused on political empowerment and commitment to ethnic activism, and the third focused on personal empowerment (Gutierrez & Ortega, 1991). Although this study supported the idea that empowerment is multifaceted and that measures need to be sensitive to ethnic and contextual variables, more attention needs to be placed on understanding empowerment issues within families whose members have disabilities and are served by multiple agencies.

Policy Considerations

This is a very important principle that cannot be ignored because of the importance that is ascribed to more traditional values held by many racial/ ethnic minority families. Addressing it, however, is also a very challenging task because the families that adhere to their "traditional culture" are apt to put full responsibility in the hands of the so-called experts (i.e., "*ellos son los que saben que hacer*"). However, from a pragmatic perspective, "*los que saben que hacer*" are truly the family members. Given this fact, policymakers must develop guidelines that underwrite the fact that reimbursements for services provided by state and/or federal departments can only be made if and when family members are involved in the development of the service plan. To verify that appropriate and relevant family involvement occurs may require that state and county policymakers establish a policy-focused department that develops the mechanism by which relevant family involvement is monitored and rated. To emphasize the importance of family involvement, the availability of future funding for the targeted project could be contingent on such ratings.

In the meantime, to accomplish such initiatives, it may be necessary to implement policies that facilitate the inclusion of family members in the therapeutic planning process. To this end, it might help if racial/ethnic minority clients, especially those new to the United States, are put in contact with service providers who provide them with a culturally appropriate and relevant explanation of what they are going to encounter as they seek help for their child. In addition, the procedures and "rituals" that are followed in

the initial sessions may focus less on paperwork (e.g., getting insurance information) and administering a series of diagnostic instruments and more
on establishing a stronger caring and respectful bond between caregivers
and family. Taking extra time during the initial assessment period helps the
families be more comfortable answering personal questions. It is also crucial that all assessment instruments be translated into the dialect of the respective community and eventually be validated for use in the community.

Children Receive Early
Screening/Identification and Intervention Services

Summary

During the past two decades that systems of care have been implemented and refined, they have emphasized services to older and more
chronically needful youths. In many locales, such as Santa Barbara County,
what attracts agency participation is the promise of being able to access
comprehensive, complex services for the most involved, needful youths
they are serving. Consequently, the average age of youths entering systems
of care services is in early adolescence (Robertson et al., 1998). However, it
has also been shown that when systems of care partner agencies include service providers who target early child development (e.g., public health
offices), then early elementary and even preschool children are identified
and provided prevention services (Rosenblatt et al., 1998). In recognition of
the need for mental health services to be provided to children, hopefully
prior to the onset of more chronic problems, the federal government recently announced a grant program to identify the needs of children with depression, even calling for preschool programs. We argue that if systems of
care are to fully address the needs of youths and their families, then, over
time, the average age of first service contact should decrease and the services be more preventive and educational compared to traditional psychotherapy services.

Research

The need for increased early identification is evident in much of the recent literature. Both epidemiological studies and clinical impressions suggest that the number and intensity of behavior problems in young children
are increasing (Wright & Leonhardt, 1998). Stallard (1993), using parent reports, noted a behavior problem prevalence of 10% in 3-year-old children.
There have been few reports on the prevalence of behavior problems in infants and toddlers, but one study suggests that 3 out of 100 children younger
than 3 years of age had emotional problems and needed help (Luk, Leung,
Bacon-Shone, & Leih-Mak, 1991). In addition, few studies have followed infants and preschool children longitudinally; yet the accumulating body of

evidence suggests that a significant number of young children with emotional and behavioral problems continue to have difficulties during their school-age years and later (Wright & Leonhardt, 1998). Finally, most developmental models of emotional and behavioral disorders emphasize the importance of preschool factors such as a child's temperament and parental care and supervision in the latter development of conduct disorders (Loeber & Farrington, 1998).

In spite of such evidence, it is apparent that much work in this area is still needed. Duncan, Forness, and Hartsough (1995) conducted archival record searches to gather data regarding the diagnostic and treatment histories of 85 children and adolescents served in two exemplary school-based day treatment programs in California. Findings suggest a significant lag time between first symptoms, referral for services, and treatment; marked instability of psychiatric diagnoses over time; and lack of concordance between psychiatric diagnoses and characteristics of serious emotional disturbance as defined in the Individuals With Disabilities Education Act. The data raise serious concerns regarding the availability of prevention and early intervention services even in locales striving to develop a coordinated system of care approach to treatment. They also raise questions about the integrity and congruity of the psychiatric and educational diagnostic systems used by school and mental health personnel.

Policy Considerations

During the 1990s, numerous systems of care for children and adolescents with emotional and behavioral disorders were initiated. However, as significant as this reform has been, these efforts have focused primarily on the needs of older children and adolescents. The needs of younger children have been largely ignored, especially for those from birth to age 6 and their families (Knitzer, 1996). In fact, the majority of the population younger than 6 years of age in need of mental health services receive no services at all. To effectively intervene with young children, service providers must deal with their numerous developmental issues within a broader ecological context emphasizing a cultural framework (Wright & Leonhardt, 1998). Both developmental and cultural competencies are crucial for service providers' effective assessments and interventions with young children and their families. However, there is a paucity of well-trained clinicians available to provide services. Also, there has been little consideration of or planning for appropriately training children's mental health professionals in system of care development efforts (Wright & Leonhardt, 1998).

An analysis of the historical perspective of health and social services for young children has revealed that they tended to be fragmented and often lacking in depth and comprehensiveness (Wright & Leonhardt, 1998). For example, Head Start, which was established in the 1960s, provides early intervention services to children from disadvantaged socioeconomic backgrounds as a means of improving their chances for success in school. Parent education programs burgeoned in the 1970s, and the 1980s brought new knowledge of children's school and social success. In the 1980s and 1990s, new understandings regarding the capacities of infants developed along with information regarding the critical importance of the first weeks and months of children's lives (Bowlby, 1989). This has led to an increased emphasis on early parent-child interactions and growth of programs aimed at parents and their young children.

Implicit in these professional trends is a clear message for system of care service providers and policymakers. Developmental competence is an essential skill when working with young children and their families (Wright & Leonhardt, 1998), and programs must be designed to develop such a skill. Professionals must consider multisystem involvement just as they do with older children. Focusing attention on both environmental and biological factors impacting the lives of young children may result in less psychological and educational impairment, hence lowering public and private costs. The importance of designing *early* childhood mental health partnerships is imperative, particularly ones that are sensitive to service needs at different developmental stages. This is especially true with respect to racial/ethnic minority children in need of services who are prone to enter the mental system *later* in life through the probation department rather than directly through the mental health department (Casas et al., 1998). For these children, early intervention could help prevent the development of more serious emotional and behavioral problems later in life.

Children Are Ensured a Smooth Transition of Services Across the Life Span

Summary

Whereas the transition from high school to adulthood of youths without disabilities has been extensively researched (Malloy, Cheney, & Cormier, 1998; Wagner, 1995), few studies have focused on youths with EBD. However, the poor outcomes for these youths are well documented and include high dropout and unemployment rates, lack of ability to function independently in adulthood, and high incidence of illegal activities and/or high-risk behaviors (Clark, Unger, & Steward, 1999). Many youths with EBD disrupt or sever their ties with mental health services as they transition to adulthood. Many agencies and systems disagree with one another regarding eligibility criteria for this population once they become adults. The best implemented service plan for a child or adolescent has the potential to be for naught if transition issues related to school (to postsecondary education), work (from work-skills programs to actual employment), and mental health services (from family-focused systems of care to adult services) are not planned for at an early age and carefully monitored.

Research

Youths and their families who participate in Santa Barbara County's MISC have numerous emotional and behavioral concerns that require a variety of mental health services. Partner agencies in the MISC independently enroll their most involved youths in this system of care. Unfortunately, there is a paucity of research on the needs and characteristics of youths with EBD and their transition to adulthood (Clark et al., 1998; Wagner, 1995). However, poor outcomes for these youths are well documented and include high dropout and unemployment rates, lack of ability to function independently in adulthood, lower grades and more course failures, higher grade retention, and high incidences of illegal activities and/or high-risk behaviors (Wagner, 1995). These outcomes have a great impact on the stress levels of families (Brannan, Heflinger, & Bickman, 1997). Realizing that parents are under strain is important not only for documenting the needs of family members but also to inform treatment planning and service delivery for the student. As Morningstar (1995) suggests, parents and even extended family are powerful partners in career and transition planning. By gaining their support and trust, school personnel can collaborate with these individuals to best meet the needs of their youths.

Unfortunately, the process that encompasses the individualized educational plan (IEP) process does not always involve the family in such a collaborative way (Malloy et al., 1998). Morningstar, Turnbull, and Turnbull (1995) suggest that most transition plans do not provide family or team members with specific steps that would facilitate their students' successful entrance into the adult world. Providing students with vocational support is critical to their future development. Wood and Cronin (1999) suggest that students with EBD who work during high school have more successful adult employment outcomes. In addition, Wagner (1995) found that students with disabilities who took vocationally oriented classes were less likely to drop out than were disabled students who did not take these classes. This literature, in general, speaks to the need of family involvement and collaboration, and vocational training for youths with EBD to ensure that such youths do not disrupt their ties with mental health services as they transition to adulthood.

Policy Considerations

For certain racial/ethnic minority individuals, making transitions from one service level to another may be quite traumatic. This would be especially true for children who, over their life history, may have been forced to make transitions that were not under their control and, for all intents and purposes, they may have not understood. For example, transitions involving (a) immigration to the United States because of political reasons (i.e., to avoid being killed), (b) entering and living in the United States under great stress because of lack of immigration documents, (c) moving regularly from one geographical region to another for economic reasons, (d) having to develop the means to communicate and navigate one's self in different and often alienated worlds, and (e) having to understand and master the transitional variables that comprise one's identity as a racial/ethnic minority and as a "so-called" American. Mental health and social service professionals within a system of care need to be trained and supervised to ensure that factors such as these are taken into consideration in helping clients make transitions across their life span.

CONCLUSION

Children and adolescents of color are often underserved or inappropriately served by public and private sector mental health agencies in the United States. A service delivery model, referred to as "systems of care," has been proposed as a promising way to expand and improve mental health services to all children and adolescents who have serious emotional disorders. Because the systems of care paradigm emphasizes cultural competence in service delivery, it also provides a promising mechanism through which to assume the responsibility of meeting the mental health needs of racial/ethnic minority youths and their families. This chapter addressed the inequalities that exist for minority youths in obtaining mental health services, outlined trends and themes present in previous research on this topic, and highlighted key policy-related elements of systems of care to consider when serving racial/ethnic minority youths and their families. In this discussion, we drew extensively on the experience of staff and researchers working in the Santa Barbara County Multiagency Integrated System of Care (MISC), a collaboration among family members, health and safety net agencies, education, and community-based organizations. The MISC is one of more than 40 sites nationwide to receive a federal grant from the Center for Mental Health Services to develop and evaluate a system of care. Between 1994 and 1999, the MISC program was implemented and has proved to be a system of care that looks promising, but as noted above, there are several policy-related issues that need to be continuously addressed (i.e., staff training, assessment instruments, and parent involvement). The Santa Barbara community has embraced the system of care principles so strongly, especially in reference to its ability to better serve racial/ethnic minority children and families, that this model and the service system it has spawned are now completely self-funded using Medicaid and other revenue sources. The system of care principles discussed in this chapter have been embraced not only by mental heath agencies but also increasingly by all public and private agencies in Santa Barbara County. Readers who want to obtain additional and more detailed information about Santa Barbara

County's system of care program can do so by accessing *www.educa-tion.ucsb.edu/~sbmisc*, the program's Web site.

In addition to identifying and discussing the principles and elements that give meaning and shape to systems of care, this chapter directed attention to research perspectives and policy implications that need to be considered and addressed when implementing this service model. With these issues in mind, attention is here directed to some final thoughts relative to the future direction of research as well as policy implications that focus directly on the training of mental health workers who are both culturally competent and able to navigate successfully through a system of care.

Although the body of empirical literature examining the outcomes of individualized services for at-risk youths continues to grow, there is a paucity of research specifically documenting the process of wraparound implementation. The concept of individualizing services from multiple resources in a flexible manner (Burchard & Clarke, 1990) represents a paradigm shift in the field of mental health services away from the more manualized, uniform symptom-based interventions. This shift toward highly individualized approaches creates a complicated research task because the intervention—the independent variable—becomes more complex (Friedman, 1993). Because many individualized strategies are often organized under the rubric of wraparound services, there is a need for researchers to be able to examine the integrity of these service-planning processes to the guiding theory and to make more appropriate comparisons across studies. This, however, presents researchers and program evaluators with a dilemma. Friedman (1993) points out that if treatment integrity is defined as using the exact same intervention in a well-controlled manner with all of the involved subjects, then individualized wraparound-based interventions are in direct conflict with the need to maintain treatment integrity. Friedman and Burns (1996) state,

> The key to effective treatment within a system is not simply the presence or even the quality or effectiveness of individualized components; rather it is the ability of the system, in partnership with the child and family, to develop and implement genuinely individualized and responsive service plans.... Unless a program theory reflects this, it is not accurately reflecting the theory of a system of care, and unless an evaluation measures the extent to which this is being done, there is no way of determining if a system of care has really implemented the principles, values, and practices emphasized in its theory. (p. 129)

This underscores the need for scientific research that illuminates and clarifies the processes of planning individualized interventions in order to develop empirical methods for documenting their provision and resulting clinical outcomes. Particularly, a valid method of evaluating the quality and integrity of the service planning processes within systems of care is needed to assess the fidelity of wraparound plans, service implementation, and the efficacy of the system of care movement. Furthermore, there is a pressing need for the development of an empirical database that justifies the emphasis within a system of care on short-term care and on nontraditional therapeutic care. Along this line, new theories dealing with behavioral and emotional change will soon become obvious (Kiesler, 2000).

With respect to policy and educational implications, there is no question that if racial/ethnic minority populations are to be effectively treated in a system of care, graduate training and education in psychology and the mental health field will need a substantial overhaul. Given the philosophy and thrust of a managed, integrated system of care, the training and supervision of nondoctoral providers, who presumably, from a cost-effective perspective, would be much more numerous than doctoral providers in such a system, will be required. From another perspective, given the nature of a system of care, doctoral programs will need to train psychologists to design and deal with feedback loops in treatment. To this end, they will need to document the presenting problems, the treatment given, and outcomes observed as a principle underpinning of continuous quality improvement of treatment (Pallak, 1996). Needless to say, this will not be nor can it be "business as usual."

REFERENCES

Abe-Kim, J. S., & Takeuchi, D. T. (1996). Cultural competence and quality of care: Issues for mental health service delivery in managed care. *Clinical Psychology: Science and Practice, 3,* 273-295.

American Psychiatric Association. (1994). *Diagnostic and statistical manual for mental disorders* (4th ed.). Washington, DC: Author.

Aneshensel, C. S., & Sucoff, C. A. (1996). The neighborhood context of adolescent mental health. *Journal of Health and Social Behavior, 37,* 293-310.

Atkinson, D. R., & Lowe, S. M. (1995). The role of ethnicity, cultural knowledge, and conventional techniques in counseling and psychotherapy. In J. G. Ponterotto, J. M. Casas, L. A. Suzuki, & C. M. Alexander (Eds.), *Handbook of multicultural counseling* (pp. 387-414). Thousand Oaks, CA: Sage.

Bickman, L. (1996). A continuum of care. More is not always better. *American Psychologist, 51,* 689-701.

Boles, A. J., III, & Curtis-Boles, H. A. (1996). Culturally competent health and human services for emotionally troubled children and youths: Only through intensive case management. In P. Manoleas (Ed.), *The cross-cultural practice of clinical case management in mental health* (pp. 211-232). New York: Haworth.

Bowlby, J. (1989). The role of attachment in personality development and psychopathology. In S. I. Greenspan & G. H. Pollock (Eds.), *The course of life: Vol. 1. Infancy* (pp. 229-270). Madison, CT: International Universities Press.

Branna, A. M., Heflinger, C. A., & Bickman, L. (1997). The caregiver string questionnaire: Measuring the impact on the family of living with a child with serious emotional disturbance. *Journal of Emotional and Behavioral Disorders, 5,* 212-222.

Bruns, E., Burchard, J., & Yoe, J. (1995). Evaluating the Vermont system of care: Outcomes associated with community-based wraparound services. *Journal of Child and Family Studies, 4,* 321-339.

Bui, K. T., & Takeuchi, D. T. (1992). Ethnic minority adolescents and the use of community mental health care services. *American Journal of Community Psychology, 20*, 403-417.

Bullock, L. (1999). *A historical chronology of the CCBD*. Reston, VA: CCBD Mini-Library Series.

Burchard, J. (1988). *Project Wraparound: Training clinical psychologists through a revised service delivery system for severely emotionally disturbed children and adolescents.* Burlington: University of Vermont, Department of Psychology.

Burchard, J., & Clarke, R. (1990). The role of individualized care in a service delivery system for children and adolescents with severely maladjusted behavior. *Journal of Mental Health Administration, 17*, 48-60.

California Department of Education. (1999). *Statewide enrollment in California public schools for the year 1998-99.* Sacramento: California Department of Education, Educational Demographics Unit.

Casas, J. M. (1985). A reflection on the status of racial/ethnic minority research. *The Counseling Psychologist, 13*, 581-598.

Casas, J. M., Pavelski, R., Furlong, M. J., & Zanglis, I. (2001). Addressing the mental health needs of Latino youths with emotional and behavioral disorders: Practical perspectives and policy implications. *Harvard Journal of Hispanic Policy.* Cambridge, MA: Harvard University.

Casas, J. M., Wood, M., Alvarez, M., Furlong, M. J., Warholic, S., & Walton, R. (2000). Do we serve equitably? Services associated with clinical outcomes of Hispanic and non-Hispanic White youths with emotional and/or behavioral disturbances in a system of care. Occasional paper No. 55, Latino studies series. East Lansing, MI: Michigan State University, Julian Samora Research Institute.

Caseau, D., Luckasson, R., & Kroth, R. (1994). Special education services for girls with serious emotional disturbance: A case of gender bias? *Behavioral Disorders, 20*, 51-60.

Clark, H. B., Unger, K. V., & Steward, E. S. (1999). Transition of youths and young adults with emotional/behavioral disorders into employment, education, and independent living. *Community Alternatives: International Journal of Family Care, 5*, 19-46.

Clarke, R., Schaefer, M., Burchard, J., & Welkowitz, J. (1992). Wrapping community-based mental health services around children with a severe behavioral disorder: An evaluation of Project Wraparound. *Journal of Child and Family Studies, 1*, 241-261.

Cohen, R., Parmelee, D., Irwin, L., Weisz, J., Howard, P., Purcell, P., & Best, A. (1990). Characteristics of children and adolescents in a psychiatric hospital and a correctional facility. *Journal of the American Academy of Child and Adolescent Psychiatry, 29*, 909-913.

Cross, T., Bazron, B., Dennis, K., & Isaacs, M. (1989). *Towards a culturally competent system of care.* Washington, DC: CASSP Technical Assistance Center, Georgetown University Child Development Center.

DeChillo, N., Koren, P. E., & Schultze, K. H. (1994). From paternalism to partnership: Family and professional collaboration in children's mental health. *American Journal of Orthopsychiatry, 64*, 564-576.

Dominquez de Ramirez, R., & Shapiro, E. S. (1998). Teacher ratings of Attention Deficit Hyperactivity Disorder symptoms in Hispanic children. *Journal of Psychopathology and Behavior Assessment, 20*, 275-291.

Duncan, B. B., Forness, S. R., & Hartsough, C. (1995). Students identified as seriously emotionally disturbed in school-based day treatment: Cognitive, psychiatric, and special educational characteristics. *Behavioral Disorders, 20*, 238-252.

Dunst, C. J., & Paget, K. D. (1991). Parent-professional partnerships and family empowerment. In M. J. Fine (Ed.), *Collaboration with parents of exceptional children* (pp. 25-44). Brandon, VT: Clinical Psychology Publishing.

Freund, P. D. (1993). Professional role(s) in the empowerment process: "Working with" mental health consumers. *Psychosocial Rehabilitation Journal, 16*, 65-73.

Friedman, H. L. (1993). Adolescent social development: A global perspective: Implications for health promotion across cultures. *Journal of Adolescent Health, 14*, 588-594.

Friedman, R. M., & Burns, B. J. (1996). The evaluation of the Fort Bragg demonstration project: An alternative interpretation of the findings. *Journal of Mental Health Administration, 23,* 128-136.

Gutierrez, L., & Ortega, R. (1991). Developing methods to empower Latinos: The importance of groups. *Social Work With Groups, 14,* 23-43.

Gutierrez-Mayka, M., & Contreras-Neira, R. (1998). A culturally receptive approach to community participation in system reform. In M. Hernandez & M. R. Isaacs (Eds.), *Promoting cultural competence in children's mental health services* (pp. 133-148). Baltimore, MD: Paul H. Brookes.

Hallenbeck, B., Kauffman, J., & Lloyd, J. (1993). When, how and why educational placement decisions are made: Two case studies. *Journal of Emotional and Behavioral Disorders, 1,* 109-117.

Hernandez, M., Isaacs, T. N., & Burns, D. (1998). Perspectives on culturally competent systems of care. In M. Hernandez & M. R. Isaacs (Eds.), *Promoting cultural competence in children's mental health services* (pp. 1-29). Baltimore, MD: Paul H. Brookes.

Hoernicke, P. A., Kallam, M., & Tablada, T. (1994). Behavioral disorders in Hispanic American culture. In R. L. Peterson & S. Ishii-Jordon (Eds.), *Multicultural issues in the education of students with behavioral disorders* (pp. 115-125). Cambridge, MA: Brookline.

Hough, R. L., Landsverk, J. A., Karno, M., & Burnam, M. A. (1987). Utilization of health and mental health services by Los Angeles Mexican Americans and non-Hispanic Whites. *Archives of General Psychiatry, 44,* 702-709.

Isaacs-Shockley, M., Cross, T., Bazron, B. J., Dennis, K., & Benjamin, M. P. (1996). Framework for a culturally competent system of care. In B. A. Stroul (Ed.), *Children's mental health: Creating systems of care in a changing society* (pp. 23-39). Baltimore, MD: Paul H. Brookes.

Katz-Leavy, J., Lourie, I., Stroul, B., & Zeigler-Dendy, C. (1992). *Individualized services in a system of care.* Washington, DC: CASSP Technical Assistance Center, Georgetown University Child Development Center.

Kauffman, J., Cullinan, D., & Epstein, M. (1987). Characteristics of students placed in special programs for the seriously emotionally disturbed. *Behavioral Disorders, 12,* 175-184.

Kauffman, J., & Lloyd, J. (1995). A sense of place: The importance of placement issues in contemporary special education. In J. Kauffman, J. Lloyd, D. Hallahan, & T. Astuto (Eds.), *Issues in educational placement: Students with emotional and behavioral disorders* (pp. 94-102). Hillsdale, NJ: Lawrence Erlbaum.

Keefe, S. E., & Casas, J. M. (1980). Mexican-Americans and mental health: A selected review and recommendations for mental health service delivery. *American Journal of Community Psychology, 8,* 303-326.

Kiesler, C. A. (2000). The next wave of change for psychology and mental health in the health care revolution. *American Psychologist, 55,* 481-487.

Knitzer, J. (1982). *Unclaimed children.* Washington, DC: Children's Defense Fund.

Knitzer, J. (1993). Children's mental health policy: Challenging the future. *Journal of Emotional and Behavioral Disorders, 1,* 8-16.

Knitzer, J. (1996). Meeting the mental health needs of young children and their families. In B. A. Stroul (Ed.), *Children's mental health: Creating systems of care in a changing society* (pp. 553-572). Baltimore, MD: Paul H. Brooks.

Koren, P. E., DeChillo, N., & Friesen, B. J. (1992). Measuring empowerment in families whose children have emotional disabilities: A brief questionnaire. *Rehabilitation Psychology, 37,* 305-321.

Lewis, O. (1966). The culture of poverty. *Scientific American, 215,* 19-25.

Loeber, R., & Farrington, D. P. (1998). *Serious and violent juvenile offenders: Risk factors and successful interventions.* Thousand Oaks, CA: Sage.

Luk, S., Leung, P. W., Bacon-Shone, J., & Chung, S. (1991). Behavior disorder in pre-school children in Hong Kong: A two-stage epidemiological study. *British Journal of Psychiatry, 158,* 213-221.

Malloy, J. M., Cheney, D., & Cormier, G. M. (1998). Interagency collaboration and the transition to adulthood for students with emotional or behavioral disabilities. *Education and Treatment of Children, 21*, 303-320.

Marín, B. V., Marín, G., Padilla, A. M., & De la Rocha, C. (1983). Utilization of traditional and nontraditional sources of health care among Hispanics. *Hispanic Journal of Behavioral Sciences, 5*, 65-80.

Mattison, R., Humphrey, F., Kales, S., Handford, H., Finkenbinder, R., & Hernit, R. (1986). Psychiatric background and diagnoses of children evaluated for special class placement. *Journal of the American Academy of Child Psychiatry, 25*, 514-520.

Mattison, R., Morales, J., & Bauer, M. (1992). Distinguishing characteristics of elementary schoolboys recommended for SED placement. *Behavioral Disorders, 17*, 107-114.

Meyers, J. C. (1994). Financing strategies to support innovations in service delivery to children. *Journal of Clinical Child Psychology, 23*(Suppl.), 48-54.

McClure, G., Ferguson, H., Boodoosingh, L., Turgay, A., & Stavrakaki, C. (1989). The frequency and severity of psychiatric disorders in special education and psychiatric programs. *Behavioral Disorders, 14*, 117-126.

McDermott, P. A., & Spencer, M. B. (1997). Racial and social class prevalence of psychopathology among school-age youths in the United States. *Youth & Society, 28*, 387-414.

Morningstar, M. E., Turnbull, A. P., & Turnbull, H. R. (1995). What do students with disabilities tell us about the importance of family involvement in the transition from school to adult life? *Exceptional Children, 62*, 249-260.

Neel, R. S., Meadows, N., Levine, P., & Edgar, E. B. (1988). What happens after special education: A statewide follow-up study of secondary students who have behavioral disorders. *Behavioral Disorders, 13*, 209-216.

Nuttal, E. V., Sanchez, W., Osorio, L. B., Nuttal, R. L., & Varvogli, L. (1996). Assessing the culturally different linguistically different child with emotional and behavioral problems. In M. J. Breen & C. R. Fiedler (Eds.), *Behavioral approach to assessment of youths with emotional and behavioral disorders* (pp. 451-501). Austin, TX: Pro-Ed.

Pallak, M. S. (1996). The toughest transition: Outcome strategies and patient functioning. In N. A. Cummings & M. Pallak (Eds.), *Surviving the demise of solo practice: Mental health practitioners prospering in the era of managed care* (pp. 219-238). Madison, CT: Psychosocial Press/International Universities Press.

Parsons, R. J. (1991). Empowerment: Purpose and practice principle in social work. *Social Work With Groups, 14*, 7-21.

Ponterotto, J. G., & Casas, J. M. (1991). *Handbook of racial/ethnic minority counseling research.* Springfield, IL: Charles C Thomas.

Ponterotto, J. G., Casas, J. M., Suzuki, L. A., & Alexander, C. M. (Eds.). (1995). *Handbook of multicultural counseling.* Thousand Oaks, CA: Sage.

Pumariega, A., & Cross, T. (1997). Cultural competence in child psychiatry. In J. Noshpitz & N. Alessi (Eds.), *Basic handbook of child and adolescent psychiatry* (Vol. 4, pp. 473-484). New York: John Wiley.

Pumariega, A. J., & Vance, H. R. (1999). School-based mental health services: The foundation of systems of care for children's mental health. *Psychology in the Schools, 36*, 371-378.

Robertson, L. M., Bates, M. P., Wood, M., Rosenblatt, J. A., Furlong, M. J., & Casas, J. M. (1998). Educational placements of students with emotional and behavioral disorders served by probation, mental health, public health, and social services. *Psychology in the Schools, 35*, 333-345.

Rogler, L. H., Malgady, R. G., Constantino, G., & Blumenthal, R. (1987). What do culturally sensitive mental health services mean? The case of Hispanics. *American Psychologist, 42*, 565-570.

Ronnau, J. (1995). Family advocacy services: A strengths model of case management. In B. J. Friesen & J. Poertner (Eds.), *From case management to service coordination for children with emotional, behavioral, or mental disorders* (pp. 287-300). Baltimore, MD: Paul H. Brooks.

Rosen, L., Heckman, T., Carro, M., & Burchard, J. (1994). Satisfaction, involvement, and unconditional care: The perceptions of children and adolescents receiving wrap-around services. *Journal of Child and Family Studies, 3,* 55-67.

Rosenblatt, A., & Attkisson, C. C. (1993). Integrating systems of care in California for youth with severe emotional disturbance: III. Answers that lead to questions about out-of-home placements and the AB377 Evaluation Project. *Journal of Child & Family Studies, 2*(2), 119-141.

Rosenblatt, J., Robertson, L., Bates, M., Wood, M., Furlong, M., & Sosna, T. (1998). Troubled or troubling: Cluster analysis of youths in a system of care without system level referral constraints. *Journal of Emotional and Behavior Disorders, 6,* 42-54.

Ruiz, P. (1993). Access to health care for uninsured Hispanics: Policy recommendations. *Hospital and Community Psychiatry, 44,* 958-962.

Santa Barbara County MISC. (2000). *Santa Barbara County monthly evaluation reports.* Available at: www.education.ucsb.edu/~sbmisc

Silver, S., Duchnowski, A., Kutash, K., Friedman, R., Eisen, M., Prange, M., Brandenburg, N., & Greenbaum, P. (1992). A comparison of children with serious emotional disturbance served in residential and school settings. *Journal of Child and Family Studies, 1,* 43-59.

Sinclair, E., & Alexson, J. (1992). Relationship of behavioral characteristics to educational needs. *Behavioral Disorders, 17,* 296-304.

Sindelar, P., King, M., Cartland, D., Wilson, R., & Meisel, C. (1985). Deviant behavior in learning disabled and behaviorally disordered students as a function of level and placement. *Behavioral Disorders, 10,* 105-112.

Singh, N. N. (1998). Cultural diversity: A challenge for evaluating systems of care. In M. H. Epstein, K. Kutash, & A. Duchnowski (Eds.), *Outcomes for children and youths with emotional and behavioral disorders and their families* (pp. 425-455). Austin, TX: Pro-Ed.

Sluyter, G. V. (1994). Creating a vision for mental health services: A survey of states. *Administration and Policy in Mental Health, 21,* 247-250.

Sondheimer, D., Schoenwald, S., & Rowland, M. (1994). Alternatives to the hospitalization of youths with serious emotional disturbance. *Journal of Clinical Child Psychology, 23,* 7-13.

Stallard, P. (1993). The behavior of 3-year-old children: Prevalence and parental perception of problem behavior: A research note. *Journal of Child Psychology and Psychiatry and Allied Disciplines, 34,* 413-421.

Stroul, B. A. (1993). *Systems of care for children and adolescents with severe emotional disturbances: What are the results?* Washington, DC: CASSP Technical Assistance Center, Georgetown University Child Development Center.

Stroul, B. A. (1996). *Children's mental health: Creating systems of care in a changing society.* Baltimore, MD: Paul H. Brooks.

Stroul, B., & Friedman, R. (1986). *A system of care for severely emotionally disturbed children and youths.* Washington, DC: CASSP Technical Assistance Center, Georgetown University Child Development Center.

Stroul, B. A., & Friedman, R. M. (1996). *A system of care for children and adolescents with severe emotional disturbance.* Washington, DC: National Technical Assistance Center for Child Mental Health, Georgetown University Child Development Center.

Sue, D. W., Bingham, R. P., Posché-Burke, L., & Vasquez, M. (1999). The diversification of psychology: A multicultural revolution. *American Psychologist, 54,* 1061-1069.

Takeuchi, D. T., Bui, K. V., & Kim, L. (1993). The referral of adolescents to community health centers. *Journal of Health and Social Behavior, 34,* 153-164.

Takeuchi, D. T., Sue, S., & Yeh, M. (1995). Return rates and outcomes from ethnicity-specific mental health programs in Los Angeles. *American Journal of Public Health, 85,* 638-643.

Takeuchi, D. T., Uehara, E., & Maramba, G. (1999). Cultural diversity and mental health treatment. In A. V. Horwitz (Ed.), *A handbook for the study of mental health: Social contexts, theories, and systems* (pp. 550-565). New York: Cambridge University Press.

U. S. Surgeon General. (1999). *United States Surgeon General's report on mental health.* Washington, DC: Department of Health, Education, and Welfare, Public Health Service, National Institute of Mental Health.

Wagner, M. M. (1995). Outcomes for youths with serious emotional disturbance in secondary school and early adulthood. *The Future of Children, 5,* 90-112.

Westendorp, F., Brink, K., Roberson, M., & Ortiz, I. (1986). Variables which differentiate placement of adolescents into juvenile justice or mental health systems. *Adolescence, 21,* 23-37.

Wood, S. J., & Cronin, M. E. (1999). Students with emotional/behavioral disorders and transition planning: What the follow-up studies tell us. *Psychology in the Schools, 36,* 327-345.

Wordes, M., Bynum, T. S., & Corley, C. J. (1994). Locking up youths: The impact of race on detention decisions. *Journal of Research in Crime and Delinquency, 31,* 149-165.

Wright, H. H., & Leonhardt, T. V. (1998). Service approaches for infants, toddlers, and preschoolers: Implications for systems of care. In M. Hernandez & M. R. Isaacs (Eds.), *Promoting cultural competence in children's mental health services* (pp. 229-250). Baltimore, MD: Paul H. Brookes.

Correspondence concerning this chapter should be addressed to J. Manuel Casas, Graduate School of Education, University of California, Santa Barbara, CA 93106 (e-mail address: casas@education.ucsb.edu).

Chapter 16

FOSTERING ORGANIZATIONAL CHANGES TO REALIZE THE REVOLUTIONARY POTENTIAL OF THE MULTICULTURAL MOVEMENT

An Updated Case Study

MICHAEL D'ANDREA

JUDY DANIELS

PATRICIA ARREDONDO

MARY BRADFORD IVEY

ALLEN E. IVEY

DON C. LOCKE

BEVERLY O'BRYANT

THOMAS A. PARHAM

DERALD WING SUE

IF WE WERE to take a time capsule and flash forward to the middle of the 21st century, we would be very impressed (and perhaps even surprised) with the tremendous changes that occurred in our society. Besides being taken back by the ways in which new technologies have impacted all aspects of life in the year 2050, the continued feminization of the workforce, and the graying of America, many of us would truly be amazed at the types of changes that have occurred as a result of the cultural-racial transformation of the U.S. citizenry. What we are likely to find in the year 2050 are public school systems operating from much different curricula than what educators are currently using. These curricula changes would specifically reflect the need to better accommodate the unique challenges that students and workers face in a highly complex, technological society, a society that is comprised of a majority of persons who come from diverse cultural, ethnic, and racial backgrounds (D'Andrea & Daniels, 2000).

Assuming that the democratic principles upon which the United States was founded continue to guide the way our government operates in the future, we are likely to find that governmental agencies and their policies and practices have undergone substantial changes that were designed to guarantee the rights of every citizen in our country. This is especially true for individuals from cultural-racial groups that have traditionally been disenfranchised from the political process in the past (i.e., African Americans, Asian Americans, Latinos/Latinas, and Native Americans/Alaskan Natives/Native Hawaiians).

We would also note significant changes in the way business is conducted in the year 2050. These changes would include a workforce that is much more culturally-racially diverse than it was at the turn of the 21st century, with persons of color the dominant group, and the prevalence of new advertising strategies and marketing practices that are purposefully aimed at attracting a multicultural, multiracial consumer base (Arredondo, 1996).

These predictions are partially based on the fact that many organizational leaders have already begun to take note of demographic trends and are developing and implementing multicultural education programs and diversity training initiatives in schools, businesses, and governmental agencies across the country (Arredondo, 1996; Herring, 1997). At the dawning of the 21st century, it is apparent that many leaders in public education, business and industry, and government are becoming increasingly cognizant that they will either have to advocate for institutional changes that reflect greater sensitivity and respect for the educational needs, consumer interests, and the democratic rights of persons from diverse cultural-ethnic-racial groups or run the risk of having their agencies and organizations viewed in irrelevant and ineffective terms by the majority of persons of color and multiracial backgrounds who will soon comprise the majority of this nation's citizenry.

With this backdrop in mind, it is safe to say that the rapid cultural-racial diversification of the United States will not only result in an unprecedented transformation of this nation's demography but that it will also forge substantial changes in the way our societal institutions have historically operated. Given the historic legacy of racial tensions and the various forms of cultural oppression that continue to exist in this country, it is naive to think that the transformation to a multicultural, multiracial society will occur without heightened stress, increased manifestations of interpersonal conflicts, and a rising potential for violence (Ponterotto & Pedersen, 1993;

Sandhu & Aspy, 1997). Because many professional counselors and psychologists work within educational institutions, businesses, government, and community settings, they are well-positioned to: (a) assist individuals learn ways to effectively deal with the demographic changes that are predicted to occur in this nation in the coming decades and (b) advocate for the types of institutional-organizational changes that need to occur if the United States is to realize its potential in becoming a vibrant and inclusive democratic society. Despite their role as change agents, many counselors and psychologists continue to be ill-prepared to address the revolutionary challenges that underlie the multicultural movement in this country (Sue, Ivey, & Pedersen, 1996). Like this nation's public school systems, governmental structures, and businesses, the fields of counseling and psychology must also make changes that are necessary to transcend their own legacy of ethnocentrism, oppression, and racism. Failing to do so will increasingly place counselors and psychologists at risk of becoming viewed as irrelevant, unethical, and ineffective by persons from diverse backgrounds and groups (D'Andrea & Daniels, 2000; Lewis, Lewis, Daniels, & D'Andrea, 1998).

The multicultural transformation of the United States not only is a challenge, but it is also a positive opportunity for us all. The positive dimensions of the new society far outweigh the problems and difficulties that many persons consciously or unconsciously associate with the demographic changes that are occurring in the United States. We are slowly, but deliberately heading toward a time in which the joys of equality of opportunity will be ours. From this will come new perspectives to enrich business, education, and counseling and make each more effective within the context of a multicultural 21st century society. The mass media has already begun to show us some of the many positives of multiculturalism as it has begun to move from an all-White frame of reference.

For the fields of counseling and psychology, there is great opportunity to transcend their legacy of ethnocentrism, cultural oppression, and racism through the transformative potential of the multicultural movement. In light of these possibilities, this chapter is designed to serve a threefold purpose. First, it describes in detail the revolutionary potential of the multicultural movement. Second, this chapter provides an update of an ongoing case study that was initially described in the first edition of the *Handbook of Multicultural Counseling* (Ponterotto, Casas, Suzuki, & Alexander, 1995). In the first edition, D'Andrea and Daniels (1995) discussed an organizational development initiative that was implemented by members of the National Institute for Multicultural Competence (NIMC; formerly the National Multicultural Ad Hoc Committee) to advance "the principles of multiculturalism and reduce existing elements of racism within the fields of counseling and psychology" (p. 18). Third, the reader is provided an analysis of how organizational initiatives such as those implemented by the NIMC are essential in the revolutionary process of democratizing our society in general and the fields of counseling and psychology in particular.

THE REVOLUTIONARY
POTENTIAL OF MULTICULTURALISM

The potential to promote a greater level of democracy in our nation

There are several reasons why multiculturalism can accurately be called a revolutionary force in the United States. The most obvious and concrete factor underlying the revolutionary potential of the multicultural movement is the unprecedented shift in the demographic composition of the U.S. citizenry. While the United States has always been a multicultural and multiracial country, the melting pot ideology has argued for sameness and equality in the face of racial segregation and other forms of social stratification. However, within a few short decades, a nation that has primarily been built on the traditions, values, and worldviews of persons who come from non-Hispanic, White, European groups will be transformed into a society in which most of its citizens come from non-White, non-European, non-English-speaking backgrounds (Sue & Sue, 1999).

Besides the significant numerical changes that are occurring in the cultural-racial makeup of the U.S. population, the shifting demographic patterns will predictably be accompanied by increasing demands for greater economic, political, and social equity among groups of persons who have historically been disenfranchised and discriminated against in our country. Thus multiculturalism, despite its revolutionary potential, will remain a force without substance unless the demographic changes are accompanied by a willingness to share power (Ivey, 1995).

The beauty of the multicultural movement and the progress that has been made is not simply in the changing demography, although that is impressive. Rather, the energy and passion of a cultural crusade and the possibility of real and sustained progress must inspire individual leaders to consolidate their efforts and direct energy toward achieving mutually agreed upon goals. Such was the case in the coming together of several multicultural counseling leaders who united to form the National Institute for Multicultural Competence (NIMC). Each is a force in his or her own right. Derald Sue, a leader in the Asian American psychological and counseling community for more than two decades, was setting a standard with his scholarship (e.g., *Counseling the Culturally Different* by D. W. Sue & D. Sue, 1980, 1990, 1999) and advocacy. Thomas Parham, a leader in the African American psychological and counseling community and former president of the Association for Multicultural Counseling and Development (AMCD), was charting a new course with his work in identity development and his advocacy for multicultural competence. In fact, it was his AMCD presidential initiative that invited the development of the 1992 competency standards (Sue, Arredondo, & McDavis, 1992). Patricia Arredondo, a Latina counselor educator, was combining her academic interests with strategies to promote diversity within the culture of corporate America. Mary Bradford Ivey, a nationally recognized multicultural school counselor, is one of the pioneers who developed and field-tested school-based interventions that were designed to promote children's knowledge and respect for human diversity. Allen Ivey, Fellow with the American Psychological Association (APA), former president of APA's Division 17 (Counseling Psychology) and author of the *Microskills Training and Multicultural* series, began to incorporate multicultural issues into his writing and advocacy more than twenty years ago. Don C. Locke is a force for inclusion within the structure of the American Counseling Association (ACA), as well as a scholar who has consistently advocated for increased multicultural understanding. Similarly, Michael D'Andrea and Judy Daniels, while anchoring themselves in the corner of progressive Whites, were writing about and advocating for increased emphasis on confronting issues of racism, oppression, and White privilege. And Beverly O'Bryant, a past president of the American School Counseling Association (ASCA) who was an advocate for inclusion within the ASCA, was also president-elect of the American Counseling Association (ACA) when members of the NIMC approached her regarding the need to promote organizational changes within the counseling profession. Her receptivity and support for the ideas that the NIMC members presented led to the advancement of numerous changes in the ACA, all of which reflected a heightened sensitivity and respect for multiculturalism. The synergy created by the coming together of these individuals is what propelled the NIMC, and they have shown that each is better individually and collectively because of their affiliation and work in the NIMC.

The need to build on past achievements in promoting democracy and justice in the United States

Progress has certainly been made in terms of promoting a greater sense of social justice among culturally and racially different persons as many overt policies and practices aimed at maintaining an apartheidlike atmosphere in the United States (i.e., segregated schools, lack of access to public accommodations, denial of voting rights, etc.) have been dismantled since the 1954 school desegregation case and the 1960s Civil Rights Movement. However, it is equally clear that the United States continues to fall short of guaranteeing the promise of democracy and equal opportunities for millions of gay and lesbian persons, women, physically challenged individuals, older adults, poor persons, and individuals from different cultural-ethnic-racial groups. This largely occurs as a result of the perpetuation of more sophisticated and institutionalized forms of cultural oppression and racism in this country (Jones, 1997; Ridley, 1995).

Whether it is manifested by major corporations like Texaco; racially based police profiling policies; the disproportionate number of non-White youngsters who are tracked in special education classes; the overrepresentation of persons of color who are on death row, in prison, on parole or probation; or the escalating number of hate crimes that have been directed toward gay and lesbian persons over the past 10 years; various forms of individual and institutionalized discrimination and injustice continue to flourish in this nation (Banks & McGee Banks, 1997; D. W. Sue & Sue, 1999). Because it is not likely that such forms of injustice will be tolerated by an increasingly diverse society and since the myth of the "melting pot" has long ago lost its venerable luster as an acceptable explanation of the cultural assimilation process, the cultural-racial transformation of this country's citizenry will predictably be accompanied by increasing demands for greater levels of democracy and equity in all of our societal institutions. Unlike the civil rights movement of the 1960s, which was largely aimed at eradicating more concrete forms of racial and cultural discrimination (i.e., working to de-segregate public schools, guaranteeing voting rights to all persons), the challenge of the multicultural movement in the 21st century is to ameliorate more sophisticated and insidious forms of cultural-racial discrimination, oppression, and injustice that are deeply embedded in the institutions and organizations that constitute the infrastructure of our society (Jones, 1997).

Clearly, the challenge of guaranteeing greater democratic involvement among persons who have historically been disenfranchised in this country is a daunting task. Although the demographic transformation of the U.S. has the potential to foster a greater level of democracy in our nation as increased demands for social, educational, economic, and political equity will predictably be raised by visible spokespersons from groups that have historically been disenfranchised in this country, there is no guarantee that this nation will take the steps that are necessary to move toward a greater level of democracy and cultural inclusion. The true test in whether demographic diversification will lead to the realization of this country's democratic potential will largely be determined by the degree to which justice loving individuals are able to successfully address and eradicate unfair institutional policies and practices that continue to be perpetuated in our society (Lee & Walz, 1998).

Certainly, the task of promoting a greater level of democracy within the context of a multicultural, multiracial society will be stressful and not come easily in the coming decades. Many persons in the dominant cultural-racial group, who continue to benefit from the social, economic, and cultural arrangements that have traditionally been established in the United States, will implicitly and explicitly demonstrate resistance for a greater democratization of our societal institutions. Such resistance will not only impede this nation's ability to realize its full potential as a democratic society, but it will also continue to compromise the mental health and spiritual well-being of millions of persons from White and non-White backgrounds in our country (West, 1999).

Dr. Martin Luther King, Jr. repeatedly discussed the links that exist between a nation's mental health, spiritual well-being, and genuine commitment to promote justice and democracy among all of its citizens

(Washington, 1986). Because we agree with Dr. King's assessment of the intimate interconnection between these factors, we believe that counselors and psychologists can and should play an important role in helping to promote the democratization of our schools, workplaces, and communities in a culturally diverse 21st century society.

In fact, many counselors and psychologists do demonstrate both an awareness of and the commitment to work in a socially responsible manner by acting as change agents who strive to promote a more just society. This sort of commitment has been manifested in numerous projects that have been implemented by the members of Divisions 9 (Society for the Psychological Study of Social Issues), 27 (Society for Community Research and Action), 35 (Psychology of Women), 44 (Society for the Psychological Study of Lesbian and Gay Issues), and 45 (Society for the Psychological Study of Ethnic Minority Issues) of the American Psychological Association (APA), members of the Association for Multicultural Counseling and Development (AMCD) as well as a newly formed professional organization called "Counselors for Social Justice" (CSJ) in ACA. Numerous multicultural advocates have noted that the increased use of proactive-contextual-environmental interventions that many persons in these professional organizations are implementing in their work not only positively impact large numbers of persons from different groups and backgrounds (Lewis et al., 1998), but they also represent a better fit for the needs of individuals who come from culturally and racially diverse client populations that have effectively and systematically been disenfranchised and disempowered (Sue et al., 1996; D. W. Sue & Sue, 1999).

The potential to liberate counselors and psychologists from the epistemological hegemony of modern Western psychological thought

For many psychologists and counselors, the notion of directing efforts toward promoting social changes that foster a greater level of democracy in the schools and universities, businesses, communities, and governmental agencies where they work is a foreign concept. This reaction is in part due to the fact that the fields of psychology and counseling have historically encouraged practitioners to primarily direct their attention to clients' intrapsychic problems and needs in the confines of their offices. As a result of adopting this limited role identity, many mental health practitioners spend an inordinate amount of time and energy assisting individuals to develop new insights and/or behavioral strategies that are useful for clients to move beyond immobilizing states of depression, irrational phobias, low levels of self-esteem, and ineffective interpersonal problem-solving styles. Although such psychological interventions have proven to be effective when used among persons from some ethnic-racial groups in our society, they often do not fit the culturally constructed meaning of mental health, coping, and helping strategies that are embedded in the values, worldviews, and traditions of individuals who come from other cultural backgrounds (D'Andrea, 2000).

Several new theoretical frameworks that have recently been introduced to the fields of counseling and psychology have built on the historical legacy left by the pioneers in the field. This includes the work of the Association of Black Psychologists (ABPsy), the early work of the AMCD (formerly organized by Samuel Johnson as the Association for Non-White Concerns [ANWC]), major contributions by Robert Williams, who directed the Minority Mental Health Program at Washington University, and Thomas Gunnings and Gloria Smith, who directed the Urban Counseling Program at Michigan State University and advocated for a systemic counseling approach.

In their more contemporary manifestation, the multicultural counseling competencies (Arredondo et al., 1996; Sue et al., 1992), the empowerment counseling framework (McWhirter, 1994), and the psychology for liberation model (Ivey, 1995) represent practical alternatives to many of the traditional counseling and psychotherapeutic approaches that have dominated the fields of counseling and psychology during the 20th century. Some of the strengths that are noted to make these new helping models more appealing to culturally and racially diverse clients include (a) the expressed need for counselors and psychologists to acquire an extensive knowledge base about human diversity and (b) the emphasis that is placed on helping clients deal with the toxic contextual factors that compromise the psychological health and personal well-being of millions of persons in this nation. Researchers have noted that when counselors and psychologists operate from a more expansive professional role identity, which includes accepting the responsibility of fostering positive environmental changes in their clients' lives, these practitioners tend to be viewed in more positive and relevant terms among clients who have historically been discriminated against and oppressed in this country (Lewis et al., 1998).

Beyond pressing counselors and psychologists to reassess the role they have traditionally played in promoting the psychological health of their clients, the multicultural movement has the potential to stimulate even more fundamental and pervasive changes in the way counselors and psychologists have traditionally been conditioned to construct meaning of mental health and human development. By encouraging counselors and psychologists to (a) move beyond their own ethnocentric ways of thinking and acting (Daniels & D'Andrea, 1996), (b) emphasizing the legitimacy of multiple interpretations of reality (Sue & Sue, 1990, 1999; White & Parham, 1990), and (c) demonstrating greater respect and acceptance of the different ways that individuals from diverse cultural-racial groups construct meaning of terms like *mental health, psychological maturity,* and *personal well-being,* multiculturalism has the potential to challenge the epistemological and intellectual hegemony of modern western psychological thought (D'Andrea, 2000). By moving beyond the limits of western psychological thinking and acquiring new knowledge about the worldviews, values, and traditions of persons from culturally and racially different groups, counselors and psychologists are able to develop more expansive (and perhaps more accurate) ways of making sense of their clients' and their own lives. In doing all of this, the multicultural counseling competencies (Arredondo et al., 1996; Sue et al., 1992) are critical guideposts for effective and ethical practice.

Given the imperial nature and almost infallible status that western psychological theories have acquired during the 20th century as well as the intellectual conditioning that counselors and psychologists typically undergo in their professional training programs, it is very difficult for many mental health practitioners to genuinely entertain the legitimacy of different interpretations of reality or to accept the validity of other types of indigenous healing methods (Lee, 1996). To even suggest that the fourth edition of *Diagnostic and Statistical Manual of Mental Disorders, Fourth Edition* (*DSM-IV*; American Psychiatric Association [APA], 1994) represents a culturally biased diagnostic nosology and therefore does not provide accurate descriptions of the psychological and spiritual difficulties many persons from different cultural-racial groups experience in their lives, is readily dismissed as nonsense by many persons in the fields of counseling and psychology (Dana, 1993). Although this sort of ethnocentrism continues to dominate the thinking of many counselors and psychologists in the United States, it seriously restricts one's ability to conceptualize alternative explanations of human development. It also leads to the outright dismissal of other legitimate cultural constructions of mental health and psychological well-being.

In light of the inevitable demographic transformation of the U.S., counselors and psychologists must decide if they are going to continue to impose their own ethnocentric beliefs about mental health, coping strategies, and helping interventions among culturally different clients (many of whom have formulated very different meanings of these terms); or they can demonstrate greater open-mindedness by critically analyzing the cultural relativity and limitations of the theories and research findings that represent the bedrock of psychological thinking in our society. Should counselors and psychologists follow the former course of action, it is predicted that they will be increasingly viewed as irrelevant by many of the culturally and racially different persons that they are called upon to serve (Parham, 1993, 1996). It has also been noted that this course of action is likely to undermine the long-term viability of the counseling and psychology professions in this country (D'Andrea, Locke, & Daniels, 1997).

On the other hand, if counselors and psychologists (as well as the training programs that prepare them for the work they will do in the future) demonstrate a commitment to become culturally competent practitioners by developing a heightened level of cultural awareness, knowledge, and skills (Arredondo et al., 1996; Sue et al., 1992), they will be much better positioned to work effectively and ethically among persons from different client populations. In making this commitment, counselors and psychologists are also likely to experience a greater sense of personal liberation in their own thinking as they move beyond the cultural-biased epistemology that has dominated western psychological thought during most of the 20th century.

The potential to revolutionize the fields of counseling and psychology

By building a more culturally inclusive epistemology and dismantling the intellectual hegemony of western psychological thought in the U.S., the fields of counseling and psychology will inevitably undergo a number of revolutionary changes that reflect substantial alterations in the way counseling theorists, researchers, educators in graduate training programs, and leaders in our national professional organizations respond to the challenges of multiculturalism. This includes expanding the traditional definition of counseling, legitimizing alternative helping roles (advocacy, consulting, change agent, etc.; Atkinson, Morten, & Sue, 1998), utilizing indigenous, non-Western healing practices (Lee, 1996), and considering spirituality as an important domain of psychology (Sue, Bingham, Porche-Burke, & Vasquez, 1999). These changes will be the direct result of a newly emerging postmodern-multicultural paradigm in the mental health professions (D'Andrea, 2000). Some of the more obvious changes that are predicted to go hand in hand with this emerging new paradigm are the following:

- The deconstruction and reconstruction of traditional counseling and psychology theories that have been used to explain human development, mental health, and psychopathology (Santiago-Rivera, Vazquez, & Aviles-Davison, 1999)
- The development and implementation of new theories of counseling that result in more efficacious outcomes when working to promote the mental health of large numbers of persons from diverse client populations in the 21st century (Lewis et al., 1998)
- Greater acceptance and legitimation of a broad range of research methods (i.e., qualitative and quantitative research strategies) that can be used to (a) effectively evaluate the impact of traditional counseling and psychological theories (theory-testing research) with persons from diverse groups and (b) formulate new psychological theories (theory-building research) that reflect a more culturally inclusive epistemology (S. Sue, 1999)
- The evolution of new professional training models that are intentionally designed to foster counselors' and psychologists' multicultural competence (Arredondo et al., 1996; O'Bryant, 1999; Sue et al., 1992)
- Changes in many of the organizational traditions, policies, and practices that reflect various cultural biases and racial privileges often taken for granted by numerous leaders and members of our professional associations. Such organizational changes include but are not limited to active recruitment and retention projects that are designed to hire a greater percentage of persons from diverse cultural-racial backgrounds for meaningful organizational decision-making positions in APA and ACA; an increased demonstration of APA's and ACA's commitment for multiculturalism at state, regional, and national conferences and conventions; clearer and more explicit articulation of counselors' and psychologists' ethical responsibilities when working with persons from diverse cultural-racial backgrounds in

future revisions of ACA's and APA's Ethical Standards; and broad-based formal organizational endorsement and support from APA and ACA and all of
their divisions and associations for the multicultural counseling competencies that have been developed by AMCD (Arredondo et al., 1996; Sue et al.,
1992)

For some persons in the fields of counseling and psychology, the above
mentioned points represent common sense changes that must occur if the
mental health professions are to remain viable and relevant within the context of multicultural, multiracial 21st-century society. However, as history
has shown, these fields have often been guilty of benign neglect at best and
overt resistance at worst in terms of effectively addressing the mental
health needs and psychological well-being of culturally and racially diverse
persons in this nation (D'Andrea & Daniels, 1995; Locke, 1998). Numerous
persons have written about the various ways in which such important factors as ethnocentrism (Daniels & D'Andrea, 1996; Wrenn, 1962, 1985), individual and institutional racism (Jones, 1997; Kiselica, 1999; Ridley,
1995), and White privilege (McIntosh, 1989; Sue & Sue, 1999) continue to
serve as barriers that prevent many of the changes listed above from occurring in the fields of counseling and psychology. While the gradualist approach that these professional fields have generally taken in responding to
the increasing cultural-racial diversification of our nation has resulted in
some changes, they have not come without strong lobbying from multicultural advocates. Given the level of resistance that continues to exist in
these fields and the slow pace with which changes have been made in terms
of responding to the challenges of multiculturalism, it is important that
multicultural advocates increase their level of collaboration as they plan
and implement effective strategies that are aimed at fostering the sort of
changes that are described above.

The fields of counseling and psychology have, in fact, established a
number of formal organizational entities (i.e., AMCD and AGLBIC in ACA;
Divisions 35, 44, and 45 in APA) that are designed to address issues related
to multiculturalism and human diversity. Additionally, there are specific
psychological associations that address various areas of multicultural competency outside of ACA and APA. This includes the Association of Black
Psychologists (ABPsy), the Asian American Psychological Association, the
National Hispanic Psychological Association, and the Society of Indian
Psychologists. Other initiatives have also helped to frame and further the
discourse on multicultural issues in counseling and psychology. Most notable in this regard was the establishment of the Winter Roundtable Conference of Crosscultural Counseling and Psychotherapy founded by Samuel
Johnson at Teachers College, Columbia University in 1983.

All of these formal organizational vehicles are indeed necessary to help
usher in the changes that need to occur in the mental health professions in

the 21st century. However, these organizational entities are not immune from problems that reduce their potential to promote the sort of revolutionary changes that need to occur in the fields of counseling and psychology in the coming decades. Some of these problems are as follows:

- Having proposals for organizational changes encumbered by institutionally sanctioned policies and procedures
- Being stymied by philosophical and political differences that are manifested among participating members in these organizational entities
- Ineffective leaders who appear to be motivated by personal gain and/or supporting the existing status quo rather that advocating for revolutionary changes in the fields of counseling and psychology (D'Andrea & Daniels, 1995)

Consequently, while it is vital to support organizational entities that are intentionally designed to advocate for issues related to multiculturalism and human diversity, it is also important that individuals who understand the revolutionary potential of the multicultural movement to work collaboratively outside the restrictions of formal organizational entities.

In the first edition of the *Handbook of Multicultural Counseling* (Ponterotto et al., 1995), D'Andrea and Daniels present a case study that describes a series of organizational development strategies that were used by a group of multicultural advocates to foster positive changes in the fields of counseling and psychology. These intervention strategies were fundamentally designed to stimulate a greater level of multicultural competence among individual counselors and psychologists as well as within the professional associations to which they belong. In the following section of this chapter, we offer a brief overview of the general strategies that were used by the members of the National Institute for Multicultural Competence (NIMC; formerly the National Ad Hoc Multicultural Committee) to promote changes in the mental health professions that were originally reported in the first edition of the *Handbook of Multicultural Counseling*. We also summarize the successes this group experienced as a result of implementing these organizational development strategies from 1993 to 1995. We then provide an update of the progress the NIMC has made from 1995 to 2000 regarding this ongoing project.

FORMULATING THE NATIONAL
AD HOC MULTICULTURAL COMMITTEE

Recognizing the various forms of resistance that continue to exist in the fields of counseling and psychology as well as considering the strengths and limitations of existing organizational entities that are designed to address issues related to multiculturalism and human diversity in these professions, a number of multicultural scholars and advocates formulated an independent group called the National Multicultural Ad Hoc Committee in the Summer of 1993. The formation of this committee was in response to a call for such action by more than 100 persons who participated in a national summit meeting that was entitled, "Dealing with Racism in the Counseling Profession" in the Spring of 1993. This meeting was held at the annual ACA Convention in Atlanta and resulted in a core group of persons voluntarily agreeing to work together as members of the National Multicultural Ad Hoc Committee. Founding members of this committee included Patricia Arredondo (Arizona State University), Michael D'Andrea and Judy Daniels (University of Hawaii), Mary Bradford Ivey and Allen Ivey (Microtraining and Multicultural Development), Don C. Locke (North Carolina State University), Thomas Parham (University of California, Irvine), and Derald Wing Sue (California School of Professional Psychology and California State University, Hayward).

Operating as an autonomous group to promote multiculturalism and confront racism

To avoid being encumbered by organizational policies, practices, and traditions that can be used to effectively diffuse calls for significant political, epistemological, and structural changes within professional associations, the members of the National Multicultural Ad Hoc Committee agreed that they should operate as an autonomous entity to foster positive changes within the fields of counseling and psychology in general and within ACA and APA in particular. Besides lobbying support for the development and implementation of organizational changes that reflected greater respect and sensitivity for human diversity, the committee members agreed that their efforts should also direct attention to the different forms of racism and White privilege that continue to be perpetuated in the mental health professions (D'Andrea & Daniels, 1995). D'Andrea (1992) described some of the more notable ways that racism and White privilege operated in the fields of counseling and psychology at the time the National Multicultural Ad Hoc Committee was formulated. This included the following observations:

- Less than 1% of the chairpersons of graduate counseling and psychology training programs in the United States come from non-White groups (99% of all chairpersons in these training programs are White males).
- No Latino, Latina, Asian American, or Native American Indian person had ever been elected president of either ACA or APA up to that time.
- Only one African American person had been elected as president of APA or served in that capacity in ACA.

- None of the most commonly used textbooks in counselor education training programs in the United States listed "racism" as an area of attention in their Tables of Contents or indices.

- A 12-year computerized literature review of social science periodicals indicated that only 6 of the 308 articles published in the three leading professional counseling journals (*The Counseling Psychologist, Journal of Counseling and Development,* and *Journal of Counseling Psychology*) from 1980 to 1992 focused on the impact of racism on clients' mental health and psychological development.

- In 1992, all of the editors of the journals sponsored by ACA and APA (with the exception of one African American editor with the *Journal of Multicultural Counseling and Development*) were White persons.

- Despite more than 15 years of efforts invested in designing a comprehensive set of multicultural counseling competencies and standards, the organizational governing bodies of both ACA and APA resisted adopting them as formal guidelines for professional training, development, and practice.

Implementing organizational development strategies

To promote multiculturalism and confront the ways in which institutionalized racism and White privilege continue to be perpetuated in the fields of counseling and psychology, the members of the National Multicultural Ad Hoc Committee used four fundamental organizational development strategies in their work. These included:

1. *Mobilization strategies.* These strategies involved developing opportunities in which the rank-and-file members of counseling and psychology organizations could meet to discuss the types of problems and barriers that prevent their professional associations from advancing the spirit and principles of multiculturalism.

2. *Education strategies.* These strategies included efforts to create opportunities in which counselors and psychologists could increase their theoretical and practical understanding of multiculturalism and institutional racism. Such efforts included scholarly activities that were intentionally designed to expand the traditional epistemology upon which the fields of counseling and psychology are based. This was done, in part, by developing, publishing, and presenting new information in the fields of counseling and psychology that foster the evolution of more comprehensive theoretical frameworks and new conceptual paradigms in the mental health professions.

3. *Organizational strategies.* These strategies involved lobbying, consulting, and collaborating with leaders and members of professional counseling and psychology associations about concrete ways to implement systemic changes that reflect greater understanding, sensitivity, and respect for cultural and human diversity.

4. *Institutionalizing strategies.* These strategies included actions that would lead to the formal adoption of multicultural organizational development initiatives (D. W. Sue, 1995) within our national professional organizations (i.e., policy changes, the establishment of new organizational rituals,

revision of professional ethical standards). (D'Andrea & Daniels, 1995, pp. 24-25)

Implementing strategies into practice from 1993 to 1995

From 1993 to 1995, the members of the National Multicultural Ad Hoc Committee primarily directed their time and energy to four main projects in attempting to create changes in ACA that reflected greater sensitivity and respect for multiculturalism and human diversity. First, to build on the momentum that was created at the Atlanta meeting during the 1993 ACA Convention, members of the National Multicultural Ad Hoc Committee organized a series of national leadership conferences that were held at ACA headquarters in Alexandria, Virginia. The first national leadership meeting was held in August 1993, a second meeting was convened in December 1993, and ensuing annual meetings were held in 1994 and 1995. These meetings were designed to (a) mobilize rank-and-file members of ACA who expressed an interest in planning and implementing strategies to foster changes in the counseling profession that reflected a greater level of understanding, sensitivity, and respect for cultural and human diversity (*Mobilization Strategies*) and (b) identifying specific persons who would lobby, consult, and collaborate with ACA leaders regarding concrete changes that professional association could make to demonstrate a greater level of commitment for multiculturalism (*Organizational* and *Institutionalizing Strategies*).

Second, to further mobilize and educate additional persons in the counseling profession regarding the need to promote multiculturalism and eradicate various forms of racism that continue to be perpetuated in the fields of counseling and psychology, a major multicultural forum was planned for the 1994 ACA Convention in Minneapolis. Over 800 persons attended this major event in April 1994. During this forum, counselors in the association witnessed the establishment of a new organizational ritual that was called the "First Annual Ohana Ceremony (*Institutionalizing Strategy*). The word *ohana* is a Hawaiian term that means "extended and caring family" (McDermott, Tseng, & Maretzki, 1980, p. 11). By incorporating a Hawaiian tradition into the forum program, the members of the National Multicultural Ad Hoc Committee hoped to (a) institutionalize an organizational ritual in which counselors who are nationally recognized for their work as multicultural counseling experts could be honored by their colleagues in a public manner (*Institutionalizing Strategy*) and (b) promote counselors' awareness of a group of Native Americans (e.g., Native Hawaiians) who are frequently omitted from discussions about multicultural counseling and development (*Education Strategy*) (D'Andrea & Daniels, 1995).

During this forum, several counseling practitioners were asked to discuss ways in which they put multicultural counseling theory into practice in the schools and communities where they worked. This segment of the forum provided the audience an opportunity to learn about practical counseling strategies and techniques that were found to be effective when working with persons from culturally and racially diverse client populations (*Education Strategy*).

The members of the National Multicultural Ad Hoc Committee also used half of the time allowed for the 1994 Forum to encourage persons in the audience to get directly involved in ongoing efforts to create systemic changes in ACA that reflected the spirit and principles of multiculturalism. To accomplish this task, several resolutions were distributed and discussed during the forum (*Organizational* and *Institutionalizing Strategies*). These resolutions called upon ACA's Governing Council, president, president-elect, and executive director to implement a number of multicultural organizational development initiatives in the association that included the following:

- Requiring all persons who were contracted by ACA to provide professional development workshops and learning institutes to submit a description of the ways in which they would address multicultural and diversity issues in their training services
- Guaranteeing the ongoing inclusion of multicultural training for ACA leaders, practitioners, researchers, and educators at all association regional meetings, annual summit leadership conferences, and national conventions in the future
- Requesting ACA's support in providing two full-day multicultural professional development training workshops annually for members of the association's primary policy-making body [ACA's Governing Council]
- Adding a new column in the association's monthly newletter is specifically designed to disseminate information about issues related to multiculturalism and human diversity to the 56,000 members in the organization
- Establishing a new organizational tradition in which the president and executive director of ACA would make an annual report at the association's national conventions regarding progress the organization was making in terms of placing persons from underrepresented groups in management and decision-making positions at ACA headquarters
- Gaining support from ACA for the National Multicultural Ad Hoc Committee to coordinate another major forum at the 1995 ACA Convention in Denver, Colorado (D'Andrea & Daniels, 1995).

It is important to note that the forum that was held in 1994 in Minneapolis represented the first time an invited featured event on multiculturalism and racism was sponsored by ACA at its annual convention. The presence of then president-elect Beverly O'Bryant as only the second African American president of ACA in its 45-year history provided receptivity, advocacy, and support for the introduction of change mechanisms within the organizational structure of this professional counseling association. As president of the association the following year, President O'Bryant continued to provide guidance and immediate access to organizational processes, support through the parlimentary procedures, and organizational commitment to support future national leadership meetings that focused on issues related to multiculturalism and diversity.

Assessing the impact of the multicultural organizational development project: 1993–1995

In assessing the impact of the above mentioned organizational development efforts, D'Andrea and Daniels (1995) reported on three specific outcomes that occurred as a result of the National Multicultural Ad Hoc Committee's efforts to promote multiculturalism in ACA from 1993 to 1995. First, the National Multicultural Ad Hoc Committee was asked to coordinate the Opening Session of the 1995 ACA Annual Convention in Denver. By using the theme "Many Voices Into One Voice: Promoting Human Dignity and Development Through Diversity," committee members were able to further implement their organizational development model among a large group of professional counselors. This included using the 3-hour time period allowed for the Opening Session to discuss numerous issues related to multicultural and diversity counseling among the more than 3,000 ACA members who attended this event *(Mobilization* and *Education Strategies)*; inviting members of the association to work together to lobby for changes within ACA that reflected a greater level of commitment for multiculturalism and human diversity (*Organizational Strategy*); and calling upon ACA leaders to implement organizational changes that reflected greater understanding, respect, and acceptance of multiculturalism (*Institutionalizing Strategy*).

Second, the editor of the monthly newsletter published by ACA, titled *Counseling Today*, agreed to include a new column in all future editions of that professional periodical that would specifically address issues related to multicultural and diversity counseling. The members of the National Multicultural Ad Hoc Committee requested that the column be titled "Promoting Human Dignity and Development Through Diversity" to help build on the theme of the 1994 Multicultural Forum at the ACA Annual Convention in Minneapolis and the Opening Session of the 1995 ACA Convention in Denver. It is important to note that National Multicultural Ad Hoc Committee member and former ACA President Beverly O'Bryant played an important role in having this new column formally incorporated into *Counseling Today*.

Third, the ACA Governing Council approved two new organizational policies in 1994 that were in direct response to lobbying efforts by the National Multicultural Ad Hoc Committee. The first policy change stated that a group of master multicultural trainers would be identified to provide training to all Governing Council members as well as the entire ACA headquarters staff during the 1995–1996 fiscal year. The second policy change indicated that all persons contracted to provide professional development training services and/or workshops for ACA in the future must explicitly outline in their proposals ways in which their training addresses issues related to multiculturalism and human diversity.

MAKING THINGS HAPPEN

The members of the National Multicultural Ad Hoc Committee recognized that the above mentioned organizational changes represented positive steps toward promoting an increased commitment and sense of respect for human diversity within this nation's largest professional counseling association. However, the committee members also acknowledged that many more organizational changes would need to occur if the fields of counseling and psychology are to (a) remain viable parts of this country's mental health care and educational systems and (b) demonstrate a heightened level of understanding, respect, acceptance, and commitment to address the revolutionary challenges and realize the positive potential that underlie the cultural-racial transformation of the United States in the 21st century.

D'Andrea and Daniels (2000) predict that counselors and psychologists will generally fall into one of three categories that reflect different ways in which they respond to the challenges of multiculturalism in the coming decades. In describing these three categories, D'Andrea and Daniels suggest that many counselors and psychologists will continue to stay on the sidelines remaining content to watch things happen as the revolutionary changes that accompany the cultural-racial transformation of the United States continue to unfold. They also predict that an increasing number of mental health professionals, who are genuinely committed to the ideals and revolutionary potential that underlie the multicultural movement, will strive to make things happen by lobbying support for substantial organizational changes within professional counseling and psychology associations. It is further noted that some counselors and psychologists will fall into a category of persons who wonder what happened as they awake to a world that has been transformed by the dramatic cultural-racial shift in the demographic makeup of this nation's citizenry by the middle of the 21st century.

In an effort to join with those persons who are committed to "make things happen" in the fields of counseling and psychology, the members of the National Multicultural Ad Hoc Committee expanded their organizational plans and directed new efforts to promote multiculturalism in the mental health professions over the next five years. What follows is a discussion of the ways in which members of this group continued to catalyze changes within the mental health professions from 1995 to 2000, changes that allow these professions to become better positioned to realize much of the revolutionary potential of the multicultural movement that was described earlier in this chapter.

EXPANDING OUR WORK WITHIN THE ACA

Helping leaders in the ACA acquire new multicultural competencies

To follow up with the mandate to provide professional training for members of the ACA Governing Council, regional and state leaders, and staff persons at ACA headquarters, it was necessary to develop an educational format that would effectively increase participants' multicultural awareness, knowledge, and organizational skills (*Educational Strategy*). National Multicultural Ad Hoc Committee members Patricia Arredondo (Arizona State University) and Don C. Locke (North Carolina State University) worked with Janet Jones (a long-time multicultural advocate and leader in ACA) and Bob Barret (founding president of the Association for Gay, Lesbian, and Bisexual Counseling [AGLBIC]) to develop an innovative multicultural training model that was designed to meet the professional development needs of ACA leaders and members of the headquarters staff. The training model was specifically aimed at fostering an increased level of understanding, respect, and acceptance of gay, lesbian, and bisexual persons as well as heightening the participants' knowledge about a broad range of issues related to racism, ethnicity, and cultural identity. This professional development training framework was delivered to over 200 ACA leaders and headquarters staff persons who participated in a series of training sessions offered during the 1995–1996 and 1996–1997 fiscal years.

Building partnerships and seeking organizational endorsement for the multicultural counseling competencies

An increasing number of counselors and psychologists are becoming aware that they will need to acquire a broad range of multicultural counseling competencies if they are to work effectively and ethically among persons from culturally and racially diverse client populations in the future. Despite the fact that AMCD has developed (Sue et al., 1992) and refined (Arredondo et al., 1996) a comprehensive set of multicultural counseling competencies, the members of the National Multicultural Ad Hoc Committee were aware that none of the organizational divisions in either ACA or APA had formally endorsed the multicultural competencies by 1997. Thus, in an effort to help institutionalize multiculturalism in the counseling profession, members of the National Multicultural Ad Hoc Committee implemented a strategy that was designed to build partnerships with other leaders in ACA in an effort to gain formal endorsement of the multicultural counseling competencies from various divisions within this professional association.

The successful election of Patricia Arredondo as AMCD president in 1996 (the first Latina/o president of that organization) marked the culmination of an effort that had begun some five years earlier to increase diversity within AMCD. At that time, she was appointed secretary of AMCD during

Thomas Parham's presidential administration, thereby providing her an opportunity to serve on the AMCD Board of Directors and become a visible leader within that association. By being elected president of AMCD in 1996, Patricia Arredondo was well-positioned organizationally to solicit formal endorsement of the multicultural counseling competencies from a number of ACA divisions. As a result of her advocacy and partnership-building efforts and the continued consultation and support she received from the National Multicultural Ad Hoc Committee, Patricia Arredondo was able to successfully gain the formal endorsement of the multicultural counseling competencies from seven ACA divisions between 1996 and 1997 (*Institutionalizing Strategy*). These formal organizational endorsements came from the American School Counseling Association (ASCA), the Association of Counselor Educators and Supervisors (ACES), the Association for Gay, Lesbian and Bisexual Counseling (AGLIBIC), the International Association for Marriage and Family Counseling (IAMFC), the National Career Development Association (NCDA), the National Employment Counseling Association (NECA), and, of course, AMCD. The significance of these endorsements is underscored by the fact that no ACA division (with the exception of AMCD) had formally endorsed the multicultural counseling competencies up to that point in time.

The 1996 and 1997 multicultural town hall meetings

Besides providing professional development training services to enhance the cultural competence of ACA leaders and lobbying for the formal endorsement of the multicultural competencies from organizational entities in the association, the National Multicultural Ad Hoc Committee continued its commitment to mobilize the rank-and-file members of ACA in ways that provided them opportunities to directly participate in the multicultural movement. To accomplish this goal, the committee members submitted proposals to hold multicultural town hall meetings at the 1997 and 1998 annual ACA conventions.

These town hall meetings served multiple purposes including offering opportunities for ACA members to (a) describe successful multicultural counseling and development projects that they implemented in their work settings (*Mobilization* and *Education Strategies*), (b) openly discuss questions and concerns they had about various issues related to the multicultural counseling movement (*Education Strategy*), and (c) talk about ways in which the members of the association could help promote changes within the counseling profession that reflect an increased level of understanding, respect, and acceptance for multiculturalism and human diversity (*Organizing* and *Institutionalizing Strategies*).

Assisting in the development of ACA's multicultural and diversity agenda

In the Fall of 1997, several members of the National Multicultural Ad Hoc Committee were invited to participate in a leadership conference that was convened by ACA President Courtland Lee in Indianapolis, Indiana. The purpose of this leadership conference was to develop a comprehensive multicultural and diversity agenda that included numerous guidelines for promoting organizational changes that would distinguish ACA from all other professional mental health associations in the United States in terms of its commitment for multiculturalism and human diversity (*Organizing* and *Institutionalizing Strategies*). Not only did several members of the National Multicultural Ad Hoc Committee play important roles in this leadership conference, but President Lee used many of the training materials and other organizational development resources that the committee had developed during the Indianapolis conference.

Working with allies to address issues of social justice

Members of the National Multicultural Ad Hoc Committee recognized that, if they were to increase the impact they were having in the counseling profession, they would need to continue to develop new partnerships with persons who shared a similar commitment to realize the revolutionary potential of multiculturalism. As noted earlier in this chapter, the multicultural movement holds tremendous potential to promote a more democratic and just society. To realize this potential, members of the National Multicultural Ad Hoc Committee began consulting with a number of ACA members about the need to promote the professional counselor's role as social justice advocate. These consultation efforts led to a call for a meeting with other mental health professionals who were interested in developing a formal organizational entity designed to foster an expanded definition of the role of the professional counselor. This expanded role definition would include a clear description of the important interconnection that exists between the work counselors do to stimulate human development and the need to promote social justice and ameliorate various forms of oppression in our society.

Given the growing interest in this area, several members of the National Multicultural Ad Hoc Committee including Judy Daniels (University of Hawaii), Michael D'Andrea (University of Hawaii), Allen Ivey and Mary Bradford Ivey (Microtraining and Multicultural Development) worked with Judy Lewis (Governor's State University) to convene a special meeting of counselors from across the United States who were interested in discussing the counselor's role as social justice advocate. More than 40 persons attended a meeting that was held on November 16, 1998, at ACA headquarters in Alexandria, Virginia, to discuss these issues. This meeting resulted in the formation of a new affiliate group in the ACA called "Counselors for Social Justice" (CSJ; Guerra, 1999).

Although members of the National Multicultural Ad Hoc Committee played a pivotal role in the formation of CSJ, the genesis for this new organizational entity can be traced to the efforts of numerous persons who

acknowledged the important role counselors can play in fostering positive environmental conditions that promote the mental health and psychological well-being of large numbers of persons in our society. In this regard, Aubrey (1977) pointed out that the counselor's role as environmental change agent is clearly embedded in the historical development of the counseling profession. Aubrey's views on this topic have recently been reinforced by renewed attention that has been directed toward the counselor's role as social change agent (Lee & Walz, 1998) and client advocate (Lewis & Bradley, 2000). These roles have been noted to be particularly important to implement when working with clients who have historically been marginalized and oppressed in our society and underlie the principles upon which CSJ is founded.

BUILDING ON OUR INTERNAL STRENGTHS

In Summer 1997, members of the National Multicultural Ad Hoc Committee met for a two-day "think tank" meeting in Irvine, California. This meeting was designed to have the committee members take time to (a) assess the central challenges facing the multicultural movement; (b) evaluate the progress the committee had made since 1993 in terms of promoting organizational changes in the counseling profession that reflected a greater level of understanding, respect, and acceptance for multiculturalism; (c) discuss the need to support our own individual and collective development as multicultural theorists, researchers, practitioners, and advocates; and (d) outline new strategies for future action. A second think-tank meeting was held in 1998, also in Irvine, California, to continue discussions about these issues.

Several decisions were made during these think-tank meetings that influenced the committee's focus and direction in the coming months. These included:

- Defining and clarifying the overall purpose of the committee and the continuing role it should play in promoting multiculturalism and confronting various forms of racism in the fields of counseling and psychology
- Making a concerted effort to contribute to the building of a new epistemological base that would complement an evolving paradigm shift occurring in the mental health professions
- Discussing ways that this group could create new opportunities that would inspire a greater array of counselors and psychologists to become involved in meaningful planning for organization changes in the fields of counseling and psychology
- Describing strategies for expanding our organizational development efforts in APA as well as in ACA.

Name change: The National Institute for Multicultural Competence (NIMC)

As a result of defining and clarifying the overall purpose of the committee and discussing the members' long-term commitment to continue to work together to build on their past successes to foster additional organizational changes within the fields of counseling and psychology, it was decided that the time had come to change the name of the committee. Some of the underlying reasons for doing so included the need to (a) identify ourselves as an autonomous organization that is committed to long-term and substantial changes in the mental health professions, (b) reflect our collective commitment to continue to work to promote multicultural competence among individual counselors and psychologists, and (c) renew our commitment to foster more expansive multicultural organizational development initiatives in a variety of settings in the future. As a result of these considerations, it was unanimously agreed during the 1998 think-tank meeting that the National Multicultural Ad Hoc Committee would hence forth be called the National Institute for Multicultural Competence (NIMC).

Helping to build a new epistemological base

During the think-tank meetings, time was set aside for the NIMC members to discuss a variety of theoretical and research issues they were grappling with in their own work. Upon reflecting on the various theoretical and investigative projects in which members of the NIMC were involded, it becamse increasingly apparent that the collective research and writing skills of the persons in this group represented a unique and powerful asset that could be used to help transform the fields of counseling and psychology. It was hypothesized that, by using our research and writing skills to expand the existing epistemological base upon which the mental health professions have traditionally operated, the NIMC could have a tremendous impact in promoting behavioral changes among large numbers of counselors and psychologists in the future. For this reason, the members of the NIMC agreed to continue the practice of scheduling regular times during their think-tank meetings when they could engage in collaborative and supportive discussions about new theoretical models and research projects.

Although numerous persons have discussed the importance of building these sorts of collaborative and supportive endeavors among allies in the multicultural counseling movement (D'Andrea & Daniels, 2000; Kiselica, 1999), very little has been written about the successful implementation of these types of professional collaborative support groups. Not only did the NIMC members find these supportive collaborations helpful in stimulating new insights about various theoretical and research ideas with which they were grappling, but they also helped to enhance the members' creativity and productivity in working in these areas. Thus, besides publishing numerous journal articles and book chapters that directly address a variety

of issues related to human diversity from 1993 to 2000, NIMC members were responsible for publishing 12 new or revised books during this time period (Arredondo, 1996; Ivey, Ivey, & Simek-Mogan, 1997; Ivey & Ivey, 1999; Ivey, Pedersen, & Ivey, 2001; Lewis, Lewis, Daniels, & D'Andrea, 1998; Locke, 1998; Parham, 1993; Parham, White, & Ajamu, 1999; Pedersen & Locke, 1996; Sue & Sue, 1999; Sue et al., 1996; Sue et al., 1998). NIMC members also routinely collaborated with the editor of *Counseling Today* (a periodical published monthly by the ACA) regarding the publication of a regular column that focuses on multiculturalism and human diversity issues. As a result, 60 articles dealing with a wide range of issues related to multicultural and diversity counseling were published in *Counseling Today* from July 1994 to January 2001. Table 16.1 lists all the articles printed in this professional outlet during that time period.

Developing culture-specific counseling videos

Working in conjunction with leaders in Division 45 of APA, the NIMC recently completed another project that adds to the existing epistemological foundation upon which the fields of counseling and psychology are built. This project, titled "Innovative Approaches To Culture-Specific Counseling," was designed to address common questions and issues that practitioners have raised about the use of culture-specific counseling strategies. These videos include demonstrations of counseling techniques with African American, Asian American, Hispanic American, Native American Indian, and White European American clients. Allen Ivey (Microtraining and Multicultural Development) and Patricia Arredondo (Arizona State University) recruited several members of the NIMC and other multicultural experts with the intent of developing a set of videos that demonstrate some of the ways that practitioners can effectively and ethically implement culture-specific techniques in clinical settings. These videotapes provide counselors and psychologists with new ways of conceptualizing multicultural counseling and therapy as a variety of culture-specific counseling strategies are portrayed in five live 30- minute demonstrations.

EXPANDING OUR WORK IN THE APA

While most of the NIMC work since 1993 focused on ways to create organizational changes within ACA, members of the group agreed to expand their efforts by developing and implementing strategies to promote multiculturalism within APA. Most of the persons who comprised the NIMC have been long-time APA members. Several of us have also been actively involved in promoting multiculturalism in APA as active members of Divison 17 (Counseling Psychology) and Division 45 (Society for the Psychological Study of Ethnic Minority Issues). However, with the election of

TABLE 16.1 Summary of Multicultural and Diversity Columns Published in *Counseling Today*

Date	Title	Author(s)	Page No(s).
Sept 1994	Helping disadvantaged women	D'Andrea, M.	46
Oct 1994	Promoting the dignity of gay, lesbian, and bisexual students	D'Andrea, M.	24
Nov 1994	Supporting multicultural and diversity counseling within ACA	Arredondo, P., & D'Andrea, M.	24-25
Dec 1994	The impact of the November elections on counselors and the counseling profession	Arredondo, P., & D'Andrea, M	23, 29
Mar 1995	Caring for the caregivers in Denver: A special event for AIDS counselors	D'Andrea, M.	24, 25, 27
Apr 1995	Multicultural counseling at a crossroads	D'Andrea, M., & Arredondo, P.	48-49
Apr 1995	Revising ACA's Ethical Standards for a multicultural society	D'Andrea, M.	8
Aug 1995	AMCD clarifies the question of multicultural counseling competencies	D'Andrea, M.	45
Sept 1995	Developing a multicultural approach to group work: New challenges for professional counselors	D'Andrea, M., & Arredondo, P.	49-50
Jan 1996	Counselors react to the Million Man March	Arredondo, P., & D'Andrea, M.	44-45
Oct 1996	Counseling leaders and students call for increased multicultural counseling training	D'Andrea, M., & Arredondo, P.	25, 33
Nov 1996	Promoting multiculturalism and diversity in organizational settings	D'Andrea, M., & Arredondo, P.	59, 61, 65
Dec 1996	ACES formally endorses multicultural counseling competencies	D'Andrea, M., & Arredondo, P.	29, 30
Jan 1997	ACA leaders work together to address multicultural and diversity issues in the profession	D'Andrea, M., & Arredondo, P.	22-23
Apr 1997	And now we begin: Multicultural competencies gaining approval	Ivey, M. B., & Ivey, A. E.	40, 42
May 1997	The connection between multiculturalism and oppression	Arnold, M.S.	39, 42
July 1997	Multiculturalism and the counseling profession: Past achievements and future challenges	D'Andrea, M., & Arredondo, P.	33, 35
Aug 1997	Responding to President Clinton's call for a discussion about race in the United States	Daniels, J., & D'Andrea, M.	38, 44
Sept 1997	Enhancing diversity of ACA a goal of Courtland Lee's presidency	D'Andrea, M.	44
Oct 1997	Developing a comprehensive multicultural and diversity agenda for ACA	Arredondo, P., & D'Andrea, M.	43
Nov 1997	Providing culturally-sensitive grief counseling services to Filipino clients	D'Andrea, M., & Arredondo, P.	63
Dec 1997	Respectful Counseling: A new way of thinking about diversity counseling	D'Andrea, M., & Daniels, J.	30, 31, 34
Feb 1998	Q&A on the Multicultural Counseling Competencies	Arredondo, P., & D'Andrea, M.	38
Mar 1998	The art and heart of diversity practitioners	Arredondo, P.	42
May 1998	The counselor's role as social activist: Observations from the ACA 1998 World Conference	D'Andrea, M., & Arredondo, P.	37, 41

Date	Title	Author	Pages
Aug 1998	Increasing the impact of counseling in the 21st century	D'Andrea, M., & Arredondo, P.	36
Oct 1998	Learning to work upstream: Using social action and advocacy strategies in ACA	D'Andrea, M., & Arredondo, P.	34
Nov 1998	When White counselors work with African American clients: Some notes from the field	D'Andrea, M.	26-27
Dec 1998	Developing successful cross-cultural relationships with immigrants and refugees	Arredondo, P.	30-31
Jan 1999	Providing culturally competent disaster relief counseling services: Notes from the field	Arredondo, P., & D'Andrea, M.	38-39
Feb 1999	Integrating cultural and contextual issues into the interview: The community genogram	Ivey, A. E., & Ivey, M. B.	38, 40
Mar 1999	The challenge to change: A report from the 1999 National Multicultural Counseling Summit	D'Andrea, M., & Arredondo, P.	16, 22
Apr 1999	Media portrayals of multiculturalism and diversity	Arredondo, P., & D'Andrea, M.	23, 25
May 1999	Alternative needed for DSM-IV in a multicultural-postmodern society	D'Andrea, M.	44, 46
June 1999	Expanding counselors' thinking about the problem of violence	Daniels, J., Arredondo, P., & D'Andrea, M.	12, 17
July 1999	Give peace a chance: Developing violence prevention programs in schools	Daniels, J., Arredondo, P., & D'Andrea, M.	12,,31
Sept 1999	Bullying and school violence: The tip of the iceberg	Weinhold, B.	18
Aug 1999	Using cultural audits as tools for change	D'Andrea, Daniels, J., & Arredondo, P.	14
Oct 1999	Using focus groups and interviews to foster multicultural development	Arredondo, P., Daniels, J., & D'Andrea, M.	14
Nov 1999	How do Jews fit into the multicultural counseling movement?	Arredondo, P., & D'Andrea, M.	14, 36
Dec 1999	ACES conference highlights improvement and improvisation	Arredondo, P., & D'Andrea, M.	14
Jan 2000	Resolutions for the new millennium	Arredordo, P., & D'Andrea, M.	14, 28-29
Feb 2000	Using sports as a barometer of attitudes toward diversity	Arredondo, P., Daniels, J., & D'Andrea, M.	14, 39
Mar 2000	Institutional agendas for cultural competency: RACE 2000	Arredondo, P., & D'Andrea, M.	12
Apr 2000	Convergence of multiple identities presents new challenges	D'Andrea, M., & Arredondo, P.	12, 40
May 2000	Census 2000—Implications for counselors and educators	Arredondo, P., & D'Andrea, M.	12
June 2000	'Label-ese' as a form of control	Arredondo, P., McCarthy, J., & D'Andrea, M.	21, 30, 32
July 2000	Assessing multicultural competence—A professional issue of relevance	Arredondo, P., & D'Andrea, M.	30, 35
Aug 2000	Speaking truth to power: Dealing with difficult challenges	D'Andrea, M., & Arredondo, P.	30, 37
Sept 2000	Multiculturalism, presidential politics and counselors	D'Andrea, M., & Arredondo, P.	36, 38
Oct 2000	Cultural and linguistic diversity as a new community experience	D'Andrea, M., & Arredondo, P.	32, 34
Nov 2000	How cultural diversity affects predominately white towns	Ellis, C., Arredondo, P., & D'Andrea, M.	25
Dec 2000	The impact of Spanish-speaking newcomers in Alabama towns	Middleton, R., Arredondo, P., & D'Andrea, M.	24
Jan 2001	Politics, the election and the counseling profession	D'Andrea, M., & Arredondo, P.	24, 28

Derald Sue as the 1999–2000 president of Division 45, the NIMC had one of its own members in a major leadership position within APA.

Sue's presidency represented a milestone in promoting multiculturalism in APA. Like many of his predecessors who have done an outstanding job of advancing the principles and goals of multiculturalism in APA, President Sue worked hard to increase the level of understanding, respect, and acceptance for cultural-racial diversity in this nation's largest professional psychological association. In doing so, he routinely turned to the other members of the NIMC for consultation in planning strategies that would foster multicultural organizational development outcomes in APA. Besides providing suggestions about the types of activities that could promote these sorts of organizational outcomes, the NIMC remained a constant source of support for the bold and innovative initiatives that unfolded during Sue's 1999–2000 tenure as president of Division 45.

Many of these initiatives represented similar organizational development strategies that were found to be effective in ACA, among them (a) building meaningful organizational partnerships with allies and leaders in other APA divisions who were willing to work together to plan and implement activities that were intentionally designed to stimulate increased multicultural awareness, knowledge, and skills among the members of APA (*Organization* and *Institutionalizing Strategies*) and (b) assisting in the coordination of an unprecedented Opening Session at the 1999 Annual APA Convention that was aimed at increasing members' cultural sensitivity and understanding as well as encouraging greater direct involvement in the multicultural movement (*Education, Mobilization* and *Organization Strategies*).

The same theme (i.e., "Many Voices Into One Voice") used in the Opening Session of the 1995 ACA Convention was also adapted by the APA Convention Planning Committee for the Opening Session of the 1999 APA National Convention. The 1999 APA Opening Session incorporated a broad range of culturally diverse rituals, ceremonies, and speakers into the program and had Rev. Jesse Jackson, Sr. as the featured presenter for this major event. This Opening Session clearly represented one of APA's greatest demonstrations of support for multiculturalism in the association's history.

In addition to these achievements, President Sue played a major role in planning and coordinating the First National Multicultural Summit. This historic meeting, which was held in January 1999 in California, was attended by more than 500 multicultural theorists, researchers, trainers, and practitioners from across the United States (*Education, Mobilization*, and *Organization Strategies*). With APA as one of the cosponsors of this historic event, the association took another step in acknowledging its awareness and respect for the multicultural movement and the impact that it is having in the field.

Among the outcomes of the National Multicultural Summit were the publication of two major articles in the December 1999 issue of *American Psychologist* (D. W. Sue et al., 1999; S. Sue, 1999) and the production of four videotapes of the keynote speakers' presentations at the Summit. In one of these videotaped keynote presentations, NIMC member Thomas Parham outlined numerous challenges facing the profession and underscored the need for counselors, psychologists, and other mental health professionals to move toward multicultural competence (*Education* and *Institutionalizing Strategies*).

As president of Division 45, Sue also recruited members of the NIMC to serve on a committee that was charged with the task of writing an expanded version of the Multicultural Counseling Competencies initially developed by AMCD (Arredondo et al., 1996; Sue et al., 1992). While the original competencies represent generic standards that mental health practitioners are encouraged to acquire before working with persons from culturally diverse client populations, the newly developed APA guidelines comprise a set of standards for psychologists in professional psychology training programs, those involved in research, and psychological practitioners who primarily work in clinical settings. The development of the Guidelines for Multicultural Competencies in Education, Training, and Research represent a joint venture between Divisions 17 and 45 of APA. By working with leaders from several other APA Divisions in developing this expanded version of the multicultural competencies, NIMC members were able to gain broad-based support for the need to institutionalize these competencies in the profession. At the present time, the new multicultural guidelines are being circulated among various APA Divisions for their review and formal endorsement *(Organization* and *Institutionalizing Strategies*).

Last, Sue lobbied for the addition of several NIMC members on the Examination for Professional Practice in Psychology Test Item Task Force (EPPS). The purpose of this task force is to develop test items to be used in state and provincial psychology licensure examinations. Members of the NIMC were specifically selected to participate on this task force to assist in the development of new test items that are designed to measure an individual's multicultural awareness, knowledge, and skills. By participating on this important organizational task force, NIMC members were able to make additional inroads in institutionalizing multicultural considerations in the field of psychology (*Education* and *Institutionalizing Strategies*).

CONCLUDING COMMENTS

The organizational development strategies that were used by the members of the NIMC over the past seven years emerged as a result of the members' (a) belief in the revolutionary potential of the multicultural

movement, (b) commitment to work to help transform the fields of counseling and psychology, and (c) dedication to positively impact our society at
large. Four fundamental strategies were consistently used by the NIMC to
help realize the tremendous potential of multiculturalism. By implementing these strategies, the NIMC members hoped to further humanize and
democratize the mental health professions. These strategies included the
use of education, mobilization, organization, and institutionalizing strategies in their work. The NIMC used opening sessions at national counseling
and psychology conventions, town hall meetings, and professional development workshops to mobilize and organize thousands of persons from different specialty areas and cultural-racial backgrounds in ACA and APA.

Sometimes, the primary purpose of these organizational efforts was to
educate leaders and members of the counseling and psychology professions
about various issues related to human diversity, racism, and the tremendous potential of the multicultural movement.

Other times, the interventions were designed to promote the democratization of the helping professions. This was accomplished by creating new
organizational vehicles in which persons whose voices often go unheard
within traditional institutional structures are able to (a) respectfully express their views about the challenges they face working as mental health
practitioners within the context of a multicultural society and (b) offer input regarding their thoughts on the types of changes our professional associations need to make to remain relevant and viable in the 21st century.

The members of the NIMC also worked in a collaborative and supportive manner to dismantle the intellectual hegemony of Western psychological thought and expand the epistemological foundation on which the fields
of counseling and psychology are based. In doing so, we did and continue to
publish numerous articles and books that reflect our individual and collective thinking, theoretical insights, and research findings in a variety of
professional outlets. We also participated in a cooperative endeavor that resulted in the development of new educational audio-video tapes that model
cultural-specific approaches to counseling and therapy.

All of these achievements evolved out of an expressed willingness of
nine multicultural counselors and psychologists to work together to create
positive changes in our society in general and within our professional organizations in particular. Although we come from different cultural-racial
backgrounds and frequently express differing views about various aspects
of the multicultural movement, we share a common vision and commitment regarding the need to build a better society in the 21st century—a society that manifests a greater level of democracy and reflects a heightened
understanding, sensitivity, respect, and acceptance of human differences.

Our discussion about the success and challenges experienced by the
NIMC would not be complete without mention of the process dynamics
involved in sustaining the group. Hilliard (1997) teaches us that counselors

and psychologists are healers, and as such, should conduct their affairs with a recognition of the qualities that distinguish them. He reminds us that healers need to subdue pride and arrogance, aspire to perfection, and be open to all (a good listener). All of the NIMC members have been diligent and courageous in their efforts to achieve congruence between these attributes and the ways in which they conduct their professional affairs and interpersonal relations.

The updated information about the work the NIMC has undertaken since 1993 describes some of the organizational development strategies we have found to be useful in promoting positive changes in ACA and APA. However, in order to have a larger scale impact in the fields of counseling and psychology, these efforts need to be expanded and complemented by other professionals who are committed to making positive things happen in our profession and society. It is hoped that this updated case study provides other multicultural advocates with concrete ideas about some of the strategies they might find useful in creating organizational changes in ACA and APA. We also hope that it might serve as a source of inspiration for those persons who are interested in fostering the development of a more democratic, humane, and respectful nation in the coming decades.

REFERENCES

Arredondo, P. (1996). *Successful diversity management initiatives: A blueprint for planning and implementation*. Thousand Oaks, CA: Sage.

Arredondo, P., Toporek, R., Brown, S. P., Jones, J., Locke, D. C., Sanchez, J., & Stadler, H. (1996). Operationalization of the multicultural counseling competencies. *Journal of Multicultural Counseling and Development, 24*, 42-78.

Atkinson, D. R., Morten, G., & Sue, D. W. (1998). *Counseling American minorities* (5th ed.). Boston: McGraw-Hill.

Aubrey, R. (1977). Historical development of guidance and counseling and implications for the future. *Personnel & Guidance Journal, 55*, 288-295.

Banks, J. A., & McGee Banks, C. A. (Eds.). (1997). *Multicultural education: Issues and perspectives* (3rd ed.). Needham Heights, MA: Allyn & Bacon.

Dana, R. H. (1993). *Multicultural assessment perspectives for professional psychology*. Boston: Allyn & Bacon.

D'Andrea, M. (1992). The violence of our silence: Some thoughts about racism, counseling, and development. *Guidepost, 35*(4), 31.

D'Andrea, M. (2000). Postmodernism, constructivism, and multiculturalism: Three forces reshaping and expanding our thoughts about counseling. *Journal of Mental Health Counseling, 22*, 1-16.

D'Andrea, M., & Daniels, J. (2000). Facing the changing demographic structure of our society. In D. C. Locke, J. E. Myers, & E. L. Herr (Eds.), *The handbook of counseling* (pp. 529-539). Thousand Oaks, CA: Sage.

D'Andrea, M., & Daniels, J. (1995). Promoting multiculturalism and organizational change in the counseling profession: A case study. In J. G. Ponterotto, J. M. Casas, L. A. Suzuki, & C. M. Alexander (Eds.), *Handbook of multicultural counseling* (pp. 17-33). Thousand Oaks, CA: Sage.

D'Andrea, M., Locke, D. C., & Daniels, J. (1997, April). *Dealing with racism: Counseling strategies.* A workshop presented at the annual meeting of the American Counseling Association, Orlando, FL.

Daniels, J., & D'Andrea, M. (1996). MCT theory and ethnocentrism in counseling. In D. W. Sue, A. E. Ivey, & P. B. Pedersen (Eds.), *A theory of multicultural counseling and therapy* (pp. 157-174). Pacific Grove, CA: Brooks/Cole.

Daniels, J., & D'Andrea, M. (2000, March). *Counseling for social justice.* Paper presented at the annual meeting of the American Counseling Association, Washington, DC.

Guerra, P. (1999, June). Counselors for social justice becomes organizational affiliate. *Counseling Today, 41,* 1, 25.

Herring, R. D. (1997). *Counseling diverse ethnic youth.* Fort Worth, TX: Harcourt Brace.

Hilliard, A. G. (1997). *SBA: The reawakening of the African mind.* Gainesville, FL: Makare.

Ivey, A. E. (1995). Psychotherapy as liberation: Toward specific skills and strategies in multicultural counseling and psychotherapy. In J. G. Ponterotto, J. M. Casas, L. A. Suzuki, & C. M. Alexander (Eds.), *Handbook of multicultural counseling* (pp. 53-72). Thousand Oaks, CA: Sage.

Ivey, A. E., & Ivey, M. B. (1999). *Intentional interviewing and counseling: Facilitating development in a multicultural society.* Pacific Grove, CA: Brooks/Cole.

Ivey, A. E., Ivey, M. B., & Simek-Morgan, L. (1997). *Counseling and psychotherapy: A multicultural perspective.* Boston: Allyn & Bacon.

Ivey, A. E., Pedersen, P. B., & Ivey, M. B. (2001). *Group counseling: A multicultural perspective.* Pacific Grove, CA: Brooks/Cole.

Jones, J. M. (1997). *Prejudice and racism* (2nd ed.). New York: McGraw-Hill.

Kiselica, M. S. (Ed.). (1999). *Prejudice and racism: During multicultural training.* Alexandria, VA: American Counseling Association.

Lee, C. C. (1996). MCT theory and implications for indigenous healing. In D. W. Sue, A. E. Ivey, & P. B. Pedersen (Eds.), *A theory of multicultural counseling and therapy* (pp. 86-98). Pacific Grove, CA: Brooks/Cole.

Lee, C. C., & Walz, G. (1998). *Social action: A mandate for counselors.* Alexandria, VA: American Counseling Association.

Lewis, J., & Bradley, L. (Eds.). (2000). *Advocacy in counseling: Counselors, clients, and community.* Greensboro, NC: ERIC Counseling and Student Services Clearinghouse.

Lewis, J. A., Lewis, M. D., Daniels, J. A., & D'Andrea, M. J. (1998). *Community counseling.* Pacific Grove, CA: Brooks/Cole.

Locke, D. C. (1998). *Increasing multicultural understanding: A comprehensive model.* Thousand Oaks, CA: Sage.

McDermott, J. F., Tseng, W., & Maretzki, T. W. (1980). *People and cultures of Hawaii: A psychocultural profile.* Honolulu: University of Hawaii Press.

McIntosh, P. (1989, July/August). White privilege: Unpacking the invisible knapsack. *Peace and Freedom,* pp. 8-10.

McWhirter, E. H. (1994). *Counseling for empowerment.* Alexandria, VA: American Counseling Association.

O'Bryant, B. J. (1999). College counseling center directors' perceptions of effective techniques for increasing student retention of high risk college freshmen utilizing an individualized counseling model. *Dissertation Abstracts International, 265,* 99-268.

Parham, T. A. (1993). White researchers conducting multicultural counseling research: Can their efforts be "mo betta"? [Reaction]. *The Counseling Psychologist, 21,* 250-256.

Parham, T. A. (1996). MCT theory and African-American populations. In D. W. Sue, A. E. Ivey, & P. B. Pedersen (Eds.), *A theory of multicultural counseling and therapy* (pp. 177-191). Pacific Grove, CA: Brooks/Cole.

Parham, T. A., White, J., & Ajamu, A. (1999). *The psychology of blacks: An African centered perspective.* Upper Saddle River, NJ: Prentice Hall.

Pedersen, P. B., & Locke, D. C. (Eds.). (1996). *Cultural and diversity counseling.* Greensboro, NC: ERIC Counseling and Student Services Clearinghouse.

Ponterotto, J. G., Casas, J. M., Suzuki, L. A., & Alexander, C. M. (Eds.). (1995). *Handbook of multicultural counseling.* Thousand Oaks, CA: Sage.

Ponterotto, J. G., & Pedersen, P. B. (1993). *Preventing prejudice.* Newbury Park, CA: Sage.

Ridley, C. R. (1995). *Overcoming unintentional racism in counseling and therapy: A practitioner's guide to intentional intervention.* Thousand Oaks, CA: Sage.

Sandhu, D. S., & Aspy, C. B. (1997). *Counseling for prejudice prevention and reduction.* Alexandria, VA: American Counseling Association.

Santiago-Rivera, A.L., Vazquez, L. A., & Aviles-Davison, R. (1999, October). *The deconstruction and reconstruction of counselor education curriculum: Meeting the needs of diversity for the 21st century.* Paper presented at the annual meeting of the Association for Counselor Education and Supervision, New Orleans.

Sue, D. W. (1995). Multicultural organizational development: Implications for the counseling profession. In J. G. Ponterotto, J. M. Casas, L. A. Suzuki, & C. M. Alexander (Eds.), *Handbook of multicultural counseling* (pp. 474-492). Thousand Oaks, CA: Sage.

Sue, D. W., Arredondo, P., & McDavis, R. J. (1992). Multicultural competencies/standards: A call to the profession. *Journal of Counseling and Development, 70,* 477-486.

Sue, D. W., Bingham, R. P., Porche-Burke, L., & Vasquez, M. (1999). The diversification of psychology: A multicultural perspective. *American Psychologist, 54,* 1061-1069.

Sue, D. W., Carter, R. T., Casas, J. M., Foad, N. A., Ivey, A. E., Jensen, M., LaFromboise, T., Manese, J. E., Ponterotto, J. G., & Vasquez-Nuttall, E. (1998). *Multicultural counseling competencies: Individual and organizational development.* Thousand Oaks, CA: Sage.

Sue, D. W., Ivey, A. E., & Pedersen, P. B. (Eds.). (1996). *A theory of multicultural counseling and therapy.* Pacific Grove, CA: Brooks/Cole.

Sue, D. W., & Sue, D. (1980). *Counseling the culturally different: Theory and practice.* New York: John Wiley.

Sue, D. W., & Sue, D. (1990). *Counseling the culturally different: Theory and practice* (2nd ed.). New York: John Wiley.

Sue, D. W., & Sue, D. (1999). *Counseling the culturally different: Theory and practice* (3rd ed.). New York: John Wiley.

Sue, S. (1999). Science, ethnicity, and bias: Where have we gone wrong? *American Psychologist, 54,* 1070-1077.

Washington, J. M. (Ed.). (1986). *A testament of hope: The essential writings of Martin Luther King, Jr.* New York: Harper & Row.

West, C. (1999). *The Cornel West reader.* New York: Basic Civitas Books.

White, J. L., & Parham, T. A. (1990). *The psychology of Blacks: An African-American perspective.* Englewood Cliffs, NJ: Prentice Hall.

Wrenn, C. G. (1962). The culturally encapsulated counselor. *Harvard Educational Review, 32,* 444-449.

Wrenn, C. G. (1985). Afterword: The culturally encapsulated counselor revisited. In P. B. Pedersen (Ed.), *Handbook of cross-cultural counseling and therapy* (pp. 323-329). Westport, CT: Greenwood.

Correspondence regarding this chapter may be sent to Michael D'Andrea, Department of Counselor Education, University of Hawaii, 1776 University Avenue, Honolulu, HI 96822 (e-mail address: Michael@hawaii.edu).

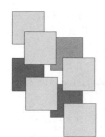

Part III

COUNSELOR ROLES IN UNDERSTANDING AND FIGHTING OPPRESSION

A central theme evident throughout this *Handbook* is the important role of counselors in advocating for social justice issues. The need for counselors to be proactive in fighting racism, sexism, homophobia, and so forth can be gleaned from the life histories in Part I and from the discussion of ethics and professional issues in Part II. This third section of the *Handbook* addresses directly the need for counselors to be aware of their own racial/ethnic socialization, their potential unearned privilege based on race, and the impact of racism on society and on counseling practice.

In Chapter 17, Neville, Worthington, and Spanierman present a detailed and illuminating discussion of the interrelated constructs of White privilege and color-blind racial attitudes. These authors clearly define their constructs and link them to multicultural counseling competence. The relationships of White privilege and color-blind racial attitudes to training and research are highlighted. Finally, the authors enumerate specific color-conscious policies and practices that will be essential to the advancement of the counseling profession. To effectively prepare counselors and psychologists for work in an increasingly multicultural society, the profession generally, and training programs specifically, must address the core constructs presented here.

Two renowned scholars who have devoted their professional careers to understanding and fighting racism are D'Andrea and Daniels. In Chapter 18, these authors summarize the results of 16 years of research on White racism. Using qualitative methods, namely, interviews and participant observation, the authors identified transcendent patterns and themes explaining how White persons, particularly White mental health professionals and university students, react to racism in U.S. society. D'Andrea and Daniels's chapter flows well from the related constructs of White privilege and color-blind racial attitudes presented by Neville et al. in Chapter 17.

Part III concludes with Chapter 19 by Utsey, Bolden, and Brown in which they discuss the history and impact of racism on African Americans in the United States. Building on the historic and visionary work of Fanon, Bulhan, and Freire, the authors propose a psychology of liberation modality for mental health professionals working with African Americans confronting societal racism and oppression. Writing through the lens of both historians and visionary healers, Utsey et al. provide the reader with an essential conceptual foundation for working with issues of racism.

Part III of the *Handbook* provides the practitioner and researcher with an essential understanding of racism in the United States. Topics and issues are discussed that have been relatively ignored in most training programs. We expect that this cadre of chapters will have a major impact on counseling training in coming years, and in fact we see these three chapters serving as an excellent scholarly base for a graduate course on racism and mental health.

Chapter 17

Race, Power, and Multicultural Counseling Psychology

Understanding White Privilege and Color-Blind Racial Attitudes

HELEN A. NEVILLE
ROGER L. WORTHINGTON
LISA B. SPANIERMAN

OVER THE PAST 30 years, counseling psychology has made tremendous progress in moving the field from one that adheres to a culturally encapsulated framework toward one that embraces a multiculturally relevant framework. Many social factors have influenced this transformation, including the impact of the civil rights, Black Power, Chicano, Native American, and women's movements of the 1960s and 1970s. These movements transformed the curriculum on college campuses through the establishment of various ethnic studies and women's studies departments. These movements also influenced production of knowledge within specific disciplines. For example, the field of psychology witnessed the development of organizations and units related to racial and ethnic psychology during this period (e.g., Association of Black Psychologists, Asian American Psychological Association, and Association for Multicultural Counseling and Development) as well as journals designed to promote theoretical and empirical research on racial and ethnic issues (e.g., *Journal of Black Psychology* and *Journal of Multicultural Counseling and Development*).

Early developments such as the above along with recent demographic trends have had a profound impact on continual advancements in the field. We now have a cluster of second- and third-generation multicultural psychology scholars. These advancements have resulted in increased professional leadership (e.g., presidents of the APA, the ACA, and specific divisions within each of the national organizations) and in tangible outcomes, such as the creation of the Multicultural Psychology Summit, establishment of the APA journal *Cultural Diversity and Ethnic Minority Psychology,* and in increased publications on racial and ethnic minority populations in mainstream journals. For example, *Journal of Counseling Psychology* doubled its publications on racial and ethnic issues from 6% between 1976 and 1986 to 12% between 1988 and 1997 (Perez, Constantine, & Gerard, 2000), and in *The Counseling Psychologist,* 34%, or 5 out of 16 of its major articles published in 1997–1999, focused solely on race and ethnicity (Heppner, 2000).

Counseling psychology's efforts to better attend to multicultural issues in training has led to the commonly held assertion that multicultural counseling is the fourth force in counseling psychology (Pedersen, 1991). Although full integration of diversity into counseling psychology activities (e.g., training activities, curricula, and research on a variety of topics such as counseling process, vocational psychology, and measurement) has yet to be actualized, the field has witnessed great strides in terms of increased awareness and stronger commitment to multicultural issues, especially issues related to race and ethnicity. For example, the overwhelming majority of counseling psychology programs offer a multiculturally focused course and there has been swift growth in curricula developments in this area (see Heppner, Casas, Carter, & Stone, 2000, for a review of advancements in these areas; see Constantine & Gloria, 1999, for a description of the strengths and limitations of multicultural predoctoral training).

The subfield of multicultural counseling psychology, itself, has rapidly developed in terms of both theoretical and empirical advancements. One area witnessing the greatest progression has been in the conceptualization and measurement of multicultural counseling competencies. Although there are several models delineating competencies in the area, most focus on issues related to race and ethnicity and incorporate three broad domains: (a) awareness of one's own values, beliefs, and prejudices; (b) knowledge about cultural realities of various ethnic groups (e.g., worldview, racial identity); and (c) possession of culturally relevant intervention skills and techniques (Arredondo, 1999; Constantine & Ladany, Chapter 25, this volume). This research has influenced the broader field of counseling psychology as evident by the adoption of Sue, Arredondo, and McDavis's (1992a, 1992b) list of multicultural counseling competencies by Division 17 of the American Psychological Association and six divisions within the American Counseling Association (Ponterotto, Fuertes, & Chen, 2000). Adoption of multicultural competencies coupled with subsequent training efforts are methods designed to increase the prospect that psychologists are providing ethical services to a wide range of populations in clinical and academic settings, a moral principle included in the 1992 revised APA Code of Ethical Principles.

It is fairly clear that multicultural counseling competencies (MCC) play an important role in the professional development of counseling psychologists. The purpose of this chapter is to build on the theoretical MCC work to date by articulating two emerging constructs that are conceptually related to MCC but have received little attention in the multicultural psychology literature: White privilege and color-blind racial attitudes. Conceptualizations of White privilege have been part of the flourishing interdisciplinary scholarship in Whiteness studies (cf. Fine, Weis, Powell, & Wong, 1997; Kincheloe, Steinberg, Rodriguez, & Chennault, 1998) and articulations of color-blindness have been the focus of popular books and an APA monograph (e.g., American Psychological Association, 1997; Carr, 1997). Consistent with conceptualizations of MCC, a base premise of our work is the understanding that, "in all cases, the counselor, client and counseling process are influenced by the state of race relations in the larger society" (Sue et al., 1992b, p. 479). That is, we situate our discussions of White privilege and color-blind racial attitudes within the context of racism (a reflection of race relations in the United States). Specifically, the chapter is divided into three main sections. In the first section, we first briefly define racism and then operationalize White privilege and color-blind racial attitudes. Our primary premise undergirding this section is that the United States is a racially stratified society in which "peoples and nationalities have been *racialized*, that is, converted into superior and subordinate "races" (Cha-Jua & Lang, 1999, p. 28) and that White privilege and color-blind racial attitudes are products of this system. We follow the explication of these key terms with discussions in Section 2 of the application of White privilege and color-blind racial attitudes to multicultural counseling psychology training and research. In the concluding section, we focus on countering the impact of White privilege and color-blind racial attitudes in the profession by implementing color-conscious policies and practices.

RACISM AND ITS COROLLARIES: WHITE PRIVILEGE AND COLOR-BLIND RACIAL ATTITUDES

Racism

Racism is a complex and multifaceted social system. Traditional psychological conceptualizations of racism have centered on "a set of ideas or beliefs [that] . . . are regarded as having the potential to lead individuals to develop prejudice" (Bonilla-Silva, 1996, p. 466). Racism thus has been viewed as an ideology or expression of racialism (i.e., belief in inherent superiority and inferiority of groups of people based on racial classification) and racial animus (i.e., hatred, hostile feelings) by individuals, groups of people, or society in general. Racial ideology, as such, is a core component of racism. Racism, however, is not limited to a set of ideas held by individuals or groups. There is also a structural component of racism that is rooted in the way our society is organized in terms of economics, politics, and social institutions and has real consequences on the material conditions of people. Sociologist Joseph Whitmeyer further defines structures as "the networks of (interactional) relationships among actors as well as the distributions of socially meaningful characteristics of actors and aggregates of actors" (cited in Bonilla-Silva, 1996, p. 469). Acknowledgment of the interactional role of individuals and groups (i.e., actors) in creating, maintaining, resisting, and changing race relations is critical in understanding the dynamic nature of both ideological and structural dimensions of racism.

The recursive relationship between ideological and structural racism manifests itself as a set of systemic practices and corresponding ideological beliefs (i.e., stereotypes of racial superiority and inferiority) resulting in and perpetuating a racial hierarchy in which White individuals as a group are garnered privileges from which racial and ethnic minority groups are systematically excluded (Thompson & Neville, 1999). Racism is a "critical component in the organization of modern American society" characterized most critically by the "superior position of whites and the institutions— ideological as well as structural—which maintain it" (Wellman, 1993, pp. 54-55). Layered within each of the structural and ideological components are multiple interlocking types of racism that exist on macro (e.g., institutional level or policies, practices, and norms that perpetuate inequality) and micro levels (e.g., individual- or group-level racial prejudice) (see Jones, 1997, and Thompson & Neville, 1999, for a more detailed discussion).

The racial discourse in psychology has focused on the "disadvantaged," or those who have endured under macro and micro levels of racism. However, there is a dialectic of racism—one cannot understand "disadvantaged" without having a critical understanding of "advantaged," or in this instance, those who benefit from the system of racial oppression. Our focus is on the power component of the racism dialectic. Our intent is not to deny the profound impact of racism on the lives of people of color, nor the multitude of ways in which racial and ethnic minorities resist racial oppression. Instead, we intend to articulate an underdeveloped element of the racism dialectic in the counseling psychology literature, *White privilege.* We are also interested in understanding another underexamined corollary of racism, *color-blind racial attitudes,* or the denial of the existence of racism and subsequent benefits provided to Whites and disadvantages to people of color.

White Privilege

> White privilege means having entry to structures and institutions that mete out important economic opportunities, having access to neighborhoods, jobs, credit, and tax benefits that by and large are off limits or available in limited fashion to minorities; it means being presumed competent, intelligent, and hardworking; it means not being discriminated against daily by anyone ranging from a restaurant attendant to a car salesperson. (Lazos Vargas, 1998, p. 1527)

> I have come to see white privilege as an invisible package of unearned assets, which I can count on cashing in each day, but about which I was "meant" to remain oblivious. . . . The pressure to avoid it is great, for in facing it I must give up the myth of meritocracy. . . . Some privileges make me feel at home in the world. Others allow me to escape penalties or dangers which others suffer. . . . I [can] measure up to the cultural standards and take advantage of the many options I [see] around me to make what the culture would call a success of my life. . . . Whites are taught to think of their lives as morally neutral, normative, and average, and also ideal, so that when we work to benefit others, this is seen as work which will allow "them" to be more like "us." . . . Moreover, though privilege may confer power, it does not confer moral strength. (McIntosh, 1988, pp. 1-13)

Educator Peggy McIntosh is arguably one of the most cited authorities on White privilege. Her pathbreaking work in the 1980s outlined specific White and male privileges; she also provided a language for social scientists to discuss the nebulous advantages of being White in the United States. Since her work and also that of historian David Roediger's in the early 1990s, there has been a remarkable surge of interest and theoretical writings on the general topic of Whiteness (cf. Kincheloe et al., 1998). By unveiling the privileges associated with Whiteness, researchers have created a space for public dialogue on what it means to be White in a racial hierarchy. In this section, we draw on the insights from the interdisciplinary literature (ranging from educators to critical race theorists) to further explicate the core components and function of White privilege. Our goal is to provide a concrete understanding of White privilege to help contextualize our later discussion on the implications of race and power in the field of counseling psychology.

According to *Webster's Dictionary*, privilege is defined as "the right or immunity enjoyed by a person or persons beyond the common advantages of others; the principle or condition of enjoying special rights or immunities" (Finnegan, Heisler, Miller, & Usery, 1981, p. 1187). This broad definition of privilege can be extended to the concept of racial privilege, or more specifically, White privilege. White privilege results from an identifiable racial hierarchy that creates a system of social advantages or "special rights" for Whites based primarily on race rather than merit. Thus, as suggested by several social scientists (e.g., Bonilla-Silva, 1996; Helms, 1995), within this racial hierarchy, Whites are assumed to be entitled to more than an equitable share in the allocation of resources and opportunities. It is defined as an expression of power arising from receipt of benefits, rights, and immunities and is characterized by unearned advantages and a sense of entitlement that results in both societal and material dominance by Whites over people of color. These unearned advantages are invisible and often unacknowledged by those who benefit. The usurped power is conferred, maintained, and reinforced by a culturally constructed set of symbols and protocols (or societal norms) acting as sanctions for the expression of privilege.

We next elaborate on each of the following interrelated core components and processes of White privilege:

- Differentially benefits Whites
- Embodies both macro- (e.g., systems) and micro- (e.g., individual) level expressions
- Consists of unearned advantages
- Offers immunity to selected social ills
- Embodies an expression of power
- Is largely invisible and unacknowledged
- Contains costs to Whites

A basic assumption of the definition of White privilege is that Whiteness in and of itself confers both real and perceived powers that are not conferred on people of color on the same basis. However, *benefits afforded to Whites differ greatly depending on other social group membership.* For example, White women do not receive the same level of economic advantages as do White men; White gay men and lesbians do not receive the same level of social advantages as heterosexual men and women; and White working-class and poor individuals do not receive the same level of educational advantages as their middle-class and wealthy counterparts.

Similar to racism, White privilege is multidimensional and can be constructed on both *macro and micro levels.* Macrolevel privileges are structural in nature and typically refer to the myriad benefits, rights, and immunities afforded Whites within U.S. institutions (e.g., health care, schools). These benefits often manifest themselves as social advantages one generally has access to on the basis of one's racial group membership. Microlevel privileges center on advantages often observed on an individual or group level. Overwhelmingly, these advantages evidence themselves intrapsychically and interpersonally (e.g., sense of entitlement to resources).

Macrolevel White privilege is often expressed in terms of *unearned advantages,* in which individuals wittingly or unwittingly reap the benefits of the racial status quo. According to *Changing America: Indicators of Social and Economic Well-Being by Race and Hispanic Origin* (Council of

Economic Advisors for the President's Initiative on Race, 1998) and the National Center for Education Statistics (1997), on average, Whites are more likely than members of racial-ethnic minority groups to experience the following:

- Attendance at primary and secondary schools with smaller class sizes
- Accessibility to computer technology in public schools and at home during primary and secondary schooling
- Graduation from a 4-year college or university
- Higher salaries
- Continued employment during a downturn in the economy
- Health insurance coverage and consequently access to health care
- Recovery from certain life-threatening illnesses (e.g., cancer)
- More favorable housing conditions (e.g., less crowding, less crime, less litter and deterioration, and fewer problems with public services)
- Smaller percentage of household income spent on housing
- Unimpeded access to home mortgage loans and home ownership
- Ownership of stocks, mutual funds, and IRA/Keogh accounts
- Substantial net worth

This list of advantages is obviously not exhaustive, and our intent is not to elaborate on the myriad institutional privileges that exist in the racial hierarchy but to illustrate macrolevel types of White privilege.

Although Whites are not entirely *"immune" from social ills*, macrolevel racial privilege may help mitigate against negative life experiences for some Whites. One area where we see racial privilege providing Whites, especially White middle-class persons, some sense of protection is in the criminal justice system. On average, compared to people of color, Whites receive less stringent sentencing for committing similar offenses. For example, in "1995: whites accounted for 52% of all crack users, African Americans: 38%. However, of those sentenced for crack offenses—88% were African American, 4.1% were white" (Goldberg & Evans, 1998, back page). Similarly, a recent national report compiled by the Leadership Council on Civil Rights and the Building Blocks for Youth organizations found that African American youths were 6 times more likely to be incarcerated than White American youths for committing similar offenses, even when the youths had similar previous criminal records (Texeira, 2000). Taken together, these data paint a stark difference in the enforcement of laws and in sentencing practices against African American compared to White offenders; racial privilege thus provides Whites as a group some protection against facing imprisonment for nonviolent offenses.

A core dimension of White privilege is that it is an *expression of power*, which influences and maintains both macro and micro levels of privilege. As such, we view White privilege as not only an attitude or belief characterized by status and entitlement but also as an active expression of power (conscious or unconscious) that serves to maintain status and increase access to desired goals. Pinderhughes (1989) identifies power as "an often unspoken but central dynamic in cross-cultural encounters" (p. 109) that exists on various levels, including individual, interactive, and societal. White privilege is an expression of racially conferred power that operates at all three levels. "Power is a stance that undergirds certain ... societal values: status, perfection, possession, achievement, competition, independence, and so forth" (Pinderhughes, 1989, p. 112). As a cornerstone of the racial hierarchy in the United States, *power* is associated with notions of mastery, strength, authority, dominance, superiority, influence, and control (Finnegan et al., 1981; Pinderhughes, 1989).

Also, the *invisible, unacknowledged* nature of White privilege is achieved as a result of culturally laden symbols and protocols, which reflect the racial hierarchy and the societal value system that favor Whiteness, and the sociocultural norms, values, modes of communication, and standard operating procedures that govern everyday life; in essence, White privilege has become naturalized via hegemony. These racially biased symbols are consistent with the function of the ideological dimension of racism in that they shape false representations and stereotypes of various racial groups:

> The trope of race in both contemporary American [sic] life and academic studies is a reverberation of modernism (West, 1993). The modernist perspective views identities as marked territories or boundaries which must be categorized into socially ordered pairs. This facilitates the systematic process of naming positions of centrality and periphery, subject and object. Once named, the rhetoric of oppression serves to strategically sustain privilege. (Jackson, 1999, p. 42)

As a result, White privilege is institutionalized, based in White ethnocentric definitions of self and other, good and evil, right and wrong, and normal and abnormal.

Amoja Three Rivers (1991) reminds us that prevailing cultural aphorisms promote notions of Whiteness as positively valued and blackness as negatively valenced, making racial bias almost inescapable (e.g., "pure as the driven snow" [associating purity with Whiteness]; "the pot calling the kettle black" [associating guilt and deceit with blackness]; dark day, black heart, black mood [associating depression, sadness, and doom with darkness]; heavenly White light [associating sanctification with Whiteness]; the Dark Ages [associating darkness with economic and social depression]; "it's black and White" [associating color with the contrast between wrong and right]; and countless others). Even politically incorrect terms tend to reflect this pattern (e.g., "White trash," which despite its offensive, derogatory meaning, relies on the implied contrast between the decency associated with Whiteness and the repulsiveness associated with garbage). More subtly, the use of the term "American" implies reference to White

European Americans and aspects of the European American dominant cultural system, which abets the marking of territories and socially ordered pairs (i.e., Jackson, 1999, above) by reinforcing a self-reflected sense of self and belonging for Whites, while simultaneously promoting a sense of marginalization and contrasted self for people of color in the United States (not to mention people from South and Central American nations, Mexico, the Caribbean, and Canada). These simple, everyday uses of language reflect a deeply rooted racial and ethnic hierarchy, and are as problematic as the outdated use of masculine pronouns when referring to women or gender unspecified individuals, and yet they continue—hidden, invisible, unacknowledged. More obviously, stereotypes abound about Black and Latino men being violent and lazy. On the other hand, White people are constructed and portrayed as the cultural ideal. White men as a group are stereotyped as hard working and enterprising. These opposing images of Whites as hard working and deserving, and people of color as lazy (i.e., ideological representations in the form of culturally prescribed symbols and protocols) are used to define the very nature of human existence and the so-called natural order, which ultimately support, and advance privilege. As a result, privilege becomes self-reinforcing, and as invisible as the cultures within which human life is given meaning.

Extending findings on perceptions of privilege and discrimination based on gender (i.e., Postmes, Branscombe, Spears, & Young, 1999), we assert that self-serving attributions (i.e., the tendency to attribute successes internally and failures externally) make it difficult for Whites to acknowledge the privilege associated with their group membership, because people are generally reluctant to acknowledge that their positive outcomes might be externally controlled as a function of their group's privileged position. In addition, Postmes et al. (1999) found that failure to acknowledge privilege (among males), in part, was also a function of motives to maintain a positive self-image, a finding we suggest has implications for the individual form of White privilege as well. Ultimately, self-serving and group-preserving motives promote an ethnocentric preference for symbols and protocols within individuals and institutions that both *reflect* and *maintain* a system of privilege based on the racial hierarchy, as described above.

A sense of *personal entitlement* is also a psychological outcome of racial privilege. Closely linked to the meritocracy myth or the belief that anyone who works hard can achieve social and economic success (a cultural symbol), some Whites may feel that as an "individual," they are entitled to good jobs and economic advancement because they worked hard and they deserve the benefits (self-serving, face-saving attribution). These attitudes are juxtaposed with negative views about racial and ethnic minorities who are perceived as less deserving of the same rewards (Rains, 1998). Illustratively, in the movie *Rosewood*—John Singleton's 1996 acclaimed drama on the Black Florida community that was destroyed by racially motivated violence in 1921—one of the White townspeople rationalized the racial mob violence by blaming Black residents' economic autonomy, personal dignity, and the perceived "undeserved" material wealth of community members. The following quote exemplifies this position, "Sylvester [a Black resident] has a piano; I don't even have a piano." Although the character doesn't know how to play the piano, the assumption undergirding this simple statement supports the racism-related attitude that Blacks have more than they deserve, while simultaneously supporting the notion that Whites, regardless of class, are entitled to greater material wealth than any Black person. Although this is a fictional account, the sentiment captures attitudes widely discussed by people of color.

Another specific expression of racial privilege closely linked to cultural symbols is the guarantee that one's human dignity will not be called into question by power structures or those who benefit from racial privilege because of one's racial group membership. Joshua Solomon's 1990s racial transformation from a White college student to a Black male illuminates this point. Inspired by Griffith's 1959 book *Black Like Me*, an account of a White journalist who chemically altered his skin color to explore life as a Black man in the segregated South, Solomon set out to explore contemporary race relations. After chemically darkening his skin color, Solomon sojourned to the South. On his second day of living as a Black male, he observed,

> I hardly started on my journey, but I was already furious, almost to the point of paralysis. I began to cry as I recounted the events of the last two days, the drip-drop of indifference and fear from the White people I had encountered. Their lack of patience, their downright contempt . . . I was sick of being black. I couldn't take it anymore. I wanted to throw up. Enough is enough, I thought. I didn't need to be hit over the head with a baseball bat to understand what was going on here. Usually, I'd made friends pretty easily, I was nice to them and they were nice to me. Now people acted like they hated me. Nothing changed but the color of my skin. (Solomon, 2000, pp. 463-464)

After two days, Solomon ended his experiment, commenting, "Maybe I was weak, maybe I couldn't hack it. I didn't care. This anger was making me sick and the only antidote I knew was a dose of White skin" (p. 464). Solomon's journey piercingly exemplifies how White American cultural symbols permeate social interactions and serve to affirm or repudiate one's basic humanity based on perceived racial classification. People of color do not have the privilege of reverting to White skin to obtain relief from experiencing the dehumanization associated with the microaggressions Solomon encountered. However, people of color maintain self-worth and dignity by relying on established networks of racially or ethnically similar communities and resources, networks that are steeped in culturally relevant symbols that affirm one's basic humanity.

Although racial privilege provides unearned advantages to Whites, it also creates a structure of costs. These *costs to Whites* who seemingly benefit from racial privilege are rarely explicated in the interdisciplinary literature. Developmental psychologist Beverly Tatum (1992) captures the link between racial privilege and disadvantage to Whites:

> In the context of U.S. society, [racism as a] system of advantage clearly operates to benefit Whites as a group. However, it is assumed that racism, like other forms of oppression, *hurts members of the privileged group* as well as those targeted by racism. While the impact of racism on Whites is clearly different from its impact on people of color, racism has *negative ramifications for everyone.* (p. 3, emphasis added)

We argue that the costs of racism that Tatum alludes to are dynamic and like racism exist on macro (e.g., the narrowing of the human capital base or resources in a given society) and micro levels (e.g., negative psychological consequences). A complete explication of the costs of White privilege to Whites is beyond the scope of this chapter; we have thus limited our discussion to outlining the core tenets of the psychological costs of White privilege and so do not include a discussion on macrolevel costs. The psychological costs manifest differently in terms of whether an individual (a) denies the existence of White privilege and how he or she wittingly or unwittingly benefits or (b) acknowledges White privilege and acts on or ignores this awareness.

For the privileges afforded to Whites to be preserved, it is critical that the masses of Whites remain oblivious to racism and White privilege. Whites are thus socialized to deny that race-based privileges exist and often believe that individual and group achievements are based solely on merit (Crowfoot & Chesler, 1996; Haney & Hurtado, 1994; McIntosh, 1988). On the basis of this socialization, many Whites are either unable to acknowledge (dysconscious denial) or choose to ignore (conscious denial) the privileges afforded them as a result of their racial group membership. Liberatory educator Joyce King (1991) defines dysconsciousness as "an uncritical habit of mind" and an "impaired consciousness or distorted way of thinking about race" (p. 135); thus dysconscious denial is not outside the consciousness of individuals. Furthermore, dysconsciousness or "uncritical ways of thinking about racial inequity[,] accept certain culturally sanctioned assumptions, myths, and beliefs that justify the social and economic advantages White people have as a result of subordinating diverse others" (King, 1991, p. 135).

Although many Whites benefit from dysconsciousness, some also suffer a variety of psychological costs based on an uncritical examination of race, racism, and racial privilege, including cognitive costs such as distortions of self, other, and reality. Earlier, we commented on how White privilege can create an inflated sense of self or even a delusion of superiority. We contend that such a deluded or inaccurate sense of self is antithetical to positive mental health, because "to be mentally healthy is to be aware of self and others, and accepting of self and others, and to enjoy a stable identity. Mentally healthy people are capable of perceiving reality accurately" (Thompson & Neville, 1999, p. 175). Some White individuals may also cognitively distort how they view others, resorting to limited and/or inaccurate knowledge based on stereotypes. Consequently, based on their inaccurate perceptions, some Whites may dislike or be fearful of people of color, thus expressing a heightened sense of anxiety. Again, based on the aforementioned "working definition" of mental health, inaccurate perceptions of others also undermines positive mental health.

An increased knowledge about the systemic nature of White privilege coupled with the adoption of positive racial and ethnocultural identities may help to decrease racially based cognitive distortions (a cost of White privilege). However, a new set of psychological costs (primarily affective in nature) may emerge from this heightened awareness. Upon "learning" about or acknowledging their unfair racial advantages, White individuals may begin to feel guilt or shame, perhaps wanting to rescind some of their unearned power. For example, during a graduate-level multicultural psychology course, a veteran counseling psychology instructor observed White students identifying the race-based advantages they have received (Thompson & Neville, 1999). The instructor commented that oftentimes during this "discovery" White students initially expressed feelings of shock, followed by emotional bouts with guilt and shame. Some students cried, whereas others attempted to reconcile the cognitive dissonance that they were experiencing related to unearthing the fact that America was not truly a democracy and that their achievements had not been solely based on merit. Regardless of the specific affective response to the class content, the process of grappling with White privilege was a painful journey for many students.

Other affective costs include fear and loss related to relinquishing unearned privileges. It seems important for educators to help students examine what it means to lose power and the feelings associated with such losses. Religious Studies scholar Sharon Welch (1999) contends that many diversity training activities result in White participants feeling guilty, ashamed, and exposed rather than being accountable for change. To counter the intensity of these negative emotions, which for some can be immobilizing, she suggests that multicultural educators help Whites examine how they can use their conferred power within a racial hierarchy to make changes in the distribution of social and economic power.

White people who challenge the racial hierarchy through race-defying behavior (e.g., talking about the ill effects of racism, working toward racial inclusion within the power structures, and establishing meaningful friendships with people of color) may suffer a number of negative consequences from other Whites, ranging from personal admonishments, ostracism, social isolation, and even bodily harm. Negative actions against people perceived as "race traitors" destabilize efforts among Whites to challenge the racial status quo. There are countless historical examples illustrating this process, including the brutal murders of John Brown and Viola Liuzzo for their abolitionist and civil rights work, respectively.

Less brutal forms of social control are used to "reel in" Whites who actively challenge racism and White privilege. These everyday costs include things like being labeled irrational by peers, losing friends, and in employment, being censored in meetings, receiving negative evaluations, and encountering career advancement impediments. Ellsworth (1997) describes this process as the "double binds of whiteness," in which racial privilege provides the social space for Whites to name and define the oppressive characteristics associated with Whiteness; however, by unveiling White privileges, antiracist Whites are susceptible to losing the very privileges they have explicated.

Some intellectuals have advocated abolishing the social construction of the White race altogether, suggesting that the loss of racial privileges to Whites is a minimal cost considering the potential broader positive social ramifications. For example, Noel Ignatiev, founding editor of the magazine *Race Traitor*, argues that

> for those in power, the [loss of] privileges granted Whites are a small price to pay for the stability of an unjust social system. While not all forms of injustice can be collapsed into Whiteness, undermining White race solidarity opens the door to fundamental social change in other areas. For so-called Whites, treason to the White race is the most subversive act I can imagine. (Ignatiev, 2000, p. 492)

In summary, White privilege is an often unnamed and unnoticed complex system of relationships among individuals, groups, and systems that exists in a racial hierarchical society, in which Whites are conferred power and advantages and people of color are confronted with (and resist) systematic social and economic disadvantages. Depending on nonracial social identities (e.g., class, gender, and sexual orientation), Whites differentially experience racial privileges on both macro levels (e.g., educational and economic) and micro levels (e.g., intrapsychically and interpersonally). Although Whites primarily benefit materially from racism, they are also confronted with a myriad of costs associated with White privilege (a corollary of racism), primarily on micro levels (e.g., psychological and interpersonal stress). To combat and eliminate White privilege, the unacknowledged culturally laden symbols and protocols that reflect and maintain the racial hierarchy need to be clearly identified and expunged.

Color-Blind Racial Attitudes (CoBRA)

Similar to White privilege, color-blind racial attitudes (CoBRA) are rooted in the structure of society. Essentially, to adopt a color-blind racial perspective is to deny the existence of ideological and structural racism and to believe that race does not play a meaningful role in people's lived experiences. We fully believe that we should live in a society in which race does not matter; however, this strand of color-blindness is an ideal morality for an ideal society. And, unfortunately, we do not live in an ideal or just society. To ignore, deny, distort, or evade this reality is the core of CoBRA. Although there are numerous theories outlining the criteria of a just society, political philosopher Amy Gutmann (1996) succinctly notes that "there is almost no theory of justice . . . by which the United States today can be judged as a just or nearly just society," and, according to Gutman, "a just society would secure everybody's basic liberties (regardless of race, religion, gender or sexual preference [sic], for example) and also secure basic opportunities (such as good education, adequate health care, and physical security) for everyone" (pp. 126-127). In this section, we further elaborate on the construction of CoBRA by outlining four main tenets, with a focus on micro-level expressions.

Tenet 1: CoBRA are new forms of racial attitude expressions that are separate from, but related to racial prejudice. Over the past 20 years, the nature of racism, or at least our understanding of racism, has begun to take a different shape. Far from the so-called Jim Crow racism of open bigotry, support of legal segregation, and the open assertion of the innate superiority of Whites (Bobo & Kluegel, 1997), a more modern "laissez-faire racism" has taken shape, characterized by (a) persistent negative stereotyping, (b) a tendency to blame minorities themselves for racial disparities in earnings, employment, and social status, and (c) resistance to meaningful efforts to ameliorate problematic social conditions and institutions (Bobo, Kluegel, & Smith, 1997). McConahay (1983, 1986) anticipated this shift when he conceptualized the notion of "modern racism" as a form of post Civil Rights Movement expressions of individual racism, as captured in the shift described above. An important precept of modern racism is that race, race relations, and racism are dynamic in nature and thus are in constant flux. We argue that society has changed significantly over the nearly 20 years since the first articulations of modern racism and that we are advancing to new or "ultramodern" forms of racism expressions. In agreement with sociologist Eduardo Bonilla-Silva (2000), CoBRA have "replaced Jim Crow racism as the central racial ideology supporting the 'new [or ultramodern] racism' " (p. 904) as articulated by Bobo and his colleagues (1997).

Historians Sundiata Cha-Jua and Clarence Lang (1999) theorize that the change in racism expressions reflects changes in the broader structure of race relations in the United States, a process they refer to as racial formation. The new racial formation is characterized by several social dynamics, including the marginalization of Black and Latino workers and racialized incarceration. Political assaults against equal inclusion of African Americans and Latinos in institutions of higher education also reflects these social changes, as exemplified by the public attacks against race-based scholarships in several states and legislation designed to dismantle affirmative action in education (e.g., Proposition 209 in California and the Hopwood Case in Texas) (cf. Smith, 1999). This structural retrenchment in higher education reflects changes in broader racial beliefs and attitudes (see Cha-Jua & Lang, 1999, for further discussion of structural changes in expressions of racism).

There is some empirical support documenting a shift in racial attitudes over time. Using the Gallup survey data, sociologists Schuman and Krysan (1999) examined White individuals' beliefs about racial disadvantage among African Americans over a 32-year period (1963–1995). Results suggest that White Americans' beliefs about the racial disadvantage have changed dramatically over time. In 1963, nearly half of the respondents (49%) indicated that Whites were responsible for the present social conditions of Blacks; this belief sharply declined over the years: In 1968, 28% of the participants blamed Whites for the social conditions of Blacks, and by 1995 only 20% assigned the blame to Whites. The significant decline in blaming Whites for racial disadvantage, is best understood when also considering the significant increase in beliefs that blame Blacks themselves for their present condition: 51% in 1963, 72% in 1968, and 80% in 1995. Essentially, these findings indicate a meaningful shift away from identifying structural issues causing disadvantage to blaming individuals for their own disadvantage. Current expressions of "blame the victim" ideology can also be found in results from other large surveys. For example, in the 1998 General Social Survey, nearly half (47%) of the White American respondents polled agreed with the statement "Blacks just don't have the motivation or will power to pull themselves up out of poverty" (Schuman & Krysan, p. 847; see Sears, Hetts, Sidanius, & Bobo, 2000, for further documentation of the change in individual expressions of racial attitudes).

We agree with Bobo and Kluegel (1997) that there is a tendency to blame minorities themselves for racial disparities in social and economic arenas and that this tendency does indeed reflect new dimensions of racial attitudes not clearly articulated in the psychology literature. Whereas Bobo and Kluegel focus on naming and describing this new form of racism ("laissez-faire racism"), we are mainly interested in naming and describing the racial perspective or interpretive lens from which new forms of racism are manifested. We contend that the emergence of the color-blind racial rhetoric in popular discourse at this historical moment appears to be connected to shifts in racial attitude expression. CoBRA are thus related to but distinct from individual racism in several meaningful ways. Individual racism refers to the belief in the superiority/inferiority of groups of people based on race (i.e., racialism) and on corresponding behaviors that are insensitive and/or discriminating (Sears et al., 2000). CoBRA refers to the denial that racism exists on either ideological or structural levels. Thus, color-blind racial attitudes do not necessarily reflect notions of inferiority/ superiority and are restricted to beliefs as opposed to actions. However, adopting a color-blind racial perspective may unwittingly promote racial discrimination as it "easily leads to a misrepresentation of reality in ways which allow and sometimes even encourage discrimination against minority members" (Schofield, 1986, p. 238). Moreover, color-blind racial ideology serves as the new rationalization for racial oppression (Carr, 1997; Cha-Jua & Lang, 1999).

Tenet 2: CoBRA are a cognitive schema, reflecting a conceptual framework and corresponding affect. Consistent with theoretical and empirical research on racial stereotypes (cf. Mackie & Hamilton, 1993), we argue that CoBRA reflect a complex interaction between cognitions and affect which influence the encoding, interpretation, and retrieval of race-related information. Essentially, CoBRA reflect a larger cognitive schema about race in the United States (i.e., race is unimportant in terms of social and economic experiences); feelings are attached to this schema and its corresponding beliefs (e.g., belief in a just world, meritocracy) and thus can provide people with a sense of security, albeit false. A cognitive schema suggesting that race is unimportant coupled with feelings of anxiety about race (e.g., fear of being called a racist for Whites or fear of using the "race card" for people of color) may lead individuals to deny the influence of race or racism in a given situation. These individual schemas are also reflective in broader social cognitions or cultural beliefs that racism is a thing of the past and that we live in a meritocracy, a society in which people who work hard regardless of their social location will reap the benefits society has to offer and that poor and disenfranchised people experience social disadvantages due to lack of motivation and hard work. Recent findings provide initial empirical support for the influence of racial stereotyping (Abreu, 1999) and racial cognitive schemas (Gushue & Carter, 2000) on race-related information processing.

Although adoption of a color-blind cognitive schema may influence individual behavior, the resulting behavior almost certainly will not be color-blind. For an adult to treat someone as if race didn't matter, one must first be aware that race *does matter* and attempt to counter his or her own assumptions or prejudices. Moreover, "treating different people differently and celebrating their cultural uniqueness appears to be a more equitable way to achieve social justice than attempting to adopt a color-blind stance" (APA, 1997, p. 8). Thus, adopting color-conscious behaviors and policies is needed to combat racial injustice and promote racial equality (Gutmann, 1996). Color-consciousness or the acknowledgement that racial discrimination exists is the obverse of color-blindness. However, unlike CoBRA, color-consciousness can reflect behaviors or actions designed to promote justice and fairness.

Tenet 3: CoBRA are multidimensional. CoBRA are complex and reflect multiple beliefs. In her groundbreaking research on White women and race, sociologist Ruth Frankenberg (1993) articulated two interrelated patterns of CoBRA: (a) color evasion, or "emphasizing sameness as a way of rejecting the idea of White racial superiority" (p. 144), and (b) power evasion or the belief that everyone regardless of race or ethnicity has the same opportunities to economic and social success; consequently, "any failure not to achieve is therefore the fault of people of color themselves" (p. 14). Color evasion relates to critical race theorist Sylvia Lazos Vargas's (1998) notion of the homogeneity assumption which is "embedded in the cultural assumption that we are all one [U.S.] people. . . . To proclaim difference is negative, because somehow it is un-American and threatens our belief in a strongly unified American whole" (p. 1502).

In one of the few quantitative studies in the area, Neville and her colleagues (2000) developed a scale to assess color-blind racial attitudes (Color-Blind Racial Attitude Scale, or CoBRAS), and results from a series of five studies suggest that CoBRA are multidimensional. Consistent with Frankenberg's (1993) work, two factors emerged from the CoBRAS that were conceptually related to power evasion. Specifically, denial or "blindness" to racial privilege (i.e., evasion of White privileges in society) and institutional discrimination (i.e., evasion of institutional discrimination against people of color and rejection of the belief that social policies are needed to eradicate the negative consequences of institutional forms of discrimination) were uncovered. Although items were included in the original CoBRAS to assess color evasion attitudes, a factor consistent with this construct did not emerge, and in fact, all of the items tapping into color evasion were subsequently deleted from the revised scale. A third factor, however, was found that related to denial of blatant forms of racial discrimination (e.g., racism is not an important problem today). Results suggest that greater levels of the multiple dimensions of color-blind racial attitudes as measured by the CoBRAS were related to a greater endorsement of belief in a just world ideology and racial and gender prejudice.

Tenet 4: CoBRA are differentially expressed in White and people of color populations. Much debate has occurred about who can be racist. Some scholars suggest that racism is reserved for Whites only because as a group they wield social and political power; others suggest that people of color hold racial prejudices and thus can be racist. Our intent here is not to weigh in on that debate but, rather, to highlight another distinction between individual racism and color-blindness. Anyone can adopt a color-blind racial perspective, irrespective of race or ethnicity. However, the degree to which groups, on average, adhere to these beliefs differs and, moreover, the implications of adopting a color-blind perspective vary depending on one's sociorace. Initial empirical evidence suggests that Whites, on average, adopt significantly higher color-blind racial attitudes than racial and ethnic minorities (Carr, 1997; Neville et al., 2000). For example,

Carr (1997) asked college students if they agreed with the following state-ment: "I am color-blind when it comes to race." Over three quarters of the White respondents (77%) agreed with the statement, compared to 40% of their Black counterparts. Follow-up questions revealed that students irre-spective of race tended to equate color-blind to mean that "they did not dis-criminate and were not prejudiced or that race means nothing to them" (p. 149). However, the majority of Black students who stated they did not adopt a color-blind racial perspective were offended by the concept, many arguing that "it is impossible to be African American and color-blind in America [sic]" (p. 149). Several participants differentiated color-blind racial attitudes from anti-racism beliefs: "To say that you do not discriminate and are not prejudiced is one thing, to say that you do not do this because you are 'color-blind' is something else" (p. 150).

Although Whites and people of color can adopt CoBRA, the function and consequences of this racial ideology are quite different among racial groups. For Whites, adopting a color-blind racial perspective may help alle-viate dissonance resulting from the belief in a meritocracy while acknowl-edging unearned advantages afforded Whites as a by-product of living in a racial hierarchical system. Denial of racial privileges may result in inaction in terms of working toward racial justice; thus, denial of racism and its cor-ollaries both reduces uncomfortable feelings and sustains a system of racial privilege in which Whites benefit.

Our conceptualization of the function of CoBRA to Whites, particu-larly the goal of Whites as a socioracial group to protect its group interests, is consistent with social dominance theory (SDT) (Sidanius, 1993; Sidanius & Pratto, 1999). SDT consists of the following three interrelated core components:

> First, societies are typically organized as group-based hierarchies, with a dominant group enjoying a disproportionate share of positive value (e.g., power, wealth, education) and at least one subordinate group suffering a disproportionate share of negative value (e.g., low-status jobs, poor health). Second, politics can be thought of as an exercise in *intergroup* competition over scarce material and symbolic resources. Third, one of the primary functions of values and ideologies . . . is to legitimize the dis-proportionate allocation of desired social outcomes to the dominant group and to maintain the structural integrity of the system of group-based so-cial hierarchy. (Sidanius, Singh, Hetts, & Federico, 2000, pp. 195-196)

Sidanius's (1993) systematic research provides data to support SDT. For ex-ample, in a large-scale study with nine samples across the globe, Sidanius, Levin, Liu, and Pratto (2000) recently found that people in high-status groups adhere to higher degrees of social dominance and anti-egalitarian be-liefs compared to lower status groups.

The theoretical link between CoBRA and SDT is important in under-standing individual- and group-level racism. However, the question remains, how does CoBRA function and operate in real-life interactions outside the abstraction. Legal scholar Pamela Smith (1999) insightfully captures the insidious function of adopting a color-blind racial perspective in destabilizing efforts to confront and change racist structures in the academy:

> There is always an excuse for racist behavior that is practiced by White students, White colleagues, and White administrators. A racial flyer is not really a racial flyer; it is merely a prank. . . . Racial meetings are not really racial meetings, just students venting—even though their behavior and complaints speak in racist terms. Given White denial, these excuses, and in fact any excuses, are preferable to White colleagues concluding that students who share their socio-economic class, politics, race, and rhetoric of community and inclusiveness are racist. To conclude otherwise would force many to look at some of their own behavior, including denying racism exists. . . . Denial becomes the chosen behavior for many Whites. As noted above, 'it's as if [they] think they can deny it out of existence.' Unfortunately, denying racism does not impact its existence, especially for those who are the recipients of racialized behavior. (pp. 94-95)

More closely related to the counseling psychology profession is the following harrowing story of a first-time African American graduate instructor. During the initial class meeting, an international student remarked that he wished the graduate instructor was not teaching the class because he'd had difficulty with a Black professor in the past and did not like Black people. When the graduate instructor attempted to process this event with the predominantly White class three weeks later, the class as a whole denied that the student made the comment. After the student confirmed the accuracy of the instructor's recollection, the class members proceeded to proffer that the exchange was not a critical incident in the class. The situation is obviously more complex than presented here, but the brief summation illustrates the function of CoBRA for Whites. By first denying that a racial incident occurred, students protected themselves from feeling anxious (for having to confront racism) and guilty (for not having intervened). They also protected themselves against feelings of dissonance and, moreover, were able to justify their inaction by minimizing the importance of the incident.

With the exception of racial identity research, rarely are the racial attitudes of people of color theoretically or empirically examined. We assert that the function of people of color adopting a color-blind racial perspective is quite different from their White counterparts. Instead of working to protect one's group interest, embracing a color-blind racial perspective for racial and ethnic minorities may actually work against one's individual and group interest. Social psychologists have extended the Marxist concept *false consciousness* to further elucidate this process: "holding false beliefs that are contrary to one's personal or social interest . . . contribute to the maintenance of the disadvantaged position of the self or the group" (Jost & Banaji, 1994, p. 3). If people of color accept the racial status quo, believing it is just and natural, then the maintenance of racial privilege is likely to occur. "However, opposition to perpetual dominance of Whites, for example, reveals itself in opposition to false consciousness, rejection of the status quo, and the systematic deconstruction of legitimizing myths and system justifications" (Jones, 1997, p. 230).

On a psychological level, a person of color with high levels of CoBRA may not have the skills or social networks in place to effectively cope with the accumulation of microaggressions or blatant racial discrimination within new environments. Illustratively, an Asian American graduate student in a psychology program located in a small town communicated to us that she was contemplating dropping out of the program after the first year. The student had lived in a racially, ethnically, and culturally diverse environment most of her life, in which cultural differences were appreciated and celebrated. Because of the perceived racial and cultural harmony in her community, she assumed that racism, for the most part, was a thing of the past and that consequently race was unimportant. After moving to the relatively racially/ethnically homogeneous campus community, she encountered subtle forms of racism in her interactions with peers; she began to feel isolated from others. Only after consciously linking her experiences on campus to racism was she able to problem-solve ways to cope with, resist, and change her experiences in her learning environment. This insight played a significant role in her decision to continue her studies in the program.

In summary, CoBRA is the dominant ideology associated with contemporary expressions of new or ultramodern forms of racism. On a structural level, the denial of the existence of racism as a dominant racial ideology serves an important function in maintaining dominance for Whites and the subordination of people of color (i.e., White privilege). On an individual level, CoBRA reflect cognitive schemas influencing the encoding and interpretation of racial stimulus. Although most of the literature on CoBRA to date has been theoretical in nature, the few empirical studies suggest that individual expressions of CoBRA are complex and multidimensional.

Applications of White Privilege and CoBRA in Multicultural Counseling Psychology Theory and Practice

The social transformations resulting from the civil rights and other social movements of the 1960s provided space in psychology to produce scholarship on race and racism. These changes resulted in the development of new theories articulating the role of sociorace on human behavior. Most of the initial theoretical writings on race in counseling psychology focused on racial identity and on operationalizing multicultural counseling competencies. Understanding the impact of racial and other forms of systemic oppression on the material conditions and interpersonal interactions among people served as the basis for which initial multicultural competency models were articulated (Arredondo, 1999). In the past decade there has been production of new theories related to the field of multicultural counseling, including Ridley and colleagues' (1994, 2000) perceptual cultural schemata model and Leong's (1996) integrative model of cross-cultural counseling, each with varying degrees of emphasis on racial oppression (see Ponterotto et al., 2000, for a description of new theoretical models). Conceptualizations of White privilege (WP) and color-blind racial attitudes (CoBRA), both corollaries of racial oppression, have recently emerged in the social science literature and appear to have significant implications for training in the field of counseling psychology. In this section, we build on the definitions of WP and CoBRA provided earlier in the chapter and apply them to multicultural counseling psychology theory and practice. Specifically, we outline the applications of these concepts to relevant theory, training, and research.

APPLICATION OF WP AND CoBRA TO MULTICULTURAL PSYCHOLOGY THEORY

Multicultural Counseling Competency Models

Explicating the context undergirding the development of multicultural counseling competencies documents, Arredondo (1999) observed that professionals "recognized that counseling as an interpersonal practice provokes a range of dynamics given the nation's sociopolitical reality. People, the counselor and client, come together in an institutional setting in a sociopolitical reality to address any number of life-impacting dilemmas or issues" (p. 103). As briefly summarized in the beginning of this chapter, most multicultural counseling competencies models include three broad areas of multicultural competence: awareness, knowledge, and skills. Arredondo and her colleagues (1996) clearly articulated the importance of understanding systems of power as a manifestation of competencies across the three core domains. The following explanatory statements within the cultural awareness competency domain exemplify this point:

> Can specifically identify, name, and discuss privileges that they personally receive in society due to their race, socioeconomic background, gender, physical abilities, sexual orientation, and so on. . . . Can provide a reasonable specific definition of racism, prejudice, discrimination, and stereotype. Can describe a situation in which they have been judged on something other than merit. (cited in Arredondo, 1999, p. 107)

Consistent with Arredondo et al.'s (1996) articulation of essential expressions of MCC, we contend that knowledge about systems of racial oppression and specifically WP and CoBRA are critical components of the knowledge dimension of MCC. Without this critical consciousness (as opposed to dysconsciousness), it is difficult to expect counseling psychology professionals to disrupt White privilege in clinical environments and within our profession. In addition to obtaining a critical level of knowledge about WP and CoBRA, it is also important for multiculturally competent counselors to become aware of their affective reactions to the racial system in the United States and the multiple ways in which they have been impacted by the system. The awareness of one's own experience with WP or CoBRA is important to explore as it may influence the degree to which one is able to accurately attend to or process cognitive information on racial oppression (Gushue & Carter, 2000). Thus, we argue that developing MCC in the area of WP and CoBRA is an iterative process in which one is exposed to content information on racial oppression, is provided with the opportunity to process his or her affective responses to this information, and then is re-exposed to content information and so forth. The assumption is that not everyone will be ready to accurately encode, interpret, and integrate the new race-related content at initial critical exposure.

Racial Identity Theories

There are a number of psychological theories that are conceptually related to WP and CoBRA. Earlier, we briefly outlined the link between CoBRA and social dominance theory. In this section, we speculate about the connection between both WP and CoBRA to racial identity theories. We have delimited our discussion to Helms's (1990, 1995) racial identity theories because she has well-articulated parallel theoretical models for Whites and people of color, thus aiding in the conceptual cohesion to our discussion. Because Helms's models are described extensively in the extant literature and also within this volume (see Fischer & Moradi, Chapter 20, this volume), we assume basic knowledge of Helms's conceptual frameworks on the part of the reader and thus do not outline the models here.

White privilege as a consequence of a racial hierarchical social structure serves as a central premise of Helms's racial identity theories (Helms & Cook, 1999). Thus, racial identity itself reflects the psychological consequences of being socialized as a member of a group that either benefits from or is hindered by the social order. Using Helms's terminology, White privilege is experienced and expressed as a function of an individual's racial identity ego status and information-processing strategies (i.e., Helms, 1995). Specifically, White individuals who embrace higher levels of *Contact* status espouse "satisfaction with the racial status quo" and are "oblivious to racism and one's participation in it," whereas *Immersion/Emersion* status individuals search for an understanding of the ways by which one benefits from racism, and *Autonomy* status individuals develop the capacity to "relinquish the privileges of racism" (Helms, 1995, p. 185). Further, with respect to racial identity attitudes, Helms (1995) characterizes the fundamental developmental issue for Whites as "the abandonment of entitlement" (p. 184) or intrapsychic and interpersonal White privilege:

> As a consequence of growing up and being socialized in an environment in which members of their group (if not themselves personally) are privileged relative to other groups, Whites learn to perceive themselves (and their group) as entitled to similar privileges. In order to protect such privilege, individual group members, and therefore the group more generally, learn to protect their privileged status by denying and distorting race-related reality and aggressing against perceived threats to the racial status quo. Consequently, healthy identity development for a White person involves the capacity to recognize and abandon the normative strategies of White people for coping with race. (p. 188)

The task of abandoning perceived racial entitlement is not a core developmental task for racial and ethnic minorities. However, in establishing a positive, healthy racial identity, people of color must shed the internalization of the racial inferiority/superiority ideology associated with White privilege. CoBRA attitudes appear to be more closely linked to the racial identity development process of both people of color and Whites. Specifically, denial, distortion, and minimization of racism and socioracial concerns, central aspects of CoBRA, are the core information processing strategies used in the least sophisticated status for both people of color (i.e., Conformity) and Whites (i.e., Contact; Helms & Cook, 1999). The expression of CoBRA is thus a critical manifestation of initial racial identity statuses.

APPLICATION OF WP AND CoBRA
TO COUNSELING PSYCHOLOGY TRAINING

Teaching

Interestingly, given that racial oppression and its various manifestations in society and within our profession served as a rationale for the articulation of MCCs, with notable exception (e.g., Helms & Cook, 1999) there is remarkably little serious attention to these power relationships in current multicultural counseling survey texts. If one of the goals of developing MCC is to become informed of the nature of racism and its corollaries on clinical practice, then in-depth analyses of this complex social process should be covered in every introduction-level course on multicultural counseling psychology. Consistent with the above, Welch (2000) insightfully argues for the development of "power literacy" as a key component of multicultural competencies. She operationalizes "power literacy" skills as the ability to (a) "recognize social conflict and imbalances of power between social groups"; (b) "think and act systemically"; and (c) be accountable for one's actions, that is, "to use power truthfully" (Welch, 2000, pp. 1-2). There are a number of good books that could be (and have been) included in such courses to supplement current survey texts and that can help promote power literacy, including *Understanding Race, Ethnicity and Power: The Key to Efficacy in Clinical Practice* (Pinderhughes, 1989) and *Using Race and Culture in Counseling and Psychotherapy: Theory and Process* (Helms & Cook, 1999); we recommend that new multicultural survey texts include at least one chapter defining racism and its corollaries as well as fully integrating these processes throughout the treatise.

Most empirical literature in the area has found (a) a significant relationship between increased levels of multicultural counseling training and greater self-reported MCC and (b) support for the effectiveness of multicultural counseling courses in increasing trainees' MCC (see Ponterotto et al., 2000, for a review of the extant literature). On the basis of the counseling psychology literature, it seems that multicultural instruction could also decrease endorsement of WP and higher levels of CoBRA. Gushue and Carter's (2000) findings, however, remind us of the importance of how racial messages are delivered, explained, and processed. Thus, in addition to content, it seems important for educators to attend to method of instruction, especially considering students' individual level or racial identity and overall classroom racial identity level may influence the processing of race-related content (Gushue & Carter, 2000; Helms & Cook, 1999). There are excellent texts discussing pedagogical techniques to decrease defensiveness and retrenchment in White students and to promote affirmation and exploration in all students (see Welch, 1999). Simply discussing readings in class will not adequately address the defensiveness around the topic of power, and power relationships within a racially stratified society. Perhaps viewing videos, participating in in-class simulation exercises, engaging in dialogues with racially and ethnically diverse panels, and/or completing cultural exploration projects may help alleviate some of the defensiveness.

Clinical Training

Although a variety of multicultural scholars have noted the importance of racial identity ego statuses (or racial identity attitudes) in the practice of multicultural counseling (e.g., Helms, 1990; Ottavi, Pope-Davis, & Dings, 1994; Ponterotto et al., 2000), little attention has been given to specifically hypothesizing the relations of WP or CoBRA to counselor training and practice. Helms (1995) suggests that multiculturally competent White counselors (those exhibiting more advanced racial identity ego statuses) are more likely to acknowledge and assess their own experiences and expressions of White privilege. White counselors who have assessed the extent to which they may view their "lives as morally neutral, normative, and average, and also ideal, so that when [they] work to benefit others, this is seen as work which will allow [clients] to be more like [them]" (McIntosh, 1998, p. 152) are more likely to reduce the potential impact of White privilege in the counseling process. However, training students to recognize personal privilege is not an easy task because many White students are unlikely to view racism as embedded in systems of advantage, and racial privilege is often invisible to them (Lawrence, 1998). Ottavi et al. (1994) recommended that White racial identity attitudes be considered in the conceptualization and planning of interventions to improve multicultural counseling competencies. Similarly, we recommend that White privilege be assessed and challenged during the process of counselor training. Counselors who examine their own privileged status are (a) less likely to succumb to racial stereotypes, (b) more likely to view problems of clients of color from a systemic, contextual perspective, (c) more likely to seek knowledge and understanding of the worldviews of their clients of color, (d) less likely to impose ethnocentric notions of normativeness on clients of color, (e) more likely to recognize and reduce the influence of racial power dynamics, and (f) less likely to avoid verbalizing racial and cultural material in counseling sessions.

This latter counseling characteristic is directly related to CoBRA. It stands to reason that counselors with relatively high endorsement of CoBRA (regardless of race or ethnicity) will be (a) less likely to conceptualize the potential influence of race or ethnocultural factors on the client's presenting concern and thus (b) less likely to verbally express race-related information in counseling sessions. Counselors who endorse lower levels of CoBRA are probably more likely to include relevant racial content in sessions, which in turn has been found to enhance the counseling process and outcome (Thompson, Worthington, & Atkinson, 1994), including the working relationship and satisfaction with counseling (Wade & Bernstein, 1991).

Beyond counselor factors, we are aware that there are a host of client factors that impact the process and outcome of counseling (Bergin & Garfield, 1994). In terms of White privilege, we would be remiss to neglect addressing it in terms of client characteristics. Indeed, when racial and ethnic minority clients are considered, a myriad of racial and cultural factors come to the fore (e.g., racial identity development, acculturation, cultural mistrust, worldview, help-seeking attitudes, indigenous healing practices and beliefs, etc.) as focal concerns that influence counseling process and outcome. Similarly, White privilege, conceptualized as a variant in the mental health of White clients (Helms, 1995), should be a focal concern when addressing the needs of White clients. There are inevitably a host of negative consequences for Whites attributable, at least in part, to White privilege. These conditions can be legitimate central foci of counseling, as well as considerations about how White privilege may impact counseling.

APPLICATION OF WP AND CoBRA
TO FUTURE DIRECTIONS IN RESEARCH

Both WP and CoBRA are emerging constructs in counseling psychology and thus there is a dearth of extant empirical literature. Almost any research on these interrelated ideas will make a meaningful contribution to the budding topic area. However, research on the following especially will help to theoretically ground and empirically support the influence of WP and CoBRA on intrapsychic and interpersonal interactions: (a) qualitative research examining expressions of White privilege in individuals and in systems (see D'Andrea & Daniels, Chapter 18, this volume); (b) qualitative studies, perhaps using life narratives or grounded theory, to describe the process of abandoning WP among White allies; (c) studies designed to further articulate and measure the personal costs of White privilege to Whites; (d) research examining the meaning and consequences of adopting a color-blind racial attitude perspective for various racial and ethnic groups, using both qualitative and quantitative methodologies; (e) investigations exploring the relationship between internalized WP and entitlement expression (for Whites) and CoBRA (for all groups of people) to personality related constructs, including racial identity attitudes and social dominance orientation; (f) studies evaluating the effectiveness of training strategies to decrease internalization of WP and CoBRA; and (g) research exploring the relationship between internalized WP and CoBRA on self-reported and observed MCC. In light of the recent developments in MCC research, future investigations along these lines must include external measures of competencies (e.g., observed ratings, case conceptualization skills; Worthington, Mobley, Franks, & Tan, 2000) and control for the potential effects of social desirability in self-report assessments (Constantine & Ladany, 2000).

CREATING COLOR-CONSCIOUS
POLICIES AND PRACTICES IN
COUNSELING PSYCHOLOGY:
A PROFESSIONAL IMPERATIVE

Policies with the explicit goal of promoting social justice and racial inclusion (e.g., color-conscious policies) are an essential ingredient in the eradication of White privilege within our profession and, ultimately, our society. Ecological or contextual models provide us with the best framework within the psychology field to impact the greatest amount of change. Contextual intervention models consider interventions within multiple systems, including macro- (e.g., racial ideology, values, political economic structure), exo- (e.g., profession and organization level), meso- (e.g., interaction among specific departments or institutions), and microsystem (e.g., specific program area or department) and individual (e.g., counseling psychology professional).

Operating within a general ecological framework, Sue (2000) outlines a personal identity model designed to promote cultural competence (with a goal toward creating social justice). Four central questions frame his conceptualization: How do we as individuals become culturally competent? How do we become multiculturally competent as a counseling psychology profession? How do we promote cultural competence in our national professional organizations (e.g., APA, ACA)? How do we move our society to become culturally competent? Using this general framework, outlined next are suggested interventions to promote cultural competencies, specifically the eradication of White privilege and the embracing of a color-blind racial ideology.

Individual Interventions

Many individual counseling psychology training programs have implemented color-conscious policies in their racial and ethnic minority student recruitment efforts. In addition to recruiting racial and ethnic minority students to individual programs, we also believe it is critical to implement retention strategies. For example, creating a pluralistic learning environment by attending to both the physical environment and the learning opportunities in the program will assist in both recruitment and retention efforts (see Ponterotto, Alexander, & Grieger, 1995, and Pope-Davis, Liu, Nevitt, & Toporek, 2000, for discussions and assessment options in examining multicultural environments at the program level). The following strategies may also help counter White privilege and color-blind racial ideology within individual programs:

- Creating safe spaces for faculty and students to dialogue about the program, its curriculum, and the environment in general and related to power issues, especially around race and ethnicity (it is important to bear in mind that with greater racial and ethnic minority faculty and student representation in the program there will most likely come greater conflict around racial issues; this conflict can be used to create the impetus to promote positive changes within the program)
- Writing a diversity position statement to be included on all program-related publicity materials; such a statement can be used to communicate the program's commitment to diversity and social justice
- Significantly increasing the incorporation of social justice (e.g., social action research and practice) and also race- and ethnicity-related topics into existing courses
- Including a formal evaluation of students' multicultural competencies in counseling psychology (research, clinical practice, and teaching, if applicable)

Profession- and Organization-Level Interventions

Sue (2000) outlined important color-conscious strategies to enhance social justice issues within our profession as psychologists in general and counseling psychologists specifically, including the following: (a) adopting ethical codes that more explicitly incorporate guidelines to providing ethical services to racial and ethnic minority populations and also to a broad range of cultural groups (Ridley, Liddle, Hill, & Li, Chapter 14, this volume, further articulate culture-centered ethical guidelines); (b) critically examining the standard practices within professional organizations (e.g., APA, ACA), ensuring that policies, programs, practices, and so forth help create equal access and opportunities for racial and ethnic minorities and that there is a commitment to ending discrimination within the organizations; and (c) altering performance appraisal systems that determine which individuals and programs are promoted so that they promote racial and ethnic minority inclusion. Performance appraisal systems could be extended to evaluating programs for accreditation and in state licensing requirements, such that all programs have to demonstrate multicultural training effectiveness to become accredited and all states require multicultural psychology training to sit for licensure. (We recognize that some states have this as an official requirement, such as Massachusetts, but that the majority of states do not.)

Interventions to Impact Society

The profession of psychology in general and counseling psychologists specifically have countered, and can continue to counter, White privilege and color-blind racial ideology in society. For example, the APA (1997) produced a monograph outlining the negative implications of adopting a color-blind racial perspective. The APA and the ACA as organizations can further create and/or support legislation designed to counter the onslaught of anti-Affirmative Action rulings as well as support and publicize research documenting the ill effects of structural and ideological oppression on racial and ethnic minorities' physical, economic, and mental well-being. Both the APA and the ACA are powerful institutions that have the capability of challenging ideological representations of people of color and of lobbying for equitable distribution of resources in society, which in turn most likely will have a tremendous impact on the lived experiences of racial and ethnic minorities.

CONCLUSION

In this chapter, we identified core tenets of the interrelated constructs White privilege and color-blind racial attitudes. After grounding the analysis of the constructs within the interdisciplinary literature, we provided a conceptual link between WP and CoBRA and multicultural competencies in counseling psychology. It is our contention that a critical analysis of how race and power influences counseling psychology research, training, and practice is important as we prepare professionals to make the field more inclusive and attend to the health concerns of our increasingly multiracial, multilingual, and multicultural society. In addition to increasing counseling psychologists' awareness of and knowledge about WP and CoBRA, we advocate for the adoption of color-conscious practices at multiple systemic levels, including micro (e.g., program level) and macro levels (e.g., profession and organizational), as a method of countering the hegemony of White privilege and color-blind racial ideology. We must not stop with extending MCC to include specific processes related to racial oppression, but further conceptualizations of the complex interaction among multiple systems of oppression on individual and group life experiences also seem warranted. Such conceptualizations will begin to capture the complexity of the human condition and the interconnections of social oppressions.

REFERENCES

Abreu, J. (1999). Conscious and nonconscious African American stereotypes: Impact on first impression and diagnostic ratings by therapists. *Journal of Consulting & Clinical Psychology, 67,* 387-393.

American Psychological Association. (1997). *Can—or should—America be color-blind? Psychological research reveals fallacies in a color-blind response to racism* [Pamphlet]. Washington, DC: Author.

Arredondo, P. (1999). Multicultural counseling competencies as tools to address oppression and racism. *Journal of Counseling & Development, 77,* 102-108.

Arredondo, P., Toporek, R., Brown, S. P., Jones, J., Locke, D. C., Sanchez, J., & Stadler, H. (1996). Operationalization of the multicultural counseling competencies. *Journal of Multicultural Counseling & Development, 24,* 42-78.

Bergin, A. E., & Garfield, S. L. (Eds.). (1994). *Handbook of psychotherapy and behavior change* (4th ed). New York: John Wiley.

Bobo, L., & Kluegel, J. R. (1997). Status, ideology, and dimensions of Whites' racial beliefs and attitudes: Progress and stagnation. In S. A. Tuch & J. K. Martin (Eds.), *Racial attitudes in the 1990s: Continuity and change* (pp. 93-120). Westport, CT: Praeger.

Bobo, L., Kluegel, J. R., & Smith, R. A. (1997). Laissez-faire racism: The crystallization of a kinder, gentler, antilock ideology. In S. A. Tuch & J. K. Martin (Eds.), *Racial attitudes in the 1990s: Continuity and change* (pp. 15-44). Westport, CT: Praeger.

Bonilla-Silva, E. (1996). Rethinking racism: Toward a structural interpretation. *American Sociological Review, 62,* 465-480.

Bonilla-Silva, E. (2000). The essential social fact of race. *American Sociological Review, 66,* 899-906.

Carr, L. G. (1997). *Color-blind racism.* Thousand Oaks, CA: Sage.

Cha-Jua, S. K., & Lang, C. (1999). Strategies for Black liberation in the era of globalism: Restronouveau civil rights, militant Black conservatism, and radicalism. *The Black Scholar, 29,* 25-47.

Constantine, M. G., & Gloria, A. M. (1999). Multicultural issues in predocotoral intern-
    ship programs: A national survey. *Journal of Multicultural Counseling and Develop-
    ment, 27*, 42-53.
Constantine, M. G., & Ladany, N. (2000). Self-report multicultural counseling compe-
    tence scales: Their relation to social desirability attitudes and multicultural case con-
    ceptualization ability. *Journal of Counseling Psychology, 47*, 155-164.
Council of Economic Advisors. (1998, September). *Changing America: Indicators of social
    and economic well-being by race and Hispanic origin.* Available: http://Whitehouse.
    gov/WH/EOP/CEA/html/publications.htm
Crowfoot, J. E., & Chesler, M. A. (1996). White men's roles in multicultural coalitions. In
    B. J. Bowser & R. G. Hunt (Eds.), *Impacts of racism on White Americans* (2nd ed.,
    pp. 202-229). Thousand Oaks, CA: Sage.
Ellsworth, E. (1997). Double binds of whiteness. In M. Fine, L. Weis, L. C. Powell, & L. M.
    Wong (Eds.), *Off White: Readings on race, power, and society.* New York: Routledge.
Fine, M., Weis, L., Powell, L. C., & Wong, L. M. (Eds.). (1997). *Off White: Readings on race,
    power, and society.* New York: Routledge.
Finnegan, M., Heisler, R., Miller, M., & Usery, S. (Eds.). (1981). *New Webster's dictionary
    of the English language: College edition.* New York: Belair.
Frankenberg, R. (1993). *White women, race matters: The social construction of White-
    ness.* Minneapolis, MN: University of Minnesota Press.
Goldberg, E., & Evans, L. (1998). *The prison industrial complex and the global economy.*
    Berkeley, CA: Agit.
Gushue, G. V., & Carter, R. T. (2000). Remembering race: White racial identity attitude
    and two aspects of social memory. *Journal of Counseling Psychology, 47*, 199-210.
Gutmann, A. (1996). Responding to racial injustice. In K. A. Appiah & A. Gutman, *Color-
    conscious: The political morality of race* (pp. 106-183). Princeton, NJ: Princeton Uni-
    versity Press.
Haney, C., & Hurtado, A. (1994). The jurisprudence of race and meritocracy: Standardized
    testing and "race-neutral" racism in the workplace. *Law and Human Behavior, 18*,
    223-248.
Helms, J. E. (Ed.). (1990). *Black and White racial identity: Theory, research, and practice.*
    Westport, CT: Praeger.
Helms, J. E. (1995). An update of Helms's White and people of color racial identity models.
    In J. G. Ponterotto, J. M. Casas, L. A. Suzuki, & C. M. Alexander (Eds.), *Handbook of
    multicultural counseling* (pp. 181-198). Thousand Oaks, CA: Sage.
Helms, J. E., & Cook, D. A. (1999). *Using race and culture in counseling and psychother-
    apy: Theory and process.* Boston: Allyn & Bacon.
Heppner, P. P. (2000, May). Personal communications with Helen A. Neville.
Heppner, P. P., Casas, J. M., Carter, J., & Stone, G. L. (2000). The maturation of counseling
    psychology: Multifaceted perspectives, 1978–1998. In S. D. Brown & R. W. Lent (Eds.),
    Handbook of counseling psychology (3rd ed., pp. 3-49). New York: John Wiley.
Ignatiev, N. (2000). Treason to Whiteness is loyalty to humanity: An interview with Noel
    Ignatiev of *Race Traitor Magazine.* In J. Pera, R. Delgado, P. A. Harris, & S. Wildman
    (Eds.), *Race and races: Cases and resources for a multiracial America* (pp. 489-492).
    St. Paul, MN: West Group, American Casebook Series.
Jackson, R. (1999). White space, White privilege: Mapping discursive inquiry into the self.
    Quarterly Journal of Speech, 85, 38-54.
Jones, J. M. (1997). *Prejudice and racism* (2nd ed.). New York: McGraw-Hill.
Jost, J. T., & Banaji, M. R. (1994). The role of stereotyping in system-justification and the
    production of false consciousness. *British Journal of Social Psychology, 33*, 1-27.
Kincheloe, J. L., Steinberg, S. R., Rodriguez, N. M., & Chennault, R. E. (Eds.). (1998). *White
    reign: Deploying Whiteness in America.* New York: St. Martin's.
King, J. E. (1991). Dysconscious racism: Ideology, identity, and the miseducation of teach-
    ers. *Journal of Negro Education, 60*, 133-146.
Lawrence, S. M. (1998). Unveiling positions of privilege: A hands-on approach to under-
    standing racism. *Teaching Psychology, 25*, 198-200.
Lazos Vargas, S. L. (1998). Deconstructing homo[geneous] Americanus: The White ethnic
    immigrant narrative and its exclusionary effect. *Tulane Law Review, 72*, 1493-1596.

Leong, F. T. L. (1996). Toward an integrative model for cross-cultural counseling and psychotherapy. *Applied and Preventive Psychology: Current Scientific Perspectives, 5,* 189-209.

Mackie, D. M., & Hamilton, D. L. (Eds.). (1993). *Affect, cognition, and stereotyping: Interactive processes in-group perception.* San Diego: Harcourt Brace Jovanovich.

McConahay, J. B. (1983). Modern racism and modern discrimination: The effects of race, racial attitudes, and context on hiring decisions. *Personality and Social Psychology Bulletin, 9,* 551-558.

McConahay, J. B. (1986). Modern racism, ambivalence, and the Modern Racism Scale. In J. F. Dovidio & S. L. Gaertner (Eds.), *Prejudice, discrimination, and racism* (pp. 91-125). New York: Academic Press.

McIntosh, P. (1988). *White privilege and male privilege: A personal account of coming to see correspondences through work in women's studies* (Working Papers Series No. 189). Wellesley, MA: Wellesley College, Center for Research on Women.

McIntosh, P. (1998). White privilege: Unpacking the invisible knapsack. In M. McGoldrick (Ed.), *Re-visioning family therapy: Race, culture, and gender in clinical practice* (pp. 147-152). New York: Guilford.

National Center for Education Statistics. (1997, January). *Integrated postsecondary education data system (IPEDS): "Fall Enrollment" survey.* Washington, DC: Author.

Neville, H. A., Lilly, R. L., Duran, G., Lee, R., & Browne, L. (2000). Construction and initial validation of the Color-Blind Racial Attitudes Scale (CoBRAS). *Journal of Counseling Psychology, 47,* 59-70.

Ottavi, T. M., Pope-Davis, D. B., & Dings, J. G. (1994). Relationship between White racial identity attitudes and self-reported multicultural counseling competencies. *Journal of Counseling Psychology, 41,* 149-154.

Perez, R. M., Constantine, M. G., & Gerard, P. A. (2000). Individual and institutional productivity of racial and ethnic minority research in the *Journal of Counseling Psychology. Journal of Counseling Psychology, 47,* 223-228.

Pinderhughes, E. (1989). *Understanding race, ethnicity and power: The key to efficacy in clinical practice.* New York: Free Press.

Ponterotto, J. G., Alexander, C. M., & Grieger, I. (1995). A multicultural competency checklist for counseling training programs. *Journal of Multicultural Counseling and Development, 23,* 11-20.

Ponterotto, J. G., Fuertes, J. N., & Chen, E. C. (2000). Models of multicultural counseling. In S. D. Brown & R. W. Lent (Eds.), *Handbook of counseling psychology* (3rd ed., pp. 639-669). New York: John Wiley.

Pope-Davis, D. B., Liu, W. M., Nevitt, J., & Toporek, R. L. (2000). The development and initial validation of the Multicultural Environmental inventory: A preliminary investigation. *Cultural Diversity and Ethnic Minority Psychology, 6,* 57-64.

Postmes, T., Branscombe, N. R., Spears, R., & Young, H. (1999). Comparative processes in personal and group judgments: Resolving the discrepancy. *Journal of Personality and Social Psychology, 76,* 320-338.

Rains, F. V. (1998). Is the benign really harmless? Deconstructing some "benign" manifestations of operationalized White privilege. In J. L. Kincheloe, S. R. Steinberg, N. M. Rodriguez, & R. E. Chennault (Eds.), *White reign: Deploying Whiteness in America* (pp. 77-101). New York: St. Martin's.

Ridley, C. R., Chih, D. W., & Olivera, R. J. (2000). Training in cultural schemas: An antidote to unintentional racism in clinical practice. *American Journal of Orthopsychiatry, 70,* 65-72.

Ridley, C. R., Mendoza, D. W., Kanitz, B. E., Angermeier, L., & Zenk, R. (1994). Cultural sensitivity in multicultural counseling: A perceptual schema model. *Journal of Counseling Psychology, 41,* 125-136.

Schofield, J. W. (1986). Causes and consequences of the color-blind perspective. In J. F. Dovidio & S. L. Gaertner (Eds.), *Prejudice, discrimination, and racism* (pp. 231-253). New York: Academic Press.

Schuman, H., & Krysan, M. (1999). A historical note on Whites' beliefs about racial inequality. *American Sociological Review, 64,* 847-855.

Sears, D. O., Hetts, J. J., Sidanius, J., & Bobo, L. (2000). Race in American politics: Framing the debates. In D. O. Sears, J. Sidanius, & L. Bobo (Eds.), *Racialized politics: The debate about racism in America* (pp. 1-43). Chicago: University of Chicago Press.

Sidanius, J. (1993). The psychology of group conflict and the dynamics of oppression: A social dominance perspective. In S. Iyengar & W. J. McGuire (Eds.), *Explorations in political psychology* (pp. 183-219). Durham, NC: Duke University Press.

Sidanius, J., Levin, S., Liu, J., & Pratto, F. (2000). Social dominance orientation, anti-egalitarianism and the political psychology of gender: An extension and cross-cultural replication. *European Journal of Social Psychology, 30,* 41-67.

Sidanius, J., & Pratto, F. (1999). *Social dominance: An intergroup theory of social hierarchy and oppression.* New York: Cambridge University Press.

Sidanius, J., Singh, P., Hetts, J. J., & Federico, C. (2000). It's not Affirmative Action, it's Blacks: The continuing relevance of race in American politics. In D. O. Sears, J. Sidanius, & L. Bobo (Eds.), *Racialized politics: The debate about racism in America* (pp. 191-235). Chicago: University of Chicago Press.

Smith, P. J. (1999). Teaching the retrenchment generation: When Sapphire meets Socrates at the intersection of race, gender, and authority. *William and Mary Journal of Women and the Law, 6,* 53-214.

Solomon, J. (2000). Skin deep: Reliving "Black like me": My own journey into the heart of race-conscious America. In J. Pera, R. Delgado, P. A. Harris, & S. Wildman (Eds.), *Race and races: Cases and resources for a multiracial America* (pp. 461-464). St. Paul, MN: West Group, American Casebook Series.

Sue, D. W. (2000, February). *Multicultural competence: Individual, professional, and organizational development.* Keynote address presented at the 17th Annual Teachers College Winter Roundtable on Cross-Cultural Psychology and Education.

Sue, D. W., Arredondo, P., & McDavis, R. J. (1992a). Multicultural competencies and standards: A call to the profession. *Journal of Multicultural Counseling and Development, 20,* 64-88.

Sue, D. W., Arredondo, P., & McDavis, R. J. (1992b). Multicultural counseling competencies: A call to the profession. *Journal of Counseling & Development, 70,* 477-486.

Tatum, B. D. (1992). Talking about race, learning about racism: The application of racial identity development in the classroom. *Harvard Educational Review 62,* 1-24.

Texeira, E. (2000, May 22). Justice is not color blind, studies find. *Los Angeles Times,* pp. B1, B8.

Thompson, C. E., & Neville, H. A. (1999). Racism, mental health, and mental health practice. *The Counseling Psychologist, 17,* 155-223.

Thompson, C. E., Worthington, R., & Atkinson, D. R. (1994). Counselor content orientation, counselor race and black women's cultural mistrust and self-disclosures. *Journal of Counseling Psychology, 41,* 155-161.

Three Rivers, A. (1991). *Cultural etiquette: A guide for the well-intentioned.* Indian Valley, VA: MARKET WIMMIN.

Wade, P., & Bernstein, B. L. (1991). Culture sensitivity training and counselor's race: Effects on black female clients' perceptions and attrition. *Journal of Counseling Psychology, 38,* 9-15.

Welch, S. D. (1999). *Sweet dreams in America: Making ethics and spirituality work.* New York: Routledge.

Welch, S. D. (2000). *Training multiculturally competent professionals.* Unpublished document.

Wellman, D. T. (1993). *Portraits of White racism* (2nd ed.). New York: Cambridge University Press.

Worthington, R. L., Mobley, M., Franks, R. P., & Tan, J. A. (2000). Multicultural counseling competencies: Verbal content, counselor attributions, and social desirability. *Journal of Counseling Psychology, 47,* 460-468.

Correspondence regarding this chapter may be addressed to Helen A. Neville, E&CP/Black Studies, 16 Hill Hall, University of Missouri, Columbia, MO 65211 (e-mail address: NevilleH@missouri.edu).

Chapter 18

EXPANDING OUR THINKING ABOUT WHITE RACISM

Facing the Challenge of Multicultural Counseling in the 21st Century

MICHAEL D'ANDREA

JUDY DANIELS

IN SELECTING THE TITLE of this chapter we recognized that many of the persons for whom it was intentionally written might be put off by the term "White racism" and that they would avoid reading the information that is contained within the following pages. We also understand that there are a substantial number of White counselors and mental health professionals who are genuinely apathetic and disinterested in the ways that White racism negatively impacts the lives of millions of persons in the United States and thus would not likely be motivated to read a chapter that focuses on this topic.

Our concerns about the way many White counselors, psychologists, social workers, university administrators, professors, and undergraduate and graduate students respond to the term "White racism" is based on the interactions we have had with thousands of persons in these fields over the past 20 years. This includes individuals who have been involved in our ongoing research on White racism and numerous professional encounters with colleagues and graduate students that focused on multicultural issues in general and the problem of racism in particular (D'Andrea & Daniels, 1999a, 1999b, 1999c). As a result of these experiences, we have noted that the vast majority of White persons included in our research typically reacted in one of three general ways when the topic of White racism was raised for discussion. These common responses included the expression of heightened anger, apathy, and intellectualized detachment (D'Andrea, Locke, & Daniels, 1997). Given the negative impact that racism continues to have on the lives of millions of persons of color who are victimized by this problem (Bowser & Hunt, 1996; Jones, 1997), it is distressing to note the frequency with which mental health professionals, educators, administrators, and graduate students respond to the problem of White racism in such angry, hostile, apathetic, and detached ways.

Despite the negative and apathetic reactions many White persons are likely to exhibit when confronted with the problem of White racism, there are several reasons why we feel compelled to continue to write about this controversial and unpopular topic. First, given the tragic historical legacy White racism has had in the United States and the negative consequences that continue to result from the ongoing perpetuation of this social pathology, we believe that White racism represents one of the most important moral problems our nation faces in the 21st century.

Second, recognizing that the United States is rapidly being transformed from a nation that has traditionally been composed of a majority of persons who primarily came from White European backgrounds to a country in which most of its citizens will come from non-White, non-European, non-English-speaking groups (D'Andrea & Daniels, 2001), it is predicted that mental health professionals will increasingly be called upon to effectively deal with the multiple problems that are directly linked to the perpetuation of White racism in a multicultural, multiracial society.

Third, by reporting on the insights and knowledge we have gained as a result of conducting research on White racism for the past 16 years, we hope to promote a more expansive understanding of the different ways that this serious societal problem continues to be deeply embedded in our societal structures and perpetuated by many mental health professionals.

With this backdrop in mind, we begin our discussion of White racism by defining a number of basic terms that are important to understand when embarking on a serious discussion of this difficult and emotionally laden topic. This includes defining such foundational terms as race, racial minority, persons of color, and White racism.

After defining these terms, we shift our attention to describing the ways in which White racism continues to operate as a pervasive pathological force that oppresses large numbers of persons from diverse cultural and racial backgrounds in this country. This discussion includes examining the various ways that structural racism is deeply embedded in our societal institutions, resulting in a broad range of negative consequences for the overall health and well-being of millions of persons of color in the United States.

Last, we describe some of the common reactions many White counselors, psychologists, educators, university administrators, professors, and undergraduate and graduate students have exhibited regarding the problem of racism. This includes reporting on the findings of our research and describing some of the typical defense mechanisms that White counselors, psychologists, educators, administrators, professors, and undergraduate and graduate students commonly employed during discussions related to White racism.

DEFINITION OF TERMS

Race

The term "race" is one of the most confusing and ambiguous terms that is used in the field of multicultural counseling (Helms & Cook, 1999). On the one hand, most persons think they know what is meant by the term "race" as they easily classify themselves and others according to certain physical characteristics (usually skin color) that are visually apparent. In differentiating individuals according to race, many people classify themselves and others into one of five major racial groups in the United States: African Americans, Asian Americans, Euro-Americans/Caucasians, Native American Indians, and Latinos/Latinas. However, as Helms and Cook (1999) stress,

> race has no consensual biological or physiological definition. . . . Any physical characteristic that one assumes can be used to differentiate one "racial" group from another can generally be found in other racial groups as well. In fact, it has been argued that the range of within-group variability among members of supposedly discrete racial categories with respect to various physiological traits (e.g., blood types, skin colors) exceeds that of between-group variability regarding the same traits. (p. 15)

Although we now know that distinguishing individuals into one of the five major racial groups that were listed above according to certain observable physical characteristics is an extremely flawed and inaccurate way to classify people, such classifications are indeed frequently made by persons in both the general and professional publics. Although these classifications are not necessarily accurate from a biological perspective, they nonetheless represent a general tendency to classify individuals according to socially constructed beliefs about racial differences. These socially constructed beliefs frequently result in inaccurate generalizations about persons and foster the development of positive or negative stereotypes about individuals who are identified as belonging to a certain race. Such socially constructed generalizations and stereotypes help perpetuate conscious and unconscious cognitions about the superiority and inferiority of different groups as well as the legitimacy or illegitimacy of the diverse values, worldviews, and behavioral styles that are manifested by persons who are associated with different racial groups. Notions of White superiority and the inherent inferiority of non-White persons represent powerful social constructions that have historically been nurtured and sustained by the dominant cultural-racial group in the United States (hooks, 1995; West, 1999).

Dominant Cultural Group
Members and Persons of Color

In the United States, the dominant cultural-racial group consists of individuals who by and large have descended from western European countries. These persons have been identified as belonging to the White or Caucasian race, a socially constructed racial identity that distinguishes members of the dominant group in the United States from other persons who are viewed and treated in inferior terms largely as a result of their skin color and cultural group affiliation. To guarantee these persons' position as the dominant cultural-racial group in the United States, historical beliefs about their superiority have not merely been ingrained into their consciousness (through ideological mechanisms such as manifest destiny) but are also institutionalized in a broad range of economic, educational, governmental, and political policies and practices.

The institutionalization of such policies and practices helps guarantee the privileged positionality of persons from the dominant cultural-racial group while simultaneously disenfranchising and oppressing individuals from non-White minority group backgrounds. By institutionalizing ideological beliefs about their own value and superiority and devaluing the essential humanity of persons from non-White backgrounds, members of the dominant cultural-racial group are able to maintain their own privileged positionality at the expense of the economic, personal, psychological, and spiritual well-being of non-White persons in this country (West, 1999).

Multiculturalists have used different terms to refer to individuals who comprise the dominant cultural group in the United States and persons identified as members of non-White minority groups in this country. Terms like Euro-Americans, Anglos, Anglo-Americans, Whites, and White Americans have all been used in the professional literature when referring to the dominant cultural-racial group in the United States. For the purpose of this chapter, the terms "Whites" and "White Americans" are used interchangeably when referring to the dominant cultural-racial group in this nation.

Although the term "non-White minority group members" has effectively been used to connote the lack of power that characterizes the lives of persons from various cultural-racial groups in the United States (Sue, Ivey, & Pedersen, 1996), we find this term problematic in that it implicitly directs attention to the current numerical status of non-White persons in our nation. While it is agreed that persons from non-White, non-European backgrounds currently hold a minority status (politically, socially, and numerically) in our society, the cultural-racial transformation of the United States will predictably result in an obsolescent use of this term. Given the demographic trends that point to the fact that persons from non-White, non-European backgrounds will constitute a numerical majority in a few short decades in the United States, it is stressed that the unprecedented demographic change in the overall makeup of our citizenry will predictably be accompanied by calls for more economic, political, and social power and equity in our society (D'Andrea et al., Chapter 16, this volume). In light of these considerations, we have chosen to use the terms "persons of color" and "non-White, non-European persons" interchangeably in this chapter when referring to individuals who are not a part of the dominant cultural-racial group.

Racism and White Racism

Rollock and Gordon (2000) note that definitions of racism tend to center on three elements: (a) attention directed to "racial" (phenotypic and observable) differences among individuals as members of distinct groups; (b) belief systems concerning the inherent inferiority or superiority of various racial groups; and (c) patterns of behavior that differentially affect the esteem, social opportunities, and life chances of individuals from racial groups that are directly associated with the above mentioned belief systems (pp. 5-6).

When thinking about the meaning of the term "racism," we have noted that many White persons typically fixate on the types of hateful and disrespectful behaviors commonly manifested by individuals from one racial group toward persons of a different racial group. It has been pointed out that such behaviors are easy to identify as being racist not only because of the hatred and disrespect that underlie them but also because of the overt and intentional ways in which they are manifested (Locke, 1992). Despite the negative consequences that predictably result from these overt and intentional racist acts, it has been repeatedly argued that the real power of this social pathology is rooted in the different ways in which it has been institutionalized within the infrastructure of our society (hooks, 1995; Jones, 1997; West, 1999). In writing about this aspect of racism, Chesler (1976) points out that this destructive social pathology is manifested whenever "institutional procedures help create or perpetuate sets of privileges for Whites and exclusions or deprivations for racial minority groups. This usually requires an ideology of explicit or implicit superiority or advantage of one racial group over another, plus institutional power to implement that ideology in social operations" (p. 22).

The issue of power is an important factor that underlies the existence of racism in any society. As members of the dominant racial group who are granted numerous privileges and power by their positionality in a society that continues to be stratified by race (and gender), we have noted that White persons commonly exhibit certain behaviors and emotional

dispositions and fail to exhibit other types of behaviors and emotional reactions that effectively help perpetuate this social pathology. Although attention is often directed to those individuals who manifest overt and
intentional racist behaviors, it is very important to understand that most of
the racism that exists in the United States is perpetuated by millions of
well-meaning, liberal-thinking White persons who react with passive acceptance and apathy to the pervasive ways in which this problem continues
to be embedded in our institutional structures. From the results of our extensive research in this area, we have concluded that most of the racism
that continues to be perpetuated in the United States is, in fact, fueled by
broad-based passive acceptance among the majority of White persons who
unintentionally allow this social pathology to persist by their silent and
complicit acceptance of various ongoing forms of institutional oppression
and racism. Because most of the persons who contribute to the perpetuation of racism through their silent and passive complicity come from
White, European backgrounds, we use the term "White racism" to more accurately identify the type of racism that is pervasive in our country.

THE PERVASIVE NATURE OF WHITE RACISM
IN OUR CONTEMPORARY SOCIETY:
UNDERSTANDING STRUCTURAL RACISM

White racism is not just something that is manifested by a relatively
small number of White persons who belong to the Ku Klux Klan or other
hate groups in the United States. It is not just a phenomenon that is reflected in routine acts of police brutality that disproportionately target persons of color or highly publicized and offensive racial statements made by
celebrities (e.g., professional athletes, college coaches, and government officials). White racism is a pervasive force in our society that is deeply embedded in our societal structures and entrenched in the ideological and
epistemological paradigms used by the dominant cultural-racial group in
the United States to construct meaning of reality (West, 1999).

Despite the tremendous moral courage and sacrifices that civil rights
advocates demonstrated in confronting the problem of White racism during
the 1960s and 1970s, and contrary to the arguments of some individuals
who suggest that White racism no longer represents a meaningful barrier
that negatively impacts the personal well-being of non-White persons in
our nation (D'Souza, 1995), the economic-educational-social-political realities of our society provide overwhelming evidence that underscores how
White racism continues to thrive in our society. Certainly, White racism
has evolved since slavery was an acceptable social-economic practice in the
United States. As this nation's history reveals, the impact of White racism
and its various manifestations changed in several ways over time (see West,
1999):

- Positive changes that occurred during the Reconstruction era that provided brief hope for racial justice as efforts were made to dismantle the formal and informal manifestations of White racism
- The period of Jim Crown segregation that effectively undermined progressive efforts to foster the enfranchisement of persons of color
- Calls for revolutionary changes in the state of race relations in the United States during the 1960s and 1970s that stimulated heightened fear and anger among many White persons in our society
- A resurgence of overt and covert forms of racism that was largely fueled by conservative leadership in our government during the 1980s and 1990s.

White racism remains a major societal problem that will not disappear without concerted effort by all justice-loving persons in this country. For this reason, it is important to avoid being content with the progress that has undeniably been achieved in the past. By being satisfied with the past progress that has been made in this area, many persons develop what Agger (1998) refers to as a "false consciousness" (p. 124) regarding the negative impact that White racism continues to have on the lives of millions of persons in our nation. To avoid becoming complacent and operating from this sense of false consciousness, it is vital for all White persons (and White mental health professionals and graduate students in particular) to become more knowledgeable of the complex ways that this serious problem is manifested in our nation and work to ameliorate this pervasive form of social pathology.

Our research and professional experiences have taught us that many White mental health professionals, educators, administrators, professors, and undergraduate and graduate students who manifest anger or apathy when the issue of White racism is raised for discussion are generally not knowledgeable of the complex ways in which this problem exists in our nation. To help expand White counselors', psychologists', social workers', and students' thinking about the different ways that racism is manifested in the United States, the following section describes numerous examples of racial discrimination as they continue to be reflected in many of the policies and practices of our social structures. These powerful and self-sustaining dimensions of White racism are referred to as *structural racism*.

Economic Manifestations of Structural Racism

When looking at the ways in which structural racism is manifested, there is no better place to start than by examining the serious discrepancies and injustices that are reflected in this nation's economic structures. Economic structures include but are not limited to banking institutions, mortgage and loan companies, societal mechanisms that have been developed to facilitate entry into the workforce (e.g., governmental programs that provide job placement and career development opportunities, private training and employment agencies, and educational institutions), and public and private policies regarding employees' salary scales. Numerous researchers have reported on the various ways that White racism continues to be reflected in many policies, practices, and outcomes that are intricately tied to these economic structures.

For instance, recognizing that banks, mortgage companies, and other types of financial loan agencies represent the primary means by which most people in the United States are able to secure the monetary assistance necessary to start a business or buy a home, Meyers (1995) examined how racial factors influence the approval of loan applications. The results of this investigation indicated that racial discriminatory practices were responsible for approximately 70% of the rejections of loan applications that were submitted by persons of color annually in the United States. This sort of economic discrimination greatly limits the ability of non-White persons to realize their economic potential in a country that maintains the view that anyone can become economically successful if one works hard enough. For the purpose of the present discussion, this research finding represents a powerful example of one of the primary ways that structural racism is maintained economically by members of the dominant cultural-racial group in the United States.

How Structural-Economic Racism Impacts the Quality of Life and Overall Health of Persons of Color

Additional evidence that underscores other ways that structural racism is perpetuated economically in the United States is reflected in national unemployment rates, annual family incomes, and poverty levels that have been reported by numerous researchers. These investigations resulted in the following findings:

1. The unemployment rates for African Americans have consistently remained twice as high as White unemployment rates (11% vs. 5%) during the 1990s (D'Andrea & Daniels, 2001; U.S. Bureau of the Census, 1998).
2. Structural barriers (e.g., poor education, lack of job training programs) that contribute to the disproportionate number of African Americans who remain chronically unemployed have been directly tied to the poverty rate for these persons, which remains nearly three times higher than that of White Americans (33.1% vs. 12.2%) (Sue & Sue, 1999; U.S. Bureau of the Census, 1998).
3. The median net worth of Hispanic American households in 1997 was $16,500, well below the $56,400 median for all households in the United States (Russell, 1998).
4. The annual income level of Native American Indians is only 62% of the U.S. average, with a poverty rate nearly three times higher than for persons in the dominant cultural-racial group in this country (U.S. Bureau of the Census, 1998).

Given the clearly established links that exist between individuals' socioeconomic status and health-related problems, it should come as no surprise that millions of poor African Americans, Asian Americans, Hispanic Americans, American Indians, Native Hawaiians, and Alaskan Natives continue to be at risk for a broad range of physical and psychosocial difficulties. As a result of synthesizing the findings of several researchers, it has been demonstrated that the disproportionate number of persons of color who experience a broad range of physical and psychosocial difficulties is directly related to the economic disenfranchisement of non-White persons in our society in general (D'Andrea & Daniels, 2001). These structurally based economic and health problems contribute to the fact that infant mortality rates for babies who are born to non-White mothers are two and three times higher than infants born to White females in this country. The above mentioned structurally based economic discrepancies have also been linked to shorter longevity rates for poor non-White persons in comparison to their White counterparts (hooks, 1995; West, 1999).

In addition to these tragic health-related problems, structural racism has also been linked to the disproportionate number of non-White persons who are incarcerated in this nation's correctional system. The racial disparities that continue to be reflected in our justice system were underscored by Sue and Sue (1999), who reported that "about 1/3 of African American men in their 20s are in jail, on probation, or on parole. This rate has increased by over 30% during the past five years" (pp. 235-236).

Thus in summarizing these findings, it is accurate to acknowledge that the perpetuation of White racism is directly related to the fact that non-White babies are dying at higher rates than White infants, persons of color live shorter lives due to a host of health-related problems, and a disproportionate number of young African American males forfeit their dreams of leading productive and satisfying lives as the result of being imprisoned in this country's growing correctional industrial complex.

Rather than responding to the high non-White unemployment rates and the crippling levels of poverty that adversely impact persons of color during a time of so-called economic prosperity by creating new job training and educational opportunities, policymakers have reacted to these forms of structural racism by creating more institutional structures that further promote racism during the 1990s (hooks, 1995; West, 1999). One example of such action involves the large amount of government spending currently being directed toward building and maintaining new prisons in the United States. As a result of the tremendous increase in this spending during the 1990s, a large percentage of state and federal expenditures is being directed toward creating new jails and prisons in this country. Tragically, the building of these new prison structures has often taken place in economically impoverished non-White communities where schools are deteriorating and there is a deficit of the sort of educational resources (e.g., books and computers) necessary to effectively prepare students of color to enter an increasingly competitive, technological, global economy (West, 1999).

Educational Manifestations of Structural Racism

Recognizing the important link that exists between the economic disenfranchisement of non-White persons and discriminatory educational practices that are directed toward students of color, civil rights leaders dedicated much time and energy during the 1960s and 1970s to address these forms of structural racism. As a result of their tireless efforts, definite improvements have been made in the overall quality of life for many persons from non-White groups in this country. Among the gains that have been made include improvements in the provision of educational services and outcomes among students of color. As Gay (1997) points out,

> Unquestionably, some significant progress has been made in the last thirty years in the social conditions of schooling and academic achievement of students of color. This is evident in increasing rates of high school graduation; some steady but small improvements in proficiency levels in the academic core subjects (math, science, reading, writing, social studies); and the enactment of federal legislation (such as the Indian Education Act, Chapter 1, and the Bilingual Education Act), which pays for supplementary instructional services for educationally and economically disadvantaged children in kindergarten through grade twelve to assure them equal access to high quality academic achievement. (p. 197)

It is important to emphasize that these achievements did not come easily. These positive changes were largely realized through the courageous efforts of civil rights and social justice advocates who refused to allow the legacy of White racism to continue to go unchecked in this nation's public school systems. Despite the gains that were achieved from the 1960s to the early 1980s, numerous governmental policies and practices established during the Reagan-Bush presidential years have undermined much of the progress that was made in these areas in the past (hooks, 1995; West, 1999). These include the following (Gay, 1997, p. 197):

1. The disqualification of more than 750,000 children (the majority of whom come from non-White backgrounds) from Chapter 1 programs during the mid and late 1980s
2. The relaxation of various requirements that schools were expected to follow in complying with antidiscrimination laws in order to receive federal funds
3. The institution of new funding arrangements benefitting private schools at the expense of urban and inner-city schools
4. Drastic cuts in the funding of bilingual, migrant, Indian, and gender equity educational initiatives

Thus, although the work of civil rights and social justice advocates led to a number of positive changes that benefitted persons of color from the late 1960s to the early 1980s, the strength and resurgence of structural racism continues to be manifested in a number of ways in this country's governmental and educational institutions. Consequently, as we enter the beginning of the 21st century, it has been reported that most elementary and secondary schools in the United States remain racially segregated (Banks & McGee Banks, 1997). In addition to the continuing problem of racial segregation in our schools, several other aspects of our public education system are described below to further explain how structural racism is currently perpetuated in this country.

First, it has been reported that the high school graduation rates for White persons aged 25 or older in the United States is 83.3%, compared with 71.2% for similar-aged African Americans and 54.7% for Hispanic Americans (U.S. Bureau of the Census, 1998). As one might expect, the discrepancies that reportedly exist between the graduation rates of persons from different racial groups correlates with similar discrepancies in school drop out rates. Consequently, while approximately 7.3% of the total number of White school-aged youngsters drop out of school each year in this country, 12.3% of all African American students, and a staggering 30.7% of all school-aged Hispanic American youths reportedly drop out of our public education system annually (Banks & McGee Banks, 1997).

A second form of structural racism that continues to be manifested in our educational institutions relates to the ongoing racial disparities that are manifested in academic achievement. Again, it is important to acknowledge that improvements have clearly been made in the overall performance of persons of color on standardized educational tests from 1983 and the present time (U.S. Department of Education, 1994). Despite these reported improvements, it is equally important to point out that non-White students' test scores continue to remain significantly lower than those generated by White students in this country (Banks & McGee Banks, 1997).

Several theories have been offered to explain the disparities that exist in the academic achievement of students from different racial groups. Some mental health professionals have advanced the belief that innate differences in the intellectual ability of individuals from diverse racial and cultural groups represent an important factor that underlies differences in school success (Jensen, 1969). This perspective has recently been revived in the writings of a number of White social scientists (Herrnstein & Murray, 1994). On the other hand, multicultural advocates argue that differences in school achievement can more accurately be explained by the ongoing use of culturally and racially biased educational assessment instruments (Sue & Sue, 1999), the widespread misdiagnosis of learning problems, which results in the overrepresentation of non-White students in special education classes across the United States (Grossman, 1998; Oswald, Coutinho, Best, & Singh, 1999), and other types of educational inequities that continue to be institutionalized in this nation's public school system. To underscore some of the ways that structural racism continues to underlie much of the inequity that persists in our public education institutions, Banks and McGee Banks (1997) identify sharp disparities in per capita spending for White and non-White students, differences in the quality of instructional services offered, and the availability (and unavailability) of educational resources such as computers in school districts primarily composed of White versus non-White students.

The Manifestation of Structural Racism in the Mental Health Professions

When one directs time and attention to examining the various ways that structural factors contribute to the maintenance of racism in our country, it becomes easier to understand how the vast majority of White persons in the United States (including most White counselors, psychologists, administrators, professors, and undergraduate and graduate students) serve as co-conspirators in this complex problem when they fail to say or do anything that would help ameliorate the problem of racism in our society. Although stating that "most White counselors and psychologists" are guilty of being racist predictably angers many colleagues in the field, there is ample evidence supporting such a statement.

Several multicultural experts have written extensively about the numerous ways that counselors and other mental health professionals have fostered the perpetuation of racism and cultural oppression in our society (Parham, White, & Ajamu, 1999; Ridley, 1995; Sue et al., 1996; Sue & Sue, 1999). These include the overuse of monocultural ethnocentric counseling theories and practices (Sue & Sue, 1999), the use of dominant cultural values as normative standards of mental health for persons from all cultural-racial groups (Parham et al., 2000), and inappropriate diagnostic labels routinely imposed on non-White clients as a result of using culturally biased psychological instruments and other forms of assessment techniques (Ridley, 1995).

Rollock and Gordon (2000) describe additional ways in which White racism continues to impact the delivery of psychological services in this country. These researchers point out that the availability of ethno-culturally diverse therapists and other mental health service providers, the comfort and attitude of these personnel when working with ethno-culturally diverse populations, their attention to prevention in contrast to treatment and remediation, and the appropriateness (and inappropriateness) of using Western psychological models among persons from culturally and racially diverse client populations all reflect ways in which unintentional and covert forms of White racism continue to be manifested in this nation's mental health professions.

The ethnocentric biases upon which traditional counseling and psychotherapeutic theories have been based (Sue et al., 1996), the perpetuation of culturally biased counseling practices (Sue & Sue, 1999), and the general tendency of White mental health professionals to avoid dealing with the ways that clients' racial background and experiences impact their sense of personal well-being (D'Andrea & Daniels, 1999b) all contribute to the perpetuation of White racism in the fields of counseling and psychology. Beyond these theoretical and clinical practices, an even more fundamental, insidious, and pervasive form of White racism continues to operate in the mental health professions. This pervasive form of racism has been referred to as "epistemological racism" (Scheurich & Young, 1997, p. 6).

In discussing this term, Scheurich and Young (1997) explain that racism is generally fueled by conscious or unconscious thoughts about White superiority that are deeply rooted in the epistemology that characterizes our Western civilization. This epistemology not only shapes our thinking about human development, mental health, and helping strategies but in a more basic sense leads us to construct meaning of reality in culturally and racially biased ways. Many persons (including counselors, psychologists, university administrators, professors, and undergraduate and graduate students) generally accept the assumptions and premises of our modern Western epistemology as "common sense," which are thought to represent universal beliefs about the world. However, as postmodern (Gergen, 1994) and multicultural theorists (Parham et al., 1999; Sue & Sue, 1999; Wrenn, 1985) have repeatedly pointed out, such thinking results in narrow, ethnocentric, and culturally encapsulated constructions of the world.

Given the fact that the United States is rapidly becoming a multicultural society, it is important that mental health professionals, educators, and administrators avoid falling prey to the sort of intellectual incarceration that accompanies an unequivocal acceptance of the epistemology with which the fields of counseling, education, and psychology have historically operated. An unequivocal acceptance of any single epistemology is particularly disrespectful and dangerous at a time when this country is undergoing unprecedented changes in the cultural-racial makeup of its citizenry. In fact, our culturally and racially diverse nation is increasingly becoming populated by persons who adhere to different epistemological beliefs and interpretations of the world. These beliefs include different constructions of educational excellence, personal success, psychological health, collective well-being, and helping strategies.

Despite the cultural and racial differences that make up the U.S. populace, we have noted that many White administrators, educators, and mental health professionals continue to impose assumptions and beliefs about education, human development, and psychological health that emerge from a culturally and racially biased epistemology. When these persons do so, they are guilty of perpetuating the sort of epistemological racism (Scheurich & Young, 1997) and cultural oppression (Jones, 1997) that has negatively impacted millions of persons of color throughout the history of the United States.

HOW DO MOST WHITE MENTAL HEALTH PROFESSIONALS, EDUCATORS, AND UNDERGRADUATE AND GRADUATE STUDENTS RESPOND TO THE PROBLEM OF WHITE RACISM?

In light of the numerous ways that racism continues to assault the health and well-being of millions of persons of color in our nation, it might be expected that a relatively large number of White mental health professionals, educators, and undergraduate and graduate students would enthusiastically support calls for corrective action. Minimally, such enthusiastic support might include (a) demonstrating strong feelings of aversion toward this broad-based social pathology, (b) expressing support for efforts that are aimed are ameliorating this problem, and (c) being willing to discuss the specific things that White mental health professionals, administrators, educators, and undergraduate and graduate students can do to address the problem of racism in our universities, communities, and nation as a whole. Because many counselors, psychologists, administrators, educators, and college students are often viewed as being liberal-thinking, well-intentioned persons, these expectations seemed reasonable to us before we conducted our research.

However, as a result of our 16-year study of the psychology of White racism, we did not find much enthusiastic support for the elimination of this problem among the majority of persons who were included in our research. It was particularly disturbing to note that the vast majority of White counselors, psychologists, university administrators, professors, and undergraduate and graduate students we studied did not typically exhibit attitudes and behaviors considered useful in ameliorating the problem of White racism in our society. Given the frequency with which these attitudes and behaviors were repeatedly manifested, we were able to classify them into three general response patterns. Before providing a detailed description of these response patterns, however, we briefly discuss our research focus and methodology as they were somewhat different from the types of investigative approaches employed by other researchers in the past.

Research Focus and Methodology

There are two noticeable differences in our research focus and methodology worth mentioning here. First, rather than focusing on the ways in which White racism impacts persons of color in the United States (as has been the case in most of the studies done in this area in the past), we intentionally directed our attention to the reactions that White persons have toward the problem of racism in the United States.

Another distinguishing feature regarding our approach to studying the psychology of White racism involved the multiple methods used to investigate this complex phenomenon. By using a naturalistic inquiry research approach as well as semistructured interviews, participant observation, and field study techniques, we were able to record the different cognitive, affective-attitudinal, and behavioral reactions that a large number of White persons exhibited when discussing issues related to racism in our nation. To date, we have interviewed and observed more than 1,200 White persons who reside in the northeastern, southeastern, midwestern, southwestern, and far western parts of the United States. These persons come from a broad range of socioeconomic backgrounds: doctors, lawyers, state legislators, law enforcement personnel, ministers, businesspersons, teachers, psychologists, social workers, university administrators, professors, undergraduate and graduate students, and unemployed persons. Although we specifically sought to study the reactions that a broad range of White persons had to the problem of racism in our country, we intentionally positioned ourselves to direct particular attention to the ways that White counselors, psychologists, university administrators, educators, and undergraduate and graduate students responded to this social pathology. As a result, more than 600 of our interviews and observations were done among these persons.

The data that were generated in our 16-year study revealed common patterns and themes in the way White persons typically reacted to the serious problem of racism in our society. It is important to point out here, however, that in describing these three response patterns we do not intend to diminish the unique variability in which many persons responded to this serious problem. Nonetheless, given the limitations that are associated with writing a single chapter on this topic, it is our intent to provide an overview of three of the most commonly observed ways in which White counselors, psychologists, university administrators, professors, and undergraduate and graduate students responded to this destructive form of social pathology in our research. It should also be pointed out that in describing the unique characteristics that distinguish these response patterns, we frequently use direct quotes from a number of the persons who were included in our study. For a more detailed description of our research methodology and results, the interested reader is encouraged to review three recently published works in this area (D'Andrea & Daniels, 1999a, 1999b, 1999c).

RESPONSE PATTERN 1:
OVERT EXPRESSIONS OF ANGER

Given the negative impact that racism continues to have on the health and well-being of millions of persons in the United States, it was surprising to observe the frequency and intensity with which overt expressions of anger were commonly expressed by many White mental health professionals, administrators, professors, and undergraduate and graduate students who were included in our research. It is important to further point out that the sort of anger that was typically expressed was not usually directed to the numerous ways in which racism continues to be perpetuated in our country nor in response to the tragic human suffering that this problem causes many persons in our society.

Rather, these reactions often appeared to be fueled by a heightened sense of frustration over what was repeatedly referred to as the "politically correct climate" that currently exists in our society. When expressing their feelings about this sort of "politically correct" atmosphere, many of the persons we studied did so in sarcastic and depreciating ways. These individuals commonly stated that they believed much of the politically correct sentiment that has developed in the United States is directly connected to the rising popularity of multiculturalism in our country.

One White counselor educator made a statement that reflected a common view that was shared by numerous other persons in our research. In expressing a heightened sense of frustration with the state of race relations in this country, this individual stated that he felt that "many non-White people prejudge me in negative ways without getting to know me. I also feel that there are lots of instances when different kinds of reverse racism occurs and negatively affects lots of White people like me." The latter comment reflected the respondent's thoughts about affirmative action programs and the negative consequences he believes White persons experience as a result of implementing this sort of policy to promote racial justice in our society.

Another theme that was associated with the angry reactions many White persons exhibited in our research involved the expression of a genuine sense of blamelessness regarding the problem of racism. This sentiment was manifested in various ways such as acknowledging that slavery was indeed wrong but adding that "I didn't have anything to do with it," agreeing that racism continues to be manifested in our society but implicitly relinquishing any sense of responsibility for this problem since "it is usually perpetuated by people who are sick or belong to hate groups," and angrily insisting that "I cannot think of a time in my life when I intentionally acted in a racist way."

In attempting to explain these statements and the angry feelings that typically accompanied them from a psychological perspective, we have concluded that they represent the sort of defense mechanisms that many White persons commonly use to avoid dealing with the stress and discomfort that normally accompanies discussions about White racism. More specifically, we have noted that White persons frequently rely on the use of projection and denial to cope with the uncomfortable feelings that are predictably generated in these sorts of discussions.

Projection was commonly manifested in numerous conversations and interviews we conducted with White persons in our research. In this regard, individuals frequently directed blame for this problem on historical situations like the institutionalization of slavery in the 1800s and legal segregation policies in the 1900s. Comments about the historical roots of racism in the United States would typically be followed by a frustrated statement in which many respondents acknowledged that since they had no part in such obvious racist behaviors they are not responsible for the problem. Other White persons in our study were quick to express their anger by indicating numerous times in which they felt persons of color acted in prejudical, discriminatory, and racist ways toward them. These projections were frequently accompanied by a general denial that they were responsible for the perpetuation of racism in our contemporary society or by stating that the problem of racism was really not as bad as a lot of people said it was.

In attempting to explain the sort of anger, projections, and denial that were commonly manifested in our research from a psychological perspective, it is suggested that these types of defensive reactions are often designed to serve a twofold purpose by: (a) helping individuals avoid the uncomfortable process of exploring ways in which they might unintentionally be contributing to the perpetuation of structural racism in this country and (b) alleviating these persons from the responsibility of examining how they benefit from the types of privileges and power that are differentially bestowed on persons in our society as a result of their racial positionality (McIntosh, 1989; West, 1999).

RESPONSE PATTERN 2:
GENERALIZED APATHY

The second response pattern that we frequently noticed White counselors, psychologists, university administrators, professors, and undergraduate and graduate students exhibiting toward the problem of racism involved a generalized sense of apathy. In fact, we found this response pattern to be the one most commonly manifested by the majority of White persons we studied.

As the term suggests, this response pattern is characterized by a lack of interest in the problem of White racism and an absence of a genuine sense of concern about the ways in which millions of persons of color continue to be negatively impacted by this problem. Despite the tremendous negative impact that continues to result from this social pathology, most of the White counselors, psychologists, university administrators, professors, and undergraduate and graduate students in our study demonstrated a lack of motivation to work to ameliorate this problem in their universities, workplaces, and communities.

Most of the White mental health professionals, university administrators, professors, and undergraduate and graduate students who demonstrated a general sense of apathy regarding this problem have been identified as operating from what is called a "liberal disposition of White racism" (D'Andrea & Daniels, 1999c, p. 71). Although commonly acknowledging that they are liberal in their political-social views, persons who operate from this psychological disposition typically demonstrate a lack of understanding and empathy regarding the suffering that White racism continues to cause many persons of color in the United States. It should also be pointed out that, even when provided with information that is intentionally designed to increase their awareness of the negative impact that this problem presents, few persons moved beyond the generalized apathy that characterizes the liberal disposition of White racism (D'Andrea & Daniels, 1999b). In short, such persons were consistently observed to lack the motivation to intentionally act in ways that are designed to ameliorate the problem of White racism in either their personal or professional lives (D'Andrea & Daniels, 1999c).

Similar to the individuals who exhibited the angry response patterns described earlier, the White persons who manifested generalized apathy and disinterest regarding the problem of racism were able to effectively avoid being confronted with the types of racially based privileges and power they experience as a result of being a part of the dominant cultural-racial group in the United States. Avoidance of such confrontation was primarily achieved by maintaining disinterest and noninvolvement in issues or conversations about White racism in their personal or professional lives. This included demonstrating an unwillingness to become engaged in discussions or other types of learning about the unfair treatment and suffering that continues to be imposed on millions of persons of color in the United States as a result of the perpetuation of various forms of structural racism. By avoiding opportunities to learn about the complex ways that White racism continues to be perpetuated in our society, many White persons are able to (a) deny the extent to which racism exists as a social-political reality in this country and (b) abdicate any sense of responsibility for dealing with this serious problem.

Besides the use of denial, we have identified two additional factors that play important roles in fostering the sort of generalized apathy commonly exhibited by many White persons in the fields of counseling, education, and psychology. The first factor involved a reluctance to say or do things that might offend other White persons or cause controversy in their work settings. As one White professor explicitly stated, "I do not get involved in dealing with racism because it might put off some people and I just don't want to alienate them." A similar sentiment was frequently noted among many other White persons included in our research. As a result of feeling personally obligated to conform to the existing status quo and fearing the repercussions that might ensue from demonstrating the courage of one's own conviction to deal with the problem of racism, many White counselors, psychologists, university administrators, professors, and undergraduate and graduate students avoid making any commitment to address this problem in their work.

The second factor that contributes to the apathy that most of the White mental health professionals, administrators, educators, and students we studied demonstrated relates to the lack of organizational incentives that are in place to reward individuals for working to ameliorate the problem of White racism. Most organizations do not provide incentives for counselors, psychologists, administrators, professors, and students to actively work to address the problem of racism in educational institutions, mental health agencies, businesses, and communities. Not only is there a lack of incentives to do such work, but individuals who have made an effort to address this problem reported that they frequently experienced negative repercussions in doing so. These negative repercussions ranged from a general lack of interest that was manifested by organizational leaders and coworkers to increased feelings of alienation from their co-workers to being reprimanded by supervisors for "acting too much like an activist" in their work. A combination of the lack of organizational incentives that are discussed above and the tendency to be fearful of creating controversy and alienating others nurture a sense of learned helplessness that many White counselors, psychologists, administrators, professors, and undergraduate and graduate students exhibited in our research.

RESPONSE PATTERN 3:
INTELLECTUAL DETACHMENT

The third response pattern discussed in this chapter is called "intellectual detachment." In our research we noticed that many White persons (and especially White professionals) were quite knowledgeable of the different ways that racism has historically been perpetuated in the United States. What was particularly interesting about these persons was that they were not only knowledgeable about the various ways racism is manifested in our society and the negative impact that it has on persons of color, but they also possessed a good understanding of other forms of oppression (e.g., sexism, heterosexism, classism, ageism, and ableism). In articulating their views about racism and other forms of oppression, these individuals did so with a genuine sense of passion that clearly distinguished them from the persons who exhibited the sort of angry and apathetic response patterns described earlier.

Although these persons clearly possessed a great deal of knowledge about the various forms of oppression that continue to exist in our society and passionately stated the need to effectively address these oppressive factors, they were rarely observed to take direct action in dealing with these problems in personal or professional ways. While having the opportunity to share their insights about the problem of White racism in the United States provided a chance to demonstrate their intellectual competence in this area, the knowledge they had about this subject was usually not connected to any pragmatic action to ameliorate White racism in the places where they lived and worked. Thus, these White counselors, psychologists, university administrators, professors, and undergraduate and graduate students tended to fit the stereotypic image of those individuals who "talk the talk" about racism but are unwilling to "walk that talk" in any meaningful, change-producing way.

CONCLUSION

Given the unprecedented changes that are occurring in the demography of the United States, White mental health professionals, administrators, and educators will increasingly be pressed to provide services that effectively address the needs and concerns of persons from culturally and racially diverse populations. One of the major problems that these professionals will predictably face involves the various ways in which White racism continues to negatively impact the health and well-being of millions of persons of color in this country.

Having conducted an extensive study of the ways that White counselors, psychologists, university administrators, professors, and undergraduate and graduate students typically react to this problem, we found that angry, apathetic, and detached responses frequently characterize the ways in which most of these persons deal with this destructive phenomenon. By presenting this information we hope to stimulate an expanded understanding of the various ways that White racism continues to be perpetuated in our society and encourage an increased level of discussion about the types of things mental health professionals, educators, university administrators, professors, and undergraduate and graduate students can do to more effectively deal with this important problem in the future.

The rapid cultural-racial transformation of the demography of the United States demands that immediate attention and resources be developed to address the problem of White racism in our professional training programs, clinical practices, research endeavors, university campuses, and communities. To do less will result in the mental health and educational systems becoming increasingly perceived as irrelevant institutions by culturally and racially different persons in our nation. More important, continued inattention to this problem will reinforce the sort of moral paralysis that many White counselors, psychologists, university administrators, professors, and undergraduate and graduate students have historically demonstrated when it comes to dealing with the problem of White racism. By making the commitment to confront the negative impact that White racism continues to have in our nation, we must be willing to act with

courage in advocating for the dignity, health, development, and well-being
of all citizens of the United States. In doing so, we will truly help build a
more just society in the 21st century.

REFERENCES

Agger, B. (1998). *Critical social theories: An introduction.* Boulder, CO: Westview.

Banks, J. A., & McGee Banks, C. A. (Eds.). (1997). *Multicultural education: Issues and per-spectives* (3rd ed.). Needham Heights, MA: Allyn & Bacon.

Bowser, B. J., & Hunt, R. G. (Eds.). (1996). *Impacts of racism on white Americans* (2nd ed.). Thousand Oaks, CA: Sage.

Chesler, M. A. (1976). Contemporary sociological theories of racism. In P. A. Katz (Ed.), *Towards the elimination of racism* (pp. 21-72). New York: Pergamon.

D'Andrea, M., & Daniels, J. (1999a). Building on our knowledge of racism, mental health, and mental health practice: A reaction to Thompson and Neville. *The Counseling Psychologist, 27,* 224-238.

D'Andrea, M., & Daniels, J. (1999b). Exploring the psychology of White racism through naturalistic inquiry. *Journal of Counseling and Development, 77,* 93-101.

D'Andrea, M., & Daniels, J. (1999c). Understanding the different psychological dispositions of White racism: A comprehensive model for counselor educators and practitioners. In M. Kiselica (Ed.), *Confronting prejudice and racism during multicultural training* (pp. 59-88). Alexandria, VA: American Counseling Association.

D'Andrea, M., & Daniels, J. (2001). Facing the changing demographic structure of our society. In D. C. Locke, J. Myers, & E. Herr (Eds.), *The handbook of counseling* (pp. 529-539). Thousand Oaks, CA: Sage.

D'Andrea, M., Locke, D. C., & Daniels, J. (1997, April). *Dealing with racism: Counseling strategies.* A workshop presented at the annual meeting of the American Counseling Association, Orlando, FL.

D'Souza, D. (1995). *The end of racism.* New York: Free Press.

Gay, G. (1997). Educational equality for students of color. In J. A. Banks & C. A. McGee Banks (Eds.), *Multicultural education: Issues and perspectives* (3rd ed., pp. 195-225). Needham Heights, MA: Allyn & Bacon.

Gergen, K. J. (1994). Exploring the postmodern: Perils or potentials. *American Psychologist, 49,* 412-416.

Grossman, H. (1998). *Ending discrimination in special education.* Springfield, IL: Charles C Thomas.

Helms, J. E., & Cook, D. A. (1999). *Using race and culture in counseling and psychotherapy: Theory and practice.* Boston: Allyn & Bacon.

Herrnstein, R., & Murray, C. (1994). *The bell curve: Intelligence and class structure in American life.* New York: Free Press.

hooks, b. (1995). *Killing rage: Ending racism.* New York: Holt.

Jensen, A. (1969). How much can we boost IQ and school achievement? *Harvard Educational Review, 39,* 1-123.

Jones, J. M. (1997). *Prejudice and racism* (2nd ed.). New York: McGraw-Hill.

Locke, D. C. (1992). *Increasing multicultural understanding.* Newbury Park, CA: Sage.

McIntosh, P. (1989, April). White privilege: Unpacking the invisible knapsack. *Peace and Freedom,* pp. 10-12.

Meyers, S. L. (1995). Racial discrimination in housing markets: Accounting for credit risk. *Social Science Quarterly, 76,* 543-561.

Parham, T. A., White, J., & Ajamu, A. (1999). *The psychology of blacks: An African centered perspective.* Upper Saddle River, NJ: Prentice Hall.

Oswald, D. P., Coutinho, M. J., Best, A. M., & Singh, N. N. (1999). Ethnic representation in special education: The influence of school-related economic and demographic variables. *Journal of Special Education, 32,* 194-206.

Ridley, C. R. (1995). *Overcoming unintentional racism in counseling and therapy: A practitioner's guide to intentional intervention.* Thousand Oaks, CA: Sage.

Rollock, D., & Gordon, E. W. (2000). Racism and mental health into the 21st century: Perspectives and parameters. *American Journal of Orthopsychiatry, 70,* 5-13.

Russell, C. (1998). *Racial and ethnic diversity* (2nd ed.). Ithaca, NY: New Strategist.

Scheurich, J. J., & Young, M. D. (1997). Coloring epistemologies: Are our research epistemologies racially biased? *Educational Researcher, 26,* 4-16.

Sue, D. W., Ivey, A. E., & Pedersen, P. B. (Eds.). (1996). *A theory of multicultural counseling and therapy.* Pacific Grove, CA: Brooks/Cole.

Sue, D. W., & Sue, D. (1999). *Counseling the culturally different: Theory and practice* (3rd ed.). New York: John Wiley.

U.S. Bureau of the Census. (1998). *Populations profile of the United States.* Washington, DC: Government Printing Office.

U.S. Department of Education. (1994). *Digest of education statistics.* Washington, DC: Government Printing Office.

West, C. (1999). *The Cornel West reader.* New York: Basic Civitas Books.

Wrenn, C. G. (1985). Afterword: The culturally encapsulated counselor revisited. In P. B. Pedersen (Ed.), *Handbook of cross-cultural counseling and therapy* (pp. 323-329). Westport, CT: Greenwood.

Correspondence regarding this chapter may be sent to Michael D'Andrea, Department of Counselor Education, University of Hawaii, 1776 University Avenue, Honolulu, HI 96822 (e-mail address: Michael@hawaii.edu).

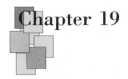

Chapter 19

VISIONS OF REVOLUTION FROM THE SPIRIT OF FRANTZ FANON

A Psychology of Liberation for Counseling African Americans Confronting Societal Racism and Oppression

SHAWN O. UTSEY
MARK A. BOLDEN
ANDRAE L. BROWN

But the war goes on: and we will have to bind up for years to come the many, sometimes ineffaceable, wounds that the colonist onslaught has inflicted on our people.

—From *The Wretched of the Earth*
by Frantz Fanon (1963, p. 249)

RACISM AND OPPRESSION in the United States is insidious, pervasive, and ubiquitous, and for those who experience it daily, the consequences can be deadly. By definition racism does not exclusively victimize any one particular racial group, but historically its impact has been especially brutal for African Americans. Since arriving on these shores White Americans have been relentless in developing, implementing, and enforcing social, economic, and institutional policies based on rigid racial and cultural group distinctions. Consequently, racism has become embedded in the social, psychological, and institutional structure of White America (Essed, 1990; Jones, 1997). Although racism is not limited to the United States of

America, it has enjoyed a tremendous amount of acceptance and, to some degree, respectability throughout the history of this country.

For African Americans, the chronic strain associated with the experience of racism and oppression has been implicated in the development of several stress-related diseases—for example, high blood pressure, stroke, cancer, cardiovascular disease, substance abuse and alcoholism, and depression (see Burke, 1984; McCord & Freeman, 1990; Outlaw, 1993; Smith, 1985). The negative influence of racism in all of its forms and manifestations (both overt and subtle: direct and indirect) permeates every aspect of African American life, and as such, significantly infringes upon the quality of life for this segment of the population (Essed, 1990; Jones, 1997; Semmes, 1997; Smith, 1985). In fact, the stress associated with the experience of everyday racism ranks high on the list of problems African Americans bring to the counseling process (National Institute of Mental Health, 1983, cited in Priest, 1991). Given the pervasiveness of racism and oppression in the lives of African Americans and its deleterious effects on the psychological and somatic health of this population, it seems intuitive that counselors have an ethical obligation to develop effective strategies for addressing these issues with their African American consumers.

There have been numerous attempts by psychologists and other mental health practitioners to address, in the context of counseling and psychotherapy, the deleterious effects of racism and oppression on the psychological well-being of African Americans (i.e., Abernethy, 1995; Lee, 1999; Priest, 1991; Smith, 1985). For the most part, these interventions prescribed traditional counseling techniques and strategies to address issues related to the racism and oppression experienced by African Americans. However, traditional approaches to psychology and psychotherapy are part of the problem in that they maintain the status quo by encouraging the oppressed to adapt to an oppressive social structure (Bulhan, 1985; Ivey, 1995). What is needed is a culturally relevant approach to counseling that facilitates the liberation of African Americans from societal racism and oppression through consciousness raising and a collective action toward self-determination.

In this chapter, we integrate a psychology of liberation from a Fanonian perspective in offering a more effective modality for counselors and other mental health practitioners working with African Americans confronting societal racism and oppression. In the first section, we introduce Frantz Fanon the person and provide some background information so that the reader may understand his personal and professional development as a revolutionary leader and freedom fighter, mental health practitioner, and visionary for the full development of the human spirit. In the next section, for the purposes of establishing a context for understanding the experiences of African Americans with racism and oppression, a sociohistory of the "Black experience" in the United States is provided. Following the sociohistory of the African American experience, we discuss the impacts of racism and oppression with regard to prolonged exposure and acute racism-reactions. Next, we present the tenets for a psychology of liberation as discussed in the works of such revolutionary visionaries as Fanon, Bulhan, and Freire. Finally, we propose several levels of action for counselors seeking to facilitate authentic liberation for their African American clients.

FRANTZ FANON:
PROPHET OF REVOLUTION

Frantz Fanon remains a luminary in the fields of revolution, liberation, and psychology. His impact on the world continues to reverberate from his groundbreaking and revolutionary analysis of the impacts of oppression delineated in *Black Skin, White Masks* (Fanon, 1967) and *The Wretched of the Earth* (Fanon, 1963). Fanon was interested in the application of psychology to healing the "tormented psyches" of those whom he referred to as the "wretched of the earth." Although Fanon's life ended at age 36, he gained immortality through his applied theoretical contributions to revolutionary reconceptualizations of the plight of oppressed people, the effects and process of colonization, decolonization, and neocolonization, and the inevitability of African liberation. In the context of liberation, Fanon's work embodied and vocalized not only the Algerian spirit during the Algerian war but spoke to the plight of all African descended people throughout the diaspora, transforming him into a clarion call for the voiceless.

Fanon was born July 20, 1925, on the Caribbean island of Martinique into a middle-class Black family. He was the middle child of eight siblings and the youngest of four boys. By most accounts, Frantz had a close relationship with his mother, whom he viewed as the stability and strength behind the family. However, there was a strained relationship between Fanon and his father; he felt his father had deserted the family, leaving his mother to raise all eight children alone (Bulhan, 1985). As a child, Fanon was described as creative, strong willed, crafty, courageous, and a natural leader. His commitment to liberation was evident quite early in his development, as reflected in his intense interest in the liberation of France from German occupation (Bulhan, 1985). In fact, at age 17, Fanon left home to join the armed services in the fight for France's liberation.

Fanon was well aware of the insidious nature of racism and oppression on the island of Martinique (Fanon, 1963, 1967). He observed the overt acts of racism, harassment, and sexual exploitation at the hands of the French army who occupied the Caribbean island for most of his adolescence. Fanon experienced personal encounters with racism and bigotry when he was stationed in North Africa for military duty in the French army (Bulhan, 1985; Fanon, 1963). There Fanon suffered humiliation based on his color at the hands of White soldiers from French, Italian, and German forces (Bulhan,

1985). Fanon also observed that the African soldiers, often referred to as wild savages, were treated even worse than the Antillean soldiers. These experiences in the military, and later in medical school, along with the influence of several leading revolutionary thinkers would serve to transform Frantz into the "prophet of revolution" that the world would come to know, love, and respect.

Fanon's development as a revolutionary scholar and leader was greatly influenced by his teacher and mentor Aime Cesaire. Cesaire coined the term negritude and began to advocate that Blacks abandon their efforts to assimilate into French culture and instead embrace their African roots. Being among the most vocal critics of Western civilization at the time, Cesaire was relentless in his attacks on French culture, describing it as a civilization that is sick and morally decayed (Bulhan, 1985). Cesaire's influence on Fanon was primarily at the level of critique and analysis of the role of Black consciousness in the liberation of the oppressed—negritude. Fanon later broke with Cesaire because he felt the negritude movement lacked a mechanism of transformation required for the liberation of the oppressed and alienated (Bulhan, 1985). This departure with Cesaire and the negritude movement demarcates Fanon's move toward a true revolutionary praxis for the liberation of oppressed people in the African diaspora.

Having completed medical school, Fanon returned to Martinique for a brief time where he practiced medicine as a general practitioner. He worked in France for a while before going to Algiers for what would become his defining work in psychiatry and revolution. In Algiers, Fanon witnessed the brutality of the torture and repression heaped upon the indigenous population by the French armed forces (Fanon, 1963). While there, Fanon had begun secretly working on behalf of the Algerian liberation movement "Front de Liberation Nationale" (FLN); he would later be expelled from Algeria for his efforts toward the liberation of the Algerian people from French colonialism and oppression (Bulhan, 1985). Fanon's participation in the Algerian struggle for liberation made him the target of several assassination attempts. While traveling in Mali, Fanon suddenly became ill, and in December 1960 he was diagnosed with leukemia. A year later, after completing his most controversial work, *The Wretched of the Earth,* Fanon died in Bethesda, Maryland. His remains were flown back to Algeria to be buried beneath the soil he struggled to liberate (Bulhan, 1985).

A SOCIOHISTORY OF THE AFRICAN *MAAFA*

A psychology for the liberation of African Americans from the destructive forces of White supremacy and domination must be grounded in the social and historical experiences of this population. Fanon (1963) believed that all problems of the human condition existed inside the context of sociohistory and culture. Furthermore, he posited that theories that ignore the role of an oppressive social structure tend to blame the victim for their own oppression as well as underestimate their power to transform the forces responsible for their personal and collective misery. For the purposes of providing a sociohistorical context of the African American condition under a system of White supremacy and domination, as currently exists in the United States, it is necessary to begin with a discussion and overview of the African *Maafa*.

Maafa is Kiswahili for "Great Disaster" and refers to the forced dislocation of millions of Africans from their families, communities, and cultural reality and their subsequent enslavement under a violently brutal system of chattel slavery that existed throughout the Western Hemisphere (Ani, 1994). During the Maafa, Africans were captured and, enslaved, marched to the west coast of the African continent where massive ships awaited them for transportation to strange and foreign lands. During these infamous middle passages, men, women, and children were chained together in the hull of the enslavement ships in squalid conditions (e.g., human waste, vermin, unbearable heat, death, and disease) for a journey that often lasted between 8 and 12 weeks (Everett, 1991). Upon arrival at various destinations, the enslaved Africans were separated from husbands, wives, and children and then sold into a system of perpetual servitude that in the history of humanity remains unequalled in its violence and brutality (Everett, 1991; Stampp, 1956).

Chattel slavery in the United States was a unique and complex economic and social institution whose operation and maintenance required the total submission and complete obedience of the enslaved African. A necessary ingredient for maintaining the system of chattel slavery that existed in the United States was the absolute debasement and dehumanization of the enslaved Africans. The African was viewed as an inferior being, occupying a status no different from that of domesticated animals (Everett, 1991; Stampp, 1956). Another important component of the enslavement process was to effectively sever the African from any cultural ties with Africa (e.g., language, religion, and music) while at the same time voiding them of any sense of personhood (Akbar, 1984, 1996; Morgan, 1985; Pinkney, 1993).

Under the institution of chattel slavery, all aspects of the enslaved lives were dictated according to the rigid social, psychological, and physical controls implemented by the slavoracy (Akbar, 1984; Everett, 1991; Stampp, 1956). According to Stampp (1956), the collective strategy for the maintenance of such absolute control was carried out by several methods. First, slaveholders had to establish and maintain strict discipline, whereby the enslaved must willingly obey at all times. In addition, the enslaved needed to accept their personal inferiority and status in perpetual servitude as the natural order of things. To instill a sense of awe in the enslaved African, the slaveholders often demonstrated their enormous power and control over the enslaved to the degree that it produced a constant state of fear in the communities of the enslaved (Stampp, 1956). Finally, a most effective and lasting method of control was to instill in the enslaved a sense of general helplessness and complete dependence on their masters for all their needs (Akbar, 1984; Morgan, 1985).

Whites relied on social, scientific, and biblical rationalizations to protect themselves from any sense of collective guilt that might result from the inhumane treatment of other human beings and to justify the brutal and horrific systematic enslavement of African people as a source of forced labor (Stampp, 1957; Pinkney, 1993). For example, by distorting the biblical story of Noah the American slavocracy attempted to convince themselves and the American public that Africans, as evidenced by their black skin, were the descendants of Ham who had been cursed by God for transgressions against Noah, his father (Thompson, 1977). Another rationale used to justify the enslavement of African people was that in addition to their innate inferiority the Africans were a separate and subhuman species of humankind for whom perpetual servitude was the natural order (Thompson, 1977). It was reasoned that the Africans, who were "uncivilized" and "barbaric," would in fact benefit from their servitude under the highly "civilized" and "cultured" White race (Pinkney, 1993). Such justifications for the forced servitude of Africans, though obviously flawed and irrational, would eventually become permanently incorporated into the psychological and social consciousness of White America (Jones, 1997; Pinkney, 1993) and Black America (Akbar, 1984, 1996; Wilson, 1990).

Although chattel enslavement legally ended at the conclusion of the Civil War in 1865, the status of African Americans changed little over the next few decades (Pinkney, 1993). For a brief time during Reconstruction, and under the watchful eye of the Union Army, African Americans did enjoy a few privileges associated with being full participants in a free society (Pinkney, 1993). However, shortly thereafter, the Union Army left, and almost immediately "black codes" were enacted to restrict the rights of African Americans and maintain White supremacy as the law of the land (Everett, 1991; Pinkney, 1993).

Many of the myths developed and maintained about the innate inferiority and deficient moral character of African Americans to justify keeping them in bondage were now used to keep them from being full participants in American society. African Americans were segregated from Whites in education, employment, and public accommodations (Pinkney, 1993). There were laws against interracial marriages; just the thought of intimate relations with a White woman could prove fatal for an African American male (Everett, 1991; Pinkney, 1993). According to Stampp (1957) and Pinkney (1993), Whites strictly enforced the racial codes of conduct governing the behavior of African Americans, often by means of unspeakable acts of violence (e.g., lynching, burnings, castration, beatings, and intimidation) (Everett, 1991; Stampp, 1957). There are several historical accounts (e.g., Tulsa, Oklahoma; Rosewood, Florida) of the mass murder of African

Americans and the wholesale destruction of thriving Black communities by mobs of Whites seeking to avenge alleged infractions of the racial codes of conduct.

With the death of Reconstruction, Whites wasted no time institutionalizing White supremacy. Race became the dominant factor in the social, economic, and political structure of American society (Pinkney, 1993; Semmes, 1997). Several major Supreme Court rulings served as the vehicle that officially relegated African Americans to a subordinate status in society. For example, in 1883 the Court ruled that the Civil Rights Act of 1875, which made it a crime to deny any citizen equal access to public accommodations, was unconstitutional (Pinkney, 1993). Additionally, in the 1896 *Plessy v. Ferguson* case, the Court ruled that racially segregated facilities mandated by law were not in violation of the Thirteenth and Fourteenth Amendments to the U.S. Constitution. The majority opinion of the Court declared that the inherent racial inferiority of African Americans could not be undone by any provisions in the Constitution (Pinkney, 1993).

During the first half of the 20th century, America would experience many changes, but the status of African Americans would remain relatively static. Although African Americans would engage in constant struggle for their civil and human rights, and in some cases win major concessions to undo government-sponsored segregation (Pinkney, 1993), little could be done to change White America's perception of African Americans as being innately inferior and subhuman. The tenets of White supremacy had become so well ingrained in the consciousness of White America that they soon found expression in almost all aspects of American life (Akbar, 1984; Feagin, 1991; Pinkney, 1993). By the time Jim Crow had been dismantled and African Americans were, in theory, entitled to equal protection under the law and access to public accommodations, racism and White supremacy had become a permanent fixture in the psychological, social, political, and economic landscape of American society.

RACISM AND OPPRESSION:
INSTRUMENTS OF WHITE SUPREMACY AND DOMINATION

If you do not understand White Supremacy (Racism)—what it is, and how it works—everything else that you understand, will only confuse you.

(Fuller, 1969, p. A)

White Supremacy

Several renowned scholars have examined the psychological and cultural mechanisms of White supremacy and global domination emanating out of the European worldview and survival thrust (Ani, 1994; Fuller, 1969; Kambon, 1998; Welsing, 1991; Wilson, 1998). White supremacy is defined by Sutherland (1993) as the "varied manifestations of violence imposed on people of African descent by Europeans for the satisfaction of the Europeans' maleficent psychohistorical needs" (p. 5). Welsing (1991) defined White supremacy as a system of power and domination, determined consciously or subconsciously, and embedded in the logic, thought, speech, action, perceptions, and affective response of people who classify themselves White. According to Fuller (1969), White supremacy permeates cultural, economic, ideological, military, political, psychological, religious, and social structures in the service of European global conquest and domination.

The system of White supremacy and domination is perpetuated and maintained through violence, cultural hegemony, and the myth of European superiority (Ani, 1994; Fanon, 1963; Kambon, 1998; Sutherland, 1993). The European worldview, which values rugged individualism, dominance over nature, competition, materialism, and aggression, is congruent with a White supremacy orientation toward relations with others (Ani, 1994; Kambon, 1998; Myers, 1993). According to Welsing (1991), it is the culture/system of White supremacy and its thrust toward the global domination of "people of color" that produces the phenomenon called racism. Fuller (1969) posits that in spite of any self-professed economic and political independence on the part of individuals of color, all "non-White" people are victims of White supremacy.

Racism

Essed (1990) defines racism as "a complex aggregate of prejudice and discrimination based on an ideology of racial domination and oppression" (p. 11). Fanon (1964) recognized that traditional racism, grounded in vulgar notions of the biological inferiority of certain racial groups, usually dark-skinned people, had become transformed into a more sophisticated and insidious form of cultural racism. Jones (1997) describes racism as "resulting from the transformation of race prejudice and/or ethnocentrism through the exercise of power against a racial group defined as inferior, by individuals and institutions with the intentional or unintentional support of the entire culture" (p. 280).

Jones (1997) posits that the experience of racism is multidimensional and can be classified using the following tripartite typology: (a) *individual racism*—experienced on a personal level, (b) *institutional racism*—racism embedded in the policies of a given institution, and (c) *cultural racism*—the cultural practices of one group lauded as superior to that of another. Essed (1990) extends the individual realm of racism to include *collective racism*. Collective racism occurs when organized (or semi-organized) Whites/non-Blacks seek to restrict the rights of Blacks—for example, when a Black family moves into a White community and is met with open hostility by its new neighbors.

Oppression

Freire (1970) views oppression as an act or acts of violence that by its very nature interferes with a person's ability to evolve as a complete human being. He defines oppression as any attempt by an individual and/or group of individuals to exploit and/or block/hinder a person's and/or group's pursuit of self-determination. The highest form of oppression is what Bulhan (1985) termed "autocolonialism," which occurs when the victims of White supremacy, consciously or unconsciously, participate in their own oppression.

Not only is oppression achieved and maintained by violence, but the violence gradually permeates all aspects of the social order, whereby it impacts the everyday lives of the oppressed (Fanon, 1963, 1967). In the course of time, such violence becomes normalized, camouflaged, subtle, and at some point embedded in the institutional and psychological reality of society. The violence of oppression, once established in the culture, consumes and dehumanizes both the oppressed and the oppressor (Bulhan, 1985; Fanon, 1963, 1964).

IMPACTS OF RACISM AND OPPRESSION

A normal Negro child, having grown up within a normal family, will become abnormal on the slightest contact with the White world.

(Fanon, 1967, p. 142)

According to Wilson (1998), the most nefarious tool of White supremacy and domination is psychic violence. Psychic violence is unrelenting in its impact on the collective African American psyche and is perpetrated through the media and other cultural outlets in words, symbols, images, and misinformation that instill a sense of false consciousness, self-alienation, and self-hatred in the minds of its victims. Given that African Americans are confronted daily with a constant onslaught of psychic violence by a hostile, anti-Black society, many are at risk of experiencing some form of psychological, emotional, social, cultural, and/or spiritual decomposition. Consequently, the dislocation and distortion of the African spirit/reality and the imposition of an alien spirit/reality and worldview (European) will produce behaviors that are self-defeating, self-destructive, and counter to the liberation of African people (Akbar, 1984; Ani, 1994; Kambon, 1992, 1998; Wilson, 1998).

In the context of American society, the institutionalized violence of racism and White supremacy is so sinister and ubiquitous that its victims are very often unable to fully recognize it in all its forms, even when personally experienced (Akbar, 1984; Feagin, 1991; Jones, 1997). Firmly held notions of Black inferiority and White superiority have consummated the cultural legacy of racism in American society. Anti-Black sentiments are casually, commonly, and openly expressed daily in American society, both directly and through cultural symbolism (Ani, 1994; Wilson, 1998). To the extent that African Americans internalize these anti-Black attitudes and accept their subordinate status in society, as prescribed to them under a social order of White supremacy, the most damning and irreversible effect will occur: self-alienation (Akbar, 1984; Fanon, 1963, 1967; Wilson, 1990, 1998).

Impacts of Prolonged
Exposure to Racism and Oppression

Paulo Freire (1970) coined the phrase "fear of freedom" to describe the psychological process whereby the oppressed are bound by the parameters of the relationship between themselves and their oppressor. The term *prescription*, used to characterize the relationship between the oppressor and the oppressed, represents the imposition of the oppressor's reality onto the reality structure of the oppressed (Freire, 1970). Having adopted the reality of the oppressor, the oppressed are fearful of freedom. To achieve freedom would require the oppressed to reject the reality of the oppressor and replace it with their own. Having adapted to the social order of domination and subordination, the oppressed are resigned to accept their oppression as destiny (Akbar, 1984, 1996; Freire, 1970).

Fanon (1967) prescribed a sociogenetic approach to a psychology of liberation for the oppressed based on the concepts of *internalization* and *objectification* (Fanon, 1967). In this framework, internalization is the process wherein external, sociohistorical reality becomes incorporated into the psyche of the oppressed. Objectification, on the other hand, is the process whereby man, through his own efforts, achieves congruence between himself and his external reality. Fanon understood that through the mechanisms of oppression, specifically a social structure based on the domination of others, a person is unable to achieve self-objectification and is prone to internalize the negative identities associated with the psychological assaults heaped upon him or her by the social institutions seeking to maintain their oppression.

According to Fanon (1967), a person's obsessions, anxieties, inhibitions, and contradictions are not the result of the unconscious but the manifestation of the internalization of conflict in the social order as well as restrictions imposed on one's liberty. Fanon posited that the denial and/or abdication of liberty is directly related to psychopathology with regard to its definition, etiology, and symptom expression. According to this perspective, psychopathology is the manifestation of sociohistorical and cultural conflict in persons with a low threshold for tolerance. In this regard, psychopathology is the person-specific response to a pathogenic social order.

Fanon (1963) believed that adopting the cultural reality of the oppressor and abandoning one's own resulted in a profound sense of alienation for the oppressed. He proposed the following five aspects of alienation as a reaction to conditions of oppression:

1. Alienation from the self—to be alienated from one's personal identity
2. Alienation from the significant other—estrangement from one's family or group
3. Alienation from the general other—characterized by violence between Blacks and Whites
4. Alienation from one's culture and history—estrangement from one's language and history
5. Alienation from creative social praxis—denial and/or abdication of self-determination and of socialized and organized activity, which is at the core of the realization of human potential.

Similar to Fanon, Akbar (1984) proposed that African Americans who adopt the worldview of the oppressor experience alienation. He developed an Africentric classificatory system of four mental disorders that result from the assimilation of an alien worldview by people of African descent (see Kambon, 1998). The first, *Alien-Self Disorder*, is characterized by a conscious-level rejection of one's African reality, a denial of the reality of racism, and the active attempt of African Americans to emulate a European worldview/reality. The second, *Anti-Self Disorder*, shares some characteristics with Alien-Self Disorder but has the added element of covert and overt hostility toward all things African. The third, *Self-Destructive Disorder*, reflects the ineffective and destructive attempts of African Americans to cope with the unnatural conditions of White supremacy and domination. The fourth, *Organic Disorder*, refers to the physiological and/or biochemical diseases having their etiology in the oppressive conditions typical for the victims of White supremacy (e.g., ecological racism, poor nutrition, and substandard health care).

Kambon (1998), another Africentric scholar, proposed that African Americans who are alienated from their "natural African self-consciousness" experience *Cultural Misorientation* (CM), which, according to Kambon, is the net result of the European cultural oppression experienced by African Americans that disconnects them from their natural African cultural reality. African Americans who prescribe to an individualistic orientation, express and/or exhibit anti-African/Black behavior, manifest self-depreciating or self-destructive tendencies, or are exploitive and/or hostile to other African Americans are seen by Kambon as suffering from the mental disorder Cultural Misorientation. According to Kambon,

African Americans can experience CM in varying degrees of severity (i.e., minimal, moderate, or severe CM). In the context of White supremacy, CM, although a mental disorder characterized by an anti-African self-consciousness, is viewed as normal and mentally healthy behavior.

Acute Racism Reactions

In addition to the impacts of long-term exposure to racism and oppression, African Americans are at risk of experiencing a number of acute racism reactions. We propose that there are six racism-related reactions that characterize African Americans' response to the psychological and physiological processes associated with the experience of racism and oppression. Although the reactions may occur simultaneously, each response is distinctive in its functionality and interpretation by the respondent. The racism-related reactions are as follows: (a) race-related trauma, (b) racism-related fatigue, (c) anticipatory racism reaction, (d) race-related stress/distress, (e) racism-related frustration, and (f) racism-related confusion. The following sections provide further explanations of the racism-related reactions and examples of their physical and psychological manifestation.

Race-Related Trauma

Race-related trauma is the spiritual, psychological, and physiological devastation that African Americans experience following exposure to stressors involving the direct personal experience, that is, victim, witness, learning of the actual or attempted death/injury to one's person, or other threat to one's physical integrity on the basis of their race, skin color, or as a result of the vicious and aggressive encroachment of oppression and White supremacy. Symptoms associated with race-related trauma include recurring thoughts and/or nightmares regarding the traumatic event, anxiety, fear, sleeplessness, and depression. Race-related trauma is not a pathological reaction per se but a logical and predictable response to racism and oppression.

Events that potentially trigger the onset of a race-related traumatic episode include being victimized with regard to housing or employment discrimination, race-based exclusion from goods and services, humiliation and degradation in public places, witnessing and/or experiencing mob violence (i.e., lynching, being attacked by a hate group), and being harassed, detained, arrested, and/or beaten by the police or other law enforcement personnel. Notable race-related events that have traumatized the collective psyche of African Americans include the dragging death of James Byrd in Jasper, Texas; witnessing the videotaped beating of Rodney King; the brutal beating and sodomy of Abner Louima by New York City police; the murder of Eleanor Bumpers by New York City police; or the murder of Amadou Diallo, also by New York City police (note that this list is hardly exhaustive). These horrific events, once heard by the masses, cause fear, anger, outrage, and shock in the African American community.

Racism-Related Fatigue

Racism-related fatigue is the tremendous psychological and physiological exhaustion that African Americans experience as a result of and in response to the chronic exposure to racism and oppression. Racism-related fatigue is a physiological manifestation of the constant, sweltering, and grinding toll that the individual experiences in combating racism, oppression, and White supremacy daily. The more determined the struggle against racism and oppression, the more taxing on one's ability to maintain focus in daily routine tasks, concentrate, or participate in activities that require physical exertion.

Similar to the physical fatigue one experiences as a result of exhaustive training and the chronic fatigue that women experience while pregnant, racism-related fatigue is just as exhaustive and debilitating, making daily chores and routine tasks challenging and at times impossible. The causality of racism-related fatigue often goes unrecognized because of its coupling with the daily challenges of life—balancing family, school, intimate relationships, and financial obligations—and work environments.

Anticipatory Racism Reaction

An *anticipatory racism reaction* is a defense mechanism that African Americans develop after being the victim/recipient and or combatant of racial discrimination and racially motivated hostility. The development of the anticipatory racism reaction is necessary and functional as it forces the individual to remain aware at all times in all situations involving Whites, based on their previous interracial experiences. Although functional for self-protection and environmental awareness, the extreme amount of energy that the individual expends while attempting to maintain this high level of awareness increases his or her anxiety, becoming too taxing and burdensome to sustain.

The fear and threat of being attacked results in a state of hypervigilance for African Americans who are constantly confronted with personal and shared experiences with racism and oppression (Essed, 1990; Feagin, 1991). Even in a perceived nonthreatening environment, the mechanisms of anticipatory racism reaction are unable to disengage, consequently making the situation uncomfortable for others. The effort which the individual must exert in anticipation of a race-related incident occurring may be more anxiety producing and stressful than the anticipated encounter itself (Essed, 1990).

Race-Related Stress/Distress

Chronic exposure to racism and oppression has been shown to have a deleterious effect on the psychological and physical well-being of African Americans (Utsey, 1997; Utsey & Payne, 2000). Racism is viewed as a major source of stress in the lives of African Americans, thereby resulting in increased incidences of stress-related diseases (Outlaw, 1993). Stress is recognized as a person-environment encounter that is appraised as relating to one's well-being and taxes or exceeds the person's resources to cope with a situation (Lazarus & Folkman, 1984, cited in Outlaw, 1993). In this regard, encounters with racism and oppression result in an acute source of stress for African Americans.

Symptoms associated with *race-related stress/distress* include the onset of tension headaches, muscle tightness, inability to concentrate, intrusive thoughts regarding a specific racism encounter, and a general sense of anxiety and tension. Moreover, race-related stress/distress may result in greater susceptibility to minor (e.g., common cold, flu) and major (e.g., hypertension, cancer) illnesses due to a weakened immune system.

Racism-Related Frustration

Racism-related frustration occurs when African Americans believe that they are powerless over the treatment they receive because of their race. This experience often results in feelings of anger, irritability, aggravation, disappointment, dissatisfaction, and lack of fulfillment and satisfaction. Encounters with racism and oppression that are neither traumatic nor life-threatening are still bothersome and upsetting. The individual involved in the incident recognizes that the encounter is both unnecessary and frivolous but must be entertained and managed until a conclusion is reached. If the situation is not resolved, closure cannot occur, and the individual will remain frustrated until a new racism encounter is experienced and the existing frustration is magnified.

Racism-Related Confusion

Racism-related confusion is a reaction that occurs when an individual in the midst of an onslaught of racist exchanges continues to ask, "Who am I?" (Fanon, 1963). In addition to this consuming question and search for identity in an oppressive society, the oppressed, now psychologically and physically fatigued, are left to function in bewilderment. Other questions now need answering: "What is going on?" "Who's problem is this?" and the unanswerable "Why me?" While in this state of racism-related confusion, the oppressed begin to look at events and individuals differently. Things that were once certain are now uncertain; positions known are now unknown. As the oppressed are continuously attacked and placed in compromising positions, they now question their own involvement and skills and internalize the plight of deserving victims.

A PSYCHOLOGY OF LIBERATION
FROM A FANONIAN PERSPECTIVE

Eurocentric Psychology:
Instrument of Oppression

Several scholars have noted the historical complicity of Western/Euro-American psychology in the service of White supremacy and domination (for an in-depth review of the history of racism in psychology, see Guthrie, 1998; Thomas & Sillen, 1972). Psychology was, and continues to be, used to justify the domination of Black people and other oppressed groups. It has been through the malevolent lens of Western/Euro-American psychology that African Americans have been, and continue to be, maligned and portrayed as psychologically, emotionally, and morally deviant. Therefore, Eurocentric psychology (i.e., Western/Euro-American) must be placed within its historical context of the conquest, domination, and demonization of African people. Moreover, given that Eurocentric psychology is a tool of White supremacy and domination, it is not amenable to the liberation of oppressed people.

Traditional psychological theories as well as contemporary psychotherapy function as an instrument of social control rather than a mechanism for social change (Bulhan, 1985; Ivey, 1995). The focus of modern psychotherapies is one of self-compromising adjustment to the status quo of oppression as opposed to a praxis for liberation, which by definition encourages resistance from the domination of an oppressive social structure (Bulhan, 1985; Comas-Díaz, Lykes, & Alarcon, 1998). Traditional Western psychotherapy has as its goal personal adjustment, adaptation, developing increased self-worth, competence, and individual autonomy. In traditional approaches to counseling and psychotherapy, the responsibility is with the individual to effect change in one's own life in order to increase one's personal happiness. The individual is seen as the primary facilitator for establishing the conditions amenable to healthy psychological and social functioning. Moreover, traditional forms of counseling and psychotherapy are ineffective for use with oppressed populations because they tend to ignore an individual's status in the social order.

Approaches to counseling and psychotherapy that focus solely on an individual's social and psychological well-being do not serve the interest of those who are oppressed. Counselors and other mental health workers are ill advised to focus on the individual rights and needs (i.e., autonomy, self-esteem, etc.) of persons from oppressed groups; instead, the focus should be on obtaining the collective liberty of the group (Bulhan, 1985). An individual focus in working with persons who are oppressed perpetuates a sense of defenselessness and is counter to developing a necessary sense of collective struggle among oppressed people (Akbar, 1996). Individualism for the oppressed is a form of alienation and/or the betrayal of self or the collective group (Fanon, 1967; Kambon, 1998). Therapeutic interventions and techniques that are geared toward reducing symptoms, changing behavior, and modifying the personalities of individuals should be discouraged when working with oppressed populations. In contrast, strategies and techniques that are based on a psychology of liberation must seek to effectively change the social structures responsible for the oppression of Black people (Bulhan, 1985; Comas-Díaz et al., 1998).

A Psychology of Liberation

> Power and liberty are of course never given; they are demanded, taken, and assumed. For if and when "given," they are at best conditional, often superficial, and readily "taken away."
>
> (Bulhan, 1985, p. 276)

A psychology of liberation requires a paradigmatic shift for psychologists and other mental health practitioners (healers) for developing more appropriate interventions for working with oppressed populations (Bulhan, 1985; Comas-Díaz et al., 1998; Ivey, 1995; Parham, White, & Ajamu, 1999). Efforts toward the liberation of African Americans must be directed at changing causes, not just a reduction in associated symptoms. Moreover, healers seek to help the oppressed empower themselves to solve their own problems as opposed to fostering dependency and powerlessness (Freire, 1970). Instead of encouraging the individualization of oppression-related syndromes, healers must push for a collective action among the oppressed that has as its goal the deconstruction of the oppressive social order (Bulhan, 1985; Wilson, 1998). Essential to the deconstruction of the oppressive social structure is raising the awareness of oppressed persons regarding the nature and consequences of their oppression, including the historical and societal context of White supremacy and domination (Freire, 1970; Comas-Díaz et al., 1998).

A psychology of liberation does not focus on the immediate and private distress of individuals but encourages members of oppressed groups to view their predicament as a collective experience requiring a collective response (Bulhan, 1985). Individuals are helped to understand how collectivism, interdependence, and intersubjectivity are the natural order of human behavior (Kambon, 1992, 1998; Myers, 1993). In working with the oppressed, healers must place all diagnostic conceptualizations and interventions in a sociohistorical context (Bulhan, 1985; Comas-Díaz et al., 1998; Fanon, 1963, 1967; Nobles, 1990; Parham et al., 1999). Furthermore, effective work with the oppressed must be based on them defining their own problems, seeking their own solutions, and choosing their own means of effecting change (Bulhan, 1985; Ivey, 1991).

Self-determination is an essential ingredient for the authentic liberation of any people. It is the process and capacity to make choices, exercise control over one's behavior, and to ultimately influence one's destiny (Bulhan, 1985; Freire, 1970). In the context of psychotherapy, it follows that a main goal of the therapeutic intervention with people who are oppressed is to foster, encourage, and facilitate self-determination. The quest for self-determination requires the process of identifying and defining the self through an internal, historical lens, identifying and defining the nature of the problem (White supremacy), and identifying and proactively working toward the solution of the problem (Bulhan, 1985; Comas-Díaz et al., 1998; Freire, 1970; Parham et al., 1999). The generational mission is fulfilled when the generation works toward the solution but is betrayed when the problem persists unchallenged (Fanon, 1963).

Interventions based on a psychology of liberation are only concerned with change. This change is usually aimed at the social institutions and organizational structures that oppress (Bulhan, 1985). The organized efforts of the oppressor and his or her institutions must be countered with the reorganization of the institutions and activity of the oppressed (Bulhan, 1985; Fanon, 1963). The counselor/healer seeks to empower through organizing and mobilizing people in an effort to effect change in the social structures that are responsible for the oppression of the client (Bulhan, 1985; Fanon, 1963). Goals must be defined, programs developed to carry out the aims of the goals, and the oppressed called to collective action in implementing changes to the oppressive social structure (Bulhan, 1985). Healers must ground their interventions in the development of a comprehensive plan, including strategies and tactics for achieving liberation (Bulhan, 1985).

A psychology of liberation encourages the empowerment of the oppressed through organized and socialized activity aimed at the restoration of personal biographies and a collective history that had formally been distorted and denied or been placed within the context of the oppressive social structure (Fanon, 1963). Under conditions of oppression, reciprocity and equality are nonexistent (Ani, 1994; Kambon, 1998). Under conditions of oppression life becomes morbid and the individual and collective sanity of the people is tenuous given the infringement on the time, space, energy, and identity of those being oppressed (Bulhan, 1985).

It becomes difficult, near impossible, for the person to develop a sense of self-integrity when they continuously experience psychological and emotional assaults from the violence of their oppression (Fanon, 1963, 1964). Given the constant onslaught of the violence of White supremacy experienced by the oppressed it is appropriate and often necessary for counselors to assist with immediate relief from the effects of the insult and injury experienced in the face of racism and oppression (Bulhan, 1985;

Comas-Díaz et al., 1998). However, this is not done at the expense of effecting change to the oppressive social structures that belie their problems in the first place. Hence, the authentic liberation of African Americans from the oppressive social order of the United States requires the articulation and application of an anti-oppressive model of psychological health and well-being (Ivey, 1995; Semmes, 1996). Such a model should be articulated by African American healers and grounded in an Africentric framework (Kambon, 1992, 1998).

The Working Alliance:
The Liberator and the Liberatee

A psychology of liberation must break with the paradigm that maintains a therapist-patient power inequity, lack of reciprocity in the therapeutic relationship, and elitism that parallels the existing oppressive social structure (Bulhan, 1985). A situation in which the therapeutic relationship is itself a mirror of the social order that maintains oppression cannot result in healing for the oppressed but simply serves to preserve the status quo of oppression. In fact, terms such as patient and client should be discarded because they perpetuate the power inequity and dependency inherent in traditional counseling relationships (Ivey, 1995). For the purposes of this discussion, we use the term "person(s) seeking liberation" to refer to individuals of African descent in the process of struggling for their liberation.

Given that the primary task of the healer/clinician is to restore liberty to the oppressed, the therapist must maintain an active role in the therapeutic process. The context and site of action for the therapist's work is society and the oppressive social structure that denies the oppressed liberation (Bulhan, 1985; Fanon, 1963). It is important that persons seeking liberation be afforded their own space, time, and respect for their privacy and that no immediate demands be made on the persons' liberty nor questions raised regarding their personal appearance. The persons are accepted for who they are but challenged to evaluate their current state of existence in an oppressive social order (Bulhan, 1985; Comas-Díaz et al., 1998).

In work with members of oppressed groups, attention must be given to the therapeutic alliance and problems inherent in the relationship between the therapist and client (Bulhan, 1985). White therapists may be prone to view the Black client as defined solely by the pathology of oppression. Another common pitfall is to avoid discussions of race and oppression altogether, invoking the illusion of color blindness. Black therapists may experience their own sense of conflict around their Blackness and attempt to avoid discussions of race or they may overidentify in an effort to work through their own insecurities around their group membership status. Another source of difficulty for the Black therapist is the potential for mistrust stemming from their social class status.

African-Centered Approaches
to the Liberation of African Americans

An Africentric framework, as applied to the liberation of African Americans, places the needs and interests of African-descended people at its center. It allows African Americans to draw upon the "best African cultural practices" (Sutherland, 1993; T'Shaka, 1995) for self-preservation, self-determination, and ultimately liberation. Africentric psychology is realized in systemic-based practices that seek to find the divine expression within the relationships of humans to each other, to their environment, and to the Creator (Myers, 1998). The key components of Africentric psychology are balance, reciprocity, harmony, rhythm, collectivism, a focus on spirit/spirituality, and connecting humans with their environment and the universe (Kambon, 1998; Myers, 1999).

The philosophical assumptions of Africentric psychology are grounded in an African worldview and are best articulated according to its ontological, epistemological, and axiological framework. According to Myers (1999), in the African ontological perspective the nature of reality is both spiritual and material. At the epistemological center of the African worldview is the notion that self-knowledge is the foundation for all knowledge. It is through symbolic imagery and rhythm that the individual knows. The axiological perspective of the African worldview holds that interpersonal relationships among people are the most important component in the realm of human values. In the African worldview, there is a union of opposites, and all things are interrelated through human and spiritual networks (Myers, 1999).

The Africentric approach uses a both/and approach to epistemology; it is holistic, rational and intuitive, thus developing whole thought based on cognitive, affective, and emotive factors. The Africentric paradigm is also a practice-based paradigm and does not exist solely in the realm of mere thought. Asante (1990) notes that Africentricity "seeks agency and action" (p. 19). The usefulness of Africentricity for the African in America is grounded in the African culture, which is a dynamic expression of African reality. Therefore, based in this diasporic context, the Africentric paradigm employs healthy cultural practices derived from Africa and those that African Americans have developed while on these shores. An example of soul expression unique to African Americans is the advent of jazz. Jazz epitomizes Africentrism because it consciously employs values that reflect African philosophy—that is, spontaneity, rhythm, harmony, and rational and intuitive processes (Hester, 1999).

Africentrism in the therapeutic context focuses on consubstantiation, the interconnectedness of divine or universal spirit within all entities (Nobles, 1990). With spirit as a focal point, one goal for an Africentric approach to therapy is to illuminate the spirit (Kambon, 1998; Nobles, 1990), which in the Fanonian context requires a raising of consciousness. Raising consciousness is the most important part of therapy because it allows for spirit illumination through self-determination and cultural connection, which corresponds to the self-knowledge and self-development indicative of praxis (Freire, 1971), the dialectical approach (Fanon, 1963), an Africentric, holistic approach that employs collective struggle. Fanon (1963) notes that

> the claim to a natural culture in the past does not only rehabilitate that nation and serve as a justification for the hope of a national culture. In the sphere of psycho-affective equilibrium it is responsible for an important change in the native. (p. 170)

Consciousness raising and spirit illumination are both collective and individual responsibilities that occur through rituals of harmony. Harmony requires the African American community to proactively participate in maintaining the "equilibrium," the point of healthy interaction, with the Creator, the community of spirits, ancestors, elders, both adults and children, nature, history, present conditions, and future aspirations (Nobles, 1990). Rituals exemplify how culture is used as a tool for healing, revitalizing, and liberating (Ani, 1990; Arewa, 1998; Stewart, 1999).

Rituals allow the African American to strengthen the connection with positive ancestors, develop more community-mindedness and create the sacred time-space (Ani, 1990) that allows the transcendent, transformative nature of spirit to exist (Agyei & Akoto, 1998). Stewart (1999) notes that "through ritualization . . . that which is alien and alienates and dislocates being and spiritual vitality becomes harmonized and ordered through the ceremonial invocation of the spirit and power of divine reality" (p. 23). Thus, rituals establish an African sense of time that insulates African American reality from the limitations of the European ethos (Ani, 1994) and reconnects the African American to the realm of spirit.

It has been noted that consciousness raising and ritual are two approaches to revolutionary liberation for the African. Consciousness raising should develop what Sutherland (1997) calls an authentic struggler who strives "for the liberation of productive forces and the enhancement of African person's psychological, military, economic, cultural, social, spiritual, and political progress" (p. 59). Akoto notes that

> historical consciousness . . . involves the adoption of new criteria for life; where Afrikan centered values and definitions dictate the rhythm of one's life. This new consciousness corresponds in part to Fanon's "Fighting phase" where the formerly culturally alienated are completely reenculturated in such a way that their identification with their own culture is complete, and their commitment to battle for its existence and development is conceived. (p. 25)

This is consistent with the Fanonian context of a psychology of liberation that requires the multimodal liberation of all spheres (i.e., politics, law, religion, government, economics, family relationships, productivity, and history) where the institutional mechanisms of oppression operate. To this end, we recommend five levels of action toward the liberation of African Americans.

The first level of action needed is a program of community psychoeducation to provide a framework for understanding White supremacy, oppression, and the impacts of slavery so that African Americans understand the nature and context for their relationship to the oppressor (see Akbar, 1996; Ani, 1994; Armah, 1979; Fanon, 1963, 1967; Welsing, 1991). This becomes vitally important so that African Americans understand that many of the conditions endemic in the Black community (e.g., poverty, crime, alcohol and substance abuse, and stress-related diseases) are the result of White supremacy and oppression, not some innate weakness in the character structure or personalities of African-descended people. This first step and all the others can be achieved through community forums held at cultural institutions, community agencies, and churches and should achieve the goal of preventing race-related confusion. This step would allow the community to address the following questions: "What is the condition of African Americans, and why are African Americans in this condition?"

The next level of the psychoeducation process is for the community to understand, revitalize, and embrace the traditional African concepts of reciprocity, harmony, and order, which will allow African Americans to understand their extended family relationship to each other while simultaneously preventing the continued practice of self-negation and auto-colonialism (see Armah, 1979; Agyei & Akoto, 1998; Fanon, 1963, 1967; Nobles, 1990; T'Shaka, 1995). This step should not only teach culture but use culture to teach (i.e., using libations to begin meetings, seeking spiritual advice from elders for decision-making processes, developing a healthy village to raise a healthy child, etc.). This step will allow African Americans to answer the questions "Who were we before we lost our way, and who will we be under our new way?"

The third level of action requires the community to conceptualize its optimal functioning based upon African-centered health, which should decrease incidences related to the organic disorders and some stress-related acute-racism reactions (e.g., hypertension, diabetes, cancer, and stroke). Semmes (1996) notes the influence of racism and oppression on the dietary habits of African Americans, specifically the widespread consumption of unhealthy foods having their origin in the enslavement experience (i.e., "soul food"). Moreover, the lack of adequate exercise among African Americans results in poorer health and shorter life expectancies. Institutional racism has led to a scarcity of adequate medical care available in the African

American community (McCord & Freeman, 1990; Semmes, 1996). Much of the misinformation regarding proper nutritional and health care practices can be addressed through consciousness raising and psychoeducation. Collective action is required to dismantle the institutional racism that denies African Americans access to preventive health care.

The fourth level of action requires the use of material and human resources to promote economic stability that will achieve the liberation of African Americans by attending to basic biological needs, the ability to be self-sufficient, and the production of the necessary goods for the self-determination of the community (see Akbar, 1996; Kambon, 1998; Wilson, 1998—i.e., recirculating money in the Black community, starting and supporting Black-owned businesses, working toward being a productive member of the African American community, preventing capitalistic materialism, etc.). Moreover, economic stability allows for political consciousness and the ability to effect radical change based on a viable means of African-centered politics, which is predicated on a strong economic base (Wilson, 1998). Along with political consciousness, economic development should be guided by the principles of African cosmology so as to understand how the divine order affects our notion of production and reciprocity with the earth's natural resources. Harmonizing the collective efforts of African Americans would "provide the economic platform for launching the African American community into the mainstream of international trade and commerce and thereby to permit it to provide substantially greater employment and economic opportunities for its constituents" (Humphreys, 1994, cited in Wilson, 1998, p. 591).

The final and most important level of action is spiritual liberation. The African spirit has been the most viable strength of African liberation (Ani, 1990; Stewart, 1999). Thus, accessing this strength through ritual is imperative for the liberation of African Americans. African American spirituality pervades all domains of life, and due to the African survival thrust (Kambon, 1992, 1998) the spirit has protected and preserved the African American as much as the African American has used spirituality as a source of survival (Stewart, 1999). African metaphysical systems are one way to access the spirit (Ani, 1990). In addition, the Black church has historically served as a source of strength for preserving the African spirit (Asante, 1990; Stewart, 1999). Another practical way to access the spirituality, or spiritness (Nobles, 1990), of African Americans is to establish rites of passage (Arewa, 1998).

Rites of passage create community and allow for the elders to become an integral part of the African American liberation by imparting their wisdom and experience to the youth. Rites of passage are a ritualistic approach to adult development that imparts education, vocational development, ethical responsibility, moral maturity, and internal/spiritual identification for the youth. Rites of passage help each individual understand one's purpose in life and how that purpose will facilitate community, which is a way to achieve Fanon's "generational mission." Ultimately, rites of passage let one understand one's true nature, which implies that it can be used as a way to access self-determination and transcend the boundaries of spiritual incarceration brought about by the imposition of Christian missionaries.

Spiritual liberation will result in a communal effort toward achieving the freedom of African Americans through the common denominator of consubstantiation. Spiritual liberation is guided by spirit and sees spirit in all areas of struggle. Consequently, it seeks to distinguish the deep structure from the surface structure, the spiritual from the physical, the macro universe from the micro-man, and subsumes all of the previous processes of liberation. African American liberation may only exist when all Africans have the freedom to express the soul in sacred-time-space. This along with the aforementioned goals is intertwined and inseparable, as is the African to the African spirit and the inevitability of African liberation (see Ani, 1990; Fu-Kiau, 1991; Nobles, 1990; Stewart, 1999). In short, spiritual liberation is the ultimate level of consciousness raising.

In addition to strengthening the spiritual nexus, the plight of oppressed Africans in the diaspora and on the continent must be recognized and viewed as one struggle (Nobles, 1998; Sutherland, 1993; Wilson, 1998). Dual liberation struggles (T'Shaka, 1995), of continental and diasporic African liberty, allow the proper self-analysis of African Americans as non-minorities, by virtue of the global African community. Dual liberation also allows Africans in America and throughout the diaspora to internalize a global consciousness that supersedes tribalism, the glorification of geographically based ethnic differences (i.e., identify as African American, Jamaican, Haitian, etc., as opposed to African), and "saline consciousness" (Soyinka, 1990), the notion that Africa and Africans exist only within the confines of the coastlines and that only people and events within Africa are African. As the ravages of White supremacy are a global phenomenon, it is necessary for African Americans to understand, and acknowledge that, at the core, they are an African people.

SUMMARY AND CONCLUSION

The work of Frantz Fanon has not received adequate attention in the psychological literature with regard to applied approaches to counseling and psychotherapy. Fanon provided a framework for conceptualizing a psychology of liberation for African people throughout the diaspora who are oppressed (Bulhan, 1985). In this chapter we argued that African Americans continue to suffer deleterious effects related to their chronic exposure to invidious forms of societal racism and oppression. Furthermore, we noted that, although psychologists and other clinicians have attempted to address issues related to the racism and oppression experienced by African Americans, traditional approaches to psychotherapy have failed to provide the praxis necessary for their true and complete liberation.

A psychology of liberation requires a paradigmatic shift among psychologists and other mental health practitioners so as to develop more appropriate interventions for working with oppressed populations. Efforts should be directed at changing causes, not just symptom reduction. Counselor-activists must seek to empower the oppressed, thus allowing them to solve their own problems as opposed to fostering dependency and powerlessness. Moreover, instead of encouraging the individualization of oppression-related syndromes, counselors must push for a collective action among the oppressed that has as its goal the deconstruction of the oppressive social order. An Africentric approach to counseling African Americans toward liberation is recommended, given its consistency with Fanon's belief in a culturally relevant praxis for the liberation of the oppressed.

REFERENCES

Abernethy, A. D. (1995). Managing racial anger: A critical skill in cultural competence. *Journal of Multicultural Counseling and Development, 23*, 96-102.

Agyei, K., & Akoto, A. N. (1998). *The Sankofa movement: Re-Afrikanization and the reality of war.* Hyattsville, MD: Oyoko InfoCom.

Akbar, N. (1984). *Chains and images of psychological slavery.* Jersey City, NJ: New Mind Productions.

Akbar, N. (1996). *Breaking the chains of psychological slavery.* Tallahassee, FL: Mind Productions & Associates.

Ani, M. (1990). *Let the circle be unbroken: The implications of African spirituality in the diaspora.* New York: Nkonimfo Publications.

Ani, M. (1994). *Yurugu: An African-centered critique of European cultural thought and behavior.* Trenton, NJ: African World Press.

Arewa, C. S. (1998). *Opening to spirit: Contacting the healing power of the chakras & honoring African spirituality.* London: Thorson's.

Armah, A. K. (1979). *Two thousand seasons.* Chicago: Third World Press.

Asante, M. K. (1990). *Kemet, Afrocentricity, and knowledge.* Trenton, NJ: African World Press.

Bulhan, H. A. (1985). *Frantz Fanon and the psychology of oppression.* New York: Plenum.

Burke, A. W. (1984). Is racism a causatory factor in mental illness? *International Journal of Social Psychiatry, 30*, 1-3.

Comas-Díaz, L., Lykes, M. B., & Alarcon, R. D. (1998). Ethnic conflict and the psychology of liberation in Guatemala, Peru, and Puerto Rico. *American Psychologist, 53*, 778-792.

Essed, P. (1990). *Everyday racism: Reports from women of two cultures.* Claremont, CA: Hunter House.

Everett, S. (1991). *History of slavery.* Secaucus, NJ: Chartwell Books.

Fanon, F. (1963). *The wretched of the earth.* New York: Grove.

Fanon, F. (1964). *Toward the African revolution.* New York: Grove.

Fanon, F. (1967). *Black skin, White masks.* New York: Grove.

Feagin, J. R. (1991). The continuing significance of race: Antiblack discrimination in public places. *American Sociological Review, 56*, 101-116.

Freire, P. (1970). *The pedagogy of the oppressed.* New York: Continuum.

Fu-Kiau, K. K. B. (1991). *Self healing power and therapy: Old teachings from Africa.* New York: Vantage.

Fuller, N. (1969). *The united independent compensatory code/system/concept: A textbook/workbook for thought, speech and/or action for victims of racism (White supremacy).*

Guthrie, R. V. (1998). *Even the rat was White: A historical view of psychology* (2nd ed.). Boston: Allyn & Bacon.

Hester, K. E. (1999). Parallel streams of consciousness. In K. E. Hester (Ed.), *Issues involving innovative Afrocentric art forms: The call and response journal of the Africana Studies and Research Center at Cornell Univesity.* Ithaca, NY: Hesteria.

Ivey, A. E. (1995). Psychotherapy as liberation: Toward specific skills and strategies in multicultural counseling and therapy. In J. G. Ponterotto, J. M. Casas, L. A. Suzuki, & C. M. Alexander (Eds.), *Handbook of multicultural counseling* (pp. 53-72). Thousand Oaks, CA. Sage.

Jones, J. M. (1997). *Prejudice and racism* (2nd ed.). New York: McGraw-Hill.

Kambon, K. K. K. (1992). *The African personality in America: An African-centered framework.* Tallahassee, FL: Nubian Nations Publications.

Kambon, K. K. K. (1998) *African/Black psychology in the American context:* Tallahassee, FL: Nubian Nation Publications.

Lee, C. C. (1999). Counseling African American men. In L. E. Davis (Ed.), *Working with African American males* (pp. 39-53). Thousand Oaks, CA: Sage.

McCord, C., & Freeman, H. P. (1990). Excess mortality in Harlem. *New England Journal of Medicine, 322,* 173-177.

Morgan, J. C. (1985). *Slavery in the United States: Four views.* Chapel Hill, NC: McFarland.

Myers, L. J. (1993). *Understanding an Afrocentric world view: Introduction to an optimal psychology* (2nd ed.). Dubuque, IA: Kendall/Hunt.

Myers, L. J. (1998). The deep structure of culture: Relevance of traditional African culture in contemporary life. In J. D. Hamlet (Ed.), *Afrocentric visions: Studies in culture and communication* (pp. 3-14). Thousand Oaks, CA: Sage.

Nobles, W. (1990). African philosophy: Foundation of Black psychology. In R. L. Jones (Ed.), *Black psychology* (pp. 47-63). Berkeley, CA: Cobb & Henry.

Nobles, W. (1998). To be African or not to be: The question of identity or authenticity— Some preliminary thoughts. In R. L. Jones (Ed.), *African American identity development* (pp. 185-206). Hampton, VA: Cobb & Henry.

Outlaw, F. H. (1993). Stress and coping: The influence of racism on the cognitive appraisal processing of African-Americans. *Issues in Mental Health Nursing, 14,* 399-409.

Parham, T. A., White, J. L., & Ajamu, A. (1999). *The psychology of Blacks: An African centered perspective* (3rd ed.). Upper Saddle River, NJ: Prentice Hall.

Pinkney, A. (1993). *Black Americans* (4th ed.). Englewood Cliffs, NJ: Prentice Hall.

Priest, R. (1991). Racism and prejudice as negative impacts on African American clients in therapy. *Journal of Counseling and Development, 70,* 213-215.

Semmes, C. E. (1996). *Racism, health, and post-industrialism: A theory of African American health.* Westport, CT: Praeger.

Smith, E. M. J. (1985). Ethnic minorities: Life stress, social support, and mental health issues. *The Counseling Psychologist, 13,* 537-579.

Soyinka, W. (1990). *The African world and the ethnocultural debate.* In M. K. Asante & K. W. Asante (Eds.), African culture (pp. 13-38). Trenton, NJ: African World Press.

Stampp, K. M. (1956). *The peculiar institution: Slavery in the antebellum South.* New York: Random House.

Stewart, C. F. (1999). *Black spirituality and Black consciousness: Soul force, culture, and freedom in the African American experience.* Trenton, NJ: African World Press.

Sutherland, M. (1997). *Black authenticity: A psychology for liberating people of African descent.* Chicago: Third World Press.

Thomas, A., & Sillen, S. (1972). *Racism and psychiatry.* New York: Carol Publishing.

Thompson, A. O. (1977). Race and color prejudice and the origin of the transatlantic slave trade. *Caribbean Studies, 16,* 29-59.

T'Shaka, O. (1995). *Return to the African mother principle of male and female equality: Volume 1.* Oakland, CA: Pan Afrikan Publishers and Distributors.

Utsey, S. O., & Payne, Y. (2000). Psychological impacts of racism in a clinical versus normal sample of African American men. *Journal of African American Men, 5,* 57-72.

Utsey, S. O. (1997). Racism and the psychological well being of African American men. *Journal of African American Men, 3,* 69-87.

Welsing, F. C. (1991). *The Isis papers: The keys to the colors.* Chicago: Third World Press.

Wilson, A. N. (1990). *Black-on-Black violence: The psychodynamics of Black self-annihilation in service of White domination.* New York: Afrikan World Infosystems.

Wilson, A. N. (1998). *Blueprint for Black Power: A moral political and economic imperative for the twenty-first century.* New York: Afrikan World Infosystems.

Correspondence regarding this chapter may be addressed to Shawn O. Utsey, College of Education and Human Services, Seton Hall University, 40 South Orange Avenue, South Orange, NJ 07079 (e-mail address: Utseysha@shu.edu).

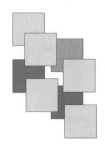

Part IV

PSYCHOLOGICAL MEASUREMENT
OF MULTICULTURAL CONSTRUCTS

The first edition of the *Handbook* devoted extensive attention to describing theories or models of racial and ethnic identity development. In many respects, those presentations are still current, as the models have not witnessed significant revision. Rather than revisit these models descriptively, we decided in this second edition to extend the theoretical discussion by assessing the status of instrumentation designed to operationalize the constructs. Therefore, Part IV presents state-of-the-art critiques of quantitative instruments assessing racial identity, ethnic identity, acculturation, and worldview. The section also includes up-to-date reviews of instruments designed to assess two vibrant research areas in multicultural counseling: prejudice/racism and multicultural competence. We believe this section of the *Handbook* will be an invaluable aid to researchers as they attend to the careful selection of valid and reliable instrumentation.

Fischer and Moradi in Chapter 20 begin Part IV by critiquing racial identity measures used to study heterogeneity in various racial/ethnic groups. Both popular and more emergent instrumentation is reviewed. Importantly, the authors take care to define and distinguish the constructs of racial identity and ethnic identity. The authors conclude the chapter by outlining 9 important directions for racial identity research.

In Chapter 21, the pioneering theoretician and researcher Cross and his coauthor Vandiver introduce their new racial identity measure, the Cross Racial Identity Scale (CRIS), which is designed to operationalize Cross's revised theory of Nigrescence. The chapter begins with a review of the theory's latest developments and concludes with a systematic review of the CRIS development. We expect that the CRIS will shortly become the most widely used racial identity scale for use with African Americans. Cross and Vandiver close their chapter with 10 suggestions for needed research on the CRIS and the Cross model.

In Chapter 22, authored by Kim and Abreu, we move from a focus on racial and ethnic identity to one centered on the process of acculturation. Acculturation is one of the most frequently studied topics in multicultural counseling. There are numerous instruments used to assess acculturation, and there is extensive confusion over what exactly acculturation is, how it should be measured, and what valid instruments are available for use with different racial and ethnic groups. Kim and Abreu take a giant step toward resolving this confusion and toward presenting a clear path for needed acculturation research. The authors carefully define acculturation and then describe leading acculturation measurement models. The core of the chapter centers on a systematic organization and critique of leading acculturation measures for various racial and ethnic groups. A landmark contribution of this chapter is the authors' ability to categorize acculturation measures according to linearity and construct dimensions.

Ibrahim, Roysircar-Sodowsky, and Ohnishi address the construct of worldview in Chapter 23. They highlight the critical link between worldview and counseling assessment and diagnosis. Leading worldview instruments are reviewed, and research findings both between and within groups on worldview are integrated. This chapter serves as both a review of the research on worldview in counseling and a critique of leading worldview instruments. The authors close with insightful suggestions for needed research on the topic of worldview in counseling.

As highlighted in earlier sections of this *Handbook,* the topic of prejudice and racism is central to the mission of multicultural counselors. In recent years, particularly, there has been a rapid growth of counselor interest in studying and combating prejudice. The first step in designing prevention and intervention programs aimed at reducing all forms of bias is to assess a program's validity and reliability. In Chapter 24, Burkard, Medler, and Boticki review recent developments in self-report measures of racial and anti-gay prejudice. Leading instruments in these areas are critiqued in depth. A major strength of this chapter is the comprehensive and balanced coverage given each instrument critique. The authors also present detailed coverage of emerging issues in prejudice measurement, including the distinction between implicit and explicit prejudice, and the value in studying linguistic intergroup bias.

In Chapter 25, Constantine and Ladany provide a state-of-the-art review of quantitative and qualitative assessment in multicultural counseling competence. The authors are comprehensive in their coverage, reviewing leading self- and observer-report measures, portfolio assessments, and collective training program evaluations. Importantly, they present an alternative conceptualization of multicultural competence that addresses many of the limits linked to previous models of competence. The authors end their chapter with a discussion of specific practice and research implications linked to the development of multicultural competence.

Given the large number of chapters and the extensive content presented in Part IV, we thought it prudent to provide some integration of the material for the reader. Therefore, Part IV closes with Chapter 26 by Alexander and Suzuki, who provide an integration of measurement issues in multicultural counseling, highlighting key components of the material. They conclude by providing direction for needed research on instrumentation in multicultural counseling.

Clearly, as multicultural-focused research takes on an increasingly central role in counseling, the instruments reviewed in this section coupled with the focused research suggestions of the various authors will provide valuable tools to students and seasoned researchers alike.

Chapter 20

RACIAL AND ETHNIC IDENTITY

Recent Developments and Needed Directions

ANN R. FISCHER
BONNIE MORADI

TO SELECT MEASURES of racial and ethnic identity to include in this review, we sought to identify a framework that would allow us to conceptualize clearly racial and ethnic identity, in light of the limited consensus about what these terms mean, how they are alike, how they are different, and how they relate to constructs such as acculturation. First, we attempted to distinguish between racial and ethnic identity and ultimately adopted Helms's (1996) conceptualization, such that identity models

> be considered "racial" models if they describe reactions to societal dynamics of "racial" oppression (i.e., domination or subjugation based on racial or ethnic physical characteristics commonly *assumed* [emphasis in original] to be racial or genetic in nature) . . . [and] be considered "ethnic" models if acquisition or maintenance of cultural characteristics (e.g., language, religious expression) are defining principles. (p. 144)

This was a helpful distinction, but it then became apparent that Helms's (1996) description of "ethnic identity" echoed closely what many refer to as "acculturation." Phinney (1990) noted that these terms often are used synonymously but recommended that researchers distinguish between acculturation as a group-level process (i.e., at a sociological level of analysis) and as an individual difference variable in group members'

AUTHORS' NOTE: Many thanks to David Tokar for feedback on a draft of this chapter.

341

retention of cultural characteristics. She suggested that the latter is an appropriate description of "ethnic identity," which she framed as "*an aspect of* [emphasis added] acculturation, in which the concern is with individuals and the focus is on how they relate to their own group as a subgroup of the larger society" (p. 501). Further clouding the distinctions among these constructs, Landrine and Klonoff (1996) cast a broad net in suggesting that concepts such as racial identity and African self-consciousness can be conceptualized as dimensions of African American acculturation.

So . . . we are starting from an ambiguous state in the literature as a whole. The most useful conceptual overview we found was that of Phinney (1990), who identified three traditions of theory and research on ethnic identity: (a) those arising from social identity theory (e.g., Luhtanen & Crocker, 1992; Sellers, Smith, Shelton, Rowley, & Chavous, 1998), typically addressing a sense of belonging or "groupness," which is theorized to help maintain an individual's positive self-concept (Tajfel & Turner, 1979); (b) those with an identity formation focus (e.g., Phinney, 1992; Cross & Vandiver, Chapter 21, this volume), generally assuming "a process similar to ego identity formation that takes place over time, as people explore and make decisions about the role of ethnicity in their lives" (Phinney, 1990, p. 502); sense of belonging and/or attitudes toward one's ethnic group and perhaps some "countergroup(s)" make up the usual content of identity formation research; and (c) those working within an "acculturation" framework, whose focus centers on ethnic involvement, or on individuals' acquisition, retention, and maintenance of cultural characteristics. This review addresses measurement of constructs falling roughly within the first two traditions (social identity and identity formation). Kim and Abreu's Chapter 22 in this book presents research on measurement of acculturation. In general, we selected instruments whose scores appeared to reflect the meaning and importance of race or ethnicity to an individual at a given time.

As we struggled with our charge to review the recent literature on the most widely used measures (see previous reviews by Kohatsu & Richardson, 1996, and Sabnani & Ponterotto, 1992), we became aware that doing so might perpetuate a problem in the racial and ethnic identity literature. In particular, the majority of measurement research focuses only on Black/African American or White racial identity. It would seem logical, therefore, to write a chapter reflecting this preponderance of literature. Though inadvertent, such a focus ultimately would marginalize other constructs and replicate much of psychology's selective dialogue around race and ethnicity. Therefore, we have structured this chapter to encompass a larger (though not exhaustive) domain of racial and ethnic identity measurement, ideally to build awareness of and interest in less popular constructs and instruments. Following Sabnani and Ponterotto's (1992) format, we start with a brief description of each instrument's theoretical base, which—in many cases—is well-known and not discussed in detail.

Next, we briefly describe the instrument's development and then focus on psychometric properties and overall evaluation.

AFRICAN AMERICAN RACIAL IDENTITY

Multidimensional Inventory of Black Identity
(MIBI; Sellers, Rowley, Chavous, Shelton, & Smith, 1997)

Theoretical base. The MIBI is based on the Multidimensional Model of Racial Identity (MMRI; Sellers, Shelton, et al., 1998; Sellers, Smith, et al., 1998), which posits four dimensions of African American racial identity. Racial *salience* varies across situations and is the mechanism through which other dimensions of racial identity influence persons' experiences. Racial *centrality* reflects the extent to which race is a core part of one's self-definition. *Ideology* is divided into four types of philosophies about how members of one's race should behave: (1) nationalist (emphasizing the importance and uniqueness of African American heritage), (2) oppressed minority (focusing on connections between African Americans and other oppressed groups), (3) assimilationist (highlighting the connections between African Americans and American society), and (4) humanist (emphasizing connections among all humans). Finally, *regard* reflects positive or negative feelings or judgments about one's race and is divided into public (perception of others' judgments about one's racial group) and private (feelings about others and self as members of the racial group).

Development. The MIBI was developed rationally and factor-analytically to assess the centrality, ideology, and regard dimensions of the MMRI (due to the context-dependent nature of the salience dimension, it is not assessed by the MIBI; Sellers et al., 1997). The authors generated some items and selected other items from existing measures of racial, ethnic, and social identity (for a total of 71 items), reflecting the aforementioned stable dimensions of racial identity and their components (Sellers et al., 1997). All items are rated on a 7-point Likert-type scale (*strongly disagree* to *strongly agree*), with higher scores on each scale reflecting greater endorsement of the relevant dimension. A Kaiser-Meyer-Olkin test, conducted on the intercorrelations of the initial 71 items, suggested that a factor analysis of the total set of items would be inappropriate. Still, Sellers et al. (1997) conducted three analyses, in which they defined an a priori target structure (conforming to the MIBI item-subscale structures) and then, in general, selected items for the final scale based on the extent to which they behaved as intended; however, in several cases, they prioritized theoretical over empirical considerations and assigned items to subscales based strictly on the proposed structure (even if the item loaded most highly on a different subscale). This procedure resulted in 51 items: a 36-item Ideology scale (each type of ideology is assessed by 9 items), an 8-item Centrality scale, and a 7-item Regard scale that assesses only Private Regard (items intended to assess Public Regard were deemed to be inadequate). This series of analyses is questionable and does little to clarify the actual structure of MIBI data. Sellers and colleagues (Sellers, Shelton, et al., 1998; Shelton & Sellers, 2000) have described two revised versions of the MIBI; however, these authors provided no information about how revisions were made.

Psychometric properties. Sellers et al. (1997) reported internal consistency estimates in the .70s for five of the six subscales (Public Regard was not included, and Private Regard α = .60). For the updated MIBI, Sellers, Shelton, et al. (1998) reported slightly improved estimates; they ranged from .71 to .81, excluding Public Regard. Although eliminated from the original scale development study, a 3-item Public Regard scale yielded internal consistency estimates of .11 and .18 (Rowley, Sellers, Chavous & Smith, 1998); however, these authors did not provide information about the development of this scale.

Regarding convergent validity, Centrality scores were related positively to Private Regard and Nationalist ideology and negatively to Assimilationist and Humanist ideology (Sellers et al., 1997; Sellers et al., in press). Centrality and Nationalist ideology scores each were related positively to having an African American best friend, taking Black studies courses, and level of interracial contact (Sellers et al., 1997). For students with high Centrality, Private Regard was related positively to level of self-esteem (Rowley et al., 1998) and negatively to alcohol use (Sellers, Caldwell, Zimmerman, & Hilkene, 1999). Finally, Sellers, Shelton, et al. (1998) reported that, in general, MIBI scales correlated moderately and in the expected directions with subscales of the MEIM and RIAS (both reviewed below), but they provided limited methodological details, so confident interpretation is difficult.

Evaluation. An important strength of the MIBI is that it operationalizes multiple dimensions of racial identity so that centrality of racial identity to one's self-concept, evaluation of oneself and other African Americans, and racial ideology are assessed separately (Rowley et al., 1998). However, further development and evaluation of the MIBI by independent investigators is needed, with particular attention to reliability of the Public Regard scale and the structure of the MIBI. We recommend that researchers use exploratory factor analytic procedures and conventional criteria for selecting and rotating factor solutions (e.g., Kaiser's criterion, Cattell's scree test, factor intercorrelations). Results from such analyses may suggest some item-to-scale reassignment since Sellers et al. (1997) assigned some items to the theoretically relevant scale despite items' higher loadings on other scales. This process may in turn improve internal consistency reliability for some scales; however, it also begs the question of content validity. In addition, confirmatory factor analytic procedures may allow researchers to examine the fit of the proposed hierarchical structure (i.e., 3 interrelated higher-order dimensions of centrality, regard, and ideology, with further subdivisions of regard and ideology) to obtained MIBI responses. Finally, examination of the MIBI's applicability to nonstudent populations is needed.

African Self-Consciousness Scale (ASCS; Baldwin & Bell, 1985)

Theoretical base. The ASCS is based on Baldwin's (a.k.a. Kobi K. K. Kambon) Africentric theory which proposes that African Self-Consciousness (ASC) is a core component of Black personality. Baldwin (1981) proposed that ASC consists of four competency dimensions: (1) recognition of oneself as African and an understanding of the meaning of this identity, (2) prioritizing African survival and development, (3) respect for and participation in African life and institutions, and (4) recognition of and opposition to racial oppression. These competency dimensions may be expressed in six "manifest" areas: education, family, religion, cultural activities, interpersonal relations, and political orientation.

Development. From approximately 130 items (origin unspecified), Baldwin and Bell (1985) retained 42 items based on five judges' ratings of appropriateness. ASCS items are rated on an 8-point Likert-type scale (1–2 = *strongly disagree* to 7–8 = *strongly agree*), with higher scores indicating a greater level of ASC. However, some researchers' use of other response formats (i.e., 4-point, 7-point, or dichotomous formats) complicates integration of available psychometric data on the ASCS.

Psychometric properties. Acceptable internal consistency estimates (ranging from the high .70s to low .90s) have been reported. Baldwin and Bell (1985) reported a 6-week test-retest reliability of .90. Stokes, Murray, Peacock, and Kaiser (1994) conducted a principal axis factor analysis on ASCS data (using a 7-point response format) from a community sample. They reported that examination of the scree plot suggested a four-factor solution loosely resembling the four competency dimensions described by Baldwin (1981). Myers and Thompson (1994) provided limited information about their factor analysis of ASCS data (response format unspecified) from another community sample but reported that they interpreted a 7-factor solution, with 4 of these factors reflecting the proposed competency dimensions. In a sample of drug-addicted men (ASCS response format unspecified), Dixon and Azibo (1998) conducted a principal components analysis with varimax rotation and selected a 4-factor solution based on examination of the scree plot. They retained only items with factor load-ings > .50; 2 of the 4 factors were not interpreted because they each had only 2 items which met this stringent criterion. The authors interpreted the 2 remaining factors as value for and value against Africentricity.

Mixed support for the construct validity of the ASCS has been reported in the literature. For example, total scores were related positively to pro-fessors' ratings of students' ASC, level of self-reported Black conscious-ness (Baldwin & Bell, 1985), interest in/affiliation with African American people/culture, and reported experiences of discrimination (Cheatham, Tomlinson, & Ward, 1990), but negatively to the number of affirming expe-riences with White people. Also consistent with expectations, in south-eastern states, students in historically or primarily Black colleges had higher ASCS scores than those in primarily White colleges (Baldwin, Duncan, & Bell, 1987; McCowan & Alston, 1998); surprisingly, however, the opposite pattern was found in a northern state (Cheatham et al., 1990). Contrary to theory, some studies have found ASCS scores to be unrelated or negligibly related to endorsement of an Africentric philosophy and value system (Brookins, 1994), self-esteem (e.g., Chambers et al., 1998), or body-esteem (Makkar & Strube, 1995; however, please see our comments on in-terpretation of links with mental health constructs in the "Directions for Future Research" section).

Evaluation. Some important strengths of the ASCS include internal consis-tency reliability and temporal stability. However, we echo Kambon's (1996) call for more validity research. We encourage researchers to ground their re-search questions in the propositions of Africentric theory. Integration of factor analytic results was made difficult by the limited detail typically pro-vided about response formats, statistical procedures, and rationales for those procedures. However, taken together, these factor analyses raise questions about the dimensionality of the ASCS. Thus, we suggest that re-searchers conduct exploratory factor analyses using multiple criteria and conventional decision rules to determine the number and item composi-tion of factors, as well as extraction and rotation methods. Such analyses can be followed by scale revisions (as necessary) and use of confirmatory factor analyses to examine the fit of the revised scale structure to data from various samples.

We encourage researchers using the ASCS to consider the risk of Type I and Type II error. In some studies, relations of a multitude of variables to ASCS scores were examined without adjustment to protect against Type I error. Also, continuous ASCS scores sometimes were converted into cate-gorical variables, resulting in range restriction, which in turn increases the possibility of Type II error. Finally, in the absence of an empirical compari-son of the benefits and disadvantages of various response formats, we en-courage researchers to use the original 8-point Likert-type format, for consistency.

Racial Identity Attitudes Scale
(RIAS; Helms & Parham, 1996)

Theoretical base. The three versions of the RIAS are based on Cross's (1971) five-stage model of Nigrescence but assess only the first four stages. As described in detail by Helms (1990), these stages reflect a progressive movement away from a pro-White, anti-Black stance to greater flexibility in attitudes toward Black and White people and cultures.

Development. The RIAS was originally developed by converting Hall, Cross, and Freedle's (1972) Q-sort measure into a 5-point Likert-type (1 = *strongly disagree* to 5 = *strongly agree*) paper-and-pencil questionnaire (Helms, 1990). This (also referred to as Short Form A or RIAS-A) and all subsequent versions of the RIAS utilize this response format and contain four subscales corresponding to the Pre-Encounter, Encounter, Immersion-Emersion, and Internalization stages. Based on factor-analytic results (about which limited methodological information was reported), Helms and Parham (1996) made revisions to the RIAS-A; the resulting instrument has been referred to as Short Form B or RIAS-B (short). Yanico, Swanson, and Tokar (1994) reported that correlations between corresponding subscales of the RIAS-A and RIAS-B (short) ranged from .24 to .97 and paralleled the range of item overlap across corresponding subscales. To improve internal consistency of the RIAS-B, Helms and Parham (1996) developed the Long Form or RIAS-B (long). They also provided a table containing some clarification about the item composition of subscales for the three versions of the RIAS (we noted a few differences between this table and the RIAS-B [short] table in Helms, 1990). It appears that across versions of the RIAS (a) different numbers of items are included and scored, (b) some items have been reassigned from subscale to subscale, and (c) some items are scored for more than one subscale (and this changes across versions). For each version, subscale scores are obtained by calculating a mean of subscale item ratings, with higher scores indicating greater endorsement of racial identity attitudes assessed by the subscale.

Psychometric properties. Our review will focus on the latest two versions of the RIAS. Estimates of internal consistency reliability for RIAS-B (short) have been poor to moderate. For example, White et al. (1997) reported alphas of .62, .41, .69, and .72; Yanico et al. (1994) reported alphas of .59, .45, .63, and .59; and Helms and Parham (1996) reported alphas of .69, .50, .67, and .79 for Pre-Encounter, Encounter, Immersion-Emersion, and Internalization, respectively. Yanico et al. (1994) reported substantial range restriction for Pre-Encounter and Internalization items, with most respondents expressing disagreement with Pre-Encounter and agreement with Internalization items. These authors also examined the structure of the RIAS-B using a principle axis factor analysis with a varimax rotation and squared multiple correlations as initial communality estimates. Using conventional criteria for determining the number of factors, Yanico et al. (1994) reported that a 3-factor solution was most interpretable yet somewhat problematic. Several items had negligible loadings on their assigned subscales or substantial cross-loadings, and the solution accounted for only 20% of the variance. White et al. (1997) found that Black male activists (involved in Black male rites-of-passage programs) had higher Encounter, Immersion-Emersion, and Internalization scores than did nonactivists; however, there was no Pre-Encounter score difference between groups.

Analyses of the psychometric properties of the RIAS Long Form have been more extensive. As with the RIAS-B (short form), internal consistency reliabilities for the Long Form have ranged from poor to moderate. For example, Carter et al. (1997) reported alphas of .77, .41, .59, and .79; Neville, Heppner, and Wang (1997) reported alphas of .86, .27, .60, and .58; and Helms and Parham (1996) reported alphas of .76, .51, .69, and .80 for Pre-Encounter, Encounter, Immersion-Emersion, and Internalization subscales, respectively. Lemon and Waehler (1996) used a 60-item version of the RIAS and reported 1-month test-retest reliability coefficients of .61, .60, .66, and .52 for Pre-Encounter, Encounter, Immersion-Emersion, and Internalization subscales, respectively. However, a shorter test-retest interval may be more appropriate, given that RIAS subscales are purported to measure a developmental process. In addition, Tokar and Fischer (1998) also reported range restriction in responses to Pre-Encounter and Internalization items that mirrored those reported by Yanico et al. (1994) for the RIAS Short Form B.

Tokar and Fischer (1998) used confirmatory factor analysis to test the 4-factor RIAS Long Form structure proposed by Helms and Parham (1996) and found a poor fit to the data (χ^2/df = 5.11; SRMR = .012; GFI = .65; CFI = .48; TLI = .45). Next, they performed an exploratory principle axis factoring with a varimax rotation (since the orthogonal and oblique solutions were nearly identical). Using conventional criteria for determining the number of factors, these authors reported that a 3-factor solution (roughly reflecting Pre-Encounter, Immersion-Emersion, and Internalization statuses) was most interpretable. This solution accounted for 26% of the variance and contained several items that failed to load substantially on their assigned subscales. Similarly, for a sample of adolescents, Stevenson (1995) conducted a principal components analysis with varimax rotation. He specified a four-factor solution but reported that examination of the scree plot and item-factor loadings suggested that a three-factor solution corresponding to Pre-Encounter, Immersion-Emersion, and Internalization subscales (as with Tokar & Fischer, 1998) was most meaningful and accounted for 22% of the variance.

In terms of convergent and discriminant validity of the RIAS Long Form, Pre-Encounter scores have been related positively to perceived general and culture-specific stress (Neville et al., 1997), self-derogation (Lemon & Waehler, 1996), suppressed anger, and tendency to use social

comparison as a basis for self-definition (Fischer, Tokar, & Serna, 1998).
Immersion-Emersion scores have been related positively to expressed
anger, reactionary anger, contact with other African Americans (Fischer
et al., 1998), and identification with one's ethnic origin (Lemon & Waehler,
1996). Encounter and Internalization scores also have been linked positively to identification with one's ethnic origin, and Internalization scores
have been linked positively to self-esteem (Lemon & Waehler, 1996).
Finally, in a sample of community members and students, Fischer et al.
(1998) found that social desirability affected relations of Pre-Encounter (but
not other subscales') scores to criterion variables, suggesting that at least
some previously reported evidence of convergent validity is not simply a
product of socially desirable response patterns. Looking more closely at
social desirability and the structure of the RIAS Long Form, Fischer
et al.'s (1998) series of confirmatory factor-analytic model comparisons revealed the presence of social desirability method effects; those effects contaminated the Pre-Encounter construct structurally but not Immersion-
Emersion or Internalization.

Evaluation. First, it was not always clear which version of the RIAS was
used in some studies, making integration across studies difficult. Relatedly, given the changes in subscales' item composition and scoring procedures throughout the development of the three versions of the RIAS, we
were aware of the possibility that error variance due to miscalculation of
subscale scores may exist across studies. We encourage researchers who intend to use any of the RIAS instruments to refer to Helms and Parham's
(1996) table of subscales' item composition for clarification about scoring
and to report clearly the version of the RIAS used, paying particular attention to the number of items *scored* (vs. number of items that make up the
scale) and to items that are scored for more than one subscale.

It was encouraging to see that studies evaluating psychometric properties of the RIAS Short Form B and Long Form have included nonstudent and
student participants. Taken together, these studies have suggested some
improvement in the internal consistency of Long Form subscales over
those of the Short Form B. However, for the Encounter, Immersion-
Emersion, and Internalization subscales, internal consistency continues to
be problematic. Thus, further subscale development is warranted. In addition, it may be fruitful to follow Helms's (1996) call for the use of "balanced" (in terms of item content) split-half procedures as an alternative
method of assessing internal consistency of racial identity measures. Also,
the fact that RIAS Short Form B and Long Form data have not generally adhered to the proposed 4-factor structure raises questions about the suggested subscale composition and scoring procedures (Ponterotto, Fuertes,
& Chen, 2000). Finally, RIAS Long Form subscales generally related as expected to criterion variables, although the meaningfulness of some of these
relations is tempered by the presence of range restriction for Pre-Encounter
and Internalization items (and social desirability for Pre-Encounter). As

Helms (1996) suggested, researchers need to intentionally recruit participants endorsing Pre-Encounter and not endorsing Internalization items.

WHITE RACIAL IDENTITY

White Racial Identity Attitudes Scale
(WRIAS; Helms & Carter, 1990)

Theoretical base. The WRIAS is based on Helms's (1984) theory of White
racial identity (WRI) development, which assumes that White people may
undergo a developmental process of making meaning about their identities
as White people, particularly in terms of how they think about and respond
to African Americans. The first three stages (Contact, Disintegration, Reintegration) reflect a progression toward the abandonment of a racist identity (Phase I of the model); the final two stages (Pseudo-independence and
Autonomy) involve movement toward a nonracist White identity (Phase
II). Helms (1990 and later) has since reframed the developmental progression of WRI in terms of ego statuses rather than as stages and has added a
sixth status. However, the WRIAS is based on the original theory and thus
contains five subscales.

Instrument development. Helms and Carter (1990) provided minimal information about scale construction (i.e., no information about the processes of item development, evaluation, or selection). Responses are made
on a 5-point Likert-type scale (*strongly disagree* to *strongly agree*); higher
scores indicate attitudes reflecting the stage for which each subscale is
named. Each item was reported to have correlated $\geq .30$ with its intended
subscale and nonsignificantly with a social desirability scale.

Psychometric properties. Internal consistency estimates for some of the
WRIAS subscales have been less than ideal, with the Contact subscale the
most troublesome. Behrens (1997) reported estimates of .50 (Contact), .77
(Disintegration), .78 (Reintegration), .67 (Pseudo-independence), and .61
(Autonomy) in a meta-analysis of data from 22 previous studies. In terms of
structural validity, the WRIAS subscales frequently have evidenced a pattern of intercorrelations which are consistent with theory but which
also have been so high as to suggest redundancy. For example, when inter-
scale correlations were corrected for attenuation due to measurement
error, Behrens's meta-analysis revealed Disintegration-Reintegration and
Pseudo-independence-Autonomy correlations nearing 1.00. In an exploratory factor analysis by the WRIAS authors (Helms & Carter, 1990),
an 11-factor structure was reported to have emerged. In an independent
examination, Swanson, Tokar, and Davis's (1994) item- and exploratory
factor analyses revealed little support for the WRIAS's proposed structure
(e.g., most items correlated more highly with other subscales than with

their own; a five-factor structure reflected a first bipolar factor, with subsequent factors not reflecting intended subscales). Pope-Davis, Vandiver, and Stone (1999) subjected a combination of WRIAS and ORAS-P (this instrument is reviewed below) items and item parcels to a joint exploratory factor analysis, summarizing their findings as revealing a three-factor structure for the WRIAS. However, a series of unusual analytic and interpretive strategies (e.g., interpreting results of a joint factor analysis in terms of single instruments) makes results of this study difficult to integrate into the WRIAS literature. Carter (1996) also proposed construct validity evidence through a cluster analysis, but he did not present error terms, on which decisions about the number of clusters to retain should be based; thus, we cannot endorse those findings as reflecting positively (or negatively) on the WRIAS. Finally, Jome (2000) evaluated the WRIAS subscales' relations to social desirability response set, finding small or nonsignificant zero-order correlations, supporting discriminant validity. In a series of confirmatory model comparisons, Jome found that method effects due to social desirability were present in the data but that these effects did not substantially alter key parameters (i.e., WRIAS status constructs did not appear to be contaminated by social desirability).

Behrens (1997) explored possible reasons that confirmatory factor analyses often have produced inadmissible solutions; the typical culprit has been a nonpositive definite phi matrix, indicating that the latent factors (WRIAS subscales) are too highly related to be considered separate constructs. Carter (1996) argued that high subscale intercorrelations may reflect sample- or environment-specific issues. However, the fact that Behrens's findings were based on 22 samples renders that possibility unlikely.

Behrens (1997) noted a paradox in the literature: The WRIAS's psychometric properties seem weak overall, yet its subscales often behave with convergent validity criteria in accord with theory—predicting external variables such as comfort working with African American colleagues (Block, Roberson, & Neuger, 1995), inter- and intrapersonal skills (Taub & McEwen, 1992; Tokar & Swanson, 1991), and self-reported multicultural counseling competencies (Neville et al., 1996). As a resolution to this paradox, Rowe, Behrens, and Leach (1995) posited the "reduced dimensionality hypothesis," meaning that this pattern of results may reflect the fact that the WRIAS is best conceptualized as tapping a single dimension of Whites' positive to negative racial attitudes, particularly toward African Americans (cf. Swanson et al., 1994). Results of Behrens's confirmatory factor analyses (with previous studies' data) were partially consistent with this hypothesis. A one-factor model did not fit the data well, but it did fit better than multiple-factor models, notably the five-factor model most closely resembling the instrument's foundation. A similar pattern in another independent sample was found by Jome (2000), who also tested the reduced dimensionality hypothesis more directly, by assessing relations of WRIAS subscales with specific pro- and anti-Black attitudes, intergroup anxiety, and two measures of racism. Results indicated that the WRIAS subscales behaved precisely as pro- and antiminority variables.

Evaluation. The literature suggests that the WRIAS has strengths but also suffers from serious limitations, as used thus far. Part of its weakness probably stems from its widespread use soon after its initial construction, which was not well-documented; further refinements to the WRIAS, if made, are not widely available. Helms (1996) argued that problems revealed with the scale may reflect problems with sampling, since the WRIAS is intended to reflect a wide range of identity statuses, including those that only a very few Whites are theorized ever to attain and which are dependent partly on interracial contact. Thus, she admonished researchers to use the WRIAS in broader samples, including those with participants who are known to have had a variety of race-related experiences. Consistent with this speculation, Jome (2000) found White participants' degree of prior social contact with African Americans to predict Disintegration and Reintegration negatively and to predict Pseudo-independence and Autonomy positively. However, these results also are consistent with the reduced dimensionality hypothesis, which challenges the model as a good measure of Helms's (1984) theory.

Unfortunately, we must echo Behrens's (1997) call to exercise extreme caution when using the WRIAS for group-level analyses. (Carter, 1996, and Helms, 1996, recently have advocated use of the WRIAS profiles with individuals, though they still recommended comparing individual data to norms.) In general, consistent with Goodstein and Ponterotto's (1997) analysis, it appears that the WRIAS assesses "how Whites react to an 'other' group and not how they identify with one another" (p. 287). If one is interested in assessing Whites' attitudes toward other racial groups, better instruments are available for that explicit purpose (and the WRIAS is focused only on "Blacks").

Oklahoma Racial Attitude Scale
(Behrens, Leach, Franz, & LaFleur, 1999; Choney & Behrens, 1996)

Theoretical base. Rowe, Bennett, and Atkinson (1994) proposed a model of White racial consciousness (WRC), "the awareness of being White and what that implies in relation to those who do not share White group membership" (pp. 133-134). The construct resembles Helms's (1984) WRI but was designed to be conceptually cleaner. First, it focuses on describing clusters of attitudes at a given point in time and avoids the assumption of a developmental progression (though it does hypothesize mechanisms of change). Second, because of its explicit focus on attitudes, not identity, it avoids "the burden of additional complexity and surplus implications associated with the abstraction 'identity'" (Choney & Behrens, 1996, p. 226). If the WRIAS is measuring—largely—Whites' attitudes toward African

Americans, and if such attitudes are of interest, Rowe et al. (1994) reasoned, then formalizing a model for those attitudes would be a useful
contribution.

The WRC model takes its cue from Phinney's (1989) work on stages of
ethnic identity development, positing that attitudes vary along the dimensions of exploration (of one's attitudes about race) and commitment (to
one's attitudes). Nonachieved WRC types are those characterized by dependence on other people's opinions (*Dependent*) and by minimizing or ignoring racial/ethnic issues (*Avoidant*). The *Dissonant* type is transitional
and involves uncertainty and quest for resolution to apparent conflicts between recent events and prior racial attitudes. Achieved WRC types have
engaged in some levels of both exploration and commitment, including
Dominative (ethnocentric attitudes, rationalization of racial/ethnic oppression), *Conflictive* (less overt ethnocentrism or racism; opposition to ra-
cial/ethnic discrimination coupled with opposition to programs aimed at
reducing such discrimination), *Reactive* (awareness of White privilege and
oppression of others; idealization of or parental attitudes toward members
of non-White groups), and *Integrative* (comfort with racial issues; recognition of White privilege and oppression but without unhelpful "liberal
guilt"). Based on empirical findings with an early version of the ORAS, the
model and instrument both have been revised to collapse *Dominative* and
Integrative types of attitudes into a single bipolar dimension (Behrens et al.,
1999).

Instrument development. Choney and Behrens (1996) initially pooled 52
items reflecting racial attitudes proposed in the WRC model. Most of the
items were written rationally by the authors and by researchers in multicultural counseling who were familiarized with the model; other items
were adapted from racism scales. Responses are made on a 5-point Likert-
type scale (*strongly disagree* to *strongly agree*), with higher scores reflecting attitudes more similar to the type represented. The authors and their
colleagues have refined the scale over a period of years, with a number of ad-
ministrations of progressively revised versions of the ORAS-P (Preliminary) and ORAS. Subscale composition has been revised based on standard
criteria (e.g., item-subscale correlations, factor loadings).

Psychometric properties. The focus here is on the updated ORAS (rather
than the ORAS-P), since that is likely to be the instrument of choice for
researchers interested in this WRC model. Using the current 34-item version of the ORAS in a large sample of White undergraduates from geographically diverse regions of the United States, Behrens et al. (1999) reported
internal consistency estimates of .84 for Integrative/Dominative, .83 for
Conflictive, .72 for Reactive, .78 for Dependent, .73 for Dissonant, and .60
for Avoidant. No subscales correlated significantly with social desirability.
Results of a confirmatory factor analysis (with correlated factors) in the

same sample indicated a moderate fit of the proposed ORAS model to the data (AGFI = .86, RMSR = .08, χ^2/df = 1.86). Using an archival data set for cross-validation (i.e., the old data contained all items from the reduced 34-item ORAS), confirmatory factor analysis (with identical model specification) again yielded fit index values not meeting conventional criteria for goodness of fit but which were not extremely out of range (AGFI = .80, RMSR = .10). Additional studies of construct validity are underway (Behrens, personal communication, March 27, 2000).

Evaluation. The major strengths of the ORAS as we see it are its (a) clear grounding in theory, (b) appropriate and well-documented development process, and (c) extensive and careful refinements over a period of years. We encourage researchers to follow the lead of this team in terms of their adherence to appropriate instrument development, refinement, and evaluation procedures. We note, however, that although the structure of the current ORAS is plausible, our reading of the data presented in Behrens et al. (1999) suggests that it is far from a perfect fit to the revised model. Thus, we reiterate these researchers' own calls for further research on the ORAS. In particular, they noted that a clear scoring method, normative data, and additional cross-validations of the ORAS's structure are needed. One conceptual issue to consider is the wording of the ORAS items. In particular, most items refer to Whites' attitudes toward "minorities," which is understood to mean racial and ethnic minority group members. As a point of observation, some authors have noted that the term "minority" may perpetuate a racial hierarchy with Whites on top, given its connotation of "less than" (Atkinson, Morten, & Sue, 1998).

NATIVE AMERICAN/INDIAN ETHNIC IDENTITY

We found only a few published descriptions of Native American/Indian ethnic identity instruments, and those we found generally had been used only once. We note promising elements in the methods of Lysne and Levy (1997), who modified Phinney's (1992) MEIM (reviewed below) to apply to Native American Indians in particular and to measure identity exploration (α = .74 in a sample of 101 rural reservation-dwelling, primarily Plains Indian adolescents) and commitment (α = .88) separately. Bates, Beauvais, and Trimble (1997) developed a very broad identity questionnaire, including assessment of participation in traditional Indian activities, friendship patterns, self- and parental identification as Indian, and acculturative status in Native American Indians in the western United States (tribal groups unspecified). In a sample of 120 children and adolescents from a partnership tribe (of Ottawa and Chippewa), Zimmerman, Ramirez-Valles, Washienko, Walter, and Dyer (1996) presented preliminary convergent validity data for a composite of a 5-item cultural affinity scale(α = .70), a 9-item Native

American Indian family activities checklist, and a single identity item. Although it is early to make definite judgments about these methods, we encourage readers to turn to these sources and contribute to this literature on Native American populations. We especially appreciated Zimmerman et al.'s (1996) excellent sampling and attention to tribe-specific features, which reminds us of the enormous variability within Native American Indian populations.

ASIAN AMERICAN ETHNIC IDENTITY

Similarly, we found only a few published descriptions of instruments specifically oriented toward Asian Americans, and they each, unfortunately, were unclear about how items were generated and (if) refined. One sample is the work of Oyserman and Sakamoto (1997), who provided a sketchy description of a new Asian American Identity Scale (12 items; α = .72), apparently derived rationally and used in a mixed sample of Chinese Americans, Korean Americans, and other Asian Americans and based loosely on a model of African American identity (Oyserman, Gant, & Ager, 1995). Subscales include components of connectedness (importance of ethnic customs/traditions and ethnic pride; α = .77), familialism (importance of family; α = .64), interdependent achievement (i.e., individual achievement as reflecting on one's ethnic group; α = .72), and awareness of racism toward one's group (α = .63). The subscales generally behaved in accord with theory, in terms of relations with collective self-esteem, collectivism, work ethic, and positive feelings about the model minority label but not in terms of links with individualism (perhaps due to range restriction; the sample endorsed individualism over collectivism).

As with the Native American Indian measures, we encourage readers also to explore the following sources and to add to this nascent literature: Rosenthal and Feldman's (1992) 7-item Chinese ethnic pride scale (α = .76 for Chinese Americans and α = .83 for Chinese Australians); and Kwan and Sodowsky's (1997) Internal-External Ethnic Identity Measure (16 internal [psychological] items, α = .79; 19 external [behavioral] items, α = .86 in a sample of Chinese immigrants). Further, we echo the caution to avoid consideration of Asian Americans as a homogeneous group. For example, Oyserman and Sakamoto (1997) specifically excluded Asian Indians from their sample because they were studying the model minority stereotype and considered it not to be routinely applied to Asian Indians.

LATINA/LATINO ETHNIC IDENTITY

We found several instruments that were called measures of "ethnic identity" for Latina/o populations. However, many of them actually assessed cultural preference, familiarity, and/or affiliation (e.g., Fèlix-Ortiz, Newcomb, & Myers, 1994; Garcia, 1982; Garcia & Lega, 1979). In a study that seemed to measure what we defined as ethnic identity, Gao, Schmidt, and Gudykunst (1994) asked 88 Mexican American telecommunication workers to rate agreement (on a 7-point Likert-type scale) with statements that being a Mexican American "is central to who I am," "is important to my self-definition," and "defines me." Gao et al. (1994) reported $\alpha = .73$ for these three items, but validity evidence is unclear at best. Dividing their sample into high and low ethnic identity groups, these authors explored validity by analyzing group differences on 22 separate variables; even without adjusting for Type I error, they found only 3 significant differences, one of which was inconsistent with prediction.

Greater clarification of and consensus about the similarities and differences among variables such as ethnic identity, affiliation, familiarity, preference, and acculturation in theory, instrumentation, and terminology is needed. In addition, we encourage researchers to pay close attention to within-group variables (e.g., culture, nationality) that may shape ethnic identity for various Latina/o groups.

JEWISH IDENTITY

We found a few studies that defined and measured Jewish identity in ways that were consistent with our conceptualization of ethnic identity. For example, Zack (1973) described a 10-item Jewish American Identity measure (α of .90 in a sample of 164 Jewish students in New York). Zack (1973) also described a series of factor analyses, conducted on data from 1,006 Jewish college students from various parts of the United States, who completed the Jewish identity and a similar American identity measure. The results of this study were difficult to interpret due to some unusual statistical procedures and reporting. However, it seems that the Jewish and American identity items emerged as two distinct factors, the corresponding scale scores for which were unrelated ($r = .07$). In another study, Amyot and Sigelman (1996) used 4 questions to assess "strength of Jewish identification" (e.g., "Would you agree or disagree that when it comes to a crisis, Jews can only depend on other Jews?" and "How important would you say that being Jewish is in your life?"). They reported that for a sample of 510 Jewish participants, religiosity and social contact with other Jewish persons each were unique positive predictors of Jewish identification as measured by these items. However, no other psychometric data were provided.

Overall, we were encouraged to find some studies addressing Jewish ethnic identity (above; see also Cohen, 1988; Kivisto & Nefzger, 1993). Across these few studies, however, operationalization of Jewish identity has remained largely atheoretical. Further, limited psychometric information is available about the instruments cited. Clearly, more research is needed to address theoretical issues within and assessment of Jewish identity, including attention to diversity within Jewish populations.

MULTIGROUP MEASURES

Multigroup Ethnic Identity Measure
(MEIM; Phinney, 1992)

Theoretical base. Phinney's work on ethnic identity can be situated generally within both the social identity and developmental paradigms. Based on reviews of the literature, Phinney (1992) delineated several major components of ethnic identity (self-identification/ethnicity, ethnic behaviors and practices, affirmation and belonging) and conceptualized the process of coming to one's ethnic identity in developmental terms. Borrowing from Erikson (1968), she hypothesized that identity *achievement* occurs from a combination of *exploration* of one's ethnicity and its meanings, along with *commitment* or a clear sense of oneself as an ethnic person. Identity *diffusion* involves lack of exploration and/or commitment and is considered to reflect an unsuccessful resolution to ethnic identity issues. The MEIM addresses both the content (e.g., belongingness) and a history of the process (i.e., exploration and commitment) of one's ethnic identity development.

Instrument development. Using an existing general ego identity development instrument as a starting point, Phinney and Ambarsoom (1987) created a measure of ethnic exploration and commitment (crossing these variables to classify participants into ethnic identity statuses), but they provided no information about item development. Phinney and her colleagues have conducted several revisions of the scale, based on item analyses and inclusion of content generated by adolescents during ethnic identity interviews (e.g., Phinney, 1992; Phinney & Alipuria, 1990). In the current version, responses are made on a 4-point Likert-type scale (*strongly disagree* to *strongly agree*), and higher scores indicate stronger ethnic identity. The 14-item MEIM may be scored as a global measure of ethnic identity, or as a set of subscales: Affirmation/Belonging (5 items), Identity Achievement (7 items), and Ethnic Behaviors (2 items). The additional 6-item Other-Group Orientation subscale generally is regarded as tapping a construct related to but distinct from ethnic identity (Phinney, 1992) and thus is not reviewed here.

Psychometric properties. Internal consistency estimates for the overall 14-item scale have been acceptable to quite good in a variety of samples—for example, α of .85 for Mexican American college students (Cuéllar, Nyberg,

Maldonado, & Roberts, 1998); .92 for White college women (Taub, 1995) and for Navajo undergraduates (McNeil, Kee, & Zvolensky, 1999); .83 in a mixed sample of Latino, African American, and White adolescents (Phinney, Cantu, & Kurtz, 1997); around .80 for separate samples of Asian Americans, African Americans, and Latinos (Phinney, Ferguson, & Tate, 1997); .77 to .80 for rural, lower-income White and African American high school students (Markstrom & Hunter, 1999); and .70 in a mixed sample of African Americans and African nationals (Phinney & Onwughalu, 1996). As expected, internal consistency estimates for the (shorter) subscales have been somewhat weaker (e.g., Affirmation/Belonging αs typically have ranged from the mid-.70s (Phinney, 1992, in a sample of ethnically diverse high school students) to the mid-.80s (e.g., Cuéllar et al., 1998; Abu-Ali & Reisin, 1999, in a sample of Muslim adolescent girls), and Achievement αs have ranged from < .65 (even with 2 items having low item-subscale correlations dropped; Abu-Ali & Reisen, 1999) to the mid-.80s (Mack et al., 1997). The Ethnic Behaviors subscale contains only 2 items and most often is included as a part of the globally scored 14-item MEIM or not at all.

Construct validity data also have been fairly good. Global and subscale scores have been related in theoretically predicted ways to variables such as Mexican Americans' acculturation (Cuéllar et al., 1997), vocational maturity in both majority and minority students (Perron, Vondracek, Skorikov, Tremblay, & Corbière, 1998), African Americans' and Latinos' self-esteem (Goodstein & Ponterotto, 1997; Lorenzo-Hernández & Ouellette, 1998 [with a slightly modified MEIM]; Phinney & Onwughalu, 1996; Phinney, Cantu, & Kurtz, 1997), and African Americans' racial and general ego identity (Goodstein & Ponterotto, 1997; Markstrom & Hunter, 1999; Smith & Brookins, 1997). Further, MEIM scores typically (but not always; Murray, Kaiser, & Taylor, 1997; Ponterotto, Gretchen, Utsey, Stracuzzi, & Saya, 2000) are higher for ethnic minority than ethnic majority populations (e.g., Markstrom & Hunter, 1999; Perron et al., 1998; Phinney, 1992; Phinney, Cantu, & Kurtz, 1997), and some evidence has suggested that scores increase for minority individuals over time (Perron et al., 1998; and for international students with increasing length of U.S. residence [Phinney & Onwughalu, 1996]). However, a few surprising findings challenge construct validity. For example, Phinney and Devich-Navarro (1997) found MEIM scores not to predict self-concept or—startlingly—African American and Mexican American adolescents' ways of being (or not being) bicultural, as revealed in semistructured interviews.

The data on MEIM's structural validity is much less clear. Phinney's (1992) presentation of the MEIM contained reports of exploratory factor analyses in ethnically diverse samples of high school and college students, ostensibly demonstrating a single ethnic identity factor (and another other-group orientation factor); however, no information on methods of rotation or of choosing factor solutions (beyond proportion of variance accounted for) was provided. Roberts et al. (1999) recently reported a principle components analysis of the 14-item scale (excluding Other-Group Orientation items) in another ethnically diverse sample of adolescents, but these results are even more difficult to interpret, due to limited information about and unclear rationales for statistical/methodological procedures made in this analysis and in follow-up confirmatory factor analyses.

Two independent investigations of the MEIM's structure in ethnic minority samples have been published. First, Reese, Vera, and Paikoff (1998) replicated several of Phinney's (1992) analyses in a sample of pre-adolescent African American children living in poverty. Principle components analysis of data for the set of 20 items resulted in a single ethnic pride factor accounting for a modest proportion of the variance. McNeil et al. (1999) forced a two-factor structure on MEIM data from 160 Navajo undergraduates in principal axis factoring and concluded that results supported a single ethnic identity factor (and a second other-group orientation factor). In a sample of primarily White high school students, Ponterotto et al. (2001) also forced two factors in a principal components analysis with promax rotation, which resulted in factor loadings quite similar to Phinney's (1992). Next, these authors reported results of confirmatory factor analyses (using item parcels to reduce the indicators-to-latent-variable ratios), which evidenced unimpressive fits for a single-factor model (χ^2/df = 4.4, GFI = .87, AGFI = .80, RNI = .86, RMSR = .09) and fits ranging from unacceptable to encouraging for both correlated and uncorrelated two-factor models (for both models, χ^2/df = 2.8, GFI = .92, AGFI = .88, RNI = .93, RMSR = .08).

Evaluation. The MEIM appears to be a relatively solid instrument, but more research on several aspects of its performance is needed. First, we recommend further investigation of its structure in various samples, with careful attention to rationales for types of analyses (e.g., principle axis vs. principle components) and for analytic decisions (e.g., number of factors or components to retain). Along with clearer reporting, we would like to see more genuinely exploratory factor analyses of MEIM data (vs. specifying *a priori* the number of factors, which is closer to a confirmatory analysis in spirit).

Second, we were pleased to see some good internal consistency and construct validity data for the MEIM, but we are curious about the unstudied possible role of socially desirable responding in the scale's links with validity criteria. For example, the studies supporting construct validity all involved correlational paper-and-pencil methodology. The one study with the most surprising findings (Phinney & Devich-Navarro, 1997), which—if replicated—presents a challenge to the MEIM, used interview methodology. Perhaps the MEIM shares social desirability or positive affectivity variance with validity criteria, leading to spuriously created relations (cf. Fischer et al.'s, 1998, findings with RIAS data).

Phinney (1992) concluded that although "each group has its unique history, traditions, and values . . . a sense of identification with, or belonging to, one's own group, is common to all human beings" (p. 158) and therefore has focused her research program (including the MEIM) on that general identity phenomenon. We find this to be a reasonable rationale but echo Phinney's suggestion to consider both universal and culture-specific factors in ethnic identity.

Collective Self-Esteem Scale
(CSES; Luhtanen & Crocker, 1992)

Theoretical base. The CSES focuses on evaluations of "aspects of the self-concept that relate to race, ethnic background, religion, feelings of belonging in one's community, and the like" (Luhtanen & Crocker, 1992, p. 302), which are referred to variously as *social identity*, as *collective identity*, or as the *"we"* facet of the self. Luhtanen and Crocker (1992) developed the CSES primarily as a tool for investigating the potential roles of collective (vs. personal) self-esteem in moderating group-level basic social psychological processes (e.g., in-group-serving attributions). They also concentrated their efforts on measuring collective self-esteem (CSE) based on *ascribed* (e.g., ethnicity, class, sex) rather than on *achieved* (e.g., occupation, interest) group membership, in part because achieved identities usually come into being because of individual achievements or desires.

Instrument development. Based on various conceptions of the collective self, Luhtanen and Crocker (1992) wrote 43 items intended to reflect the following four domains: (1) *membership* CSE, assessing sense of how worthy a member of my social group I am, (2) *private* CSE, reflecting my personal evaluation of my group, (3) *public* CSE, or judgments of the public's view of my group, and (4) importance of this group *identity* to my self-concept. Participants rate their agreement on a 7-point Likert-type scale (1= *strongly disagree*, 7= *strongly agree*), such that higher scores indicate greater CSE. In a sample of 82 ethnicity-unspecified college students, a principal components analysis with orthogonal rotation suggested a 4-component solution, according to Luhtanen and Crocker (1992), but the authors provided no justification for choosing this solution. Based on a series of conventional item selection criteria (highest factor loadings, item-total correlations, and inclusion of some reverse-scored items), the scale was reduced to 16 items (4 for each subscale), with each long-short subscale correlation in the .90s.

An important methodological note is that different instructions have been and may be used with the CSES, varying in two major ways. First, participants may be primed for—or directly instructed to respond to items keeping in mind—a particular group membership (e.g., "your ethnic group"), or they may be asked to respond in general terms (e.g., with reference to "your social groups"). In a racially diverse sample, Crocker, Luhtanen, Blaine, and Broadnax (1994) found substantial but not exceptionally high correlations between CSES subscale scores obtained under different administration procedures (items completed twice per person, once with respect to "your race" and once in general terms).

Second, if instructions are general, sample group memberships may include either ascribed or achieved memberships ("gender, race, religion, nationality, ethnicity, and socioeconomic class" in the original vs. "sorority, club, team, political organization" in a revision; both in Luhtanen & Crocker, 1992). The authors of one study, however, reasoned that the *membership* construct did not make sense in the context of an ascribed group (Hispanics) and thus omitted that subscale (Ethier & Deaux, 1990).

Psychometric properties. In terms of structural validity, Luhtanen and Crocker (1992) reported 2 examinations of the reduced 16-item CSES with predominantly White samples (and general instructions). Rather than exploring the optimal structure of responses, they specified a 4-factor solution a priori in principal components analyses. The four components corresponded clearly to the four intended domains and subscales, but this analysis largely reflected confirmatory ("What would four components look like?") rather than exploratory ("How many components best represent these data?") procedures. Studies 1 through 3 also included confirmatory factor analyses, in which none of the models tested (1-factor, 4-factor correlated and uncorrelated, or second-order general factor subsuming 4 first-order factors) demonstrated good fits to the data according to conventional criteria (although the 4-factor correlated and hierarchical models came quite close in Study 1, which had the largest sample). In an independent examination, Verkuyten (1995) created a short form of 10 items (without providing rationale for item selection) and found support for factor invariance across ethnic groups (majority Dutch and minority Turkish, Moroccan, and Surinamese) in the Netherlands, suggesting that the structure of responses to those items was similar across these groups.

Regarding internal consistency and construct validity, we review only studies clearly specifying that participants respond to the CSES in terms of racial or ethnic identity. Internal consistencies for the subscales generally have been acceptable to good (particularly considering that each subscale is only 4 items), ranging from an occasional low in the low .60s (e.g., Lay, 1992, in a sample of Greek Canadians and Italian Canadians) to an occasional high in the .90s (e.g., Ethier & Deaux, 1990, in a sample of Ivy-league Hispanic students). More typically, however, αs have hovered in the .70s or .80s, and the pattern of reliabilities does not seem to indicate any one particularly problematic (or stellar) subscale.

A number of studies have supported the CSES's construct validity as a measure of ethnic identity. Some of the most direct evidence comes from links of Public scores with endorsement of stereotypical beliefs about African Americans (in a sample of African Americans—see Arroyo & Zigler, 1995) and with perceptions of own-group societal status (with minority Chinese Netherlanders—see Verkuyten & Lay, 1998); Public scores also were higher in higher-status northern Italians than in lower-status southern Italians (Maas, Ceccarelli, & Rudin, 1996). Further, the Private and Identity subscales were substantially related to Hispanic students' ratings of importance of ethnicity to their identity (Ethier & Deaux, 1990). Quinton, Cowan, and Watson (1996) found Private + Identity composite scores to be negatively related to Latinos' support of anti-immigrant legislation (California's Proposition 187) but positively related to Whites' support, while Ruttenberg, Zea, and Sigelman (1996) found total scores to predict Jewish students' religious (but not Jewish organizational) involvement. Also supporting construct validity, racial or ethnic minority participants typically have scored more highly than majority participants on the Identity subscale (e.g., Quinton et al., 1996); in one study, the African American-White difference was close to two standard deviations (Crocker et al., 1994). Finally, CSE variables sometimes have been linked in predicted ways with personal mental health variables (e.g., Crocker et al., 1994; Verkuyten & Lay, 1998) and sometimes have not (e.g., Arroyo & Zigler, 1995). In terms of discriminant validity, Luhtanen and Crocker (1992; Study 2) reported no significant links between CSES subscales and social desirability, but the generalizability of this finding is unknown, particularly since the sample was predominantly (86%) White, and the CSES was administered with general instructions.

Evaluation. The CSES appears to have a number of strengths, including typically good reliabilities and support for construct validity. One important piece of information missing from the published literature, though, is how the items originally were developed. And, as is the case with many instruments in this review, we recommend more clearly reasoned and presented explorations of the CSES's factorial validity in various samples. A few conceptual issues are, first, because of its intended applicability to a range of social identities, the cross-group cautions we described regarding the MEIM also hold for the CSES. Second, based on logic and on Crocker et al.'s (1994) results, we recommend that researchers specify the reference group of interest (e.g., "being Native American/Indian," "your ethnicity" vs. the general "your social groups"). Third, we encourage researchers to think carefully about how well the constructs of CSE reflect their specific research questions. For example, of the four subscales, *identity* and *private* CSE are probably the most similar to what multicultural researchers often want to know about (i.e., the significance of and attachment to ethnicity in one's overall sense of self).

CONCLUSIONS AND
RECOMMENDATIONS FOR FUTURE RESEARCH

It is encouraging to see such a large and continually growing body of literature on racial and ethnic identity development, which may be a sign of counseling psychology's commitment to improving assessment and understanding of the roles that such identity processes play in people's lives. The following are some thoughts on directions for future research:

1. Advancing knowledge of the nature and functioning of racial and ethnic identity processes is crucial, and we encourage researchers to maintain the highest standards for their work, with more careful attention to measurement issues. In particular, it is critical that authors *reason* through and *report their reasoning* for each developmental and analytic decision (e.g., how exactly were items originally developed? why principal axis factoring over principle components? why a given number of factors? why a given rotation?).

2. Although there do seem to be similar identity processes occurring across racial and ethnic groups, we also would like to see more (and more systematic) efforts to assess group-specific identity issues (especially for Native American Indian, Asian American, Latino, multiracial, and Jewish groups). However, this raises the unresolved issue of how specific is specific enough, considering that each of the "groups" we mention is itself an overbroad classification (e.g., Korean American ethnic identity is not the same as Vietnamese American ethnic identity).

3. An important conceptual issue to keep in mind is that results of construct validity investigations generally have multiple interpretations, especially early in an instrument's life (or when the same instrument has been used repeatedly without needed refinements). In particular, if theory would predict that scores on Instrument A should be positively related to scores on Validity Criterion B, and results do not pan out, does that reveal a problem with the theory or with the instrument?

4. Related to Item 3, we encourage researchers to think carefully about their theoretical rationales for predictions. For example, many investigators have hypothesized that racial and ethnic identity constructs should be linked to mental health variables. However, Cross (1995) and others (e.g., Goodstein & Ponterotto, 1997) reminded readers that social/collective identity is just *one part* of an individual's identity, along with personal identity. We suggest that when evaluating construct validity of racial or ethnic identity measures, it is not logical to hold rigidly to links with personal self-esteem or other global mental health variables as validity criteria. Thus, the fact that racial and ethnic identity measures sometimes have been linked in predicted ways with personal mental health and sometimes have not is difficult to distill into a singular judgment. We argue that such links *may* support construct validity, but their absence is not necessarily damaging to validity of the instruments in question.

5. We should be conducting theory-driven research. To this end, readers are encouraged to detach as much as possible from "thinking in instruments" and strive instead to "think in constructs." In other words, researchers should ideally shift their planning from "What measures are available for

me to include in this questionnaire packet?" to "What do I really want to know, or what does theory predict, *specifically?*" Our experience and reading of the literature has suggested that it is tantalizingly simple to become familiar with instruments by their names (e.g., "this is a measure of ethnic identity"), rather than by what data suggest are their actual measured constructs (e.g., "this seems to be measuring self-reported importance of ethnicity to one's overall self-concept").

6. Although there are a great many strengths, there also are a number of limitations to the usefulness of paper-and-pencil measures of racial and ethnic identity:

   a. How should scores be interpreted? For example, Cross (1995) has implied that, for African Americans, endorsement of Pre-Encounter-type statements may indicate anti-Black attitudes, or it may indicate low race-salience (see Cross & Vandiver, Chapter 21, this volume.)

   b. When researchers provide close-ended questions for participants' ratings, are the "right" (socially desirable) responses pulling strongly for endorsement? (Certainly, an important question is "socially desirable to whom?") For example, research (Tokar & Fischer, 1998; Yanico et al., 1994) has indicated that Pre-Encounter—one of the RIAS subscales most frequently predicting variables of interest—evidences little variability, such that what is typically covarying with other scores is degree of *disagreement* (strong disagreement vs. disagreement), not agreement versus disagreement. Thus, we recommend reporting more clearly basic descriptive statistics (minimally, examination of frequency distributions).

   c. In the case of many paper-and-pencil racial and ethnic identity instruments, it is just not clear what is being measured. For example, what is going on when MEIM scores don't predict ethnic identity management strategies culled from one-on-one interviews (Phinney & Devich-Navarro, 1997)?

   d. In response to Item c, we wonder if scores may reflect, in part, basic personality processes. For example, in a related domain (gender, which—like racial and ethnic identity—is posited to be heavily influenced by external and societal circumstances and experiences), Tokar, Fischer, Schaub, and Moradi (2000) found that many empirical links between masculine gender-role variables and counseling-related variables were completely mediated by personality (especially neuroticism). Thus, positive or negative affectivity, for example, may be an unacknowledged source of common variance.

   e. For these reasons, researchers are encouraged to consider developing and using alternate (e.g., qualitative) methods of assessing identity (cf. Ponterotto, Fuertes, & Chen, 2000), not necessarily instead of but in addition to paper-and-pencil instruments.

7. Several popular measures (e.g., MEIM and CSE) are devoid of attention to the roles of power and oppression, which can be extraordinarily significant in the way we make meaning of our lives, and we encourage researchers to think about them as they develop research questions. We hope readers will explore some of the excellent conceptual work on power and subordination (e.g., Apfelbaum, 1979; Freire, 1972; Ivey, 1995).

8. Another important issue for future work is context. For example, a number of authors (e.g., Root, 1996; Sellers, Smith, et al.'s, 1998, multidimensional

model of racial identity) have acknowledged that—although ethnicity may be made chronically salient to those in political or numerical minority groups—the salience of ethnicity can vary tremendously (temporally, situationally) within one person. Thus, rather than thinking about racial or ethnic identity as necessarily stable, we hope researchers will continue thinking about conditions under which it may be more or less salient or may contain different feelings or beliefs.

9. In terms of theorizing, a number of the instruments reviewed here were based on models conceptualizing more and less "advanced" ways of experiencing one's racial or ethnic identity. But what happens beyond the highest or most optimal statuses posited (e.g., Integration in Helms's theorizing; high levels of exploration and commitment in Phinney's work)? Dr. Seuss's *On Beyond Zebra* (Geisel, 1955) asks what kinds of letters (and hence things and ideas) come after "Z." Similarly, if we hypothesized that there were more, what might we find? Interviewing people who have done a great deal of racial and ethnic identity exploration, growth, and change over their lifetimes could help shed light on what kinds of processes may evolve.

REFERENCES

Abu-Ali, A., & Reisen, C. A. (1999). Gender role identity among adolescent Muslim girls living in the US. *Current Psychology: Developmental, Learning, Personality, Social, 18*, 185-192.

Amyot, R. P., & Sigelman, L. (1996). Jews without Judaism? Assimilation and Jewish identity in the United States. *Social Science Quarterly, 77*, 177-189.

Apfelbaum, E. (1979). Relations of domination and movements for liberation: An analysis of power between groups. In W. G. Austin & S. Worchel (Eds.), *The social psychology of intergroup relations.* Pacific Grove, CA: Brooks/Cole.

Arroyo, C. G., & Zigler, E. (1995). Racial identity, academic achievement, and the psychological well-being of economically disadvantaged adolescents. *Journal of Personality & Social Psychology, 69*, 903-914.

Atkinson, D. R., Morten, G., & Sue, D. W. (1998). *Counseling American minorities* (5th ed.). Boston: McGraw-Hill.

Baldwin, J. A. (1981). Notes on an Africentric theory of Black personality. *Western Journal of Black Studies, 5*, 172-179.

Baldwin, J. A., & Bell, Y. R. (1985). The African Self-Consciousness Scale: An Africentric personality questionnaire. *Western Journal of Black Studies, 9*, 61-68.

Baldwin, J. A., Duncan, J. A., & Bell, Y. R. (1987). Assessment of African Self-Consciousness among Black students from two college environments. *Journal of Black Psychology, 13*, 27-41.

Bates, S. C., Beauvais, F., & Trimble, J. E. (1997). American Indian adolescent alcohol involvement and ethnic identification. *Substance Use and Misuse, 32*, 2013-2031.

Behrens, J. T. (1997). Does the White Racial Identity Attitude Scale measure racial identity? *Journal of Counseling Psychology, 44*, 3-12.

Behrens, J. T., Leach, M. M., Franz, S., & LaFleur, N. K. (1999, August). *Revising the Oklahoma Racial Attitudes Scale: Work in progress.* Paper presented at the annual meeting of the American Psychological Association, Boston.

Block, C. J., Roberson, L., & Neuger, D. A. (1995). White racial identity theory: A framework for understanding reactions toward interracial situations in organizations. *Journal of Vocational Behavior, 46*, 71-88.

Brookins, C. C. (1994). The relationship between Afrocentric values and racial identity attitudes: Validation of the Belief Systems Analysis Scale on African American college students. *Journal of Black Psychology, 20*, 128-142.

Carter, R. T. (1996). Exploring the complexity of racial identity attitude measures. In G. R. Sodowsky & J. Impara (Eds.), *Multicultural assessment in counseling and clinical psychology* (pp. 193-223). Lincoln, NE: Buros Institute of Mental Measurement.

Carter, R. T., DeSole, L., Sicalides, E. I., Glass, K., & Tyler, F. B. (1997). Black racial identity and psychosocial competence: A preliminary study. *Journal of Black Psychology, 23,* 58-73.

Chambers, J. W., Kambon, K., Birdsong, B. D., Brown, J., Dixon, P., & Robbins-Brinson, L. (1998). Africentric cultural identity and the stress experience of African American college students. *Journal of Black Psychology, 24,* 368-396.

Cheatham, H. E., Tomlinson, S. M., & Ward, T. J. (1990). The African Self-Consciousness construct and African American students. *Journal of College Student Development, 31,* 492-499.

Choney, S. K., & Behrens, J. T. (1996). Development of the Oklahoma Racial Attitudes Scale–Preliminary Form (ORAS-P). In G. R. Sodowsky & J. Impara (Eds.), *Multicultural assessment in counseling and clinical psychology* (pp. 225-240). Lincoln, NE: Buros Institute of Mental Measurement.

Cohen, S. M. (1988). *American assimilation or Jewish revival?* Bloomington: Indiana University Press.

Crocker, J., Luhtanen, R., Blaine, B., & Broadnax, S. (1994). Collective self-esteem and psychological well-being among White, Black, and Asian college students. *Personality & Social Psychology Bulletin, 20,* 503-513.

Cross, W. E., Jr. (1971). The Negro-to-Black conversion experience: Toward a psychology of Black liberation. *Black World, 20,* 13-27.

Cross, W. E., Jr. (1995). The psychology of Nigrescence: Revising the Cross model. In J. G. Ponterotto, J. M. Casas, L. A. Suzuki, & C. M. Alexander (Eds.), *Handbook of multicultural counseling* (pp. 93-122). Thousand Oaks, CA: Sage.

Cuéllar, I., Roberts, R. E., Nyberg, B., & Moldanado, R. E. (1998). Ethnic identity and acculturation in a young adult Mexican origin population. *Journal of Community Psychology, 25,* 535-549.

Dixon, P., & Azibo, D. A. (1998). African self-consciousness, misorientation behavior, and a self-destructive disorder: African Amercian male crack-cocaine users. *Journal of Black Psychology, 24,* 226-247.

Erikson, E. (1968). *Identity: Youth and crisis.* New York: Norton.

Ethier, K., & Deaux, K. (1990). Hispanics in ivy: Assessing identity and perceived threat. *Sex Roles, 22,* 427-440.

Fèlix-Ortiz, M., Newcomb, M. D., & Myers, H. (1994). A multidimensional measure of cultural identity for Latino and Latina adolescents. *Hispanic Journal of Behavioral Sciences, 16,* 99-115.

Fischer, A. R., Tokar, D. M., & Serna, G. S. (1998). Validity and construct contamination of the Racial Identity Attitude Scale–Long Form. *Journal of Counseling Psychology, 45,* 212-224.

Freire, P. (1972). *Pedagogy of the oppressed.* New York: Herder & Herder.

Gao, G., Schmidt, K. L., & Gudykunst, W. B. (1994). Strength of ethnic identity and perceptions of ethnolinguistic vitality among Mexican Americans. *Hispanic Journal of Behavioral Sciences, 16,* 332-341.

Garcia, J. A. (1982). Ethnicity and Chicanos: Measurement of ethnic identification, identity, and consciousness. *Hispanic Journal of Behavioral Sciences, 4,* 295-314.

Garcia, M., & Lega, L. I. (1979). Development of a Cuban ethnic identity questionnaire. *Hispanic Journal of Behavioral Sciences, 1,* 247-261.

Geisel, T. S. [pseud. Dr. Seuss]. (1955). *On beyond zebra.* New York: Random House.

Goodstein, R., & Ponterotto, J. G. (1997). Racial and ethnic identity: Their relationship and their contribution to self-esteem. *Journal of Black Psychology, 23,* 275-292.

Helms, J. E. (1984). Toward a theoretical explanation of the effects of race on counseling: A Black and White model. *The Counseling Psychologist, 12,* 153-165.

Helms, J. E. (1990). *Black and White racial identity: Theory, research and practice.* Westport, CT: Greenwood.

Helms, J. E. (1996). Toward a methodology for measuring and assessing racial as distinguished from ethnic identity. In G. R. Sodowsky & J. C. Impara (Eds.), *Multicultural assessment in counseling and clinical psychology* (pp. 143-192). Lincoln, NE: Buros Institute of Mental Measurement.

Helms, J. E., & Carter, R. T. (1990). Development of the White Racial Identity Inventory. In J. E. Helms, *Black and White racial identity: Theory, research and practice* (pp. 67-80). Westport, CT: Greenwood.

Helms, J. E., & Parham, T. A. (1996). The Racial Identity Attitudes Scale. In R. L. Jones (Ed.), *Handbook of tests and measurements for Black populations* (Vol. 1, pp. 167-174). Hampton, VA: Cobb & Henry.

Ivey, A. E. (1995). Psychotherapy as liberation. In J. G. Ponterotto, J. M. Casas, L. A. Suzuki, & C. M. Alexander (Eds.), *Handbook of multicultural counseling* (pp. 53-72). Thousand Oaks, CA: Sage.

Jome, L. M. (2000). *Construct validity of the White Racial Identity Attitude Scale.* Unpublished doctoral dissertation, University of Akron, Akron, OH.

Kambon, K. K. K. (1996). An introduction to the African Self-Consciousness Scale. In R. L. Jones (Ed.), *Handbook of tests and measurements for Black populations* (Vol. 1, pp. 207-216). Hampton, VA: Cobb & Henry.

Kivisto, P., & Nefzger, B. (1993). Symbolic ethnicity and American Jews: The relationship of ethnic identity to behavior and group affiliation. *Social Science Journal, 30,* 1-12.

Kohatsu, E. L., & Richardson, T. Q. (1996). Racial and ethnic identity assessment. In L. A. Suzuki, P. J. Meller, & J. G. Ponterotto (Eds.), *Handbook of multicultural assessment* (pp. 611-650). San Francisco: Jossey-Bass.

Kwan, K. K., & Sodowsky, G. R. (1997). Internal and external ethnic identity and their correlates: A study of Chinese-American immigrants. *Journal of Multicultural Counseling and Development, 25,* 51-67.

Landrine, H., & Klonoff, E. A. (1996). *African American acculturation: Deconstructing race and reviving culture.* Thousand Oaks, CA: Sage.

Lay, C. H. (1992). Athens' failed bid for the Olympic Games: The role of ego-involvement and affect on the collective self-esteem of Greek-Canadians. *European Journal of Social Psychology, 22,* 375-385.

Lemon, R. L., & Waehler, C. A. (1996). A test of stability and construct validity of the Black Racial Identity Attitude Scale, Form B (RIAS-B) and the White Racial Identity Attitude Scale (WRIAS). *Measurement and Evaluation in Counseling and Development, 29,* 77-85.

Lorenzo-Hernández, J., & Ouellette, S. C. (1998). Ethnic identity, self-esteem, and values in Dominicans, Puerto Ricans, and African Americans. *Journal of Applied Social Psychology, 28,* 2007-2024.

Luhtanen, R., & Crocker, J. (1992). A collective self-esteem scale: Self-evaluation of one's social identity. *Personality & Social Psychology Bulletin, 18,* 302-318.

Lysne, M., & Levy, G. D. (1997). Differences in ethnic identity in Native American adolescents as a function of school context. *Journal of Adolescent Research, 12,* 372-388.

Maas, A., Ceccarelli, R., & Rudin, S. (1996). Linguistic intergroup bias: Evidence for in-group-protective motivation. *Journal of Personality & Social Psychology, 71,* 512-526.

Mack, D. E., Tucker, T. W., Archuleta, R., DeGroot, G., Hernandez, A. A., & Cha, S. O. (1997). Interethnic relations on campus: Can't we all get along? *Journal of Multicultural Counseling and Development, 25,* 256-268.

Makkar, J. K., & Strube, M. J. (1995). Black women's self-perceptions of attractiveness following exposure to White versus Black beauty standards: The moderating role of racial identity and self-esteem. *Journal of Applied Social Psychology, 25,* 1547-1566.

Markstrom, C. A., & Hunter, C. L. (1999). The roles of ethnic and ideological identity in predicting fidelity in African American and European American adolescents. *Child Study Journal, 29,* 23-38.

McCowan, C. J., & Alston, R. J. (1998). Racial identity, African self-consciousness, and career decision making in African American college women. *Journal of Multicultural Counseling and Development, 26,* 28-38.

McNeil, D. W., Kee, M., & Zvolensky, M. J. (1999). Culturally related anxiety and ethnic identity in Navajo college students. *Cultural Diversity and Ethnic Minority Psychology, 5,* 56-64.

Murray, C. B., Kaiser, R., & Taylor, S. (1997). The O. J. Simpson verdict: Predictors of beliefs about innocence or guilt. *Journal of Social Issues, 53,* 455-475.

Myers, M. A., & Thompson, V. L. S. (1994). Africentricity: An analysis of two culture specific instruments. *Western Journal of Black Studies, 18,* 179-184.

Neville, H. A., Heppner, M. J., Louie, C. E., Thompson, C. E., Brooks, L., & Baker, C. E. (1996). The impact of multicultural training on White racial identity attitudes and therapy competencies. *Professional Psychology: Research and Practice, 27,* 83-89.

Neville, H. A., Heppner, P. P., & Wang, L. (1997). Relations among racial identity attitudes, perceived stressors, and coping styles in African American college students. *Journal of Counseling and Development, 75,* 303-311.

Oyserman, D., Gant, L., & Ager, J. (1995). A socially contextualized model of African American identity: Possible selves and school persistence. *Journal of Personality and Social Psychology, 69,* 1216-1232.

Oyserman, D., & Sakamoto, I. (1997). Being Asian American: Identity, cultural constructs, and stereotype perception. *Journal of Applied Behavioral Science, 33,* 435-453.

Perron, J., Vondracek, F. W., Skorikov, V. B., Tremblay, C., & Corbière, M. (1998). A longitudinal study of vocational maturity and ethnic identity development. *Journal of Vocational Behavior, 52,* 409-424.

Phinney, J. S. (1989). Stages of ethnic identity in minority adolescents. *Journal of Early Adolescence, 9,* 34-49.

Phinney, J. S. (1990). Ethnic identity in adolescents and adults: Review of research. *Psychological Bulletin, 108,* 499-514.

Phinney, J. S. (1992). The Multigroup Ethnic Identity Measure: A new scale for use with diverse groups. *Journal of Adolescent Research, 7,* 156-176.

Phinney, J. S., & Alipuria, L. (1990). Ethnic identity in college students from four ethnic groups. *Journal of Adolescence, 13,* 171-183.

Phinney, J. S., & Ambarsoom, H. (1987). *Ethnic identity in young adults from three ethnic groups.* ERIC Document No. ED 283 057.

Phinney, J. S., Cantu, C. L., & Kurtz, D. A. (1997). Ethnic and American identity as predictors of self-esteem among African American, Latino, and White adolescents. *Journal of Youth and Adolescence, 26,* 165-185.

Phinney, J. S., & Devich-Navarro, M. (1997). Variations in bicultural identification among African American and Mexican American adolescents. *Journal of Research on Adolescence, 7,* 3-32.

Phinney, J. S., Ferguson, D. L., & Tate, J. D. (1997). Intergroup attitudes among ethnic minority adolescents: A causal model. *Child Development, 68,* 955-969.

Phinney, J. S., & Onwughalu, M. (1996). Racial identity and perception of American ideals among African American and African students in the United States. *International Journal of Intercultural Relations, 20,* 127-140.

Ponterotto, J. G. (1998). Charting a course for research in multicultural counseling training. *The Counseling Psychologist, 26,* 43-68.

Ponterotto, J. G., Fuertes, J. N., & Chen, E. C. (2000). Models of multicultural counseling. In S. D. Brown & R. W. Lent (Eds.), *Handbook of counseling psychology* (3rd ed., pp. 639-669). New York: John Wiley.

Ponterotto, H. G., Gretchen, D., Utsey, S. O., Stracuzzi, T., & Saya, R., Jr. (2001). *A critique and confirmatory test of the Multigroup Ethnic Identity Measure (MEIM).* Manuscript under review.

Pope-Davis, D. B., Vandiver, B. J., & Stone, G. L. (1999). White racial identity attitude development: A psychometric examination of two instruments. *Journal of Counseling Psychology, 46,* 70-79.

Quinton, W. J., Cowan, G., & Watson, B. D. (1996). Personality and attitudinal predictors of support of Proposition 187—California's anti-illegal immigrant initiative. *Journal of Applied Social Psychology, 26,* 2204-2223.

Reese, L. E., Vera, E. M., & Paikoff, R. L. (1998). Ethnic identity assessment among inner-city African American children: Evaluating the applicability of the Multigroup Ethnic Identity Measure. *Journal of Black Psychology, 24,* 289-304.

Roberts, R. E., Phinney, J. S., Masse, L. C., Chen, Y. R., Roberts, C., & Romero, A. (1999). The structure of ethnic identity of young adolescents from diverse ethnocultural groups. *Journal of Early Adolescence, 19,* 301-322.

Rosenthal, D. A., & Feldman, S. S. (1992). The relationship between parenting behavior and ethnic identity in Chinese-American and Chinese-Australian adolescents. *International Journal of Psychology, 27,* 19-31.

Root, M. P. P. (1996). A bill of rights for racially mixed people. In M. P. P. Root (Ed.), *The multiracial experience: Racial borders as the new frontier* (pp. 3-14). Thousand Oaks, CA: Sage.

Rowe, W., Behrens, J. T., & Leach, M. M. (1995). Racial/ethnic identity and racial consciousness: Looking back and looking forward. In J. G. Ponterotto, J. M. Casas, L. A. Suzuki, & C. M. Alexander (Eds.), *Handbook of multicultural counseling* (pp. 218-235). Thousand Oaks, CA: Sage.

Rowe, W., Bennett, S. K., & Atkinson, D. R. (1994). White racial identity models: A critique and alternative proposal. *The Counseling Psychologist, 22,* 129-146.

Rowley, S. J., Sellers, R. M., Chavous, T. M., & Smith, M. A. (1998). The relationship between racial identity and self-esteem in African American college and high school students. *Journal of Personality and Social Psychology, 74,* 715-724.

Ruttenberg, J., Zea, M. C., & Sigelman, C. K. (1996). Collective identity and intergroup prejudice among Jewish and Arab students in the United States. *Journal of Social Psychology, 136,* 209-220.

Sabnani, H. B., & Ponterotto, J. G. (1992). Racial/ethnic minority-specific instrumentation in counseling research: A review, critique, and recommendations. *Measurement and Evaluation in Counseling and Development, 24,* 161-187.

Sellers, R. M., Caldwell, C., Zimmerman, M., & Hilkene, D. (1999, June). *Racial identity and substance abuse in a sample of academically at-risk African American high school students.* Paper presented at the biennial meeting of the Society for Community Research and Action, New Haven, CT.

Sellers, R. M., Rowley, S. A. J., Chavous, T. M., Shelton, J. N., & Smith, M. A. (1997). Multidimensional Inventory of Black Identity: A preliminary investigation of reliability and construct validity. *Journal of Personality and Social Psychology, 73,* 805-815.

Sellers, R. M., Shelton, J. N., Cooke, D. Y., Chavous, T. M., Rowley, S. A. J., & Smith, M. A. (1998). A multidimensional model of racial identity: Assumptions, findings, and future directions. In R. L. Jones (Ed.), *African American identity development: Theory, research, and intervention* (pp. 275-302). Hampton, VA: Cobb & Henry.

Sellers, R. M., Smith, M. A., Shelton, J. N., Rowley, S. A. J., & Chavous, T. M. (1998). Multidimensional Model of Racial Identity: A reconceptualization of African American racial identity. *Personality and Social Psychology Review, 2,* 18-39.

Shelton, J. N., & Sellers, R. M. (2000). Situational stability and variability in African American racial identity. *Journal of Black Psychology, 26,* 27-50.

Smith, E. P., & Brookins, C. C. (1997). Toward the development of an ethnic identity measure for African American youth. *Journal of Black Psychology, 23,* 358-377.

Stevenson, H. C. (1995). Relationship of adolescent perceptions of racial socialization to racial identity. *Journal of Black Psychology, 21,* 49-70.

Stokes, J. E., Murray, C. B., Peacock, M. J., & Kaiser, R. T. (1994). Assessing the reliability, factor structure, and validity of the African Self-Consciousness Scale in a general population of African Americans. *Journal of Black Psychology, 20,* 62-74.

Swanson, J. L., Tokar, D. M., & Davis, L. E. (1994). Content and construct validity of the White Racial Identity Attitude Scale. *Journal of Vocational Behavior, 44,* 198-217.

Tajfel, H., & Turner, J. C. (1979). An integrative theory of intergroup conflict. In W. Austin & S. Worchel (Eds.), *The social psychology of intergroup relations* (pp. 34-48). Pacific Grove, CA: Brooks/Cole.

Taub, D. J. (1995). Relationship of selected factors to traditional-age undergraduate women's development of autonomy. *Journal of College Student Development, 36,* 141-151.

Taub, D. J., & McEwen, M. K. (1992). The relationship of racial identity attitudes to autonomy and mature interpersonal relationships in Black and White undergraduate women. *Journal of College Student Development, 33,* 439-446.

Tokar, D. M., & Fischer, A. R. (1998). Psychometric analysis of the Racial Identity Attitude Scale–Long Form. *Measurement and Evaluation in Counseling and Development, 31,* 138-149.

Tokar, D. M., Fischer, A. R., Schaub, M., & Moradi, B. (2000). Masculine gender roles and counseling-related variables: Links with and mediation by personality. *Journal of Counseling Psychology, 47,* 380-393.

Tokar, D. M., & Swanson, J. L. (1991). An investigation of the validity of Helms' (1984) model of White racial identity development. *Journal of Counseling Psychology, 38,* 296-301.

Verkuyten, M. (1995). Self-esteem, self-concept stability, and aspects of ethnic identity among minority and majority youth in the Netherlands. *Journal of Youth and Adolescence, 24,* 155-175.

Verkuyten, M., & Lay, C. (1998). Ethnic minority identity and psychological well-being: The mediating role of collective self-esteem. *Journal of Applied Social Psychology, 28,* 1969-1986.

White, A. M., Potgieter, C. A., Strube, M. J., Fisher, S., & Umana, E. (1997). An African-centered, Black feminist approach to understanding attitudes that counter social dominance. *Journal of Black Psychology, 23,* 398-420.

Yanico, B. J., Swanson, J. L., & Tokar, D. M. (1994). A psychometric investigation of the Black Racial Identity Attitude Scale–Form B. *Journal of Vocational Behavior, 44,* 218-234.

Zack, I. (1973). Dimensions of Jewish-American identity. *Psychological Reports, 33,* 891-900.

Zimmerman, M. A., Ramirez-Valles, J., Washienko, K. M., Walter, B., & Dyer, S. (1996). The development of a measure of enculturation for Native American youth. *American Journal of Community Psychology, 24,* 295-310.

Correspondence regarding this chapter may be addressed to Ann R. Fischer, Department of Psychology, University of Akron, Akron, OH 44325-4301 (e-mail address: ann10@uakron. edu).

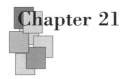

Chapter 21

NIGRESCENCE THEORY AND MEASUREMENT

Introducing the Cross Racial Identity Scale (CRIS)

WILLIAM E. CROSS, JR.
BEVERLY J. VANDIVER

IN 1971, CROSS INTRODUCED his Nigrescence model that outlined the stages of individual Black consciousness development, associated with involvement in the Black Power Movement of the late 1960s. Over time the model has been expanded into a comprehensive theory, including the explication of eight exemplars of Black identity, of which six have been operationalized in a new measure of Black racial identity. The first part of the chapter presents an overview of the expanded Nigrescence theory, and the second introduces the Cross Racial Identity Scale (CRIS; Vandiver, Cross, Fhagen-Smith, et al., 2000). Suggestions for future research include longitudinal studies, clinical utility of the CRIS, and further validation of Nigrescence Theory.

INTRODUCTION

Nigrescence Theory has come a long way from its origins—the Black Power days of the 1970s. Then, the emphasis was limited to mapping the stages of identity change that accompanied an individual's involvement in the Black Power Movement. This was followed in the 1980s with studies showing the relevance of the stage concept to an analysis of Black identity in ordinary Black life and beyond the pale of social movement dynamics

(Helms, 1990). Today, the theory has been expanded to address six issues: (a) the structure of the (Black) self-concept in which personal identity is differentiated from reference group orientation; (b) the vast universe of Black identities and the critical decision concerning which exemplars to include or leave out of a study; (c) identity socialization covering infancy through adolescence and early adulthood; (d) adult identity conversions, or resocialization experiences, which were the original focus of the Nigrescence model; (e) identity recycling, or the process by which Black adults experience continued identity enrichment and enhancement across the life span; and (f) identity functions, or the repertoire of Black identity enactments Black people evidence within and across situations.

The theory presupposes the existence of a spectrum of Black identities (e.g., not every Black identity is alike); thus, eight identity types are presented as exemplars of this spectrum, which permeates each level of Nigrescence Theory. Testing the theory required the operationalization of these exemplars or Black identity types, which resulted in the development of a Black racial identity scale. After a review of the six levels of the theory, this chapter describes the Cross Racial Identity Scale (CRIS; Vandiver, Cross, Fhagen-Smith, et al., 2000), which was five years in the making and measures six of the eight Black identity exemplars that are crucial to the integrity of the theory. With the introduction of the CRIS, it is now possible to directly test various aspects of the expanded Nigrescence Theory.

OVERVIEW OF THE
SIX LEVELS OF NIGRESCENCE THEORY

Level 1:
Nigrescence and the Structure of the (Black) Self-Concept

Nigrescence Theory rests on the assumption that the self-concept has two components, a general personality or personal identity (PI) component and a reference group orientation (RGO) or social identity component. Given that both components are multidimensional, it might be more accurate to refer to each as a *matrix*. The PI Matrix refers to the multitude of traits, psychological processes, and deep-structure personality dynamics that are commonplace in the psychological makeup of all human beings (state of alertness, emotions, cognitive skills, interpersonal competencies, level of anxiety, worry or happiness, and general self-esteem, as cases in point). PI is frequently operationalized through the use of trait measures such as the Minnesota Multiphasic Personality Inventory (MMPI; Meehl & Dahlstrom, 1960) or various versions of the Big-Five Adjective Checklist (e.g., Brand & Egan, 1989), achievement motivation scales, and, of course, self-esteem scales. Trait descriptions (e.g., a Black person is described as gregarious, risk taking, mercurial, daring, or shy) reflect the general personality, or PI, component of the overall self-concept. Phenomeno-logically, a person experiences this aspect of the self as "my personality" (e.g., the self as personality). A key precept of Nigrescence Theory is that personality plays a minor role in the definition of Black identity because Blackness is viewed as a *social identity* or reference group variable, and not a personality variable. Nigrescence Theory may lead to hypotheses about the *relationship* between personality and group identity variables, as in the prediction that racial group hatred is linked to diminished self-esteem (e.g., racial self-hated). However, in Nigrescence Theory, group identity (e.g., Black identity), is *never* defined through the use of PI variables. For example, knowing that a person has high or low self-esteem or is gregarious or shy tells little to nothing about the *content and dynamics* of a person's racial-cultural frame of reference. The person just described could be Black or White, Jewish or Protestant, male or female, gay or heterosexual, and so forth.

The RGO Matrix defines the complex of social groups used by the person to make sense of oneself as a social being (e.g., what it means to be Black, male, gay, disabled, West Indian, or middle class). This *social identity awareness* is different from one's sense of being a "personality" (e.g., a Black person is shy, hypersensitive, mathematically inclined, or sexually adventuresome), as underscored in the previous paragraph. The social groups can be *ascribed* by society (e.g., society imposes such categories as gender, race, and social class in depicting a person as, for example, male, Black, and middle class), or by the *individual,* independently of whether or not society generally associates the individual with the group or groups personally selected—for example, the person could be Black but also (a) an expert on Russian Studies, (b) a member of the Jewish faith, and (c) an internationally known mountain climber. The sum of all these socially ascribed and individually affirmed reference groups constitutes one's RGO Matrix, with each reference group or social category occupying a separate *cell* in the matrix.

In Nigrescence Theory, it is understood that to study *Black identity* refers to the way a person thinks about (cognitive component of identity), feels (evaluative component of identity that also includes tastes and preferences), and acts (behavioral component of identity) in reference to one cell or a subset of cells in a person's RGO Matrix. A Black identity that is heavily influenced by only one cell of the matrix reflects a categorical or highly bounded sense of Blackness, as for example, in some forms of narrow nationalism or reactionary assimilationism. On the other hand, a bicultural Black perspective connects at least two cells (the cell coded American and the cell representing one's sense of Africanity, as in an "African American" social identity). As a last example, a Black identity that is multiculturally oriented connects three or more cells (e.g., Black identity as interconnectivity or multiplicity). Regardless of the identity configuration and the number of cells engaged, it bears repeating that the study of Black identity does not begin to exhaust the total number of cells contained in a person's RGO Matrix. One last and related issue: An unknown percentage of Black people give little credence to the fact that they are Black. Such persons can be categorized as Black, in a nominal sense; otherwise, their RGO Matrix is organized around social cells or categories that have nothing or very little to do with race and Black culture (e.g., an assimilated Black person). There is no such thing as an assimilated Black identity, but a Black person may exhibit an assimilated identity.

Level 2:
Nigrescence and the Universe of Black Identity Types

The second supposition of Nigrescence Theory is that Black people reflect a vast array of identity profiles or types, and this "universe of identity types" cannot possibly be captured in one or even a series of studies. Scholars and students of Black identity are usually put in the position of having to articulate a rationale for including or excluding x, y, or z exemplars from the total universe of Black identity types. The criteria for selection of exemplars addressed in Nigrescence Theory is based on the following question: What types of Black identities increase the probability that the person will join with other Blacks to (a) engage in struggles against the problems and challenges that beset Black people and (b) engage in the search, codification, dissemination, protection, and celebration of Black culture and history? Put more straightforwardly, who will step forward, when there are problems, and who will partake in the discovery, protection, and celebration of Black culture? One of the objectives of Nigrescence Theory is to isolate the shared characteristics of such identities, using psychological theories and methods. Because African Americans are the products of two dominant cultural influences, Nigrescence Theory is eclectic in what theories or methods to employ, as a purely Afrocentric approach would be insensitive to the forces that shape the "American" side of the Black psyche, and the reverse would be true, if only a Eurocentric approach is undertaken.

In effect, Nigrescence Theory is not value neutral; however, it is a theory that conveys respect for whatever identity a participant may reveal in the course of a research investigation. Because knowledge and discourse analysis is inherently dialectical, the theory is used as much to interrogate the opposite types of identities as those that compliment our rationale. This means that when a Nigrescence perspective is used to scan the universe of Black identity types, one looks for (a) those identities that do not lead to the engagement of Black problems and Black culture and (b) those that do, with the expectation that in each instance will be revealed a cluster of identities, and not one singular exemplar for each category

Identity types that reflect nonengagement are called Pre-Encounter exemplars, and the ones that do *engage* are referenced as Internalization exemplars. The label Pre-Encounter is derived from the fact that there is always the possibility that a person who currently holds an identity that signals nonengagement will have an experience, a racial-cultural epiphany, an "encounter" that causes the person to go through a conversion experience, which results in the displacement of the nonengaged identity by a new identity that does engage Blackness. Thus, Pre-Encounter identities are, in a manner of speaking, at risk of an Encounter, which, if experienced, can lead to an identity metamorphosis. The critical marker of the effects of identity conversion is that thereafter the person will engage Black problems (the oppressive aspects of Black life) as well as Black culture (the non-oppressive and proactive side of the Black experience). There are no Encounter types, but Nigrescence Theory dissects the characteristics of the contexts, situations, and experiences that can trigger an Encounter experience. Immersion-Emersion is used in Nigrescence Theory to highlight those identity exemplars that provide a curious mixture of extreme or militant pro-Blackness and livid anti-Whiteness. In the context of an identity conversion, such Immersion-Emersion exemplars are markers of the transition from a nonengaged to a variant of the engaged type of identity. Finally, Nigrescence Theory tries to discover why some Black people show long-term interest in Black problems and Black culture, whereas others evidence a more attenuated interest. Exemplars of sustained commitment are labeled Internalization Commitment. When Nigrescence Theory is applied to the study of Black identity change, the categories Pre-Encounter, Encounter, Immersion-Emersion, Internalization, and Internalization-Commitment are viewed as *stages*. However, when the focus is on the socialization experiences, covering infancy through early adulthood, that result in the production of the exemplars described below, then the exemplars are viewed as bounded and fairly stable identity or distinctive reference group orientations A more in-depth differentiation between reference group orientation and stages will be undertaken shortly. For the purposes of this chapter, only the Nigrescence exemplars for Pre-Encounter, Immersion-Emersion, and Internalization are highlighted:

- *Pre-Encounter Assimilation* describes the type of Black person whose social identity is organized around her or his sense of being an American and an individual. Little significance is accorded racial group identity; consequently, race and Black culture are not engaged. The person may actually work with White groups to destroy what are perceived as "race-based" programs, and the person often shows disdain for Black culture, all-Black groups, and multiculturalism. In its more passive version, the person simply does not engage Blackness.

- *Pre-Encounter Miseducation* depicts the type of Black person who accepts, as truthful, facts, images, and historical information about Black people that are, in fact, stereotypical and forms of cultural-historical misinformation. Because she/he sees so little strength in the Black community as a whole, the miseducated person may hesitate to engage Black problems and

Black culture. The person will compartmentalize his/her stereotypic perceptions so that such negative group images do not affect her/his personal self-image (e.g., "That's the way they act, but I am different, exceptional").

- *Pre-Encounter (Racial) Self-Hatred* characterizes the type of Black person who experiences profound negative feelings and deep-structure self-loathing because of the fact she or he is Black. Such personal dysfunctionality and group hatred clearly limit the positive engagement of Black problems and Black culture.

- *Immersion-Emersion Anti-White* describes Black people who are nearly consumed by a hatred of White people and White society and all that it represents and will engage Black problems and Black culture but are frequently predictably unpredictable, volatile, and full of fury and pent-up rage.

- *Immersion-Emersion Intense Black Involvement* is descriptive of a person who is typically simplistic, romantic, oceanic, and obsessively dedicated to all things Black. The person engages Blackness in a nearly cultlike fashion and is subject to Blacker-than-thou social interactions with other Blacks and evidences an either/or mentality about complex issues.

- *Internalization Nationalist* is a type of Black individual who stresses an Africentric perspective about oneself, Black people, and the surrounding world. There is no question that such persons engage Black problems and Black culture.

- *Internalization Biculturalist* is an exemplar of a Black person who gives equal importance to "Americanness" as well as Africanity (e.g., the comfortable fusion of White and Black cultures), and engages Black issues and culture but also openly engages aspects of the mainstream culture. This person can be as dedicated as anyone else but also enjoys and feels part of mainstream events, celebrations, and issues.

- *Internalization Multiculturalist* is a type of Black person whose identity fuses or reticulates linkages between three or more social categories (multiplicity) or frames of reference. Whether it is the person's perceptions of a situation or the need to make a key identity decision, nearly equal weight is given to the multiple categories that drive the person's sense of identity. Although the person feels very much a part of the Black community and the Black struggle, he or she easily appreciates a wide range of cultural events and activities. As a result, a person with a Multiculturalist identity eschews solutions that rely on single-group interests and prefers solutions, instead, that address multiple oppressions.

The second part of this chapter introduces a new identity measure that incorporates separate subscales for most of the exemplars described above. At one point in the history of the scale development process, the team searched for a subscale that might globally capture the notion of engagement. Had it been produced it would have been called a race-salience scale (e.g., a scale that measures the degree to which race and Black culture are important to an individual). The effort was eventually dropped, and while there were both empirical and logical reasons that supported this decision, at this point it is relevant to the current discussion to mention the conceptual concerns. Measures of race salience or race centrality (Sellers, Smith, Shelton, Rowley, & Chavous, 1998) are only useful if they are sensitive to all three of the last exemplars noted above (e.g., Black Nationalist, Biculturalist, and Multiculturalist). Each of these is a valid expression of Black identity; however, the definition for salience is different for each type of identity, with nationalism representing a singular salience, biculturalism representing a form of dual salience, and multiculturalism reflecting multiple saliences. Likewise, the Racial Self-Hatred exemplar takes one in still another direction in reflecting a singular *negative* salience. A unidimensional or bipolar measure of salience could not possibly address all these concerns. The only salience measure that could work would have to be *multidimensional.* It was concluded that it might be just as easy, if not easier, to construct a separate scale for each exemplar than to struggle with a multidimensional race-salience or race-centrality measure.

Consequently, a key premise of Nigrescence Theory is that the best way to conceptualize Black identity *variability* is through ideology, or, more specifically, through the explication of ideological types. From the universe of Black identities, Nigrescence Theory describes a specific set of exemplars. These different interpretations of what it means to be Black, these differing RGO stances, are at the heart of the theory, and the operationalization of these distinctive categories was behind the development of the CRIS.

Level 3:
Nigrescence Theory and Traditional Socialization

In a recent chapter titled "Patterns of African American Identity Development," Cross and Fhagen-Smith (2001) traced the development of various types of social identities found among any large group of Black people. Their analysis focused on the identity profiles defined above: Assimilation, Racial Self-Hatred, Miseducation, Anti-White, Militantly Pro-Black (e.g., Intense Black Involvement), Black Nationalist, Biculturalist, and Multiculturalist. The socialization pattern for each of these identity types is traced across the developmental phases of infancy, early childhood, preadolescence, adolescence, and early adulthood. As is somewhat self-evident, some of the profiles focus, to varying degrees, on race and Black culture (Nationalist, Biculturalist, and Multiculturalist), whereas others play down the significance of race and culture (Assimilation) and/or reflect varying degrees of racial self-loathing (Racial Self-Hatred) and Black cultural stereotyping (Miseducation). Black persons who enter adult life with either a Nationalist, Biculturalist, or Multiculturalist type of Black identity, are said *not* to be in need of an identity conversion because the content and dynamics of their upbringing have resulted in self-concepts that are already race and Black culture sensitive. When Nigrescence Theory focuses on the outcomes of differing socialization experiences, the identity outcomes are called racial-cultural reference group orientations or identity statuses (Helms, 1995) rather than stages.

Level 4:
Nigrescence as Resocialization or Conversion Experience

Those Black persons who reach late adolescence with either an Assimilation, Miseducation, or Racial Self-Hatred profile are said to be *at risk* or in need of a Nigrescence conversion experience (Cross, Strauss, & Fhagen-Smith, 1999; Cross & Fhagen-Smith, 2001). Assimilation individuals are at risk because their race-insensitive orientation may someday fail to explain a highly charged personal, racial experience, and an identity conversion can replace their low race salience identity with one that accords considerable significance to race and Black culture. The risk factors for the other two profiles are somewhat more self-evident. Individuals with a Miseducation profile need Nigrescence as a corrective for internalized, negative stereotypes and distorted interpretations of Black history. As to the self-hatred profile, Cross and Fhagen-Smith (2001) were "hesitant to suggest that a conversion experience can, in and of itself, cure (racial) self-hatred" (p. 22). However, on the heels of a conversion experience, a person is said to become more aware of what additional actions are needed (individual or group counseling, psychotherapy, etc.) to complement the positive effects of one's change in frame of reference. Regardless of the identity profile with which an individual may enter the conversion experience (e.g., Assimilation, Miseducation, and Racial Self-Hatred), the "output" or resulting range of new or converted Black identities will now match, exactly, the range of reference group orientations that are achieved by others through their formative socialization process (e.g., how they were raised between infancy, childhood, adolescence, and early adulthood). Thus, having a Nationalist, Biculturalist, or Multiculturalist type of Black identity can result from a person's *traditional* upbringing or as the result of a *conversion* experience. One last point related to conversions: When the focus of Nigrescence Theory is identity change in the context of an adult identity conversion, the exemplars are treated as stage-related exemplars or simply stages.

Level 5:
Nigrescence and Recycling

Thomas Parham (1989) has noted that Black persons with well-developed Black identities will periodically pass in and out of certain Nigrescence stages. He explained that such persons are not confused or unstable, rather they are experiencing what he called "Nigrescence recycling." No single Black person has all the answers to identity questions that typically confront Black people at different points across the life span. Rather, each life span challenge or "question" must be "processed" and worked-through, and the result is a deeper understanding and appreciation of one's Blackness. According to Cross and Fhagen-Smith (2001), recycling does not fundamentally alter the type of Black identity with which one enters the recycling episode (e.g., Nationalist, Biculturalist, or Multiculturalist); however, the effect is to strengthen and enrich whatever is the identity in question. Recycling highlights some of the same identity types that are also the focus of conversion and formative socialization experiences. That is, recycling episodes operate to strengthen and give deeper meaning to whatever is at the core of one's already well-formed identity, be it Nationalist, Biculturalist, or Multiculturalist.

Level 6:
Nigrescence and Identity Functions

According to Cross and colleagues (Cross & Strauss, 1998; Cross, Strauss, & Fhagen-Smith, 1999), once a Black identity has been internalized, that is, once an individual has settled on either a Nationalist, Biculturalist, or Multiculturalist type of Black identity, that identity will be revealed during everyday social interactions with others, regardless of ethnicity or race (e.g., Whites, other Blacks, and Latino/as), as a series of identity enactments, operations, or what can be called identity functions: buffering; code switching; bridging; bonding; or acting as an individual (individualism). Due to limited space, the only social interactions or situations noted next are those involving White or Black people:

- *Buffering* involves any psychological act of protection, which Black people employ when they encounter Whites who are explicitly acting in a racist and insulting manner.
- In required, predictable, daily social interactions with, say, fellow White employees or classmates that are characterized as reasonably friendly and somewhat trustworthy, Blacks will typically *code-switch* and act according to the cultural norms set by the White majority (act in a cultural way that helps Whites relax and be comfortable). Code switching makes everyday activities (on the job or in the classroom, etc.) go smoothly. The Black person "fronts," code-switches, or acts "White" in a temporary sense. Code switching is actually a display of bicultural competence in that the Black person can switch back and forth between a person's "natural" Black way of communicating and the communication style favored by the mainstream situation.
- When in the presence of a White person toward whom the Black person feels profound trust, love, affection, and cross-cultural connectivity, *bridging* is the way Black identity is enacted. One's racial-cultural differences are at the heart of the friendship and interactions; consequently, the interactions involve *psychological* bridging between the White person's frame of reference and that of the Black person and vice versa. For example, if the White person is Jewish, his or her Jewishness and the Black person's Blackness will frequently take center stage in their friendship, and, as such, friendship and closeness are achieved through difference, not by avoiding it. In contradistinction to color blindness, bridging makes difference foundational, explicit, and intrinsically engaging.

- Whereas buffering, code switching, and bridging capture the way Black identity is enacted in situations involving Whites, *bonding,* or attachment activities, describes positive, proactive Black-on-Black interactions (negative interactions are not considered here). Repeated, daily, positive interactions with other Blacks, from the mundane to the significant, have the accumulative effect of sustaining a Black person's sense of connection or *attachment* to Black people and the Black experience.
- Finally, *individualism,* or "just being me," can mean that, in the situation in question, the Black person is more in tune with the self as personality than with the self as a social category or reference group member. Also, the person may tend to see whoever is in the situation not as a Black or White person but as simply a person. Individualism is at the heart of *color-blind* social interactions.

Accordng to Nigrescence Theory, a person's use of these race and culture sensitive enactments is mediated by ideology. Because they give almost no significance to race and Black culture, people with an Assimilation identity stress individualism in their interactions with Whites and other Blacks and make *infrequent* use of the other more race- and culture-sensitive enactments. On the other hand, a person who is anti-White, or has an hardcore Afrocentric ideology, may seldom, if ever, bridge to White people and will rely, instead, on buffering and code switching, and, of course, bonding. Biculturalist- and Multiculturalist-oriented types will engage all the functions in their daily interactions with Whites and Blacks. Implicit in this component of Nigrescence Theory is a rejection of the use of multiple selves to explain Black identity at the level of a single event. Rather than equate each identity function with a distinctive self, Black identity is said to be stable; and all the functions that the person's ideology dictate are always in a state of readiness, to be triggered by an *external* cue (a White person approaches a Black person) and/or by an *internal* drive (an internal need to hear live jazz triggers a person to read the newspaper to see what jazz groups are coming to town in the near future).

Summary

A central proposition of Nigrescence Theory is that the Black self-concept has two key dimensions: a personal identity component (PI) and a social identity or reference group component (RGO). The focus of Nigrescence Theory is on RGO and not PI because Black identities constitute case studies in *social identity.* The relationship between the two domains is addressed by Nigrescence Theory, but the core of the theory is on the various ways Black people make sense of themselves as social beings rather than as a constellation of personality traits.

Another premise of Nigrescence Theory is that there is more than one type of Black identity, which has resulted in the delineation of a *range* of identity exemplars. To explain the developmental origins of this range, three patterns of Black identity development have been incorporated into Nigrescence Theory:

1. Traditional socialization experiences that take place across infancy, childhood, adolescence, and adulthood, resulting in a wide range of Black identity types
2. Resocialization stemming from an identity conversion experience
3. Recycling, or the process by which a person's Black-focused sense of self may be continually enriched, challenged, and allowed to grow throughout the life span.

The theory also addresses the multiple ways that Black identity is *enacted* in everyday interactions with both White and Black people. These everyday identity functions involve stigma management (buffering); switching back and forth between one social interaction style to another (code switching); the achievement of psychological closeness with Whites (bridging); and the continuous sense of connectivity to other Blacks, the Black community, and the Black experience (bonding). The theory highlights how Black people may simply see themselves as acting as an individual in situations involving either Whites or other Blacks. Specific *functions* (e.g., enactment profile) are associated with each identity type, in which a person's racial-cultural ideology causes one to value none, few, or all of the race- and culture-sensitive functions.

A final assumption of Nigrescence Theory is that great variability exists in the way Black people make meaning of and interpret their social sense of self. Because it is impossible to represent every type of Black identity in existence, a specific set of identity exemplars are in Nigrescence Theory. In most instances, empirical explorations of the theory require that all or most of the exemplars be effectively operationalized.

DEVELOPMENT OF THE CRIS

The CRIS was developed in six phases over a 5-year period. The initial item development and content validation of the scale was conducted in Phase 1. The goals of Phases 2 through 4 were to establish a minimum reliability estimate of .70 for the subscale scores and establish construct validity through exploratory factor analysis. In Phases 5 and 6, the goals of scale development were to achieve a minimum reliability estimate of .80 for subscale scores and to replicate construct validity through exploratory and confirmatory factor analyses. An in-depth account of the scale development of the CRIS for Phases 2 through 6 is provided by Vandiver, Cross, Worrell, et al. (in press) and Vandiver and Worrell (in press). Phases 2 through 4 are detailed by Vandiver (in press), Vandiver, Fhagen-Smith, et al. (in press), and Worrell, Cross, and Vandiver (in press). An in-depth examination of Phases 5 and 6 is provided by Vandiver, Cross, Worrell, et al. (in press).

In addition to the specific goals of each phase, an overarching goal in developing the CRIS was to create orthogonal subscales. A common problem of attitudinal/personality scales is the lack of independence among the subscales. Can distinct constructs be independently measured when the constructs also share a common thread or theme? The Nigrescence process reflects the degree of accepting a salient Black identity. In addition, identities within a stage share a common link to each other. To maximize the independence of the CRIS subscales, the goal of item development was not to describe all theoretical aspects of an identity but to capture the core essence of each identity that would delineate it from the others.

Item and Subscale Development

During the scale development process, items were written to characterize seven Nigrescence identities for Stages 1, 3, 4, and 5, which resulted in three Pre-Encounter (Assimilation–PA, Miseducation–PM, and Self-Hatred–PSH), two Immersion-Emersion (Intense Black Involvement–IEIBI and Anti-White–IEAW), and two Internalization (Black Nationalist–IBN and Multiculturalist–IMCI) subscales. Encounter was not measured because of the difficulty of measuring its transitory nature and the infinite number of individual events that could be perceived as encounter experiences. Stages 4 (Internalization) and 5 (Internalization-Commitment) were combined as one stage because of the significant overlap between them. An activist ideology is incorporated in the Internalization subscales to capture the essence of Internalization-Commitment.

Pre-Encounter constructs. Based on the Nigrescence model, two Pre-Encounter subscales were initially developed, but three eventually emerged out of the scale development process (Vandiver, Fhagen-Smith, et al., in press). Items for Pre-Encounter Assimilation were written to describe an individual who was pro-American and did not view being Black as important. Being Black was not addressed in any of the items. Nationality was the focus.

Originally, the content of the Pre-Encounter Anti-Black items depicted aspects of miseducation and self-hatred because both were viewed as integral to the anti-Black identity (Cross, 1991). However, empirical findings from Phases 2 and 3 revealed that the two sets of Anti-Black items appeared to reflect two separate anti-Black identities. Thus, the Anti-Black items were separated to create two subscales: Miseducation and Self-Hatred (Vandiver, Fhagen-Smith, et al., in press). The Pre-Encounter Miseducation items focused on the negative stereotyping of the Black community as lazy and criminal. Pre-Encounter Self-Hatred items highlighted the personal dislike of being Black.

Immersion-Emersion constructs. Two immersion features were independently operationalized: pro-Blackness and anti-Whiteness. Items for the Intense Black Involvement subscale focused on the extreme acceptance of anything Black as good. The Anti-White items were straightforward, emphasizing the hatred of Whites.

Internalization constructs. Of the three Internalization identities described by Cross (1991, 1995), only items for the Black Nationalist and Multiculturalist identities were created. The Biculturalist identity was not included as a subscale because of its overlap with the Multiculturalist identity. The content of the Black Nationalist items focused on Black empowerment. To distinguish the Black Nationalist from the Immersion-Emersion identities, in which emphasis is either on an extreme pro-Black or anti-White stance, the term *Black Nationalist* was initially used to anchor each of the items, but the generic use of the term was not effective in delineating the Black Nationalist items from the Immersion-Emersion pro-Black identity (Intense Black Involvement; see Vandiver, Cross, Worrell, et al., in press; Vandiver, Fhagen-Smith, et al., in press). To ameliorate the overlap in the content of the subscales, two alterations were made: (a) The IEIBI subscale was temporarily removed from the CRIS (Vandiver, Fhagen-Smith, et al., in press), and (b) the content of the Black Nationalists items changed from a general Black Nationalist ideology of empowerment to a specific Nationalist ideology: Afrocentricity. Thus, at the end of Phase 5, the Internalization Black Nationalist subscale (IBN) was renamed Internalization Afrocentric (IA; Vandiver, Cross, Worrell, et al., in press).

The Multiculturalist subscale focused on the twin aspects of positively accepting being Black and the acceptance of others from diverse cultural groups, including gays, lesbians, and progressive Whites. To differentiate the multicultural perspective from the Pre-Encounter Assimilation identity, the acceptance of diverse cultural groups was made explicit. This was achieved by the referencing of specific racial minority groups, Whites, gays, and lesbians in a parenthetical statement at the end of each IMCI statement.

Content Validity

Based on Cross's writings (1991, 1995) and the research team's discussion regarding the essence of the Nigrescence constructs, a pool of 250 items was generated. After numerous discussions over a three-month period, 126 items were selected from the initial pool for a content validity study. A list of 75 experts in the field of multicultural psychology, who are knowledgeable about the revised Nigrescence Theory, was identified and solicited in rating items, which best reflected the Nigrescence constructs for inclusion in the scale. Of these 75 experts, 45 agreed to participate as judges, and 44% (20/45) returned their item analysis of the CRIS. The judges were asked to rate on a 10-point Likert-type scale the degree each item appeared to measure six racial identities (initially, Pre-Encounter Anti-Black was one subscale, not two). An item rated 1 indicated that it was a poor indicator of the designated construct, and an item rated 10 denoted that it was excellent in capturing one of the identities. It was possible for an item to be rated as characterizing more than one identity.

Three criteria were used to select items from the judges' ratings: (a) An item had to receive at least a 6-point rating, (b) 75% of the judges had to agree, and (c) fewer than 25% of the judges rated the item as measuring multiple constructs. In addition, items rated 5 by the majority of the judges were considered if qualitative comments had been provided in revising or rewording the items. Based on these criteria and discussion by the CRIS research team, 57 items were selected for the initial CRIS. Future iterations of the CRIS were based on the theoretical constructs in relation to the empirical findings of the items.

Demographic Features of the Samples

Data about the CRIS were collected over a 4-year period from five different samples of African American college students attending two predominantly White universities, one in the mid-Atlantic area and the other in the New England area, in which African Americans were 3% and 8% of the student body, respectively. Table 21.1 provides a general description of the five samples, with sample sizes ranging from 119 to 336. Participants' ages ranged from 17 to 59, with 21 the mean age across samples (mean $SD = 3.66$). Typically, there were approximately twice as many females as males, and the majority of the participants were working toward a bachelor's degree, with an equivalent number at each academic class level. In general, the samples were equivalent on demographic features (Vandiver, Fhagen-Smith, et al., in press; Vandiver, Cross, Worrell, et al., in press).

Summary of the Results

Descriptive statistics. Table 21.2 provides a summary of the subscale intercorrelations and reliability estimates of the subscale scores for the CRIS across Phases 2 through 6. The reliability estimates for the CRIS subscale scores ranged from .59 to .90 and improved across the phases. IEAW scores always resulted in reliability estimates in the .80 range, whereas the scores on PM, IEIBI, IA, and IMCI resulted in more variable reliability estimates. However, at the conclusion of Phase 6, all of the reliability estimates for the CRIS subscale scores, except for PM (.78), were above .80 (Vandiver, Cross, Worrell, et al., in press).

Subscale intercorrelations ranged from −.51 to .63, with a majority of the values dropping below .30 from Phase 2 to Phase 6 as the items were

TABLE 21.1 Demographic Features of Samples Used in CRIS Scale Development for Phases 2 Through 6

	Phase 2 (57)[a]	Phase 3 (76)	Phase 4 (64)	Phase 5 (64)	Phase 6 (52)
Sample Size	119	142	150	296	336
Gender					
Female	78[b]	92	99[c]	212[d]	212[e]
Male	31	50	48	76	119
Age					
Range	17–47	17–40	17–35	17–43	17–59
Mean	21	21	21	21	21
SD	4.60	3.75	2.69	3.29	3.96

NOTE: CRIS = Cross Racial Identity Scale.
a. Number of items on the CRIS for each phase.
b. Ten participants did not specify their gender.
c. Three participants did not specify their gender.
d. Eight participants did not specify their gender.
e. Five participants did not specify their gender.

TABLE 21.2 Summary of Subscale Intercorrelations and Reliability Estimates on the CRIS Scores From Phases 2 Through 6[a]

	PA	PM[b]	PSH[b]	IEIBI[c]	IEAW	IA[d]	IMCI	α
PA								.68 – .86 (.82)[e]
PM	.28 – .48 (.32)[c]							.73 – .90 (.78)
PSH	.07 – .16 (.10)	.13 – .26 (.23)						.71 – .89 (.86)
IEIBI	−.34 – −.05 (−.17)	−.06 – .22 (.08)	−.05 – .14 (.05)					.63 – .84 (.75)
IEAW	−.31 – −.16 (−.26)	−.07 – .04 (−.01)	.01 – .21 (.12)	.32 – .49 (.44)				.83 – .91 (.89)
IA	−.50 – −.12 (−.20)	.01 – 16 (.08)	−.16 –.14 (−.01)	.50 – .63 (.55)	.37 – .43 (.41)			.65 – .83 (.78)
IMCI	.09 – .22 (.11)	−.08 – .13 (−.03)	−.26 – .03 (−.11)	.04 –.11 (.10)	−.51 – −.10 (−.31)	−.17 – .30 (.03)		.59 – .86 (.80)
No. of items	5 – 14	5 – 11	6 – 10	5 – 17	5 – 11	5 – 12	5 – 13	

NOTE: CRIS = Cross Racial Identity Scale; PA = Pre-Encounter Assimilation; PM = Pre-Encounter Miseducation; PSH = Pre-Encounter Self-Hatred; IEIBI = Immersion-Emersion Intense Black Involvement; IEAW = Immersion-Emersion Anti-White; IA = Internalization Afrocentric; IMCI = Internalization Multiculturalist Inclusive.
a. Sample sizes ranged from 119 to 336.
b. Separate scores not computed for PM and PSH until the end of Phase 2.
c. Included in Phases 2 through 4.
d. Initially named IBN = Internalization Black Nationalist until Phase 6.
e. Median value of range.

revised. However, despite item revisions, the relationships between IEAW, IEIBI, and IA continued to be moderate ($r > .30$), and was the primary reason why IEIBI was temporarily removed from the CRIS after Phase 3 (Vandiver, Fhagen-Smith, et al., in press). At the end of Phase 6, the subscale inter-correlations between IEAW and IA and IMCI were .41 and .37, respectively (Vandiver, Cross, Worrell, et al., in press).

Factorial validity. Exploratory factor analyses (EFA) have been conducted on the scores of two samples (Vandiver, Cross, Worrell, et al., in press; Vandiver, Fhagen-Smith, et al., in press) and confirmatory factor analysis (CFA) has been conducted on the scores of one sample (Vandiver, Cross, Worrell, et al., in press). In Phase 4, the initial EFAs indicated that two solutions (5- and 6-factor structures) were viable, depending on whether IEIBI items were included in the analysis. When IEIBI items were included in the EFA, IEIBI and IA loaded on the same factor. Both subscales appeared to be measuring the same construct: a pro-Black ideology. Also, on the 5-factor solution, IMCI and IEAW items loaded on the same factor but inversely. Those who rated themselves higher on the Multiculturalist subscale also rated themselves lower on the Anti-White subscale. Further empirical analyses of the IEIBI and IA items and the IEAW and IMCI items did not offer any clues on how to disentangle these constructs from the other. Thus, the decision was made to temporarily not measure IEIBI, and its items were removed from the scale. The removal of IEIBI items from the EFA resulted in a 6-factor solution in which the remaining CRIS items loaded on separate factors by subscale (Vandiver, Fhagen-Smith, et al., in press). The EFA conducted in Phase 5 replicated a 6-factor solution of the CRIS items, providing further support that the CRIS subscales reflected six fairly independent constructs (Vandiver, Cross, Worrell, et al., in press).

In Phase 6, the 6-factor structure of the CRIS was tested against competing models (1-factor through 5-factor) through confirmatory factor analysis (CFA). In contrast to the 1- to 5-factor models, the 6-factor model had a comparative fit index greater than .90 (Bentler, 1995) and the root mean square residual of approximation was below .05 (MacCallum, Browne, & Sugawara, 1996; Vandiver, Cross, Worrell, et al., in press). The CFA provided further support for the 6-factor model.

THE CROSS RACIAL IDENTITY SCALE

The CRIS (Vandiver, Cross, Fhagen-Smith, et al., 2000) consists of 40 items, in which 30 items make up the 6 subscales: Pre-Encounter Assimilation (PA); Pre-Encounter Miseducation (PM); Pre-Encounter Self-Hatred (PSH); Immersion-Emersion Anti-White (IEAW); Internalization Afrocentric (IA); and Internalization Multiculturalist Inclusive (IMCI). Each subscale has 5 items and all items are rated on a 7-point rating scale, 1 for

TABLE 21.3 Sample CRIS Items by Subscale

1. Pre-Encounter Assimilation
    I think of myself primarily as an American and seldom as a member of a racial group.

2. Pre-Encounter Miseducation
    Blacks place more emphasis on having a good time than on hard work.

3. Pre-Encounter Self-Hatred
    I sometimes have negative feelings about being Black.

4. Immersion-Emersion Anti-White
    I hate White people.

5. Internalization Afrocentric
    Black people will never be free until we embrace an Afrocentric perspective.

6. Internalization Multiculturalist Inclusive
    I believe it is important to have both a Black identity and a multicultural perspective, which is inclusive of everyone (e.g., Asians, Latinos, gays, lesbians, Jews, and Whites).

NOTE: CRIS = Cross Racial Identity Scale.

strongly disagree to 7 for *strongly agree.* To highlight what typifies and distinguishes one subscale from another, Table 21.3 lists an item from each subscale. Ten additional items, which are not scored and are not part of any subscale, are mixed among the subscales to minimize response bias and to diminish the obviousness of the CRIS items. With regard to administration, Vandiver, Cross, Worrell, et al. (in press) have recommended that from both a theoretical and empirical standpoint, all of the subscales of the CRIS should be administered in assessing an individual's racial identity.

Scoring

Because the CRIS is a multidimensional scale, respondents will obtain scores on all of the subscales; otherwise, the unique aspects of each identity would be obscured in a total CRIS score or in a stage score. The ratings of the 5 items on each subscale are summed to create a subscale score, resulting in a minimum subscale score of 5 and a maximum score of 35. To ensure appropriate comparisons among the subscale scores, one of two procedures is recommended. One, a mean score can be computed for each subscale by dividing the subscale score by the number of subscale items. In this case, 5 is the divisor for all of the subscales. The mean subscale scores can then be compared using the 7-point rating scale. Two, the raw scores can be transformed into standard or z scores, which permits comparisons of scores on different subscales. Because z scores are cumbersome to use (i.e., negative values and decimal values), a more convenient standard score transformation is recommended (Anastasi & Urbina, 1997). The standard score distribution based on a mean of 10 and standard deviation of 3 is recommended to ensure the ease of comparability among all users of the CRIS.

Interpretation

The creation of 6 reliable and valid subscales, which are fairly independent of each other, does not mean that the interpretation of each subscale score should be done in the absence of the other subscale scores. Orthogonal CRIS subscales were created to ensure the precise measurement of the different identities; therefore, the psychometric properties of a scale should not be the sole indicator of the interpretation of its scores. To interpret the CRIS scores, they must be connected to the revised Nigrescence Theory. Cross (1991) did not view the racial identity of Blacks as unidimensional. By virtue of delineating identities within each stage, he highlighted the complexities of racial identity. This complexity is reflected in the respondents obtaining a score on each CRIS subscale. Thus, each CRIS subscale score is interpreted in the context of the other subscale scores. Helms (1995) has noted that "an individual may exhibit attitudes, behaviors, and emotions reflective of more than one stage" (p. 183), and in the case of the CRIS, individuals may have attitudes associated with more than one identity.

However, as Worrell et al. (in press) have observed, "Multiple scores for each individual create a classification dilemma" (p. 9). For example, how is a score on PA interpreted in relation to an equivalent score on IA or IEAW? An ideal way to interpret the CRIS is to plot either standard subscale or mean scores and examine them in relation to each other. Figure 21.1 depicts an example of a possible CRIS profile based on the 6 subscale scores. However, the ability to use and interpret the subscale scores in this fashion requires validation not only of individual subscales, but of diverse profiles. Empirical work using cluster or profile analysis has been recommended to examine the validity and utility of different profiles (Vandiver, Cross, Worrell, et al., in press; Worrell et al., in press).

Statistical Analyses

The selection of statistics for examining the CRIS is based on two criteria: the scale of measurement and the multidimensional nature of the CRIS. It is recommended that the CRIS subscale scores be treated as continuous or interval variables because the CRIS rating scale represents a quantitative attribute (Tabachnick & Fidell, 1996). Thus, converting the CRIS scores into dichotomous variables by creating high and low cutoffs is discouraged. Power and complexity are lost when interval variables are reduced to a categorical level (Anastasi & Urbina, 1997). Each CRIS score means more than a

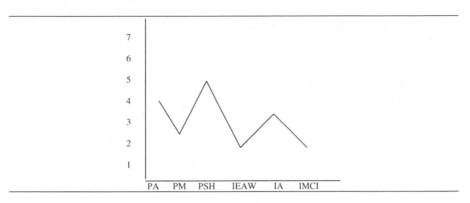

Figure 21.1. Possible CRIS Profile

high or low score, which also underscores the second criterion for the selection of statistics. As stated earlier, the CRIS scores are meaningless if interpreted independently of each other. The primary reason for creating orthogonal subscales was to ensure that each construct was measuring a different, not the same, construct. The validation of each subscale was based on the CRIS as a whole, not each subscale as a separate entity; therefore, the CRIS subscale scores need to be treated as a multivariate set of variables (Vandiver, Cross, Worrell, et al., 2000; Worrell et al., 2000).

Based on the criteria cited, it is recommended that the CRIS scores be used as a set of independent or dependent variables, not as individual independent or dependent variables. As a set of independent or dependent variables, recommended analyses of the CRIS scores, depending on the research question, currently include standard multiple regression analysis, cluster analysis, profile analysis, canonical correlation, multivariate analysis of variance with post hoc discriminant analysis, factor analysis, and structural equation modeling. No specialized hierarchical or sequential analyses are recommended, such as sequential multiple regression, because no assumptions are made regarding the hierarchy or sequence of the CRIS scores (Tabachnick & Fidell, 1996).

CONCLUDING REMARKS

The CRIS is now ready for use by other researchers interested in the study of Black identity with the expanded Nigrescence Theory (Worrell et al, in press) as its basis. The introduction of the measure does not presume that the theoretical and scale development process of Nigrescence is complete (Worrell et al., in press). Future work on Nigrescence Theory and the CRIS is recommended to strengthen the validity and clinical utility of both. In the process of revising the theory and developing the scale, new challenges emerged (Worrell et al., 2000) and form the basis for the following 10 research recommendations:

1. *Pre-Encounter exemplars.* Pre-Encounter Assimilation is only one of many examples of low race salience identities, in which Blacks do not base their daily existence on race or Black culture. Future research is needed to explore the possible identification of other nonpathological examples of Pre-Encounter.

2. *Miseducation.* With the delineation Miseducation and Self-Hatred as separate anti-Black identities during the scale development process (Vandiver, Fhagen-Smith, et al., in press), more research is needed to understand the Miseducation identity and the psychological mechanisms that result in some Black individuals negatively perceiving Black people as a group, while positively evaluating themselves as individuals. Are there community and personal costs of such compartmentalization? And if so, what are they? Perhaps miseducation is a greater problem to the political health of the Black community than racial self-hatred, in that miseducation may be more rampant.

3. *Pro-Black and anti-White perceptions.* Based on anecdotal data, attributes such as "calm," "relaxed," and "positive" are believed to describe individuals with an internalized Afrocentric identity. However, the calm rationality attributed to those with an Afrocentric ideology could not be differentiated from the intense and exaggerated emotionality and cognition of the Immersion identities of Intense Black Involvement and Anti-White (Vandiver, Fhagen-Smith, et al., in press). A link appears to exist between the pro-Black and anti-White perspectives, regardless of the attributes used to distinguish them (Vandiver, Cross, Worrell, et al., in press; Vandiver, Fhagen-Smith, et al., in press; Worrell et al., in press). Additional research is warranted to understand the theoretical and empirical link between these two perspectives. Are these really independent constructs, or are they bipolar attributes of one construct?

4. *Levels of multiculturalism.* While constructing the Internalization Multiculturalist Inclusive subscale, a variation of the construct was identified (Vandiver, Fhagen-Smith, et al., in press): Internalization Multiculturalist Racial, in which Blacks prefer to affiliate with other people of color to the exclusion of Whites and nonethnic cultural groups such as gays and lesbians. Because this variation of an internalized Multiculturalist identity was discovered during the final validation of the CRIS, the subscale and theoretical underpinning are still in the early phases of development. Theoretical and empirical examination of the Multiculturalist Racial identity and subscale will be a priority for future research.

5. *Identity theories.* As no one personality theory explains all possible aspects of personality, no one identity theory explains entirely the identity makeup of all human beings. Nigrescence Theory is not presumed to describe all aspects of Black racial identities and related functions. It is hoped that the revision and expansion of Nigrescence Theory will stimulate the development of complementary and competing theories of Black racial and cultural identities. Specifically, a multicultural or multifocused theory of identity is needed, where Black identity is understood in relation to other socially constructed attributes such as gender, social class, and sexual orientation, to name a few. Continuing to look at Black racial identity

in a singular way obscures the complexity of identity and human nature, thereby limiting the understanding of Blacks as individuals and as members of diverse reference groups.

6. *Longitudinal research.* To understand the developmental and recycling aspects of Nigrescence, longitudinal research is necessary (Worrell et al., in press). Are specific racial identity profiles stable over time? Is the sequence of Nigrescence mediated by the variations in socialization (childhood vs. adulthood)?

7. *Continued validation research.* Reliability and validity are not fixed entities of a scale but "properties of the scores obtained from the use of a measure—under certain conditions and with a particular group of participants, rather than the properties of the instruments per se" (Goodwin & Goodwin, 1999, p. 409). Therefore, the validity and reliability of the CRIS have not been established but are estimated based on its use with African American college students attending schools in only two geographical areas of the United States. "Multiple types of evidence" (Goodwin & Goodwin, 1999, p. 410), such as research with noncollege African American populations from diverse geographical locations, are necessary to infer that the validity of the CRIS scores are meaningful and appropriately used in the measurement and interpretation of the specified Black racial identities (Goodwin & Goodwin, 1999; Vandiver, Cross, Worrell, et al., in press; Worrell et al., in press).

8. *Clinical utility.* Continued validation of the CRIS is imperative if it is to have any utility beyond an academic or research exercise. For the CRIS scores to have meaning in the counseling process (e.g., Cooper & Lesser, 1997; Franklin, 1999; Schaumann, 1998), the education of Blacks (e.g., Gainor & Lent, 1998; Peart-Newkirk, 1998), and the psychological empowerment of Blacks (e.g., Myers, 1998), further validity work—discriminant, convergent, and predictive—is warranted. Can different identity profiles or clusters be delineated based on group affiliation or preference (Black Muslims vs. NAACP vs. political party)? Are Blacks who have a racial identity profile dominated by Miseducation or Self-Hatred more prone to depression, low self-esteem, and other mental health problems than individuals with other racial identity clusters?

9. *Demographic research.* Research with a focus on the demographic features (e.g., gender, social class, and sexual orientation) is recommended to understand the nature of racial identity in relation to the salience of other cultural identities within the Black population. What influence does gender have on the racial identity of Blacks (Pimentel, 1999)? Do the racial identity profiles of African American males and females differ? If so, what variables mediate the differences? Does racial designation influence the racial identity profiles (Parham & Williams, 1993)? What relationship does racial identity profiles have with social class (Carter & Helms, 1987) and age (Plummer, 1996)? These are just a sample of the myriad of questions to be examined about Black racial identity and other cultural aspects.

10. *Scoring.* As the CRIS is used, continued exploration is necessary in determining the best way to score it. Although preliminary scoring, interpretation, and analyses have been offered, the actual process will not be known until various scoring and statistical procedures are compared. Scoring procedures may vary depending on what questions about racial identity are asked or how they are asked.

REFERENCES

Anastasi, A., & Urbina, S. (1997). *Psychological testing* (7th ed.). Upper Saddle River, NJ: Prentice Hall.

Bentler, P. M. (1995). *EQS structural equation programs manual.* Encino, CA: Multivariate Software.

Brand, C. R., & Egan, V. (1989). The "Big Five" dimensions of personality? Evidence from ipsative, adjectival self-attributions. *Personality & Individual Differences, 10,* 1165-1171.

Carter, R. T., & Helms, J. E. (1987). The relationship between racial identity attitudes and social class. *Journal of Negro Education, 57,* 22-30.

Cooper, M., & Lesser, J. (1997). How race affects the helping process: A case of cross racial therapy. *Clinical Social Work Journal, 25,* 323-335.

Cross, W. E., Jr. (1971, July). The Negro-to-Black conversion experience. *Black World,* 13-27.

Cross, W. E., Jr. (1991). *Shades of Black: Diversity in African-American identity.* Philadelphia: Temple University Press.

Cross, W. E., Jr. (1995). The psychology of Nigrescence: Revising the Cross model. In J. G. Ponterotto, J. M. Casas, L. A. Suzuki, & C. M. Alexander (Eds.), *Handbook of multicultural counseling* (pp. 93-122). Thousand Oaks, CA: Sage.

Cross, W. E., Jr., & Fhagen-Smith, P. E. (in press). Patterns of African American identity development: A life span perspective. In B. Jackson & C. Wijeyesinghe (Eds.), *New perspectives on racial identity development.* New York: New York University Press.

Cross, W. E., Jr., & Strauss, L. (1998). The everyday function of Black identity. In J. K. Swim & C. Stangor (Eds.), *Prejudice: The target's perspective* (pp. 268-279). New York: Academic Press.

Cross, W. E., Jr., Strauss, L., & Fhagen-Smith, P. E. (1999). African American identity development across the life span: Educational implications. In R. H. Sheets & E. R. Hollins (Eds.), *Racial and ethnic identity in school practices: Aspects of human development* (pp. 29-47). Mahwah, NJ: Lawrence Erlbaum.

Franklin, A. J. (1999). Invisibility syndrome and racial identity development in psychotherapy and counseling African American men. *The Counseling Psychologist, 27,* 761-793.

Gainor, K. A., & Lent, R. W. (1998). Social cognitive expectations and racial identity attitudes in predicting the math choice intentions of Black college students. *Journal of Counseling Psychology, 45,* 403-413.

Goodwin, L. D., & Goodwin, W. L. (1999). Measurement myths and misconceptions. *School Psychology Quarterly, 14,* 408-427.

Helms, J. E. (1990). An overview of Black racial identity theory. In J. E. Helms (Ed.), *Black and White racial identity: Theory, research, and practice* (pp. 9-47). New York: Greenwood.

Helms, J. E. (1995). An update of Helms's White and people of color racial identity models. In J. G. Ponterotto, J. M. Casas, L. A. Suzuki, & C. M. Alexander (Eds.), *Handbook of multicultural counseling* (pp. 181-198). Thousand Oaks, CA: Sage.

MacCallum, R. C., Browne, M. W., & Sugawara, H. M. (1996). Power analysis and determination of sample size for covariance structure modeling. *Psychological Methods, 1,* 130-149.

Meehl, P. E., & Dahlstrom, W. G. (1960). Objective configural rules for discriminating psychotic from neurotic MMPI profiles. *Journal of Consulting and Clinical Psychology, 24,* 375-387.

Myers, M. E. (1998). An exploration of racial identity and social support in African American women confronting discrimination. *Dissertation Abstracts International: Section B: The Sciences & Engineering, 59(6-B),* 3068.

Parham, T. A. (1989). Cycles of psychological Nigrescence. *The Counseling Psychologist, 17,* 187-226.

Parham, T. A., & Williams, P. T. (1993). The relationship of demographic and background factors to racial identity attitudes. *Journal of Black Psychology, 19,* 7-24.

Peart-Newkirk, N. J. (1998). The psychosocial correlates of academic success, satisfaction, and retention among African-American graduate students. *Dissertation Abstracts International: Section B: The Sciences & Engineering, 58(9-B),* 5196.

Pimentel, A. M. (1999). *Racial identity development in African Americans: Feminist critiques and reconceptualizations.* Unpublished manuscript, Harvard University, School of Education, Human Development Program.

Plummer, D. L. (1996). Black racial identity attitudes and stages of the life span: An exploratory investigation. *Journal of Black Psychology, 22,* 169-181.

Schaumann, E. M. (1998). The effects of racial identity attitudes on the therapeutic alliance in cross-racial dyads. *Dissertation Abstracts International: Section B: The Sciences & Engineering, 58(12-B),* 6826.

Sellers, R. M., Smith, M. A., Shelton, J. N., Rowley, S. A. J., & Chavous, T. M. (1998). Multidimensional model of racial identity: A reconceptualization of African American racial identity. *Personality & Social Psychology Review, 2,* 18-39.

Tabachnick, B. G., & Fidell, L. S. (1996). *Using multivariate statistics* (3rd ed.). New York: HarperCollins.

Vandiver, B. J. (in press). Psychological nigrescence revisited: Introduction and overview. *Journal of Multicultural Counseling & Development.*

Vandiver, B. J., Fhagen-Smith, P. E., Cokely, K. O., Cross, W. E., Jr., & Worrell, F. C. (in press). Cross' nigrescence model: From theory to scale to theory. *Journal of Multicultural Counseling & Development.*

Vandiver, B. J., Cross, W. E., Jr., Fhagen-Smith, P. E., Worrell, F. C., Caldwell, L., Swim, J., & Cokley, K. (2000). *The Cross Racial Identity Scale.* Unpublished scale.

Vandiver, B. J., Cross, W. E., Jr., Worrell, F. C., & Fhagen-Smith, P. E. (in press). Validating the Cross Racial Identity Scale. *Journal of Counseling psychology.*

Vandiver, B. J., & Worrell, F. C. (Eds.) (in press). Psychological nigrescence revisited: Theory and research. *Journal of Multicultural Counseling & Development.*

Worrell, F. C., Cross, W. E., Jr., & Vandiver, B. J. (in press). Nigrescence theory: Current status and challenges for the future. *Journal of Multicultural Counseling & Development.*

Correspondence regarding this chapter may be sent to William E. Cross, Jr., Department of Psychology–Social Personality Program, Graduate Center, 6th Floor, Office 6301.11, City University of New York, 365 Fifth Avenue, New York, NY 10016-4309 (e-mail address: Wcross@gc.cuny.edu).

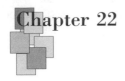

Chapter 22

ACCULTURATION MEASUREMENT

Theory, Current Instruments, and Future Directions

BRYAN S. K. KIM
JOSÉ M. ABREU

THE GROWING NUMBER of ethnic minorities in the United States represents a challenge to counselors and other mental health practitioners trained to implement therapeutic interventions designed primarily for European Americans. Indeed, ethnic minorities are expected to constitute 50% of the U.S. population by the year 2050 (U.S. Bureau of the Census, 1990), a statistic that multicultural researchers use to highlight the increasing need for understanding issues related to diversity, and to promote more culturally relevant services for non-European American populations (e.g., Atkinson, Morten, & Sue, 1998). The study of acculturation, for example, has helped us better understand the dynamic process of minority adaptation to the dominant U.S. culture (Rogler, Cortes, & Malgady, 1991; Vega & Rumbaut, 1991). In turn, this understanding has allowed us to establish within-group differences among several ethnic groups that yield plausible explanations as to why minority individuals may respond positively or negatively to various counseling approaches (Pomales & Williams, 1989; Gim, Atkinson, & Whiteley, 1990).

The potential usefulness of acculturation theory and measurement to counselors and other professional helpers has been well-established (Atkinson et al., 1998; Moyerman & Forman, 1992; Saldana, 1995).

AUTHORS' NOTE: We thank Dr. Donald R. Atkinson, University of California at Santa Barbara, for his helpful comments on an earlier draft of this chapter. Many of the ideas presented in this chapter originated during our discussions with Dr. Atkinson.

Atkinson et al. (1998) identified "acculturation" as one of four concepts (the other three are racial/ethnic identity, socioeconomic differences, and cultural mistrust) that can assist counselors in conceptualizing the needs of ethnic minority clients. After reviewing the extant research covering the relationship between acculturation and counseling process variables, Atkinson et al. concluded that

> these studies provide consistent documentation that acculturation is related to how racial/ethnic minority clients perceive and respond to counseling services. In general, they suggest that less acculturated racial/ethnic minorities are more likely to trust and express a preference for and a willingness to see an ethnically similar counselor than their more acculturated counterparts. . . . In summary, acculturation is a measure of within-group diversity that is related to a number of counseling process variables. Counselors working with an ethnic minority client should be aware not only of the client's ethnic background but the extent to which the client identifies with and practices the culture of his/her ancestors. (p. 31)

Not surprisingly, a Delphi survey of researchers in the field of cross-cultural counseling revealed a consensus among these experts in predicting that the concept of acculturation would play an increasingly important role in theory and research publications during the 1990s (Heath, Neimeyer, & Pedersen, 1988). A search of the PsychInfo literature database appeared to confirm this prediction. Using "acculturation" as the key word for the search, we found 1,736 citations for articles published between 1990 and 1999. Among these publications, there were 11 articles documenting the development of new acculturation instruments, a remarkable number given that 22 acculturation instruments already existed prior to 1990.

The purpose of this chapter is to provide the reader with an up-to-date guide to acculturation theory and instrumentation. The first two sections provide an operational definition of acculturation and an overview of theoretical models of measurement. In the third section, 33 acculturation instruments developed for specific as well as general ethnic groups are reviewed with respect to construct dimension, measurement model, reliability, and validity. The fourth and final section highlights the strengths and limitations of current models of acculturation measurement, posits future directions for needed research, and proposes a conceptual framework intended to integrate the major construct dimensions of acculturation.

DEFINING ACCULTURATION

The process of acculturation has been defined and redefined many times over the past sixty years. Redfield, Linton, and Herskovits (1936), for example, outlined this process in the following manner: "Acculturation comprehends those phenomena which result when groups of individuals sharing different cultures come into continuous first-hand contact, with subsequent changes in the original culture patterns of either or both groups" (p. 149).

Three decades later, Graves (1967) coined the term *psychological acculturation* to describe the effects of acculturation at the individual level of study, a concept that Szapocznik, Scopetta, Kurtines, and Aranalde (1978) elaborated by proposing that psychological acculturation involved changes in two personal dimensions: behaviors and values. According to Szapocznik et al., the behavioral dimension of acculturation includes language use and participation in other cultural activities, and the values dimension reflects relational style, person-nature relationships, beliefs about human nature, and time orientation. Padilla (1980) further expanded the conceptualization of acculturation by suggesting that this process also involved cultural awareness and ethnic loyalty. Cultural awareness refers to an individual's attunement to the cultural manifestations of native and host cultures. Ethnic loyalty, on the other hand, is an indication of preferences for one culture over the other, and includes an individual's level of ethnic pride and identity.

Definitions of acculturation have continued to grow progressively more integrative and comprehensive (e.g., Berry, 1980; Cuellar, Arnold, & Maldonado, 1995). Berry (1980), for example, identified six dimensions of psychological functioning directly affected by acculturation: language, cognitive styles, personality, identity, attitudes, and acculturative stress. Berry posited that as an individual moves through the acculturation process, changes occur in each of these areas. More recently, Cuellar et al. (1995) defined acculturation in terms of changes at three levels of functioning: behavioral, affective, and cognitive. They stated,

> The behavioral level includes many types of behaviors, including verbal behavior or language. Language development obviously includes aspects beyond the behavioral and is understood to include cognitive aspects and related processes. Also at the behavioral level are customs, foods, and such cultural expressions as the music one chooses to listen to or dance to. At the affective level are the emotions that have cultural connections. For example, the way a person feels about important aspects of identity, the symbols one loves or hates, and the meaning one attaches to itself are all culturally based. At the cognitive level are beliefs about male/female roles, ideas about illness, attitudes toward illness, and fundamental values. (p. 281)

As evident in this brief review, acculturation has evolved into a complex psychosocial phenomenon comprising many aspects of human functioning. When juxtaposed next to Redfield et al.'s (1936) early definition, the latest conceptualization of acculturation by Cuellar et al. (1995) clearly reflects this evolution. Importantly and concomitant with the development of acculturation as a construct, various models of measurement also have evolved.

ACCULTURATION MEASUREMENT MODELS

Early acculturation theorists (Berry & Annis, 1974; Szapocznik et al., 1978) conceptualized acculturation as a process taking place along a single, or unilinear,[1] continuum. According to the unilinear model, acculturation occurs when a person moves from one end of a continuum, reflecting involvement in the culture of origin, to the other end of the same continuum, reflecting involvement in the host culture. Szapocznik, Kurtines, and Fernandez (1980) noted that these theories

> conceptualized immigrants as adopting host-culture behavior and values while simultaneously discarding those attributes of their culture of origin. Thus, acculturation has been viewed as a process in which there is an inverse linear relationship between an individual's involvement with his/her original and host cultures. (p. 353)

A number of authors (Mendoza, 1984, 1989; Padilla, 1980; Ramirez, 1984; Szapocznik & Kurtines, 1980) have pointed out the limitations of the unilinear model, especially its inability to represent true biculturation, that is, high adherence to *both* indigenous and host cultures. According to Ramirez (1984), a bicultural person is an individual who "has had extensive socialization and life experiences in two or more cultures and participates actively in these cultures" (p. 82). Szapocznik and Kurtines (1978) noted that biculturalism is an important aspect of acculturation because the preexistence of a minority community could lead to the process of an individual retaining the culture of origin while accommodating to the host culture.

Szapocznik and his colleagues (Szapocznik & Kurtines, 1980; Szapocznik, Kurtines, & Fernandez, 1980) are credited with the development of the first bilinear measurement model of acculturation. After studying adaptation patterns of Cuban Americans, Szapocznik and colleagues noted that the earlier acculturation theories could not account for biculturalism because they did not allow the conceptualization of involvement in both the indigenous culture and the dominant culture on *separate* continua. They proposed a bilinear model in which one continuum represented either cultural involvement or marginality while the other continuum reflected either monoculturalism or biculturalism. Similarly, Mendoza and Martinez (1981) advanced a measurement model that attempted to account for biculturalism. The authors identified four typological patterns of acculturation: (a) cultural incorporation (adaptation of both indigenous and dominant cultures), (b) cultural transmutation (alteration

of indigenous and dominant culture to create a unique subcultural entity),
(c) cultural resistance (maintenance of indigenous culture while resisting
dominant culture), and (d) cultural shift (substitution of indigenous culture
with dominant culture). To measure these statuses, Mendoza (1989) created a bilinear instrument consisting of two continua, one reflecting dominant cultural assimilation and the other reflecting native cultural
extinction.

A measurement model similar to Mendoza's (1989) and frequently
cited by researchers of acculturation was developed by Berry and his colleagues (Berry, 1990, 1994; Berry & Kim, 1988; Berry, Kim, Power, Young, &
Bajaki, 1989; Berry, Trimble, & Olmeda, 1986), who proposed four acculturation "attitudes": integration, assimilation, separation, and marginalization. These attitudes express the combined level of adherence to host and
indigenous cultures, with each culture represented by a separate continuum. *Integration* occurs when an individual sustains an active interest in
the indigenous culture while maintaining daily interactions with members
of the dominant or host group, an attitude representing biculturalism.
Thus, a person with this acculturation attitude desires to become proficient in the culture of the dominant group while retaining proficiency in
the indigenous culture. *Assimilation* occurs when an individual maintains
daily interactions with members of the host group but has no interest in remaining conversant with the native culture. An assimilated individual ab-
sorbs the culture of the dominant group while rejecting the indigenous
culture. *Separation* occurs when much value is placed in the culture of origin and its members, whereas contact with members of the host culture is
avoided. An individual with a separation attitude is not interested in learning the culture of the dominant group and wants to maintain and perpetuate the culture of origin. Finally, *marginalization* represents the attitude of
an individual with no interest in maintaining or acquiring proficiency in
any culture, native or host. Marginalization is perhaps the most problematic of the four acculturation attitudes since, by definition, a marginalized
individual generally would not be expected to relate well to others.

Extending the theory of acculturation, there has been some movement
toward a multilinear measurement model that includes measuring acculturation along various domains of social functioning. Rather than just measuring a general level of acculturation along the continua of adherence to
indigenous and host cultures, the multilinear model extends the bilinear
model to include acculturation measurements in various settings that reflect different cultures. Ramirez (1984) asserted that acculturation involves
changes in "different life-domains of the different cultures with which the
person interacts. For example, at the same time, a person may be developing
in the familial domain of one culture, the educational domain of another,
and the work domain of still another" (p. 92). This complex model of acculturation potentially could lead to a fuller measurement model and better

explain the complexities of the adaptation processes experienced by ethnic minorities in the United States.

REVIEW OF ACCULTURATION INSTRUMENTS

Efforts were made to identify all of the acculturation instruments published in professional psychological and sociological journals. Through the use of the PsychInfo database and the reference sections of published articles on acculturation, we identified instruments with the word "acculturation" as part of their titles (e.g., African American Acculturation Scale; Landrine & Klonoff, 1994) as well as those that purported to measure acculturation (e.g., Cultural Life Style Inventory; Mendoza, 1989). This search procedure yielded 33 instruments: 2 designed for use with African Americans, 3 with Asian Americans, 23 with Hispanic Americans (general Hispanics, Cuban Americans, Mexican Americans, and Puerto Rican Americans), 3 with Native Americans, 1 with Native Hawaiians, and 1 with all ethnic minority groups. In this section, each of these acculturation instruments is reviewed with respect to measurement model (unilinear, bilinear), acculturation dimensions covered (behaviors, values, knowledge, cultural identity), and psychometrics (reliability, validity), followed by a brief summary evaluation.

Each instrument was first classified in terms of whether it represents a unilinear or bilinear model of measurement. Within the unilinear classification, we also made a distinction between instruments based on a single culture, identified as *monocultural unilinear*, from those based on two cultures, which we identified as *dual-cultural unilinear*. Instruments based on a monocultural unilinear model measure acculturation along a single continuum, with one endpoint representing low involvement in one's culture, while the other end reflects high adherence to the same culture. Instruments based on a dual-cultural unilinear model also measure acculturation along a single continuum, but one end of the continuum reflects high involvement in the indigenous culture and the other end high involvement in the host culture; the middle of the continuum represents equal adherence to both indigenous and host cultures (i.e., biculturalism). Instruments utilizing two separate continua to measure acculturation were classified as *bilinear*. The bilinear system of measurement yields two independent scores, one representing level of adherence to the culture of origin and the other reflecting adherence to the host culture.

After linearity classification, the dimensions covered by each instrument are presented. This information was obtained by conducting a content analysis of each instrument and determining the type of acculturation dimension measured by each of the items in the instrument. The number of items under each dimension was then divided by the total number of items to obtain a percent value per dimension. After inspecting the item content across all of the instruments reviewed, we identified four basic dimensions: behaviors, values, knowledge, and cultural identity. Examples of the behavior dimension are friendship choice and preferences for spoken language and mass media. Examples of the values dimension are attitudes and beliefs about social relations and cultural customs and traditions. An example of the knowledge dimension is having an understanding of culture-specific information such as the historical significance of a cultural festivity. Examples of the cultural identity dimension are specific cultural identification determined by oneself (e.g., American or Spanish American) and attitudes and comfort toward one's own and the dominant group (e.g., rejection of and discomfort toward one's own culture).

Finally, evidence of reliability and construct validity are reported for each instrument. This information was obtained from the original article describing the instrument and its psychometric properties, and any review articles evaluating the psychometric properties of the instrument (e.g., Ponterotto, Baluch, & Carielli, 1998). For the reader's convenience, instrument summaries are presented in Table 22.1.

AFRICAN AMERICANS

The literature on acculturation makes scant reference to African Americans. According to Landrine and Klonoff (1994), this neglect is the result of traditional psychology's view that African Americans are not part of an ethnic group, making issues of ethnicity and culture irrelevant. These authors point out that there is now empirical evidence for a distinct African American minority culture, making the acculturation construct just as applicable to African Americans as it is to other minority groups in the United States.

Consistent with Landrine and Klonoff's (1994) observations, a literature search yielded only two instruments designed to measure African American acculturation: the African American Acculturation Scale (AAAS; Landrine & Klonoff, 1994) and the Scale to Assess African American Acculturation (SAAAA; Snowden & Hines, 1999). Both the AAAS and the SAAAA use the dual-cultural unilinear model of measurement, with a continuum of scores ranging between immersion in the African American culture to immersion in the White culture.

The AAAS is composed of 74 items that were differentially endorsed by African Americans and other ethnic groups from an initial list of 189 items generated by the authors and seven African Americans from diverse geographical regions (Landrine & Klonoff, 1994). Among the items in the AAAS, 57% measure behavior, 30% measure values, 12% measure cultural identity, and 1% measure knowledge. These items are distributed across 8 subscales: (1) preference for African American things, (2) traditional family

TABLE 22.1 Critique of Acculturation Instruments

Ethnic Group	Linearity	Construct Dimensions (%)	Reliability	Construct Validity
African Americans				
AAAS (Landrine & Klonoff, 1994)	D-U	B = 57; V = 30; CI = 12; K = 1	Alpha (number corresponds to the subscale number in the text): 1) .90, 2) .71, 3) .78, 4) .81, 5) .81, 6) .76, 7) .79, 8) .72; Split-half (all items): .93	Criterion
SAAAA (Snowden & Hines, 1999)	D-U	B = 70; V = 20; CI = 10	Alpha: .75	Criterion, factor analysis
Asian Americans				
ASCA (Yao, 1979)	D-U	Inst. A: V = 83; CI = 17 Inst. B: B = 100	Alpha: Instrument A = .58, Instrument B = .75	None reported
SL-ASIA (Suinn et al., 1987)	D-U	B = 76; CI = 24	Alpha: .68 to .91 with a modal range in the .80s	Criterion, concurrent, factor analysis
AVS (Kim et al., 1999)	M-U	V = 100	Alpha: .81 to .82; 2-week test-retest: .83	Concurrent, discriminant, factor analysis
Hispanic Americans				
ABS (Triandis et al., 1982)	D-U	B = 100	None reported	Criterion, factor analysis
CHBS (Martinez et al., 1984)	D-U	B = 100	1.58-day test-retest: .92	Criterion, concurrent
AS (Caetano, 1987)	D-U	B = 83; CI = 8.5; V = 8.5	Alpha: .91; Split-half: .87	Criterion, factor analysis
SASH (Marin et al., 1987)	D-U	B = 100	Alpha: Overall = .92, Language Use = .90, Media Preference = .86, Ethnic Preference in Social Relations = .78	Criterion, factor analysis
SASH-Y (Barona & Miller, 1994)	D-U	B = 100	Alpha: Overall = .94, Hispanic = .92, Non-Hispanic = .85; Split-half: Overall = .96, Hispanic = .95, Non-Hispanic = .87	Criterion, factor analysis

(Continued)

TABLE 22.1 (Continued)

Ethnic Group	Linearity	Construct Dimensions (%)	Reliability	Construct Validity
AMHA (Epstein et al., 1996)	D-U	B = 100	Not applicable	Concurrent
BASH (Norris et al., 1996)	D-U	B = 100	Alpha: Overall = .90, Mexican American = .92, Puerto Rican American = .80	Criterion
BSASH (Marín & Gamba, 1996)	Bil	B = 100	Alpha: Hispanic Domain: Mexican American = .93, Central American = .87; Non-Hispanic Domain: Mexican American = .97, Central American = .95	Criterion, concurrent, factor analysis
Cuban Americans				
BAS (Szapocznik et al., 1978)	D-U	B = 100	Alpha: .97; 4-week test-retest: .96; Correlation between Spanish and English forms: 88	Criterion, concurrent, factor analysis
VAS (Szapocznik et al., 1978)	D-U	V = 100	Alpha: .77, 4-week test-retest: .86; Correlation between Spanish and English forms: .46	Criterion, concurrent, factor analysis
BIQ (Szapocznik et al., 1980)	Bil	B = 100	Alphas: Hispanicism = .93, Americanism = .89, Biculturalism = .94 Cultural Involvement = .79; 6-week test-retest: .50, .54, .79, .14, respectively	Concurrent
Mexican Americans				
AMCA (Olmedo et al., 1978; Olmedo & Padilla, 1978)	D-U	B = 55; V = 45	2- to 3-week test-retest: Overall = .84, Chicano = .89; Anglo = .66	Criterion, factor analysis
ARSMA (Cuellar et al., 1980; Montgomery & Orozco, 1984)	D-U	B = 70; CI = 25; Demo = 5	Alpha: .81 to .92, 5-week test-retest: .72 to .80; Interrater: .89	Criterion, concurrent, factor analysis

Instrument		Sample	Reliability	Validity
PAS (Padilla, 1980)	D-U	CA: CI = 47, B = 40, K = 13; EL: B = 64, CI = 36	Alpha: Cultural Awareness = .98, Ethnic Loyalty = .83	Criterion, factor analysis
CAS (Franco, 1983)	D-U	B = 50; CI = 10; Demo = 40	Alpha: .77; 5-week test-retest: .97; Interrater: .93	Concurrent, factor analysis
B/MEI (Ramirez, 1984)	D-U	B = 86; CI = 4; Demo = 10	Alpha: .79 for personal history, .68 for multicultural participation	Criterion
LASMA (Deyo et al., 1985)	D-U	B = 100	Coefficient of reproducibility: .96; Coefficient of scalability: .81	Criterion
Media-AS (Ramirez et al., 1986)	D-U	B = 100	Lack of significant difference between pretest and posttest scores.	Criterion
LAECA-AS (Burnam et al., 1987)	D-U	B = 85; CI = 11; Demo = 4	Alpha: .91 to .97	Criterion, factor analysis
CLSI (Mendoza, 1989)	Bil	B = 62; CI = 38	Alpha: .84 to .91, 2-week test-retest: .88 to .95 English-Spanish parallel form: .77 to .80	Criterion, concurrent, factor analysis
ARS (Montgomery, 1992)	D-U	B = 75; CI = 25	Alpha: Overall = .94, and .92, .86, .92, .90, .92 for the five factors	Criterion, factor analysis
ARSMA—II (Cuellar et al., 1995)	Bil	AOS: B = 85, CI = 15; MOS: B = 76, CI = 24	Alpha: AOS = .77, MOS = .84; Split-half: AOS = .77, MOS = .84; 1-week test-retest: AOS = .94, MOS = .96	Criterion, concurrent, factor analysis
Puerto Ricans				
BSPR (Cortes et al., 1994)	Bil	B = 56; V = 22; CI = 22	Alpha: American = .78, Puerto Rican = .73	Criterion, factor analysis
Native American Indians				
NFAS (Boyce & Boyce, 1983)	D-U	B = 85; CI = 5; K = 10	Alpha: .65; 3-month test-retest: .88	None reported
NCAS (Boyce & Boyce, 1983)	D-U	Not applicable	Interrater: .53	Criterion
RPOS (Hoffman et al., 1985)	D-U	Not published	None reported	None reported
Native Hawaiians				
NMHS (Rezentes, 1993)	M-U	B = 57; V = 14; CI = 10; K = 19	Correlation between each item and total score ranged from .36 to .76	None reported
All ethnic groups				
Multicultural-AS (Wong-Rieger & Quintana, 1987)	Bil	Not published	None reported	None reported

403

practices and values, (3) traditional health beliefs, practices, and folk disorders, (4) traditional socialization, (5) traditional foods and food practices, (6) religious beliefs and practices, (7) interracial attitudes, and (8) superstitions. Reported alpha coefficients for the 8 subscales were, respectively, .90, .71, .78, .81, .81, .76, .79, and .72. The split-half reliability for the entire scale is .93. According to Landrine and Klonoff (1994), the AAAS has evidence of criterion-related validity in its scores' correlation with ethnicity and in the form of significant score differences on 4 of the 8 subscales and the total score between respondents who indicated they live in a Black neighborhood (i.e., less acculturated) and respondents who indicated they did not live in a Black neighborhood (i.e., more acculturated).

Much shorter in length compared to the AAAS, the 10-item SAAAA focuses on media preferences, social interaction patterns, and attitudes about ethnic identity. Among the items, 7 (70%) measure behaviors, 2 (20%) measure values, and 1 (10%) measures cultural identity. Reported alpha coefficient was .75. According to Snowden and Hines (1999), evidence for criterion-related validity was observed in the correlations between female respondents' scores and religious affiliations, age, income, likelihood of marriage, place of residence, and employment rates, and in the correlations between male respondents' scores and marital status, income, educational attainment, place of residence, religious affiliation, and employment; the authors noted that the use of these demographic information as criteria for construct validity are consistent with theory and research on African American acculturation. Also, exploratory factor analysis results provided additional evidence of the SAAAA's construct validity.

Evaluation

The AAAS and the SAAAA are the first measures of African American acculturation and represent a promising start to the study of acculturation among African Americans. However, further studies on their reliability and validity are needed. The initial reports of internal consistency for some of the AAAS subscales and for the SAAAA were rather low, indicating poor performance. Also, studies are needed to examine the instruments' stability over time (test-retest reliability). Both instruments evidenced some criterion-related validity, but evidence of concurrent and discriminant validity is also needed. In addition, confirmatory factor analytic studies are necessary to confirm the subscales of the AAAS.

ASIAN AMERICANS

Three acculturation instruments developed for Asian Americans were found, one specifically designed for Chinese Americans, the other two for Asian Americans in general. The Acculturation Scale for Chinese

Americans (ASCA; Yao, 1979) is composed of two scales, designated by the author as Instruments A and B. Both scales are based on the dual-cultural unilinear model of measurement. The 24-item Instrument A measures beliefs and attitudes about family relations, interpersonal relations, sex education, women's status, social/economic/political issues, and America and its people. Instrument B, which has 16 items, measures an individual's feelings about social isolation, English proficiency, adaptation to the American lifestyle, and future life prospective. All 24 items were generated by the author based on intrinsic and extrinsic cultural traits of Chinese Americans. With reference to Instrument A, we determined that 83% of the items measure values and the remaining 17% cultural identity; all items in Instrument B (100%) measure behaviors. The internal reliabilities for Instruments A and B are .58 and .75, respectively. Yao (1979) did not report any evidence of construct validity.

The Suinn-Lew Asian Self-Identity Acculturation Scale (SL-ASIA; Suinn, Rickard-Figueroa, Lew, & Vigil, 1987) has been the most widely used acculturation scale for Asian Americans. It is a 21-item instrument modeled after the Acculturation Rating Scale for Mexican Americans (the ARSMA is described later; Cuellar, Harris, & Jasso, 1980) and is based on the dual-cultural unilinear model of measurement. The SL-ASIA items reflect language use, friendship choice, food preference, media preference, participation in cultural activity, generation and geographic history of life experiences, and ethnic/racial identity; 76% of the items measure behavior, and 24% measure cultural identity. Internal consistency for the SL-ASIA ranges from .68 to .91, with a modal range in the .80s (Ponterotto et al., 1998). Correlations between SL-ASIA scores and generation status, length of residence in the U.S., self-rating of ethnic identity, and country of residence have been reported as evidence of criterion-related validity (Ponterotto et al., 1998). Also, evidence for concurrent validity was observed in the correlation between SL-ASIA scores and attitudes toward mental health services, preferred source of help, scores on Brief Symptom Inventory and Holland career codes, and locus of control orientation (Ponterotto et al., 1998). Exploratory factor analysis has provided further evidence of construct validity; it should be noted, however, that the exact factor structure underlying SL-ASIA has not been confirmed (Ponterotto et al., 1998).

The Asian Values Scale (AVS; Kim, Atkinson, & Yang, 1999) is the newest addition to instruments measuring Asian American acculturation. The AVS is designed to measure an individual's adherence to Asian cultural values endorsed more highly by Asian Americans than by European Americans. It was developed from an initial set of 112 items describing 14 Asian value dimensions and contains 36 items describing 12 Asian value dimensions that discriminated between first-generation Asian Americans and European Americans. The AVS is based on the monocultural unilinear system of measurement, and 100% of its items measure the value dimension of acculturation. Reported alpha coefficients ranged from .81 to .82, and the 2-week test-retest reliability coefficient was .83. With respect to construct validity, confirmatory factor analysis results demonstrated that AVS is a reliable indicator of Asian values acculturation when compared to two other measures of acculturation, thus providing evidence of concurrent validity. Confirmatory factor analysis results also showed evidence of discriminant validity in the low correlation obtained between the AVS and an indicator of behavioral acculturation. Evidence of discriminant validity was also evidenced in the form of a slower rate of change, across generation status, for AVS scores than the scores from a behavioral measure. Results from an exploratory factor analysis on the constructs measured by the AVS provided further evidence of AVS's construct validity.

Evaluation

Generally, both the SL-ASIA and AVS appear to have adequate evidence of psychometric reliability and validity. Evidence of reliability over time, however, is needed for the SL-ASIA. With respect to construct validity, the SL-ASIA has satisfactory criterion-related validity, but further studies are needed to gather evidence of discriminant validity. Further studies are also needed to examine AVS's criterion-related validity. The ASCA does not appear to have acceptable levels of reliability and lacks evidence of construct validity.

HISPANIC AMERICANS

Hispanics constitute the largest and most rapidly growing immigrant group in the United States. Thus, it was not surprising that a literature search yielded 23 instruments designed for Hispanic Americans of various nationalities, by far the largest number of acculturation measures developed for any one ethnic group. This notable number of instruments posed a logistical challenge to us, and we struggled to find a viable schema to organize our review in a cogent manner. We settled on a chronological approach based on measurement model, with unilinear instruments presented first, followed by the bilinear measures. In Table 22.1, acculturation instruments are grouped under intended user national-origins.

Unilinear Measures

Eighteen acculturation instruments for Hispanic Americans that were based on the dual-cultural unilinear model of measurement were found, all published between 1978 and 1996. As noted earlier, the dual-cultural unilinear measurement model is based on a single continuum, with one end reflecting high adherence to the indigenous culture and the other indicating high adherence to the dominant culture.

In 1978, three acculturation measures were introduced: Behavioral Acculturation Scale (BAS; Szapocznik, Scopetta, Kurtines, & Aranalde, 1978), Value Acculturation Scale (VAS; Szapocznik et al., 1978), and Acculturation Measure for Chicano Adolescents (AMCA; Olmedo, Martinez, & Martinez, 1978). The 24 items comprising the BAS were chosen by way of differential endorsements by Cuban Americans and European Americans and through factor analysis. All 24 items tap into the behavioral dimension of acculturation, with 9 items measuring language use, 10 items measuring preference for types of music, dance, readings, food, television, radio, and recreation, 3 items measuring preferred ways of celebration, and 2 items measuring ways of relating to others. Coefficient alpha, 4-week test-retest reliability, and parallel language form reliability coefficients are .97, .96, and .88, respectively. Evidence of criterion-related validity for the BAS was observed in the form of correlations between its scores and the length of residence in the United States, whereas BAS's concurrent validity was evident in its scores' correlation with the VAS scores (described next); factor analysis from which the BAS items were derived also provided further evidence of construct validity.

The 10-item VAS, developed using identical selection criteria as the BAS, measures relational value orientation. We determined that all 10 items of the VAS measure the value dimension of acculturation. The VAS's coefficient alpha, 4-week test-retest reliability, and parallel language form reliability coefficients are .77, .86, and .46, respectively. A direct relationship between VAS scores and length of residence in the United States provided evidence of criterion-related validity. Evidence of concurrent validity was obtained in the form of a correlation between VAS and BAS scores; factor analysis from which VAS items were derived also provided further evidence of construct validity.

As the name indicates, the AMCA was designed for Chicano adolescents. This 20-item instrument is composed of semantic and sociocultural variables, from which "the acculturation score for a given individual is defined as the linear combination of semantic and sociocultural variables which provides the best least squares estimate of the individual's score on a dichotomous variable in which Chicanos are assigned a value of zero and Anglos a value of one" (Olmedo et al., 1978, p. 165). Of AMCA's 20 items, 55% measure the behavior dimension of acculturation, and 45% measure the value dimension. According to Olmedo et al. (1978), the AMCA has a 2- to 3-week test-retest reliability coefficients of .89 for a Chicano sample, .66 for an Anglo sample, and .84 overall, and evidence of construct validity based on the results of an exploratory factor analysis and a double cross-validation procedure that yielded validity coefficients from .66 to .80; no evidence of internal consistency was reported. Further study of the AMCA provided evidence of criterion-related validity in the form of correlations with ethnic group membership and generation status (Olmedo & Padilla, 1978).

Two instruments were introduced in 1980: Acculturation Rating Scale for Mexican Americans (ARSMA; Cuellar et al., 1980) and Padilla Acculturation Scale (PAS; Padilla, 1980). The 20-item ARSMA taps into language familiarity and usage, ethnic interaction, ethnic pride and identity, cultural heritage, and generational proximity. Among the items in the ARSMA, 70% measure the behavior dimension of acculturation and 25% reflect cultural identity; the remaining 5% are demographic items. The ARSMA has alpha coefficients ranging from .81 to .92, 5-week test-retest reliability coefficients ranging from .72 to .80, and an interrater reliability coefficient of .89, obtained by having two raters independently administer the ARSMA to 26 psychotic Mexican American patients in the same week (Cuellar et al., 1980; Montgomery & Orozco, 1984). ARSMA scores have evidence of criterion-related validity in the form of correlatinons with generation status, age, and socioeconomic status; correlations with BAS and independent ratings of acculturation provided evidence of concurrent validity (Cuellar et al., 1980; Montgomery & Orozco, 1984). The ARSMA has further evidence of construct validity based on factor analysis (Cuellar et al., 1980; Montgomery & Orozco, 1984).

The PAS is a 26-item instrument having two subscales, Cultural Awareness (15 items) and Ethnic Loyalty (11 items). According to Padilla (1980), these subscales were developed using the normality and linearity of regression criteria from an initial set of 108 items measuring cultural awareness and 77 items measuring ethnic loyalty. Among the items in the Cultural Awareness subscale, 47% measure the cultural identity dimension of acculturation, 40% measure the behavioral dimension, and 13% measure the knowledge dimension. Among the items in the Ethnic Loyalty subscale, 64% measure behaviors, and 36% measure cultural identity. The alpha coefficients reported for the Cultural Awareness and Ethnic Loyalty subscales are .98 and .83, respectively. There is evidence of criterion-related validity as PAS scores have been shown to correlate with generation status, educational attainment, income level, and ethnic density of neighborhood; construct validity was also evidenced via factor analysis.

The Acculturation and Biculturalism Scale (ABS; Triandis, Kashima, Hui, Lisansky, & Marín, 1982), modeled after the AMCA, ARSMA, BAS, PAS, and VAS, was developed using a general Hispanic American sample. The 15-item ABS is composed of two subscales, Acculturation and Bicultural. The 9-item Acculturation subscale measures length and place of residence, media preferences, and social preferences. The Bicultural subscale has 6 items that tap into media preference and social preference. Triandis et al. (1982) differentiated acculturation and biculturalism by noting that the former refers to a cultural shift in which elements of the majority culture progressively predominate, whereas the latter refers to a cultural orientation in which elements of both minority and majority cultures are increasingly found in equal proportions. All 15 items (100%) in the ABS measure the behavioral dimension of acculturation. Triandis et al. did not report any data on the ABS's reliability but noted evidence of criterion-related validity in that its scores correlated with generation status. Also, Triandis et al. reported that the subscales were derived from factor analysis results, thus providing further evidence of construct validity.

The 10-item Children's Acculturation Scale (CAS; Franco, 1983) assesses the acculturation status of Mexican American children; it is designed to be completed by parents, teachers, and counselors. The ABS is derived from an initial set of items generated from the literature, communication with experts in the field, other acculturation scales, and interviews with Mexican Americans. Five CAS items (50%) measure the behavior dimension of acculturation, and 1 other item (10%) measures cultural identity; the remaining items are demographic in nature. The CAS's coefficient alpha, 5-week test-retest reliability, and interrater reliability (two raters administered the CAS to 12 first-graders) were .77, .97, and .93, respectively. A direct correlation between CAS and ARSMA scores provides evidence of concurrent validity, and additional evidence of construct validity was obtained via exploratory factor analysis.

The Bicultural/Multicultural Experience Inventory (B/MEI; Ramirez, 1984) was developed using a Mexican American sample. The B/MEI is a 57-item instrument based on the experiences of 8 individuals who were identified as being bicultural-multicultural persons. It consists of three parts: demographic-linguistic information, socialization and educational (personal) history, and multicultural participation. Among the items in the B/MEI, 86% measure the behavior dimension of acculturation and 4% measure the cultural identity dimension; the remaining items request demographic information. The B/MEI has coefficient alphas of .79 for personal history and .68 for multicultural participation. An association between B/MEI scores and the psychohistory of participants and their behavior in a group setting has been offered as evidence of criterion-related validity.

The 30-item Children's Hispanic Background Scale (CHBS; Martinez, Norman, & Delaney, 1984) taps into Spanish language use and exposure (23 items), preference for Spanish language media and church service (5 items), and food preference (2 items). We determined that all 30 items reflect the behavioral dimension of acculturation. The CHBS has a 1.58-day (an average) test-retest coefficient of .92, evidence of concurrent validity in its correlation with a bilingual classification scale, and evidence of criterion-related validity in its correlation with socioeconomic status and generation status; no internal reliability coefficient was reported.

As the name indicates, the Language-Based Acculturation Scale for Mexican Americans (LASMA; Deyo, Diehl, Hazuda, & Stern, 1985) is a measure of language use among Mexican Americans. The LASMA contains 4 items measuring preference for and the use of either Spanish or English; all of these items tap into the behavioral dimension of acculturation. The

LASMA has coefficients of reproducibility and scalability of .96 and .81. It has evidence of criterion-related validity based on correlations between LASMA scores and generation status, place of residence (barrio vs. suburb), family income, educational attainment, and age.

Similar to the LASMA, the Media Acculturation Scale (Media-AS; Ramirez, Cousins, Santos, & Supik, 1986) is a 4-item instrument developed with a Mexican American sample that measures language preference and use; all of these items tap into the behavioral dimension of acculturation. With respect to its reliability, Ramirez et al. (1986) reported a lack of significant chi-square difference between pretest and posttest scores. Also, the authors reported evidence of criterion validity in the form of correlations between Media-AS scores and respondent's frequency in listening to a local Spanish-language radio station, generation status, age, education level, and income.

A year after the publication of the Media-AS, three acculturation instruments were published: Acculturation Scale (AS; Caetano, 1987), Los Angeles Epidemiological Catchment Area Acculturation Scale (LAECA-AS; Burnam, Telles, Karno, Hough, & Escobar, 1987), and Short Acculturation Scale for Hispanics (SASH; Marín, Sabogal, Marín, Otero-Sabogal, & Perez-Stable, 1987). The 12 items comprising the AS were developed using a general Hispanic sample. These items were chosen based on the results of a factor analysis, which provided evidence of construct validity. Among the items in the AS, 83% measure behaviors, 8.5 % measure cultural identity, and 8.5 % measure values. The AS has coefficient alpha of .91 and split-half reliability of .87. It also has evidence of criterion-related validity in its correlation with generation status, length of years in the United States, and age.

The LAECA-AS is a 26-item instrument based on a Mexican American sample from Southern California. This instrument was modeled after the ARSMA and the BAS, thus it contains items such as language preference and use, preference for cultural activities, and friendship choice. Among the items in the LAECA-AS, 85% measure the behavioral dimension, and 11% the cultural identity dimension of acculturation; the remaining items request demographic information. Coefficient alpha for the LAECA-AS was reported in the range of .91 to .97. Criterion-related validity was evidenced in correlations between LAECA-AS scores and generation status and age; further evidence of construct validity was based on the results of exploratory factor analysis.

The SASH is a 12-item instrument that measures language use, media preference, and ethnic preference in social relations constructs; all of the items in these three constructs measure the behavioral dimension of acculturation. It has an overall coefficient alpha equal to .92, and coefficient alphas of .90, .86, and .78 for language use, media preference, and ethnic preference in social relations, respectively; factor analysis results supporting these three constructs provided support for SASH's construct validity.

Evidence of criterion-related validity is based on its correlation with generation status, time in the United States, respondent's own evaluation of acculturation level, age of arrival in the United States, and an overall acculturation index (based on length of residence, generation status, and self-identification).

Published five years after the three previous instruments, the Acculturation Rating Scale (ARS; Montgomery, 1992) is a 28-item instrument designed for Mexican Americans and modeled after the ARSMA and the BAS. The ARS identifies one's ethnic preference (i.e., Mexican vs. Anglo orientation) as well as one's perceived satisfaction versus marginality. Factor analysis results showed that the ARS items reflect comfort with Spanish language use and media and Mexican traditions, comfort with English language media and Anglo American traditions, one's preference for ethnic identity, self-rated ethnic identity, and comfort with thinking and speaking English. Among the items, 75% measure the behavior dimension and 25% the cultural identity dimension of acculturation. The ARS has an overall coefficient alpha of .94 and coefficient alphas of .92, .86, .92, .90, and .92 for the five factors, respectively, and evidence of criterion-related validity in its correlation with level of education and generation status.

The Short Acculturation Scale for Hispanic Youths (SASH-Y; Barona & Miller, 1994) is a 12-item instrument modeled after the SASH and the CHBS. The SASH-Y contains items related to Spanish language use and media preference; all 12 items tap into the behavioral dimension of acculturation. The SASH-Y has an overall alpha and split-half reliability coefficients equal to .94 and .96, respectively, and coefficient alphas of .92 and .85 and split-half reliability coefficients of .95 and .87 for the Hispanic and non-Hispanic samples, respectively. A correlation between SASH-Y scores and SES was offered as evidence of criterion-related validity, and additional evidence of construct validity was noted based on the results of exploratory factor analysis.

The Acculturation Measure for Hispanic Adolescents (AMHA; Epstein, Botvin, Dusenbury, Diaz, & Kerner, 1996) is another instrument designed for Hispanic nonadults. It is a brief 1-item behavioral scale in which a respondent indicates the language he or she uses with his or her parents. It has evidence of concurrent validity in its correlation with the LAECA-AS.

The Brief Acculturation Scale for Hispanics (BASH; Norris, Ford, & Bova, 1996), the last of the unilinear measures reviewed in this section, is composed of the 4 language-use behavioral items taken from the 12-item SASH. Coefficient alpha was .90 for a combined Mexican American and Puerto Rican sample, .92 for Mexican American sample only, and .80 for Puerto Rican American sample only. The BASH has evidence of criterion-related validity as its scores are correlated with generation status, length of time in the United States, subjective measure of acculturation, place of birth, and interview language preference.

Evaluation

As this section illustrates, there are numerous instruments designed to measure acculturation among Hispanic Americans. Most of these instruments have adequate internal consistency, but only a handful have information on stability over time. More research on reliability is needed for those instruments. With respect to construct validity, most of the measures have evidence of criterion-related validity (e.g., correlation with generation status) and many have evidence of construct validity based on factor analysis. However, most instruments lack information on other types of validity such as discriminant validity.

Bilinear Measures

Five bilinear measures of Hispanic American acculturation were identified. These instruments are bilinear because they were designed to measure the adaption process on two continua, one that reflects adherence to Hispanic culture, the other reflecting adherence to U.S. culture. This measurement model allows for the assessment of the degree to which a person adheres to each culture independent of the other culture. Publication dates for these instruments ranged from 1980 to 1996.

The 33-item Bicultural Involvement Questionnaire (BIQ; Szapocznik, Kurtines, & Fernandez, 1980) was developed for Cuban Americans and has two subscales, Hispanicism and Americanism. BIQ subscale scores are based on ratings to a unique set of 12 items, plus a common set of 9 items. All items in the BIQ measure the behavioral dimension of acculturation. A Biculturalism index can be calculated by subtracting the Americanism score from the Hispanicism score. Summing up Hispanicism and Americanism scores yields a Cultural Involvement value. Coefficient alphas are .93 for Hispanicism, .89 for Americanism, .94 for Biculturalism, and .79 for Cultural Involvement. Respectively, 6-week test-retest reliability coefficients are .50, .54, .79, and .14; it should be noted that the lack of test-retest reliability may be a function of small sample size ($n = 16$). All BIQ subscales evidence some degree of concurrent validity in correlations obtained between Biculturalism and Cultural Involvement scores and bicultural teacher ratings of participant acculturation.

The Cultural Life Style Inventory (CLSI; Mendoza, 1989) is a 29-item measure derived from an initial set of 83 items generated by experts in Mexican and Anglo cultures. The items that differentiated between Mexican Americans and Anglo Americans were selected for the final instrument. According to Mendoza, "independent estimates of cultural resistance (CR), cultural incorporation (CI), and cultural shift (CS) can be obtained by computing the proportion of items on the scale that are answered in a CR, CI, or CS fashion" (p. 382). The results of an exploratory factor analysis for the entire instrument showed that the items tap into intrafamily language, extrafamily language, social affiliation and activities, cultural familiarity and activities, and cultural identification and pride; these results also demonstrated support for CLSI's construct validity. Among these items, 62% measure the behavior dimension and 38% the cultural identity dimension of acculturation. For the entire scale, estimates of internal consistency ranged from .84 to .91, 2-week test-retest reliability ranged from .88 to .95, and reliability coefficients between English-Spanish parallel forms ranged from .77 to .80. Correlations between CLSI scores and participant generation status, exposure to mainstream culture, and intended length of residence in the United States provided evidence of criterion-related validity, and a correlation between CLSI scores and other people's evaluation of participant acculturation provided evidence of concurrent validity.

Developed by Cortes, Rogler, and Malgady (1994) using factor analysis, the Bicultural Scale for Puerto Ricans (BSPR) consists of a 9-item Puerto Rican Cultural Involvement subscale and a 9-item American Cultural Involvement subscale. The subscales are identical to each other except for the reference culture, and both tap into language preferences and usage, values, ethnic pride, food preferences, child-rearing practices, and interpersonal relations. The authors noted that high scores on both subscales, while indicating high adherence to each culture separately, also are indicative of biculturalism; in turn, low scores on both subscales are indicative of low biculturalism, or marginality. Among the items in the instrument, 56% measure the behavior dimension, 22% the value dimension, and another 22% the cultural identity dimension of acculturation. The BSPR's coefficient alphas are .78 for American orientation and .73 for Puerto Rican orientation. The BSPR has evidence of construct validity based on factor analysis; criterion-related validity was obtained via correlations with generation status, age at arrival in the United States, and number of years in the United States.

The Acculturation Rating Scale for Mexican Americans–II (ARSMA-II; Cuellar et al., 1995), a bilinear version of the ARSMA, consists of two subscales, the 17-item Mexican Orientation Scale (MOS), and the 13-item Anglo Orientation Scale (AOS). In addition to yielding independent (bilinear) mean scores for MOS and AOS, high scores on both MOS and AOS are indicative of biculturalism, whereas low scores on both subscales are indicative of marginalization. Furthermore, a single (unilinear) value along a continuum ranging from very Mexican oriented to very Anglo oriented can be computed by simply subtracting the MOS mean from the AOS mean. Among the items in the MOS, 76% measure the behavioral dimension and 24% measure the cultural identity dimension of acculturation. Among the items in the AOS, 85% measure the behavioral dimension and 15% measure cultural identity. The ARSMA-II has coefficient alphas of .84 for MOS and .77 for AOS, split-half reliability coefficients of .84 for MOS and .77 for AOS, and 1-week test-retest reliability coefficient of .96 for MOS and .94 for AOS. The ARSMA-II has evidence of criterion-related validity in its correlation with generation status and socioeconomic status, additional construct validity based on factor analysis results, and concurrent validity in correlations with ARSMA scores.

The latest addition to the instruments measuring Hispanic American acculturation is the Bidimensional Short Acculturation Scale for Hispanics (BSASH; Marín & Gamba, 1996). The BSASH has a 12-item subscale representing a continuum on the use of the Spanish language and another 12-item subscale representing a continuum on the use of English; in addition to indicating one's adherence to both cultures separately, the theory underlying the measure suggests that high scores on both subscales are indicative of biculturalism, whereas low scores on both subscales indicate marginalization. The items in the BSASH were derived from an initial set of 60 items (30 representing the Hispanic domain and 30 reflecting the non-Hispanic domain) measuring language use, media preference, participation in cultural activities, and ethnicity of social relations; all items tap into the behavioral dimension of acculturation. Final item selection was based on a factor analysis. Coefficient alphas for the Hispanic domain subscale were reported at .93 and .87, and for the non-Hispanic domain at .97 and .95, for Mexican American and Central American samples, respectively. Evidence of criterion-related validity has been reported in the form of correlations with generation status, length of residence in the United States, educational attainment, age at arrival in the United States, proportion of life in the United States, and ethnic self-identification. Correlations with the SASH provided some indication of concurrent validity; additional evidence of construct validity was obtained via factor analysis.

Evaluation

The five bilinear measures reviewed in this section represent the most sophisticated measures of Hispanic acculturation. All of the instruments allow for the measurement of adherence to host and culture-of-origin on separate continua, and most allow for an index of acculturation based on a mathematical computation of scores from both continua (e.g., in ARSMA-II, acculturation = AOS – MOS). However, despite the fact that these instruments are capable of specifying an individual's acculturation status such as biculturalism and marginalization, they lack normative data necessary to categorize a respondent to one of these statuses. Future studies should focus on establishing normative scores among Hispanic Americans for the various acculturation statuses measured by these instruments. With respect to instrument psychometrics, most have acceptable levels of internal consistency and stability over time. In addition, most of the instruments have at least some evidence of construct validity. Nonetheless, more research is needed, particularly to obtain evidence of discriminant validity.

NATIVE AMERICANS

Three acculturation instruments for Native Americans were found, two designed for Navajos and one for American Indians in general. Both acculturation measures for Navajos were developed by Boyce and Boyce (1983). The 20-item Navajo Family Acculturation Scale (NFAS; Boyce & Boyce, 1983) was developed by asking Navajo informants about the questions they would use to distinguish children raised in traditional versus modern family backgrounds; traditional background is indicative of low acculturation, whereas modern background is indicative of high acculturation. This scale measures the following aspects of Navajo family acculturation: modernity of the physical home environment, involvement of the family in the elements of a traditional lifestyle, and the extent of family contact with the Anglo world. The NFAS is based on the dual-cultural unilinear system of measurement; among its 20 items, 85% measure the behavior dimension, 10% measure the knowledge dimension, and 5% measure the cultural identity dimension of acculturation. Coefficient alpha and 3-month test-retest reliability were reported at .65 and .88, respectively. Boyce and Boyce did not report any evidence of construct validity for the NFAS.

The Navajo Community Acculturation Scale (NCAS; Boyce & Boyce, 1983) is a 1-item measure on which communities are rated on a 7-point scale from most traditional (i.e., low acculturation) to most modern (i.e., high acculturation). It has interrater reliability equal to .53 and some evidence of criterion validity based correlations with distance to an urban center, population size, and presence of paved road. Similar to the NFAS, the NCAS represents a dual-cultural unilinear measurement model, with one end of the continuum reflecting involvement in the traditional Native American Indian culture and the other end reflecting adherence to the modern U.S. culture.

The Rosebud Personal Opinion Survey (RPOS; Hoffman, Dana, & Bolton, 1985) contains 32 items that comprise the following subscales: (a) social behavior, membership, and activities; (b) value orientation and cultural attitudes; (c) blood quantum; (d) language preference and usage; (e) educational and occupational status. The RPOS is based on the dual-cultural unilinear model of measurement, and most of its items apparently tap into the behavioral dimension of acculturation (the calculation of percentages was not possible because we could not contact the authors to obtain a copy of the instrument). Hoffman et al. (1985) did not report any reliability and validity data for the RPOS.

Evaluation

In general, there appears to be a great need for more research that aims to improve or establish the psychometric properties of instruments designed to measure Native American acculturation. The three instruments reviewed in this section represent the beginning efforts in this endeavor.

NATIVE HAWAIIANS

One measure of Native Hawaiian acculturation was identified: Na Mea Hawai'i Scale (NMHS; Rezentes, 1993), a 21-item instrument that measures "how Hawaiian a person is by contemporary Hawaiian standards" (p. 384). From an initial set of 34 items that were rationally derived based on interviews with Native Hawaiians, 21 items that differentiated Native Hawaiians from Caucasians and Japanese Americans were retained. The instrument measures an individual's knowledge or participation in Hawaiian language, food, major events, arts and crafts, family values, cultural affiliation, history, religious or spiritual beliefs, and customs. The NMHS is based on the monocultural unilinear measurement model; 57% of its items tap into the behavioral dimension, 14% into the value dimension, 19% into the knowledge dimension, and 10% into the cultural identity dimension of acculturation. The author reported low to moderate range of intercorrelations between the items (.36 to .76), but no evidence of construct validity; coefficient alpha was not reported.

Evaluation

Comparable to the acculturation instruments for Native American Indians, the NMHS represents an initial effort in the development of a reliable and valid measure of Native Hawaiian acculturation. Given that little previous research has been conducted to study Native Hawaiians, a significant ethnic minority in the Hawaiian Islands and on the West Coast mainland, this initial effort is commendable. However, the NMHS requires more development, such as research to establish construct validity as well as to increase internal consistency and examine stability over time.

ALL ETHNIC GROUPS

The Multicultural Acculturation Scale (Multicultural-AS; Wong-Rieger & Quintana, 1987) consists of 12 behavioral items measuring changes in cognition (language, skills, and history), behaviors (cultural activities, work, and residence), and self-identity (friends and self-labeling) among ethnic minorities. It was developed from an initial set of 50 items that discriminated between modes of acculturation and addressed adaptation issues that are relevant to many groups. The Multicultural-AS measures the behavioral and cultural identity dimensions of acculturation (the calculation of percentages was not possible because we could not contact the authors to obtain a copy of the instrument) and is based on the bilinear measurement model. Scoring yields an Ethnic Orientation Index (EOI) and an American Orientation Index (AOI). Applying the same computational strategy used to score the ARSMA-II, an Overall Acculturation Index (OAI) can be calculated by subtracting the EOI from the AOI. Unfortunately, the authors of the Multicultural-AS did not report any reliability or validity data.

Evaluation

The Multicultural-AS represents an initial effort to develop an acculturation instrument that can be used with all ethnic groups. However, while this goal is commendable, more research is sorely needed to establish this instrument's reliability and validity.

CURRENT STATE OF
ACCULTURATION MEASUREMENT AND
SUGGESTIONS FOR FUTURE DIRECTIONS

In general, a number of psychometric strengths were noted in the acculturation measures reviewed in this chapter. We found that most instruments had acceptable levels of reliability, particularly along the line of internal consistency. Indeed, over 70% of instruments reporting reliability data had coefficient alpha of .80 or greater, indicating adequate internal consistency. Ninety percent of the instruments with stability over time data also reported acceptable levels of test-retest reliability. Most instruments had some form of construct validity, and in particular, evidence of criterion-related validity, such as associations with generation status and place of birth, were reported for 70% of all instruments. In addition, 36% of all instruments had evidence of concurrent validity, indicating a significant association with at least one other measure of acculturation. Another source of strength is the apparent focus on measuring behaviors, an important dimension of acculturation. We determined that at least half of the items in over 85% of the instruments reviewed tapped into the behavioral dimension of acculturation and that 36% of the instruments were exclusively composed of behavioral dimension items, reflecting behaviors such as language use, choice of friendship, and food preferences.

Despite these strengths, the current state of acculturation measurement has a number of limitations. For example, many instruments reported acceptable levels of internal consistency, but nearly three quarters of all instruments (74%) had no evidence of test-retest reliability. Thus, more research is needed to establish instrument stability over time. Another psychometric limitation is the lack of construct validity information. Less than two thirds of all instruments reported any evidence of construct validity stemming from factor analysis, and more than half did not provide any evidence of concurrent or discriminant validity. As Heppner, Kivlighan, and Wampold (1999) noted, concurrent and discriminant validity indices and factor analytic results are necessary because they provide important information regarding how precisely an instrument measures the intended construct. The apparent lack of validity studies reported in the acculturation literature is an indication that more research is needed to better establish the validity of current and future instruments.

Another weakness can be ascribed to the measurement model used by most acculturation measures, for 23 of the 33 (70%) instruments we reviewed fit the dual-cultural unilinear model of measurement. This system of measurement, based on a single continuum with the ends representing high adherence to either indigenous or host-culture, has been criticized by many researchers (Cortes et al., 1994; Marín, 1992; Rogler et al., 1991; Ruelas, Atkinson, & Ramos-Sanchez, 1998). Rogler et al. (1991) stated that many developers of acculturation instruments incorrectly "assume increments of involvement in the American host society culture necessarily entail corresponding decrements of disengagement from the immigrant's traditional culture" and that "items presented this way constrain the respondent's choice of alternative answers according to a model of zero-sum competition between the two cultures" (p. 587). Marín (1992) and Cortes et al. (1994) pointed out that unilinear models do not allow the independent determination of the degree to which an individual is involved in each culture, that is, *acculturation* to the dominant culture and *enculturation* to the indigenous culture.

The need to recognize the separate effects of enculturation to the indigenous culture from acculturation to the dominant culture was underscored in a recent study by Ruelas et al. (1998), who reported a significant positive association between enculturation and Mexican American perceptions of counselor credibility. Importantly, the decrease in credibility was associated with *loss* of Mexican culture, rather than *acquisition* of Anglo culture (i.e., acculturation). More specifically, when ARSMA-II's Mexican Orientation Scale (MOS) and Anglo Orientation Scale (AOS) scores were correlated *separately* with ratings of counselor credibility, only the MOS scores related significantly to credibility ratings of counselors. The results suggested that it was the loss of Mexican culture, not the acquisition of Anglo culture, that accounted for diminished perceptions of counselor credibility. Reflecting on their findings, Ruelas et al. noted that had they used a unilinear measure of acculturation—rather than the bilinear ARSMA-II—their results would have led them to conclude that perceptions of counselor credibility were inversely related to U.S. acculturation, a rather misleading inference.

Given the problems raised by dual-cultural unilinear instruments, we suggest that future acculturation measures move away from this model of measurement. One relatively straightforward approach to develop bicultural instruments is to *expand* the existing monocultural unilinear measures. As noted previously, these measures are based on a single continuum and reflect adherence to indigenous cultures (e.g., AVS and NMHS). Upgrading these instruments to fit a bilinear model of acculturation could be accomplished by establishing a second continuum designed to measure adherence to the host or majority culture. This would require the development of scale items tapping into characteristics that distinguish European Americans from ethnic minority persons.

More generally, we recommend that developers of future acculturation measures also consider utilizing multilinear models, in which acculturation to various cultural settings such as school, work, and home are measured on separate continua.

One final and important limitation in the current state of acculturation measurement is related to the issue of construct dimensions. Most of the instruments that were reviewed focus primarily on behaviors. Although this focus represents a strong point, as behaviors denote an important dimension of acculturation, it also has resulted in a lack of attention to other dimensions, such as values, cultural identity, and knowledge. This oversight becomes particularly salient when considering that some acculturation researchers (e.g., Kim et al., 1999; Marín, 1992; Padilla, 1980; Szapocznik et al., 1978) have emphasized the importance of acculturation dimensions not limited to specific behaviors. For example, Marín (1992) suggested that changes in cultural values might be more significant than behavioral changes because values represent an individual's worldviews as well as patterns of social interactions.

Even among the instruments that measure dimensions other than behavior, the additional dimensions are mixed in with behavior, thus causing ambiguity as to what is actually being measured. The acculturation score obtained from the BSPR (Cortes et al., 1994), for example, is composed of items from the behavioral, value, and cultural identity dimensions, making it difficult to infer which aspect of acculturation is reflected by the score. Unaccounted "mixing" of dimensions is problematic, especially when considering that various acculturation dimensions do not represent a uniform index of acculturation. This issue was raised by Betancourt and Lopez (1993), who noted that the behavioral dimension of acculturation represents an indirect measure of cultural values, implying that changes in behaviors and values do not reflect an identical phenomenon. In addition, there is now some research evidence that behavioral acculturation and value acculturation have different rates of change. A study by Kim et al. (1999) revealed that Asian American acculturation along the value dimension occurred much slower than acculturation along the behavioral and cultural identity dimensions. They found that scores on the AVS (Kim et al., 1999), a measure of value acculturation, did not change significantly across first-generation, second-generation, and third-generation Asian

Americans, whereas the scores on the SL-ASIA (Suinn et al., 1987), a measure of behavioral and cultural identity dimensions, changed significantly across these generations. These findings suggest that a single acculturation score reflecting both value and behavioral dimensions (as well as other dimensions) may lead to erroneous or misleading conclusions about a respondent's acculturation status. Accordingly, instrument developers may want to be particularly careful so as to not mix items from different acculturation dimensions when designing new (or revising existing) instruments. Another possibility is the development of instrument subscales with items reflecting a specific acculturation dimension.

Although dimensions of acculturation have played an important role in the evolving definitions of acculturation as a psychosocial construct (e.g., Berry, 1980; Cuellar et al., 1995; Padilla, 1980; Szapocznik et al., 1978), we could find no formal and consistent guideline to classify these dimensional aspects of acculturation. In describing instrument content analysis in a preceding section of this chapter, we observed that items in existing measures fit nicely into behavior, values, knowledge, or cultural identity categories. By way of elaborating on this observation, we would like to propose a formal model for categorizing the dimensions of acculturation. Our model closely follows the functional definition developed by Cuellar et al. (1995), who defined acculturation in terms of changes at three levels of functioning: behavioral, affective, and cognitive.

Along the behavioral level of functioning, we propose the acculturation dimension of *behavior* consisting of friendship choice, preferences for television programs and reading, participation in cultural activities, contact with indigenous culture (e.g., time spent in country of origin), language use, food choice, and music preference. Along the cognitive level of functioning, we propose two dimensions, *values* and *knowledge.* The values dimension of acculturation refers to attitudes and beliefs about social relations, cultural customs, and cultural traditions, along with gender roles and attitudes and ideas about health and illness. The knowledge dimension of acculturation refers to culturally specific information such as names of historical leaders in the culture of origin and the dominant culture, and historical significance of culturally specific activities. Along the affective level of functioning, we propose the *cultural identity* dimension of acculturation. Cultural identity refers to attitudes toward one's cultural identification (e.g., preferred name is in Spanish), attitudes toward indigenous and dominant groups (e.g., feelings of shame toward the indigenous culture and pride toward the dominant group), and level of comfort toward people of indigenous and dominant groups. In summary, we propose that the definition of acculturation includes four dimensions (behavior, values, knowledge, and cultural identity) operating at three levels of functioning.

In classifying "cultural identity" as one of four dimensions of acculturation, we should point out that this concept largely overlaps with the construct of "ethnic identity"; indeed, "acculturation" and "ethnic identity" are constructs that are not well differentiated in the literature (Sodowsky & Maestas, 2000; see Fischer & Moradi's Chapter 20, this volume, for an excellent discussion on ethnic and racial identity). We should also note that the proposed four dimensions of acculturation are not orthogonal to each other. For example, the behavioral and knowledge dimensions may be correlated, since behavior is likely to be preceded by knowledge, a principle that also applies to other pairs of dimensions. These provisos notwithstanding, we hope the proposed 4-dimensional model of acculturation will lead to more sophisticated studies of acculturation (e.g., examine the rate of acculturation along each dimension) as well as more informative counseling process and outcome research (e.g., examine the relationship between each dimension and reaction to counselor interventions).

CONCLUSION

Given the continued influx of immigrants and high birth rates among ethnic minority groups in the United States, acculturation is likely to continue to be a relevant psychosocial process during the new millennium. The development of reliable and valid measures is an important area in the study of acculturation. Although the growing number of acculturation instruments is encouraging, our review and critique of these measures indicated that many do not have adequate evidence of reliability and validity. In addition, most measures also lag behind advancements in acculturation theory. For acculturation to be examined more accurately, we feel that more psychometric studies on existing instruments are needed and that future acculturation measures need to converge more closely with acculturation theory. This chapter is an attempt to encourage this process.

NOTE

1. We use the term *linearity* (e.g., unilinear, bilinear, multilinear) to refer to acculturation continua, such as levels of involvement in one's culture of origin and the dominant culture, and use the term *dimension* to refer to the factors comprising acculturation, such as behaviors, values, knowledge, and cultural identity.

REFERENCES

Atkinson, D. R., Morten, G., & Sue, D. W. (1998). *Counseling American minorities* (5th ed.). Boston: McGraw-Hill.

Barona, A., & Miller, J. A. (1994). Short Acculturation Scale for Hispanic Youths (SASH-Y): A preliminary report. *Hispanic Journal of Behavioral Sciences, 16*, 155-162.

Berry, J. W. (1980). Acculturation as varieties of adaptation. In A. M. Padilla (Ed.), *Acculturation: Theory, models, and some new findings* (pp. 9-25). Boulder, CO: Westview.

Berry, J. W. (1990). Psychology of acculturation: Understanding individuals moving between cultures. In R. W. Brislin (Ed.), *Applied cross-cultural psychology* (pp. 232-253).
Newbury Park, CA: Sage.

Berry, J. W. (1994). Acculturation and psychological adaptation: An overview. In A. Bouvy,
F. J. R. van de Vijver, P. Boski, & P. Schmitz (Eds.), *Journeys into cross-cultural psychology* (pp. 129-141). Amsterdam: Swets & Zeitlinger.

Berry, J. W., & Annis, R. C. (1974). Acculturative stress: The role of ecology, culture and differentiation. *Journal of Cross-Cultural Psychology, 5,* 382-406.

Berry, J. W., & Kim, U. (1988). Acculturation and mental health. In P. R. Dasen, J. W. Berry,
& N. Sartorius (Eds.), *Health and cross-cultural psychology: Toward applications*
(pp. 207-236). Newbury Park, CA: Sage.

Berry, J. W., Kim, U., Power, S., Young, M., & Bajaki, M. (1989). Acculturation attitudes in
plural societies. *Applied Psychology: An International Review, 38,* 185-206.

Berry, J. W., Trimble, J. E., & Olmeda, E. L. (1986). Assessment of acculturation. In W. J.
Lonner & J. W. Berry (Eds.), *Field methods in cross-cultural research* (pp. 291-324).
Newbury Park, CA: Sage.

Betancourt, H., & Lopez, S. R. (1993). The study of culture, ethnicity, and race in American
psychology. *American Psychologist, 48,* 629-637.

Boyce, W. T., & Boyce, J. C. (1983). Acculturation and changes in health among Navajo
boarding school students. *Social Science Medicine, 17,* 219-226.

Burnam, M. A., Telles, C. A., Karno, M., Hough, R. L., & Escobar, J. I. (1987). Measurement
of acculturation in a community population of Mexican Americans. *Hispanic Journal
of Behavioral Sciences, 9,* 105-130.

Caetano, R. (1987). Acculturation and drinking patterns among U.S. Hispanics. *British
Journal of Addiction, 82,* 789-799.

Cortes, D. E., Rogler, L. H., & Malgady, R. G. (1994). Biculturality among Puerto Rican
adults in the United States. *American Journal of Community Psychology, 22,* 707-
721.

Cuellar, I., Arnold, B., & Maldonado, R. (1995). Acculturation Rating Scale for Mexican
Americans–II: A revision of the original ARSMA scale. *Hispanic Journal of Behavioral Sciences, 17,* 275-304.

Cuellar, I., Harris, L. C., & Jasso, R. (1980). An acculturation scale for Mexican American
normal and clinical populations. *Hispanic Journal of Behavioral Sciences, 2,* 199-217.

Deyo, R. A., Diehl, A. K., Hazuda, H., & Stern, M. P. (1985). A simple language-based acculturation scale for Mexican Americans: Validation and application to health care research. *American Journal of Public Health, 75,* 51-55.

Epstein, J. A., Botvin, G. J., Dusenbury, L., Diaz, T., & Kerner, J. (1996). Validation of an acculturation measure for Hispanic adolescents. *Psychological Reports, 79,* 1075-1079.

Franco, J. N. (1983). An acculturation scale for Mexican-American children. *Journal of
General Psychology, 108,* 175-181.

Gim, R. H., Atkinson, D. R., & Whiteley, S. (1990). Asian-American acculturation, severity of concerns, and willingness to see a counselor. *Journal of Counseling Psychology,
38,* 57-62.

Graves, T. D. (1967). Psychological acculturation in a tri-ethnic community. *Southwestern Journal of Anthropology, 23,* 337-350.

Heath, A. E., Neimeyer, G. J., & Pedersen, P. B. (1988). The future of cross-cultural counseling: A delphi poll. *Journal of Counseling and Development, 67,* 27-30.

Heppner, P. P., Kivlighan, D. M., Jr., & Wampold, B. E. (1999). *Research design in counseling* (2nd ed.). Pacific Grove, CA: Brooks/Cole-Wadsworth.

Hoffman, T., Dana, R. H., & Bolton, B. (1985). Measured acculturation and MMPI-168 performance of Native American adults. *Journal of Cross-Cultural Psychology, 16,* 243-
256.

Kim, B. S. K., Atkinson, D. R., & Yang, P. H. (1999). The Asian Values Scale: Development,
factor analysis, validation, and reliability. *Journal of Counseling Psychology, 46,* 342-
352.

Landrine, H., & Klonoff, E. A. (1994). The African American Acculturation Scale: Development, Reliability, and Validity. *Journal of Black Psychology, 20,* 104-127.

Marín, G. (1992). Issues in the measurement of acculturation among Hispanics. In K. F. Geisinger (Ed.), *Psychological testing of Hispanics* (pp. 235-251). Washington, DC: American Psychological Association.

Marín, G., & Gamba, R. J. (1996). A new measurement of acculturation for Hispanics: The Bidimensional Acculturation Scale for Hispanics (BAS). *Hispanic Journal of Behavioral Sciences, 18*, 297-316.

Marín, G., Sabogal, F., Marín, B. V., Otero-Sabogal, R., & Perez-Stable, E. J. (1987). Development of a short acculturation scale for Hispanics. *Hispanic Journal of Behavioral Sciences, 9*, 183-205.

Martinez, R., Norman, R. D., & Delaney, H. D. (1984). A children's Hispanic background scale. *Hispanic Journal of Behavioral Sciences, 6*, 103-112.

Mendoza, R. H. (1984). Acculturation and sociocultural variability. In J. L. Martinez, Jr., & R. H. Mendoza (Eds.), *Chicano psychology* (2nd ed., pp. 61-74). New York: Academic Press.

Mendoza, R. H. (1989). An empirical scale to measure type and degree of acculturation in Mexican-American adolescents and adults. *Journal of Cross-Cultural Psychology, 20*, 372-385.

Mendoza, R. II., & Martinez, J. L. (1981). The measurement of acculturation. In A. Baron, Jr. (Ed.), *Explorations in Chicano psychology* (pp. 71-82). New York: Praeger.

Montgomery, G. T. (1992). Comfort with acculturation status among students from south Texas. *Hispanic Journal of Behavioral Sciences, 14*, 201-223.

Montgomery, G. T., & Orozco, S. (1984). Validation of a measure of acculturation for Mexican Americans. *Hispanic Journal of Behavioral Sciences, 6*, 53-63.

Moyerman, D. R., & Forman, B. D. (1992). Acculturation and adjustment: A meta-analytic study. *Hispanic Journal of Behavioral Sciences, 14*, 163-200.

Norris, A. E., Ford, K., & Bova, C. A. (1996). Psychometrics of a brief acculturation scale for Hispanics in a probability sample of urban Hispanic adolescents and young adults. *Hispanic Journal of Behavioral Sciences, 18*, 29-38.

Olmedo, E. L., Martinez, J. L., Jr., & Martinez, S. R. (1978). Measure of acculturation for Chicano adolescents. *Psychological Reports, 42*, 159-170.

Olmedo, E. L., & Padilla, A. M. (1978). Empirical and construct validation of a measure of acculturation for Mexican Americans. *Journal of Social Psychology, 105*, 179-187.

Padilla, A. M. (1980). The role of cultural awareness and ethnic loyalty in acculturation. In A. M. Padilla (Ed.), *Acculturation: Theory, models, and some new findings* (pp. 47-84). Boulder, CO: Westview.

Pomales, J., & Williams, V. (1989). Effects of level of acculturation and counseling style on Hispanic students' perceptions of counselor. *Journal of Counseling Psychology, 36*, 79-83.

Ponterotto, J. G., Baluch, S., & Carielli, D. (1998). The Suinn-Lew Asian Self-Identity Acculturation Scale (SL-ASIA): Critique and research recommendations. *Measurement and Evaluation in Counseling and Development, 31*, 109-124.

Ramirez, A. G., Cousins, J. H., Santos, Y., & Supik, J. D. (1986). A media-based acculturation scale for Mexican-Americans: Application to public health education programs. *Family and Community Health, 9*, 63-71.

Ramirez, M., III (1984). Assessing and understanding biculturalism-multiculturalism in Mexican-American adults. In J. L. Martinez, Jr., & R. H. Mendoza (Eds.), *Chicano psychology* (2nd ed., pp. 77-93). New York: Academic Press.

Redfield, R., Linton, R., & Herskovits, M. J. (1936). Memorandum on the study of acculturation. *American Anthropologist, 56*, 973-1002.

Rezentes, W. C. (1993). Na Mea Hawai'i: A Hawaiian acculturation scale. *Psychological Reports, 73*, 383-393.

Rogler, L. H., Cortes, D. E., & Malgady, R. G. (1991). Acculturation and mental health status among Hispanics: Convergence and new directions for research. *American Psychologist, 46*, 585-597.

Ruelas, S. R., Atkinson, D. R., & Ramos-Sanchez, L. (1998). Counselor helping model and participant ethnicity, locus of control, and perceived counselor credibility. *Journal of Counseling Psychology, 45*, 98-103.

Saldana, D. H. (1995). Acculturative stress: Minority status and distress. In A. M. Padilla (Ed.), *Hispanic psychology: Critical issues in theory and research*. Thousand Oaks, CA: Sage.

Snowden, L. R., & Hines, A. M. (1999). A scale to assess African American acculturation. *Journal of Black Psychology, 25*, 36-47.

Sodowsky, G. R., & Maestas, M. V. (2000). Acculturation, ethnic identity, and acculturative stress: Evidence and measurement. In R. Dana (Ed.), *Handbook of cross-cultural and multicultural personality assessment* (pp. 131-172). Mahwah, NJ: Lawrence Erlbaum.

Suinn, R. M., Rickard-Figueroa, K., Lew, S., & Vigil, P. (1987). The Suinn-Lew Asian Self-Identity Acculturation Scale: An initial report. *Educational and Psychological Measurement, 47*, 401-407.

Szapocznik, J., & Kurtines, W. M. (1980). Acculturation, biculturalism, and adjustment among Cuban Americans. In A. M. Padilla (Ed.), *Acculturation: Theory, models and some new findings* (pp. 000-000). Boulder, CO: Westview.

Szapocznik, J., Kurtines, W. M., & Fernandez, T. (1980). Bicultural involvement and adjustment in Hispanic-American youths. *International Journal of Intercultural Relations, 4*, 353-365.

Szapocznik, J., Scopetta, M. A., Kurtines, W., & Aranalde, M. A. (1978). Theory and measurement of acculturation. *Interamerican Journal of Psychology, 12*, 113-120.

Triandis, H. C., Kashima, Y., Hui, C. H., Lisansky, J., & Marín, G. (1982). Acculturation and biculturalism indices among relatively acculturated Hispanic young adults. *Interamerican Journal of Psychology, 16*, 140-149.

U.S. Bureau of the Census. (1990). *Statistical abstract of the United States: 1990* (110th ed.). Washington, DC: Government Printing Office.

Vega, W. A., & Rumbaut, R. G. (1991). Ethnic minorities and mental health. *Annual Review of Sociology, 17*, 351-383.

Wong-Rieger, D., & Quintana, D. (1987). Comparative acculturation of southeast Asian and Hispanic immigrants and sojourners. *Journal of Cross-Cultural Psychology, 18*, 345-362.

Yao, E. L. (1979). The assimilation of contemporary Chinese immigrants. *Journal of Psychology, 101*, 107-113.

Correspondence regarding this chapter may be sent to Bryan S. K. Kim, Department of Psychology, University of Maryland, College Park, MD 20742-4411 (e-mail address: bkim@psyc.umd.edu).

Chapter 23

WORLDVIEW

Recent Developments and Needed Directions

FARAH A. IBRAHIM

GARGI ROYSIRCAR-SODOWSKY

HIFUMI OHNISHI

HISTORY OF WORLDVIEW IN COUNSELING AND PSYCHOTHERAPY

Grieger and Ponterrotto (1995) note that worldview is one of the most popular constructs in the multicultural counseling literature. This construct was first proposed by Sue (1978) with the use of two cognitive constructs, Locus of Control (Rotter, 1966) and Locus of Responsibility (Jones et al., 1972). Ibrahim (1984) conceptualized worldview from the perspective of beliefs, values, and assumptions that are derived from a cultural context. She based her construct on an existential values model (Kluckhohn, 1951, 1956; Kluckhohn & Strodtbeck, 1961) proposed for anthropological studies in the United States. In collaboration with Kahn, Ibrahim developed the Scale to Assess Worldview© (Ibrahim & Kahn, 1984, 1987) to provide a measure for her proposed worldview construct, in an effort to use the construct in an applied manner in cross-cultural and multicultural transactions. Ibrahim (1991) notes that worldview assessment can be done for an individual, a family, a social group, or a nation or society. Dana (1993) further expanded on Ibrahim's concept of worldview to include group identity, individual identity or self-concept, values, beliefs, and language, as worldview pertains to the client's perceptions of counseling services, service providers, and service delivery. The constructs delineated by Sue, Ibrahim, and

Dana, respectively, provide a blueprint for effective multicultural counseling and psychotherapy.

Knowledge and assessment of worldview, as it relates to both the client and the counselor, have been included in the multicultural competency statement issued by the Association for Multicultural Counseling and Development (AMCD) and the American Counseling Association (ACA) in 1991 (Sue, Arredondo, & McDavis, 1992). Effective multicultural training incorporates assessment and understanding of both client and counselor worldviews. Although the term worldview has been used widely in the understanding of between-group and within-group differences, its specific meaning or assessment may not mean the same to all involved in using the term, for example, as used by Fisher, Jome, and Atkinson (1998) and Claiborn (1986). Differences are also noted in the respective conceptualizations of worldview by Sue (1978), Ibrahim (1984), and Dana (1993). Our writing will focus on discussing the implications for the assessment of the construct of worldview and its use in counseling and psychotherapy, not only for between-group comparisons but also for within-group variations.

HISTORY OF DIAGNOSIS IN COUNSELING AND PSYCHOTHERAPY

Diagnosis in counseling and psychotherapy has been a significant concern and a difficult issue within cultures and is a major concern between cultures, especially when people from one social-cultural context diagnose individuals from social-cultural contexts they are not educated about or familiar with (Castillo, 1997; Lonner & Ibrahim, 1996). Diagnosis is further complicated if the professional is unaware of cultural assumptions that are the socializing forces for people within a culture, and how wellness, mental health, and illness are defined culturally. Worldview, as conceptualized by Ibrahim, can be a key variable in understanding a client's cultural assumptions and how they influence his or her cognitive structures and affective structures and reactions. Worldview is the mediating variable that provides an explanatory principle used by the mental health professional in defining a problem and its severity that confront the client (Ibrahim, 1991, 1999). Clarification of worldview highlights the meaning of the presenting problem for the client and assists the counselor or therapist in understanding the meaning and the implications of the problem for the client and the processes to be used in the resolution of the problem.

Counseling and psychotherapy in the United States have their roots both in European cultures from which evolved the psychodymanic movement and in the reinforcement theories of American behaviorism. Counseling is influenced by Western cultures, and this has implications for treatment at the global level as we confront a world that is rapidly shrinking and transforming due to advances in Information Age technology. Torrey (1986) notes that healing systems have existed in all societies of the world. In addition, Marsella and White (1982) state that all systems of healing are basically derived from theories of learning (these principles are common to all cultures) advocated by modern psychology. Considering this perspective, it is clear that all theories of counseling have within them psychological concepts and healing methods that have some relevance and meaning for most cultures. However, applying these theories without identifying and understanding the client's cultural group and the specific client's beliefs, values, and assumptions is tantamount to cultural malpractice. In addition, given the history of colonialization, most cultures of the world emulate Western models of healing and treatment. In an attempt to make these systems of health services culturally sensitive and appropriate to the client and his or her setting, it is critical that the client's beliefs, values, and assumptions that guide the client's cognitive structures and behaviors are clarified to provide assistance within the client's context and world. Clarification of worldview can provide one way of making the counseling process useful and ethical. Knowledge of worldview can assist in all phases of counseling and psychotherapy, from diagnosis to treatment planning and execution to evaluation of the usefulness of the intervention by keeping the whole process within the client's belief and value perspective. Other variables to consider that interface with worldview, when providing ethical services in a multicultural setting, are the client's cultural identity, social context (societal norms, educational level, social class), gender, religion, life stage, sexual orientation, age, linguistic status, and ability and disability status (Ibrahim, 1991, 1999a). Thus, we are proposing that worldview interacts with all client variables and, consequently, must be addressed in the conceptualization of diagnosis, presenting problem, and treatment in multicultural and cross-cultural counseling.

Castillo (1977) highlighted the developmental history of the diagnostic process in the mental health field. He chronicled the earlier history of *Diagnostic and Statistical Manual (DSM)*, noting that this manual is not culture free and is based in a specific cultural and intellectual tradition. *DSM–I* (American Psychiatric Association, 1952) is a variation of *International Classification of Diseases (ICD)* (World Health Organization, 1948) and had its roots in a biopsychosocial model of mental health (Castillo, 1977). According to Castillo, *DSM–I* was etiological in structure; that is, diagnostic categories were "defined based on the assumed causes of the disorders rather than their symptoms" (p. 7). Mental illness was conceived of on a continuum of pathology and was presumed to be the result of trauma. Counseling and therapy were directed to undoing the pathogenic causes of the problem, instead of treating the symptoms or the biomedical issues underlying the disease. *DSM–II* (American Psychiatric Association, 1968) moved away from psychological and social etiological factors to biomedical factors. This, according to Castillo, was the beginning of the paradigm shift. This shift led to changes in the psychiatric field that started to focus on disease-centered psychiatry.

DSM–III (American Psychiatric Association, 1980) represented a paradigm shift to a disease-centered model (Dana, 1998). This version did not allow for any problems as a result of psychological trauma or other forms of adaptation to the environment. *DSM–IV* (American Psychiatric Association, 1994), although committed to the disease model, signaled another shift to an acceptance of other factors that may be functioning in the client's world and may influence the problems confronted by the client (Dana, 1998). *DSM–IV* may be more client centered in its approach. Using the framework of culture-bound syndromes, *DSM–IV* allows for accepting the cognitive framework a client uses to understand his or her experiences and identifies these cognitions and experiences as culturally and socially defined (Castillo, 1977; Roysircar-Sodowsky & Kuo, 2000). The critical element in this historical development is the recognition and acceptance that the problem confronted by the client has meaning in a cultural and social context along with the client's understanding of the problem. Thus, *DSM–IV* encourages counselors and therapists to assess clients extensively on Axis 4, which allows the assessment of psychosocial factors related to the presenting problem, and to formulate treatment on the basis of these Axis 4 factors (Roysircar-Sodowsky & Kuo, 2000). Current research on mental health suggests that health and ill health cannot be viewed in a vacuum (Ibrahim & Ohnishi, 2001). The problems or symptoms experienced by the client must be understood within the client's cultural and social world along with the client's understanding of the problem. This supports the stance taken by multicultural psychologists and counselors over the past 30 years (Jackson, 1995). Dana (1998) acknowledges that *DSM–IV* and its movement toward viewing the client in a cultural context is positive; however, he believes that *DSM–IV* is insufficient for the therapist to provide ethical and culturally sensitive diagnosis and therapeutic interventions to clients. Therefore, multicultural counseling psychology trainers are providing guidelines for culturally based clinical assessment (Ibrahim, 1993a, 1999a, 1999b; Roysircar-Sodowsky & Kuo, 2000).

Castillo (1977) proposed that a cultural assessment is essential because of the role and impact of culture in structuring a clinical problem. He also noted that mental disorders are far too complex and cannot be explained away from a disease model. He added that the "psychic unity of humankind" (p. 55) that was previously the underlying premise of the disease model was no longer valid and that it is inappropriate to take a universal approach to assessment, diagnosis, and treatment. Cultural assumptive schemas shape individual and group realities in terms of experiences, emotions, and behaviors. These schemas, we propose, must be systematically incorporated into the counseling and psychotherapy process for it to be culturally sensitive and meaningful to the client. To provide a sound and culturally relevant diagnosis and treatment, the first step should include a multimethod assessment that includes beliefs, values, assumptions, and worldview (for detailed recommendations, see Berry, Poortinga, Segall, & Dasen, 1992; Dana, 1998; Grieger & Ponterotto, 1995; Ibrahim, 1999a; Ibrahim, Ohnishi, & Wilson, 1994; Lonner & Ibrahim, 1996; Roysircar-Sodowsky & Kuo, 2000; Sodowsky & Johnson, 1994; Sodowsky, Kuo-Jackson, & Loya, 1996).

ASSESSMENT OF WORLDVIEW

Worldview pertains to the lenses we wear to see the world (Ivey, Ivey, & Simek-Morgan (1997). It represents our beliefs, values, and assumptions about people, relationships, nature, time, and activity in our world (Ibrahim & Kahn, 1987; Ibrahim & Owen, 1994). Multicultural counseling researchers and professionals emphasize that accurate assessment of worldview is a necessary step in understanding the client's frame of reference for the therapy process (Carter, 1991; Dana, 1993; Grieger & Ponterotto, 1995; Ibrahim, 1991; Ibrahim, Ohnishi, & Wilson, 1994; Sue & Zane, 1987). Worldview also provides the information on the client's and the professional's subjective reality (Ibrahim, 1985). This information is critical in expanding the professional's knowledge base and in developing meaningful skills that can assist in developing a culturally sensitive and humanistic intervention (Hickson, Christie, & Shmukler, 1990). Sadlak and Ibrahim (1986) and Cunningham-Warburton (1988) found that when a shared frame of reference was established between the counselor and the client, using the SAWV instrument, counselor effectiveness and perceived self-efficacy led to successful engagement in counseling. Shared worldview implies finding a common ground in terms of beliefs, values, and assumptions (Ibrahim, 1991). The SAWV can be successfully used as a training tool to enhance cross-cultural counselor effectiveness in dealing with some basic existential dilemmas that people face to cope with life's challenges and questions. The scale can also be used with different cultures to compare groups as well as to compare differences within each cultural group and to gain important information on cross-cultural differences and similarities (Ibrahim & Owen, 1994) (also see section on Recent Worldview Research and Instrumentation). The SAWV addresses some universal concerns of humankind and thus compensates for the deficits of limited, Western-based assessment research (Sue, Ito, & Bradshaw, 1982; Triandis & Brislin, 1984; Triandis, Malpass, & Davison, 1973). The scale also attempts to address a lack of attention to individual differences, a major drawback in the cross-cultural research of the 1970s and 1980s (Atkinson, 1985; Hilliard,

1985; Kwan & Sodowsky, 1997; Kwan, Sodowsky, & Ihle, 1994; Smith, 1977; Sue, 1982).

The SAWV is a 45-item instrument with a Likert-type response format. The scale has adequate reliability and validity (Ibrahim & Kahn, 1987; Ibrahim & Owen, 1994). Ibrahim's (1984) conception of worldview uses Kluckhohn's universal values orientation categories as a base to understanding the beliefs, values, and assumptions inherent in the construct of worldview. Her concept is operationalized by Ibrahim and Kahn (1987) in the SAWV instrument. Recent research with the SAWV (Ibrahim & Owen, 1994) provides four empirically supported worldviews:

1. *Optimistic Worldview.* This worldview is characterized by values in three areas: Human Nature, Activity Orientation, and Relationship With Nature. There is a belief that human nature is essentially good, that human activity must focus on inner and outer development (i.e., spiritual and material), and that there is a need to be in harmony with nature, with an acceptance of the power of nature.

2. *Traditional Worldview.* The emphasis here is on Social Relationships, Time, and Relationship With Nature. Social relationships are defined by accepting that relationships are primarily lineal-hierarchical, with some exceptions for collateral-mutual relationships. Time is mostly future oriented, with some emphasis on the past. There is a belief that humans can subjugate and control nature.

3. *Here-and-Now Worldview.* This worldview reflects assumptions of the value dimensions of Activity and Time. Activity focuses primarily on spontaneity. Time's emphasis is mainly on present time, with some attention to the past.

4. *Pessimistic Worldview.* This perspective reflects assumptions from three value areas: Human Nature, Social Relationship, and Relationship With Nature. Human nature is considered primarily bad, with some allowance made for a combination of good and bad qualities. There is an acceptance of the power of nature. The preferred relationship orientation is collateral-mutual.

Discussion on the use of the SAWV as an assessment measure and the meaning of the results can be found in Ibrahim and Kahn (1987), Ibrahim (1991, 1993a, 1999a), and Ibrahim, Ohnishi, and Wilson (1994). In addition, the SAWV can be used qualitatively to help identify beliefs, values, and assumptions that undergird a client's cognitions, feelings, and behavior. Using the instrument qualitatively in an interview format would be useful for individuals who are not able to take pencil-and-paper tests, such as the linguistically different, people with disabilities, and people who prefer a more informal approach in counseling versus people who are structured and seek a formal diagnostic profile. This approach would ensure that the cultural dimension of basic beliefs and assumptions has not been overlooked either in the diagnostic or therapeutic process (Ibrahim, Ohnishi, & Wilson, 1994).

RECENT WORLDVIEW
RESEARCH AND INSTRUMENTATION

This section reviews studies that have used worldview as a construct from 1985 to recent times. There are four objectives for this review. First, studies that address worldview from the Clyde Kluckhohn (1951, 1956) and the Kluckhohn and Strodtbeck (1961) paradigm are presented. Second, studies are discussed that investigate other value-based assumptions that are used as explanatory principles by people. Third, there is a focus on studies that have included race, nationality, socioeconomic, and gender variables. Fourth, we present both a cross-cultural focus (interest in different societies around the world) and a multicultural focus (interest in American racial and minority groups and their resultant experience of oppressed status). We refer the reader to the following tables that appear further on in the chapter: Table 23.1 for a summary of the reviewed studies and Table 23.2 for information on worldview instruments that were used in studies referenced in this writing. While ours is not an exhaustive review, we have made an attempt to select studies and instruments that represent our four stated objectives.

EXISTENTIAL VALUES ORIENTATION

Studies based on the Kluckhohn and Strodtbeck model of existential values orientation represent the majority of the studies reviewed here. Instrumentation in these studies were predominantly the Intercultural Values Inventory (IVI: Kohls, Carter, & Helms, cited in Carter, 1990; Carter & Helms, 1990) and the Scale to Assess Worldviews (SAWV: Ibrahim & Kahn, 1984, 1987; Ibrahim & Owen, 1994). Two studies (Carter, 1990; Carter & Parks, 1992) used the IVI. The SAWV was used in 15 studies (Berkow, Richmond, & Page, 1994; Cheng, O'Leary, & Page, 1995; Chu-Richardson, 1988; D'Rozario, 1996; Gerber, 1998; Gordon, 1997; Hansman, Grant, & Jackson, 1999; Hickson, Christie, & Schmukler, 1990; Ibrahim, Freitas, & Owen, 1993; Lo, 1996; Lockney, 1999; Ngumba, 1996; Sodowsky, Maguire, Johnson, Ngumba, & Kohles, 1994; Thompson, 1977; Toczyska, 1996). Three additional studies used the SAWV–Short Form, which reduces the original rationally/judgmentally derived five values orientations with 15 subscales into two dominant factors (Ihle & Roysircar-Sodowsky, in press; Ihle, Sodowsky, & Kwan, 1996; Kwan, Sodowsky, & Ihle, 1994). One study (Betancourt, Hardin, & Manzi, 1992) distilled constructs from the Kluckhohn and Strodtbeck model and presented them in vignettes. The Betancourt et al. study, Kwan et al. study, and the Ihle and Sodowsky studies focused more on within-group differences, whereas the other studies focused more on differences between cultural, nationality, or racial groups. Finally, one study (Cooke, Klopf, & Ishii, 1991) looked into differences between Eastern and Western perspectives for Japanese and American participants. These studies are presented under major themes that we developed from our understanding of the studies.

Differences Between Racial, Ethnic, and Nationality Groups

Carter (1990) and Carter and Parks (1992) showed differences between Anglo Americans and African Americans, and among "second-generation European Americans," respectively. The participants in Carter and Parks's (1992) study self-assigned their White ethnicity as Polish, German, Irish, Italian, Mixed European, and American. Participants who designated themselves "American" believed that they were Americans culturally. Thus, Carter and Parks raised the question of shared values among Americans, suggesting that while individuals living in the United States may represent diverse ethnic groups they hold shared values that describe "American-ness." However, more representative sampling may be needed to determine consistent values associated with a multicultural U.S. society. As the body of empirical literature continues to grow, studies that focus on isolating elements of the American worldview will become important. Given the implications across studies that many societies differ from Americans in their respective worldviews (see Table 23.1 for differences shown between White Americans and other cultural groups), many of the studies were conducted as a point of contrast with White American value assumptions or to imply the influence of Western societies or of modernization on people of developing nations.

Cheng et al. (1995) investigated value differences among Irish, American, and Taiwanese counseling students in Ireland, the United States, and Taiwan, respectively. The Taiwanese counselor trainees, who answered the SAWV in English, endorsed a greater number of value orientations than the American and Irish counselor trainees, and these values were significantly different from those of their Western counterparts. Similarly, Berkow, Richmond, and Page (1994) measured significant value differences between American and Fijian counseling students and between male and female trainees.

Sodowsky et al. (1994) compared values orientation of graduate students composed of mainland Chinese, Taiwanese, Africans from West and East Africa, and White Americans all attending a midwestern U.S. university. Traditional worldviews of the international students' respective original cultures (mainland China, Taiwan, and sub-Saharan Africa) were examined as points of comparison with these international students' self-reported contemporary worldviews. The international students indicated some values that seemed different from those espoused by their respective traditional belief systems. The mainland Chinese and Taiwanese

(text continues on page 438)

TABLE 23.1 Authors, Sample Sizes, Dependent Variables (DVs), and Findings on Worldview/Orientations

---

Existential Values Orientation

1. Carter (1990)

Ns: 799: 293 African Americans and 506 White American college students

DV(s):   Intercultural Values Inventory (IVI); Kohls, Carter, & Helms, as cited in Carter, 1984)

Findings: Significant differences between Whites and African Americans:
1. *Human Nature* (Evil): African Americans > Whites
2. *Person/Nature* (Subjugation): African Americans > Whites
3. *Time* (Past): African Americans > Whites
4. *Activity* (Being-in-becoming): African Americans > Whites; (Being): Whites > African Americans
5. *Social Relations* (Lineal): African Americans > Whites; (Collateral): Whites > African Americans; (Individualistic): Whites > African Americans

2. Sodowsky, Maguire, Johnson, Ngumba, and Kohles (1994)

Ns: 224 graduate students: 106 White Americans, 58 mainland Chinese, 20 Taiwanese, and 40 Africans from West and East Africa (SubSahara region)

DV(s):   Scale to Assess Worldviews (SAWV; Ibrahim & Kahn, 1987)

Findings: Significant differences found among nationality groups:
1. *Human Nature* (Evil): Chinese, Taiwanese, Africans > Whites
2. *Human Relationships* (Lineal): Chinese, Taiwanese, Africans > Whites; Taiwanese, Africans > Chinese; (Collateral-mutual): Chinese, Taiwanese, Africans > Whites; (Individualistic): Whites > Chinese, Taiwanese, Afrieans; Chinese > Taiwanese, Africans
3. *Relationship to Nature* (Control of Nature): Chinese, Taiwanese, Africans > Whites; Chinese > Africans
4. *Time Orientation* (Past): Africans > Whites, Chinese, Taiwanese; (Prcscnt): Africans > Whites; Chinese > Whites, Taiwanese. (Future): Chinese, Taiwanese > Whites and Africans
5. *Activity Orientation* (Being): Whites > Africans; (Doing): Chinese, Taiwanese, Africans > Whites

3. Ngumba (1996)

Ns: 220 university students: 75 students of African nationalities, 61 African Americans, and 84 White Americans

DV(s):   SAWV, Student Adaptation to College Questionnaire; African Self-Consciousness Scale

Findings: 1. a. *Human Nature* (Evil): Africans > Whites; African Americans > Whites; (Good): Whites > African Americans; African Americans > Africans; (Good-Bad): Africans > African Americans, Whites
       b. *Human Relationships:* (Lineal) Africans > Whites; (Collateral-Mutual): Africans, African Americans > Whites
       c. *Time* (Past): Africans > Whites; (Future): African Americans > Whites
2. Gender differences: *Human Nature* (Good); *Human Relationships* (CollateralMutual), (Lineal); *Activity* (Being-in-Becoming)
3. Academic adjustment related to: *Human Nature* (Evil); *Social Relations* (Individualistic); Time (Present)
4. African Self-Consciousness: Africans > African Americans
5. Academic Adjustment: Whites > Africans; African Americans > Africans

---

(continued)

TABLE 23.1 (Continued)

4. Berkow, Richmond, and Page (1994)
Ns: 213 counseling students: 104 Fijians and 109 Americans
DV(s):   SAWV
Findings: 1. *Nature* (Harmony with Nature): female Fijians > male Fijians, male
           Americans, female Americans; Fijian groups > Americans
           2. *Human Relationships* (Lineal): Fijians > Americans; (Collateral-Mutual):
           Fijians > Americans
           3. *Time* (Past): Fijians > Americans
           4. *Time* (Future): Fijians > Americans

5. Cheng, O'Leary, and Page (1995)
Ns: 130 counseling students: 64 Americans, 37 Chinese, and 29 Irish
DV(s):   SAWV
Findings: 1. *Human Nature* (Evil): Chinese > Irish, Americans; (Good-Bad): Chinese >
           Irish, American; (Good): Irish > Americans, Chinese
           2. *Human Relationship* (Lineal): Chinese > Americans > Irish; (Individual-
           istic): Chinese > Irish, Americans
           3. *Relationship with Nature* (Harmony): Chinese > Americans; (Subjugating):
           Chinese > Irish, Americans
           4. *Time* (Past): Chinese > Americans > Irish; (Present): Americans < Chinese,
           Irish; (Future): Chinese > Americans > Irish
           5. *Activity* (Doing): Chinese, Americans > Irish; (Being): female > male

6. Hickson, Christie, and Shmukler (1990)
Ns: 200: 100 White and 100 Black South African (SAF) adolescent students
DV(s):   SAWV
Findings: 1. *Human Nature* (Evil): Black South African > White; (Good): White >
           Black South African
           2. *Human Relationships:* (Lineal, collateral-mutual, individualistic): Black
           South African > White
           3. *Relationship with Nature* (Control): Black > White
           4. *Time* (Past, Future): Black > White
           5. *Activity* (Being): White > Black
           6. Significant *F* values reported for race, age, and sex:

Race:	Human Nature (Evil, Good); Human Relationships (Lineal, Collateral-Mutual); Relationship with Nature (Control); Time (Past, Future)
Age:	Human Nature (Evil, Good)
Sex:	Human Relationship (Lineal, Individualistic); Relationship with Nature (Harmony); Time (Future)
Race × Sex:	Human Nature (Evil): Human Relationship (Individualistic)
Age × Sex:	Human Nature (Good-Evil); Human Relationship (Lineal); Time (Present); Activity (Being-in-Becoming)
Race × Age Sex:	Human Nature (Evil); Human Relationship (Lineal, Individualistic); Time (Present)

7. Carter and Parks (1992)
Ns: 434 White American students: 67 Polish, 136 Germans, 59 Irish, 43 Italian,
           65 Mixed Europeans, and 64 "Americans"
DV(s):   Intercultural Values Inventory
Findings: 1. Significant difference for SES
           2. Significant differences between Germans, Irish, Americans, Polish,
           Italians, Mixed Europeans
           a. *Lineal, Past, Harmony with Nature:* Irish > other groups
           b. *Present, Doing, Being:* Americans, Polish, Germans > Italians, Irish,
           Mixed Europeans who generally endorsed the good-evil human nature
           and the harmony person-nature orientation

TABLE 23.1 (Continued)

---

8. Ihle, Sodowsky, and Kwan (1996)
   Ns: 180 women: 47 White American clients, 66 White American counselors,
             and 67 Chinese international students
   DV(s):   Modified SAWV factored-analyzed to two scales (SAWV-Short Form,
             Sodowsky, as reported by Ihle et al., 1996)
   Findings: 1. *Endeavoring Self:* White American clients > White American counselors;
               Chinese > White American counselors; Taiwanese > mainland Chinese
           2. *Harmonizing Self:* Chinese < White American counselors

9. Ihle and Roysircar-Sodowsky (in press)
   Ns: 210 clients and counselors (105 counselor-client dyads)
   IV(s):   SAWV-Short Form; Organicism Paradigm Inventory (worldview); Masculine
             gender role and Feminine gender role
   DV(s):   Nurturant Counseling Role Expectancy-Client, Counselor; Self-Reliant
             Counseling Role Expectancy-Client, Counselor
   Findings: 1. Clients: *Harmonizing* negatively correlated with *Nurturant* Role Expec-
               tancy; *Endeavoring* positively correlated with *Nurturant* and *Self-Reliant*
               Role Expectancies; *Harmonizing* and *Endeavoring* each significantly pre-
               dicted *Nurturant* Expectancy; *Endeavoring* significantly predicted *Self-
               Reliant* Expectancy
           2. *Counselors: Organicism* worldview correlated with *Masculine* Gender
               Role and *Feminine* Gender Role; *Endeavoring* correlated with *Masculine*
               Gender Role and negatively correlated with *Feminine* Gender Role;
               Organicism: Counselors > clients
           3. Negative Pearson correlations of client-counselor difference scores on
               Organicism and *Harmonizing* indicated that many clients had lower
               scores and many counselors had higher scores on these two worldview
               orientations

10. Kwan, Sodowsky, and Ihle (1994)
   Ns: 221 Chinese International students: 171 mainland Chinese, 44 Taiwan, and
             16 Hong Kong
   DV(s):   SAWV-Short Form: Endeavoring Self (ES) and Harmonizing Self (HS)
   Findings: *ES:* Chinese and Taiwanese > Hong Kong; Individual differences: ES (84.71%
           of respondents) > HS (15.79% of respondents)

11. Furn (1986)
   Ns: 378 American college students
   DV(s):   SAWV
   Findings: Gender differences
           1. *Human Nature* (Good or Evil): Female > Male
           2. *Social Relationships* (Lineal-Hierarchical): Female > Male
           3. *Activity Orientations* (Being or Being-in-Becoming): Female > Male
           4. *Nature* (Subjugation and Control of Nature): Male > Female
           5. *Time* (Present): Male > Female

12. D'Rozario (1996)
   Ns: 103 Singaporean international and 108 U.S. college students
   DV(s):   SAWV, Expectations about Counseling-Brief Form, Counselor Effectiveness
             Rating Scale
   Findings: Nationality and gender differences
           1. *Worldview* (Optimistic): Singaporean = Americans; (Traditional) Male >
               Female
           2. *Human Nature* (Bad): Singaporean > Americans; Male > Female
           3. *Social Relationships* (Lineal-Hierarchical): Singaporean > Americans;
               (Lineality and Individualism) Male > Female
           4. *Activity Orientations* (Being-in-Becoming): Americans > Singaporean
           5. *Expectations of personal commitment to counseling:* Americans >
               Singaporean

(continued)

TABLE 23.1 (Continued)

      6. *Expectations of directive, empathic, and self-disclosing counseling styles* : Singaporeans > Americans; Male > Female
      7. *Motivation toward counseling:* Female > Male

13. Thompson (1997)
Ns: 35 interethnic couples
DV(s):   SAWV, Battery of Interpersonal Capabilities, Dyadic Adjustment Scale
Findings: Marriage satisfaction predicted by:
      1. *Worldview* (Traditional): Wife = Husband
      2. *Interpersonal Flexibility* Wife/Husband

14. Gordon (1997)
Ns: 99 deaf adolescents
IV(s):   Deaf cultural identity (Deaf Cultural Identity Scales), gender
DV(s):   SAWV, Semantic Differential Scales
Findings: Cultural identity and gender differences:
      1. *Positive evaluation of self, present time orientation:* bicultural identity > Other Identities
      2. *Higher levels of self-esteem, human activity* (Being-in-Becoming): Bicultural identity > Other Identities
      3. *Potency of sense of self, present time orientation, positive relationships with others:* Male > Female

15. Boatswain (1997)
Ns: 88 African American and Afro-Caribbean managers and higher level professionals
IV: SAWV
DV: Minnesota Job Satisfaction Questionnaire
Findings: Job satisfaction differences:
      1. *Human Relations* and *Activity Orientation* discrepancy among staff/ Job Satisfaction

16. Betancourt, Hardin, and Manzi (1992)
Ns: Experiment 1: 79 students
        Experiment 2: 126 students
DV(s):   Vignettes designed from Kluckhohn and Strodtbeck model of cultural variations (control v. subjugation of nature); attribution values; helping perspectives
Findings: <u>Experiment 1</u>
      1. > Control oriented > perceived controllability of causal attributions of *successful* outcomes in social settings; > subjugation-oriented < perceived controllability of causal attributions; > control-oriented > perceived controllability concerning failure in achievement events
      2. > Control-oriented related to (+) feelings toward actor in success situations > (+) feelings of subjugation-oriented participants
      3. > Control-oriented related to (-) feelings toward actor in failure situation > subjugation-oriented participants' (+) feelings toward failing actor
      <u>Experiment 2</u>
      1. > Control: objectivity equals to > help; empathy equals to < help; > subjugation: empathy equals to > help; objectivity equals to < help

17. Cooke, Klopf, and Ishii (1991)
Ns: 403: 240 Japanese and 163 Americans
DV(s):   "Eastern Thought" (ET)—Questionnaire to Measure Eastern and Western Thought
Findings: 1. *ET:* Japanese > Americans
      2. By gender between cultures: *ET:* Japanese > American
      3. By gender within culture: *ET:* American females > American males
      4. Non-significance for Japanese females v. males: *ET.*

TABLE 23.1 (Continued)

Other Explanatory Principles

18. Frey and Roysircar-Sodowsky (in press)

Ns: 268: 125 White American and 143 South, Southeast, and Central American international graduate students

IV(s):   Modified Polarity Scale (Normative and Humanist Worldviews); American-International Relations (Acculturation; Perceived Prejudice) Dissociative Experiences Adapted Scale

Findings: 1. *Normative:* International > White
2. *Humanist:* International > White
3. *Whites: Acculturation* significantly correlated with *Normative* and *Humanist.*
4. *International: Perceived Prejudice* significantly correlated with *Normative* and *Humanist; Normative* significantly predicted ratings of dissociative experiences

19. Bowman (1996)

Ns: 186: 81 Native American Indians and 105 Anglo Americans

DV(s):   Sense of Coherence

Findings: 1. SOC (-) correlated with depression ($r = -.49$, Native Americans; $r = -.66$, Anglo Americans)
2. Anxiety ($r = -.43$, Native American Indians; $r = -.64$, Anglo Americans)
3. Physical symptoms scores ($r = -.29$, Native Americans; $r = -.41$, Anglo Americans)

20. Potash, Crespo, Patel, and Ceravolo (1990)

Ns: 99 students: 39 Americans and 69 Brazilians

DV(s):   Sentence Completion Test

Findings: 1. *Positive Work Ethic:* Americans > Brazilians
2. *Positive Attitude About Future:* Americans > Brazilians
3. *Positive Attitudes About Interracial Marriages:* Brazilians > Americans
4. *Positive Attitudes Toward Sex:* Brazilian women > American women

Justice Beliefs

21. Furnham (1993)

Ns: 1,659 psychology students from 12 countries

DV(s):   Just World Beliefs (JWB); gross domestic product (GDP) of a country
Unjust World Belief (UJWB); power distance norms; individualism; gender

Findings: 1. *Rank-orderings of countries by JWB and UJWB,* India = #1: JWB, UJWB; Israel = #12: JWB, UJWB
2. *Gender differences:* Israel: males > females (JWB). Zimbabwe: females > males (JWB). America, Israel, South Africa: males > females (UJWB)
3. *Significant correlations:* JWB and power distance, $r = .75$; UJWB and GDP, $r = .84$; JWB and UJWB not significantly correlated

22. Dalbert and Yamauchi (1994)

Ns: 232: 171 Hawaiian and 61 German university students

DV(s):   Belief in a Just World Scale; Justice Judgment in Hawaii; Justice Judgment in Germany

Findings: 1. *Just worldview:* Hawaiians > Germans
2. *Germans:* Justice Judgments and Just World Beliefs associated with similarities between *father's occupation* and immigrant worker; > Just World Beliefs > Justice Judgments
3. *Age:* > age > just situation for foreign worker > belief in a just world > just situation for German workers
4. *Hawaiians: Age and parents' immigrant status:* younger students of parents who were immigrants > just situation for immigrants

(continued)

TABLE 23.1 (Continued)

5. Nonimmigrant Hawaiian families < just situation for immigrants; > belief in a just world > just situation for immigrants

23. Calhoun and Cann (1994)

Ns: 140 undergraduate students: 73 European Americans, 65 African Americans, and 6 other ethnic groups

DV(s):   World Assumptions Scale; Just World Scale

Findings: 1. *Personal just worldview* > others' just worldview; "benevolent (world)": personal > others; benevolent (self): personal > others
2. *Ethnic group main effects:* "Luck": European Americans > ethnic groups; "Benevolence" (world and of others): European Americans > ethnic groups; "Self-worth": ethnic groups > European Americans

24. Umberson (1993)

Ns: 3,617 Blacks and Whites (mean age = 53.6)

DV(s):   Worldviews (measures of vulnerability (V), justice (J), and personal efficacy (PE)); psychological distress (depression). Interview self-report of worldviews measures

Findings: 1. *Race:* Blacks < Whites (V, PE); Blacks > Whites (J)
2. *Gender:* Women > men (V); women < men (PE, J)
3. *Marital status:* Divorced < married (PE, J)
4. Lower income and education: negatively related to V and J and positively related to PE

participants completed a Chinese translation of the SAWV. Mainland Chinese, Taiwanese, and Africans endorsed similarly several orientations that included Human Nature as "evil," Relationships With People as "lineal-hierarchical" and "collateral-mutual," Relationship With Nature as "control over nature," and Activity orientation as "doing." White Americans were distinguished from these Southeast Asian and African students by their endorsing Relationships With People as "individualistic" and an Activity orientation as "being." Somewhat similar to the Sodowsky et al. findings, Ngumba (1996) showed that international students from the continent of Africa, compared with White students, endorsed Human Nature as evil, Time as past, and Social Relationships as lineal-hierarchical and collateral-mutual. Studying South African White and South African Black students, Hickson, Christie and Schmukler (1990) arrived at similar findings as Sodowsky et al. and Ngumba, showing differences by *race.* In addition, Hickson et al. (1990) indicated that for males, Race × Gender, and Age × Gender were associated with the "lineal-hierarchical" and "individualistic" Social Relationships orientation. South African males, Whites versus Blacks, of a particular age were predisposed to these particular endorsements.

Ibrahim, Freitas, and Owen (1993) compared Americans and Brazilians. The Brazilians' worldview was more Traditional as compared to the Americans' worldview, showing a preference for lineal-hierarchical Social Relationships and a Time focus on the past and the future. The Americans in comparison to the Brazilian sample appeared more spontaneous and modern in their assumptions. Thompson (1997) studied degree of similarity with regard to the Traditional worldview, degree of similarity of interpersonal flexibility, and marital satisfaction in interethnic couples from Hawaii and Southern California. Similarity among interethnic couples on the Traditional worldview and their difference in interpersonal flexibility predicted marital satisfaction. Lockney (1999) studied worldview and acculturation level of Latino/a and White Americans and their perceptions of the other group's worldview. The worldviews of White Americans and Latino/a Americans were significantly different. In addition, highly acculturated Latino/a Americans *were not* similar to White Americans in their worldview. Both groups saw each other in a stereotypic manner.

In Chile, Gerber (1998) studied Roman Catholics of five social classes to test the hypotheses that contextual variables, specifically social class, influences the resolution of psychosocial, developmental identity crises. There were worldview differences by social class. In addition, the closer one's worldview was to Euro-American perspectives, the more positive the resolution was of developmental crises. Lo (1996) examined how worldview is influenced by Westernization and professionalism among professionals in Taiwan. Chinese professionals saw Human Nature as a combination of good and bad, preferred collateral-mutual Social Relationships, believed in living in harmony with nature, and focused on the future and the present. Overall, Chinese professionals favored the Optimistic worldview. Lo (1996) contended that a Western influence was evident in the participants' view of human nature and social relations. Sodowsky et al. (1994) and Kwan et al. (1994) have also commented on the influence of modernization and Western thoughts on the Taiwanese. D'Rozario (1996) focused on Singaporean and U.S. college students' worldview, expectation for counseling, and perceptions of counselor effectiveness based on directive and nondirective counseling styles. There were significant differences in worldview between the two samples. Additionally, based on different worldviews, different expectations for counseling were expressed.

Institutional Settings and Values Orientation

Toczyska (1996) researched the relationship of worldview to the perception of organizational culture among managers and nonmanagers from dominant and nondominant groups in the workplace. The dominant culture (i.e., Whites) indicated a belief in the goodness of Human Nature, in social relations based on Individualism, and in a Relationship With Nature based on harmonious coexistence. Time and Activity dimensions indicated separate subcultures, showing differences between managers and nonmanagers. Gordon (1997) investigated the worldview, self-concept, and cultural identity of deaf adolescents. Cultural identity influenced the ways deaf adolescents evaluated their sense of self together with Time and Activity dimensions. Chu-Richardson (1988) studied worldview, learning style, and locus of control as factors of institutional culture differentiating academically successful and unsuccessful students and faculty. Successful students and the faculty had similar worldview, learning style, and locus of control. Unsuccessful students had divergent worldview, learning styles, and locus of control, lending credence to the argument that the dominant culture in an academic environment may not be tolerant of culturally different students.

Hansman, Grant, and Jackson (1999) studied the implications of student worldview in graduate professional preparation programs. The sample consisted of graduate students mostly within a school of education. The dominant worldview of the sample in descending order was: Optimistic, Traditional, Pessimistic, and Here-and-Now. Although Optimistic was the predominant worldview, analysis by age, gender, and race indicated variations. While males and females ranked their worldviews similarly, males scored higher on all worldviews except Here-and-Now, and females had the highest Pessimistic score. A higher standard deviation was noted for African Americans (6.6) versus European Americans (3.6), suggesting more diversity in African American worldviews. African American scores indicated higher pessimism, less optimism, and higher traditionalism than did European American scores.

Differences Within Cultural Groups

Using the SAWV–Short Form, Kwan et al. (1994) revealed significant differences among Chinese students. The mainland Chinese and Taiwanese students, in comparison to the Hong Kong students, endorsed the Endeavoring Self as an expression of worldview. The Endeavoring Self characterizes a practical, realistic, persistent, and active approach to life. Ihle et al. (1996) investigated differences between White American women counselors and women clients and Chinese international women students, using the above-mentioned SAWV–Short Form. With regard to differences among women, White American clients endorsed the Endeavoring Self moreso than the White American counselors. Chinese women also endorsed the Endeavoring Self higher than White women counselors. Mainland Chinese endorsed the Endeavoring Self more than the Taiwanese. White American counselors endorsed the Harmonizing Self higher than the Chinese. The Harmonizing Self characterizes an expressive approach to life, individualism in one's naturalness, and harmony with personal needs. The similarities of the findings between these two studies (Kwan et al., 1994, and Ihle et al., 1996) revealed that Chinese students endorsed the Endeavoring Self over the Harmonizing Self.

Ihle et al. (1996) also examined age, income, and marital and educational status with regard to within group differences among White American women participants. Lower income and younger age predicted an Endeavoring orientation for White American clients. A Harmonizing orientation was predicted by increased income and education and the married status of women counselors.

In another study, Ihle and Roysircar-Sodowsky (in press) showed that for clients, the majority of whom were White Americans, the Harmonizing worldview negatively predicted their Nurturant Counseling Role Expectancies; their Endeavoring worldview positively predicted both their Nurturant Expectancies and Self-Reliant Counseling Role Expectancies. However, neither worldview, that is, Harmonizing and Endeavoring, predicted the mostly White counselors' counseling role expectancies. For clients, the implication was that while they may come to counseling seeking nurturance, they are independent individuals and survivors who may want to be actively involved in the therapy process. With regard to a third worldview orientation, Organicism, investigated in the study, the counselors had significantly higher organicism scores than the clients. The metaphor for the organismic worldview is the complex organic growth process that underlies the structural development of a phenomenon (Johnson, Germer, Efran, & Overton, 1988; Lyddon & Adamson, 1992). Thus, the counselors were more humanistic in their orientation than their clients.

Other Examples of Existential Values Studies

Betancourt et al. (1992) studied participants' perceptions of "control over nature" versus "subjugation to nature" in relation to vignettes of successes or failures. "Control-oriented" participants attributed greater degrees of controllability of success than "subjugation-oriented" participants. Vignettes of individuals needing help were also presented to measure participants' objective or empathic responses. Control-oriented participants were associated with objective responses of help, whereas subjugation-oriented participants were associated with empathic responses of help.

Worldview has also been conceptualized as Eastern and Western thought. A Western worldview is influenced by Judeo-Christianity that is practiced in Western cultures, and an Eastern worldview is influenced by Hinduism, Buddhism, Taoism, and Confucianism that are practiced in Eastern cultures. The Eastern view is seen as primarily monistic and the Western view as dualistic. The Eastern perspective is concerned with experiences of unity with nature, oneself, and others. The Western view is concerned with individualism, autonomy, and the need to control and survive. These two worldviews represent distinctive existential themes. Cooke,

Klopf, and Ishii (1991) examined Eastern and Western worldviews of American and Japanese undergraduate students. Significant differences were reported between the worldviews of the American and Japanese students and along gender lines. The Americans endorsed Western thought, the Japanese endorsed Eastern thought, and American females revealed a stronger preference for Eastern thought than American males did. No significant differences were reported between Japanese males and females on Eastern or Western worldview. Cooke et al. suggested that worldview is influenced by dominant socialization elements such as the religion and the type of rationality practiced in society and thus manifests itself as a unique worldview presentation.

A summary of some of the previously mentioned studies (specifically, Hickson et al., 1990; Ngumba, 1996; Sodowsky et al., 1994) using the SAWV revealed that African and African American participants consistently endorsed particular orientations with regard to Time (past), Human Nature (evil), and Relationships With People (lineal-hierarchical, collateral-mutual). Similarly, Chinese participants in two studies using the SAWV (Cheng et al., 1995; Sodowsky et al., 1994) endorsed similar orientations with regard to Human Nature (evil), Relationships With People (lineal-hierarchical), Time (future), and Activity (doing). Ibrahim and Owen (1994) define such value orientations as Traditional.

Although group trends were noted, individual differences did exist and findings of each study must be appreciated in the light of their unique settings and outcome. People's relationships with nature and with other people seem to reappear across studies and thus suggest their continued importance. Perhaps of interest is the apparent lack of significant endorsement of values by White participants except for a belief in a relationship orientation of "individualistic" and in an activity orientation of "being." It may remain a task of future studies to narrow down and re-operationalize existential worldview constructs for White participants. It may also be suggested that White Americans tend to be less aware of their values orientation than people from non-White cultures. We also tentatively suggest that White Americans may be guided by Optimism and by changing, contemporary values.

WORLDVIEWS AS OTHER EXPLANATORY PRINCIPLES

Seven studies (Bowman, 1994; Calhoun & Cann, 1994; Dalbert & Yamauchi, 1994; Frey & Roysircar-Sodowsky, 2000; Furnham, 1993; Potash, Crespo, Patel, & Ceravolo, 1990; Umberson, 1993) presented other value-based principles that explain the world and its phenomena for people. These perspectives, taken together, suggest a wider framework of worldview expressions that can distinguish individuals and cultures.

Justice Beliefs

Three studies (Calhoun & Cann, 1994; Dalbert & Yamauchi, 1994; Furnham, 1993) investigated just and unjust world beliefs (JWB and UJWB) (Rubin & Peplau, 1973). With regard to JWB, people share fundamental assumptions about the benevolence and predictability of the world and people's worthiness within it. They tend to view their world in excessively positive ways, despite objective contradictory criteria. The more people believe in a just world, the more they will rationalize inequalities and be less sympathetic and more judgmental toward immigrants and the disadvantaged. Because of these views, JWB and UJWB are linked to socioeconomic and sociopolitical conditions for different societies.

Furnham (1993) investigated JWB and UJWB with psychology students from colleges and universities from 12 countries: Hong Kong, West Germany, United States, South Africa (Whites), Australia, Great Britain, Greece, India, New Zealand, West Indies, Zimbabwe, and Israel. JWB and UJWB were related with "power distance" and individualism. Power distance was described as social norms that define class distinctions based on degrees of equality, entitlement, and superiority or inferiority. JWB was positively related to and UJWB inversely related to gross domestic product (GDP) of each culture, such that higher or lower GDP of a country was believed to predict levels of JWB or UJWB, respectively.

Dalbert and Yamauchi (1994) investigated JWB with Hawaiian and German university students, focusing on between-group attitude differences regarding immigrants in these societies. Participants' parental experiences of immigration influenced participants' perceptions of JWB toward immigrants in their respective societies in Hawaii and Germany. For the German group, if occupational similarities existed between the father's occupation and that of the immigrant, Germans ranked the immigrant's situation as just, and an increase in age was associated with increased perceptions of JWB. These findings were similar to Furnham's (1993) findings that JWB was significantly related to the construct of "power distance." On the other hand, for the Hawaiian group, lower age and immigrant status of participants' parents equated with perceptions of justness for immigrants' conditions. However, generally for both groups, greater belief in a just world was associated with perceptions of justness of immigrants' conditions, regardless of sociodemographic variables.

Calhoun and Cann (1994) studied differences between American majority and minority group members. Comparisons of JWB were made between European Americans and U.S. minority groups. Instruments were modified to include personal pronoun stems to measure perceptions of a participant's personal world as well as the world in general with regard to justness. Belief in a personal just world was associated with beliefs in justness for others. In a related study, Umberson (1993) defined worldview as degrees of personal efficacy, justice, and vulnerability, as these variables were understood along lines of minority and majority status for White American and African American men and women. The study had an interview format. Significant differences were reported between majority and minority members. Female participants had higher vulnerability scores and lower justice and efficacy scores than males. Divorced persons reported lower personal efficacy and justice than married individuals. Increased age was associated with lower levels of vulnerability and increased personal efficacy. Lower income and lower education were negatively associated with lower vulnerability and justice but positively associated with personal efficacy.

Consistency and Conformity

Three studies defined worldview from the perspectives of Sense of Coherence (Bowman, 1996), cross-cultural attitudes (Potash, Crespo, Patel, & Ceravolo, 1990), and Normativism and Humanism (Frey & Roysircar-Sodowsky, in press). Sense of Coherence (SOC) is believed to be a worldview in which individuals expect that problems will be resolved, and life in general is meaningful, understandable, and manageable. Consistency of experience is a determining factor of one's SOC rather than the positive or negative impact (e.g., poverty vs. affluence) of experiences per se. Bowman (1996) studied SOC with Native American Indian and Anglo American college students and showed that levels of socioeconomic status, size of family, and environmental factors were significant for levels of SOC.

Potash et al. (1990) measured worldview differences between Brazilian and American students, using a projective inventory containing sentence stems that referred to sexuality, money, work ethic, authority, interracial marriage, and morality. Brazilians had more positive attitudes about interracial marriages than Americans. Brazilian women reported more positive attitudes about sex than American women.

Normativism parallels the construct of collectivism in that humans are viewed as struggling to meet their potential through conformity to societally set values and norms; Humanism parallels the construct of individualism, in that humans are viewed as active, creative, thinking, desiring, and loving (de St. Aubin, 1996). Frey and Roysircar-Sodowsky (in press) showed that, for White Americans, acculturation was significantly correlated with Normative and Humanist worldviews. However, for international graduate students from South Asia, Southeast Asia, and Central America, their perception of prejudice in U.S. society significantly correlated with Normativism and Humanism, and their Normative scores significantly predicted their rating troubling dissociative experiences as possibly being due to acculturative stress.

In summary, studies that are efforts to understand worldview apart from an existential values orientation model present facets of worldview that are viable and worthy of further study. Constructs, such as organicism as opposed to mechanism, normativism and humanism, just world beliefs, degrees of personal efficacy, justice, and valuability, sense of coherence, and cultural attitudes contribute to an understanding of the diverse sources that shape individual and collective worldviews.

Worldview constructs have been linked with sociodemographic (gender, age, occupation, income) and sociocultural (immigrant status, race, nationality, majority versus minority status, religion) variables. Individuals may present worldviews that are a composite of demographic, socioeconomic, and cultural influences gained from the immediate environment and personal experiences. These influences do not exist in isolation but are potentially influential in shaping the way an individual perceives the world. To have a better understanding of the studies reviewed here, readers need to be informed of the worldview measures that have been referenced. Table 23.2 provides a summary of seven worldview instruments.

WORLDVIEW:
NEEDED DIRECTIONS IN RESEARCH AND PRACTICE

At this juncture, after discussions on clinical and research assessments of worldview, several issues point to future directions regarding the use of the construct of worldview. There is ambiguity in the literature regarding what specifically worldview is and how it can be assessed. The term worldview is widely used to label various constructs, in addition to it being used in a folksy manner in the common vernacular and popular media. The primary issue facing the profession is to arrive at a cohesive understanding of worldview and a standard definition that can be used in professional communications and when doing psychotherapy and assessment. To reiterate, as used in cross-cultural and multicultural counseling, worldview is a set of beliefs, values, and assumptions that undergirds a person's behavior and emotional reactions. It provides an implicit frame of reference for interpretation of the world and its experiences and is derived from one's social and cultural world (including family, primary group, secondary social cultural groups, community, and nation) (Ibrahim, 1984, 1993, 1999a).

It is clear that for counseling and psychotherapy purposes, any operational definition of worldview must be as comprehensive as our definition and address variables that influence attitudes, behavior, decision making, and emotions. Current theories and instruments either have overlapping dimensions, as indicated by this review, or have a completely different understanding of the concept. Particularist models of worldview make it difficult for practitioners to concretely apply the construct in their work. Meta-analytic research could focus on determining the overlap between the different instruments so that identified common themes may be applied qualitatively for clinical assessment. To some extent, our section on Recent Worldview Research and Instrumentation attempted a qualitative

TABLE 23.2 Worldview Instruments Referenced in This Chapter

Instrument:	Intercultural Values Inventory (IVI)
Authors:	Kohls, Carter, and Helms, cited in Carter (1990); Carter and Helms (1990)
Description:	A 150-item self-report based on five Kluckhohn and Strodtbeck existential values orientation of Human Nature, Person-Nature, Time, Activity, and Social Relations; each orientation represented by 3 subscales of 10 items each for a total of 15 subscales; yes-no format with subscale scores ranging from 0 to 10; items on how to live life and rear children; originally developed as a training tool for Americans living abroad
Psychometrics:	Subscale Cronbach's alphas ranging from .54 to .79; Criterion-related validity on differentiation between U.S. racial and White ethnic groups; convergent validity with Black racial identity attitudes (Carter & Helms, 1987)
Instrument:	Scale to Assess Worldviews (SAWV)
Authors:	Ibrahim and Kahn (1987); Ibrahim and Owen (1994)
Description:	A 45-item self-report based on five Kluckhohn and Strodtbeck existential values orientation of Human Nature, People-Relationships, Nature-Relationships, Time, and Activity; each orientation represented by 3 subscales of 3 items each for a total of 15 subscales; 5-point Likert-type scale, from *strongly agree* to *strongly disagree*, with subscale scores ranging from 3 to 15
Psychometrics:	Multidimensional scaling used for instrument development; full scale split-half reliability reported as .95 and .96, and odd-even item reliability reported as .95 and .96; content validity indicated by a minimum of 60% agreement among 20 judges; Lipjhart agreement scores of 501 participants on all 45 items reported as .98; recent conceptualization of four empirically supported worldview dimensions: Optimistic, Traditional, Here-and-Now, and Pessimistic; criterion-related validity on differentiation between ethnic, nationality, racial, age, and gender groups in the U.S. and abroad; convergent validity with attitudes scales.
Instrument:	SAWV-Short Form
Authors:	Sodowsky, as reported in Ihle and Roysircar-Sodowsky (in press); Ihle, Sodowsky, and Kwan (1996); and Kwan, Sodowsky, and Ihle (1994)
Description:	A 20-item self-report based on the Kluckhohn and Strodtbeck existential values orientation; Harmonizing Self takes an expressive approach to life, and Endeavoring Self focuses on present needs and ambitions for the future; each subscale with 10 items; a 6-point Likert-type scale, from "I do not believe at all" to "I believe strongly," with subscale scores ranging from 10 to 60
Psychometrics:	Two factors obtained through exploratory factor analysis of responses to the original SAWV and confirmatory factor analyses on responses to the SAWV Short Form; the two factors' and full-scale Cronbach's alphas reported as .79, .77, and .77, respectively, with interfactor correlation of .15; criterion-related validity on differentiation within the White cultural group and within international groups; convergent validity with scales measuring gender role, another worldview construct, and counseling role expectancies
Instrument:	Organicism-Mechanism Paradigm Inventory
Authors:	Johnson, Germer, Efran, and Overton (1988)

TABLE 23.2 (Continued)

Description:	Distinction made between reality as growth and development (Organicism) and reality as cause and effect (Mechanism); a unidimensional self-report, with 26 forced-choice items, and scores ranging between 0 and 26; a respondent's score is the total number of organismic statements checked; 13 items deal with epistemology, ontology, causality, and change, and 13 items cover pragmatic matters related to conjugal relationships, parenting, occupations, and various interpersonal relationships
Psychometrics:	Guttman split-half reliability of .87 and Cronbach's alpha of .77; Criterion-related validity showing relationships with personality traits, gender role, counselor preference, and client-counselor differences
Instrument:	Modified Polarity Scale (MPS)
Authors:	de St. Aubin (1996); adapted the original Polarity Scale (PS; Tompkins, 1965)
Description:	Distinction made between Humanism, which places priority on individualistic values of equality, open-mindedness, and independence, and Normativism, which places priority on collectivistic values of social recognition, politeness, and self-discipline. The 80-item self-report MPS is a transformation of the original Polarity Scale's 40-paired ipsative items; a 5-point Likert-type scale measuring degrees of agreement to disagreement; 2 subscales with 40 items each and with scores ranging from 0 to 200; one's personal ideology can include both Humanism and Normativism patterns
Psychometrics:	Cronbach's alphas of .78 for Humanism and .81 for Normativism; split-half reliabilities of .66 and .63, respectively; nonsignificant correlation between the 2 subscales; convergent and discriminant validity of the MPS and the PS with social, political, and racist attitudes shown by studies in the United States and abroad
Instrument:	Just World Belief Scale
Authors:	Rubin and Peplau (1973)
Description:	Measures attitudes of benevolence with people and the world, justness of the world despite hardships, possibilities of control, randomness of events, self-worth, and luck; 16-item self-report measuring polar conceptions of just or unjust worldviews; 9 items for just world beliefs, and 7 items for unjust world beliefs
Psychometrics:	Cronbach's alphas ranging from the upper .60s to the upper .70s; inconsistent factor analysis results (Whatley, 1989), and, therefore, total score is typically used
Instrument:	Variations in Value Orientations
Authors:	Kluckhohn and Strodtbeck (1961)
Description:	A 22-item interview that requires the rank ordering of two or three solutions to four values orientations
Psychometrics:	There is no report of reliability. Significant within-culture trends and between culture differences were found. Data were insufficient for an analysis of variations *within* each culture group. Extensive ethnographic data tended to support the findings of the schedule and many of the predicted relationships. For clinical assessment, practitioners may modify the interview, perhaps finding ways to assess degree of valuation and introducing urban-based items as substitutes for rural situations. The comprehensiveness and generality of the value orientations and the possible variations have great potential utility in clinical work

analysis of empirical worldview studies, using a meta-analytic framework. Our initial identification of common themes in worldview research may invite other professionals to pursue the notion of developing a thematic worldview assessment scheme for clinical assessment. The ecological validity of worldview instruments must also be determined prior to their applications in clinical work.

Another critical issue that is emerging in the literature is the concept of immutability or mutability of worldview. Kluckhohn and Strodtbeck (1961) had originally presented the issue of whether value orientations were immutable or mutable. Ibrahim and Kahn (1984, 1987) consider worldview to be an immutable frame of reference, typically not available for social engineering or manipulation, and violation of this premise would constitute cultural malpractice in counseling and psychotherapy. Some theorists consider worldview a mutable phenomenon; we refer to Fisher et al. (1998), who stated that when a counselor acquires cultural knowledge about the client, a "shared worldview" results between the counselor and the client. Fisher et al. further explained that this cultural information can be "filed away" by the counselor and brought to bear when "formulating culturally-relevant rationales for client distress" (p. 551). Our position is that cultural knowledge and culturally based case conceptualizations are not adequate signs of a client-counselor "shared worldview" of beliefs, values, and assumptions. Ibrahim (1984, 1985, 1991) has discussed how a shared worldview can be created between a client and a counselor. This shared worldview is the common ground created in terms of similar values and beliefs that the counselor and client share. This perspective, when applied in research, showed an increase in clients' perception of counselor effectiveness and credibility (Cunningham-Warburton, 1988; Sadlak & Ibrahim, 1986). Some researchers and theorists (Claiborn, 1986; Fisher et al., 1998; Trevino, 1996) who use the social influence model of perceived counselor credibility and power or who are proponents of strategic therapy consider worldview a mutable construct that must be changed or shaped during counseling. Focusing on changing client worldview, especially in multicultural and cross-cultural encounters, may constitute an ethical violation and cause major harm. Worldview changes, however, may occur as a result of major traumatic events or a near-death experience (Furn, 1987). Counseling and psychotherapy in a multicultural context ethically requires that the counselor stay within the bounds of the client's cultural value system and not focus on changing it. Indeed, ethical practice requires that one provides services within the client's cultural, social, and personal schemas and that value conflicts are not created (Dana, 1998; Ibrahim, 1999; Roysircar-Sodowsky & Kuo, 2001; Sodowsky et al., 1996). We believe that change in psychotherapy is focused on changing maladaptive attitudinal responses, perceptions, and behaviors that have been learned and are ineffective coping mechanisms or strategies for the client; it does not focus on reconstructing basic beliefs and values that are at the core of a client's cultural and gender identity. As women immigrants in the United States from formerly colonized nations, we are well experienced in the trauma of religious conversion, assimilation, and English language domination, all of which, we propose, cause diaspora in those who are subjugated and influenced to change culturally (Ibrahim & Ohnishi, 2001).

In essence, worldview is immutable, unless the client wishes to change his or her basic value system. Such a client request also raises an ethical dilemma for the therapist because of the emotional upheaval and resultant life changes that will ensue for the client. The best example of a cultural worldview change process is the cultural crisis faced by immigrants and people with dual identities. This is in large part due to a cultural change process that occurs as a result of the transition from one culture to another, and it can last over the life span of the immigrant (and across several generations within an immigrant family and/or within an ethnic minority group) (Ibrahim & Ohnishi, 2001; Portes & Rumbaut, 1990; Roysircar-Sodowsky & Maestas, 2000).

A major issue for us is the misunderstanding of the construct of worldview and the consequent misuse of the SAWV. The latter issue pertains to a confusion over what the SAWV assesses. The confusion appears to be over whether the scale is assessing Kluckhohn's (1951) value orientations and whether those value orientations represent worldview. As noted earlier, worldview is composed of a person's grounded cultural, personal-social beliefs, and values in four specific domains: Optimism, Traditionalism, Here-and-Now, and Pessimism (Ibrahim & Owen, 1994). The original article on the psychometric properties of the instrument clearly (Ibrahim & Kahn, 1984) indicated that the judgmentally derived instrument from the Kluckhohn paradigm did not stand up to empirical scrutiny due to the degree of variability in values included (5 value areas and 15 subscales all assessing different assumptions). In its stead, a multidimensional scaling analysis provided a framework for assessing worldview that combined values from the five domains (Ibrahim & Kahn, 1987). In addition, as previously noted, Ibrahim and Owen (1994) presented another empirical analysis of the instrument that indicated four distinct worldview domains. Researchers continue to do research on the original Kluckhohn categories by using the SAWV, although there is no empirical validation that the SAWV assesses values, as conceptualized by Kluckhohn. The SAWV does not purport to assess Kluckhohn's (1951) original value orientations. It does not include all values or dimensions that were proposed by Kluckhohn. Researchers who want to investigate the Kluckhohn model might wish to use Kluckhohn and Strodtbeck's (1961) Variations in Value Orientations, which is an interview instrument with 22 familiar scenarios that purport to assess the rank ordering of solutions for each orientation (see Table 23.2 for a summary of this instrument).

Another critical issue pertains to training and competence in counseling and psychotherapy. Simply being aware of the construct of worldview and its potential is not enough. As noted in several multicultural competency and ethical statements (Ibrahim & Arredondo, 1986; Sue et al., 1992; Sodowsky et al., 1996), training and education must be undertaken to assess and use the concept of worldview in counseling and psychotherapy. However, individuals must achieve a minimum level of multicultural competence before they proceed to apply the worldview construct in therapeutic work. In addition, we, as professionals, must continually focus on clarifying and assessing our own worldview. Worldview is not explicit to a person. It is implicit, and usually with reflection, maturity, supervision, and consultation, we can clarify it over the life span.

Other issues that remain unresolved at this juncture are the relationships of worldview to self-concept and to personal, cultural, racial, and gender identities. Theorists and some initial research, as reviewed in this writing, have suggested that these dimensions are related. However, stronger empirical evidence is needed. Several other dimensions that may enhance our understanding of people and their worldview pertain to the relationships of worldview to developmental stage; the age at which worldview becomes fixed; wellness, religion or spirituality; trauma; near-death experiences; and cultural identity (i.e., perception of own group and other groups, isolation and alienation, acceptance and rejection of self and others, and acculturation issues). The interface of worldview with the cultural dynamics of family structure, child rearing, and attachment issues warrants investigation. Worldview needs to be studied along with cultural dimensions of power, authority, and social hierarchies; human rights issues; and impact of modern technology on social relationships. Also needed are analyses of ethnic group worldview, community worldview, and national worldview and their respective impact on an individual.

Within counseling and psychotherapy, several issues still await resolution. These pertain to which theoretical framework would be most useful and for which specific worldview; issues of counseling process as they relate to worldview; engagement in counseling and empathically creating a shared worldview as a base for reaching a client's subjective reality and culture; and counselor and client worldview differences and their impact on the counseling relationship, process, and outcome. Some preliminary work has been done with the construct of worldview in counseling process research (D'Rozario, 1996; Ihle et al., 1996; Ihle & Roysircar-Sodowsky, in press; Ohnishi & Ibrahim, 1999) and in marriage and family therapy (Ibrahim, 1999; Ibrahim & Schroeder, 1990; Thomas, 1998; Thompson, 1997). Further research is needed to establish the usefulness of the construct in process research. Important issues for the future also include further clarifying others' perceptions of different ethnic groups and their respective worldviews. Preliminary research points out that we may hold exaggerated stereotypes regarding ethnic groups different from ourselves (Lockney, 1999). More research is needed on the worldview of various cultural groups so that counselors start applying this information in their applied work specific to the normative nature of the information and its representation in a specific cultural group and in a particular individual.

Research on applications of the worldview construct in business and industry must be expanded to address the needs of the increasing multicultural workforce. Preliminary research suggests differences in worldview are not just between cultural groups but also among various levels of employment (managers, supervisors, and employees) and job satisfaction (Boatswain, 1997; Toczyska, 1996). In addition, recommendations exist that support the use of the worldview construct in business and industry to increase sensitivity to the beliefs, values, and assumptions of all the cultural groups in the workforce, and to increase productivity and job satisfaction (Ibrahim, 1993b). Additional research must be conducted to establish the usefulness of understanding worldview and its appropriate application in business and industry. This extension in the use of the worldview construct would be welcomed by counseling psychologists who provide consultation services to business and industry.

REFERENCES

American Psychiatric Association. (1952). *Diagnostic and statistical manual-I.* Washington, DC: Author.

American Psychiatric Association. (1968). *Diagnostic and statistical manual-II.* Washington, DC: Author.

American Psychiatric Association. (1980). *Diagnostic and statistical manual-III.* Washington, DC: Author.

American Psychiatric Association. (1994). *Diagnostic and statistical manual-IV.* Washington, DC: Author.

Atkinson, D. R. (1985). A meta-review of research on cross-cultural counseling and psychotherapy. *Journal of Multicultural Counseling and Development, 13,* 138-153.

Berkow, D. N., Richmond, B., & Page, R. C. (1994). A cross-cultural comparison of worldviews: American and Fijian counseling students. *Counseling and Values, 38,* 121-135.

Berry, J. W., Poortinga, Y. H., Segall, M. H., & Dasen, P. R. (1992). *Cross-cultural psychology.* Cambridge, UK: Cambridge University Press.

Betancourt, H., Hardin, C., & Manzi, J. (1992). Beliefs, value orientation, and culture in attribution processes and helping behavior. *Journal of Cross-Cultural Psychology, 23*(2), 179-195.

Boatswain, B. (1997). The relationship between cultural values and job satisfaction among African-American managers and higher level professionals. *Dissertation Abstracts International, 58-11B,* 62-64.

Bowman, J. (1996). Cross-cultural validation of Antonovsky's Sense of Coherence scale. *Journal of Clinical Psychology, 52,* 547-549.

Calhoun, L. G., & Cann, A. (1994). Differences in assumptions about a just world: Ethnicity and point of view. *Journal of Social Psychology, 134,* 765-770.

Carter, R. (1990). Cultural value differences between African Americans and White Americans. *Journal of College Student Development, 31,* 71-79.

Carter, R. T. (1991). Cultural values: A review of empirical research and implications for counseling. *Journal of Counseling and Development, 70,* 361-369.

Carter, R., & Helms, J. E. (1987). The relationship of Black value-orientation to racial identity attitudes. *Measurement and Evaluation in Counseling and Development, 19,* 185-195.

Carter, R. T., & Helms, J. E. (1990). The Intercultural Values Inventory (ICV). In Educational Testing Service, *Tests in microfiche test collection.* Princeton, NJ: Educational Testing Service.

Carter, R. T., & Parks, E. E. (1992). White ethnic group membership and cultural values preferences. *Journal of College Student Development, 33,* 499-506.

Castillo, R. J. (1977). *Culture and mental illness: A client-centered approach.* Pacific Grove, CA: Brooks/Cole.

Cheng, H., O'Leary, E., & Page, R. C. (1995). A cross-cultural comparison of the worldviews of American, Chinese (from Taiwan), and Irish graduate counseling students and implications for counseling. *Counseling and Values, 40,* 45-54.

Chu-Richardson, P. B. (1988). Worldview, learning style, and locus of control as factors of institutional culture differentiating academically unsuccessful students, academically successful students, and faculty. *Dissertation Abstracts International, 49,* 2152.

Claiborn, C. D. (1986). Social influence: Toward a general theory of change. In F. J. Dora (Ed.), *Social influence processes in counseling and psychotherapy* (pp. 65-74). Springfield, IL: Charles C Thomas.

Cooke, P. A., Klopf, D., & Ishii, S. (1991). Perceptions of worldview among Japanese and American university students: A cross-cultural comparison. *Communication Research Reports, 8,* 81-88.

Cunningham-Warburton, P. (1988). *A study of the relationship between cross-cultural training, the Scale to Assess Worldview, and the quality of care given by nurses in a psychiatric setting.* Unpublished doctoral dissertation, University of Connecticut.

de St. Aubin, E. (1996). Personal ideology polarity: Its emotional foundation and its manifestation in individual value systems, religiosity, political orientation, and assumptions concerning human nature. *Journal of Personality and Social Psychology, 71,* 152-165.

Dalbert, C., & Yamauchi, L. A. (1994). Belief in a just world and attitudes toward immigrants and foreign workers: A cultural comparison between Hawaii and Germany. *Journal of Applied Social Psychology, 24,* 1612-1626.

Dana, R. H. (1993). *Multicultural assessment perspectives for professional psychology.* Boston: Allyn & Bacon.

Dana, R. H. (1998). *Understanding cultural identity in intervention and assessment.* Thousand Oaks, CA: Sage.

D'Rozario, V. A. (1996). Singaporean and United States college students' worldviews, expectations of counseling, and perceptions of counselor effectiveness based on directive and nondirective counseling style. *Dissertation Abstracts International, 56,* 2564.

Fisher, A. R., Jome, L. M., & Atkinson, D. R. (1998). Reconceptualizing multicultural counseling: Universal healing conditions in a culturally specific context. *The Counseling Psychologist, 26,* 525-588.

Frey, L. L., & Roysircar-Sodowsky, G. (in press). Differences in acculturation, worldview, and ratings of dissociative experiences: A study of White American and international students. *Cultural Diversity and Ethnic Minority Psychology.*

Furn, B. G. (1986). The psychology of women as a cross-cultural issue: Perceived dimensions of worldviews. *Dissertation Abstracts International, 48-01A,* 0234.

Furn, B. G. (1987). Adjustment and the near death experience: A conceptual and a therapeutic model. *Journal of Near Death Studies, 6,* 4-19.

Furnham, A. (1993). Just world beliefs in twelve societies. *Journal of Social Psychology, 133,* 317-329.

Gerber, M. H. (1998). Worldview, social class, and psychosocial development. *Dissertation Abstracts International, 60,* 2983.

Gordon, R. D. (1997). Worldview, self-concept, and cultural identity patterns of deaf adolescents: Implications for counseling. *Dissertation Abstracts International, 58,* 4448.

Grieger, I., & Ponterotto, J. G. (1995). A framework for assessment in multicultural counseling. In J. G. Ponterotto, J. M. Casas, L. A. Suzuki, & C. M. Alexander (Eds.), *Handbook of multicultural counseling* (pp. 357-374). Thousand Oaks, CA: Sage.

Hansman, C. A., Grant, D. F., & Jackson, M. H. (1999). Implications of students' worldviews in graduate education. *Education, 119,* 551-559.

Hickson, J., Christie, G., & Shmukler, D. (1990). A pilot study of Black and White South African adolescent pupils: Implications for cross-cultural counseling. *South African Journal of Psychology, 20,* 170-177.

Hilliard, A. B. (1985). Multicultural dimensions of counseling and human development in an age of technology. *Journal of Non-White Concerns in Personnel and Guidance, 13,* 17-27.

Ibrahim, F. A. (1984). Crosscultural counseling and psychotherapy: An existential-psychological perspective. *International Journal for the Advancement of Counseling, 7,* 159-169.

Ibrahim, F. A. (1985). Effective cross-cultural counseling and psychotherapy: A framework. *The Counseling Psychologist, 13,* 625-638.

Ibrahim, F. A. (1991). Contribution of cultural worldview to generic counseling and development. *Journal of Counseling and Development, 70,* 13-19.

Ibrahim, F. A. (1993a). Existential worldview theory: Transcultural counseling. In J. McFadden (Ed.), *Transcultural counseling: Bilateral and international perspectives* (pp. 25-58). Alexandria, VA: American Counseling Association.

Ibrahim, F. A. (1993b, August). *Paradigm shift in organizational development theories.* Paper presented at the annual meeting of the American Psychological Association, New York.

Ibrahim, F. A. (1999a). Transcultural counseling: Existential worldview theory and cultural identity. In J. McFadden (Ed.), *Transcultural counseling* (2nd ed., pp. 23-58). Alexandria, VA: American Counseling Association.

Ibrahim, F. A. (1999b, August). *Integration of culture, gender and vulnerable population information in the counseling psychology curriculum: The University of Connecticut experience.* Paper presented at the symposium "A Multicultural Curriculum for Counseling Psychology" at the annual meeting of the American Psychological Association, Boston.

Ibrahim, F. A., & Arredondo, P. M. (1986). Ethical standards for cross-cultural counseling: Preparation, practice, assessment, and research. *Journal of Counseling and Development, 64,* 349-351.

Ibrahim, F. A., & Arredondo, P. M. (1990). Essay on law and ethics: Multicultural counseling. In B. Herlihy & L. Golden (Eds.), *American Association for Counseling and Development: Ethics casebook* (4th ed.). Alexandria, VA: AACD Press.

Ibrahim, F. A., Frietas, K., & Owen, S. V. (1993, August). *Comparison of Brazilian and American worldviews.* Paper presented at the annual meeting of the American Psychological Association, New York.

Ibrahim, F. A., & Kahn, H. (1984). *Scale to Assess Worldview© (SAWV).* Unpublished document.

Ibrahim, F. A., & Kahn, H. (1987). Assessment of worldviews. *Psychological Reports, 60,* 163-176.

Ibrahim, F. A., & Ohnishi, H. (2001). Posttraumatic stress disorder and the minority experience. In D. Pope-Davis & H. Coleman (Eds.), *The intersection of race, class, & gender: Implications for multicultural counseling* (pp. 89-126). Thousand Oaks, CA: Sage.

Ibrahim, F. A., Ohnishi, H., & Wilson, R. P. (1994). Career assessment in a culturally diverse society. *Journal of Career Assessment, 2,* 276-288.

Ibrahim, F. A., & Owen, S. V. (1994). Factor analytic structure of the Scale to Assess Worldview©. *Current Psychology: Developmental • Learning • Personality • Social, 13,* 201-209.

Ibrahim, F. A., & Schroeder, D. G. (1990). Cross-cultural couple counseling: A developmental psychoeducational intervention. *Journal of Comparative Family Studies, 21,* 193-207.

Ihle, G. M., & Roysircar-Sodowsky, G. (in press). Client-counselor discrepant values: Worldviews, gender role identities, and counseling role expectancies. *Professional Psychology: Research and Practice.*

Ihle, G. M., Sodowsky, G. R., & Kwan, K. (1996). Worldviews of women: Comparisons between White American clients, White American counselors, and Chinese international students. *Journal of Counseling and Development, 74,* 300-306.

Jackson, M. L. (1995). Multicultural counseling: Historical perspectives. In J. G. Ponterotto, J. M. Casas, L. A. Suzuki, & C. M. Alexander (Eds.), *Handbook of multicultural counseling* (pp. 3-16). Thousand Oaks, CA: Sage.

Johnson, J. A., Germer, C. K., Efran, J. S., & Overton, W. F. (1988). Personality as the basis for theoretical predilections. *Journal of Personality and Social Psychology, 55,* 615-624.

Jones, E. E., Kanouse, D., Kelley, H. H., Nisbett, R. E., Valins, S., & Weiner, B. (Eds.). (1972). *Attribution: Perceiving the causes of behavior.* Morristown, NJ: General Learning Press.

Kluckhohn, C. (1951). Values and value orientations in the theory of action. In T. Parsons & E. A. Shields (Eds.), *Toward a general theory of action* (pp. 388-433). Cambridge, MA: Harvard University Press.

Kluckhohn, C. (1956). Towards a comparison of value-emphasis in different cultures. In L. D. White (Ed.), *The state of social sciences* (pp. 116-132). Chicago: University of Chicago Press.

Kluckhohn, F. R., & Strodtbeck, F. L. (1961). *Variations in value orientations.* Evanston, IL: Row, Petersen.

Kwan, K.-L. K., & Sodowsky, G. R. (1997). Internal and external ethnic identity and their correlates: A study of Chinese American immigrants. *Journal of Multicultural Counseling and Development, 25,* 51-67.

Kwan, K. K., Sodowsky, G. R., & Ihle, G. M. (1994). Worldviews of Chinese international students: An extension and new findings. *Journal of College Student Development, 35,* 190-197.

Lo, Y.-H. (1996). The role of culture and subculture in worldviews: The impact of Western influence and profession in Taiwan. *Dissertation Abstracts International, 57,* 2948.

Lockney, J. P. (1999). Worldview: Accuracy of interpersonal perceptions on diversity. *Dissertation Abstracts International, 60-06B,* 3018.

Lonner, W. J., & Ibrahim, F. A. (1996). Appraisal and assessment in cross-cultural counseling. In P. B. Pedersen, J. G. Draguns, W. J. Lonner, & J. Trimble (Eds.), *Counseling across cultures* (4th ed., pp. 293-322). Thousand Oaks, CA: Sage.

Lyddon, W. J., & Adamson, L. A. (1992). Worldviews and counseling preference: An analogue study. *Journal of Counseling and Development, 71,* 41-47.

Marsella, A. J., & White, A. (Eds.). (1982). *Cultural conceptions of mental health.* Higham, MA: Reidel.

Ngumba, E. W. (1996). The relationship between worldview, African self-consciousness, and adjustment of African and African-American students: A comparative study. *Dissertation Abstracts International, 57,* 2877.

Ohnishi, H., & Ibrahim, F. A. (1999). Culture-specific counseling strategies for Japanese nationals in the United States of America. *International Journal for the Advancement of Counseling, 21,* 189-206.

Portes, A., & Rumbaut, R. G. (1990). *Immigrant America.* Berkeley: University of California Press.

Potash, H. M., Crespo, A. F., Patel, S., & Ceravolo, A. (1990). Cross-cultural attitude assessment with the Maile-Holsapple Sentence Completion Test. *Journal of Personality Assessment, 55*(3/4), 657-662.

Rotter, J. B. (1966). Generalized expectancies for internal versus external control of reinforcement. *Psychological Monographs, 80,* 1-28.

Roysircar-Sodowsky, G., & Kuo, P. Y. (2001). Determining cultural validity of personality assessment: Some guidelines. In D. Pope-Davis & H. Coleman (Eds.), *The intersection of race, class, & gender: Implications for multicultural counseling* (pp. 213-240). Thousand Oaks, CA: Sage.

Roysircar-Sodowsky, G., & Maestas, M. V. (2000). Acculturation, ethnic identity, and acculturative stress: Evidence and measurement. In R. H. Dana (Ed.), *Handbook of cross-cultural and multicultural personality assessment* (pp. 131-172). Mahwah, NJ: Lawrence Erlbaum.

Roysircar-Sodowsky, G., & Maestas, M. V. (in press). Assessment of acculturation and cultural variables. In K. S. Kurasaki, S. Okazaki, & S. Sue (Eds.), *Asian American mental health: Assessment theories and methods.* Dordrecht, The Netherlands: Kluwer Academic.

Rubin, Z., & Peplau, L. (1973). Belief in a just world and reactions to another's lot: A study of participants in the national draft lottery. *Journal of Social Issues, 31,* 65-90.

Sadlak, M. J., & Ibrahim, F. A. (1986, August). *Cross-cultural counselor training: Impact on counselor effectiveness and sensitivity.* Paper presented at the annual meeting of the American Psychological Association.

Smith, E. J. (1977). Counseling black individuals: Some stereotypes. *Personnel and Guidance Journal, 55,* 390-396.

Sodowsky, G. R., & Johnson, P. (1994). Worldviews: Culturally lessened assumptions and values. In P. Pedersen & J. C. Carey (Eds.), *Multicultural counseling in schools: A practice handbook* (pp. 59-79). Needham Heights, MA: Allyn & Bacon.

Sodowsky, G. R., Kuo-Jackson, Y. P., & Loya, G. J. (1996). Outcome of training in the philosophy of assessment: Multicultural counseling competencies. In D. Pope-Davis & H. Coleman (Eds.), *Multicultural counseling competencies: Assessment, education and training, and supervision* (pp. 3-42). Thousand Oaks, CA: Sage.

Sodowsky, G. R., Maguire, K., Johnson, P., Kohles, R., & Ngumba, W. (1994). Worldviews of White American, Mainland Chinese, Taiwanese, and African students in a midwestern university: An investigation into between-group differences. *Journal of Cross-Cultural Psychology, 25,* 309-324.

Sue, D.W. (1978). Worldviews and counseling. *Personnel and Guidance Journal, 56,* 458-462.

Sue, D. W., Arredondo, P. M., & McDavis, R. J. (1992). Multicultural counseling competencies: A call to the profession. *Journal of Multicultural Counseling and Development, 20,* 64-88.

Sue, S., Ito, J., & Bradshaw, C. (1982). Ethnic minority research: Trends and directions. In C. E. Jones & S. J. Korchin (Eds.), *Minority mental health* (pp. 47-61). New York: Praeger.

Thomas, A. J. (1998). Understanding culture and worldview in family systems: Use of the multicultural genogram. *Family Journal, 6,* 24-33.

Tompkins, S. S. (1965). Affect and the psychology of knowledge. In S. S. Tomkins & C. E. Izard (Eds.), *Affect, cognition, and personality: Empirical studies* (pp. 72-97). New York: Springer.

Thompson, M. L. (1997). Traditional worldview, interpersonal flexibility, and marital satisfaction among interethnic couples. *Dissertation Abstracts International, 5807A,* 2864.

Toczyska, M. A. (1996). Worldview and perception of organizational culture: Factors distinguishing dominant cultures from subcultures and managers from non-managers in northeastern United States workplaces. *Dissertation Abstracts International, 57,* 1737.

Torrey, E. F. (1986). *Witch doctors and psychiatrists.* New York: Harper & Row.

Trevino, J. G. (1996). Worldview and change in cross-cultural counseling. *Counseling Psychologist, 24,* 198-216.

Triandis, H. C., & Brislin, R. W. (1984). Cross-cultural psychology. *American Psychologist, 39,* 1006-1016.

Triandis, H. C., Malpass, R. S., & Davison, A. R. (1973). Psychology and culture. *Annual Review of Psychology, 60,* 355-378.

Umberson, D. (1993). Sociodemographic position, worldviews, and psychological distress. *Social Science Quarterly, 74,* 575-589.

Whatley, M. A. (1989). Belief in a Just World Scale: Unidimensional or multidimensional? *Journal of Social Psychology, 129,* 547-551.

World Health Organization. (1948). *International classification of diseases, sixth edition (ICD-6).* Geneva: Author.

Correspondence regarding this chapter may be sent to Farah A. Ibrahim, Program Director, Counseling Psychology, Howard University, 2441 Fourth Street, NW, Washington, DC 20059 (e-mail address: Ffibrahim@aol.com).

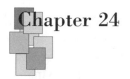

Chapter 24

Prejudice and Racism

Challenges and Progress in Measurement

ALAN W. BURKARD

BARBARA R. MEDLER

MICHAEL A. BOTICKI

COUNSELORS AND PSYCHOLOGISTS are increasingly designing and implementing prejudice prevention programs in schools, communities, and organizations. Critical to the development of these programs is the evaluation of outcomes and research on treatment-intervention efficacy. Clearly, measures that operationalize prejudice are an important need if counseling practitioners and researchers are to understand the attitudes of clients/research participants and the effects of prejudice reduction programs on changing negative attitudes.

Prejudice toward a variety of groups based on social categories (e.g., gender, ethnicity, race, sexual orientation, and socioeconomic class) has been overtly expressed with little or no societal repercussions throughout most of the 20th century. Allport (1954) wrote about a world that witnessed African Americans being lynched, the rise of the KKK and Nazism, and the political oppression of McCarthyism. White Americans in particular seemed to feel uninhibited in the overt expression of their racist and homophobic attitudes. During this period in psychological research, prejudice was often measured as a unidimensional concept (e.g., Social Distance Scale; Bogardus, 1933), predominately through self-report paper-and-pencil assessments (Biernat & Crandall, 1999).

The Civil Rights Movement, Affirmative Action, the emergence of multiculturalism in our schools, and shifting demographic trends in the United States have all led to significant changes of societal norms involving prejudice toward out-group members. Consequently, the nature and

457

expression of prejudice and racism also appears to have evolved. Although hate crimes are still a major concern in the United States (Sue & Sue, 1999), "newer" forms of prejudice that are subtle and covert seem to represent the predominate attitude, particularly among White Americans (e.g., Banaji & Greenwald, 1994; Gaertner & Dovidio, 1986; Katz & Taylor, 1988; McConahay, 1986). Although this newer form of racism has been conceptualized in different ways (see Gaertner & Dovidio, 1986; Jacobson, 1985; McConahay, 1986; Sears, 1988), the term *implicit prejudice* (Banaji & Greenwald, 1994; Greenwald & Banaji, 1995) is used here for several conceptual reasons addressed later in this chapter.

The intent of this chapter is to review three categories of prejudice measures that practitioners and researchers can use in practice or research. Given that a recent comprehensive review of self-report racial prejudice measures was completed by Biernat and Crandall (1999), this chapter focuses on new developments in self-report measures of racial and anti-gay prejudice. Anti-gay prejudice is an important clinical and research area, and to date, only a few critical reviews of instruments measuring negative attitudes toward gay men and lesbian women have appeared in the literature (Herek, 1994; O'Donohue & Caselles, 1993; Schwanberg, 1993). Emerging prejudice measurement issues are the final focus, specifically addressing theoretical developments and the implications for prejudice measurement. Concluding comments address future needs in prejudice measurement and the application to counseling practice and research.

SELF-REPORT MEASURES OF RACIAL PREJUDICE

QUICK DISCRIMINATION INDEX

Description and Development

In a review of the literature, Ponterotto et al. (1995) identified three concerns with current measures of prejudice. First, some measures were composed of a small number of items that represented moderate psychometric properties, whereas other measures that had adequate psychometric properties were unduly lengthy and impaired practical utility. Second, prejudice measures have typically focused on cognitive aspects of people's attitudes rather than seeking to tap into affective aspects of respondents' attitudes. Finally, measures of prejudice were often solely based on White racism toward African Americans. In view of these criticisms, Ponterotto et al. developed the Quick Discrimination Index (QDI) to address both cognitive and affective aspects of prejudice, provide a measure applicable to diverse racial and ethnic populations, and provide an instrument with both practical utility and psychometric soundness.

The QDI is composed of 30 items in a Likert-type format, with responses that range from strongly disagree (1) to strongly agree (5). Several items are reverse scored to control for a response bias. Based on the Lix Readability Index (Anderson, 1983), the QDI was assessed at the ninth-grade reading level (Utsey & Ponterotto, 1999). Consistent with the original intent of the QDI, this data suggests that the instrument is best used with adolescent and adult populations. Although a full-scale score can be reported, the QDI is best interpreted as a three-factor structure based on 23 of the 30 items (Ponterotto et al., 1995; Utsey & Ponterotto, 1999). The three factors are believed to measure cognitive attitudes toward racial diversity, interpersonal-affective attitudes regarding racial diversity, and general attitudes toward women's equality. Sample items are "It is as easy for women to succeed in business as it is for men," "My friendship network is very racially mixed," and "I feel that I could develop an intimate relationship with someone from a different race."

Psychometric Properties

Ponterotto et al. (1995) conducted three independent studies in the initial development of the QDI. Forty items were written for Study 1, and through a factor analysis and examination of criterion-related validity (based on Walsh and Betz's, 1990, Group-Differences Approach) the QDI was reduced to 25 items. Based on the evidence from Study 1, 2 items were rewritten, and 5 new items were written to further develop the second and third factors. Studies 2 and 3 of Ponterotto et al. and the Utsey and Ponterotto (1999) investigation represent the current data concerning the QDI's psychometric properties.

Reliability. Studies 2 and 3 of Ponterotto et al. (1995) reported the following Cronbach's alpha for the full scale and each of the factors, respectively: (a) .88 and .88 for the full scale, (b) .80 and .85 for Factor 1, (c) .83 and .83 for Factor 2, and (d) .65 and .76 for Factor 3. For three independent samples, Utsey and Ponterotto (1999) reported the following ranges of Cronbach's alpha: (a) .85 to .90 for Factor 1, (b) .70 to .79 for Factor 2, and (c) .70 to .77 for Factor 3. This evidence suggests that the QDI subscales have stable internal consistency coefficients across samples. A test-retest procedure was conducted in Study 2 of Ponterotto et al. (1995). The sample consisted of 37 undergraduates, and the retest procedure was completed at a 15-week interval. The coefficients of stability were .90, .82, and .81, respectively, for the three factors.

Validity. Based on a principal components analysis with a varimax rotation, seven factors were identified with eigenvalues greater than 1.0 in Study 2 of Ponterotto et al. (1995). Upon further analysis, and using a cut-off criterion of .40 for factor loadings, a three-factor oblique extraction accounting for 41% of the total scale variance emerged as the best interpretable factor structure for the QDI, a finding consistent with the results of Study 1 in Ponterotto et al. A confirmatory factor analysis conducted in Study 3 supported the three-factor oblique extraction as the best interpretation of the QDI factor structure. Utsey and Ponterotto (1999) conducted a confirmatory factor analysis of the QDI with three independent samples using an aggregate procedure recommended by Bagozzi and Heatherton (1994). The results indicated that the three-factor oblique structure remained fairly stable across these samples.

To examine the criterion-related validity of the QDI, Ponterotto et al. (1995) analyzed correlational patterns of QDI scores with various individual demographic variables among a sample of adolescents and adults from the New York metropolitan area. Analyses resulted in significant findings for gender, race, respondent residence (e.g., urban, suburban), and political affiliation, whereas income level and childbearing status were insignificant. All findings were consistent with those expected by the researchers and supported the criterion-related validity of the QDI based on the Group-Differences approach described by Walsh and Betz (1990).

In Study 3, Ponterotto et al. (1995) examined convergent and discriminant validity by correlating QDI factor scores with scores from the New Racism Scale (NRS; Jacobson, 1985), the Multicultural Counseling Awareness Scale (MCAS; Ponterotto et al., 1993), and the Social Desirability Scale (SDS; Crowne & Marlowe, 1960). All three factors of the QDI were significantly correlated with the NRS (cognitive factor, $r = .44$; interpersonal-affective factor, $r = .44$; and the women's equality factor, $r = .30$), demonstrating that the QDI factors correlated with another measure of racism-oppression. The cognitive factor of the QDI significantly correlated with both factors of the MCAS. Only the interpersonal-affective factor of the QDI correlated with the knowledge/skills factor of the MCAS ($r = .34$), whereas the women's equity factor correlated with the awareness factor of the MCAS ($r = .39$). These general findings support the convergent validity of the QDI. Finally, the absence of significant correlations with the SDS suggests no contamination from social desirability and establishes some discriminant validity.

Evaluation

Ponterotto et al. (1995) set out to create a prejudice measure that had practical utility across racial groups without sacrificing the psychometric properties of the measure. Additionally, given that most measures of prejudice solely address the cognitive aspects of prejudice (Ponterotto & Pedersen, 1993), Ponterotto et al. attempted to measure affective components of racial prejudice. The QDI does appear to have stable psychometric properties at this time across the samples studied. The initial internal consistency and coefficient of stability suggest that the QDI factors have moderate to strong reliability. The findings from Ponterotto et al. (1995) and Utsey and Ponterotto (1999) suggest that QDI factor structure is also relatively stable with samples across diverse geographical locations.

In general, additional validity studies should be completed on the QDI. Investigations to date have primarily explored the factor structure of the QDI, significantly contributing to the development of construct validity evidence. Contrary to one of the goals of the original scale, it is questionable if the QDI factor structure is applicable to racially diverse populations. A rough average from Studies 2 and 3 of Ponterotto et al. (1995) and Utsey and Ponterotto (1999) show that 79% of the combined samples from these investigations were composed of White participants, many of whom were college students. It will be important that future research replicate factorial studies with demographically diverse samples (e.g., age, ethnicity, race, gender, and educational level) if the QDI is to be generalized to diverse populations. Also important to the development of the construct validity of the QDI is additional research exploring group differences, correlational investigations with similar constructs, and convergent/discriminant validity analyses with racially and ethnically diverse populations.

Although some initial criterion-related validity evidence is presented by Ponterotto et al. (1995), certainly further research is needed to explore the dimensions and conceptual correlates of the QDI subscales. This becomes a critical issue, given the development of dual-process models of prejudiced attitudes (Devine, 1989; Devine & Monteith, 1999). From a dual-process perspective, the QDI would seem to be appropriately classified as an explicit measure of prejudice. Further research that examines the relationship between behavioral expressions of prejudice and QDI scores will be important to the development of criterion-related validity.

MIVILLE-GUZMAN
UNIVERSALITY-DIVERSITY SCALE

Description and Development

Vontress (1988, 1996) asserted the notion that people are simultaneously similar to and different from each other, and that the awareness and acceptance of this notion is critical to relationship development between culturally different individuals. This ability to accept both similarities and differences in others is seen as fundamental to a counselor's work with a culturally different client (Vontress, 1996). Recognizing the implications of Vontress's writings, Miville (1992) worked to conceptually define and operationalize the universal-diverse orientation (UDO) construct. UDO is defined as "an attitude of awareness and acceptance of both the similarities and differences among people" (Miville et al., 1999, p. 292). The emphasis of the UDO construct is on the simultaneous acceptance of cultural (e.g., age, ethnicity, gender, race, and sexual orientation) similarities and differences in others. The Miville-Guzman Universality-Diversity Scale (M-GUDS) was developed by Miville et al. (1999) to operationalize the UDO construct, and to assess an individual's level of UDO.

The M-GUDS uses a 6-point Likert-type format to measure UDO, with responses that range from strongly agree (6) to strongly disagree (1). The 45-item M-GUDS is currently interpreted as a single factor, and the total scores range from 45 to 270. High scores on the M-GUDS indicate a higher simultaneous appreciation of the similarities and differences in individuals culturally different than ourselves. The M-GUDS requires about 15 to 25 minutes to complete. Sample items are "I can best understand someone after I get to know how he/she is both similar and different from me" and "It's really hard for me to feel close to a person from another race" (reverse scored).

Psychometric Properties

In developing the M-GUDS, Miville (1992) constructed an initial set of 78 items equally distributed across the three hypothesized factors of the M-GUDS (e.g., relativistic appreciation, diversity of contact, and sense of connectedness). These initial items were administered to an undergraduate sample (N = 33). Following an examination of item-subscale total-score correlations, Miville determined that 45 items would be retained for the further development of the final scale. All current psychometric data on the 45-item M-GUDS are reported in Miville et al. (1999), which represents four studies related to the initial construction and validation of the instrument.

Reliability. Across the four initial studies, Miville et al. (1999) reported coefficient alphas of .89 to .94 for the full-scale score on the M-GUDS. To assess the temporal stability of the instrument, Miville et al. conducted a test-retest procedure. Based on a retest interval of 1-2 weeks in Study 1 (n = 23), the coefficient of stability for the M-GUDS was .94. The test developers indicated that due to the small sample size this coefficient of stability should be interpreted with caution.

Validity. Content validity of the M-GUDS was established through five judges' (counseling psychology doctoral students) ratings of item clarity and domain appropriateness (Miville et al., 1999). Items were retained if they received a mean clarity rating of 4 (on a 1 to 5 scale) and if the majority of the judges agreed on the subscale assignment based on provided subscale definitions.

To examine the construct validity of the M-GUDS, Miville, Romans, Johnson, and Lone (1998) conducted an exploratory factor analysis of the 45-item scale. The results of this analysis suggested that a significant proportion of variance from the M-GUDS scores can be accounted for by a single general factor. A subsequent examination of subscale correlations showed significant intercorrelations between .65 and .69 (Miville et al., 1999). Based on the pattern of the factor structure and subscale inter-correlations, Miville et al. (1999) suggested that a unidimensional factor is the best interpretation of the M-GUDS.

Although criterion-related validity was not a focus of Miville et al.'s (1999) investigations, some evidence of criterion-related validity is available using Walsh and Betz's (1990) Group-Differences Approach. Among a sample of White university students, it was found that men's M-GUDS scores where significantly lower than women's scores, indicating that men are less appreciating of similarities and differences than women. No gender differences emerged among a sample of African American university students. For both African American and White university students, Miville et al. also examined the racial composition of respondents' childhood neighborhoods and high schools. Racial composition of childhood neighborhoods and high schools were not significantly correlated with M-GUDS scores for African American students. In contrast, higher scores on the M-GUDS were found for those White respondents who reported living in predominantly White neighborhoods and attending high schools that were predominantly White in racial composition.

Across a series of four studies, Miville et al. (1999) examined the concurrent, convergent, and discriminant validity of the M-GUDS. An examination of the correlation patterns between the M-GUDS and several other scales yielded significantly positive correlations with androgyny, empathy toward others, healthy aspects of narcissism, positive attitudes toward feminism, positive aspects of African American and White racial identity. Significantly negative correlations emerged with dogmatism (closed-mindedness), negative attitudes toward gays and lesbians, and the more negative aspects of African American and White racial identity attitudes. Among White respondents, it was also found that M-GUDS scores did not correlate significantly with SAT verbal scores, the Fantasy and Personal Distress subscales of the Empathy Scale (Davis, 1980), or social desirability scores. Each of these sets of correlational findings were in the predicated direction. Five findings emerged from these four studies that were contrary to the original predications. Positive correlations were found between the M-GUDS and White racial identity Contact Subscale scores ($r = .45$) and SAT Quantitative scores ($r = -.21$) for a sample of White undergraduates, and ACT ($r = .25$), grade point average ($r = .24$), and social desirability ratings ($r = .26$) were significantly correlated with a sample of African American undergraduates.

Evaluation. Measurement of racial prejudice has often focused on negative attitudes toward out-groups, leaving little room for understanding aspects and dimensions of nonprejudiced racial attitudes. UDO, as measured by the

M-GUDS, represents an important movement in the direction of understanding dimensions of nonprejudiced racial attitudes. As a new instrument, the M-GUDS lacks extensive psychometric examination; however,
the current evidence on construct validity is particularly promising. Certainly, the M-GUDS warrants further research and validation in the field of
counseling.

The internal consistency of the scale is satisfactory and was consistent
across samples in the four Miville et al. (1999) investigations. Additional reliability evidence was provided through a test-retest procedure. It should be
noted that the sample size was small ($n = 23$) for the test-retest procedure,
and these findings need to be replicated with larger samples. As indicated
by the scale's authors, the factor structure and subscale correlations suggest
that the M-GUDS is best interpreted as a unidimensional scale. The combination of the factor analysis, the correlational evidence with other scales
representing similar constructs, and the convergent/discriminant validity
provide evidence that the M-GUDS has initially strong construct validity.
A few correlations between scores on other scales and M-GUDS scores
were contrary to the predicted direction (e.g., White participants' scores on
SAT Quantitative subscale, African American students' grade point aver-
ages, ACT scores, and social desirability scores). Replication of these findings will be important to determine if this was an artifact of the samples, or
a stable pattern needing conceptual clarification. It is important to note
that three of four investigations on the M-GUDS focused on samples consisting of White undergraduates, and the fourth sample was composed of
African American undergraduate students. Consequently, researchers will
need to examine the generalizability of the M-GUDS to populations outside a university setting that represent more diversity. This should include
confirmatory factor analysis studies across demographically diverse samples (e.g., racial/ethnicity, gender, and socioeconomic status).

MOTIVATION TO
CONTROL PREJUDICE REACTIONS

Description and Development

Researchers in cognitive and social psychology are increasingly recognizing the dissociation between automatic and controlled social judgment
processes (Devine, 1989; Devine & Monteith, 1999; Greenwald & Banaji,
1995). The independence of these two social judgment processes was demonstrated in a study of an unobtrusive measure of racial prejudice (Fazio,
Jackson, Dunton, & Williams, 1995). An important finding of this study
was that an unobtrusive measure did not significantly correlate with participants' Modern Racism Scale (MRS; McConahay, 1986) scores, despite

the fact that participants in this investigation were selected based on MRS scores falling within the lowest and highest 10% of a large sample.

Dunton and Fazio (1997) considered these findings from the Motivation and Opportunity as Determinants (MODE) model of attitude-behavior processes perspective (see Fazio, 1990, for a complete review of the MODE model) and concluded that "any controlled component within a mixed sequence of automatic and controlled processes, requires that the individual be both motivated to engage in the necessary cognitive effort and have the opportunity to do so" (p. 317). In essence, any automatic or implicit process that is activated in social judgment situations (e.g., homophobia, racism, and sexism) involving out-group members may be mediated by the motivation to control such processes. The Motivation to Control Prejudice Reactions (MCPR) scale was developed to measure this important individual difference construct specifically with respect to racial prejudice.

The current MCPR (Dunton & Fazio, 1997) consists of 17 items developed to measure two dimensions of the motivation to control prejudiced reactions. Following a factor analysis with a varimax rotation, two factors (i.e., concern with acting prejudiced and restraint to avoid dispute) emerged as the best interpretation of the scale. Respondents are directed to indicate the degree to which they agree or disagree with each item-statement on a Likert-type scale, which ranges from –3 (*strongly disagree*) to +3 (*strongly agree*). The MCPR can be completed in approximately 5 to 10 minutes. Sample items are "In today's society it is important that one not be perceived as prejudice in any manner" and "I think that it is important to speak one's mind rather than to worry about offending someone."

Psychometric Properties

Psychometric data on the MCPR are reported in Dunton and Fazio (1997), Fazio et al. (1995), and Fazio and Dunton (1997). Four independent samples for the initial development of the MCPR (Dunton & Fazio, 1997) consisted of (a) 55 students, (b) 418 undergraduates in a mass survey, (c) 429 undergraduates in a mass survey, and (d) 207 paid participants recruited through advertisements in campus or local town newspapers who agreed to participate in psychological research.

Reliability. Coefficient alphas across the four samples were reported to range from .74 to .81 (Dunton & Fazio, 1997). Individual coefficient alphas were not reported for the two subscales in any investigations.

Validity. Using a principal components analysis with a varimax rotation, five factors were identified that had eigenvalues greater than one (Dunton & Fazio, 1997). The combined total of these factors accounted for 56% of the variance. To test the stability and replicability of the factor structure,

Dunton and Fazio (1997) employed a factor comparability procedure recommended by Everett (1983). An examination of the factor score coefficient matrix that was derived from two independent samples suggested that a two-factor structure was stable and replicable across these samples. The first factor, measuring concern with acting prejudiced, accounted for 23.1% of the variance. The second factor, measuring restraint to avoid dispute, accounted for 11.6% of the variance. A correlation between the two factors has not been reported in the research publications on the MCPR scale.

The criterion-related validity of the MCPR was examined in a series of studies reported in Fazio et al. (1995), Dunton and Fazio (1997), and Fazio and Dunton (1997). Fazio et al. (1995) found that higher scores on the MCPR were statistically related to less prejudiced attitudes as measured by the Modern Racism Scale (MRS). An interaction effect also emerged. As scores on the MCPR decreased, the statistical relationship between scores on the MRS and an indirect measure of racial prejudice involving social judgment reaction time increased. Specifically, high MCPR scores (higher motivation to control prejudice) were correlated with high MRS scores, and the interaction between these two scales was statistically significant and predicted positive attitudes on an unobtrusive measure of racial attitudes.

Dunton and Fazio (1997) replicated the Fazio et al. study in order to examine the influence of the two identified factors of the MCPR (e.g., concern for acting prejudiced, restraint to avoid dispute) in predicting racially prejudiced attitudes, as measured by the MRS and an unobtrusive measure. They found that positive racial attitudes scores on the unobtrusive measure could be predicted from the interaction between high scores on the Concern with Acting Prejudiced (CAP) factor and low scores on the MRS. This indicated that if an individual has low explicit prejudiced attitudes and a high motivation to control prejudiced reactions they are likely to have less implicit racially prejudiced attitudes. Similar to the prior findings on the full scale MCPR, the interaction between low scores on the CAP factor and negative racial attitudes, as measured by the MRS, were predictive of negative racial attitudes, as measured by the unobtrusive priming procedure. In contrast, an interaction between the MRS and the Restraint to Avoid Dispute (RAD) factor did not predict scores on an unobtrusive measure priming procedure. Dunton and Fazio suggested that the prediction of negative racial attitudes by an unobtrusive measure can best be accounted for by the CAP factor of the MCPR scale.

Additional research by Fazio and Dunton (1997) found that individuals with high MCPR scores tended to use race less in a similarity judgment task. As in prior investigations, type and speed of social judgments varied based on an interaction between MCPR scores and a behavioral task involving perception of race. These relationships varied in the predicted direction.

This study provided further evidence of the criterion-related validity of the MCPR.

Evaluation

The MCPR scale is the first instrument of its kind to measure an individual's motivation to control expressions of prejudice. This measure represents an important conceptual development in understanding individual differences in social judgment processes. Given that the scale is composed of 17 items, it is efficient and easy to use in research. The MCPR has been specifically used as a moderating variable between an explicit and implicit measure of racial prejudice, and further study is needed before the MCPR is used outside this specific research context.

Although the MCPR has acceptable levels of internal consistency, further research is needed to examine the internal consistency and temporal stability of the full scale and subscales. Dunton and Fazio (1997) and Fazio and Dunton (1997) presented strong evidence of the MCPR's construct validity through a factor analysis and experimental investigations using the MCPR as a moderator variable. It is important that additional studies explore the construct validity of the MCPR by analyzing discriminant and convergent validity patterns and by further analyzing the underlying factor structure using confirmatory factor analyses with other samples. The studies presented in this review focused on White participants, and it remains unclear conceptually and empirically if these social judgment processes are applicable to individuals outside diverse racial backgrounds. Finally, Schmidt, Hunter, and Urry (1976) found that sample sizes of 200 or more were needed to reflect accurate validity levels in the population 90% of the time. The experimental investigations had small sample sizes; consequently, it is important that sample sizes be increased in future validity studies.

An important issue to resolve is the use of the total MCPR scale score or the subscale scores. In the investigation by Dunton and Fazio (1997), the CAP factor was found to significantly contribute to the prediction of unobtrusive measure scores, whereas the RAD factor did not contribute to the prediction equation. Certainly, further study is needed, but it currently appears that the CAP factor is primarily responsible for the interaction effect between MRS scores and the unobtrusive measure of racial prejudice.

Theoretically, the motivation to control prejudice reactions represents an important conceptual advancement with respect to prejudice reduction. Current and past prejudice reduction efforts have focused on attempts to reduce negative stereotypes or prejudicial attitudes (Ponterotto & Pedersen, 1993). MCPR represents an operational definition of an individual differences construct that is thought to affect both controlled and automatic social judgment processes, and that may be an appropriate target for future prejudice reduction efforts.

THE MODERN HOMOPHOBIA SCALE

Description and Development

To keep pace with the more subtle forms of prejudice expressed in contemporary society, conceptual and empirical advances have been made with respect to the measurement of racist attitudes. Similar advances have been slower to evolve with respect to the measurement of prejudice toward lesbian women and gay men. Recognizing this need, Raja and Stokes (1998) sought to develop a contemporary measure of prejudiced attitudes toward lesbian women and gay men to address three concerns. First, noting that older measures of racism and sexism have been updated to reflect the relatively more subtle forms of prejudice that appear to be expressed today (Swim, Aikin, Hall, & Hunter, 1995), Raja and Stokes (1998) identified a need to "update the content of some of the older homophobia scales" (p. 115) in a similar manner. Second, older measures of antigay prejudice ask about "homosexuals" or "homosexuality" in general, rather than differentiating between attitudes toward gay men and lesbian women (e.g., Kite & Deaux, 1986; Larsen, Reed, & Hoffman, 1980). Finally, Raja and Stokes (1998) sought to operationally differentiate personal discomfort and institutional discrimination toward lesbian women and gay men.

The Modern Homophobia Scale (MHS) consists of two subscales: the attitudes toward lesbians subscale (MHS-L) and the attitudes toward gay men subscale (MHS-G). The MHS consists of 46 total items (24 of which comprise the MHS-L and 22 of which comprise the MHS-G). Items are presented in an agree-disagree format on a 5-point Likert-type scale ranging from 1 (*do not agree*) to 5 (*strongly agree*). Sample items from the MHS-L are "Employers should provide health care benefits to the partners of their lesbian employees," "I wouldn't mind working with a lesbian," and "Female homosexuality is a psychological disease." Sample items from the MHS-G are "I wouldn't mind going to a party that included gay men," "Male homosexuality is a psychological disease," and "I would not vote for a political candidate who was openly gay."

Psychometric Properties

Psychometric data for the MHS are reported in Raja and Stokes (1998), and the sample for the development of the MHS consisted of 322 undergraduate students.

Reliability. Coefficient alphas for the MHS-L and MHS-G were reported to be .95 for each of the two subscales. Coefficient alphas for each of the three MHS-L factors were reported as follows: (a) .89 for Factor 1, institutional homophobia toward lesbians; (b) .92 for Factor 2, personal discomfort when associating with lesbians; and (c) .90 for Factor 3, the belief that female homosexuality is deviant and changeable. The coefficient alphas for each of the three MHS-G factors were reported as follows: (a) .91 for Factor 1, personal discomfort when associating with gay men; (b) .85 for Factor 2, the belief that male homosexuality is deviant and changeable; and (c) .90 for Factor 3, institutional homophobia toward gay men.

Validity. Since Raja and Stokes (1998) intended to measure attitudes toward gay men and attitudes toward lesbian women separately, separate factor analyses were performed for the two subscales. A principal factors extraction and oblique rotation were implemented. After restricting the range of item-to-total correlations, eliminating items not meeting criteria recommended by Schmitt (1993), and including only those factors with coefficient alphas of greater than .80, three factors were identified as best representing the items for each of the two MHS subscales. The three combined factors for the MHS-L accounted for 47.3% of the variance in MHS-L scores, and the three combined factors for the MHS-G accounted for 44.9% of the variance in MHS-G scores. High intercorrelations among the factors were noted. Correlations among the MHS-L factors were reported to range from .60 to .74, and correlations among the MHS-G factors were reported to range from .71 to .82. Correlations between MHS-L and MHS-G factors were reported to range from .57 to .90.

To further explore the construct validity of the MHS, correlational patterns between scores on the MHS and certain respondent variables were examined. In comparing MHS-L and MHS-G scores by gender of respondent, Raja and Stokes (1998) found that a gender difference in responding emerged in the predicted direction. Male respondents endorsed more negative attitudes as compared to female respondents, although they indicated more positive attitudes toward lesbians than toward gay men. Conversely, female respondents endorsed more positive attitudes toward gay men than toward lesbian women.

A consistent finding that has emerged across studies of the correlates of antigay prejudice is that persons who report having had contact with gay male and lesbian individuals tend to endorse more positive attitudes toward these persons as compared to persons who report that they have had no such contact (Herek & Glunt, 1993). As expected, Raja and Stokes (1998) found that female respondents who indicated that they had at least one lesbian friend-acquaintance endorsed statistically significantly lower personal discomfort factor scores as compared to female respondents who indicated that they had no lesbian friends-acquaintances. Similarly, male respondents who indicated that they had at least one gay male friend-acquaintance had less personal discomfort (as measured by the personal discomfort factor of the MHS-G) as compared to male respondents who indicated that they had no gay male friends-acquaintances.

Criterion-related validity was examined by correlating scores on the MHS-L and MHS-G with scores on an existing measure of homophobia, the Index of Homophobia (IHP; Hudson & Ricketts, 1980) and with a measure of traditional beliefs about women's roles, the Attitudes Toward Women Scale (ATWS; Helmreich & Spence, 1978). As expected, higher scores on the MHS-L and MHS-G, indicating greater endorsement of antigay beliefs, were found to be significantly related to higher scores on the IHP, also indicating greater endorsement of antigay beliefs. Higher scores on the MHS-L and MHS-G were also found to be statistically significantly associated with higher scores on the ATWS, indicating more traditional beliefs about women's roles. Further evidence of criterion-related validity was established by examining correlations between negative affective reactions to vignettes containing a gay male, lesbian, or heterosexual target and scores on the MHS-L and MHS-G. A statistically significant relationship was found between negative affective reactions and higher MHS scores for participants whose target character was a gay or lesbian person, indicating that the MHS-L and MHS-G may accurately predict negative affective reactions to lesbian women and gay men.

Raja and Stokes (1998) expected that lower levels of homophobia, as measured by both the MHS and IHP, would be associated with higher levels of socially desirable responding, as measured by the Impression Management scale of the Balanced Inventory of Desirable Responding (BIDR-IMP; Paulhus & Reid, 1991). Contrary to prediction, higher BIDR-IMP scores were found to be related to greater levels of homophobia, as measured by both the IHP and MHS.

Evaluation

The MHS represents a more contemporary approach to defining and measuring heterosexual persons' negative attitudes toward lesbian women and gay men. A strength of the measure is that, in keeping with contemporary measures and theoretical formulations of other forms of prejudice, it attempts to "tap into" the more subtle prejudicial beliefs that may be represented among the general population today. Another strength of the measure is that it represents an attempt at conceptually and operationally differentiating heterosexuals' attitudes toward lesbian women and their attitudes toward gay men. Moreover, it represents an initial attempt to make a distinction between a personal discomfort dimension of negative attitudes toward lesbian women and gay men and a cultural-institutional dimension having to do with one's beliefs about these individuals' fundamental rights in society.

Since the MHS is a relatively new measure, psychometric data reported here are limited to those reported by the instrument developers based on the sample on which the measure was constructed. The scale developers report satisfactory estimates of internal consistency for the instrument; however, additional research is needed to examine the internal consistency and temporal stability of the instrument. Solid evidence of the construct validity of the MHS was provided by the test developers through separate factor analyses of subscales, and an examination of correlational patterns with other conceptually related measures (e.g., ATWS and IHP). Moreover, during initial validation of the MHS, the frequent finding that male respondents tend to endorse stronger antigay attitudes as compared to female respondents was replicated, as was the expectation of an interaction between sex of respondent and sex of target, with women endorsing more negative attitudes toward lesbians than toward gay men and men endorsing more negative attitudes toward gay men than toward lesbian women.

Since the validation studies reported here are limited to the sample upon which the measure was constructed, it will be important that additional validation studies of the MHS are undertaken across demographically diverse samples. The high intercorrelations among the MHS-L and MHS-G factors suggest significant construct overlap and redundancy. This finding may suggest that a general homophobia factor may account for the intercorrelations between the MHS factors. Future investigations should include confirmatory factor analyses to test the generalizability of the MHS factor structure across samples as well as higher-order factor analyses to test for a general factor of homophobia and the underlying factor structure. It will be important to subject the relationship between the MHS-L and MHS-G to further statistical examination, as the correlations between the two subscales were not reported by Raja and Stokes (1998). Further examination of the finding of a positive relationship between greater endorsement of antigay prejudice and more socially desirable responding is certainly in order, since this finding may have important implications to the study and prevention of negative attitudes toward lesbian women and gay men.

EMERGING ISSUES IN PREJUDICE MEASUREMENT

LIMITS OF SELF-REPORT MEASURES

One predominant concern in the measurement of prejudice has been the reactivity of self-report measures (Crosby, Bromley, & Saxe, 1980). In essence, respondents can vary their scores on measures of prejudice by discerning the content of the items of the scale and making a decision whether to provide a response that is more reflective of their attitudes or one that represents a deliberately managed response to present themselves in a favorable light. From the empirical evidence on the MCPR scale presented earlier in this chapter, we see that some individuals are motivated to control their prejudiced responses (Dunton & Fazio, 1997). This suggests that self-report measures of prejudice are inherently limited and that construct validity may be compromised (Sniderman & Tetlock, 1986).

The reactivity of self-report measures has led some researchers to question the validity of measuring prejudice with this methodology (Crosby et al., 1980; Gaertner & Dovidio, 1986). This would seem to be an extreme position, and evidence presented by Fazio et al. (1995) and Dunton and Fazio (1997) would seem to suggest that self-report measures do have a place in the assessment of explicit prejudice. In a comprehensive review of self-report prejudice measures, Biernat and Crandall (1999) expressed a strongly favorable view of self-report as a measurement tool, asserting their "faith that the heart of modern-day racial attitudes can be successfully measured through self-report" (p. 298). Yet multiculturalism has taught our field to question its "faith" in traditional assumptions. Although measurement of prejudice through self-report measures may be an important assessment tool, it may also represent a conceptually and empirically limited perspective.

More recent prejudice attitude research has resulted in the development of conceptual models and measures that recognize both automatic and controlled processes (Devine & Monteith, 1999), or what is also referred to as implicit and explicit prejudice processes (Greenwald & Banaji, 1995). Thus, if counselor educators and researchers are to move forward in understanding and measuring prejudice and in developing appropriate interventions, prejudice must be seen as a multidimensional construct and measured as such. One specific implication for counseling researchers that follows from this more contemporary view of prejudice is that alternative methodologies to self-report measures may be important to prejudice assessment. We strongly disagree with Biernat and Crandall's (1999) "faith" perspective and feel that alternative and novel measurement approaches must be encouraged and explored to help facilitate better understanding of the nature of prejudice and to assist practitioners in the design of appropriate prejudice reduction programs.

IMPLICIT PREJUDICE

The assumption underlying self-report measures of prejudice is that the processes involved in prejudice are explicit by nature. Even more recent conceptual or operational definitions of prejudice, such as modern racism (McConahay, 1986), symbolic racism (Sears, 1988), and modern homophobia (Raja & Stokes, 1998) assume that attitudes are accessible consciously and that individuals are able to consciously manage their prejudice in response to members of target groups.

Contrary to the assumption of explicit prejudice processes underlying traditional self-report measures of prejudice, recent research efforts in the area of social cognition suggest that the expression of prejudice involves simultaneous implicit and explicit processes (Devine, 1989; Devine & Monteith, 1999; Greenwald & Banaji, 1995). Although a full theoretical treatment of explicit and implicit prejudice is not appropriate here (see Devine & Monteith, 1999; Greenwald & Banaji, 1995), a conceptual definition for implicit prejudice will be facilitative in understanding relevant measurement issues. Greenwald and Banaji (1995) suggest the following definition: "Implicit attitudes are introspectively unidentified (or inaccurately identified) traces of past experience that mediate favorable or unfavorable feeling, thought, or action toward social objects" (p. 8). In essence, past experiences that are not remembered through explicit memory, and which are inaccessible through introspection or self-reflection, affect some behavior.

Evidence of implicit prejudice has been presented primarily in experimental studies (e.g., Devine, 1989; Fazio et al., 1995; Gilbert & Hixon, 1991). Such evidence suggests that the expressions of implicit and explicit prejudice are concurrent but independent social cognitive processes. Thus, it may be that explicit measures of prejudice measure conscious content of prejudicial attitudes, and implicit measures of prejudice measure people's social judgment processes with respect to those attitudes (von Hippel, Sekaquaptewa, & Vargas, 1997). Although the initial evidence suggests that implicit and explicit prejudice are independent processes, Bargh (1989, 1994) has argued that operational definitions of implicit prejudice have not been held to stringent criteria in delineating these underlying processes. This lack of definitional clarity has served as a measurement confound and has, on occasion, led to empirically and conceptually unclear results.

One of the difficulties in the measurement of implicit prejudice is one of practical utility. Judgment latencies have often been used as an individual differences measure of implicit social cognition (e.g., Devine, 1989; Dunton & Fazio, 1997; Fazio et al., 1995). These measurement techniques are computer and technology dependent. Within the context of counseling, educational workshops, or supervision, counselors would rarely find judgment latencies a practical tool in the measurement of implicit racism. Essentially, measures of implicit prejudice that are conceptually and empirically valid and have practical utility are needed.

BRIDGING THE GAP:
LINGUISTIC INTERGROUP BIAS

Maas, Salvi, Arcuri, and Semin (1989) developed a model of in-group/out-group prejudice behavior called Linguistic Intergroup Bias (LIB), which is based on Semin and Fiedler's (1988) psycholinguistic model. Semin and Fiedler's model identified four distinct linguistic categories that could be used to describe people. These linguistic categories varied in descriptive complexity from concrete, behaviorally focused descriptions of people, to abstract, trait-focused descriptions (e.g., descriptive action verb, interpretative action verb, state verb, and adjectives). Maas et al. (1989) applied this model to stereotyping in-group and out-group members. They found that concrete, behavioral descriptions (descriptive action verbs) were used by participants when identifying stereotype-incongruent behaviors; whereas, participants used more abstract, trait-focused descriptions (adjectives) when identifying stereotype-congruent behaviors.

Recently, von Hippel et al. (1997) suggested that LIB could be used as a conceptual basis for measuring implicit racial prejudice. Adapting the LIB stimulus materials from Maas et al. (1989), von Hippel et al. developed a booklet containing a series of various ersatz newspaper articles (e.g., basketball slam-dunk contest winner, employee embezzling money from a computer firm, spelling-bee winner planning to attend MIT, jewelry thief that lived in subsidized housing). Stereotype congruency-incongruency was controlled through these newspaper articles by pairing either an African American or White photograph with the various articles. Consistent with Maas et al.'s application of Semin and Fiedler's (1988) model, below each article-photograph pairing were four descriptive statements, varying in complexity from abstract to concrete, describing the person portrayed in the article. Participants rated the accuracy of the description based on a 10-point scale anchored from 1 (describes very poorly) to 10 (describes very well).

In two specific studies involving White undergraduate students, von Hippel et al. (1997) found support for the LIB measurement technique. In both experimental studies, it was found that implicit prejudice toward African Americans, as measured by LIB, predicted differential responses of perceived threat by African American and Caucasian targets. More specifically, White respondents' scores on an explicit measure of prejudice (MRS) predicted higher perceived threat in Caucasian targets rather than African American targets, whereas the findings from the LIB measure resulted in higher ratings of perceived threat from African American targets as opposed to Caucasian targets. The scores on the explicit measure would seem to reflect more socially desirable responses and support the notion that LIB is measuring an independent social judgment process. This evidence would seem to suggest that LIB may be a valuable measure of implicit prejudice.

There are some important implications with respect to implicit prejudice measurement that can be drawn from von Hippel et al.'s (1997) research on LIB. One of the difficulties of measures of implicit prejudice is that they have often been reliant on fairly sophisticated computer equipment that has little practical utility for multicultural counselors and educators. LIB, as operationally defined by von Hippel et al., represents an important paper-and-pencil measure of implicit racism that is relatively simple to administer and score. In this sense, von Hippel et al.'s technique has great practical utility without sacrificing conceptual integrity. It appears to be a promising measure of individual differences with respect to implicit prejudice. At this stage of development, however, LIB is experimental and needs further research and development. All aspects of the psychometric properties of the instrument need to be subjected to empirical examination.

CLARIFYING CONCEPTUALIZATIONS
AND OPERATIONAL DEFINITIONS

Although some initial investigations are indicating that explicit and implicit prejudicial attitudes and processes are independent (e.g., Devine, 1989; Fazio et al., 1995; von Hippel et al., 1997), not all studies support this finding (Wittenbrink, Judd, & Park, 1997). One of the major difficulties in comparing results of implicit prejudice is a lack of consistency across studies in the criteria used to operationalize the concept. Bargh (1989, 1994) identified a variety of methods through which implicit prejudice has been operationalized in research. A definitional confound may account for the empirical differences across investigations. It is important that future research conduct criterion-related validity studies to explore how or if implicit prejudice measures are conceptually related and empirically correlated.

A second related issue is the contrast between content and process issues in the measurement of prejudice. In examining the focus of past prejudice attitude scales, von Hippel et al. (1997) have suggested that these scales have tended to focus on the content of prejudice rather than the underlying processes. This would suggest that responses to self-report instruments are an outcome of a social judgment process, and this may in part account for the differences found between explicit and implicit measures of prejudice. Several recent models of attitude measurement (see Fazio et al., 1995) have focused on prejudice judgment processes. Counseling researchers should familiarize themselves with these models and explore how these contemporary conceptual models may be used to better understand the role of prejudiced attitudes and behavioral expression.

There are important conceptual and definitional issues that are specific to the measurement of antigay prejudice. In contrast to other forms of prejudice, such as racism, prejudice toward gay men and lesbians potentially involves the evaluation of a target person with respect to two social dimensions: gender and sexual orientation. Others have argued that the literature on negative attitudes toward gay men and lesbians has not typically taken into account the complexity of those attitudes; thus sex differences that emerge in studies of anti-gay prejudice are still not well understood (Kite & Whitley, 1996). Specifically, it is not clear for what reasons heterosexual men tend to endorse greater degrees of anti-gay prejudice as compared to heterosexual women, although support for traditional gender roles for women was identified as an important mediating variable in a meta-analysis of sex differences in antigay prejudice (Kite & Whitley, 1996). Another issue related to gender of respondents in anti-gay prejudice research is that in some studies an interaction between sex of respondent and sex of target has emerged (Herek, 1994; Kite & Whitley, 1996). Specifically, in some studies heterosexual men endorse more negative attitudes toward gay men than toward lesbians, whereas heterosexual women endorse more negative attitudes toward lesbians than toward gay men. However, this has not been a consistent finding across studies (Herek, 1994).

The development of the MHS represents an important conceptual step forward in beginning to think about attitudes toward lesbian women and attitudes toward gay men as separate constructs entirely. It has long been argued that attitudes toward gay men and lesbian women should be examined separately, and others have developed psychometrically sound measures that allow for this differential examination (Herek, 1994). However, the items comprising such scales are based on similar conceptualizations of the two constructs (Herek, 1994). It is possible that the specific belief structure and social judgment processes underlying negative attitudes toward lesbian women is different from the belief structure and underlying social judgment processes underlying negative attitudes toward gay men. Advances that have been made with respect to implicit prejudice could be helpful in further delineating such distinctions.

An interesting finding from the initial validation studies of the MHS was that socially desirable responding was associated with higher rather than lower homophobia scores. This finding could suggest that, in contrast to other forms of prejudice, anti-gay prejudice may be considered to be the most desirable form of responding with respect to gay and lesbian individuals. This is a possibility, given the fact that many states have yet to pass legislation protecting gay men and lesbians from discrimination in such areas as housing and employment (Herek, 1993, 1994). Further investigation of this finding is recommended, as it has potentially important implications for educators and researchers in the area of anti-gay prejudice prevention and reduction.

CONCLUSION

This chapter critically reviewed several contemporary developments in the measurement of prejudice. As a group, the instruments reviewed represent important definitional developments in understanding the nature and measurement of prejudice. Clearly, one of the important conceptual trends is the recognition of implicit and explicit prejudice as concurrent but separate social judgment processes. This advancement in prejudice theory has led to the development of both innovative self-report and novel measurement instruments, which have implications for practice and research. In bringing this chapter to a close, we offer some final summary comments about the direction of future research and implications for educational and clinical practice.

The first general area of discussion concerns several issues important to continuing the development of theory and measurement of prejudice. The following areas represent important research directions. First, the LIB procedure and self-report measures reviewed for this chapter must continue to be the focus of validity and reliability studies. Although evidence for each measure had some initial supporting evidence, these findings need to be replicated with other samples, especially with samples outside the context of a university environment. Second, Ponterotto et al. (1995) and Miville et al. (1999) have recognized the need to explore conceptual and empirical meanings of prejudice in diverse groups; however, few investigators have actually explored prejudicial processes beyond African American and White relations. Clearly, White prejudice toward African Americans constitutes a major societal problem in the United States (Sue & Sue, 1999) as well as globally (Ponterotto & Pedersen, 1993). To develop a more complete understanding of prejudicial processes and attitudes, however, research must expand beyond the confines of African American and White relations. For example, heterosexual and gay/lesbian relations have been underresearched, as have race relations between other racial/ethnic populations (e.g., Asian Americans, Hispanic/Latino Americans, and Native American Indians). A related concern involves prejudice toward bisexual individuals. There is a great need for the development of theoretical conceptualizations and operational definitions of prejudice toward members of this neglected group in prejudice research. Finally, prejudice is rapidly being recognized as a multidimensional construct both in terms of process (e.g., explicit and implicit) and content (e.g., homophobia, racial discrimination, and universal-diverse orientation). New dimensions of prejudice and corresponding measures continue to be developed and published. For

example, Neville, Lilly, Duran, Lee, and Browne (2000) recently operationalized color-blindness attitude to racism and racial issues through the
Color-Blind Racial Attitudes Scale. Research efforts should incorporate
these new developments, and seek to clarify conceptually and empirically
the various dimensions of prejudice.

The second direction in prejudice research concerns the methodological processes used for measurement. In particular, implicit prejudice may
challenge counseling researchers to examine and use alternative or novel
measurement methodologies. Counseling researchers may want to familiarize themselves with technology-based measures, such as reaction latencies and priming procedures (see Dovidio & Fazio, 1992), as well as
psychophysiological measures of prejudice (see Guglielmi, 1999). Although these measurement strategies may be outside the domain of common practice in counseling research, stretching ourselves into these
alternative measurement methodologies may prove to be productive in facilitating our understanding of prejudice and its various behavioral expressions. Another consideration is the development of additional alternative
measures. For example, Greenwald and Banaji (1995) indicated that projective techniques have proved useful in the measurement of achievement
motivation (Spangler, 1992), and that projectives may be useful in the
assessment of implicit prejudice. It appears that we are only limited by our
creativity.

In the introduction to this chapter, we recognized the commitment of,
and challenges for, counseling educators and practitioners in reducing various forms of prejudice. In that endeavor, measurement of prejudice marks
our progress in changing prejudicial attitudes and facilitates understanding
and clarification of prejudicial processes. For those of us who are practitioners, some of these ideas may appear abstract and obtuse. However, the
initial evidence based on measures of implicit prejudice reviewed in this
chapter suggests that prejudice reduction efforts targeted solely toward explicit prejudice attitudes may not address implicit dimensions of prejudice.
In this sense, measurement can help inform practice. The recent advances
in conceptualization and measurement of prejudice discussed in this chapter clearly represent creative efforts and a beginning toward understanding
the multidimensional nature of prejudice and the implications that this understanding may have for changing these attitudes.

REFERENCES

Allport, G. W. (1954). *The nature of prejudice.* Cambridge, MA: Addison-Wesley.
Anderson, J. (1983). Lix and Rix: Variations on a little-known readability index. *Journal of Reading, 26,* 490-496.
Bagozzi, R. P., & Heatherton, T. G. (1994). A general approach to representing multifaceted personality constructs: Application to state self-esteem. *Structural Equation Modeling, 1,* 35-67.

Banaji, M. R., & Greenwald, A. G. (1994). Implicit stereotyping and unconscious prejudice. In M. P. Zanna & J. M. Olson (Eds.), *The psychology of prejudice: The Ontario Symposium* (Vol. 7, pp. 55-76). Hillsdale, NJ: Lawrence Erlbaum.

Bargh, J. A. (1989). Conditional automaticity: Varieties of automatic influence in social perception and cognition. In J. S. Uleman & J. A. Bargh (Eds.), *Unintended thought* (pp. 3-51). New York: Guilford.

Bargh, J. A. (1994). The four horseman of automaticity: Awareness, intention, efficiency, and control in social cognition. In R. S. Wyer, Jr., & T. K. Srull (Eds.), *Handbook of social cognition* (2nd ed., Vol. 1, pp. 1-40). Hillsdale, NJ: Lawrence Erlbaum.

Biernat, M., & Crandall, C. S. (1999). Racial attitudes. In J. P. Robinson, P. R. Shaver, & L. S. Wrightsman (Eds.), *Measures of social psychology attitudes: Volume 2. Measures of political attitudes* (pp. 297-411). San Diego: Academic Press.

Bogardus, E. S. (1933). A social distance scale. *Sociology and Social Research, 17,* 265-271.

Crosby, F., Bromley, S., & Saxe, L. (1980). Recent unobtrusive studies of Black-and-White discrimination and prejudice: A literature review. *Psychological Bulletin, 87,* 546-563.

Crowne, D. P., & Marlowe, D. (1960). A new scale of social desirability independent of psychopathology. *Journal of Consulting Psychology, 24,* 349-354.

Davis, M. (1980). A multidimensional approach to individual differences in empathy. *JSAS Catalog of Selected Documents in Psychology, 10,* 85.

Devine, P. G. (1989). Stereotypes and prejudice: Their automatic and controlled components. *Journal of Personality and Social Psychology, 56,* 5-18.

Devine, P. G., & Monteith, M. J. (1999). Automaticity and control in stereotyping. In S. Chaiken & Y. Trope (Eds.), *Dual-process theories in social psychology* (pp. 339-360). New York: Guilford.

Dovidio, J. F., & Fazio, R. H. (1992). New technologies for the direct and indirect assessment of attitudes. In J. M. Tanur (Ed.), *Questions about questions: Inquiries into the cognitive bases of surveys* (pp. 204-236). New York: Russell Sage Foundation.

Dunton, B. C., & Fazio, R. H. (1997). An individual difference measure of motivation to control prejudiced reactions. *Personality and Social Psychology Bulletin, 23,* 316-326.

Everett, J. E. (1983). Factor comparability as a means of determining the number of factors and their rotation. *Multivariate Behavioral Research, 18,* 197-218.

Fazio, R. H. (1990). Multiple processes by which attitudes guide behavior: The MODE model as an integrative framework. In M. P. Zanna (Ed.), *Advances in experimental social psychology* (Vol. 23, pp. 75-109). New York: Academic Press.

Fazio, R. H., & Dunton, B. C. (1997). Categorization by race: The impact of automatic and controlled components of racial prejudice. *Journal of Experimental Social Psychology, 33,* 451-470.

Fazio, R. H., Jackson, J. R., Dunton, B. C., & Williams, C. J. (1995). Variability in automatic activation as an unobtrusive measure of racial attitudes: A bona fide pipeline? *Journal of Personality and Social Psychology, 69,* 1013-1027.

Gaertner, S. L., & Dovidio, J. F. (1986). The aversive form of racism. In S. L. Gaertner & J. F. Dovidio (Eds.), *Prejudice, discrimination, and racism* (pp. 61-89). New York: Academic Press.

Gilbert, D. T., & Hixon, J. G. (1991). The trouble with thinking: Activation and application of stereotypic beliefs. *Journal of Personality and Social Psychology, 60,* 509-517.

Greenwald, A. G., & Banaji, M. R. (1995). Implicit social cognition: Attitudes, self-esteem, and stereotypes. *Psychological Review, 102,* 4-27.

Guglielmi, R. S. (1999). Psychophysiological assessment of prejudice: Past research, current status, and future directions. *Personality and Social Psychology Review, 3,* 123-157.

Helmreich, R. L., & Spence, J. T. (1978). Work and family orientation questionnaire: An objective instrument to assess components of achievement motivation and attitudes toward family and career. *Catalogue of Selected Documents in Psychology, 8,* 35.

Herek, G. M. (1993). The context of antigay violence: Notes on cultural and psychological heterosexism. In L. Garnets & D. C. Kimmel (Eds.), *Psychological perspectives on lesbian and gay male experiences* (pp. 89-107). New York: Columbia University Press.

Herek, G. M. (1994). Assessing heterosexuals' attitudes toward lesbians and gay men. In B. Greene & G. M. Herek (Eds.), *Lesbian and gay psychology: Theory, research, and clinical applications* (pp. 206-228). Newbury Park, CA: Sage.

Herek, G. M., & Glunt, E. K. (1993). Interpersonal contact and heterosexuals' attitudes toward gay men: Results from a national survey. *Journal of Sex Research, 30,* 239-244.

Hudson, W. W., & Ricketts, W. A. (1980). A strategy for the measurement of homophobia. *Journal of Homosexuality, 5,* 357-372.

Jacobson, C. R. (1985). Resistance to affirmative action: Self-interest or racism. *Journal of Conflict Resolution, 29,* 306-329.

Katz, P., & Taylor, D. (Eds.). (1998). *Eliminating racism: Profiles in controversy.* New York: Plenum.

Kite, M. E. (1984). Sex differences in attitudes toward homosexuals: A meta-analytic review. *Journal of Homosexuality, 10,* 69-81.

Kite, M. E., & Deaux, K. (1986). Attitudes toward homosexuality: Assessment and behavioral consequences. *Basic & Applied Social Psychology, 7,* 137-162.

Kite, M. E., & Whitley, B. E., Jr. (1996). Sex differences in attitudes toward homosexual persons, behaviors, and civil rights: A meta-analysis. *Personality and Social Psychology Bulletin, 22,* 336-353.

Larsen, K. S., Reed, M., & Hoffman, S. (1980). Attitudes of heterosexuals toward homosexuality: A Likert-type scale and construct validity. *Journal of Sex Research, 16,* 245-257.

Maas, A., Salvi, D., Arcuri, L., & Semin, G. (1989). Language use in intergroup contexts: The Linguistic Intergroup Bias. *Journal of Personality and Social Psychology, 57,* 981-993.

McConahay, J. B. (1986). Modern racism, ambivalence, and the modern racism scale. In J. F. Dovidio & S. L. Gaertner (Eds.), *Prejudice, discrimination, and racism* (pp. 91-125). Orlando, FL: Academic Press.

Miville, M. L. (1992). *Measuring and defining universal orientation.* Unpublished master's thesis, University of Maryland at College Park.

Miville, M. L., Gelso, C. J., Pannu, R., Liu, W., Touradji, P., Holloway, P., & Fuertes, J. (1999). Appreciating similarities and valuing differences: The Miville-Guzman Universality-Diversity Scale. *Journal of Counseling Psychology, 46,* 291-307.

Miville, M. L., Romans, J. S. C., Johnson, D., & Lone, R. (1998, August). *Exploring correlates of well-functioning using the Miville-Guzman Universality-Diversity Scale.* Poster session presented at the 106th Annual Convention of the American Psychological Association, San Francisco.

Neville, H. A., Lilly, R. L., Duran, G., Lee, R. M., & Browne, L. (2000). Construction and initial validation of the Color-Blind Racial Attitudes Scale (CoBRAS). *Journal of Counseling Psychology, 47,* 59-70.

O'Donohue, W., & Caselles, C. E. (1993). Homophobia: Conceptual, definitional, and value issues. *Journal of Psychopathology and Behavioral Assessment, 15,* 177-195.

Paulhus, D. L., & Reid, D. B. (1991). Enhancement and denial in socially desirable responding. *Journal of Personality and Social Psychology, 60,* 307-317.

Ponterotto, J. G., Burkard, A. W., Rieger, B. P., Grieger, I., D'Onofrio, A., Dubuisson, A., Heenehan, M., Millstein, B., Parisi, M., Rath, J. F., & Sax, G. (1995). Development and initial validation of the Quick Discrimination Index (QDI). *Educational and Psychological Measurement, 55,* 1016-1031.

Ponterotto, J. G., & Pedersen, P. B. (1993). *Preventing prejudice: A guide for counselors and educators.* Newbury Park, CA: Sage.

Ponterotto, J. G., Rieger, B. P., Barrett, A., Harris, G., Sparks, R., Sanchez, C. M., & Magids, D. (1993, September). *Development and initial validation of the Multicultural Awareness Scale (MCAS).* Paper presented at the Ninth Buros-Nebraska Symposium on Measurement and Testing: Multicultural Assessment, Lincoln.

Raja, S., & Stokes, J. P. (1998). Assessing attitudes toward lesbians and gay men: The Modern Homophobia Scale. *Journal of Gay, Lesbian, and Bisexual Identity, 3,* 113-134.

Schmidt, F. L., Hunter, J. E., & Urry, V. W. (1976). Statistical power in criterion-related validity studies. *Journal of Applied Psychology, 61,* 473-485.

Schmitt, N. (1993). *Test construction.* Unpublished manuscript, Michigan State University.

Schwanberg, S. L. (1993). Attitudes toward gay men and lesbian women: Instrumentation issues. *Journal of Homosexuality, 26,* 99-136.

Sears, D. O. (1988). Symbolic racism. In P. Katz & D. Taylor (Eds.), *Eliminating racism: Profiles in controversy* (pp. 53-84). New York: Plenum.

Semin, G. K., & Fiedler, K. (1988). The cognitive functions of linguistic categories in describing persons: Social cognition and language. *Journal of Personality and Social Psychology, 54,* 558-568.

Sniderman, P., & Tetlock, P. (1986). Symbolic racism: Problems of motive attribution in political analysis. *Journal of Social Issues, 42,* 423-447.

Spangler, W. D. (1992). Validity of questionnaire and TAT measures of need for achievement: Two meta-analyses. *Psychological Bulletin, 112,* 140-154.

Sue, D. W., & Sue, D. (1999). *Counseling the culturally different: Theory and practice* (3rd ed.). New York: John Wiley.

Swim, J. K., Aikin, K. J., Hall, W. S., & Hunter, B. A. (1995). Sexism and racism: Old-fashioned and modern prejudices. *Journal of Personality and Social Psychology, 68,* 199-214.

Utsey, S. O., & Ponterotto, J. G. (1999). Further factorial validity assessment of scores on the Quick Discrimination Index (QDI). *Educational and Psychological Measurement, 59,* 325-335.

von Hippel, W., Sekaquaptewa, D., & Vargas, P. (1997). The linguistic intergroup bias as an implicit indicator of prejudice. *Journal of Experimental Social Psychology, 33,* 490-509.

Vontress, C. E. (1988). An existential approach to cross-cultural counseling. *Journal of Multicultural Counseling and Development, 16,* 78-83.

Vontress, C. E. (1996). A personal retrospective on cross-cultural counseling. *Journal of Multicultural Counseling and Development, 24,* 156-166.

Walsh, W. B., & Betz, N. E. (1990). *Tests and assessment* (2nd ed.). Englewood Cliffs, NJ: Prentice Hall.

Wittenbrink, B., Judd, C. M., & Park, B. (1997). Evidence for racial prejudice at the implicit level and its relationship with questionnaire measures. *Journal of Personality and Social Psychology, 72,* 262-274.

Correspondence regarding this chapter may be addressed to Alan W. Burkard, School of Education, Schroeder Health Complex 138, Marquette University, Milwaukee, WI 53201 (e-mail address: alan.burkard@marquette.edu).

New Visions for Defining and Assessing Multicultural Counseling Competence

Madonna G. Constantine

Nicholas Ladany

AS THE POPULATION of the United States becomes increasingly culturally diverse, it is critical that counseling psychologists are able to meet the mental health needs of a broad range of clients (Sue & Sue, 1999). Consequently, researchers and educators in counseling and counseling psychology programs are underscoring the importance of counselors demonstrating multicultural counseling competence in working with diverse cultural populations (Constantine, Ladany, Inman, & Ponterotto, 1996; Ponterotto, Fuertes, & Chen, 2000; Quintana & Bernal, 1995; Ridley, Mendoza, & Kanitz, 1994). Multicultural counseling competence has been defined as counselors' attitudes/beliefs, knowledge, and skills in working with individuals from a variety of cultural (e.g., racial, ethnic, gender, social class, and sexual orientation) groups (Sue, Arredondo, & McDavis, 1992; Sue et al., 1998).

Over the past couple of decades, the field of counseling psychology has witnessed profound growth in its attention to multicultural issues in counseling, training, and supervision (e.g., Constantine, 1997; Hills & Strozier, 1992; Ladany, Inman, Constantine, & Hofheinz, 1997; Pedersen, 1991; Ponterotto, 1998; Quintana & Bernal, 1995). In particular, Ridley et al. (1994) recommended that training in multicultural issues have a core philosophical foundation, followed by narrower objectives that are ultimately evaluated. Although many counseling psychology programs have begun to actively integrate multicultural issues into their academic curriculum, few of these programs are able to accurately assess the effectiveness of the multicultural counseling training they provide (Coleman, 1996; Constantine et al., 1996; Pope-Davis & Dings, 1995). Furthermore, few resources exist that identify specific outcomes related to cultural competence in providing psychological services to diverse client groups (Allison, Echemendia, Crawford, & Robinson, 1996; Ridley et al., 1994).

The potential challenges associated with evaluating multicultural counseling competence may rest in the methods used to measure this construct. As such, there is a need for critical analysis of the assessment methods that have been used to date. Moreover, it is possible that the difficulties related to accurate assessment of multicultural counseling competence may lie in the contemporary theoretical conceptualizations of this construct. To this end, this chapter discusses current methods of assessing multicultural competence, including salient limitations of some of these methods. An enhanced and expanded conceptualization of multicultural counseling competence is then offered. Future practice, research, and training implications for the development and measurement of multicultural counseling competence are also discussed.

CONTEMPORARY METHODS TO ASSESS MULTICULTURAL COMPETENCE

This section reviews methods to evaluate multicultural competence in therapists and in training programs. In particular, self-report, portfolio, and observer-rated indices of multicultural counseling competence will be presented along with methods to assess the presence of multicultural issues in training programs. Limitations of these approaches are then discussed.

Self-Report Measures of Multicultural Counseling Competence

Sue et al.'s (1982) position paper has served as the basis for the development of several self-report instruments designed to measure the multicultural competencies of counselors. These scales include the (a) Multicultural Awareness/Knowledge/Skills Survey (MAKSS; D'Andrea, Daniels, & Heck, 1991); (b) Multicultural Counseling Inventory (MCI; Sodowsky, Taffe, Gutkin, & Wise, 1994); and (c) Multicultural Counseling Knowledge and Awareness Scale (MCKAS; Ponterotto, Gretchen, Utsey, Rieger, & Austin, 2000). The following subsections are devoted to a brief description of these scales.

Multicultural Awareness/ Knowledge/Skills Survey (MAKSS)

The MAKSS (D'Andrea et al., 1991) is a 60-item self-report scale that has been used primarily to evaluate the effectiveness of multicultural counseling training. It consists of three subscales measuring Awareness,

Knowledge, and Skills. The Awareness subscale is composed of items assessing awareness of personal attitudes toward people of color, the Knowledge subscale measures knowledge about populations of color, and the Skills subscale consists of items designed to assess cross-cultural communication skills (Ponterotto & Alexander, 1996). It uses a 4-point rating scale, with responses ranging from 1 (*very limited*) to 4 (*very good*) for most of the items; 1 (*very limited*) to 4 (*very aware*) for three of the items; and 1 (*strongly disagree*) to 4 (*strongly agree*) for the remaining items. Scores in each subscale range from 20 to 80; hence, MAKSS total scale scores range from 60 to 240.

Evidence of content validity for the MAKSS was demonstrated (a) through matching MAKSS items with specific instructional objectives of a multicultural training course and (b) by comparing items on the MAKSS Awareness subscale to an Awareness subscale of another multicultural instrument (D'Andrea et al., 1991). Criterion-related validity was achieved in that MAKSS scores increased after participation in a multicultural training course, and construct validity was established through item-to-scale correlations and scale-specific exploratory factor analysis (D'Andrea et al., 1991). In the validation sample, coefficient alphas for the subscales ranged from .75 to .96 (D'Andrea et al., 1991).

Multicultural Counseling Inventory (MCI)

The MCI (Sodowsky et al., 1994) is a 40-item, 4-point Likert-type (1 = *very inaccurate,* 4 = *very accurate*) scale designed to "operationalize some of the proposed constructs of multicultural counseling competencies" (Sodowsky et al., 1994, p. 139). It consists of four subscales that assess Multicultural Counseling Awareness (10 items, possible range of scores = 10 to 40), Multicultural Counseling Knowledge (11 items, possible range of scores = 11 to 44), Multicultural Counseling Skills (11 items, possible range of scores = 11 to 44), and Multicultural Counseling Relationship (8 items, possible range of scores = 8 to 32). MCI total scale scores range from 40 to 160. The MCI Awareness subscale measures issues such as multicultural sensitivity, multicultural interactions and experiences, general cultural understanding, and multicultural advocacy. The Knowledge subscale is composed of items that measure phenomena such as multicultural case conceptualization and treatment strategies and knowledge of cultural information. The Skills subscale consists of items assessing multicultural and general counseling skills, and the Relationship subscale contains items measuring aspects of counselors' interpersonal processes with racial and ethnic minority clients.

Evidence of the MCI's content validity was derived through expert raters' accuracy of classifying items into their appropriate subscale categories and through expert evaluation of item clarity; criterion-related validity was established in that individuals with multicultural training or more professional experience working with culturally diverse populations obtained higher MCI scores (Ponterotto & Alexander, 1996; Sodowsky et al., 1994). Based on findings from previous studies, a mean Cronbach's alpha of .87 has been reported for the entire MCI scale, and mean Cronbach's alphas of .78, .77, .80, and .68 have been reported for the Awareness, Knowledge, Skills, and Relationship subscales, respectively (Sodowsky et al., 1998).

Multicultural Counseling Knowledge and Awareness Scale (MCKAS)

The MCKAS (Ponterotto, Gretchen, et al., 2000) is a 32-item, 7-point Likert-type (1 = *not at all true*, 7 = *totally true*) measure of (a) general knowledge related to multicultural counseling and (b) subtle Eurocentric worldview bias. The MCKAS, a revised version of the Multicultural Counseling Awareness Scale–Form B (Ponterotto et al., 1996), consists of two factors: Knowledge (20 items, possible range of scores = 20 to 140) and Awareness (12 items, possible range of scores = 12 to 84). Scores for the entire scale range from 32 to 224. Initial studies examining the psychometric properties of the MCKAS indicate (a) coefficient alphas of .85 for each of the subscales and (b) that it has good content, construct, and criterion-related validity (Ponterotto, Gretchen, et al., 2000).

Limitations of Self-Report Scales

Self-report multicultural counseling competence instruments have enjoyed moderate use in the counseling literature, and they seem to be an important first step in assessing multicultural competence. However, several limitations have been noted regarding their usage. One such criticism is that the inventories tend to measure "anticipated" rather than actual behaviors or attitudes correlated with multicultural competence (Pope-Davis & Dings, 1995; Sue, 1996). Lending support to this contention, Constantine and Ladany (2000) and Ladany et al. (1997) found no significant relationships between self-reported and an aspect of demonstrated multicultural counseling competence (i.e., written multicultural case conceptualization ability).

Investigators (e.g., Ponterotto, 1998; Ponterotto & Alexander, 1996; Pope-Davis & Dings, 1995) have also identified the need for more validity-based information regarding self-report multicultural counseling competence instruments. In particular, some researchers have noted a lack of uniformity regarding what these scales actually assess (Pope-Davis & Dings, 1995; Sue, 1996). For example, in an investigation comparing the MCI and the MCAS–B (the previous version of the MCKAS), Pope-Davis and Dings (1994) found that although these two scales were to some degree positively correlated, they seemed to measure fundamentally different constructs. Furthermore, although multicultural competence instruments have the common goal of assessing perceived multicultural counseling competence, these measures tend to vary in the number of factors thought to comprise this overall construct. For example, D'Andrea et al. (1991) offered a three-factor model (i.e., awareness, knowledge, and skills) of multicultural competence. Sodowsky et al. (1994) proposed both a four-factor model (i.e., awareness, knowledge, skills, and relationship) and a higher order model (i.e., general multicultural counseling) of multicultural counseling competence, and Ponterotto, Gretchen, et al. (2000) reported a two-factor model (i.e., knowledge and awareness) of multicultural counseling competence. Thus, although the multicultural scales have similar objectives, there seems to be a lack of clarity about what they actually assess.

Social desirability is also a potential limitation associated with self-report multicultural counseling competence instruments (Pope-Davis & Dings, 1995; Sue, 1996). Sodowsky (1996) suggested that the completion of multicultural competence measures be accompanied by a measure of social desirability or impression management (Paulhus, 1991). In previous studies, Sodowsky et al. (1994) and Ponterotto et al. (1996) reported minimal correlations between a measure of social desirability and their self-report multicultural counseling competence instruments. Subsequently, however, Sodowsky, Kuo-Jackson, Richardson, and Corey (1998) found a significant positive relationship between the MCI full-scale score and a measure of social desirability (i.e., multicultural social desirability). In addition, Constantine and Ladany (2000) found significant relationships between a general social desirability measure and some subscales of self-report multicultural counseling competence scales. As these researchers indicate, social desirability attitudes may need to be statistically accounted for when examining correlates of self-report multicultural counseling competence.

There are several other limitations of self-report multicultural measures. For example, although many multicultural instruments claim to assess respondents' ability to work with a range of cultural groups, a review of each scale's items suggests that they are primarily assessing perceived competence in working with people of color (Constantine & Ladany, 2000). To sufficiently assess a broad range of multicultural issues, various approaches will need to be developed to measure counselors' abilities or competencies regarding working with other cultural groups (e.g., women, men, the impoverished, and persons with disabilities) (Constantine & Ladany, 2000; Lowe & Mascher, Chapter 36, this volume). Moreover, many approaches to assessing multicultural counseling competence appear to be rooted in the assumption that such competence is demonstrated primarily in individual counseling situations. Future measures of multicultural counseling competence may need to include procedures that assess such competence in the context of larger systems (e.g., families, groups, and organizations) and noncounseling interventions (e.g., outreach, consultation, and advocacy).

Finally, current self-report multicultural scales have used the predominant tripartite definition of multicultural counselor competence (i.e., counselors' attitudes/beliefs, knowledge, and skills in working with culturally diverse clients) as their primary theoretical foundation. Except for Sodowsky et al. (1994), who expanded the three general multicultural counseling competence domains to include a fourth factor (i.e., multicultural counseling relationship), this historical conceptualization has remained essentially unchallenged by multicultural scholars and practitioners in counseling and psychology (Constantine & Ladany, 2000). Hence, future conceptualizations that support and/or refute the existing constructs believed to underlie the multicultural counseling competence construct are needed.

Portfolio Approaches to Assessing Multicultural Counseling Competence

Portfolio approaches have emerged as methods of assessing students' multicultural counseling competence in counselor training programs (Coleman, 1996). A portfolio is a collection of work that explicates an individual's efforts, progress, and achievements in a given area (Arter & Spandel, 1992). Coleman (1996) asserted that portfolios reflect counselors' competence within the domains of multicultural awareness, knowledge, and skills and across the four main treatment modalities stressed in the context of academic and applied training programs: individual, group, family, and consultation. In other words, portfolios display the interactions between the three multicultural domains and within the aforementioned therapeutic modalities. The types of evidence that could be presented to illustrate competence with regard to these domains and modalities would vary, depending on issues such as the contexts in which portfolio approaches are used and counselors' skill levels.

A primary strength of portfolio approaches is that competency judgments would be grounded in a broad range of behaviors, as opposed to more limited manifestations of culturally competent behavior (e.g., watching a trainee's videotaped session with a culturally diverse client). Portfolios can also function as a stimulus for discussion of multicultural issues and can demonstrate that an individual has mastered specific concepts. Portfolios can serve as a way to integrate information from different therapeutic domains and can demonstrate how particular educational processes are effective at building competence (Coleman, 1996). Despite the many benefits of portfolio approaches, some limitations to their use have been identified. Among these shortcomings are the following: (a) Developing portfolios is time-consuming and takes more time to develop and review than other instruments, and (b) they lack reliable methods for scoring and evaluation (Coleman, 1996; Collins, 1992; O'Neill, 1992).

Methods to Assess
Multicultural Issues in Training Programs

The Multicultural Competency Checklist (MCC; Ponterotto, Alexander, & Grieger, 1995) is a 22-item instrument designed to assist faculty members in counseling psychology and counselor education programs to assess their status with regard to providing multicultural training for their students. This checklist is intended to be completed by the director of training or the collective program faculty. The MCC focuses exclusively on racial and ethnic diversity issues in training programs and is organized along six categories: minority representation, curriculum issues, counseling practice and supervision, research considerations, student and faculty competency evaluation, and physical environment. It has been identified as a useful tool for encouraging discussion and exploration of multicultural issues within training programs in general. Research using the MCC has indicated that, in general, counseling training programs are attending to multicultural issues (Ponterotto, 1997), although the integration of multicultural issues is sometimes perceived as occurring more frequently by faculty than students (Constantine et al., 1996).

Another multicultural instrument, the Multicultural Environmental Inventory–Revised (MEI–R; Pope-Davis, Liu, Nevitt, & Toporek, 2000), assesses counseling graduate students' perceptions of their academic training milieu in terms of its multicultural focus. The MEI–R consists of 27 Likert-type items that are organized into four factors: Curriculum and Supervision, Climate and Comfort, Honesty in Recruitment, and Multicultural Research. The MEI–R can be used to provide academic programs with information about potential areas of enhancement regarding attention to multicultural issues. Initial psychometric information regarding the MEI–R suggests that it has sound construct validity. Despite their psychometric promise, however, the utility of instruments such as the MEI–R and the MCC as valid indices of training programs' attention to multicultural issues may be hampered by similar limitations associated with self-report measures (e.g., reporting of anticipated versus actual phenomena, potential social desirability attitudes of respondents).

Observer Ratings of
Multicultural Counseling Competence

The Cross-Cultural Counseling Inventory–Revised (CCCI–R; LaFromboise, Coleman, & Hernandez, 1991) is a 20-item, 6-point Likert-type (1 = *strongly disagree,* 6 = *strongly agree*) instrument that was developed for use by supervisors to assess their trainees' cross-cultural counseling competence. This one-factor scale was developed based on the cross-cultural counseling competencies identified by the Education and Training Committee of Division 17 of the American Psychological Association (Sue et al., 1982). The CCCI–R consists of items that represent three areas: cross-cultural counseling skill, sociopolitical awareness, and cultural sensitivity. This scale is reported to demonstrate good content, construct, and criterion-related validity (Sabnani & Ponterotto, 1992) and excellent reliability (i.e., a coefficient alpha of .95 was noted in the CCCI–R's validation sample) (LaFromboise et al., 1991). A unique limitation of observer ratings of trainee multicultural competence is that the raters, typically supervisors, must themselves be multiculturally competent, a state of affairs that may not exist in some training programs (Constantine, 1997; Priest, 1994).

Multicultural case conceptualization ability, another form of observer-rater multicultural counseling competence, is defined as counselors' ability to conceptualize clients' concerns by differentiating and integrating multicultural knowledge pertaining to their problems (Constantine & Ladany, 2000; Ladany et al., 1997). Counselors who are able to differentiate and integrate information related to their clients are believed to be more skillful in working with them (Blocher, 1983). Conceptualizing clients from a multicultural perspective indicates that counselors can (a) understand and integrate the impact of various cultural factors on clients' presenting issues and (b) suggest an appropriate treatment plan for working with clients based on this knowledge. Client conceptualizations may become increasingly sophisticated as counselors make associations between and among hypothesized etiologies of presenting issues and, accordingly, integrate these data into treatment plans. Counselors' multicultural case conceptualization ability has been presumed to represent an appropriate manifestation of their demonstrated multicultural counseling competence in several previous studies (e.g., Constantine & Ladany, 2000; Ladany et al., 1997). Moreover, Sodowsky et al. (1994) asserted that case conceptualization ability, as an aspect of the counseling process, may be one way of reflecting counselors' multicultural counseling competence. However, it is important to note that an "academic" multicultural conceptualization is still removed from specific multicultural performance skills.

In the next section, we present a revised conceptualization of multicultural counseling competence by identifying factors believed to impact counselors' multicultural competence in most therapeutic encounters. We believe that addressing such factors would be helpful across a variety of therapeutic contexts, including individual, couples, family, and group counseling.

AN ALTERNATIVE CONCEPTUALIZATION
OF MULTICULTURAL COUNSELING COMPETENCE

Competency has been defined as the degree to which therapists adhere to procedures relative to identified criteria or standards (Beutler, Crago, & Arizmendi, 1986). Competent therapists in general are presumed to possess a host of competent behaviors, including (a) a theoretical orientation to guide their interactions, (b) the skillful use of interventions or techniques to bring about the conditions necessary for change or to promote desired changes in behavior, and (c) an awareness of when to apply (or not apply) these interventions (Shaw & Dobson, 1988; Yeaton & Sechrest, 1981). When applying the notion of competence to the area of multicultural counseling, multiculturally competent therapists are expected to possess (a) multicultural attitudes/beliefs in relation to working with culturally diverse individuals, (b) knowledge about the impact of various cultural group memberships on clients, and (c) appropriate intervention skills in the delivery of psychological services to culturally diverse clients. Although multicultural counseling competence has been traditionally conceptualized as consisting of these three components, the multicultural literature has generally not fully addressed how client-counselor interactions may impact manifestations of counselors' multicultural competence.

Fischer, Jome, and Atkinson (1998) discussed a framework that emphasized the importance of understanding culture in counseling within a framework of "common factors" in psychotherapy or counseling. These common factors include the therapeutic relationship, a shared worldview between clients and counselors, meeting clients' expectations, and using interventions that are deemed appropriate by both clients and counselors. Fischer et al. acknowledged that although common characteristics of the helping process exist across cultures, counselors must be sensitive and responsive to culturally specific contexts in counseling. Influenced by their framework, we contend that to understand fully how multicultural counseling competence can be achieved, a broader conceptualization of this construct is needed. To this end, we propose that multicultural counseling competence consists of six dimensions: (1) counselor self-awareness, (2) general knowledge about multicultural issues, (3) multicultural counseling self-efficacy, (4) understanding of unique client variables, (5) an effective counseling working alliance, and (6) multicultural counseling skills. Counselors are deemed to be multiculturally competent depending on the levels at which the six dimensions are achieved. That is, lower ability on any of the six domains corresponds to a lower overall level of multicultural counseling competence. We also assert that no counselor may ever achieve 100% multicultural counseling competence because of the inexact nature of many therapeutic interventions and the seemingly infinite number of variables that could impact any of the six multicultural counseling competence dimensions. That said, we believe that a primary goal of counselors must be ongoing strivings to achieve greater multicultural competence.

The first proposed dimension of multicultural counseling competence is *self-awareness*, which involves counselors' ability to understand their own multiple cultural identities as well as how their personal biases about others influence their ways of being and operating in a wide range of interpersonal situations. Self-awareness also involves understanding how socialization processes have impacted the development of counselors' values and attitudes. Self-awareness is typically achieved through various forms of self exploration, such as experiential and didactic activities, consultation, supervision, and personal therapy. Self-awareness is also believed to be beneficial to counselors in using themselves as therapeutic change agents.

The second dimension is *general knowledge about multicultural issues*, which involves the ongoing acquisition of knowledge about psychological and social issues pertaining to living in a multicultural society. Knowledge may be gleaned from theoretical, empirical, journalistic, and popular literature sources and includes the ability to critique these sources from a multicultural perspective. Additionally, counselors with general knowledge about multicultural issues are aware of both subtle and overt forms of prejudicial attitudes and discriminatory behavior reflected in society at large as well as within and throughout the counseling and psychology professions. Finally, therapists who possess general multicultural knowledge are able to distinguish between universal issues related to a particular cultural group (i.e., etic knowledge) and individual differences within this particular cultural group (i.e., emic knowledge).

Multicultural counseling self-efficacy is the third dimension of multicultural competence. Multicultural counseling self-efficacy pertains to counselors' confidence in their ability to perform a set of multicultural counseling skills and behaviors successfully (Constantine & Ladany, 2000). This definition follows Bandura's (1982) self-efficacy theory, which posits that self-efficacy expectations are related to the actual performance of these skills and behaviors. An important distinction must be made between self-efficacy expectations and self-perceptions of multicultural competence (i.e., counselors' belief that they possess multicultural competence) across realms other than multicultural counseling skills (e.g., multicultural knowledge, counselor self-awareness, etc.). Self-efficacy is directly tied to specific behaviors, whereas beliefs about dimensions such as knowledge and self-awareness are self-perceptions. Both multicultural self-efficacy and self-perceptions could be inaccurate, and both may or may not be linked to the provision of true multiculturally competent counseling services.

The *understanding of unique client variables* dimension of multicultural counseling competence refers to counselors' understanding of how a host of personal (e.g., cultural group memberships, background, socialization, personality traits, and values) and situational (e.g., clients' presenting concerns, therapeutic expectations, motivation to change, and willingness to self-disclose) factors converge to impact a specific client in a specific therapeutic context. Hence, a thorough understanding of how specific cultural group memberships (e.g., race and sex) may relate to clients' therapeutic concerns, for example, is necessary to fulfill this dimension. Clients bring a wealth of information to counseling, and counselors constantly make decisions regarding whether or not to focus on any given piece of data. However, the full range of unique client variables needs to be continually recognized and conceptualized for counselors to fully understand the impact of these factors in therapeutic contexts.

The fifth dimension of multicultural competence is forming an *effective counseling working alliance.* Bordin (1979), based on the work of Greenson (1967) and others, conceptualized the therapeutic relationship as a working alliance between a counselor and a client. He postulated that the therapeutic working alliance was pantheoretical and consisted of three primary components: (1) mutual agreement between the client and therapist about the goals of counseling (e.g., decreasing depression, improving interpersonal functioning), (2) mutual agreement between the client and therapist about the tasks of counseling (e.g., discussing multicultural issues in counseling), and (3) an emotional bond between the client and therapist (e.g., mutual caring and trust). Applying Bordin's (1979) model to multicultural counseling situations, we believe that counselors' multicultural competence is reflected in the extent to which multicultural issues are addressed in the context of the working alliance. For example, counselors who initiate discussions of racial or ethnic issues when warranted may be viewed as having some degree of multicultural counseling skills. However, the extent to which counselors and clients discuss these issues is tied to the strength of the working alliance in that if they agree that a discussion of such differences is important, they will proceed to have this discussion. Subsequently, the alliance is enhanced and strengthened. Conversely, if only one member of a counseling dyad believes that such a discussion is important, then the alliance is weakened. In sum, multicultural competence in counselors is reflected in the extent to which working alliances with culturally diverse clients can be formed and strengthened. Working alliances then become the foundations upon which multicultural counseling skills are deemed effective or ineffective.

The sixth dimension, *multicultural counseling skills,* refers to counselors' ability to effectively address multicultural issues in the context of therapeutic situations. Multiculturally skilled counselors are viewed as proficient in applying multiculturally sensitive therapeutic techniques in counseling while understanding how multicultural issues may affect various aspects of the therapeutic process. Thus, therapists who possess adequate multicultural counseling skills are able to effectively identify and process multicultural issues when appropriate. This ability is crucial to both counseling process and outcome.

Future Implications for the Development and Assessment of Multicultural Counseling Competence

Practice and Research Implications

As the aforementioned model illustrates, the development of multicultural counseling competence is influenced by many factors that relate to the therapeutic alliance, particularly on the part of clients. Previous research has found that therapist-offered relationship variables are relatively poor predictors of therapeutic outcome when compared with client variables (Hartley, 1985). Hence, within the multicultural counseling realm, it is critical that future researchers identify specific client variables that may contribute to or impede desired treatment outcomes. In addition, although competence in one area of cultural issues (e.g., working with African American clients) may generalize to other areas of multicultural competence (e.g., working with Latino clients), generalization to other areas is not absolute (Ancis & Ladany, 2001). Thus, empirical validation of how the integration of both etic and emic approaches may impact multicultural counseling competence, particularly with regard to treatment processes and outcomes, is also needed (Ponterotto, Fuertes, et al., 2000). There is also a strong need for empirical testing of existing theoretical models of multicultural counseling competence.

In relation to the evaluation of multicultural counseling competence, it is important that multimethod approaches are identified and instituted (Ladany & Muse-Burke, in press; Ponterotto, Fuertes, et al., 2000). Examples of these methods include a combination of the following: (a) self-report ratings, (b) multiple ongoing opportunities to have counseling work evaluated by peers and more experienced colleagues or supervisors (e.g., observer ratings), and (c) portfolios. It is also vital that ratings of multicultural counseling competence consider the difficulty level of clients, and corrections may need to be made for more challenging clients because counselors may demonstrate decreased skill when working with such clients (Shaw & Dobson, 1988). Conversely, counselors' ability to work consistently (and effectively) with a broad range of populations may represent, in part, their level of multicultural counseling competence. Nonetheless, difficulties in how to account for potential differences in difficulty levels among clients may also present challenges to raters of multicultural counseling competence.

Training Implications

Numerous studies have explored various constructs that may be related to counselors' perceived multicultural counseling competence. Many of these investigations (e.g., Constantine, Juby, & Liang, in press; Ladany, Brittan-Powell, & Pannu, 1997; Neville et al., 1996; Ottavi, Pope-Davis, & Dings, 1994; Pope-Davis, Reynolds, Dings, & Nielson, 1995; Sodowsky et al., 1998) have examined demographic (e.g., race, ethnicity, gender, and age), training (e.g., multicultural coursework taken, number of client contact hours with people of color), and psychological variables (e.g., racial identity attitudes, racism) as predictors of self-reported multicultural counseling competence. Extrapolating ideas from the results of such studies may be helpful in identify training variables that could contribute to their multicultural counseling competence.

Because professional competence is normally obtained through formal academic training and supervised experiences (Hogan, 1979), it is important that these training opportunities accurately reflect the proposed competencies that are being taught. Similarly, the development of multicultural counseling competence through various training venues is presumed to mirror the types of competencies that counselors will need in working with various cultural populations. With regard to the multicultural counseling area, standards of competence are often based on conceptual or theoretical writings rather than being supported by empirical research. Thus, it is unclear the extent to which the competencies emphasized in training programs can be successfully applied to actual professional practice situations. Future researchers may wish to identify effective in-session therapeutic phenomena in relation to culturally diverse clients and attempt to replicate these factors in the context of multicultural training situations.

A multitude of individual factors must be considered in the context of evaluating multicultural counseling competence in supervisees. For example, theoretical orientation, value system, cultural group memberships, and previous experiences, to name a few, on the part of both supervisors and trainees will undoubtedly affect how rating instruments are completed. Consequently, supervisors who rate trainees' multicultural counseling competence may evaluate observed behavior against various aspects of their own personal standards (e.g., what they might have done in the same situation). In using personal criteria to make therapeutic judgments, the potential for low interrater reliability exists among multiple rating sources (Shaw & Dobson, 1988). Thus, evaluations of counselor competence require specific predetermined standards and criteria, along with explicit procedures for conducting such evaluations. However, standards for professional practice have not been well articulated in applied mental health fields. Although standards for the provision of multiculturally competent services have been identified (e.g., Arredondo et al., 1996; Sue et al., 1992), there is a need to test the utility of these competencies to real-life therapeutic situations.

It is also important to note that external evaluations of competence may create anxiety among trainees and are often challenging to make (Shaw

& Dobson, 1988). Nonetheless, "evaluating and making judgments about other people is an essential and unavoidable part of living" (Klein & Babineau, 1974, p. 788). In training settings, students' exposure to evaluations of their multicultural counseling competence in and of itself may raise their anxiety because of the challenges and controversies often associated with discussing racial, ethnic, and other cultural issues. Hence, in such settings, it may be important for trainers to underscore the ethical principle of helping professionals that speaks to the recognition that such personnel must only provide services for which they are qualified by training and experience. It is possible that merely the desire to be ethical in their professional behavior may encourage more resistant trainees to embrace the importance of being multiculturally competent. Furthermore, the identification of means in which to best facilitate multicultural counseling competence in trainees is sorely needed.

Furthermore, because some counselors may overestimate their level of multicultural counseling competence due to factors such as social desirability (e.g., Constantine & Ladany, 2000), so too may supervisors overestimate or underestimate their trainees' level of multicultural counseling competence based on their general like or dislike of their trainees (e.g., halo effects). Some research evidence exists that suggests that trainees' general counseling competence is influenced by supervisors liking their trainees (Carey, Williams, & Wells, 1988; Dodenhoff, 1981). Thus, it will be important for trainees to obtain multiple indices of supervisor-rated multicultural counseling competence in order to get information from varied "objective" sources regarding their multicultural counseling competence. However, a phenomenon that could complicate this issue relates to the finding that some counselors-in-training and recent counseling graduates may have received more exposure to multicultural training than their supervisors (Constantine, 1997). Hence, these counselors may be more multiculturally competent than the supervisors who are responsible for rating them in this domain, making these supervisors' ratings suspect.

CONCLUSIONS

Multicultural counseling competence is a complex variable that may have multidimensional conceptualizations and meanings. There is a need for counseling psychology practitioners and scientists to work in concert to better understand the nature of this construct so as to improve therapeutic services to culturally diverse populations. Empirical validation of various models of multicultural counseling competence will also be necessary to effectively operationalize this construct. The accurate measurement of multicultural counseling competence will continue to present challenges to counselors, educators, supervisors, trainees, and researchers, even with the most reliable and valid assessment procedures. Nevertheless, it is important that dynamic and valid assessment indices be formulated so as to capture the essence of this important construct.

REFERENCES

Allison, K. W., Echemendia, R. J., Crawford, I., & Robinson, W. L. (1996). Predicting cultural competence: Implications for practice and training. *Professional Psychology: Research and Practice, 27,* 386-393.

Ancis, J. R., & Ladany, N. (2001). A multicultural framework for counselor supervision. In L. J. Bradley and N. Ladany (Eds.), *Counselor supervision: Principles, process, and practice* (3rd ed.) (pp. 63-90). Philadelphia: Brunner-Routledge.

Arredondo, P., Toporek, R., Brown, S. P., Jones, J., Locke, D., Sanchez, J., & Stadler, H. (1996). Operationalization of the multicultural counseling competencies. *Journal of Multicultural Counseling and Development, 24,* 42-78.

Arter, J. A., & Spandel, V. (1992). Using portfolios of student work in instruction and assessment. *Educational Measurement: Issues and Practice, 11,* 36-44.

Bandura, A. (1982). Self-efficacy mechanism in human agency. *American Psychologist, 37,* 122-147.

Beutler, L. E., Crago, M., & Arizmendi, T. G. (1986). Therapist variables in psychotherapy process and emotions. In A. E. Bergin & S. L. Garfield (Eds.), *Handbook of psychotherapy and behavior changes* (pp. 257-310). New York: John Wiley.

Blocher, D. H. (1983). Towards a cognitive-developmental approach to counseling supervision. *The Counseling Psychologist, 11,* 27-34.

Bordin, E. S. (1979). The generalizability of the psychoanalytic concept of the working alliance. *Psychotherapy: Theory, Research, and Practice, 16,* 252-260.

Carey, J. C., Williams, K. S., & Wells, M. (1988). Relationships between dimensions of supervisors' influence and counselor trainees' performance. *Counselor Education and Supervision, 28,* 130-139.

Coleman, H. L. K. (1996). Portfolio assessment of multicultural counseling competency. *The Counseling Psychologist, 24,* 216-229.

Collins, A. (1992). Portfolios for science education: Issues in purpose, structure, and authenticity. *Science Education, 76,* 451-463.

Constantine, M. G. (1997). Facilitating multicultural competency in counseling supervision: Operationalizing a practical framework. In D. B. Pope-Davis & H. L. K. Coleman (Eds.), *Multicultural counseling competencies: Assessment, education and training, and supervision* (pp. 310-324). Thousand Oaks, CA: Sage.

Constantine, M. G., Juby, H. L., & Liang, J. J. (in press). Examining self-reported multicultural counseling competence and race-related attitudes in White marital and family therapists. *Journal of Marital and Family Therapy.*

Constantine, M. G., & Ladany, N. (2000). Self-report multicultural counseling competence scales and their relation to social desirability and multicultural case conceptualization. *Journal of Counseling Psychology, 47,* 155-164.

Constantine, M. G., Ladany, N., Inman, A. G., & Ponterotto, J. G. (1996). Students' perceptions of multicultural training in counseling psychology programs. *Journal of Multicultural Counseling and Development, 24,* 241-253.

D'Andrea, M., Daniels, J., & Heck, R. (1991). Evaluating the impact of multicultural counseling training. *Journal of Counseling and Development, 70,* 143-150.

Dodenhoff, J. T. (1981). Interpersonal attraction and direct-indirect supervisor influence as predictors of counselor trainee effectiveness. *Journal of Counseling Psychology, 28,* 47-52.

Fischer, A. R., Jome, L. M., & Atkinson, D. R. (1998). Reconceptualizing multicultural counseling: Universal healing conditions in a culturally specific context. *The Counseling Psychologist, 26,* 525-588.

Greenson, R. R. (1967). *The technique and practice of psychoanalysis.* New York: International Universities Press.

Hartley, D. E. (1985). Research on the therapeutic alliance in psychotherapy. In R. E. Hales & A. J. Frances (Eds.), *Annual review of psychiatry* (Vol. 4, pp. 532-543). Washington, DC: American Psychiatric Association Press.

Hills, H. I., & Strozier, A. L. (1992). Multicultural training in APA-approved counseling psychology programs: A survey. *Professional Psychology: Research and Practice, 23,* 43-51.

Hogan, D. B. (1979). *The regulation of psychotherapists* (Vol. 1). Cambridge, MA: Ballinger.

Klein, R. H., & Babineau, R. (1974). Evaluating the competence of trainees: It's nothing personal. *American Journal of Psychiatry, 131,* 788-791.

Ladany, N., Brittan-Powell, C. S., & Pannu, R. K. (1997). The influence of supervisory racial identity interaction and racial matching on the supervisory working alliance and supervisee multicultural competence. *Counselor Education and Supervision, 36,* 284-304.

Ladany, N., Inman, A. G., Constantine, M. G., & Hofheinz, E. W. (1997). Supervisee multicultural case conceptualization ability and self-reported multicultural competence as functions of supervisee racial identity and supervisor focus. *Journal of Counseling Psychology, 44,* 284-293.

Ladany, N., & Muse-Burke, J. L. (2001). Understanding and conducting supervision research. In L. J. Bradley & N. Ladany (Eds.), *Counselor supervision: Principles, process, and practice* (3rd ed.) (pp. 304-529). Philadelphia: Brunner-Routledge.

LaFromboise, T. D., Coleman, H. L. K., & Hernandez, A. (1991). Development and factor structure of the Cross-Cultural Counseling Inventory–Revised. *Professional Psychology: Research and Practice, 22,* 380-388.

Neville, H. A., Heppner, M. J., Louie, C. E., Thompson, C. E., Brooks, L., & Baker, C. E. (1996). The impact of multicultural training on White racial identity attitudes and therapy competencies. *Professional Psychology: Research and Practice, 27,* 83-89.

O'Neill, J. (1992). Putting performance to the test. *Educational Leadership, 49,* 14-19.

Ottavi, T. M., Pope-Davis, D. B., & Dings, J. G. (1994). Relationship between White racial identity attitudes and self-reported multicultural counseling competencies. *Journal of Counseling Psychology, 41,* 149-154.

Pedersen, P. B. (Ed.). (1991). Multiculturalism as a fourth force in counseling [Special issue]. *Journal of Counseling and Development, 70,* 4-250.

Ponterotto, J. G. (1997). Multicultural counseling training: A competency model and national survey. In D. B. Pope-Davis & H. L. K. Coleman (Eds.), *Multicultural counseling competencies: Assessment, education and training, and supervision* (pp. 111-130). Thousand Oaks, CA: Sage.

Ponterotto, J. G. (1998). Charting a course for research in multicultural counseling training. *The Counseling Psychologist, 26,* 43-68.

Ponterotto, J. G., & Alexander, C. M. (1996). Assessing the multicultural competence of counselors and clinicians. In L. A. Suzuki, P. J. Meller, & J. G. Ponterotto (Eds.), *Handbook of multicultural assessment* (pp. 651-672). San Francisco: Jossey-Bass.

Ponterotto, J. G., Alexander, C. M., & Grieger, I. (1995). A multicultural competency checklist for counseling training programs. *Journal of Multicultural Counseling and Development, 23,* 11-20.

Ponterotto, J. G., Fuertes, J. N., & Chen, E. C. (2000). Models of multicultural counseling. In S. D. Brown & R. W. Lent (Eds.), *Handbook of counseling psychology* (3rd ed., pp. 639-669). New York: John Wiley.

Ponterotto, J. G., Gretchen, D., Utsey, S. O., Rieger, B. P., & Austin, R. (2000). *A construct validity study of the Multicultural Counseling Awareness Scale (MCAS).* Unpublished manuscript.

Ponterotto, J. G., Rieger, B. P., Barrett, A., Sparks, R., Sanchez, C. M., & Magids, D. (1996). Development and initial validation of the Multicultural Counseling Awareness Scale. In G. R. Sodowsky & J. C. Impara (Eds.), *Multicultural assessment in counseling and clinical psychology* (pp. 247-282). Lincoln, NE: Buros Institute of Mental Measurements.

Pope-Davis, D. B., & Dings, J. G. (1994). An empirical comparison of two self-report multicultural counseling competency inventories. *Measurement and Evaluation in Counseling and Development, 27*, 93-102.

Pope-Davis, D. B., & Dings, J. G. (1995). The assessment of multicultural counseling competencies. In J. G. Ponterotto, J. M. Casas, L. A. Suzuki, & C. M. Alexander (Eds.), *Handbook of multicultural counseling* (pp. 287-311). Thousand Oaks, CA: Sage.

Pope-Davis, D. B., Liu, W. M., Nevitt, J., & Toporek, R. L. (2000). The development and initial validation of the Multicultural Environmental Inventory: A preliminary investigation. *Cultural Diversity and Ethnic Minority Psychology, 6*, 57-64.

Pope-Davis, D. B., Reynolds, A. L., Dings, J. G., & Nielson, D. (1995). Examining multicultural competencies of graduate students in psychology. *Professional Psychology: Research and Practice, 26*, 322-329.

Priest, R. (1994). Minority supervisor and majority supervisor: Another perspective on clinical reality. *Counselor Education and Supervision, 34*, 152-158.

Quintana, S. M., & Bernal, M. E. (1995). Ethnic minority training in counseling psychology: Comparisons with clinical psychology and proposed standards. *The Counseling Psychologist, 23*, 102-121.

Ridley, C. R., Mendoza, D. W., & Kanitz, B. E. (1994). Multicultural training: Reexamination, operationalization, and integration. *The Counseling Psychologist, 22*, 76-102.

Sabnani, H. B., & Ponterotto, J. G. (1992). Racial/ethnic minority-specific instrumentation in counseling research: A review, critique, and recommendations. *Measurement and Evaluation in Counseling and Development, 24*, 161-187.

Shaw, B. F., & Dobson, K. S. (1988). Competency judgments in the training and evaluation of psychotherapists. *Journal of Consulting and Clinical Psychology, 56*, 666-672.

Sodowsky, G. R. (1996). The Multicultural Counseling Inventory: Psychometric properties and some uses in counseling training. In G. R. Sodowsky & J. C. Impara (Eds.), *Multicultural assessment in counseling and clinical psychology* (pp. 283-324). Lincoln, NE: Buros Institute of Mental Measurements.

Sodowsky, G. R., Kuo-Jackson, P. Y., Richardson, M. F., & Corey, A. T. (1998). Correlates of self-reported multicultural competencies: Counselor multicultural social desirability, race, social inadequacy, locus of control racial ideology, and multicultural training. *Journal of Counseling Psychology, 45*, 256-264.

Sodowsky, G. R., Taffe, R. C., Gutkin, T. B., & Wise, S. L. (1994). Development of the Multicultural Counseling Inventory: A self-report measure of multicultural competencies. *Journal of Counseling Psychology, 41*, 137-148.

Sue, D. W. (1996). Multicultural counseling: Models, methods, and actions. *The Counseling Psychologist, 24*, 279-284.

Sue, D. W., Arredondo, P., & McDavis, R. J. (1992). Multicultural counseling competencies and standards: A call to the profession. *Journal of Multicultural Counseling and Development, 20*, 64-68.

Sue, D. W., Bernier, J. E., Durran, A., Feinberg, L., Pedersen, P., Smith, E. J., & Vasquez-Nuttall, E. (1982). Position paper: Cross-cultural counseling competencies. *The Counseling Psychologist, 10*, 45-52.

Sue, D. W., Carter, R. T., Casas, J. M., Fouad, N. A., Ivey, A. E., Jensen, M., LaFromboise, T., Manese, J. E., Ponterotto, J. G., & Vasquez-Nuttall, E. (1998). *Multicultural counseling competencies: Individual and organizational development.* Thousand Oaks, CA: Sage.

Sue, D. W., & Sue, D. (1999). *Counseling the culturally different: Theory and practice* (3rd ed.). New York: John Wiley.

Yeaton, W. H., & Sechrest, L. (1981). Critical dimensions in the maintenance of successful treatments: Strengths, integrity, and effectiveness. *Journal of Consulting and Clinical Psychology, 49*, 156-167.

Correspondence concerning this chapter should be addressed to Madonna G. Constantine, Department of Counseling and Clinical Psychology, Teachers College, Columbia University, 525 West 120th Street, Box 92, New York, NY 10027 (e-mail address: mc816@columbia.edu).

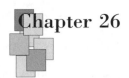

Chapter 26

MEASUREMENT OF MULTICULTURAL CONSTRUCTS

Integration and Research Directions

CHARLENE M. ALEXANDER
LISA A. SUZUKI

THIS CHAPTER EXAMINES issues of measurement of multicultural constructs covered in this section (i.e., racial and ethnic identity, the Cross Racial Identity Scale, acculturation, worldview, prejudice and racism, and multicultural counseling competence). As noted by all the authors, the ability to accurately and reliably measure multicultural constructs is central to the role and function of a psychologist. A good measure can be used for appropriate diagnosis, classification, intervention, education, and research. The measurement of multicultural constructs has continued to grow as the professions in counseling recognize the need to address the concerns of a growing minority population. Some of the strongest criticisms leveled against the counseling profession have been concerns regarding bias in assessment procedures and the lack of appropriate measures available. Another concern is that researchers continue to perpetuate poor measurement practices in the development and use of multicultural instruments and assessment procedures. This chapter summarizes the literature found in this section and provides the reader with information regarding the integration of current research practices and future directions.

MEASUREMENT OF
RACIAL AND ETHNIC IDENTITY

The chapter by Fischer and Moradi provides a comprehensive review of recent developments in the area of racial and ethnic identity. One major finding is that there is little consensus about the meaning of racial and ethnic identity, with limited attention given to measures and constructs not focused on Black/African or White ethnic identity. The authors identified the following: 3 measures of Black/African ethnic identity, 3 measures of White ethnic identity, 2 measures of Native American ethnic identity, 1 Latina/Latino ethnic identity measure, 1 Jewish identity measure, and 2 multigroup ethnic identity measures. The chapter does an excellent job of drawing attention to populations and instruments that have received limited attention in the literature.

Readers are provided with a theoretically sound way to define and evaluate measures of ethnic identity for specific populations and multigroup populations as well as a glimpse of the comprehensive state of the research regarding Black/African and White ethnic identity measures and the limited (in some cases, measures have only been used once) studies addressing other underrepresented populations. As noted by the authors, to continue to focus on only two groups will perpetuate much of psychology's selective dialogue around race and ethnicity.

The authors also point to the limited utility of pencil-and-paper measures. Self-report attitudinal research needs to be supplemented with behavioral observations and interventions to verify the validity of measurement outcomes as well as to explore the discrepancies that exist between attitudes and behavior.

Multicultural counseling practice will benefit from continued exploration of the racial identity development of both counselors and clients. Knowledge regarding self-actualization, self-esteem, and preference for counselor characteristics, to name a few, have been facilitated by the development of racial identity attitude scales. Future investigations can only enhance the knowledge base. As our understanding of racial identity becomes more sophisticated and complex, it is likely that other variables will be included to explore interactions with different racial minority groups and measures of other psychological constructs.

NIGRESCENCE THEORY
AND MEASUREMENT

The chapter by Cross and Vandiver provides the reader with a unique look at the development of the Cross Racial Identity Scale (CRIS). The reader has a clear sense of the role of reference group orientation (RGO) versus general personality (PI) in the development of this instrument. Further, understanding Black identity as a range of identity development patterns from traditional socialization experiences, resocialization, and recycling can be quite complex in its application.

Cross and Vandiver, in developing the CRIS, set as their goal the development of orthogonal subscales. The lack of orthogonal subscales has been a source of major criticism of other identity measures. The development of this scale was carefully thought out and executed over the course of 5 years, and the authors are to be commended for their care and persistence in the development of this instrument. The CRIS consists of six reliable and valid subscales that are independent of each other. One concern, however, is the omission of items to measure the Encounter stage (Stage 2) and the blending of items to represent both the Internalization (Stage 4) and Internalization-Commitment (Stage 5) stages. This omission and integration limits the researcher's ability to accurately and reliably measure the theory of Nigrescence, thus limiting one's capacity to assign individuals in a systematic way to represent properties of the entire theory. However, the psychometric properties of the measure presented should entice researchers to use this measure with confidence.

ACCULTURATION

The chapter by Kim and Abreu summarizes the evolution of the acculturation construct as a "complex psychosocial phenomenon comprising many aspects of human functioning." Although initially viewed as a linear construct, current understanding supports a more multidimensional (e.g., bilinear, multilinear) framework.

The authors provide a comprehensive review of a number of published acculturation instruments classified according to linearity, content focus, and levels of reliability and validity. They also note information regarding group-specific versus multigroup instruments. This review provides the reader with a concise way of examining the strengths and weaknesses of 33 instruments identified in the literature. Even though each instrument is viewed with its own unique profile of strengths and weaknesses, a number of significant psychometric limitations are noted for all scales. These included, in some cases, limited validity and reliability studies and/or a lack of normative data. Also, there appeared to be few scales that address non-behavioral aspects of acculturation (i.e., values, cultural identity, and knowledge).

Although many scales have evolved to address the construct of acculturation, there appear to be many issues limiting the potential applicability of scores to actual counseling. This chapter by Kim and Abreu provides readers with a glimpse of how to examine instruments in the area based on their psychometric and conceptual rigor with regard to the process of acculturation.

WORLDVIEW

The chapter by Ibrahim, Roysircar-Sodowsky, and Ohnishi highlights the complexity of understanding and assessing worldview. As noted, this construct is defined as "a set of beliefs, values, and assumptions that undergrids behavior and emotional reactions; provides an implicit frame of reference for the interpretation of the world and its experiences; and is derived from a person's social and cultural world (including family, primary group, secondary social cultural groups, community, and nation)." These authors note that to be useful the construct must be comprehensive, and the literature identifies a number of variables that impact worldview. These include gender, age, occupation, immigrant status, race, nationality, majority versus minority status, and religion. Another complexity is the finding that within-racial/ethnic group differences exceed between-racial/ethnic group differences on most assessed psychological constructs, and worldview is not an exception. Thus, "findings of each study must be appreciated in light of their unique settings and outcome." Ibrahim, Roysircar-Sodowsky, and Ohnishi indicate that worldview cannot be understood in a vacuum but, rather, needs to be examined in conjunction with other contextual variables. Given the complexity of the worldview construct, it is no wonder there are limitations in our understanding of this construct.

With regard to assessment of this worldview, there are limitations based on the particular definitions applied during the development of the scale. In addition, the usage of primarily self-report, Likert-type scale items is also limiting (i.e., SAWV). Although most counselors use scales like the SAWV as a quantitative measure, the authors report that the scale can be used qualitatively to help the clinician in understanding the client's beliefs, values, and assumptions that underlie their cognitions, feelings, and behaviors.

Ibrahim, Roysircar-Sodowsky, and Ohnishi highlight 25 studies related to worldview. Of these 25, 17 studies were conducted with students primarily at the university level. This poses a major limitation in the literature given that university samples are often identified as "samples of convenience" and not necessarily reflective of a particular racial/ethnic group population.

Other limitations noted by the authors include questions regarding the immutability or mutability of worldview and the misuse of instruments stemming in part from definitional problems. Difficulties with the psychometric properties of particular scales like the SAWV are also reported.

PREJUDICE AND RACISM

Burkard, Medler, and Boticki review important literature related to the measurement of racial and anti-gay prejudice. These authors, like those cited before in this section, note the complexity of the constructs under scrutiny and the lack of agreement on an operational definition of these terms. Burkard, Medler, and Boticki note the importance of both implicit and explicit prejudice that exist concurrently but separately as social judgment processes. With regard to assessment, they cite summative reviews conducted by scholars in this area that identify significant limitations regarding test development practices and psychometric properties of particular instruments. In addition, the research has concentrated primarily on White racism in relation to African Americans.

The chapter examines a number of scales like the Quick Discrimination Index that was developed to address both cognitive and affective components of attitudes. Despite the construction of a number of scales, the authors continue to cite limitations in terms of limited sampling and psychometric properties of the scales (e.g., applicable factor structures for various racial/ethnic groups). There exists a clear need to expand our understanding of prejudice and racism. The majority of research on these constructs has relied on self-report instruments, and there is now a strong need to link measurement outcomes to clinically meaningful behavior.

MULTICULTURAL COUNSELING COMPETENCE

This chapter by Constantine and Ladany reviews current methods of assessing multicultural counseling competence, presents an alternative conceptualization of multicultural counseling competency, and presents recommendations for future practice, training, and research in this area.

The authors provide a comprehensive review of contemporary methods of assessing multicultural counseling competency, most of which are based on Sue et al.'s (1982) position paper. The authors' review includes individual self-report measures, the multicultural competency checklist, observer ratings, multicultural case conceptualization ability, and the portfolio method to multicultural competency evaluation. The authors further present an alternative conceptualization of multicultural counseling competency based on three dimensions: (a) awareness of the self, others, and the self in relation to others; (b) unique client variables; and (c) responsiveness to clients regarding multicultural issues. The evaluation of multicultural competency is dependent on an individual's level of achievement on each of these three dimensions.

This chapter provides readers with a new and unique way to conceptualize multicultural counseling competency, one that is closely related to the therapeutic alliance and includes the role of empathy and other salient characteristics. In making recommendations for future directions, this chapter encourages supervisors and academicians to closely examine their level of multicultural competency and regard for students in determining how these variables negatively or positively affect the evaluation of multicultural competency.

CONCLUSIONS

The primary goal of this chapter was to bring attention to the importance of accountability and assessment in the measurement of multicultural constructs. Although instruments have been developed, studies of their reliability and validity need to be conducted in a more systematic manner. As each chapter in this section has detailed, even though much research has been done, much is still needed to increase our complex understanding of these areas. However, as with any evolving instrument, the measures cited here require additional work to ensure greater understanding of the results obtained.

To this end, we would like to recommend that researchers make greater efforts to obtain representative samples of different racial and ethnic groups. Clearly, as stated in a number of these chapters, limitations exist when the primary focus is on students in higher education as they may not be reflective of the larger racial/ethnic populations.

Further, we also need to become more sophisticated with regard to our research designs and statistical techniques. As noted by many authors, the constructs are often not linear. Future research should ensure that what we are examining may in fact be curvilinear, multilinear, or bidirectional.

Future theory development should explore the advantages and disadvantages of stage theories versus statuses. Statuses seem to imply less of a hierarchical structure than stage theories. However, the method of assigning individuals to stages/statuses on instruments being developed needs further exploration. Certainly, one method to assess the utility of a measure is to examine the method of describing properties of the individual. For some of the measures reviewed in Part IV, greater attention is needed in this area. For example, what does it mean to assign participants to stages on a measure that is intended to be descriptive of a particular theoretical stage, while simultaneously recommending the use of profile analysis to describe an individual or sample? Should a different method be employed in future research that represents the complexity of ethnic identity development?

Researchers also need to note the importance of cultural context and develop an understanding of individual differences in applied settings. While examination of group differences is interesting and can yield helpful information, clinicians need guidance on utilizing assessment information during the intervention process.

Further, we encourage researchers to develop measures that take into account nontraditional variables that reflect the complexity of cultures—for example, immigrant status, refugee status, history of trauma, and creative forms of cultural expression can be studied in conjunction with the more general features of the research. The continued development and refinement of measures of racial identity development in any of these areas will enhance our understanding of this construct and its impact on appropriate clinical intervention strategies.

The chapters in Part IV highlight the exciting work that has been done to bring greater understanding of significant multicultural constructs. It appears that, based on what has been concluded thus far, an infinite amount of potential work remains. Lest we engage in too much critical scrutiny, it is vital that we acknowledge the work that has been conducted by scholars in the past as we document a path to future generations of researchers. As our assessment practices become more sophisticated, there is an even greater chance of the understanding of these constructs leading to meaningful psychological practices for all racial and ethnic communities.

REFERENCE

Sue, D. W., Bernier, J. E., Durran, A., Feinberg, L., Pedersen, P., Smith, E. J., & Vasquez-Nuttall, E. (1982). Position paper: Cross-cultural counseling competencies. *The Counseling Psychologist, 10,* 45-52.

Correspondence concerning this chapter may be sent to Charlene M. Alexander, Department of Counseling Psychology and Guidance Services, Teachers College 622, Ball State University, Muncie, IN 47306-0585 (e-mail address: calexander@bsu.edu).

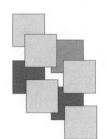

PART V

THEORY AND RESEARCH DESIGN
IN MULTICULTURAL COUNSELING:
LATEST DEVELOPMENTS

Part V of the *Handbook* presents substantive chapters on theory and research methods in multicultural counseling. The section opens with
Chapter 27, in which Fuertes and Gretchen review the state of theory and
model development in multicultural counseling. The past decade has witnessed vibrant scholarly attention to theory development in multicultural
counseling. This is a particularly exciting area because in the early decades
in multicultural counseling scholarship less attention was devoted to theory development. Strong theories lead to well designed research and improved clinical practice. Fuertes and Gretchen review nine promising new
theories of multicultural counseling. Importantly, the authors identify
themes that transcend the developing theories. Such integrative information will facilitate improved theory explication. Finally, the authors provide insightful and specific directions for further theoretical and empirical
work in the area.

In Chapter 28, Atkinson, Bui, and Mori provide a penetrating analysis
of the psychology profession's increasing momentum toward establishing
"Empirically Supported Treatments" (EST). The EST movement attempts
to identity the most effective treatments for specific problems regardless of
potential mediating variables such as counselor and client cultural influences. Relying on a thorough and well-integrated review of the literature,
Atkinson et al. present a convincing argument that one cannot ignore cultural variables in the identification of effective treatments. The authors

fear that the EST movement may have deleterious consequences for the multicultural counseling emphasis now so central to the mental health professions and advocate increased attention to common factors approaches to assessment and treatment.

One theme inherent in this *Handbook* revolves around the complexity of counseling in a culturally heterogeneous society. As such, research in multicultural counseling is challenging on a number of fronts. For decades, consistent with the psychology profession generally, counseling research has relied most heavily on quantitative methods rooted in positivist and postpositivist research paradigms. Although of certain value, these methods are naturally limited in their ability to descriptively capture the complexity of the process of multicultural counseling. In recent years, there has been a growing acceptance, and in fact, an embracing of qualitative research methods rooted in more constructivistic and critical theory paradigms. In Chapter 29, Morrow, Rakhsha, and Castañeda provide a comprehensive and accessible overview of qualitative research methods for multicultural counseling. They tap an interdisciplinary literature to provide clear descriptions of various qualitative paradigms and then present specific guidelines for how to conduct qualitative research in multicultural contexts.

Part V closes with a comprehensive analysis of quantitative research for multicultural counseling by Quintana, Troyano, and Taylor in Chapter 30. They review specific challenges to conducting quantitative research in a multicultural context and elaborate on the new construct for research called "Cultural Validity." This form of validity ensures the appropriateness of the research with respect to the cultural context. Importantly, the authors review threats to and solutions for establishing cultural validity for each stage of the quantitative research process.

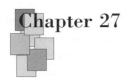

Chapter 27

EMERGING THEORIES OF
MULTICULTURAL COUNSELING

JAIRO N. FUERTES
DENISE GRETCHEN

A REVIEW OF THE multicultural counseling literature reveals that a number of scholars continue to develop new theories and concepts in an effort to advance the treatment of ethnically and racially diverse clients. This chapter reviews and critiques several of these "emerging" theories of multicultural counseling and presents an integrated discussion that includes research ideas and recommendations. We define "emerging" theories as those published within the past 7 years that have the potential to inform research and practice in multicultural counseling. We limit our review to those theories that focus on individual counseling of racially and ethnically diverse clients. Other chapters in this Handbook focus on related topics and modalities (e.g., family counseling, career development, supervision, multicultural competence, racial and ethnic identity, and worldview theory).

This chapter extends the work of Ponterotto, Fuertes, and Chen (2000), who reviewed seven major theoretical contributions to the multicultural counseling literature. At the conclusion of their chapter, Ponterotto et al. (2000) identified four additional theories worthy of future exploration: (a) Ho's (1995) perspective on internalized culture; (b) Gonzalez, Biever, and Gardner's (1994) social constructionist approach to multicultural counseling; (c) D.W. Sue, Ivey, and Pedersen's (1996) theory of multicultural counseling; and (d) Coleman's (1995, 1997) coping with diversity counseling model. This chapter reviews and critiques these four emerging theoretical formulations plus five additional theories found as part of our literature

AUTHORS' NOTE: We would like to thank the editors of this *Handbook*, Ann R. Fischer, and Vincent C. Alfonso for their excellent and supportive feedback on this chapter. Authorship is alphabetical. The authors contributed equally to this chapter.

review: (a) Steenbarger's (1993) multicontextual model; (b) Herring and
Walker's (1993) synergistic model; (c) Locke's (1998) model of multicultural
understanding; (d) Hanna, Bemak, and Chung's (1999) counselor wisdom
paradigm; and (e) Ramirez's (1999) multicultural model of psychotherapy.

Our literature review consisted of electronic searches of the ERIC and
PSYCHLIT databases and manual searches of the following counseling
journals: *Journal of Counseling Psychology, The Counseling Psychologist,
Journal of Counseling and Development, Journal of Multicultural Coun-
seling and Development, Journal of Consulting and Clinical Psychology,
American Psychologist, Professional Psychology: Research and Practice,
Cultural Diversity and Ethnic Minority Psychology,* and *Psychotherapy.*
Due to space limitations, the reviews presented here are limited to a minimal presentation of each theory, and we refer the reader to the original refer-
ences for in-depth reading.

The outline of our chapter is as follows: (a) a review and critique of nine
theoretical formulations (the order of our presentation in this section is
random), (b) an integrative discussion of themes found throughout the
models, and (c) a discussion of implications for future theoretical and empirical activity in this area.

REVIEW AND
CRITIQUE OF SELECTED THEORIES

D. W. Sue, Ivey, and Pedersen's (1996)
Theory of Multicultural Counseling

We begin by reviewing a metatheory (i.e., a theory about theories) of
multicultural counseling proposed by Sue, Ivey, and Pedersen (1996). Its six
propositions describe a broad and culture-based conceptualization of counseling. Table 27.1 includes a brief summary of these six propositions. This
table also includes information relative to the other eight theories reviewed
in this chapter. Sue et al.'s treatise captures the philosophical and spiritual
essence of the multicultural movement in counseling. It encourages us to
see culture(s) as deeply imbedded in the consciousness of all human beings
and central in all psychological functioning. It extends the conceptualization of human beings as cultural beings to the client and the counselor in
therapy, including the synergistic by-product called the therapeutic relationship. It also accounts for the importance of context in psychological development and functioning, as well as in the counseling enterprise (see
Table 27.1).

Sue et al. acknowledge the value of more traditional Western psychological perspectives, but allow for the exploration of other psychological
perspectives regarding human relationships. They also consider how culture influences the processes and goals of counseling. In acknowledging the

(text continues on p. 514)

TABLE 27.1 Summary of Emerging Multicultural Counseling Theories

Theory	*Basic Assumptions, Constructs, and Processes*
D. W. Sue, Ivey, and Pedersen's (1996) Theory of Multicultural Counseling	Their six propositions are the following: 1. Each Western and non-Western theory represents a different worldview. 2. The totality and interrelationships of client-counselor experiences and contexts must be the focus of treatment. 3. A counselor or client's racial/cultural identity will influence how problems are defined and dictate or define appropriate counseling goals or processes. 4. The ultimate goal of a culture-centered approach is to expand the repertoire of helping responses available to counselors. 5. Conventional roles of counseling are only some of many alternative helping roles available from other cultural contexts. 6. There is an emphasis on the importance of expanding personal, family, group, and organizational consciousness in a contextual or relation-to-self-orientation.
Gonzalez, Biever, and Gardner's (1994) Social Constructionist Approach	The eight propositions of their model are the following: 1. Therapist as learner: Therapist must be sensitive to the unique nuances of clients' understandings of the influences of their culture. 2. Entertain all ideas: Therapist should allow for more than one answer to a problem and for more than one way to arrive at a solution. 3. Maintenance of curiosity: Therapist strives to avoid learning too quickly or assuming he or she has an answer prior to asking a question. 4. Collaboration between client and therapist: Implicit in this way of working is a confidence in the client's ability to incorporate or expand various descriptions and explanations that may be useful in generating solutions to their problem. 5. Maintain a focus on the client's presenting problem: The client's self-stated problem *is* the problem. 6. Therapist's understandings as "grist for the mill": Therapist's understandings of a client's story are introduced as tentative hypotheses rather than better stories, better descriptions, or better options. 7. Create a space for the client's story: A person from an ethnic minority group frequently understands and explains his or her world significantly different than a person from a majority culture. 8. Seeing opportunities instead of barriers: Emphasize opportunities in the form of strengths, skills, and competencies rather than emphasizing barriers in the form of weaknesses, deficits, and incompetence.
Ho's (1995) Perspective on Internalized Culture	Multicultural counselors consider the following: 1. All counseling necessarily entails cultural awareness. 2. Assess both the counselor's and client's worldview and cultural identity. 3. Consider the unique life experiences of the client and adjust approach accordingly. 4. Becoming apologetic and timid with minority clients does a disservice to them.

(continued)

TABLE 27.1 (Continued)

Theory	Basic Assumptions, Constructs, and Processes
	5. Counselors must enhance their own awareness of cultural diversity and their own culture. 6. Counselors subject their understanding of "internalized culture" to critical scrutiny. 7. Counselor's self-understanding is critical to multicultural training. 8. Counselors must have an in-depth knowledge of the culture of clients different than their own.
Coleman's (1995, 1997) Coping with Diversity Counseling Model	Counselors and clients will deal with diversity in six possible ways. The result is a 6 × 6 matrix between client and counselor, with respective adaptation strategies leading to either convergence or divergence in the counseling relationship: 1. *Assimilation:* The individual strives to acquire values and beliefs of a single cultural group. The goal of this strategy is to become indistinguishable from other members of that group. 2. *Acculturation:* Involves seeing a particular value of pay-off in learning how to become competent in the second culture but also recognizing that one will probably not be accepted into that culture. 3. *Alternation:* Involves learning how to become competent in two or more cultures. 4. *Multiculturalism/integration/pluralism:* Places an equal emphasis on maintaining one's culture of origin and developing second culture competence. 5. *Fusion:* Engage in activities that allow a culturally diverse group of people the opportunity to develop new standards of behavior that are appropriate for a particular context. 6. *Separation:* Focus on the incompatibility between cultural groups and the desirability of developing positive intracultural relationships.
Ramirez's (1991, 1999) Multicultural Model of Psychotherapy	The multicultural therapist or counselor has seven major tasks during therapy: 1. Match clients in an atmosphere of acceptance by providing a nonjudgmental, positive, accepting atmosphere devoid of conformity or assimilation pressures. 2. Formally assess preferred styles by administering three personality inventories that assess the client's preferred cognitive and cultural styles. 3. Conduct a life history interview, which identifies a time or times when the pressure to conform or assimilate caused a suppression of a preferred style for the client. 4. Conduct a self-assessment, which can determine areas of match and mismatch with the client, allowing the therapist to flex in order to better match the client. 5. Introduce the client to the major concepts of both the flex theory of personality and the multicultural model of psychotherapy and give homework assignments to client on basis of the model. 6. Compare data obtained from the readministration of the paper-and-pencil inventories and from the observation instruments to those obtained in the initial stage of therapy.

TABLE 27.1 (Continued)

Theory	Basic Assumptions, Constructs, and Processes
	7. Encourage clients to become change agents, which empowers them to gain control over their destinies and become more committed to multiculturalism by helping others faced with mismatch.
Hanna, Bemak, and Chung's (1999) Counselor Wisdom Paradigm	Wisdom is defined as "a particular set of cognitive and affective traits that are directly related to the possession and development of life skills and understanding necessary for living a life of well-being, fulfillment, effective coping, and insight into the nature of self, others, environment, and interpersonal interactions." The *wise multicultural counselor:* 1. Is highly empathic and compassionate 2. Does not automatize skills or approaches 3. Is deeply insightful 4. Is not easily fooled or deceived 5. Has extensive self-knowledge and awareness 6. Learns from mistakes 7. Can readily reframe cultural contexts 8. Knows a wide range of coping strategies 9. Properly frames problems 10. Can cut to the essence of situations and conditions 11. Is extremely tolerant and accepting 12. Is adept at self-transcendence 13. Sees the interdependence and connections among people and things
Locke's (1998) Model of Multicultural Understanding	Presents seven principles that serve as the guiding philosophy for the model of multicultural understanding: 1. Culturally diverse individuals and groups should be the primary source of information about their situation, condition, or direction. 2. Multiculturalism encourages the treatment of culturally diverse group members with dignity, respect, and responsibility. 3. Ethnically diverse populations are heterogeneous. 4. Educational institutions should have well-defined policy statements and curricula regarding the significance, purpose, and thrust of their multicultural efforts. 5. Multicultural efforts must focus on normal behaviors and wellness, rather than on abnormal behaviors and illness. 6. Multiculturalism requires that educators and counselors be aware of the systemic dimensions of racism and alienation and thereby attempt to understand the experiences, lifestyles, and values of students and clients. 7. Educators and counselors must be trained who are capable of demonstrating effectiveness with individuals from culturally diverse ethnic groups.
Herring and Walker's (1993) Cross-Cultural Specific Model (CSS)	Their theory of counseling includes the following components: 1. Realistically comprehend client expectations: The motivation to seek counseling typically means the client has exhausted both inner resources and social support systems.

(continued)

TABLE 27.1 (Continued)

Theory	Basic Assumptions, Constructs, and Processes
	2. Realistically assess clients: Counselors must determine the degree to which clients' cultural backgrounds contribute to their perceptions of their problems. 3. Establish desired client goals: Client change occurs when the client reaches self-understanding of feelings in relation to the client's perceptions of social realities and when the cultural differences between counselor and client are understood and accepted. 4. Determine an appropriate therapeutic process. This should be based on an awareness of differences among clients and the importance of the effects of family and cultural factors on the way clients view the world.
Steenbarger's (1993) Multicontextual Model	Presents a three-stage model of counseling characterized by the following: 1. *Engagement* involves an assessment of the strengths and weaknesses of the client and an assessment of fit between these characteristics and the client's environment. This is an open-minded inquiry that leads to a collaborative plan for client treatment. 2. *Discrepancy* has at its core the "realignment" of the person-context interface through education, consciousness raising, and is ecological and consultative. 3. *Consolidation* which is characterized by practice, feedback, and the establishment of fit and appropriate social structures.

unique role of varied sociopolitical realities (such as racism, sexism, and homophobia), the authors list events, such as the liberation of consciousness and personal freedom, as adequate goals or outcomes of therapy.

We see this metatheory as a philosophical treatise, whose tenets call for a paradigm shift in the way counselors conceptualize and practice multicultural counseling. Its tenets have the potential to inform theories of multicultural counseling by focusing future conceptual and empirical efforts on client culture and context as the central framework of helping and therapy.

A refreshing addition to Sue et al.'s MCT theory is an entire chapter devoted to implications for research. In this chapter, Casas and Mann (1996) provide a critical examination of percepts and terms in MCT theory. We summarize their criticisms here because our own critique of MCT theory overlaps a great deal with their chapter. Casas and Mann (1996) note that MCT theory seems to be two theories presented as one. Thus, it has some theoretical inconsistency. The theory claims at various points to be a metatheory on the one hand, and a theory of counseling on the other. Until the authors decide which of these two foci will be the subject of the theory, it will be difficult to know which avenues of research are needed to substantiate the theory.

Another criticism of MCT theory is that the authors fail to define some core concepts around which the proposed theory revolves. For example, Casas and Mann (1996) state that it is unclear which definition of culture the authors are referring to in their model, since numerous conceptualizations of culture exist in the literature (e.g., Hughes, 1976; Kluckhohn & Strodtbeck, 1961; Nash, 1989; Steward, 1972). Other undefined terms that are important to MCT theory include racism, culture-bound, and ethnocentrism. Casas and Mann (1996) suggest that MCT theorists should continue to define these terms and present examples that can help one apply the terms within the counseling process.

Other criticisms noted by Casas and Mann (1996) include MCT's lack of discussion regarding the philosophical assumptions underlying the theory. MCT theory seems largely based on the ubiquitous conceptualization of multiculturalism. This suggests that every facet of one's identity and circumstance contributes to one's culture, thus allowing individuals to belong to multiple cultures (Carter, 1995). MCT theory also includes elements of raced-based (Carter, 1995) multiculturalism, including a number of references to racism and the oppression of racial/ethnic minorities by traditional counseling approaches. Understanding the context for which MCT theory was developed is helpful but not suficient. Explicit assumptions and motivations behind MCT theory need to be explained to provide directions for researchers who want to expand it (Casas & Mann, 1996).

Gonzalez, Biever, and Gardner's (1994) Social Constructionist Approach

Gonzalez et al. (1994) draw clear parallels between multicultural counseling and social constructionist perspectives and suggest the latter offers a way of meeting the objectives of the former. Social constructionism is described as a mechanism for gleaning racially or culturally based material from the client's reality to help the counselor understand the role of these factors in the client's life. Gonzalez et al. explain some of the basic tenets of social constructionism and multiculturalism and discuss issues of mutual concern for both adherents, such as developing effective methods of psychotherapy, diagnosis, and assessment. Gonzalez et al. then discuss the clinical applications of social constructionism, with an emphasis on multicultural understanding. These clinical applications form the bulk of their model and detail the therapist's role and therapeutic process, and are listed in Table 27.1.

Social constructionism appears to provide a potential mechanism for understanding the culture and context of the client and the role of these factors in helping the client understand and interpret his or her reality. However, Gonzalez et al. highlight several challenges that await practitioners using the social constructionist approach. These include: (a) incorporating ideas presented by clients that make sense for them but that are not yet articulated in the psychological literature; (b) relinquishing the therapist's more privileged "expert" position in the therapy room to one that accepts *all* understandings as potentially practical and valuable; and (c) not relying on socially constructed documents like the *DSM* to express personal and social health.

Gonzalez et al. are persuasive in presenting the social constructionist approach as respectful of the client's perspective and reality. The social constructionist perspective may prove useful as a guide to fostering nonjudgmental attitudes like openness and inquisitiveness in multicultural counseling. It appears to provide one mechanism for training counselors to understand the role of culture and context in their client's life. The authors note the counselor should be more interested in exploring the client's theories about the nature and meaning of his or her problems and less interested in fitting the client into an "established" or preferred theory that explains the client's problems.

Adequate use of this approach, however, may depend on the counselor's own understanding of his or her cultural background and willingness to understand another person's perspective. The authors seem to suggest that all therapists who use this perspective may be able to work with all types of clients without awareness of macrosystemic variables like cultural values and worldviews. This seems like a narrow view of therapy and an oversimplification of counseling. Clearly, clients' lives are complex, and they are at times in need of emotional support and alternative perspectives. This model assumes, perhaps unfairly, that clients are always articulate, self-aware and verbal. Some clients may be unable to articulate their problems when they come to therapy. In addition, the model presents the counselor as rather passive, which may prove unhelpful to some members of racial/ethnic groups who expect a more directive counseling approach (Sue, Zane, & Young, 1994).

Ho's (1995) Perspective on Internalized Culture

Understanding and transcending internalized culture are central components in Ho's (1995) treatise on multicultural counseling. Internalized culture functions like a cognitive map to guide one's social actions through the social terrain. It is a psychological variable that includes cultural influences operating within the individual that shape personality formation and various aspects of psychological functioning. According to Ho, internalized culture influences the formation of our worldviews, which are broadly defined as a set of presuppositions underlying our views about the world and our place in it.

The basic mechanism Ho proposes for effective multicultural counseling is the idea of counselors "transcending" their own culture and thus transcending their potential for cultural egocentrism. Table 27.1 outlines eight points multicultural counselors should consider while keeping Ho's assertion in mind. Ho asserts counselors should subject their own "cognitive map" (i.e., internalized culture) to critical scrutiny to help sensitize them against overgeneralization and stereotyping. He offers two additional psychological concepts that may liberate the counselor from the rigidity of looking at clients solely in terms of their cultural membership. The first, cultural identification, acknowledges that individuals may differ widely in the extent to which they identify with the cultural heritage of their group or those of other groups. The second, cultural orientation, reaffirms a measure of autonomy in individual preference for various cultural patterns. Cultural identification and cultural orientation are instrumental to the development of self-identities and worldviews. Thus, Ho suggests counselors must take into account their clients' cultural identification and cultural orientation to understand clients more deeply.

Ho encourages us to think of the role of culture in counseling from a psychological (or individual level) not an anthropological (group membership) perspective. He incorporates concepts from many different areas of science including anthropology, social psychology, and cognitive psychology. In addition, he writes about the need for counseling programs to place greater emphasis on multicultural issues. He makes emphatic statements about the importance of program-level reform when training counselors to work with diverse populations. He states that requiring courses in multicultural counseling are not enough for training programs to be effective. He believes training programs should adhere to a theoretical orientation that gives *full* recognition to the importance of cultural and multicultural processes.

Ho also suggests multicultural courses go beyond helping counselors understand and work with clients from different cultural or ethnic backgrounds and assist counselors in articulating how their lives have been shaped by their own culture. Thus, self-understanding is a goal that should be integral to multicultural training. We appreciate Ho's attempt to widen the lens of transcending an individual's culture to the systemic level of counselor training programs. Clearly, he echoes the work of others (e.g., Ponterotto, 1998) advocating institution-wide changes to better develop multicultural competence in counseling trainees.

However, Ho is not clear in discussing how it is that we transcend culturocentrism and differences in culture. He suggests that having a sense of "internalized culture" can sensitize the counselor against overgeneralization and stereotyping, but he fails to explain how one is able to achieve internalization. He seems to suggest that counselors' own appreciation of their internalized culture may provide them with awareness of the impact of culture on the counseling process.

Arbona (1995) discusses the absence of a precise definition of culture and the lack of attention to the social context as the major weakness of Ho's model. Ho does not specify which aspects of culture influence behavior nor

does he discuss the relationship between internalized culture and the social
relations or sociopolitical realities that may either support or challenge the
client's conception of culture. While we appreciate the difficulty in being
clear while writing about internal psychological processes, we agree with
Arbona (1995) that a major weakness of Ho's theory is that he does not adequately define the basic units of his analyses, including the definition
of culture. With so many definitions of culture available in the literature
in multicultural counseling (cf. Pedersen, 1997), we were left wondering
exactly what Ho meant when he used the word. We certainly would have
liked more concrete definitions of the constructs he presented and explicit
clinical examples for his ideas.

In addition, terms included in the discussion, such as enculturation, acculturation, bienculturation, and mulitenculturation, were not defined
and left us unsure of their meaning, level of overlap, and level of distinctiveness. Again, we would have liked more definitions and examples of the processes he outlines in his theory.

Coleman's (1995, 1997) Coping
With Diversity Counseling Model

Coleman (1995, 1997) focuses on the coping strategies individuals
use when faced with cultural diversity, and suggests that participants will
deal with diversity in six possible ways: assimilation, acculturation, alternation, multiculturalism/integration/pluralism, fusion, and separation.
These strategies for coping with diversity are outlined in Table 27.1.
Coleman briefly discusses the coping, adaptation, and social patterns of individuals operating from each of these six perspectives and ties this presentation to possible events in counseling. The result is a six-by-six matrix
between client and counselor, with respective adaptation strategies leading
to either convergence or divergence in the counseling relationship.
Coleman suggests that conflict in multicultural counseling relationships
is often the result of divergence in the strategies used by counselors and clients to cope with cultural diversity. His model suggests that some strategies are compatible, some are not compatible, and others are subject to
individual variation.

The rationale for Coleman's model stems from the belief that the nature and quality of the individual's coping strategies may have a significant
effect on the nature and etiology of the presenting problem, the individual's
expectations of the counselor, the therapy relationship, and the outcome of
counseling. How a client copes with cultural diversity will also be an important variable in developing an effective therapeutic alliance. Since a
counselor will also use the strategy he or she uses with the client's cultural
group within the counseling relationship, the counseling relationship will
naturally be affected by both client's and counselor's strategies for coping with diversity. Therefore, the type of goals that are developed for

counseling should reflect the strategy the client uses to cope with cultural diversity.

The strength of Coleman's model lies in the ecosystemic perspective he presents to understand the strategies individuals use to cope with cultural diversity. He explains the client's level of acculturation in more detail than the models on which he based his own (i.e., Atkinson, Thompson, & Grant, 1993; Helms, 1984). He extends Helms's (1984) model by describing in terms of process, rather than outcome, the strategies an individual in certain stages of ethnic identity may be using. Coleman's model makes an important contribution to improving the effectiveness of counseling interventions with clients. He places appropriate focus on the relationship between culture and behavior and helps counselors understand the effect that a person's strategy for coping with cultural diversity might have on various aspects of the counseling process. He uses interesting clinical examples to illustrate his ideas, particularly in describing the potential difficulty of managing a counseling relationship with someone from a culture with a history of suffering social and political oppression.

Although he recognizes his model is in the early phase of development and calls for a systematic examination of its validity, several issues need to be examined. Coleman cites D. H. Ford's (1987) and M. E. Ford's (1992) Living System Framework (LSF) for describing the interaction between the self-system (i.e., biology, cognition, emotions, and behavior) and the individual's environment. Specifically, Coleman makes use of their construct of behavioral episode schemas as a description of personality. He cites no empirical research on the LSF and the reader is left to wonder about the validity of this model. Basing a new model on a model that may not have adequate validity is problematic, and Coleman might have provided more evidence for his use of the LSF.

In addition, he neglects to inform the reader exactly *how* behavioral episode schemas are formed. He uses circular logic when he says that the strategy or strategies an individual develops to cope with cultural diversity is/are behavioral episode schemas. Are we to assume, then, that strategies for coping with diversity are schemas and schemas are strategies for coping with diversity? Coleman (1995) defines a behavioral episode schema as "a learned pattern of behavior that is stimulated within particular contexts" (p. 725). Are we to assume the six strategies of coping with diversity are also defined this way? Coleman could have dedicated more time to explaining the behavioral episode schema because it is one of the core constructs in his model. His excellent use of clinical examples throughout his model could have illuminated this seemingly complex construct.

Ramirez's (1999) Multicultural Model of Psychotherapy

Ramirez's (1999) cognitive-behavioral model aspires to help clients develop a flexible, multicultural personality that adjusts to the environment.

One of the goals of his theory of psychotherapy is to help clients feel free to express their uniqueness in the form of their preferred cognitive and cultural styles. Multicultural therapy should help clients identify the self that may have been suppressed earlier in life and recognize how pressures from others and/or from society have forced them to try to be someone other than their unique self. Multicultural therapy should help in the development of cultural and cognitive flexibility, which can facilitate the development and expression of the unique self. In addition, the model teaches clients and counselors concepts like the flex theory of personality so that they can create change in their environment. Clients are encouraged to become active change agents to help develop a society of social justice, peace, and cooperation.

Ramirez makes several assumptions about clients and counselors. He outlines seven major tasks during therapy for the multicultural counselor. These tasks are listed in Table 27.1. He assumes that every client has the potential for multicultural development and that the therapist should respect the client's origins. He posits that therapists have preferred cognitive and cultural styles and that they should be aware of their preferred styles. In addition, therapists should make use of opportunities for multicultural growth offered by the client's immediate environment.

Ramirez has presented a comprehensive, clear, and well-organized model of psychotherapy and counseling that recognizes the interaction and tension between the individual and the dominant Euro-American culture. He presents helpful guidelines and outcomes to guide counselors in the helping process. The advantages of his model lie in his emphasis on therapist self-awareness and cultural exploration and the empowerment of clients to become change agents.

Ramirez notes that many models of psychotherapy ignore the powerful impact of the therapist's personality on the outcome of therapy. He cites relevant research to illustrate this point (Sue, 1990; Sue & Zane, 1987) and devotes an entire chapter to how the therapist can examine his or her preferred cultural and cognitive styles. He encourages therapists to follow a systematic approach for determining how their preferred styles and ability to flex have been shaped by socialization and life experiences. Activities include self-assessment exercises that examine the therapist's life history and cultural and cognitive flexibility.

Ramirez also encourages clients to become multicultural educators, peer counselors, and ambassadors. He believes that clients should become active change agents to enhance their own multicultural development in addition to helping develop a society that will be responsive and sensitive to the individual differences of its population. This represents a departure from traditional forms of psychotherapy and counseling that see the work in therapy as initiated and maintained by the therapist. He provides several rich case examples that highlight the potential positive effects an activist frame of mind can have on the self-esteem, mood, and relationships of clients. This can benefit clients who have previously felt like victims of oppression and who were powerless to effect change in their world.

Encouraging clients to become active change agents can have some disadvantages that Ramirez does not explore. Clients may feel pressured to change and perhaps "please" the counselor. It implies the client may somehow be at fault for not being a proactive "change agent" before and thus partly responsible for the current state of affairs. This is a large burden for clients to analyze and may place undue stress on those who are vulnerable to feelings of guilt or who are so depressed they are unable to be active in the way Ramirez suggests.

Another concern with Ramirez's model is its rather prescriptive structure and manualized approach. The model may have limitations for ethnic minority clients and counselors who may not appreciate or benefit from its structure. On the other hand, some clients and counselors may appreciate these very features (e.g., the prescribed administration of personality inventories, lecture to clients on theory, homework assignments, and strict 16-session format). These activities may be especially useful to therapists who appreciate structured, introspective exercises. Ramirez could have dedicated some discussion to the types of clients and counselors for whom his model is appropriate. Instead, he seems to make the assumption that his model will work for all types of therapeutic relationships.

Hanna, Bemak, and Chung's (1999) Counselor Wisdom Paradigm

Hanna et al. propose that effective multicultural counselors go beyond textbook knowledge, and suggest that "wisdom" as an operative concept provides a new paradigm to bring the field to a higher plateau of effectiveness in multicultural counseling practice and training. They present a definition of wisdom and describe the qualities of a wise multicultural counselor. The definition and list can be found in Table 27.1.

Hanna et al. introduce the concept of *dialectical thinking* as an important characteristic of wisdom. Dialectical reasoning recognizes and uses the interplay of opposing views in human thought processes (Tolman, 1983), including opposing cultural viewpoints. In counseling, dialectical thought contemplates and uses the many theories of counseling and therapy in the contexts of individual, family, and group approaches as appropriate to a client's given situation and needs.

Hanna et al. make several assumptions about multicultural counseling. They posit that it is possible for mental health professionals to enhance their effectiveness by understanding and developing their own wisdom. They also assume that clients in the United States believe that counselors or healers have wisdom. Wisdom may be the factor that makes the difference between effective helping and merely going through the motions. They also assume that aspects associated with wisdom, such as depth, fluidity, and richness of understanding, are vital in multicultural settings. Integrating rich and diverse experiences may help a person to recognize both the universal core of humanity in each individual and the unique cultural heritage and attributes of that person.

We applaud these authors for venturing into new territory for multicultural counseling. They are to be commended for presenting a decidedly non-Western approach to counseling that is, in our view, refreshing. They clearly define wisdom and differentiate it from important concepts like intelligence and metacognition. The reader is left with an understanding of wisdom that is based in empirical research and sound theoretical development. In addition, Hanna et al.'s discussion of wisdom, culture, and dialectical thinking is exciting. Theory development in multicultural counseling needs to move toward capturing the complexity of diversity in psychotherapy and Hanna et al. make a valiant effort to address this. They note that dialectical thinking (i.e., incorporating a number of approaches appropriate to a client's given situation and needs) has the capacity to see through the limits of a narrow mindset or single interpretive framework. They further note that members of the dominant culture may not be as inspired to shift to dialectical thinking due to the complacency that often comes with being in the majority and the mindset that prevails. This is an important point and serves as a springboard for counselors willing and able to engage in the deep self-exploration that wisdom entails.

Wisdom is an interesting concept and we appreciate how Hanna et al. encourage training programs to begin to teach it and foster it in their students. They cite research that indicated graduate training has generally not been successful at producing counselors or therapists who are more effective than paraprofessionals with relatively little training (Christensen & Jacobson, 1994; Dawes, 1994; Humphreys, 1996; Peterson, 1995). Their answer to this lack of differentiation between mental health professionals lies in how programs have neglected to develop wisdom in their students. They recommend programs actively teach dialectical thinking, have students engage in awareness techniques adapted from different forms of therapy (e.g., Gestalt, Existentialism), and incorporate experiential learning approaches that borrow from techniques in religious sects like insight-meditation in Buddhism. Although their suggestions may seem radical to some, we agree that sole use of GRE scores and purely academic or scholarly assignments by programs with goals of training students to be *effective counselors* may not be very helpful or "wise."

Our criticism of their model is predicated on our understanding that wisdom is a lofty goal to aspire to. Hanna et al. admit that wisdom contains qualities of "master" counselors. We agree with this parallel and feel that Hanna et al. could have linked their discussion of wisdom with developmental models of counseling. Thus, wisdom may develop in stages, just as counselors progress from beginner to semiprofessional to professional to master. For example, Hanna et al. might have illustrated the specific components of wisdom that develop in beginning trainees. They also could have included a breakdown of how programs can foster wisdom in students at this level of development. Programs would then need to explain the criteria needed for a beginning trainee to progress to an intermediate stage of development and wisdom. The transitions from being a good counselor to a wise counselor were not clearly outlined and we were left wondering how, exactly, one *becomes* wise.

Locke's (1998) Model of Multicultural Understanding

Locke's (1998) model is designed to provide a solid foundation for exploring ethnic differences and includes elements of personal awareness and information necessary to engage in positive helping relationships with culturally diverse individuals. He presents seven principles as the guiding philosophy for his model of multicultural understanding. These principles are listed in Table 27.1. Locke asserts that the differences existing between members of the dominant culture and members of ethnically diverse cultures are real. Counselors and educators must be aware of these differences and how they complicate interactions between themselves and their students and clients. He believes increased knowledge of multicultural issues contributes to better relationships between educators and counselors and their students and clients.

The four components of Locke's model are (a) an awareness of self that includes knowing one's own personal biases, values, interests, and worldview; (b) an awareness of world events and how members of various cultures translate those events into personal meaning; (c) an understanding of the dominant culture of the United States (i.e., Anglo-Saxon) from the perspectives of the individual, family and community; and (d) an ability to evaluate different cultural practices and determine how these practices affect the helping relationship.

Locke presents one of the clearest explanations of culture we have come across. He defines culture as "a construct that captures a socially transmitted system of ideas that shape behavior, categorize perceptions, and gives names to selected aspects of experience" (p. 3). He then discusses 10 elements of his model that separates culture into discrete, understandable variables (e.g., acculturation, poverty and economic concerns, history of oppression, language and the arts, racism and prejudice, sociopolitical factors, child-rearing practices, religious practices, family structure and dynamics, cultural values and attitudes about time, human relations, human activity, human nature and the supernatural). Clinicians who gather information from their clients following Locke's model will be left with a rich, detailed picture of how culture may influence presenting problems.

We also resonate to Locke's inclusion of how counselors should make efforts to understand global influences from a client's culture. He believes counselors have a responsibility to their clients to be knowledgeable in world affairs. Locke presents a valid argument for this, noting that knowledge of a client's culture of origin provides the helper with a more complete picture of that client's worldview. What was not clear, however, was exactly how to do this. The reader must assume that a counselor should watch the news, read the newspaper, and/or converse with members of different ethnic groups to gather information about current events. Is this enough? Locke does not discuss the issue of whether or not to talk with one's client about the impact of world events on his or her well-being in session. We would have liked a more detailed explanation of this component of his model, including how a counselor might bring up such issues with a client in a counseling session.

Another aspect of Locke's model that is worth noting is that he uses the White Anglo-Saxon culture as the backdrop for understanding culturally diverse individuals and groups. Some theorists and scholars have criticized counseling theories for basing helping interventions on the values of White Anglo-Saxon Americans (e.g., Carter, 1995; Pinderhughes, 1989). For example, Pinderhughes (1989) notes that the use of the White middle-class yardstick has resulted in inappropriate and even destructive service delivery to persons of certain backgrounds. She asserts, along with other scholars, that cultural insensitivity marked by the persistence of the White middle-class model has been labeled not only as inappropriate, but problematic, dysfunctional, disrespectful, unethical, and a sign of incompetence of the service deliverer or clinician (Draguns, 1981; Leighton, 1982; Sue, 1978).

Our understanding of Locke is that he recognizes and accepts the criticisms of scholars such as Pinderhughes and offers his model as a solution to cultural insensitivity. Thus, Locke believes the best way to avoid being insensitive to culturally diverse individuals is to understand the dominant culture they have to contend with every day of their lives. What is missing from his model, however, is his rationale for choosing this as the starting point (i.e., understanding White Anglo-Saxon values) from which one develops cultural sensitivity.

Herring and Walker's (1993) Cross-Cultural Specific Model (CSS)

Herring and Walker present their model as a representation of synergistic counseling. They view counseling theory from the point of view of the client's culture rather than the traditional European North American frame of reference. The helping professional should not subscribe to any one central view of human nature but remains open-minded and selectively incorporates counseling strategies in response to the cultural milieu of the client.

The Cross-Cultural Specific (CSS) model allows the counselor to choose those techniques that are most appropriate to the client's cultural and environmental existence. Synergistic counseling is defined broadly as a theory of counseling that selects what technique or strategy is most appropriate for the client within the context of that client's environmental and cultural status. Thus, the interaction of the client and the client's environment can be incorporated in the topic content, problems presented, and expectations for the helping relationship and helping process. Their theory of counseling includes four components that are listed in Table 27.1.

Herring and Walker discuss the basic philosophical issues upon which the CSS model is built, including a theory of personality, the nature of humans, and the role of the environment. Thus, the synergistic counselor bases therapy on syntality instead of a traditional theory. Syntality involves incorporating a group's cultural and environmental personality into the counseling process. Thus, the helping professional does not subscribe exclusively to any one central view of human nature but remains open-minded and selectively incorporates counseling strategies in response to the cultural milieu of the client, with the exception of the basic motivation for personal security.

Synergistic models emphasize therapeutic processes rather than how the individual is organized. Issues such as basic drives, motivations, and innate characteristics are not primary loci of therapy. Rather, a counselor must assist the client in discerning those external forces that exert either a real or perceived influence on the client's behavior. Environmental influences are derived from physical, social, and cultural elements. However, helping professionals are urged to remember that ethnic groups contain tremendous intragroup variations and to select specific native or non-native techniques that may be appropriately incorporated into the counseling process.

We appreciate Herring and Walker's focus on encouraging counselors to adjust to and work within the client's worldview. They assert that the counseling profession must broaden its base of cultural knowledge and be willing to develop new structures, policies, and strategies. The CSS model presents a dynamic integration of different concepts and techniques that fit the professional's unique personality and style. It integrates parts of the psychodynamic, humanistic, and cognitive-behavioral approaches in its eclectic focus. In addition, the cultural and environmental worldview of the client is recognized and respected.

We also recognize, however, that there are drawbacks to eclecticism. According to Garfield (1980), practitioners who call themselves eclectic risk criticism for being unsystematic. When eclecticism is unsystematic, practitioners may try to use what they consider to be the best techniques from a variety of theories without basing their selection on a coherent theory of personality. Such practitioners will not be able to find a consistent rationale for treatment planning, assessment, therapeutic intervention, and ultimately for empirical testing of their approach.

Herring and Walker include a section in their article that describes seven different currently available synergistic models. Although Herring and Walker recommend the reader consult the direct references for more in-depth discussions, there is the risk of developing a "cafeteria style" approach. Thus, practitioners may consult these references and think they are selecting the proper techniques from each model. Herring and Walker do not provide examples and guidance for those who may want to explore the other approaches they mention in their article. An expanded discussion of an unsystematic approach to researching and utilizing these synergistic models would have been helpful.

While we realize that focusing on the client's culture in psychotherapy is important, we also realize there are some caveats to this position. A client's worldview may include maladaptive coping patterns that are fueled by or blended with culture. Herring and Walker should have emphasized that counselors distinguish maladaptive coping patterns from healthy cultural values and beliefs, which might be harnessed to help the client make positive change. Also, Herring and Walker's focus on the client and counselor working together through a process of counseling that is most effective for them makes an assumption that all clients are able to do this. Some clients might feel threatened by such close "collaboration" with a counselor, particularly if they view counselors as experts who are judged competent based on the nature of the directives they give to the client. Such a client may feel a counselor is not competent because he or she is asking for the client's help in conceptualizing goals and solutions. Herring and Walker also present their model as holistic and imply it is effective for all clients in all situations. They fail to discuss the limitations of their model with clients at different levels of acculturation and ethnic or racial identity development.

Steenbarger's (1993) Multicontextual Model

Steenbarger (1993) presents a multicontextual model of counseling that bridges concepts of brevity and diversity. He cites studies that suggest counselors, as a whole, do not view brief treatments as appropriate for a diverse array of clients and conditions (e.g., Burlingame & Behrman, 1987). However, he also cites studies that point to an explosion of interest and research on brief therapy (e.g., Budman & Gurman, 1988; Garfield, 1989; Wells & Giannetti, 1990). Thus, Steenbarger realizes brief and multicultural counseling therapies have their differences, but recognizes they are not impossible to blend into a more comprehensive system of therapy for diverse clients.

Steenbarger begins his treatise with a review of themes associated with brief counseling, such as time-consciousness, criteria of client inclusion, therapeutic focus, therapist and client activity and involvement. He also reviews some basic assumptions of multicultural counseling, such as validation of client identity and worldviews, attention to the social context of presenting complaints, and attentiveness to client distrust. He then presents a three-stage model of counseling, which is outlined in Table 27.1.

Steenbarger acknowledges the differences inherent in brief and multicultural counseling. However, he proposes that by conceptualizing the dimensions of time (brief to long-term), as interacting with those of change target (individuals to groups and systems) and scope (educational and supportive), it is possible to derive a multicontextual model of intervention. The intersection of these dimensions captures several intervention frameworks. The first includes brief, system change strategies, such as consciousness-raising activities to combat racism. The second framework includes short-term, person-change strategies, such as informational and competency-building interventions for clients in workshop, theme group, and psychoeducational course formats. The third framework is a long-term, system-change strategy, emphasizing ongoing, collaborative efforts that can have a reconstructive impact on the client's milieu. The final framework includes long-term, person-change strategies that allow clients to explore the individual, social, and cultural facets of selfhood in an accepting context.

Steenbarger attempts to capture the complexity of multicultural counseling. The four dimensions of his model (system change, individual change, brief, and long-term) form a cross section of continua that casts a rather wide net around different strategies for change in counseling. Thus, he emphasizes strategies that fit between persons and their life contexts. He encourages counselors to actively create experiences of inclusion, value, empowerment, and trust. Also, he suggests that brief multicultural counseling need not stop at short-term, individual change strategies like group and individual therapy. It can encompass broader reconstructive strategies like social advocacy and organizing individuals into groups pressing for change.

Steenbarger also appropriately limits his model and explains who will benefit the most from a multicontextual approach. He asserts that the "health" of the environment, as much as that of individual clients, will determine the extent that brief work will be viable for disempowered clients. In a multicontextual framework, the choice of brevity is not dictated by client factors alone. Counseling is most likely to be of short duration when (a) disruption at the client-context interface is circumscribed; (b) clients and contexts possess significant resources and the capacity to use these constructively; and (c) clients and contexts can rapidly engage counselors in change efforts. This is in contrast to traditional brief therapy that is deemed ideal for relatively high-functioning clients experiencing focal problems of recent onset. Thus, Steenbarger addresses a point other models overlook—namely when and with whom his particular model works.

Some of the underlying assumptions of Steenbarger's multicontextual model are not fully explained. For example, he notes that multicontextual counseling emphasizes the assessment of person-environment fit;

however, he does not cite or present literature on person-environment fit. There is a large body of literature on person-environment fit that could have been utilized to explain this assumption (e.g., Dawis & Lofquist, 1984; Holland, 1992; Spokane, 1987). Steenbarger's model includes an important focus on creating experiences in which clients can effectively engage and alter the hostile physical, social and cultural contexts (e.g., neighborhoods, workplaces, relationships, communities). Steenbarger might have expanded his discussion of this point to include ideas from other areas, such as the literature on organizational change and career development. He provides only cursory examples of how, exactly, counselors can work with clients to effect change in their environments (e.g., workshops, groups, in-service training sessions, and brochures) and seems unaware that organizations are often highly resistant to change.

More important, Steenbarger seems not to have considered the psychological risk and potential impact of frustration on the client as he or she attempts to change or create social structures that can meet his or her needs. Clients run the risk of assuming it may be their fault they could not change or create social structures. At the very least, his model needs to include components of how a counselor prepares and supports a client when faced with setbacks, bureaucracy, racism, and general organizational stagnation.

GENERAL DISCUSSION

Thus far, we have provided the reader with our understanding and critique of each emerging model of multicultural counseling. The nine models we explored each provide unique and important contributions to the literature. In this section, we highlight some general themes and trends that, in our view, permeate all the theories. We outline eight observations and reactions underlying the conceptual and operative tenets of these works to provide our readers with a framework for understanding the current state of multicultural counseling theory development. Our eight observations are listed in Table 27.2 and explained in more detail below.

Emerging theories of multicultural counseling are at various stages of theoretical and empirical development.

Some of the nine emerging theories are more comprehensive and explicit in their assumptions and techniques than are others. In addition, some are more developed and ready for immediate use by practitioners and researchers than others. We have summarized our analysis of these theories along three criteria: comprehensiveness, operationalization for testing (or heuristic value), and clinical utility. Our ratings on each criterion are presented in Table 27.3. It is important to note that "low" ratings on any of these dimensions do not speak to the quality of ideas or usefulness of the theory. Rather, they indicate that some theories are more developed than

TABLE 27.2 Observations Based on an Analysis of the Selected Emerging
Models

1. Emerging theories of multicultural counseling are at various stages of theoretical and empirical development.

2. There is more than one way to conceptualize and deliver multicultural counseling.

3. There is an emphasis on exploring multicultural constructs that inform *all* counseling.

4. Effective counselors understand the complex, idiographic nature of client identity and worldview.

5. These theories supplement, rather than supplant, other counselor techniques and skills.

6. These theories focus on the sociopolitical and environmental context of clients' presenting complaints.

7. Counselor sociopolitical and racial/cultural self-awareness are important.

8. These theories provide mixed views of the "matching hypothesis."

TABLE 27.3 Analysis of Emerging Theories

	Comprehensiveness as a Counseling Model	Operationalization for Testing	Operationalization for Clinical Utility
Ramirez	High	High	High
Ho	Low	Low	Low
Locke	Medium	Medium	Medium
Herring and Walker	Medium	Low	Low
Steenbarger	Low	Medium	Low
Coleman	Medium	High	Medium
Gonzalez et al.	Medium	Medium	Medium
Hanna et al.	Low	Medium	Low
Sue et al.	Low	Low	Low

others. A theory like Ho's, which is ranked "low" on all three dimensions, has tremendous potential to influence our understanding of multicultural counseling. It is simply at an earlier stage of development (i.e., conceptualization) compared to older models, like Ramirez's.

A comprehensive theory encompasses and accounts for a wide range of data. We see Ramirez's (1999) model as the most comprehensive theory in the current review (see Table 27.3). It has a well-established and supported theoretical base, and specific counselor interventions are tied to well-described counseling outcomes.

Our second criterion is operationalization for testing. A theory has heuristic value if it stimulates and guides conceptual and empirical investigations. All of the theories reviewed identify potential venues for further theoretical and empirical inquiry (see Table 27.3). Coleman, Ramirez, Locke, Steenbarger, Gonzalez et al., and Hanna et al. present useful conceptualizations of multicultural practice with considerable heuristic value, and the reader is directed to the original articles for excellent research ideas. Ho, Herring and Walker, and Sue et al. offer helpful conceptualizations of multicultural counseling and related constructs that might lead to further theory development, perhaps to "mini-theories" of counseling (Gelso, 1996) with explanatory and potential empirical value.

Our final criterion is clinical utility. A theory has high clinical utility if it can reasonably be translated into practice by counselors. Some authors, like Coleman (1995, 1997), Gonzalez et al. (1994), and Locke (1998), give specific suggestions that might be implemented with diverse clients. For example, Coleman's strategies for coping with cultural diversity may help counselors utilize new techniques to establish stronger relationships with ethnic minority clients. Gonzalez et al. (1994) dedicate sections of their theory to clinical applications, and outline the therapists' role and that of the therapeutic process. Locke (1998) outlines ten specific components of culture that counselors should inquire about with their clients, and provides specific questions that may be used to garner such information. Parenthetically, we caution the reader against "trying out" ideas and techniques that on the one hand have limited empirical backing, and on the other, for which the reader has had no practicum or applied training or supervision.

A review of these theories indicates that there is a need to "operationalize" or translate useful concepts into deliverable techniques and services for ethnic minority clients. To varying degrees, the practice component is missing from many of these theories, and a lack of clarity about their prescribed use and limitations is also evident. The link between theoretical tenets and process or outcome is weak, and the role of the counselor and client could be better delineated. The therapy relationship, considered one of the best and most consistent indicators of counseling outcome, is not attended to as centrally as we would have liked.

In addition, we feel that these theories missed an important component of service delivery: that most counselors have an eclectic theoretical and technical disposition. By and large, these theorists do not discuss how their approaches fit with more established or "traditional" approaches and techniques in counseling (e.g., client-centered therapy). Thus, readers of these theories might wonder how and when to integrate these newer formulations with their current approaches to counseling. We suggest future multicultural theoretical advancement focus on (a) communicating specific suggestions to practitioners on how they can integrate a theory into their work; (b) offering comprehensive and explicit recommendations for relating practice guidelines to treatment and outcome variables; and (c) providing guidelines for empirical validation of theoretical constructs.

There is more than one way to conceptualize and deliver multicultural counseling.

The multicultural counseling movement is rich, diverse, and not predicated on one theory or construct, person, or philosophical tradition. A review of the theories supports our observation. For example, Sue et al. suggest that there is no single effective approach across all populations and life situations. Gonzalez et al.'s constructivist theory suggests that the many possible understandings of behaviors, interactions, or events are determined by social and cultural contexts. Ho suggests counselors need an intimate understanding of a client's internalized assumptions and views that may originate from multiple cultural belief systems. Herring and Walker also assert there is no one distinctive approach to multicultural counseling in their presentation of seven different synergistic models of counseling. Hanna et al. note that the skill of counselor dialectical thinking will lead to an appreciation of multiple meanings.

Many of the theoretical formulations presented here hold promise as effective therapeutic techniques with ethnic minority clients, just as traditional counseling theories and techniques have all shown value to practice (Wampold, 2000). Each theory's value and use, however, will ultimately be determined by empirical studies that demonstrate their effectiveness with certain clients and presenting problems. The recent conceptualization of multicultural counseling offered by Fischer, Jome, and Atkinson (1998) might be extended by research that examines a global or unifying conceptualization of multicultural counseling emphasizing common factors extracted from the nine diverse approaches presented in this chapter.

There is an emphasis on exploring multicultural constructs that inform all counseling.

Among the emerging theories reviewed in this chapter, there is a focus on multicultural constructs and counselor skills that have the potential to inform all counseling, rendering all counseling, to varying degrees, multicultural. For example, Gonzalez et al. indicate that every encounter between counselor and client is a multicultural interaction. Ho (1995) writes that all counseling involves internalized "cultural processes" and that "all encounters between any two individuals are, in a sense, cross-cultural encounters" (p. 15). Locke (1998) reminds us that "culture inevitably influences personality orientation, acculturation, manifestations of behavior, effectiveness of procedures, and the language used" (p. 15). Ramirez's model views every client in counseling as having the potential for multicultural development.

Based on the above observations, one may conclude that multiculturalism as a unique movement loses its relevance. We believe that the opposite is true. All counselors need to be multiculturally competent and recognize themselves, among many things, as cultural and racial beings (Sue et al., 1998). Counselors should realize their potential for cultural encapsulation and enrich their service delivery to be more culturally informed and sensitive. All counselors need to incorporate into their conceptualization and treatment planning client data such as values, beliefs, family cultural and traditional history, and level of acculturation. These foci would be lost without the power of multicultural theory, research, and practice informing counseling process and outcome.

However, while all counseling can be conceived as multicultural, some forms of counseling may still be thought of as "more multicultural." For example, the relevance of multicultural competence and sensitivity may be more acute when significant differences exist between the client and counselor (e.g., on race, level of acculturation, and socioeconomic status). Multicultural competence may also be more necessary when client presenting issues focus on culturally relevant domains, such as coping with racism, effective interpersonal contact with diverse populations or colleagues, acculturation, and racial identity issues.

Effective counselors understand the complex, idiographic nature of client identity and worldview.

The models presented here emphasize the unique qualities of each client. Thus, instead of being representative of cultural groups, clients are conceived of as individuals who may prescribe to some or all of the cultural values of one or more group(s) with varying levels of intensity. Discerning the complexity of internalized aspects of cultural membership and clients' interpretation and meaning of their values and beliefs is emphasized beyond the simple appreciation of client group membership or affiliation. There is an increasing emphasis on client phenomenology and an appreciation of the role that family, small group, and macrolevel cultural and political systems have in defining or impinging on the individual. From these perspectives, counselors are being asked to balance their appreciation of the individual client while understanding how the individual's cultural affiliations make unique contributions to personality and worldview.

These theories supplement, rather than supplant, other counselor techniques and skills.

These theories supplement, strengthen, and broaden the skills available to practitioners. Most counselors tend to be eclectic (Sharf, 1999) and will probably use these new theories and techniques in conjunction with those that they already use. Counselors who desire to be more competent and effective with minority clients may choose to enhance their approach to therapy by reading and receiving training and supervision that is guided by multicultural theory. While this may add to counselor competence, in our view, it does not necessarily run counter to training received in other theoretical modalities, such as psychodynamic or cognitive-behavioral techniques. Thus, counselors may be able to retain their theoretical preference or style, and at the same time become more multiculturally competent and effective. The theories reviewed here place the cultural experience of the person at the center of the counseling enterprise and as such provide the counselor with an additional lens with which to appreciate the nature and complexity of client concerns. Thus, for example, a cognitive-behavioral counselor can utilize techniques like systematic desensitization and script analysis while viewing the process and goals of therapy as informed through the lens of a preferred multicultural counseling theory.

These theories focus on the sociopolitical and environmental context of clients' presenting complaints.

A client's external environment contains important information that can help counselors understand the etiology of his or her symptoms and problems. While an appreciation of internalized events and intrapsychic phenomena is important, these theories urge counselors to thoroughly explore environmental variables. A renewed appreciation for the person-environment fit underlying client behavior permeates many of these emerging theories. For example, Sue et al. (1996) write that "a person's identity is formed and continually influenced by his or her context.... [T]he totality and interrelationships of experiences and contexts must be the focus of treatment" (p. 15). Sue et al. also assert counselors must understand clients' cultural and sociopolitical contexts in order to adequately assess and treat them.

Other authors also emphasize the importance of environmental context. Steenbarger (1993) perceives client distress as due to "hostile physical, social, and cultural contexts (neighborhoods, workplaces, relationships, families, communities) in which power is maldistributed and misused.... [A]n open-ended inquiry attempts to capture the multiple interfaces between clients and their various contexts.... [M]ulticontextual counseling demands that the counselor actively engage the client's life contexts" (p. 11). Herring and Walker suggest that clients' interpretation of environmental presses can inform the focus of counseling and the quality of the therapy relationship as well as the overall helping process. Locke suggests counselors remain cognizant of world events and how clients from various cultures may personally interpret those events. Ramirez urges counselors to encourage their clients to use the environment toward growth and multicultural development.

There are also indirect suggestions by Ramirez, Sue et al., and Coleman that the counselor examine the therapy hour as a culturally constructed context or environment. This reminds us of Schneider's (1987) reconceptualization of Lewin's classic field theory. Schneider suggests that all work or social environments have a culture, and that such culture is the product of the interaction between the attributes of the people in it and the behavior that they engage in $(E = f, P \times B)$. The authors of some of these theories remind us that the counseling hour is a cultural environment and urge counselors to carefully attend to the context they create with their clients. They also call on counselors to ensure that such a context is multicultural and reflective of both the counselors' and clients' input and worldviews.

Counselor sociopolitical and racial/cultural self-awareness are important.

These theories tend to be counselor focused and emphasize the role of counselor multicultural competence and sensitivity. Sue et al. describe counselor self-awareness as the *sine qua non* of effective counseling and a professional and ethical obligation of every counselor.

Coleman specifically suggests that counselors demonstrate facility in using alteration or integration strategies to cope with client cultural diversity. Ho emphasizes counselor psychological "decentering" to remedy cultural encapsulation and ethnocentrism. Locke and Hanna et al. emphasize self-knowledge and personal growth as key to increasing counselor sensitivity to client's meaning of culture. Ramirez (1999) notes that his model "encourages the therapist to become aware of his unique culture and cognitive styles and to learn how to flex in order to best match the unique styles of clients" (p. 45).

The theorists highlighted in this chapter have attempted to operationalize an aspect of the Sue et al. (1998) multicultural competency model—counselor awareness of own assumptions, values, and biases. Sue et al. (1998) note that prevention of ethnocentrism is a key ingredient to effective cross-cultural counseling. Counselors need to understand their own worldviews, how they are the product of their cultural conditioning, and how it may be reflected in their counseling and work with racial and ethnic minorities. Each theorist in this chapter has emphasized, to varying degrees, the importance of cultural self-awareness in counselors. They adhere to the old adage "counselor, know thyself," and seem concerned, above anything else, with counselors not allowing the deleterious effects that biases, personal and social values, or "hang ups" might have on their effectiveness as helpers.

These theories provide mixed views of the "matching hypothesis."

Some of the authors emphasize matching of counselors and clients on various components. However, those authors who underscore the importance of matching tend to be discussing matching on skills and psychological constructs, and not on specific race or ethnic qualities. For example, Coleman (1997) implies counselors and clients match on the strategies they use to cope with cultural diversity to avoid conflict. He doubts a counselor can work effectively with a client from a different culture "unless one has true peer relationships with members from a different cultural group" (p. 199). Ramirez's (1999) model "encourages the therapist to become aware of his unique culture and cognitive styles and to learn how to flex in order to best match the unique styles of clients" (p. 45). The exception here is Locke (1998), who clearly suggests minority clients be paired with "well-trained *ethnic- and language-matched* helpers so that a claim can be made for its acceptance and effectiveness" (p. 17, italics added).

Other authors in this chapter de-emphasize, directly or indirectly, the importance of matching. For example, Sue et al. (1996) suggest that counselor-client dissimilarity may be beneficial in that differences may stimulate interpersonal learning and solidify the counseling relationship. Gonzalez et al. imply that any therapist can work with any client, as long as the therapist adheres to social constructionist ideas. Herring and Walker only emphasize that the counselor and client understand and accept their differences in order for effective counseling to begin. Steenbarger insists multicultural counselors try to understand the point of view and feelings of someone whose values and cognitive styles may be very different than those their own. Ho (1995) is clear in his position on this point:

> Human beings have the amazing capability to integrate diverse cultural influences into a cognitive whole at increasingly higher levels. Extending this argument to counseling would *negate* the claim, sometimes made by misguided mental health professionals, that persons in need of help can or should be helped only by professionals belonging to the same ethnic or cultural group. (p. 18, italics added)

Ultimately, the importance and value of matching counselors and clients on specific attributes or on level of development and other variables should be based on compelling data that show "matching" improves counseling process or outcome for ethnic minority clients.

FUTURE THEORETICAL AND EMPIRICAL RESEARCH

We encourage the reader to follow through on the excellent and helpful recommendations for research that are offered by each of the authors in their respective articles. These recommendations are timely and pertain specifically to each of the theoretical contributions made by the author. In the section below, we provide a more general research agenda stimulated by our collective reading of the theories presented above.

Theory Validation and Extension

The most immediate and exciting opportunities for research lie in the area of theory validation/extension, especially testing selected hypotheses in field settings. Many of the questions raised in our critiques indicate these theories have promise for informing cultural-centered practice and for advancing science. The empirical validation of these models seems ideal for dissertations focusing on multiculturalism—especially those focusing on applied therapy approaches, the therapy relationship, and process and outcome variables.

The field of multicultural counseling is poised for data showing that ethnic minority clients benefit from culture-centered theories and techniques. It is essential, however, that researchers identify and include along with traditional measures of outcome (e.g., symptom reduction) indices that are culturally or racially based (e.g., racial identity, acculturation, and interpersonal tolerance or sensitivity). Studies may also be designed to show the relative effectiveness of these theories and techniques with respect to process (e.g., the working alliance) and outcome (e.g., in preventing clinically contraindicated client termination from treatment or improving client satisfaction). Field studies are needed to demonstrate that multicultural concepts, constructs, and techniques, when used competently by therapists, improve counseling process and outcome for ethnic minority clients. Comparative analyses may be conducted to highlight the unique contribution of multicultural theories versus non-culturally-based interventions to process and outcome variables. We also agree with Sue, Zane, and Young (1994), who suggested that applied research in multicultural counseling study the client, therapist, and situational circumstances that are associated with positive outcomes and progress in therapy.

Events in Counseling

Research can also examine events in counseling, and qualitative studies seem particularly appropriate for such an endeavor (cf. Fuertes, Bartolomeo, & Nichols, 2001; Ponterotto & Casas, in press). In-session, exploratory research may inform current theories of multicultural counseling and highlight the ever-elusive description of moment-to-moment process, counselor interventions and consequences, and other counselor-client interactions (cf. Thompson & Jenal, 1994, for an excellent example of this type of research). Idiographic research may highlight how treatment actually unfolds in multicultural counseling and may lead to hypotheses that may be appropriate for study from a nomothetic, hypothetico-deductive framework. We also agree with Essandoh (1996), who suggested that theories of multiculturalism and counseling be developed with and from minority clients' views and perspectives. We also support suggestions by Meara, Schmidt, and Day (1996), who recommended that ethical multicultural counseling and research be guided by virtue ethics grounded in the values and wisdom from local communities where services are provided.

Counselor Variables

We note the continued focus on counselor variables (e.g., competencies, multiple and flexible roles, cognitive processes) in the development of multicultural counseling theory, and we contend that this focus should continue. It seems particularly important to study, in a qualitative way, how counselors cope with ambiguity and difficult multicultural cases and the process by which they decide to seek supervision or consultation for these difficulties. It also seems important to study how counselors in multicultural counseling negotiate culturally based conflicts or ruptures in the therapy relationship and how counselors empower themselves and clients to be culturally affirming and sensitive. Research may also examine how ethnic minority counselors adapt multicultural theory in working with minority clients and how this process is either facilitated or made more complex by the counselor's ethnic/cultural perspective.

Client Variables

We know from the literature that client variables, such as problem solving skills and motivation, are key to positive outcomes in counseling (Lambert & Bergin, 1994). Multicultural researchers might choose to focus on culturally based client dynamics and variables (e.g., bicultural vs. monocultural identity status) and if/how these are associated with therapy outcome. For example, researchers may study what some of the best indicators of counseling outcome are for racially and ethnically diverse clients. They may examine the cultural values, perspectives, and worldviews that ethnic minority clients tend to bring to counseling, and how these can be recognized and used to help the client move forward. Multicultural counseling researchers might examine how culture, worldview, and resources in the community might be used to improve client problem solving and motivation for change.

The Therapy Relationship

There has been some theoretical and empirical work devoted to the formation and role of the therapy relationship in multicultural counseling. Nevertheless, it appears that much more research can be devoted to the analysis of the relationship and how theories of multicultural counseling may inform the development of trust, focus, and even a sense of partnership between the counselor and the client. For example, a general question that may be examined is how multicultural theory facilitates how counselors and clients derive and accept a feasible plan of treatment. Theory development might be advanced from the "ground up" by research that examines the process by which counselors deal with race differences with their clients, how they establish and maintain the therapy relationship with their clients, and how counselor receptiveness to reports of racism strengthen the working relationship. An entire research program may also be directed at examining the level of overlap or influence between theories of multicultural counseling and the "real" relationship in counseling, the working alliance, and the transference-countertransference configuration in the counseling relationship (Gelso & Hayes, 1998).

Values/Culture and Personality

A fascinating area of potential research is the role of culture or cultural values and beliefs on personality functioning. Researchers and practitioners of multicultural counseling might choose to study how certain values and beliefs (e.g., orientation to time or authority) aid the coping and adjustment process of clients or how these values and beliefs might be used by the client to resist the process of helping or change in counseling. Leong (1996) recently extended Kluckhohn and Murray's (1950) tripartite conceptualization of personality into a theory of counseling that accounts for both clients' and counselors' individual, group, and universal levels of being and interacting in counseling. In our view, an important amount of work that may advance his compelling theory of counseling would be a thorough and careful delineation of the types of values, beliefs, and behaviors that comprise each of these levels and the development of a method by which these might be assessed.

CONCLUSION

This chapter extends the work of Ponterotto et al. (2000) by identifying and reviewing nine theories of multicultural counseling. We pointed out eight themes that emerge from these nine theories and identified potential venues for future research in the areas of multicultural counseling and multicultural counseling theory development. We hope that our discussion of these theories will inspire service providers to be more thoughtful and better prepared in working with ethnic minority populations. We also hope to stimulate a critical review of these theories as well as critical evaluations and extensions of our interpretations and research ideas.

As a caveat, we note that these theories have a decidedly North American (i.e., United States) focus, reflecting an American multicultural perspective. We recognize this is likely a narrow and limited view of the helping process and that there is potential for a more global and inclusive multicultural psychology. Theoretical and technical approaches to helping that are indigenous to countries and cultures outside of the United States can inform the current state of American multicultural theories of counseling. The challenge will be for current multicultural researchers to travel, study, and broaden their search for knowledge in a more international framework. This search may enrich and advance psychological science to better serve the increasingly diverse immigrant populations in the United States.

REFERENCES

Arbona, C. (1995). Culture, ethnicity, and race: A reaction. *The Counseling Psychologist, 23,* 74-78.

Atkinson, D. R., Thompson, C. E., & Grant, S. K. (1993). A three-dimensional model for counseling racial/ethnic minorities. *The Counseling Psychologist, 21,* 257-277.

Budman, S. H., & Gurman, A. S. (1988). *Theory and practice of brief therapy.* New York: Guilford.

Burlingame, G. M., & Behrman, J. A. (1987). Clinical attitudes toward time-limited and time-unlimited therapy. *Professional Psychology: Research and Practice, 18,* 61-65.

Carter, R. T. (1995). *The influence of race and racial identity in psychotherapy: Toward a racially inclusive model.* New York: John Wiley.

Casas, J. M., & Mann, D. (1996). MCT theory and implications for research. In D. W. Sue, A. E. Ivey, & P. B. Pedersen (Eds.), *A theory of multicultural counseling and therapy* (pp. 139-154). Pacific Grove, CA: Brooks/Cole.

Christensen, A., & Jacobson, N. (1994). Who (or what) can do psychotherapy: The status and challenge of nonprofessional therapies. *Psychological Science, 5,* 8-14.

Coleman, H. L. K. (1995). Strategies for coping with cultural diversity. *The Counseling Psychologist, 23,* 722-741.

Coleman, H. L. K. (1997). Conflict in multicultural counseling relationships: Source and resolution. *Journal of Multicultural Counseling and Development, 25,* 195-200.

Dawes, R. M. (1994). *House of cards: Psychology and psychotherapy built on myth.* New York: Free Press.

Dawis, R. V., & Lofquist, L. H. (1984). *A psychological theory of work adjustment.* Minneapolis: University of Minnesota Press.

Draguns, J. (1981). Cross-cultural counseling and psychotherapy: History, issues, current states. In A. Marsella & P. Pedersen (Eds.), *Cross-cultural counseling and psychotherapy* (pp. 3-27). New York: Pergamon.

Essandoh, P. K. (1996). Multicultural counseling as the "fourth force": A call to arms. *The Counseling Psychologist, 24,* 126-137.

Fischer, A. R., Jome, L. M., & Atkinson, D. R. (1998). Reconceptualizing multicultural counseling: Universal healing conditions in a culturally specific context. *The Counseling Psychologist, 26,* 525-588.

Ford, D. H. (1987). *Humans as self-constructing living systems.* Hillsdale, NJ: Lawrence Erlbaum.

Ford, M. E. (1992). *Motivating humans: Goals, emotions, and personal agency beliefs.* Newbury Park, CA: Sage.

Fuertes, J. N., Bartolomeo, M., & Nichols, C. M. (2001). Future research directions in the study of counselor multicultural competency. *Journal of Multicultural Counseling and Development, 29,* 3-12.

Garfield, S. L. (1980). *Psychotherapy: An eclectic approach.* New York: John Wiley.

Garfield, S. L. (1989). *The practice of brief psychotherapy.* New York: Pergamon.

Gelso, C. J. (1996). Applying theories in research: The interplay of theory and research in science. In F. T. L. Leong & J. T. Austin (Eds.), *The psychology research handbook: A guide for graduate students and research assistants* (pp. 359-368). Thousand Oaks, CA: Sage.

Gelso, C. J., & Hayes, J. A. (1998). *The psychotherapy relationship: Theory, research, and practice.* New York: John Wiley.

Gonzalez, R., Biever, J. L., & Gardner, G. T. (1994). The multicultural perspective in therapy: A social constructionist approach. *Psychotherapy, 31,* 515-524.

Hanna, F. J., Bemak, F., & Chi-Ying Chung, R. (1999). Toward a new paradigm for multicultural counseling. *Journal of Counseling and Development, 77*, 125-134.

Helms, J. E. (1984). Toward a theoretical model of the effects of race on counseling: A Black and White model. *The Counseling Psychologist, 12*, 153-165.

Herring, R. D., & Walker, S. S. (1993). Synergetic counseling: Toward a more holistic model with a cross-cultural specific approach. *TCA Journal, 22*(2), 38-53.

Ho, D. Y. F. (1995). Internalized culture, culturocentrism, and transcendence. *The Counseling Psychologist, 23*, 4-24.

Holland, J. L. (1992). *Making vocational choices: A theory of vocational personalities and work environments* (2nd ed.). Odessa, FL: Psychological Assessment Resources.

Hughes, C. C. (1976). *Custom made: Introductory readings in cultural anthropology.* Chicago: Rand-McNally.

Humphreys, K. (1996). Clinical psychologists as psychotherapists: History, future and alternatives. *American Psychologist, 51*, 190-197.

Kluckhohn, C., & Murray, H. A. (1950). Personality formation: The determinants. In C. Kluckhohn & H. A. Murray (Eds.), *Personality in nature, society, and culture* (pp. 35-48). New York: Alfred A. Knopf.

Kluckhohn, F. R., & Strodtbeck, F. L. (1961). *Variations in value orientations.* Westport, CT: Greenwood.

Lambert, M. J., & Bergin, A. E. (1994). The effectiveness of psychotherapy. In A. E. Bergin & S. L. Garfield (Eds.), *Handbook of psychotherapy and behavior change* (4th ed., pp. 143-189). New York: John Wiley.

Leighton, A. (1982). Relevant generic issues. In A. Gaw (Ed.), *Cross-cultural psychiatry* (pp. 83-108). Littleton, MA: Wright-PSG.

Leong, F. T. L. (1996) Toward an integrative model for cross-cultural counseling and psychotherapy. *Applied and Preventive Psychology, 5*, 189-209.

Locke, D. C. (1998). *Increasing multicultural understanding* (2nd ed). Newbury Park, CA: Sage.

Meara, N. M., Schmidt, L. D., & Day, J. D. (1996). Principles and virtues: A foundation for ethical decisions, policies, and character. *The Counseling Psychologist, 24*, 4-77.

Nash, M. (1989). *The cauldron of ethnicity in the modern world.* Chicago: University of Chicago Press.

Pedersen, P. B. (1997). Recent trends in cultural theories. *Applied and Preventive Psychology, 6*, 221-231.

Peterson, D. R. (1995). The reflective educator. *American Psychologist, 50*, 975-983.

Pinderhughes, E. (1989). *Understanding race, ethnicity, and power: The key to efficacy in clinical practice.* New York: Free Press.

Ponterotto, J. G. (1998). Charting a course for research in multicultural counseling training. *The Counseling Psychologist, 26*, 43-68.

Ponterotto, J. G., Fuertes, J. N., & Chen, E. C. (2000). Models of multicultural counseling. In S. D. Brown & R. W. Lent (Eds.), *Handbook of counseling psychology* (3rd ed., pp. 639-669). New York: John Wiley.

Ponterotto, J. G., & Casas, J. M. (in press). *Handbook of racial/ethnic minority counseling research* (2nd ed.). Springfield, IL: Charles C Thomas.

Ramirez, M., III. (1999). *Multicultural psychotherapy: An approach to individual and cultural differences* (2nd ed.). Boston: Allyn & Bacon.

Schneider, B. (1987). E = f (P, B): The road to a radical approach to person-environment fit. *Journal of Vocational Behavior, 31*, 353-361.

Sharf, R. S. (1999). *Theories of psychotherapy and counseling: Concepts and cases* (2nd ed.). Belmont, CA: Wadsworth/Thomson Learning.

Spokane, A. R. (1987). Conceptual and methodological issues in person-environment fit research [Special issue]. *Journal of Vocational Behavior, 31*, 217-361.

Steenbarger, B. N. (1993). A multicontextual model of counseling: Bridging brevity and diversity. *Journal of Counseling and Development, 72*, 8-15.

Steward, E. C. (1972). *American cultural patterns.* La Grange Park, IL: Intercultural Network.

Sue, D. W. (1978). World views and counseling. *Personnel and Guidance Journal, 58*, 458-462.

Sue, D. W., Arredondo, P., & McDavis, R. (1992). Multicultural counseling competencies and standards: A call to the profession. *Journal of Counseling and Development, 70,* 477-485.

Sue, D. W., Carter, R. T., Casas, J. M., Fouad, N. A., Ivey, A. E., Jensen, M., LaFrombiose, T., Manese, J. E., Ponterotto, J. G., & Vazquez-Nutall, E. (1998). *Multicultural counseling competencies: Individual and organizational development.* Thousand Oaks, CA: Sage.

Sue, D. W., Ivey, A. E., & Pedersen, P. B. (Eds). (1996). *A theory of multicultural counseling and therapy.* Pacific Grove, CA: Brooks/Cole.

Sue, D. W., & Sue, S. (1990). *Counseling the culturally different* (2nd ed.). New York: John Wiley.

Sue, S., & Zane, N. (1987). The role of cultural techniques in psychotherapy: A critique and reformulation. *American Psychologist, 42,* 37-45.

Sue, S., Zane, N., & Young, K. (1994). Research on psychotherapy with culturally diverse populations. In A. E. Bergin & S. L. Garfield (Eds.), *Handbook of psychotherapy and behavior change* (4th ed., pp. 783-871). New York: John Wiley.

Thompson, C. E., & Jenal, S. T. (1994). Interracial and intraracial quasi-counseling interactions when counselors avoid discussing race. *Journal of Counseling Psychology, 41,* 484-491.

Tolman, C. (1983). Further comments on the meaning of "dialectic." *Human Development, 26,* 320-324.

Wells, R. A., & Giannetti, V. J. (Eds.). (1990). *Handbook of the brief psychotherapies.* New York: Plenum.

Wampold, B. E. (2000). Outcomes of individual counseling and psychotherapy: Empirical evidence addressing two fundamental questions. In S. D. Brown & R. W. Lent (Eds.), *Handbook of counseling psychology* (3rd ed., pp. 711-739). New York: John Wiley.

Correspondence regarding this chapter may be sent to Jairo N. Fuertes, PES Room 1000, Fordham University at Lincoln Center, 113 West 60th Street, New York, NY 10023-7478 (e-mail address: VT320@aol.com).

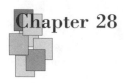

Chapter 28

MULTICULTURALLY SENSITIVE EMPIRICALLY SUPPORTED TREATMENTS—AN OXYMORON?

DONALD R. ATKINSON

UYEN BUI

SAKURAKO MORI

TWO MAJOR MOVEMENTS in professional psychology, the Empirically Supported Treatment (EST) movement and the Multicultural Counseling (MC) movement, are on a collision course, and one or both may be significantly altered by the encounter. The purpose of this chapter is to review problems with existing criteria for identifying ESTs, provide documentation that supports the inclusion of MC constructs when identifying effective treatments, and argue for de-emphasizing research on effective treatments and emphasizing research on common factors in future MC studies. We begin by providing a brief history of the EST movement.

HISTORY OF THE EST MOVEMENT

Interest in identifying and codifying efficacious psychotherapy treatments can be traced back more than 50 years in the professional psychology literature (Kazdin, 1996). Goldfried and Wolfe (1998) point to a review of research by Snyder (1950) as the first to ask if psychotherapy, in general, contributes to personality change. By the 1960s, however, researchers and reviewers were interested in determining if specific types of treatment were effective with specific types of problems. In recent years, there has

AUTHORS' NOTE: The second and third authors made equal contributions to this chapter.

been a heightened interest within professional psychology in validating the efficacy of specific psychotherapy interventions and in establishing a professionwide standard for recognizing validated treatments.

In 1993, Division 12 of Clinical Psychology of APA (American Psychological Association) reacted to this movement by forming the Task Force on Promotion and Dissemination of Psychological Procedures (hereafter referred to as the Task Force). The Task Force was created to develop criteria for determining efficacy of treatments, disseminate examples of treatments, and provide recommendations regarding education about empirically validated treatments (EVTs).[1] To understand why the Task Force was formed, it is important to examine the sociopolitical climate that existed in the United States in the late 1980s and early 1990s that produced pressures within the psychology profession to formalize identification of ESTs.

Pressure for Establishing ESTs

In the late 1980s and early 1990s, medical costs were rising much faster than the rate of inflation, and costs associated with mental health care were rising even faster than those for physical health care. Managed care was seen as a possible solution to these rising costs because it emphasized prevention and cost containment; as a result, Health Maintenance Organizations (HMOs) and other forms of managed care grew rapidly in the early 1990s. In order to hold costs down, HMOs put pressure on mental health providers to provide effective and cost efficient treatments. HMOs began to develop and publish their own guidelines for clinical practice in order to limit the kinds and lengths of mental health services they would reimburse. HMOs were also calling on the mental health professions to identify effective treatments in order to further justify limiting reimbursement to selected treatments (just as they were doing for physical health care).

The HMO guidelines tended to promote psychopharmacological treatments over psychotherapeutic treatments because a substantial body of evidence already existed supporting the efficacy of drug treatments for some mental disorders. It has been argued that pharmacotherapy research got a head start on identifying ESTs because it is generously funded by drug companies, and because pharmacotherapy researchers can easily produce data from randomized, double-blind, placebo-controlled studies to demonstrate the efficacy of their treatments (Crits-Christoph, Frank, Chambless, Brody, & Karp, 1995). By comparison, psychotherapy research generally has been underfunded because there are no large companies with vested interest in supporting such research; researchers must instead compete for grants from the federal and state governments and private foundations to fund psychotherapy research. Furthermore, psychotherapy outcomes are often less immediate and less obvious than drug treatment outcomes.

According to Glass and Arnkoff (1996), psychiatric organizations began to publish information about efficacious psychopharmacological treatments in the early 1990s. At that time, the American Psychiatric Association began publishing books and guidelines on treatments that are empirically supported and the Agency for Health Care Policy and Research of the U.S. Department of Health and Human Services began publishing clinical guidelines for the treatment of depression in primary care. Thus the movement to disseminate findings on empirically supported psychosocial treatments can be viewed in part as a reaction to counter the biological bias that was developing in the early 1990s (Glass & Arnkoff, 1996).

A national health care policy and program was seen by some as another part of the solution to rising health care costs. It is important to note that at the time a task force for identifying efficacious treatments was being conceived by APA in 1992, the U.S. Congress was debating the establishment of national health care (Beutler, 1998). According to Beutler, psychotherapy was threatened because it was in danger of not being covered by any of the proposed plans. It became clear that in order for psychologists to survive and be competitive in the managed health care and national health care environments, psychotherapy treatments had to be proven to be at least as effective as existing psychopharmacological treatments.

Establishment of Division 12 Task Force

Given these conditions, the movement to identify empirically validated treatments emerged quite quickly within Division 12 of APA. The idea of constituting a committee to identify ESTs was conceived in 1992 (Beutler, 1998). In 1993, David Barlow, president of the Division of Clinical Psychology of APA, pursued a number of initiatives to increase the knowledge of the effectiveness of psychological interventions (Crits-Christoph, 1998). One of the initiatives was the formation of the Task Force; the Task Force published its first report in 1995 in *The Clinical Psychologist.*

The Task Force appealed to members of Division 12 for support of its efforts in urgent tones: "If clinical psychology is to survive in this heyday of biological psychiatry, APA [American Psychological Association] must act to emphasize the strength of what we have to offer—a variety of psychotherapies of proven efficacy" (Task Force, 1995, p. 3). The main goal of the Task Force was to "consider methods for educating clinical psychologists, third party payers, and the public about effective psychotherapies" (Task Force, 1995, p. 3). In identifying ESTs the Task Force focused on whether a treatment was effective for a specific problem or disorder and not on whether certain treatments were in general effective (Crits-Christoph, 1998). In addition to identifying ESTs, the Task Force made several recommendations concerning training and practice. Task Force members reasoned that students need to be trained in ESTs to be prepared and competitive in the current market.

Because of the arbitrariness of defining treatment efficacy, the Task Force proposed two categories: well-established treatments, and probably

TABLE 28.1 Criteria for Empirically Validated Treatments

Well-Established Treatments

  I. At least two good group design studies demonstrating efficacy in one or more of the following ways:
  A. Superior to pill or psychological placebo or to another treatment
  B. Equivalent to an already established treatment in experiments with adequate statistical power (about 30 per group; cf. Kazdin & Bass, 1989)
  OR
 II. A large series of single case design experiments ($n > 9$) demonstrating efficacy. These experiments must have
  A. Used good experimental designs
  B. Compared the intervention to another treatment as in IA

FURTHER CRITERIA FOR BOTH I AND II

 III. Experiments must be conducted with treatment manuals.
 IV. Characteristics of the client samples must be clearly specified.
  V. Effects must have been demonstrated by at least two different investigators or investigatory teams.

Probably Efficacious Treatments

  I. Two experiments showing the treatment is more effective than a waiting-list control group
  OR
 II. One or more experiments meeting the Well-Established Treatment Criteria I, III, and IV but not V
  OR
 III. A small series of single-case design experiments ($n > 3$) otherwise meeting Well-Established Treatment Criteria II, III, and IV

SOURCE: Reproduced from Chambless et al. (1996), Task Force on Promotion and Dissemination of Psychological Procedures, Division 12, American Psychological Association.

efficacious treatments. Treatments that did not meet the criteria for either of the two categories were labeled experimental treatments (Task Force, 1995). The criteria for designating specific effective treatments for specific problems are provided in Table 28.1. Using these criteria the Task Force identified 18 treatments as "well-established" and 7 treatments as "probably efficacious." Division 12 has also appointed a permanent standing committee to update the criteria. Since the initial report published in 1995, there have been two updates on empirically validated therapies, one in 1996 (Chambless et al., 1996) and the other in 1998 (Chambless et al., 1998).

Although the work of the Task Force was completed by and for psychologists, the EST movement is likely to affect a variety of mental health workers, including professional counselors, clinical social workers, marriage and family therapists, and possibly even psychiatrists. Therefore, we use the generic terms psychotherapist and counselor interchangeably when referring to professionals who may use ESTs. When referring to the application of psychological interventions, we use counseling and psychotherapy interchangeably.

GENERAL CRITICISMS OF THE EST MOVEMENT

Although various forces inside and outside psychology converged in the mid 1990s to promote the identification and codification of ESTs by the Task Force, acceptance of the EST movement by psychologists has not been universal. A number of authors have found fault with the assumptions underlying identification of ESTs, the criteria used to identify them, and the narrow focus on treatment to the exclusion of nontreatment factors in the psychotherapy and counseling process. In the following sections we review some of these criticisms.

Criticisms Related to the
Assumptions Underlying ESTs

The rationale for the development of the Division 12 list of ESTs rests on several implicit assumptions, the first of which is that identification of such a list "is advantageous to the psychotherapy community" (Wampold, 1997, p. 21). Another is that for each mental disorder, there exists a hierarchy of treatments ranging from least efficacious to most efficacious (implicit in Criterion I-A and II-B). Still another is that psychotherapies that satisfy the criteria contain some unique characteristic that differentiate them from other treatments and make them effective (Wampold, 1997). While it may be advantageous to the psychotherapy community to identify a list of particularly efficacious treatments to be used with specific mental disorders, the assumptions that some treatments are more effective than others and that each treatment contains a unique characteristic that accounts for its effectiveness can be challenged based on past meta-analyses of psychotherapy effectiveness.

A number of meta-analyses have demonstrated that psychotherapy in general is more effective than no treatment (Lambert & Bergin, 1994). However, attempts to prove one treatment more effective than another have either shown "little or no difference between therapies" (Lambert & Bergin, 1994, p. 156) or are open to criticism of researcher bias in favor of one of the therapies, that is, that "treatments administered by advocates of a treatment are administered more skillfully or more faithfully than are the other treatments" (Wampold, 1997, p. 35). Wampold goes so far as to argue that "efficacy research, as currently conducted, cannot test [the] assumption . . . that some treatments are better than others" (p. 30) because advocates for the less efficacious treatment can always argue that the unique, essential characteristics of their treatment were not adequately represented. On the other hand, there is reason to believe that all psychotherapy treatments may share certain essential characteristics that make them effective. Over 65 years ago, Rosenzweig (1936) suggested that nonspecific, implicit factors common to all forms of psychotherapy account for their relatively comparable effects. This theme that common factors, not unique characteristics, account for the relatively similar effectiveness of psychotherapy approaches was expanded further by Frank (1961, 1973, 1982) and others. Thus, it can be argued that research demonstrating that particular treatments are superior to a placebo or are equivalent to an established treatment are actually demonstrating the efficacy of common factors, while research attempting to establish the superiority of one treatment over another are invariably flawed and therefore unwarranted.

Criticisms of Division 12 EST Criteria

In addition to resting on questionable assumptions, the EST criteria themselves have been criticized by a number of authors. We will review a few of the most significant criticisms raised against the criteria.

Bohart, O'Hara, and Leitner (1998) point out that the criteria are based on a disorder-driven medical model and are not applicable to therapies whose main focus is not on "curing disorder" but on promoting personal growth. This exclusive focus on remediation of problems should be of concern to counseling psychologists, community psychologists, family therapists, and any mental health professional who seeks to prevent problems and promote growth as well as remediate problems. Treatment modalities that do not conform to the Task Force assumptions about the nature of psychotherapy could easily be disfranchised.

Crits-Christoph (1998) has suggested that randomized clinical trials (i.e., group experimental designs) have been significantly overemphasized as the standard for determining which treatments are efficacious (although, in all fairness, the criteria do include one other methodology option, 9 or more single-case experiments). As a consequence, the list of empirically supported therapies are overrepresented by cognitive (41%) and behavioral (41%) treatments because they are readily amenable to experimental research designs (Henry, 1998). Thus, despite the prevalence of other treatment modalities in actual clinical practice (such as psychodynamic therapy and family therapy), these modalities are not represented in the Division 12 list of ESTs.

Some of the criticisms focus on the design limitations inherent in randomized clinical trials. Elliott (1998) points out that the heavy reliance on randomized clinical trials to validate treatments "ignores serious method problems which have been identified in their usual implementation (selective attrition, limited range of outcome measures, absence of long-term follow-up data, allegiance effects)" (pp. 120-121). Randomized clinical trials also often have questionable external validity; their findings frequently cannot be fully generalized to actual clinical settings (Goldfried & Wolfe, 1998). Further, Elliott points out that the criteria do not reflect the current "state of the art" with respect to psychotherapy research in that (a) "the power requirements for a comparative treatment study to detect a medium effect size (ES = .5 sd) greatly exceed the 30 patients per groups cited in the criteria" (p. 120) and (b) empirical validation is based on statistical significance rather than clinical significance or effect size.

The criterion of *two* good group design studies (or nine or more single subject studies) demonstrating treatment efficacy can be criticized given the profession's penchant for publishing only significant results (Atkinson, Furlong, & Wampold, 1982). Chance alone would dictate that 1 out of every 20 studies conducted under similar circumstances should result in significant findings. Although two very well designed studies might demonstrate the effectiveness of a particular treatment over a pill, placebo, or another treatment at the .05 level of significance, what assurance is there that numerous other published and (and particularly) unpublished studies have found no effect in favor of the treatment?

To ensure treatment reliability, the EST criteria specify that all "experiments must be conducted with treatment manuals." While it is desirable to standardize treatments for the purposes of research, the use of manuals has been criticized from a clinical practice point of view because the complexity of treatment and scope of exchanges between therapist and patient cannot be standardized in manuals (Kazdin, 1991, p. 293). More will be said about this in the next section, which identifies important variables in psychotherapy that the Division 12 criteria completely ignore.

Criticism Related to
Important Variables the Criteria Ignore

A number of authors have criticized the EST criteria for focusing exclusively on treatments and ignoring other variables that research has suggested are important contributors to psychotherapy process and outcome. To wit, the criteria have been criticized for ignoring client variables, therapist variables, and relationship variables. This criticism is particularly germane to the current chapter because it relates to variables that multicultural counseling theorists and researchers have identified as ingredients that are essential to bridging potential barriers when the client and counselor are ethnically and/or culturally different.

Client variables. Garfield (1996) has pointed out that not all clients identically diagnosed require identical treatments. Certain client characteristics can determine how well the client will respond to a particular treatment, suggesting that for clients who share the same diagnosis, the same treatment could be more effective with some clients than with others. These characteristics include, but are not limited to, the client's personality (Garfield, 1996), defensive tendencies, coping styles (Beutler & Baker, 1998), life situation (Garfield, 1996), levels of social support (Beutler & Baker, 1998), life stress (Wampold, 1997), severity of the problem (Beutler & Baker, 1998), previous therapy, expectations about therapy, perception of therapist (Garfield, 1996), and racial/ethnic and cultural background (Doyle, 1998).

Therapist variables. Although it can be argued that any "treatment" effect is a function of both the technique and the therapist who applies the technique, by including manualized treatment as a criterion the Task Force is obviously attempting to isolate the treatment effect from any effect due to the therapist (Garfield, 1996). In fact, the Task Force appears to have treated therapist effect as a nuisance variable. Yet as suggested by Wampold (1997), outcome variances due to therapist differences tend to be large when the effects of therapist variables are not specifically controlled. In fact, there is evidence that the therapist effect may be even larger than the effect due to treatment alone. Lambert (1989) reviewed the literature on the therapist's contribution to psychotherapy process and outcome and concluded the following:

> (a) In addition to clinical wisdom and anecdotal evidence, there is empirical support for the notion that the individual therapist can have a substantial effect on process and outcome, one that often exceeds that attributable to technique and one that justifies thoughtfulness and care in making referrals; (b) this effect which has been shown to be both positive and negative can be observed across a variety of patient diagnoses and levels of symptom severity. (p. 480)

Therapist variance usually refers to factors that affect competence, such as the criteria used to select therapist-trainees, the quality of the training and supervision they receive, and the criteria used to determine therapist competence (Crits-Christoph, 1998). To the list of therapist characteristics that critics of the Task Force say were ignored in developing the EST criteria, we would like to add multicultural counseling competence. In the last two decades multicultural counseling competence has emerged as an important source of variance in multicultural counseling situations. We will offer further documentation of the importance of this therapist characteristic in a later section.

Relationship variables. A number of authors have lamented the fact that the Task Force ignored the role of relationship variables in identifying effective treatments. As suggested earlier, the fact that a variety of psychotherapies have been found effective with the same client problem (Beckham, 1990; Elkin et al., 1989) suggests the existence of common factors that account for a treatment effect. Garfield (1996) points out that there is little disagreement that a good therapeutic alliance between therapist and client is one of the common factors of psychotherapy. We propose that being paired with an ethnically similar counselor contributes significantly to a good therapeutic alliance; being paired with a culturally similar counselor contributes even more to a positive therapeutic alliance. Similarly, it can be argued that racial/ethnic identity development compatibility between the client and counselor contributes to a positive therapeutic alliance. In the next section we review some of the theory and research that we believe support the importance of ethnic and cultural similarity, and ethnic identity development compatibility, between counselor and client, and that provide further evidence that client, counselor, and relationship variables cannot be ignored when defining effective treatment.

CRITICISMS OF THE EST MOVEMENT
FROM A MULTICULTURAL PERSPECTIVE

With two major exceptions, there has been surprisingly little published reaction to the EST movement from advocates of the MC movement. In this section, we review the concerns raised earlier by Doyle (1998) and S. Sue (1999) and then document why a number of specific client, counselor, and relationship variables must be taken into account when determining effective treatments for ethnic minorities. As evidence to support our position, we cite professional policy statements, multicultural counseling postulates, and multicultural research findings.

Client Characteristics

In their initial report on ESTs, the Task Force made no mention of the need to test ESTs with specific ethnic groups. In a subsequent report (Chambless et al., 1996), the Task Force rectified this oversight by noting that "the efficacy of EVTs has not been established with ethnic minority populations" and calling on researchers to "begin to conduct rigorous outcome research on diverse cultural groups" (p. 7). Their suggestions for doing so included specifying the ethnicity of subjects in all studies, creating incentives to promote more research with minorities, and examining effect sizes for different ethnic groups. However, these recommendations were limited to extending research on currently recognized ESTs to ethnic minority populations. According to Chambless et al. (1996),

> Strictly speaking, then, the efficacy of EVTs has not been established with ethnic minority populations. . . . Obviously, those treatments that have been validated for one population may be valid for another. However, as scientists, we cannot assume that the effects will be similar. (p. 7)

Doyle (1998) was among the first to criticize the Task Force for not having taken ethnicity and culture into consideration in identifying ESTs. Doyle pointed out that even though culture plays a critical role in the assessment, etiology, symptoms, and treatment of mental health problems, the applicability of specific treatment procedures to culturally diverse populations has received scant research attention. In fact, there are no empirical studies that convincingly demonstrate the outcome efficacy of psychotherapy with racial/ethnic minority populations (S. Sue, 1995). Doyle noted that the ethnicity and race of the sample were specified in only 15% of 33 empirically valid treatment studies published since 1985. In this 15%, which included 248 participants, 92% were White. Minor improvement was observed in the 1996 revision of the Task Force report (Chambless et al., 1996): 24% of the 21 additional post-1985 studies mentioned the race/ethnicity of the participants. The majority of subjects in these studies, however, also were predominantly White (86%), thus precluding the opportunity to analyze differential treatment effectiveness across race and ethnicity (Doyle, 1998). This significant lack of attention to racial, ethnic, and cultural influences suggests a research bias because racial/ethnic minorities make up approximately 25% of the entire population in the U.S., a percentage that is projected to increase to almost 50% by 2050.

More recently, S. Sue (1999) has drawn attention to the failure to test EST effectiveness with ethnic/cultural minorities. S. Sue has argued convincingly that in order to make causal inferences, psychological science needs to emphasize both internal validity and external validity. He goes on to point out, however, that a bias exists in psychological research that favors internal validity over external validity. As a result, carefully controlled studies are carried out on samples drawn from a very limited population (often European American college students) with little regard to how generalizable the outcomes are to other ethnic and/or cultural groups. Furthermore, S. Sue suggests that the burden of proving that the outcomes of studies with European Americans *are not* generalizable to other groups (and, paradoxically, that outcomes with ethnic/cultural groups *are* generalizable to European American populations) is left to MC counseling researchers.

Building on the concerns expressed by Doyle (1998) and S. Sue (1999), we offer the following discussion as a rationale for including specific ethnic/cultural variables in the determination of effective treatments.

Symptom Manifestations

In identifying ESTs, the Task Force purposely linked specific treatments to specific mental disorders. Therefore, psychotherapists need to make specific clinical diagnoses prior to selecting specific ESTs. However, mental and emotional health and illnesses are defined differently in each culture based on the worldview and philosophy of that culture (Das, 1987). Hence, the role of cultural variables in determining what constitutes "normal" and "abnormal" behavior should never be ignored or discounted in diagnosing and counseling cultural minority clients. Unfortunately, nowhere in the criteria for validating treatments or the list of ESTs is there any recognition that culture determines what constitutes abnormal behavior. By simply linking specific treatments with specific disorders, the Task Force has ignored the relationships among culture, symptom manifestation, and treatment.

Although ignored by the Task Force in identifying ESTs, the important role that culture plays in identifying mental disorders has been recognized in the latest edition of *Diagnostic and Statistical Manual of Mental Disorders (DSM)*. For the first time in the manual's history, *DSM-IV* (American Psychiatric Association, 1994) acknowledged the need to take ethnic and cultural considerations into account when making mental disorder diagnoses:

> Diagnostic assessment can be especially challenging when a clinician from one ethnic or cultural group uses the *DSM-IV* Classification to evaluate an individual from a different ethnic or cultural group. A clinician who is unfamiliar with the nuances of an individual's cultural frame of reference may incorrectly judge as psychopathology those normal variations in behavior, belief, or experience that are particular to the individual's culture. . . . Applying Personality Disorder criteria across cultural settings may be especially difficult because of the wide cultural variation in concepts of self, styles of communication, and coping mechanisms. (American Psychiatric Association, 1994, p. xxiv)

In addition to acknowledging cultural differences in normal and abnormal behavior, *DSM-IV* included information about specific cultural features that might be manifested in many of the classified disorders. A new section was added to most of the diagnostic categories that provides information about how a particular diagnosis might manifest itself for a particular cultural group, as well as data on the differential prevalence of the disorder among cultural groups. Furthermore, a list of 25 "culture-bound syndromes" was included in Appendix I of *DSM-IV*. These syndromes were described as patterns of aberrant behavior that "are generally limited to specific societies or culture areas and are localized, folk, diagnostic categories that frame coherent meanings for certain repetitive, patterned, and troubling sets of experiences and observations" (American Psychiatric Association, 1994, p. 844). This is a strong endorsement of the role that culture plays in determining abnormal behavior by both the authors of *DSM-IV* and the American Psychiatric Association.

Although recognition of the important role that culture plays in diagnosing mental disorders represents a major step forward, we need to point out that *DSM-IV* still reflects the Western philosophy of dualism between mind and body and between thoughts and emotions. Also, *DSM-IV* still divides mental disorders into disorders of mood, anxiety, and soma (Mukherji, 1995). Contrary to this model, a great majority of ethnic minorities strongly emphasize the interconnectedness of mind, body, and spirit. Their psychological disturbances are thus often experienced in a somatopsychological mode (Lewis-Fernandez & Kleinman, 1994). Somatic complaints, such as headaches, stomachaches, back and chest pains, seizures, and paralyses, are probably the most prevalent expressions of emotional and mental problems around the world (Mukherji, 1995). By somaticizing symptoms, culturally unacceptable psychic conflicts can be disguised (Kuo & Kavanagh, 1994). The therapist's lack of understanding of these cultural influences can lead to inaccurate diagnoses by either overpathologizing the cultural minority client or underestimating the severity and complexity of the client's emotional distress (S. W. Sue & D. Sue, 1999).

In summary, how individuals manifest psychological problems is in large part a function of their cultural upbringing. *DSM-IV* (hardly a bastion of mental health liberalism) acknowledges that culture affects how individuals manifest psychological problems and has implications for the diagnoses they should receive. A logical extension of this argument is that an individual's culture plays a role in determining if and how his or her psychological problems should be treated. The Task Force makes no mention of the role that symptom manifestation might play in identifying ESTs. Given the importance of culture in determining abnormal behavior in *DSM-IV*, it seems short-sighted that the Task Force would completely ignore this variable in establishing criteria for identifying ESTs.

Acculturation

In a later section, we describe how essential it is that client and psychotherapist beliefs about the causes and cures for psychological problems be similar. Because such beliefs are a function of culture, and adherence to such beliefs a function of acculturation, client acculturation is an important variable to consider when selecting a treatment. Acculturation was defined, and models of acculturation presented, in some detail in Chapter 20. In this section, we briefly review the theoretical, professional, and research support for taking acculturation into consideration when selecting treatments for ethnic minority clients.

Acculturation is a critical variable because it is closely related to the client's psychological functioning. Lowered mental health status frequently results from acculturative stress (Berry, 1998). Many racial/ethnic minority individuals experience such mental health concerns as "threats to cultural identity, powerlessness, feelings of marginality, a sense of inferiority, loneliness, hostility, and perceived alienation and discrimination" as they acculturate (Sandhu, 1997). Furthermore, relationships between acculturation levels and gang membership, delinquency, alcohol and drug abuse, major depression, dysthymia, phobia, and eating disorders have been documented by research (Casas, 1995). Berry (1998) points out that refugees in particular face considerable risk in their adjustment processes due to the involuntary, migratory, and often temporary nature of their relocation. Their difficult pre-acculturation experiences, such as war, famine, deprivation, humiliation, massive exclusion, and domination, frequently lead them to develop posttraumatic stress, amnesia, depression, and anxiety.

The need to take acculturation into consideration when working with cultural minority clients has been recognized by the American Psychological Association's (1993) Guidelines for Providers of Psychological Services to Ethnic, Linguistic, and Culturally Diverse Populations (hereafter referred to as Diversity Guidelines):

> Psychologists recognize ethnicity and culture as significant parameters in understanding psychological processes. . . . Psychologists' practice incorporates an understanding of the client's ethnic and cultural background. This includes the client's familiarity and comfort with the majority culture. . . . The kinds of mainstream social activities in which families participate may offer information about the level and quality of acculturation to American society. (p. 46)

Although a number of studies and research reviews (e.g., Casas & Casas, 1994; Moyerman & Forman, 1992; Rogler, Cortes, & Malgady, 1991) have examined the relationship between acculturation and measures of mental health or mental illness, little research has looked at the relationship between acculturation and counseling process and outcome. Atkinson, Morten, and D. W. Sue (1998) reviewed the research that has looked at this relationship and concluded that,

> although few in number, these studies provide consistent documentation that acculturation is related to how racial/ethnic minority clients perceive and respond to counseling services. In general, they suggest that less acculturated racial/ethnic minorities are more likely to trust and express a preference for and a willingness to see an ethnically similar counselor than are their more acculturated counterparts. . . . In summary, acculturation is a measure of within-group diversity that is related to a number of counseling process variables. Counselors working with an ethnic minority client should be aware not only of the client's ethnic background but the extent to which the client identifies with and practices the culture of his/her ancestors. (p. 31)

Thus, theory has described, the APA has recognized, and research has supported the important role that acculturation can play in the counseling process. We believe that future attempts to identify effective treatments with immigrant populations would be remiss if they ignored the role of acculturation in counseling and psychotherapy.

Counselor Characteristics–
Multicultural Counseling Competence

As suggested earlier, a number of authors have criticized the EST movement for failing to acknowledge the role that counselor characteristics, particularly therapeutic competence, play in treatment outcome. Among those counselor competencies that the Task Force overlooked is multicultural counseling competence. Although there has been no research to date that links multicultural counseling competence to counseling outcome, there is considerable agreement within the profession that counselors must be multiculturally competent in order to work effectively with any client, but particularly ethnic minority clients. In this section, we review the professional mandate for multicultural counseling competence and argue that this counselor characteristic plays a major role in determining treatment effectiveness with cultural minority clients.

Although the need for multiculturally competent counselors was recognized as early as the mid 1960s, it was not until the 1980s that a professionally sanctioned definition of multicultural counseling competence was developed. In 1981, the Education and Training Committee of Division 17 (Counseling Psychology) of the American Psychological Association developed a position paper defining competencies for counselors when counseling racial/ethnic minority clients. The Division 17 position paper identified 11 multicultural counseling competencies that were subsumed under three dimensions: beliefs/attitudes (four competencies), knowledges (four competencies), and skills (three competencies). Although Division 17 did not formally endorse the 1981 position paper, the paper was published in *The Counseling Psychologist* in 1982 (D. W. Sue et al., 1982), and it served as a catalyst for subsequent attempts by Division 17 and the American Counseling Association (ACA) to refine these competencies (Arredondo et al., 1996; D. W. Sue, Arredondo, & McDavis, 1992; D. W. Sue et al., 1998).

Ten years after the position paper developed by the Division 17 Education and Training Committee appeared in print, D. W. Sue et al. (1992) published an expanded list of multicultural counseling competencies. This revised list consisted of 31 multicultural competencies organized within a 3 by 3 matrix. One side of the matrix identified three counselor characteristics judged to be essential ingredients of multicultural counseling competence; these three characteristics are (a) counselor awareness of own values and biases, (b) counselor awareness of client's worldview, and (c) culturally appropriate intervention strategies. The other side of the matrix consisted of the three dimensions of multicultural counseling competence identified in D. W. Sue et al. (1982): (a) attitudes/beliefs, (b) knowledges, and (c) skills. The following is an example of a multicultural counseling competence in the cell generated by crossing the attitudes/beliefs dimension with the awareness of own values and biases characteristic: "Culturally skilled counselors have moved from being culturally unaware to being aware and sensitive to his/her own cultural heritage and to valuing and respecting differences."

As one of their purposes in publishing the matrix of 31 multicultural counseling competencies, D. W. Sue et al. (1992) called for the establishment of multicultural standards by the American Association for Counseling and Development (precursor to the ACA). Neither the APA nor the ACA has established multicultural standards; however, the 31 competencies identified by D. W. Sue et al. (1992) have been endorsed by three divisions (17, 35, 45) of the APA and five divisions (ACES, AADA, AGLBIC, ASCA, ASGW, IAMFC) of the ACA (D. W. Sue, personal communication, August 26, 1997).

Although the APA as an umbrella psychological organization has not yet endorsed the D. W. Sue et al. (1992) multicultural counseling competencies, the APA's Board of Ethnic Minority Affairs did publish the Diversity Guidelines (American Psychological Association, 1993) in which the need for multicultural competence is clearly stipulated. These guidelines provide general principles and suggestions to psychologists when working with ethnic, linguistic, and culturally diverse populations. Among other principles and suggestions, the APA's (1993) Diversity Guidelines state that

> psychologists seek out educational and training experiences to enhance their understanding and thereby address the needs of these [ethnic/racial] populations more appropriately and effectively. . . . Psychologists recognize the limits of their competencies and expertise. Psychologists who do not possess knowledge and training about an ethnic group seek consultation with, and/or make referrals to, appropriate experts as necessary. (p. 46)

The APA has also stipulated the need for multicultural competence in the organization's ethical code. Its (1992) Ethical Principles of Psychologists and Code of Conduct states that

> psychologists are cognizant of the fact that the competencies required in serving, teaching, and/or studying groups of people vary with the distinctive characteristics of those groups. In those areas in which recognized professional standards do not yet exist, psychologists exercise careful judgment and take appropriate precautions to protect the welfare of those with whom they work. (p. 1599)

Very clearly, there is considerable agreement within both APA and ACA that psychologists and counselors need to possess multicultural counseling competence when they work with ethnic minority clients. However, the criteria developed by the Task Force to be used to identify ESTs make no reference to therapist competency, let alone therapist multicultural counseling competence. In fact, by requiring that treatment efficacy be established exclusively through the use of treatment manuals, the Task Force appears to be purposely attempting to reduce or eliminate the influence of therapist competence in identifying ESTs. Based on the widespread professional recognition of the important role that multicultural competence plays when working with ethnic minority clients, we propose that the multicultural competence of the counselor should always be taken into consideration in selecting treatments to use with ethnic minority clients.

Relationship Characteristics

As suggested earlier, Garfield (1996) chastised Task Force members for not acknowledging the importance of the working alliance between client and therapist when they identified ESTs. In this section, we identify some of the relationship variables that can contribute significantly to building a strong working alliance with a client.

Linguistic Similarity

It seems axiomatic that in order for psychotherapy treatments to be effective, the psychotherapist and client must speak the same language. Linguistic similarity between counselor and client is especially important for ethnic minority clients who are recent immigrants and who speak English as a second or third language. Contrary to a common American assumption that everyone readily understands English, an acquisition of foreign language proficiency, especially in adult years, requires a relatively long period of strenuous study, strong linguistic ability, and an extensive knowledge of the adopted culture (Takahashi, 1989). The English skills of recent immigrants are, therefore, likely to be negatively affected when they are under a considerable amount of stress. Furthermore, psychological expressions tend to be much freer and more spontaneous in one's first language than in a second or third language, which frequently promotes the use of intellectual defense and control (Pitta, Marcos, & Alpert, 1978). Since utilization of an interpreter can easily cause distortions of the client's actual messages (to say nothing of the threat to confidentiality), sharing the same native tongue with the client can be a major advantage.

Research indicates that language match between therapist and client is associated with more sessions and more positive therapeutic outcomes than when therapist and client are not matched on language. Flaskerud (1986) examined the relationship between a culturally sensitive approach to mental health service and ethnic minority utilization of services (as measured by dropout rates and total number of counseling sessions) and found language match between psychotherapists and clients to be one of the best predictors of utilization (Flaskerud, 1986). In a major study involving data from 600,000 clients seen over 15 years, S. Sue, Fujino, Hu,

Takeuchi, and Zane (1991) found that among clients for whom English was a second language, both language and ethnic match were predictors of length and outcome of treatment.

The APA Board of Ethnic Minority Affairs recognized the importance of language similarity in the psychotherapy process and cautioned that

> problems may arise when the linguistic skills of the psychologist do not match the language of the client. In such a case, psychologists refer the client to a mental health professional who is competent to interact in the language of the client. If this is not possible, psychologists offer the client a translator with cultural knowledge and an appropriate professional background. When no translator is available, then a trained paraprofessional from the client's culture is used as a translator/culture broker. (APA, 1993, p. 46)

The importance of language similarity is so fundamental that any document identifying ESTs should begin with a statement that, in order to be effective, treatment must be provided in the client's language of choice.

Racial/Ethnic Similarity

Although ethnic and racial similarity provides no guaranty of cultural and linguistic similarity, there is ample evidence that research participants prefer an ethnically similar psychotherapist. Atkinson and Lowe (1995) conducted a major review of research on preference for counselor ethnicity and concluded that "for both the simple choice and paired-comparison methodologies, there is consistent and strong evidence that, other things being equal, ethnic minority participants prefer an ethnically similar counselor over an ethnically dissimilar counselor" (p. 392). Atkinson and Lowe found that the ethnic similarity effect also manifested itself with other measures of counseling process and outcome. Their review of research on perceptions of counselor credibility led to the tentative conclusion that "for some individuals within each of the ethnic minority groups, counselor similarity/dissimilarity is an important factor in determining perceived counselor credibility" (p. 395). In summarizing their review of research linking counselor-client ethnic similarity to mental health utilization, Atkinson and Lowe concluded that the major archival studies by Flaskerud (1986), Flaskerud (1991), and S. Sue et al. (1991) "provide substantial evidence that treatment . . . [utilization is] . . . enhanced by matching therapist and client on the basis of language and ethnicity" (p. 397).

Further evidence that treatment outcome is enhanced by providing ethnically similar counselors has been provided by two more recent studies. In the study conducted by Russell, Fujino, S. Sue, Cheung, and Snowden (1996), ethnically matched counselors rated their clients' psychological functioning higher than did mismatched counselors for African American, Asian American, and Mexican American clients. Similarly, Ricker, Nystul, and Waldo (1999) found that ethnic similarity between counselor and client was also related to positive outcomes as measured by the degree of symptom relief in time-limited counseling.

Thus, ethnic similarity between psychotherapist and client has been found to be related to both treatment process and outcome. For some clients, having an ethnically similar psychotherapist determines whether they will stay in counseling, and if they do, whether counseling is likely to be effective or not. Suggesting that ESTs can be selected and effectively implemented with ethnic minority clients without considering the ethnic match between counselor and clients seems professionally irresponsible. No EST can be effective if the client drops out of counseling because he/she feels uncomfortable with an ethnically different counselor.

Racial/Ethnic Identity
Development Compatibility

Although ignored by the Task Force, the compatibility of the client's and counselor's stage (or state) of ethnic identity development may play an important role in psychotherapy effectiveness. Helms (1990) has proposed a Black/White interaction model that analyzes how the counselor's and client's stages of racial/ethnic identity development interact and can affect the working alliance between the psychotherapist and client. Furthermore, Helms hypothesizes that the compatibility of client and counselor stage of racial identity development is directly related to outcome. For the sake of brevity, we do not describe all aspects of the interaction model, but we do provide a few examples of how counselor and client ethnic identity compatibility can affect counseling process and outcome. Furthermore, because Fischer and Moradi have described the Black Racial Identity Development (BRID) and the White Racial Identity Development (WRID) models in some detail in Chapter 20, we assume the reader has some knowledge of the stages of both Black and White ethnic identity development.

Focusing on the Black and White races, Helms (1990) suggests that "when both counselor and client stages of racial consciousness are assessed and used to predict the counseling process, four types of relationships are possible: parallel, crossed, progressive, and regressive" (p. 140). Briefly, a *parallel relationship* exists when the counselor and client share the same racial attitudes about Blacks and Whites. A *crossed relationship* exists, on the other hand, when they hold contradictory attitudes about Blacks and Whites. A *progressive relationship* exists when the counselor's stage of racial consciousness is at least one stage more advanced than the client's. A *regressive relationship* exists when the client is at least one stage more advanced than the counselor. Helms further suggests that whereas a progressive relationship will promote client racial identity development, a regressive relationship will likely end in termination.

Beyond her general predictions for progressive and regressive relationships, Helms's predictions about the quality of the counseling relationship and the likelihood of a positive outcome are unique to each combination of counselor-client race and each combination of attitudes toward Blacks and Whites. For example, when a White counselor in the Disintegration stage of WRID is counseling a Black client in the Internalization stage of BRID, Helms predicts that the counseling outcome is likely to be premature termination with the client seeking a counselor who "is more in tune with his/her needs" (p. 143). Another example is when both counselor and client are at opposite stages, such as a Black counselor in the Immersion stage, where he or she may feel obligated to reeducate the client about Blackness, and a White client is at the Pre-encounter stage, where he or she feels negatively about Black people. This interaction may actually have a positive influence on counseling outcome if the counselor can act as a positive role model to help the client develop positive feelings about Blacks (Helms, 1990). Thus, there are specific implications of parallel and crossed relationships, and these will differ depending on whether the counseling dyad is intra- or cross-racial.

Although the Black/White Interaction Model itself has received relatively little research attention, a number of studies have demonstrated that counselor and client racial identity development stages/states do play an important role in counseling process and outcome. In one of the early studies of racial identity development, Parham and Helms (1981) found that Pre-encounter attitudes on the part of Black college students were directly related to their preference for a White counselor and inversely related to their preference for a Black counselor. In a later study, Helms and Carter (1991) found that the Internalization attitudes of Black male and female college students were directly related to preference for White male counselors. Helms and Carter (1991) also found that White students' preferences for White counselors were related to their Disintegration attitudes. In one of the few studies to look at counseling outcome, Bradby and Helms (1990) found that satisfaction with counseling among Black clients was a function of their Encounter and/or Internalization attitudes.

Evidence has also been found that racial identity development attitudes held by counselors may influence counseling process and outcome. In a recent study by Burkard, Ponterotto, Reynolds, and Alfonso (1999), the researchers found that White racial identity attitudes significantly impacted counselor trainee ratings of the counseling relationship in same-racial and cross-racial counseling dyads (Burkard et al., 1999). Although the findings are preliminary, the authors suggest that White racial identity may influence the ability of a counselor to form a productive working relationship with a client.

In one of the few studies that directly addressed the Black/White Interaction Model, Carter (1990) examined how the racial identity attitudes held by counselors and clients were related to counseling process and found the strongest evidence of a relationship for dyads involving White counselors and White clients. He also found some evidence that White counselor and Black client racial identity attitudes were related to counselor intentions and client reactions in counseling.

Although it is premature to imply that the Black/White Interaction Model has been empirically validated, there is enough research support to suggest that racial identity development attitudes on the part of the counselor and client play an important role in counseling process and outcome. The EST movement, by focusing exclusively on the efficacy of the type of treatment, has ignored the important contributions of racial identity development attitudes to counseling outcome. In a regressive relationship, for example, an ethnic minority client will probably terminate counseling no matter how effective a particular EST has been found to be with European Americans. Furthermore, by stressing the importance of treatments, the Task Force has indirectly implied that counselors need not assess and identify their own attitudes on White racial identity; thus the EST movement may actually impede this self-awareness process. Counselors may rationalize that because ESTs are "empirically validated" they will be effective regardless of their own and their clients' racial identity development attitudes.

Compatibility of Beliefs About Causes of Psychological Problems

Perhaps the most important similarity or compatibility that needs to exist between client and psychotherapist is compatibility of beliefs about the causes of psychological problems. When the client and psychotherapist are ethnically/culturally different, their etiology beliefs are likely to be different. Psychotherapists' beliefs about the causes of psychological problems are shaped by the cultural values in the United States and by the scientific method. D. W. Sue and D. Sue (1999) point out that in Western science, the experimental design is viewed as the ultimate method to address questions about a variety of human conditions. These authors assert that the analytical and reductionistic characteristics of experimental design, which are reflected in a strong emphasis on objectivity, autonomy, and independence, have led to the clear detachment of the individual from the society and of science from spirituality.

Although these underlying assumptions of Western science have improved many aspects of our daily living conditions, most non-Western cultures operate from perspectives which are quite different from those of Westerners. In direct opposition to the Western cultural norm, minimal distinctions are made between secular and spiritual lives in the majority of non-Western societies (Lee & Armstrong, 1995). Because religious traditions often condition the worldview of the people in these societies (Das, 1987), all aspects of human development and interactions tend to be affected by their spiritual beliefs (D. W. Sue & D. Sue, 1999). Thus, either spirit possession or violation of some religious or moral principles are often used to account for the people's psychological distress and disorders (Das, 1987).

Torrey (1972) pointed out that although beliefs about the causes of mental illness vary greatly between Western and non-Western cultures, each holds validity within its respective culture:

> Biological causes widely believed in by people in Western cultures include genetic damage, inborn constitutional factors, biochemical and metabolic imbalances, infections, drug toxicity, and damage to the brain. . . . Experiential causes, especially experiences in childhood, are the hallmark of American psychiatry. . . . Metaphysical causes are the most important ones in most of the world: the loss of the soul; the intrusion of a spirit into the body (spirit possession); sorcery, angering a deity. . . . Though most investigators dismiss theories of causation in other cultures as "just magic and spirits," those who have looked more closely have found a complex and coherent belief system equally as sophisticated as our own. (pp. 21-22)

A number of authors have documented the unique etiology beliefs of specific cultural groups. In traditional Chinese medicine, the imbalance of cosmic forces and lack of willpower explain why someone becomes sick (Hahn, 1995). Attachment to personal desires and worldly things are considered by Buddhists as a main cause of human suffering (Axelson, 1993). Some American Indians believe mental illness results when cultural values and community respect are ignored (LaFromboise, 1998). The "Taboo violation" beliefs held by the Iroquois about the causes of illnesses are not atypical. Examples of the societal and cultural prohibitions established by Iroquois tradition include "the killing of a bear or otter without first properly thanking the spirits of these animals, not "feeding" one's hunting charm, not avoiding a "witch" plant, profane singing of sacred songs, ridiculing the False Faces, neglecting to purge one's body in the spring or fall, eating food prepared by a menstruating woman, failing to thank or beseech properly a spirit force, neglecting the ghost of a relative, and failing to properly rejoice at any of the gifts given to humans by the Creator" (Herrick, 1983, p. 147). In summary, inexplicable misfortune (D. W. Sue & D. Sue, 1999), fate (Lee & Armstrong, 1995), shameful thoughts and actions, and familial inheritance (Flaskerud, 1986) are frequently cited as origins of psychological problems among many ethnic minority groups.

Medical anthropologists have known for at least three decades that the prospect of healing mental illness is seriously impaired if the patient's beliefs about the causes of the problem are at odds with their healer's beliefs about causation. According to Torrey (1972), "it can be shown that people in various cultures have different beliefs regarding what causes [mental] illness. Insofar as the therapists of that culture share these beliefs, or can persuade the people to accept their theories of causation, they will be effective" (p. 21). Consider the following scenario, which could take place in California, Minnesota, Texas, or in a number of other U.S. states:

> A 62-year-old Hmong woman is referred to a mental health counselor (let's say a male) by a medical doctor because she is acutely depressed after being diagnosed as having breast cancer. Through an interpreter, the counselor learns that the woman is somewhat sad about her diagnosis, which she assumes means that she will die soon, but is very depressed because her placenta is buried in Cambodia and she fears that after death her soul will not be able to find it. According to Hmong beliefs, in order for the soul to reunite with its ancestors (a prerequisite to being reborn as the soul of a new baby), it must first find the placental "jacket" and put it on (Fadiman, 1997). Without its jacket, the soul is destined to wander naked and alone throughout eternity. The counselor, on the other hand, believes that her depression is the result of irrational self-statements she is making related to the breast cancer diagnosis.

In this situation, it seems highly unlikely that the client will stay in counseling, let alone improve from it, if the counselor ignores the woman's beliefs about the causes of her depression. Basically, the Western-trained counselor has two choices: (a) attempt to convince the woman that his explanation of why she is depressed is more valid than hers or (b) refer the client to a psychotherapist/healer who shares her beliefs about the causes of her depression. If he chooses the former, the client is likely to drop out of counseling and self-refer to a shaman from the Hmong culture who shares her beliefs about what will happen after she dies.

The APA Board of Ethnic Minority Affairs recognized the important role that clients' beliefs can play in symptom manifestation: "Psychologists respect clients' religious and/or spiritual beliefs and values, including attributions and taboos since they affect world view, psychosocial functioning, and expressions of distress" (APA, 1993, p. 46). We believe that psychologists should not only respect clients' beliefs and values but that psychologists should take clients' beliefs about the causes of a psychological problems into account when selecting treatments. In the next section we examine how beliefs about the solutions to psychological problems might also affect choice of treatment.

Compatibility of Beliefs About
Cures for Psychological Problems

Culture plays a vital role not only in promoting beliefs about the causes of psychological difficulties but also in establishing beliefs about effective treatment for these problems. In traditional societies, beliefs about how psychological problems are resolved often involve a ceremony or treatment in which a spirit is expunged or the client atones for some infraction of cultural standards. These ceremonies and treatments are usually carried out by an indigenous healer or shaman who shares with the client the cultural beliefs about how problems are caused and cured (Das, 1987). Witch doctors, magic men/women, sorcerers (Lee & Armstrong, 1995), diviners, fortune-tellers (Kuo & Kavanagh, 1994), physiognomists, temple-based ritual experts (Kleinman & Sung, 1979) and other religious leaders, herbalists, acupuncturists, curanderos, root doctors, and voodoo practitioners (Flaskerud, 1986) are some examples of such healers. The value of the therapeutic approaches taken by these traditional healers tends to be discounted by mental health professionals because they are "backward," "primitive," or "unsophisticated" from the contemporary Western perspective (Lee & Armstrong, 1995). In addition, the techniques utilized by Western psychotherapists are frequently considered to be "scientific" and sound, whereas those employed by therapists elsewhere are labeled as "magical" (Torrey, 1972) and "unscientific."

Continuing the scenario depicted earlier of the Hmong woman diagnosed as having breast cancer,

> the woman believes that the only way she can prevent her spirit from wandering naked and alone throughout eternity is to seek out the assistance of a *txiv neeb* (Hmong shaman), who will negotiate with the spirits to ensure that her soul finds her placenta after death. The psychologist, being familiar with published examples of ESTs in Chambless et al. (1996), offers to treat her with cognitive therapy, a well-established treatment for depression.

Regardless of how many published studies may have "validated" cognitive therapy as a treatment for depression, application of this EST in this situation is no more likely to be successful than if a Hmong shaman recommended sacrificing a chicken to treat a Wall Street broker for anxiety disorder.

Although our example of the Hmong woman being treated for depression with an EST may seem extreme, it is important to recognize that large numbers of Asian and South American immigrants (as well as smaller numbers of immigrants from other parts of the world) are coming to the United States each year who maintain their indigenous beliefs about the causes of, and cures for, psychological problems. Furthermore, some of these beliefs are retained in varying degrees among subsequent generations after immigration. The central fact that is most frequently ignored by Western psychotherapists is that the services provided by these traditional healers have successfully addressed a variety of physical and psychological problems of people in the respective culture for many centuries (Lee & Armstrong, 1995). Having been developed within specific cultural contexts, these traditional healing practices are built on their culturally derived philosophy. Therefore, the people tend to trust the efficacy of these practices, and, in turn, their willingness to commit to the treatment regimen produces positive therapeutic outcomes (Atkinson et al., 1998).

Several APA and ACA policy statements have acknowledged that cultural beliefs should be taken into consideration in treatment selection. The APA Board of Ethnic Minority Affairs recognized the need to match treatments to clients' beliefs as evidenced by the following statement in the APA's (1993) Diversity Guidelines: "Psychologists consider not only differential diagnostic issues but also the cultural beliefs and values of the client and his/her community in providing intervention" (p. 46). One of the multicultural counseling competencies identified by D. W. Sue et al. (1992) and endorsed by divisions in both the APA and the ACA clearly links treatment choice to culture: "Culturally skilled counselors are not adverse to seeking consultation with traditional healers or religious and spiritual leaders and practitioners in the treatment of culturally-different clients when appropriate" (p. 79).

As we have tried to suggest, each immigrant group comes to this country with its own unique beliefs about the cures for psychological problems that include culturally based treatments. Although we have serious reservations about the validity and utility of establishing a professionally sanctioned list of ESTs, we believe that if a register of well-established treatments and probably efficacious treatments is to be created, it should include culturally based treatments as well. Even though the Task Force has failed to acknowledge the significance of any indigenous healing methods, it is imperative to recognize that counseling as practiced in the West is only one of many potentially effective therapeutic modes. The importance of understanding the "alternative reality" and cultural relativism in validating treatments for racial/ethnic minorities cannot be overstressed (Lee & Armstrong, 1995).

IMPLICATIONS OF THE
EST MOVEMENT FOR THE MC MOVEMENT

The EST movement has important, and potentially very negative, implications for the theory, research, teaching, and practice of multicultural counseling.

Implications for Theory and Research

As our review of the EST movement suggests, there are powerful forces within psychology (e.g., Division 12 leadership) and outside psychology (e.g., the insurance industry) advocating for the codification of effective treatments for specific psychological problems. The most obvious way for MC theoreticians and researchers to respond to this pressure is to advocate for validating ESTs with specific ethnic/cultural groups (indeed, S. Sue,

1999, has already recommended that greater stress be placed on external validity in outcome research). Chambless et al. (1996) anticipated this concern and agreed that we need to examine the effectiveness of each EST with each cultural group. Beyond pushing the EST movement to replicate EST research with ethnic/cultural minorities, MC proponents might advocate for research on culturally specific healing strategies, first with members of the culture from which the healing strategy emerged and next with other cultural groups (including European Americans).

The argument in favor of this response is that if culturally adapted and/or culturally specific treatments are to gain respectability in the future, they will need to be empirically validated according to the criteria established by the Task Force. For multicultural counseling researchers caught up in the publish or perish pressures of most major universities, this response to the EST movement would provide a research bonanza; every EST and every culturally specific healing strategy would need to be validated with at least one ethnic group and tested with every ethnic group. When one considers all the various permutations and combinations of cultural groups and ESTs, multicultural researchers should have no problem generating EST studies indefinitely.

Yet despite initially having some appeal to MC researchers, we see several problems with this response to the EST movement. First, even if ESTs had to be validated with each and every ethnic group, and even if culturally specific treatments were included in the process, this approach still reinforces the myopic emphasis on treatment. In effect, the roles of other important culturally related client, counselor, and relationship characteristics would still be overlooked in determining effective treatments. We believe that to be truly multiculturally sensitive, any means of identifying effective treatments would need to take into account factors like client acculturation, language similarity, racial/ethnic similarity, ethnic identity compatibility, and mental health belief similarities. Merely validating manualized ESTs with ethnic minority populations does not do this. Second, when taken to the extreme, this response to the EST movement could mean the proliferation of an unlimited number of esoteric ESTs, many of which might only be effective for a small number of clients. Although this might be more desirable than implying that the current list of ESTs is applicable to all clients, carried to the extreme it could trivialize the MC movement by suggesting that culturally specific counseling strategies really just reflect client individual differences.

Implications for Training

The EST movement is exerting considerable pressure on the psychology profession to require training in ESTs. Crits-Christoph et al. (1995) surveyed clinical psychology training programs and found that most responding programs provided training in one or more ESTs but that there was wide variability among programs, with some offering training in none of the ESTs. In its 1995 report, the Task Force cited the results of this study as evidence that "in one APA-approved program in five, empirically-validated treatments may be under-emphasized" (p. 6) and as justification for their recommendation that APA site visitors make "training in empirically-validated treatments a criterion for APA accreditation" (p. 8). That same year the Accreditation Committee's *Guidelines and Principles for Accreditation of Programs in Professional Psychology* (American Psychological Association, 1995) was published, specifying that accredited programs must provide (a) course instruction in "formatting and implementing intervention strategies (including training in empirically supported procedures)" and (b) practicum experiences that "provide a wide range of training and educational experiences through applications of empirically supported intervention procedures" (p. 7). Very clearly, pressure is being exerted by Task Force members and the APA Accreditation Committee to require psychology programs to provide more training in ESTs.

However, increased emphasis on ESTs in doctoral training may lead to a decreased emphasis on multicultural competency training. Most training programs have few degrees of freedom for adding courses and experiences beyond those mandated by the Accreditation Committee and state licensing boards (to say nothing of the anticipated effects of the prescription privilege movement on curricula). Although training programs are also expected to recognize "the importance of cultural and individual differences and diversity in the training of psychologists" (American Psychological Association, 1995, p. 9), they are not required to provide training in specific techniques or alternative counseling roles for specific ethnic groups. Programs that do provide training in culturally specific techniques and alternative roles may have to reduce those efforts in favor of providing more training in ESTs. If training in culturally responsive techniques and alternative counseling roles must be curtailed in favor of more comprehensive EST training, it is reasonable to assume that the multicultural competence of training program graduates will suffer. Pope-Davis, Reynolds, Dings, and Ottavi (1994) found that "educational variables accounted for a significant amount of variance of self-reported multicultural counseling competencies" (p. 468). Thus, increased attention to ESTs could result in decreased multicultural competence in trainees.

If the current list of ESTs is expanded to include treatments validated with diverse populations as well as European American populations, it is not hard to imagine that at some point the list of ESTs will become so large that programs will be able to provide only minimal training for most. In that situation it is a pretty safe bet that ESTs validated with minority populations will receive minimal attention, whereas those validated with the majority population will receive greater attention.

Implications for Practice

The Task Force has suggested that until such time as ESTs are validated for diverse populations, practitioners should continue to offer psychotherapy to ethnic minorities based on the ESTs identified for European Americans:

> Given the lack of efficacy data, should we continue offering psychotherapy to diverse populations? Yes. We have a responsibility to provide services, even without definitive research findings on which to base services. Of greater importance is the need to alleviate suffering to the best of our ability and to the best of our knowledge, *based on generalization from white samples.* (Chambless et al., 1996, p. 8; italics added)

This statement reflects an ethnocentric bias by suggesting that EST research and application can trickle down from White samples to ethnic minority populations. However, it also provides practitioners with a justification for using ESTs with ethnic minority clients without regard to their English-language proficiency, level of acculturation, stage of identity development, or mental health beliefs.

As the study by Pope-Davis et al. (1994) suggests, trainees who do not receive training in multicultural counseling are not likely to become multiculturally competent practitioners. If, as we have suggested, training in ESTs is emphasized at the expense of training in multicultural competence, we will be producing practitioners who will lack even the awareness that ESTs should be applied within a culturally sensitive context. Practitioners who are trained in ESTs very likely will use them with their ethnic minority clients, even if they have not been validated with their clients' ethnic group. Consequently, the counselor could easily overlook possible conflicts that the treatment might have with the client's cultural beliefs, and this may result in diminished treatment effectiveness and/or premature termination by the client. By way of contrast, studies by Rogler, Malgady, and Rodriguez (1989), S. Sue, Zane, and Young (1994), and Szapocznik et al. (1989) suggest that culturally sensitive interventions may actually increase service utilization, length of treatment, client's satisfaction, and therapy outcomes.

PUTTING EFFECTIVE
TREATMENTS IN PERSPECTIVE

By focusing on treatment as the active ingredient in psychotherapy, the EST movement has overemphasized the importance of treatment and ignored the role of other variables in psychotherapy. The MC movement, on the other hand, has drawn attention to the role of other variables in providing psychotherapy for ethnic minority clients. In effect, the MC movement has suggested that ethnic and cultural factors account for as much or more of the variance in psychotherapy outcome with ethnic minority clients as does the treatment provided. We are concerned that by urging the Task Force (and future iterations of the Task Force) to validate ESTs with ethnic populations, MC advocates may unwittingly reinforce the EST movement's overemphasis on treatment and discounting of client, counselor, and relationship variables. It has taken the MC movement over three decades to convince the mental health professions that client, counselor, and relationship variables contribute to effective counseling with ethnic clients. It would be unfortunate if these variables are lost in our zeal to demand validation of ESTs with ethnic populations.

We are not suggesting that research on the effectiveness of ESTs or culturally specific techniques with ethnic populations should be curtailed. However, we do want to suggest that the role of ESTs be kept in perspective. A theoretical explanation for psychotherapy effectiveness that keeps psychological treatments in proper perspective is the common factors theory. From a common factors viewpoint, treatments (or techniques or rituals) are just one of several factors that contribute to psychological healing. Examples of other common factors are the therapeutic relationship, a shared worldview, and client expectations (Fischer, Jome, & Atkinson, 1998). It can be hypothesized that some of the variables we reviewed earlier (similar language, ethnic identity compatibility, similar race/ethnicity, compatibility of beliefs about the causes of, and solutions to, psychological problems) make significant contributions to these common factors. For example, language similarity and racial/ethnic similarity may promote the establishment of a strong therapeutic relationship. Compatibility of beliefs about the causes of and solutions to psychological problems is an important part of a shared worldview. Ethnic identity compatibility and compatibility of beliefs about the causes of and solutions to psychological problems may help to raise client expectations.

In a review of research with important implications for all of professional psychology, Wampold (2000) used the findings of meta-analyses to examine two major questions about counseling and psychotherapy effectiveness: Does counseling and psychotherapy produce positive outcomes? Are the outcomes due to common factors or specific ingredients in the counseling and psychotherapy provided? With respect to the first question, he concluded that "the absolute efficacy of psychotherapy is unambiguous" (p. 734). With respect to the second question he determined that "the evidence appears to support a model of psychotherapy in which the common factors are paramount" (p. 734). His findings also provide important support for MC counseling and the variables examined in the current chapter.

> The evidence strongly favors letting clients select a psychological treatment that makes sense to them and permitting therapists to adapt treat-

ments to be consonant with the attitudes, values, and culture of the client, rather than having third-party payers or health maintenance organizations mandate a particular treatment. Whereas the specific ingredient model assumes that an empirically valid treatment is universally applicable for a disorder, a common factor model . . . prescribes that the treatment be consistent with the meaning system of the client, which provides a persuasive rationale for culturally specific treatments. (pp. 735-736)

For a thorough analysis of the research addressing the common factors versus specific ingredients controversy, the reader is referred to Wampold (2000). For more information about the implications of common factors theory for MC, the reader is referred to Fischer et al. (1998)

CONCLUSION

The EST and MC movements are both exercising considerable influence on professional psychology as we enter the new millennium. Unfortunately, however, these two movements have fairly distinct and somewhat antithetical goals. The goal of the EST movement is to identify the most effective treatments for specific problems, regardless of other factors that might affect psychotherapy outcome. The goal of the MC movement is to draw attention to ethnic and cultural influences (particularly as manifested by client, counselor, and relationship characteristics) on counseling process and outcome. Our review of the professional, theoretical, and empirical support for the role of ethnic and cultural influences on counseling process and outcome provides, in our opinion, compelling evidence that client, counselor, and relationship characteristics must be taken into account in establishing psychotherapy effectiveness.

The effect of the current EST movement is to overemphasize the importance of treatment and ignore the role of other variables in psychotherapy. This has important and possibly catastrophic consequences for the MC movement. In particular, MC theoreticians and researchers may respond to the EST movement by simply expanding treatment outcome research to include diverse populations. We believe this would be a mistake because it would de-emphasize the important role of client, counselor, and relationship variables, ignore the complexity of multicultural influences on counseling outcome, and fractionalize the MC movement into numerous esoteric cultural/treatment camps. Recognition of specific treatments for specific cultural groups is important, but it is only one piece of the total puzzle. We urge advocates of the MC movement to look carefully at the common factors approach to psychotherapy, which views treatment as one of several components found in all effective psychotherapy, as an alternative to embracing the EST movement. Such an approach will allow us to draw attention to the important multicultural variables that affect psychotherapy, rather than lead to the proliferation of countless culturally specific ESTs that ignore other client, counselor, and relationship variables.

NOTE

1. The Task Force initially referred to treatments that met their criteria for validation as Empirically Validated Treatments (EVTs). When confronted with criticism that treatments are never fully validated, the Task Force members began using the term Empirically Supported Treatments (ESTs; see Chambless & Hollon, 1998). We use EST except when quoting from early Task Force documents.

REFERENCES

American Psychiatric Association. (1994). *Diagnostic and statistical manual of mental disorders* (4th ed.). Washington DC: Author.

American Psychological Association. (1992). Ethical principles of psychologists and code of conduct. *American Psychologist, 47*, 1597-1611.

American Psychological Association. (1993). Guidelines for providers of psychological services to ethnic, linguistic, and culturally diverse populations. *American Psychologist, 48*, 45-48.

American Psychological Association. (1995). *Guidelines and principles for accreditation of programs in professional psychology.* Washington, DC: Author.

Arredondo, P., Toporek, R., Brown, S. P., Jones, J., Locke, D. C., Sanchez, J., & Stadler, H. (1996). Operationalization of the multicultural counseling competencies. *Journal of Multicultural Counseling and Development, 24*, 42-78.

Atkinson, D. R., Furlong, M. J., & Wampold, B. E. (1982). Statistical significance, reviewer evaluations, and the scientific process: Is there a (statistically) significant relationship? *Journal of Counseling Psychology, 29*, 189-194.

Atkinson, D. R., & Lowe, S. (1995). The role of ethnicity, cultural knowledge, and conventional techniques in counseling and psychotherapy. In J. G. Ponterotto, J. M. Casas, L. A. Suzuki, & C. M. Alexander (Eds.), *Handbook of multicultural counseling* (pp. 387-414). Thousand Oaks, CA: Sage.

Atkinson, D. R., Morten, G., & Sue, D. W. (1998). *Counseling American minorities* (5th ed.). Boston: McGraw-Hill.

Axelson, J. A. (1993). *Counseling and development in a multicultural society* (2nd ed.). Pacific Grove, CA: Brooks/Cole.

Beckham, E. E. (1990). Psychotherapy of depression research at a crossroads: Directions for the 1990's. *Clinical Psychology Review, 10*, 207-228.

Berry, J. W. (1998). Acculturative stress. In P. B. Organista, K. M. Chun, et al. (Eds.), *Readings in ethnic psychology* (pp. 117-122). Florence, KY: Taylor & Francis.

Beutler, L. E. (1998) Identifying Empirically Supported Treatments: What if we didn't? *Journal of Consulting and Clinical Psychology, 66*, 113-120.

Beutler, L. E., & Baker, M. (1998). The movement toward empirical validation: At what level should we analyze, and who are the consumers? In K. S. Dobson & K. D. Craig (Eds.), *Empirically supported therapies: Best practice in professional psychology* (pp. 43-65). Thousand Oaks, CA: Sage.

Bohart, A. C., O'Hara, M., & Leitner, L. M. (1998). Empirically violated treatments: Disenfranchisement of humanistic and other psychotherapies. *Psychotherapy Research, 8*, 141-157.

Bradby, D., & Helms, J. E. (1990). Black racial identity attitudes and white therapist cultural sensitivity in cross-racial therapy dyads: An exploratory study. In J. E. Helms (Ed.), *Black and White racial identity: Theory, research and practice* (pp. 165-175). Westport, CT: Greenwood.

Burkard, A. W., Ponterotto, J. G., Reynolds, A. L., & Alfonso, V. C. (1999). White counselor trainees' racial identity and working alliance perceptions. *Journal of Counseling & Development, 77*, 324-329.

Carter, R. T. (1990). The relationship between racism and racial identity among White Americans: An exploratory investigation. *Journal of Counseling and Development, 69*, 46-50.

Casas, J. M. (1995). Counseling and psychotherapy with racial/ethnic minority groups in theory and practice. In B. Bongar & L. E. Beutler (Eds.), *Comprehensive textbook of psychotherapy* (pp. 311-335). New York: Oxford University Press.

Casas, J. M., & Casas, A. (1994). The acculturation process and implications for education and services. In A. C. Watiella (Ed.), *The multicultural challenge in health education* (pp. 23-49). Santa Cruz, CA: ETR Associates.

Chambless, D. L., Baker, M. J., Baucom, D. H., Beutler, L. E., Calhoun, K. S., Crits-Christoph, P., Dainto, A., De Rubeis, R., Detweiler, J., Haaga, A. F., Johnson, S. B., McCurry, S., Mueser, K. T., Pope, K. S., Sanderson, W. W., Shoham, V., Stickle, T., Williams, D. A., & Woody, S. R. (1998). An update on Empirically Validated Therapies II. *The Clinical Psychologist, 51,* 3-16.

Chambless, D. L., & Hollon, S. D. (1998). Defining empirically supported therapies. *Journal of Consulting and Clinical Psychology, 66,* 7-18.

Chambless, D. L., Sanderson, W. C., Shoham, V., Johnson, S. B., Pope, K. S., Crits-Christoph, P., Benjamin, M. B., Woody, S. R., Sue, S., Beutler, L., Williams, D. A., & McCurry, S. (1996). An update on empirically validated therapies. *The Clinical Psychologist, 49*(2), 5-18.

Crits-Christoph, P. (1998). Training in empirically validated treatments. In K. S. Dobson & K. D. Craig (Eds.), *Empirically supported therapies: Best practice in professional psychology* (pp. 3-25). Thousand Oaks, CA: Sage.

Crits-Christoph, P., Frank, E., Chambless, D. L., Brody, C., & Karp, J. F. (1995) Training in empirically validated treatments: What are clinical psychology students learning? *Professional Psychology: Research and Practice, 26,* 514-522.

Das, A. K. (1987). Indigenous models of therapy in traditional Asian societies. *Journal of Multicultural Counseling and Development, 15,* 25-37.

Doyle, A. B. (1998). Are empirically validated treatments valid for culturally diverse populations? In K. S. Dobson & D. D. Craig (Eds.), *Empirically supported therapies: Best practice in professional psychology* (pp. 93-103). Thousand Oaks, CA: Sage.

Elkin, I., Shea, M. T., Watkins, J. T., Imber, S. D., Stotsky, S. M., Collins, J. F., Glass, D. R., Pilkonis, P. A., Leber, W. R., Docherty, J. P., Fiester, S. J., & Parloff, M. B. (1989). National Institute of Mental Health treatment of depression collaborative research program. General effectiveness of treatment. *Archives of General Psychiatry, 46,* 971-982.

Elliott, R. (1998). Editor's introduction: A guide to the empirically supported treatments controversy. *Psychotherapy Research, 8,* 115-125.

Fadiman, A. (1997). *The spirit catches you and you fall down.* New York: Farrar, Straus & Giroux.

Fischer, A. R., Jome, L. M., & Atkinson, D. R. (1998). Reconceptualizing multicultural counseling: Universal healing conditions in a culturally specific context. *The Counseling Psychologist, 26,* 525-588.

Flaskerud, J. H. (1986). The effects of culture-compatible intervention on the utilization of mental health services by minority clients. *Community Mental Health Journal, 22,* 127-141.

Flaskerud, J. H. (1991). Effects of an Asian client-therapist language, ethnicity and gender match on utilization and outcome of therapy. *Community Mental Health Journal, 27,* 31-42.

Frank, J. D. (1961). *Persuasion and healing.* Baltimore, MD: Johns Hopkins University Press.

Frank, J. D. (1973). *Persuasion and healing* (Rev. ed.). Baltimore, MD: Johns Hopkins University Press.

Frank, J. D. (1982). Therapeutic components shared by all psychotherapies. In J. H. Harvey & M. M. Parks (Eds.), *The master lecture series: Vol. 1. Psychotherapy research and behavior change* (pp. 5-37). Washington, DC: American Psychological Association.

Garfield, S. L. (1996). Some problems associated with "validated" forms of psychotherapy. *Clinical Psychology: Science & Practice, 3,* 218-229.

Glass, C. R., & Arnkoff, D. B. (1996). Psychotherapy integration and empirically validated treatments: Introduction to the special series. *Journal of Psychotherapy Integration, 6,* 183-189.

Goldfried, M. R., & Wolfe, B. E. (1998). Toward a more clinically valid approach to therapy research. *Journal of Consulting and Clinical Psychology, 66,* 143-150.

Hahn, R. A. (1995). *Sickness and healing: An anthropological perspective.* New Haven, CT: Yale University Press.

Helms, J. E. (1990). Counseling attitudinal and behavioral predispositions: The Black/White Interaction Model. In J. E. Helms (Ed.), *Black and White racial identity: Theory, research, and practice* (pp. 135-143). Westport, CT: Greenwood.

Helms, J. E., & Carter, R. T. (1991). The relationship of Black and White racial identity attitudes and demographic similarity to counselor preference. *Journal of Counseling Psychology, 38,* 446-457.

Henry, W. P. (1998). Science, politics, and the politics of science: The use and misuse of empirically validated treatment research. *Psychotherapy Research, 8,* 126-140.

Herrick, J. W. (1983). The symbolic roots of three potent Iroquois medical plants. In L. Romanucci-Ross, D. E. Moerman, & L. R. Tancredi (Eds.), *The anthropology of medicine: From culture to method* (pp. 134-155). New York: Praeger.

Kazdin, A. E. (1991). Treatment research: The investigation and evaluation of psychotherapy. In M. Hersen, A. E. Kazdin, & A. S. Bellack (Eds.), *The clinical psychology handbook* (2nd ed., pp. 293-312). New York: Pergamon.

Kazdin, A. E. (1996). Validated treatments: Multiple perspectives and issues: Introduction to the series. *Clinical Psychology: Science & Practice, 3,* 216-217.

Kazdin, A. E., & Bass, D. (1989). Power to detect differences between alternative treatments in comparative psychotherapy outcome research. *Journal of Consulting and Clinical Psychology, 57,* 138-147.

Kleinman, A., & Sung, L. H. (1979). Why do indigenous practitioners successfully heal? *Social Science & Medicine, 13B,* 7-26.

Kuo, C. L., & Kavanagh, K. H. (1994). Chinese perspectives on culture and mental health. *Issues in Mental Health Nursing, 15,* 551-567.

LaFromboise, T. (1998). American Indian mental health policy. In D. R. Atkinson, G. Morton, & D. W. Sue (Eds.), *Counseling American minorities* (5th ed., pp. 137-158). Boston: McGraw-Hill.

Lambert, M. J. (1989). The individual therapist's contribution to psychotherapy process and outcome. *Clinical Psychology Review, 9,* 469-485.

Lambert, M. J., & Bergin, A. E. (1994). The effectiveness of psychotherapy. In A. E. Bergin & S. L. Garfield (Eds.), *Handbook of psychotherapy and behavior change* (4th ed., pp. 143-189). New York: John Wiley.

Lee, C. C., & Armstrong, K. L. (1995). Indigenous models of mental health intervention: Lessons from traditional healers. In J. G. Pontcrotto, J. M. Casas, L. A. Suzuki, & C. M. Alexander (Eds.), *Handbook of multicultural counseling* (pp. 441-456). Thousand Oaks, CA: Sage.

Lewis-Fernandez, R., & Kleinman, A. (1994). Culture, personality, and psychopathology. *Journal of Abnormal Psychology, 103,* 67-71.

Moyerman, D. R., & Forman, D. (1992). Acculturation and adjustment: A metaanalytic study. *Hispanic Journal of Behavioral Sciences, 14,* 163-200.

Mukherji, B. R. (1995). Cross-cultural issues in illness and wellness: Implications for depression. *Journal of Social Distress and the Homeless, 4,* 203-217.

Parham, T. A., & Helms, J. E. (1981). The influence of Black students' racial identity attitudes on preferences for counselor's race. *Journal of Counseling Psychology, 28,* 250-257.

Pitta, P., Marcos, L., & Alpert, M. (1978). Language switching as a treatment strategy with bilingual patients. *American Journal of Psychoanalysis, 38,* 255-258.

Pope-Davis, D. B., Reynolds, A. L., Dings, J. G., & Ottavi, T. M. (1994). Multicultural competencies of doctoral interns at university counseling centers: An exploratory investigation. *Professional Psychology: Research and Practice, 25,* 466-470.

Ricker, M., Nystul, M., & Waldo, M. (1999). Counselors' and clients' ethnic similarity and therapeutic alliance in time-limited outcomes of counseling. *Psychological Reports, 84,* 674-676.

Rogler, L., Cortes, D. E., & Malgady, R. G. (1991). Acculturation and mental health status among Hispanics. *American Psychologist, 467,* 585-597.

Rogler, L. H., Malgady, R. G., & Rodriguez, O. (1989). *Hispanics and mental health: A framework for research*. Malabar, FL: Krieger.

Rosenzweig, S. (1936). Some implicit common factors in diverse methods in psychotherapy. *American Journal of Orthopsychiatry, 6*, 412-415.

Russell, G., Fujino, D. C., Sue, S., Cheung, M. K., & Snowden, L. R. (1996). The effects of therapist-client ethnic match in the assessment of mental health functioning. *Journal of Cross-Cultural Psychology, 27*, 598-615.

Sandhu, D. S. (1997). Psychocultural profiles of Asian and Pacific Islander Americans: Implications for counseling and psychotherapy. *Journal of Multicultural Counseling and Development, 25*, 7-22.

Snyder, W. U. (1950). Clinical methods: Psychotherapy. *Annual Review of Psychotherapy, 1*, 221-234.

Sue, D. W., Arredondo, P., & McDavis, R. J. (1992). Multicultural counseling competencies and standards: A call to the profession. *Journal of Multicultural Counseling and Development, 20*, 64-87.

Sue, D. W., Bernier, J. E., Duran, A., Feinberg, L., Pedersen, P., Smith, E. J., & Vazquez-Nuttall, E. (1982). Cross-cultural counseling competencies. *The Counseling Psychologist, 10*, 45-52.

Sue, D. W., Carter, R.T., Casas, J. M., Fouad, N. A., Ivey, A. E., Jensen, M., LaFromboise, T., Manese, J. E., Ponterotto, J. G., & Vazquez-Nutall, E. (1998) Multicultural competencies: Developing culturally appropriate intervention strategies. In P. Pedersen (Ed.), *Multicultural counseling competencies: Individual and organizational development* (pp. 81-92). Thousand Oaks, CA: Sage.

Sue, D. W., & Sue, D. (1999). *Counseling the culturally different: Theory and practice* (3rd ed.). New York: John Wiley.

Sue, S. (1995). The implications of diversity for scientific standards of practice. In S. C. Hayes, V. M. Follette, R. M. Dawes, & K. E. Grady (Eds.), *Scientific standards of psychological practice: Issues and recommendations* (pp. 265-279). Reno, NV: Context.

Sue, S. (1999). Science, ethnicity, and bias: Where have we gone wrong? *American Psychologist, 54*, 1070-1077.

Sue, S., Fujino, D. C., Hu, L., Takeuchi, D. T., & Zane, N. (1991). Community mental health services for ethnic minority groups: A test of the cultural responsiveness hypothesis. *Journal of Consulting & Clinical Psychology, 59*, 533-540.

Sue, S., Zane, N., & Young, K. (1994). Research on psychotherapy and behavior change. In S. L. Garfield et al. (Eds.), *Handbook of psychotherapy and behavior change* (4th ed., pp. 783-817). New York: John Wiley.

Szapocznik, J., Santisteban, D., Rio, A., Perez-Vidal, A., Santisteban, D., & Kurtines, W. M. (1989). Family effectiveness training: An intervention to prevent drug abuse and problem behaviors in Hispanic adolescents. *Hispanic Journal of Behavioral Sciences, 11*, 4-27.

Takahashi, Y. (1989). Suicidal Asian patients: Recommendations for treatment. *Suicide & Life-Threatening Behavior, 19*, 237-245.

Task Force on the Promotion and Dissemination of Psychological Procedures. (1995). Training in and dissemination of empirically validated psychological treatments: Report and recommendations. *Clinical Psychologists, 48*, 1, 3-23.

Torrey, E. F. (1972). *The mind game: Witchdoctors and psychiatrists*. New York: Emerson Hall.

Wampold, B. E. (1997). Methodological problems in identifying efficacious psychotherapies. *Psychotherapy Research, 7*, 21-43.

Wampold, B. E. (2000). Outcomes of individual counseling and psychotherapy: Empirical evidence addressing two fundamental questions. In S. D. Brown & R. W. Lent (Eds.), *Handbook of counseling psychology* (pp. 711-739). New York: John Wiley.

Correspondence regarding this chapter may be sent to Donald R. Atkinson, Graduate School of Education, University of California at Santa Barbara, Santa Barbara, CA 93106 (e-mail address: don@education.ucsb.edu).

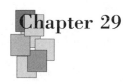

Chapter 29

QUALITATIVE RESEARCH METHODS FOR MULTICULTURAL COUNSELING

SUSAN L. MORROW
GITA RAKHSHA
CARRIE L. CASTAÑEDA

Written documents are limited in what they can teach about life and survival in the world. Blacks are quick to ridicule "educated fools," [who] have "book learning" but no "mother wit," knowledge, but not wisdom.

—Geneva Smitherman (1977, p. 76)

MULTICULTURAL QUALITATIVE research in counseling attempts to ground research in the lived experiences of those whose lives we investigate. In this chapter, we hope to introduce you to a discovery process in which mother wit and wisdom play a huge role, where "personal experience is considered very good evidence," and "distant statistics are certainly not as important as the actual experience of a sober person" (Gwaltney, 1980, p. 7).

Writing a chapter about qualitative research in multicultural counseling is a tricky task. It is, in a sense, a bicultural endeavor. From the dominant-culture (quantitative) paradigm, we could supply you with evidence in support of the validity, relevance, and importance of qualitative research in generating multiculturally authentic knowledge, appealing to your logic, reason, and inclusionary value system and impelling you to object to discriminatory research practices of the past. We could also provide you with scholarly supporting evidence stating that knowledge produced within "so-called objective modes of knowing" (Belenky, Clinchy,

Goldberger, & Tarule, 1986, p. 6) validates a skewed reality that reinforces "social relations of domination" (Collins, 1990, p. xii). Or, from the more marginalized but colorful perspective (qualitative research), we could invite you become a "connected knower" (Belenky et al., 1986), embracing the tenets of qualitative research that emphasize mutuality, value subjectivity, and insist on studying people in the context of their social, historical, and political surroundings.

Each approach—one being more academic, structured, linear, and certain and the other more practical, intuitive, circular, and packed with ambiguity and discovery—complements the other, and each has its particular strengths, much like two individuals in their culturally different kitchens, each a "situated knower" as she or he cooks. One learns recipes from a book, following explicit, step-by-step instructions through "received knowledge" (Belenky et al., 1986). The other, with a "sixth sense about everything concerning food" (Esquivel, 1992, p. 5), calls on generations of experience, practical knowledge, and passion about culinary aromas, tastes, and colors, much like Tita in *Como agua para chocolate* (*Like Water for Chocolate*; Esquivel, 1992). The two kitchens reveal unique socialization processes that nurture and legitimize different ways of knowing. In the first, the knower's position is assumed to be distant from the known, and logic and experimentation are held as the "primary authority for truth" (Slife, 1998, p. 208). This mode of thought and exchange of knowledge has been legitimized as "scientific" in traditional social science research. The second is more narrative and "requires that the story be told, not torn apart in analysis, and trusted as core belief, not 'admired as science' " (Collins, 1990, p. 210). The authority of this knowledge lies in experiencing the story, not in abstraction from it (Collins, 1990).

Although traditional research methods have assembled a wealth of knowledge within the field of counseling, the "compass" used to guide such knowledge has been a Eurocentric paradigm that reflects the perspectives of White, middle-class males (Stanfield, 1994; Sue, 1999; Sue, Kurasaki, & Srinivasan, 1999). Intuitively, the multicultural researcher questions the effectiveness of such paradigms when applied to marginalized populations (Padilla & Lindholm, 1995; Slife, 1998; Sue et al., 1999). How can the worldviews of people of color be understood when the researcher's "compass" is directed by the polarities of a Eurocentric worldview? In addition, Sue (1999) criticized conventional research for its failure to adequately address issues of external validity. Qualitative methods can address these dilemmas. For the qualitative researcher, the participants in a study *are* the researcher's "compass." The participants direct the nature and direction of the researcher's journey, and meanings are made of the data from the ground up, that is, from the lived experiences of the individuals and cultures under investigation. Granted, the researcher has an impact on the route the participant takes and even the pace of the participant's journey; for this reason, the researcher is considered the primary instrument in the research process.

Qualitative methods centralize the context of the research phenomenon and the people who experience it. Rather than working from a paradigm that conceptualizes a participant's culture as a problem or "nuisance variable," the researcher recognizes that culture is a significant piece of a person's identity that should not be controlled or averaged. Sue (1999) suggested that researchers not limit their studies to comparing ethnic groups and reporting the differences but that they actually study individual ethnic groups and gain an understanding of the nature of these differences. A major component in this undertaking would be the consideration of environmental context (Suzuki, Prendes-Lintel, Wertlieb, & Stallings, 1999). Suzuki et al. (1999) asserted, "People of color have been inappropriately pathologized at times based upon a lack of understanding of the context in which the participants existed" (p. 223).

Research in counseling has traditionally been influenced by ethnocentric research traditions, which have neither been bias free in their depiction of minority cultures nor inclusive in their research paradigms and ways of validating knowledge (Belenky et al., 1986; Stanfield, 1994). On the contrary, these practices may have institutionalized "epistemological racism" (Scheurich & Young, 1997), however unintentionally, by creating the impression that the dominant research paradigm is "universalistic rather than particularistic" (Stanfield, 1994, p. 177). Such mistaken impressions result in rigid and narrow understandings of what constitute valid paradigms in capturing knowledge of multiple cultures. Thus, it is particularly important to become deliberative in the choice of research paradigms in order to bring formerly marginalized realities to the center.

"Hidden within the 'scientific' bias of psychology is a narrow perspective determined by privilege. And privilege, indeed, has a thundering voice" (Espín, 1997, p. 10) that maintains the power structures which, in turn, silence the voices of those on the margins. Espín pointed out that the "issue of inclusion is not about . . . generous reaching out to those who are less privileged, out of a duty to help them. It is about *the nature of knowledge* in the discipline of psychology" (p. 11).

Qualitative research traditions address issues of context, power, and voice as core concerns, particularly related to marginalized peoples. Thus, multicultural counseling research can benefit immensely from the inclusion of qualitative methods as it attempts to address problems of external validity, everyday wisdom, culture and context, privilege, power, and oppression. In addition, qualitative methods are particularly suited to the study of individual meanings in social context and to research on phenomena and experiences that previously have not been investigated, about which there is little research, or where there are contradictory findings in the literature.

We want to stress that by critiquing traditional research methods we do not mean to imply that quantitative researchers cannot or do not attend to issues such as those noted above. However, the exclusive dependence on a single paradigm has the potential to limit one's understanding of multicultural counseling issues. To understand more fully how qualitative research can complement traditional counseling research methods, we turn now to an examination of various paradigms for qualitative research that can benefit multicultural counseling.

RESEARCH PARADIGMS
FOR MULTICULTURAL COUNSELING

A research paradigm is a broad umbrella encompassing one's belief about reality, how we know that reality, the methods by which we investigate reality, and what we value. Quantitative and qualitative research are sometimes referred to as research paradigms. However, within qualitative research alone there are multiple paradigms that guide the formulation of the research questions, the choice of research design, and the analysis and interpretation of data. What follows is a brief and, we hope, painless approach to the paradigms guiding qualitative research. There seem to be as many ways of classifying paradigms as there are scholars who write about them, and the classification that follows is only one possible way of looking at paradigms. For purposes of simplicity, we refer to four overarching paradigms: conventional, interpretivist-constructivist, poststructural, and ideological-emancipatory.

Conventional Paradigm

The dominant paradigm in counseling research today is postpositivism. Built on the foundations of logical positivism (which espoused an objective reality that can be known, a belief that the social world can be studied in the same way as the natural world, an objective scientific method of inquiry, and a clear relationship between cause and effect), postpositivists believe that although there may be one objective reality it can be only imperfectly known. Whereas positivists believed in the separateness of researcher and "subject," postpositivists acknowledge that researcher subjectivity is a reality to be dealt with; thus, objectivity, while desirable, is seen as something to aspire to. There are other specific differences between positivism and postpositivism; however, for the sake of convenience we refer to them as the *conventional paradigm* (Hoshmand, 1994). Virtually all quantitative research until recently was based on a positivist and then postpositivist paradigm, and anthropological and sociological qualitative research also adhered to a postpositivist paradigm.

Today, a minority of qualitative studies are conducted from a postpositivist paradigm.

Interpretivist-Constructivist Paradigm

Interpretive research is a term sometimes given to all qualitative research (Mertens, 1998). However, interpretivism-constructivism is also a more specific paradigm guiding research. This paradigm assumes that knowledge is both individually and socially constructed; that is, instead of reality being something that is "out there," separate from the knower, it is constructed in the human mind in the context of interactions with others. Thus, each individual's reality is unique. The researcher is acknowledged as the instrument of the research, and subjectivity is acknowledged and even embraced. Researcher and participants are viewed as coconstructors of knowledge in the research endeavor. The purpose of research in this paradigm, then, is to uncover the meanings people construct or to understand how those meanings are constructed. Constructivism has become increasingly common in quantitative research in counseling, and it is a dominant paradigm within qualitative research.

Poststructuralist Paradigm

Like constructivism, the poststructuralist paradigm views reality as socially constructed, with an emphasis on *social*. Poststructuralism as an academic endeavor emerged from literary criticism and emphasized such concepts as the meaning of text lies not in the author or the text itself but in the reader's interaction with the text. Likewise, reality is constructed in interaction with others, and language or "discourse" is the medium by which that reality is constructed. Language both emerges from and "recreates hierarchies of power" (Morrow & Smith, 2000, p. 203). There are multiple meanings, multiple realities, and no objective reality. In addition, no one reality is seen as better than any other. It is believed that language is the key to challenging dominant meaning systems; therefore, changing the discourse will dismantle structures of power.

Ideological-Emancipatory Paradigm

Morrow and Smith (2000) included the ideological-emancipatory paradigm along with poststructuralism under the term postmodernism because poststructuralist and ideological-emancipatory paradigms are similar in their views of how knowledge is constructed. However, the ideological theorist holds that there is, in fact, a reality "out there" that perpetuates oppression and privilege. The goal of ideological research is to dismantle the structures of power in order to achieve liberation. Liberatory research actively addresses issues of power within the research context, and the research process itself embraces activism and social change. The primary subparadigms within the larger ideological-emancipatory paradigm include critical (Foster, 1994; Kincheloe & McLaren, 1994; Tierney, 1994), feminist (Bernal, 1998; Collins, 1990; Fine, 1994; Lather, 1994; Olesen, 1994), queer (Leck, 1994; Tierney, 1994), and ethnic (Collins, 1990; Foster, 1994; Stanfield, 1994) paradigms, all of whose goal is liberation. Because of their importance to multicultural counseling research, a subset of the ideological-emancipatory paradigm—ethnic and liberatory paradigms—deserves further articulation.

Ethnic and Liberatory Paradigms

Ethnic and liberatory paradigms are particularly important to multicultural counseling research because of the common experience of oppression among people of color as well as women, lesbian-gay-bisexual-transgendered (LGBT) individuals, people with disabilities, and others. These subparadigms may be viewed from three perspectives: ethnic models and paradigms, liberation psychology and psychotherapy, and African American and Chicana feminist-womanist epistemologies.

Ethnic paradigms. Historically, multicultural counseling research, even that conducted by people of culture, has been grounded in a Euro-American positivist or postpositivist research paradigm. Scheurich and Young (1997) referred to this phenomenon as *epistemological racism.* This results, according to Stanfield (1994),

> in Afrocentrists' contradicting themselves by claiming to be producing knowledge sensitive to the experiences of African-descent peoples as a unique cultural population even as they insist on using Eurocentric logics of inquiry that reduce the knowable to the measurable or to evolutionary or linear variables. (p. 182)

Alternatively, ethnic paradigms must call "into serious question the vast warehouse of knowledge that researchers of European descent have been accumulating and legitimating as ways of knowing and seeing" (p. 183). Indigenous ethnic models for qualitative research are "grounded directly in the experiences of people of color" (p. 183) and centralize non-European notions of time, space, property, ancestors, oral communication, folklore, spirituality, and relationships with nature. Thus, ethnic paradigms or "race-based epistemologies" (Scheurich & Young, 1997) begin with the inquiry forms and value systems of the particular culture under question and investigate from indigenous perspectives.

Liberation psychology and psychotherapy. Central to the psychology of liberation (and psychotherapy as liberation; Ivey, 1995) is Freire's notion of *praxis*—"action and reflection upon the world in order to change it" (hooks, 1994, p. 14). It may be alien for many of us educated in traditional academic systems to embrace the concept that the central purpose of research and counseling is the practice of freedom. Essential to the process of research as "cultural action for freedom" (Freire, 1970) is the notion that the object of research must be, first, a conscious subject (critically self-aware) and, second, a mutual participant in the research process. The researcher does not "liberate" or "empower" the participant; rather, through a process of mutual exchange, both researcher and researched participate in *conscientização* (becoming conscious of oneself in the context of oppressive social, political, and cultural structures); breaking silence; throwing off colonization and domination; and participating in liberatory action (Comas-Díaz, 1994, 1999).

African American and Chicana feminist-womanist epistemologies. Both African American and Chicana feminists have articulated ways of knowing that can contribute to our formulation of a multiculturally oriented paradigm for qualitative research. Patricia Hill Collins (1990) identified the central characteristics of Black feminist thought as rooted in the everyday life experiences of African American women. Among these characteristics are wisdom that is based in concrete experience, a "belief in connectedness and use of dialogue" (p. 212), an ethic of caring, and an ethic of personal responsibility. These themes are repeated and expanded by Chicana feminists, whose "historical voice is one of resistance, resilience, humor and wit" (Martinez, 1996, p. 114). Bernal (1998) stressed that Chicana feminist research places Chicanas at the center of inquiry; frames research questions "in ways that give voice to these women" (p. 559); addresses intersections of race, ethnicity, class, and gender; acknowledges different opportunity structures for Chicanas from those of White women and Chicanos; and "validates and addresses experiences that are intertwined with issues of immigration, migration, generational status, bilingualism, limited English proficiency, and the contradictions of Catholicism" (p. 561). Feminist women of color have pointed out the "matrix of domination" (Collins, 1990, p. 225)—formed by race, gender, and class—under which women of color live their lives and have criticized the underattention given to socioeconomic class by feminists and even scholars of color.

Identifying a Paradigm for Your Research

Most people newly introduced to paradigmatic issues in qualitative research wonder why qualitative researchers make such a big deal about paradigms. Quantitative researchers don't seem to spend the same kind of time and energy debating these issues. Because quantitative research is so often grounded in a common paradigm (postpositivism), quantitative researchers do not have to specify that paradigm. However, qualitative researchers base their inquiry on any of a number of paradigms, which must be articulated in order to present the assumptions underlying the research. These assumptions also inform the audience about the standards to be used to judge the research, so articulating one's paradigm is not just an exercise in theorizing.

To identify one's paradigm, one should consider three types or levels: the paradigm of the soul, or one's personal mental model (Smith, 1997); the paradigm that best fits the research topic and question; and the paradigm of the discipline. Undoubtedly, even during the brief foray above into various paradigms, each reader was able to identify a paradigm that seemed to "fit" the best. One's paradigm of the soul is that which feels natural, comfortable, like home. Often, this paradigm guides one's research interests and questions so that the second level, the paradigm that best fits the research topic and question, evolves quite naturally. However, the paradigm of the discipline can be quite a bit more challenging. Consider, for example, that the paradigm of your soul, that with which you resonate most strongly, is that of liberation psychology. You may even be a social activist, challenging oppression and working for social change. Your research interests are in the area of how counseling and therapy can be conducted in a way that clients of color throw off internalized colonization and internalized racism, thereby increasing self-esteem and becoming activists themselves. However, the field (your thesis or dissertation committee, the journals in which you hope to publish) is currently dominated by postpositivism and would criticize your research as lacking objectivity and as being "not real science." Resolving these dilemmas is not easy, and we recommend having a wise mentor to assist in the process of finding a solution that will permit you, the researcher, to follow your heart while still conducting research that has the potential to contribute to the field in which you are situated.

WHY QUALITATIVE RESEARCH FOR MULTICULTURAL COUNSELING?

Multicultural quantitative researchers have worked to address many of the criticisms of traditional research. Qualitative research has several characteristics that make it a "natural" approach to conducting multicultural counseling research:

- It includes context as an essential component of the research.
- It addresses the researcher's processes of self-awareness and self-reflection.
- It is uniquely able to capture the meanings made by participants of their experiences.
- It can be used within the paradigms of participants, using the stories, folk wisdom, and common sense of ordinary people.

- Scholars in the field of multicultural counseling and psychology have called for expanded methodological possibilities to address questions that cannot be answered using traditional methods.

- Its methods provide the opportunity for voices that were previously silenced to be heard and lives that were marginalized to be brought to the center.

- It provides an opportunity to explore previously unexplored or undefined constructs, many of which appear in multicultural counseling.

QUALITATIVE RESEARCH METHODS

The task for multicultural qualitative researchers in counseling and psychology is a complex one. On the one hand, we are positioned in a discipline that, as a whole, is based in a traditional postpositivist approach to research, which has been criticized by multiculturalists for a number of shortcomings. On the other hand, some of the paradigms (e.g., ideological perspectives) embraced by qualitative researchers in related disciplines such as education suit multicultural research quite well. However, these approaches can embrace standards of rigor so far afield from conventional models of science that the majority of researchers may find them unpalatable. As qualitative methods achieve acceptance in counseling research, its proponents have many tasks, including setting standards by which qualitative research in counseling should be evaluated (rigor or trustworthiness), articulating those standards (given the state of the field, qualitative researchers have a responsibility to conduct excellent research *and* teach the reader what excellence is), and providing training in multicultural qualitative research for students and mentors in the field.

Conducting qualitative research in multicultural counseling is a political endeavor. In addition to investigating issues that may raise controversy, the stances and methods of the researcher must be chosen with care. In the qualitative methods that follow, some (such as grounded theory) may be quite acceptable in conventionally oriented research environments, whereas others (e.g., action research) may raise outcries from those whose notions of scientific rigor emphasize objectivity and replicability. Action research challenges our traditional notions of intervention and measurement, yet provides an opportunity to conduct community-based research in a manner that empowers and engages participants. Conventional research scientists may admire a complex, testable theoretical model emerging from a qualitative study much more than a narrative that depicts the lives of real people, whereas a narrative approach may be better suited to epistemologies of color. The following methodological approaches, then, should be considered in the overall context of the research being conducted.

Multiple Methods in Qualitative Research

Just as there are many paradigms or worldviews underlying science, qualitative research as a discipline is made up of multiple methodological approaches. Three approaches—grounded theory, narrative research, and action research—are described here, all of which have been used successfully in multicultural counseling or multicultural research in general.

Grounded Theory

Richie et al. (1997) used a grounded-theory or constant-comparative method (Glaser & Strauss, 1967; Strauss, 1987; Strauss & Corbin, 1990) to investigate the career development of highly achieving African American-Black and White women. The purpose of the grounded-theory approach is to develop a conceptual model (or theory) that is "grounded" in the data. This study resembles conventional quantitative approaches in that it states research hypotheses, compares two groups (Black and White women) matched on demographic variables, attends to internal consistency by the use of more than one analyst of data, and attends to traditionally quantitative standards of rigor such as internal and external validity. In addition, the standards of qualitative rigor employed in the study are excellent and will be addressed below.

Richie et al.'s (1997) study included nine African American-Black and nine White nationally prominent, highly successful women representing a variety of professions, marital and family statuses, and age. The research team employed rigorous steps to develop an interview protocol based on an extensive literature review and in-depth research-team discussion. Efforts were made to use language that would communicate with participants, thus avoiding standard psychological terminology. Questions were semi-structured and open-ended, providing some standardization while permitting the flexibility necessary in qualitative interviewing to allow the participant's unique perspective to be gleaned. The interview protocol and process were piloted, and feedback from the pilot was incorporated into the final protocol. Interview topics included information about the current job; stressors, challenges, and limitations; successes and failures; background and current influences; and retrospective and summary questions.

Interviews were conducted by a team of two interviewers, one African American-Black and one White. Interviews lasted 60-90 minutes, and interviewers took field notes as well as audiotaping the interviews. Audiotapes were transcribed, reviewed by the investigators for accuracy, and sent to participants to check on accuracy.

Using the grounded-theory method, data were analyzed as follows. Each transcript was analyzed by a pair of analysts, who extracted meaning units (words, phrases, sentences, or even larger blocks of text) that represented certain concepts related to the research questions. These concepts, or *codes,* were given names. The process of identifying concepts or codes from the original data is called *open coding.* A master list of 3,000 concepts or codes (e.g., "early lack of self confidence," Richie et al., 1997, p. 136) were compiled from the data. These codes were compared with one another by the full research team (thus the alternative term for this method, *constant comparison*) and, based on their similarities, were arranged into 123 separate categories. Using the second step in the analytic process, *axial coding,* the team then examined the relationships between categories, creating higher-level categories (e.g., "wanting to change the world," p. 136). Finally, during *selective coding,* the theoretical model was refined based on a key category or *"core story,* consisting of participants' career behaviors, attitudes toward work, and relationships in both professional and personal life, that is enacted within *sociocultural, personal background,* and *current contextual conditions:* in addition, *actions and consequences* result and, in turn cycle back to exert influence on the contextual conditions, thus creating a dynamic, constantly evolving person-environment interaction" (Richie et al., 1997, p. 137).

It should be noted that Glaser, one of the two original articulators of grounded theory, was extremely critical of Strauss and Corbin's (1990) departure from the original conceptualization of grounded theory. In a scathing treatise, Glaser (1992) hotly challenged Strauss's departure from the inductive model that was integral to grounded theory. An example of the departure from a more inductive stance is Strauss and Corbin's identification of the grounded theory paradigm model, which includes causal conditions, phenomenon, context, intervening conditions, action/interaction strategies, and consequences. Although these categories may indeed have fit Richie et al.'s (1997) data, Morrow (1992) found them to be confining and artificial. Thus we, the authors of this chapter, recommend developing the grounded-theory model based on inductive categories alone.

Richie et al. (1997) illustrated the "core," inductively formed category as "the beliefs about themselves expressed by the women in the study—the essence of how they see themselves in the world and who they are in relation to others and to their work" (p. 138). They presented their results with an excellent balance of interpretive information and quotes from participants. Their integration of the Strauss and Corbin model flows from the core category and is richly illustrated with the words of participants as well, an essential characteristic of qualitative research results.

Strengths of this study include triangulation or multiple data sources (audiotaped interviews and field notes), exhaustive formulation and testing of the interview protocol, in-depth training of research-team members, regular research-team meetings throughout the analysis, attention to power dynamics among research-team members, peer debriefing, and the use of multiple analyzers of data. In addition, the data were extensive, and the research team immersed themselves in the data as demonstrated by having saturated the codes and categories (all of the codes and categories were fully explained by the existing data; the categories and model are complex; and all of the codes were accounted for by the emergent theoretical model).

There are several advantages of the grounded-theory approach to qualitative research in multicultural counseling. First, it provides a highly structured format for conducting rigorous research, which is important in a field that has only recently embraced qualitative methods. It is also intelligible to the quantitative community in ways that other approaches are not. Its processes and outcome (a model, which may be testable using quantitative approaches) "make sense" in the predominantly quantitative scholarly community in which counselors and psychologists conduct their research. This approach may be seen by traditional researchers as more credible than many others that may offer possibilities for a more people-based or community-based perspective.

Narrative Research

Narrative research offers the possibility of connecting with the stories of people's lives. The various epistemologies articulated by women and feminists of color (e.g., Collins, 1990) make clear the importance of stories and of the common-sense wisdom of everyday people. Imbedded in this perspective are the ideas that people make sense of their lives through telling stories; that the stories of individual people are inextricable from the stories of their ancestors and extended families; and that presenting research results in storied form provides results that are powerful, true to the meanings of participants, and accessible to those whose lives are under investigation.

However, identifying a single approach to narrative research for this chapter proved to be an impossible task. Polkinghorne (1995) described two approaches to narrative research: *paradigmatic* and *narrative.* In the former, the researcher elicits data in the form of stories from participants, then uses any of a number of analytic approaches or paradigms to analyze those data. The results may appear in the form of a theoretical framework or conceptual model (such as in grounded theory), a set of themes, or another story or narrative. In the narrative type of narrative research, any data may be used, from stories to responses to interview questions to field notes or documents. It is the analysis that is narrative, focusing on plot, character, and other aspects of stories or novels. The outcome (results) is typically a narrative, much like stories told to children with an obvious lesson imbedded. In reality, researchers conduct various composites of these and other possibilities. Two are described in this section.

In a study of homeless youths in New Orleans, Finley and Finley (1999) used narrative as data, analytic process, and results. Their data consisted of researchers' observational experiences on the streets of New Orleans, "free live poetry" readings, informal conversational interviews, and limited documentary data (a diary, school records). The investigators analyzed the data by telling the participants' stories to each other, trying to make sense of the participants as individuals and as people on the street. Results were presented in the form of short stories that imbued certain narrative qualities to the research writing, with a particular emphasis on character, situation, and action. As storytellers, the researchers "compressed time to recapture the meanings of past events in current contexts while foreshadowing future possibilities" (p. 319, based on Franklin, 1986). Finally, the researchers wrote with a purpose of requiring readers to interact with the text by remaining deliberately ambiguous, suggesting rather than concluding. Their results are presented as a story of Roach, one of the street kids.

Conducting research from a narrative perspective has strong cultural implications. For some cultures, such as the Maori of Aotearoa (New Zealand), oral traditions are at the heart of the transmission of culture. This is true, as well, of many cultures of color in the United States. The U.S.-trained counselor has been schooled to see storytelling as a distraction from the actual "work" of counseling and may find it disconcerting when clients of color use stories as a medium for the counseling enterprise. However, Alexander and Sussman (1995), Ivey (1995), and others have emphasized the importance of folk tales and storytelling in therapy. Qualitative researchers, too, will find that, by asking broad questions of interviewees about their lives, they will elicit data that are full, rich, complex, and contextualized. Wright (1999), in her research titled *He Ara Whakaora I Whaia E Wtahi Wahine I Tukinohia* or *Long Term Effects of Childhood Sexual Abuse Among Maori Women: A Healing Path for Abused Women*, cited the importance of a narrative approach to respect the oral traditions of Maori women.

Wright interviewed 13 Maori women who had experienced sexual abuse as children. These participants were from various regions of Hawaii, where the research was conducted, ranging in age from 21 to 57. The interview process included formal introductions (*whakawhanaungatanga*) to make links between the researcher and participant, followed by a discussion of the mechanics of the research. Wright found that this initial rapport building quickly created a sense of trust she had not experienced in her prior research with non-Maori participants. This initial session was accompanied by refreshments and lasted about an hour and a half. The investigator then conducted in-depth interviews of a conversational style (*korero*) familiar to Maori women, with each interview lasting approximately 90 minutes and each woman being interviewed between two and five times. The interviews were in the form of a structured conversation around the topics of family of origin; relationship, educational, and work history; health and medical issues; sexual and sexual abuse history; chemical dependency; dynamics of disclosure of abuse; and issues regarding healing. "The topics were broad enough to allow the participants to say what they wanted to, and digress or emphasize any aspect of their life stories" (p. 100). Wright also interviewed five Maori counselors who worked with sexual abuse survivors.

As Wright noted, "analysis of the transcripts was consciously minimal" because she wished to "understand the material rather than manipulate it" (p. 104). She attempted to accept each participant's "interpretation of her world as valid" (p. 104). The investigator excluded any information that was not directly related to the research, then grouped themes from the data that both were and were not represented in the literature on sexual abuse survivors. Her depiction of the results is descriptive rather than interpretive, and each woman's story is depicted according to the topics discussed in the interviews, with a minimum of interpretive remarks by the investigator and extensive quotes by participants. The quotes are lengthy and clearly "tell the story" of each woman. In the final chapter of the dissertation, Wright draws on the data to propose a Maori-based model for healing from childhood sexual abuse that is culturally congruent and is displayed as a *koru* or spiral-shaped, undeveloped fern frond.

Conventional researchers may struggle with what might be considered a descriptive, rather than analytic, approach to the stories of these survivors. However, narrative psychology (Bruner, 1990; Kerby, 1991; McAdams, 1996; Polkinghorne, 1988, 1996; Sarbin, 1986) emphasizes that human meaning-making is inherently narrative and encourages psychological researchers to turn their focus to stories. Therapy is seen as a renegotiation of stories, with the therapist's role that of helping the client construct new, healing, and more adaptive life stories. Storytelling is inherent in many approaches to qualitative research, including life-history and oral-history research. Although these approaches have not yet been embraced by counseling and psychological research, they offer the possibility of a research form and process that is more true to multicultural counseling research than many other perspectives.

Action Research

Consistent with the psychology and psychotherapy of liberation (Comas-Díaz, 1999; Freire, 1970, 1972; hooks, 1994; Ivey, 1995), action research—or participatory action research (Carr & Kemmis, 1984)—has at its heart a commitment to social justice and change. Participatory action research assumes that the participants themselves are the experts on their context and situation. The researcher's stance is more as consultant than research expert. In participatory action research, those who would traditionally be considered participants are involved in every aspect of the research, from conceptualization to design, through implementation, analysis, and presentation of results. The point of participatory action research is not simply to investigate a phenomenon; it is to engage individuals in intervening in systems and structures that oppress them, documenting the process of change as it occurs. Intervention and investigation become a mutual feedback process, with one affecting the other. Properly conducted, participatory action research is a "deliberate, personally or group owned and conducted, solution-oriented investigation" (Herr, 1995, p. 47) that "helps practitioners theorize their practice, to revise their theories self-critically in the light of practice and to transform their practice into praxis (informed, committed action)" (Carr & Kemmis, 1984, p. 169).

As a school social worker, Herr (1995) was concerned about the low retention rates of students of color in her school. Herr, a White woman, approached two colleagues, one African American male teacher and one Hispanic male administrator (all three were first-generation college graduates), and the three brainstormed until the "stories" project emerged, in which student's stories of their experiences at school were gathered. As the practitioner-researchers (social worker and teacher) asked students of color the question, "What is it like being a student of color here," the students moved from being research participants to social change agents.

Originally, Herr and her colleague interviewed students individually in their "spare time." At one point, because of time demands and to add breadth to the research, they began meeting with students in groups. As students began to share their stories with one another, they asked to meet regularly in an ongoing group. The researchers tape-recorded these group sessions, but the group process evolved without their intervention. African American, Jewish, Hispanic, and Asian students participated. As the students dissected their experiences, they began to distinguish which of those experiences were racist and became "the experts of their own experiences" (p. 51).

This experience giving voice to their experiences served as a catalyst for students to frame their experiences in the larger culture, analyze the school environment and curriculum, educate themselves and others, form a minority awareness committee, and conduct forums for discussions of racism on campus. Their growing empowerment was based in their ownership of the social-action process. The researchers intervened only to ask the group questions that would expand their thinking about certain issues and to attend to safety issues as they "shepherd[ed] young activists through the realities of working for social change" and resisting "the well worn, hierarchical roles of adults with students while continuing to create collaborative relationships across these standard power lines" (p. 54).

Participatory action research embodies the integration of science and practice in a profound way, where the boundaries between researchers and participants, and between practitioners and researchers, are blurred. The researchers in this project did not "empower" the students; they simply provided the means and the process by which the students empowered themselves. At the heart of liberation psychology and counseling is the idea that individuals are the agents of their own empowerment and liberation.

We have addressed only three of many, many approaches to conducting qualitative research. Others are qualitative case study, phenomenology, analytic interpretation, ethnography, and so on. The reader is referred to Creswell (1998), Mertens (1998), Morrow and Smith (2000), and many of the resources cited in this chapter for additional research designs.

Ingredients of Qualitative Research

There are several key aspects that distinguish qualitative research, which we explain briefly here. Four key components are the importance of context, subjectivity, an *emic* approach, and researcher reflexivity.

Context. Quantitative research has at times been criticized for "context stripping." Through more sophisticated statistical analyses, quantitative researchers are better able to take context into consideration. However, qualitative research has at its core a commitment to understand the individual in the context within which she or he lives—the family, school, workplace, community, and society. This is a critical factor in multicultural counseling research.

Subjectivity. In addition to examining context, qualitative research values the subjective experiences of individuals. This is particularly important in the multicultural arena, where individual variability may be quite broad compared with research conducted on more homogeneous populations.

Emic perspective. Sue (1999) noted that much traditional research fails at achieving external validity because it fails to take into account the realities of people of color. An *etic*, or culture-general or universal, approach—typical of traditional research methods—tends to ignore the cultural variables that play such an important role in people's lives. An *emic* approach (Morrow & Smith, 2000; Sue et al., 1999), on the other hand, attends to culture-specific variables.

Researcher as instrument. In addition to valuing the subjective experiences of research participants, researcher subjectivity is acknowledged and dealt with. The researcher is the primary instrument of the research and thus has a responsibility to make her or his own assumptions, experiences, and biases known. In addition, the process of self-reflection is a crucial one to be certain that the meanings conveyed are those of the participants, not just the researcher. The collaborative process of meaning making between and among researcher and participants is valued (Heshusius, 1994; Moustakas, 1990; Smith, 1980).

There are several important differences between quantitative and qualitative approaches that become immediately apparent when one is first exposed to qualitative research. Some of the most obvious involve sample size, generalizability, and the research question itself.

Sample size. Initially, the novice reader or researcher notices that sample sizes in qualitative studies are generally considerably smaller than those used in quantitative studies. A quantitative investigation may survey hundreds, thousands, or even millions of participants, whereas a qualitative case study uses an N of one. There are several reasons for this discrepancy. First, quantitative approaches require some kind of statistical analysis for generalizability, which depends for its power on numbers. Qualitative research, on the other hand, uses words as power, and the analysis is rational and mental, not statistical. Shontz (1985) noted,

> An investigator who collects 9 bits of information from each of 900 persons has a total information base of 8100 bits. An investigator who obtains 900 bits of information from 9 persons has an information base of the same size. The second, however, is in a better position to make statements about the states, conditions, or actions of single individual beings rather than group norms. (p. 510)

Generalizability. Questions of numbers lead invariably to questions of generalizability. "If you can't generalize from your study, why do it at all?" is a common question. Once one begins to examine all the possible reasons to conduct research, however, it becomes clear that generalizability is only one of many valid purposes. In addition, one may wish to learn about the meanings that people attribute to their experience; understand processes (such as counseling) from the client's or participant's point of view; or learn about the "whys" and "hows," not just the "whats," of a phenomenon. Qualitative methods may be used to uncover discrepancies and contradictions in the quantitative literature. Because quantitative instruments are most often developed from the theoretical literature, these instruments may not reflect the worldviews of those who are being studied, particularly if those under investigation are different from the mainstream culture. Thus, the imposition of categories from the literature may mask underlying meanings. A qualitative investigation can go directly to the source for those meanings, and subsequent instrument construction can be much more congruent with the meanings and worldviews of participants.

The research question. A closely related issue, then, is the purpose of the research question. Both quantitative and qualitative researchers may hope to describe phenomena and uncover causes for things. In addition, however, quantitative researchers seek to predict and control, compare and contrast, whereas qualitative researchers hope to understand, uncover meanings, and construct theory. Because of the different purposes of qualitative and quantitative approaches, individual variability is treated differently in the two paradigms. In a quantitative paradigm, individual variability is treated, first of all, statistically. It is averaged and referred to as deviation, as "nuisance" or "noise." In contrast, qualitative researchers seek out and embrace variability. Differences only serve to enhance the complexity and depth of understanding of human behavior. Thus, qualitative research lends itself quite nicely to the study of individual and cultural differences, and a well-constructed and properly conducted qualitative study will capture those differences in a way that respects variability instead of averaging it.

Of course, there are numerous other differences between qualitative and quantitative methods from those noted here. However, this brief introduction to the different ways of thinking in the two paradigms may help to explain the sense of overwhelm experienced during one's first foray into the field of qualitative research. It should be noted that quantitative and qualitative methods can also be used in concert in any of a number of ways; however, Behrens and Smith (1996) warned that it is difficult to master one methodological paradigm, much less two. In addition to the key characteristics of qualitative research and some of the basic differences between qualitative and quantitative research, qualitative research has unique standards of "goodness," credibility, or trustworthiness.

Rigor or Trustworthiness in Qualitative Research

Qualitative research uses standards of rigor that are quite different from those employed in quantitative methods. However, our goals are the same: to produce credible research that will answer questions about human beings and that can be translated into practice. Qualitative methodologists have adopted numerous approaches to talking about how to conduct credible research. Guba and Lincoln (1989) wrote about "parallel criteria" in which the various steps taken in qualitative research (e.g., internal and external validity) can be talked about in quantitative terms. However, most qualitative researchers recognize that standards of rigor in qualitative research stand alone. A few of the core standards include immersion in the field, sufficient data, triangulation, immersion in the data, participant checks, search for disconfirming evidence, management of researcher subjectivity, thick description, an audit trail, and authenticity criteria.

Immersion in the field. The "field" may be an actual site in which the investigator gathers data, or it may be the interview process itself. However, regardless of how the field is defined, the researcher must spend sufficient time to insure that the questions being asked are appropriate and that she or he understands as fully as possible the worldviews of participants. Thus, when entering a field of research that differs substantially from one's own life experiences (as often happens in multicultural counseling research), the researcher may spend weeks or months "hanging out" in the culture, relating to people in the culture, and gaining tacit (unspoken) knowledge before actually gathering data.

Sufficient data. Closely related to immersion in the field is gathering sufficient data. When one asks, "How many participants do I need for my study?" one is really asking a question about how much data is enough. Remember that anthropologists and sociologists spend months or even years gathering data, hoping to provide an adequate description of the cultures in which they conduct research. Thus, an interview-based study can be quite paltry as a data source if the researcher is not conscientious. There is no magic number of participants that will ensure sufficient data; instead, the researcher collects data to the point of redundancy, that is, until additional data provide no new information.

Triangulation. Triangulation of data sources is one way to contribute to sufficient data. Triangulation refers to multiple data sources, such as interview, observation, focus groups, or documentary evidence. Two or more (triangulation does not need to be three) data sources permit the investigator to have multiple lines of sight on the phenomenon under investigation and strengthen the credibility of the data. It is also possible to triangulate by theory or method.

Immersion in the data. In addition to immersing oneself in the field, one must also immerse oneself in the data once collected. Once again, the investigator must spend enough time in the data to ensure that she or he understands clearly what is being said and until new forays into the data do not reveal anything new (redundancy or saturation of one's themes or categories of analysis).

Participant checks. An important aspect of rigor in qualitative research involves going back to participants to clarify and expand meanings, gather additional data, check one's emerging analysis, and ensure that what the researcher is describing fits with the participants' realities. This can be done by giving an interview transcript back to participants to check and expand, conducting followup interviews, sending a draft of results to participants for comment, or conducting focus-group interviews.

Disconfirming evidence. Humans appear hardwired to confirm their preexisting assumptions, schema, and views of reality (Mahoney, 1991). Thus, the qualitative researcher deliberately searches for evidence to disconfirm her or his emerging analysis. This may be done by seeking out cases that contradict the emerging analysis, asking participants for additional information that may disconfirm what one is finding in the analysis, or by seeking disconfirming evidence within the existing data set.

Researcher subjectivity. Researcher subjectivity has been addressed in part above. Researchers manage their biases, assumptions, and emotions through the use of a self-reflective journal, a peer research team, and careful examination of the ways in which their subjectivity affects the collection and analysis of data.

Thick description. Thick description is particularly important in multicultural counseling research. Counseling research runs the risk of "psychologizing" the participant and phenomenon under investigation, that is, treating the individual participant and her or his experience as if it is an individual, intrapsychic phenomenon. Thick description means that the participants and phenomena are seen in context, and the results of the investigation must always reflect the historico-socio-political context of people's lives. Thus, even an interview-based study must be conducted and presented with the context of the interviewees' lives as a central feature of the research.

Audit trail. In the broad sense, an audit trail includes every transcript, every tape, and every bit of raw data that is part of the study. In addition, the conscientious researcher keeps a chronological audit trail—a step-by-step description of the research processes and products—for examination by colleagues when requested. Because the actual data are often confidential, it may be difficult to make raw data available to peers or advisers for examination; however, the audit trail should contain enough information that the examiner can affirm that the research was conducted in a rigorous manner.

Authenticity and emancipatory paradigm criteria. There are other standards of rigor in multicultural qualitative research that should be considered. Authenticity criteria reflect the social impact of a study as well as its contribution to the education and consciousness-raising of participants and audience (Guba & Lincoln, 1989). Emancipatory paradigm criteria (Mertens, 1998) include attention to voice, community, reciprocity, and sharing power and privilege. These authenticity and emancipatory paradigm criteria are central to multicultural counseling research because many participants of such research, and the phenomena that are investigated, relate to issues of power, silencing of voice, and oppression. Liberatory criteria can contribute to the empowerment of those whose lives we investigate.

The Conduct of Qualitative Research

The conduct of multicultural qualitative research, from the earliest foray into the field through the presentation of results, is a project requiring patience, awareness, and understanding of issues of power and privilege (particularly one's own in relation to participants). In the remainder of this chapter, we address research processes, with a particular focus on multicultural concerns in qualitative research.

Entry Into the Field

In qualitative research, one enters the field not as an expert but as a learner. Lofland and Lofland (1984) wrote of the issues involved in "getting along with the folk" (p. 36) by attending to the researcher's stance and style. The *stance* of the researcher should be one of trust mixed with a healthy dose of skepticism—that is, trusting in the goodness and trustworthiness of participants while at the same time understanding that they may have good reason not to be completely forthcoming to the researcher. It goes without saying that the multicultural qualitative researcher maintains a stance of respect. The *style* of the researcher is one that is nonthreatening in dress, demeanor, and behavior. The investigator may adopt a style of "acceptable incompetence" by asking questions as if in a student role. Reciprocity and mutuality characterize the qualitative research endeavor (Patton, 1990) just as in the multicultural counseling relationship.

The researcher may need to identify a "gatekeeper" if she or he is not an insider or member of the community to which participants belong. By establishing a relationship with an individual who is a community member, the researcher can be more certain of being welcomed into the community. In addition, this practice protects participants from insensitive researchers. As mentioned earlier, if the researcher is unfamiliar with the culture of participants, it is important to spend significant time immersing oneself in the culture, learning the language and folkways of participants, and understanding the tacit knowledge, social relationships, and patterns of respect before attempting to gather data.

Gathering Qualitative Data

Typical data-gathering strategies include observation, interviews, and collecting or observing physical data. In multicultural research, language may be an important issue in gathering data. Interview questions must be posed in a language that is familiar and comfortable to participants and, where actual language differences exist, must be translated competently according to accepted standards in the field (Sue et al., 1999). In addition, care should be taken with the use of translators: first, they must be competent in both languages not only in a general sense but related to the topic of the interview. Second, the use of insiders to the community as translators may stress relationships because of confidentiality, the inappropriateness of using younger-generation members as translators for elders, and so on. Interviews often take a more collectivist orientation in multicultural research, where there is a give and take of information, social exchange, and reciprocity (Sue et al., 1999). Emotional content may be difficult for participants from cultures that do not encourage affect. Family or group interviews may be more comfortable for participants than individual, and the group interview has the advantage of being a vehicle for empowerment as group members find they are not alone and have the opportunity to gain support and even generate social action. Care should be taken when taking photographs, observing cultural ceremonies, and handling artifacts, as such activities may violate religious or cultural norms.

Sampling in qualitative research is *purposeful,* not random. There are many kinds of sampling procedures, including strategies to maximize or minimize variation between participants (maximium-variation sampling or homogeneous sampling), sampling politically important cases, extreme-case sampling, sampling cases that will confirm or disconfirm emerging themes, as well as many others (Patton, 1990). Thoughtful attention to the sampling purposes and processes is integral to conducting good qualitative research.

Qualitative observation or participant observation necessitates the development of one's observational skills. One must make decisions about one's placement on two continua: participant to observer, and insider to outsider (Spradley, 1980). These two continua are sometimes, but not always, intertwined. As an observer, the researcher attempts to use as broad a lens as possible to view the phenomenon or culture under investigation, alternated with focusing in intensely and specifically as needed. Extensive field notes are taken, sometimes in the setting (if this will not impair rapport) to provide an outline for later detailing of the observation. Immediately after leaving the setting, the observer attempts to fill in the outline in great detail, attending to data of all the senses, recalling specific words and nonverbal communications of participants, as well as the observer's own subjective experiences in the setting. These field notes become part of the complete data set for subsequent analysis.

The researcher should become familiar and practiced with interview procedures. The interview is framed as a conversation with a purpose (Kvale, 1996; Spradley, 1979), and rapport building occurs during all phases. Interviews may be structured, semistructured, or unstructured, depending on the subject and context of the research. In addition, they may be standardized across participants or quite flexible, depending on the researcher's paradigm. Interviews should include informing the participant about the purpose of the research, attending to issues of risk and confidentiality (informed consent), building rapport, asking global questions, asking for clarification and specificity, and asking interviewees what other things they think the interviewer should ask to fully understand the phenomenon.

In addition to individual interviews, focus groups (discussion groups with a research purpose) can go more in-depth with a phenomenon, enabling participants to make meaning together and serve as catalysts for one another's remembering (Morgan, 1993). The focus-group facilitator should be knowledgeable about group dynamics and able to facilitate the group in such a way that everyone is heard, participants are treated with respect, and the group contributes to the understanding and growth of all its members. Focus groups may be one- or two-session meetings in which the researcher merely checks her or his emerging analysis, or they may be ongoing (6, 8, or more sessions), in which real depth may be achieved and the participants have the opportunity to become co-analysts with the investigator (Morrow, 1992).

Finally, physical data may be limited only by the researcher's imagination and include published and unpublished manuscripts, autobiographies, journals (either archival or written for the investigation), art and other media, artifacts, and so on. It may be possible to ask participants to talk about the meaning of these data; in other cases, guidelines exist to assist the investigator in conducting analysis (e.g., Ball & Smith, 1992).

Data analysis actually begins informally with the initial foray into the field and continues through data collection and writing. However, there comes a time when formal analysis begins.

Analyzing Qualitative Data

Researchers typically adopt a specific analytic approach based on the paradigm underlying the research as well as the overall research design. Such analytic strategies include coding-categorizing approaches such as grounded theory (Strauss & Corbin, 1990); combing the data for themes, which typifies phenomenological or ethnographic studies (Erickson, 1986); and examining the "storied" aspects (plot, character, etc.) of the data as in narrative research (Polkinghorne, 1995). In this chapter we present a generic approach that best characterizes a coding-categorizing or theme-based analysis.

Data analysis begins informally as soon as data collection begins. During an interview, the researcher formulates ideas and questions that may be used in the interview itself or saved for the earliest possible opportunity to make notes once the interview is complete. The researcher's field journal is an essential tool in which not only the sights, sounds, and other sensory experiences are noted, but hunches, analytic memos, and other analysis activities are recorded. It is often helpful to use this journal to write "the finding of the day" (C. Edelsky, personal communication, October 7, 1986).

The next phase is to immerse oneself in the data. The immersion process begins with transcribing interviews and field notes. There is no substitute for transcribing one's own data, as the combined audio-tactile-visual input engages the analytic process in a unique way. By reading and rereading transcripts, replaying tapes, and re-viewing artifacts, the investigator becomes so familiar with the data that she or he can almost instantaneously find a quote by a participant out of mounds of data and verify or disconfirm an emerging theme.

Using an inductive, ground-up (or data-up, to be more precise) approach to data analysis, the investigator next searches for small meaning units (a word, a phrase, a sentence)—called codes—that represent a particular concept. Alternatively, the researcher identifies a theme (a statement or working hypothesis) that captures what is being said by the participant. It is important that these early codes or themes are very concrete and are expressed, as nearly as possible, in the words of the participants. These early codes or themes are the basic building blocks of the analysis, and the researcher typically reviews all the data repeatedly until no new codes or themes emerge.

These analytic data are managed in any of a number of ways—through traditional cut-and-paste methods, where multiple copies of transcripts and other data are physically cut in strips and put in envelopes with other quotes that represent the same concept; by coding on Post-it® notes that are affixed to large poster boards; by listing codes or themes on a word processor; or by using a qualitative data analysis software package (Weitzman & Miles, 1995). Personal preference, availability, cost, and other factors will influence one's choice of data management techniques.

The next step is to group the various concepts (codes or themes) into categories or "families." One typically checks and rechecks the original data during this process to be sure that the assignment to categories reflects the total data in context, not just a collection of "proof texts." These families of data will, in turn, belong to larger, extended families or overarching categories. One can represent this hierarchical type of analysis as a pyramid, with the original codes or themes on the bottom, mid-range categories at the middle levels, and overarching categories or themes at the top. Those at the bottom are most concrete and specific and reflect the language of participants most closely, whereas those at higher levels are increasingly abstract and inclusive, fewer in number, and less closely reflective of actual participant language. The researcher should take care, however, that more abstract categories or themes still reflect the meanings of participants and do not shift to "counselorese." A helpful guideline is that participants can examine the emerging analysis and agree that the categories or themes reflect their meanings, if not their actual words.

Additional steps are necessary to ensure a rigorous analysis. Throughout the analysis, the investigator continues to return to the actual data to ensure that the interpretation accurately reflects participants' meanings in context. In addition, one searches for disconfirming evidence; that is, as a category or theme emerges, one looks for a way to disprove or "complexify" it by re-examining the data, establishing alternative hypotheses, and testing each one against the data. When data are found that do not support a particular working hypothesis, the hypothesis is reconceptualized—and sometimes additional data collected—to provide the best fit between the data and interpretation. The investigator seeks to "saturate" all the categories or themes by making sure that all the data are accounted for in the emerging analytic model or framework. There are no "outliers" in qualitative analysis—that is, it is not acceptable to exclude divergent or minority perspectives.

In multicultural qualitative research, it is important to use analytic strategies that ensure that the meanings of participants are fairly presented. These strategies include immersion in the culture, having members of the culture (either research team members or actual research participants) participate in the data analysis, employing extensive participant checks, and using follow-up focus groups to evaluate the interpretation of results.

Finally, qualitative analysis continues even through the writing of the results. During this time, inconsistencies may come to light, causing the investigator to fine-tune the analysis. This analysis-in-writing completes the synthesis of data collection, analysis, and writing that characterize qualitative research.

Ethical Considerations

In addition to research ethics that guide the treatment of human research participants (found in professional codes of ethics and Institutional Review Board guidelines), several considerations apply particularly to multicultural qualitative research. The first relates to confidentiality. Issues of confidentiality may be particularly salient for certain groups around sensitive topics such as sexuality, family relations, politics of a community, spiritual practices, and other issues. The researcher should be well schooled in what these issues are likely to be. Second, informed consent procedures should be tailored to the participants and community in which they are situated. The standard informed consent document may be alienating to participants, and a more conversational, verbal form of informed consent may be more appropriate (Sue et al., 1999). Third, issues of researcher privilege should be addressed and strategies designed to establish mutuality and a nonexploitive relationship with participants. Finally, and perhaps most important, how do we as researchers give back to communities we investigate? Monetary rewards may sometimes be offensive to participants, given cultural values. The research process should be examined in an effort to make it empowering, educative, healing, growthful, or otherwise rewarding. Often, the process of "telling one's story" is sufficient reward, as is the knowledge that one is contributing to a larger good. When disseminating results, will the investigator restrict her or his presentation to scholarly audiences, or will the results be returned to the community in a useful way?

In this synopsis of qualitative research methods, we illustrated just three of many qualitative research designs in order to show how these approaches may be used in multicultural counseling research. In addition, we identified the core underpinnings of qualitative research as well as some important features that distinguish qualitative research from quantitative methods. We then identified central standards of rigor or "goodness" in qualitative research and concluded this section by touching on the conduct and process of qualitative research. In the conclusion and summary that follows, we examine further some of the implications of qualitative research for multicultural counseling.

IMPLICATIONS AND CONCLUSIONS

Qualitative methods provide an opportunity to use the very skills valued by multicultural counselors—talk, interview, self-reflection, open-ended questioning, curiosity about cultures, and considering individuals in context—to conduct research. These approaches to inquiry also offer us liberatory paradigms in which to contribute to the empowerment of both clients and research participants. One of the most exciting potentials for qualitative research comes in the integration of research and practice. Learning to conduct qualitative research can change how counselors listen and how we ask questions, as well as how we think about such things as diagnosis, assessment, and even counseling and therapy. In Morrow's (1992) investigation of survival and coping by women who had been sexually abused as children, Meghan, one participant—after participating in an interview, a 10-week focus group, and a year-long additional group in which four participants became co-analysists of the data with the researcher—noted,

> As I thought about what was important about it all, I think the thing that was so powerful in terms of empowerment was participating in the grounded theory-generating process. That was the key to the empowerment. It wasn't really the ten weeks. It was really the five of us. . . . I am an individual voice in all other settings. The focus group provided some support, but was still a collection of individual voices. . . . But [this] was a shared voice, a shared paradigm. It provided a system into which my experience fit that I had a part in creating. That creates the experience of being understood. (pp. 321-322)

When research becomes the kind of experience described by Meghan, when it contributes to participants' empowerment and healing, when it expands participants' and researchers' personal and social meanings, it is therapeutic in the most profound sense.

Collaborative research with participants has the potential to "give back" to community in ways that have not been explored. Qualitative research—like multicultural counseling—has the potential for mutuality, empowerment, and liberation. Both qualitative research and multicultural counseling embrace the complexity of people's lives. Qualitative research in multicultural counseling offers real possibilities for addressing some of the shortcomings of the past and adding richness and depth to the research endeavor. Finally, qualitative research is immensely accessible to counselors *and* to clients, who may read research findings and, in doing so, find the stories of their lives.

REFERENCES

Alexander, C. M., & Sussman, L. (1995). Creative approaches to multicultural counseling. In J. G. Ponterotto, J. M. Casas, L. A. Suzuki, & C. M. Alexander (Eds.), *Handbook of multicultural counseling* (pp. 375-384). Thousand Oaks, CA: Sage.

Ball, M. S., & Smith, G. W. H. (1992). *Analyzing visual data.* Newbury Park, CA: Sage.

Behrens, J. T., & Smith, M. L. (1996). Data and data analysis. In D. C. Berliner & R. C. Calfee (Eds.), *Handbook of educational psychology* (pp. 945-989). New York: Simon & Schuster.

Belenky, M. F., Clinchy, B. M., Goldberger, N. R., & Tarule, J. M. (1986). *Women's ways of knowing.* New York: Basic Books.

Bernal, D. D. (1998). Using a Chicana feminist epistemology in educational research. *Harvard Educational Review, 68,* 555-582.

Bruner, J. (1990). *Acts of meaning.* Cambridge, MA: Harvard University Press.

Carr, W., & Kemmis, S. (1984). *Becoming critical: Knowing through action research.* Victoria: Deakin University Press.

Collins, P. H. (1990). *Black feminist thought: Knowledge, consciousness, and the politics of empowerment.* New York: Routledge.

Comas-Díaz, L. (1994). An integrative approach. In L. Comas-Díaz & B. Greene (Eds.), *Women of color* (pp. 287-318). New York: Guilford.

Comas-Díaz, L. (1999, January). *The evolution of multiculturalism: Past, present, and future.* Paper presented at the National Multicultural Conference and Summit, Newport Beach, CA.

Creswell, J. W. (1998). *Qualitative inquiry and research design: Choosing among five traditions.* Thousand Oaks, CA: Sage.

Erickson, F. (1986). Qualitative methods in research on teaching. In M. Wittrock (Ed.), *Handbook of research on teaching* (3rd ed., pp. 119-161). New York: Macmillan.

Espín, O. M. (1997). *Latina realities: Essays on healing, migration, and sexuality.* Boulder: Westview.

Esquivel, L. (1992). *Like water for chocolate.* New York: Doubleday.

Fine, M. (1994). Dis-stance and other stances: Negotiations of power inside feminist research. In A. Gitlin (Ed.), *Power and method: Political activism and educational research* (pp. 13-35). New York: Routledge.

Finley, S., & Finley, M. (1999). Sp'ange: A research story. *Qualitative Inquiry, 5,* 313-337.

Foster, M. (1994). The power to know one thing is never the power to know all things: Methodological notes on two studies of Black American teachers. In A. Gitlin (Ed.), *Power and method: Political activism and educational research* (pp. 129-146). New York: Routledge.

Franklin, J. (1986). *Writing for story.* New York: Penguin.

Freire, P. (1970). *Cultural action for freedom.* Cambridge, MA: Harvard Educational Review.

Freire, P. (1972). *Pedagogy of the oppressed* (M. B. Ramos, Trans.). New York: Herder & Herder.

Glaser, B. G. (1992). *Emergence vs. forcing: Basics of grounded theory analysis.* Mill Valley, CA: Sociology Press.

Glaser, B. G., & Strauss, A. L. (1967). *The discovery of grounded theory: Strategies for qualitative research.* New York: Aldine.

Guba, E. G., & Lincoln, Y. S. (1989). *Fourth generation evaluation.* Newbury Park, CA: Sage.

Gwaltney, J. L. (1980). *Drylongso: A self-portrait of Black America.* New York: Vintage.

Herr, K. (1995). Action research as empowering practice. *Journal of Progressive Human Services, 6*(2), 45-58.

Heshusius, L. (1994). Freeing ourselves from objectivity: Managing subjectivity or turning toward a participatory mode of consciousness? *Educational Researcher, 23,* 15-22.

hooks, b. (1994). *Teaching to transgress: Education as the practice of freedom.* New York: Routledge.

Hoshmand, L. L. T. (1994). *Orientation to inquiry in a reflective professional psychology.* Albany: State University of New York Press.

Ivey, A. E. (1995). Psychotherapy as liberation: Toward specific skills and strategies in multicultural counseling and therapy. In J. G. Ponterotto, J. M. Casas, L. A. Suzuki, & C. M. Alexander (Eds.), *Handbook of multicultural counseling* (pp. 53-72). Thousand Oaks, CA: Sage.

Kerby, A. P. (1991). *Narrative and the self.* Bloomington: Indiana University Press.

Kincheloe, J. L., & McLaren, P. L. (1994). Rethinking critical theory and qualitative research. In N. K. Denzin & Y. S. Lincoln (Eds.), *Handbook of qualitative research* (pp. 138-157). Thousand Oaks, CA: Sage.

Kvale, S. (1996). *InterViews: An introduction to qualitative research interviewing.* Thousand Oaks, CA: Sage.

Lather, P. (1994). Fertile obsession: Validity after poststructuralism. In A. Gitlin (Ed.), *Power and method: Political activism and educational research* (pp. 36-60). New York: Routledge.

Leck, G. M. (1994). Queer relations with educational research. In A. Gitlin (Ed.), *Power and method: Political activism and educational research* (pp. 77-96). New York: Routledge.

Lofland, J., & Lofland, L. H. (1984). *Analyzing social settings: A guide to qualitative observation and analysis.* Belmont, CA: Wadsworth.

Mahoney, M. J. (1991). *Human change processes: The scientific foundations of psychotherapy.* New York: Basic Books.

Martinez, T. A. (1996). Toward a Chicana feminist epistemological standpoint: Theory at the intersection of race, class, and gender. *Race, Gender, and Class, 3*(3), 107-128.

McAdams, D. P. (1996). Personality, modernity, and the storied self: A contemporary framework for studying persons. *Psychological Inquiry, 7,* 295-321.

Mertens, D. M. (1998). *Research methods in education and psychology: Integrating diversity with quantitative and qualitative approaches.* Thousand Oaks, CA: Sage.

Morgan, D. L. (1993). *Successful focus groups: Advancing the state of the art.* Newbury Park, CA: Sage.

Morrow, S. L. (1992). *Voices: Constructions of survival and coping by women survivors of child sexual abuse.* Unpublished doctoral dissertation, Arizona State University, Tempe.

Morrow, S. L, & Smith, M. L. (2000). Qualitative research for counseling psychology. In S. D. Brown & R. W. Lent (Eds.), *Handbook of counseling psychology* (3rd ed., pp. 199-230). New York: John Wiley.

Moustakas, C. (1990). *Heuristic research: Design, methodology, and applications.* Newbury Park, CA: Sage.

Olesin, V. (1994). Feminisms and models of qualitative research. In N. K. Denzin & Y. S. Lincoln (Eds.), *Handbook of qualitative research* (pp. 158-174). Thousand Oaks, CA: Sage.

Padilla, A. M., & Lindholm, K. J. (1995). Quantitative educational research with ethnic minorities. In J. A. Banks & C. A. McGee-Bansk (Eds.), *Handbook of research on multicultural education* (pp. 97-113). New York: Macmillan.

Patton, M. Q. (1990). *Qualitative evaluation and research methods* (2nd ed.). Newbury Park, CA: Sage.

Polkinghorne, D. E. (1988). *Narrative knowing and the human sciences.* Albany NY: State University of New York Press.

Polkinghorne, D. E. (1995). Narrative configuration in qualitative analysis. *Qualitative Studies in Education, 8,* 5-23.

Polkinghorne, D. E. (1996). Explorations of narrative identity. *Psychological Inquiry, 7,* 363-367.

Richie, B. S., Fassinger, R. E., Linn, S. G., Johnson, J., Prosser, J., & Robinson, S. (1997). Persistence, connection, and passion: A qualitative study of the career development of highly achieving African American-Black and White women. *Journal of Counseling Psychology, 44,* 133-148.

Sarbin, T. R. (Ed.). (1986). *Narrative psychology: The storied nature of human conduct.* New York: Praeger.

Scheurich, J. J., & Young, M. D. (1997). Coloring epistemologies: Are our research epistemologies racially biased? *Educational Researcher, 26*(4), 4-16.

Shontz, F. C. (1985). A future for research on rehabilitation and adjustment to disability. *Rehabilitation Counseling Bulletin, 33,* 163-176.

Slife, B. D. (1998). Raising the consciousness of researchers: Hidden assumptions in the behavioral sciences. *Adapted Physical Activity Quarterly, 15,* 208-221.

Smith, M. L. (1980). *Solving for some unknowns in the personal equation.* CIRCE Occasional Paper, University of Illinois, Urbana.

Smith, M. L. (1997). Mixing and matching: Methods and models. *New Directions for Evaluation, 74,* 73-85.

Smitherman, G. (1977). *Talkin and testifyin: The language of Black America.* Boston: Houghton Mifflin.

Spradley, J. P. (1979). *The ethnographic interview.* New York: Holt, Rinehart & Winston.

Spradley, J. P. (1980). *Participant observation.* Fort Worth, TX: Harcourt Brace Jovanovich.

Stanfield, J. H., II. (1994). Ethnic modeling in qualitative research. In N. K. Denzin & Y. S. Lincoln (Eds.), *Handbook of qualitative research* (pp. 175-188). Thousand Oaks, CA: Sage.

Strauss, A. L. (1987). *Qualitative analysis for social scientists.* Cambridge, UK: Cambridge University Press.

Strauss, A., & Corbin, J. (1990). *Basics of qualitative research: Grounded theory procedures and techniques.* Newbury Park, CA: Sage.

Sue, S. (1999). Science, ethnicity, and bias: Where have we gone wrong? *American Psychologist, 54,* 1070-1077.

Sue, S., Kurasaki, K. S., & Srinivasan, S. (1999). Ethnicity, gender, and cross-cultural issues in clinical research. In P. C. Kendall, J. N. Butcher, & G. N. Holmbeck (Eds.), *Handbook of research methods in clinical psychology* (pp. 54-71). New York: John Wiley.

Suzuki, L., Prendes-Lintel, M., Wertlieb, L., & Stallings, A. (1999). Exploring multicultural issues using qualitative methods. In M. Kopala & L. A. Suzuki (Eds.), *Using qualitative methods in psychology* (pp. 213-234). Thousand Oaks, CA: Sage.

Tierney, W. G. (1994). On method and hope. In A. Gitlin (Ed.), *Power and method: Political activism and educational research* (pp. 97-115). New York: Routledge.

Weitzman, E. A., & Miles, M. B. (1995). *Computer programs for qualitative data analysis: A software sourcebook.* Thousand Oaks, CA: Sage.

Wright, D. H. (1999). *He ara whakaora i whaia e wtahi wahine i tukinohia* [Long-term effects of childhood sexual abuse among Maori women: A healing path for abused women]. Unpublished doctoral dissertation, University of Waikato, New Zealand.

Correspondence regarding this chapter may be sent to Susan L. Morrow, Department of Educational Psychology, 1705 E. Campus Center Drive, Room 327, University of Utah, Salt Lake City, UT 84112-9255 (e-mail address: morrow@gse.utah.edu).

Chapter 30

Cultural Validity and Inherent Challenges in Quantitative Methods for Multicultural Research

STEPHEN M. QUINTANA
NICOLAS TROYANO
GENELLA TAYLOR

SOMEDAY, WE HOPE, all research will be multicultural and we will not need the qualifier "multicultural" when referring to research. Presently, we have the opportunity to transform multicultural research from being maligned for its purportedly descriptive, atheoretical, and politically motivated nature (Betancourt & Lopez, 1993; see S. Sue, 1999) to becoming the standard for research in every domain of psychology. The way we overcome challenges endemic to multicultural research could become a model for how these challenges are overcome in other areas of psychological research and thereby, psychological research could become more useful, more relevant, and more authentic in our global community (Betancourt & Lopez, 1993).

GOALS OF MULTICULTURAL RESEARCH

Culture has long been considered a vital determinant of human behavior (Betancourt & Lopez, 1993). The importance of cultural factors led one pioneer of modern Western psychology, Wilhelm Wundt, to argue that an individually focused psychology be complemented by a *Völkerpsychologie*, or "cultural psychology" (Titchener, Leahey, & Furumoto, 1997). Most psychological theories and research in the United States, however, have focused on individualistic and context-independent explanations of human psychological activity (Marsella, 1998).

Culture, therefore, has often been treated by modern psychological research as a nuisance variable to be ignored or eliminated in order to uncover the workings of purportedly universal processes responsible for human cognition and behavior (Shweder, 1990). Furthermore, in the United States, the leading producer of psychological research, White Americans have dominated intellectual discourse and have monopolized the utilization, as well as the delivery, of applied psychological services (Marsella, 1998). This domination of research, training, and delivery of psychology has fostered a tradition that allowed Whites to be considered normal being the reference point for all other groups (Steinberg & Fletcher, 1998). S. Sue (1999) noted "researchers tend to question the generality of findings only when the research involves ethnic minority populations . . . but we fail to ask the same request when the research involves White populations" (p. 1072). Hall (1997) stated that psychological researchers have historically excluded or underrepresented diverse populations in their work. Graham (1992) reviewed empirically based research in four major APA journals from 1970 to 1989 and found that only 3.6% of the studies involved African American participants. Ponterotto (1988) examined research articles in the *Journal of Counseling Psychology* from 1976 to 1986 and found that only 5.7% used ethnic minority participants. Often, the inclusion of ethnic minority samples increased when the focus of research was on pathology relative to normal development during adolescence (MacPhee, Kreutzer, & Fritz, 1994). The message is clear: researchers define normalcy with White populations and deviance with ethnic minority groups.

Our focus in this chapter is to provide recommendations for creating culturally valid quantitative research that can help the field of counseling better serve the increasingly diverse population of the United States as well as offer relevant knowledge to our global community. We believe that quantitative research can serve as an important tool for advancing multiculturalism on many fronts. The application of quantitative methods to cultural studies has been criticized by some (e.g., Gergen, Gulerce, Lock, & Misra, 1996) who suggest that quantitative methods may be incapable of yielding findings that reflect the complexity of human behavior, cognition, and affect as well as that reflect the importance of context in understanding human psychological activity. Some may reflexively equate quantitative research with traditional, conservative, and Eurocentric views of science and therefore conclude that quantitative research cannot be appropriate for historically oppressed groups. We acknowledge the previous and ongoing misuses of quantitative research as well as important limitations. Nonetheless, we believe that quantitative research is an important tool, and like any tool, its utility depends on the skill and intentions of whoever wields it.

To draw a parallel, for centuries the legal system in the United States was used to keep the system of racial oppression in place. But since the civil rights movement, the legal system has often served as an instrument to work toward dismantling the system of racial oppression—even though the opposite has often been true as well. Similarly, although past and present quantitative research has either ignored or stigmatized minority groups, it is imperative that quantitative research help challenge the continued oppression of historically stigmatized groups. We believe that quantitative research, analogous to the legal system, may be an important tool to persuade those who are fair-minded about the value, relevance, and utility of multicultural theories. Because quantitative research addresses issues with traditional and conservative procedures it is particularly persuasive to the scientific community (S. Sue, 1999).

The goals of quantitative multicultural research should be to create useful knowledge that can, for example, help inform social policies and multicultural practices; evaluate and refine multicultural theories; identify and describe cultural processes and differences; and promote social justice. Before these goals are more fully realized, there are several challenges inherent to multicultural research that need to be addressed.

CHALLENGES IN MULTICULTURAL RESEARCH

Demographic Variables Serving as Proxies for Psychological Variables

Most multicultural research investigates the implications of demographic characteristics (e.g., racial or acculturation status) on psychological constructs (e.g., racial or ethnic identity). Several problems often result from this integration of demographic and psychological variables. The first is that demographic variables are often confused with psychological constructs (Hermans & Kempen, 1998; Okazaki & Sue, 1995; S. Sue, 1999). Demographic variables such as race or sex are often used as proxies, or substitutes for other variables (Steinberg & Fletcher, 1998). For example, research on race and IQ scores has led some to conclude that racial differences in IQ scores are *because* of race (e.g., Herrnstein & Murray, 1994). Others (e.g., Flynn, 1999; Helms, 1992) argue that factors other than racial status (e.g., social class, racism, other environmental factors) are responsible for observed racial differences on IQ. In this example, race serves as a proxy variable for these other factors, such as social class, which are associated with race but are more directly responsible for IQ differences. Frequently, ethnic status may be a proxy variable for social class in psychological research because of the disproportionate representation of ethnic and racial minority populations in lower social class statuses (Quintana, Vogel, & Ybarra, 1991).

The use of proxy variables is only appropriate when research is strictly for the purpose of prediction—predicting who might be, for example, at risk for academic or social problems. The purpose of most research is, however, not prediction, but explanation. Rather, researchers usually attempt to explain obtained differences based on the predictor variables included in the study. The use of proxy variables is inappropriate when the purpose of research is to posit explanations about the obtained results. All too often, study results are inappropriately attributed to the proxy variable of racial or ethnic status when the variables that truly account for the results are not directly measured in the study (Steinberg & Fletcher, 1998). The solution is to identify and measure those underlying variables as ways to avoid proxy variables (S. Sue, 1999). An excellent example is the increasing reliance on clients' racial identity attitudes, instead of clients' racial status, to predict attitudes toward culturally different counselors—previously, clients' racial status was used as a proxy for clients' racial attitudes (Carter, 1995). Similarly, the use of acculturation status, instead of ethnic status, has been an important shift in multicultural research on, for example, the validity and interpretability of MMPI (and MMPI-2) for Mexican American and other Hispanic subgroups (Velasquez, Ayala, & Mendoza, 1999). We strongly encourage researchers to measure the variables that are directly related to the dependent or criterion variables in the study.

The shift away from using demographic characteristics as proxies for psychological variables is an important development in the sophistication of multicultural research. This shift could potentially represent movement away from misleading monolithic and stereotypic generalizations to theoretically grounded research and understanding. To illustrate, the use of proxy variables may lead to conclusions such as: all Black clients want to work with Black therapists. In contrast, measuring variables directly related to the criterion variable implicates the following, more useful and less stereotypic conclusion: Clients' level of racial identity development influences their racial preference for counselors. We believe that the viability and utility of multicultural research in the future is fundamentally based on the increasing discovery, identification, and measurement of the psychological characteristics that underlie the demographic characteristics.

External Validity Based on Demographic Characteristics

Demographic characteristics have been used traditionally to determine the external validity or generalizability of study results. Multicultural research has attempted to increase the external validity of extant psychological research and theory by including sociodemographic groups that have been historically underrepresented in psychological research (S. Sue, 1999). S. Sue noted that the inclusion of these groups represents an important, albeit underappreciated, contribution of multicultural research. Clearly, we need to evaluate the validity of current psychological theory and research for historically underrepresented groups.

To improve the level of external validity, there have been recent efforts to improve the demographic representativeness of the United States for samples used in psychological research and in generating norms for standardized tests (e.g., WAIS-III; Kaufman & Lichtenberger, 1999). These efforts allow for more accurate population norms to be estimated. These norms allow for an unbiased estimate for an "average" person and for an unbiased estimate for an average score if the entire population were sampled. However, if we were interested in estimating how an "average" person from a particular group would respond, we would need to compute separate analyses for that group. Hence, efforts to include more representative samples allow the research to be generalized to the aggregate population. In order for the research to be generalized to specific subgroups, separate analyses have to be conducted specific to those groups (Quintana & Atkinson, 1999). In short, the inclusion of historically underrepresented groups in psychological research is an important, albeit very limited, step in the process of evaluating the validity of research findings and instruments for multicultural populations (Quintana & Atkinson, 1999).

For psychological theory and research to be generalizable to all subgroups within the United States, there must be separate investigations of each theory and research finding on what must be thousands of relatively distinct subgroups within the United States (S. Sue, 1999). We see this strategy as unrealistic. We also view the de facto alternative strategy previously followed in psychological research—uncritically generalizing research on dominant populations to other groups—as unethical and unscientific.

The current strategy for establishing external validity is a form of generalization based on the statistical theory of random sampling (Heppner, Kivlighan, & Wampold, 1999). However, the critical assumption of this theory—that participants were selected randomly—is grossly violated in most research which often uses samples of convenience (e.g., local college students in introductory psychology courses). Even when underrepresented ethnic groups are included in psychological research these groups are rarely representative of the larger ethnic population because the samples of ethnic groups tend to be selected according to convenience (e.g., university students of color). Although some studies use sophisticated sampling techniques that approach satisfying the assumption of random sampling (e.g., see Bowman, 1999; Caldwell, Jackson, Tucker, & Bowman, 1999), these studies typically still violate the assumption of random sampling. The ethical requirement that participation in most psychological research be voluntary creates systematic sampling bias even in studies with sophisticated sampling procedures. Hence, the current strategy for establishing external validity is not only unrealistic but also compromised by the failure of most research to satisfy a critical assumption.

We propose an alternative approach to external validity: that (a) external validity be based on conceptual rather than on strict statistical considerations and that (b) generalizability be based in part on psychological characteristics rather than exclusively on demographic characteristics. Researchers need to address the conceptual reasons for why each theory and hypothesis being investigated is suited for the sampled population. For example, racial identity theory is particularly well suited for many African Americans, not because of their racial genotype, but because of their interracial and intraracial experiences. Moreover, particular features of their interracial experiences, including the experiences of racism and intraracial bonding (Cross, Strauss, & Fhagen-Smith, 1999) seem to be the psychological features of African Americans that allow racial identity theory to be generalized to this population. It is significant that racial identity theory, with superficial modifications, has been found to have validity for a variety of stigmatized ethnic and racial populations (see Frable, 1997). Consequently, generalization of racial identity theory has little to do with racial heritage, per se, and much more to do with certain psychological experiences shared among these stigmatized and oppressed groups.

We see four potential advantages for external validity with a greater emphasis on conceptual rather than statistical generalization, and with a greater emphasis on psychological rather than demographic characteristics. First, conceptual forms of generalization could promote better theory building by giving more consideration to the theoretical reasons why a model may be applicable for a particular population. We believe this kind of generalization is important for all research, even research testing theories developed by White theorists for White populations. There is an important cultural context of many psychological theories—this context represents implicit assumptions of these theories. To illustrate, many theories of career development formulated for White populations assume that some of the structural features associated with racism (Ogbu, 1994) are not present (Leong & Brown, 1995). Similarly, many counseling theories make implicit assumptions about the cultural values of clients and counselors. It would be very important for the development of psychological science for all theorists to make assumptions explicit about why a theory is particularly well suited for a particular cultural group.

Second, the use of psychological characteristics, rather than demographic characteristics, could minimize the use of inappropriate generalizations to an entire population. Given that most samples included in psychological research are not truly representative of the larger population, it seems misleading to suggest the findings are generalizable to the entire demographic group. On the other hand, if we took seriously the caveats made at the end of many journal articles that the results are only generalizable to the populations represented by the study samples, we could not generalize the results much beyond the actual participants in each study. Researchers should articulate which psychological characteristics within the sample are relevant to understanding the generalization and limits thereof for the results of the study.

Third, using psychological rather than exclusively demographic characteristics as a basis for generalization, researchers could avoid using racial status as an explanation for psychological phenomena and properly focus on psychological antecedents for psychological outcomes. A fourth benefit might be also avoiding token representation of ethnic minority populations in order to obtain grants or satisfy journal editors. For example, convenient sampling of highly acculturated members of ethnic and racial minority populations would seem to satisfy criteria established by some granting agencies and journal policies for including diverse samples, but sampling of highly acculturated groups would fail to represent the important psychological characteristics of larger ethnic and racial populations. We believe our proposal for external validity could contribute to upholding high standards of scientific research rather than what we perceive as rather token efforts to satisfy minimally existing guidelines for including diverse populations. Culturally diverse groups potentially bring unique psychological characteristics and experiences that need to be better incorporated into psychological theory and research. If we better understand the impact of these psychological characteristics, we can build a better scientific foundation for our theories.

The Role of Values and Political Views in Research

A third challenge for multicultural research is the role of values, including political views, in research. Long before anyone coined the term multicultural, research has been biased by political views. As others have commented (e.g., Flynn, 1999; Kendler, 1999; D. W. Sue, Bingham, Porché-Burke, & Vasquez, 1999), psychological research has been tainted by race politics. Early psychological research clearly could be considered scientific racism. Much of the traditional psychological research has perpetuated hegemony to help justify disproportionate distribution of social, political, and economic power among ethnic and racial groups. These political agendas are pursued through nearly every component of research including the formulation of theory, design of measures, experimental procedures, and interpretation of results. Many psychological theories, as formulated, have been blatantly Eurocentric, suggesting difference from Eurocentric norms is pathological and ignoring the important role of racism and discrimination in the lives of stigmatized populations (D. W. Sue & D. Sue, 1990). Measures have been designed to reflect Eurocentric, individualistic values; for example, a separation-individuation construct (e.g., Hoffman, 1984) was operationalized, equating independence with adjustment and interdependence with immaturity (Quintana & Kerr, 1993). Eurocentric and racist bias has also been associated with procedures used to conduct research. The Tuskegee medical experiment represents a dramatic example of racist experimental procedures in which treatment and even knowledge of their disease was withheld from Black men who had syphilis (Scott-Jones, 1994). Obviously bias can influence the interpretation of data (Gil & Bob, 1999). In contrast to traditional conceptions, data are not self-evident and must be interpreted. Several researchers (Jensen, 1980; Herrnstein & Murray, 1994) examining the racial differences in IQ exemplify how apparent racial bias can lead to biased interpretation of results. The intentional and unintentional pursuit of these political agendas in psychology compromises the purported neutrality or objectivity of quantitative research.

Some multicultural research has also been accused of placing political goals ahead of the scientific goals of generating knowledge. These accusations seem to have taken the form of overinterpreting data as confirming or supporting a multicultural theory prematurely (e.g., Rowe, Bennett, & Atkinson, 1994). Occasionally, authors who purport to advocate for a population may perpetuate misleading characterizations about the group. For example, in her landmark work on women's moral development, Gilligan implied that women would score lower than men on Kohlbergian measures of moral development, even though meta-analyses (e.g., Thoma, 1986) indicate otherwise: despite probable gender bias women score at least as high as men on Kohlbergian forms of moral development. Similarly, ethnic and racial minority children are often described as self-loathing because of ethnic stigmatization even though research has indicated that there are no differences between stigmatized and nonstigmatized groups for general self-esteem (Crocker & Major, 1989; Cross & Vandiver, Chapter 21, this volume). We encourage all theorists, multicultural and monocultural, to better incorporate existing data in order to provide accurate characterizations of various cultural groups. To illustrate, we have great respect for the way in which Cross's (1995) theory of racial identity development has evolved in response to developments in empirical research and theory (see Cross & Vandiver, Chapter 21, this volume).

The current political context can also make it difficult for theorists and researchers to explore counterproductive patterns within stigmatized populations. Some multicultural researchers may resist 'airing dirty laundry' about their own group out of concerns that (a) they are acting on internalized racism, (b) their findings may be taken out of context and misused for racist purposes, or (c) colleagues may be critical. There has been interesting work by social psychologists on stereotype threat (Steele, 1997) and on self-handicapping (Midley, Arunkumar, & Urdan, 1996) that enhances understanding of stigmatized populations and provides potential implications for redressing important problems. Personal and political values can and do have an important role in psychological research. The challenge is for researchers to design research that can seriously test critical and fundamental aspects of their preferred theories. Similarly, when reviewing research, it is important to balance supportive evidence with potentially contradictory evidence. If this kind of scientific integrity had been followed more closely, much of the previous research stigmatizing minority populations would have been more seriously challenged. As multicultural researchers, we need to uphold high standards for scientific integrity in part because others who disagree with us are quick to find fault in our work. More important, we have a critical obligation to evaluate our theories and research with high standards of scientific integrity and not just assume they are authentic representations of the populations we investigate. Our research represents an important medium for the voices of the populations we investigate—our analyses and interpretation of data represent the translations of these many voices.

Cross-Cultural Research

Most multicultural research has been cross-cultural in nature. By cross-cultural we mean (a) research that investigates psychological constructs, measures, and theories that developed within one culture and extended to other cultural groups, and (b) research that attempts to compare one cultural group to another. Pike (1954) coined the term "etic" to refer to the application of a theoretical framework to empirical constructs across cultures. There are particular challenges in this kind of research—contemporary researchers admit that traditional cross-cultural research was plagued by blatant ethnocentrism (Rogler, 1999; Segall, Lonner, & Berry, 1998). Contemporary cross-cultural research continues to be affected by insidious, albeit more subtle forms of cultural and ethnocentric bias (D. W. Sue et al., 1999; Rogler, 1999). Ethnocentrism takes several forms: (a) assumption of decontextualized universal psychological constructs, (b) emphasis on translations based on linguistic equivalence rather than on equivalence of cultural meaning, and (c) use of nonindigenous "experts" to formulate theory and research procedures.

Most psychological theories derived in North America and Europe make an assumption of universality: The theory will be applicable across contexts. At first, major theorists such as Freud and Piaget assumed that their theories would have universal application, irrespective of cultural context. The linguistic translation of popular instruments—for example, the MMPI and Weschler intelligence scales—are examples of the assumption of universality of personality, psychopathology, and intelligence.

When instruments are modified for cross-cultural work, typically efforts are made to establish only linguistic equivalence for the application to a new cultural context. Cross-cultural researchers (Leong, 1997; Lonner & Ibrahim, 1996) have identified three other forms of equivalence necessary for applying an instrument cross-culturally: functional, conceptual, and metric. Functional equivalence refers to whether psychological phenomena have similar functions across cultures. For example, in the United States some behaviors which are positively valued (e.g., assertiveness, acceptance of compliments, and showing pride in one's work) may be considered rude in some collectivistic cultures. These behaviors, then, have different functions in different cultures. Conceptual equivalence refers to whether a psychological concept has an equivalent in another culture. For example, there is not conceptual equivalence for intelligence between the United States and other cultures because in some cultures noncognitive factors (e.g., social skills and hard work) are given greater emphasis in defining intelligence (see Okagaki & Sternberg, 1993). Metric equivalence implies that the way in which concepts are quantified (e.g., Likert-type ratings) are equivalent across cultural groups. Metric equivalence would be threatened in cross-cultural research, for example, when the cultures differ in the cognitive style between dialectic and deductive tendencies used because those using dialectic reasoning tend to favor middle ground explanations and ratings while those using deductive may be more polarized in their response style (Peng & Nisbett, 1999). These four forms of equivalence address the cross-cultural construct validity of an instrument developed in one culture and used in another.

It is important to note that the psychometric properties of an instrument—its reliability and cross-cultural construct validity—are not properties of an instrument. Rather, psychometric qualities are properties specific to a particular sample and are, consequently, greatly affected by the context of the study procedures. Participants' interpretation of the context of a study greatly affects their response to measurement instruments (Schwartz, 1999). One of us (S. Quintana) recalls an experience administering a measure of cultural knowledge to students in a class on a historically Black campus. During this administration, the participants openly discussed their suspicion that the author of the instrument was not African American. This discussion suggested that their experience of taking the instrument was strongly affected by the perceived cultural nature of the instrument. Problems recruiting ethnic and racial minority populations for participation in research have been noted (Bowman, 1999; Cauce, Ryan, & Grove, 1998). Minority participants react to the cross-cultural nature of studies—reflected in the design, purpose, and instrumentation of the study—and this participant reactivity is likely to compromise the validity and reliability of the cross-cultural research even for those instruments with demonstrated reliability and validity in other contexts.

The third form of ethnocentrism characteristic in cross-cultural research results from decisions for study design and focus to be determined in a cross-cultural manner. Too often, the experts for translating theory into measurement instruments are European-descent researchers. If used at all, local experts' participation is usually limited to technical aspects of the study (e.g., translation of measures, conducting interviews) and does not usually include involvement during the conceptualization phase of the research. Local experts of the target culture could offer important insights into how the study is conceptualized, how constructs are measured, and how the results are to be interpreted (Bowman, 1999).

These forms of ethnocentrism are often manifest in research in which psychological theory and/or methods developed in one cultural group are then transported to another. One common subgroup of cross-cultural research involves comparing one cultural group to another, usually when the methods and theory were developed for one of those groups and extended to other cultures. There are some specific problems associated with this fairly common design in which cultural groups are directly compared (see Rogler, 1999; Segall et al., 1998).

Typically, cross-cultural research involves exploration of differences between cultural groups. The pattern of findings in cross-cultural studies, particularly differences in means between cultural groups, are subject to many explanations (van de Vijver & Leung, 1997). Differences may be due to some culture related variables including acculturation or cultural values, may be related to noncultural variables such as social class, or be associated with some contextual factors independent of general characteristics associated with the larger ethnic group. These contextual factors may be characteristics of the setting of the study (e.g., recruitment from an ethnic studies class) or of the environment in which the study occurs (e.g., university campus with recent racial conflict). It is, therefore, critical that findings of ethnic or cultural differences be empirically or conceptually attributed to the specific factors that are responsible for those findings. Clearly, a study that includes measurement of these specific factors would provide a better explanation of the reasons for the finding of ethnic differences. A study that includes measurement of all of these specific variables should be able to demonstrate that no ethnic or racial differences exist independent of these psychological variables. In essence, when differences across ethnic groups remain, these differences may indicate that critical specific psychological variables were not adequately measured.

There are limited benefits of finding mean differences between cultural groups. One benefit of finding mean differences across groups includes providing more descriptive information about group differences. The finding of mean differences, however, is limited when the research is attempting to justify alternative approaches for underrepresented cultural groups. For example, the finding of mean differences on an assessment does not imply, per se, that the assessment is biased. Rather, there may be legitimate reasons for group differences to emerge. For example, girls have been shown to score higher than boys on measures of social understanding and these differences have been shown to be related to gender differences in social skills (Selman, 1980). The finding of gender differences in this example suggests that, instead of being biased, the instrument shows sensitivity to important differences between these groups. The implications of group differences may be somewhat limited in the sense that differences, per se, may not suggest that an instrument or a theory is necessarily inappropriate for one of the groups studied.

In contrast, findings of group differences in *relationships* (e.g., group differences in size of correlational relationships between variables) may have important practical and theoretical implications. For example, the finding that a social skills intervention has differential impact according to gender (i.e., the relationship between treatment and outcome is different between boys and girls) could imply that a different intervention would be necessary for each gender group. Too often, we find researchers attempting to infer, inappropriately, a group difference in relationships among variables simply because the relationship among variables was significant for one group, but not for another.

To briefly reiterate, cross-cultural research is particularly susceptible to ethnocentric bias. Psychologists' pursuit of universally generalizable constructs has lead them to disregard cultural context and to assume that the dominant cultures within the United States define normalcy. Most of the efforts to translate instruments for another culture are to establish linguistic equivalence across cultures, but problems with establishing equivalence have been noted (Rogler, 1999). Moreover, it is fairly rare for researchers to address conceptual, functional, and metric forms of equivalence when translating an instrument from one culture to another. Ethnocentrism also affects the procedural aspects of study design in the sense that experts on local culture are used primarily for their linguistic services, including translations as well as administration. They should, however, assist in study design, conceptualization of the measurement strategy, or in interpretation of the findings (Rogler, 1999). We present some suggestions below for addressing these and other challenges that are common to multicultural research.

CULTURAL VALIDITY
OF MULTICULTURAL RESEARCH

To date, five kinds of research validity have been articulated: Internal, External, Construct, Hypothesis, and Statistical Conclusion (Heppner, Kivlighan, & Wampold, 1999). We would like to propose an extension to this list of validities to include *Cultural Validity*, which specifically addresses the cultural aspects of research. First, we discuss a conceptualization of the standard forms of validity with respect to multicultural research.

The validity of all research, multicultural or monocultural, is in essence based on the representativeness of the research. Each research project attempts to *represent* accurately and effectively (a) an important aspect of a psychological theory (i.e., hypothesis validity; Wampold, Davis, & Good, 1990) that is being explored or evaluated, (b) a target population to which the findings will be generalized (external validity), (c) theoretical constructs (construct validity), which the study procedures attempt to operationalize, (d) causal relationships, which are attributed to some feature internal to the study design (internal validity), and (e) the nature of the empirical relationships reflected in the data (statistical conclusion validity). Hypothesis validity is supported when study hypotheses represent important aspects of the theory and when the results can be evaluated as supporting or contradicting theoretical predictions. Given the fairly recent introduction of multicultural theory into psychology (e.g., D. W. Sue, Ivey, & Pedersen, 1996), theoretically driven multicultural research is in its infancy (Fuertes & Gretchen, Chapter 27, this volume). Nonetheless, multicultural research has made important contributions to understanding the external validity of psychological research (S. Sue, 1999). Indeed, multicultural theory and research evolved from concerns over poor external validity (i.e., generalizability) of extant psychological research to ethnic and racial minority populations. Traditional psychological research has been notably unconcerned with conducting research on samples that accurately represent the larger U.S. populations (S. Sue, 1999). Findings based on research with predominately White populations, many times college sophomores, have been uncritically accepted as generalizable to other populations in the U.S. and the world (Marsella, 1998; S. Sue, 1999).

Construct validity of any research is threatened when the measures used in a study either underrepresent the theoretical constructs or include variance from other unrelated constructs (Heppner et al., 1999). Theoretical constructs used in multicultural research, such as racial identity development, are often complex phenomena that may be underrepresented with simple paper-and-pencil questionnaires. Moreover, even simple questions assessing, for example, ethnic status may be confounded with other constructs (e.g., social class status). Finally, many of the research questions investigated in multicultural research do not lend themselves to designs with sufficient experimenter control to maintain internal validity. Researchers, for example, cannot randomly assign racial status to participants and therefore often must rely on observational designs with several inherent threats to internal validity (see Cook & Campbell, 1979). Statistical conclusion validity refers to the validity of the conclusions based on the statistical procedures such that findings are detected appropriately. This form of validity does not seem to be inherently challenging for multicultural research, except for difficulties in recruiting sample sizes large enough to yield sufficient statistical power.

These five articulated research validities fail to address the appropriateness of the research with respect to the cultural nature of the investigation. Leong and Brown (1995) may have been the first to introduce the concept of cultural validity: "Cultural validity is concerned with the construct, concurrent, and predictive validity of theories and models across cultures, that is, for culturally different individuals" (p. 144). Consequently, we propose that cultural validity could be a standard with which to evaluate quantitative multicultural research. Leong and Brown correctly, we believe, focus the definition of cultural validity on construct validity (concurrent and predictive validity are subsumed under construct validity). As described above, it is particularly challenging to ascertain cultural equivalence in the measurement of constructs across cultures (Helms, 1992). Nonetheless, our application of the concept of cultural validity to quantitative research includes important aspects of external and of hypothesis validity that have implications for the cultural validity of the research. We would also like to borrow insights from qualitative researchers in how they evaluate the validity of research. For example, the utility, or what we call "utility validity," of the multicultural research for addressing social justice and redressing previous stigmatization of multicultural populations is an important aspect of the cultural validity of the research. Consequently, we define cultural validity as

> the authentic *representation* of the cultural nature of the research in terms of how constructs are operationalized, participants are recruited, hypotheses are formulated, study procedures are adapted, responses are analyzed, and results are interpreted for a particular cultural group as well as the *usefulness* of the research for its instructional utility in educating readers about the cultural group being investigated, its practical utility in yielding practice as well as theoretical implications about the cultural group, and its service utility in "giving back" to the community in important ways.

As is common when discussing aspects of validity, we will focus on threats to cultural validity. We also describe possible ways of addressing these threats in the context of the stages of conducting research. It may not be surprising that the most pernicious threat to cultural validity is ethnocentrism enacted during each phase of the research.

Cultural Validity in Study Design and Procedures

Ethnocentrism threatens cultural validity during planning stages of a research project. One threat is if the researcher uses uncritically an ethnocentric theory to conceptualize research to be conducted for a different cultural group. One example is the application of locus of control theory to ethnic and racial minority populations (Caldwell et al., 1999). The locus of control model is based on an implicit cultural value of internal control or mastery over one's environment particularly characteristic of the individualistic culture within the United States. The application of the locus of control paradigm to a more collectivistic cultural group may result in further stigmatization in this group's cultural values, even potentially stigmatizing their adaptive recognition that certain aspects of the environment, such as exposure to racism, are not within the control of an individual. Cultural validity is also threatened when the researcher's personal beliefs about the topic of the study are embedded within an ethnocentric viewpoint. These viewpoints may include either racism or internalized racism depending on whether the researchers are investigating their own cultural group.

There are some advantages for cultural validity when a researcher is investigating a topic with which he or she is intimately involved. When the researcher personally identifies with the participants in the study, it may be less likely that the participants' experiences will be objectified. In situations where researchers are studying their own group, they may be particularly careful to represent accurately the critical experiences being investigated. Moreover, the researchers in this situation may bring particular depth to the topic, which is rarely equaled in other situations. When first exploring the understanding of race and ethnicity for children of color, I (S. Quintana) began with Latinos as this group was most familiar to me. I found myself wanting to take extra care in conceptualizing this research, in part because I was working with children, but also because I wanted the results to be authentic for this group. Of course, the potential disadvantage to investigating participants or topics close to the heart of the researcher is the danger of overidentifying with the participants and forcing one's own preconceptions onto the research.

Cultural validity could also be enhanced by consulting with cultural communities before commencing the study. Before initiating a study of children's ethnic understanding, I (S. Quintana) consulted with members of the community and also pilot tested the procedures before finalizing the study. Prior to extending my model of children's understanding of ethnicity to other groups (i.e., African Americans and Guatemalan children's understanding of race and international children's understanding of nationality), I collaborated with researchers indigenous to these groups. Although this collaboration was an invaluable step in the design of these research projects, while writing this chapter we realized I could have made a greater effort to include the community at more substantive and earlier aspects of research projects.

There is another step necessary to cultural validity in conceptualizing a quantitative research project. A thorough review of extant theory and research is essential for quantitative research. Although many begin reviewing psychological literature, multicultural research can also be informed by related disciplines such as sociology, anthropology, ethnic studies, and gender studies, to name a few. The challenge here is to translate what may be personal knowledge or experiences into theoretical formulations. This process is valuable because it can indicate potential directions for investigation as well as provide possible explanations for various psychological events. When conceptualizing how to investigate children's understanding of ethnicity, I (S. Quintana) found a theory of perspective-taking ability that could be readily extended to the ethnic domain. This theory provided directions to explore that I could not have formulated without it.

Hypothesis validity as described by Wampold et al. (1990) requires that research be conceptualized such that the study addresses a key or critical aspect of a theory. Useful theoretical knowledge is obtained when research explores the predictions derived from a theory that are not anticipated or predicted by other theoretical models (see Quintana & Maxwell, 1999). In some cases, research could directly evaluate two competing theoretical predictions, thereby providing supportive evidence for one theory while providing potentially disconfirming evidence against the other. Research is of limited value which explores areas which could be anticipated by a number of theories or could have been anticipated by atheoretical or intuitive commonsense reasoning. It is important, therefore, to choose a topic that may stem from personal experience, is formulated by consultation with members of the community that will be the focus of the study, is informed by theoretical and empirical research, and will focus on an area of theoretical, personal, and community importance.

At times, the theoretical conceptualizations may be culturally incongruent for the target population. Roland (1996) describes a two-step process to correct for the cultural embeddedness of a theory that is going to be extended to another cultural group: (1) decontextualize the theory and (2) recontexualize the theory based on the new target group. Decontextualization of a theory is to assess the culturally embedded features of the theory and identify the underlying processes. For example, assertiveness training seems embedded in a particular cultural context of individualism and appears inconsistent with some collectivistic cultures. The theory underlying assertiveness training may be decontextualized by understanding that assertiveness training is the instruction of culturally sanctioned forms of communication with the particular content of the instruction, assertiveness, the cultural expression of this communication. To recontextualize this approach, it would be important to identify forms of communication that are culturally sanctioned for the target group. A culturally congruent intervention could then be adapted for a different cultural group from the culturally embedded assertiveness intervention. Cultural validity often requires that current psychological theories be decontextualized and then recontextualized in order to extend them for other cultural groups. A summary of threats to cultural validity and some strategies to improve cultural validity appears in Table 30.1.

Once a topic is chosen and appropriately recontextualized for the target group, a critical decision is the selection of measurement instruments. Across all scientific domains, the development of new measurement tools may foreshadow important discoveries. Many multicultural processes cannot yet be investigated until appropriate empirical instruments are developed. Consequently, study hypotheses are greatly affected by available instruments to measure the theoretical constructs of interest. Even when an instrument is available, it may not measure the theoretical construct in the manner expected by theory. When considering an instrument, we advise researchers to inspect closely the items and not to accept on faith that the instrument measures what is purported by the name of the instrument (see Part III of this volume).

We also strongly recommend that multiple measures of a theoretical construct be used. There are several advantages related to statistical power and construct validity for using multiple measures. It is important that critical forms of multiplism (see Houts, Cook, & Shadish, 1986; Quintana & Maxwell, 1999) be used in selecting the range of instruments. The important concept of critical multiplism for our purposes is that a construct is operationalized in multiple ways, using multiple methods and multiple dimensions of a construct. For example, the use of multiple self-report questionnaires usually fails to satisfy the concept of critical multiplism because self-report questionnaires do not control for the impact of response bias (how respondents complete the questionnaires) on the results. The common practice of using multiple subscales from one instrument also fails to satisfy critical multiplism. One aspect of critical multiplism is to have measures vary across the method of operationalization, such as self-report, behavioral observation, projective, or other methods. Another particularly important form of critical multiplism is to have instruments operationalize different dimensions of a theoretical construct. Critical multiplism allows measures to more authentically and completely represent the often complex aspects of cultural phenomena.

In order to increase the cultural validity of a study involving multiple instruments, researchers must attend to potential ethnocentric bias embedded in the instruments. It may be necessary to go through the two-step process of decontextualization and recontextualization described above to modify the instruments to be culturally valid for the target cultural groups. Moreover, we encourage researchers to go beyond using self-report questionnaires to measure important cultural constructs. The prototypical self-report questionnaire may be culturally incongruent for many of the historically stigmatized groups we investigate. The language or general form of communication (e.g., forced choice formats) used in questionnaires may reflect a decontextualization or abstract nature that is foreign or culturally incongruent in some cultural groups. The abstract nature of a task in which participants complete paper-and-pencil questionnaires alone may also be incongruent for some cultural groups. We believe that individual interviews offer promise for being culturally congruent for many of the historically stigmatized groups. First, interviews allow cultural groups to respond to items in their own words and do not force participants to translate their often complicated responses into the obscure language of, for example, likert ratings, which are favored by psychologists but rarely used outside research contexts. The interview process can foster rapport between interviewers and participants and may facilitate participants engaging

TABLE 30.1 Cultural Validity During Planning Phase of Research

Threats to Cultural Validity	Ways to Improve Cultural Validity
Use of ethnocentric theory to conceptualize research	Apply multicultural theory or indigenous theories to conceptualize research
Failure to conceptualize adequately cultural phenomena being investigated • Failure to conceptualize which relevant psychological processes underlie demographic variables • Failure to conceptualize why a theory is appropriate for target cultural group • Formulate only atheoretical hypotheses	Integrate theories from other disciplines (e.g., sociology, anthropology, political studies, ethnic studies) Consult with cultural communities to help formulate relevant research questions and methodology Translate demographic characteristics (e.g., racial status) into psychological characteristics (e.g., experience of stigmatization)
Ethnocentric personal beliefs of researcher influence conceptualization of study Researchers overidentify with participants	Focus on groups with which the researchers personally identify (but do not over-identify) Decontextualize ethnocentric theories and recontextualize according to new cultural context Integrate personal experiences with theoretical principles

meaningfully in the study processes. Additionally, the interview process allows researchers to more authentically represent the voices of the participants by providing illustrative quotes. Interviews could also address the mistrust that some stigmatized groups may feel toward traditional research. Finally, interview measures allow researchers to report results that are easily understood outside of the psychological community. In order to increase the cultural validity of a study, we encourage researchers to be creative and search for meaningful ways to measure psychological processes associated with cultural processes. Table 30.2 lists threats to and ways to enhance cultural validity.

Once measures are selected and appropriately contextualized, researchers need to plan strategies for recruitment of participants. When planning participant recruitment, researchers need to consider to which populations the research may be generalized. A key to enhancing cultural validity (see Table 30.3) is to recruit a sample that represents this larger population. As mentioned, it is important for researchers to specify why the study questions are particularly relevant for the targeted population. Although it is common to report demographic characteristics (e.g., racial

TABLE 30.2 Cultural Validity of Measurement Instruments

Threats to Cultural Validity	Ways to Improve Cultural Validity
No instrument available to measure cultural phenomena being investigated	Adapt ethnocentric instruments by decontextualizing and recontextualizing for cultural group
Existing instruments have ethnocentric bias	Use interviews or other procedures that may increase cultural congruence of instruments with sample
Instruments fail to measure cultural phenomena purported to measure	
Instruments are not culturally congruent for sample	Pilot test instruments on sample of target population
<ul><li>Language or dialect of instrument is inappropriate</li><li>Response format is inappropriate</li><li>Abstract or decontextualized nature of items inappropriate for cultural group</li></ul>	Use multiple measures to represent complexity of cultural phenomena
Instruments inadequately represent cultural phenomena	

heritage) in order to describe the sample, it is also important to survey the psychological characteristics (e.g., experience of stigmatization) that make this population particularly relevant for the purposes of the study.

The logistics of participant recruitment are also key to maintaining cultural validity. It is believed by some (Bowman, 1999; Ward, 1992) that stigmatized groups may be reluctant to participate in psychological research, but others (e.g., Cauce et al., 1998) question if this belief is myth. Cauce et al. provide excellent recommendations for recruitment strategies including offering incentives for participation, soliciting support from respected community leaders, making personal contact with participants, and conducting the research in the community or participants' preferred environments. They also suggest that the participants should not be stigmatized during the recruitment, which could be avoided simply by choosing an appropriate title ("Seattle 500 study" vs. "Cocaine During Pregnancy study"). Moreover, the researchers should take care to foster rapport and build relationships with participants during the conduct of the study. In one study of Latino youths (Quintana, 1994), parents of participants indicated their consent to participate was positively influenced by a desire to expose their children to Latino graduate students whom they felt could be positive role models to their children. In short, the recruitment and conduct of the study should respect the cultural integrity of participants—those participants who have to accommodate to the researchers' cultural orientation

TABLE 30.3 Cultural Validity for Participant Recruitment

Threats to Cultural Validity	Ways to Improve Cultural Validity
Sample fails to represent target cultural population	Recruit sample that represents target population
Participants have to accommodate to culture of researcher	Make recruitment procedures congruent with cultural group
Participants are stigmatized by research process	Recruit samples to represent psychological characteristics (e.g., reference group orientation) of target population
Potential participants are reluctant to participate due to cultural mistrust	
Samples are recruited to represent only demographic characteristics of target population	

may be reactive and thereby their responses may reflect the study context rather than contexts with which they are more familiar.

Cultural Validity in Data Analyses

With only rare exceptions, data analyses should be conducted according to conceptual principles and should not be data driven. Analyses which are guided by a conceptual framework allow results to be interpreted meaningfully. When data analyses are not guided by conceptual principles, results may be difficult to interpret, or worse, may be misinterpreted to imply inappropriately characteristics about cultural groups. When analyses are data driven (e.g., stepwise regression), there are serious problems with how well the study findings will be replicated in other samples. Exploratory analyses may be justified in some cases, but usually only those with large sample sizes (see Quintana & Maxwell, 1999).

Data analyses should not only evaluate study hypotheses, but should evaluate rival hypotheses that provide alternative explanations of the study findings. Results suggesting that study hypotheses are supported do not imply that alternative hypotheses are disconfirmed. Many of the problems with cultural validity in previous research, particularly that research consistent with a "blame the victim" orientation, failed to conceptualize alternative models (e.g., role of racism) to account for study results. Consequently, whenever possible, alternative cultural conceptualizations should be statistically evaluated along with study hypotheses in order to enhance cultural validity (see Quintana & Maxwell, 1999, for construction and evaluation of alternative models). Methodological sources for rival hypotheses may stem from problems with the cultural nature of construct validity, including the use of a culturally biased instrument. Similarly, some findings may be specific to statistical procedures used and alternative statistical procedures may implicate very different interpretations. Hence, data analyses should be used, when possible, to evaluate rival interpretations based on conceptual, methodological, and statistical sources.

Within multicultural and other kinds of research, there is some confusion over the relationship between variable type (e.g., categorical or continuous) and forms of statistical analyses (nonparametric and parametric analyses). Recent statistical research has suggested that linearity of the variables is more important variable type, per se (see Quintana & Maxwell, 1999) in the use of statistical procedures based on the general linear model (e.g., correlational, regression, or structural equations analyses). For example, dichotomous categorical variables (e.g., sex) can be entered as predictor variables into a regression analysis because these kinds of variables can be linearly represented (recall from geometry that two points define a line). For those categorical variables with multiple categories (e.g., N categories), multiple (i.e., $N-1$) dichotomous variables can be coded and analyzed using standard linear statistical procedures. For example, a race variable with three different racial groups (e.g., Black, White, and Asian) would be a categorical variable. In this instance, two separate dichotmous variables could be coded to represent this tripartite categorical variable. One dichotomous variable would be presence or absence of Black heritage and the second could be presence or absence of Asian heritage (the White participants would be coded as absence of both Black and Asian racial heritage). Finally, some categorical variables which may be roughly or coarsely linear (e.g., developmental stages) may be analyzed using linear statistical procedures. The use of statistical procedures based on the general linear model, particularly multivariate procedures, tend to be more advanced, flexible, and often more powerful than other statistical procedures.

There are, therefore, many innovative ways to include cultural and racial factors within statistical analyses that go beyond traditional use of ethnic or racial status as a categorical or control variable (Steinberg & Fletcher, 1998). Indeed, Knight and Hill (1998) and Steinberg and Fletcher (1998) articulate numerous ways to investigate cultural differences, cultural bias, and the ways in which cultural factors can be integrated into statistical analyses. Cultural variables that act as moderators in an empirical relationship among psychological variables indicate, for example, that for each cultural group the nature of the relationship among psychological variables is significantly different. A description of the statistical procedures for detecting moderator and mediator relationships is beyond the scope of this chapter, but several sources are available that provide more technical details (Baron & Kenny, 1986; Knight & Hill, 1998). Statistical innovation allows for the evaluation and comparison of relatively complex conceptual multicultural models. The key to cultural validity in data analyses is the way in

TABLE 30.4 Cultural Validity for Data Analyses

Threats to Cultural Validity	Ways to Improve Cultural Validity
Analyses fail to evaluate cultural hypotheses	Evaluate cultural hypotheses as well as rival hypotheses
Analyses fail to evaluate rival or alternative cultural, methodological, statistical, or theoretical explanations	Investigate moderator effects of cultural variables
Analyses are data driven	Use appropriate procedures to represent cultural variables statistically

which cultural variables are included in the statistical procedures (see Table 30.4).

Cultural Validity in the Evaluation and Discussion of Study Results

We believe that the litmus test for cultural validity is the cultural utility of the results (see Table 30.5). The potential for important implications for multicultural practice and theory as well as for social justice are based on the representativeness of (a) cultural features in the planning of the study design, (b) cultural processes in the translation of personal and theoretical conceptions in the study hypotheses, (c) cultural dimensions in the measurement instruments selected for the study, (d) cultural context of participants in recruitment and conduct of the study procedures, and (e) empirical relationships among cultural variables in the statistical procedures. Studies that appropriately represent culture in each of these aspects are more likely to offer utility of a cultural nature. Cultural utility could offer direct benefits to participants, suggest important reformulation of a multicultural theory, generate knowledge about one or more cultural groups for consumers of the research, introduce implications for intervention or prevention programs, and more generally, offer a service to the cultural community.

A study should be designed to provide some direct benefits for participants. Most proposals submitted to institutional review boards include evaluation of benefits as well as risks for participants. When research involves historically stigmatized groups it seems critical that particular care be taken to prevent these groups from being further stigmatized through participation in the research process. Instead, the study should offer direct benefits to participants from their actual participation or through the outcomes of the study. Studies which implement an intervention or prevention program may provide benefits to participants, depending, of course, if the program is effective. Some studies engage participants in meaningful

TABLE 30.5 Cultural Validity During Interpretation of Results

Threats to Cultural Validity	Ways to Improve Cultural Validity
Limited utility of results for participants, theory, and practice	Design study to benefit participants directly
Research exploits communities	Engage participants in meaningful way (e.g., ask participants for input in interpretation of data)
	Individualize procedures and reports of results for participants
	Integrate service to community in research as a way of "giving back"
	Represent participants' "voices" authentically when interpreting data

ways and thereby offer each participant some greater self-awareness or knowledge. Again, the use of individualized interviewing procedures could make the study personally meaningful and rewarding to participants. Participants may also derive benefits by sharing results of the study—learning more about the topic of the study, about themselves in relation to others, and often about the nature of psychological research. Attention to cultural characteristics helps researchers to engage participants meaningfully in the study process as well as to inform them about the study and thereby provide culturally relevant benefits.

The results of a study may yield instructional value to theoreticians and other consumers of the research. Although informative, research that simply supports an existing theory may be of limited instructional value if it does not add any new knowledge. Research that reformulates or refines existing theories may offer more in the way of instructional value. In this sense, the research tells us more than what we could know based on the theory alone. It is particularly important for multicultural theories to be informed and modified by research results. The beginning phases of most research paradigms are marked by a search for support and validation. As the multicultural research paradigm develops, multicultural theories are likely to be more firmly grounded in research results and, if productive, the research will implicate significant changes in these theories. Analogously, research will be particularly instructive to practitioners when it suggests innovation in the way in which culturally diverse populations are served. In turn, these modifications and innovations will make multicultural theory and practice more useful in representing and addressing cultural phenomena. Research may also offer instructional value if readers of the research obtain new insights into the cultural population or phenomenon being investigated.

Finally, research should offer some service to the larger cultural community as a way of giving back to the community. Researchers personally benefit tremendously from the research they conduct on historically stigmatized cultural groups. Research also benefits the researcher's graduate education, salary, grant funding, promotions, reputation, and investigative curiosity, to name but a few of the substantial rewards. The benefits for participants as well as the participants' communities are more diffuse and difficult to identify. It is important that researchers maintain awareness of the considerable self-interest and enrichment that they obtain from conducting research. Keeping this perspective may encourage us to maintain more of a balance in the relative rewards from research that they obtain compared to benefits obtained by the ethnic and racial communities in which research is conducted. One particular imbalance in the research process is that researchers may exercise psychological hegemony over participants. By this we mean that researchers may influence the ways in which participants' voices are expressed or heard. Researchers control how participants express their reality through the selection of study hypotheses, measurement instruments, data analyses, and interpretations of results. We should, therefore, strive to make the research as authentic as possible in representing the communities we are studying and to maintain awareness of how much the research reflects our own bias, agenda, and personal interest.

REFERENCES

Baron, R. M., & Kenny, D. A. (1986). The moderator mediator variable distinction in social psychological research: Conceptual, strategies, and statistical considerations. *Journal of Personality and Social Psychology, 51*, 1173-1182.

Betancourt, H., & Lopez, S. R. (1993). The study of culture, ethnicity, and race in American psychology. *American Psychologist, 48*, 629-637.

Bowman, P. J. (1999). Race, class and ethics in research: Belmont principles to functional relevance. In R. L. Jones (Ed.), *Black psychology* (3rd ed., pp. 747-766). Berkeley, CA: Cobb & Henry.

Caldwell, C. E., Jackson, J. S., Tucker, M. B., & Bowman, P. J. (1999). Culturally competent research methods. In R. L. Jones (Ed.), *Black psychology* (3rd ed., pp. 101-127). Berkeley, CA: Cobb & Henry.

Carter, R. T. (1995). *The influence of race and racial identity in psychotherapy.* New York: John Wiley.

Cauce, A. M., Ryan, K. D., & Grove, K. (1998). Children and adolescents of color, where are you? Participation, selection, recruitment, and retention in developmental research. In V. C. McLoyd & L. Steinberg (Eds.), *Studying minority adolescents: Conceptual, methodological, and theoretical issues* (pp. 147-166). Mahwah, NJ: Lawrence Erlbaum.

Clark, R., Anderson, N. B., Clark, V. R., & Williams, D. R. (1999). Racism as a stressor for African Americans: A biopsychological model. *American Psychologist, 54*, 805-816.

Cook, T. D., & Campbell, D. T. (1979). *Quasi-experimentation: Design and analysis issues for field settings.* Chicago: Rand McNally.

Crocker, J., & Major, B. (1989). Social stigma and self-esteem: The self-protective properties of stigma. *Psychological Review, 96*, 608-630.

Cross, W. E., Jr. (1995). The psychology of Nigresence: Revising the Cross model. In J. G. Ponterotto, J. M. Casas, L. A. Suzuki, & C. M. Alexander (Eds.), *Handbook of multi-cultural counseling* (pp. 93-122). Thousand Oaks, CA: Sage.

Cross, W. E., Jr., Stauss, L., & Fhagen-Smith, P. (1999). African American identity development across the life span: Educational implications. In R. H. Sheets & E. R. Hollins (Eds.), *Racial and ethnic identity in school practices: Aspects of human development* (pp. 29-47). Mahwah, NJ: Lawrence Erlbaum.

Darou, W. G., Hum, A., & Kurtness, J. (1993). An investigation of the impact of psychosocial research on a native population. *Professional Psychology: Research and Practice, 24,* 325-329.

Fairchild, H. H., Yee, A. H., Wyatt, G. E., & Weizmann, F. M. (1995). Redressing psychology's problems with race. *American Psychologist, 50,* 46-47.

Flynn, J. R. (1999). Searching for justice. *American Psychologist, 54,* 5-20.

Frable, D. E. S. (1997). Gender, racial, ethnic, sexual, and class identities. *Annual Review of Psychology, 48,* 139-162.

Gergen, K. J., Gulerce, A., Lock, A., & Misra, G. (1996). Psychological science in cultural context. *American Psychologist, 51,* 496-503.

Gill, E., & Bob, S. (1999). Culturally competent research: An ethical perspective. *Clinical Psychology Review, 19,* 45-55.

Graham, S. (1992). "Most of the subjects were White and middle class": Trends in published research on African Americans in selected APA journals, 1970–1989. *American Psychologist, 47,* 629-639.

Greenfield, P. M. (1997). You can't take it with you: Why ability assessments don't cross cultures. *American Psychologist, 52,* 1115-1124.

Hall, C. C. I. (1997). Cultural malpractice: The growing obsolescence of psychology with the changing U.S. population. *American Psychologist, 52,* 642-651.

Helms, J. E. (1992). Why is there no study of cultural equivalence in standardized cognitive ability testing? *American Psychologist, 47,* 1083-1101.

Helms, J. E. (1994). How multiculturalism obscures racial factors in the therapy process. *Journal of Counseling Psychology, 41,* 162-165.

Heppner, P. P., Kivlighan, D. M., & Wampold, B. E. (1999). *Research design in counseling* (2nd ed.). Belmont, CA: Brooks/Cole.

Hermans, H. J. M., & Kempen, H. J. G. (1998). Moving cultures: The perilous problems of cultural dichotomies in a globalizing society. *American Psychologist, 53,* 1111-1120.

Herrnstein, R. J., & Murray, C. (1994). *The bell curve: Intelligence and class structure in American life.* New York: Simon & Schuster.

Hoffman, J. A. (1984). Psychological separation of late adolescents from their parents. *Journal of Counseling Psychology, 31,* 170-178.

Houts, A. C., Cook, T. D., & Shadish, W. R. (1986). The person-situation debate: A critical multiplist perspective. *Journal of Personality, 54,* 52-87.

Jensen, A. J. (1980). *Bias in mental testing.* New York: Free Press.

Kaufman, A. S., & Lichtenberger, E. O. (1999). *Essentials of WAIS-III assessment.* New York: John Wiley.

Kendler, H. H. (1999). The role of value in the world of psychology. *American Psychologist, 54,* 828-835.

Knight, G. P., & Hill, N. E. (1998). Measurement equivalence in research involving minority adolescents. In V. C. McLoyd & L. Steinberg (Eds.), *Studying minority adolescents: Conceptual, methodological, and theoretical issues* (pp. 183-210). Mahwah, NJ: Lawrence Erlbaum.

Leong, F. T. L. (1997). Cross-cultural psychology: Comment on Fouad, Harmon, and Borgen (1997) and Tracey, Watanabe, and Schneider (1997). *Journal of Counseling Psychology, 44,* 355-359.

Leong, F. T. L., & Brown, M. T. (1995). Theoretical issues in cross-cultural career development: Cultural validity and cultural specificity. In W. B. Walsh & S. H. Osipow (Eds.), *Handbook of vocational psychology* (2nd ed., pp. 143-180). Mahwah, NJ: Lawrence Erlbaum.

Lillard, A. (1998). Ethnopsychologies: Cultural variations in theories of mind. *Psychological Bulletin, 123,* 355-359.

Lonner, W. J., & Ibrahim, F. A. (1996). Appraisal and assessment in cross-cultural counseling. In P. B. Pedersen & J. G. Draguns (Eds.), *Counseling across cultures* (4th ed., pp. 293-322). Thousand Oaks, CA: Sage.

MacPhee, D., Kreutzer, J. C., & Fritz, J. J. (1994). Infusing a diversity perspective into human development courses. *Child Development, 65,* 699-715.

Marsella, A. J. (1998). Toward a "global-community psychology": Meeting the needs of a changing world. *American Psychologist, 53,* 1282-1291.

Mays, V. M., Bullock, M., Rosenzweig, M. R., & Wessells, M. (1998). Ethnic conflict: Global challenges and psychological perspectives. *American Psychologist, 53,* 737-742.

Midley, C., Arunkumar, R., & Urdan, T. C. (1996). "If I don't do well tomorrow, there's a reason": Predictors of adolescents' use of academic self-handicapping strategies. *Journal of Educational Psychology, 88,* 423-434.

Ogbu, J. U. (1994). From cultural difference to differences in cultural frame of reference. In P. M. Greenfield & R. R. Cocking (Eds.), *Cross-cultural roots of minority child development* (pp. 365-392). Hillsdale, NJ: Lawrence Erlbaum.

Okagaki, L., & Sternberg, R. J. (1993). Parental beliefs and children's school performance. *Child Development, 64,* 36-56.

Okazaki, S., & Sue, S. (1995). Methodological issues in assessment research with ethnic minorities. *Psychological Assessment, 7,* 367-375.

Peng, K., & Nisbett, R. E. (1999). Culture, dialectics, and reasoning about contradiction. *American Psychologist, 54,* 741-754.

Pike, K. L. (1954). *Language in relation to a unified theory of the structure of human behavior.* Dallas, TX: Summer Institute of Linguistics.

Ponterotto, J. G. (1988). Racial/ethnic minority research in the *Journal of Counseling Psychology:* A content analysis and methodological critique. *Journal of Counseling Psychology, 35,* 410-418.

Quintana, S. M. (1994). A model of ethnic perspective taking ability applied to Mexican-American children and youth. *International Journal of Intercultural Relations, 18,* 419-448.

Quintana, S. M., & Atkinson, D. (1999, August). *Principles for empirical support for intervention programs: Implications for multicultural counseling.* Symposium presentation at the annual convention of the American Psychological Association, Boston.

Quintana, S. M., & Kerr, J. (1993). Relational needs in late adolescent separation-individuation. *Journal of Counseling & Development, 71,* 349-354.

Quintana, S. M., & Maxwell, S. E. (1999). Implications of recent developments in structural equations modeling for counseling psychology. *The Counseling Psychologist, 27,* 485-527.

Quintana, S. M., Vogel, M. C., & Ybarra, V. C. (1991). Meta-analysis of Latino students' adjustment in higher education. *Hispanic Journal of Behavioral Sciences, 13,* 155-168.

Rogler, L. H. (1999). Methodological sources of cultural insensitivity in mental health research. *American Psychologist, 54,* 424-433.

Rogoff, B., & Chavajay, P. (1995). What's become of research on the cultural basis of cognitive development? *American Psychologist, 50,* 859-877.

Roland, A. (1996). How universal is the psychoanalytic self? In R. P. Foster, M. Moskowitz, & R. A. Javier (Eds.), *Reaching across boundaries of culture and class* (pp. 71-90). Northvale, NJ: Jason Aronson.

Rowe, W., Bennett, S. K., & Atkinson, D. R. (1994). White racial identity models: A critique and alternative proposal. *The Counseling Psychologist, 22,* 129-146.

Scarr, S. (1989). Constructivism and socially sensitive research. *American Psychologist, 44,* 849.

Schwartz, N. (1999). Self-reports: How the questions shape the answers. *American Psychologist, 54,* 93-105.

Scott, N. E., & Borodovsky, L. G. (1990). Effective use of cultural role taking. *Professional Psychology: Research and Practice, 21,* 167-170.

Scott-Jones, D. (1994). Ethical issues in reporting and referring in research with low-income minority children. *Ethics and Behavior, 4,* 97-108.

Segall, M. H., Lonner, W. J., & Berry, J. W. (1998). Cross-cultural psychology as a scholarly discipline: On the flowering of culture in behavioral research. *American Psychologist, 53,* 1101-1110.

Selman, R. L. (1980). *The growth of interpersonal understanding: Developmental and clinical analyses.* San Diego: Academic Press.

Shweder, R. (1990). Cultural psychology: What is it? In J. W. Stigler, R. A. Shweder, & G. Herdt (Eds.), *Cultural psychology: Essays on comparative human development.* New York: Cambridge University Press.

Steele, C. M. (1997). A threat in the air: How stereotypes shape intellectual identity and performance. *American Psychologist, 52,* 613-629.

Steinberg, L., & Fletcher, A. C. (1998). Data analytic strategies in research on ethnic minority youth. In V. C. McLoyd & L. Steinberg (Eds.), *Studying minority adolescents: Conceptual, methodological, and theoretical issues* (pp. 279-294). Mahwah, NJ: Lawrence Erlbaum.

Sue, D. W., Bingham, R. P., Porché-Burke, L., & Vasquez, M. (1999). The diversification of psychology: A multicultural revolution. *American Psychologist, 54,* 1061-1069.

Sue, D. W., Ivey, A. E., & Pedersen, P. B. (1996). *A theory of multicultural counseling and therapy.* Pacific Grove, CA: Brooks/Cole.

Sue, D. W., & Sue, D. (1990). *Counseling the culturally different.* New York: Wiley Interscience.

Sue, S. (1999). Science, ethnicity, and bias. *American Psychologist, 54,* 1070-1077.

Suzuki, L. A., & Valencia, R. R. (1997). Race-ethnicity and measure intelligence: Educational implications. *American Psychologist, 52,* 1103-1114.

Thoma, S. (1986). Estimating gender differences in the comprehension and preference of moral issues. *Developmental Review, 6,* 165-180.

Titchener, E. B., Leahey, T. H., & Furumoto, L. (1997). E. B. Titchener and structuralism. In L. T. Benjamin, Jr. (Ed.), *A history of psychology: Original sources and contemporary research* (2nd ed., pp. 168-202). New York: McGraw-Hill.

Van de Vijver, F., & Leung, K. (1997). *Methods and data analysis for cross-cultrual research.* Thousand Oaks, CA: Sage.

Velasquez, R., Ayala, G. X., & Mendoza, S. A. (1999). *Psychodiagnostic assessment of U.S. Latinos with MMPI, MMPI-2, and MMPI-A: A comprehensive resource manual.* East Lansing, MI: Julian Samora Research Institute.

Wampold, B. E., Davis, B., & Good, R. H. (1990). Hypothesis validity of clinical research. *Journal of Consulting and Clinical Psychology, 58,* 360-367.

Ward, C. O. (1992). Cross-cultural methods for survey research in Black urban areas. *Journal of Black Psychology, 3,* 72-87.

Weisz, J. R., & McCarty, C. A. (1999). Can we trust parent reports in research on cultural and ethnic differences in child psychopathology? Using the bicultural family design to test parental culture effects. *Journal of Abnormal Psychology, 108,* 598-605.

Yee, A. H., Fairchild, H. H., Weizmann, F., & Wyatt, G. E. (1993). Addressing psychology's problems with race. *American Psychologist, 48,* 1132-1140.

Zuckerman, M. (1990). Some dubious premises in research and theory on racial differences: Scientific, social and ethical issues. *American Psychologist, 45,* 1297-1303.

Correspondence regarding this chapter may be sent to Stephen M. Quintana, Department of Counseling Psychology, 1000 Bascom Mall, University of Wisconsin at Madison, Madison, WI 53706 (e-mail address: Quintana@education.wisc.edu).

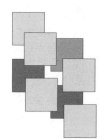

Part VI

CAREER, FAMILY, SCHOOL, AND REFUGEE COUNSELING

The chapters in Part VI of the *Handbook* focus, respectively, on career counseling, family counseling, school counseling, and refugee counseling. The section opens with Chapter 31, where Byars and McCubbin review and discuss trends in multicultural career development research. Their comprehensive review spanned the 1994–1999 time frame and focused on research designs, theoretical models, specific topics, sample characteristics, instrumentation, and statistical procedures. The authors provide a thorough synthesis of these trends while also offering eight descriptive and specific directions for needed theoretical and empirical work in the area.

In Chapter 32, Adachi Sueyoshi, Rivera, and Ponterotto provide an applied perspective on the practice of multicultural career counseling. Using real cases and actual genogram models, the authors demonstrate the potential value of family genogram work in multicultural career counseling.

The focus of Chapter 33 by Sanchez is on the family in multicultural counseling, specifically ethnic minority families who develop maladaptive behavior patterns as a result of stressful life transitions. The author introduces the term "cultural sensibility," which refers to variables that affect the counselor's ability to implement appropriate counseling interventions. Factors impacting cultural sensibility include counselor worldview, practice and experience, and language. Sanchez describes a multicultural family practice framework that he and his staff have developed over the past 12 years in Chico, California. Using real cases from their campus-based family clinic, Sanchez vividly demonstrates his counseling model in action.

Chapter 34 focuses on children, the schools, and the roles of the school counselor. Sciarra reviews the long-standing debate on the most appropriate role for the school counselor (academic or personal counseling), and he addresses reasons for noted achievement disparities across groups. Building from his extensive experience as a bilingual school counselor in New York City's South Bronx, Sciarra demonstrates through a vivid case study how the counselor can serve as an advocate for rigorous academic training for all students. The author views the role of the school counselor as a multicultural consultant working within the school, family, and community.

Part VI closes with Chapter 35, where Prendes-Lintel outlines a pragmatic and effective working model for counseling recent refugees. The author reviews the stages of the translocation experience, and she discusses the psychological trauma often accompanying the process. Anchored in her extensive clinical and administrative experience working with refugees, Prendes-Lintel demonstrates her working model through the use of actual cases. As the United States continues to be a haven for refugee settlement, professional counselors will be increasingly called on to address the trauma and adjustment needs of these individuals.

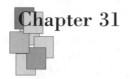

Chapter 31

TRENDS IN CAREER DEVELOPMENT RESEARCH WITH RACIAL/ETHNIC MINORITIES

Prospects and Challenges

ANGELA M. BYARS
LAURIE D. MCCUBBIN

RESEARCH IS A process of inquiry used to understand our world. It is one activity of science that shapes what questions are posed, how variables of interest are operationalized and measured, the methods invoked to study and observe such variables, the analytical procedures used to describe and interpret variables, and even how the results of this research process are communicated in publications. The scientific research in a given discipline, therefore, reflects the priorities of that field and informs the practice of that profession.

Heppner, Kivlighan, and Wampold (1999) outlined the implications of the role of science for the discipline of counseling. Specifically, they discussed the following issues as significant factors shaping the research conducted in the counseling profession: (a) the goals of science in counseling, (b) methodological diversity, (c) the need to examine and expand our assumptions regarding human nature, and (d) our responsibility for applying research tools (p. 8). It is science, then, that develops the knowledge base on which the counseling profession rests. Clearly, if the scientific research informing counseling represents knowledge of only a few cultural groups, then the cultural validity of counseling practice is controvertible (see Quintana, Troyano, & Taylor, Chapter 30, this volume).

Leong and Brown (1995) defined cultural validity as concerning "the construct, concurrent, and predictive validity of theories and models across other cultures, that is, for culturally different individuals" (p. 144). African Americans, Asian Americans and Pacific Islanders, Latino/as, and Native Americans, collectively referred to as racial/ethnic minorities (R/EMs), represent various diverse, cultural groups in the United States. An example of cultural validity inquiry applied to R/EMs' career behavior might be an investigation of how well Super's (1990) construct of vocational self-concept predicts career choice for Native Americans and Latino/as, as well as for European Americans. Establishing the cultural validity of career-related processes is an important means of determining the relevance of such processes to R/EMs. As a function of unique and shared social, political, economic, and educational experiences relative to their integration into U.S. society and institutions, R/EMs may vary greatly from traditional European American samples on which many career theories and research are based. Accordingly, these unique experiences have significant implications for the development of their career behavior. The examination of R/EMs' career development and behavior, however, has often been absent in vocational psychology research.

Based on Leong and Brown's (1995) examination of vocational psychology research with R/EMs, we assert that the lack of cultural diversity in samples and the lack of culturally-relevant constructs have been two of the significant threats to validity in a great deal of vocational research. In addition, the cultural validity of career theories has been constrained due to the limited range and contexts of career behavior covered (Hackett & Lent, 1992). Carter and Cook (1992) summarized the criticisms levied against career theories as follows: (a) Many were based and developed on European American middle-class males; (b) they were founded on European American cultural values; (c) they ignored sociopolitical realities and psychological experiences of R/EMs; (d) they ignored prevailing economic and social contexts in which R/EMs exist; and (e) they ignored cultural institutions that promote and support the expression of R/EMs' vocational talents often unrecognized in dominant contexts. Simply stated, the worldviews, experiences, and unique cultural contexts of R/EMs have been grossly omitted from the majority of vocational research. Indeed, vocational psychology has been challenged to advance the field's understanding of the meaning of work for a broader range of individuals by examining both the cultural validity of career theories and by including more culturally specific variables (e.g., acculturation) within vocational research (Leong & Brown, 1995).

Smith (1983) stated that one impediment to the development of a theory, or theories, of R/EMs' career development has been the definition of the meaning of career development. Some of the tenets of career development and career choice theories, as identified by Smith (1983), are the concept of "dignity of work," the existence of a "free and open labor market" with a variety of career choices, and a planfulness about one's career development (pp. 186-187). These tenets typically overlook the dynamic and continuous interplay between the individual and his/her environment. Crites (1975) added that many gaps in the research literature and inconclusive data on R/EM groups preclude the development of a model to explain and understand the career development of these populations. Within quantitative paradigms, for instance, psychology's overvaluing of internal validity (i.e., causal and correlational effects of one variable on another) relative to external validity (i.e., generalizability of results from sample to population) often has led to cultural bias in research (Sue, 1999). These challenges have stimulated the much needed career research on R/EMs that Smith (1983) called for nearly 20 years ago within the field of vocational psychology.

In this chapter, we review the research and theoretical literature in vocational psychology on racial and ethnic minorities. The purpose of this chapter is to (1) provide an overview of the major contributions to career research with R/EMs from 1994 to 1995, updating and extending Leung's (1995) review of the career development literature for R/EMs published in the first edition of the *Handbook of Multicultural Counseling*; (2) summarize trends in the theoretical and empirical literature on R/EMs in vocational psychology since Leung's publication; (3) synthesize the implications of these research trends; and (4) propose directions for future innovative, inclusive, and informed research on the career behavior of R/EMs. For the purposes of this writing, we focus our discussion on the four traditionally identified R/EM groups in the United States: African Americans, Asian Americans and Pacific Islanders, Latino/as, and Native Americans.

The decision to contain our review of the vocational literature to these four groups was made to be consistent with seminal publications in vocational psychology that selected these populations as the focus of study (cf. Leong, 1995). Although we use the preceding terms to refer to the major U.S. R/EM groups in aggregate form, we recognize the considerable cultural variations within each group. For example, within Asian American and Pacific Islander populations, there are Japanese, Chinese, Koreans, Laotians, Hawaiians, Filipinos, Vietnamese, and Asian Indians, among others. Native Americans represent 200 Alaskan Native groups and 318 federally recognized tribes such as Hopi, Oneida, Cherokee, Sioux, and Navajo (Bureau of Indian Affairs, 1993). Among African (or Black) Americans, there are persons whose cultural heritage extends from the Caribbean, Latin America, and Europe, as well as from Africa. Latino/a ethnic groups include people who are Central and South American, Puerto Rican, Cuban, and Mexican. Each racial and ethnic group possesses its own norms, cultural beliefs and values, language, and sociopolitical history that distinguish it from others. Despite this diversity, these groups share historical racial discrimination relative to their social, economic, and political status in the United States

(Leung, 1995). This shared experience may have a significant impact on their career behavior.

RECENT ADVANCES IN
MULTICULTURAL VOCATIONAL PSYCHOLOGY

Since 1994, several major publications have addressed critical issues for the career development of R/EMs. In 1994, *Journal of Vocational Behavior* devoted a special issue to the topic of racial and ethnic identity and career behavior. Vocational psychology researchers contributing to this special issue outlined ways in which the internalized, psychosocial consequences of socialization as an R/EM might contribute to their perception of work, perceived opportunities and barriers in career choice, and work values. Also in 1994, Fitzgerald and Betz authored a chapter in the edited book *Convergence in Career Development Theories*, examining the influences of gender, race, class, and sexual orientation on career development. The authors asserted that these cultural variables provide significant contexts within which career choice occurs. In the following year, several significant critiques and reviews of the research literature with R/EMs were published in the field of vocational psychology.

Leong (1995) edited the pivotal book *Career Development and Vocational Behavior of Racial and Ethnic Minorities.* Contributing authors to this book critically examined multiple factors associated with career development, assessment, and interventions for R/EMs. A primary thesis throughout the chapters in this edited volume was the necessity for vocational research and practice to explicitly attend to the cultural contexts within which career-related experiences occur. These cultural contexts are moderated by the "history, education, and social, political, and economic experience" of R/EMs (Osipow & Littlejohn, 1995, p. 251). Inattention to these variables renders vocational frameworks applied to R/EMs culturally irrelevant. The authors suggested that attention to cultural contexts would facilitate movement beyond traditional monocultural assumptions of career to more culturally valid and relevant theories and research on R/EMs' career behavior.

Leong and Brown's (1995) chapter in the second edition of *Handbook of Vocational Psychology* reviewed cross-cultural issues in theories of career development vis-à-vis two theoretical dimensions: cultural validity and cultural specificity. Cultural validity, as previously stated, addresses the degree to which theories and models validly predict and explain behavior for individuals across various cultures. Cultural specificity, on the other hand, relates to the consideration of concepts, constructs, and models particular to certain cultural groups in explaining and predicting their behavior. For instance, acculturation may be a significant influence on the career development of Native Americans, Asian Americans, and Latino/as given the relationship of this variable to cultural values and work values (cf. Leong, 1986). Based on the assertions of Leong and Brown, research incorporating both cultural validity and cultural specificity considerations will promote more informed within-group analysis that can explicate the heterogeneity among R/EMs.

Fouad and Bingham (1995) authored another chapter in the same edition of *Handbook of Vocational Psychology* in which they offered a culturally appropriate counseling model for career interventions with R/EMs. They examined the role that cultural variables play, like worldviews and racial and ethnic identity, in R/EMs' career decision making, underscoring the importance of incorporating both culture-specific and culture-general considerations in every phase of career intervention.

In the first edition of *Handbook of Multicultural Counseling,* published in 1995, Leung's chapter on career development and interventions with R/EMs discussed variables on which vocational behavior of these groups were convergent and divergent. Similar to the Fouad and Bingham (1995) conclusion, Leung's (1995) examination of the research literature and career interventions further advocated for vocational research and counseling that include both culture-general and culture-specific considerations.

General Trends and Findings: 1994–1995

An examination of the research reviewed in these major publications shows that much of the literature followed the cultural validity dimension of inquiry detailed by Leong and Brown (1995). That is, a predominance of the work was dedicated to establishing the applicability of traditional career development theories and related constructs to culturally different groups. For example, considerable research has been conducted on the validity of various constructs from Holland's (1985a) career choice model, such as congruence, with African Americans (Brown, 1995). Collectively, these publications highlighted the persistent deficit in the vocational literature on R/EMs relative to culture-specific factors, including social and historical experiences of these ethnic groups.

Conceptual and empirical work in vocational psychology is needed to address the current and historical social status of R/EMs relative to career-related concepts. The potential impact of R/EMs' historical and current social status on career development may be moderated by several factors. Some experiences may be shared across the groups as a function of the general context of oppression and discrimination; these experiences and associated cognitive processes vary for individuals within the groups; and complex interactions of social class, acculturation, and assimilation with race and ethnicity may further moderate culture-specific influences (Byars & Hackett, 1998).

A primary identified focus for future research emerging from these aforementioned publications was the development of multicultural career perspectives. Advocates for such multicultural perspectives that might advance the field of vocational psychology called for increased examination of cultural and contextual factors related to career choice. That is, the profession was challenged to move research beyond examination of the process and products of career development to an examination of the dynamic cultural contexts in which these processes and products occur. New variables for future study included the investigation of more subtle variables such as self-concept, racial and cultural identity, self-efficacy, and factors underlying social learning (Osipow & Littlejohn, 1995).

What impact have these suggested directions for research had on the empirical work exploring R/EMs' vocational behavior? What type of research has been conducted since 1994 examining the cultural validity and cultural specificity dimensions of career-related constructs and theories? The next section reviews current trends in multicultural career-related research with R/EMs.

CURRENT TRENDS IN
MULTICULTURAL VOCATIONAL RESEARCH

We conducted an extensive literature review of the research on career development and R/EMs from 1994 through 1999. This time frame was selected based on two factors. First, as previously stated, we endeavored to update and extend Leung's (1995) examination of career development of R/EMs since the first edition of *Handbook of Multicultural Counseling.* Second, given that many manuscripts are written in the year prior to the time they appear in print, some publications from 1994 may not have been available for inclusion in Leung's (1995) chapter. Therefore, inclusion of publications from 1994 in our literature review might add to a more complete examination of the career development literature with R/EMs to date.

Publications that focused on multicultural career related issues and/or had samples consisting of U.S. R/EMs were reviewed and analyzed for this chapter. The literature search was conducted via four databases: Psychlit, ERIC, Sociofile, and Social Work abstracts. Each publication was analyzed using the following factors: nature of research design (e.g., quantitative, qualitative, conceptual/theoretical), journal or publication type, theoretical framework, topical focus, sample size, sample demographics, ethnic groups within the samples, instrumentation, and statistical procedures used. These factors were selected based on adaptations from Koegel, Donin, Ponterotto, and Spitz (1995).

Research Design

Of the 79 articles chosen for this review, 54 (68%) were quantitative studies and 12 (15%) were qualitative studies (1 study incorporated both, or mixed, methodologies), 4 were literature reviews, and 9 were conceptual/ theoretical papers with no empirical research involved. One trend noted in the research designs included in the studies under review is the use of qualitative methods. More qualitative research is being conducted focusing on multicultural issues and career development compared with research trends in the past. Koegel et al. (1995) found that only 2.5% of articles focusing on multicultural career issues were qualitative empirical investigations from 1985 to 1992 in three career journals. The increase observed in qualitative multicultural research from Koegel et al.'s publication to this current review may also be due to the wider range of journal and publication sources included in this literature search. Nonetheless, recognition of the need for greater use of qualitative methods in the area of multicultural career research to elucidate process variables is increasing (Fouad & Bingham, 1995; Leong & Brown, 1995).

Journal/Publication Type

The journal that published the greatest number of research articles on multicultural career related issues was *Journal of Vocational Behavior* with 12 articles (15%). *Journal of Multicultural Counseling and Development* and *Journal of Career Development* each published 9 articles (22%). Both *Career Development Quarterly* and *Journal of College Student Development* published 5 articles each. Other journals that focused on particular groups of ethnic minorities, such as *Hispanic Journal of Behavioral Sciences* and *Journal of Negro Education*, published articles related to career development issues as well. Articles on the topic were also found in the sociological literature and the social work field. Table 31.1 summarizes these results. Although a preponderance of career-related publications was found in journals related to counseling psychology and education, these trends indicate that multidisciplinary perspectives are informing career research.

Theory and Heuristic Models

Of the 79 articles selected, 25 (32%) did not have a particular theory guiding the research. Among the mainstream career theories that were studied, Holland's (1985a) model of career choice is still the most widely studied approach, with self-efficacy theory (Bandura, 1986, 1997) following. Other major theories included in the research were Krumboltz's Social Learning Theory (Mitchell & Krumboltz, 1990), Social Cognitive Career

TABLE 31.1 Summary of Journal/Publication Names in Literature Review

Name of Journal or Publication	Number of Articles
Journal of Vocational Behavior	12
Journal of Career Development	9
Journal of Multicultural Counseling and Development	9
Career Development Quarterly	5
Journal of College Student Development	5
Journal of Counseling and Development	3
Journal of Negro Education	3
Journal of Counseling Psychology	2
Professional School Counseling	2
Journal of Employment Counseling	2
Journal of Applied Behavioral Science	2
Hispanic Journal of Behavioral Sciences	2
APA conference paper/other conferences	2
Measurement and Evaluation in Counseling and Development	1
Journal of Black Studies	1
College Student Journal	1
Journal of Vocational Educational Research	1
Journal for the Education of the Gifted	1
Social Science Quarterly	1
Journal of Research on Adolescence	1
Journal of Social Work Education	1
Journal of Clinical Psychology	1
Journal of Applied Social Psychology	1
Journal of Black Psychology	1
American Educational Research Journal	1
Journal of Adolescence	1
New Directions for Community Colleges	1
Families in Society	1
Sociological Quarterly	1
Innovative Higher Education	1
Sociological Perspectives	1
Urban Girls book chapter	1
Journal of Career Assessment	1
Youth & Society	1
Total Number of Publications	79

Theory (Lent, Brown, & Hackett, 1994), and Super's (1990) Life Span Life Space developmental approach, particularly his concept of career maturity.

Racial identity theories served as the theoretical foundation for the largest number of publications, with 9 articles focusing on this topic (11%). These articles tended to use two theories jointly in the studies, such as Cross's (1971) model of racial identity along with Gottfredson's (1981) theory of circumscription and compromise (Evans & Herr, 1994). Racial identity theory was also linked in studies with Holland's model (Jackson & Neville, 1998), feminist identity development theory (Weathers, Thompson, Robert, & Rodriguez, 1994), nigrescence (Parham & Austin, 1994), and

TABLE 31.2 Theories and Heuristic Models Found in Publications

Name of Theory/Heuristic Model	Frequency
Atheoretical	25
Holland	9
Self-Efficacy	6
Social Learning Theory—Krumboltz	5
Super's Developmental Approach	4
Social Cognitive Career Theory	3
Vocational Identity	1
Trait and Factor	1
Gottfredson	1
Developmental	5
Grounded Theory	3
Racial Identity[a]	9
Acculturation	4
Model Minority Thesis	3
Wilson's Declining Significance of Race Thesis	1
Lorie's Qualitative Study of Teacher Motivation	1
Cultural Discontinuity Thesis	1
Racial Bias	1
Heuristic Model of African American Students' Career Development	1
Nigrescence	1
Feminist Identity Development	1

NOTE: Four articles were not included as they were literature reviews or conceptualizations for career centers.

a. Some studies combined two theories particularly for Racial Identity, and one study combined three theories.

acculturation (Lucero-Miller & Newman, 1999). Acculturation and the model minority thesis (Tang, 1997; Wong, Lai, Nagasawa, & Lin, 1998) were found in the literature when looking specifically at Asian Americans (e.g., Leong & Chou, 1994; Lew, Allen, Papouchis, & Ritzler, 1998). These trends are outlined in Table 31.2.

The theoretical and heuristic models included in these publications show a significant trend toward studying culture-specific phenomena such as racial bias, cultural discontinuity, the model minority thesis, and acculturation (e.g., Oyserman & Sakamoto, 1997). Although research is still being conducted to validate mainstream theories, culture-specific theories are also being examined. This shift toward cultural specificity in research is changing what constructs are being researched and how research questions are posed. In addition, this trend has increased the number of within-group studies. For example, instead of investigating how Latino/as vary from European Americans on career self-efficacy, one study examined how well acculturation and (English) language usage predicted this construct for a sample of Latino/a clients in a community agency setting (Miranda &

TABLE 31.3 Focus of Research in Publications

Topic of Focus	Frequency
Occupational Perceptions, Expectations, Interests, Aspirations	18
Racial Identity	9
Self-Concept/Self-Efficacy	8
Evaluation of Career Services	7
Application/Validation of Culture-Specific Theory	6
Work-Related Values/Preferences	5
Acculturation	5
Validation of Mainstream Career Theory	4
Career Maturity	3
Career Decision Making	3
Mentoring	3
Contextual Factors (e.g., family)	2
Gender Differences	2
Workplace/Occupational Stress	2
Career Choice	1
Developmental	1
Career Patterns	1
Racial Bias	1
Career Planning	1
Personality and Career Commitment	1
Job Satisfaction	1

Umhoefer, 1998). Rather than examining R/EMs in contrast to mainstream (i.e., European American) society, research seems to be shifting toward understanding the specific worldviews of various cultural and ethnic groups.

Topical Foci

The list of topics was adapted and modified from the literature review conducted by Koegel et al. (1995) and is summarized in Table 31.3. The most common topical focus was on occupational perceptions, expectations, interests, and aspirations (n = 18). The second most common factor was racial identity (n = 9). Common topics identified in career development research were consistently found validating mainstream career theories and constructs, such as self-efficacy (Ancis & Phillips, 1996; Daniels, D'Andrea, & Gaughen, 1998; Gloria & Hird, 1999; Hackett & Byars, 1996; Luzzo, Funk, & Strang, 1996; Luzzo, McWhirter, & Hutcheson, 1997; Tang, Fouad, & Smith, 1999), work-related values (Vacha, Walsh, & Kapes, 1994), and career maturity (Jackson & Healy, 1996; Naidoo, Bowman, & Gerstein, 1998). There were also many topics focusing on the validation of culture-specific theories such as racial identity (e.g., McCowan & Alston, 1998), acculturation (e.g., Miranda & Umhoefer, 1998), and racial bias in the work-place (e.g., Holder & Vaux, 1998). The culture-specific factors, however, tended to focus on African Americans and Asian Americans. Less research is being conducted examining culture-specific factors for Latino/as and Native Americans.

Sample Trends

Sample Size

The sample sizes in the publications reviewed varied from over 1,000 to as few as 2 participants. The majority of samples found in the quantitative studies ranged between 100 and 199 participants, approximately 31% ($n = $ 21). The second most frequent sample size was in the range of 1 to 49 participants, 21% ($n = 14$), which included the majority of the qualitative studies. In 8 of the studies, the number of participants ranged from 50 to 99. There were 11 studies with between 200 and 499 participants, 4 with participants in the 500–999 range, and 8 with samples comprising over 1,000 participants.

Sample Description, by Educational Level and Age Group

Samples were largely selected from educational settings. College undergraduates constituted the majority of these samples, representing approximately 45% ($n = 30$) of participants in the studies. The second most common age group consisted of adults, 24% ($n = 16$). Studies with adult samples were conducted in the community either through an agency setting or by studying a particular occupation group, such as lawyers or nurses. Elementary school samples were used for 4 studies, junior high school samples for 5, and high school samples for 10.

There continues to be a focus on early childhood to late adolescence in the career-related research with R/EMs. This trend may reflect the convenience and ease in gaining access to these populations. However, it should be noted that a number of studies were conducted with adult samples that ranged in size from 2 to 238. Most of those studies using adult samples were conducted with African Americans.

Racial and Ethnic Minority Group Composition of Samples

For the empirically based publications, the representation of R/EM groups across all studies was as follows: African Americans = 49, Asian Americans = 19, Latino/as = 27, and Native Americans = 11. Within each study, the number of R/EM groups varied greatly. Seven studies included R/EM groups wherein the comparison group was White/European American, and 6 others included a comparison between two R/EM groups (e.g., Asian Americans and African Americans). There were 24 studies that included three or more racial and ethnic groups.

The 33 studies that included a single ethnic group represented primarily African Americans (n = 20) and Latino/as (n = 7). Five single ethnic group studies were identified for Asian Americans and only 1 with Native Americans. With the exception of African Americans, R/EM groups were mostly studied in comparison to other ethnic groups.

Instrumentation

Over 89 separate instruments were used in the research. Some of the most frequently used career measures were My Vocational Situation (Holland, 1980), Career Decision-Making Self-Efficacy Scale (Taylor & Betz, 1983), and Self-Directed Search (Holland, 1985b). Measures of cultural processes included the Racial Identity Attitude Scale (Parham & Helms, 1985) and Attitudes Toward Women Scale (Spence & Helmreich, 1972). The majority of the remaining measures assessed social and environmental factors that may influence career processes such as the Social Support Appraisal Scale (Holder & Vaux, 1998), Suinn-Lew Asian Self-Identity Acculturation Scale (Suinn, Rickard-Figueroa, Lew, & Vigil, 1987), and Personal Discrimination Scale (Watts & Carter, 1991).

Statistical Procedures

Examination of the statistical procedures used in the studies indicates that 56% of the researchers applied analysis of variance and multivariate techniques. This finding is similar to Koegel et al.'s (1995) analysis wherein nearly 50% of researchers in the studies they reviewed used these same techniques. Among the studies we reviewed that used analysis of variance techniques, 13 used ANOVA methods and another 6 used either ANCOVA, MANOVA, or MANCOVA. The most common multivariate analysis used was a multiple regression technique (n = 18). Overall, researchers used a range of other data analytic methods, including descriptive statistics (n = 14), Pearson correlations (n = 12), chi-square (n = 4), factor analysis (n = 2), and structural equation modeling (n = 1).

Although research examining the degree to which participants differ on several variables continues to be significant (e.g., ANOVA techniques), the notable number of studies incorporating multiple regression analyses (23%) indicate that a significant amount of research purposed to clarify explanatory relationships among research variables. Interestingly, many of these studies investigated the predictiveness of culturally specific variables, such as acculturation, to various career-related constructs (e.g., Lucero-Miller & Newman, 1999).

SYNTHESIS AND IMPLICATIONS OF TRENDS

Fitzgerald, Fassinger, and Betz (1995) asserted that the study of women's career development has enriched the overall discipline of vocational psychology by promoting the examination and inclusion of variables previously ignored in vocational issues, such as the influence of family on career choice. Similarly, the study of R/EMs has focused the field more on contextual variables, like perceived supports and barriers, and cultural variations in the meaning of work. Findings from the research trends we examined highlight the impact of such research with R/EMs on the field. There were three overarching trends in the publications reviewed.

First, there was continued examination of the cultural validity of mainstream career constructs and theories, such as Holland's model of career choice (e.g., Park & Harrison, 1995; Ryan, Tracey, & Rounds, 1996). Research addressing cultural validity of extant career theories and constructs was predominantly conducted with African Americans (e.g., Jackson & Neville, 1998; Naidoo, Bowman, & Gerstein, 1998) and Latino/as college students (e.g., Fisher & Padmawidjaja, 1999). Evaluations of cultural validity were likely to be conducted within race-comparative frameworks; that is, the construct, concurrent, predictive validity of variables were often examined across different racial and ethnic groups within the same study. This is evidenced by the fact that slightly more than half (35 out of 68) of the research conducted compared R/EMs to another racial or ethnic group.

Although a few studies examined Asian Americans as a single R/EM group (e.g., Liu, 1998; Tang, Fouad, & Smith, 1999), they were most likely to be compared to White/European Americans on vocational constructs, especially on the variable of acculturation and the "model minority thesis." This research suggested two issues. First, the career research seemed to focus on Asian Americans' vocational behavior in terms of their adaptation to or adoption of White/European values (e.g., levels of acculturation). Second, examination of the "model minority thesis" appeared to attempt validation of Asian Americans as a legitimate minority, countering the erroneous perception that members of these racial and ethnic groups have uniformly integrated into the labor force and other U.S. social institutions successfully. This point is underscored by Leong and Serafica's (1995) assertion that "subtle racial discrimination and occupational stereotyping may present barriers to their entry and advancement in certain occupational fields" (pp. 87-88).

Vocational issues of Native Americans were hugely understudied. Out of 79 publications, we identified only 6 that examined the career behavior of this group (Daniels, D'Andrea, & Gaughen, 1998; Ensher & Murphy,

1997; Luzzo, McWhirter, & Hutcheson, 1997; McWhirter, Larson, & Daniels, 1996; Strong, 1998; Wood & Clay, 1996). The inattention to Native Americans in the vocational literature may be due to difficulty in accessing samples identified as Native American. This point is especially significant when considering that the majority of career research is carried out with college populations (Fitzgerald & Betz, 1994) where enrollments of Native Americans are small, though growing (Johnson, Swartz, & Martin, 1995).

Second, the deliberate attention to culturally specific variables, such as acculturation, perceived discrimination, and racial/ethnic identity, was noted. Rather than comparisons of R/EMs to White/European American behavior and cultural standards, research attended to the specific world-views of R/EMs. However, this trend happened primarily for African Americans. As previously stated, research with Asian American and Latino/a samples often examined the influence of acculturation levels on career behavior. Nonetheless, the study of culture-specific dimensions of career behavior has (a) added to the number of within-group studies, examining variance among members of a single R/EM group on career constructs; (b) increased the recognition and study of cultural contexts, such as sociopolitical and institutional factors, shaping career choice; and (c) increased attention given to person-environment transactions regarding individuals' experience of their cultural contexts and the consequential perceptions of themselves and their environments as a function of these experiences.

Another outgrowth of the incorporation of culture-specific variables in career research has been the concurrent diversity in instrumentation measuring these variables. Measures such as the Asian American Career Development Questionnaire (Tang, Fouad, & Smith, 1999), Career Locus of Control (Luzzo, Funk, & Strang, 1996), and Workplace Racial Treatment Scale (Holder, 1994) are examples of both culture-specific and sociocultural contextual variables.

The third trend observed in the research was the informing and conducting of vocational research from multidisciplinary perspectives. Nearly one third of publications on the career behavior of R/EMs appeared in noncounseling or psychology-related periodicals or books. The broad vocational research from different social sciences, including sociology and education, may expand how and what we look at in career development. That is, multidisciplinary perspectives may better inform the various, myriad components and expressions of career behavior. This trend may extend vocational psychology research beyond the traditional study of career behavior up to initial choice, expand the populations studied from typical college students, and increase the methods and analytic procedures used to study various vocational processes. The need for increased diversity in methods and analytic procedures applied to the study of career is supported by our findings of studies dominated by quantitative designs with multivariate and analysis of variance statistical procedures.

PROSPECTIVE DIRECTIONS FOR FUTURE RESEARCH

The increase in career-related research with R/EMs has yielded a two-fold result. First, the research has offered exciting prospects for more in-depth conceptualization and theorizing of R/EMs' career behavior. In particular, the growing study of influences from contextual variables on African Americans, Asian Americans and Pacific Islanders, Latino/as, and Native Americans has greatly contributed to the extant understanding of career behavior for these groups. These advances have been supported by incorporation of both cultural validity and cultural specificity consider-ations. Second, vocational psychology is being prompted to venture further into the subjective meaning of work across culturally diverse groups. This charge can be met both by addressing culture-specific variables as well as methodological diversity. The call for diversity of measures, methods, and methodologies is underscored by Fouad (1999), who noted that in an annual review of career research over a 3-year period the typical study applied a cor-relation analysis between two variables that often explained between only 10% to 15% of the variance.

The discipline of vocational psychology, then, has the formidable task of conducting research that is culturally valid and more accurately reflec-tive of the racial/ethnic diversity that exists both in our society and in the labor force. Yet it is not enough to examine the cultural validity of cur-rent paradigms and move toward more culturally specific models of ca-reer behavior. Transformation from monocultural paradigms that excluded R/EMs from study without development of new, informed, multicultural paradigms leaves the field ripe for reentrenchment into old ways of know-ing and doing. To that end, we pose the following suggestions for directions in future conceptual and empirical work on R/EMs' career behavior:

- *Development of culturally valid theories and models of career develop-ment for R/EMs.* Much of the vocational quantitative research with R/EMs was not driven by theory. The significant number of atheoretical studies (32%) may speak to the lack of culturally relevant models and theories in vocational psychology needed to inform our understanding of the career be-havior of R/EMs. Such models may better articulate how the psychological, social, and cultural contexts and consequences of one's R/EM status can im-pact vocational processes. For example, a cultural systems framework may advance understanding of the influences that various social systems have on career choice and be more relevant for R/EMs who share a collectivist worldview. As Carter and Cook (1992) noted, "Work is a functional aspect of life in that individuals contribute their skills and labor to their cultural soci-eties and the maintenance of their families. Consequently, careers may rep-resent a 'collective' identity rather than an 'individual' identity" (p. 199).
- *More within-group research studies (Byars & Hackett, 1998; Leong & Brown, 1995).* Attention to within-group variance among R/EM groups can further help to explicate cultural differences on career behavior. We do not advocate for within-group designs as alternatives to between-group studies;

clearly, both are necessary to advance vocational psychology's understanding of the career development of R/EMs (Leong & Brown, 1995). Yet, as discussed in the preceding analysis of the treatment of Asian Americans in the literature, race-comparative frameworks can promote a focus on studying "the other." However, even though race-comparative studies, when conducted properly, are not to be discounted for their value, they should not be the preferred method of choice, as they currently appear to be (Graham, 1992), to the exclusion of intragroup studies of R/EMs. We refer the reader to Quintana et al. (Chapter 30, this volume) for related discussion on this topic.

- *Advance multidisciplinary research efforts.* Vocational research may be well served by conducting collaborative studies informed by several disciplines, such as sociology and economics, as well as psychology. This approach has two foreseeable benefits. First, it may promote the investigation of more complex research questions and the inclusion of more dynamic variables heretofore underexplored in vocational psychology (e.g., effects of global economy, work supply and demand) and inspire more creative ways of collecting and assessing data/variables. Second, this multidisciplinary work may facilitate more strategic, sound, and systematic research programs that use multimethod approaches to investigate variance in larger demographic variables beyond race/ethnicity and gender, including SES and geographic location. Likewise, Leong and Brown (1995) encouraged the formation of large, national research teams that would increase sample sizes of studies in addition to increased examination of the effects of SES and geographic location on career development.

- *Increase research on diverse populations.* D. W. Sue, Parham, and Santiago (1998) observed that the characteristics of the workforce have dramatically changed as a function of what the authors call the "changing complexion of the workforce," the "feminization of the workforce," and the "graying of the workforce." In addition to racial and ethnic diversity, vocational research lacks diversity in studying the career behavior of adults, children, those entering the workforce directly from high school, and the working poor, as well as others who have significant restrictions on their freedom to choose a career (e.g., people with mental and cognitive challenges). Vocational theories and research must expand to include these demographic challenges. Without this attention to vocational behavior of a wider range of people, vocational psychology will inadvertently promote culturally biased paradigms that include the work of some groups as valuable and dignified and exclude the work of others as invaluable and undesirable.

- *Investigate multiple social identities.* Vocational research must move beyond acknowledgment of the complexity of multiple identities and roles to the study of the simultaneous and interrelated effects of these variables with various life domains—gender, race/ethnicity, class, and so forth—with work. These various identities are partially distinct social hierarchies that uniquely position individuals to the distribution of power, privilege, and prestige (Ransford & Miller, 1983). Traditional treatment of cultural variables like race/ethnicity and gender as separate, independent factors affecting the psychosocial status of R/EMs oversimplifies the relationships among these variables (King, 1988). Instead, these variables are interdependent, dynamic, and multiplicative, with no one variable superseding the other. Zinn and Dill (1994) suggested that the experience of any of the social constructions of race, gender, and class is dependent on the intersection of these variables with all forms of discrimination and inequality. Integrative models of cultural variables and vocational behavior may clarify how these factors potentially moderate relationships among career constructs (e.g., career decision making). Relatedly, Hackett and Byars (1996) encouraged career researchers and practitioners to attend to the role of individuals' efficacy for coping with the psychosocial effects of being ethnically and culturally different. The importance of this type of work is illustrated in a study done by Holder and Vaux (1998) examining African American professionals' job satisfaction in a predominantly White/European American environment. The authors found that job satisfaction was related to African Americans' management of racial stressors in the workplace.

- *Establishment of longitudinal career-related studies.* Although vocational researchers have long called for longitudinal research on careers (Byars & Hackett, 1998; Fouad, 1999; Leong & Brown, 1995; Smith, 1983), few studies focusing on the career behavior of R/EMs have been longitudinal (e.g., Dawkins, 1989). Research is lacking that identifies how specific mechanisms operate over time that may facilitate or inhibit the career development of African Americans. Such mechanisms would include coping abilities, types of role models available, the differential effects and experience of racism, sexism and classism, achievement motivation, goal-oriented behavior, and persistence. As Smith (1983) points out, this line of research should also ascertain if there are new variables in the striving behavior of R/EMs.

- *Incorporate the concept of praxis into research.* In examining culturally valid research and practice with African Americans, Parham, White, and Ajamu (1999) suggested that praxis is the "attempt to insure that maximum congruence is achieved between thought and practice" (p.119). The value of praxis is in promoting the development of culturally centered theories, methods, and paradigms that give meaning to the cultural experiences of R/EMs. Praxis applied to the study of career-related processes for R/EMs may further the examination of culturally relevant research with these populations in the following ways. First, praxis encourages the examination of topics that is informed by the communities studied. Participation of R/EM communities in the development of research projects can promote more culturally relevant work by identifying the vocational concerns that are salient in such communities. Researchers may assess the critical issues that are priorities in a community and allow the focus of a study to emerge from this assessment. This may also serve to empower R/EM groups to identify and utilize their own cultural and social institutions that can support the career development of members who belong to their racial or ethnic community (e.g., churches and civic or fraternal organizations). Second, praxis underscores the need to include samples that are reflective of R/EM groups beyond race/ethnic, gender, and class demographics. Last, praxis may advance methodologies effective in capturing the cultural phenomena under study. Incorporation of praxis in vocational research may help the field more accurately reflect the R/EM groups studied and increase the practical applicability of such research to these groups.

- *Expanded use of qualitative approaches to the study of vocational behavior.* Suzuki, Meller, and Ponterotto (1996) suggested that the validity and acceptance of nonlinear cultural perspectives and subjective evidence are increasing as the visibility of non-Western cultural contexts grows. Qualitative research designs may add to the understanding of the specific worldviews of R/EMs and encourage more dynamic research questions (e.g., Richie et al., 1997). For example, Boyd-Franklin (1991) found that African American women in group therapy expressed guilt about achievement, especially those who had attained a high level of education or professional status. A qualitative study may investigate the following questions: "How are feelings of guilt about vocational success experienced among African American women?" "What are the consequences of these guilty feelings on vocational achievement motivation or strivings?"

CONCLUSION

The literature is replete with statistics indicating the burgeoning numbers of R/EMs in the U.S. population in general and the labor market in particular (e.g., D. W. Sue et al., 1998). In addition to responding to this challenge to be more inclusive and culturally relevant in vocational research, we believe that the field of vocational psychology is also presented with another challenging opportunity relative to career research with R/EMs. Vocational psychology evolved out of a response to societal needs with an emphasis on promoting social justice and promoting individuals' access to resources and opportunities for meaningful work (e.g., Frank Parsons). The discipline can continue this rich tradition by furthering the study of R/EMs' career behavior and conducting more culturally inclusive research. Certainly, the viability, potential, and future of vocational psychology is intricately tied to the discipline's striving toward a vocational psychology of not only R/EMs but of all people.

REFERENCES

Ancis, J. R., & Phillips, S. D. (1996). Academic gender bias and women's behavioral agency and self-efficacy. *Journal of Counseling and Development, 75*, 131-138.

Bandura, A. (1986). *Social foundations of thought and action: A social cognitive theory.* Englewood Cliffs, NJ: Prentice Hall.

Bandura, A. (1997). *Self-efficacy: The exercise of control.* New York: Freeman.

Boyd-Franklin, N. (1991). Recurrent themes in the treatment of African American women in group psychotherapy. *Women and Therapy, 11*, 25-40.

Brown, M. T. (1995). The career development of African Americans: Theoretical and empirical issues. In F. T. L. Leong (Ed.), *Career development and vocational behavior of racial and ethnic minorities* (pp. 7-36). Mahwah, NJ: Lawrence Erlbaum.

Bureau of Indian Affairs. (1993). *Federally recognized tribes.* Washington, DC: U.S. Department of Interior, Bureau of Indian Affairs.

Byars, A. M., & Hackett, G. (1998). Applications of social cognitive theory to the career development of women of color. *Applied and Preventive Psychology, 7*, 255-267.

Carter, R. T., & Cook, D. A. (1992). A culturally-relevant perspective for understanding the career paths of visible racial ethnic group people. In H. D. Lea & Z. B. Leibowitz (Eds.), *Adult career development: Concepts, issues, and practices* (2nd ed., pp. 192-217). Alexandria, VA: National Career Development Association.

Crites, J. O. (1975). Foreward. In J. S. Picou & R. E. Campbell (Eds.), *Career behavior of special groups: Theory, research, and practice* (pp. ix-x). Columbus, OH: Merrill.

Cross, W. E., Jr. (1971). Negro to Black conversion experience: Toward a psychology of Black liberation. *Black World, 20,* 13-27.

Daniels, J., D'Andrea, M., & Gaughen, K. J. S. (1998). Testing the validity and reliability of the Perceived Employability Scale (PES) among a culturally diverse population. *Journal of Employment Counseling, 35,* 114-124.

Dawkins, M. P. (1989). The persistence of plans for professional careers among Blacks in early adulthood. *Journal of Negro Education, 58,* 220-231.

Ensher, E. A., & Murphy, S. E. (1997). Effects of race, gender, perceived similarity and contact on mentor relationships. *Journal of Vocational Behavior, 50,* 460-481.

Evans, K. M., & Herr, E. L. (1994). The influence of racial identity and the perception of discrimination on the career aspirations of African American men and women. *Journal of Vocational Behavior, 44,* 173-184.

Fisher, T. A., & Padmawidjaja, I. (1999). Parental influences on career development perceived by African American and Mexican American college students. *Journal of Multicultural Counseling and Development, 27,* 136-152.

Fitzgerald, L. F., & Betz, N. E. (1994). Career development in cultural context: The role of gender, race, class, and sexual orientation. In M. L. Savikas & R. W. Lent (Eds.), *Convergence in career development theories: Implications for science and practice* (pp. 103-117). Palo Alto, CA: Consulting Psychologists Press.

Fitzgerald, L. F., Fassinger, R. E., & Betz, N. E. (1995). Theoretical advances in the study of women's career development. In W. B. Walsh & S. H. Osipow (Eds.), *Handbook of vocational psychology: Theory, research and practice* (2nd ed., pp. 67-109). Mahwah, NJ: Lawrence Erlbaum.

Fouad, N. A. (1999, August). Methodological diversity in vocational psychology. In G. Hackett & J. Lichtenberg (Chairs), *Issues related to methodological diversity in counseling psychology research.* Symposium conducted at the annual meeting of the American Psychological Association, Boston.

Fouad, N. A., & Bingham, R. P. (1995). Career counseling with racial and ethnic minorities. In W. B. Walsh & S. H. Osipow (Eds.), *Handbook of vocational psychology: Theory, research, and practice* (2nd ed., pp. 331-365). Mahwah, NJ: Lawrence Erlbaum.

Gloria, A. M., & Hird, J. S. (1999). Influences of ethnic and nonethnic variables on the career decision-making self-efficacy of college students. *Career Development Quarterly, 48,* 157-174.

Gottfredson, L. S. (1981). Circumscription and compromise: A developmental theory of occupational aspirations [Monograph]. *Journal of Counseling Psychology, 28,* 545-579.

Graham, S. (1992). Most of the subjects were White and middle class: Trends in published research on African-Americans in selected APA journals, 1970–1989. *American Psychologist, 47,* 629-639.

Hackett, G., & Byars, A. M. (1996). Social cognitive theory and the career development of African American women. *Career Development Quarterly, 44,* 322-340.

Hackett, G., & Lent, R. W. (1992). Theoretical advances in career psychology. In S. D. Brown & R. W. Lent (Eds.), *Handbook of counseling psychology* (2nd ed., pp. 419-451). New York: John Wiley.

Heppner, P. P., Kivlighan, D. M., & Wampold, B. E. (1999). *Research design in counseling* (2nd ed.). Belmont, CA: Wadsworth.

Holder, J. C. (1994). *Workplace racial treatment scale.* Unpublished measure, Southern Illinois University.

Holder, J. C., & Vaux, A. (1998). African American professionals: Coping with occupational stress in predominantly White work environments. *Journal of Vocational Behavior, 53,* 315-333.

Holland, J. L. (1980). *My vocational situation.* Palo Alto, CA: Consulting Psychologists Press.

Holland, J. L. (1985a). *Making vocational choices: A theory of vocational personalities and work environment* (2nd ed.). Englewood Cliffs, NJ: Prentice Hall.

Holland, J. L. (1985b). *Self-directed search.* Odessa, FL: Psychological Assessment Resources, Inc.

Jackson, G. C., & Healy, C. C. (1996). Career development profiles and interventions for underrepresented college students. *Career Development Quarterly, 44*, 258-269.

Jackson, C. C., & Neville, H. A. (1998). Influence of racial identity attitudes on African American college students' vocational identity and hope. *Journal of Vocational Behavior, 53*, 97-113.

Johnson, M. J., Swartz, J. L., & Martin, W. E., Jr. (1995). Applications of psychological theories for career development with Native Americans. In F. T. L. Leong (Ed.), *Career development and vocational behavior of racial and ethnic minorities* (pp. 103-136). Mahwah, NJ: Lawrence Erlbaum.

King, D. K. (1988). Multiple jeopardy, multiple consciousness: The context of a Black feminist ideology. *Signs: Journal of Women in Culture and Society, 14*, 42-72.

Koegel, H. M., Donin, I., Ponterotto, J. G., & Spitz, S. (1995). Multicultural career development: A methodological critique of 8 years of research in three leading career journals. *Journal of Employment Counseling, 32*, 50-63.

Lent, R. W., Brown, S. D., & Hackett, G. (1994). Toward a unified social cognitive theory of career/academic interest, choice, and performance [Monograph]. *Journal of Vocational Behavior, 45*, 79-122.

Leong, F. T. L. (1986). Counseling and psychotherapy with Asian Americans: Review of the literature. *Journal of Counseling Psychology, 33*, 196-206.

Leong, F. T. L. (Ed.). (1995). *Career development and vocational behavior of racial and ethnic minorities.* Mahwah, NJ: Lawrence Erlbaum.

Leong, F. T. L., & Brown, M. T. (1995). Theoretical issues in cross-cultural career development: Cultural validity and cultural specificity. In W. B. Walsh & S. H. Osipow (Eds.), *Handbook of vocational psychology: Theory, research, and practice* (2nd ed., pp. 391-426). Mahwah, NJ: Lawrence Erlbaum.

Leong, F. T. L., & Chou, E. L. (1994). The role of ethnic identity and acculturation in the vocational behavior of Asian Americans: An integrative review. *Journal of Vocational Behavior, 44*, 155-172.

Leong, F. T. L., & Serafica, F. C. (1995). Career development of Asian Americans: A research area in need of a good theory. In F. T. L. Leong (Ed.), *Career development and vocational behavior of racial and ethnic minorities* (pp. 67-102). Mahwah, NJ: Lawrence Erlbaum.

Leung, S. A. (1995). Career development and counseling: A multicultural perspective. In J. Ponterotto, M. Casas, L. Suzuki, & C. Alexander (Eds.), *Handbook of multicultural counseling* (pp. 549-566). Thousand Oaks, CA: Sage.

Lew, A. S., Allen, R., Papouchis, N., & Ritzler, B. (1998). Achievement orientation and fear of success in Asian American college students. *Journal of Clinical Psychology, 54*, 97-108.

Liu, R. W. (1998). Educational and career expectations of Chinese-American college students. *Journal of College Student Development, 39*, 577-588.

Lucero-Miller, D., & Newman, J. L. (1999). Predicting acculturation using career, family, and demographic variables in a sample of Mexican American students. *Journal of Multicultural Counseling and Development, 27*, 75-93.

Luzzo, D. A., Funk, D. P., & Strang, J. (1996). Attributional retraining increases career decision-making self-efficacy. *Career Development Quarterly, 44*, 378-386.

Luzzo, D. A., McWhirter, E. H., & Hutcheson, K. G. (1997). Evaluating career decision-making factors associated with employment among first-year college students. *Journal of College Student Development, 38*, 166-172.

McCowan, C. J., & Alston, R. J. (1998). Racial identity, African self-consciousness, and career decision making in African American college women. *Journal of Multicultural Counseling and Development, 26*, 28-38.

McWhirter, E. H., Larson, L. M., & Daniels, J. A. (1996). Predictors of educational aspirations among adolescent and gifted students of color. *Journal of Career Development, 23*, 91-109.

Miranda, A. O., & Umhoefer, D. L. (1998). Acculturation, language use, and demographic variables as predictors of the career self-efficacy of Latino career counseling clients. *Journal of Multicultural Counseling and Development, 26*, 39-51.

Mitchell, L. K., & Krumboltz, J. D. (1990). Social learning approach in career decision making: Krumboltz's theory. In D. Brown & L. Brooks (Eds.), *Career choice and development: Applying contemporary theories in practice* (2nd ed., pp. 145-196). San Francisco: Jossey-Bass.

Naidoo, A. V., Bowman, S. L., & Gerstein, L. H. (1998). Demographics, causality, work salience, and the career maturity of African American students: A causal model. *Journal of Vocational Behavior, 53*, 15-27.

Osipow, S. H., & Littlejohn, E. M. (1995). Toward a multicultural theory of career development: Prospects and dilemmas. In F. T. L. Leong (Ed.), *Career development and vocational behavior of racial and ethnic minorities* (pp. 251-262). Mahwah, NJ: Lawrence Erlbaum.

Oyserman, D., & Sakamoto, I. (1997). Being Asian American: Identity, cultural constructs, and stereotype perception. *Journal of Applied Behavioral Science, 33*, 435-453.

Parham, T. A., & Austin, N. L. (1994). Career development and African Americans: A contextual reappraisal using the Nigrescence construct. *Journal of Vocational Behavior, 44*, 139-154.

Parham, T. A., & Helms, J. (1985). Relation of racial identity attitudes to self-actualization and affective states of Black students. *Journal of Counseling Psychology, 32*, 431-440.

Parham, T. A., White, J. L., & Ajamu, A. (1999). *The psychology of Blacks: An African centered perspective* (3rd ed.). Upper Saddle River, NJ: Prentice Hall.

Park, S. E., & Harrison, A. A. (1995). Career-related interests and values, perceived control, and acculturation of Asian-American and Caucasian-American college students. *Journal of Applied Social Psychology, 25*, 1184-1203.

Ransford, H. E., & Miller, J. (1983). Race, sex, and feminist outlooks. *American Sociological Review, 48*, 46-59.

Richie, B. S., Fassinger, R. E., Linn, S. G., Johnson, J., Prosser, J., & Robinson, S. (1997). Persistence, connection, and passion: A qualitative study of career development of highly achieving African American-Black and White women. *Journal of Counseling Psychology, 44*, 133-148.

Ryan, J. M., Tracey, T. J., & Rounds J. (1996). Generalizability of Holland's structure of vocational interests across ethnicity, gender, and socioeconomic status. *Journal of Counseling Psychology, 43*, 330-337.

Smith, E. J. (1983). Issues in racial minorities' career behavior. In W. B. Walsh & S. A. Osipow (Eds.), *Handbook of vocational psychology* (Vol. 1, pp. 161-222). Hillsdale, NJ: Lawrence Erlbaum.

Spence, J. T., & Helmreich, R. (1972). The Attitudes Toward Women Scale: An objective instrument to measure attitudes toward the rights and roles of women in contemporary society. *Journal Supplement: Abstract Service Catalog of Selected Documents in Psychology, 2*, 66.

Strong, W. C. (1998, April). *Low expectations by teachers within an academic context.* Paper presented at the annual meeting of the American Educational Research Association, San Diego, CA.

Sue, D. W., Parham, T. A., & Santiago, G. B. (1998). The changing face of work in the United States: Implications for individual, institutional, and societal survival. *Cultural Diversity and Ethnic Minority Psychology, 4*, 153-164.

Sue, S. (1999). Science, ethnicity, and bias: Where have we gone wrong? *American Psychologist, 54*, 1070-1077.

Suinn, R. M., Rickard-Figueroa, K., Lew, S., & Vigil, P. (1987). The Suinn-Lew Asian Self-Identity Acculturation Scale: An initial report. *Educational and Psychological Measurement, 47*, 401-407.

Super, D. E. (1990). A life-span, life-space approach to career development. In D. Brown & L. Brooks (Eds.), *Career choice and development: Applying contemporary theories in practice* (2nd ed., pp. 197-261). San Francisco: Jossey-Bass.

Suzuki, L., Meller, P., & Ponterotto, J. (Eds.). (1996). *Handbook of multicultural assessment.* San Francisco: Jossey-Bass.

Tang, J. (1997). The model minority thesis revisited: (Counter) evidence from the science and engineering fields. *Journal of Applied Behavioral Science, 33*, 291-315.

Tang, M., Fouad, N. A., & Smith, P. L. (1999). Asian Americans' career choices: A path model to examine factors influencing their career choices. *Journal of Vocational Behavior, 54,* 142-157.

Taylor, K. T., & Betz, N. E. (1983). Applications of self-efficacy theory to the understanding and treatment of career indecision. *Journal of Vocational Behavior, 23,* 63-81.

Vacha, H. T., Walsh, B. D., Kapes, J. T., Dresden, J. H., Thomson, W. A., Ochoa-Shargey, B., & Camacho, Z. (1994). Gender differences on the values scale for ethnic minority students. *Journal of Career Assessment, 2,* 408-421.

Watts, R. J., & Carter, R. J. (1991). Psychological aspects of racism in organizations. *Group and Organization Studies, 16,* 328-344.

Weathers, P. L., Thompson, C. E., Robert, S., & Rodriguez, J., Jr. (1994). Black college women's career values: A preliminary investigation. *Journal of Multicultural Counseling and Development, 22,* 96-105.

Wong, P., Lai, C. F., Nagasawa, R., & Lin, T. (1998). Asian-Americans as model minority: Self-perceptions and perceptions by other racial groups. *Sociological Perspectives, 41,* 95-118.

Wood, P. B., & Clay, W. C. (1996). Perceived structural barriers and academic performance among American Indian high school students. *Youth & Society, 28,* 40-61.

Zinn, M. B., & Dill, B. T. (Eds.). (1994). *Women of color in U.S. society.* Philadelphia: Temple University Press.

Correspondence regarding this chapter may be sent to Angela M. Byars, Department of Counseling Psychology, University of Wisconsin–Madison, 304 Education Building, 1000 Bascom Mall, Madison, WI 53706-1398 (e-mail address: abyars@mail.soemadison.wisc.edu).

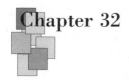

Chapter 32

THE FAMILY GENOGRAM
AS A TOOL IN MULTICULTURAL
CAREER COUNSELING

LINA ADACHI SUEYOSHI
LOURDES RIVERA
JOSEPH G. PONTEROTTO

RECENTLY, PONTEROTTO, Rivera, and Adachi Sueyoshi (2000) introduced the Career-in-Culture Interview, a 23-item semi-structured interview protocol for use in multicultural career counseling. The interview protocol is rooted in recent developments in the theories of social cognitive career development (Lent, Brown, & Hackett, 1994) and multicultural counseling and therapy (Sue, Ivey, & Pedersen, 1996). An important component of the Career-in-Culture Interview is the construction of a career-focused family genogram. Ponterotto et al. (2000) did not elaborate on, nor demonstrate the use of, the family genogram as part of their interview presentation. The purpose of this chapter is to expand on that work by describing and illustrating how the use of a genogram may be a culturally appropriate and useful technique in the career counseling process.

THE FAMILY GENOGRAM:
RATIONALE AND DESCRIPTION

Traditional personal and career counseling, grounded in Western, Euro-American values and culture, may be incompatible with the needs and values of some culturally diverse clients. In particular, the emphasis on the

AUTHORS' NOTE: We thank Professor Spencer G. Niles of Pennsylvania State University for his guidance and encouragement in expanding our work on the family genogram.

655

individual, verbal and emotional expressiveness, ambiguous or unstructured approach to problem-solving, long-term goals and solutions, and monolingual orientation (Leong, 1995; Sue & Sue, 1999) may prove conflictual to the counseling expectations of some culturally diverse clients. Moreover, a lack of attention to economic and social barriers, acculturation and racial/minority identity development, as well as insufficient norms for culturally diverse populations on personal and career assessments (Betz & Fitzgerald, 1995; Leung, 1995) may also be problematic. We maintain that a culturally sensitive incorporation of a family genogram into intake counseling sessions may serve as a valuable tool in career counseling.

The genogram, or multigenerational graphic representation of a client's family of origin (Okiishi, 1987), has been used in various modalities, including family therapy (McGoldrick & Gerson, 1985; McGoldrick, Gerson, & Shellenberger, 1999), career counseling (Heppner, O'Brien, Hinkelman, & Humphrey, 1994; Moon, Coleman, McCollum & Nelson, 1993; Okiishi, 1987; Splete & Freeman-George, 1985), and family-based multicultural career counseling (Borodovsky & Ponterotto, 1994). The wide application of its usage suggests that it is versatile and can be modified for use in diverse settings with different clients.

We believe the family genogram may be particularly useful and effective in a career counseling interview with culturally different clients for several reasons. First, it depicts parental and familial influences and therefore does not assume an individualistic orientation to career decisions and lifestyles. Not only does it examine familial influences on the client as perceived by the client her/himself, but it can also elicit family involvement if the family is invited to help complete the genogram. Second, it is visual and relies less on verbal communication and expressiveness. In an initial intake interview, this may prove helpful in gauging the client's language ability and comfort level with verbalization, self-expression, and counseling. Third, it presents information in an organized and structured way, and gives the client something "concrete" to take back with him/her (see discussion in Sue & Zane, 1987, on "gift giving" in multicultural counseling).

Moreover, a brief explanation of the purpose of the genogram, as well as the career counseling process, may be beneficial for culturally different clients who are uncomfortable and unfamiliar with the ambiguous and unstructured nature of some Western counseling approaches. For cultures that place a value on hierarchical relationships, an active and directive counselor may be more appropriate and consistent with cultural norms and values (Sue & Sue, 1999). Finally, genograms can potentially tap into acculturation and racial/minority identity development, two critical components of personal development (Sue et al., 1998). In describing family influences, the client can be encouraged to discuss cultural influences and differences within the family. Understandably, different generations may display different degrees of acculturation and cultural identification.

Okiishi (1987) proposed three steps in the construction of a genogram in the career counseling process: (1) construction of a genogram, (2) identification of occupations, and (3) exploration with the client (e.g., role models, reinforcements, and possible barriers, both posed by family members or perceived by client). He also suggests confronting possible omissions, inconsistencies, and disregarded alternatives as an additional, but not necessary, step. Although these three (or four) steps outline the basic stages in the construction of a genogram in career counseling, it can also be modified for use in a multicultural career counseling context. Questions that assess level of acculturation, language preference and ability, and racial/ethnic identity development of both the client and other family members may be particularly helpful (see Ponterotto et al., 2000). An exploration of barriers not only external but also internal and familial may also raise a client's concerns regarding experiences with racism, discrimination, and oppression.

GENOGRAM ILLUSTRATION

To help illustrate the preparation of the family genograms, we present samples in Figures 32.1, 32.2, 32.3, and 32.4. The first two genograms, those of J. A. and H. A., involve the participants describing their genograms in a narrative fashion. Both of these participants were advanced doctoral students (nonclients) in psychology who were familiar with the counseling process and genogram work. These students were able easily to describe their genograms in a flowing narrative without counselor prompts.

The third and fourth genogram illustrations, those of Mike and Dave, are presented in counselor-client dialogue fashion. These clients (actual cases from a community college counseling center) were less familiar with Western counseling approaches and had never worked with genograms prior to the session. In these cases, we demonstrate how the counselor can guide the client in the use of the genogram. These genograms also include the counselor's notes to herself, which are presented in parenthetical italics throughout the illustrations.

J. A.'s Genogram

J.A. is a 25-year-old female of Japanese American heritage whose genogram is shown in Figure 32.1.

Constructing my family genogram has been helpful in seeing the various careers and educational background of my relatives and extended family, and how this may have impacted my decision to pursue a doctoral degree in counseling psychology. As depicted in the genogram, male family members' careers were rather diverse and included such occupations as stone company owner, designer/art director, trader, bicycle shop owner,

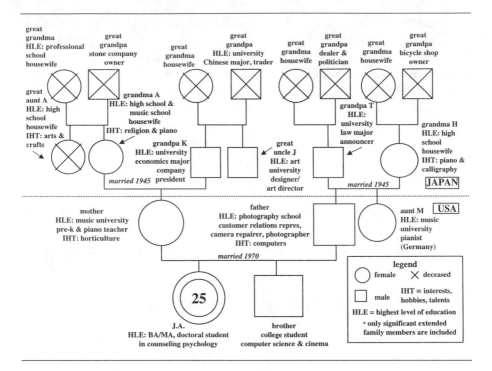

Figure 32.1. J. A.'s Career Family Genogram

and company president. With respect to the women in the family, all were traditional "housewives" (household chores being primary duty) until my parents' generation (e.g., my mother is an assistant teacher and my aunt is a professional pianist). However, many of these housewives also had other interests/hobbies that they were actively engaged in and consumed a significant amount of their time. This is particularly true for my grandparents' generation. For example, Grandma H is a piano teacher and an accomplished calligrapher, who has won several awards, and Grandma A is a devoted Buddhist whose life revolves around religious activities and prayers. Although it is not clear whether the women in my great grandparents' generation had any particular hobbies/interests, I have been told that their jobs always involved more than "just housework" and included significant duties, such as taking care of all the finances and making important household decisions. I know that this was true for the wives of the stone company owner and bicycle shop owner. All this seems to indicate that both the men and women in my extended family had equally important and exciting lives and jobs. But for the women who had other interests/hobbies on the side, their lives may have been slightly more rich and varied. I also think it was these women who instilled in me the importance of both finding and cultivating something meaningful in one's life.

    The educational background of my relatives ranges from high school to university to professional/vocational school, and reveals a rather privileged and educated group. Both my grandmothers and great aunt received, what was considered at the time, the highest level of education for women. This was high school education and special instruction in traditional Japanese arts (e.g., calligraphy, flower arrangement, and embroidery) and/or piano. Both grandfathers and a great-grandfather graduated from universities with majors in economics, law, and Chinese. On the creative side, there is a great uncle who has his degree from an art university, an aunt and mother who went to music universities, and a father who received his associate's degree from photography school. In this way, education has been something that has been valued and sought after since my grandparents generation, and maybe earlier. This is how I feel I came to place an importance on education and have been able to receive the necessary support from my family to be in graduate school. In fact, my maternal grandparents are probably my biggest fans, always rooting me on and never letting me lose sight of my goal.

It is interesting to note that although it was common for occupations to be handed down to the next generation, especially in Asian culture, this did not happen in my extended family. The reasons for this may be that there were no "traditional family careers" my grandparents (and perhaps, my great-grandparents) were obligated to carry out (i.e., careers changed with every generation), and/or my grandparents had many siblings and were not the oldest. Because of this, my grandparents may have, in fact, been encouraged to pursue careers/interests that were different from my great-grandparents. And this is exactly what my grandparents did. My parents took this a step further and left their native country of Japan to come to the United States. They did this to pursue their own interests rather than those of their parents. In this way, they truly "role modeled" the importance of following one's dreams and convictions. They also continue to stand by us, constantly encouraging and supporting the career and educational interests of my brother and me.

Among my family, I am probably the most "bicultural" because I have been able to, and still continue to, spend every year in both cultures. As a child, I spent nine months of the year with my parents and brother in the United States, and the remaining three months with my grandparents and relatives in Japan. Moreover, it is my conscious effort to be in touch with both cultures, when I can physically be in only one at a time, that also keeps me bicultural. My parents, who migrated less frequently but still retain all the traditional Japanese customs of their time and prefer the Japanese language, can be considered "traditional Japanese," and my brother, at least for the time being, prefers to be identified as "more American." By completing a genogram, I feel I have gained a better understanding and appreciation for the role of family and culture in one's career development.

H. A.'s Genogram

The genogram presented in Figure 32.2 was prepared by H. A., a 36-year-old female of Puerto Rican American descent. Once again, in the participant's own words, we present her processing of the genogram exercise.

My genogram focuses on family members who stood out in my mind as being particularly important to me as a child and who continued to play a significant role in my life as I made educational and career decisions. Fur-

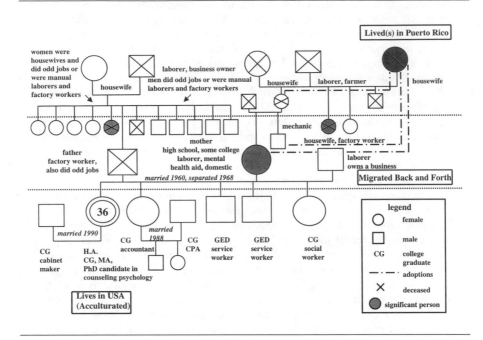

Figure 32.2. H. A.'s Career Family Genogram

thermore, my genogram is divided into three categories to reflect family members who never left Puerto Rico (PR), those who migrated back and forth between PR and the mainland USA, and those who have made their lives on mainland USA and will most likely return to PR only to visit. This categorization also reflects the level of acculturation that has taken place, with those living in the mainland USA being the most acculturated.

As can be seem from my genogram, there are no traditional occupations that were held by members of my family. My family came from *el campo* (countryside), and it was not until my mother's generation that formal education was available to them. The men were mostly laborers and the women housewives. Most of my mother's and father's generation would migrate back and forth between PR and the mainland for employment opportunities, which tended to be in factories. However, it was the roles they played within the family and the community that influenced my educational and career goals. Although there were some men in my family who had played a significant role in my life, it was the roles that the women played that were the most significant and had a prominent influence in my life. Perhaps the reason why they were so compelling and influential was that despite the traditional values, roles, and expectations that these women adhered to, they were and are very strong and determined women who managed to take on leadership roles and responsibilities outside their traditional roles. These women did not have "careers" or, in some cases, not even "jobs" they could be identified with, yet they nonetheless served as strong role models and influences in my professional development.

First among these women is my maternal (step) great-grandmother, a strong, feisty woman who was seen by many in her hometown as the pillar of the community. I remember visiting her during summer vacation and sitting with her on the porch as people passed by her home and asked for her blessing as they went by. I am told that in some way or another all these people were related to us. However, "related" could mean that she was godmother to a child in the family, helped raise some of them for short periods of time while the parents worked on the mainland, or, as in my case, had adopted and raised my grandmother, and when she died, had adopted my mother and her brother. I always respected her ability to give and share and care for so many people.

The other significant women in my life were two aunts, one from each side of the family, and my mother. For me, these three women represent a dichotomy, for although they adhered to the traditional roles expected of them within the family they also managed to work outside these roles, assuming less traditional responsibilities yet never taking credit for them as being on a par with male roles. For example, my aunt who worked for a while as a taxicab driver but saw this as a necessity and not as an ability to do the same type of work as a man. Or the aunt, who, speaking no English, would come to New York City every summer, leaving her children at home with my grandmother, so that she could earn extra money working in a factory to provide for her children during the rest of the year. And finally my mother, who working different jobs managed to raise five children, being both mother and father to us.

Comments on the Cases of J. A. and H. A.

As noted earlier, the cases of J. A. and H. A. are somewhat unique in that both individuals are highly educated professionals working in the counseling profession and so needed little prompting or guidance in preparing or processing in narrative form their family genograms. Of particular interest to the two genograms are the following observations. Both J. A. and H. A., female professionals, had strong women role models in their extended families. Historically, within the families, women have held positions of leadership and importance while also maintaining "traditional" female roles as defined by the respective cultures. It was easy to see the impact of these "strong" women on both J. A. and H. A. Also, both participants are bicultural and bilingual. As can be seen from the genograms depicted in Figures 32.1 and 32.2, J. A. has strong connections to both Japan and the United States. Interestingly, H. A. partitions her genogram into three sections reflecting life in Puerto Rico, life in the United States, and life in the migratory status common to many Puerto Ricans who travel back and forth between the island and the mainland, given the proximity of the lands. Discussions of the genograms and immigration/migration histories helped the participants more fully understand varying acculturation levels within the families.

Each of the two cases is also unique in certain respects. J. A. talks about the family's long tradition of higher education, whereas this was not the case with H. A.'s family. Interestingly, both genograms led to discussions of sterotyping, with both cases breaking traditional career stereotyping to some degree. Contrary to Asian stereotypes, J. A. highlighted the freedom some children had in selecting their own career paths while H. A. highlighted the nontraditional roles of women given cultural expectations. As noted in the genogram narratives, both J. A. and H. A. found the activity quite insightful despite their already high level of personal insight as counseling professionals.

We now turn to two actual cases, those of "Mike" and "Dave") (fictitious names), where more counselor involvement and probing is used. For both of these cases the senior author of this chapter was the counselor.

Mike's Genogram

Mike is a 22-year-old Chinese American male student at an urban community college in New York. He has been seeing a Japanese American counselor at the school for academic advising. In a previous session, he revealed to the counselor that his goal at the current school was to obtain an associate's degree in engineering science and then go on for a bachelor's degree in the same field. The following dialogue is an edited transcription designed to highlight the relevant points that were raised in the session with Mike:

> Counselor: Last time we met, you told me you wanted to pursue a career in engineering. You seemed to be certain that this was what you wanted to do, but why don't we spend some time today exploring how this interest came about? A genogram is a graphic representation of one's family history. It can be used to track family careers, relationships, influences, and expectations. Would you like to try this?
>
> Mike: Okay.
>
> Couns.:   All right, let's start with you and your siblings. You are which one of how many siblings?
>
> Mike: Well, I'm the oldest, then there are two sisters after me, and then my youngest brother.
>
> Couns.:   In a genogram we use circles to represent female family members and squares to represent male family members. So I'll put you down as a square and follow that with two circles to represent your two sisters and finally your brother as a square, in that order from oldest to youngest. *(I depict him and his siblings at the bottom of the page on the same horizontal plane.)* Are they presently in school? *(Because his siblings are younger than him, I inquire if they are in school rather than focusing on careers.)*
>
> Mike: Yes, the sister immediately behind me (S) is a hospitality management major at another college, the sister after her (R) is in high school, and my brother (V) is in junior high school.
>
> Couns.:   Do your two youngest siblings have any particular interests or careers they're thinking about pursuing at this time? *(Importance of inquiring about career interests of siblings even if they are still young.)*
>
> Mike: No, not yet.
>
> Couns.:   Okay, now we'll move along to your mother and father. Let's start with your mother. She is which one of how many siblings? *(I depict his*

mother, father, and their siblings above Mike and his siblings on the same horizontal plane.)

Mike: She is the second oldest of seven siblings, five girls and two boys.

Couns.:   Okay, let's start with the oldest sibling. What does she do?

Mike: She owns a store in Panama.

Couns.:   Okay, a store owner who lives in Panama. I'll write this information down next to her circle. Who is next? What does that person do, and where does he/she live? *(Now I also inquire about where the sibling lives because I realize he/she may be living in places other than the United States or China.)*

Mike: Next is my mother and she lives here (U.S.). She sews clothes now, but also helped with my father's business at one time.

Couns.:   Okay, so she's a seamstress or a person who sews *(I help client come up with an appropriate job title.)* I'll also note that she helped your father's business. What is his business?

Mike: He owns a store and a restaurant in Mexico. He lives with us but travels back and forth between the two places. *(Panama, New York, Mexico . . . I am starting to see that his family is spread out geographically.)*

Couns.:   In Mexico? Okay, I'll note that here, but we'll come back to him later. Who's next after your mother?

Mike: Another sister in Panama who owns a store. Then there's a brother who owns a gas station and restaurant in Mexico. Then a sister who lives in Panama, but I'm not sure what she does. After her there is a sister, living in the United States and working in a factory, and finally, a brother in Mexico who owns a hotel and restaurant.

Couns.:   This is very interesting. With the exception of two aunts, a factory worker, and an aunt you are unsure about, your relatives on your mother's side are all in the business field. *(Importance of pointing out similarities and patterns.)*

Mike: Yes, they are. *(He proceeds to describe his father's occupation as well as his father's siblings' occupations, all who similarly own or help out in a family business.)*

Couns.:   How do you think this might have influenced your decision to pursue a career in engineering?

Mike: Actually, it didn't. I was not encouraged or discouraged from helping my father's business. I just wasn't interested in it. I was always attracted to machines, electronics, and computers ever since I was little. My parents always pressured us to do well in school, but they didn't say anything about our careers.

Couns.:   So, they are supportive of your career decision, whatever that may be?

Mike: Yes.

Couns.:   That's great. This goes against the Asian tradition about being the oldest son and having to carry on the family occupation or an occupation chosen by one's parents. Is that the same for your siblings? *(This question challenges and taps into parents' acculturation level—e.g., Westernized, traditional Asian.)*

Mike: Yes. They can do whatever they want, too.

Couns.:   So, your parents are very open and Americanized?

Mike: Yes.

Couns.:   Going back to the genogram, how about your grandparents? Where are they, and what do/did they do?

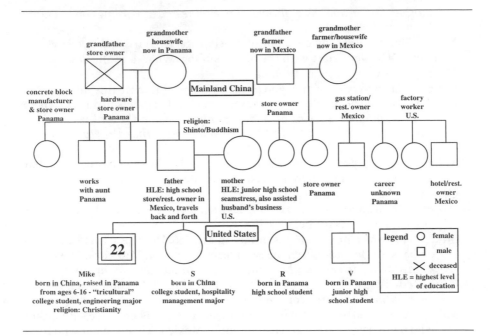

Figure 32.3. Mike's Career Family Genogram

Mike: My grandparents on my mother's side were farmers in China. Now they are living in Mexico with one of my relatives. My grandfather on my father's side owned a store, and my grandmother stayed at home. My grandfather passed away, but my grandmother lives in Panama with another relative.

Couns.:   So, looking over your genogram we see this pattern of family businesses, which actually started from your grandfather's generation. Can you go further back to your great-grandparents?

Mike: No, I don't know anything about them. *(Most people can go back three generations, but may have difficulty going beyond this [McGoldrick et al., 1999].)*

Couns.:   It also appears that most of your relatives are now either in Panama or Mexico. Your father and one aunt are the only two family members in the United States. How did this happen?

Mike: Well, my family was originally in Panama, too. That's where I grew up for 10 years of my life. Then we moved to the United States, and my father moved his business to Mexico. As for the rest of my relatives, they all decided to immigrate to either Panama or Mexico after my father and uncle were able to set up successful businesses there.

Couns.:   Any particular reason why Panama and Mexico?

Mike: They just thought it would be easier to set up businesses there.

Couns.:   So, everyone starting from your parent's generation are first-generation Chinese immigrants?

Mike: Yes, I guess you can say that. But I actually see myself as more Spanish than Chinese or American. Although I was born in China and am currently living in the States, I grew up in Panama, so I feel closer to that culture than either Chinese or American culture.

Couns.:   That's understandable. But it also sounds like you are tricultural. *(I help client acknowledge and embrace all three cultures.)*

Mike: Tricultural, like three cultures? That's an interesting way of calling it. I like that.

The counselor continued to explore Mike's tricultural Panamanian-Chinese-American identity with him, including visible (Asian Chinese) versus invisible (Panamanian) identities, or the way "others" define him versus the way he defines himself or "wishes" to define himself. The counselor also went on to address the relationship between identity and language (feeling more Panamanian when speaking Spanish), situational aspects of language and identity (English at school, Chinese at home, Spanish with friends), and the relationship between identity and religion (while Mike's parents are Buddhist and Shinto, Mike considers himself Christian, a religion that is consistent with the Hispanic culture). Also briefly discussed was Mike's family educational history. The highest level of education attained by Mike's parents' generation was high school, and it is Mike's generation (him, his siblings, and cousins) who will be the first generation to attend college.

Dave's Genogram

Dave is a 19-year-old Albanian American male student at the same urban community college as Mike. He was referred for academic advisement and personal counseling. Dave has met with the Japanese American counselor for several weeks and has expressed uncertainty over his college major and career goal. The following dialogue, again an edited transcription of the session, summarizes the major issues and concerns that were elicited in the construction of Dave's family career genogram (Figure 32.4):

Counselor: The last few times we have met, you raised concern over the lack of a career goal or interest. Would you like to try an exercise where we can explore your family's career history. Maybe your indecisiveness is related to this. It will also help me better understand how you view the world of work. The exercise requires constructing a family genogram. Do you know what this is?

Dave: No, what is it?

Couns.:   A genogram is similar to a family tree, where we map out your family, both nuclear and extended family, and their careers. *(Inform client exactly what construction of genogram entails.)*

Dave: Yeah, I know what a family tree is, but I've never even done one of those.

Couns.:   Would you like to try doing a genogram together?

Dave: All right.

Couns.:   Okay, let's start with your grandparents, or your most remote relatives that you can remember. Let's begin with your mother's side. Who were they, and what did they do?

Dave: I only know as far back as my grandparents. My grandmother was German, and she immigrated to the United States. My grandfather was American, but I don't remember what he did. I only know he was an alcoholic and died from lung cancer. I also know that he had a wife who wasn't my grandmother.

Couns.:   You mean your grandmother was a second wife or mistress? *(Importance of clarifying family relationships, keeping in mind that emotionally loaded material may elicit resistance and/or strong reactions. A certain level of trust and understanding, as was already established between Dave and the counselor, may also be necessary when asking such direct and personal questions.)*

Dave: Maybe. They make a strange couple.

Couns.:   Do you know what your grandmother did?

Dave: No, I don't know what she did. I only know she works in a grocery store now. Do people actually know this stuff? I've never given much thought to this before. I know practically nothing about my grandparents.

Couns.:   Well, there are going to be some things about your family you know and some things you don't. No one is going to know everything, but every bit of information that you can provide will be helpful. *(Normalizing the experience and letting the client know he is not expected to know everything about his family.)* Besides, you can always go back and change or fill in the gaps later. I'm going to be giving you a copy of this genogram later, so you won't need to remember or record any of this now. *(Genogram as a tangible "gift" from counselor to client [see Sue & Zane, 1987].)* How about your grandparents on your father's side?

Dave: They're both from Albania and immigrated to the United States. My grandfather worked in a restaurant, and he had a lot of money in Albania, but it was nothing here. My grandmother was pretty much a housewife. Including my dad, my grandparents had six children together. I wish I knew more about my Albanian culture, but I just don't. I don't even speak the language. And it'd be hard for me to find out more about my Albanian culture because my grandparents are now both dead. My only living grandparent is my grandmother on my mother's side. Well, there is my father and his brothers and sisters.

Couns.:   Yes, who are they, and what did they do?

Dave: My father is the oldest of six children. He was a pattern designer but is now on disability. Then there is a brother (uncle) who is a plane mechanic, formerly for the Army, now for Federal Express. Then an uncle who is in a psychiatric ward and who I've seen only once. No one talks about him, it's like a big secret. Then there are three aunts after him who are pretty much housewives, although one aunt also works as a librarian and another aunt is in retail part-time.

Couns.:   Recently you've mentioned an interest in psychology and a possible career in that field. Do you think having an uncle in a psychiatric ward might have something to do with that? *(I note employment/unemployment history and psychological and medical problems in family and inquire about possible connections.)*

Dave: No, I doubt it.

Couns.:   Okay. How about your uncles-in-law, the husbands of your aunts? *(Importance of inquiring about nonblood kin.)*

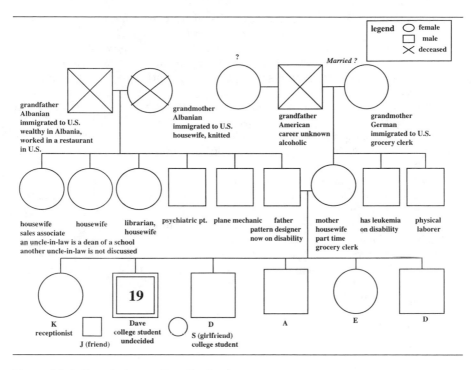

Figure 32.4. Dave's Career Family Genogram

Dave: One of them is dean of a school, another uncle-in-law is not talked about like my other uncle, and the other one I don't know.

Couns.:   Okay, how about on your mother's side?

Dave: This genogram is coming slow, are we almost done?

Couns.:   Yes, we are almost done. I just have a few more questions left about your mother's side and you and your siblings. Is something unclear or bothering you about this, or did you have something else you wanted to talk about today? *(Inquiring and clarifying what client's real concern is: an ambivalence with the genogram exercise or client's wish to discuss another matter.)*

Dave: No, I'll continue if it's not going to take much longer. I just didn't know where this was going.

Couns.:   That's a valid concern. I know it might not be clear where this is all going now, but once we get everyone down it will make sense. I promise to fill you in with everything and answer all your questions later. *(Acknowledging the process may appear ambiguous but that all will be clarified later.)* Okay, can we proceed?

Dave: Yeah.

Couns.:   You were about to tell me about your mother's side.

Dave: Yes, on my mother's side, there is my mother and two uncles. My mother was a housewife but she works part-time in a grocery store now. One of her brothers has leukemia and is on disability, and the other brother is a physical laborer.

Couns.:   Any cousins or people outside the family who may have had an impact on you? *(Importance of inquiring about significant other people—e.g., teachers, friends, neighbors, clergy.)*

Dave: No, not really. I mean, my cousins are all young, but I have a couple of friends and two brothers, D and A, who I really admire and respect. My brothers and my friend John are smart and real, not phony like other people I know. They don't care what others think and just do their own thing. And my girlfriend Susan is also a smart, hard-working student at another college.

Couns.:   Any others, or anyone older than you who you look up to as a role model?

Dave: No, I can't think of anyone else.

Couns.:   Now we're finally up to you and your siblings. You are which one of how many siblings?

Dave: I'm the second oldest of six children.

Couns.:   Let's start with the oldest, is this sibling your sister or brother, and what does he/she do?

Dave: It's a sister and she's a receptionist at a fitness club.

Couns.:   Then comes you . . .

Dave: Yes, then comes me, and I'm here. Then there are two brothers after me, D and A. And then my youngest sister, E, and my youngest brother, D. They're all in school, but I'm the only one in college.

Couns.:   Do they know what they want to be or do?

Dave: Well, my brother, D, wants to be a mechanic. He always knew he wanted to be a mechanic, and that's what he's been setting himself to do. I so wish I had something like that.

Couns.:   So what kind of career dreams or fantasies did you have as a child?

Dave: Well, I wanted to be a fighter pilot at one time. But I also wanted to be a race car driver, a detective, and archaeologist, too. But those were just that, fantasies of a kid. Would I be any of these now? No. Even my dad wanted to be a pilot, but his father wouldn't let him.

Couns.:   So, maybe it's not so much about not having any interests but more about not having support.

Dave: Maybe. I'm so confused, I don't even know what I want to do tomorrow.

Couns.:   This is not an easy process, and it can take some time before you figure out what you really want to do, and that is okay. The important thing is that you are starting on that journey now. Looking over your genogram, do any relatives or any of their careers stand out to you?

Dave: Well, none of them had any so-called "careers" or careers that I'd be interested in.

Couns.:   That's one way of looking at it. It seems like you didn't really have anyone in your immediate or extended family who you could look up to in terms of careers, whether it be role models, support, or just exposure to different careers. This would explain why you may be undecided about your college major and career goal. *(I help validate and attribute client's indecisiveness to a lack of career role models, support, and exposure.)* Not everyone has or needs all these things, but it can be a hard process without them. Fortunately, you seem to have some really good friends and brothers who you can relate and turn to. I think it would be helpful for us in our next session to explore the various careers you were interested in as a child and see what made them so appealing to you and if any of these are still possibilities. And if you like, I can also arrange for you to take a career interest inventory, which assesses one's interests in work and different work settings, and we can see what that comes up with. How does that sound?

Dave: I could do that.

Comments on the Cases of Mike and Dave

Constructing a career family genogram with Dave raised several issues, which were very different from Mike's. First, Dave expressed some concern about not knowing much about his family career history. The counselor handled this situation by having Dave focus on what he did know about his family and reassuring him that he was not expected to know everything. The counselor also informed him that he would be able to revise any of the information that he provided, which gave Dave the opportunity to confirm the information with his family. Second, Dave displayed some resistance and skepticism with the exercise. The counselor dealt with this by confronting and clarifying the resistance directly. Third, when Dave could not identify any family members who had an influence on him, the counselor proceeded to inquire about people outside the family. The counselor did this not just to have a more thorough and complete career genogram of Dave but to also find out and highlight his resources and supports. Just as it is important for clients to see what is lacking or absent in their career genograms, it is equally important for them to see what is present and available to them, especially any strengths and assets.

The counselor incorporated the same family career genogram exercise with both Mike and Dave but with different purposes. With Mike, it was used to clarify and understand where and how his interest in engineering developed, but with Dave, it was used to investigate and understand his indecisiveness and confusion regarding a college major and a career. Just as the family career genogram can be used to understand and conceptualize the problem, it can also be used to determine appropriate interventions. Follow-up sessions with Mike, for example, might involve supportive counseling to help him actualize his goal of becoming an engineer, but for Dave, they may involve assistance with career exploration and commitment.

Although Dave expressed some discomfort and resistance with the genogram halfway through his session, both Dave and Mike found the experience interesting and valuable overall. While Mike was surprised to see how much he knew about his family, Dave was disappointed at how little he knew about his. However, both seemed to feel that the construction of a family career genogram piqued their interest and curiosity in their family history. Both also planned to interview family members to gather more information and "fill in the gaps." In this way, the construction of a family career genogram can and has elicited discussion on various topics such as migration history, language use and preference, acculturation, racial/ethnic identity development, religion, socioeconomic status, education, medical and psychological problems, employment/unemployment history, and career role models, all of which influence one's career decision (Ponterotto et al., 2000).

As with any counseling assessment or tool, the genogram is not without problems or limitations. Some possible limitations offered by Okiishi (1987) are that it may be too cumbersome or time-consuming for some counselors as well as clients, that it may be inappropriate for individuals who are emotionally and geographically distant and disconnected from their family, and that it leaves out significant role models and influences outside the family. Still another limitation is that construction of a family genogram may be too personal for some clients in an initial career session.

CONCLUSION

This chapter explored the use of the family genogram in career counseling. Incorporating actual case examples, the authors demonstrated the usefulness of the genogram with participants diverse in demographic and cultural backgrounds, and in presenting concerns. The family genogram, used by a culturally competent counselor (see Sue et al., 1998), can serve as a valuable clinical tool in career counseling. We hope this chapter together with the previously presented Career-in-Culture Interview (Ponterotto et al., 2000) facilitates a broadened, more culturally expansive perspective on career development.

REFERENCES

Betz, N. E., & Fitzgerald, L. F. (1995). Career assessment and intervention with racial and ethnic minorities. In F. T. L. Leong (Ed.), *Career development and vocational behavior of racial and ethnic minorities* (pp. 263-279). Mahwah, NJ: Lawrence Erlbaum.

Borodovsky, L. G., & Ponterotto, J. G. (1994). A family-based approach to multicultural career development. In P. Pedersen & J. C. Carey (Eds.), *Multicultural counseling in schools: A practical handbook* (pp. 195-206). Boston: Allyn & Bacon.

Heppner, M. J., O'Brien, K. M., Hinkelman, J. M., & Humphrey, C. F. (1994). Shifting the paradigm: The use of creativity in career counseling. *Journal of Career Development, 21*, 77-86.

Lent, R. W., Brown, S. D., & Hackett, G. (1994). Toward a unified social cognitive theory of career/academic interest, choice, and performance (monograph). *Journal of Vocational Behavior, 45*, 79-122.

Leong, F. T. L. (Ed.). (1995). *Career development and vocational behavior of racial and ethnic minorities.* Mahwah, NJ: Lawrence Erlbaum.

Leung, S. A. (1995). Career development and counseling: A multicultural perspective. In J. G. Ponterotto, J. M. Casas, L. A. Suzuki, & C. M. Alexander (Eds.), *Handbook of multicultural counseling* (pp. 549-566). Thousand Oaks, CA: Sage.

McGoldrick, M., & Gerson, R. (1985). *Genograms in family assessment.* New York: W. W. Norton.

McGoldrick, M., Gerson, R., & Shellenberger, S. (1999). *Genograms: Assessment and intervention* (2nd ed.). New York: W. W. Norton.

Moon, S. M., Coleman, V. D., McCollum, E. E., & Nelson, T. S. (1993). Using the genogram to facilitate career decisions: A case study. *Journal of Family Psychotherapy, 4*, 45-56.

Okiishi, R. W. (1987). The genogram as a tool in career counseling. *Journal of Counseling and Development, 66*, 139-143.

Ponterotto, J. G., Rivera, L., & Adachi Sueyoshi, L. (2000). The Career-in-Culture Interview: A semi-structured protocol for the cross-cultural intake interview. *Career Development Quarterly, 49,* 85-96.

Splete, H., & Freeman-George, A. (1985). Family influences on the career development of young adults. *Journal of Career Development, 12,* 55-64.

Sue, D. W., Carter, R. T., Casas, J. M., Fouad, N. A., Ivey, A. E., Jensen, M., LaFromboise, T., Manese, J. E., Ponterotto, J. G., & Vazquez-Nutall, E. (1998). *Multicultural counseling competencies: Individual and organizational development.* Thousand Oaks, CA: Sage.

Sue, D. W., Ivey, A. E., & Pedersen, P. B. (1996). *A theory of multicultural counseling and therapy.* Pacific Grove, CA: Brooks/Cole.

Sue, D. W., & Sue, D. (1999). *Counseling the culturally different: Theory and practice* (3rd ed.). New York: John Wiley.

Sue, S., & Zane, N. W. (1987). The role of culture and cultural techniques in psychotherapy: A critique and reformulation. *American Psychologist, 42,* 37-45.

Correspondence regarding this chapter may be sent to Lina Adachi Sueyoshi, PES Room 1008, Fordham University at Lincoln Center, 113 West 60th Street, New York, NY 10023 (e-mail address: sueyoshi@fordham.edu).

Chapter 33

MULTICULTURAL FAMILY COUNSELING

Toward Cultural Sensibility

ARTHUR R. SANCHEZ

El Olvido[1]
(forgetfulness)
(segun las madres)

> *It is a dangerous thing*
> *to forget the climate of*
> *your birthplace; to choke out*
> *the voices of dead relatives when*
> *in dreams they call you by*
> *your secret name; dangerous*
> *to spurn the clothes you were*
> *born to wear for the sake of fashion;*
> *to use weapons and sharp instruments you*
> *are not familiar with; dangerous*
> *to disdain the plaster saints before*
> *which your mother kneels praying for you with*
> *embarrassing fervor that you survive in*
> *the place you have chosen to live; a costly,*
> *bare and elegant room with no pictures*
> *on the walls; a forgetting place where*
> *she fears you might die of exposure.*
> *Jesus, Maria y Jose.*
> *El olvido is a dangerous thing.*

—Judith Ortiz Cofer (1987)

AUTHOR'S NOTE: I extend my sincere gratitude, respect, and warm thanks to Professor Bill Rector, who introduced me to the phenomenologist perspective, which is the basis for my counseling convictions, to my graduate students without whom therapy could not have occurred, to school psychologist Rose Wanken for her family referrals, to Professor Eddie Vela whose review of the manuscript was invaluable, and especially to the families who honored us by allowing us into their courageous lives.

THE FOLLOWING CHAPTER is divided into five major sections. The first section contains four subsections that introduce the concept of culture, its relationship to family and to counseling, and its use as an intervention. The second section ties counselor cultural sensibility to three related variables: counselor worldview, counselor practice and experience, and counselor use of language. The third section presents a conceptual framework for family counseling along with four orientations that have influenced its theoretical context. The fourth section introduces specific methods and procedures for organizing and conducting family counseling sessions. It is divided into seven subsections, the first of which addresses the collection of presession family data, followed by six subsections that specify procedures for organizing and conducting the sessions. The procedures, in part, include initiating the counseling process, assessing the family-identified problem(s) and therapeutic interventions. The section culminates with two case study summaries. The final section provides a summary of the chapter.

TOWARD CULTURAL SENSIBILITY

Culture Introduced

The image of a kneeling mother praying for the survival of her children who she views as having exposed themselves dangerously by relinquishing their past, and their culture, elicits poignantly provocative reflections. Judith Ortiz Cofer's (1987) poem offers the reader an opportunity to reflect and ponder the essential nature and importance of one's culture by suggesting an inherent mortal danger of culture forgotten, *"segun las madres"* (according to mothers). With respect to culture lost, culture forgotten, for whom does this poem's warning resonate? It resonates undoubtedly for those who face the challenges of immigration, acculturation, and/or assimilation. As they journey into a new way of living, they face difficult decisions and choices between what has always been a way of living and what is now needed to accommodate their new environment. Past practices often make way for new ones. Albeit perhaps not as drastic, everyone sooner or later faces similar life decisions and choices that manifest in changes to previously held culture-based practices. Perhaps the poem's forewarning of "culture forgotten" calls out to everyone.

Culture is, however, an elusive concept, one in which volumes have been devoted to defining. For the purposes of this chapter, culture includes the codes, rules, beliefs, and practices that orient, educate, and motivate families and individuals toward a range of socially acceptable behaviors. Does it follow that everyone has a culture? To the extent that one is embedded within a wider social context, the answer is "yes."

Whether conscious or not, we behave according to a set of principles that guides our daily activities. Individual and group/family principles combine to make up our cultural lens. Accordingly, no one is acultural. Student anecdotes commonly repeated in my "multicultural" counseling courses make this point clear. As a precursor to understanding others, each student develops an awareness and understanding of his/her own cultural background through workbook assignments. The workbook assignments are designed to facilitate culture-of-origin explorations (e.g., family rituals, celebrations, rules, and myths) that each student summarizes into a set of cultural values that represent his/her culture. When first presented with the workbook assignment, many Euro-American students anxiously suggest that they don't have a culture or don't know what it is. However, with each workbook learning objective, students begin to have flights of associations that awaken in them a sense of cultural identity and quickly begin to appreciate the notion that no one is acultural.

Family and Culture

Indeed, the poem resonates meaningfully for most readers. However, it resonates more strongly for some than for others. The mother prays earnestly for the family and its members who are facing the transitional struggles associated with immigration, acculturation, and/or assimilation. These struggles may be particularly relevant to ethnic minorities. Why more relevant for ethnic minorities? There are at least two reasons. First, for ethnic minorities, attempts to negotiate these life transitions are likely to be confounded by the social and institutional practices of racial prejudice and discrimination. Second, ethnic minorities tend to have distinct cultural boundaries that contrast their group identity from the majority culture and often in a mutually exclusive manner (Falicov, 1988). The greater the contrast, the more change and adjustment required and the greater the threat to family stability.

What repercussive dangers does the mother fear? Anecdotes of individuals within the community or within the family accused of presumably forgetting or losing their culture are abundant. Ethnic groups have adopted derogatory labels to characterize these individuals. Let us for a moment reflect on "group norm theory" as reported in the work of Allport (1954). According to Allport, groups develop and establish norms that define the boundaries of acceptable behaviors for its membership and provide the group with a distinct identity (in-group). Outsiders (out-group) are viewed as those who behave outside established norms and are devalued. Implicit and explicit reinforcers regulate in-group member behaviors. According to a general systems perspective (Becvar & Becvar, 1988), subtle and/or direct pressures correct member behaviors that extend beyond the range of acceptable norms. These pressures are attempts to maintain group homeostasis and preserve identity. The principles apply to ethnic groups and families as well. Behaviors that go beyond ethnic and/or family norms become threats to ethnic and family loyalties, ethnic and family identities, perceived family stability, and cultural consonance.

It follows that the mother's fears, in part, reflect fears of compromised cultural and family loyalties and disconnection with familial relations—relations that have provided the family sustenance through the generations. She also fears for her child's potential loss of self. Children at particular risk of cultural loss have "ensemble" self-identities in which one's self-other boundary is fluid. In contrast, children with more "contained" self-boundaries tend to have a more rigid self-other boundary and thus may be less likely to suffer cultural loss (Sampson, 1988).

Culture and Counseling

Another danger exists, one central to the underpinnings of the counseling framework presented later in this chapter. As noted, culture provides the guideposts that direct our daily living. It provides a lens for filtering our internal and external world experiences, and it guides our behavior. It provides the framework for observing and identifying problems and orients us toward methods of problem resolving. Forgetting or losing culture is like losing a much needed compass on an ocean voyage. One's ability to navigate is compromised. The families I have observed in counseling posture themselves much like they have lost their compass. Sometimes, the compass (cultural guidepost, rituals, and practices) has been abandoned or lies dormant. Cultural dissonance, which manifests in dysfunctional behaviors that threaten family identity, stability, and member safety and compromises the family's ability to navigate through difficult times, often characterizes these cases. The initial counseling strategy is to revitalize cultural practices that lay dormant, ones that aid family stability, promote cooperation, and provide for member protection.

On the other hand, families who are negotiating acculturative adjustments have no compass available. It is my observation that culture is absent a "rule" (guidepost) on how to negotiate the accommodation of a new culture into the existing one. Let us suppose that from a general systems perspective culture and family are self-regulating, self-correcting entities whose tendencies are toward the maintenance of homeostasis. Acculturation, by definition, threatens cultural/family stability, particularly in those cases where the boundaries between the host culture and the culture of origin provide for distinct group rules, values, and customs.

Some families, individuals, and even ethnic groupings, in response to acculturation, resist cultural change by maintaining their lives within ethnic/cultural enclaves as commonly observed in some Asian, Latino, and Native American Indian communities. Other individuals and families opt for assimilation as their model of cultural transition and abandon, for the most part, practices, customs, and values of their culture of origin. Bicultural or multicultural abilities are adopted by others such that they are able to move smoothly between cultures. Each of these responses to acculturation is idiomatic of familial and personal histories, which provide personal meaning to the experience and decisions of the individuals.

In any case, ethnic minorities' attempts to survive, succeed, and/or evolve within the context of the majority culture are likely to produce stressful challenges for families and their members (Falicov, 1988; Sluzki, 1979; Szapocznik, Santisteban, Kurtines, Perez-Vidal, & Hervis, 1984). Negotiating these periods of stressful adjustment requires the creation of new cultural practices and strategies (morphogenesis) that help guide family transitions while minimizing threats to overall family cohesion.

When and for whom is culture an important variable to consider in counseling? The answer is a resounding "Always" and "Everyone." However, counseling theories, until recently, were products of ethnocentric thinking that innately did not question the use of Western cultural indicators of mental health as the norm. Consequently, monocultural imperviousness appeared as the professional norm until ethnic minority professionals and larger numbers of women entered the field. It was not until recently that other cultural paradigms were introduced as mediating forces in counseling. Fortunately, cultural relativistic thinking emerged in the 1980s and 1990s as a professional norm (Ariel, 1999).

Culture as Intervention

As we enter the new millennium, families face a rapidly changing world. Technological advances to a large degree drive many changes. Advancing technologies offer society and families new opportunities for socioeconomic and educational growth, as well as health advancements, but not without posing new challenges. In many ways we are entering uncharted waters. The journey offers new opportunities and new discoveries but also presents new dangers. Societal as well as familial ability to evolve and establish new cultural and moral guidelines to keep pace with, as well as to navigate, the changes is marginal at best. Nevertheless, the central goal of the family—to socialize, educate, and provide safety for its members—remains. Against the backdrop of a rapidly changing world, families face the everyday challenges associated with maintaining a household as well as the transitional challenges associated with navigating family and individual life-cycle development. Ethnic minority families face the added complexities of navigating the challenges that arise from immigration, acculturation, and/or assimilation processes (Falicov, 1988; Sluzki, 1979; Szapocznik et al., 1984).

This chapter is designed to assist counselors in working with ethnic minority families who develop maladaptive patterns of behaviors resulting from an inability to successfully negotiate and navigate one or more of life's transitional challenges. The methods presented here, however, are useful in working with any family who struggles with life transitions. Family symptoms often reflect, but are not limited to, intercultural conflicts, intergenerational conflicts, sibling conflicts, marital conflicts, parental inadequacy, inadequate social skill development, and abuse. A systematic conceptual framework that incorporates culture as an essential family counseling variable is presented. The model focuses on ethnic minority families who enter counseling as a result of either a breakdown or interruption in family cultural practices that normally provide stability and navigation through stressful life events and/or an inability to successfully deal with acculturative life challenges. Primary counseling interventions involve the reintroduction of abandoned cultural practices and/or the establishment of new practices. The method incorporates culturally sensitive and culturally responsive procedures.

COUNSELOR CULTURAL SENSIBILITY

The following subsections address variables that may influence a counselor's ability to implement culture-sensible/sensitive counseling methods. The three subsections address what constitutes a counselor's worldview, practice and experience, and use of language.

Worldview

"Worldview" constitutes our psychological orientation in life and determines how we think, behave, make decisions, and define events (Sue, 1978). It includes one's group and individual identities, beliefs, values, and language that construct a reality for perceiving life events (Dana, 1993). Worldview also provides the framework for defining mental health, appropriate service providers, and acceptable methods of intervention.

Counselors must have an awareness and understanding of their own cultural background to be culturally sensitive to clients of a different culture (Pinderhughes, 1989). They must also understand how their combined cultural values and theoretical orientation provide a counseling worldview that shapes how they observe, assess, define, and approach client problems. Potential misunderstandings and miscommunications increase when worldviews between counselor and client diverge and may lead to premature termination of counseling services (Dana, 1993). Counselor and client ecological fit is dependent on the counselor's ability to observe clashes between his/her worldview and the client's and to make corrective adjustments that promote understanding and rapport. A comprehensive review of majority and minority worldviews is found in Dana (1993).

Today's counselors find themselves in a paradoxical situation when it comes to working with clients whose cultural background is different from theirs. It is impractical, if not impossible, to gain complete knowledge of a group's cultural intricacies, much less its within-group variability. So what do counselors often do? For one, counselors may maintain a monocultural perspective and in effect minimize cultural differences. This, however, is likely to lead to misunderstandings and possibly misdiagnoses of their clients' problems. Alternatively, counselors may depend on generalizations about cultural groups and run the risk of ethnic/racial stereotyping, which is likely to lead to misunderstandings and inappropriate interventions (Falicov, 1988). Of course, neither option is desirable.

Another solution to this dilemma is found in the combined writings of Schwartzman (1983) and Ariel (1999). Schwartzman asserts that families are like individuals who develop unique personalities. Each family develops a unique family culture that incorporates antecedent sociocultural experiences. Schwartzman concludes that it is misguided for counselors to observe clients from the abstraction of a general cultural perspective. Ariel uses Schwartzman's argument to challenge the notion that cultural continuity exists from one generation to the next. Ariel argues that each successive generation shapes its antecedent cultural referents to satisfy its present needs, which results in some distinctiveness from previous generations. Both authors argue that families are better served if counselors interact with families in a way that is sensitive to characteristics that are unique to the particular family.

Nevertheless, counselors still need a point of reference to assess their interactions with families. Can counselors use generalized cultural referents and at the same time avoid the pitfall of stereotyping? Yes, with the exception of referents derived from racial prejudice. It is not the generalized cultural referents that pose a problem but how counselors choose to use them. Generalized cultural referents need not become counseling stereotypes. Used effectively, they are essential heuristics for recognizing, assessing, and prompting relevant therapeutic inquiries and have the added safeguard against what Wrenn (1962) refers to as cultural encapsulation. Several points can be concluded so far:

- *Culturally sensitive* counselors have an awareness and understanding of their own cultural values and background.
- *Culturally responsive* counselors understand how their cultural values and theoretical orientation combine and form a counseling worldview that shapes how they observe, assess, define, and intervene on client problems.
- *Culturally sensitive* counselors have knowledge of research-based cultural referents that define and influence the behaviors of a given ethnic or cultural group and use them as reference points.
- *Culturally sensible* counselors interact with family clients to assess the relativity of cultural-group referents to the particular family.
- *Culturally sensible* counselors are alert to divergence between their worldview and their clients' and make corrective adjustments that promote understanding and rapport.

Practice and Experience

As noted, "cultural sensibility" requires counselors to first have an awareness of their "counseling worldview" (cultural values + professional orientation) and knowledge of the cultural referents (ethnic cultural values) associated with their clients' ethnic grouping. Developing an awareness and knowledge base for each ethnic grouping plus the noted family transitional points of reference presents overwhelming challenges for a counselor, not to mention putting them into practice. There is no substitute for ongoing practice and experience. "Cultural sensibility" is an ongoing, evolving learning process that has no end.

Point in fact, the specific family counseling framework presented in this chapter formally took shape over a 12-year period and continues to evolve. It began while teaching a doctoral-level family practicum for 2 years and then over the past 10 years teaching a family practicum to master's-level students in a marriage and family therapy program.

Counselor/Client Language

A counselor's language (grammar/words) as well as how he/she observes a client's use of language directly affects the counselor's observations of the counseling phenomena (Dell, 1980). Dell (1980) describes how Western language in general influences observed reality:

> Grammar is inherently metaphysical because it delineates how aspects of "reality" are related. Western languages, for example, which provide an analysis of phenomena into subjects and predicates, lead their speakers to believe that this grammar objectively reports the true structure of the world. . . . In contrast, Hopi language has a relational grammar that describes the world in terms of process. A similar grammar underlines systems theory and provides family therapists with an accurate and useful epistemology of families and other social systems. (p. 124)

Language is the vehicle by which we communicate our worldview. Using the client's language assists in understanding his/her worldview. This means noticing how clients frame their presenting problems with specific word use and understanding the metaphors they use to describe their experiences. One's capacity to listen and observe from this perspective is enhanced by using an epistemology that is least restrictive. For example, normative language, associated with medical model and *DSM-IV* epistemologies, is restrictive because it requires the use of labels to define pathology. Labels are convenient descriptors but tend to overgeneralize and undermine unique personal characteristics that provide meaning for a person's experience.

CONCEPTUAL FRAMEWORK FOR FAMILY COUNSELING

Theoretical Context

Family counseling is a natural fit when working with ethnic minorities (Ariel, 1999). Approaches to multicultural and family counseling are, in general, consistent with the belief that an adequate understanding of an individual's behaviors necessitates an observance of the social, cultural, and familial context within which the individual's behaviors manifest. Family counseling methods have, however, ranged from the individually oriented modalities with intrapsychic emphases (e.g., psychoanalytic, behaviorist, humanistic, and cognitive) to modalities based on General Systems and Cybernetic theories (e.g., structural, strategic, and systemic) that emphasize interpersonal interactions (Becvar & Becvar, 1988).

The next four subsections introduce four orientations that have influenced the present family counseling framework. These subsections also provide brief descriptions and rationales for their respective relevance. Each orientation is viewed as compatible with multiculturalism in general and has been found to be easily adapted to the present framework because of its respective emphases on context and relativity in understanding human phenomena.

General Systems Theory

General Systems Theory (Becvar & Becvar, 1988) is incorporated into the current counseling framework for several reasons:

- It provides a general framework for conceptualizing a group of related elements (family members) with an emphasis on how they interact to create and maintain a whole entity (family).

- It is a way of thinking about counseling that places the individual within a larger context (family/culture).

- It provides a perspective for observing the counseling session as well as family/individual problems from a content and/or process emphasis. Content refers to specific items of discussion, and process is the manner in which the discussion is being negotiated (Worden, 1999).

- Its terminology (language/grammar) fosters an ecological and process view of the world that tends to be consistent with non-Western cultures (Dell, 1980).

- It also provides the general underpinnings of a number of different family therapy approaches and provides the family counselor with a complement of therapeutic options for observation, assessment, and intervention of client problems.

Social Constructionism

Social Constructionism is additive and complementary to General Systems Theory (Worden, 1999) and multiculturalism. It is also consistent with the assertions of Schwartzman (1983) and Ariel (1999) discussed earlier. In their book *The Social Construction of Reality*, Berger and Luckmann (1985) present the argument that one's reality is socially constructed through interactions with others and social consensus. Add the word "culture" and you have the notion of sociocultural construction of reality. Social Constructionism has also influenced a shift from problem-centered family approaches to solution-focused family approaches as observed in narrative therapies (Berg & DeShazer, 1993; White & Epston, 1990). In brief, narrative therapy observes the family and its members within the context of "constructed narratives" or realities. An emphasis is placed on constructing new narratives or realities to replace narratives saturated with problem-focused events. In effect, the counselor and the family co-construct narratives that free the families from impasse. This is germane to counseling interventions previously suggested where counselors co-construct with the family new cultural practices that help guide its transitions while minimizing threats to overall stability.

Feminist Perspective

It is important to note that feminist authors and practitioners have engendered a major change in the field of systemic family counseling (Waters, Carter, Papp, & Silverstein, 1992). Feminists challenged the use of mutual/circular causality as a generalized therapeutic principle, particularly when applied to family abuse. Their actions resulted in a human quality being added to systems thinking. An example of this is child sexual abuse by an adult. The child cannot be a mutual contributor to the abusive situation. In essence, the feminist and cultural perspectives have called into question the apersonal application of general systems principles (based on physics and biology models) to human systems (Waters et al., 1992).

Ecosystemic Considerations

The ecosystemic perspective maintains a person-in-environment focus (Ho, 1987) that is concerned with the interactive adaptations and ecological fit between family and its environment (Falicov, 1988). Cultural dissonance, family imbalance, conflict, and stress are viewed as byproducts of a pronounced lack of fit between family behaviors and environmental requirements (Falicov, 1988; Ho, 1987).

ORGANIZING AND
CONDUCTING THE FAMILY COUNSELING SESSIONS

This section provides information for organizing the family session interviews along with step-by-step procedures for conducting ongoing counseling sessions. The section is divided into seven subsections. The first addresses the collection of presession family data, followed by six that specify procedures for organizing and conducting the sessions. The procedures, in part, include initiating the counseling process, assessing the family-identified problem(s), and therapeutic interventions. The section culminates with two case study summaries.

Presession Family Data

Counselors commonly collect client historical information prior to the first interview, although the amount and variety of information varies by counselor orientation and setting. Intake forms solicit information related to the nature of the presenting problem, its history, duration, and prior service. The counselor's use of prior family data can make the counseling sessions more efficient. Cultural information is collected, reviewed, and presession cultural points of reference (family life cycle, acculturation, migration) identified before conducting the first session. Collecting cultural-familial information enhances counseling efficiency and promotes a culture-sensible counseling framework by (a) presupposing a culturally sensitive counseling posture before sessions begin by framing family concerns within a cultural context (e.g. acculturation, migration), (b) promoting cultural responsiveness by providing a vehicle to select which cultural variants are relevant considerations, and (c) helping the counselor avoid overgeneralized inquiries that undermine rapport, particularly with highly assimilated families who may confuse the counselor's effort with ethnic stereotyping.

Family life cycle, immigration, relocation, and acculturation (family) are presession family process assessment considerations that can be used to inform initial as well as ongoing treatment decisions. Each is germane to this chapter's therapeutic modality, which focuses on family process, family transition, and family adaptiveness as the path to family healing and growth. The family's resource network—extended family and community (school, church, etc.)—is another important presession consideration. Grieger and Ponterotto (1995) suggest additional noteworthy assessment variables that address client counseling readiness: client's psychological mindedness, family's psychological mindedness, client's attitudes toward counseling, and family's attitudes toward counseling. Intracultural variations related to acculturation and ethnic identity are assessed as sessions progress.

Numerous resources review family life cycle, immigration, and acculturation constructs. I note those that are quite useful and provide good
places to begin. Carter and McGoldrick's (1989) edited volume presents a
thorough review of the relevant issues. It also incorporates a family-as-
system approach and provides several chapters specific to ethnicity
and family. Sluzki (1979) presents an excellent migration-stage model with
specific stage indicators for recognizing and assessing potential family conflicts specific to the process of migration. Dana (1993) presents a comprehensive review of worldview as well as available acculturation measures.

Although some acculturation/ethnic-identity models claim to be generalizable across cultures, I have found that emic-based constructs provide
more utility when working with specific ethnic groups. For example, Sue's
(1978) worldview model for Asian Americans with a cognitive perceptual
emphasis, Helms's (1984) model for African Americans with sociopolitical
emphases, Ruiz, Casas, and Padilla's (1977) or Cuellar, Harris, and Jasso's
(1988) bicultural models for Latinos with bicultural emphases, and
LaFromboise, Coleman, and Gerton's (1993) alternation model for Native
American Indians with a heritage consistency emphasis are each designed
by professionals within the specific ethnic groupings. However, in the absence of assessment instruments, family or individual generation can be a
good reference point to gauge acculturation level.

Initiating the Counseling Process

Family counseling begins once intake data is collected, reviewed, and
cultural reference points identified. In opening the first session, consideration is given to greeting the family and spending some relaxed time warm-
ing the members to the immediate process. In most cases, it will be the
family's first experience with family counseling. Anticipations and expectations are usually discussed as part of the warm-up period. This is an
opportunity to observe family interactions and family etiquette, noting
who emerges as the family spokesperson. During the relaxed discussion, it
can be useful, when deemed appropriate, to discuss family background in
an attempt to have members share their preferred ethnic label (e.g., Black,
African American, Chicano, Hispanic). An ethnic label provides specific
personal meaning for the individual who has chosen it. Differing ethnic
labels used between family members can signal intercultural tensions.

The overall goal of the first session is to provide the family with emotional support, a sense of being understood, meaningful insight, and an alternate view of the presenting problem. It is also a goal of the first session to
"punctuate the sequence" (Watzlawick, Beavin, & Jackson, 1967) of family
interactions and interrupt the behavioral sequence that contributes to the
maintenance of the problem (Fisch, Weakland, & Segal, 1982).

Family Interview Questions

Numerous theoretic models are available for designing family interview questions. I have settled on the Mental Research Institute's model (Fisch et al., 1982) primarily for its straightforward and efficient use of questions. The questions provide both an organized way for prompting family interaction and a guideline for problem assessment. These questions are as follows:

1. *What is the concern that brings your family in to counseling?*
2. *How is it you decided to come in for counseling at this time as opposed to earlier or later?*
This question is used to get at the family's level of motivation for counseling. Sometimes, the question is asked toward the end of the session.
3. *How is the situation you just described a problem for you?*
This question is used to identify specific behavioral effects of the problem on each family member. Sometimes, the answers are used to customize individual interventions and a means to monitor change.
4. *What is your best guess as to why the problem continues?*
This question is used to identify what Fisch et al. (1982) refer to as the complainant, the client, and/or the identified patient. A complainant is the person who identifies another member as the problem. An identified patient is the person who others are calling the problem. A client is viewed as a person who is both complainant and identified patient. It is believed that a "client" or a "complainant" is most motivated to end the problem and therefore most likely to assist the counselor's work.
5. *What have you or anyone else done to try to resolve the problem?*
Attempted solutions that have failed are avoided as future interventions. How people apply common logic to resolve a problem is seen as contributing to the maintenance of the problem.
6. *If the situation began to get better, what would be a small but significant sign this was occurring?*
The answers give the family members and the counselor specific therapeutic goals.

The questions, as used in this chapter, are intended as guidelines and can be adapted to fit the present need. They can also be addressed via counseling techniques such as family drawings, sculpting, and sociodramas. Often, they are adapted to a circular question format, which emphasizes relationships and is reflexive. Circular questions ask each family member to comment on or speculate about other family members' relationships with regard to the family problem. For example, the counselor might ask a family member to comment on who he/she believes would be most relieved between one family member and another (excluding him/herself) if the problem were to be resolved. Circular questioning can help identify family coalitions as well as relational shifts resulting from cultural disruptions (Fleuridas, Nelson, & Rosenthal, 1986; Penn, 1982). It is a very useful method when assessing relational shifts resulting from acculturation. Understanding differences in family member relationships before and after the problem emerged is important to reestablishing family cultural consonance.

Family size and length of sessions will influence the number of sessions it takes to complete the questions. The framework presented in this chapter uses a 90- to 120-minute session. Questions are usually completed within one to one and a half sessions but may require revisiting as sessions progress.

Reframing Presenting Problem

Usually, the initial complaint is reported through a designated family representative. Designation of the family spokesperson is normally based on the cultural values of the family. Acculturation can disrupt normal cultural patterns of family organization and functioning and create numerous unpredictable family configurations. Who speaks for the family in counseling may not be the normal family spokesperson. Recent immigrant families with distinct cultural boundaries that define authority hierarchy may be predictable based on generalized patterns of culture-specific behaviors. However, counselors should be aware that each family culturally constructs a unique posture that provides direction for family adaptations and role assignments. How a family negotiates and accommodates acculturation is a product of its unique but culturally biased posture and the demands of its new environment. Counselors should spend some time having the family educate them with respect to roles in the family.

Family-presenting problems are what families report as the main complaint (Fisch et al., 1982), and usually target a particular family member (identified patient). However, family problems are seldom straightforward. What the counselor assesses as the family problem and what the family complains about can be significantly discrepant. Nevertheless, families expect relief based on their notion of the concern, seldom realizing that it is their view of the problem that contributes to its maintenance. Changing the family's perception of the problem requires reframing identified patient problems as family problems. A reframe takes the problem out of its present context and places it in a new equally valid context and creates a shift in perspective. The identified patient usually experiences a great deal of relief as a result. Reframes work best when couched in the client's language.

When new environmental demands require family reorganization and accommodation, a family's prolonged inability to make the necessary adjustments cultivates family cultural dissonance. Family symptoms and their companion complaints signal the family's inability to successfully negotiate the transition. Complaints are more often than not directed at one person (identified patient) who is perceived as the threat to family cohesion (cultural consonance) and stability. However, agreement about the complaint may vary among family members (Fisch et al., 1982). How counselors solicit family member views of the problem depends on the family's adherence to cultural values. Encouraging members to speak openly without consideration of family values may unwittingly undermine the family hierarchy. One way to avoid this pitfall is to reframe the problem as a "family problem," using the rationale that the symptom disrupts family functioning and affects everyone. The complainant's acceptance of the reframe is enhanced if counselors make the complaint synonymous with care and concern for the identified patient and the family as a whole. It is less likely to be rejected if the primary authority figure(s) in the family had been involved in the decision to seek family counseling. Once there is a shift from identified patient problem to identified family problem, the counselor can frame the solicitation of input from all members as necessary, since the problem affects everyone and so everyone's help is needed to resolve it.

Externalizing the Problem

A family unable to negotiate required life transitions will develop problems resulting from shifts in the family's normal coalitions, cultural loyalties, and/or normal patterns of communication and interactions. Family symptoms often reflect intercultural conflicts, intergenerational conflicts, sibling conflicts, marital conflicts, parental inadequacy, inadequate social skill development, unresolved loss, or abuse. As family frustration builds, within-family fighting takes center stage. Fighting and bickering may target an identified patient, focus between the primary caretakers, focus on the marital dyad, or alternate among members. Fights are often metaphors that describe specific breakdowns in previously held family coalitions and/ or unresolved loss.

The counseling strategy is to redirect family frustration and fighting toward a common target outside the family. This is done by framing the "identified family problem" as resulting from external (e.g., acculturation, relocation, unresolved loss) pressures (Szapocznik et al., 1984; White & Epston, 1990). Externalizing the problem channels family maladaptive energies toward a common external target. Szapocznik et al. (1984) have developed a useful family training model that externalizes family intercultural conflicts and trains families on how to manage acculturation demands. The authors suggest that when intergenerational conflict appears as a symptom counselors should assess intercultural conflict as a possible confound of family life-cycle adjustment.

Family Genogram

Notwithstanding the legal traditions that establish society's range of acceptable norms, family health is understood from the family's point of view of what it sees as its goals, and how well it believes it is accomplishing them (Becvar & Becvar, 1988). Accordingly, Becvar and Becvar (1988) define family health

> as the family's success in functioning to achieve its own goals . . . [and] the observance of shared rituals and traditions . . . [as having] a natural network of relationships outside the family. . . . Well-functioning families speak clearly and concurrently so that both verbal and nonverbal levels match. . . . In healthy families the members celebrate each other. They enjoy uniqueness and togetherness as individuals and as a family. They fight, but always they belong. (pp. 109-112)

The genogram is a useful vehicle for assessing family health and can be designed to solicit family data specific to the family problem(s), assess related family-of-origin problems, assess family-of-origin models for problem solving, and develop a reference for designing and implementing therapeutic interventions. Inquiries concerning family history are tailored to the family's identified problem(s) and its legacy within the families of origin. Special attention is given to problem-solving methods modeled in the families (father/mother) of origin as they will have shaped current family methods.

It is particularly important during the genogram process to inquire about the observance of cultural and family rituals. Disruptions of family rituals are associated with the transmission of pathology from one generation to the next (Wolin & Bennett, 1984) and are clear signs of family dysfunction. Rituals are one of culture's vehicles for transmitting values, attitudes, historical information, and goals from one generation to the next (Evenson & Evenson, 1991). Rituals take the form of celebrations or practices that are repetitive in nature. They occur daily (eating meals together), weekly (attending religious practice), monthly (outings), yearly (birthdays), and periodically (family reunions, religious/cultural rites of passage). They may also follow cultural and religious calendars marking significant historical events. In essence, rituals are celebrations of family heritage that provide unity, loyalty, stability, and reinforce individual identity while promoting an overall sense of belonging and family identity. Families adapt cultural and family rituals to satisfy present needs and therefore should be considered from the point of view of family members for whom they provide special meaning. Questions should be designed to assess cultural consonance as well as periods of cultural disruptions.

Family unresolved loss also is an important consideration during the genogram process (McGoldrick & Boundy, 1996). Loss can be viewed as physical death, spiritual interruptions, or relational interruptions. Migration and relocation should be reviewed for the types of loss the family has suffered during the process. Adjustments and accommodations made as a result of acculturation demands can also create family loss. Loss due to migration and acculturation are easily dismissed and ignored by families because of their intangible nature. Denial, overcompensation, and unexplainable symptoms (e.g. depression, grieving absent of reason) can signal unresolved loss (Sluzki, 1979). Questions should address the family's cultural beliefs and practices for addressing family loss (see McGoldrick & Boundy, 1996, for a useful genogram resource guide).

I have found it beneficial to implement the genogram in or around the third family session. It may take an additional session to go through the process, depending on family size and length of sessions. The family is introduced to the method in the session prior to its implementation. Genogram use has the added benefit of getting the family members working together to construct the family tree. Most family members enjoy the experience and actively engage in the process. It is not surprising to see previously reluctant family members come alive during the genogram process. Children find joy in discovering that their parents were once children too. Parents often discover that their children have not been passive observers of family life. Overall, it can be an insightful and humanizing family experience to review and discover family legacies. The following is a partial listing of possible therapeutic options and reframes that may emerge against the backdrop of the family legacy:

- Opportunities to reframe the present family context as encouraging compared to family history: for families who see their current situation as hopeless but when compared to family history they shine; at minimum, the family is empowered, having insight that has eluded the previous extended family network.
- Opportunities to externalize the problem and divert tensions: useful in situations where prior families of origin modeling was inadequate; parental guilt is redirected toward learning new skills.
- Opportunities to reframe family goals as attainable: the presenting problem is framed in part as abandoned cultural practices; their reintroduction as family practices makes goal appear attainable and reinforces family togetherness.
- Opportunities to realign disrupted and interrupted healthy family coalitions: useful when cultural loyalties are disrupted and normal hierarchies have been shifted to dysfunctional ones; they are important for reestablishing family protectorships from parents (sometimes extended network) down through the youngest child.
- Opportunities to create new family rituals: for cases of unresolved loss from migration or acculturation; they are also useful in celebrating new family identity without the problem or in symbolically burying a past problem.

A central goal of conducting the genogram is to set the stage for reintroducing abandoned cultural practices and to assist in the co-creation of new ones that satisfy pressing family needs. The genogram provides the narrative that brings to life family functioning and identity. The family's personalized theme emerges and provides personalized meaning to family adaptations. When families experience trauma, they develop a protective pattern of behavior to ensure safety. At times, the protective patterns of behavior are rigidly held and get in the way of the family's need to grow and develop.

Family Rituals Reestablished and New Ones Co-Created

Family rituals are conducted either during or between sessions as family "homework," depending on their design. Between-session rituals are processed in the session following their completion.

Reestablishing Family Rituals

Family cooperation in reestablishing abandoned cultural practices is generally a smooth process if the problem has been reframed as a family problem, it has been externalized, reframes identifying ritual disruptions as contributing to the maintenance of the problem are accepted, and a sense of family identity and belonging via the genogram has been rekindled. Families can brainstorm what and where to begin, although it is practical to begin with establishing daily and weekly practices. Getting family members to eat meals together without distractions is a good start. Another example is having parents connect with the educational experience of their children by having them participate in the child's daily educational requirements. Even parents with limited formal education have much to offer in the way of informal education. Depending on family size and age of family members, preparation of evening meals can involve the whole family. Weekly practices usually take the form of outings, special meals, visits with extended family, and religious/spiritual activities. Reuniting with grandparents or other relatives who are identified as stabilizing family agents are also good choices.

Co-Creating New Rituals

Co-created new family rituals are designed to address the new emerging sense of family belonging. Counseling and therapy have set the stage for this process, having introduced to the family new ways of looking at family history, legacies, and periods of cultural consonance. Counseling methods and techniques used to explore the family problem such as family drawing exercises have been so successful and enjoyable that families have incorporated them into other aspects of family life after leaving therapy.

Compromised family hierarchies and coalitions, resulting from the identified family problem, cause a great deal of "spiritual pain" (Madanes, 1990) to families. They are considered in this section based on the assumption that reestablishing previous coalitions in the face of compromised loyalties requires collaborative participation in the healing and reshaping of new ones. I have found Cloe Madanes's (1990) model for intervening and

transforming family violence to love to be a very useful guideline for healing family member pain and awakening the spiritual life of the family that
so often is compromised by family trauma. Particularly insightful and useful is the concept of a healing ritual that provides a therapeutic framework
for family members' repentance, reparations, and forgiveness. Madanes's
(1990, 1995) model is designed for working with family violence such as
dominance, physical abuse, and sexual abuse but can be tailored to address
any family problem that has compromised the family spirit. Spirituality is
an aspect of life that scientists and psychologists have generally kept at a
distance, if not ignored. However, it is a vital component of ethnic and cultural activities. I have commonly used the term "spiritual pain" when
working with families and have found it to resonate quite well without any
complaints to its usage. The following are some considerations adapted
from Madanes's model and presented in order of importance, each requiring
the co-creation of a family ritual/celebration to accompany it:

1. Correcting parental, sibling, and extended hierarchies to establish how
   each family member has an important contribution to make with regard to
   family member protection and overall family stability. Have the family
   members discuss the roles and responsibilities each has in protecting the
   family, beginning with the parents (extended family included where appropriate) and discuss why the roles are important. Then have the children develop a ritual that celebrates the parents' role as primary protectors. The
   family then develops a ritual that can be generalized to each family member that recognizes his/her importance in the family. These rituals should
   be viewed as ways to honor family members, much like birthdays do.
2. In cases where spiritual practices are not associated with organized religious practices, have the family members discuss what spirituality means
   to them and have them develop rituals that celebrate and reinforce the family belief.
3. Counselors tailor a healing ritual specifically designed to address the variety of concerns the family has dealt with during the sessions—those that
   have caused the family spiritual pain. This usually requires an entire session to complete. An example is presented later under "case summaries."

The final rituals to be created are directed at bringing closure to the
externalized problem(s) and to celebrate new family identity without the
problem. The process begins by asking the family to come up with a ceremony that symbolically buries the externalized problem. Families usually
come up with very creative ideas that provide particular meaning to them.
For example, families have drawn, sculpted with clay, or made a collage of
the problem and gone to a special place to bury it. Encouraging a special
place is useful because the place can then be a symbolic place the family returns to for hope and reassurance when faced with future challenges. Counselors need to monitor this process closely to keep the family from
unwittingly moving off the externalized problem and back to the identified
person/problem that brought the family into counseling.

The family is now ready to create a final ritual to celebrate the family's new sense of belonging and family identity. It is useful for counselors to use methods already demonstrated as successful during previous sessions to assist the family's work. The ritual often produces a tangible product that is displayed in a place of honor in the family home.

Case Summaries

The following case summaries are brief accounts of interventions that were employed using the present framework. The families were seen through a Marriage Family Therapy Training Program. Families were seen for 9 and 12 sessions, respectively. The counseling format used a team approach (3-4 students + supervisor) with live supervision. Supervision and observations were conducted via a one-way mirror and in-room telephone connection. The assigned team roles were therapist (counselor), historian, two hypothesizers, and director (supervisor) (see Bernstein & Burge, 1988). At times, a team member from behind the one-way mirror would enter the counseling room to assist the assigned therapist. Family names have been changed to protect client privacy.

The following listed issues were common presession and ongoing counseling considerations, which shaped the counseling interventions and treatment. Each was viewed as compromising the overall family culture balance stemming from rigid family member responses to family problems and interruptions to normal family cultural practices, which aided the maintenance of their problems. Central to the theme of this chapter, therapy focused on reestablishing healthy family cultural practices as the vehicle for helping the families negotiate more effectively the needed transitions:

- The families had issues related to family migration and/or relocation.
- There were unresolved loss issues related to separation from the family of origin, which included unresolved trauma.
- Overcompensations resulted from unresolved loss and trauma.
- The families had disruptions in family-of-origin and current family rituals that created an imbalance in family culture.
- Compromised family structure and hierarchies were evident.
- The families were struggling with a required family transition.
- The events surrounding the family problems had caused spiritual pain for the family.

Case 1

The Jackson family was referred to counseling services by a local school psychologist who had been consulting with Ms. Jackson concerning her older son's recent drop in schoolwork performance. Ms. Jackson is an

African American mother with two children. The children's father (African American) had been incarcerated approximately five years earlier. However, for all practical purposes, Ms. Jackson had been a single parent since the birth of her first son (10 years old), who was now the identified patient. She reported having worked very hard to maintain a well-paying job and to provide for her children who she loved very much. The family had relocated as part of her effort. She was highly motivated to provide her sons with future opportunities.

Her other son was age 7 and had no reported school or behavior problems. The problem presented in the first session by Ms. Jackson was her deep concern and bewilderment concerning her elder son's recent school problem that, up to then, had been persisting for approximately 3 months. Ms. Jackson had tried a variety of interventions "to get her son back on track." These began with discussions about the problem and her concern, her helping with his school work, and progressed to restrictions on play and other social activities. No behavior problems were reported other than his academic performance. It was noticed during the first session that her depth of worry and concern was unusually high given the nature of the problem. She attributed it to her deep love and concern for her son. Toward the end of the first session, the problem was reframed by the therapist as a "family problem" since it was affecting the family atmosphere and normal family activities. A genogram was conducted during the second session. The source and depth of Ms. Jackson's concern (actually fears) were quickly revealed during the process. Ms. Jackson gave accounts of the family histories, hers and her ex-husband's. Ms. Jackson was the only person from both families who had completed high school and had attended two years of college and attained an Associate of Arts degree. Both family histories were characterized by a number of incarcerations, patterns of unemployment, substance abuse, and broken families. Through her initiation, the family was presently estranged from the extended family network. It became clear that Ms. Jackson had been and continued to be doing everything she could to immunize her sons from their family legacies. This included interrupting previously held kinship connections and extended family rituals. She was very frightened that if she was not vigilant her worst fears would come true.

Consequently, her son's drop in school performance activated a disproportionate emotional response and evoked rigid adherence to the family boundaries. Normal family activities and rituals were interrupted during this period. Her son's behavior was reframed by the therapy team as a "signal" that the family's overcompensated response to past family histories, although once necessary for family survival, had now become too restrictive and rigid. As a consequence, her son's demeanor in the sessions changed from disengaged to engaged, as if a burden had been lifted from his shoulders. The family's reported history was targeted as the external problem that was now sabotaging its ability to adapt and change and had caused an unresolved spiritual pain in the family. Before she would loosen her grasp, we had to convince her that her son was safe from the perceived dangers of the family's past. We accomplished this by contrasting her success against her family's and spent a bit of time discussing how she managed to do so well in the absence of role models. She spoke of her deceased grandmother's help as a young girl that provided her a foundation and the fact that she was so determined. This elicited sadness and guilt on her part for her sons' disconnection from their extended family. However, by spending time with her successes (solution focused) we were able to assure her that she had developed a wonderful home and foundation (like her grandmother had provided her) to protect her children and that, from our perspective, her children were going to do quite well as a result and that perhaps now was a good time for her and the family to reunite. We were then able to convince Ms. Jackson to allow us, as her family intermediary, to carry some of her burden (concern/worry) at least while the team worked on the family problem. Ms. Jackson showed a great deal of relief.

In subsequent sessions, the family was engaged in future-oriented family drawings. These included Ms. Jackson's personal wishes for herself that she had put on hold. Other future-oriented family and individual goals were embedded in the family exercises. During the counseling sessions we were also able to convince the school counselor and the son's teacher to relax their vigilance concerning his problem to give us time to work with the family. As the family's energies were redirected toward family and desired personal goals (which included reconnecting the family with relatives), Ms. Jackson's response to her son's problem relaxed and his school performance made a remarkable recovery within a 3-week period.

The final five sessions were involved in designing and implementing new family rituals that reinforced future family and individual goals. Family-of-origin practices, particularly those that included her grandmother, were used as guidelines for establishing new family rituals. Interventions also included getting both of her sons connected with African American male role models through a local Big Brother program.

Case 2

A local school psychologist also referred the Collins family for our services. The Collins family was a blended family consisting of two children (Keri, 12 years old, and Annie, 9 years old) from the father's (Michael) previous marriage, one son (Pablo, 10 years old) from the mother's (Sonya) previous marriage, and two children from their current marriage (Sara, 4 years old, and Joseph, 18 months old). The father was born in the United States of distant Irish ancestry, and the mother was born and raised in Mexico. She had moved to the United States on her own to connect with her sisters (who had migrated several years earlier) while divorced and pregnant with Pablo, who was born in the United States. Michael and Sonya had been married six years. During all but the last eight months of this period, his daughters Keri and Annie lived with their biological mother in another state. Child Protective Services, who were prosecuting their biological mother's live-in male partner for sexually abusing the two girls, placed them back with their father. The school counselor prior to the referral had seen both girls. After the referral, they were assigned individual counselors who would provide regular weekly counseling (via our services) at their school site under my supervision. The school psychologist was aware of the circumstances for the children's placement with their father's new family. Michael and Sonya confided to the school psychologist that the girls' presence in the home was disrupting the family, which prompted her to make the referral to our services.

Mr. and Mrs. Collins, during the telephone calls preceding counseling as well as during the first session, presented the problem as stemming from the girls fighting and lying and generally disrupting family harmony. During the first session they both were openly adamant that if the girls' behavior didn't change they would not be allowed to stay. Their frustration and annoyance were made quite clear. The father indicated that he did not want this family to end up like his previous one. Their stepmother indicated that she didn't trust the girls around her younger daughter and baby. The team was aware and extremely sensitive to the precarious situation the two girls were in given the trauma of the abuse and losing their mother. After assessing the problem, the team took a 20-minute session intermission to discuss the case before returning to the closing phase of the session.

During the discussion, the team (4 students + myself) became polarized, with two members wanting to rescue the children from what they felt were two insensitive parents. As the director/supervisor, I suggested that to help the two girls we needed to join with Michael and Sonya in a manner that allowed us to influence their behavior toward the girls and that compromising our relationship with the parents would negatively affect the girls by inflaming an already frustrated couple. We began the closing phase of the session by reframing their frustration as stemming from the deep love and concern they had for the two girls and for the family as a whole, which was accepted by both. We also were able to reframe the problem as a family problem, which, given their level of concern, was readily accepted. The team suggested that since the problem had been persisting for so long that it was unlikely to resolve it without some bit of work and time. We added that we could see the level of their frustration had nearly met its limit but that we wanted them not to try to do anything more to resolve the problems until we completed our assessment. We indicated that it would be useful to us if they could just make notes of the problems during the week so we could review them in the next session. They agreed and indicated that there should be plenty of examples.

In an attempt to lower the parents' level of frustration and reaction to the girls, we asked Keri and Annie to pick a day during the week in which they would pretend a fight (rules were established) and pretend a lie. The parents were to guess and record the events and to report their findings in the following session, which they agreed they would do. This intervention is what strategic family therapy refers to as "prescribing the symptom" (Madanes, 1981; Watzlawick, Jackson, & Beavin, 1967). The rationale is based on the notion that turning the problem behavior into a game distracts the principles from the source of tension normally associated with the behavior. The intervention in turn punctuates the normal behavioral sequence of events surrounding the problem behavior and provides for alternative response patterns. In effect the intervention creates a paradox in which it is hard to get frustrated at something that is now by design intentional.

In the next session, the parents indicated that they had not observed any major problems since their last visit. When they were asked to guess what day during the week their daughters acted out the prescribed symptoms, they guessed incorrectly. There was a noticeable difference in their levels of frustration, and they reported that for some reason it was a better week. They did, however, continue with their ultimatum for the girls but with less intensity. By using future-oriented solution-focused inquiries, we were by the end of the second session able to hear both Michael and Sonya use terms that included the girls as a part of the future family. The last 10 minutes of the session were spent discussing the problems as stemming from the family not knowing how to handle the added responsibility of a suddenly larger family with the added financial burden (externalized problem). It was decided that we would conduct the genogram in the following session.

The genogram was tailored to inquire into family-of-origin modeling of love and discipline within each family's history. Michael was one of 3 siblings and Sonya one of 12 siblings, with both parents present in each respective household. The most substantial information shared during the genogram was Sonya revealing that she had been molested as a child by an uncle but had never revealed the abuse until she became involved with Michael. She had revealed this to him when it was discovered that his daughters had been molested. She had not discussed it again until the genogram. She revealed that her parents, having 12 children, were unable to attend to her emotional needs and that her embarrassment over the abuse also contributed to her unresolved anguish. The revelation significantly changed the family dialogue and allowed the team to use it as a bridge between her and her stepdaughters. Michael talked with tears in his eyes about his sadness for his wife and daughters having experienced their tragedies. All dialogue from Michael and Sonya from then on was characterized by terms of family inclusion when talking about the two girls.

The genogram also revealed that both family trees had legacies of closed communications and constricted emotional expression between family members but particularly between parents and children. There were clear signs that Sonya had unresolved losses with regard to her flight from Mexico and her ex-husband and that Michael had unresolved losses stemming from his divorce. These issues were dealt with during the latter sessions when we met with the couple separately for two sessions. However, the combined losses (parents' and children's) were noted as causing a spiritual pain in the family.

Over the next two weeks, the girls' fighting had nearly completely diminished. Counseling efforts were centered on reestablishing family roles of protectorships beginning with the parents as primary family protectors and down through the children. Family discussions were held on the importance of roles and also maintaining family rituals. As a ritual, the children decided that once a week they would do something special for their parents. To initiate the ritual, Pablo and Keri baked a cake, with the other children helping, to honor the parents' roles as primary protectors. The event was reported as a fun experience for both the adults and children. Each child was assigned a day to honor his/her position in the family, with a personal drawing (done in session) placed on the refrigerator for that day.

A family healing forgiveness ritual was conducted during the sixth session. It was tailored from Step 8 of Cloe Madanes's (1990) model for intervening on family violence and molest. The Madanes model is a 16-step therapy procedure that helps families address violence within the family (e.g., abuse) by discussing the problem openly, discussing how the problem has caused "spiritual pain" for all members of the family, having the family members express repentance and sorrow to the victim for not protecting him/her, reestablishing a family member protector hierarchy, and restoring love within the family.

During the checking-in period of the sixth session, Michael and Sonya reported that both girls had voluntarily divulged that they had taken some money from their aunt (Sonya's sister). Both parents were proud of the girls' honesty, and the girls lit up with smiles. The counselor in the session indicated that the girls felt safe that they were now part of the family. Sonya's response was "I hope so."

The in-session ritual began with an explanation that the family's love, hard work, and commitment had demonstrated that they were ready to take the next step, which was introduced as the "forgiveness ritual." The ritual was tailored so each member could apologize to others in the family for matters that specifically applied to his/her situation. The members were told that each would have to participate and that it would be difficult but important for all to do so (we excluded the two youngest, although the second youngest was present throughout the ritual). We began with Keri because we were convinced she would set a good tone for the others, and she did just that. We were very careful in designing her and her sister's apologies so as not to blame the victims. She was instructed to beg for forgiveness by getting on her knees and apologizing to her father "for not knowing how to behave in the new family and not being able to help out like she would have liked to."

Having the family members get on their knees is based on the belief that apologies paired with a humiliating posture will best convey the sincerity, seriousness, and commitment to the moment (Madanes, 1990). As is often observed, kneeling commonly appears in many religious practices. However, the format of having clients get on their knees should be adjusted to match the cultural and religious practices of the particular family. Asking families about their traditional and religious practices for healing wrongful acts can provide the counselor with this information. Nevertheless, it is my experience that, in cases where it is clear that hierarchical protector roles have broken down and have contributed to a family member being victimized, family member protectors, especially parents, harbor a great deal of guilt for not being able to protect their child regardless of blame or fault. In these cases, kneeling, although it may appear out of context to conflict with hierarchical family relationships, provides a means for parental and/or guardian relief from overwhelming guilt and an opportunity to correct the family protector hierarchy, which is central to family health and unity. It is up to the family and the counselor to decide whether or not the family's problem is threatening enough to family survival to warrant extreme interventions such as kneeling.

It is important to note that Keri's wording, while an apology, places the responsibility on the parents to teach her. She was then asked to perform this with Sonya and then to the whole family. It was done in a tearful and moving manner. Her sister went next, using the identical words. Their father's turn was next. He was asked to apologize to each daughter for not being able to protect her from the abuse. He took turns kneeling in front of each daughter; it is impossible to capture here his sincere heartfelt words as he added much more than directed. Both girls were in tears and embraced him when he finished.

To bring the whole family into the process, we felt that it was very important to include Pablo in the process. Consequently, the next step was to have him and his stepfather together kneel in front of the females and apologize for men in general who are usually the perpetrators. It was made very clear that it was not because he had done anything wrong. It was very interesting because in order for Pablo to understand, Michael had to help explain what they were doing; in doing so, he went first and then told Pablo to just say what was in his heart—it was quite a touching moment.

The challenge of the ritual came when it was Sonya's turn. She was asked to apologize to Keri and Annie for not trusting them. It is difficult to capture the true nature of the impasse: Sonya began twice, and before completing the first apology she went back to her seat and said she couldn't do it. She said she couldn't do it because of her English, so we said to do it in Spanish—but she still couldn't. It was very moving because after both attempts Michael went over to reassure and comfort her while the children sat and waited. Before her third attempt, while she was sitting, she reflected that Keri reminded her of herself at her age and revealed again that she thought something had happened to them. She also reflected how terrible it was and then said she felt bad she wasn't able to do anything. I immediately called in over the loudspeaker and indicated that now she could do something. Her husband then added, "It's not just for them, it's for you too"—and with that a few seconds later she made her final try. As she knelt down in front of both girls with one hand on each of the girls' knees, she explained how sorry she was for them and that she knew what they were going through. She added that she didn't want them to live with the same embarrassment she had lived with through the years. After a series of heartfelt words, she said, "All we can do is work together." The girls were in tears as was she; one by one, starting with her husband, each moved toward her and embraced; this was followed by a family embrace with Sonya in the middle. The session ended with a homework assignment for the family to create something together to represent the bad feelings of the past 8 months and to go to a special place and bury it. They reported the next week that they had made a collage, gone to a special place, and burned and buried it.

The family was seen for another six sessions during which we worked on future goals and had two half-sessions addressing marital issues. Marital issues centered on unresolved loss (noted earlier) that added pressure to the marriage. One session was dedicated to helping the family with the anticipated court date. The two girls continued individual counseling. Later reports indicated that the family was doing quite well.

CLOSING COMMENTS

Culture has been presented as a conceptual model for observing, assessing, and intervening in family problems. Culture provides the path to family health and is the essence by which families subsist from generation to generation. Culture has a profound influence on how we construct our realities and, in turn, how we think about, observe, and act upon our environments. Traditions and rituals are culture's vehicles for transmitting values, attitudes, and goals and act to reinforce a sense of stability, belonging, and identity for family members. The model of family therapy presented in this chapter is based on the notion that family problems requiring outside professional assistance often stem from disruptions in traditional family cultural practices. The model is also based on the belief that a family's inability to negotiate adaptations to new environment demands, such as those resulting from acculturation, requires the creation and adaptation of new family rituals.

Hence this chapter's goal has been to assist counselors in working with ethnic minority families who develop maladaptive patterns of behaviors resulting from an inability to successfully negotiate and navigate one or more of life's transitional challenges. As noted, the methods also are useful in working with any family who struggles with life transitions. The model is useful in addressing family symptoms resulting from intercultural conflicts, intergenerational conflicts, sibling conflicts, marital conflicts, parental inadequacy, inadequate social skill development, and abuse. The model focuses on ethnic minority families who enter counseling as a result of a breakdown or interruption in family cultural practices that normally provide stability and navigation through stressful life events and/or an inability to successfully deal with acculturative life challenges. Primary counseling interventions involve the reintroduction of abandoned cultural practices and/or the establishment of new practices. The method incorporates culturally sensitive and culturally responsive procedures.

In closing, it is humbling, from a professional perspective, to realize that the vast majority of families and individuals have never been served by a professional counselor and yet most manage quite well. Could it be culture's healing powers working its daily inconspicuous magic? If so, *el olvido* (forgetfulness) indeed can be a dangerous thing.

NOTE

1. "El Olvido" by Judith Ortiz Cofer from *Terms of Survival.* Copyright © 1987 by Arte Publico Press, University of Houston. Reprinted with permission.

REFERENCES

Allport, G. W. (1954). *The nature of prejudice.* Reading, MA: Addison-Wesley.

Ariel, S. (1999). *Culturally competent family therapy: A general model.* Westport, CT: Praeger.

Becvar, D. S., & Becvar, R. J. (1988). *Family therapy: A systemic integration.* Boston: Allyn & Bacon.

Berg, I. K., & deShazer, S. (1993). Making numbers talk: Language in therapy. In S. Friedman (Ed.), *The new language of change: Constructive collaboration in psychotherapy* (pp. 5-24). New York: Guilford.

Berger, P. L., & Luckmann, T. (1985). *The social construction of reality.* New York: Doubleday.

Bernstein, R. M., & Burge, S. K. (1988). A record-keeping format for training systemic therapists. *Family Process, 27,* 339-349.

Carter, B., & McGoldrick, M. (1989). *The changing family life cycle: A framework for family therapy.* Boston: Allyn & Bacon.

Cofer, J. O. (1987). El olvido [Poem]. In *Terms of survival.* Houston, TX: Arte Publico Press.

Cuellar, I., Harris, I. C., & Jasso, R. (1980). An acculturation scale for Mexican American normal and clinical populations. *Hispanic Journal of Behavioral Science, 2,* 199-217.

Dana, R. H. (1993). *Multicultural assessment perspectives for professional psychology.* Boston: Allyn & Bacon.

Dell, P. F. (1980, April). The Hopi family therapist and the Aristotelian parents. *Journal of Marital and Family Therapy,* pp. 123-129.

Evenson, M. L., & Evenson, T. L. (1991, April). *Creative family rituals as a way of maintaining wellness.* Paper presented at the annual meeting of the American Association for Counseling & Development, Reno, NV.

Falicov, C. (1988). Learning to think culturally. In H. A. Liddle, D. C. Breulin, & R. C. Schwartz (Eds.), *Handbook of family therapy training and supervision* (pp. 335-357). New York: Guilford.

Falicov, C. (1995). Training to think culturally: A multidimensional comparative framework. *Family Process, 34*, 373-388.

Fisch, F., Weakland, J. H., & Segal, L. (1982). *The tactics of change: Doing therapy briefly.* San Francisco: Jossey-Bass.

Fleuridas, C., Nelson, T. S., & Rosenthal, D. M. (1986). The evolution of circular questions: Training family therapists. *Journal of Marital and Family Therapy, 12*, 113-127.

Grieger, I., & Ponterotto, J. G. (1995). A framework for assessment in multicultural counseling. In J. G. Ponterotto, J. M. Casas, L. A. Suzuki, & C. M. Alexander (Eds.), *Handbook of multicultural counseling* (pp. 357-374). Thousand Oaks, CA: Sage.

Helms, J. E. (1984). Toward a theoretical explanation of the effects of race on counseling: A Black and White model. *The Counseling Psychologist, 12*, 153-165.

Ho, M. K. (1987). *Family therapy with ethnic minorities.* Newbury Park, CA: Sage.

LaFromboise, T., Coleman, H. L. K., & Gerton, J. (1993). Psychological impact of biculturalism: Evidence and theory. *Psychological Bulletin, 114*, 395-412.

Madanes, C. (1981). *Strategic family therapy.* San Francisco: Jossey-Bass.

Madanes, C. (1990). *Sex, love, and violence.* New York: W. W. Norton.

Madanes, C. (1995). *The violence of men.* New York: W. W. Norton.

McGoldrick, M., & Boundy, D. (1996). *The legacy of unresolved loss.* New York: Newbridge Communications.

McGoldrick, M., & Gerson, R. (1985). *Genograms in family assessment.* New York: W. W. Norton.

Penn, P. (1982). Circular questioning. *Family Process, 21*, 267-280.

Pinderhughes, E. (1989). *Understanding race, ethnicity, and power.* New York: Free Press.

Ruiz, R. A., Casas, J. M., & Padilla, A. M. (1977). *Culturally relevant behavioristic counseling.* Presentation to the Mental Health Research Center, Los Angeles.

Sampson, E. E. (1988). The debate on individualism: Indigenous psychologies of the individual and their role in personal and societal functioning. *American Psychologist, 43*, 15-22.

Schwartzman, J. (1983). Family ethnography: A tool for clinicians. In C. J. Falicov (Ed.), *Cultural perspectives in family therapy* (pp. 137-149). Rockville, MD: Aspen Systems.

Sluzki, C. (1979). Migration and family conflict. *Family Process, 18*, 379-390.

Sue, D. W. (1978). World views and counseling. *Personnel and Guidance Journal, 56*, 458-462.

Szapocznik, J., Santisteban, D. A., Kurtines, W. M., Perez-Vidal, A., & Hervis, O. (1984). Bicultural effectiveness training: Treatment intervention for enhancing intercultural adjustment in Cuban American families. *Hispanic Journal of Behavioral Sciences, 6*, 317-344.

Waters, M., Carter, B., Papp, P., & Silverstein, O. (1992). *The invisible web: Gender patterns in family relationships.* New York: Guilford.

Watzlawick, P., Beavin, J., & Jackson, D. (1967). *Pragmatics of human communication.* New York: W. W. Norton.

White, M., & Epston, D. (1990). *Narrative means to therapeutic ends.* New York: W. W. Norton.

Wolin, S. J., & Bennett, L. A. (1984). Family rituals. *Family Process, 12*, 401-420.

Worden, M. (1999). *Family therapy basics.* Pacific Grove, CA: Brooks/Cole.

Wrenn, C. G. (1962). The culturally encapsulated counselor. *Harvard Educational Review, 32*, 444-449.

Correspondence regarding this chapter may be sent to Arthur R. Sanchez, Psychology Department, California State University at Chico, Chico, CA 95929 (e-mail address: asanchez@csuchico.edu).

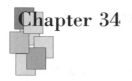

Chapter 34

SCHOOL COUNSELING IN A
MULTICULTURAL SOCIETY

DANIEL T. SCIARRA

ON NOVEMBER 29, 1999, then-President Bill Clinton signed into law the Elementary School Counseling Demonstration Act allocating $20 million for the hiring of new elementary school counselors. How much recent celebrated incidents of violence in schools had to with the passage of this legislation is open to speculation. However, while incidents like Columbine and their consequences continue to make front-page headlines, the continued lack of educational attainment and achievement among large numbers of minority youth goes relatively unnoticed. Therefore, this chapter is dedicated to delineating the role of the school counselor in a multicultural society as one who can play a crucial role in promoting higher academic achievement and consequently higher quality jobs for low-income and underrepresented minority groups.

I begin by addressing the contemporary debate surrounding the role of the school counselor between those who favor a more mental health focus and those who favor an achievement focus (i.e., increasing the academic performance of all children). Next, while not discounting the need for school counselors to be trained in and attend to psychological health issues, I provide a portrait of education in the United States, the disparities in achievement among racial groups, and the reasons for such disparities. Then, using a case example, I demonstrate how school counselors can play a crucial role in helping students achieve their potential by being skilled multicultural consultants both with parents and school staff. I follow this with a section dedicated to how school counselors can play leading roles in developing multicultural awareness within their schools and then conclude the chapter with a section on postsecondary preparation targeted to the needs of low-income and minority students.

THE ROLE OF THE SCHOOL COUNSELOR:
A DEBATED ISSUE

In early 1997, The Education Trust, a nonprofit organization dedicated to promoting high academic achievement for all students, sent a Request for Proposal (RFP) to more than 700 counseling programs in the United States. The RFP was for a competitive grant funded by the DeWitt Wallace-Reader's Digest Fund to transform the training of school counselors. Ultimately, six universities would receive upwards of a half a million dollars over three years to "build new models for graduate-level preparation of school counselors—models that will produce professionals better equipped to serve the diverse student population of the 21st century" (The Education Trust, 1997, p. 1). After the appearance of an article in *Counseling Today* (Guerra, 1998) publicizing the seemingly benign and laudable initiative by The Education Trust, a firestorm of debate was unleashed primarily through CESNET (the Internet listserve for counselor educators). Fueling the debate was The Education Trust's (1997) criticism of the current training of school counselors, which included the following points: (a) Current programs do not place the academic preparation of all students at the center of the counselor's responsibilities; (b) there is a lack of connection between how counselors are trained and the services they need to provide; (c) training school counselors in isolation from other school personnel does not promote the school counselor as collaborator; (d) school counselors-in-training take a core of generic counseling courses that does not provide them with competencies specific to the school setting; and (e) school counselors' training primarily has a mental health focus.

Although debate around the role of the school counselor is nothing new, The Education Trust's initiative did delineate more clearly the lines of controversy between those who advocate for a mental health model of training for school counselors and those who favor a more programmatic approach for increasing the academic preparation of all students. Proponents of the mental health model point to, among other things, increased violence in schools, a rising suicide rate among adolescents, and an overwhelming report of child abuse cases, all of which require school counselors to be trained in issues of mental health (Guerra, 1998). The other side argues that because counselor caseloads across the nation tend to range from 300 to 500 students it is impossible for school counselors to provide ongoing mental health counseling, so students in need of such services should be referred for long-term counseling in the community. Then, school counselors can dedicate their efforts in a proactive, programmatic fashion toward advocacy for those students who are underachieving. A major part of the problem, according to The Education Trust, is that school counseling students were being trained in universities by professors who had little or no experience in schools and therefore taught only from the familiar focus of mental health counseling. In response, one counseling professor compared The Education Trust to health insurance companies that are allowed to dictate treatment because they are paying for it without having the medical expertise to make such determinations (Hanna, 1998).

Because emotions have run so high in this debate, it is likely that neither side appreciates the other's positive and valid points. Having been a school counselor, I can affirm that when emotional crises arise within a school, the point person will always be the school counselor. It certainly would be a sad day if school counselors had to respond to a child in emotional turmoil stemming from, say, a family problem, suicidal ideas, or being a victim of abuse and violence by saying they were not trained for such "mental health" problems. Although this was not the intent of The Education Trust, it must be emphasized that school counseling has to remain contemporary by training its students in dealing (albeit on a short-term basis) with the psychological and developmental challenges of growing up in the new millennium. However, I do believe that the fundamental impetus behind The Education Trust's grant became lost amid its own criticism of how school counselors are currently trained and the rebuttal to that criticism.

My school counseling experience took place in the nation's poorest congressional district (U.S. Bureau of the Census, 1990), popularly known as the South Bronx, in New York City. Therefore, I resonated profoundly with what I perceived to be the fundamental thrust behind The Education Trust's RFP: to train school counselors in such a way that they would be better equipped to play a significant role in closing the achievement gap between more affluent SES Whites and low-income and underrepresented students. The school in which I worked was 80% Latino and 20% African American and ranked continually among the lowest 5 of 181 intermediate schools throughout the New York City school system. Simply put, students were not achieving up to their potential. I saw The Education Trust's invitation as a beacon of hope in the midst of a dismal situation because it invited school counselors-in-training to become cognizant also of systemic forces which can keep low-income, minority individuals from high academic achievement and educational attainment. A chapter titled "School Counseling in a Multicultural Society" and written for the second edition of *Handbook of Multicultural Counseling* cannot ignore this significant and potentially devastating achievement gap that currently exists in the United States among different racial groups. The purpose of this chapter is to make counselors aware of the tremendous educational disparities that exist among various cultural groups and to suggest concrete ways by which school counselors can intervene to close the achievement gap.

EDUCATION IN AMERICA

Simply put, African American, Latino, and Native American Indian students continue to lag far behind their White and Asian peers on many educational measures (College Board, 1999). There is an urgent need to deal with the lack of educational attainment among these three groups because they presently compose nearly 33% of the under-18 population in the United States and are projected to comprise 40% by 2030 (U.S. Bureau of the Census, 1996). In other words, if the educational achievement gap is not closed for African Americans, Latinos, and Native American Indians, almost half of this country's youths will be ill prepared to meet the increasingly more technologically complex demands of the workplace. The practical consequences are that (a) U.S. companies will find themselves more and more unable to find qualified workers and (b) many young people from these three groups will continue to work in low-paying service jobs. Without high academic achievement, such students' access to high-quality education and consequently to quality high-paying jobs, is severely limited.

Educational Attainment

The good news is that across all underrepresented groups educational attainment has increased. For example, in the mid 1990s, underrepresented minorities achieved about 13% of bachelor's degrees awarded in the United States, up from 9% in the early 1980s. However, during the same period, the percentage of Whites receiving bachelor's degrees rose from 23% to 31%. Thus, about twice as many Whites in their mid-20s earned bachelor's degrees as did African Americans, Latinos, and Native American Indians (College Board, 1999). One must also consider that during this period the under-18 population of these three major underrepresented groups grew by 6% while that of Whites declined. Educational attainment on the high school level has also increased. By 1995, the percentage of Black 25- to 29-year-olds who had graduated from high school (or earned an equivalency diploma) reached 87% (equal to Whites' and up from 77% in 1980). Neither Latino nor Native American Indians fared as well. The percentage of young Latino adults completing high school actually decreased from 59% in 1980 to 57% in 1995. However, when immigrant status is controlled for, the situation is less dismal. For example, in 1990, 78% of Mexican American adults born in the United States graduated from high school, compared to 38% of young adult Mexican immigrants (U.S. Bureau of the Census, 1990). In contrast, 88% of young adult Asian immigrants had graduated from high school, compared to 95% of native-born Asian Americans. And in 1990, only 63% of young Native American Indian adults graduated from high school (U.S. Bureau of the Census, 1990). Thus, it appears that immigration status can be a factor in educational attainment in some populations but not in others.

Educational Achievement

Statistics concerning educational attainment (i.e., the number of those earning degrees) do not tell the whole story. Data about educational

TABLE 34.1 Percentage of Twelfth-Grade Students Within the Proficient and
Advanced Achievement Ranges on the NAEP 1998 Reading Test,
1996 Math Test, and 1996 Science Test

	Proficient			Advanced		
	Reading	Math	Science	Reading	Math	Science
White	40	18	24	7	2	3
Black	17	4	4	1	0	0
Hispanic	24	6	6	2	0	1
Asian	33	26	19	6	7	3
Native American	24	3	10	3	0	0

SOURCE: From the *1996 Science Performance Standards: Achievement Results for the Nation and the
States* (Washington, DC: National Assessment Governing Board) by M. L. Bourque, 1997; *NAEP 1998
Reading Report Card for the Nation and the States* (Washington, DC: U. S. Department of Education) by
P. L. Donahue (1999); *NAEP 1996 Mathematics Report Card for the Nation and the States* (Washington,
DC: U. S. Department of Education) by C. M. Reece (1997).

achievement (i.e., developing superior academic skills and subject mastery
at each level of education) have to be considered as they reveal who will gain
access to high-quality advanced education and high-quality career options
(College Board, 1999). About 30 years ago, the federal government began
tracking long-term achievement trends through its National Assessment
of Educational Progress (NAEP) testing program. NAEP data reveal that relatively small percentages of African American, Hispanic, and Native
American Indian high school seniors have scores that show them well prepared for college (see Table 34.1).

Table 34.1 reveals that on the NAEP reading test about 25% of Hispanic
and Native American Indian 12th graders reached the Proficient level and
only 2%-3% the Advanced level in contrast to 50% of Whites who reached
or exceeded the Proficient level and 7% the Advanced level.[1] Only 1 out of
10 African American, Latino, and Native American Indian 12th graders
scored at the Advanced level of all three tests and at the Proficient level on
both the math and science tests, in spite of constituting one third of the age
group (College Board, 1999). These scoring patterns are similar to fourth-
and eighth-grade students who are also tested by the NAEP. Thus, the wide
achievement gaps begin to appear at an early age and probably develop
within the first three years of school (College Board, 1999). Doing well in
elementary school is of paramount importance, and few low achievers
in elementary school become high achievers in high school. The fact of the
matter is that African American and Latino 12th graders read and do math
at the same levels as White 8th graders (National Assessment of Educational Progress, 1996a). Although 49% of low achievers in high school still
go on to some form of postsecondary education, proficiency gaps persist
among African American, Latino, and White college graduates,
with Whites significantly outperforming the others. Thus, even the small

percentage of African Americans and Latinos armed with baccalaureate degrees can find themselves excluded from top-quality jobs because of inferior math and reading skills.

Why Do Gaps in Educational Achievement Exist Across Racial Groups?

Educational scholars do not lack for theories as to why tremendous gaps in achievement exist for underrepresented minorities. Ranging from the *Bell Curve* (Herrnstein & Murray, 1994) explanation that children of color lack ability to more systemic explanations of socioeconomic status, discrimination, and an ethnocentric philosophy of education, researchers, politicians, and the average taxpayer continue to expend huge amounts of psychological energy debating this question. However, when one begins to examine certain trends among different groups, explanations emerge that ought to concern the counseling profession as a whole and school counselors in particular.

Different Students Are Taught Different Things

In the United States, some students follow a college preparatory track and others take more vocational credits. However, when African American, Latino, and White students follow the same rigorous mathematics curriculum (Algebra I, Geometry, Algebra II, and pre-Calculus or Calculus), their math scores improve equally well (National Assessment of Educational Progress, 1994). Students, regardless of race, who complete advanced math and science score higher on the Scholastic Aptitude Test (SAT; College Board, 1994). NAEP math scores are also higher for eighth graders enrolled in Algebra as opposed to those in pre-Algebra and eighth-grade Math.

Moreover, a more or less rigorous curriculum is related to socioeconomic status as the percentage of eighth-grade Title I (i.e., schools with a high percentage of low-income students) school students enrolled in Algebra is 16%, compared to 26% of students in more affluent schools (National Association of Educational Progress, 1996b). Across the board, low-income students are less likely to have Algebra integrated into the Math curriculum and less likely to be enrolled in a college preparatory track (U.S. Department of Education, 1995b). High-income students compose 65% of those enrolled in a college preparatory track, compared to 49% of middle-income and 28% of low-income students. Furthermore, socioeconomic status cannot be divorced from issues of race. The RAND Corporation projections for the year 2015 show that Whites and Asians will continue to constitute the overwhelming majority of youths from high-income families and that Latinos and African Americans[2] will constitute the overwhelming majority of low-SES students (Karoly, 1998). In fact, African American and Latino students without a parent who has at least a high school education are expected to grow from 60% in 1990 to 78% in 2015 (College Board, 1999). In terms of race, current data show 22.6% of Latinos and 25.7% of African American 10th graders enrolled in a college preparatory track compared to 34% of White and 42% of Asian 10th graders (U.S. Department of Education, 1998). Furthermore, the percentage of African American, Latino, and Native American Indian high school graduates completing Algebra II, Geometry, Biology, Chemistry, Physics, and Calculus ranks far below the percentage of Whites and Asians who complete these courses.

These data suggest that, unless something is done, large numbers of Black, Latino, and Native American Indian youngsters will be involved in an educational curriculum that tracks them for lower academic achievement. However, if this trend can be stopped, the number of the highly educated from underrepresented minorities will increase and reverse the aforementioned year 2015 projections. In other words, more African American, Latino, and Native American Indian children will have parents with more education than is currently projected. Research over the years indicates that more highly educated parents provide earlier and more varied cognitive assistance to their children, which results in an early home life environment reflective of a preschool (College Board, 1999).

Quality of Instruction Is Not the Same for All Students

Not only do schools teach different subject matter to different children as shown above, but schools vary greatly in terms of resources and quality of teaching. In school districts where 30% or more of the students are poor, 59% of teachers report lacking reading resources as compared to only 16% of teachers in districts with no poor students (Educational Testing Service, 1988). Equally disconcerting data exist for math resources, with 48% of teachers in disadvantaged urban schools and 44% in extreme rural schools reporting a lack of resources compared to only 15% of teachers in advantaged urban schools (Mullis, 1991). However, in high-poverty schools with adequate resources, students score higher on NAEP tests (The Education Trust, 1999).

Furthermore, high-poverty schools have a higher percentage of underqualified teachers.[3] For example, in schools where more than 49% of students receive free lunch, 31% of English teachers and 40% of math teachers are underqualified, compared to 19% and 28% in schools where less than 20% of students receive free lunch (National Commission on Teaching and America's Future, 1996). These inequities are also true for racial differences. In schools that are 90% to 100% White, 86% of teachers are certified and 69% have a B.A. or B.S. degree in their field of teaching, compared to only 54% and 42% in schools that are 90% to 100% non-White (Oakes, 1990). Ferguson (1997) has shown the long-range effects of high- and low-scoring teachers on student achievement (see Figure 34.1). Districts with

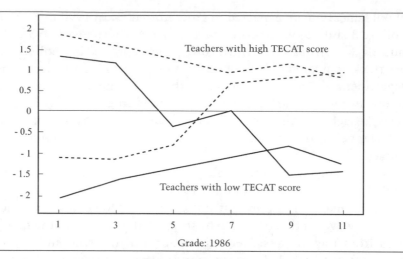

Figure 34.1. Effect of Teachers' Test Scores on District-Average Mathematics Test Scores Across Grades: Texas, Selected Districts, 1985–1986[a]

SOURCE: From "Can Schools Narrow the Test Score Gap?" by R. F. Ferguson, in *The Black-White Test Score Gap* (p. 356), edited by C. Jencks and M. Phillips, 1998, Washington, DC: Brookings Institution. Copyright 19-- by the Brookings Institution. Adapted with permission.

a. Sample comprises 3 districts with unusually high teacher scores on the Texas Examination for Current Administrators and Teachers (TECAT) and unusually low student scores on mathematics achievement tests; 4 districts with low teacher scores and high student scores; 37 districts with high scores for both teachers and students; and 25 districts with low scores for both teachers and students. For TECAT scores, "high" and "low" mean one standard deviation or more above and below, respectively, the Texas mean; for mathematics scores, the respective criteria are 0.50 standard deviations above and below the Texas mean. Standard deviations for both teachers' and students' scores are from the distribution of district-level means. In each case, the ratio of this standard deviation to that for individuals statewide is 3 to 1.

high-scoring teachers and low-scoring first and third graders have been able to raise student achievement progressively above the mean from the seventh grade on. The exact opposite is true for districts with high-scoring first and third graders and low-scoring teachers. By the seventh grade, these students are scoring consistently below the mean.

Connected to this lack of quality instruction is the fact that standards are different and lower standards tend to prevail for those in disadvantaged schools. For example, "A" students in high-poverty schools (schools where 76% to 100% of students receive free or reduced lunch) score at about the same level as "C" and "D" students in affluent schools (schools where 0% to 10% of the students receive free or reduced lunch) (U.S. Department of Education, 1994a). Students in poor schools seemingly are not held to the same standard of learning as those in affluent schools; in other words, expectations for such students are lower and result in inflated grades.

Low-Income and Minority Students Can and Do Meet High Standards

In spite of the troublesome data reported above, our nation has many examples of school systems in which low-income and underrepresented minority youths have improved their academic achievement when given the same rigorous academic curriculum and not allowed to take an over-abundance of non-college-preparatory courses. For example, El Paso, Texas, a high-poverty school district, in school year 1995–1996 enrolled 94% of Latinos in Algebra with a 55% passing rate compared to 59% enrollment and 31% passing rate in school year 1992–1993 (The Education Trust, 1999). This same school district saw pass rates for African American and Latino students in 3rd, 8th, and 10th grades increase from 32% and 36%, re-spectively, in 1992–1993 to 75% and 80%, respectively, in 1997–1998! (The Education Trust, 1999). Similar gains were made for reading pass rates in-creasing from 58% (African Americans) and 54% (Latinos) to 86% and 84%, respectively. In New York City, where 80% of students live at or near the poverty line, the number of African American 9th graders passing regents science increased from 4,496 in 1994 to 9,433 in 1995 and Latinos from 2,209 to 8,764 (Board of Education of the City of New York, 1995). City Uni-versity of New York (CUNY), whose enrollment consists mainly of gradu-ates from New York City high schools, has seen a significant increase in college preparatory units completed among its first-time enrollees. For ex-ample, 88% of first-time enrollees completed sequential math in 1996 compared to only 65% in 1991, and 73% in 1996 had completed Lab Science compared to only 55% in 1991 (Reynolds & Crew, 1997). What this means is that more New York City high school students are being enrolled in and passing college preparatory courses.

While there are many other examples where underrepresented minori-ties living in poverty have shown significant gains in academic achieve-ment, it is hoped that these few examples will serve to convince the reader that the school counselor can and should play a pivotal role in promoting academic achievement, especially among those students who traditionally have been tracked for courses known to limit their achievement potential. The school counselor's traditional role has been as gatekeeper, allowing some and not others into courses that can either promote or limit academic achievement (Hart & Jacobi, 1992). As evident in the case below, the school counselor can move from gatekeeper to advocate (i.e., one who works toward providing the necessary supports for minority students to follow a rigorous academic curriculum).

THE ROLE OF THE SCHOOL COUNSELOR IN PROMOTING ACADEMIC ACHIEVEMENT

Case Example

Mr. Smith, long-time and dedicated Math teacher, has come to Ms. Goodwin, the school counselor for the ninth grade, about one of his Latino students, Ramon Martinez, because he feels that Ramon should not be in ninth-grade Algebra and more appropriately belongs in remedial Math. Mr. Smith is quite eloquent in his presentation, saying he has tried to help Ramon by inviting him to come for extra help, but Ramon has failed to do so. The Math teacher feels that Ramon is not capable of keeping up with the rest of the class and predicts that the student will receive a failing grade. Mr. Smith is troubled by this possibility as he knows that a failure may retard Ramon's educational attainment, and the teacher is cognizant of the high dropout rate among Hispanics due to failing grades. He asserts that he cannot slow down the rest of the class down because of one student and feels that it is in the best interest of all that Ramon be removed from his class. He has come to Ms. Goodwin in her traditional role of school counselor (i.e., the one who "appropriately" places students in college preparatory courses). She is relatively new at her job and feels a bit intimidated by Mr. Smith, a well-respected veteran teacher in the school. On the other hand, Ms. Goodwin's training has made her aware of the long-term achievement consequences for someone who does not learn Algebra and learn it well. She realizes that putting Ramon in remedial Math may earn him a higher grade but also knows that it may mean tracking him for low Math achievement and therefore closes off opportunities of a higher quality education and job opportunities. She starts from the premise that given the right conditions Ramon *can* learn Algebra. She garners enough strength to tell Mr. Smith her view and suggests she look further into Ramon's situation before changing his class. Mr. Smith is a bit taken aback by her response and indicates that rarely has a school counselor disagreed with his opinion. Ms. Goodwin does not want to alienate Mr. Smith since her training emphasized having good working relationships with teachers. She negotiates with Mr. Smith by asking for a week's time to assess Ramon's social and educational history before making a decision. Shaking his head and probably wondering where Ms. Goodwin received her training as a school counselor, Mr. Smith agrees somewhat hesitantly and leaves the office.

The counselor felt good about her intervention with Mr. Smith, yet she had mixed feelings about the extra work she had given herself. It would have been easier to simply change Ramon's class. Ms. Goodwin put such feelings aside and began, amidst all the other things she had to do that day, to work on Ramon's case. She began with the school record, which showed average grades since the beginning of school with a slight decline in intermediate school. His Math grades were not particularly strong, but a comment from a sixth-grade teacher caught Ms. Goodwin's eye: "Ramon seems to perform and learn better in group activities." Other than this, the school record showed nothing extraordinary as most teachers considered Ramon "likeable" and not a behavioral problem. Ms. Goodwin's next step was to meet with Ramon. She had had no previous contact with Ramon, and he appeared a bit shy and somewhat afraid that he was in trouble. Ms. Goodwin, drawing on all of her good relationship-building skills learned in her recent counseling program, explained to Ramon that she wanted to know about his Math class since Mr. Smith had informed her of his progress. Ramon simply said that he did not like the class and did not like Mr. Smith because he constantly called on Ramon or sent him to the board without his knowing the answers. Ramon often felt embarrassed and asked Ms. Goodwin if she could change his class to an easier one. Ms. Goodwin began to feel the systemic forces impinging upon her—a student with low self-esteem and a learned helplessness, most likely stemming from his low socioeconomic and racial background, and a school system that traditionally tracked students, albeit in subtle ways. Oh! It would be all so easy to just change Ramon's class. As with Mr. Smith, Ms. Goodwin drew from her stronger side and explained to Ramon the importance of learning Algebra and its connection to higher SAT scores and the ability to do more complex operations demanded by the current job market. Ramon appeared unimpressed and said he was not planning on going to college. Ms. Goodwin challenged by saying that in today's society there were no good-paying jobs without the ability to perform complex operations and that Algebra was an essential ingredient in helping a student achieve that kind of cognitive complexity.

Ms. Goodwin laid out a plan for Ramon. He could attend an after-school Math Club that provided tutoring in a small group setting. It was composed of almost all Latinos, and cultural appreciation activities were also part of the group. Ms. Goodwin reasoned that this would be good for Ramon's self-esteem and remembered how Ramon did seem to do better in group activities. She would also talk to Mr. Smith about the possibility that Ramon could do more group work in class and suggest that he call on Ramon when the teacher was fairly sure that Ramon knew the answer. Finally, Ms. Goodwin would consult with the school psychologist and refer Ramon for testing just to rule out any learning disability that might be interfering with his achievement in Mathematics. Ramon appeared somewhat agreeable to Ms. Goodwin's plan except the after-school program which he would not be able to attend because he had a part-time job after school at the local gas station to help out his mom. Ms. Goodwin felt deflated, but her multicultural counseling preparation permitted her to appreciate Hispanic loyalty to family. Also, the fact that Ramon came from a single-parent family and was the eldest male among six siblings created the expectation that he help out his mom. Fortunately, Ms. Goodwin remembered something coming across her desk about one of the local technology companies starting some sort of internship program on Saturdays. It was designed for students needing to work and wanting to learn about technology. After informing herself further about the program, Ms. Goodwin believed that Ramon would qualify for the program and calculated that he would earn almost as much in one day in this internship as he did working four days a week at the gas station. When Ramon heard this, his first reaction was that they had better talk with his mom.

Ms. Goodwin sensed that Ramon's external locus of control might prevent him from seriously talking with his mother. Therefore, she asked Ramon if it would be okay for her to call home and discuss it with his mother. Ramon said okay but warned Ms. Goodwin that his mother did not speak English. Ms. Goodwin knew a little Spanish, so she attempted the phone call with the hope of inviting Sra. Martinez to school and since the counselor knew she could find a translator. With her broken Spanish, Ms. Goodwin alleviated Sra. Martinez's fear that Ramon was in trouble and explained she simply wanted to discuss how Ramon could do better in school. In response to Ms. Goodwin's invitation to come to school, Sra. Martinez explained that it was very difficult since she had three small children at home and one who was chronically ill. Ms. Goodwin remembered one of her former counseling professors saying that if school counselors limited their role within the school and the hours of 8 a.m. to 3 p.m., they would never intervene properly in the academic lives of their more disadvantaged students. Ms. Goodwin responded by asking Sra. Martinez if the counselor could come to her home and discuss Ramon's situation. Sra. Martinez responded readily "*Como no! Con eso, no hay problema!*" [Of course! That's no problem!]. Ms. Goodwin asked a Spanish-speaking, male paraprofessional to accompany her both for translation purposes and because Ramon lived in an unfamiliar neighborhood.

THE SCHOOL COUNSELOR
AS MULTICULTURAL CONSULTANT

In the case of Ramon, Ms. Goodwin was acting as a consultant with the student, Ramon, the teacher, Mr. Smith, and the parent, Sra. Martinez. Eventually, a school psychologist as well as an administrator might also be involved. Ms. Goodwin operated from the assumption that Ramon can and will learn Algebra. For school counselors dedicated to promoting higher achievement among underrepresented minorities, consultation will become an ever increasingly important part of their job. Furthermore, school counselors, because of their training in relationship building and behavior change, are well suited for the role of consultant.

Definition of Consulting

"Consultation can be regarded as a form of counseling in which the consultee's goal is to change another person's behavior, and counseling can be regarded as a special form of consultation, where the consultee seeks the services of the consultant to change his/her own behavior" (Ramirez, Lepage, Kratochwill, & Duffy, 1998, p. 484). Consulting is a "function of providing help on the content, process, structure of a task or series of tasks where the consultant is not actually responsible for doing the task itself but is helping those who are" (Beckhard, 1969, p. 93). By adopting this position, Ms. Goodwin, in our case example, can deal with the precariousness of the situation. Ms. Goodwin can admit selflessly that neither Ramon nor

Mr. Smith is her problem nor is it her role to teach or tutor Ramon in Math, as this would be going beyond the boundaries of her job as a school counselor. Yet she is called upon to suggest ways to help Mr. Smith, Ramon, and Ramon's mother as to how Ramon might maximize his achievement in Algebra.

Models of Consultation

Schein (1969, 1978) has proposed three basic models of consultation:

1. *Purchase of expertise model.* In this model, the consultant is viewed as an expert hired to solve a problem that the organization has diagnosed and communicated to the consultant. After such communication has taken place, the responsibility for solving the problem rests with the consultant using his/her expertise. In this model, the success of the consultation is dependent on the accuracy of the diagnosis made by the organization (Rockwood, 1993).

2. *Doctor-patient model.* In this model, the consultant is charged with diagnosing the problem and prescribing a solution. The organization's responsibility is to provide sufficient and necessary data that will help the consultant make a proper diagnosis (Rockwood, 1993).

3. *Process consultation model.* In this model, the focus is less on the content of the problem and more on how problems are solved (Rockwood, 1993). Process consultation involves the client throughout the entire process of diagnosis, generation of solutions, and implementation of interventions. Unlike the above two models, process consultation emphasizes a collaborative relationship between consultant and client.

All three models can be appropriate for a given consultation. One of the consultant's first tasks is to determine what role is the most appropriate given the nature of the consultee. For example, with the Math teacher Ms. Goodwin might use a process consultation model and with Ramon's mother a doctor-patient model. Among underrepresented groups, consultants should consider forms of acculturation and levels of cultural identity development in determining which consultation model should be employed. For someone with a withdrawn acculturative form (see Sciarra, 1999, for a description of differing acculturative forms and levels of cultural identity development) and a conformist level of cultural identity, a doctor-patient model may be more effective. In contrast, for someone with a bicultural form and an integrationist level of cultural identity, a process-oriented consultation is more indicated.

Consultation Through the Identification of Learning and Personality Styles

Because of the cultural basis of learning and personality styles, school counselors need to be acutely sensitive to the possible mismatches between a traditional Eurocentric teaching style and students from diverse cultural backgrounds. Vazquez (1998) has suggested a tripartite procedure for adapting instruction to cultural traits (see Figure 34.2). In this model, once a student trait is identified, it is passed through questions of context, content, and mode leading to a reorganized instructional strategy. A multiculturally skilled school counselor can be helpful to teachers in identifying these traits.

School counselors-in-training most likely take a course in tests and measurement which introduces the student to the fundamentals of measurement and the use of tests appropriate to their field of training (Council for Accreditation of Counseling and Related Education Programs [CACREP], 1996). Some of this training can be used for the identification of learning and personality styles. Peeke, Steward, and Ruddock (1998) have suggested the use of the Myers-Briggs Type Indicator (MBTI; Myers-Briggs, 1962) for such identification. For example, a Sensing-Thinking learning style is indicative of someone who is good with facts and detail, is organized and sequential in doing tasks, adapts well to reestablished guidelines, strives for efficiency and accuracy, and is goal oriented (Silver & Hanson, 1982). In contrast, an Intuitive-Feeling learning style interprets facts and details to see the broader picture, is creative in expressing ideas, likes to try different ways of doing a task, can adapt to new situations, is not confined by convention, and is concerned with creativity (Silver & Hanson, 1982).[4] At times, a student may have already undergone a complete and formal assessment done by a school psychologist. A good place to start is always the school record as it could contain valuable information to understanding further the learning and personality styles of a student who is underachieving. In the case scenario, Ms. Goodwin discovered something that suggested Ramon would work better in a group setting. In fact, research suggests that Hispanics, particularly those with lower levels of second-culture acquisition, might achieve better in group settings (Concha, Garcia, & Perez, 1975; Vazquez, 1979). If a psychological evaluation has been done, school counselors should do their best in trying to access it. At times, there are problems with confidentiality, but the dedicated and knowledgeable school counselor ought to pursue the evaluation's access in the most ethical manner.

Ms. Goodwin, in the case scenario, also identified Ramon's external locus of control, meaning that the control of his destiny rested on forces outside himself (Sue & Sue, 1999). Sue (1978) represented graphically culturally based worldviews developed through the psychological orientations of locus of control and locus of responsibility (see Figure 34.3). Considerable research has been done on these orientations to suggest they are culturally based (Garcia & Levenson, 1975; Levenson, 1974; Sanger & Alker, 1972; Strickland, 1973). The mainstream Eurocentric bias in this country is in favor of IC-IR orientation—rugged individualism which holds people responsible for controlling their own environment. If

THREE-STEP PROCEDURE FOR ADAPTING INSTRUCTION TO CULTURAL TRAITS

Step 1	Step 2	Step 3
Teacher observes/identifies student trait.	Trait is passed through "filter" of three questions to identify which aspect of teaching (content, context, mode) should be affected.	Teacher verbalizes/ writes out the new instruction strategy.
1. Carlos is very concerned about pleasing his family.		*1.* I'll tell Carlos that I'll inform his parents when he does really good work. (Carlos should work with great effort and expectation and thus for him the context is changed).
2. Sammy and Joanna seem disinterested when given individual work and more "turned on" when interacting with others.	**Content** *a.* Does any aspect of the trait suggest the kind of material I should be teaching?	2. I'll provide more activities that allow Sammy and Joanna to work on projects with others in small groups. (Mode is changed since the means of instruction has shifted to include more student input.)
3. Ben seems intimidated and shy when I ask him questions to which he may not know the answer.	**Context** *b.* Does any aspect of the trait suggest the physical or psychological setting I should create in the classroom?	3. I'll ask Ben questions in class that I'm fairly sure he can answer correctly, and work with him individually in areas in which he is less knowledgeable. (This strategy affects both the mode of instruction and the psychological context for Ben.)
4. Charlotte does better when the material I teach involves people interacting with one another; she is not strongly "object" oriented.	**Mode** *c.* Does any aspect of the trait suggest the manner in which I should be teaching?	*4.* I'll teach more math concepts in the context of people dealing with one another, as in buying, trading, borrowing. (The mode is basically changed to suit Charlotte's preferred style of learning.)

Figure 34.2. Three-Step Procedure for Adapting Instruction to Cultural Traits

SOURCE: From table by J. A. Vazquez (p. 3), *The Prevention Researcher*, 5(1), 1998. Copyright © 1998 by Integrated Research Services. Reprinted with permission.

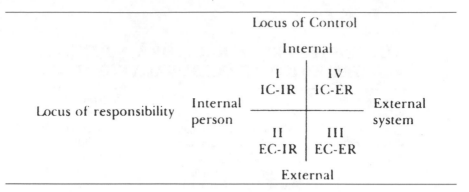

Figure 34.3. Graphic Representation of Worldviews
SOURCE: From "Eliminating Cultural Oppression in Counseling: Toward a General Theory" by D. W. Sue, 1978, *Journal of Counseling Psychology, 25,* p. 422. Copyright © 1978 by the American Psychological Association. Reprinted with permission.

Ms. Goodwin imposed this orientation upon Ramon, she would have simply counseled him to work hard because it will bring him success, to be the master of his own fate, and to be concerned only about the future (Sue & Sue, 1999). However, Ms. Goodwin sensed Ramon's external locus of control (understandable as a member of a racial minority and living in very poor socioeconomic conditions), as he feels little control over his situation and simply wishes *her* to change his class. On the contrary, Ms. Goodwin acts to manipulate some aspects of Ramon's environment with the hope of creating conditions more conducive to higher academic achievement. Since Ramon does evidence some internal locus of responsibility (works diligently at a part-time job; senses the need to help his mother), there is a good chance that with some systemic adjustments, Ramon could respond with a good effort in improving his Algebra skills.

It is hoped that through the identification of learning and personality styles, school counselors will come to recognize academic problems among low-income, underrepresented minority children more in terms of achievement and less in terms of ability. Undoubtedly, there are those cases where a student's ability is limited because of serious developmental delays. These should be recognized and confirmed early on through psychological testing. However, the data presented in the first half of this chapter clearly indicate that for low-income underrepresented minorities, the problem is underachievement, which can be remedied through the fundamental belief that all children can learn if certain systemic and environmental variables are adjusted to create the right learning environment.

Consultation With Parents

Consulting with parents not only provides valuable information concerning a child's psychosocial history but also serves the more important purpose of involving them in their child's education. Research has shown that when parents are involved in their children's education, promote a positive learning environment at home, and have positive academic expectations, there is a significant impact on student achievement (Henderson, 1987). However, when dealing with immigrant or low-income or underrepresented minority parents, their involvement and collaboration with the school becomes more challenging.

In the case of Ramon, we saw how a single, low-income parent might find it logistically very difficult to attend a within-school consultation. Sometimes, school personnel can construe this as parents not caring about their child's education. This reaction can be insensitive. For example, Casas et al. (1986) found that parents of Hispanic at-risk students had the highest educational aspirations for their children when compared to parents of Anglo at-risk, Anglo successful, and Hispanic successful students. However, when these same parents were asked about their realistic expectation (versus aspiration) for their children, 43% said high school graduation would be the highest educational attainment for their child compared to 85% of parents of Anglo successful students and 79% of parents of Hispanic successful students who said their children would receive at least a college degree. Thus, school counselors can collaborate with parents of at-risk children by having them maintain high expectations for their children. Research has found that East Asian parents, more than any other group, teach their children that educational success is based more on effort than on innate ability (College Board, 1999).

In the case scenario, the school counselor, rather than dismiss Sra. Martinez's inability to come to school as evidence of not caring about her son's education, made the decision that if the parent can't come to the school, the school can go to the parent. This kind of flexibility is demanded of school counselors if they take seriously their job of promoting higher academic achievement. In my own work as a school counselor in a very poor Latino neighborhood, I held parent meetings in the community rooms of the large apartment complexes surrounding the school. Parents from nondominant cultural backgrounds can oftentimes experience the school building as intimidating and culturally alienating. The power differential between the school and parent is accentuated in the case of those parents who are from underrepresented minority groups. This differential can be reduced by meeting with parents in a place more familiar to them. School counselors should see this as going beyond the confines of traditional counseling to establish working relationships, much the same way a counselor would do with any client from a nondominant cultural background. Multiculturally skilled counselors understand this and can transpose this skill into multicultural school consultation with parents. Schools in New York City with high achievement profiles hold parent meetings on Saturdays, and one principal indicated how he stays sometimes until 11 p.m. if that's the time the parent can make it (Lehrer, personal communication, December 1999).

Language problems also exist when dealing with immigrant parents whose knowledge of English may be minimal or even nonexistent. School counselors must monitor carefully their countertransference to parents who don't speak English or speak it poorly. There is a tendency of language problems to generate a perception of inferiority toward those who are not English-dominant (Sue & Sue, 1999). School counselors who work in a multicultural environment are encouraged to learn the language of the most popular group they serve. If this is not feasible, they should at least learn a few words for the purposes of establishing some immediate connection to parents from a diverse cultural background. Counselors should not underestimate the positive effect that even a few words can have toward building a working relationship with a parent. In the case scenario with Ramon's mother, Ms. Goodwin used her limited knowledge of Spanish to establish a connection with Sra. Martinez and eventually gain access to her home. For the home visit, Ms. Goodwin resorted to the use of a translator. Translators are sometimes the only solution, but counselors need to be aware of the pitfalls in using translators (Sciarra & Ponterotto, 1991).

Part of multicultural counseling competence is knowledge of the client's culture (Arredondo et al., 1996). This, of course, applies to school counselors working with students and their families who come from diverse cultures. However, I believe that school counselors need to be vitally connected to the neighborhoods where the schools in which they work are located. During my years as a school counselor, I lived for part of the time in the school's neighborhood, which was different racially, ethnically, and socioeconomically from my own cultural background. I am a White, middle-class Italian. I cannot emphasize enough what this experience did for the development of my own multicultural competence. This immersion experience (see also Pope-Davis, Breaux, & Liu, 1997) helped me attain a biculturalism and establish smoother working relationships in the community. The reader can only imagine a student's reaction to seeing me on a Saturday in the local grocery market or on the playground chatting informally with their family members. While I realize that for many multicultural school counselors, living in the neighborhood where they work might not be feasible, I do mean to emphasize that they must spend as much time as possible immersed in the environment where their schools are located or where the majority of their students come from. This, more than anything else, will promote their multicultural competence by reducing the cultural divide between their students' background and their own. As mentioned in the case example, school counselors who limit their role to the school on Monday through Friday from 8 a.m. to 3 p.m. and leave for an environment totally distinct from that of their students will have great difficulty establishing connections in the community so necessary to perform productive consultations with parents.

Networking in the Community

Research indicates that immigrant groups, Hispanics in particular, use informal networks to access services and build trusting relationships (De LaRosa, 1998; Delgado, 1997, 1998; Delgado & Humm-Delgado, 1982). My own experience confirms this. When I worked as a psychology intern and psychologist at a community mental health center located in a predominantly Spanish-speaking neighborhood, I performed numerous intake interviews that included the standard referral question "How is it that you came to this center?" Answers usually had something to do with a friend or extended family member telling them about how they could get help. While one might argue that this is what occurs in any population, the informal networking is particularly noteworthy when it involves mental health services since many people find it difficult to admit they receive such services.

Another example involved my work, which I have already referred to on several occasions, as a school counselor in the South Bronx. Much of the success I had in working with the parents was due to establishing networks with community leaders involved in churches, social service organizations, and youth groups dedicated to various activities (martial arts, sports, entrepreneurship, etc.). Since these leaders already had the parents' trust, it became useful to rely on them as liaisons with the goal of eliciting the parents' trust and collaboration in working with the school on behalf of their children. A vivid memory of mine involved a local Catholic priest, Father Joe ("*El Padre José*"), who used to visit the school frequently and enjoyed a close relationship with the principal. While some staff members resented his presence, I decided to befriend Father Joe as a potential part of my network for dealing with some students who were having difficulties. Since a large majority of the neighborhood's Latino population was Catholic, I thought the collaboration of Father Joe could be particularly valuable. Even though issues of confidentiality had to be respected, I came to view Father Joe as a professional collaborator with whom I could plan more sensitive interventions for some of the students and their families. In the case example with Ramon, Ms. Goodwin did something similar by asking a trusted teacher's aide living in the community and from the same cultural background as Sra. Martinez to accompany her to see Ramon's mother.

As mentioned previously, school counselors, when working cross-culturally, must spend as much time as possible in the local communities where their students come from. Part of this time can be dedicated to establishing networks with local community leaders. School counselors should not assume that the relationship between the school and the parent is a given; rather, it must be earned through brokering. It would be a mistake to assume that parents from underrepresented minority groups would automatically place their trust in a predominantly White-run institution like a school. School counselors, more than any other staff members in the school, should be adept at understanding the need for building a trusting relationship before effective work can be done. In my own experience, I too often saw many White teachers talk to non-White parents from the assumption that the parents should believe without hesitation what they were telling them about their child. I saw school staff demanding collaboration from parents, condemning them for not collaborating, and when they did collaborate, talking to parents in a condescending fashion less as collaborators and more as someone to obey orders. For this reason, school counselors, because of their training in communication skills and multiculturalism, can play a key role in developing and fostering multicultural sensitivity among the entire school staff.

Consultation With Teachers and Other School Staff

If higher achievement for all students is to become a priority for school counselors, then consulting with teachers and other school staff will increasingly become a more important part of the school counselor's role in a multicultural society. However, since consultation is not seen as a high priority for counselors, little emphasis is placed on consultation in school counselor training programs (Carey, Reinat, & Fontes, 1990). Perhaps in the strict mental health model, school counseling services are seen as ancillary to the main functions of the school, namely teaching and the promotion of higher academic achievement (Gysbers & Henderson, 2000). In the case of Ramon, we saw the challenges facing a relatively new school counselor dealing with a veteran and highly respected teacher. Ms. Goodwin was in a very precarious situation. On the one hand, she needed to establish good working relationships with teachers; on the other hand, she felt the need to challenge Mr. Smith's solution of placing Ramon in remedial Math class. Can she be faithful to her role as student advocate and also not alienate Mr. Smith? The key to success lies in Ms. Goodwin's ability, after talking with all the necessary parties, to present a plan that is good for Ramon and makes sense to Mr. Smith. If Mr. Smith is a good and caring teacher (just perhaps unaware of the long-term consequences of his actions), one has to hope that he will come to respect the good and caring actions of Ms. Goodwin. However, there is no guarantee as to teachers' flexibility, which makes the point of how challenging the role of school counselor as consultant can be.

PROMOTING MULTICULTURAL
AWARENESS WITHIN THE SCHOOL

School counselors, because of their training in issues of diversity and hopefully their self-awareness around such issues, can be especially equipped to promote multicultural awareness within the school. Through encounters with other staff members, a school counselor should always be ready to introduce issues of race and culture into the conversation in a knowledgeable and nonthreatening fashion. In our case example, Ms. Goodwin remarked to the teacher, Mr. Smith, how she is familiar with the research regarding Math achievement among Hispanics. She asked Mr. Smith to be patient while she investigated Ramon's situation a bit more. Ms. Goodwin must avoid a power struggle with Mr. Smith while at the same time staying faithful to her commitment to minority achievement. However, in addition to the opportunities presented by individual encounters, school counselors can adopt a leading role in developing a programmatic approach toward enhancing multicultural relations within the school.

Johnson (1995) proposed that school counselors be instrumental in establishing a Multicultural Advisory Council dedicated to identifying issues and concerns that are part of the school system. This Council should be culturally diverse and include a cross section of roles and responsibilities (administrators, teachers, parents, students, and community leaders). After the identification of concerns, the Council can work toward establishing goals and objectives. For example, if a concern was multicultural awareness among school staff, the Council might recommend a series of staff development workshops provided by a leading multiculturalist. For the Council to do effective work, it must be sanctioned and supported by the principal and perhaps even the superintendent of the district. Resistance should be expected from school staff since they are no different from the rest of society when asked to examine issues of diversity within themselves and the system in which they work.

If concerns are more with the student body, there are a number of interventions that should feel familiar to counselors. For example, the establishment of conflict mediation and peer mediation programs (Johnson, 1995) can give many students an alternative to violence for solving racial conflicts. Both small group counseling and classroom guidance units are excellent modalities for developing multicultural awareness. Small groups that are racially and culturally diverse give students the opportunity to share their heritage with the other members. Since both the small groups and classroom guidance lessons can follow a structured curriculum and school counselor caseloads can be in the several hundreds, multicultural teams composed of staff members (professional and nonprofessional) who are particularly interested in these issues should be formed (Robinson, 1992). During my own years as a school counselor, I constantly sought ways to reach all students through employing others paraprofessionally. One program of which I am particularly proud used selected eighth-grade students (the school was Grades 5 through 8) to work with me in facilitating group guidance lessons for incoming fifth graders in order to help their adjustment to intermediate school. This group of eighth graders would in turn serve as individual mentors for the fifth graders. Rather than be overwhelmed by their enormous caseloads and give up hope of working with all students, counselors are urged to be creative in using other resources within the school to multiply their services. Rather than seeing themselves as having to provide all services to all students, school counselors should see themselves as program directors (Gysbers & Henderson, 2000) who work closely with and supervise others who are providing paraprofessional counseling services.

Finally, the enhancement of multicultural appreciation within the school cannot be effectively accomplished without including education for the parents (Johnson, 1995). An earlier section of this chapter talked about strategies for involving newly arrived parents from underrepresented groups. An even bigger challenge may be working with mainstream parents to appreciate the culturally changing population of their children's school. Too often I hear of White parents, reluctant to have their children attend a racially diverse school, making choices about schools based on racial homogeneity. Undoubtedly, it takes a highly developed White racial identity on the part of parents to understand that their children will benefit from being in a racially diverse school. A White student of mine, who had attended racially diverse schools her whole life, remarked how troubled she was by the fact that her own children, because of where they were currently living, would probably attend predominantly White schools! Why not do for parents what is done for the students? As students learn to appreciate other cultures by learning about them in small groups and classroom guidance sessions, school counselors can organize informational workshops for parents about the representative cultures within the school. It makes little sense to work with the students around multicultural appreciation, if upon returning home, they are hearing negative comments from their parents about cultural diversity.

These are just some of the ways by which school counselors working in a multicultural society can begin to take a leading role in enhancing multicultural awareness and appreciation within the school. Throughout this exposition, the assumption has been that school counselors will themselves enjoy a highly developed racial identity that allows them to commit heart and soul to helping others understand cultural diversity not as a threat but as a source of enrichment. If such an identity is not present, school counselors will be unable to meet the educational challenges of working in a multicultural society.

POSTSECONDARY PREPARATION

Although the emphasis on the consulting role of school counselors is relatively recent, that of preparing students for life after high school is much more traditional. Since the focus of this chapter has been on higher academic achievement for underrepresented groups, space must be given to working with the special challenges presented by low-income minority students in preparing them for postsecondary schooling and/or work. For example,

> an eighth-grade Honduran student came into my office to discuss her career plans. She said she wanted to be a pediatrician. While I remarked to myself "A lofty aspiration," I wanted to support her in every way possible. Perhaps my own sexism wanted to clarify if she really meant a medical doctor or a pediatric nurse. She responded boldly "Not a nurse, a medical doctor!" And then almost in the same breath added "But I don't want to go to four years of college!"

This example reveals a high career aspiration based on very little reality, and I suspect this student's experience of pediatricians was mostly through the television. Because of her socioeconomic background, she lacked exposure to real-life role models who would explain the academic preparation involved in becoming a pediatrician. Thus, it is imperative for school counselors, especially those on the elementary level, to give students from underrepresented groups as much real-life exposure to quality careers as possible. This can be done by having career role models come to the school and speak with the children. Counselors should strive to have speakers representative of the different racial groups in the school and also have a career development program composed of goals and objectives for each year beginning in Grade 1 all the way to Grade 12 (see Gysbers & Henderson, 2000, for examples of career development programs by goals and objectives). One school in Los Angeles County requires, as part of its career development program, all fifth graders to visit a college campus, and the school provides transportation. A friend of mine recently told me about his son who, back in the seventh grade, visited the Notre Dame campus, and from that moment he never had to struggle with his son over doing homework. Last year, his son received early admission to Notre Dame. Other exposure activities can include field trips to local corporations that have opportunities for quality careers. Grant money is also available for promoting higher educational attainment among racial groups. For example, the W. K. Kellog Foundation has made money available for a multiyear initiative called *ENLACE*. Targeted to Latino youth, *ENLACE* seeks to establish partnerships between higher and secondary education institutions and promote both the creation and adoption of educational models known to enhance the academic performance and educational achievement of Latinos.

The goal for school counselors working with children from underrepresented groups must be to excite them about future career options and provide them with accurate and realistic information for the work involved in attaining such careers. The fact remains that not all such students will attend college after graduation. Therefore, school counselors must also be attentive to those students who will be transitioning from school to work after high school by making sure they are acquiring the necessary knowledge and skills to obtain jobs that pay more than the minimum wage.

School-To-Work Transition Program

In 1994, the federal government passed the School-To-Work Opportunities Act (STWOA) with the goal of helping all students, but most especially non-college-bound youths, negotiate a more productive transition from school to work. As mentioned in the data section at the beginning of this chapter, the number of students from underrepresented groups who attend postsecondary schooling, while on the rise, is still significantly lower than for middle-income-and-above White and Asian students. Thus, it would seem that the STWOA could make a significant contribution to this population. Although a complete description of the STWOA is beyond the scope of this chapter,[5] it will suffice to highlight the aspects particularly relevant for school counselors working with underrepresented youths.

The STWOA emphasized that, besides general employability skills (attendance, promptness, motivation, initiative, etc.), high school graduating students need to possess industry-specific skills making them attractive to employers (Worthington & Juntunen, 1997). It indirectly criticized the current educational system for not providing students with such skills. Thus, the STWOA recommended that local industry become more involved in the school system by providing curriculum suggestions and paid internships for students while in school. The STWOA is not without its critics who contend that private industry should not dictate curriculum and that it returns us to a tracking system by deciding early on who is college bound and who is not. However, becoming involved in the school-to-work transition does not cut off access to postsecondary education because these students take enough academic credits to at least attend a 2-year community college. What the STWOA does is allow the school to identify at-risk students and try to prepare them better for quality jobs not requiring a college education. In this sense, the STWOA can make the difference for non-college-bound youths between a minimum-wage service job and a good-paying quality job that demands certain academic and technology skills. This is especially important when one considers that African American workers (both men and women) earn 77% and Latino workers 67% of the median weekly earnings of White workers (U.S. Department of Labor, 1996).

Perhaps the most attractive dimension of the STWOA for low-income youths is the paid internship provided by private companies in the local area. Not only do these internships provide on-the-job training which increases future employability, but they also satisfy the immediate need felt by many low-income youths to earn money. Remember the case of Ramon, who worked after school at a gas station to help out his single mother? Ms. Goodwin realized the possibility of Ramon working in a paid internship on

Saturdays at a local industry. The economic and psychological needs of many low-income youths make it difficult for them to delay the gratification of earning money. Unfortunately, for many of these youths, even a minimum-wage job seems like an attractive alternative to staying in school. The paid internship provided by the STWOA can circumvent this reason for dropping out of school. Critics contend that the internship is a variation of the traditional apprenticeship, which again tracks a student for a particular career. However, research has shown that students who obtain employment after graduation in the field for which they have been trained do better (Stern et al., 1994).

School counselors should investigate the status of the STWOA in their local districts. The original monies were distributed through state education departments, and all school districts in the state were welcomed to apply for their share of the funds. Each school system had to submit a plan for the implementation of the fundamental dimension of the STWOA. If a student says seriously that he/she wants to go to college, it is the responsibility of the school to make that happen. However, the school also has a responsibility to those who may not be college bound. The STWOA is a piece of legislation designed for those most at risk for not participating in the earning potential of quality jobs. School counselors, especially those on the secondary level who work with underrepresented youths, are encouraged to make the STWOA a part of their overall career development program.

SUMMARY

This chapter has made a case for reconceptualizing the role of the school counselor from one who offers ancillary services to one who forms a critical part of the school's academic team. Undoubtedly, school counselors will have to continue to be trained in issues of mental health, but this training should not alienate them from the school's primary function, which is to promote higher academic achievement. To respond to today's educational challenge, school counselors will need additional training in cultural differences as they affect learning and in the skill of consultation. Rather than focus on a small number of the most difficult students, counselors should consider ways to multiply their effect upon the school by starting innovative programs that can reach all children. However, if forced to make choices because of overwhelming caseloads, it is hoped that counselors will dedicate their energies to those students most at risk for not achieving up to their potential. This chapter has laid out the long-term consequences of such failure and the groups most at risk for this failure. It is both a challenge and an exciting opportunity for school counselors to become involved in helping all children, regardless of color and socioeconomic status, learn and achieve educationally. This, indeed, would make a great difference in the life of a child and hopefully evoke what I heard one day from one of my African American counselees upon leaving a small group session: "Thank God for counseling!"

NOTES

1. Proficient level means students have competency over challenging subject matter while the Advanced level means the demonstration of superior performance.

2. Limited data were available for Native Americans, but, based on the 1990 census, it is projected that they will have the same social class patterns in 2015.

3. Underqualified teachers are defined as those who do not have at least a minor in the subject matter that they are teaching.

4. Space prevents a complete explanation of different learning and personality styles of the Myers-Briggs. I refer interested readers to the Myers-Briggs manual (Myers, 1962) and Silver and Hanson (1982, 1986) for its applicability to academic settings.

5. Readers interested in STWOA can consult two government documents published by the U. S. Department of Education (1994b, c): *Creating a School to Work Opportunities System* and *School to Work Opportunities: An Owner's Guide.*

REFERENCES

Arredondo, P., Toporek, R., Brown, S. P., Jones, J., Locke, D., Sanchez, J., & Stadler, H. (1996). Operationalization of the multicultural counseling competencies. *Journal of Counseling and Development, 24,* 42-78.

Beckhard, R. (1969). *Organizational development: Strategies and models.* Boston: Addison-Wesley.

Board of Education of the City of New York. (1995). *The class of 1995: Final longitudinal report.* New York: Author.

Carey, J. C., Reinat, M., & Fontes, L. (1990). School counselors' perceptions of training needs in multicultural counseling. *Counselor Education and Supervision, 29,* 155-169.

Casas, J., Furlong, M., Carranza, O., Solberg, S., & Jamaica, P. (1986). *Santa Barbara student success study.* Unpublished manuscript, University of California, Santa Barabara.

College Board. (1994). *College-bound seniors: 1994 profile of SAT and Achievement Test takers.* Washington, DC: College Entrance Examination and Educational Testing Service.

College Board. (1999). *Reaching the top: A report of the National Task Force on minority high achievement.* New York: Author.

Concha, P., Garcia, L., & Perez, A. (1975). Cooperation versus competition: A comparison of Anglo-American and Cuban-American youngsters in Miami. *Journal of Social Psychology, 95,* 273-274.

Council for Accreditation of Counseling and Related Educational Programs. (1996). *CACREP Accreditation standards and procedures manual* (Rev. ed.). Alexandria, VA: Author.

De LaRosa, M. (1998). Natural support systems of Puerto Ricans: A key dimension to well-being. *Health and Social Work, 13,* 181-190.

Delgado, M. (1997). Role of Latina-owned beauty parlors in a Latino community. *Social Work, 42,* 445-453.

Delgado, M. (1998). Puerto Rican elders and merchant establishments. *Journal of Gerontological Social Work, 30,* 33-45.

Delgado, M., & Humm-Delgado, M. (1982). Natural support systems: Source of strength in Hispanic communities. *Social Work, 27,* 83-89.

Educational Testing Service. (1988). *Teacher questionnaire from the 1988 NAEP reading assessment, grade 4.* Princeton, NJ: Author.

Ferguson, R. F. (1998). Can schools narrow the test score gap? In C. Jenko & M. Phillips (Eds.), *The Black-White test score gap* (pp. 318-374). Washington, DC: Brookings Institution.

Garcia, D., & Levenson, H. (1975). Differences between Blacks' and Whites' expectations of control by chance and powerful others. *Psychological Reports, 37,* 563-566.

Guerra, P. (1998). Revamping school counselor education: The DeWitt Wallace-Reader's Digest Fund. *CTOnline.* Available: www.counseling.org

Gysbers, N. C., & Henderson, P. (2000). *Developing and managing your school guidance program* (3rd ed.). Alexandria, VA: American Counseling Association.

Hanna, F. (February, 1998). *CESNET L: Discussion Forum for Counselor Education and Supervision* (on-line listserve). Available: cesnet-l@vm.sc.edu

Hart, P., & Jacobi, M. (1992). *From gatekeeper to advocate: Transforming the role of the school counselor.* New York: College Board.

Henderson, A. T. (1987). *The evidence continues to grow: Parent involvement in education.* Columbia, MD: National Committee for Citizens in Education.

Herrnstein, R. J., & Murray, C. A. (1994). *The bell curve: Intelligence and class structure in American life.* New York: Free Press.

Johnson, L. S. (1995). Enhancing multicultural relations: Intervention strategies for the school counselor. *The School Counselor, 43,* 103-113.

Karoly, L. A. (1998). *Investing in our children: What we know and don't know about the costs and benefits of early childhood interventions.* Santa Monica, CA: RAND.

Levenson, H. (1974). Activism and powerful others. *Journal of Personality Assessment, 38,* 377-383.

Mullis, I. (1991). *The state of mathematics achievement: NAEP's 1990 assessment of the nation and the trial assessment of the states.* Princeton, NJ: Educational Testing Service.

Myers-Briggs, I. (1962). *The Myers-Briggs Type Indicator manual.* Princeton, NJ: Educational Testing Service.

National Assessment of Educational Progress. (1994). *1992 NAEP trends in academic progress.* Washington, DC: U.S. Department of Education.

National Assessment of Educational Progress. (1996a). *1994 NAEP trends in academic progress.* Washington, DC: U.S. Department of Education.

National Association of Educational Progress. (1996b). *National mathematics results.* Washington, DC: U.S. Department of Education.

National Commission on Teaching and America's Future. (1996). *What matters most: Teaching for America's future.* Washington, DC: Author.

Oakes, J. (1990). *Multiplying inequalities: The effects of race, social class, and tracking on opportunities to learn mathematics and science.* Santa Monica, CA: RAND.

Peeke, P. A., Steward, R. J., & Ruddock, J. A. (1998). Urban adolescent's personality and learning styles: Required knowledge to develop effective interventions in schools. *Journal of Multicultural Counseling and Development, 26,* 120-136.

Pope-Davis, D. B., Breaux, C., & Liu, W. (1997). A multicultural immersion experience: Filling a void in multicultural training. In D. B. Pope-Davis (Ed.), *Multicultural counseling competencies: Assessment, education and training, and supervision* (pp. 227-241). Thousand Oaks, CA: Sage.

Ramirez, S. Z., Lepage, K. M., Kratochwill, T. R., & Duffy, J. L. (1998). Multicultural issues in school-based consultation: Conceptual and research considerations. *Journal of School Psychology, 36,* 479-509.

Reynolds, W. A., & Crew, R. F. (1997, May). *College preparatory initiative (CPI): A partnership between the New York City Public Schools and the City University of New York.* Presentation to the New York City Board of Education.

Robinson, T. (1992). Transforming at-risk educational practices by understanding and appreciating differences. *Elementary School Guidance and Counseling, 27,* 84-95.

Rockwood, G. F. (1993). Edgar Schein's process versus content consultation models. *Journal of Counseling and Development, 71,* 636-638.

Sanger, S. P., & Alker, H. A. (1972). Dimensions of internal-external locus of control and the women's liberation movement. *Journal of Social Issues, 28,* 15-129.

Schein, E. H. (1969). *Process consultation.* Reading, MA: Addison-Wesley.

Schein, E. H. (1978). The role of the consultant: Content expert or process facilitator. *Personnel and Guidance Journal, 56,* 339-345.

Sciarra, D. T. (1999). *Multiculturalism in counseling.* Itasca, IL: Peacock.

Sciarra, D. T., & Ponterotto, J. G. (1991). Counseling the Hispanic bilingual family: Challenges to the therapeutic process. *Psychotherapy, 28,* 473-479.

Silver, H. F., & Hanson, J. R. (1982). *Learning styles and strategies: Who am I as a learner? What are my assets and liabilities? How can I work more effectively with students, teachers, parents, and administrators?* Moorestown, NJ: Hanson Silver & Associates.

Silver, H. F., & Hanson, J. R. (1986). *Teaching styles and strategies: Techniques for meeting the diverse needs and styles of learners.* Moorestown, NJ: Hanson Silver & Associates.

Stern, D., Finkelstein, N., Stone, J. R., Latting, J., & Dornsife, C. (1994). *Research on school-to-work transition programs in the United States.* Macomb, IL: National Center for Research in Vocational Education.

Strickland, B. (1973). Delay of gratification and internal locus of control. *Journal of Counseling and Clinical Psychology, 40,* 338-346.

Sue, D. W. (1978). Eliminating cultural oppression in counseling: Toward a general theory. *Journal of Counseling Psychology, 25,* 419-428.

Sue, D. W., & Sue, D. (1999). *Counseling the culturally different: Theory and practice* (3rd ed.). New York: John Wiley.

The Education Trust. (1997). *Transforming school counseling: Request for planning grant proposals.* Washington, DC: Author.

The Education Trust. (1999). *Education watch: 1999 Education Trust achievement in American data disk.* Washington, DC: Author.

U.S. Bureau of the Census. (1990). *Statistical abstract of the United States: 1990* (110th ed.). Washington, DC: Government Printing Office.

U.S. Bureau of the Census. (1996). *Population projections of the U.S. by age, sex, race, and Hispanic origin: 1995-2030.* Washington, DC: Government Printing Office.

U.S. Department of Education. (1994a). *What do students' grades mean? Differences across schools.* Washington, DC: Author.

U.S. Department of Education. (1994b). *Creating a school-to-work opportunities system.* Washington, DC: Author.

U.S. Department of Education (1994c). *School to work opportunities: An owner's guide.* Washington, DC: Author.

U.S. Department of Education. (1995a). *Vocational course-taking and achievement: An analysis of high school transcripts and 1990 NAEP assessment scores.* Washington, DC: Author.

U.S. Department of Education. (1995b). *A profile of the American high school senior in 1992.* Washington, DC: Author.

U.S. Department of Education. (1998). First follow-up student study. In *National education longitudinal study of 1998.* Washington, DC: Author.

U.S. Department of Education, U.S. Department of Labor. (1994). *School-to-work opportunities: An owner's guide.* Washington, DC: Author.

U.S. Department of Labor. (1996). *Employment and earnings: Annual report.* Washington, DC: Author.

Vazquez, J. A. (1979). Motivation and Chicano students. *Bilingual Resources, 2,* 2-5.

Vazquez, J. A. (1998). Three-step procedure for adapting instruction to cultural traits. *The Prevention Researcher, 5*(1), 1-5.

Worthington, R. L., & Juntunen, C. L. (1997). The vocational development of non-college-bound youth: Counseling psychology and the school-to-work transition movement. *The Counseling Psychologist, 25,* 323-363.

Correspondence regarding this chapter may be sent to Daniel T. Sciarra, Assistant Professor, Mason Hall 212, Hofstra University, Hempstead, NY 11549 (e-mail address: cprdts@hofstra.edu).

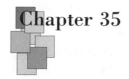

Chapter 35

A WORKING MODEL
IN COUNSELING
RECENT REFUGEES

MARIA PRENDES-LINTEL

IT HAS LONG BEEN recognized that displacement or forced migration from one sociocultural context to another has an impact on the process of adaptation/acculturation (Williams & Berry, 1991). However, more than ever before, the forcible uprooting of so many people now has been accompanied by the additional trauma of direct experiences of violence (Vernez, 1991). War, ethnic cleansings, and other terrorizing acts of displacement to civilian populations continue to have a personal effect on individuals (Widgren, 1988). In fact, up to 35% of the world's approximate 20 million refugees are estimated to be survivors of torture (Baker, 1992; Marsella, Bornmann, Ekblad, & Orley, 1994).

Personal and cultural losses result in grief for most refugees. Trauma and torture can result in varying degrees of posttraumatic stress. Changes in culture can result in acculturative stress. Posttraumatic stress disorder (PTSD) can complicate an individual's ability to adapt to a new cultural environment. In this chapter the literature on the refugee experience, stress-coping research, posttraumatic stress, acculturation/adjustment, and cultural grief is examined in order to present a working model of counseling and evaluation of recent refugees. Summaries of case vignettes are included to demonstrate the use of this model.

This chapter gives an overview of a working model utilizing the theoretical literature. This literature led to the development of an unstructured interview process, which is used in a collaborative approach with the client. It helps our counselors and clinicians to discard, verify, or correct our hypothesis and begin intervention.

STRESS AND COPING

The term "stress" was coined by Hans Selye, an Austrian endocrinologist, who identified stress as a consistent pattern of mind-body reaction, which he called the "nonspecific response of the body to any demand" [e.g., a dangerous event] (Selye, 1974, p. 14). Stress response is an adaptive reaction from the autonomic nervous system and is anticipated to last approximately 20 minutes (Mitchell & Everly, 1997). This would presumably give the individual enough time to respond to the danger presented. Following the initial response the parasympathetic system stops the stress reaction and returns the body to homeostasis. This represents the Alarm Phase and Resistance Phase of the General Adaptation Syndrome formulated by Selye (1974). The third phase of this syndrome is the Exhaustion phase, more recently characterized as the "Excess Phase," and represents the individual's constant exposure to stress-related biological changes that impair health and keep the system on constant alert (Hall, 1999).

Prolonged and chronic stress is known to have a debilitating effect on the body's neuromuscular system, sympathetic nervous system, parasympathetic nervous system, limbic system, neocortical system, neurohormonal system, and the neuroimmune system. The Diathesis Stress Model addresses the vulnerability of the individual because of stress factors. This model suggests that the eventual development of a disorder or illness in a certain individual is determined by a variety of vulnerability and resource factors.

Much of the notion of stress is also rooted in the work of Lazarus and Folkman (1984) who suggest that stress is a generic term that includes the stimuli producing stress reactions, the reactions themselves, and the various intervening processes. Intervening processes include coping, which represents environmental, behavioral, and psychological efforts to deal with excessive stress and stressful experiences (Mitchell & Everly, 1997). Coping suggests that the way an individual appraises a situation affects her or his reactions to stressful experiences. Resiliency reflects both internal and external factors that interact to play a protective role in the recovery from stress.

The Diathesis Stress Model of vulnerability and the stress-coping research offer important tools for the conceptualization and treatment of refugee physical health and mental health problems because they are less affected by cultural bias (Struwe, 1994) than are other approaches. This framework has been invaluable in understanding stress, the importance of context, and the effect of prolonged or chronic traumatic stress for refugees. Coping research facilitates understanding of how coping serves to mitigate the impact of the stress response including factors of resiliency. Further, it necessitates an understanding of the individual's perspective of events and/or situations and their perceptions of the effects on them. Use of this framework necessarily requires a collaborative approach, which is imperative in cross-cultural intervention. Collaborating resources include the refugee client and/or family, interpreters, physicians, hospital personnel, case managers, resettlement workers, school personnel including English-as-a-Second-Language teachers, native healers, religious leaders, and others with whom the refugee is significantly involved. Collaboration enhances understanding of the refugee client's personal, familial, cultural, and traumatic experience with current adjustment difficulties. Further, it maximizes identification of problem(s), possible resolutions, and realistic availability of resources.

The healthcare needs of the refugee are best met through collaborative work with physicians because of the possibility of diseases (tuberculosis), illnesses (malnutrition), torture/beatings (possible close head injuries, other injuries), sexual assault (STDs), and the overall impact of the sequelae of chronic and excessive stress (fatigue, depression, anxiety). It is important for the refugee to have a full physical to identify potential problems. Additionally, these people are often exhausted and unable to obtain relief enough to recuperate and to cope. As a result, medication is often necessary to begin the healing process.

THE REFUGEE CAREER

Berry (1988) used the term "refugee career" to classify the experiences that are related to psychological acculturation and eventual adaptation into a chronological order. Berry states a chronological perspective is necessary for the purpose of knowing where an individual refugee is, as well as to understand present and future experiences the refugee may undergo. The refugee career perspective is used here as it illustrates the refugee process and the opportunity for stressful experiences, that occur for refugees, that are separate from acculturative stress. In classifying the refugee experience chronologically, Berry suggests we can consider the characteristic psychological experiences and social problems that accompany this experience. Figure 35.1 notes Berry's (1991) six stages or phases of the refugee career and the generalized relationship and overlap of experiences occurring at these stages. It is important to note that the refugee career is not the same for all refugees. Some refugees go directly from Flight to Claimant stage and there are various combinations that occur.

Predeparture. This first phase is the one where the most traumatic events occur. These traumatizing events include wars, revolutions and resulting famines, and attendant atrocities such as ethnic cleansing, deliberate torture, and imprisonment. Berry (1991) notes that, ironically, it is these predeparture high-risk factors that are beyond the capabilities of counselors in the receiving nations to prevent because they cannot be addressed until a war or other traumatic situation is over.

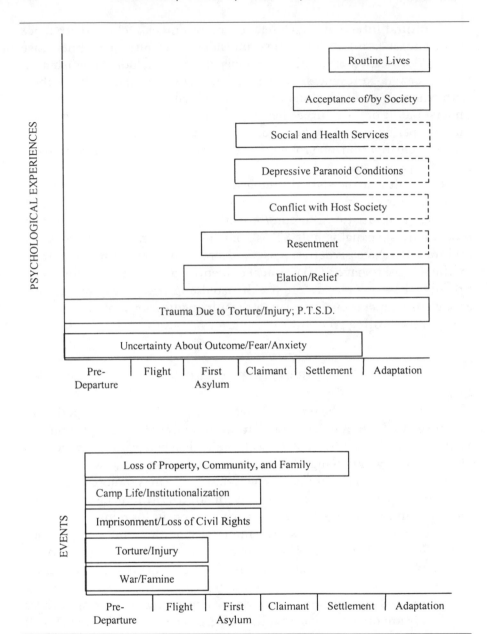

Figure 35.1. Phases, Events, and Experiences During a Refugee Career
SOURCE: Berry (1991).

Flight. During this period, the trauma continues. There is the risk of capture, starvation, torture, and death. Further, there is the possibility of loss of family through death or separation and loss of community. The refugee does not know where he/she will go or what will happen next. It is this uncertainty of events to come that has direct psychological impact.

First asylum. The refugee has a sense of elation and relief upon first arriving at the place of asylum. Once the elation subsides and the magnitude of future problems is realized, anxiety and depression can set in. For many refugees, the first asylum is the nearest refugee camp. Refugee camps differ greatly, and although some of these camps truly offer asylum, others only continue the fear and abuse the refugee had fled. Even when safety and physical needs are met, psychological needs may be unexpressed and unmet. It is critical for the counselor to have knowledge of the refugee individual's camp experience. Some refugees have been in refugee camps under aversive conditions for 7 years or more prior to moving to the Claimant stage.

Claimant. The refugee reaches the country of potential resettlement, and asylum is granted but the possibility exists for deportation. Many refugees are turned back to the home country if not accepted into the host country after they have exceeded the permitted time of asylum. This, of course, raises or at least maintains the sense of fear to often unbearable levels for the refugee. Suicide and depression are not uncommon at this point. Acculturative stress may begin to appear here because of the refugee's exposure to the culture of the receiving country or the country granting asylum.

Settlement. Formal acceptance by the host country is granted and the refugee receives the rights and freedoms of the host country including the potential for citizenship. Although resettlement finally occurs, many families are separated due to policies that undermine the needed support system. Services here are often culturally insensitive or may be too short-lived to be of value.

Adaptation. Most refugees do make satisfactory adaptations and settle into routine lives. However, caution should be used in the generalization of such statements because of the many variables involved. In some cases, repatriation is a real possibility, as with the Kosovo refugees who were supported in their repatriation by the United States government. The possibility of repatriation may complicate the decision to stay and the eventual adaptation of the refugee (Berry, 1988).

The refugee career has no set time limit—it can range from days to years. Prolonged experience offers more opportunities for ongoing stress and for trauma. The experience of the refugee occurs in the midst of individual, familial, and general life developmental stages.

EXCESSIVE REFUGEE STRESS AND TRAUMATIC STRESS

Refugees experience excessive stress from unexpected and rapid changes, losses, abuse, and trauma (Eisenbruch, 1991). Additionally the

TABLE 35.1 Major Factors Predicting Psychological Trauma

- Actual severe physical injury, disfigurement, dismemberment, or disability
- Fear of severe physical injury, disfigurement, dismemberment, or disability
- Fear of losing one's life
- Torture
- Fear of torture
- Sexual assault
- Fear of sexual assault
- Watching someone else die, experience extreme pain, or physical injury
- A belief of failed responsibility that results in harm to others
- The belief of unjustified survival or escape/avoidance from harm
- The belief of betrayal
- Death or injury to children
- The violation or contradiction of a "core belief" or "critical expectation" (e.g., God, friendship, loyalty, fairness, justice, fidelity, or competence)
- Shame associated with factors other than those listed above
- Guilt associated with factors other than those listed above
- War
- Environmental or ecological catastrophe

SOURCE: From *Critical Incident Stress Debriefing: An Operations Manual for the Prevention of Traumatic Stress Among Emergency Service and Disaster Workers* (2nd ed. rev., p. 34) by J. T. Mitchell and G. S. Everly, Jr., 1997, Ellicott City, MD: Chevron. Copyright © 1997 by Chevron Publishing Corporation. Reprinted with permission.

exposure to major factors that may predict psychological stress such as those listed in Table 35.1 increase the possibility for posttraumatic stress to occur. Awareness of the individual's refugee career informs the clinician of the chronicity of the refugee's stress and of the opportunity for trauma. It is important to be familiar with mediating factors in regard to refugee stress such as the illusion of control, particularly as it relates to trauma, and the illusion of support. According to the literature, it is not so much that an individual had control as it is that they felt they had some control (Herman, 1992, 1997; van der Kolk, 1987). The illusion of support is also not as much related to actual support but to perceived support and the relationship to connect with others (van der Kolk, 1987). These and other protective factors are also related to resiliency. Resilience involves both internal and external resources and has been defined as "the positive role of individual differences in people's response to stress and adversity" (Rutter, 1985, p. 598) and refers to individuals who have adjusted well in spite of extreme stress. Understanding these factors of individual differences in response to the devastating and transforming effects of repeated and prolonged exposure to traumatic events increasing the possibility of what Herman (1997) calls a complex PTSD reaction and van der Kolk (1987) refers to as disorders of extreme stress must also be recognized. The effects of repeated traumatic events, stress, and adversity are among the many reasons why it is imperative to have a collaborative approach with the client. The collaborative approach is important so as to better understand their individual perspectives on their refugee career experience and its meaning to the refugees themselves rather than making an assumption about how the refugee experience affects them in resettlement.

TRAUMA

According to the American Psychiatric Association, a trauma is "a psychologically distressing event outside the range of usual human experience" (APA, 1994, p. 424). Events that are traumatic overwhelm our coping mechanism. Allodi (1999) addresses the use of PTSD terminology in regard to torture as a technical and humanitarian response to a particular form of suffering. Understanding the limitations of this terminology, he states,

> PTSD is, in a technical language, the expression of the inexpressible, i.e., of the pain of the body, the experience of suffering, and the loss of the wholeness of the self in adversity. In psychological dynamics it represents an attempt to master the loss of continuity of the self in time, in intention, and in relation to others. Of course, those symptoms or criteria with technical names, such as re-experiencing, hyper-arousal, and avoidance, are metaphoric expressions. All language ultimately consists of tropes, and in the case of a living body in torture, no language expression is truly adequate; only an approximate recreation of the experiences of the body in full consciousness is possible. (p. 103)

Diagnostic and Statistical Manual IV (DSM-IV; APA, 1994) identifies a criterion that must to be met in order to diagnose PTSD. The specific criteria in the manual is readily available and known to psychologists. Struwe (1994) suggests PTSD is a special variant of stress-induced mental and physical changes. Further, in working with refugees the clinician must be aware of the ethnocultural aspects in the expression of trauma, which can readily lead to a misdiagnosis (Eisenbruch, 1991; Marsella, Bornemann, Ekblad, & Orley, 1994). Unfamiliarity with ethnocultural aspects of PTSD can lead to a misdiagnosis of psychosis or of missing the diagnosis of PTSD altogether because symptoms may be expressed only through somatic complaints. Additionally, for refugees the duration of the trauma, and the identification from single to multiple traumatic events, often lead to a diagnosis of complex and or extreme PTSD (Herman, 1997; van der Kolk, 1987).

It is no surprise, given the above discussion on the effects of stress and the refugee career, that refugees often present with somatic complaints. Prolonged and chronic stress does have a physiological impact on the body, which can result in real damage and which is, at times, irreversible (Hall, 1999; Mitchell & Everly, 1997). Also, trauma scars are often acknowledged only through somatic complaints. It is through exploring these complaints that the trauma is uncovered. The most prevalent co-occurring disorder with PTSD is depression, which is also often masked by somatic complaints. Panic attacks also occur in traumatic stress and are expressed somatically. Experience suggests that because these somatic complaints are often treated symptomatically the traumatic and depressive illness is frequently missed. Somatic complaints can also be due to the fatigue that accompanies prolonged stress.

The somatic presentation of psychological concerns is the most common way that disorders are presented. When working with refugees it is critical that an accurate history be taken addressing their premorbid condition prior to the trauma. It is important that clinicians understand the individual, cultural, and religious context of the expression of the refugee's pain. Clinicians also need to be familiar with the physiological effects of stress.

ACCULTURATION

Many refugees endure prolonged and chronic traumatic stress. The process from flight to resettlement can continue from many weeks to many years. Traumas endured in flight (i.e., physical abuse, sexual abuse, torture, starvation, separation from family, loss of home, and other violations) often continue in refugee camps. Although the external stress of threat is no longer present after refuge is obtained, the psychological stress continues as refugees struggle to make sense of their experience. Acculturation begins with the refugee's contact with the new culture. Williams and Berry (1991) state that acculturation refers to changes that groups and individuals undergo when they come in contact with another culture. Williams and Berry identify group-level changes as including such variables as economic, technological, social, cultural, and political transformation. Individual-level acculturation involves changes in behavior, attitudes, and identity. In all there is a fundamental change in the social cultural environment. Acculturative stress is probabilistic and usually occurs at a time when physical and psychological resources are already depleted. Acculturative stress adds to the growing list of overwhelming factors affecting refugees (Williams & Berry, 1991).

ACCULTURATIVE STRESS

Berry's (1988) notion of acculturative stress is grounded in the literature on stress, particularly as it was developed by Lazarus and Folkman (1984). Acculturative stress is linked to the acculturating experience and includes a variety of cultural, social, and psychological variables. The interaction involves two groups, host and refugee, at two levels, cultural and

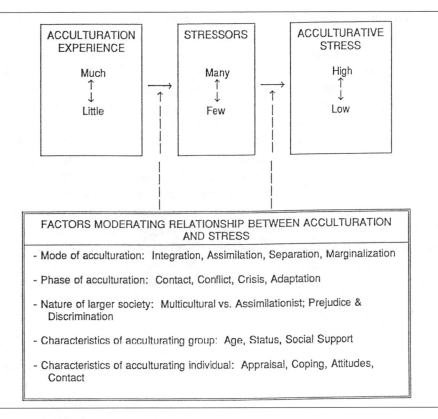

Figure 35.2. Acculturative Stress
SOURCE: Berry (1991).

individual. The interaction is further complicated by the moderating effects of these variables with the individual's personal factors (i.e., coping ability, factors existing prior to the acculturating experience, individual's appraisal of the situation). This view of acculturative stress also indicates that although problems arise during acculturation, these problems are not necessarily negative. Berry's (1988) highly variable relationship between acculturative stress and factors that moderate this relationship are illustrated in Figure 35.2. Acculturation may enhance one's life, including mental health, or may virtually destroy one's ability to carry on (Williams & Berry, 1991).

According to Berry (1988), all of this indicates a probable outcome that is not inevitable and that is itself varied and can produce a particular level of adaptation (marginalization, integration, separation, assimilation). Assimilation is the adaptive process whereby refugees discard their own cultures and customs and replace them with the customs and cultures predominant in the mainstream society of their new homeland. With separation, individuals take on none of the customs and culture of their new country and remain segregated from mainstream society. With marginalization, individuals fail to fit in with both their old customs and culture and those of their new country. With integration, people take on the best of both worlds and continue to observe the customs and preserve the culture of their native culture and also take on the values and customs of their new society. According to Berry (1991), most refugees find marginalization to be the least desirable option and integration the most desirable.

Berry also suggests a four-prong process consisting of contact, conflict, crisis, and adaptation. The refugee characteristics that were present prior to contact with the new culture and those that developed during the acculturation process are important. These characteristics may impact the refugee's ability to function effectively through the acculturation process. Contact experiences in terms of amounts, whether they are pleasant or conflictual, whether the individual's needs are met or they experience a crisis due to unmet needs, and whether the individual perceives the contacts as positive can, according to Berry (1991), set the stage for future contacts and can have an impact on the refugee's mental health during resettlement.

According to this model, the individual's response to acculturative stress is a highly complex process that cannot simply be assumed but must be understood for the individual client within the context of her or his reality or perceptions. This model is attractive because it not only gives guidelines of the complexity of this process but also mandates knowing and understanding the individual's contexts including personal strengths, weaknesses, resources, personal meaning of events, and self/other perceptions, as well as external variables and other moderating variables. It thus allows the clinician to move away from assumptions to collaboration with the client and recognition of possibilities of variability in acculturation.

Thus an individual may be from a different culture, have little or no experience with the new culture, and have a number of stressors but experience low acculturative stress. Possible reasons may be that the individual has a generally positive appraisal and attitude of life, has strong coping skills including coping with past traumatic situations that the individual has meaningfully addressed, has little actual social support but this social support is seen as strong, is settled into a multicultural society where there is greater tolerance of diversity, comes at a time of economic wellness of the new society, has met with little conflict, and has integrated the home culture with the positives of the new culture. This model requires knowing the client and the meaning of their context from the client's perspective and utilizing this information in understanding acculturation for the individual as stressful or nonstressful.

Although it is clear that the process of acculturation can be extremely stressful, according to diagnostic criteria acculturative stress does not generally meet *DSM-IV* criteria for PTSD. Although there is controversy on this subject (Friedman & Jaranson, 1994), the distinction between post traumatic stress and acculturative stress is helpful. According to *DSM-IV*,

> The essential feature of Posttraumatic Stress Disorder is the development
> of characteristic symptoms following exposure to an extreme traumatic
> stressor involving direct personal experience of an event that involves ac-
> tual or threatened death or serious injury, or other threat to one's physical
> integrity; or witnessing an event that involves death, injury, or a threat to
> the physical integrity of another person; or learning about unexpected or
> violent death, serious harm, or threat of death or injury experienced by a
> family member or other close associate (Criterion A1). The person's re-
> sponse to the event must involve intense fear, helplessness, or horror (or in
> children, the response must involve disorganized or agitated behavior)
> (Criterion A2). The characteristic symptoms resulting from the exposure
> to the extreme trauma include persistent reexperiencing of the traumatic
> event (Criterion B), persistent avoidance of stimuli associated with the
> trauma and numbing of general responsiveness (Criterion C), and per-
> sistent symptoms of increased arousal (Criterion D). The full symptom
> picture must be present for more than 1 month (Criterion E), and the dis-
> turbance must cause clinically significant distress or impairment in so-
> cial, occupational, or other important areas of functioning (Criterion F).
> (APA, 1994, p. 424)

According to this definition, acculturative stress does not generally
meet the "A" criterion of a traumatic stressor, nor the "B" criterion of intrusive or re-experiencing thoughts or nightmares about the traumatic
event. The "C" criterion of avoidant/numbing symptomatology of the
traumatic event and its related stimuli is also not met. Criterion "D,"
hyperarousal, overlaps with the symptoms that can occur in acculturative
stress. With acculturative stress, there is not the hypervigilance and startled response that are unique to PTSD. In acculturative stress there is, however, the possibility of panic attacks and other general anxiety symptoms
such as insomnia, poor concentration, and irritability. Criterion "E" is not
met because the durations of the symptoms experienced must relate to all
three criterions of B, C, and D, although it is certainly feasible that the disturbance in acculturation causes clinically significant distress. The "F" criterion, distress, is again related to Criterions B, C, and D, and therefore,
although overlapping with acculturative stress, these symptoms cannot be
diagnosed under the criterion for PTSD. They would be more consistent
with diagnosis under Adjustment Disorder, "in which the symptom pattern of Posttraumatic Stress Disorder occurs in response to a stressor that is
not extreme" (APA, 1994, p. 427). In some cases, acculturative stress may
lead to other disorders such as major depression.

The intensity of the trauma and the depth of the wounding differentiate
traumatic stress from acculturative stress. Common symptoms of acculturative stress do include disorientation, unusual fatigue, extreme mood
swings, crying easily or laughing inappropriately, constant feeling of irrita-
tion and annoyance, general nervousness and restlessness, fearfulness,
heightened anxiety, withdrawal, inappropriate levels of distress over small
matters, and antagonism or suspicion toward members of the new culture.

Berry (1991) suggests that monocultural responses to acculturation can result in an increase in dysfunctional, abusive behavior.

FAMILY ACCULTURATION/ADAPTATION

Szapocznik, Santisteban, Kurtines, Perez-Vidal, and Hervis (1984) used the concept of "bicultural" as an outcome of family adaptation and indicated that it occurs most often in pluralistic societies. These researchers recognized the intergenerational acculturation effect on families. This model addresses how families may pull in two different directions as they engage in acculturation. An example of this is the adolescent who pulls toward the new culture lured by its newness, and the parents who in fear of changes may act protectively to pull the adolescent back toward the culture of origin. Such actions can result in intergenerational conflict. Their Bicultural Effectiveness Model (Szapocznik et al., 1984) is used to reduce stress and conflict due to acculturation differences within the family structure. This model is based on the assumption that those individuals who are most successful at coping with intercultural sources of stress are those who have learned to interface effectively and strategically among various cultural environments. Findings of their studies led them to conclude that families living in bicultural contexts tend to become maladjusted when they remain or become monocultural.

Bemak (1989) related that traumatic experiences, as well as the radical adjustment to a new culture, make transition difficult for many refugees and their families. He stated that family adjustment is particularly important as members of the family are placed in varied strata of the host society. Rueschenberg and Buries (1989) stated that family acculturation is not an all-or-none phenomenon. Accordingly, adjustment to the host society can take place with the basic integrity of the family remaining intact. Further, they state that it is possible for the family to adapt externally while retaining many of its internal characteristics.

CULTURAL GRIEF

Cultural grief addresses cultural bereavement due to forced adaptation to a new culture (Eisenbruch, 1991). The many losses a refugee endures such as loss of identity, loss of loved ones, and loss of culture, are referred to as cultural grief by Eisenbruch. Cultural bereavement occurs at the personal and cultural level and augments the refugee's level of stress. Cultural grief has to be understood within a personal and cultural context. Eisenbruch states that massive social loss that refugees experience through uprooting produces grief. The term *cultural bereavement* was coined by

Eisenbruch to explain the particular grief of the refugee due to loss of social structures, cultural values, and self-identity. In order to understand the subjective experience of the refugee, we need to understand the meaning the refugee gives to the distress of the losses to understand the refugee's reaction to that loss. Doing so helps the clinician frame, identify, and treat the individual more effectively and accurately.

PROCESS OF RESETTLEMENT

Some authors have tried to link a timeline on the adaptation/ acculturation process to acculturative stress and to particular phases of acculturation, although not all authors (Williams & Berry, 1991) agree, citing there is not enough evidence to support such a simple relationship. Still such guidelines are helpful reminders of adaptation/adjustment as a process. Berry (1991) in Figure 35.1 addresses the phases of the refugee career, ending with resettlement. This section addresses refugee experiences in resettlement. These phases continue a possible chronological order to the refugee experience in resettlement. Tyhurst (1951) identified two distinct periods that tended to occur in both patients and nonpatients.

1. Initial period, lasting about 2 months after arrival. This was characterized by a subjective sense of well-being, sometimes referred to as Euphoria. This period of euphoria is, according to Sluzki (1979), often accompanied by confusion and disorientation.

2. Period of psychological arrival. This is when the refugees begin to understand their current social situation while becoming increasingly aware of language difficulties, differences in customs and values, recent separations and losses, and other problem areas. The individual may react by being obsessed with the past (especially their childhood, which is often idealized) or are so aware of the present that they dread the future. According to Sluzki (1979), the second period begins anywhere between 2 to 6 months after arrival, and it is during this time that attention is focused on day-to-day activities associated with building a new life.

Sluzki added a third period starting somewhere after two and a half years that the refugees start to reflect upon the impact of uprooting and begin to appreciate the realities of their new life.

Individuals failing to come to terms with their own realities, especially those who come with high hopes and unrealistic expectations, can become disillusioned and be at higher risk for developing emotional problems. The effect of adaptation affects all aspects of the individual as well as the family's involvement and effectiveness in such activities as parenting, work, and school.

WORKING MODEL

As the collaborative assessment with the individual client begins, information not applicable or important to the individual refugee is discarded. Subjective units of distress in which the refugee compares self to own known criteria and that of those known to him/her are also utilized to enhance the understanding of personal experience. A feedback loop in clarification of meaning and intent is critical. Information is gathered through interpreters who have been trained in working with the clinician and in confidentiality. No family members, particularly children, are used for interpretation in either treatment or assessment. Experience suggests using family members may be helpful in some situations. However, it can also be hurtful when family members present erroneous information in over- or underrepresenting the individual client's symptoms and problems out of concern or frustration. Using children to interpret makes it difficult for the adults to discuss personal information openly. Additionally, it may contribute to disrupting the parent-child hierarchy in which the parent becomes dependent upon the child for guidance and problem identification and resolution. Having trained interpreters is imperative for both individual and cultural interpretation that has greater accuracy and confidentiality and is removed from any personal agenda.

Assessment begins with an unstructured interview developed by this author based on Berry's (1988) refugee career phases and the general refugee literature, some of which was presented above. This interview (Table 35.2) focuses on important distinct phases of the refugee experience. All of the information gathered is couched around what is typical for the individual, the family, neighbors, and the surrounding community. An attempt is made to clarify and differentiate between cultural, religious, familial, and personal norms and expectations.

The administration of various instruments is useful in identifying levels of symptoms experienced. Information is obtained from these instruments to stimulate discussion with the refugee in order to clarify, explore, and further understand the expression of their experience. The instruments are also useful in gauging progress and in relating information to physicians with whom the clinician may be collaborating. Whenever possible, instruments are administered in the language of the refugee. If this is not possible, interpreters who have been trained by the clinician in the administration of tests are utilized. This type of administration breaks standardization, which must be acknowledged in the summarized findings. These instruments are helpful in the overall gathering of information and as previously stated points of discussion.

Some useful psychological tests have been developed and standardized cross-culturally (Butcher, 1991; Kinzie & Manson, 1987; Williams, 1987) and/or are adapted for use with particular populations (Marusic, Kozaric-Kovacic, Arcel, & Fonegovic-Smalc, 1998). We have found it useful to

TABLE 35.2 Unstructured Interview

History of Functioning Prior to Refugee Experience
    Developmental history
    Intellectual/school/functional history
    Social/familial/special relationships (family or friends of family and other)
    Personal characteristics
    Strengths/weakness
    Experience with prior losses
    Coping with prior losses
    Familial history of medical/psychological illnesses

History of War Experience
    Exposure to violence (self, family, and others)
    Type of event (man-made, other disaster)
    Duration (number of occurrences, length)
    Psychological experience of violence (control of personal integrity, helpless, angry, etc.)
    Support through the war experience (actual/perceived, none, family, stranger)
    How does the individual make sense of what occurred?

History of Refugee Experience
    Decision to flee:
        How was the decision made?
        Who made it?
        How did the client feel about the decision?
        What concerns/fears did the client have about leaving?
        Whom did they leave behind?
        Who came, and why?
        Who knew/who didn't?

First Asylum
    Where was the first asylum?
    What were the conditions?
    How long was the individual there?
    What was it like day to day?

Goodness of Fit Between Refugee and Community of Resettlement
    Individual developmental phase/Familial developmental phase
    Level of adjustment of individual and individual's family members
    Cultural distance between individual's home culture and that of resettlement
    Prior experience with culture of resettlement
    Language/personal/occupational skills that will transfer to site of resettlement
    Home support/familial support/community support/spiritual support of individual
    Communication from home (positive/negative, pressures for money and other demands) from home country
    Individual's previous expectations of resettlement versus current experience (propaganda)

SOURCE: Copyright © by Maria Prendes-Lintel.

administer the following instruments for baseline information. The Symptom Checklist-90-Revised (SCL-90-R; Derogatis, 1975b), although useful, is long, particularly when an interpreter is used. As a result, we often use the Brief Symptom Inventory (BSI; Derogatis, 1975a), which is a brief form of the SCL-90-R. With both the SCL-90-R and the BSI it is useful to explore earlier experiences of those symptoms that were endorsed as *quite a bit* or *extremely.* If such responses are positive, it is useful to explore under what circumstances these occurred. The BSI is seen as a relatively reliable and valid cross-cultural measure of psychological distress. However, problems with the Psychoticism subscale of both the SCL-90-R and the BSI occurred across three immigrant groups studied (Aroian, Patsdaughter, Levin, & Gianan, 1995). These authors suggested this scale be interpreted with caution when used with immigrants (Polish, Filipino, and Irish). The Psychoticism scale was based on Eysenck and Eysenck's (1968) conceptualization of psychoticism as a continuous dimension of human experience (i.e., ranging from mild interpersonal alienation to dramatic evidence of psychosis).

When working with refugees or immigrants, items on the Psychoticism scale should be carefully reviewed because items such as "Feeling lonely even when you are with people" and "Never feeling close to people" are reflective of normative conditions surrounding refugee and immigrant lives rather than symptoms of psychoticism per se. These feelings of alienation are situational. Cultural differences are also reflected when refugees and immigrants answer statements regarding friendships as they may feel these will never be as good as those from home because of the differences of culture and language. In general, it is felt that the clinician should not assume that BSI Psychoticism scores are accurate indicators of the internal psychological structure but rather may be reflective of normative refugee or immigrant conditions (Aroian et al., 1995; Sivan, Fogg, & Muftic, 1997).

The Beck Depression Inventory II (BDI-II; Beck, Steer, & Brown, 1996) is used primarily to assess depression and depressive symptoms, but it also has been applied in working with stress because it is helpful in distinguishing the incidence of traumatizing stress from that of other types of stress. Much of the symptomatology associated with traumatization stress is related, both theoretically and descriptively, to clinical depression. The Beck Depression Scale has been used in assessing depression in PTSD (Goldberger & Breznitz, 1993). The BDI-II, in addressing both cognitive and behavioral features thought to be associated with major depression, is considered to be an important diagnostic screening measure in the study of posttraumatic stress (Goldberger & Breznitz, 1993).

Several posttraumatic scales are successfully used with immigrant/ refugee groups, and some scales have been developed that are group specific. The Harvard Trauma Questionnaire (Mollica et al., 1996) is divided into four parts. The first part measures the quality and quantity of experienced trauma. The second part asks for a personal description of the most hurtful or terrifying events the individual has experienced and when the events occurred. It also asks specifically about what is the most hurtful event the individual has experienced in the country of resettlement. Part 3 is in reference to head injuries including drowning, suffocation, blows to the head, and loss of consciousness. Part 4 is a 30-item Likert-type scale inquiry into traumatic symptoms. This instrument is available in several versions, including Cambodian, Laotian, and Vietnamese.

The Civilian Mississippi PTSD Scale is a 39-item questionnaire. It was first developed by Keane, Caddell, and Taylor in 1988 to measure combat-related PTSD. Fontana and Rosenheck (1994) developed a short 11-item form of the Mississippi scale. Marusic, Kozaric-Kovacic, Arcel, and Fonegovic-Smalc used this scale in a study of the reliability and validity of three PTSD scales. Their sample was refugees and displaced persons. Their findings suggested that the 11-item Mississippi Scale might be a suitable alternative to the lengthier measuring instruments when the number of refugees is high and time is limited.

In my practice I utilize a checklist that corresponds to the three main prongs of *DSM-IV* (Intrusion, Avoidance, and Hyperarousal). This is based on self-report and I have found it very useful in identifying progress both for the refugee and for the clinician.

CASE VIGNETTES

The following summaries are of cases referred to our center. The individuals in all the cases were interviewed and assessed following the above criteria. A summary of how the literature discussed above applies follows the case summary as well as the identification of possible points for intervention. In all cases permission was obtained from the refugees to present their case for the purpose of educational discussion. Identifying data and names were changed to maintain confidentiality.

Sana—
37-year-old married Kurdish woman from Iraq

Sana and her husband and three children have been in the United States for 2 years. The family had been in a refugee camp in Syria for 3 years prior to coming to the United States. They were seemingly making a good adjustment both personally and as a family. Sana was referred as a result of trying to start herself on fire. Utilization of chronological interview of her Refugee Career revealed that Iraqi soldiers had barged into her home in Iraq and dragged her sister out of the home and killed her. She was made to watch her execution, carry off her body, and bury it without any expression of distress or grief under threat of death to herself and remaining family members. Prior to her attempt to start herself on fire, her husband had a minor car accident and the police gave him a ride to his destination. Sana's friend (another Kurdish woman) witnessed this event and notified Sana that the police had taken her husband. Sana reported she thought her worst fears had occurred—that her husband would also be taken and possibly executed. It was through this interview that the number of times she had been to the physician with medical complaints of fatigue, headaches, and overall mal-aise was made known. At home the family took care of Sana. They knew she did not feel well and were frustrated with the physician that she was not being cured. They accepted that Sana spent the majority of her time in bed and had crying spells.

Consistent with the interview, the PTSD checklist suggested PTSD symptomalogy, the BDI-II suggested Severe Depression, the BSI suggested clinical severity, and there were elevations on all scales. Case review suggested that PTSD, which had never been addressed prior to referral, was triggered by the police interaction in the new culture. The incident with the police, which was interpreted as a positive contact by the husband, was interpreted as a crisis (contact) by Sana's friend and by Sana. The impact of the crisis was fueled by Sana's traumatic past experience and her limited knowledge (low amount of contact) with the new culture. This exacerbated distress and the increased feelings of helplessness resulted in a crisis (contact) in which Sana had few resources (personal coping, who to go to for help-support, limited knowledge of English, no perceived control) available to challenge her perceptions of crisis. There were no moderating variables in regard to the level of her stress. PTSD was the primary diagnosis. Acculturative stress was also identified.

Geoffrey—
36-year-old married man from the former Soviet Union

Geoffrey was referred due to increasing difficulties concentrating at work and increased anger. He is married and the father of 8, and his income was not sufficient to raise his family. Geoffrey tried to supplement his income by doing what he used to do at home (i.e., raising vegetables and small animals, welding). None of these activities were permissible where he lives. He had difficulties making ends meet and finding housing that he could afford that could house a family of 10. Geoffrey was especially worried about his relationship with his sons. He felt the skills he valued and planned to pass to his sons were no longer relevant. He also struggled with the propaganda leading him to expectations of land for his family and a farm and his thoughts of taking his family to Hawaii for a vacation. The interview found no history of trauma and no premorbid history of psychological problems. His wife volunteered that he always thinks negatively.

Administration of the BSI suggested a magnitude of severity at clinical levels of distress, with elevations particularly on the depression and anxiety scales. The BDI-II was consistent in identifying moderate levels of depression.

Discussion of this case included predisposing factors. Geoffrey's self-reports suggested that he saw the contact with the new culture as conflicting with what his expectations had been, given the propaganda he had received. He moved away from initial hopes for integration and toward

separation, stating directly that he wanted to be resettled in a place where
there were only other refugees from the former Soviet Union. He made it
clear that he could not control what happened outside his house but that inside his house he would maintain his ways. His identity felt threatened. His
experience of conflict with the new culture also moved to crisis contact as
he struggled to make ends meet for his sizable family. He saw no way out
within the new culture. Acculturative stress, and particularly cultural bereavement, was evident.

The Hussan Family

The Hussan family from the Middle East consists of four children,
mother, and father. They are Muslims. The mother was referred to our
clinic due to her increasing sadness after court hearings and legal family
separations had already occurred. The Hussan family had fled their home
because of increased danger. The family was witness to war's bombing and
killing. After leaving home, the family lived in a refugee camp for 3 years.
Upon arrival in the United States, their older daughter, age 13, made a rapid
adjustment to the new culture. The girl talked to the boys in her school,
wanted to dress differently than her mother taught her, and even experi-
mented with various aspects of our culture. The parents were frustrated,
angry, fearful, and concerned. They resorted to the ways they had brought
from their home country to resolve the problems they saw. Following all of
their customs, they arranged for the daughter to marry (with the daughter's
permission, as is the custom). The parents themselves had been married at
ages 13 and 18. The parents felt that in marriage the daughter would be safe
from the unknown aspects of the new culture and could satisfy her sexual
urges in a marital environment. Subsequently, the new husband was
charged with sexual assault, and the daughter was removed from the home.
The local authorities carried out their legalities—while making a number
of assumptions about the parents' actions, reactions, and context—assuming malicious intent. These assumptions appeared in the records that accompanied the referrals to professionals who were requested to evaluate
various members of the family. Blatant statements handwritten across reports included one about the daughter being sold into marriage, supposedly
for a dowry. In this case, the dowry actually went to the newly married couple and not to the parents. The entire family was now torn apart, trying to
understand what occurred. The daughter, saved from feared family interactions and antiquated customs, has lost much of her identity and was being
schooled in the religion of her foster placement.

The approach used with this family further intensified the adversarial
relationship that naturally occurs in families due to stages of individual development and that has been exacerbated in this family by differences in
rate of acculturation. The interview suggested that the family had been exposed to traumatic experiences. However, the PTSD checklist did not pick

up any symptomalogy in this regard, and it was not claimed by Ms. Hussan. The BSI did not suggest a clinical magnitude of symptoms. Mild depression was noted on the BDI-II.

Discussion with Ms. Hussan further confirmed that although the family and Ms. Hussan had been exposed to trauma, the current emphasis was not on trauma from home. Emphasis was placed on the lack of experience in previous cultural contact with the resettlement country. The experience of contact, which was seen initially as conflict that disrupted smooth acculturation, was then perceived as crisis as the allegations leading to separation took place. The notion of intergenerational acculturation stress with differing rates of acculturation for parents and daughter was noted. While the daughter moved to integration with the dominant culture, the parents moved to rejection of the new culture. It was felt that the behaviors of both the daughter and the parents, although very different from one another, were within their context functional although obviously not acceptable. A concern was that maliciousness of intent to cause harm was perceived by the supportive services leading to family separation, and the extreme impact of how these differing rates of acculturation affected Ms. Hussan, her daughter, and her family. It was noted that the family had resettled in a community that had little experience with multicultural populations.

A MENTAL HEALTH ORIENTATION PROGRAM OF NEWLY ARRIVED REFUGEES: PRIMARY PREVENTION

In a primary prevention effort, I developed a mental health orientation for newly arrived refugees. Taking into consideration information in the literature on prevention regarding stress, coping, acculturation, and adjustment (Berry, 1991), I developed a program for counselors to use with newly arriving refugees. This program is framed around and adapted from the debriefing that was developed by the International Critical Incident Stress Foundation, Inc. (Mitchell & Everly, 1997). All involvement is voluntary and occurs as part of a general cultural orientation session at the resettlement agency. This orientation occurs as part of a number of cultural orientation sessions that are held at the local resettlement agency. The purpose of this orientation is to (a) validate and normalize the experience of excessive stress in their life; (b) educate the refugee in regard to stress, stress reduction, and coping; and (c) initiate contact and make mental health services accessible. Further, I begin primary prevention in this session by educating families on the effects of acculturation and addressing such issues as role reversal, parenting strategies, and child protection laws. An anecdotal study on this orientation program indicated that the mental health orientation was reported by the refugees to be one of the most helpful presentations.

In working with refugees it is imperative that one develop a list of resources who are also familiar with working with refugees. This includes physicians, psychiatrists, and school counselors, among others. Many pitfalls can occur, particularly in the early phase of resettlement, that can interfere with adjustment and with treatment. Training and the availability of consultation at all levels is necessary—from the incoming refugee, the interpreter, the case manager, the teachers, and community workers to mental health workers and physicians. Because of the severity of the stress it is often necessary to work collaboratively with physicians. At times, the physician is included in the therapy session or in family home intervention. Occasionally, a refugee sponsor or religious leader and/or other individuals important in the refugee's life may be included in the intervention as may be appropriate to the particular situation. In training case managers and other members of the health care teams, I have found it useful to share the following guidelines adapted from Sivan et al. (1997).

Sivan et al. (1997) suggest that subjective units of distress be used when the distress of the individual interferes with that person's ability to care for family, to work, or to care for self. They suggest posing the above as a question and asking the individual to rate the degree of interference on a continuum of rarely, occasionally, some of the time, most of the time, and all of the time. These subjective units of distress mean this is the client's perception of the amount of stress or difficulty that he or she is experiencing.

I have also found it helpful to include red flags, which are offered as a guide to be discarded or acted upon as information is gathered. A red flag does not mean one rushes for help but that the counselor may want to check in on how the individual or family is adjusting as greater support may be indicated in the following situations: (a) no familial support system in the same geographical location of individual resettlement; (b) poor general support system locally; (c) greater cultural distance from majority group; (d) resettlement occurring in a monoculture environment and the refugee is the other culture; (e) history of psychological difficulties pre-war; and (f) changes in known behavior (i.e., increased alcohol use).

The individual gathering the information can, according to Sivan et al. (1997), ascertain level of hardship an individual or family has experienced by asking further questions such as "Acknowledging that there is no way to measure the hardship you experienced during this war, compare the difficulty you experienced with the experiences of other people. Specifically, on a scale of 1 to 5, what was your experience during the war?" This question can also be answered on a continuum of (a) much less severe than, (b) somewhat less severe than, (c) about the same as, (d) somewhat more severe than, and (e) much more severe than that of most other people. These are again subjective units of distress, which means the clients' perceptions of the amount of stress or difficulty they are experiencing.

Finally, case managers and other resettlement team members are given the following guidelines for reference:

1. If you suspect difficulty, REFER. It is much better to be wrong than wish you had acted.
2. If the client's subjective units of distress suggest perceived difficulty by client, REFER.
3. You don't need to evaluate or judge whether you should refer or not. If you think you should, DO.

SUMMARY

In my work with refugees I have found Berry's (1988, 1991) broad framework particularly useful. In encompassing the refugee experience from the home country through flight and resettlement he gives credence as well as guidance as to where a working hypothesis can begin and where it can be discarded or modified. The highly variable relationship between acculturation and mental health outcome must be understood and allows understanding of identified problems and strengths.

Berry sees acculturation as both a process and an outcome, which can be interrupted by the effects of trauma. This has been particularly helpful in understanding that PTSD needs to be treated in order to facilitate adjustment. Berry's (1988, 1991) framework allows for recognition and understanding of cultural distress expression.

As a practitioner I am aware that at times the theories, although sounding great, do not transfer well to a level where they can be operationalized. One such area addressed in the literature is, for example, intergenerational stress. It was helpful to be able to turn to the Bicultural Effectiveness Model of Szapocznik et al. (1984) for what to do once intergenerational stress is identified. A limitation of this model is that it was developed with Cubans and may not transfer across cultural groups.

I have also found other literature, particularly the literature on stress and the use of the Diathesis Stress Model (Struwe, 1994), to be helpful in going beyond cultural expressions of distress as somatic to an understanding of the physiological effects of chronic stress on the body. Although stress is alluded to in its acute phase, the long-term effects that stress has had on some refugees who have been in camp for years (and are at times entrenched in their stress) is seldom identified in the psychological literature. The literature on cultural grief and bereavement is helpful in identifying and understanding the depth of grief in regard to cultural roles and related identity.

In working with refugees, prevention through early identification and appropriate treatment is practiced through education at all levels. Training begins for the incoming refugees with a mental health orientation and continues through training and consultation for case managers, English-as-a-Second-Language (ESL) teachers (school system), early education teachers, community health care workers, mental health workers, and physicians.

The purpose of this chapter was to offer an overview of a working model used in practice to understand the complexity of the refugee experience. Review of the literature regarding the refugee experience, stress-coping research, posttraumatic stress, acculturation/adjustment, and cultural grief was used in the development of an unstructured interview. The research base offers a place to begin formulating a hypothesis. The collaborative unstructured interview helps us as counselors and clinicians to discard, verify, or correct our hypothesis and begin the intervention process. The goal is the provision of effective interventions that go beyond sensitivity to competency in the delivery of services.

REFERENCES

Allodi, F. (1999). The body in political violence: The phenomenology of torture. *Torture, 9,* 100-105.

American Psychiatric Association. (1994). *Diagnostic and statistical manual of mental disorders* (4th ed.). Washington, DC: Author.

Aroian, K. J., Patsdaughter, C. H., Levin, A., & Gianan, M. E. (1995). Use of the Brief Symptom Inventory to assess psychological distress in three immigrant groups. *International Journal of Social Psychiatry, 41,* 31-46.

Baker, R. (1992). Psychosocial consequences for tortured refugees seeking asylum and refugee status in Europe. In M. Basoglu (Ed.), *Torture and its consequences: Current treatment approaches* (pp. 83-101). London: Cambridge University Press.

Beck, A. T., Steer, R. A., & Brown, G. K. (1996). *Beck Depression Inventory-II.* San Antonio, TX: Psychological Corporation.

Berry, J. (1988). *Understanding the process of acculturation for primary prevention* (Contract No. 278-85-0024 CH). Minneapolis: University of Minnesota, National Institute of Mental Health Refugee Assistance Program.

Berry, J. W. (1991). Managing the process of acculturation. In U.S. Department of Health and Human Services, *Mental health services for refugees* (DHHS Publication No. ADM 91-1824, pp. 189-204). Rockville, MD: National Institute of Mental Health.

Butcher, J. (1991). Psychological evaluation. In U.S. Department of Health and Human Services, *Mental health services for refugees* (DHHS Publication No. ADM 91-1824, pp. 111-122). Rockville, MD: National Institute of Mental Health.

Derogatis, L. R. (1975a). *Brief Symptom Inventory.* Minnetonka, MN: NCS.

Derogatis, L. R. (1975b). *Symptom Checklist-90-Revised.* Minnetonka, MN: NCS.

Eisenbruch, M. (1991). From posttraumatic stress disorder to cultural bereavement: Diagnosis of Southeast Asian refugees. *Social Science Medicine, 33,* 673-680.

Eysenck, H. J., & Eysenck, B. G. (1968). A factorial study of psychoticism as a dimension of personality. *Multidisciplinary Behavioral Research, All Clinical Specialties Issue,* 15-31.

Fontana, A., & Rosenheck, R. A. (1994). A short form of the Mississippi Scale for measuring change in combat related PTSD. *Journal of Traumatic Stress, 7,* 407-414.

Friedman, M., & Jaranson, J. (1994). The applicability of the posttraumatic stress disorder concept to refugees. In A. J. Marsella, T. Bornemann, S. Ekblad, & J. Orley (Eds.), *Amidst peril and pain: The mental health of the world's refugees.* Washington, DC: American Psychological Association.

Goldberger, L., & Breznitz, S. (1993) Measurement of stress and coping. In L. Goldberger & S. Breznitz (Eds.), *Handbook of stress: Theoretical and clinical aspects* (2nd ed.). New York: Free Press.

Hall, N. (1999, Fall). *Stress and disease.* Presentation at the Institute for CorTexT Research and Development, Lincoln, NE.

Herman, J. (1992). *Trauma and recovery: The aftermath of violence from domestic abuse to political terror.* New York: Basic Books.

Herman, J. (1997). *Trauma and recovery: The aftermath of violence from domestic abuse to political terror* (2nd ed.). New York: Basic Books.

Keane, T. M., Caddell, J. M., & Taylor, K. L. (1988). Mississippi Scale for combat related posttraumatic stress disorder: Three studies in reliability and validity. *Journal of Consulting and Clinical Psychology, 56,* 85-90.

Kinzie, D., & Manson, S. (1987). The use of self-rating scales in cross-cultural psychiatry. *Hospital and Community Psychiatry, 38,* 190-196.

Lazarus, R. S., & Folkman, S. (1984). *Stress appraisal and coping.* New York: Springer.

Marsella, A. J., Bornmann, T., Ekblad, S., & Orley, J. (1994). The scope of the refugee problem. In A. J. Marsella, T. Bornmann, S. Ekblad, & J. Orley (Eds.), *Amidst peril and pain.* Washington, DC: American Psychological Association.

Marusic, A., Kozaric-Kovacic, D., Arcel, L. T., & Fonegovic-Smalc, V. (1998). Validity of three PTSD scales in a sample of refugees and displaced persons. In L. T. Arcel in collaboration with G. T. Simunkovic (Eds.), *War violence, trauma and the coping process.* Denmark: International Rehabilitation Council for Torture Victims.

Mitchell, J. T., & Everly, G. S., Jr. (1997). *Critical incident stress debriefing: An operations manual for the prevention of traumatic stress among emergency service and disaster workers* (2nd ed. rev.). Ellicott City, MD: Chevron.

Mollica, R. F., Caspi-Yavin, Y., Lavelle, J., Tor, S., Yang, T., Chan, S., Pham, T., Ryan, A., & de Marneffe, D. (1996). Manual of The Harvard Trauma Questionnaire. *Torture, 1*(Supp.), 22.

Rueschenberg, E., & Buries, R. (1989). Mexican American family functioning and acculturation: A family systems perspective. *Hispanic Journal of Behavioral Sciences, 11,* 232-244.

Rutter, M. (1985). Resilience in the face of adversity: Protective factors and resistance to psychiatric disorder. *British Journal of Psychiatry, 147,* 598-611.

Selye, H. (1974). *Stress without distress.* Philadelphia: Lippincott.

Sivan, A. B., Fogg, L., & Muftic, A. (1997, August). *Refugee mental health: Development of a screening instrument. Rush Presbyterian St. Luke's Medical Center, Chicago.* Paper presented at the annual conference of the American Psychological Association, Chicago.

Sluzki, C. (1979). Migration and family conflict. *Family Process, 18,* 379-390.

Struwe, G. (1994). Training health and medical professionals to care for refugees: Issues and methods. In A. J. Marsella, T. Bornemann, S. Ekblad, & J. Orley (Eds.), *Amidst peril and pain: The mental health and well-being of the world's refugees* (pp. 311-324). Washington, DC: American Psychological Association.

Szapocznik, J., Santisteban, D., Kurtines, W., Perez-Vidal, A., & Hervis, O. (1984). Bicultural Effectiveness Training: A treatment intervention for enhancing intercultural adjustment in Cuban American families. *Hispanic Journal of Behavioral Sciences, 6,* 317-344.

Tyhurst, L. (1951). Displacement and migration, a study in social psychiatry. *American Journal of Psychiatry, 107,* 561-568.

van der Kolk, B. (Ed.). (1987). *Psychological trauma.* Washington, DC: American Psychiatric Press.

Vernez, G. (1991). Current global refugee situations and international public policy. *American Psychologist, 46,* 631-672.

Widgren, J. (1988). The uprooted within a global context. In D. Miserez (Ed.), *Refugees: The trauma of exile* (pp. 1-9). Dordrecht, The Netherlands: Martinus Nijhoff.

Williams, C. (1987). Issues surrounding psychological testing of minority patients. *Hospital and Community Psychiatry, 38,* 184-189.

Williams, C. L., & Berry, J. W. (1991). Primary prevention of acculturative stress among refugees. *American Psychologist, 46,* 632-641.

Correspondence regarding this chapter may be sent to Maria Prendes-Lintel, The Wellness Center, 1919 South 40th Street, Suite 111, Lincoln, NE 68506 (e-mail address: mlintel@aol.com).

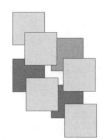

Part VII

INTERSECTION OF IDENTITIES

The two chapters in Part VII highlight the importance of considering multiple identities. Integrating their own voices and tapping an extensive and broad literature base, Lowe and Mascher in Chapter 36 call upon the multicultural counseling movement to more actively embrace gay, lesbian, bisexual, and transgender issues. Earlier in the *Handbook*, Part III discussed White privilege; here, these authors address the consequences of heterosexual privilege. Lowe and Mascher position gay and lesbian issues in the context of the evolving multicultural movement; they clearly discuss barriers to embracing intersections of identities and propose a renewed vision for the field.

In 1988, a working conference organized by APA Division 17's (Counseling Psychology) Section for the Advancement of Women was held to discuss the intersection of feminism and multiculturalism in counseling. Two of the *Handbook*'s editors (Suzuki and Alexander) were in attendance and were profoundly impacted by the process, contents, and outcome of this working conference. A year later, a follow-up symposium on the topic was held at the APA convention. It became clear to those in attendance, and to the thousands of other professionals who were to be informed of the proceedings, that discussion on the topic was essential for the field. In Chapter 37, key organizers and participants of these two proceedings capture the spirit and essence of the meetings. Bowman, Rasheed, Ferris, Thompson, McRae, and Weitzman present a critical discussion on the interface of feminism and multiculturalism. They begin by summarizing various feminist ideologies and then present perspectives on feminism held by women of color. The core of the chapter includes personal and self-revealing reflections on the topic as presented by a subgroup of the authors.

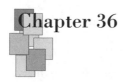

Chapter 36

THE ROLE OF SEXUAL ORIENTATION IN MULTICULTURAL COUNSELING

Integrating Bodies of Knowledge

SUSANA M. LOWE
JACKQUELYN MASCHER

WE BEGIN AND CONCLUDE this chapter with comments about our personal investment in this work.

I am an Asian American woman from a working-class background who works for a predominantly White Catholic institution (S. M. Lowe). I confront racism, sexism, and classism in my daily work. Now, more than ever, I crave opportunities to write about issues that touch me deeply because this is what holds the most meaning for me and what keeps me alive in the face of adversity. So I begin this chapter by telling you about why I want the multicultural counseling movement to embrace connections with a group of people who have been pushed to the margins of society: specifically, gay, lesbian, bisexual, and transgender individuals. Some are visible racial/ethnic minorities and others are not, but we have much to share.

The invisibility I feel as an Asian American woman in U.S. society, in which discussions on race are frustratingly reduced to Black and White, echoes the marginalization of gay men and lesbians within the multicultural counseling movement. Seldom do teachers, historians, or reporters talk about my struggle and the racism against Asians in the United States; if we are considered at all, we are mentioned as token Whites. Fortunately, I found empowerment through ethnic studies and multicultural counseling

AUTHORS' NOTE: Susana Lowe would like to thank Celeste Myers for her compassion, her wisdom, and for always teaching.

movements, which have taught me about my history and culture, my struggle, and my humanity. Yet the voices and perspectives of ethnic minority gay, lesbian, and bisexual people are conspicuously missing from the dialogue in these multicultural movements. "Oh, that's another movement," some say. Over the years, it has become increasingly intolerable for me to consider sexual orientation as part of some other movement. In an interview with a woman who identifies as African American and lesbian, I was reminded that in our work as psychologists we see whole people, not just parts of people (C. Myers, personal communication, February 2, 2000).

Years ago, I had a conversation with an Asian American psychologist and was telling him how outraged I was about an incident of homophobia that had just occurred, when he said, "Why are you so upset? This isn't *your* issue." Although he didn't know my sexual orientation, he presumed I was heterosexual. What's more, he couldn't understand why I might feel angry about an injustice done to someone else, even if it isn't something that I personally might experience. I felt such disappointment. Intellectually, I know it's unfair, but I still feel more offended when a person of color, woman, or gay person is racist, sexist, or heterosexist because we know what oppression feels like.

I feel it is imperative for us to address the racism, heterosexism, and sexism we have internalized, as they are all forms of oppression that keep us down. I am a woman of color who is heterosexual. Racism and sexism are forms of oppression that people expect me to fight against, but heterosexism is also oppression that affects me—it unfairly privileges me and pushes down family, friends, coworkers, and other people simply for the fact that they are not heterosexual. This oppression is so painfully familiar, as it is waged against people for not being White, for not being male, for not being Christian, and so on. I feel we must learn to resist partitioning movements, as this keeps people in need apart and diffuses social and political activism against all forms of systemic discrimination.

A GOOD THING

The cultural competency models for counseling recommend that psychologists and mental health practitioners examine their own cultural values and biases (Atkinson, Morten, & Sue, 1998; Helms & Cook, 1999; Sue, Arredondo, & McDavis, 1992). If counselors become consciously aware of their own worldview and prejudices, they are more likely to be able to address them (e.g., in the form of processing countertransference) before or while working with a client. Frequently, the discussion on cultural competence concerns counseling racial and ethnic minorities. We argue in this chapter that models of cultural competence should include counselor examination of values and biases with regard to a variety of minority populations, including gay, lesbian, bisexual, and transgender clients.

To strengthen as a movement and to do justice to our stated values, we must embrace our gay, lesbian, bisexual, and transgender brothers and sisters. Not all psychologists will agree. Why resist renouncing heterosexism? There is evidence in our collective histories that ethnic minorities and gays and lesbians have suffered a similar plight: restricted rights, violence, denigration, isolation, and trauma (Atkinson & Hackett, 1998; Dupre, 1997; Helms & Cook, 1999; Herek, 1998; Thompson & Neville, 1999). What is preventing us from embracing one another, resisting domination, and progressing together? A chilling connection was made when Matthew Shepard's father, in a speech to his son's convicted murderers, recalled a conversation he'd had about the death penalty with his son. He said it was Matthew's opinion that the "death penalty should be sought and that no expense should be spared to bring those responsible for [the] murder [of James Byrd, Jr.] to justice" (Cart, 1999). Yet that day, Shepard made a plea against the death penalty "to begin the healing process." Both Mr. Byrd, Jr., and Mr. Shepard were brutally tortured and killed because of their respective statuses as a Black man and a gay man in the United States of America. How can we ignore sexuality diversity among people of color, and how can we deny that racial majority gays and lesbians share a common cause? Respect, equal rights, competent health, and mental health care are our collective goals.

We place our argument within the context of growing trends in the multicultural literature. We then discuss the barriers to embracing intersections of identities and review some of the work that more integrative psychologists have done. Finally, we propose a renewed vision for the future of the multicultural movement in counseling.

THE MULTICULTURAL
COUNSELING MOVEMENT—FLUID AND EVOLVING

As with any movement that seeks to empower people who've been oppressed by a system, a sense of history is absolutely key. We need to know where we've been in order to plan a strategy for where to go. Jackson (1995) traces the history of the multicultural counseling movement from the 1950s to the mid 1990s. Pioneering the field were scholars who focused on gaining cultural understanding of the largest U.S. racial minority group, African Americans, and as the movement gained momentum, expanded their studies to include Latino Americans, Asian Americans, and Native American Indians. The multicultural movement in counseling may have reached full swing in 1991 when *Journal of Counseling and Development* published a special issue on multiculturalism as the fourth force in counseling, complementary to psychodynamic, behavioral, and humanistic approaches (e.g., Pedersen, 1990). An inspirational issue, it tackles racism as a disease (Skillings & Dobbins, 1991), examines the influence of worldview on counseling (Ibrahim, 1991), presents a model for cultural diversity training (Sue, 1991), and more. Concepts from this special issue remain compelling and relevant. However, with the exception of a contribution by Reynolds and Pope (1991), "culture" in the multicultural counseling movement seemed narrowly defined as the cultural and racial experiences of people of color in the United States.

In fact, by the early 1990s only a handful of ethnic minority counseling and clinical psychologists published articles on the importance of intersections of identities, such as sexual orientation and ethnicity (Chan, 1989; Loiacano, 1989; Greene, 1997; Morales, 1990). Greene (1997) asserted that the complex interaction between sexual orientation and ethnic identity development was roundly ignored in both the ethnic minority and gay and lesbian literatures. Varying constructions of the meaning of culture, identity, and minority status seem to have influenced thinking on who and what to include in the multicultural counseling movement. For example, Greene (1997) defines culture quite broadly, as "the behaviors, values, and beliefs that characterize a particular social group and perhaps distinguish it from others" (p. xi). She further states that factors including ethnicity, age, socioeconomic class, religion, skin color, gender, regional affiliation, and sexual orientation often serve to distinguish groups. Using her definition of culture, the multicultural movement would surely include gay and lesbian studies.

In *Counseling Diverse Populations*, Atkinson and Hackett (1995, 1998) address counseling issues for four "minority" groups: gay/lesbians; women; people with disabilities; and the elderly. This counselor training text is organized similarly to *Counseling American Minorities* (Atkinson, Morten, & Sue, 1993, 1995, 1998), a volume dedicated to counseling ethnic minorities. Atkinson and Hackett (1998) maintain that "groups who are singled out for differential and unequal treatment allows us to expand the list of minorities beyond ethnic groups." (p. 5). What ethnic minorities and other minorities have in common is that they face systematic discrimination in U.S. society. Without explicitly stating as much, these two works acknowledge the linkages between movements for ethnic minority and gay rights. Indeed, they recognize the need for psychologists in general to pay attention to the psychosocial and economic circumstances for a variety of marginalized groups.

Scholars invested in the multicultural counseling movement periodically revisit its themes and create visions for the future. A special issue of *The Counseling Psychologist* edited by Thompson and Neville (1999) challenges us to address some of the gaps in our current thinking about multicultural counseling. Thompson and Neville (1999) reinvigorate psychologists to address issues of oppression in their work, specifically to engage in fighting racism in and outside of the therapy office. In doing so, the authors question the validity of maintaining a focus on the individual without impacting the systems within which we and our clients live.

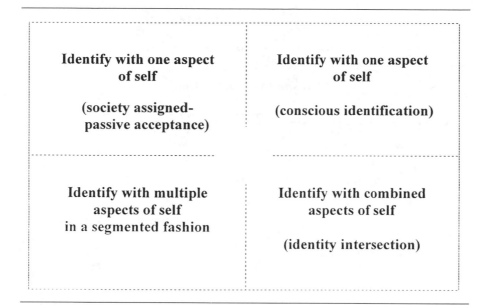

Figure 36.1. Multidimensional Identity Model

SOURCE: From Reynolds, A. L., & Pope, R. L. (1991). The complexities of diversity: Exploring multiple oppressions. *Journal of Counseling and Development.* 70(1), 174-180. Reproduced with the permission of the American Counseling Association.

Almost a decade following *JCD*'s 1991 special issue on multicultural counseling, Robinson and Ginter (1999) edited an issue titled "Racism: Healing its Effects." This issue provides compelling qualitative evidence that multicultural counseling encompasses not only issues of race, culture and ethnicity, but also multiple oppressions, intersecting and complex identities, and issues of privilege. In it, we read the personal stories of mental health professionals from a variety of ethnic, gender, class, and sexual orientation backgrounds. Through the power of their narratives, they convey the effects of racism, sexism, heterosexism, and other forms of oppression on their lives. In an analysis of the narratives, Watt (1999) reveals, among other themes, a fluidity in the construction of racial and sexual orientation identities. Robinson (1999) discusses the intersections of dominant discourses on race, sex, sexual orientation, physical ability, and class. Unlike the Multidimensional Identity Model (Reynolds & Pope, 1991), the Robinson Model on Discourses illustrates how privileged statuses stand in comparison to marginalized statuses (Robinson, 1999). We feel this marks a trend of moving beyond the intrapsychic components of minority identity, even that of multiple identities within the self, and making visible our psychological identity development as positioned in a society that differentially allocates privilege. Please see Figures 36.1 and 36.2.

To illustrate the growing trend in examining privilege as a necessary component of multicultural competency, Fine, Weiss, Powell, and Wong

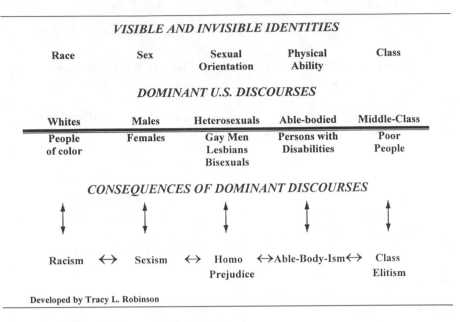

Figure 36.2. The Robinson Model on Discourses
SOURCE: From Robinson, T. L. (1999). The intersections of dominant discourses across race, gender, and other identities. *Journal of Counseling and Development, 77*(1), 73-79. Reproduced with the permission of the American Counseling Association.

(1997) edited a collection of essays that address the invisible side of the multicultural movement, that of White privilege. This collection also tackles the complexities of diversity and identity with qualitative research, narratives, and fictional essays. In it readers have an opportunity not only to examine White privilege, but also explore inter-ethnic tension, and issues between heterosexual people of color and gay, lesbian, and bisexual people. A perfect example of the uncompromising style of the more recent multicultural discourse is the chapter titled, "The White Girl in Me, the Colored Girl in You, and the Lesbian in Us: Crossing Boundaries" (Connolly & Noumair, 1997). Connolly and Noumair (1997) present critical issues first through identifying their own lenses, examining their minority as well as privileged statuses, and modeling for the reader a high level of introspection recommended by cultural competence experts (Arredondo, 1999).

Two recent events brought major visibility to the multicultural counseling movement: the 1999 annual convention of the American Psychological Association and the National Multicultural Conference and Summit, also in 1999. Research about ethnic minority mental health received legitimate attention from the leadership of APA when Richard Suinn, the first Asian American APA president, made it one of his presidential initiatives. Furthermore, the Multicultural Summit received sponsorship from three separate APA divisions: Counseling Psychology; Division on Women; Society for the Psychological Study of Ethnic Minority Issues. This conference brought together psychologists with distinct and overlapping agendas. Although there was clear dominance of ethnic minority psychology at the conference, a growing force cried out for attention to gay, lesbian, and bisexual concerns, spirituality, and rights of people with disabilities. Within sessions that focused on intersections of diversity, a lack of answers was combined with, at times, tension. Yet there was presence. There is a force that is joining these movements. In fact, the Society for the Psychological Study of Lesbian, Gay, and Bisexual Issues held its executive committee meeting concurrently with the conference, a show of support for the Multicultural Summit as a whole. The conference and summit hosted "Difficult Dialogues," a panel discussion between psychologists representing diverse ethnic, gender, and sexual orientation backgrounds talking about these diverse personal statuses. Unlike the aforementioned literature embracing the study of intersecting identities and coalition among oppressed groups, the panel discussion unveiled some of the deeply felt emotional and philosophical barriers we face in making connections a reality.

Thus, there seems to be increasing momentum to conceptualize identity as encompassing complex intersections between race, ethnicity, sexual orientation, and gender, among other factors. It also appears that psychologists are not mincing words when it comes to confronting oppression on many fronts. Scholars, particularly in counseling psychology, continue to critique our reliance on individual psychotherapy and challenge us to become more invested in structural changes and less rigid forms of helping, such as advocacy and psychoeducation. The recognition that oppression contributes in large part to the mental health stress of ethnic minority and other minority populations has had implications for counselor training. It is now more common for counselor trainees to study White privilege and racism as a necessary step toward developing competency. Will we soon notice a similar trend in analysis of heterosexual and male privilege in compulsory counselor training?

WHAT'S HOLDING US UP?

Our sense of history needs to extend beyond a review of recent trends in our professional communities. As a historical and ongoing process, colonization has resulted in the psychological, social, physical, and geographic dispersion or fragmentation of various identities (see Utsey, Bolden, & Brown, Chapter 19, this volume). As such, it has erected significant barriers to holistic, integrated, collective identities. Analyses of profound historical processes reveal much that is similar in what oppressed racial/ethnic, gendered, and nonheterosexual groups have endured (Beemyn & Eliason, 1996). To Somerville (1996), race and sexuality have been historically managed in the same ways: (a) the classification and separation of types, (b) cultural anxieties about "mixed bodies," and (c) the convergence of "unnatural and perverse" desires in psychological discourse. It is known that a significant impact of dominant groups is the miseducation of themselves and the oppressed (Helms & Cook, 1999). Not surprisingly, the collective history of nonheterosexuals is fragmented and obfuscated (McCarn & Fassinger, 1996).

Sexual identities have also formed as a matter of interaction or assimilation into the majority culture (Greene, 1997). Specifically, European communities have historically interacted with global majority cultures via Christian religion. For example, Catholicism has been very successful in expanding itself globally. Its comprehensive impact was spawned from its historical role in the colonization of numerous majority cultures. During these colonization processes, European countries in competition with one another measured their political and economic power by increased number of converts, growing Church memberships, and resources extracted from abroad. Catholicism existed, partnered with its own expansion and ability to reproduce itself (Ani, 1994), introducing an emphasis on White-male-dominated reproductive sexuality. In the Americas, the degree to which Two-Spirited, or *berdache,* identities persist among Native American Indian cultures, depends largely on the nature of the colonizing religions (Tafoya, 1997; Williams, 1993).

Compartmentalization is a familiar tactic used by dominant power structures to create the appearance of groups of numerical minorities that oppose each other. The assumption of any monolithic "community" is rhetoric (Ridge, Hee, & Minichiello, 1999), as is the idea of distinct and separate communities. Conflicting parts facilitate the objectification of others and only maintain distance between all identities (Ani, 1994). Such discourse contributes to pressures to choose one identity over another. By focusing on what the preferential affiliations of marginalized people might be, we pathologize them. The illusion of "choice" of community relegates more political power, structural privilege, and economic status to minorities than actually exists, a mentality that is bedfellow to the bootstrap. Thus, one of the major barriers we face in integrating sexual orientation and ethnic minority discourses in psychology is that we remain structurally compartmentalized; consequently, the weapon of racism within predominantly White gay movements and the weapon of heterosexism within predominantly heterosexual ethnic minority movements are used to keep us apart. The bedrock of this structural segregation, of course, is that White and straight are considered to be the norm (Jensen, 1999; Macintosh, 1992).

Rigid definitions of identity and community are especially pronounced for some of us. We know from research and countless personal narratives that visible racial and ethnic minorities who are gay, lesbian, or bisexual feel pressured to choose one of their marginalized identities over another. This dynamic has been confirmed for many Asians and Asian Americans (Chan, 1989; Sanitioso, 1999), African American men (Crisp, Priest, &

Torgerson, 1998; Icard, 1986; Loiacano, 1989), and others (Greene, 1997; Peterson, 1992). Pressure to have any primary identification can intensify in subcommunities such as church (Crisp, Priest, & Torgerson, 1998). Many fear rejection not only from society at large but also in part from their major sources of support (Liu & Chan, 1996), a situation that has been known to lead to stress and depression. Inadequate support or failed support can magnify the effects of marginalization and can serve as a second injury to a primary event of oppression (Mascher & Lowe, 1999).

There are multiple sources of oppression facing gay ethnic minorities. There is rampant racism among queer groups as well as heterosexism in visible racial and ethnic minority communities (Conerly, 1996; Loiacano, 1989). Cultural, social, and political institutions for crossover marginalizations, such as bisexual non-White populations, are rare (Conerly, 1996). There is a tremendous lack of overlap between all communities that are separated politically, culturally, and geographically, leaving members to negotiate themselves intrapsychically. While it is important to understand the subjective experience of identities in conflict, we risk pathologizing those who are caught in sociocultural double binds. In reality, the pathological splitting is located not within individuals but in the dominant culture that is so invested in separating others.

Racism in gay communities takes many forms (Garnets & Kimmel, 1993; Jones & Hill, 1996; Morales, 1990). There are few, if any, representations of ethnic minorities in gay media. White gay communities offer few psychological benefits to VREGs (i.e., visible racial or ethnic groups; Helms & Cook, 1999) in the way of social support, visible role models, overall acceptance, and participation in steering or event committees. Visible minorities are routinely denied entrance to clubs in addition to enduring violence, tokenism, invisibility, and hostility in Anglo-dominated gay spaces (Peterson, 1992; Ridge, Hee, & Minichiello, 1999).

Culturally defined rules of social and sexual relationships, when combined with privilege differences, are significant barriers that deeply affect mental, emotional, and physical well-being. Ridge et al. (1999) investigated the intersection of relationship rules and power among Southeast Asian men in an Anglo-American-dominated gay culture. Asian men reported receiving sexual attention when they were isolated but not in the context of larger social groups. Asians and Asian Americans may be drawn to escape such invisibility by mirroring Anglo-approved gay masculinities such as well-defined musculature, fashion, or demeanor (Ridge et al., 1999). Invisibility and increased isolation could lead to decreased self-efficacy in these Asian men, impacting their willingness to enter helpful contexts where information can be obtained, for example, on topics such as HIV (Sanitioso, 1999). Gender stereotypes have become linked to racial stereotypes, as in the case of "passive" gay Asian men who are relegated to submission and lower statuses in interpersonal decision making (Sanitioso, 1999).

People who do not share sociosexual rules with dominant groups are at risk of being exploited or harmed. For instance, Asian men may act out of respect, collective responsibility, investment in maintaining harmony, or saving the face of a higher status partner; any of these could be misinterpreted as passivity or consent, predisposing gay Asians to sexually risky or vulnerable situations with Anglos (Ridge et al., 1999; Sanitioso, 1999). Regional and cross-cultural differences regarding sexual orientation or gender roles, with visible racial or ethnic groups (Sanitioso, 1999), are also invisible to dominant Anglo groups. Whites and privileged others are chronically unaware of power differences, and this makes sociosexual negotiations dangerous.

Heterosexism in Latina (Espin, 1993), Black (Jones & Hill, 1996), and other VREG communities (Greene, 1997) has also been documented. Herek (1995) found that queerness tends to be accepted in Black communities by people who are highly educated, unmarried, politically liberal, registered to vote, included Blacks in their concept of gayness and could report having personal contact with nonheterosexuals. A lack of acceptance of queer identity by Blacks has been correlated with conflicting religious beliefs, attribution of choice to sexuality, and a lack of knowledge about sexual orientation (Herek, 1995).

Because entrenched gender roles in family and community have been another source of heterosexism (Garnets & Kimmel, 1993), individuals may encounter resistance as they explore variations of these roles in same-sex relationships. Liu and Chan (1996) review ways in which Confucianism, Taoism, and Buddhism could influence sexual identity in Asians and Asian Americans. For example, in Confucianism, family role structures are well-defined as heterosexual and patriarchal, rendering homosexual relationships within this worldview highly problematic. They note that among queer Asian American relationships, partners may replicate a Confucian family structure and play out the same hierarchical roles defined by Confucian worldview. Thus, constructs such as family, sexuality, and religion intersect with complexity within cultural groups, resulting in a variety of adaptation styles (Bhugra, 1997; Laird & Green, 1996). An example is if Asian American families emphasize educational achievement over social interactions, Asian American queers may pursue academic success in order to conceal their nonheterosexual identities (Morales, 1990). Morales (1990) points out that for underrepresented ethnic groups, families are not only symbols and foci of ethnicity but also represent historical links; thus queer people may form their own relationships as a unique variation on familial and cultural templates.

In our own research, we seek to understand barriers to interpersonally diverse alliances in the face of oppression (Lowe & Mascher, 2000). From semistructured interviews, interactive sessions, and workshops we have assessed how people of different backgrounds perceive barriers to interpersonal support. Preliminary findings suggest that there are many barriers to receiving support on issues of heterosexism, racism, and sexism. Among these barriers are victim uncertainty about what is helpful, social isolation, lack of safety and confidentiality to discuss issues, low self-efficacy, other people's denial about oppression, and a lack of educated or skilled people to provide needed support. We have also assessed perceived barriers to providing effective support to another person who is a victim of discrimination. For example, participants report that negative feelings such as guilt, shame, and anger prevent them from reaching out to marginalized others. They also comment on how emotional unavailability, or an inability to relate to a particular form of discrimination, inhibits their ability to help others. What is both promising and frustrating about our findings thus far is that there are many similarities in people's experiences of discrimination, whether it is racism, sexism, or heterosexism. Yet frequently people do not see one another as sources of support due to the predominant view that one "ism" is unlike the other.

Even within close trusting relationships, the topic "discrimination" often seems to be unacceptable or risky conversation. People have reported that significant others, who in most realms would provide social and emotional support, fail to comprehend the impact of oppression (Lowe & Mascher, 2000). Mays, Cochran, and Rhue (1993) have found that Black lesbian women in their research made relationship and community affiliation choices based on their perceptions, anxieties, expectations and experiences with discrimination in these contexts. In some cases, the participants reported seeking other Black partners after experiencing racism while in relationships with White women. It is important for psychologists to assess not only how discrimination affects clients individually but how oppression plays out within their relationships. For instance, do clients actually speak to significant others about discrimination, and if so, do they trust that they can relate and/or provide support?

Greene (1997) has identified a number of countertransference issues that impede psychotherapy with multiply oppressed individuals. Insecure therapists are likely to feel threatened and act out their insensitivities to real barriers or they may lack boundaries. As with other countertransferences, therapists may overaccommodate lesbigay clients of color or somehow seek to assuage their own feelings of guilt or inadequacy. Specifically, therapists working with these populations may avoid or pursue sexual or racially charged material in the session. On the other hand, lesbigay therapists of color could overlook or minimize their clients' other problems in living or may find themselves particularly vulnerable to dual role relationships (Greene, 1997). Therapists need to examine their assumptions of race, ethnicity, and sexuality as well as their own races, ethnicities, and sexualities.

In summary, the major barriers we face to the integration of sexual orientation issues in the multicultural movement include the persistence of false dichotomies in identity construction, as well as heterosexism and

racism that are deeply embedded in our society. More specifically, it is paramount that we address the heterosexism within ethnic minority communities from both a historical and contemporary perspective; in doing so, we
may uncover cultural heritages that are not as rigid as our current constructions of sexuality in the United States. For coalitions to form, it is also critical that predominantly White gay communities address the racism within,
which poses a continued threat to ethnic minority gay men, lesbians, and
bisexuals as well as alienates coalitions within the multicultural counseling movement.

FROM PARALLEL TO INTERSECTING: MATHEMATICAL IMPOSSIBILITY OR THERAPEUTIC INTERVENTION

In this section, we review a small but growing body of literature that focuses on intersections between ethnicity, sexual orientation, and a variety
of psychological concerns. We see this literature as indicative of a trend toward integration of minority psychologies, work that both acknowledges
the power of distinct identity layers as well as inquires how these identities
are interwoven.

It is because racial and sexual orientation minorities share a common
plane of marginalization that they have continued on separate paths without intersecting. Minority groups spend much time and effort justifying
their experiences and trying to gain equal rights in the context of the majority group, be it White, heterosexual, male, or economically privileged. Relatively little time or effort is spent noticing how marginalized neighbors are
fighting equally hard against a virtually identical dominant structure. Even
when there is such acknowledgment, people who are fighting for a cause
frequently experience burnout and feel it is all they can do to help "their
own." The unseen power of these dynamics is that minority groups remain
divided, fighting for fair representation and resources but doing so in a segregated fashion. Treating identities as distinct and parallel bars integration
and facilitates the routine mirroring of dominant power structures within
the movements of the oppressed.

Pathways of research on visible racial and ethnic groups, on one hand,
and gays, lesbians, and bisexuals, on the other hand, are quite similar. Until
recently, these literatures have not intersected. We witness parallel developments in the literatures on identity development (Atkinson et al., 1998;
Cass, 1979), the effects of racism and heterosexism respectively (Herek,
1998; Jones, 1997), and issues in therapy competence or lack thereof
(Greene, 1997; Helms & Cook, 1999). For instance, models of sexual orientation identity development have been largely informed by the literature
on racial identity development. After reviewing numerous models of sexual orientation development (Cox & Gallois, 1996; Sophie, 1986), it is clear

how these models have evolved relative to racial identity development models, how they have carved a parallel path, have comparable shortcomings, and so endure similar criticisms. Earlier models target the development of marginalized identities, visible racial or ethnic groups, or gay and lesbian sexualities. Identity theorists have secondarily addressed the development of privileged identities, be it White racial identity (Helms, 1995) or heterosexual identity development (Eliason, 1995).

Slowly, intersections of multiply oppressed selves have taken the stage in identity development modeling. This body of literature, however, is in its infancy. We found a variety of qualitative studies, whose results are difficult to summarize because many of them bear witness to the overall experiences of specific ethnic minority gay, lesbian, or bisexual groups. Thus the following literature is rich in laying the groundwork for more specific research questions to be investigated in the future.

In nonheterosexual identity development, Dube and Savin-Williams (1999) have found variations across ethnic groups in the timing and sequencing of developmental milestones, extent to which sexuality was disclosed to family members, and rates of heterosexual relationships. There are models of ethnic minority gay men and lesbians in general (Morales, 1990), African American lesbigay development (Loiacano, 1993), Asian American gay men and lesbians (Chan, 1989), and Latina lesbians (Espin, 1987). The Multidimensional Identity Model (Reynolds & Pope, 1991), which describes a psychological orientation toward multiple identites, is an outgrowth of Root's (1990) work in biracial identity. The Robinson Model on Discourses situates people's identities within dominant U.S. discourses of race, sex, sexual orientation, physical ability, and class (Robinson, 1999).

The tensions and pressures that multiply oppressed individuals feel among various aspects of their identities have been well documented (Greene, 1997). Because social, political, and even personal spaces do not often acknowledge whole identities, aspects of individuals become exaggerated or obscured. Peterson (1992), Loiacano (1989), and others have documented tensions in the affiliations of Black nonheterosexuals. Similarly, Chan (1989) has reported identity conflicts among Asian American lesbians and gay men. One mainstream view values the emergence of a dominant identity over another intrapsychically. In *The Textbook of Homosexuality and Mental Health* Cabaj and Stein (1996) suggest an important therapeutic goal is for lesbians or gay men of color to select a primary identification. Current research is still concerned with answering questions such as "are you black first, or are you queer?" (Conerly, 1996, p. 133).

Overwhelmingly, the "coming out" process is still considered a milestone in the development of a sexual minority identity in Whites and people of color, with a host of its own implications for psychological and emotional well-being (Garnets & Kimmel, 1993; Greene, 1997; Smith, 1997). In the United States context, being "out" is often assumed to be a

singular constellation and dichotomous. Not coming out can be seen as
an indication of immaturity, shame, secrecy, and pathology. Smith (1997)
challenges researchers and practitioners to seek alternative reasons for
coming-out behaviors in lesbigay VREGs. Of course, coming out is necessitated only in contexts where heterosexuality is assumed and valued. Although many theorists have considered the role of culture in the coming
out process, a new language is needed to emphasize the heterosexist meaning and process of it all (Smith, 1997). Furthermore, Fygetakis (1997) and
Chan (1989) suggest that there may be cultural variations on the necessity
and/or expression of "outness."

Garnets and Kimmel (1993) suggest that multiply oppressed individuals can take steps toward integrating their identities by prioritizing
commitments to numerous distinct communities. However, primary identification with any community is a complex business. According to Chan
(1993), queer Asian Americans rely in part on their perceptions of homophobia in Asian American communities and of racism in queer communities. Community identification may also depend on the nature of
affiliations with any Asian American queer communities, on changing
needs for support, and on desires to share culturally (Chan, 1993).

Other recent efforts have focused on the unique combinations of stressors and mental health issues that face queer racial and ethnic groups
(Greene, 1997). Psychologists are just beginning to explore what it means to
combine several marginalized identities and how "unsuccessful integra-
tions" are seen to lead to maladjustment or health problems (Greene, 1997).
Isolation, psychological vulnerability, and behavior that result from conflicting loyalties have been misinterpreted as psychopathology. Rather,
strategies that have been used to cope successfully in the past might be
maladaptive or self-destructive at other times or in other contexts. In fact,
such tensions should indicate resilience and coping in those contexts that
pathologize integrated individuals. Integrated multiple identities need to
be seen as desirable (Greene, 1997).

General developmental issues have been addressed for some populations of queer people of color and frequently explore experiences with racism, heterosexism, internalized oppression, and a variety of relationship
concerns. For example, Rodriguez (1996) looks at dating issues among Latino gay men, as well as gay Latino survivors of sexual abuse. Crisp, Priest,
and Torgerson (1998) research developmental issues in African American
gay men as they relate to manhood, self-concept, and self-esteem. Adams
and Kimmel (1997) explore the lives of older African American gay men,
commenting on the double jeopardy these men face in terms of racism and
homophobia. However, the continuities and discontinuities of identity
throughout youth, adolescence, midlife, and seniority of nonheterosexuals
of color has remained largely unexamined, and our understanding of life-
span development is still limited. Critical lifespan constructs, such as

adolescence, parenting, or career, have yet to be linked to sexual orientation in combination with race or ethnicity. These cross sections continue to elude us as we frame our clinical discussions.

Theory and narratives about the romantic partnerships of non-heterosexual people of color have also emerged recently. With the historical momentum of the civil rights movement, racial identity literature, and other leads in multicultural counseling, much of the groundbreaking integrative research in this area involves African Americans. Greene and Boyd-Franklin (1996) write about African American lesbian partnerships with implications for couples therapy. We have data on the relationships of African American lesbians and gay men, with special attention to partner selection, commitment, satisfaction, sexual behavior, and HIV (Peplau, Cochran, & Mays, 1997). Another critical piece of research examines the impact of perceived discrimination on the close relationships of Black lesbians with their friends, lovers, family, and community (Mays, Cochran, & Rhue, 1993).

Recent data have emerged about Black-White interracial heterosexual relationships (Wehrly, Kenney, & Kenney, 1999), but data about interracial same-sex couples are still sparse (Peplau et al., 1997). Greene and Boyd-Franklin (1996) outline several challenges to interracial lesbian couples. Pearlman (1996) outlines relational challenges to the interracial lesbian couple, with implications for therapy. One therapeutic task would be to depersonalize power struggles within these relationships in order to work through issues of racism, classism, and heterosexism as well as reframe differences in coping and resilience as an added dimension in attraction. Future work with interracial same-sex couples could have astounding sociopolitical implications and deeply affect the way we think about identity integration and coalition building.

Morales (1990) and Rodriguez (1996) examine broader clinical issues for gay Latino men. The interaction of environment and identity includes family as a basis for socialization, class, religion, *machismo*, gender roles, acculturation/not being brown enough, language, *familismo*, family dynamics, the redefinition of *familia*, socialization in multiple worlds, and HIV/AIDS. Alquijay (1997) has written about Latina lesbians and self-esteem, including the impact of socioeconomic status and lifestyle. Morales (1996) examines the effect of gender role socialization in families and couples of Latino gay men. Liu and Chan (1996) look at family issues for lesbian, gay, and bisexual Asian Americans. As is typical for clinical research, the emphasis has been on intervention rather than prevention.

By many accounts, psychotherapy has been an unsafe place for queer people of color (Garnets et al., 1991). Issues in psychotherapy have been reviewed for a number of circumscribed populations including queer Latino/as, queer African Americans, queer Native American Indians, queer Asian Americans, Jewish lesbians, Latina lesbians, Black lesbians (Dworkin,

1997; Greene, 1997; Laird & Green, 1996; Smith, 1997), and others. Authors report on therapist biases, countertransference, coming out, safety, and confidentiality, among other concerns. Clinical implications mirror the cultural competency models, which state that therapists must examine their own worldview, cultural values, and biases as well as learn about the developmental and psychosocial experiences of their gay, lesbian, or bisexual clients.

THE FUTURE OF
INTEGRATED MULTICULTURAL COUNSELING

We humbly provide some food for thought on where these integrative lines of inquiry might take us. Some suggestions are obvious extensions of the extant literature. We also hope to inspire some creative thinking as we present some of the questions we have had about the psychology of minorities, broadly defined.

Sexual and racial identities are simply not stable constructs across context and time. The integrative models of identity continue to focus on psychological factors of individuals and fail to fully accommodate the fluid nature of identities (Beemyn & Eliason, 1996) such as sexuality, race, or other social constructions. Overall, models are also individualistic by locating identity development within individuals and individual lifespans rather than in interpersonal spaces or in a collective, historical sense. For example, how is asserting gay identity within an individualist versus collectivist family/social environment similar or different from one another?

There may be intergenerational differences, cohort effects (Dube & Savin-Williams, 1999), or historical shifts (Helms, 1995) that inevitably change the meaning of identity formation. Counseling psychologists need to expand their notions of identity development to include transgenerational and historical analyses. How does coming out relate to the historical context of one's family in terms of economic status, migration, and significant historical events, such as the legalization of gay marriages? There are numerous sociopolitical pieces written in the context of queer identity that can inform more complete identity modeling, including indigenous American Indian, African, and Asian accounts (Potgeiter, 1997). Fygetakis (1997) offers versions of Greek-American tradition in the context of lesbian and gay identity.

In the context of a therapeutic relationship identities are misread, reread, and continually merged in new ways. Dworkin (1997) has written about Jewish lesbians and the implications of psychotherapy for the client, therapist, family, couples, religion, and community. She puts forth a modified self-psychology model to conduct therapy with Jewish lesbians (Dworkin, 1997). The goals, identity models, and theoretical bases for working with Jewish and other lesbians in therapy need to incorporate developmental and clinical issues with historical contexts.

Psychologists need to do much more integrating and not just of one marginalized identity with another. Psychologists need to integrate various parts of themselves, themselves with others, and psychology with politics. Identity development models have affirmed and named minority statuses and call for the integration of multiple minority statuses. The development of minority-friendly theory, separate from integration with majority status, maintains a discriminating focus on "the other" from a clinical and theoretical gaze.

Multicultural counseling psychologists have long called for the self-study in dominant populations. For privileged psychologists, this means comprehensive content-and-process approaches that involve seeking self-knowledge with as much intensity as when we study the other. For example, Whites need to be studying Eurocentrism in detail (Richardson & Molinaro, 1996). Heterosexuals, similarly, need to be considering the identity questions that are popularly asked of nonheterosexuals: For example, when did I first realize I was heterosexual? What caused my heterosexuality? To whom do I disclose my heterosexuality? Historical-developmental contexts can be particularly useful in analyzing how maladjustment, narcissism, and other problems in living rest on being White, heterosexual, or male. We also need to be clear about how the unacknowledged use of power leads to problematic relationships.

Identity development theory could use a model and language for us to reconcile the privileged and oppressed parts of ourselves. For example, I seek to integrate the privilege of my European Americanness with my lesbianism (J. Mascher), or the privilege of my heterosexuality with my Chinese Americanism (S. Lowe). The point is to embrace that which is splintered and distant from ourselves psychologically, emotionally, physically, or geographically. The most potent and integrative presence of multiple identities has come in the form of poems, essays, novels, biomythographies, or other versions of narratives (Jones & Hill, 1996) from outside mainstream multicultural psychology. In counseling psychology, the particularly powerful and integrative research will continue to be narrative driven.

As we become increasingly aware of how layers of identity impact our experiences, more research is needed to describe the nuances of minority statuses. What is the role of visible minority status in predicting the experience of oppression? Involuntary visibility can come in the form of skin color/tone and facial features, such as the shape of eyes, noses, and texture and color of hair, to name some phenotypes (Helms & Cook, 1999; Jones, 1997; Okazawa-Rey, Robinson, & Ward, 1987). But marginalized status can emanate from style of speech, language accent or proficiency in English, type of dress, or haircut/style, which may be consciously or unconsciously managed (Chan, 1993; Lee, 1991). Marginalization can also come via affiliation—neighborhood, education, choice of leisurely and political activities, career, and so on. We could speculate that direct experiences with discrimination vary on some kind of continuum from least frequently visible to most frequently visible minority status.

If there are continua that predict discrimination, what is the link between constantly visibly identified minorities and stress? What would the role of community buffers, education, economic status, and relationship support be on the resilience of such an individual? How about people who pass as White, as straight, as Christian? What are the psychological strengths and strains of passing? What happens when such a person is frequently privy to prejudice, yet has a choice to hide or ignore one's identity in a given moment or conversation? What are the consequences of letting prejudice slide so as not to be discovered as one of the marginalized? What is the nature of the psychological toll when marginalization is secretly experienced? If the availability of allies and social support is directly related to being "out" about one's minority status, it may be the case that nonvisible minorities are particularly at risk for isolation. Future research may explore how such isolation impacts identity development, especially internalization of oppression.

Perhaps those who are only intermittently identified as "other" experience something altogether different—is there a double consciousness? When one is outwardly seen as in the majority but has a minority identification (e.g., nonheterosexuality or racial minority heritage), does the person feel a sense of being majority by suspending disbelief that oppression occurs to others? What occurs to multiracial and bisexual people for whom identification with both the oppressed and the oppressor is salient? Is there a separate or fully integrated sense of minority self, one that is adversely affected every time a negative expression about the person's invisible minority status is expressed? How do these experiences vary with identity construction and development as well as level of internalized oppression? What kind of psychological resources does a person develop to cope with the less frequent or intermittent denigrations based on minority status? What are the factors affecting a person's degree of resilience or ability to cope? How effective is social support in the absence of structural or institutional changes?

It will be important to investigate the myriad interactive effects between type and amount of oppression and developmental concerns such as self-concept, relationships, global mental health, culture, and acculturation. Until and unless we have a firm understanding of the psychosocial effects of oppression, we will never approach competency in counseling.

CONCLUSION

There are clear sociopolitical implications for choosing to identify with any one community over another (Beemyn & Eliason, 1996) at any one time. In counseling theory and research, the rampant exclusion of bisexuality, biracial and multiracial issues, transnationalism, and other interstitial embodiments illustrate how problematic it is to maintain segregated paradigms of identity. However, oppressive polarizations can be generative. With less room to maneuver between categorical identities, we more quickly challenge the borders that are meant to control us (Badgett, 1996). For example, there is reluctance on the part of queer theorists to institute bisexuality as a category out of fear that bisexuality would then lose its radical, integrative edge (Rust, 1996).

There are many risks involved in embracing connections and realizing our multiple identities; we fear losing our political edges. We believe that to liberate ourselves and our communities psychologically we must resist what now have become perfunctory categorizations of our complex nature as human beings. This activism would require seeking an understanding of the intersections between marginalized as well as privileged identities, using a fluid, contextual, historical approach. We do not mean to say that these distinct identity constructs should be melded into one another; rather, we contend that it is necessary to explore how these identity components integrate collectively or disparately contribute to the human experience.

We see this as the future of the multicultural counseling movement, one that is not merely the fourth force but more like a fourth dimension, as psychologists grapple with describing the human experience integrating privileged and oppressed socialization in research and practice. Privilege, marginalization, multiple identities, contemporary and historical analysis, culture, support, coalition, antiracism, and antiheterosexism are just some of the key words about which the movement would educate people. The multicultural literature and the literature on gay, lesbian, and bisexual psychology forged the way toward more inclusive developmental paradigms; however, the growth of a movement that examines intersections of race, sexuality, gender, class, and so on will truly mark the next advancement in psychology.

Concluding Remarks

I am a European-American upper-middle-class student (J. Mascher) at a White, Jesuit institution. I am thoroughly embedded in a Eurocentric, achievement-oriented, individualistic way of life that I am finding to be increasingly maladaptive. Accordingly, I embrace the dissolution of dichotomy and seek to deconstruct the bifurcations that exist in my daily living. As such, I seek to unify various parts of me. I am female, lesbian-identified, White, athletic, academic, emotional, and other things that my culture insists be compartmentalized from one another, from other people, and from myself as a whole person. As parts of me are reconciled with other parts, my struggle is to be interactive. My urge is to keep to myself.

Politically, I am a lesbian, but I am also a White person who confronts racism and ethnocentrism. My labels do not describe me fully, of course; the word *lesbian* does not account for my full range of emotional, behavioral, and cognitive ways of being. In most contexts, I choose to call myself "lesbian" over "bisexual," "multisexual"—or simply sexual—because there is a silence in these other terms that might breed heterosexism, sexism, and racism. I am blanketed in contexts where White heterosexual men can speak first, loudest, and longest about anything and everything. I am deeply afraid. My fear lies not in loving another woman. Rather, I fear that my Whiteness and my classism will overtake me. I don't want to speak and contribute to the silence of others. How can I represent myself and other selves in this short chapter? There is so much more that needs to be said.

I find that to be a lesbian is to be loaded politically, as it is based in affiliation and coupling rather than separation and splitting. I have been told overtly and covertly that I don't belong. Professors, supervisors, and peers objectify me in offices, gesticulate to me offensively in the hallways, use sexualized language in professional conversations with me, or otherwise let me know that I am threatening to their exaggerated partial identities. And so, even as I want distance from oppression, I have the task of facing what surrounds me and acknowledging that part of it, Whiteness and classism, is part of me as well.

Sometimes, I feel that my rage is the accumulation of thousands of years of systematic global sexism, racism, and heterosexism. I know that, as psychologists, parts of us remain oblivious to these histories so that we have defined our field based on partial accounts. I know that our histories and our future directions have something to do with the professions we make, and so I'll admit my ignorance. Clearly, the contemporary work of psychologists involves self-study, where dominant groups examine themselves, and we look at where and how we have defined the beginnings of our collective work. I will deconstruct my Whiteness by renouncing privilege where I can and engaging in a process of reconstructing my European American cultural heritage, just as heterosexuals need to understand their sexualities as intimately as the rest of us. In this way, as we redefine our histories and psychologies, our intrapsychic and interpersonal coalitions and alliances will permeate the barriers that maintain professional divisions.

REFERENCES

Adams, C. L., & Kimmel, D. C. (1997). Exploring the lives of older African American gay men. In B. Greene (Ed.), *Ethnic and cultural diversity among lesbians and gay men* (pp. 132-151). Thousand Oaks, CA: Sage.

Alquijay, M. A. (1997). The relationships among self-esteem, acculturation, and lesbian identity formation in Latina lesbians. In B. Greene (Ed.), *Ethnic and cultural diversity among lesbians and gay men* (pp. 249-265). Thousand Oaks, CA: Sage.

Ani, M. (1994). *Yurugu: An African-centered critique of European cultural thought and behavior.* Trenton, NJ: Africa World Press.

Arredondo, P. (1999). Multicultural counseling competencies as tools to address oppression and racism. *Journal of Counseling and Development, 77,* 102-108.

Atkinson, D. R., & Hackett, G. (1995). *Counseling diverse populations.* Boston: McGraw-Hill.

Atkinson, D. R., & Hackett, G. (1998). *Counseling diverse populations* (2nd ed.). Boston: McGraw-Hill.

Atkinson, D. R., Morten, G., & Sue, D. W. (1993). *Counseling American minorities: A cross-cultural perspective* (3rd ed.). Boston: McGraw-Hill.

Atkinson, D. R., Morten, G., & Sue, D. W. (1995). *Counseling American minorities: A cross-cultural perspective* (4th ed.). Boston: McGraw-Hill.

Atkinson, D. R., Morten, G., & Sue, D. W. (1998). *Counseling American minorities: A cross-cultural perspective* (5th ed.). Boston: McGraw-Hill.

Badgett, M.V.L. (1996). Employment and sexual orientation: Disclosure and discrimination in the workplace. *Journal of Gay & Lesbian Social Services, 4*(4), 29-52.

Beemyn, B., & Eliason, M. (Eds). (1996). *Queer studies: A lesbian, gay, bisexual, and transgender anthology.* New York: New York University Press.

Bhugra, D. (1997). Coming out by South Asian gay men in the United Kingdom. *Archives of Sexual Behavior, 26,* 547-557.

Cabaj, R. P., & Stein, T. S. (Eds.). (1996). *Textbook of homosexuality and mental health.* Washington, DC: American Psychiatric Press.

Cart, J. (1999, December 31). Killer of gay student is spared death penalty; courts: Matthew Shepard's father says life in prison shows mercy to someone who refused to show any mercy. *Los Angeles Times,* p. A1.

Cass, V. C. (1979). Homosexual identity formation: A theoretical model. *Journal of Homosexuality, 4,* 219-235.

Chan, C. (1989). Issues of identity development among Asian American lesbians and gay men. *Journal of Counseling and Development, 68,* 16 20.

Chan, C. S. (1993). Issues of identity development among Asian-American lesbians and gay men. In L. Garnets & D. Kimmel (Eds.), *Psychological perspectives on lesbian and gay male experiences* (pp. 376-387). New York: Columbia University Press.

Conerly, G. (1996). The politics of Black, lesbian, gay, and bisexual identity. In B. Beemyn & M. Eliason (Eds.), *A lesbian, gay, bisexual and transgender anthology* (pp. 133-145). New York: New York University Press.

Connolly, M. L., & Noumair, D. A. (1997). The White girl in me, the colored girl in you, and the lesbian in us: Crossing boundaries. In M. Fine, L. Weis, L. C. Powell, & L. M. Wong (Eds.), *Off white* (pp. 322-332). Thousand Oaks, CA: Sage.

Cox, S., & Gallois, C. (1996). Gay and lesbian identity development: A social identity perspective. *Journal of Homosexuality, 30*(4), 1-30.

Crisp, D., Priest, R., & Torgerson, A. (1998). African American gay men: Developmental issues, choices, and self-concept. *Family Therapy, 25,* 161-168.

Dube, E. M., & Savin-Williams, R. C. (1999). Sexual identity development among ethnic sexual-minority male youths. *Developmental Psychology, 35,* 1389-1398.

Dupre, J. (producer and director). (1997). *Out of the past: The struggle for gay and lesbian rights in America* [Film]. Unapix Films, Inc.

Dworkin, S. (1997). Female, lesbian, and Jewish: Complex and invisible. In B. Greene (Ed.), *Ethnic and cultural diversity among lesbians and gay men* (pp. 63-87). Thousand Oaks, CA: Sage.

Eliason, M. J. (1995). Accounts of sexual identity formation in heterosexual students. *Sex Roles, 32,* 821-834.

Espin, O. (1987). Issues of identity in the psychology of Latina lesbians: Explorations and challenges. In Boston Lesbian Psychologies Collective (Ed.), *Lesbian psychologies: Explorations and challenges* (pp. 35-55). Urbana: University of Illinois Press.

Espin, O. M. (1993). Issues of identity in the psychology of Latina lesbians. In L. D. Garnets & D. C. Kimmel (Eds.), *Psychological perspectives on lesbian and gay male experiences* (pp. 348-363). New York: Columbia University Press.

Fine, M., Weiss, L., Powell, L. C., & Wong, L. M. (1997). *Off white: Readings on race, power, and society.* New York: Routledge.

Fygetakis, L. M. (1997). Greek American lesbians: Identity odysseys of honorable good girls. In B. Greene (Ed.), *Ethnic and cultural diversity among lesbians and gay men* (pp. 152-190). Thousand Oaks, CA: Sage.

Garnets, L. D., & Kimmel, D. C. (Eds.). (1993). *Psychological perspectives on lesbian and gay male experiences.* New York: Columbia University Press.

Garnets, L., Hancock, K. A., Cochran, S. D., & Goodchilds, J. (1991). Issues in psychotherapy with lesbians and gay men: A survey of psychologists. *American Psychologist, 46*(9), 964-972.

Greene, B. (Ed.). (1997). *Ethnic and cultural diversity among lesbians and gay men.* Thousand Oaks, CA: Sage.

Greene, B., & Boyd-Franklin, N. (1996). African American lesbian couples: Ethnocultural considerations in psychotherapy. In M. Hill & E. Rothblum (Eds.), *Couples therapy: Feminist perspectives* (pp. 49-60). New York: Harrington Park Press/Haworth.

Helms, J. E. (1995). An update of Helms's White and people of color racial identity models. In J. G. Ponterotto, J. M. Casas, L. A. Suzuki, & C. M. Alexander (Eds.), *Handbook of multicultural counseling* (pp. 181-198). Thousand Oaks, CA: Sage.

Helms, J. E., & Cook, D. A. (1999). *Using race and culture in counseling and psychotherapy: Theory and process.* Boston: Allyn & Bacon.

Herek, G. M. (Ed.). (1998). *Stigma and sexual orientation: Understanding prejudice against lesbians, gay men, and bisexuals.* Thousand Oaks, CA: Sage.

Herek, G. M., & Capitanio, J. P. (1995). Black heterosexuals' attitudes toward lesbians and gay men in the United States. *Journal of Sex Research, 32*(2), 95-105.

Ibrahim, F. A. (1991). Contribution of cultural worldliness to generic counseling and development. *Journal of Counseling and Development, 70,* 13-19.

Icard, L. (1986). Black gay men and conflicting social identities: Sexual orientation versus racial identity. *Journal of Social Work and Human Sexuality, 4,* 83-93.

Jackson, M. L. (1995). Multicultural counseling: Historical perspectives. In J. G. Ponterotto, J. M. Casas, L. A. Suzuki, & C. M. Alexander (Eds.), *Handbook of multicultural counseling* (pp. 3-16). Thousand Oaks, CA: Sage.

Jensen, R. (1998, July 19). White privilege shapes the U. S. *Baltimore Sun.*

Jensen, R. (1999, July 4). More thoughts on why a system of White privilege is wrong. *Baltimore Sun.*

Jones, B. E., & Hill, M. J. (1996). African-American lesbians, gay men, and bisexuals. In R. P. Cabaj & T. S. Stein (Eds.), *Textbook of homosexuality and mental health* (pp. 549-561). Washington, DC: American Psychiatric Press.

Jones, J. M. (1997). *Prejudice and racism* (2nd ed.). New York: McGraw-Hill.

Laird, J., & Green, R. J. (Eds.). (1996). *Lesbians and gays in couples and families: A handbook for therapists.* San Francisco: Jossey-Bass.

Lee, M. W. (Producer and Director). (1991). *The color of fear* [Film]. Oakland: Stir Fry Productions.

Liu, P., & Chan, C. S. (1996). Lesbian, gay, and bisexual Asian Americans and their families. In J. Laird & R. J. Green (Eds.), *Lesbians and gays in couples and families: A handbook for therapists* (pp. 137-152). San Francisco: Jossey-Bass.

Loiacano, D. K. (1989). Gay identity issues among Black Americans: Racism, homophobia, and the need for validation. *Journal of Counseling and Development, 68,* 21-25.

Loiacano, D. K. (1993). Gay identity issues among Black Americans: Racism, homophobia, and the need for validation. In L. Garnets & D. Kimmel (Eds.), *Psychological perspectives on lesbian and gay male experiences* (pp. 364-375). New York: Columbia University Press.

Lowe, S. M., & Mascher, J. (2000). *Interpersonal coping with discrimination: A qualitative analysis.* Manuscript in progress.

Macintosh, P. (1992). White privilege and male privilege: A personal account of coming to see correspondences through work in women's studies. In M. L. Andersen & P. H. Collins (Eds.), *Race, class, and gender* (pp. 70-81). Belmont, CA: Wadsworth.

Mann, D., & Casas, J. M. (1998, August). *Cultural influences on the identity formation of Asian American gay men.* Poster presented at the annual convention of the American Psychological Association, San Francisco.

Mascher, J., & Lowe, S. M. (1999, August). *Forming alliances: An intervention to combat heterosexism, racism, and sexism.* Poster presented at the meeting of the American Psychological Association, Boston.

Mays, V. M., Cochran, S. D., & Rhue, S. (1993). The impact of perceived discrimination on the intimate relationships of Black lesbians. *Journal of Homosexuality, 25*(4), 1-14.

McCarn, S. R., & Fassinger, R. E. (1996). Revisioning sexual minority identity formation: A new model of lesbian identity and its implications for counseling and research. *The Counseling Psychologist, 24,* 508-534.

Morales, E. S. (1990). Ethnic minority families and minority gays and lesbians. *Marriage & Family Review, 14*(3/4), 217-239.

Morales, E. S. (1996). Gender roles among Latino gay and bisexual men: Implications for family and couple relationships. In J. Laird & R. J. Green (Eds.), *Lesbians and gays in couples and families: A handbook for therapists* (pp. 272-297). San Francisco: Jossey-Bass.

Multiculturalism as a fourth force in counseling [Special issue]. (1991). *Journal of Counseling and Development, 70*(1).

Okazawa-Rey, M., Robinson, T., & Ward, J. V. (1987). Black women and the politics of skin color and hair. *Women and Therapy, 6*(1/2), 89-102.

Pearlman, S. F. (1996). Loving across race and class divides: Relational challenges and the interracial lesbian couple. *Women & Therapy, 29*(3), 25-35.

Pedersen, P. (1990). The multicultural perspective as a fourth force in counseling. *Journal of Mental Health Counseling, 12,* 93-95.

Peplau, L. A., Cochran, S. D., & Mays, V. M. (Eds.). (1997). *A national survey of the intimate relationships of African American lesbians and gay men: A look at commitment, satisfaction, sexual behavior, and HIV disease.* Thousand Oaks, CA: Sage.

Peterson, J. L. (1992). Black men and their same-sex desires and behaviors. In G. Herdt (Ed.), *Gay culture in America: Essays from the field* (pp. 147-164). Boston: Beacon.

Potgeiter, C. (1997). From apartheid to Mandela's constitution: Black South African lesbians in the nineties. In B. Greene (Ed.), *Ethnic and cultural diversity among lesbians and gay men* (pp. 88-116). Thousand Oaks, CA: Sage.

Reynolds, A., & Pope, R. L. (1991). The complexities of diversity: Exploring multiple oppressions. *Journal of Counseling and Development, 70,* 174-180.

Richardson, T. Q., & Molinaro, K. L. (1996). White counselor self-awareness: A prerequisite for developing multicultural competence. *Journal of Counseling and Development, 74,* 238-241.

Ridge, D., Hee, A., & Minichiello, V. (1999). "Asian" men on the scene: Challenges to "gay communities." *Journal of Homosexuality, 36*(3/4), 43-68.

Robinson, T. L. (1999). The intersections of dominant discourses across race, gender, and other identities. *Journal of Counseling and Development, 77,* 73-79.

Robinson, T. L., & Ginter, E. J. (1999). Introduction to the special issue on racism. *Journal of Counseling & Development, 77,* 3.

Rodriguez, R. A. (1996). Clinical issues in identity development in gay Latino men. In C. J. Alexander (Ed.), *Gay and lesbian mental health: A sourcebook for practitioners* (pp. 127-157). New York: Harrington Park Press.

Root, M. P. P. (1990). Resolving "other" status: Identity development of biracial individuals. In L. S. Brown & M. P. P. Root (Eds.), *Complexity and diversity in feminist theory and therapy* (pp. 185-205). New York: Haworth.

Rust, P. C. (1996). Sexual identity and bisexual identities: The struggle for self-description in a changing sexual landscape. In B. Beemyn & M. Eliason (Eds.), *Queer studies: A lesbian, gay, bisexual, and transgender anthology* (pp. 64-86). New York: New York University Press.

Sanitioso, R. (1999). A social psychological perspective on HIV/AIDS and gay or homosexually active Asian men. *Journal of Homosexuality, 36*(3/4), 69-85.

Skillings, J. H., & Dobbins, J. E. (1991). Racism as a disease. *Journal of Counseling and Development, 70,* 206-212.

Smith, A. (1997). Cultural diversity and the coming-out process: Implications for clinical practice. In B. Greene (Ed.), *Ethnic and cultural diversity among lesbians and gay men* (pp. 279-300). Thousand Oaks, CA: Sage.

Somerville, S. (1996). Scientific racism and the invention of the homosexual body. In B. Beemyn & M. Eliason (Eds.), *Queer studies: A lesbian, gay, bisexual, and transgender anthology* (pp. 241-261). New York: New York University Press.

Sophie, J. (1986). A critical examination of stage theories of lesbian identity development. *Journal of Homosexuality, 12*(2), 39-51.

Sue, D. W. (1991). A diversity perspective on contextualism. *Journal of Counseling and Development, 70*(2), 300-301.

Sue, D. W., Arredondo, P., & McDavis, R. J. (1992). Multicultural counseling competencies/standards: A call to the profession. *Journal of Multicultural Counseling and Development, 20,* 64-88.

Tafoya, T. (1997). Native gay and lesbian issues: The Two-spirited. In B. Greene (Ed.), *Ethnic and cultural diversity among lesbians and gay men* (pp. 1-10). Thousand Oaks, CA: Sage.

Thompson, C. E., & Neville, H. A. (1999). Racism, mental health, and mental health practice. *The Counseling Psychologist, 27,* 155-223.

Watt, S. K. (1999). The story between the lines: A thematic discussion of the experience of racism. *Journal of Counseling and Development, 77,* 54-61.

Wehrly, B., Kenney, K., & Kenney, M. (1999). *Counseling multicultural families.* Thousand Oaks, CA: Sage.

Williams, W. L. (1993). Persistence and change in the Berdache tradition among contemporary Lakota Indians. In L. Garnets & D. Kimmel (Eds.), *Psychological perspectives on lesbian and gay male experiences* (pp. 339-347). New York: Columbia University Press.

Correspondence regarding this chapter may be sent to Susana M. Lowe, Asian & Pacific Islander American Health Forum, 942 Market Street, Suite 200, San Francisco, CA 94102 (e-mail address: slowe@apiahf.org).

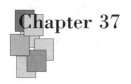

Chapter 37

Interface of Feminism and Multiculturalism

Where Are the Women of Color?

SHARON L. BOWMAN

SABA RASHEED

JUDY FERRIS

DELORES A. THOMPSON

MARY McRAE

LAUREN WEITZMAN

DURING OCTOBER 1998, a group of psychologists and psychologists-in-training attended a working conference in Ypsilanti, Michigan, organized by Division 17's (Counseling Psychology) Section for the Advancement of Women (SAW). We were to participate in developing a series of casebooks that would consider the joint advancement of feminism and multiculturalism across various areas of counseling psychology such as supervision and mentoring, career development, training, counseling and psychotherapy, and research. The intent of the working conference was to (a) bring the whole group together and develop cohesion and camaraderie and (b) give the various work groups several days to meet together and begin to structure the casebooks.

AUTHORS' NOTE: This chapter is a result of a symposium by the same name presented at the 1999 annual convention of the American Psychological Association held in Boston. The personal statements in this chapter are synopses of the symposium presentations. We also gratefully acknowledge the participation of Michele C. Boyer, Ph.D., Indiana State University, as a second discussant for the symposium and a reviewer of the chapter.

This working group included members of several constituent groups: American women of every color, international women, heterosexual, lesbian, and bisexual women, and professors, students, and practitioners. There was also a small number of men. The energy was infectious as the work began. Over time, however, insistent questions arose about the process and, more important, about the real meaning of integrating feminism and multiculturalism. It became obvious that a dialogue was needed and terms defined before any other work could be successful.

What does "feminist" mean? How is the term perceived by others? Are multiculturalists automatically feminists and vice versa? What are the power dynamics inherent in identifying as a feminist, or in assuming that gender is the most salient characteristic for all attendees? The questions were hard, and the answers did not come easily or readily by the end of the conference. As the conference ended, it seemed that the real work was only beginning. And so a symposium at APA was created around these questions; it was that symposium which led to this chapter.

We do not pretend to have the answers to the aforementioned questions; if that could easily be done, there would be no need for this chapter. What we have done here is bring the topic to the table. We invite the reader to partake in our current thinking about feminism and multiculturalism, about the interactions of White women with women of color, and about women of color interacting with each other. Our hope is that others will be stimulated to think honestly about these issues and willingly risk bringing them to their own tables.

WHAT IS FEMINISM?

Assuming that there is one feminist ideology is like assuming that there is one theory of counseling and psychotherapy. Various ideologies have different goals for society, which stem from their varied histories. What follows is an abbreviated explanation of some of the major ideologies. For a deeper understanding of the tenets of feminism, the reader is directed to Enns (1997) or Brown and Root (1990).

Liberal feminism seems to be what is commonly considered mainstream feminism. This view assumes that women are subordinate to men in all important arenas: legally, economically, and socially (Enns, 1997). Liberal feminism stems from the earliest periods of this country's history when women did not command their own destinies. Contemporary liberal feminism has continued the fight for women's ability to make their own decisions about their lives and develop their own sense of identity. This fight seems to be for women to have the option to work productively outside the home if they so choose and fulfill their own definition of the maternal role without conflict (Friedan, 1963, as cited in Enns, 1997). The image of liberal feminism, then, is that of White middle-class women who were bored with their roles in society and seeking change, an image not conducive to meeting the needs of women of different classes, races, or ethnicities who might not have the same privileges as these White women.

Radical feminism presents a completely different view of the role and "problem" of women in society (Enns, 1997). The contention seems to be that women are and have always been oppressed by men; in fact, women were the first oppressed group. This oppression occurs in all cultures. Changing the economic and social structure is not enough to change the face of women's oppression; it is important that women actively resist the expectations of mainstream society (Enns, 1997). Radical feminists may hold one of three stances. The pro-woman stance assumes that women do not need to link to men for marriage or finances, and they should acknowledge, then renounce their privileges and link with less privileged women. The anti-role stance presumes that both men's and women's traditional roles (e.g., marriage) should be forsaken and new roles created that would benefit all concerned. A third stance of radical feminism asserted that male domination over women was meant to feed the male ego. In other words, the less powerful a man feels in relation to other men, the more likely he is to dominate and oppress women. Women also play a role in perpetuating the oppression by socializing other women to "conform to social expectations and accept these limitations as natural" (Enns, 1997, p. 55). Radical feminism considers heterosexual sex punishing for women, leading some (but not all) radical proponents to push for women to move toward a lesbian perspective either sexually or politically.

Socialist feminism, like the other two ideologies, boasts a long history of fighting oppression. Proponents do not perceive oppression as universal across cultures, nor do they see sexuality as the central form of oppression. Instead, according to a socialist feminist perspective, women are oppressed by a patriarchal, capitalistic society (Enns, 1997). Women are marginalized in the workforce, earning lower wages in "unimportant" jobs. Women's "real" work is in the home, which ironically, is not seen as real work at all but as a role that women must hold. Creating universal access to child care, family leave, birth control, and education will restructure the family and reduce oppression (Enns, 1997). Of all the ideologies described in this chapter, socialist feminism gives the strongest voice to multiculturalism, purporting that oppression is a battle fought across gender, race, class, and nationality lines; one cannot assume that there is a single category of women (Anthias & Yuval-Davis, 1990, cited in Enns, 1997). Removing barriers to equality allows us to deal with oppression at its root (Tong, 1989).

Cultural feminism asserts that women's intuitive traits and connection to motherhood and other typically devalued women's roles should be embraced instead of ignored (Enns, 1997). Women's strengths include cooperation, connections to nature, pacifism, and a valuing of life. Cultural feminists believe that encouraging these values would bring about a more peaceful, nurturing society as compared to the current disordered society that is characterized by male traits of competition, domination, and destruction of nature. In other words, this approach would "humanize" society (Enns, 1997). Cultural feminism does not necessarily address issues of multiculturalism.

WOMEN OF COLOR'S PERCEPTIONS OF FEMINISM

Although White feminism's roots are in the antislavery movement, and more recently the American Civil Rights Movement, many women of color continue to perceive feminism as a very ethnocentric concept. It should not be surprising that women of color did not trust modern feminism's attempts to embrace the oppression of ethnic minorities as similar to that of women in the United States. Such attempts clearly ignored the joint effects of racism and classism on the lives of women of color by presenting White women's experiences as "universal, normative, and representative of others' experiences" (Gawelek, 1997, p. 36). It also assumes that all women, regardless of race, see gender as their primary defining variable; Brown (1990) reminds us that race or class, not gender, may be the salient organizing variable for some women of color.

American culture is very race focused; White women, as members of the privileged racial group, experience access to power that women of other races do not (Gawelek, 1997). Black, Asian American, and Chicana feminists have all been struggling with the "relationship between feminism and the ideology of cultural nationalism or racial pride, feminism and feminist-baiting with the larger [liberation] movements, and the relationship between their feminist movements and the White feminist movement" (Garcia, 1991, p. 272). Inherent in the view of oneself as a "woman of color" is both gender and race; it does not seem possible to define oneself as a woman without also considering race (Enns, 1997).

Asian American Women

Chow (1991) reports that the relatively small numbers of Asian American women in the United States and the fact that many are foreign born and may have had less exposure to the long history of the American feminist movement may render this group invisible to the broader feminist movement. In addition, the diversity across Asian cultures (Japan is not China is not India) makes it difficult to bring different groups of Asian American women together to discuss these issues. Asian cultures, in general, are based on a hierarchy of sex, age, and generation and are characterized by well-defined family roles. Such cultures may lead to a different sense of gender consciousness than is typical of White women. A feminist consciousness may be less salient for women who find classism and racism so pervasive that gender is secondary. Conversely, Asian American women who are aware of multiple oppressions may develop a feminist consciousness that transcends gender, race, class, and other cultural boundaries (perhaps another way to describe multicultural feminism).

Chow (1991) notes that Asian American women, like other ethnic minority women, have found the White feminist movement lacking in its ability to relate to the racial and class problems prevalent in Asian cultures. They also experienced sexism from Asian American men, voicing some of the same statements that have been directed toward other minority women in the past: "weakening the male ego, dilution of resources in the community, destruction of male/female relationships, setbacks for the Asian American cause, cooptation into the larger society, and eventual loss of ethnic identity for Asian Americans as a whole" (p. 258). Asian American women are presented with a dilemma: Do they deal with racial and gender identity at the personal level or with liberation for Asian Americans and/or women at the societal level? Joining White feminist groups is not always helpful because the double oppression of sexism and racism is not easily understood by White feminists. For example, historical restrictions on Asians in the United States hampered economic and demographic growth and discouraged family formation. Although many of these laws have been repealed, their effects continue to hamper the communities against which they were directed. The perception by Asian American women that White feminists do not understand these historical realities and that feminist groups are not welcoming to Asian American women also hampers Asians' willingness to participate fully in the White feminist movement.

Chicana Women

Garcia (1991) states that the Chicano movement developed in the 1960s as a "politics of protest . . . focused on a wide range of issues: social justice, equality, educational reforms, and political and economic self-determination for Chicano communities in the United States" (p. 269). The Chicana feminist movement emerged in reaction to the treatment of women in the overall Chicano movement, similar to the emergence of African American and Asian American feminist movements. The idea of social inequality was multidimensional; Chicanas wanted equality with men as they jointly struggled with the broader social movement to gain equality for their people.

Chicana feminists experienced the same issues that the other groups did: pressure from Chicano men to acquiesce to the goals of the broader movement, pressures from nonfeminist Chicanas who perceived them as sellouts to the cause, and a lack of acceptance and understanding within the White feminist movement. Chicana feminists identified such factors as "poverty, limited opportunities for higher education, high school dropouts, health care, bilingual education, immigration reform, prison reform, welfare, and U.S. policies in Central America" (Garcia, 1991, pp. 282-283) as salient concerns for their communities. Chicana feminists did not perceive these same concerns as salient for the broader feminist movement.

Black Women

Collins (1998) notes that Black feminists also faced demands from the Afrocentric movement to focus on issues of race, not gender, and if gender discrimination was acknowledged at all in the movement, it was almost always seen as secondary to issues of race. For Black women, simply the term Black feminist was a problem. Feminism has long been portrayed in the media as a "White" thing, not something that women of color do. Calling oneself a Black feminist might suggest that one identifies too strongly with the White system, and therefore is "less Black" than someone who identifies more strongly with racial issues (Collins, 1998). The term feminist suggested division within long-held racial solidarity in Black society by separating Black women from Black men. Some feminist tenets are antithetical to some Black religious traditions, another fundamental element of Black society. Some Black women totally reject the term feminist, preferring instead to use the term womanist to describe their commitment to womanhood and the Black community. Walker (1991) defines womanist, in part, as "a Black feminist or feminist of color . . . committed to the survival and wholeness of entire people, male and female" (p. xi). Whether labeled Black feminists or womanists, women are more prone to focus on public issues such as child care, poverty and welfare, health care, and affirmative action because these are the issues that affect their community. Using White women's experiences as the standard influenced feminism's struggles for economic equality, freedom from violence, and equality within the family but has not accounted for the varying experiences of women of color. Historically, women of color were denied control of their bodies. Slavery and other racist behaviors dehumanized women of color and left them vulnerable to rape and other sexual violence. At the turn of the century, there was pressure to limit the size of poor and minority women's families through birth control and sterilization, as they were seen as undesirables (Ross, 1993, cited in Enns, 1997). The current promotion of reproductive rights as freeing women to control their destinies and pursue their dreams ignores the realities for poor women and women of color. Reproductive rights for these women may mean economic survival, not self-fulfillment. For example, the majority of women seeking help with infertility or even non-U.S. adoptions are White middle- and upper-class women. There are few options for infertile racial and ethnic minority women who might also want children (Ceballo, 1999). There are also few rewards for minority women who, despite the odds, manage to produce "miracles" like large multiple births. As Ceballo (1999) notes, if a White woman has a multiple birth, media and corporate support pours in; the same cannot be said of a Black woman with a multiple birth.

When White feminism focuses on family issues, again the ethnocentric bias is evident. Assuming women of all cultures are dependent on a male breadwinner again denies the realities of the lives of many women of color. The long-held expectation that a woman will work outside the home, the likelihood of a nontraditional family structure in which the woman is the primary or sole breadwinner or on a par with the man, and the realities of poor or nonexistent child-care options lead women of color to create their own structures. Instead of seeing the family as a symbol of oppression, the family may be the main source of solace and support against external oppression. Family is one place to go to find support and understanding regarding those outside hurdles. Any sexism evident in the home may be perceived as the lesser of two evils compared to the oppression outside the home. Women of color feel compassion for the slights and slanders experienced by men of color, as they share that oppression. When White women suggest that minority women should join with them against men, they conveniently forget that White women have also been oppressors against women of color when it was convenient for them to do so (Enns, 1997; hooks, 1984).

PERSONAL REFLECTIONS ON
FEMINISM AND MULTICULTURALISM

As noted at the beginning of this chapter, we authors came together through our participation in a conference to link feminist and multicultural philosophies in counseling psychology through a series of casebooks. Each of us left the conference filled with conflicting emotions about the experience and the meaning these ideologies had for our individual understanding of our own cultures and of feminism. As we came together nearly a year later to present our views at the American Psychological Association annual convention it was clear that these emotions were still close to our hearts and that we had done a great deal of self- and other examination in the ensuing months.

What follows are highlights from the APA symposium in each presenter's own words. Discussions of history aside, these personal reactions reflect more than the conference, which was simply the catalyst that brought us together. These statements are four women's perceptions of the term "feminist," of our identities as women of color, and of the very lively struggle that we believe should happen in both feminist and multicultural circles. We question the link between feminism and multiculturalism on either a personal or a professional level. The fifth section presents the reflections of one of the discussants for the symposium, a White woman who was also Chair of the Section for the Advancement of Women. The discussions may seem redundant to the reader; this is merely a reflection of the universality of these thoughts and feelings across cultures.

Feminism and Multiculturalism:
The Common Ground (Rasheed)

A Muslim woman in the United States can experience the struggle of East meeting West. Neither Muslim nor American alone can fully define me as a human being any more than feminist or multiculturalist alone can fully define my professional identity. Each of these things contributes to my self-definition as a woman of color and a self-declared feminist.

For an orthodox Muslim woman of color to also identify as a feminist creates conflict in other feminists. The popular perception of Islam is that women and men are inherently unequal, an image fed by the media and often unthinkingly accepted by the general public. The assumption is that Muslim women are inherently oppressed and caught in a patriarchal system, forced to live sheltered lives and cover themselves from head to toe. The common wisdom further suggests that Muslim women do not hold positions of power in society. Feminists, of course, are no less susceptible to "common wisdom" than the rest of the American public.

So what happens to a Muslim woman who is also a feminist? She is challenged by both feminists and multiculturalists about her beliefs and background. She may be constantly confronted about her religion by feminists who assert that she cannot be a Muslim feminist. A feminist perspective that assumes that Muslim women have no power marginalizes women in the same ways that the Muslim religion is purported to do. It refuses to acknowledge her sense of spirituality while narrowly defining her religion from a feminist perspective. As noted earlier in the chapter, the standard is White women's, or in this instance White Christian women's, experiences. This standard ignores numerous examples of Islamic women who have contributed to Islam's rich history, including the fact that the very first person to convert to Islam was a woman, Hazart Khadija, the first wife of Prophet Muhammed (may Allah's blessing be upon them). It automatically suggests that Muslim women cannot think for themselves and do not have a choice in their affairs. These assumptions are made without seeking direct knowledge of the culture or accepting that the perspective of the person living in the system might also be valid.

This is not to suggest that Muslim women do not experience oppression in the name of religion. Muslim women do experience some of the worst forms of culturally sanctioned sexism in the world. This behavior cannot be excused by way of culture. A multiculturalist perspective that excuses this behavior on the basis of culture is an equally oppressive philosophy. For example, I once tried to join a Muslim student organization on a college campus. The group consisted solely of Muslim men from different countries. As I did not wear the traditional *hijab* (covering of the head worn by many Muslim women) and was assertive and direct in my introduction I was greeted with snide remarks and ignored throughout most of the meeting. I was even questioned as to whether I was a "real" Muslim. To excuse this behavior as simply a part of their culture ignores the affront to my identity as a woman.

Through these experiences I found it necessary to seek a voice and a place to express my feelings, my uniqueness. Both the multicultural and feminist perspectives help me do this. Without both of these perspectives, my experiences are an incomplete story, just as I am incomplete when people try to label me as either a "feminist" or a "multiculturalist." This is why I practice what I refer to as multicultural feminism. I define multicultural feminism as the recognition of the strengths of my rich cultural and religious heritage, the celebration of my female Muslim ancestors, and the awareness that I have experienced sexism that has been perpetrated by both White men and men of color.

Viewing my experiences from this perspective also affords me the opportunity to acknowledge all the people (men and women alike) who have contributed to and facilitated my empowerment. One person who has been the most influential in this process is my adviser, a White woman who is a true agent of empowerment. She has consistently demonstrated her appreciation of my cultural heritage while supporting me in my need to find a voice within my community.

Through dialogue with my mentor and others, I have learned to use multicultural feminism to frame my experiences. This framework, in turn, empowers me to do the work that I must do. Empowerment as defined by McWhirter (1998) is the process by which a marginalized person becomes aware of power dynamics and develops skills to gain control over his or her life without infringing on others' rights. Part of this process is to also empower others in my community. This empowerment, then, is the common ground that exists between multiculturalism and feminism and through which I will pursue the "best practices" of my chosen profession.

An American Indian Woman's View of Feminism (Ferris)

Picture the 1500s. A Spaniard named Solis lands on the shores of Virginia and is met by indigenous people. Who greets him? A brown man in a breechcloth adorned with shells, tattoos, and a bonnet of feathers? No, it is a Queen, a woman who offered him and his people a form of hospitality he had never known. He was housed in a mansion and treated to feasts and entertainment before being totally replenished with supplies. Solis proclaimed her "the Great Lady." This is documented history (Churchill, 1994).

Now picture the 1600s. Women leaders were common among the northeastern Indians. Documents dating back to 1584 describe Indian women as having the highest ranks, with full power to rule the people, create or enter into alliances, or go to war. In 1675, a female Sachem led 300 warriors to attack 52 of the then 90 existing English villages, completely destroying 12 of them. This too is documented history (Churchill, 1994).

But the wave of conquerors continued to flow, and they began to rewrite Indian knowledge. Female deities who had helped guide Indian thinking, including White Shell Woman, Grandmother Spider, and Sky Woman, were omitted from history. Other female figures were transformed into men. The conquerors sent their agents to Indian men to persuade them to sign away land that did not belong to them, all the while ignoring the women leaders of the community. European women wrote of their jealousy of Indian women's status in the community. Indian women, meanwhile, tucked themselves into a hard shell to ensure that their people would survive (Churchill, 1994).

Remember what your history books teach about Indians during the 1800s: They emphasize Native Americans such as Squanto and Pocahontas, who sided with the invaders. The books invert the history, portraying White aggressors as settlers and showing native settlers as aggressors. The history books say that Indians were offered money in exchange for their land, glossing over the fact that Indians were forced to cede most of their land and retreat to reservations. Indian history with Whites is filled with over 200 years of almost continuous war. Although Hollywood Westerns typically show wagon trains full of Whites circled by menacing "savages," the reality is that Indians were more likely to give the new settlers directions, show them water holes, and sell them food.

What does this have to do with feminism? Women of many Indian nations have been and are currently leaders; they are political voices. They are respected as leaders, healers, and spiritual counselors. Most important, they have the innate gift of power that comes from the creator who made them female. They are the keepers of the fire. They are the women known as Apache, Natchez, Cherokee, Nipnets, Nisenan, Hopi, Anishnabe, Kwakiutl, Tlinglet, Cheyenne, Comanche, Cocopah, Quinalt, Yurok, Menominee, Huron, Lakota, Salish, Cree, Zuni, Lummis, Dine, Odawa, and others. Throughout history they have met with one another to collaboratively make decisions. They have been role models. Yet they are seldom, if ever, recognized outside Native circles. They have traditionally been uninvited.

Today, as in days gone by, Indian women have power both in the home and in the political arena. For example, a push by the group Women of All Red Nations (WARN) was successful in blocking U.S. policy of forced sterilizations and in exposing U.S. governmental and corporate uranium contamination of reservation lands (Churchill, 1994). Many Indian women are "feminist acting."

That does not mean that many Indian women will call themselves "feminist." I refuse to take the label feminist. Tarhe once said "the longest journey in life is from the heart to the head." My heart is feminist in a pure way, but my head gets confused. Feminism is a label created by a movement of White middle-class women. They fought with their hearts, and all have benefited from their success. I know that I have benefited. But when they talk about their history, my grandmother is not present. They do not acknowledge the origin of their thoughts. They do not acknowledge that Indian society, and Indian women's status as equals to men, was one of the examples on which they based their ideas.

Even if I were to call myself feminist, I would not know which type of feminist would be the right one. If I call myself a radical feminist, my more conservative sisters might banish me, or I may be accused of hating the brother whom I love. If I match a conservative profile, the feminists who are social activists may dismiss me as nonessential or misguided. I am caught in a web of inaccurate self-portrayals. I will not call myself feminist. Instead, I embrace the heart that is feminist and will continue to stand with all my family, supporting my people, until I see some closing of the gap between the head and the heart. I close by saying that we cannot take personal responsibility for the past, as history belongs to the collective. We are, however, responsible for our own actions once we become aware. It is important, then, to embrace what is in our hearts and to use our minds to act in ways to bring us together, not push us apart.

Making Lemonade Out of Lemons:
One African American Woman's Perspective (Thompson)

As a woman of color I expected to travel over a lot of ground to incorporate feminism into my understanding of my own experience. I had rarely heard my own "voice" or seen faces like mine among those who use feminism as their point of departure. The reality for me is that race is more significant in U.S. society than being a woman. My female ancestors had always fought for equality but alongside my male ancestors. I knew the struggle was not *against* males but against a common oppressor who made race the most salient criteria for defining my existence. In my experience, men and women of color face discrimination, and men and women of European descent enjoy the privileges and power attached to membership in the dominant racial group. While my gender may be an element in discrimination against me, I have never experienced it as the sole reason for the pain of discrimination.

At the conference, feminists tended to be European American, and multiculturalists tended to be women of color. The poison of race and power that separates men and women along race lines is not lessened within a group of women. As Hurtado (1997) notes, gender alone does not determine either a superordinate or subordinate position. One must consider race, ethnicity, and class among the powerful cultural variables that create the more refined and sophisticated understanding of the tensions that underlie the experiences of a mixed group of women.

Feminist understanding of women selectively attempts to deal with the power relationships created through sexual differences used to justify gender dominance (Game & Pringle, 1983; Henley & LaFrance, 1997).

However, women of color understand that women of European American identity participate in the privilege and power of their racial group over women of color, and as such they also exercise the power to define and name, marginalize, silence, send social and political messages, and order social roles among women.

Feminism has always seemed to me to be the struggle of White women to share in the power of White men. Fundamental to sharing the power is having the power to oppress. Feminists can, indeed, be oppressors. They can be biased, racist, and prejudiced. Feminism may liberate a woman from the oppression of males who have power, but it does not liberate her from her own power to oppress. It does not necessarily mean that White women give up the privileges of power. Instead, the goal seems to be full partnership in the power and privilege. As Lorde (1984) states, "White women face the pitfall of being seduced into joining the oppressor under the pretense of sharing power. This possibility does not exist in the same way for women of color. The tokenism that is sometimes extended to us is not an invitation to join power: our racial 'otherness' is a visible reality that makes it quite clear" (pp. 118-119).

The critical error, as I see it, is for a group to assume that homogeneity on one variable (in this case, women) precludes the existence of any other variables. Gender cannot overcome the influence of other variables in the lives of women, including race, ethnicity, class, age, religion, and sexual identity. Multiculturalism challenges us to look at biases, prejudices, privileges, and quests for power. A multicultural understanding of counseling posits that in order to help ourselves we must first understand, appreciate, and attend to the diversity around us and any resulting imbalance of power.

Until we are able to do this, we cannot create a working alliance. Reandeau and Wampold (1991) place the working alliance within the context of power and involvement. In working relationships, despite the goal of collaboration, there is a real issue of who holds the power and when and how it is used in a working relationship. Until this is addressed, it will be impossible to create and maintain the alliance. Fiske (1993) acknowledges the intimate relationship between power and stereotyping. She points out that power encourages stereotyping and stereotyping maintains power by determining to whom one must attend and to whom one need not attend. Presorting women as feminists and multiculturalists creates stereotypes that preclude seeing women as multidimensional.

At the conference, as in other areas of our lives, women of color exerted their power and came together to voice their concerns. We empowered ourselves and each other to act collectively against the use of power by others and formed our own working alliance. We did not have the same experience of the conference or of life. We came from different racial and ethnic backgrounds, economic classes, political persuasions, sexual identities, and ages. We were mothers and daughters, friends and acquaintances, students and scholars who have been handed down the faith that makes possible that which was not meant to be. We have created homes, inventions, families, careers, dreams, goals, and a past, present, and future. We were feminists, multiculturalists, both, or neither. Yet we shared the common bond of what it means to be a woman of color in the United States. That experience, almost inexpressible in words, needs no explanation to those whose self-hood has been formed by its intensity in the soul. We shared a collective sense of who we are and as such drank lemonade made from the same bitter lemons.

Women of color understand that feminism was and is not necessary to liberate us. Men and women of color struggle together to liberate themselves every day. That joining together at the conference was our celebration of who we are and also an act of liberation to take responsibility to attend to ourselves. It was a sip of the power to define ourselves and a gulp of the privilege to meet as we chose. We swallowed up the time and emotional space we needed for ourselves. And when we were ready, sated, refreshed, renewed, we returned to the conference as we return to life, empowered to claim it as our own.

How Do I Talk to You, My White Sister? (McRae)

As women we share the experience of sexism, of living in a society that is basically patriarchal in its hierarchical structure. White women and women of color experience sexism at work, in our communities, at home, and in many of the policies that govern our lives. This common struggle against sexism is easily discussed, and it brings us together in various activities. Racism, however, is something that is not shared between White women and women of color. Because it is not shared it causes tension in conversations between White women and women of color.

Lorde (1984) wrote, "You fear your children will grow up to join the patriarchy and testify against you; we fear our children will be dragged from a car and shot down in the street, and you will turn your backs upon the reasons they are dying" (p. 119). This quotation is particularly salient now because of the recent incidents in New York City with Amadou Diallo and Abner Louima. These events have only brought to the eyes of the world the fears that many African American women have held for many years. We are not just women of color fighting against the patriarchy, we are women of color who live with the fear of racist acts against us and those we love. Many of those racist acts are perpetrated by people authorized to do so by the political, social, and economic power structure, which is controlled by White men and women.

When I talk about race from a Black feminist perspective, there is clearly a joining of women and men. I think about race as it impacts on my life and the lives of other women. I think about race as a mother of a young Black man, as a sister, daughter, and as an intimate partner. I am not sure how White women manage the duality of race and feminism, of White skin privilege and feminism. Do they actively and knowingly participate in the racist structure and fight against the sexist structure? Or is there a denial of the racist structure as a way of distancing themselves from that aspect of the struggle against oppression? It is hard for Black women and White women to talk about these issues if there is no understanding of where we stand on issues that affect at least one side so deeply.

Talk about racism stimulates angry feelings: feelings of superiority and inferiority, feelings about authority, power, and privilege. If we think about race from a systemic perspective, we can ask who has power and authority to make decisions and who has access to those with power and authority. A recent survey of women managers and professionals (Abelson, 1999) indicated that African American, Latina, and Asian American women lagged behind White women and men of color in the kind of jobs they hold and the pay they receive. Women of color do not have the same access to opportunities for mobility in employment as their White counterparts. This survey speaks to White skin privilege and to how race and gender constitute a double negative for women of color. And even though employment discrimination has been the experience of both White women and women of color, we can see from surveys such as this that race, White skin privilege, can make a difference. As we talk about the interface between feminism and multiculturalism, how do we address this difference in access to opportunity?

The sex stereotypes that have been ascribed to White women are passive, weak, fragile, and powerless. The sex stereotypes ascribed to African American women are independent, assertive, and aggressive. Because of our history of slavery we have been depicted as strong workers and caretakers. We have had to take charge of situations and do what had to be done for the survival of our families and ourselves. The sex stereotype literature (Heilman, Block, & Martell, 1995) suggests that women often begin to believe that the negative stereotypes ascribed to them are true. Thus, girls think they are *not* supposed to be good in math, and women are *not* supposed to do jobs that men have traditionally done. I call this internalized sexism, which is very similar to internalized racism.

If Black and White girls take on the roles stereotypically ascribed to them because of their race and gender, they will process their experiences differently. White women who have internalized perceptions of themselves as weak, passive, and powerless will have difficulty identifying with the power of White skin privilege. When in conflict, White women often take a stance that suggests they are weak: They cry; they whine; they shut down as though they have no power. This denial of power and affiliation with power allows White women to see themselves as powerless in genuine exchanges about race and a multicultural movement of social equality. Perceiving race as negative and giving its ownership to women of color allows White women to maintain distance and not acknowledge the role that they may play in perpetuating racial differences in society.

For Black women, dealing with racism means dealing with anger. Anger of exclusion, anger of unquestioned privilege, anger at racial distortions, negative stereotypes, stolen opportunities, betrayal, and co-optation. I must be free to express my anger and rage at racist acts and their impact on the lives of people I care about. Lorde (1984) refers to Black women's anger as being part of a symphony, with rhythms to listen to and learn from. Some of the research on socialization around anger suggests that while White girls are socialized to stifle their anger, Black girls learn that anger can be useful (Way, 1998). Black women express their anger as a means of setting boundaries, standing up for and taking care of themselves, and telling others what they will and will not tolerate (Braxton, 1995). When Black women express their anger at racism, is there a place for it in the discourse between Black women and White women?

Many White women do not see race and racism as problems affecting their own lives and society as a whole. Talk about race and racism creates angry feelings. Women of color are expected to talk about race and to hold on to all of the anger and rage that is stimulated by the topic. My experience of this is that women of color are expected to educate White women about race without getting *too* angry. We are expected to contain our anger while discussing the topic in a way that allows White women to hear it on an intellectual level. Black women in their roles as nurturers and caretakers take on the anger about race in the service of White women. Perhaps our backs are the bridges. In the book *This Bridge Called My Back*, a collection of writing by radical women of color, the question is asked, "How can we—this time—not use our bodies to be thrown over a river of tormented history to bridge the gap?" (Moraga & Anzaldua, 1983, p. xv). A bridge is walked upon again and again. Why should that bridge, those backs, belong to women of color? Will women of color continue to allow our backs to be used in this way? When will White women step forward to do their own thinking and conversing on these topics?

The stereotypes for White and Black women help us maintain projections of each other. If my stereotypes for White women are that they are as weak, passive, and powerless as Black women are strong, caring, and nurturing, then it allows me to project all of the weak, passive, and powerless aspects of my self to White women. White women become the "other." I am in a difficult place because I do not hold on to the weak and powerless parts of my experience as a Black woman, parts of me that are also a reality in this society. Projecting these aspects of my being onto others may keep me from getting the nurturance that I need.

White women's projections of Black women as nurturing and strong force them to lose focus of the strong and powerful parts of themselves. They can see the anger in Black women as bad or dangerous. The Black woman who is justifiably angry about racism becomes the "angry bitch" and takes on the unfeminine, undesirable, out-of-character aspects of White women. Stereotyping and projecting allows White women and women of color to maintain their places in the status quo. It keeps them locked into a systemic view and prevents them from initiating and managing systemic changes. It prevents us from recognizing racial differences as having the same legitimacy as gender differences. Consider the changes that could occur in society if racism was given the same energy as sexism has received in the past two decades. What would happen if the gender and race issues for women of color were an integral part of the feminist movement? I do not have the answers to all the questions raised here, but it is not my job alone to answer them. Integrating the various aspects of oneself, the projections of "the other," and the perceived good and bad, makes for a multidimensional person who can work from different places with different people. Becoming such a person while helping others become more multidimensional is something that I optimistically strive for, and I pray that more of you will do the same.

Toward a Multicultural Feminist Alliance (Weitzman)

There are complexities involved in creating a multicultural feminism, including the inherent difficulty that a Western psychology brings to this complexity which affects our struggle to integrate multiple and sometimes conflicting perspectives. At the core of this complexity is how we bring different life experiences to the table. I strongly endorse the need to move beyond multiculturalism as an intellectual construct. The challenge resulting from this complexity that is both wonderful and overwhelming is managing our different experiences of oppression and honoring different choices about how we approach this work. For example, some of us choose not to use the label "feminist." How do we find a common ground? How do we talk about the complexity of oppression without getting competitive about the relative difficulties of our experiences? How do we make choices to risk sharing who we are and what we think and feel? I think the answer lies in forming a working alliance among a group of highly diverse women.

There are several common elements of multiculturalism and feminism: (a) reducing power imbalances between dominant and oppressed cultures, (b) respecting diversity, and (c) overcoming oppression through empowerment. I would add that both perspectives entail an examination of the socio-cultural-political context. We interacted with each other in a much more personal and experiential way than typically happens at professional meetings. At the SAW conference, we quickly hit some bumps with each other, which were experienced as even more disappointing due to our expectations that we would share a common ground. As we were challenged to "define" multiculturalism and feminism, we found that many of us held different opinions about these concepts. These disappointments and struggles seem to me to be very much a part of our growing process.

It is critical to remember that individuals, organizations, and cultures exist within a developmental context related to issues of multiculturalism.

Albrecht and Brewer (1990) define multicultural alliances as possessing "a new level of commitment that is long-standing, deep, and built on more trusting political relationships" (p. 4). Coming together in alliance building means grappling with multifaceted issues, including who sets the agenda, what are the power differentials, what are our leadership styles, what different skills do we bring, and what are our visions. Alliance-building demands a strong commitment to being in process with each other as we face these challenges. Another important aspect of this process is movement between solidarity and alliance. Women of color talked about the important and nurturing experience of caucusing with other women of color during the conference at the end of the conference. While the need for affiliating with "people like me" is critical for experiencing understanding and support, the challenge becomes how to move back together and do the much more painful work across our differences.

Most White feminists would agree that naming our power and privilege is vital in understanding the different experiences of women of color and White women, but I believe that we often hold this as an intellectual concept and find it more difficult to actively experience or to be aware of our power/privilege differences and how they play out in our interactions. The difficulty White women have in acknowledging White skin privilege was noted by writers such as McIntosh (1988). Our interactions often come from a place of projecting our stereotypes about each other, with resulting detrimental effects on how we understand and talk to each other. As individuals we must constantly work on maintaining an awareness of both our internalized domination and internalized oppression, and how these play out in our interactions.

Divisive reactions to diversity that are common for White women include defensiveness, guilt, overpersonalization, withdrawal, feeling weary and resentful, and limiting minority women to "their issues" (Albrecht & Brewer, 1990). We need to understand our individual reactions in order to move through them. In Mindell's (1995) book, *Sitting in the Fire,* he provides an important description of how privilege can manifest: "Privilege means . . . being cool, calm, detached in communication—the privilege of not having to listen to the rage, fury, and sadness of those without power" (p. 162). It is crucial for White women to come to grips with White skin privilege and how that manifests in groups and interactions as part of developing a multicultural feminism, and I would argue that this extends to other forms of privilege as well (e.g., sexual orientation, able-bodiedness).

I would also like to emphasize the crucial role of anger and learning how to "be with" the conflict. Women of color may need to express anger and rage related to racism, which can be particularly difficult for White women to hear; we must find ways to hold each other in conflict as well as in collaboration. I've already indicated how one's difficulty being with anger can be closely linked to holding power and privilege. Mindell's (1995) metaphor of "sitting in the fire" has offered me an important way to understand this aspect of the process. He views two essential elements of "sitting in the fire" as holding an acute awareness of the power and oppression that exists on each side of a conflict and accentuating privilege (which he calls "rank") versus holding back or being polite. When we fear conflict we hold back, and I wonder what it would look like if we truly risked putting privilege out on the table. In the group work that Mindell (1995) facilitates, transformation results when people are encouraged to "take the lid off feelings," to "say anything that is true for you," and to "tolerate moments of fear and chaos" (Mindell, 1995, p. 71). He suggests that "people yell when no one is listening" and that "any community committed to healing must become a wailing wall or a screaming room" (Mindell, 1995, p. 165). If we are to become whole, we must accept the disorder that comes with acknowledging and accepting diversity. Creating an alliance triggers intense emotions including fears about intimacy and trust (Albrecht & Brewer, 1990). The depth of these emotions can be a frightening prospect, especially when complicated by our individual personal history with conflict and chaos. Even so, I firmly believe we must learn to be in conflict with each other as part of the work of creating multicultural feminism. Our socialization as women makes this difficult as do culture and race differences around how we express anger, but I'm not sure if we can move forward unless we take these risks.

INTEGRATION AND CONCLUSIONS

What is the message from these stories? There are at least two themes that run through all of the discussions. First, on a personal note, these women of color will not easily be labeled. They are not solely feminists, nor are they solely multiculturalists. Claiming one identity is perceived as requiring denial of the other identity. One of the major issues raised during the SAW conference and again discussed in our symposium was that many women of color felt forced to place one identity, feminist, before the other, multiculturalist. The voices presented here did not anticipate having to make that decision one more time while in Michigan, instead assuming that this would be a safe group. Faced with that pressure yet again led some women to push back, to speak out, and to challenge the status quo. Ironically, this group felt so empowered that they were able to break through the wall that separates women of color and White women on this issue and begin a real dialogue that changed the direction of the conference. The message? Voices raised can create direct change.

The second message in these stories relates to our professional and cultural histories. Women of color are categorized both as minorities and as women, thereby filling two Affirmative Action slots. They are often forced to choose the interests of one group over the other. Women of color often seem to choose the issues of race over the issues of gender, sometimes to the consternation of White feminist women. Not understanding why this choice is made denies the history attached to feminism, and the history attached to the interactions of Whites with other racial groups. Working through the distrust will require significant energy on the part of all concerned. We must all know our history, the positive and the negative, before we can begin to make real changes. We must ask the same of ourselves that we ask of others, and we must be willing to really hear others' experiences before we can move our relations to a new level. The message? Real dialogue in this area will be a growth point for all participants.

Feminism and multiculturalism do, indeed, have a common goal: The dream of each ideology is to shape a world in which people can operate fairly and without biases. The focus of these two ideologies need not be in conflict, but they currently operate as such. Riessman (1991) notes that knowing gender is not enough, or matching on gender is not enough—we must be equally aware of all the cultural norms involved in our interactions with others, whether we are involved in a narrative interview, a therapy session, or a social interaction. Being unaware of the cultural norms only serves to increase the divisions that each ideology hopes to diminish. As counselors and psychologists, we must be models in hearing, really hearing, the views of others, especially when those views do not correspond with our personal view of reality. Only then will we be able to move beyond the intellectual aspect of these discussions and come to some deeper understanding of the possibilities of multicultural feminism.

REFERENCES

Abelson, R. (1999, July 14). Women minorities not getting to the top. *The New York Times*, p. C4.

Albrecht, L., & Brewer, R. (1990). *Bridges of power: Women's multicultural alliances.* Philadelphia, PA: New Society.

Braxton, E. (1995). *Finding your bitch and loving her.* Pittsburgh, PA: Edge Associates.

Brown, L. S. (1990). The meaning of multicultural perspective in theory building in feminist therapy. In L. S. Brown & M. P. P. Root (Eds.), *Diversity and complexity in feminist theory* (pp. 1-21). New York: Haworth.

Brown, L. S., & Root, M. P. P. (Eds.). (1990). *Diversity and complexity in feminist therapy.* New York: Haworth.

Ceballo, R. (1999). "The only Black woman walking the face of the Earth who cannot have a baby": Two women's stories. In M. Romero & A. J. Stewart (Eds.), *Women's untold stories: Breaking silence, talking back, voicing complexity* (pp. 3-19). New York: Routledge.

Chow, E. N.-L. (1991). The development of feminist consciousness among Asian American women. In J. Lorber & S. A. Fatrell (Eds.), *The social construction of gender* (pp. 255-268). Newbury Park, CA: Sage.

Churchill, W. (1994). *Indians are us.* Monroe, ME: Common Ground Press.

Collins, P. T. (1998). *Fighting words: Black women and the search for justice.* Minneapolis: University of Minnesota Press.

Donovan, J. (1992). *Feminist theory.* New York: Continuum.

Dugger, K. (1991). Social location and gender-role attitudes: A comparison of Black and White women. In J. Lorber & S. A. Fatrell (Eds.), *The social construction of gender* (pp. 38-59). Newbury Park, CA: Sage.

Enns, C. Z. (1997). *Feminist theories and feminist psychotherapies: Origin, themes, and variations.* New York: Haworth.

Fiske, S. T. (1993). Controlling other people: The impact of power on stereotyping. *American Psychologist, 48,* 621-628.

Game, A., & Pringle, R. (1983). *Gender at work.* Sydney: Allen and Unwin.

Garcia, A. M. (1991). The development of Chicana feminist discourse, 1970-1980. In J. Lorber & S. A. Fatrell (Eds.), *The social construction of gender* (pp. 269-287). Newbury Park, CA: Sage.

Gawelek, M. A. (1997). Women's diversity: Ethnicity, race, class, and gender in theories of feminist psychology. In O. L. Espin (Ed.), *Latina realities: Essays on healing, migration, and sexuality* (pp. 33-50). Boulder, CO: Westview.

Heilman, M., Block, C., & Martell, R. (1995). Sex stereotypes: Do they influence perceptions of managers? *Journal of Social Behavior and Personality, 6,* 237-252.

Henley, N. M., & LaFrance, M. (1997). Gender as culture: Difference and dominance. In T. Roberts (Ed.), *The Lanahan readings in the psychology of women* (pp. 553-567). Baltimore: Lanahan.

hooks, b. (1981). *Ain't I a woman?* Boston, MA: South End Press.

hooks, b. (1984). *Feminist theory: From margin to center.* Boston, MA: South End Press.

Hurtado, A. (1997). Relating to privilege: Seduction and rejection in the subordination of White women and women of color. In T. Roberts (Ed.), *The Lanahan readings in the psychology of women* (pp. 445-454). Baltimore: Lanahan.

Lorde, A. (1984). *Sister outsider.* Trumansburg, NY: Crossing Press.

McIntosh, P. (1988). *White privilege and male privilege: A personal account of coming to see correspondences through work in women's studies* (Working Paper No. 189). Wellesley, MA: Center for Research on Women.

McWhirter, E. H. (1998). Empowerment, social activism, and counseling. *Counseling and Human Development, 29,* 1-13.

Mindell, A. (1995). *Sitting in the fire: Large group transformation using conflict and diversity.* Portland, OR: Lao Tse Press.

Moraga, C., & Anzaldua, G. (Eds.). (1983). *This bridge called my back: Writings by radical women of color.* New York: Kitchen Table.

Reandeau, S. G., & Wampold, B. E. (1991). Relationship of power and involvement to working alliance: A multiple-case sequential analysis of brief therapy. *Journal of Counseling Psychology, 38,* 107-114.

Riessman, C. K. (1991). When gender is not enough: Women interviewing women. In J. Lorber & S. A. Fatrell (Eds.), *The social construction of gender* (pp. 217-236). Newbury Park, CA: Sage.

Tong, R. (1989). *Feminist thought: A comprehensive introduction.* Boulder, CO: Westview.

Walker, A. (1991). *In search of our mother's gardens: Womanist prose.* San Diego, CA: Harcourt Brace Jovanovich.

Way, N. (1998). *Everyday courage: The lives and stories of urban teenagers.* New York: New York University Press.

Correspondence regarding this chapter may be sent to Sharon L. Bowman, Department of Counseling Psychology and Guidance Services, Teachers College 622, Ball State University, Muncie, IN 47306-0585 (e-mail address: Sbowman@gw.bsu.edu).

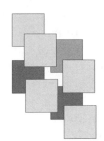

Part VIII

MULTICULTURAL ISSUES IN COUNSELOR SUPERVISION AND HIGHER EDUCATION

Part VIII opens with Chapter 38, where its author Chen presents a new interactional supervision approach to fostering multicultural competence development. In a substantive and fluid presentation, Chen reviews assumptions underlying his model, defines and reviews the constructs of intentionality and reflection central to the model, and presents a detailed case vignette highlighting the model in action.

Counseling professionals have always been integrally involved in the student service activities of this nation's colleges and universities. Although multicultural education begins very early in life, one's college years, whether for a 20- or 80-year-old student, are a vibrant and critical time for cultural exposure and discussion. Part VIII concludes with two chapters that focus on multicultural issues in predominantly White and historically Black colleges, respectively.

In Chapter 39, Grieger and Toliver review the multiple and varied roles for the counselor committed to cultural pluralism on campus. The authors begin with a thorough overview of the status of diversity on predominantly White campuses. They present the position, supported by empirical evidence, that when colleges adequately attend to diversity issues *all* students on campus benefit. Integrating an extensive body of literature, Grieger and Toliver summarize 12 variables found to be particularly salient to enhancing institutional diversity. Major discussion is then devoted to specific strategies for implementing multicultural initiatives across all key segments of the institution: the counseling center, the division of student affairs, the college administration, and the faculty and curriculum.

Chapter 40 is written by Berg-Cross, Craig, and Wessel, who work at one of this nation's most historic institutions: Howard University. The authors review multicultural issues at historically Black colleges, with a particular focus on activities centered at Howard University. The chapter covers in detail how multiculturalism has affected three main areas of academic life: curriculum, administration, and mental health services. Multicultural issues particular to Howard University and other historically Black institutions are noted.

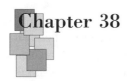

Chapter 38

MULTICULTURAL COUNSELING SUPERVISION

An Interactional Approach

ERIC C. CHEN

"Would you tell me, please, which way I ought to go from here?"
"That depends a good deal on where you want to get to,"
said the Cat.
"I don't much care where—" said Alice.
"Then it doesn't matter which way you go," said the Cat.

—*Alice's Adventures in Wonderland*
by Lewis Carroll (1865)

THE IMPORTANCE OF helping students disentangle the complexity of "that depends" embedded in multicultural counseling has been acknowledged by many counseling and psychology programs, which in recent years have provided students with training through formal coursework or informal exposure in this area (Constantine & Gloria, 1999; Ponterotto, 1997; Quintana & Bernal, 1995). The effectiveness of these training programs in raising counselors' sense of competency in working with a wide range of client groups, however, has yet to be validated (Allison, Echemendia, Crawford, & Robinson, 1996). Because the goals of supervision are to monitor client welfare and facilitate the professional competencies of the supervisee (Bernard & Goodyear, 1998), it serves as a primary mechanism for facilitating a counselor's multicultural counseling competencies (Constantine, 1997; D'Andrea & Daniels, 1997). Given the doctrine of "vicarious liability," the supervisor's primary and ultimate responsibility, professional and ethical, is to ensure that the client's welfare is not compromised as a result of the commission or omission of the counselor's behavior (Association for Counselor Education and Supervision, 1995; Bernard & Goodyear, 1998). The supervisor is ethically and legally bound to assist the counselor in building and solidifying his or her clinical competencies, and multicultural counseling competencies in particular.

Both counseling and supervision are interpersonal encounters, and the dual aspects of process and relationship in each need to be recognized. Counseling as a process is concerned with the interaction between the counselor and client, who reciprocally negotiate, shape, and define the nature of their relationship through communication at both verbal and nonverbal levels. Counseling as a relationship functions as the context within which this continuous negotiation between the counselor and client occurs. Given that supervision is also an interpersonal encounter, the dual aspects of process and relationship also merit attention. Illustrative of this common feature in both counseling and supervision encounters is the "parallel process" (Doehrmann, 1976) that has been widely recognized in supervision. For the supervisor with the goal of facilitating the development of multicultural counseling competencies, inattention to this reciprocal and intimate interaction between process and relationship is likely to result in an incomplete view of how supervision functions to facilitate the counselor's development of multicultural competencies. The dual nature serves as the guiding premise of this interactional approach.

Two additional points merit clarification. First, supervisors differ greatly in many aspects, and, as a result, they moderate and mediate the effects of supervision intervention strategies. Using an informed-case research study method (Soldz, 1990), for example, Chen and Bernstein (2000) examined the supervisory alliance as a function of communication patterns and supervisory issues in two supervisor-supervisee dyads, one characterized by high alliance and the other by low alliance, over the first three weeks of clinical supervision. One finding from their study was that the supervisory style of the supervisor in the high-alliance supervisory dyad was highly attractive, sensitive, and moderately task oriented, whereas in the low-alliance dyad, the supervisor perceived herself as moderately attractive, sensitive, and task oriented. The differences in supervisor styles may account for the different levels of complementary communication and supervision outcomes observed between these two dyads. The interactional approach presented in this chapter is developed by incorporating two bodies of literature on reflection and counselor intentionality; however, research should be conducted to assess its effectiveness as influenced by supervisor-supervisee characteristics.

Second, given space constraints, I confine discussion primarily to *counselors'* reflections of their interactions and intentionality, as opposed to those by *supervisors,* although there is some research examining supervisor intentions in the supervision process and outcome (Strozier, Kivlighan,

& Thoreson, 1993). Because the role of supervisor resembles more closely that of educator or consultant than that of counselor, this interactional approach is equally, if not more, relevant to the supervisor's own reflection in the quest for building supervisory cultural competencies as described in Ancis and Ladany (in press).

The chapter is organized into four sections and begins with a discussion of assumptions underlying this interactional approach. Drawing primarily on counseling process research and the teacher education literature, I present intentionality and reflection as two integral components of this approach, highlighting specifically the phases and steps of its application in supervision. A case vignette is then presented to illustrate this approach, followed by some closing comments.

ASSUMPTIONS

All Counseling Encounters Are Multicultural in Nature

The interactional approach presented below is predicated on two related but distinct assumptions: First, all counseling and supervision encounters are multicultural in nature, and, second, developing multicultural counseling competencies is a lifelong process. As Helms (1994) and Stone (1997) have noted, the inclusive or pluralistic versus exclusive or universalistic perspectives of multiculturalism have been a subject of interpretive debate in the counseling and psychology fields over the years. In contrast to the exclusivist who confines the definition of multiculturalism to racial and ethnic variables, the inclusivist argues for a broader definition by expanding its discussion beyond race and ethnicity to include variables such as gender, sexual orientation, physical disability, or socioeconomic status because members in each minority group share a similar experience of oppression from the majority culture. The limitation of the exclusivist view lies in its potential to discount the debilitating effects of prejudice and discrimination based on race and ethnicity vis-à-vis other types of group membership. For researchers, the exclusive version of multiculturalism is important for its parsimony and precision so that inferences can be easily drawn; for practitioners, however, the inclusivist view is more relevant, given the complexity of human experiences embedded in multiple contexts. Each counseling relationship is placed in contexts, personal and cultural, impelling it to include within its boundary various levels and divides of human experience.

Kluckhohn and Murray (1953) contended that every individual is in some respects like every other human being, like some other human beings, and like no other human beings. The diversity in each counseling encounter is increased by the rich experiences of the counselor and client, posing an additional challenge for the supervisor to recognize the contribution from the counselor and client. Counselors differ greatly in sex, race or ethnicity, sexual orientation, socioeconomic status, and professional training and experience. Despite similarities across clients in their presentation of concerns and needs, they often differ in myriad respects and require individualized counseling plans. The client presenting concerns should thus be conceptualized in appropriate sociocultural contexts prior to the development of counseling goals and strategies. The ultimate task confronting the counselor, and by extension, the supervisor, is to assess how universal human nature interacts with human differences at both the group and individual levels in shaping the client's subjective experience. The client's subjective experience, or worldview (Ibrahim & Kahn, 1987; Ibrahim, Roysircar-Sodowsky, & Ohnishi, Chapter 23, this volume), also influences his or her definition and expression of the presenting concerns in counseling. Either overreliance or underreliance on the role of culture in accounting for psychological difficulties is problematic. Even though information about a client's cultural group is of great value in counseling, it should not be assumed that a given cultural variable plays the most critical role in influencing the client's experience. Pope and Vasquez (1998) echoed this view:

> On the one hand, the clinician must become adequately knowledgeable and respectful of the client's relevant cultural or socioeconomic contexts. Therapists who ignore cultural values, attitudes, and behaviors different from their own deprive themselves of crucial information and may tend to impose their own worldview and assumptions upon clients in an exceptionally fallacious and destructive manner. On the other hand, the clinician must avoid making simplistic, unfounded assumptions on the basis of cultural or socioeconomic contexts. Knowledge about cultural and socioeconomic contexts becomes the basis for informed inquiry rather than the illusion of uniform group characteristics with which to stereotype the client. Neither variation between groups nor within groups can be discounted or ignored. (p. 210)

Although neglecting or discounting the significance of cultural variables in counseling is an example of cultural ignorance, so is inattention to the idiosyncratic dimension of the client's unique experience, an example of the counselor's "uniformity myth" (Kiesler, 1966). Moreover, this uniformity myth is also reflected in the conceptualization and research of multicultural competencies as universal rather than group specific (Helms, 1994). There is no conclusive evidence to suggest that the same counseling competencies required to deliver effective services to clients for whom racial- or ethnic-group membership is vital are transferable and equally appropriate for clients for whom other psychosocial identities are central. To avoid the pitfall of cultural blindness or uniformity bias, it is therefore incumbent upon counselors to engage their clients in this combined effort to examine how each of the cultural variables, singly and collectively, influences the experience, expression, and resolution of these concerns in counseling. Echoing the views expressed by Ridley, Mendoza, Kanitz, Angermeier, and Zenk (1994) and Leong (1996), the approach described in this chapter is premised on the assumption that all counseling and supervision encounters are multicultural in nature, although cultural factors are not necessarily in the forefront of the interpersonal encounters across different sequences. That is, depending on the nature of clients' presenting concerns, some of these cultural variables are more central than others at different phases of counseling in shaping the direction and outcome of counseling.

Developing Multicultural Competencies Is an Aspirational Goal

If all counseling is culturally contextualized, it follows that a *typical* counselor is culturally competent in the provision of quality services through the application of professional knowledge and skills to some degree with some clients. Just as no athletes excel in all kinds of sports, neither do counselors display effectiveness in all areas with all clients. Expecting counselors to be competent with all clientele as a training goal is as unrealistic as it is presumptuous. The second assumption of this approach, therefore, is that developing multicultural counseling competencies is an ongoing process, and as such it is an aspirational goal. Counselors vary with respect to their range of competencies, and, consequently, supervisors and counselors should recognize and limit their practice to areas for which they have sufficient expertise to perform in a competent manner. A constant assessment of the *boundaries* of the counselor's multicultural counseling competencies thus should be an integral part of supervision.

Professional ethics codes and guidelines (e.g., American Counseling Association, 1995; American Psychological Association, 1987, 1992, 1993) have stressed that the mental health professional should recognize his or her boundaries of competency, suggesting professional competency as a relative concept. Although most counselors reported competency in working with clients from diverse backgrounds, there was notable variability among counselors' ratings of self-perceived competency with different client groups (Allison et al., 1996). Constantine and Ladany's (2000) recent study further found that self-report multicultural counseling competency measures were significantly associated with social desirability attitudes but not with multicultural case conceptualization ability, underscoring the need for assessing the counselor's competency across various occasions through multiple means such as direct observation or videotaped session.

Since its inception in the early 1980s, the Multicultural Counseling Competency Model (MCCM; Arredondo et al., 1996; Sue, Arredondo, & McDavis, 1992; Sue et al., 1982) has been widely recognized by the counseling and psychology professions and embraced in training programs. The fundamental question of whether these competencies translate into improved counseling outcome with clients across cultures remains an un-answered empirical question (Constantine & Ladany, 2000; Ponterotto, Fuertes, & Chen, 2000). It is necessary to delineate the differences between competency and effectiveness. Competency implies capacity or ability, but it does not necessarily translate to effective performance in every counsel-ing session with every client. In a similar vein, each multicultural counsel-ing encounter is unique in itself, and, consequently, counselors need to examine factors that assist or inhibit their effectiveness in the counseling encounter. Furthermore, theoretical approaches and their accompanying intervention strategies may be effective with some clients but ineffective with others. Clearly, the appropriateness and effectiveness of counseling interventions cannot be accurately determined outside the specific coun-selor-client context. In supervision, the ultimate task confronting both the supervisor and counselor is epitomized by the recurrent question raised by Paul (1967): "*What* treatment, by *whom*, is most effective for *this* individ-ual with *that* specific problem, and under *which* set of circumstances?" (p. 111).

In an attempt to remedy the dichotomous view of multicultural coun-seling competencies and to dispel the "uniformity myth" often inherent in counselors' assumptions, I propose using the following three dimensions to evaluate multicultural counseling effectiveness: *level, phase,* and *source.* As presented in Figure 38.1, the counselor's multicultural counseling effec-tiveness and competencies, as evidenced through his or her interactions with clients, may reach different *levels* (minimum, average, or optimal) in any of the following four *phases* of counseling: developing a working alli-ance, assessment, intervention, and termination. In extending Overholser and Fine's (1990) analysis of the *sources* of clinical competency to the cur-rent approach, I argue that the counselor's cultural effectiveness, or lack thereof, in working with diverse clients is a function of the following:

1. *Factual knowledge:* clinically relevant factual information
2. *Generic clinical skills:* fundamental counseling skills necessary for the de-velopment of working alliance, assessment, intervention, and termination
3. *Theory-specific technical skills:* the use of special procedures or tech-niques in the clinical setting based on a specific theory
4. *Clinical judgment:* the ability to apply knowledge and clinical skills to counseling a particular client
5. *Interpersonal attributes:* personality characteristics and styles, past per-sonal experience, or psychosocial skills that may affect the ability to func-tion in a professional capacity

This three-dimensional framework allows for a more precise analysis of the counselor's effectiveness, suggesting strategies that would corre-spond to the learning needs of the counselor. While two counselors might display equally minimal levels of competency in developing a collaborative

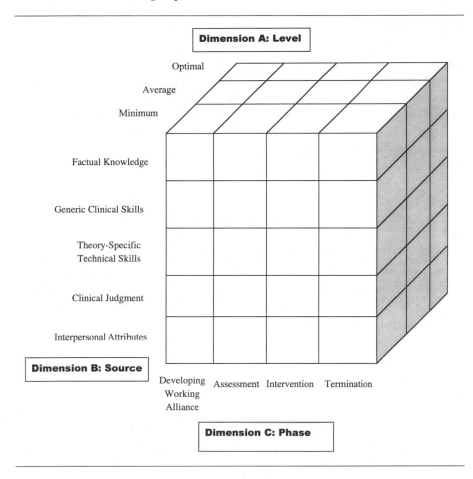

Figure 38.1. A Framework for Evaluating Multicultural Counseling Effectiveness

working alliance, for example, a careful examination may identify different sources of their ineffective performance. For one, it may reflect the weak knowledge base in regard to the client's cultural group; for the other, perhaps it arises from the counselor's inappropriate, if not harmful, use of "empty chair," an example of inattention to the limitations of theory-specific technical skill with diverse clientele. With information about the possible source of counselor incompetence, the supervisor is better equipped to assist the counselor in overcoming the roadblock to his or her cultural competency. The conceptualization presented in Figure 38.1 is in distinct contrast to the MCCM in that it expands the three components of awareness and beliefs, knowledge, and skills into more specific areas, providing more direct links and implications for guiding the supervisor in working with counselors in this endeavor.

In sum, the assumptions of counseling-in-context coupled with the focus on the boundaries of the multicultural counseling competencies function to guide the supervisor in the endeavors to increase the counselor's effectiveness with clients, ultimately facilitating the counselor's development of competencies. In a review of the process and outcome research in counseling psychology, Hill and Corbett (1993) concluded that in relation to process and outcome in counseling, the uniformity myth is still pervasive and merits our attention. Through a careful examination of the counselor's multicultural counseling competencies with respect to level, phase, and source, the supervisor is more likely to offer specific help to promote the cultural competencies of the counselor.

AN INTERACTIONAL APPROACH TO SUPERVISION

The client and the counselor each enters into the counseling context with a particular set of individual characteristics, which are primarily grounded in social-cultural contexts and life circumstances as well as by specific expectations or goals of supervision. The mistaken assumption that matching the counselor and client on group variables (e.g., sex, race, and ethnicity) would enhance the counseling relationship and outcome is seductive, as well as venerable. Empirical evidence has not corroborated this intuitive assumption, however (Ponterotto et al., 2000). One plausible explanation is that these participant characteristics are static background variables; only through the verbal discourse of both participants will they then become dynamic and meaningful. Similarly, Phinney (1996) noted the use of race or ethnicity as a categorical variable in educational and psychological research is imprecise and arbitrary, if not problematic. To fully understand how the cultural dynamics may facilitate, restrict, or override personal experience in the counseling process, the myriad cultural variables should be considered as contexts where psychological issues and experiences are embedded. Moreover, to unveil the sophisticated phenomenon in multicultural counseling process and outcome, it is thus imperative that researchers and practitioners alike take an interactional view of interpersonal transactions within the counseling session.

In a monograph on the interactional approach to counseling, Claiborn and Lichtenberg (1989) postulated that interpersonal behaviors of the counselor and client are constantly affected by each other's interpretations, expectations, and choices made during their continuous transactions. More specifically, interaction refers to the process by which interpersonal behaviors alter or change one another or generate new information that facilitates further encounters. Counseling outcome is in the end a result of this reciprocal influence process. These interpersonal transactions could be further delineated in regard to frequency, intensity, and outcome (Thomas, 1999). Interactions could be singular, periodic or intermittent, or continuous when they occur over an extended period of time. A "critical incident" is defined as a lone encounter with high emotional intensity. It is mainly the frequency of these critical incidents that ultimately influences the nature of the counseling relationship and outcome. A series of critical incidents then function as themes or patterns, which are windows into the inner working of the minds of the counselor and client. The rich subterranean lode of data as well as layers of invisible, unvoiced sentiments are often hidden underneath each critical incident waiting to be excavated through careful examination. Moreover, these incidents may often represent crossroads at which the counseling relationship is being defined, reflecting misunderstandings (e.g., Rhodes, Hill, Thompson, & Elliot, 1994), impasses (e.g., Hill, Nutt-Williams, Heaton, Thompson, & Rhodes, 1996), ruptures (e.g., Safran, Crocker, McMain, & Murray, 1990; Safran & Muran, 1996), or conflicts (e.g., Tracey, 1993) in the collaborative alliance. In the throes of conflictual moments, the counselor's ability to interact effectively with the client is of particular significance in directing the subsequent course of counseling.

As evidenced by Skovholt and Ronnestad's (1992) research, interpersonal encounters with clients exert significant influence in promoting the counselor's development. Indeed, counseling relationships, like other forms of human relationships, are richly layered, often cemented by moving or hazardous adventures. The rich and subtle interplay of this dynamic negotiation of implicit and explicit interpretations and expectations between the counselor and client plays an indispensable role in shaping the nature and outcome of the counseling engagement. This interactional approach has at its core two related yet distinct principles or concepts, intentionality and reflection, both of which are discussed in more detail below.

Intentionality

Central to this interactional approach is a recognition that each interactant is an intentional, active agent who chooses his or her behavior from a large universe of possible alternatives, thereby shaping the situational determinants of that behavior (Claiborn & Lichtenberg, 1989). Extensive research has been conducted on the role of counselor intentionality in counseling and psychotherapy (Horvath, Marx, & Kamann, 1990; Kivlighan & Angelone, 1991; Martin, Martin, Meyer, & Slemon, 1986; Stiles et al., 1996). Hill and O'Grady (1985) first proposed using counselor or therapist intentionality as a lens to examine the counseling process and outcome. Presented with voluminous client information often in considerable disarray, the counselor deliberately selects a particular response, technique, behavior, or intervention strategy to pursue from a broad spectrum of possible choices to achieve a specific goal. The counselor's behavior then elicits an internal reaction from the client, who then responds overtly to the counselor's intervention. The counselor continues to evaluate the client's overt response on the basis of other relevant historical and contextual information, such as the client's body language, family history, ethnic identity, and socioeconomic status, and then changes the intention. As the counselor's intentionality changes, the client's responses change accordingly. The counseling process and outcome are thus affected by this ongoing exchange of feedback between counselor and client. The 19 pantheoretical counselor intentions, according to Hill (1992), fall into 9 nonmutually exclusive categories: (1) *Set limits*; (2) *Assess:* get information, focus, clarify; (3) *Support:* instill hope, reinforce change; (4) *Educate:* give information; (5) *Explore:* identify and intensify cognitions, behaviors, and feelings-awareness; (6) *Restructure:* insight, resistance, challenge; (7) *Change*; (8) *Relationship*; and (9) *Miscellaneous:* cathart, self-control, therapist needs.

Horvath et al. (1990) further differentiated two overlapping but distinct meanings of counselor intentionality: the *reason* (*why* the counselor does something) and the *plan* (what the counselor has in mind *for the client*) aspects. The *reason* aspect pertains to the understanding of the element or condition that precedes the counselor's behavior as well as the rationale for choosing a behavior, response mode, skill, or intervention to use over the other alternatives with a client at any given moment during the counseling session. The *plan* aspect focuses on the intended impact on the client's cognition, affect, or behavior. Counselor intentionality plays a vital role in counseling because it mediates and influences the counselor's choice of interventions and the subsequent in-session behaviors. This role is evident in research that shows intentions are related to clients' and judges' ratings of counseling outcome (Kelly, Hall, & Miller, 1989), and account for more of the variance in immediate counseling outcome than do verbal response modes (Hill et al., 1988). It should not come as surprise then that counselor intentionality is integral to many counselor training models (e.g., Ivey's, 1971, microcounseling; Kagan's, 1976, 1980, interpersonal process recall [IPR]) and central to the counseling process and outcome research (Hill & Nutt-Williams, 2000).

In multicultural counseling, examination of counselor intentionality, or "cultural intentionality" (Ivey, 1987), is even more critical because it functions as an indicator of the counselor's sense of purposefulness or "mindfulness" (Langer, 1989) in the counselor-client transactions. Rather than operating in an automatic, habitual manner due to unwarranted assumptions or beliefs, mindful counselors are open to new information and characteristics associated with the client, and sensitive to the context when entering a new counseling relationship. Without this sense of mindfulness, counselors' interventions are likely to be guided and constrained by their reductionistic, stereotypic beliefs and assumptions, thereby severely compromising the effectiveness of these assessment and intervention strategies. Counselor intentionality also converges with Ridley et al.'s (1994) concept of cultural sensitivity as a perceptual schema, which assists the counselor in attending to culturally relevant information, organizing cultural stimuli in meaningful ways, and channeling this information to initiate and plan culturally responsive action. The counselor's cultural sensitivity is associated with the degree to which the counselor is *purposefully* applying the cultural perceptual schema to gather and organize client information to gain a meaningful understanding of the client's experience.

Reflection

The importance of reflection has been well documented in the teacher education literature (Copeland, Birmingham, De La Cruz, & Lewin, 1993; McNamara, 1990). Although there is variation with respect to its definition, consensus emerges on the centrality of reflection in facilitating the professional development of teachers (Clift, Houston, & Pugach, 1990; Zeichner & Liston, 1987). Referring to an internal process of attention and thought, the concept of reflection is rooted in John Dewey's (1938) reflective approach to scientific thinking as he asserted that "every experience affects for better or worse the attitudes which help decide the quality of further experiences" (p. 37). He further conceptualized reflection as a behavior that requires an active, persistent, and deliberate consideration of any beliefs or assumptions in light of the evidence that supports it and the immediate consequences it evokes. Underlying Dewey's (1933, 1938) view is an emphasis on *purpose* and *consequences*, reminiscent of the concept of counselor intentionality. Many contemporary writers on reflection have adopted and expanded, to varying degrees, this aspect of reflection as a navigator of future behavior. Schön (1983, 1987), for example, stressed that reflection is a mental process that involves looking back and learning from the experience to shape future behaviors. Greene (1990) further emphasized that the reflective practitioner attempts to name that which is unrecognized, seek possibilities, and imagine new alternatives.

In arguing for the use of reflection to guide the teaching practice, Van Manen (1977) outlined three levels of reflective inquiry. At the first level, reflection revolves around technical application of knowledge as a means to achieve a given end. The second level involves analyzing and clarifying experiences, meanings, values, and assumptions that function collectively as the basis of the technical intentionality. A critical reflection, the third level, centers on the connection between moral and ethical principles such as justice and equality in the application of knowledge, and an analysis of the surrounding sociocultural structures that guide and influence the assumptions and application of practical knowledge. Van Manen's analysis of reflection brings into gradual focus how, in the context of multicultural counseling, the reflective inquiry moves beyond helping the counselor become a technical expert to strive toward a higher level of practice. The counselor also learns to examine each multicultural counseling encounter as a microcosm of the dynamic yet subtle interplay of value and power at the individual, professional, and social levels. Under Van Manen's framework is an implicit plea for professionals to engage in ethical practice to eradicate all forms of prejudices inflicted on minority individuals and promote social justice.

Many counselor educators have increasingly recognized the importance of counselors' reflective inquiry as one principal tool to improve their work with clients and to develop their clinical skills and judgment (Hoshmand, 1994; Neufeldt, Karno, & Nelson, 1996; Skovholt & Ronnestad, 1992). Skovholt and Ronnestad's (1992) research, for example, identified the counselor's "reflective stance" as one major theme in counselor development.

Translated into the context of multicultural counseling, this reflective stance assists the counselor in making meaning of the complexities, uncertainties, and ambiguities of counseling encounters between two individuals across various sex, age, and sociocultural divides. Reflection, therefore, is not a brief mental replay of a series of events; rather, it involves the counselor in cycles of thoughts and actions grounded in professional experience. The ultimate goal is to move the counselor to the level of a creative artist as opposed to that of a technician, who tends to engage in routine, automatic response, guided by unwarranted assumptions or beliefs.

Sue and Sue (1999) asserted that the culturally competent mental health professional must work actively in the process of becoming aware of his or her own assumptions regarding behavior, values, biases, stereotypes, and limitations. Undergoing the process of examination of these assumptions, however central to practice, is difficult on three fronts. First, our assumptive views tend to be ingrained as part of our "core ordering processes" (Mahoney, 1991), thus resistant to change in general, as evidenced by the research findings with respect to attitude change in social psychology (Fiske & Taylor, 1991). Moreover, reflection is mainly cognitive in nature and to look back and learn from the experience requires a deliberate, concerted effort and higher level of skills, presenting a particular challenge to novice counselors. Third, the complexity of factors and issues at each of the three levels (universal, group, and individual) has further complicated the reflective process particularly for the novice counselors. Not surprisingly, many of the multicultural counseling models remain theoretical in nature, offering limited utility in guiding the reflective practice of counselors as well as the supervisors (Ponterotto et al., 2000).

Synthesis of Intentionality and Reflection in Supervision

Counselor intentionality as a covert cognitive process, or as a cultural schema (Ridley et al., 1994) in the context of multicultural counseling, is epistemologically private (Stiles et al., 1996). Supervision is thus an ideal vehicle to facilitate the reflection of counselor intentionality, as it establishes a constructive learning environment for aiding the supervisee in confronting unwarranted assumptions, increasing acquisition of knowledge, and improving mastery of skills necessary for integrating, evaluating, and applying such knowledge. The supervisor brings to the reflective inquiry his or her knowledge, experience, and skills that would lead to optimal outcome. In this way, counselor intentionality is drawn out, both with reference to the particular client and with regard to his or her own underlying cultural schemata in general, on the basis of the ambiguous situation and conditions in these salient interpersonal transactions. Reflection on critical incidents are intended to heighten awareness, confront complacency, and engender a higher level of counseling practice.

The interactional approach can be applied to different contexts (career, individual, or group counseling). In group counseling, for example, Yalom (1995) has been the most vocal advocate of the "self-reflective loop" as a critical technique for the group therapist to help group members gain self-understanding. Specifically, this "self-reflective loop" begins with an experience of emotion-laden interpersonal encounter, followed by an immediate reflection on the experience, and leads to future cognitive understanding and behavioral change. In essence, it is the emotional experience combined with cognitive understanding that provides optimal therapeutic effects. Using the concepts of intentionality and reflection as the organizing principles, I next outline the goals, steps, and characteristics of this interactional approach as applied in supervision.

The interactional approach to supervision aims to, above all, prepare reflective counselors who remain intentional or mindful of their own assumptions and views and to weave intervention strategies into the fabric of the counseling process, thus building a culturally appropriate context for change to occur. Based on their knowledge base and worldviews (Ibrahim & Kahn, 1987; Ibrahim et al., Chapter 23, this volume), counselors respond both to questions addressed to them by clients, directly and indirectly, and to contextual factors of which they have been informed. Through these critical incidents, counselors reveal much about themselves, personally and professionally, and the way in which they approach counseling. If professional and personal experience is the experimental ground upon which an individual's knowledge is constructed, counselors are then both creators and consumers of this practical knowledge. Only through this cyclical sequence of examination of personal and professional experience would counselors begin to expand a knowledge base that is practical. In this way, reflection of counselor intentionality does not strip counselors of their spontaneity; on the contrary, it increases their ability to act reflexively and "intuitively" based on these internalized principles interwoven with their response repertoire.

The second aim of this approach is to motivate counselors to become self-directed and self-monitored. As their own supervisors, they become creative in identifying strategies to improve their effectiveness when venturing into uncharted territory where limited relevant information exists to guide them and their clients in determining the propitious direction of counseling. In addition, they learn to monitor the effectiveness of their interventions through an attitude of curiosity about the meaning of the client's overt behavior and covert response. Establishing a habit of self-directed growth is more pronounced for counselors when working with diverse clients. Rather than simply practicing previously acquired knowledge and skills, they engage in this reflection of critical incidents through which many fundamental yet concealed issues are revealed. Counselors can learn to glimpse their strengths and weaknesses from these counseling encounters. Hence, each reflective act of counselors is ultimately of use to exert leverage on their will to change the behaviors in the subsequent session. The inability of counselors to broaden their perspectives and their response repertoire inevitably thwarts their efforts to increase cultural competency. Supervisors in this approach are less concerned with providing a definite, concrete solution than with expanding multiple alternative perspectives. This reflective inquiry, as a matter of fact, may raise as many questions as it answers. It is expected that counselors would have additional questions to raise, different issues to explore, and new interpretations to forge.

As Hill and Gronsky (1984) and many others have noted, multiple realities exist in counseling, depending on one's vantage point, with minimal correlations among the perspectives of counselors, clients, and observers (Caskey, Barker, & Elliott, 1984; Orlinsky & Howard, 1975). It stands to reason that the more diversity there is in each counseling relationship, the less likely the same events would be perceived consistently by the counselor and client. The third aim of this approach, therefore, is to enhance the counselor's empathic understanding of the client's subjective worldview, thus increasing the likelihood of a shared reality.

Complementary to other supervision models, such as Holloway's (1995) systems approach to supervision or Bernard's (1997) discrimination model, this approach places a premium on assisting the counselor in reflecting on critical incidents from the most recent counseling session, consisting of two phases. Prior to the beginning of each supervision session, the supervisee is expected to prepare to recall a couple of counseling episodes that are salient, meaningful, challenging, or puzzling to him or her. This requirement allows the supervisee to assume responsibility for his or her own learning, consistent with the goal of fostering professional autonomy in supervision (Bernard & Goodyear, 1998).

During the first phase of the supervision session, the supervisor uses these incidents to enhance the supervisee's reflective practice, progressing in the order outlined below. On the basis of the procedures described in Bernstein and Lecomte (1979) and Smyth (1989) for counselor training and teacher education, respectively, this process comprises four steps that are both sequential and cyclical—*Describing, Informing, Confronting,* and *Planning,* with accompanying sets of questions relative to different aspects of counselor intentionality:

1. *Describing.* What actually happened? What were you hearing your client say and observing your client do?
2. *Informing.* What was your own reaction? Why was this event important for you? What might it mean from the client's perspective?
3. *Confronting.* What was the possible range of alternatives for you to respond? How did you act the way you did from among the alternatives? How did you account for this event from your perspective? From the client's perspective? At what level—universal, group, or individual—did your response operate?
4. *Planning.* How might what happened suggest to you what you should attend to during the next session? What would you like to see happen next? To what end? What are the implications for your practice? At what level—universal, group, or individual—would you intend to influence the client's behavior?

The supervisor during this initial reflective process functions mainly as one who guides the exploration of these interpersonal transactions, similar to the role of "inquirer" as described in Kagan's (1976, 1980) IPR approach. The central tenet of IPR is that fears lead people into an approach-avoidance behavior pattern, stuck between their desire for interpersonal relationships and their fear of them. Through an exploration of these fears in the counseling relationship, the counselor interacts with the client in a more honest and effective manner. The IPR technique involves playing the videotape of the counseling session. One person plays the role of "inquirer," raising open-ended, nonevaluative questions of the counselor. The objective is to help the counselor excavate valuable information containing his or her feelings during the session and to explore the relationship between the counselor and client. The inquirer attends to certain behavioral cues or thematic shifts indicative of significant interpersonal dynamics or content issues. The inquiry questions typically revolve around any of the following areas: affect, cognition, body sensations, images, expectations, perceptions, or associations. The taped-assisted recall of covert responses, and counselor intentionality in particular, is thus complementary to this approach.

The supervisor as an inquirer refrains from offering suggestions or feedback, thus minimizing interference with the supervisee's own in-depth exploration. Accordingly, the counselor gains insight into how, amid conflicting or competing theories, principles, and strategies, he or she makes the best choice as a result of the intended effects and goals for the client and counseling. Particular attention is given to the supervisee's reason and plan aspects of intentionality (Horvath et al., 1990) in relation to the universal, group, and individual levels of the client-counselor interactions. This continuous reflective inquiry, moreover, heightens the counselor's awareness of additional or alternative characteristics associated with the client and the counseling encounter that should be taken into consideration. Depending on the developmental stage of the counselor (Stoltenberg, McNeill, &

Delworth, 1998) and the level of supervisory working alliance (Bordin, 1983; Efstation, Patton, & Kardash, 1990), the supervisor may move the level of reflection from the first level, technical rationality, to the higher levels as articulated in Van Manen (1977).

The second phase begins when a large body of information has been generated from the four aforementioned steps. The supervisor involves the supervisee in using the collected information to evaluate his or her cultural effectiveness in light of the three dimensions (level, phase, and source) of the framework described in Figure 38.1. The role of the supervisor changes from one of neutral inquirer to that of consultant, teacher, or counselor (Bernard, 1997), depending on the direction of this exploration. A considerable degree of convergence and divergence of the counselor's cultural competencies should emerge eventually from these critical incidents with clients *within* and *across* sessions. It is this constant comparison and contrast of salient interpersonal transactions in counseling that hold the promise for understanding factors, individual or cultural, that assist or inhibit the professional development of the counselor. Specifically, during this phase the supervisor exchanges feedback with the supervisee regarding his or her strengths and weaknesses, accompanied by suggestions and alternative strategies. Moreover, the supervisor involves the supervisee in identifying goals and strategies necessary to help the supervisee build or strengthen the areas of one's competencies in the remaining supervision sessions. The two-phase sequence underscores the importance of specificity, timing, and relevance in offering feedback, consistent with Hawkins and Shohet's (1989) recommendations. It should be noted that the feedback is situated in the critical incidents presented by the counselor. The supervisor stores these conclusions for later use, particularly when there are recurrent themes or patterns that point to similar areas of cultural competency or incompetence.

The complexity of human experiences, and multicultural encounters in particular, has often been reduced by researchers and practitioners alike to a simplistic, if not compartmentalized, examination of one variable at the exclusion of others, offering limited use for the counselor in practice. In response, Leong (1995) argued that an ideal multicultural counseling approach or model should have the flexibility and breadth to encompass the diversity of clients who seek counseling. Specifically, his "acid test" of evaluating a theoretical model consists of the following requirements: *integrative, sequential,* and *dynamic* features. Indicative of the integrative feature is the ideal model's recognition of human beings as active, complex adaptive systems, along with its simultaneous examination of personality at the universal, group-specific, and individual levels (Kluckhohn & Murray, 1953). A model is sequential when it attends to the moment-by-moment, temporal unfolding of the counseling process and the effects of these interpersonal encounters on the counseling outcomes. An ideal model should be dynamic to guide the practitioner to shift from the static, stagelike formulation to examination of complex interpersonal interactions within and across counseling sessions over time.

The interactional approach presented in this chapter reflects in varying degree Leong's (1996) three features. It is *integrative* because the supervision emphasis is placed on helping the counselor identify and develop case-specific recommendations that are grounded in and responsive to the client's subjective experience both personal and cultural. Not only does it attend to the idiosyncrasies of the client and the counselor, it also focuses on how these three levels interact with each other. As such, it is client focused but counselor sensitive. This approach is *sequential* in that it uses critical incidents to examine counselor-client interactions as they unfold in the counseling process rather than simply reviewing demographic characteristics associated with the client and counselor. Furthermore, this approach leans toward a more fluid, *dynamic* inquiry of interactions in counseling and away from the traditional stagelike formation of counseling process. Clearly, this interactional approach does not intend to develop standardized counseling protocol or intervention guidelines that apply to all clients, highlighting a contextualized view of counselor techniques and interventions. As Butler and Strupp (1986) noted, "The complexity and subtlety of psychotherapeutic processes cannot be reduced to a set of disembodied techniques because techniques gain their meaning, and in turn, their effectiveness from the particular interatction of individuals involved" (p. 33). The following case vignette as applied in individual supervision illuminates this approach.

CASE ILLUSTRATION

Lisa Wang, a 19-year-old Asian American female junior, is referred to Jacob, a 28-year-old, single, White, male practicum student, at the university counseling center by her professor because of a decline in her grade point average and her overall school performance. As a junior in college, Lisa is presently majoring in business. She has recently begun to feel depressed because she has realized that business is not her passion. She prefers a career in psychology because she feels she can relate well to others. She has hinted to her parents about her desire to change majors, but they responded negatively. As a traditional Asian man, Lisa's father is a dominant figure in the family and holds high expectations for his children. Lisa's family involuntarily immigrated to the United States from China for economic reasons when she was 3 years old. He expects Lisa to succeed academically to financially support the family as well as secure a "ticket" into a good marriage. Currently, Lisa's parents own and operate a Chinese restaurant. This business requires them to spend much time at the restaurant. As the first child, Lisa has always been expected to help with caring for her younger sister and brother along with keeping up with her studies.

TABLE 38.1 Using the IPR Technique, Possible Questions About Jacob's Counseling Session With Lisa

---

1. *Inquiry leads that inspire affective exploration*
   - What were your feelings for Lisa?
   - How did your feelings influence your perceptions of Lisa?
2. *Inquiry leads that encourage cognitive examination*
   - What thoughts were you having about Lisa at that time?
   - How have your impressions about Lisa changed over time?
3. *Inquiry leads about body sensations*
   - Do you recall how your body felt? Can you recall any specific parts of your body reacting more than the other parts?
   - If that physical sensation had a voice of its own, what would it have said?
4. *Inquiry leads that get at images*
   - What pictures, memories, or words were going through your mind?
   - What fantasies did you have when Lisa responded the way she did?
5. *Inquiry leads about expectations*
   - What did you want Lisa to think or feel?
   - How did you expect Lisa to respond?
6. *Inquiry leads about perceptions*
   - What effects did your perceptions of Lisa have on you?
   - What do you think Lisa's perceptions are of you?
7. *Inquiry leads into associations*
   - Did Lisa remind you of anyone else in your life?
   - What effect did that have on your behavior during the session?

As Jacob's supervisor, I started the supervision session by asking him, as usual, to recall any critical incidents in the most recent sessions with Lisa. He described episodes in this first counseling session with Lisa where she repeatedly asked for his advice on her career choices. While viewing the videotaped segment where this critical incident occurred, I raised some specific questions, as shown in Table 38.1, in keeping with the IPR technique. The following is the content of Jacob's response in the order of the four steps described previously to uncover counselor intentionality.

1. *Describing.* Salient to Jacob from this session was that on several occasions Lisa specifically asked him for guidance or advice in relation to her career pursuits. Jacob seemed to keep the career issues at arm's length and usually explored her interpersonal relationships, particularly with her family. His typical responses were "Umm-humm" and "What do you think?" or he simply asked her to elaborate on a relationship issue. Lisa initially responded with a relatively more detailed description but often continued expressing her academic and career concerns.

2. *Informing.* These interactions were important to Jacob because he recalled his anxiety during an intake session about not being able to help Lisa given cultural differences he observed existing in his relationship with her. He saw himself as highly culturally sensitive but feared that he could not offer her the concrete help she needed. Lisa's consistent advice-seeking style

further exacerbated his anxiety over the racial differences. He recalled feeling "stuck" in adjusting his theoretical orientation as a client-centered counselor to working with Lisa. Furthermore, he perceived Lisa as insecure and unassertive and was concerned that giving her "answers" would only perpetuate this style in her.

3. *Confronting.* Jacob described his behavior as a result of his intention to elicit more detailed information from Lisa to assess the nature of her depression because she was often vague and general in her account—the *reason* aspect of intentionality (Horvath et al., 1990). He was also uncomfortable in giving advice for fear that it would reinforce Lisa's dependency on him. By not responding to her request directly, he hoped to increase her confidence in expressing herself more in counseling and in other interpersonal relationships—the *plan* aspect of intentionality (Horvath et al., 1990). Furthermore, he did not respond to Lisa's questions because he conceptualized her career concerns as an example of her attempt to develop and explore her personal identity. He identified his intentionality as "get information," falling into the category of "Assess" on Hill and O'Grady's (1985) list. Despite these preceded reasons for his behavior, Jacob recalled having some fleeting doubts about whether or not to respond directly to Lisa's request given the cultural differences and in light of his awareness that she appeared more aloof and disengaged in the later part of the session. He acknowledged that his intended plan for Lisa to learn to be more assertive reflected his lack of attention to differences at both group and individual levels, particularly with reference to the cultural expectations of her to be "successful," and her attempts to balance the needs of her family with her own. His alternative hypothesis of Lisa's request for concrete advice was that because of the pressure or implicit expectations from her parents she was taking a quick problem solving approach to her perceived dilemma of balancing the needs of her family with her own. Jacob also indicated that, growing up in a Jewish family, he could empathize with Lisa's pressure to succeed academically.

4. *Planning.* Jacob became more aware that not responding to Lisa's questions had thwarted his efforts to build a collaborative working alliance with her. Through reflective inquiry, he planned to adjust his style in the next session, shifting toward giving a more specific, focused, yet tentative response, and assisting her in her problem-solving approach.

The focus of the last third of the supervision session was on our collective assessment of Jacob's skills as evidenced in his interactions with Lisa. He responded that he typically was able to respond to the challenge of clients requesting his advice or opinions. I shared with him my observation of the shift of his reflection from the appropriateness of the advice-giving skill to the values implicit in his style and the Rogerian approach in general, representing the movement from the first to the second level of reflection as described in Van Manen (1977). We both agreed that his limited effectiveness in developing a solid working relationship with Lisa reflected his difficulty in adjusting his Rogerian style to accommodate Lisa's preferred problem-solving approach. After a brief discussion of the interconnection between personal and career counseling (Hackett, 1994) as well as the meaning of work and careers across racial and ethnic groups as described in

Richardson (1993), we spent the rest of the session exploring how these issues manifested themselves in the career and personal development of Lisa as an Asian American woman and how Jacob may change his intended goals for the following session.

CONCLUSIONS

Largely due to their mechanistic, dogmatic quality, on the one hand, and the conceptual ambiguities, on the other, many of the extant multicultural frameworks in counseling and supervision often degenerate into a sterile intellectual exercise, remotely relevant to the counselor working with a particular client. The concepts of intentionality and reflection jointly constitute the keystone on which rests this integrative approach to supervision. Shifting the focus from "knowing what" to "knowing how" (Johnson, 1987), in this chapter I sketched the goals, concepts, and steps underlying this interactional approach as well as the basic assumptions on which it operates.

The confrontation with problems or issues manifested through these interpersonal counseling encounters often cause counselors to reflect on the nature of their relationship with their clients. The importance of issues at stake between the counseling participants calls forth from counselors an enormous effort of personal openness as well as fundamental considerations of personal and professional values. Though the emotional tone of the critical incident, its lack of clarity, and inattention to the contextual undercurrents do not make the incident easy to explore, it amply repays the effort required of the counselor. Through a barrage of questions, by challenges both direct and subtle, the supervisor strives to awaken in the supervisee a sense of curiosity and an appropriate response.

Unless we can begin to prepare counselors who are willing and able to assume a more central role in shaping the direction of their work with clients across cultural divides, the quest for an approach to facilitate the building of multicultural counseling competencies would remain an elusive dream. The interactional approach described here involves reflection on critical indents through which the counselor's intentions, including reasons and plans, are assessed against the subsequent client behavior. It aims to imbue clinical supervision with a spirit of collaborative inquiry, which involves the supervisor and supervisee in critical reflection of what is difficult, what is ambiguous, and what is possible in the counseling process. The interdependence of intentionality and reflection cannot be overemphasized. The synergy of counselor mindlessness and insufficient reflection continues to diminish the multicultural effectiveness of counselors. Reflection heightens the supervisee's sense of efficacy and competency, thus leading to the nurturing climate for professional and personal growth. Through this reflective inquiry, it is hoped that supervisors would assist counselors in increasing their intentionality and effectiveness as well as in promoting ethical practice in a murky field of multicultural counseling replete with numerous "it depends" (Friedlander, 1992).

REFERENCES

Allison, K. W., Echemendia, R. J., Crawford, I., & Robinson, W. L. (1996). Predicting cultural competence: Implications for practice and training. *Professional Psychology: Research and Practice, 27,* 386-393.

American Counseling Association. (1995). *Code of ethics and standards of practice.* Alexandria, VA: Author.

American Psychological Association. (1987). General guidelines for providers of psychological services. *American Psychologist, 42,* 712-723.

American Psychological Association. (1992). Ethical principles of psychologists and code of conduct. *American Psychologist, 42,* 1597-1611.

American Psychological Association. (1993). Guidelines for providers of psychological services to ethnic, linguistic, and culturally diverse populations. *American Psychologist, 48,* 45-48.

Ancis, J. R., & Ladany, N. (in press). A multicultural framework for counselor supervision. In L. J. Bradley & N. Ladany (Eds.), *Counselor supervision: Principles, process, and practice* (3rd ed.). Philadelphia: Accelerated Development.

Arredondo, P., Toporek, R., Brown, S. P., Jones, J., Locke, D. C., Sanchez, J., & Stadler, H. (1996). Operationalization of the multicultural counseling competencies. *Journal of Multicultural Counseling and Development, 24,* 42-78.

Association for Counselor Education and Supervision. (1995). Ethical guidelines for counseling supervisors. *Counselor Education and Supervision, 34,* 270-276.

Bernard, J. M. (1997). The discrimination model. In C. E. Watkins (Ed.), *Handbook of psychotherapy supervision* (pp. 310-327). New York: John Wiley.

Bernard, J. M., & Goodyear, R. K. (1998). *Fundamentals of clinical supervision* (2nd ed.). Needham Heights, MA: Allyn & Bacon.

Bernstein, B. L., & Lecomte, C. (1979). Self-critique technique training in a competency-based practicum. *Counselor Education and Supervision, 19,* 69-76.

Bordin, E. S. (1983). A working alliance based model of supervision. *The Counseling Psychologist, 11,* 35-42.

Butler, S. F., & Strupp, H. H. (1986). Specific and non-specific factors in psychotherapy: A problematic paradigm for psychotherapy research. *Psychotherapy, 23,* 30-40.

Caskey, N., Barker, C., & Elliott, R. (1984). Dual perspectives: Clients' and therapists' perceptions of therapist responses. *British Journal of Clinical Psychology, 23,* 30-40.

Chen, E. C., & Bernstein, B. L. (2000). Relations of complementarity and supervisory issues to supervisory working alliance: A comparative analysis of two cases. *Journal of Counseling Psychology, 47,* 485-497.

Claiborn, C. D., & Lichtenberg, J. W. (1989). Interactional counseling. *The Counseling Psychologist, 17,* 355-453.

Clift, R., Houston, W., & Pugach, M. (Eds.). (1990). *Encouraging reflective practice in education.* New York: Teachers College Press.

Constantine, M. G. (1997). Facilitating multicultural competency in counseling supervision. In D. B. Pope-Davis & H. L. K. Coleman (Eds.), *Multicultural counseling competencies: Assessment, education and training, and supervision* (pp. 310-324). Thousand Oaks, CA: Sage.

Constantine, M. G., & Gloria, A. M. (1999). Multicultural issues in predoctoral internship programs: A national survey. *Journal of Multicultural Counseling and Development, 27,* 42-53.

Constantine, M. G., & Ladany, N. (2000). Self-report multicultural counseling competence scales: Their relation to social desirability attitudes and multicultural case conceptualization ability. *Journal of Counseling Psychology, 47,* 102-115.

Copeland, W. D., Birmingham, C., De La Cruz, E., & Lewin, B. (1993). The reflective practitioner in teaching: Toward a research agenda. *Teaching and Teacher Education, 9,* 347-359.

D'Andrea, M., & Daniels, J. (1997). Multicultural counseling supervision: Central issues, theoretical considerations, and practical strategies. In D. B. Pope-Davis & H. L. K. Coleman (Eds.). *Multicultural counseling competencies: Assessment, education and training, and supervision* (pp. 290-309). Thousand Oaks, CA: Sage.

Dewey, J. (1933). *How we think: A restatement of the relation of reflective thinking to the educative process.* Boston: D. C. Heath.

Dewey, J. (1938). *Experience and education.* New York: Macmillan.

Doehrmann, M. (1976). Parallel processes in supervision and psychotherapy. *Bulletin of the Menninger Clinic, 40,* 3-104.

Efstation, J. F., Patton, M. J., & Kardash, C. M. (1990). Measuring the working alliance in counselor supervision. *Journal of Counseling Psychology, 37,* 322-329.

Fiske, S. T., & Taylor, S. E. (1991). *Social cognition* (2nd ed.). New York: McGraw-Hill.

Friedlander, M. L. (1992). Psychotherapeutic processes: About the art, about the science. *Journal of Counseling and Development, 70,* 740-741.

Greene, M. (1990). The passion of the possible: Choice, multiplicity, and commitment. *Journal of Moral Education, 19*(2), 67-76.

Hackett, G. (1994). Career counseling and psychotherapy: False dichotomies and recommended remedies. *Journal of Career Assessment, 1,* 105-117.

Hawkins, P., & Shohet, R. (1989). *Supervision in the helping professions.* Milton Keynes, UK: Open University Press.

Helms, J. E. (1994). How multiculturalism obscures racial factors in the therapy process: Comment on Ridley et al. (1994), Sodowsky et al. (1994), Ottavi et al. (1994), and Thompson et al. (1994). *Journal of Counseling Psychology, 41,* 162-165.

Hill, C. E. (1992). An overview of four measures developed to test the Hill process model: Therapist intentions, therapist response modes, client reactions, and client behaviors. *Journal of Counseling and Development, 70,* 728-737.

Hill, C. E., & Corbett, M. M. (1993). A perspective on the history of process and outcome research in counseling psychology. *Journal of Counseling Psychology, 40,* 3-24.

Hill, C. E., & Gronsky, B. (1984). Research: Why and how? In J. M. Whiteley, N. Kagan, L. W. Harmon, B. R. Fretz, & F. Tanney (Eds.), *The coming decade in counseling psychology* (pp. 149-159). Schenectady, NY: Character Research Press.

Hill, C. E., Helms, J. E., Tichenor, V., Spiegel, S. B., O'Grady, K. E., & Perry, E. (1988). The effects of therapist response modes in brief psychotherapy. *Journal of Counseling Psychology, 35,* 222-233.

Hill, C. E., & Nutt-Williams, E. (2000). In S. D. Brown & R. W. Lent (Eds.), *Handbook of counseling psychology* (3rd ed., pp. 670-710). New York: John Wiley.

Hill, C. E., Nutt-Williams, E., Heaton, K. J., Thompson, B. J., & Rhodes, R. H. (1996). Therapist retrospective recall impasses in long-term psychotherapy: A qualitative analysis. *Journal of Counseling Psychology, 43,* 207-217.

Hill, C. E., & O'Grady, K. E. (1985). List of therapist intentions illustrated in a case study and with therapists of varying theoretical orientations. *Journal of Counseling Psychology, 32,* 3-22.

Holloway, E. L. (1995). *Clinical supervision: A systems approach.* Thousand Oaks, CA: Sage.

Horvath, A. O., Marx, R. W., & Kamann, A. M. (1990). Thinking about thinking in therapy: An examination of clients' understanding of their therapists' intentions. *Journal of Consulting and Clinical Psychology, 58,* 614-621.

Hoshmand, L. T. (1994). *Orientation to inquiry in a reflective professional psychology.* Albany: State University of New York Press.

Ibrahim, F. A., & Kahn, H. (1987). Assessment of worldviews. *Psychological Reports, 60,* 163-176.

Ivey, A. E. (1971). *Microcounseling: Innovations in interviewing training.* Springfield, IL: Charles C Thomas.

Ivey, A. E. (1987). Cultural intentionality: The core of effective helping. *Counselor Educaiton and Supervision, 26,* 168-172.

Johnson, S. D. (1987). Knowing that versus knowing how: Toward achieving expertise through multicultural training for counseling. *The Counseling Psychologist, 15,* 320-331.

Kagan, N. (1976). *Influencing human interaction.* Mason, MI: Mason Media.

Kagan, N. (1980). Influencing human interaction—eighteen years with IPR. In A. K. Hess (Ed.), *Psychotherapy supervision: Theory, research and practice* (pp. 262-286). New York: John Wiley.

Kelly, K. R., Hall, A. S., & Miller, K. L. (1989). Relation of counselor intention and anxiety to brief counseling outcome. *Journal of Counseling Psychology, 36,* 158-162.

Kiesler, D. J. (1966). Basic methodological issues implicit in psychotherapy research. *American Journal of Psychotherapy, 20,* 135-155.

Kivlighan, D. M., & Angelone, E. O. (1991). Helpee introversion, novice counselor intention use, and helpee-rated session impact. *Journal of Counseling Psychology, 38,* 25-29.

Kluckhohn, C., & Murray, H. A. (1953). Personality formation: The determinants. In C. Kluckhohn & H. A. Murray (Eds.), *Personality in nature, society, and culture* (pp. 35-48). New York: Knopf.

Langer, E. J. (1989). *Mindfulness.* Reading, MA: Addison-Wesley.

Leong, F. T. L. (1996). Toward an integrative model for cross-cultural counseling and psychotherapy. *Applied and Preventive Psychology: Current Scientific Perspectives, 5,* 189-209.

Mahoney, M. J. (1991). *Human change processes: The scientific foundations of psychotherapy.* New York: Basic Books.

Martin, J., Martin, W., Meyer, M., & Slemon, A. (1986). Empirical investigation of the cognitive mediational paradigm for research on counseling. *Journal of Counseling Psychology, 33,* 115-123.

McNamara, D. (1990). Research on teachers' thinking: Its contribution to educating student teachers to think critically. *Journal of Education for Teaching, 16,* 147-160.

Neufeldt, S. A., Karno, M. P., & Nelson, M. L. (1996). A qualitative study of experts' conceptualization of supervisee reflectivity. *Journal of Counseling Psychology, 43,* 3-9.

Orlinsky, D. E., & Howard, K. I. (1975). *Varieties of psychotherapeutic experience.* New York: Teachers College Press.

Overholser, J. C., & Fine, M. A. (1990). Defining the boundaries of professional competence: Managing subtle cases of clinical incompetence. *Professional Psychology: Research and Practice, 21,* 462-469.

Paul, G. (1967). Strategy in outcome research in psychotherapy. *Journal of Consulting Psychology, 31,* 109-118.

Phinney, J. S. (1996). When we talk about American ethnic groups, what do we mean? *American Psychologist, 51,* 918-927.

Ponterotto, J. G. (1997). Multicultural counseling training: A competency model and national survey. In D. B. Pope-Davis & H. L. K. Coleman (Eds.), *Multicultural counseling competencies: Assessment, education and training, and supervision* (pp. 111-130). Thousand Oaks, CA: Sage.

Ponterotto, J. G., Fuertes, J. N., & Chen, E. C. (2000). Models of multicultural counseling. In S. D. Brown & R. W. Lent (Eds.), *Handbook of counseling psychology* (3rd ed., pp. 639-669). New York: John Wiley.

Pope, K. S., & Vasquez, M. J. T. (1998). *Ethics in psychotherapy and counseling* (2nd ed.). San Francisco: Jossey-Bass.

Quintana, S. M., & Bernal, M. E. (1995). Ethnic minority training in counseling psychology: Comparisons with clinical psychology and proposed standards. *The Counseling Psychologist, 23,* 102-121.

Rhodes, R. H., Hill, C. E., Thompson, B. J., & Elliott, R. (1994). Client retrospective recall of resolved and unresolved misunderstanding events. *Journal of Counseling Psychology, 41,* 473-483.

Richardson, M. S. (1993). Work in people's lives: A location for counseling psychologists. *Journal of Counseling Psychology, 40,* 425-433.

Ridley, C. R., Mendoza, D. W., Kanitz, B. E., Angermeier, L., & Zenk, R. (1994). Cultural sensitivity in multicultural counseling: A perceptual schema model. *Journal of Counseling Psychology, 41*, 125-136.

Safran, J. D., Crocker, P., McMain, S., & Murray, P. (1990). Therapeutic alliance rupture as a therapy event for empirical investigation. *Psychotherapy, 27*, 154-165.

Safran, J. D., & Muran, J. C. (1996). The resolution of ruptures in the therapeutic alliance. *Journal of Consulting and Clinical Psychology, 64*, 447-458.

Schön, D. (1983). *The reflective practitioner: How professionals think in action.* New York: Basic Books.

Schön, D. (1987). *Educating the reflective practitioner.* San Francisco: Jossey-Bass.

Skovholt, T. M., & Ronnestad, M. H. (1992). Themes in therapist and counselor development. *Journal of Counseling and Development, 70*, 505-515.

Smyth, J. (1989). Developing and sustaining critical reflection in teacher education. *Journal of Teacher Education, 40*(2), 2-9.

Soldz, S. (1990). The therapeutic interaction. In R. A. Wells & V. J. Giannetti (Eds.), *Handbook of the brief psychotherapies* (pp. 27-53). New York: Plenum.

Stiles, W. B., Startup, M., Hardy, G. E., Barkham, M., Rees, A., Shapiro, D. A., & Reynolds, S. (1996). Therapist session intentions in cognitive-behavioral and psychodynamic-interpersonal psychotherapy. *Journal of Counseling Psychology, 43*, 402-414.

Stoltenberg, C. D., McNeill, B. W., & Delworth, U. (1998). *IDM supervision: An integrated developmental model for supervising counselors and therapists.* San Francisco: Jossey-Bass.

Stone, G. L. (1997). Multiculturalism as a context for supervision: Perspectives, limitations and implications. In D. B. Pope-Davis & H. L. K. Coleman (Eds.), *Multicultural counseling competencies: Assessment, education and training, and supervision* (pp. 263-289). Thousand Oaks, CA: Sage.

Strozier, A. L., Kivlighan, D. M., & Thoreson, R. W. (1993). Supervisor intentions, supervisee reactions, and helpfulness: A case study of the process of supervision. *Professional Psychology: Research and Practice, 24*, 13-19.

Sue, D. W., Arredondo, P., & McDavis, R. J. (1992). Multicultural competencies and standards: A call to the profession. *Journal of Multicultural Counseling and Development, 20*, 64-88.

Sue, D. W., Bernier, J. E., Durran, A., Feinberg, L., Pedersen, P., Smith, E. J., & Vazquez-Nuttall, E. (1982). Position paper: Cross-cultural counseling competencies. *The Counseling Psychologist, 10*, 45-52.

Sue, D. W., & Sue, D. (1999). *Counseling the culturally different: Theory and practice* (3rd ed.). New York: John Wiley.

Thomas, R. M. (1999). *Human development theories: Windows on culture.* Thousand Oaks, CA: Sage.

Tracey, T. J. (1993). An interpersonal stage model of the therapeutic process. *Journal of Counseling Psychology, 40*, 396-409.

Van Manen, M. (1977). Linking ways of knowing with ways of being practical. *Curriculum Inquiry, 6*, 205-228.

Yalom, I. D. (1995). *The theory and practice of group psychotherapy* (4th ed.). New York: Basic Books.

Zeichner, K. M., & Liston, D. P. (1987). Teaching student teachers to reflect. *Harvard Educational Review, 57*, 23-48.

Correspondence regarding this chapter may be sent to Eric C. Chen, Division of Psychological and Educational Services, Graduate School of Education, Fordham University, 113 West 60th Street, New York, NY 10023-7478 (e-mail address: echen@fordham.edu).

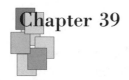

Chapter 39

MULTICULTURALISM ON PREDOMINANTLY WHITE CAMPUSES

Multiple Roles and Functions for the Counselor

INGRID GRIEGER
SUSAN TOLIVER

Whatever faculty members or administrators do about diversity, most students are living out the issues of diversity daily, personally, in a sometimes confused way, often with great pain, sometimes with eloquence and creativity.

—Diversity in Higher Education
(Musil, Garcia, Moses, & Smith, 1995), p. 60

IN THE EARLY 1990s, the California Postsecondary Education Commission (1992) asserted that colleges and universities have a responsibility to provide a campus climate that is equitable for all students and that, further, a major criterion for assessing the overall quality of an institution is its ability to provide that equitable education. The arrival of the third millennium renders that assertion even more compelling. Ever increasing diversity within the United States and economic and technological globalization challenge colleges and universities not only to educate all of their students equitably and effectively in the disciplines but also to prepare their students to function competently in a multicultural society. In fact, the mandate to educate all students to live and to work in a pluralistic society is so central that it can be argued that producing multiculturally competent graduates should be the preeminent criterion for defining academic excellence in the 21st century.

In this chapter, we first present an overview of the current status of diversity on predominantly White campuses. We then argue for multiple roles for the counselor with regard to multiculturalism on a predominantly White campus and review the empirical literature on diversity-related practices and initiatives. Using multicultural organizational development (MOD) as a framework, we suggest roles for the counselor with regard to diversity enhancement in the counseling center, the division of student affairs, the administration, and in academic affairs. Both conventional and nonconventional counselor roles are delineated, including mental health direct service provider, consultant, trainer, social change agent, administrator, educator, and collaborator. We conclude with specific recommendations for creating environments on the predominantly White campus that will permit *all* students to "live out the issues of diversity" with more "eloquence and creativity" and less "confusion and pain" (Musil et al., 1995, p. 60).

The reader should note that in this chapter the terms *multiculturalism* and *diversity* are used interchangeably, as is done in most of the professional literature on this topic.

CURRENT STATUS OF DIVERSITY ON PREDOMINANTLY WHITE CAMPUSES

The dual goals of educating all students equitably and successfully and preparing all students to function comfortably and competently with regard to diversity is particularly challenging at predominantly White four-year colleges and universities on both the undergraduate and graduate levels. As of 1994, African American and Hispanic students represented less than 4% of the total enrollment at these institutions (Carter & Wilson, 1994), and African American and Hispanic persons represented less than 5% of all faculty (Reyes & Halcon, 1990). Equally disheartening are data regarding the persistence of underrepresented populations, which indicate that African American and Hispanic students are far less likely to attain either an associate's or bachelor's degree than are their White counterparts (Carter & Wilson, 1994; Nettles, 1994; Smith et al., 1997). With regard to attendance and persistence in graduate programs, the National Center for Education Statistics (1997) reports that in 1995 only 6% of master's degrees and 3.8% of doctoral degrees were conferred upon African American students, while only 3.3% of master's degrees and 2.2% of doctoral degrees were conferred upon Hispanic students across all higher education institutions.

Clearly, on both the undergraduate and graduate levels, predominantly White institutions are not meeting the challenge of recruiting and retaining minority students. Unfortunately, recent successful challenges to affirmative action such as California's Proposition 209 and the ongoing and pervasive attacks on multiculturalism and "political correctness" on campuses and in the media strongly suggest that issues of access, education, and persistence continue unabated (D'Souza, 1991; Young, 1996). For example, at the University of California at Berkeley, college admissions for students of color plummeted dramatically between 1997 and 1998. Specifically, African American admissions dropped from 260 to 98, Hispanic admissions from 492 to 264, and Native American Indian admissions from 24 to 14 (Healy, 1998).

As disturbing as the data regarding representation and persistence are, an equally negative picture has emerged in the literature pertaining to campus climate for students of color. For example, Nixon and Henry (1992) found that 20% of minority students reported incidents of verbal or physical harassment. These investigators and others (D'Augelli, 1992; Ehrlich, 1990; Farrell & Jones, 1988; Herek, 1993) have documented incidents of physical assault, threats of violence, graffiti, hate flyers, and racist and homophobic jokes and epithets on the campus. Also noted in the literature are feelings of social isolation, alienation and marginalization, stereotyping, invisibility, discriminatory treatment by faculty and staff, language barriers, difficulty with acculturation, a paucity of student services, few faculty and administrative role models, criticism for self-segregation, and hostility regarding affirmative action (Alford, 2000; Ancis, Sedlacek, & Mohr, 2000; Dovidio, 1997; Hurtado, Carter, & Spuler, 1996; Loo & Rolison, 1986; Patterson-Stewart, Ritchie, & Sanders, 1997; Schwitzer, Griffin, Ancis, & Thomas, 1999; Sedlacek, 1998; Sidel, 1994; Tate & Schwartz, 1993; Tatum, 1997; Thomas, 1997).

Current data regarding representation, academic success, campus climate, and bias incidents targeting students of color, gays and lesbians, females, and Jewish students clearly indicate that predominantly White campuses have failed to provide safe, inclusive, empowering, and diversity-positive environments for all students (Patterson-Stewart et al., 1997; Smith et al., 1997). Sadly, even at the dawn of the 21st century, more than a dozen historically African American colleges and universities have been the victims of a campaign of racist hate mail (Willdorf, 2000), which clearly indicates that bias crimes continue to threaten all campuses.

On a more positive and promising note, there is an emerging body of literature that strongly suggests that when colleges and universities do commit themselves to diversity-positive institutional change, *all* students benefit (Appel, Cartwright, Smith, & Wolf, 1996; Astin, 1993a; Smith et al., 1997). Furthermore, there is a growing consensus about what kinds of strategies most effectively foster diversity on the campus in terms of positively impacting student success (Appel et al., 1996; Smith et al., 1997). In their extensive review of the research literature on programs in higher education undertake to facilitate diversity, Smith et al. (1997) conclude that

taken together this body of research underscores the conclusion that attending to issues of diversity is positively related to student success, and,
thus, is directly related to educational excellence. Moreover, the studies
reveal that higher education is on the right path by addressing diversity in
multiple ways at all levels of institutions. (p. 5)

MULTIPLE ROLES AND FUNCTIONS FOR THE
COUNSELOR ON THE PREDOMINANTLY WHITE CAMPUS:
A RATIONALE

It is becoming increasingly clear that providing culturally sensitive
counseling and psychotherapy is a necessary but not sufficient prerequisite
for effectively addressing multiculturalism on the campus (as well as in
other settings). In fact, it can be argued that counselors have an ethical
responsibility to move beyond in-the-office, conventional modalities of
counseling and psychotherapy if they are to adequately challenge systems
and environments that are oppressive to some of their constituents. For
example, the American Psychological Association's (1993) "Guidelines for
Providers of Psychological Services to Ethnic, Linguistic, and Culturally
Diverse Populations" states, "Psychologists attend to, as well as work to
eliminate biases, prejudices and discriminatory practices" (p. 47).

More recently, it has been suggested that multicultural competencies
must extend to personal and professional as well as organizational levels
(Sue et al., 1998). Similarly, Lee (1998) has argued for the reestablishment of
the social change agent role for counselors, emphasizing the responsibility
that counselors have to engage in social action on both the individual and
the system level. Lee (1998) has delineated two important processes that are
central to understanding counselor social change agency: empowerment
and advocacy. A three-dimensional model for counseling racial/ethnic minorities proposed by Atkinson, Thompson, and Grant (1993) also endorses
the roles of advocate and change agent for counselors, as well as other roles,
including advisor, consultant, psychotherapist, and facilitator of indigenous healing systems. Grieger and Ponterotto (1998) have suggested that in
addition to providing multiculturally competent counseling and psychotherapy, counselors must engage in multicultural organizational development (MOD), outreach and consultation, advocacy and activism, and
teaching, training, and curriculum development to challenge intolerance
and nurture culturally sensitive environments on the campus and in other
settings.

Given the growing consensus that multiculturalism must be engaged
intentionally, holistically, systemically, and at multiple levels and domains on the college campus (Grieger, 1996; Pope, 1993; Smith et al., 1997;
Stage & Hamrick, 1994), Grieger and Ponterotto's (1998) assertion that
"counselors, in particular, have a cluster of skills that are unique among

professionals" (p. 20) becomes particularly salient. Further, given the depth and breadth of findings and recommendations regarding what works to create truly diverse and multicultural campuses, the full range of counselor skills, competencies, and roles will need to be engaged.

PROMISING MULTICULTURAL
PRACTICES AND FINDINGS IN HIGHER EDUCATION

As was noted earlier, the most promising finding with regard to diversity on the predominantly White campus is that multicultural initiatives, when implemented effectively, have a positive effect on *all* students (Smith et al., 1997). These positive effects include higher levels of overall satisfaction with the institution, greater cultural awareness, higher levels of involvement, and increased levels of academic success and persistence (Astin, 1993a, 1993b; Helm, Sedlacek, & Prieto, 1998; Smith et al., 1997). Because of the significant, positive, multiple impacts of diversity initiatives on students, it is important to isolate those factors that are particularly salient.

It has been suggested that special-purpose institutions, such as historically Black colleges and universities, Native American Indian colleges, and women's colleges, serve their respective constituencies well and can serve as models of commitment to diversity (Boyer, 1997; Davis, 1994; Riordan, 1992). Among specific variables that contribute to the success of special-purpose institutions, researchers have identified the following: involvement with campus life, positive interactions with faculty, high academic expectations and support, a learning environment that builds self-efficacy, the presence of role models, and the linking of educational success to larger societal goals (Fleming, 1985; Smith, Wolf, & Morrison, 1995).

Research on the predominantly White campus has identified the following 12 variables as being particularly salient to enhancing institutional diversity:

1. A clearly articulated commitment to multiculturalism by the leadership of the institution and an emphasis on the centrality of diversity to the mission of the institution have been established (Barnhardt, 1994; Bensimon, 1995; Clewell & Ficklen, 1986; Richardson & Skinner, 1990a, 1990b; Thomas, 1997; Varlotta, 1997).

2. Multiculturalism and the commitment to the success of *all* students is a shared value across campus populations, including students, faculty, staff, and administrators (Deltz, 1992; Hurtado, Carter, & Spuler, 1996; Patterson-Stewart et al., 1997).

3. A diverse faculty and staff who serve as role models, mentors, and potential experts on diversity-related issues enjoy a visible presence on the campus (Astin, 1993a; Barnhardt, 1994; Bensimon, 1995; Smith et al., 1997; Thomas, 1997).

4. Diversity initiatives are not of a "one shot" haphazard nature; rather, they take place within a coherent framework of multicultural organizational development for institutional transformation. This includes assessment, simultaneous interventions on multiple levels (e.g., mission, policies, climate, curriculum reform, and representation), and outcomes research (Astin, 1993a; Bensimon, 1995; Richardson & Skinner, 1990a, 1990b; Smith et al., 1997; Thomas, 1997).

5. Multiculturally sensitive student services exist that competently address the needs of racial-ethnic minority, gay and lesbian, female, and other diverse student populations (Barnhardt, 1994; Clewell & Ficklen, 1986; Deltz, 1992; Nelson, 1994; Richardson & Skinner, 1990a; Thomas, 1997).

6. There is financial aid and other monetary support for the recruitment and retention of a diverse population of students, faculty, and staff (Barnhardt, 1994; Deltz, 1992; Nettles, 1990b; St. John, 1991; Thomas, 1997; Townsend, 1994).

7. Multiple and frequent opportunities exist for interaction, dialogue, contact, and collaboration among diverse student populations in the classroom, in cocurricular activities, and at social events (Astin, 1993a; Fischer & Hartmann, 1995; MacKay & Kuh, 1994; Newswanger, 1996; Pascarella, Edison, Nora, Hagedorn, & Terenzini, 1996; Smith et al., 1997; Thomas, 1997).

8. There are incentives and rewards for the implementation of faculty, staff, and curriculum multicultural development (Barnhardt, 1994; Clewell & Ficklen, 1986; Thomas, 1997).

9. Faculty actively engage issues of diversity in classroom discussions and across the curriculum (Astin, 1993a; Barnhardt, 1994; Bensimon, 1995; Musil, 1992; Smith et al., 1997; Townsend, 1994; Thomas, 1997).

10. Transition to college and first-year experiences that emphasize positive expectations for academic success are implemented for the retention of underrepresented student populations (Hummel, 1997; Hummel & Steele, 1996; "Retention Programs," 1994; Smith et al., 1997).

11. Mentoring programs are available on both undergraduate and graduate levels, which include student peers, faculty (including White faculty), and staff as mentors (Bell & Drakeford, 1992; Fleming, 1985; Fuertes, Cothran, & Sedlacek, 1991; Galbraith & Cohen, 1995; Patterson-Stewart et al., 1997; Smith et al., 1997; Thomas, 1997; Wunsch, 1994).

12. Issues relevant to (a) diversity, such as campus climate and minority student representation, (b) retention, and (c) success are assessed regularly; similarly, there is ongoing outcome research to empirically evaluate the impact of diversity initiatives (Banta, 1993; California Postsecondary Education Commission, 1992; Clewell & Ficklen, 1986; Nettles, 1990a; Sedlacek, 1994; Smith et al., 1997; Thomas, 1997).

Although providing multiculturally competent counseling and psychotherapy to all students is the most crucial and specialized role and function of the counselor, it should be clear from the forgoing review of the literature that much of what affects students' experience of diversity on the campus takes place outside the counseling session. It takes place in residence halls, in cocurricular activities, at social events, in the classroom, and as a result of students' interaction with peers, faculty, administrators, and others in their campus community. The research literature, thus, is confirmatory of the mandate for counselors on the predominantly White campus to invoke both conventional and nonconventional roles and to think holistically and systemically. Further, counselors must expand their own worldview to include not only the counseling perspective but also the perspectives, roles, and functions of other student affairs professionals, of administrators, and of faculty members.

To this end, the next section of this chapter focuses on specific strategies and rationales for implementing multicultural initiatives in the counseling center, the division of student affairs, the administration, and the curriculum and with the faculty.

IMPLEMENTING MULTICULTURAL INITIATIVES ACROSS THE PREDOMINANTLY WHITE CAMPUS

The Counseling Center

Providing effective and culturally sensitive counseling and psychotherapy to a diverse student population is the core mission of every college or university counseling center. Because of its mission, and because the predominantly White campus is in an ongoing process of change and flux with regard to the diversity of its student population, counselors in this setting are continuously called on to address new challenges and issues relevant to multiculturalism. As such, they carry a particular ethical responsibility with regard to their own ongoing professional development in the areas of operationalizing multicultural competencies, understanding racial/ethnic development, and keeping abreast of emerging models of multicultural counseling, training, supervision, assessment, and diagnosis. Although it is beyond the scope of this chapter to present each of these areas exhaustively, each is briefly touched upon, particularly as it relates to the role of the counseling center in creating a multicultural campus.

Specific delineations of multicultural competencies with regard to awareness, knowledge, and skills are well established in the counseling psychology literature, originating with the groundbreaking work of Sue, Arredondo, and McDavis (1992). These core competencies have been further operationalized and expounded on by these and other experts in the field, such that clear and accessible road maps exist for implementation by counselors (Arredondo et al., 1996; Ponterotto, Casas, Suzuki, & Alexander, 1995; Pope-Davis & Coleman, 1996; Sue et al., 1998).

Of equal salience for the counseling center practitioner is knowledge about and understanding of theories of racial identity development and their implications for overall mental health, the effectiveness of counseling, attitudes toward counseling, involvement in campus activities, racial polarization on the college campus, and career development (Cross, 1971,

1991, 1995; Delphin & Rollock, 1995; Helms, 1990, 1995; Helms & Carter, 1991; Jackson & Neville, 1998; Mitchell & Dell, 1992; Parham & Austin, 1994; Ponterotto, Anderson, & Grieger, 1986; Ponterotto, Fuertes, & Chen, 2000). In addition, Helms's interactional counseling model posits significant positive and negative impacts on the counseling relationship based on whether the counselor and the client are of a similar or dissimilar racial identity status (Carter, 1995; Helms, 1990, 1995).

Helms's interactional model is one of several emerging models that are adding depth, sophistication, and greater insight and complexity to our understanding of the process of multicultural counseling (see Fuertes & Gretchen, Chapter 27, this volume; Ponterotto et al., 2000). As noted above, Atkinson et al. (1993) posited a three-dimensional model of multicultural counseling, suggesting eight possible roles for the counselor, including change agent, adviser, psychotherapist, and consultant. The counselor's decision regarding which role would be most appropriate for a particular client is informed by the client's position on each of three dimensions: high or low level of *acculturation*, prevention or remediation as the *goal of helping*, and internal or external *locus of problem etiology*. This model has received initial empirical confirmatory support, and it appears to be quite applicable and useful for working with diverse client populations on the college campus (Atkinson, Kim, & Caldwell, 1998). Other promising emerging models for multicultural counseling include Leong's (1996) integrative model of cross-cultural counseling; Ridly, Mendoza, Kanitz, Angermeir, and Zenk's (1994) perceptual schematic model of cultural sensitivity; and Trevino's (1996) model of worldview and change.

In terms of psychotherapeutic orientation, behavioral, cognitive, and cognitive/behavioral therapy have long been regarded as useful and applicable for counseling women and persons of color (Casas, 1976; Grieger, 1982; Ponterotto et al., 1986). Of course, these approaches can only be effective when they are implemented after the worldview, level of acculturation, and other culturally relevant variables have been assessed (Atkinson et al., 1993; Grieger & Ponterotto, 1995). Currently, narrative therapy is emerging as a psychotherapeutic approach that appears to be very promising for working with diverse client populations (Semmier & Williams, 2000). Proponents of narrative therapy argue that as clients are encouraged to tell their own stories they maintain greater control over the counseling process and thus the impact of culture, bias, racism, and internalized racism can more readily emerge (Semmier & Williams, 2000). It can also be argued that narrative therapy may be a useful approach for clients dealing with homophobia, sexism, ageism, and other sociocultural biases. It should be noted, however, that multicultural research on the efficacy of narrative therapy is in its infancy. Nevertheless, because all of the approaches noted in this section are relatively short-term, as well as potentially multiculturally useful, they may be particularly relevant for use with diverse student populations at a college or university counseling center.

In addition to delineating specific multicultural competencies and conceptual models for providing culturally sensitive counseling, experts in the field have created an abundance of information to assist the counselor in gaining specific knowledge about particular student populations and their needs in the college environment and within the counseling center. Counselors thus have a wealth of relevant resources available to confront issues salient to diversity on the campus. Specifically, these issues include the following variables: racial/ethnic (Atkinson, Wampold, Lowe, Matthews, & Ahn, 1998; Barnhardt, 1994; Delphin & Rollock, 1995; Fuertes, Cothran, & Sedlacek, 1991; Gloria & Rodriguez, 2000; McNeil, Kee, & Zwolensky, 1999; Nelson, 1994), gender (Enns, 2000; Farmer, 1997; Jones, 1997), sexual orientation (D'Augelli, 1992; Fassinger, 2000; Slater, 1993), social class (Fouad & Brown, 2000), physical and learning disabilities (West et al., 1993), and the returning adult student (Hill, Thorn, & Packard, 2000; Luzzo, 1999).

Just as counseling center staff have a responsibility to further their own professional multicultural development, they carry an equal responsibility to provide multicultural training to all practicum students and interns at their site (Grieger, 1996; Ponterotto, Alexander, & Grieger, 1995). This training must address awareness, knowledge, and skills, and it must contain experiential/affective and didactic domains (Arredondo et al., 1996; Sue et al., 1992; Sue et al., 1998) as well as a wide range of diversity-related issues including race, ethnicity, gender, sexual orientation, religion, age, and ableism (Ancis & Sanchez-Hucles, 2000; Grieger, 1996; Pope, 1993).

In addition, ethical guidelines and standards for diverse populations should be presented annually, and emerging models, trends, and empirical data should be incorporated into multicultural training on a regular basis. Similarly, trainees should be encouraged to incorporate culturally relevant data into their case presentations and discussions, and each trainee should be encouraged to work with as diverse a client population as possible. In short, a college or university counseling center training site cannot view itself as meeting the challenge of producing competent clinicians unless multicultural issues are addressed coherently, sequentially, affectively, and continuously.

Another important aspect of the on-site training program is the provision of culturally sensitive clinical supervision. The relative safety of the one-on-one supervisory relationship can be viewed as a particularly valuable and productive forum in which to deepen and extend the multicultural training process. In the context of supervision, supervisees can confront their own biases, beliefs, and attitudes as countertransferential issues, more fully explore the impact of cultural variables in the counseling dyad, and enhance their own repertoire of multicultural skills. Supervisors are also called on to continuously confront their own cultural belief system and to be aware of how their worldview impinges on the supervision process (Brown & Lundrum-Brown, 1996; Chen, Chapter 38, this volume; D'Andrea & Daniels, 1997).

Counselors on predominantly White campuses must also be aware of the cultural biases inherent in traditional instruments used to assess personality and intelligence (Helms, 1992; LePage-Luis, 1997; Paniagua, 1994; Suzuki & Kugler, 1995) as well as cultural and gender biases that may be inherent in some diagnostic categories in *DSM-IV* (American Psychiatric Association, 1994). College and university counseling centers often enjoy greater flexibility with regard to assessment and diagnosis than do other, more bureaucratic agencies. As such, they have the freedom to use more culturally relevant frameworks and models for assessment, case conceptualization, and diagnosis. These should include considerations of worldview, level of acculturation, racial/ethnic identity development, emotional intelligence, language dominance, and the equivalency of psychological constructs in the client's culture (Grieger & Ponterotto, 1995; LePage-Luis, 1997; Suzuki & Kugler, 1995).

Other important multicultural roles and functions of the counseling center on a predominantly White campus include the following: providing crisis intervention and debriefing following a bias incident; offering psychoeducational programming for a diverse student population; assessing and addressing the level of utilization (or underutilization) of counseling services by underrepresented student populations; using multicultural competency as a criterion for hiring, promoting, and/or retaining staff; and engaging in scholarly research and presentations regarding diversity on the college campus. Finally, the counseling center itself must be a model of diversity. Its commitment to multiculturalism should be reflected in its mission statement, in its demographic composition, in the artwork it displays, in its written materials, and in all its policies and procedures (Grieger, 1996).

The Division of Student Affairs

Multicultural organizational development (MOD) has been proposed by Pope (1993) as a particularly useful and effective strategy for multicultural transformation in student affairs. Drawing on the seminal writings of Pope (1993) and Sue (1995), Grieger (1996) has created the Multicultural Organizational Development Checklist (MODC) as a road map for the long-term, multilayered, systemic change process for divisions of student affairs. Counselors can serve as organizational consultants and institutional change agents to divisions of student affairs that are committed to moving along a continuum from being monocultural and merely compliant to being truly multicultural.

Based on the multicultural literature, Grieger (1996) suggested 11 categories as levels of targeted change (e.g., mission, leadership and advocacy, policies, recruitment and retention, multicultural competency training, and student activities and services) and 58 specific criteria that should be met across all levels. Some of the specific strategies and interventions in which counselors can engage to facilitate MOD in the division of student affairs are as follows:

- Advocate for centrality of diversity in the mission and goals of the division and of each office within the division.
- Ensure that the student code of conduct reflects a zero-tolerance policy with regard to engaging in racist, sexist, homophobic, or otherwise intolerant behavior.
- Encourage the recruitment, retention, and promotion of women and persons of color to positions of leadership within the division.
- Educate other student affairs professionals with regard to effective strategies for retaining underrepresented student populations (e.g., mentoring, role models, special services, and transition programs).
- Create multiple and ongoing opportunities for cross-cultural interaction and dialogue among diverse student groups.
- Support and attend diversity-positive campus events.
- Consult with other departments in student affairs (e.g., career planning and placement, residential life, campus ministries, student health, campus safety and security, financial aid, and student retention) in their efforts to create student services that are fully responsive to a diverse student population.
- Advocate for establishing multicultural competency as a criterion of hiring, evaluation, and/or rewarding professional staff within the division.
- Assist other student affairs professionals and student groups in planning and presenting multicultural programs.
- Assist in the delineation of specific multicultural competencies for staff and paraprofessionals (e.g., resident advisers, campus ministers, peer educators, and peer mentors).
- Train student affairs staff and paraprofessionals in multicultural competencies appropriate to their role and function.
- Participate in the assessment and evaluation of diversity efforts within the division with regard to multicultural competency training.

Counselors should be aware that Pope and Reynolds (1997) have delineated core competencies for student affairs professionals, which can serve as a valuable resource for informing the training function. Specific core competencies proposed by Pope and Reynolds (1997) include awareness of one's own biases and assumptions; acceptance of other worldviews and perspectives; knowledge about the impact of diversity-related variables such as race, ethnicity, gender, sexual orientation, age, religion, and ability; knowledge about diverse cultures and about racial/ethnic and other identity development models for underrepresented groups; and the ability to use multicultural knowledge to make culturally appropriate interventions.

With regard to the evaluation of multicultural initiatives in student affairs, counselors should take note of the Multicultural Assessment of

Campus Programming (MAC-P) Questionnaire developed by McClellan, Cogdal, Lease, and Londoño-McConnell (1999), which has received initial empirical validation. Counselors should also be aware of an excellent resource for students titled *How to Succeed on a Majority Campus: A Guide for Minority Students* (Levey, Blanco, & Jones, 1998).

Campus Administration

Just as "it takes a village to raise a child," similarly it takes an entire campus community to educate, support, empower, and nurture a diverse student population. As already noted (Musil et al., 1995; Smith et al., 1997; Thomas, 1997), predominantly White campuses have not been exemplary in creating culturally sensitive and/or success-enhancing environments for underrepresented or oppressed student cohorts. Also noted repeatedly in the literatures of counseling psychology (Sue, 1995; Sue et al., 1998), student affairs (Grieger, 1996; McEwen & Roper, 1994; Pope, 1993), higher education (Smith et al., 1997), and corporate management (Arredondo, 1996; Sue, 1995; Toliver, 1998) is that fragmented, incoherent, and nonsystemic diversity efforts are not effective in creating and maintaining multicultural institutions.

It has been argued that MOD "represents the highest evolution of 'counselor as an agent of change,' and that counselors, in particular, are the professionals within an organization who have the constellation of skills needed to initiate and to implement this complex multidimensional system for change" (Grieger & Ponterotto, 1998, p. 24).

However, regardless of the counselor's expertise in MOD, it is impossible for an institutionwide, long-term strategic initiative to be implemented without the leadership, or the upper-echelon administrators, on board. Especially on the predominantly White campus, counselors are the most likely professionals to have the requisite knowledge and skills base to serve as "provocateurs" and advocates to challenge, educate, and motivate upper-echelon campus administrators to engage in large-scale diversity efforts.

On a logistical note, it may, however, not be feasible or advisable for the counselor to actually oversee and manage the MOD process for a number of reasons: (a) MOD is a complex and labor-intensive process that requires full-time attention and commitment; (b) "outside consultants" often have more credibility than do professionals within an organization; (c) at some colleges and universities, tension, distrust, and/or competition exist between student affairs professionals and the faculty; and (d) it may be politically and professionally risky for the counselor to be the identified manager of MOD on the campus, in that others may view him or her as a "troublemaker" (Lee, 1998).

Nevertheless, even given these considerations, at the very least counselors have an ethical obligation to assertively and continuously raise issues relevant to diversity with college administrators and to encourage systemic change. Examples of specific diversity-positive strategies that counselors can engage in vis-à-vis the campus administration are as follows:

- Encourage the promulgation of an institutional mission/vision that places multiculturalism at its core (Thomas, 1997).
- Initiate and/or serve on administration task forces and committees that address multiculturalism.
- Given the bias inherent in standardized assessment instruments used for admissions, advocate for the consideration of other criteria, including those that are noncognitive (House, 1996; Lemann, 1999; Sedlacek, 1993).
- Serve on search committees to encourage the recruitment of a diverse faculty and professional staff.
- Participate in promulgating campus policies that are diversity positive.
- Advocate for the equitable distribution of resources (monies, facilities, spaces, and personnel) to underrepresented student populations and concerns.
- Educate administrators about the needs of a diverse student population with regard to student services, cocurricular activities, the curriculum, and the need for role models.
- Advocate for the promotion of women and underrepresented populations to positions of leadership.
- Encourage the campus administration in developing a zero-tolerance stance toward any form of bias incident, harassment, or discrimination on campus.
- Advocate for campuswide competency-based diversity training.
- Advocate for empirical assessment and evaluation of diversity initiatives.
- Encourage upper-echelon administrators to provide the motivators and incentives necessary for faculty, staff, and other administrators to engage in multicultural initiatives (Barnhardt, 1994; Thomas, 1997).

It should be clear from the delineation of counselor roles across the institution that counselors on the predominantly White campus should become knowledgeable about institutional change mechanisms, especially MOD. Helpful resources that the counselor can consult include Arredondo (1996), Sue (1996), Grieger and Ponterotto (1998), and Grieger (1996).

In the remainder of this section, we turn our attention to the academic "side" of the institution, focusing on curriculum reform and faculty development with regard to multiculturalism.

Faculty and Curriculum

Whether the counselor's formal role on the predominantly White campus is one of mental health service provider within the counseling center, or whether it is one of instructor/faculty member, or a combination of both, it is incumbent upon the counselor to fully appreciate the centrality of faculty and curriculum to the mission of the institution both in terms of education within the disciplines and infusing multiculturalism across the institution.

Because interaction with faculty in the classroom is the prime activity in which all students must participate, curriculum and faculty development become key factors in any diversity effort. Typically, students can choose not to participate in cocurricular activities or in counseling, but they cannot avoid contact with the curriculum or with faculty. This holds true for undergraduate and graduate populations, for adult and traditional age populations, and even for distance learners.

Therefore, focusing on the curriculum and faculty development is essential in assuring continuity with, and the success of, diversity efforts across the campus. Furthermore, as noted earlier, counselors need to understand the nuances of multicultural diversity in all areas of the campus, perhaps especially regarding curriculum and faculty, if they are to work collaboratively and effectively with the institution's major stakeholders.

Four areas of focus addressed in this discussion of faculty and curriculum diversity are curriculum transformation, pedagogy and learning styles, faculty development, and sustaining faculty commitment and curricular change. Each of these four areas is discussed in turn.

Curriculum Transformation

Any movement toward diversity within the institution must integrate diversity at its core: the curriculum. The reasons for a diverse curriculum are several and compelling. First, colleges and universities should be on the cutting edge in terms of both the creation and the dissemination of knowledge; therefore, the new research on people of color, women, and other diverse populations must have a primal place on the campus. Second, as noted earlier, the role of higher education is to fully prepare students for the world in which they will live in every respect, including their being knowledgeable about the experiences, contributions, and perspectives of those from whom they are different. Third, much, if not most, of student training and preparation to competently inhabit increasingly diverse environments must take place in the classroom because that is when students are required to spend most of their time on campus.

Efforts to transform the curriculum must necessarily include the following:

- Infusing diversity throughout the syllabus rather than merely taking an "add on" approach or including previously excluded groups as a special topic
- Including diversity of many types: by race, ethnicity, social class, gender, difference in ability, and sexual orientation; these elements of identity should be presented as constructs that are interrelated

- Presenting elements of diversity when addressing any social group, not only persons of color; all groups are affected by race, gender, class, sexual orientation, ability, age, and other diversity-related variables
- Teaching about diversity not only in the context of social problems, such as poverty or crime, because that approach can perpetuate negative stereotypes
- Using textbooks that are inclusive with regard to the contributions of women and persons of color and that explicably engage issues of diversity as appropriate to your discipline
- When textbooks fail to fully engage diversity as appropriate to your discipline, explicitly pointing that out to students and filling in the gaps
- Developing curricula that reflect race, gender, and class as *major* themes that undergird our society, our culture, and our self-identities; to neglect these basic factors amounts to a major omission in what we teach across disciplines
- Not reinforcing prejudice by showing minorities in a primarily pejorative light
- In *every* discipline, including the contributions of women and persons of color

(For further discussion, see Collins & Andersen, 1987, and Friedman, Kolmar, Flint, & Rothenberg, 1996.)

Pedagogy and Learning Styles

How faculty deliver the message and actively engage students in the learning process matters immensely. The following are some suggestions for what to do, as well as some pitfalls to avoid:

- Use nonsexist language.
- Give equal time; empower all students to participate in classroom discussions and other activities at a level at which they are comfortable.
- At the same time, understand that factors related to culture, gender, physical challenges, and other variables may inhibit active verbal participation by some students (e.g., traditional cultural gender roles, being the only member of a particular group, and cultural constructs of relating to authority).
- Do not assume a universal, monocultural perspective; challenge the status quo by including a variety of cultural examples and perspectives.
- Vary classroom pedagogy regarding teaching/learning methodologies; appeal to different learning styles. Use the Socratic method, students-as-teachers, group work, learning by doing, seeing, and hearing. Appreciate that cultural factors may impact students' learning style and other in-class behaviors.
- Don't reinforce stereotypes. Take care that classroom behaviors, perspectives, and curriculum do not maintain status quo inequalities and biases.
- View multiculturalism as a critical skill on par with writing, thinking, and speaking in terms of defining what it means to be an educated person in a new tradition of liberal arts education.

- Create opportunities in your classroom for cross-cultural dialogue and interaction.
- Create assignments and exercises that ask students to take on a different worldview.
- Create assignments that encourage students to learn more about the contributions of women and persons of color to your discipline.
- Serve as a mentor to students of underrepresented student populations.
- Set high expectations for success in your classroom for *all* students.

Faculty Development

In a very real sense, creating a multicultural institution is about engaging in the praxis of undoing the 500-year-old hegemony of Western civilization with its elements of White racial and male superiority (see Butler & Walter, 1991). Because of this lengthy historical precedent, faculty development needs to be a long-term, ongoing process. Most of today's faculty were trained in the context of noninclusive environments, pedagogies, and curriculum. U.S.-born faculty have been socialized in a culture reflective of this monocultural hegemony. The undoing of the legacies of higher learning will require time, energy, hard work, and a shift in paradigm. The following items provide some sense of the areas for consideration for faculty development and diversity:

- Recognizing that the process of developing multicultural competencies is ongoing and long-term
- Recognizing and addressing one's own biases, prejudices, and assumptions
- Understanding where faculty, as individuals, stand with regard to how one benefits or loses because of one's own race, class, gender identity, and privileged or nonprivileged status
- Creating and participating in development seminars to learn the "how to's" of multiculturalism; there are many useful models—those at Hunter College of CUNY, the New Jersey Department of Higher Education, Memphis State University, University of Illinois at Chicago, and others
- Creating and participating in academic year ongoing and occasional workshops, summer programs, off-campus opportunities such as seminars, conferences, and sabbaticals, and negotiating release time for multicultural professional development
- Reflecting diversity in one's own scholarship—alternative perspectives, methodologies, and topics for research
- Recognizing barriers within the faculty to engaging diversity and addressing them—for example, lack of time, feeling unempowered, a sense of not knowing how, lacking resource materials, and not seeing the relevance to their particular discipline (sociology, sure, but math?); breaking old habits is very difficult
- Knowing that faculty development involves consciousness raising regarding the importance of diversity, why we need to do it, and how self and others are located regarding our diverse statuses in U.S. society and beyond

- Arming committed faculty to deal with external resistance from the administration, other faculty, students, and external constituencies in the larger community

Sustaining Faculty Commitment and Curricular Change

The following elements must be present to insure that faculty commitment to diversity and to curriculum transformation become institutionalized:

- A commitment to and a directive about diversity from top administrators, including academic deans, at the institution
- An institutional commitment to the continuing education, development, and consciousness raising of the president and other key administrators about why diversity is critically important; appreciating the depth and complexity of institutional transformation
- Diversity as a priority element in the campus strategic master plan
- Funding diversity as a regular and ongoing institutional (and/or by major offices) budget item
- Rewarding faculty for engaging diversity
- Working with those faculty most easy to "convert" first; moving toward those most resistant later
- Developing ongoing systems of continuing faculty education
- Creating support-in-diversity groups/mechanisms
- Integrating diversity throughout the campus

Efforts to sustain lasting change in academic affairs are as important as those that initiate the process of change. While diversity in the classroom and curriculum must flow from the energies and efforts of the faculty, a directive from the top and a commitment from all significant campus leaders is essential in moving toward institutional transformation. In general, the path of MOD involves a reciprocal flow of initiatives from chief administrator to faculty, to student affairs professionals and beyond. Then, and only then, can the efforts of the counselor and other professionals toward change across the institution be optimally effective.

In the final section of this chapter, we conclude by summarizing our key recommendations for creating and sustaining multicultural communities on the predominantly White campus.

SUMMARY AND CONCLUSION

In this chapter, we argued that multicultural efforts on the predominantly White campus have positive effects on *all* students. We also contended that counselors must assume multiple roles on the campus, including mental health service provider, consultant, change agent, advocate, collaborator, and teacher, in order to implement multicultural change across the institution. Throughout, we offered specific strategies and recommendations regarding targets of multicultural interventions, which include the counseling center, the division of student affairs, the campus administration, and the faculty.

We conclude by offering recommendations based on what we believe are the most critical variables for the effective and sustained implementation of multiculturalism on the predominantly White campus. They are as follows:

1. A holistic diversity model, such as multicultural organizational development (MOD), involving a systemic, coherent, multilayered change effort, should be implemented.

2. Multiculturalism and diversity must be institutionalized, that is, central to the core mission, fully funded, and reflected in the demographic composition of its various constituencies, in its policies and procedures, and pervading its culture as an institution.

3. Commitment to diversity efforts must be fully supported and embraced at the top of the administrative hierarchy.

4. Multiple and ongoing opportunities should exist for students to engage in cross-cultural interaction in a variety of settings, such as residence halls, cocurricular activities, workshops, clubs and organizations, and, especially, the classroom.

5. Mentoring, bridge and first-year-experience programs, role models, high expectations for academic success, and culturally responsive student services should be developed to create a campus environment that is hospitable and empowering to underrepresented student cohorts.

6. Both student affairs professionals and faculty must be fully engaged in campus diversity efforts and must work collaboratively to implement diversity initiatives across the institution.

REFERENCES

Alford, S. M. (2000). A qualitative study of the college social adjustment of Black students from lower socioeconomic communities. *Journal of Multicultural Counseling and Development, 78,* 2-15.

American Psychiatric Association. (1994). *Diagnostic and statistical manual of mental disorders* (4th ed.) Washington, DC: Author.

American Psychological Association. (1993). Guidelines for providers of psychological services to ethnic, linguistic, and culturally diverse populations. *American Psychologist, 48,* 45-48.

Ancis, J. R., & Sanchez-Hucles, J. V. (2000). A preliminary analysis of students' attitudes toward counseling women and women of color: Implications for cultural competency training. *Journal of Multicultural Counseling and Development, 78,* 16-31.

Ancis, J. R., Sedlacek, W. E., & Mohr, J. J. (2000). Student perceptions of campus cultural climate by race. *Journal of Counseling and Development, 78,* 180-185.

Appel, M., Cartwright, D., Smith, D. G., & Wolf, L. E. (1996). *The impact of diversity on students: A preliminary review of the research literature.* Washington, DC: Association of American Colleges and Universities.

Arredondo, P. (1996). *Successful diversity management initiatives: A blueprint for planning and implementation.* Thousand Oaks, CA: Sage.

Arredondo, P. Toporek, R., Brown, S. P., Jones, J., Locke, D. C., Sanchez, J., & Stadler, H. (1996). Operationalization of the multicultural competencies. *Journal of Multicultural Counseling and Development, 24,* 42-78.

Astin, A. W. (1993a). Diversity and multiculturalism on campus: How are students affected? *Change, 25,* 44-49.

Astin, A. W. (1993b). *What matters in college? Four critical years revisited.* San Francisco: Jossey-Bass.

Atkinson, D. R., Kim, B. S. K., & Caldwell, R. (1998). Ratios of helper roles by multicultural psychologist and Asian-American students: Initial support for the three-dimensional model of multicultural counseling. *Journal of Counseling Psychology, 45,* 414-423.

Atkinson, D. R., Thompson, C., & Grant, S. (1993). A three-dimensional model for counseling racial/ethnic minorities. *The Counseling Psychologist, 21,* 257-277.

Atkinson, D. R., Wampold, B. E., Lowe, S. M., Matthews, L., & Ahn, H. (1998). Asian American preferences for counselor characteristics: Application of the Bradley-Terry-Luce model to paired comparison data. *The Counseling Psychologist, 26,* 101-123.

Banta, T. W. (Ed.). (1993). *Making a difference: Outcomes of a decade of assessment in higher education.* San Francisco: Jossey-Bass.

Barnhardt, C. (1994). Life on the other side: Native student survival in a university world. *Peabody Journal of Education, 69,* 115-139.

Bell, E. D., & Drakeford, R. W. (1992). A case study of the Black student peer mentor program at the University of North Carolina Greensboro in Fall 1987. *College Student Journal, 126,* 81-386.

Bensimon, E. (1995). *Creating an institutional identity out of differences: A case study of multicultural organizational change.* University Park: Pennsylvania State University Press.

Boyer, P. (1997). *Native American colleges: Progress and prospects.* Princeton, NJ: Carnegie Foundation for the Advancement of Teaching.

Brown, M. T., & Landrum-Brown, J. (1996). Counselor supervision: Cross-cultural perspectives. In J. G. Ponterotto, J. M. Casas, L. A. Suzuki, & C. M. Alexander (Eds.), *Handbook of multicultural counseling* (pp. 263-286). Thousand Oaks, CA: Sage.

Butler, J. E., & Walter, J. C. (1991). Praxis and the prospect of curriculum transformation. In J. E. Butler & J. C. Walter (Eds.), *Transforming the curriculum* (pp. 325-330). Albany: State University of New York Press.

California Postsecondary Education Commission. (1992a). *Assessing campus climate: Feasibility of developing an educational equity assessment system* (Commission Report No. 92-2). Sacramento, CA: Author.

California Postsecondary Education Commission. (1992b). *Resource guide for assessing campus climate* (Commission Report No. 92-24). Sacramento, CA: Author.

Carter, D. J., & Wilson, R. (1994). *Minorities in higher education.* Washington, DC: American Council on Education.

Carter, R. T. (1995). *The influence of race and racial identity in psychotherapy: Toward a racially inclusive model.* New York: John Wiley.

Casas, J. M. (1976). Applicability of a behavioral model in serving the mental health needs of the Mexican-American. In M. R. Miranda (Ed.), *Psychotherapy with the Spanish speaking: Issues in research and service delivery* (pp. 61-65). Los Angeles: Spanish-Speaking Mental Health Resource Center.

Clewell, B. C., & Ficklen, M. S. (1986). *Improving minority retention in higher education: A search for effective institutional practices.* Princeton, NJ: Educational Testing Service.

Collins, P. H., & Andersen, M. L. (Eds). (1987). *An inclusive curriculum.* Washington, DC: American Sociological Association.

Cross, W. E. (1971). The Negro-to-Black conversion experience: Toward a psychology of Black liberation. *Black World, 20,* 13-27.

Cross, W. E. (1991). *Shades of Black: Diversity in African-American identity.* Philadelphia: Temple University Press.

844   COUNSELOR SUPERVISION/HIGHER EDUCATION ISSUES

Cross, W. E. (1995). The psychology of nigresence: Revising the Cross model. In J. G. Ponterotto, J. M. Casas, L. A. Suzuki, & C. M. Alexander (Eds.), *Handbook of multicultural counseling* (pp. 93-122). Thousand Oaks, CA: Sage.

D'Andrea, M., & Daniels, J. (1997). Multicultural supervision: Central issues, theoretical considerations, and practical strategies. In D. B. Pope-Davis & H. J. Coleman (Eds.), *Multicultural counseling competencies: Assessment, education and training, and supervision* (pp. 290-309). Thousand Oaks, CA: Sage.

D'Augelli, A. R. (1992). Lesbian and gay male undergraduates' experiences of harassment and fear on campus. *Journal of Interpersonal Violence, 1*, 383-395.

Davis, J. (1994). College in Black and White: Campus environment and academic achievement of African American males. *Journal of Negro Education, 62*, 67-79.

Delphin, M. E., & Rollock, D. (1995). University alienation and African American ethnic identity as predictions of attitudes toward, knowledge about, and likely use of, psychological services. *Journal of College Student Development, 36*, 337-346.

Deltz, R. (1992). A blueprint for Hispanic student success. *Outlook in Higher Education, 2*, 5-8.

Dovidio, J. (1997, July 25). "Aversive" racism and the need for affirmative action. *Chronicle of Higher Education*, p. A60.

D'Souza, D. (1991). *Illiberal education: The politics of race and sex on campus*. New York: Free Press.

Ehrlich, H. J. (1990). *Campus ethnoviolence and the policy options*. Baltimore: National Institute Against Prejudice and Violence.

Enns, C. Z. (2000). Gender issues in counseling. In S. D. Brown & R. W. Lent (Eds.), *Handbook of counseling psychology* (3rd ed., pp. 601-638). New York: John Wiley.

Farmer, H. S. (Ed.). (1997). *Diversity and women's career development: From adolescence to adulthood*. Thousand Oaks, CA: Sage.

Farrell, W. C., Jr., & Jones, C. K. (1988). Recent racial incidents in higher education: A preliminary perspective. *Urban Review, 20*, 211-226.

Fassinger, R. E. (2000). Gender and sexuality in human development: Implications for prevention and advocacy in counseling psychology. In S. D. Brown & R. W. Lent (Eds.), *Handbook of counseling psychology* (3rd ed., pp. 346-378). New York: John Wiley.

Fischer, B., & Hartmann, D. (1995). The impact of race on the social experience of college students at a predominantly White university. *Journal of Black Studies, 26*, 117-133.

Fleming, J. (1985). *Blacks in college: A comparative study of students' success in Black and White institutions*. San Francisco: Jossey-Bass.

Fouad, N. A., & Brown, M. T. (2000). Role of peace and social class in development: Implications for counseling psychology. In S. D. Brown & R. W. Lendt (Eds.), *Handbook of counseling psychology* (3rd ed., pp. 379-408). New York: John Wiley.

Friedman, E. G., Kolmar, W. K., Flint, C. B., & Rothenberg, P. (Eds.). (1996). *Creating an inclusive college curriculum*. New York: Teachers College Press.

Fuertes, J. N., Cothran, M., & Sedlacek, W. E. (1991). A model for increasing Hispanic involvement on U.S. campuses. *College Student Affairs Journal, 11*, 11-15.

Galbraith, M. W., & Cohen, H. (1995). *Mentoring: New strategies and challenges*. San Francisco: Jossey-Bass.

Gloria, A. M., & Rodriguez, E. R. (2000). Counseling Latino university students: Psychosociocultural issues for consideration. *Journal of Counseling and Development, 78*, 145-154.

Grieger, I. (1982). The cognitive basis of women's problems. In R. Grieger & I. Grieger (Eds.), *Cognition and emotional disturbance* (pp. 197-211). New York: Human Sciences Press.

Grieger, I. (1996). A multicultural organizational development checklist for student affairs. *Journal of College Student Development, 37*, 561-573.

Grieger, I., & Ponterotto, J. G. (1995). A framework for assessment in multicultural counseling. In J. G. Ponterotto, J. M. Casas, L. A. Suzuki, & C. M. Alexander (Eds.), *Handbook of multicultural counseling* (pp. 357-374). Thousand Oaks, CA: Sage

Grieger, I., & Ponterotto, J. G. (1998). Challenging intolerance. In C. C. Lee & G. R. Walz (Eds.), *Social action: A mandate for counselors* (pp. 17-50). Alexandria, VA: American Counseling Association and ERIC Counseling and Student Services Clearinghouse.

Healy, P. (1998, May 29). Berkeley struggles to stay diverse in post affirmative action era. *Chronicle of Higher Education*, pp. A3, A32-A33.

Helm, E. G., Sedlacek, W. E., & Prieto, D. O. (1998). The relationship between attitudes toward diversity and overall satisfaction of university students by race. *Journal of College Counseling, 11*, 111-120.

Helms, J. E. (Ed.). (1990). *Black and White racial identity: Theory, research and practice.* Westport, CT: Greenwood.

Helms, J. E. (1992). Why is there no study of cultural equivalence in standardized cognitive ability testing? *American Psychologist, 47*, 1083-1101.

Helms, J. E. (1995). An update of Helms' White and people of color racial identity models. In J. G. Ponterotto, J. M. Casas, L. A. Suzuki, & C. M. Alexander (Eds.), *Handbook of multicultural counseling* (pp. 181-198). Thousand Oaks, CA: Sage.

Helms, J. E., & Carter, R. T. (1991). Relationships of White and Black racial identity attitudes and demographic similarity to counselor preferences. *Journal of Counseling Psychology, 38*, 446-457.

Herek, G. M. (1993). Documenting prejudice against lesbians and gay men on campus: The Yale sexual orientation survey. *Journal of Homosexuality, 25*, 15-31.

Hill, R. D., Thorn, B. L., & Packard, T. (2000). Counseling older adults: Theoretical and end empirical issues in prevention and intervention. In S. D. Brown & R. W. Lent (Eds.), *Handbook of counseling psychology* (3rd ed., pp. 449-531). New York: John Wiley.

House, J. D. (1996). *College persistence and grade outcomes: Noncognitive variables as predictors for African-American, Asian-American, Hispanic, Native American, and White students.* Paper presented at the Association for Institutional Research Annual Forum.

Hummel, M. L. (1997). Eliminating the achievement gap: The 21st century program. *About Campus, 1*, 28-29.

Hummel, M. L., & Steele, C. (1996). The learning community: A program to address issues of academic achievement and retention. *Journal of Intergroup Relations, 23*, 28-33.

Hurtado, S., Carter, D. F., & Spuler, A. (1996). Latino student transition to college: Assessing difficulties and factors in successful college adjustment. *Research in Higher Education, 37*, 135-157.

Jackson, C. C., & Neville, H. (1998). Influence of racial identity models on African American college students' vocational identity and hope. *Journal of Vocational Behavior, 53*, 97-113.

Jones, S. R. (1997). Voices of identity and difference: A qualitative exploration of the multiple dimensions of identity development in women college students. *Journal of College Student Development, 38*, 376-385.

Lee, C. C. (1998). Counselors as agents of social change. In C. C. Lee & G. R. Walz (Eds.), *Social action: A mandate for counselors* (pp. 3-14). Alexandria, VA: American Counseling Association and ERIC Counseling and Student Services Clearinghouse.

Lemann, N. (1999). *The big test: The secret history of the American meritocracy.* New York: Farrow, Straus & Giroux.

Leong, F. T. L. (1996). Toward an integrative model for cross-cultural counseling and psychotherapy. *Applied and Preventive Psychology: Current Scientific Perspectives, 5*, 189-209.

LePage-Luis, P. (1997). Exploring patterns of achievement and intellectual development among academically successful women from disadvantaged backgrounds. *Journal of College Student Development, 38*, 468-478.

Levey, M., Blanco, M. W., & Jones, T. (1998). *How to succeed on a majority campus: A guide for minority students.* Belmont, CA: Wadsworth.

Loo, C. M., & Rolison, G. (1986). Alienation of ethnic students at a predominantly White university. *Journal of Higher Education, 57*, 58-77.

Luzzo, D. A. (1999). Identifying career decision-making needs of nontraditional college students. *Journal of Counseling and Development, 77*, 135-140.

MacKay, K., & Kuh, G. (1994). A comparison of student effort and educational gains of Caucasian and African American students at predominantly White colleges and universities. *Journal of College Student Development, 35*, 217-223.

McClellan, S. A., Cogdal, P. A., Lease, S. H., & Londoño-McConnell, A. (1996). Development of the multicultural assessment of campus programming (MAC-P) questionnaire. *Measurement and Evaluation in Counseling and Development, 29*, 86-99.

McEwen, M. K., & Roper, L. D. (1994). Incorporating multiculturalism into student affairs preparation. *Journal of College Student Development, 35*, 46-53.

McNeil, D. W., Kee, M., & Zwolensky, M. J. (1999). Culturally related anxiety and ethnic identity in Navajo college students. *Cultural Diversity and Ethnic Minority Psychology, 5*, 56-64.

Mitchell, S. L., & Dell, D. M. (1992). The relationship between Black students' racial identity attitudes and participation in campus organizations. *Journal of College Student Development, 33*, 39-43.

Musil, C. M. (Ed.). (1992). *The courage to question: Women's studies and student learning.* Washington, DC: Association of American Colleges. ERIC, ED 347890.

Musil, C. M., Garcia, M., Moses, Y. T., & Smith, D. G. (1995). *Diversity in higher education: A work in progress.* Washington, DC: Association of American Colleges and Universities.

National Association of Independent Colleges and Universities and National Institute of Independent Colleges and Universities. (1991). *Understanding campus climate* (ERIC Document No. ED 342-864). Washington, DC: ERIC Clearing House.

National Center for Education Statistics, U.S. Department of Education. (1997). *Digest of Education Statistics, 304.*

Nelson, W. (1994). Receptivity to institutional assistance: An important variable for African American and Mexican American student achievement. *Journal of College Student Development, 35*, 378-384.

Nettles, M. T. (Ed.). (1990a). *The effect of assessment on minority student participation.* San Francisco: Jossey-Bass.

Nettles, M. T. (1990b). Success in doctoral programs: Experiences of minority and White students. *American Journal of Education, 98*, 494-521.

Nettles, M. T. (1994). *Student achievement and success after enrolling in undergraduate public colleges and universities in selected southern states.* Commissioned paper, Southern Education Foundation, Atlanta.

Newswanger, J. F. (1996). The relationship between White racial identity attitudes and the experience of having a Black college roommate. *Journal of College Student Development, 37*, 536-541.

Nixon, H. L., & Henry, W. J. (1992). White students at the Black university: Their experiences regarding acts of racial intolerance. *Equity and Excellence, 25*, 121-123.

Paniagua, F. A. (1994). *Assessing and treating culturally diverse clients: A practical guide.* Thousand Oaks, CA: Sage.

Parham, T. A., & Austin, N. L. (1994). Career development and African Americans: A contextual reappraisal using the nigrescence construct. *Journal of Vocational Behavior, 44*, 139-1454.

Pascarella, E. T., Edison, M. I., Nora, A., Hagedorn, S., & Terenzini, P. T. (1996). Influences on students' openness to diversity and challenge in the first year of college. *Journal of Higher Education, 67*, 174-195.

Patterson-Stewart, K. E., Ritchie, M. H., & Sanders, E. T. W. (1997). Interpersonal dynamics of African-American persistence in doctoral programs at predominantly White universities. *Journal of College Student Development, 38*, 489-498.

Ponterotto, J. G., Anderson, W. H., & Grieger, I. (1986). Black students' attitudes toward counseling as a function of racial identity. *Journal of Multicultural Counseling and Development, 14*, 50-59.

Ponterotto, J. G., Alexander, C. M., & Grieger, I. (1995). A multicultural competency checklist for counseling training programs. *Journal of Multicultural Counseling and Development, 23*, 11-20.

Ponterotto, J. G., Casas, J. M., Suzuki, L. A., & Alexander, C. M. (Eds.). (1995). *Handbook of multicultural counseling.* Thousand Oaks, CA: Sage.

Ponterotto, J. G., Fuertes, J. N., & Chen, E. C. (2000). Models of multicultural counseling. In S. D. Brown & R. W. Lent (Eds.), *Handbook of counseling psychology* (3rd ed., pp. 639-669). New York: John Wiley.

Pope, R. L. (1993). Multicultural organization development in student affairs: An introduction. *Journal of College Student Development, 34,* 201-205.

Pope, R. L., & Reynolds, A. L. (1997). Student affairs core competencies: Integrating multicultural awareness, knowledge and skills. *Journal of College Student Development, 38,* 266-275.

Pope-Davis, D. B., & Coleman, H. K. (Eds.). (1996). *Multicultural counseling competencies: Assessment, education and training, and supervision.* Thousand Oaks, CA: Sage.

Retention programs: A bridge to success for at-risk students. (1994). *Journal of Developmental Education, 17,* Special issue.

Reyes, M., & Halcon, J. J. (1990). Racism in academia. In N. M. Hidalgo, C. L. McDowell, & E. V. Siddle (Eds.), *Facing racism in education* (pp. 69-83). Cambridge, MA: Harvard Education Review.

Richardson, R. C., Jr., & Skinner, E. F. (1990a). *Achieving quality and diversity: Universities in a multicultural society.* New York: Macmillan.

Richardson, R. C., Jr., & Skinner, E. F. (1990b). Adapting to diversity: Organizational influences on student achievement. *Journal of Higher Education, 61,* 485-511.

Ridly, C. R., Mendoza, D. M., Kanitz, B. E., Angermeir, L., & Zenk, R. (1994). Cultural sensitivity in multicultural counseling: A perceptual schema model. *Journal of Counseling Psychology, 41,* 125-136.

Riordan, C. (1992). Single and mixed-gender colleges for women: Educational, attitudinal and occupational outcomes. *Review of Higher Education, 15,* 327-346.

St. John, E. P. (1991). The impact of student financial aid: A review of the recent research. *Journal of Student Financial Aid, 21,* 18-32.

Schwitzer, A. M., Griffin, O. T., Ancis, J. R., & Thomas, C. R. (1999). Social adjustment experiences of African-American college students. *Journal of Counseling and Development, 77,* 189-197.

Sedlacek, W. E. (1993). Employing non-cognitive variables in admissions and retention in higher education. In *Achieving diversity: Issues in the recruitment and retention of underrepresented racial/ethnic students in higher education* (pp. 33-39). Alexandria, VA: National Association of College Admission Counselors.

Sedlacck, W. E. (1994). Issues in advancing diversity through assessment. *Journal of Counseling and Development, 72,* 549-553.

Sedlacek, W. E. (1998). Strategies for social change research. In C. C. Lee & G. R. Walz (Eds.), *Social action: A mandate for counselors* (pp. 227-240). Alexandria, VA: American Counseling Association and ERIC Counseling & Student Services Clearinghouse.

Semmier, P. L., & Williams, C. B. (2000). Narrative therapy: A storied context for multicultural counseling. *Journal of Multicultural Counseling and Development, 28,* 51-62.

Sidel, R. (1994). *Battling bias: The struggle for identity and community on college campuses.* New York: Viking/Penguin.

Slater, B. R. (1993). Violence against lesbian and gay male college students. *Journal of College Student Psychotherapy, 8,* 177-202.

Smith, D. G., Wolf, L. E., & Morrison, D. E. (1995). Paths to success: Factors related to the impact of women's colleges. *Journal of Higher Education, 66,* 245-266.

Smith, G., Gerbick, G. L., Figueroa, M. A., Watkins, G. H., Levitan, T., Moore, L. C., Merchant, P. A., Beliak, H. D., & Figueroa, B. (1997). *Diversity works: The emerging picture of how students benefit.* Washington, DC: Association of American Colleges and Universities.

Stage, F. K., & Hamrick, F. A. (1994). Diversity issues: Fostering campus-wide development of multiculturalism. *Journal of College Student Development, 35,* 331-336.

Sue, D. W. (1995). Multicultural organizational development: Implications for the counseling profession. In J. G. Ponterotto, J. M. Casas, L. A. Suzuki, & C. M. Alexander (Eds.), *Handbook of multicultural counseling* (pp. 474-492). Thousand Oaks, CA: Sage.

Sue, D. W., Arredondo, P., & McDavis, R. J. (1992). Multicultural competencies and standards: A call to the professional. *Journal of Multicultural Counseling and Development, 20,* 64-88.

Sue, D. W., Carter, R. T., Casas, J. M., Fouad, N. A., Ivey, A. E., Jensen, M., LaFromboise, T. D., Manese, J. E., Ponterotto, J. G., & Vazquez-Nutall, E. (1998). *Multicultural competencies: Individual and organizational development.* Thousand Oaks, CA: Sage.

Suzuki, L. A., & Kugler, J. F. (1995). Intelligence and personality assessment: Multicultural perspectives. In J. G. Ponterotto, J. M. Casas, L. A. Suzuki, & C. M. Alexander (Eds.), *Handbook of multicultural counseling* (pp. 493-515). Thousand Oaks, CA: Sage.

Tate, D. S., & Schwartz, C. L. (1993). Increasing the retention of American Indian students in professional programs in higher education. *Journal of American Indian Education, 33,* 21-31.

Tatum, B. D. (1997). *Why are all the Black kids sitting together in the cafeteria? And other conversations about race.* New York: Basic Books.

Thomas, G. (1997). Race relations and campus climate for minority students: Implications for higher education desegregation. In C. Herring (Ed.), *African Americans and the public agenda: The paradoxes of public policy* (pp. 171-189). Thousand Oaks, CA: Sage.

Toliver, S. D. (1998). *Black families in corporate America.* Thousand Oaks, CA: Sage.

Townsend, L. (1994). How universities successfully retain and graduate African American students. *Journal of Blacks in Higher Education, 11,* 85-89.

Trevino, J. G. (1996). Worldview and change in cross-cultural counseling. *The Counseling Psychologist, 24,* 198-215.

Varlotta, L. (1997). Invoking a university's mission statement to promote diversity, civility and free speech. *NASPA Journal, 34,* 123-133.

West, M., Kregel, J., Getzel, E. E., Ming, Z., Ipsen, S. M., & Martin, E. D. (1993). Beyond Section 504: Satisfaction and empowerment of students with disabilities in higher education. *Exceptional Children, 59,* 456-467.

Willdorf, N. (2000, January 21). Black colleges receive letters with racial slurs. *Chronicle of Higher Education,* p. A34.

Wunsch, M. A. (Ed.). (1994). *Minorities in education.* San Francisco: Jossey-Bass.

Young, C. E. (1996). UCLA "greater" because of affirmative action. *Black Issues in Higher Education, 7,* 112.

Correspondence regarding this chapter may be sent to Ingrid Grieger, Director, Counseling Center, Iona College, 715 North Avenue, New Rochelle, NY 10801 (e-mail address: IGrieger@iona.edu).

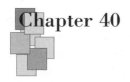

Chapter 40

MULTICULTURALISM AT HISTORICALLY BLACK COLLEGES AND UNIVERSITIES

A Case Study of Howard University

LINDA BERG-CROSS
KELLINA CRAIG
THOMAS WESSEL

THIS CHAPTER ANALYZES the intellectual trends and historical forces shaping the evolution of multicultural institutions collectively referred to as "historically black colleges and universities" (HBCUs). Using the Howard University experience, we examine how multiculturalism has affected three main areas of academic life: the curriculum, the administration, and student mental health services.

MULTICULTURALISM, CURRICULA, AND THE HISTORICALLY BLACK UNIVERSITY

While definitions of "multiculturalism" will vary widely among scholars, we have chosen to define it as follows: *Multiculturalism is a dynamic perspective that values and includes the role of culture in creating knowledge and storing memories. A multicultural perspective assumes culture has a significant bidirectional relationship with biological, characterological, familial, and societal systems.* Including these interacting systems in planning and administrating an educational institution and its curriculum is essential given the demographic shifts in our society.

849

Despite the fact that debate over the merits of multicultural education continues to be waged by scholars across a variety of disciplines, multicultural education, or some variant of it, is a necessary and permanent fixture within the American educational system (Hall, 1997). A pronouncement such as this is especially reasonable in light of past, current, and future demographic shifts. By the year 2050, a majority of the population of students enrolled in elementary education will no longer be of European descent but, instead, will reflect the ethnicities of Africa, Asia, and Central America (Landry, 1997). Those enrolled in America's colleges and universities will also reflect these trends, although to a lesser degree (U.S. Bureau of the Census, 1997).

Proponents point to the benefits that students of marginalized groups as well as majority-group students accrue from a multicultural education. The benefits cited include increased motivation for learning, easier and more relevant modes of knowledge acquisition, expanded capacities for empathy and effective problem solving, awareness of the contributions of cultures formerly omitted from previous accounts of history, the opportunity to identify with historical figures of those cultures, and a greater appreciation for ethnic and cultural diversity (Banks, 1993; Grieger & Toliver, Chapter 39, this volume; Hall, 1997; Landry, 1997).

What is of interest in the current discussion are the myriad forms that multicultural education assumes at America's colleges and universities, in particular those HBCUs established prior to 1964 whose principal mission was the education of Black Americans. Analysis of trends in multicultural education at HBCUs can reveal national trends within the academy but also highlight how its infusion into the curriculum is distinctive from that which occurs at predominantly White institutions (PWIs). It is this latter point that we focus on in this chapter.

To highlight the significance of particular points, we include excerpts from conversations with faculty, students, and administrators from Howard University and address such questions as "To what degree have HBCUs offered courses directly linked to a multicultural perspective?" and "How have multicultural perspectives been infused into traditional courses?" In the case of program development, we examine whether decisions about course development and support are linked in some way to the multicultural perspectives apparent at HBCUs.

Content and Descriptions of Course Offerings

HBCUs have been at the forefront in offering classes specifically highlighting issues relevant to African Americans and other "Black" cultures. Today, a cursory review of the course listings at the nation's largest HBCUs reveals that courses focusing on people of African descent are evident within the arts, humanities, and social sciences. A comparison of these course offerings at HBCUs with those at PWIs can yield insights about how diversity is explored by the two types of institutions.

Importantly, Howard and Stanford are exemplars of the HBCU and PWI, respectively, and as such, their course offerings are likely to be reflective of trends at other similar types of institutions. However, it should be noted that differences in the selection and offering of courses from those available at Howard and Stanford are not only possible but likely.

Howard University, founded in 1867, is the oldest and most well established of the nation's 103 HBCUs. In its 1998–2000 bulletin of courses, it lists more than 800 undergraduate courses offered through the College of Arts and Sciences. Nearly 150 of those can be characterized as having a distinctively multicultural orientation (18% of the total course offerings). This includes such courses as "Afro-Hispanic Literature in English," "Islam in Africa," and "The Holocaust in Film and Literature." In comparison, at one of the nation's most elite PWIs, Stanford University, over 1,500 courses are listed in its 1999–2000 bulletin. More than 250 of these courses can be characterized as having an explicit multicultural perspective and include courses with titles such as "Multicultural Issues in Higher Education," "The Multicultural Moment: American Literature from the Civil War to World War I," and "Latino Cultural Citizenship" (17% of total course offerings).

At first glance, then, there appears to be some parity with respect to the way that multicultural perspectives are infused throughout the course offerings of an HBCU and a PWI. Representatives of both types of institution offer a hearty dose of courses that are explicitly indicative of a multicultural perspective. However, there are two important differences to note. First, Howard's courses focus almost exclusively on Africa, the Caribbean, and the African American experience. Those at Stanford cover a much broader range of cultures. Second, there are more highly specialized courses available at Stanford as compared to Howard. This likely results from Stanford's greater number of course offerings. At Stanford, courses in history, for example, have such complex titles as "The Language of African American Names: A History of Naming Traditions," and "Flappers, Housewives, and Bra Burners: Images and Representations of Womanhood in 20th-Century America." At Howard, the history department offers courses that, while explicitly multicultural in their orientation, are broader and more traditional in their scope of inquiry. Typical offerings are titled "History of the Caribbean," "Introduction to the Black Diaspora," and "The African American Experience Up to 1877." Thus, while HBCUs have a proportionately equal number of courses centered on multicultural perspectives as PWIs, they lack the specialized depth that the larger, major PWIs can provide. Most multicultural courses at HBCUs focus on Africa, the Caribbean, and African Americans.

One longtime resident on the Howard University campus, Thomas Battle, who is currently the director of Moorland-Spingarm Research

Center, suggests that because part of the mission of the HBCU was to educate African Americans, some degree of multicultural education has always been apparent within the university's efforts to educate its student body. The multicultural focus, however, has remained fairly confined to the unique historical mission of HBCUs. According to Battle,

> Multicultural education at Howard, although an inherent aspect of its mission, assumes a different form than at predominantly White institutions. Generally speaking, at an HBCU, multicultural education entails provision and discussion of issues relevant to African Americans, formerly excluded from traditional narratives. The degree to which perspectives infused throughout the academy are truly "multi"-cultural is debatable.

For Battle and many other scholars on the Howard campus, this represents one aspect of the HBCU experience in need of improvement. In fact, he noted that this very point is central to the ongoing philosophical debate on how multicultural education should be defined at HBCUs. According to Battle, although Howard University is finally beginning to address this issue, many other HBCUs have yet to start the inevitable inclusion of a broader array of multicultural courses.

MULTICULTURALISM AND
CONTENT OF TRADITIONAL COURSE CURRICULA

Intellectual exposure to multicultural issues can also come from the faculty's specific attempts at substantive integration within traditional courses and can also be examined for differences between HBCUs and PWIs. Part of the institutional consciousness at an HBCU is awareness of the fact that culture can and does affect systems of knowledge. This is most apparent in the treatment of history but occurs in every area of inquiry. In teaching a course on history at an HBCU, one takes for granted the fact that cultural interpretations affect the historical record (e.g., the Japanese account of the politics culminating in World War II is very different from the U.S. account). HBCUs contend, however, that it is also the case that cultural reference points affect such areas of study as economics, psychology, and the performing arts.

This orientation exists in large part because individuals who are most likely to share this particular belief system are most likely to be attracted to the idea of working at an HBCU. The historical legacy and mission of HBCUs is such that the institution itself represents a solution to the oppression of one culture by another. An understanding and identification with the institution and its mission is impossible without some acceptance of the principles of a multicultural education.

Results of an informal survey conducted for this discussion nicely illustrate the type of multicultural information and perspectives that are part of traditional course offerings at Howard University. When the general psychology course is taught by one senior member of the psychology department, for example, multicultural perspectives are a part of almost every one of the units. The situation is similar in sociology and anthropology. Thus, while the traditional content is provided, students within these classes are encouraged to think critically about the epistemology and degree to which it incorporates and applies to the life experiences of those who are not White and middle-class Americans. This takes place through specific lectures geared to making this point.

One senior member of the psychology department at Howard who sometimes teaches the introductory psychology course indicated that he regularly chooses to "integrate a worldwide African perspective into the course." For example, he noted that when the subject was language he "included Frantz Fanon's views on language usage among the colonized (Bulhan, 1985; Sekyi-Out, 1997)." He said, "I found that with every unit, it was possible and necessary to relate the material to some aspect of the Black experience." In contrast, a new professor currently teaching the general psychology course noted that although the incorporation of multicultural perspectives within the course is a laudable goal, given the subject matter it is sometimes challenging to accomplish. According to this professor,

> When you're talking about the brain, and basic psychological functioning, there is very little room for discussions linked to cultural or ethnic orientation. . . . For me, incorporation of multicultural perspectives in the introductory psychology course takes the form of my presenting students with historical information about the significant contributions of African American psychologists.

The way that multicultural perspectives are incorporated into traditional courses will vary according to the professor. One factor that likely contributes to this variance is the experience of the professor with the course. In the latter case, the professor had only begun teaching the course within the past year. For the more "seasoned" professor, there may be a greater ability to see how multicultural perspectives can be effectively woven into the existing course format. We believe there should be a more systematic, campuswide plan to help instructors find the right multicultural material that would enhance the existing curricula. Such projects are afoot at other HBCUs.

Spelman College, for example, is a historically Black college for women that has developed a campuswide blueprint that is being used to build multicultural content into traditional courses (Guy-Sheftall, 1997). With funds from the Ford Foundation, the plan is to infuse multiculturalism into the entire liberal arts curriculum. They have the goal of working with a variety of diversity issues, including race/ethnicity, religion, disability, sexuality, class, and gender. The project has begun with a set of assumptions that guide curriculum modifications. The assumptions presented by Guy-Sheftall (1997) are as follows:

- Students at HBCUs need an inclusive curriculum that exposes the students to a wide variety of diverse cultural information, values, and worldviews.
- Intolerance of difference and stereotyping is present in the African American community in ways both different and similar to White Americans.
- While nearly all students at HBCUs abhor racism, they may very well endorse other "isms" (e.g., sexism and heterosexism).
- The students at HBCUs are far more heterogeneous than they appear. Diversity issues need to be addressed in a variety of contexts on campus.
- While race and class are popular multicultural topics at most HBCUs, there is an uneasy silence about other diversity issues, especially gender and sexuality.
- The curriculum at many HBCUs is still male centered and excludes (or treats inadequately) the histories and cultures of many other culture groups, such as Native American Indians, Chicanos, Asian/Pacific Americans, and Arab Americans.

In general, at PWIs, the infusion of multicultural perspectives into traditional courses is linked directly to the efforts of individual faculty members. Conversations with a small number of faculty at PWIs reveal that to the degree students are exposed to multicultural perspectives in courses not explicitly titled as such, it is most often a result of the consciousness of individual faculty members.

Administrators across the country, though, are encouraging faculty at PWIs to include more multicultural material within traditional courses. This is done, most often, by offering modest financial incentives to faculty within the humanities and social sciences. For example, faculty can, at many PWIs, submit proposals to obtain internal funding to revise existing courses. The revisions they propose are designed to include materials omitted from previous offerings of the course. Although this gesture may assume the form of simply tacking on a biography of "women of color" for a class in gender psychology, for more ambitious and committed faculty, this can entail substantial integration of multicultural materials throughout the course.

Although its mission does not mandate the infusion of multicultural perspectives into courses, a comparable vehicle for enhancement and improvement of the curriculum exists at Howard University. The Fund for Academic Excellence Grants Program was created in 1997 to promote and foster excellence in academic programs. At no place in the program description is there explicit reference to multicultural aims or goals. However, of the 153 projects funded during the first two years, 28 were specifically designed to either incorporate multicultural perspectives into existing course formats or create new courses or lecture series with an explicit multicultural content. Project titles for some of those projects are "Academic Excellence Through Africa-Centered Curriculum," "International Practica Sites for Clinical Psychology Students," and "The Ground Together: Reclaiming and Reexamining the Black Aesthetic for the Millennium." Since its inception, the program has funded more than 300 proposals, with total funding exceeding $1 million.

We assume that within selected professional schools and programs, multicultural perspectives, though no less relevant, are less apparent than at the undergraduate level at both HBCUs and PWIs. According to one new faculty member of the business school at Howard University, "the effort to incorporate such perspectives within the curriculum or into individual courses has not been undertaken as of yet." Indeed, this professor recently sought and received funding to create a course that explicitly addresses the role of diversity in marketing, consumer behavior, and commerce.

Ironically, at Howard University, the faculty of the business school is especially diverse with individuals hailing from Europe, Asia, and Africa, in addition to the United States. Yet, an examination of the titles of the courses taught in the business school reveals no explicit infusion of multicultural perspectives within any course. The lack of an explicit multicultural emphasis is particularly problematic because students consistently request such courses and want Howard to realize its potential as a leader in providing a multicultural curriculum.

Throughout the country, multiculturalism is a significant part of the graduate programs in history, English, and the social sciences. Nowhere is this more true than at HBCUs. For example, all the courses in Howard's clinical psychology program examine how family, ethnicity, religion, community, and society shape a person's attitudes, values, and behaviors and how to creatively mobilize those forces to help individual development. The main focus is to train psychologists who are able to use culture as a positive force in creating therapeutic change. In terms of research, over 95% of the clinical dissertations that have come out of Howard in the past 10 years have direct relevance for the assessment, treatment, or understanding of minority populations (Berg-Cross, Mason, & Normington, 1997). From this expanded focus on cultural diversity, the clinical program has evolved and taken a larger international view of mental health and the range of treatment possibilities.

Whether it is at the graduate level or at the undergraduate level, at a PWI or at an HBCU, the following four guidelines seem prudent for institutions seeking to infuse multicultural perspectives into the curriculum ("Advice," 1997):

1. There should be a comprehensive review across courses of which diversity issues are being addressed. Otherwise, the risk is that a disproportionate number of innovations will gravitate toward including the same type of

material and a large number of areas will be neglected (e.g., focusing on race instead of gender or facts about a culture instead of values and attitudes).

2. Curriculum additions and modifications should be grounded in the larger mission or diversity statements of the college or university.

3. Interdisciplinary coalitions and student involvement are very useful in the planning and development stages.

4. There should be explicit diversity goals in classes being revamped or designed for this purpose. In addition, there should be a method of assessing student interest and goal attainment in the course.

ESTABLISHING THE DIVERSE UNIVERSITY COMMUNITY

In this section, we hope to shed light on the ways that multicultural education, as it is manifested at HBCUs, uniquely affects such issues as student and faculty recruitment, program development, and fund-raising. To be sure, the recruitment of a diverse student population and faculty at HBCUs is quite different from efforts designed to ensure diversity at majority institutions. The degree to which multicultural perspectives are associated with the presence of a diverse student body and faculty is considered here.

Multiculturalism and Student Recruitment at HBCUs

All colleges and universities seek to maximize enrollment with the best and brightest students they can find. During the past 25 years, defining "the best" has become less a matter of individual student characteristics and more a matter of a group or class characteristic. Increasingly, the "best" undergraduate class is a diverse class. With the exception of certain religious institutions, almost all universities and colleges actively seek students from diverse ethnic, cultural, and religious backgrounds and geographic locations. HBCUs are similar in this regard, and although social pressures within and outside the HBCUs have resulted in African Americans being the largest ethnic group on these campuses, the larger HBCUs, like Howard, have always been diverse.

Howard University was founded in 1867 under the leadership of Otis Howard, an abolitionist and an amalgamationist, whose goal after the civil war was to create integration in all walks of society. The aim of Howard University was to draw pupils from all classes, conditions, and nationalities. In the early days, these goals were excitingly close to being accomplished. Americans, Brits, Celts, Indians, Asians, Greeks, and African Americans sat "side by side on the same benches" at Howard (Hoar, 1870). In 1884, a White male was valedictorian in pharmacy, a Black male was valedictorian in dentistry, and a White woman was valedictorian in medicine. However, by 1940, the university was 91% Black and less than 1% White

(Dyson, 1941). The historical transformation of Howard from a multiracial mecca to a predominantly Black university is too far afield from the main focus of this chapter to analyze here. However, it should be noted that the multicultural heritage at Howard was present at its inception and has been a guiding current, and sometimes an undercurrent, throughout the years.

Currently, the undergraduate student body at Howard University boasts a population that comes from all 50 states and more than 115 countries. Eighty-four percent of the student body are U.S. citizens, 11% are foreign born, and 5% have permanent resident visas. The federally mandated surcharge imposed on international students in the mid 1990s depressed the international enrollment, but it has begun to rebound and will soon reach Howard's more traditional 16% of the student body. Men and women are equally represented among the international students (*Howard University Self Study*, 1999). Students from all over Africa and the Caribbean make up a large proportion of the international students, and there are students from every corner of the world.

While Howard University has produced the largest percentage of the U.S. population of Black doctors, lawyers, politicians, and engineers, it has also contributed to a more diverse pool of American and international professionals. The diversity of the student body at Howard often surprises those who may be unfamiliar with the HBCU experience. Indeed, for many in this camp, the HBCU is seen as an exclusively "Black" institution with little to no diversity. In reality, the larger HBCUs tend to be very diverse.

Very often what attracts international students to HBCUs, such as Howard, is the diversity. Students who come to Howard often do so because of the expectation that a multicultural education will be provided along with traditional course and program offerings. Many students report finding a much greater presence and appreciation for cultural diversity at HBCUs. To the extent that these types of sentiments are associated with the presence of a diverse faculty and student body as well as a commitment to multicultural education throughout the university, HBCUs are quite distinct from PWIs. Because of their historical legacy of training diverse students in an atmosphere that applauds unique cultural heritages, HBCUs are uniquely positioned to bring together large groups of diverse students.

One final note about student recruitment and multicultural education is worth mentioning here. This concerns the fact that in comparison to PWIs, HBCUs have had, and continue to have, trouble attracting the brightest African American students in the numbers they would like. This is because they are often unable to compete with the lucrative financial aid packages that PWIs make available to students requiring assistance. Indeed, Whites would be attracted to HBCUs in greater numbers if they were offered equally attractive funding. Given current trends, we end this part of our discussion with the prediction that within two generations HBCUs will begin to reflect both national and local populations. As a consequence of the need for leadership in integrating the diverse student body of the future, HBCU administrators have begun to expand their mission of training for African Americans in a supportive environment to one that embraces a much broader constituency. As racism declines and the educational value of HBCUs becomes more widely known, HBCUs have the opportunity to be a premier educational setting in America, one where diverse groups feel equally confident that they "belong" to the institution.

Multiculturalism and Faculty Recruitment

At Howard, there are 1,245 full- and part-time faculty, 36% of whom are female. Among the 1,036 full-time faculty, 61% are Black, 16% are White, 9% are Asian, 1% are Hispanic, and 1% are Native American Indian. Twelve percent are unknown or unclassifiable with current codes (*Howard University Self Study*, 1999). Howard has the largest number of Black scholars in the world, and compared to national statistics, may also have the most diverse community of scholars in the world. This is apparent when one considers that in the United States only 12.2% of all full-time faculty are minorities, 9.2% are people of color, and 33.6% are women.

Within the United States, the number of African American PhDs across disciplines and relative to Whites and Asians continues to be abysmally small. Moreover, within this small set, many African Americans with doctorates opt to teach at PWIs because of the increased pay and generally easier working conditions (e.g., greater availability of staff, resources, teaching load). In this way, HBCUs are in direct competition with PWIs for desirable faculty candidates. Yet research indicates that an undersupply of minority PhDs has a statistically significant but minimal impact on minority faculty representation. Market wages exert a far greater influence on the underrepresentation of minority faculty in higher education (Turner & Myers, 1999). Within academia, clearly higher paying institutions will have greater success in attracting minorities.

For those who actively seek out the HBCU, Howard can be an especially attractive place to work. Many ethnically diverse faculty who come to Howard after having been employed at PWIs find the diversity of the student body, staff, and other faculty quite appealing. Indeed, in a study of faculty of color at eight predominantly White midwestern universities, Turner and Myers (1999) found "the persistence and the personal and professional effects of a decidedly chilly work environment. . . . Once hired, faculty of color continue to experience exclusion, isolation, alienation, and racism in uncomfortable work environments in predominantly white university settings" (p. 132).

In sharp contrast, individuals hired within the past 5 years at Howard consistently reported that they found an explicit sensitivity to multicultural perspectives. Faculty members who previously worked at PWIs indicated that in their prior institution they often found themselves in a very small minority when it came to incorporating multicultural perspectives into existing courses or altering the curriculum by developing courses with explicit multicultural goals. Because of reasons such as these, some faculty will seek out and secure employment at an HBCU.

In addition to an awareness of and appreciation for its historical legacy and mission, ethnically diverse faculty often find teaching at an HBCU especially rewarding. This is a result of the opportunities for direct mentoring of ethnically diverse students, interaction with colleagues who share similar concerns, and the ease in incorporating multicultural perspectives into teaching and research activities. These observations are echoed in the Turner and Myers (1999) study that finds faculty of color consistently stating that it is very important to be part of academic communities of color, have culturally sensitive mentors, and be in an affirming workplace.

Thus, it is likely that recruitment of a diverse faculty, including foreign nationals, does not require the same types of strategies frequently used at many of the PWIs. After assuring candidates have the requisite expertise within an area, many PWIs have tried to take advantage of Affirmative Action programs to hire minority candidates. The issues concerning faculty recruitment at HBCUs have never been that complex. Generally, they can be reduced to such basics as salary and teaching loads.

MULTICULTURAL EDUCATION AND FUND-RAISING

Fund-raising is a multicultural issue at HBCUs for three important reasons. First, a majority of the alumni of HBCUs are African Americans. Consequently, efforts to attract funds from other ethnic groups may be especially difficult given that there may be little to no name recognition within non-African American circles. Moreover, when the school is well known to the general public, there is the image that HBCUs are "only" for African Americans. If a prospective donor is especially interested in helping African Americans, this can be a useful image with which to be associated—take, for example, Bill Cosby's multi-million-dollar donation to Spelman College. However, it is just as likely that a prospective donor's interests will be in supporting "multicultural learning environments," and to the extent that they regard the HBCU as "Black" rather than "multicultural" this may be detrimental to fund-raising.

The second way that fund-raising at the HBCU evokes multicultural issues is that many potential donors who want to create multicultural environments go to PWIs to do so. Among these individuals, there is often the belief that funds earmarked for social integration and multicultural understanding can be best spent at PWIs. Accordingly, there is the assumption that multicultural education may be a more pressing issue and concern on predominantly White campuses.

In contrast to the preceding ways that HBCUs may be at a disadvantage when it comes to fund-raising, HBCUs do have an international advantage.

At many of the larger HBCUs, the international alumni and faculty provide great opportunities for fund-raising. As we move toward a more global society, those institutions that are familiar and comfortable with different cultures are poised for success. As the premier HBCU, Howard University may be especially able to take advantage of this opportunity. For example, the university currently houses the Ralph J. Bunche International Affairs Center dedicated to developing and providing service and leadership to the nation and global community. Universities and colleges with a history and appreciation of diversity and that espouse and provide multicultural education will be especially likely to benefit from the contributions of donors who also value diversity in a global society.

In summary, we have considered the way that multicultural education is manifested at an HBCU, such as Howard, and the degree to which it differs from many PWIs. Multicultural education in explicit courses designed to provide students with an appreciation for diversity occurs similarly at Howard and PWIs. Howard still focuses on a smaller group of cultures, tied to the historical mission of the university. Also, at many large PWIs, such as Stanford, there are more specialized offerings than those typically found at an HBCU. The reports of faculty who have taught at both types of institutions, across a number of disciplines, are consistent in reporting that the infusion of cultural relevancy is the distinctive curriculum hallmark of undergraduate education at an HBCU.

We have also noted that HBCUs are often forced to compete directly with PWIs in order to recruit and retain the best students and faculty. The best, we contend, is likely to be the most multiculturally diverse. HBCUs have the distinct advantage of a reputation for appreciation of diversity as well as delivery of a multicultural education to their students. In this way, the HBCU may have an even greater responsibility than the PWI to ensure the provision of a multicultural education. Although this may be somewhat daunting, it is necessary, and the existence of the HBCU may well depend on it.

We conclude this part of our discussion by pointing out that our observations have been based on the specific case of Howard University vis-à-vis Stanford. Because there is likely to be a great deal of variance within the category of HBCU and PWI, respectively, we remind the reader that attempts to generalize from case studies should be limited.

MULTICULTURAL ISSUES, COUNSELING CENTERS, AND HBCUs

While curriculum, faculty, and administrative issues are a central focus of multicultural inquiry at colleges and universities, at its heart, multiculturalism at the university is woven into the student's experience of oneself as a person-in-a-culture. It is the students' experience of their own culture and that of their peers that has a most potent influence on their motivation to understand multicultural issues as well as on their own mental health and well-being.

Like PWIs, the HBCUs have had an increasingly diverse student body over the past decade. Here, the diversity is due to a broader range of African Americans who have chosen to attend college, increased foreign enrollments, and Americans of different backgrounds (e.g., Asians, biracial, and Caucasian) who are being attracted to the value and education offered at HBCUs.

The student mental health issues concerning multiculturalism are conceptually the same at HBCUs and PWIs, although the specifics are different. They are the issues of identity, discrimination, and self-esteem. At PWIs, African Americans feel marginalized on campus, whereas at HBCUs, it is the students from lower-class families or the students of darker color or international students who feel they cannot enter the "hub" of campus life. Ironically, more than a few African American students who have attended predominantly White high schools suddenly feel "out of place" at an HBCU, the one place where they most eagerly sought a home. Their tastes in music, literature, movies, and speech patterns label them "too assimilated," and they feel they have to prove themselves "Black" over and over again. The Greek system is very strong at HBCUs, partly because it helps students define themselves in a situation where it is surprisingly difficult to do so.

CULTURE-SENSITIVE
TREATMENT MODALITIES OFFERED AT HBCUs

Traditional approaches to counseling and psychotherapy come with a historic link to the 20th-century Euro-American civilization (Pedersen, Draguns, Lonner, & Trimble, 1996). Diverse student bodies require a wider range of culture-sensitive techniques and approaches. Pedersen et al. (1996) cite several basic points about how to do effective cross-cultural counseling. Three of those points are most relevant for counseling at HBCUs. First, understanding of the counseling process is related to the culturally established modes of self-expression and the communication of distress. Second, counseling techniques have to be modified when applied to a different cultural milieu. Third, complications in the counseling process tend to increase as the gulf between the counselor and the counselee is widened. These three principles have helped guide the development of culturally relevant programs at Howard University Counseling Center.

While all counseling centers must adopt culturally informed techniques, the HBCUs have found it especially important to be flexible and adaptive in responding to the nonverbal therapeutic environment, to offer outreach services to the entire university community, to offer lots of group therapy, and to capitalize on the opportunities for multicultural training available at their centers. Each of these four foci is discussed below.

Using nonverbal approaches in a culturally informed manner. Many techniques considered fundamental to the counseling process such as eye contact, verbalization, and addressing one by name may be considered disrespectful or otherwise inappropriate by a student who is sitting with a therapist whom they view as a person of authority. Some cultures prohibit eye contact with an authority figure or elder during an interaction. For example, it is not respectful to address an elder by name in parts of India.

Verbal expression is an essential means of conducting a counseling interview. However, counselors must not rush to interpret silence as resistance in working with individuals from racial and cultural groups other than the mainstream White. Many cultures of the world do not place as much premium on talking as do the cultures in the Western hemisphere. Consider the following two brief examples (clients seen by T. Wessel):

Case Study of Ms. B

Ms. B. was an undergraduate student from Asia. She had failed in one of her clinical rotations in an allied health field. Her failure was attributed not to her knowledge or her ability in her field but to poor judgment in her interpersonal relations. She came to see me in total frustration. One of her negative evaluations by her field supervisor had to do with her insufficient verbal participation in case conferences. Essentially her supervisors were saying that she didn't talk much and interpreted that as a lack of interest and involvement. When this therapist explored further her lack of participation in classroom and group discussions, the client uttered in frustration, "I only speak if I have anything to say. In this country people talk even if they have nothing to say." She told me she just doesn't engage in superficial conversation.

Case Study of Suzie

Another client, Suzie, whom I saw early in my training as a therapist, would just come in and sit for long periods of time without saying anything. She too was an international student, hailing from an African country. She was very communicative nonverbally and very much present and involved during the therapy hour. However, she did not say much. My supervisor started referring to this client as the "sitter." I felt I was probably not doing enough to make her talk and was beginning to question my competence as a counselor. While the client seemed comfortable with her silence, I was becoming increasingly uncomfortable with it. After all, talking is what is done in counseling sessions. All our training had to do with facilitating talking. My supervisor was very understanding of my situation. She too did not seem too bothered by the silence. The "sitter" came regularly to the therapy sessions and was usually on time.

One day, at the end of the session, when she was telling me what she was going to do for the rest of the day, she said she was going to spend time with her girlfriend who worked in the government. When I asked if her friend was taking the day off, my client said "No." Of course, I had to pull teeth as usual and asked her what she would do while her friend worked. My client responded, "Just sit." Everything became clear to me then. At that moment, I felt very close to her, knowing that she had been sitting with me like she would with a close friend and I had missed it. That experience taught me a great lesson in multicultural counseling. I have since seen many clients from different cultures who were very limited in conversation and that sat well with me. A few years later, I received a nice card in the mail containing a picture of my client—the sitter—wearing a cap and gown and her handwritten note thanking me for making it possible.

Thus, therapists working with the diverse populations seen in HBCU counseling centers must learn to use their knowledge of different cultural communication patterns to accurately empathize with the client and accurately reflect the client's feelings in a nonjudgmental manner (Helms & Cook, 1999).

MULTICULTURALISM AND OUTREACH
SERVICES THAT DON'T SHOUT "THERAPY"

Recognition of racial and cultural differences between individuals is the first step in establishing a therapeutic alliance. As counselors and psychotherapists, the first thing we would like our clients to acknowledge is that there is a problem. Denial of an existing problem is the worst enemy to the psychotherapeutic process. The first phase of any therapeutic endeavor is to lead the client into admitting that there is a problem. This is no less true when it comes to resolving racial and cultural differences in the therapeutic process.

When there are obvious racial and cultural differences in the counseling dyad or in a therapy group, it is of utmost importance to address that openly. The process of addressing that issue in itself can be a model for the change process. In supervising counselors in training, we encourage our supervisees to bring up race differences very early in the therapeutic relationship. That helps the client realize the need to pay attention to, acknowledge, and address differences.

Historically, the stigma associated with seeking and receiving mental health services kept many a student in need from benefiting from these services. This was especially true among African Americans and members of other minority groups. Howard University Counseling Service has been a pioneer in helping remove the stigma and in bringing mental health services to the students and community for several decades. This was made possible through increasing the psychotherapist's awareness of multicultural issues and offering programs and services targeted at those least likely to seek professional help.

The eradication of the stigma became our mission in the early 1970s. Rather than let the counseling center sit in a corner of the campus as a clinic for the mentally ill, we launched many outreach programs and became involved in the life of the students. We helped start an academic remedial program and called it CAR (Center for Academic Reinforcement). A counseling component was added to basic skills education. We took a proactive approach, and prevention became a key word.

We got involved in training campus pals—a group of 60 student volunteers who function as peer support for incoming freshmen during the first few weeks during and after orientation. The counseling center participated in the training and orientation of residence hall assistants (RAs), campus police, and other units on campus providing support to students and also ran a tutorial program for student athletes. It became a busy place not only during the day but also in the evening. The perception that one had to be mentally ill to be seen at Howard University Counseling Service was slowly changing.

MULTICULTURALISM AND THE USE OF GROUP THERAPY

Recognizing that the group modality is a natural fit for many African Americans and other minority groups that are very group centered, efforts were undertaken to offer a variety of counseling and psychotherapy groups to the university community. First, the clinical staff needed to be trained in group work, since we had seen many group programs fail without adequate training. Many of the clinical staff received their postdoctoral training in the group modality at such prestigious institutions as National Training Laboratories, Washington School of Psychiatry, and A. K. Rice Institute.

The 1970s and 1980s saw a major growth in the number of counseling and psychotherapy groups at Howard University Counseling Service. The Black Women's Support Group, Black Men's Support Group, and groups on topics like "Race and Skin Color," "Obesity," "Prince Charming," "Body Image," and "Self-Esteem" became popular attractions among students and members of the community at large. In addition to these special interest groups, the number of ongoing weekly psychotherapy groups also increased. In becoming a part of a therapy group one realizes that one is not alone in suffering from a problem. Thus, the group modality helps break down the stigma associated with mental illness and seeking professional help for emotional problems.

Within the different types of groups, multicultural issues often become a focus of group work. There are four main diversity themes that get played out in groups. The first is how power is distributed according to one's social role in the group—group leaders typically have more power than the others.

Second, members of the majority socioracial group generally carry more power than the "minority" members represented in the group. Third, racism from the society permeates the group, and Whites are generally ceded more power and respect than other racial members. Fourth, sexism is often present with men having more power in the group than women (Helms & Cook, 1999). All of these diversity issues are explored as they emerge in the group process.

MULTICULTURALISM AND TRAINING INTERNSHIP STUDENTS IN USING CULTURE AS A PROACTIVE FACTOR IN CHANGE

HBCU counseling centers are uniquely positioned to offer multicultural training because the supervisors have spent many years consciously working on these issues and consciously progressing through the racial identity stages. Research has shown that multicultural competence is best achieved in the counseling setting when one is supervised by counselors who themselves have advanced racial identity statuses (Ladany, Brittan-Powell, & Pannu, 1997). In these progressive relationships, a trainee can identify with the supervisor (if they are at the same identity level) or emulate and learn from the supervisor (if he/she is at a more advanced level). In a regressive relationship, when the supervisee is at a more advanced level than the supervisor, the supervisory relationship was judged the worst. This type of regressive situation is least likely to occur at an HBCU.

Accredited by the American Psychological Association to offer predoctoral psychology internships, Howard University Counseling Service is a nationally known training site. Our primary training objective is to train psychologists who wish to work among disadvantaged populations. Trainees are constantly faced with the issue of diversity. It is not uncommon for students at an HBCU to be taken aback when met by a White counselor at the counseling center. Either out of respect or sheer discomfort the student may not say anything to the counselor about it and instead opt not to return. The burden is on the counselor to openly invite the client to talk about her feelings about seeing a White counselor. Even if the client is unprepared or unwilling to talk about his feelings yet, just the acknowledgment and the invitation by the therapist lays the foundation for a therapeutic alliance. The client learns his first lesson in therapy—that feelings are not to be always acted upon but are to be acknowledged, observed, and, if appropriate, talked about.

Programs across the country are trying to find ways of assessing their success in teaching clinical and counseling students multicultural concepts. There are now three well-known, self-report, empirical measures of multicultural counseling competencies: Multicultural Counseling Inventory (Sodowsky, Taffe, Gutkin, & Wise, 1994), Multicultural Awareness-

Knowledge-Skills Survey (D'Andrea, Daniels, & Heck, 1991), and Multicultural Awareness Counseling Scale (Ponterotto, Rieger, Barrett, & Sparks, 1994). The Multicultural Counseling Inventory, for example, measures four dimensions. The first, the Awareness Scale, measures how aware the trainee is of the impact of culture on problem presentation and the range of acceptable solutions and/or changes. It looks at if the trainee can recognize the cultural clashes that can occur in the therapy session as well as in the client's life. The second dimension, the Knowledge Scale, tests the academic terms and concepts that are used to discuss cultural issues in supervision (e.g., ethnicity and cultural encapsulation). The third dimension, the Skills Scale, taps into the range of techniques the trainee can use to deal with cultural issues. The fourth dimension, the Relationship Scale, assesses the self-reported trustworthiness and comfort level of the therapist when dealing with a client from a different culture group. Training centers that focus on multicultural counseling competencies may find it most helpful to customize these assessment devices to optimally reflect the skills needed in a particular community or counseling center.

SPECIALIZED PROBLEMS OF INTERNATIONAL STUDENTS

There are more than 400,000 international students studying at American universities and colleges. Universities with over 3,000 international students include Boston University (4,603), Harvard University (3,249), Purdue University at Lafayette (3,266), Columbia University (4,080), New York University (4,964), University of Illinois at Champaign (3,107), University of Michigan at Ann Arbor (3,820), University of Maryland at College Park (3,020), and University of Wisconsin at Madison (3,820) (*Open Doors*, 1997/98).

Although not among the megacenters, HBCUs are the educational institutions of choice for many international students. The international student population at Howard is on the rise primarily because Howard has served a pivotal role in training leaders for not only Black America but also for the global community. Presently, international students make up 11% of the student body, although as mentioned earlier the historic average for Howard is above 16%. The expectations are that international student enrollment will not only return to average levels but reach new heights in the next decade. The emotional issues faced by international students often go beyond separation and adjustment issues. Many problems are centered around the special challenges posed by being an "international student." These issues include the following:

- Restrictions on working. International students have their independence needs restricted when they are not permitted to work. Financial burdens are also obviously increased. Working without a permit leads to guilt, paranoia, and stress.

- Impact of failing or poor grades. International students can be forced to leave school or change their major if their grades are too low. Unlike many U.S. students who take light loads or a semester off "to get it together," the international student often does not have this luxury.

- Unwillingness to seek out psychological services. Due to cultural constraints from their home country and fear of "records," many international students with disabling depression and anxiety find it difficult to seek out help.

- Discrimination based on nationality, ethnicity, language, food preferences, and leisure styles is an ongoing, painful experience for many international students.

In summary, while there are far more similarities than differences between counseling centers at HBCUs and PWIs, the presence of a majority of "minorities" creates unique modifications of standard counseling interventions and creative training opportunities. Cultural minority counselors must acknowledge and grapple with the challenging range of diversity within the minority community, and majority-culture counselors must struggle with the additional issue of being a "minority group" within the university community. Student clients must grapple with therapists from different backgrounds. For both groups, the experience can be a difficult one, filled at times with personal trauma and intellectual confusion. More often, though, it is a transcendent experience in which all parts of the community grow in intellect and spirit by being forced to challenge stereotypes and confront the "isms" that insidiously regulate one group as inferior to another. Whether it be classism, sexism, or racism, the HBCU is at a historical juncture where it is openly and continuously starting to confront these issues; protecting its unique mission to provide an intellectual haven where minorities can experience the freedom of being a majority while welcoming diverse majority-culture faculty and students.

REFERENCES

Advice on effective curriculum transformation. (1997, Winter). *Diversity Digest*.

Banks, J. (1993). Multicultural education: Historical development, dimensions and practice. *Review of Research in Education, 19*, 3-49.

Berg-Cross, L., Mason, D., & Normington, J. (1997). The training of minority psychologists: Trends and changes during the past 15 years. *Journal of College Student Psychotherapy, 12*, 25-30.

Bulhan, H. A. (1985). *Franz Fanon and the psychology of oppression*. New York: Plenum.

D'Andrea, M., Daniels, J., & Heck, R. (1991). Evaluating the impact of multicultural counseling training. *Journal of Counseling and Development, 70*, 143-150.

Dyson, W. (1941). *Howard University: The capstone of Negro education*. Washington, DC: Graduate School of Howard University.

Guy-Sheftall, B. (1997, Winter). Teaching diversity at a historically Black college. *Diversity Digest*.

Hall, P. M. (1997). Race, ethnicity, and schooling in America: An introduction. In P. M. Hall (Ed.), *Race, ethnicity and multiculturalism: Policy and practice* (pp. 3-40). New York: Garland.

Helms, J. E., & Cook, D. (1999). *Using race and culture in counseling and psychotherapy.* New York: Allyn & Bacon.

Hoar, G. (1870, June 6). In Albert B. Hart, *Slavery and abolition* (p. 192). Report of the Committee of Congress on Education and Labor on the charges preferred against General O. O. Howard, 41st Congress, Second Session, 1870 (p. 10) (Abbreviated: Howard Investigation, 1870); Danford B. Nichols, American missionary, January 1873, XVII, 1(1).

Howard University Self Study. (1999). Washington, DC: Howard University.

Ladany, N., Brittan-Powell, C., & Pannu, R. (1997). The influence of supervisory racial identity interaction and racial matching on the supervisory working alliance and supervisee multicultural competence. *Counselor Education and Supervision, 36,* 285-305.

Landry, B. (1997). Education in a multicultural society. In P. M. Hall (Ed.), *Race, ethnicity and multiculturalism: Policy and practice* (pp. 41-62). New York: Garland.

Open doors, 1997/98. New York: Institute of International Education.

Pedersen, P. B., Draguns, J. G., Lonner, W. J., & Trimble, J. E. (Eds.). (1996). *Counseling across cultures* (4th ed.). Thousand Oaks, CA: Sage.

Ponterotto, J. G., Rieger, B. P., Barrett, A., & Sparks, R. (1994). Assessing multicultural competencies: A reivew of instrumentaion. *Journal of Counseling and Development, 72,* 316-322.

Sekyi-Out, A. (1997). *Fanon's dialectic of experience.* Cambridge, MA: Harvard University Press.

Sodowsky, G. R., Taffe, R. C., Gutkin, T. B., & Wise, S. L. (1994). Development of the multicultural counseling inventory: A self-report measure of multicultural competencies. *Journal of Counseling Psychology, 41,* 137-148.

Turner, V., & Myers, S. (1999). *Bittersweet success: Faculty of color in academe.* New York: Allyn & Bacon.

U.S. Bureau of the Census. (1997). *Education by other characteristics.* Washington, DC: U.S. Department of Commerce, Bureau of the Census.

SUGGESTED SUPPLEMENTARY READINGS

Glazer, N. (1997). *We are all multiculturalists now.* Cambridge, MA: Harvard University Press.

Kim, U., & Berry, J. (Eds.). (1993). *Indigenous psychologies: Research and experience in cultural context.* Newbury Park, CA: Sage.

Lourde, A. (1989). A question of survival: A commencement speech delivered at Oberlin College. *Gay Community News,* pp. 5-12.

Pederson, P. (1994). International students and international student advisors. In R. Brislin & T. Yoshida (Eds.), *Improving intercultural interactions: Modules for cross-cultural training programs* (pp. 115-125). Thousand Oaks, CA: Sage.

Schmidt, A. J. (1997). *The menace of multiculturalism.* Westport, CT: Praeger.

Sue, D. W., Bingham, R. P., Porche-Burke, L., & Vasquez, M. (1999). The diversification of psychology. *American Psychologist, 54,* 1061-1069.

Sue, D. W., Parham, T. A., & Bonilla-Santiago, G. (1998). The changing face of work in the United States: Implications for individual, institutional and societal survival. *Cultural Diversity and Mental Health, 4,* 153-164.

Yalom, I. D. (1995). *The theory and practice of group psychotherapy* (4th ed.). New York: Basic Books.

Correspondence regarding this chapter may be sent to Linda Berg-Cross, Program Director, CB Hall, Howard University, 525 Bryant Street, Washington, DC 20059 (e-mail address: lberg-cross@howard.edu).

INTRODUCTION TO AFTERWORD

One of the most important conferences in the history of American psychology took place in Newport Beach, California, in late January 1999. The inaugural National Multicultural Conference and Summit (NMCS) was hosted by three divisions of the American Psychological Association (APA) (Division 17, Counseling Psychology; Division 35, Society for the Psychology of Women; and Division 45, Society for the Psychological Study of Ethnic Minority Issues). Attended by approximately 550 mental health professionals and graduate students, the NMCS was aimed at motivating and empowering the APA to take a leadership role in ensuring that multicultural competence constitutes a defining variable in psychological training, research, and practice. Specific goals of the NMCS were to (a) survey the current state of the field, (b) begin difficult dialogue on issues of race, gender, and sexual orientation, (c) build alliances for advocacy and action with regard to cultural pluralism, and (d) discuss specific strategies for creating organizational change. The conference was a tremendous success and ignited multicultural efforts and activities throughout the country. At present, it is planned to have the conference every two years. The second NMCS took place in Santa Barbara, California, on January 25–26, 2001. For a detailed summary of the first NMCS, the reader is referred to Sue, Bingham, Porche-Burke, and Vasquez (1999).

Among the many presentations and panels delivered at the first NMCS was Thomas A. Parham's inspiring keynote address titled "Beyond Intolerance: Bridging the Gap Between Imposition and Acceptance." We are honored that he has consented to have his keynote appear as the Afterword to this second edition of the *Handbook*. Parham is past president of both the Association of Black Psychologists and the Association for Multicultural

Counseling and Development; he is also one of the founders of the National Institute for Multicultural Competence (see Chapter 16). A prolific scholar and gifted administrator, Parham is one of the most influential psychologists of the past half-century. The Afterword captures well the call to social justice, equity, and action echoed throughout the 40 chapters in this volume. Thomas Parham's voice brings fitting closure to the second edition of *Handbook of Multicultural Counseling.*

REFERENCE

Sue, D. W., Bingham, R. P., Porche-Burke, L., & Vasquez, M. (1999). The diversification of psychology: A multicultural revolution. *American Psychologist, 54,* 1061-1069.

AFTERWORD:
BEYOND INTOLERANCE

Bridging the Gap Between
Imposition and Acceptance

THOMAS A. PARHAM

IN THE SHORT PERIOD of time that I have with you today, allow me to be very pointed in my remarks. Allow me to be very deliberate in my attempts to penetrate your consciousness, for indeed our topic today is a serious one. In an atmosphere when multicultural competence is the issue we celebrate, I'd like to appeal to both your professional and personal side to take seriously your commitment to being a competent service provider.

Now my characterization of this conference as a celebration and festive occasion is no accident for indeed we are here to celebrate the gathering of the National Multicultural Conference and Summit and to reaffirm ourselves as culturally different healers, doing good things for people in communities across this country.

Brothers and sisters, a celebration is a time for all involved to take stock and to reflect back on those things that we as members of this profession of psychology and/or counseling are thankful for. Certainly, we are thankful for having a conference such as this to attend, where issues of multiculturalism are given center stage. Conferences like these are more than mere avenues of professional development; they serve as places of refuge when the roller-coaster of academic and professional life seems out of control. We

---

EDITORS' NOTE: Keynote address delivered at the First National Multicultural Conference and Summit, Newport Beach, California, January 28–29, 1999.

871

know we have a place where we can come to receive support, encouragement, nurturing, and an understanding ear. Similarly, we are thankful for the intellectual stimulation and professional validation we receive because too often our attempts to conceptualize client distress or research problems from a culturally centered reality are shunned, unsupported, or otherwise characterized as trivial.

Now, while our personal reflections are focused on present and past accomplishments, our celebration is also a time when all involved renew their commitment to continue their efforts and remember where we as a profession and where we as individuals still need to go. In reflecting back on a long and glorious past, I will remember with reverence the pioneers of multiculturalism who charted the course we commit ourselves to every day. Consequently, the question we ask ourselves today as we reflect back on their vision is how do we give proper credit and recognition to the legacy these pioneers have left?

Shall we read the latest text on multicultural counseling and psychology? Shall we break out our new summit posters or T-shirts? Shall we watch new videotapes on multicultural counseling and consider ourselves informed? Hmmm, I suspect the pioneers in our field will be left unsatisfied by these tributes. We must understand that giving proper credit and recognition to the ancestors and pioneers in the field requires that we must do a better job of recommitting ourselves to the principles and practices on which this discipline was founded and not simply worship the personalities of the giants in the field.

We are a collection of psychologists, counselors, and other mental health providers of different races and ethnicities, different genders, different physical abilities, different sexual orientations, and different ages. We are not simply a social club; we are members of professional organizations that have been called by the ancestors and the pioneers in this field as well as the people in our communities to be the caretakers of their minds, their souls, their spirits, and the hearts of the generations still to come. On occasion, it appears to me that we lose sight of our purpose in conferences like this one. We lose sight of our purpose because too often our participation and level of commitment are a reaction to the personalities of the conference speakers or their organizational leadership. And sadly for us, we embrace and/or react to the personalities of these individuals rather than the principles on which their presentations and leadership are based. Brothers and sisters, psychology professionals, personalities come and go, but principles and truth are like truly chewy Tootsie Rolls—they last a long time!

WHAT IS INTOLERANCE?

Our task today is to talk about moving beyond intolerance. The question remains, "How do we bridge the gap between imposition and acceptance?" It seems sensible to continue our discussion by defining the construct on which this text is based. If you were to consult your household dictionary, I suspect it might say that intolerance is defined as "active refusal to allow others to have or to put into practice beliefs (and by extension behaviors) that are different from one's own." Intolerance is much more than a difference of opinion. Intolerance is much more than a mere disagreement. Intolerance as an attitude says "I don't like something, and I don't want you to like that something either." Friends and colleagues, understand that intolerance is an active rather than a passive word, in that it implies active engagement in efforts that would prevent others from actualizing their thoughts, feelings, and behaviors in ways that differ from our own. How many of us have found the sentiment of intolerance alive and well in our own lives and institutions we inhabit? Clearly, intolerance cultivates imposition in that we seek to impose our will on others, regardless of their receptivity to be influenced.

It is important today to understand how intolerance is manifest in our everyday lives. How is intolerance practiced? My observations lead me to believe that intolerance is manifested in the normative standards created by certain segments of society which are forced upon us. If we examine our own American society and our disciplines of psychology and counseling, we find normative standards abundant. As an African American male, I grew up much like my Chicano/Latino, Asian, Native American, and poor White counterparts with a veil of imposition. That veil told me that my success in America, indeed my very worth as a human being, was related to my ability to assimilate my values, lifestyles, characteristics, and behaviors into what White middle-class culture suggested was legitimate. My experiences were not unlike many young underrepresented people who learned that the phrase "I'm OK, you're OK" is a euphemism for looking like, acting like, walking like, and talking like your White American counterparts.

Intolerance is also practiced in the attitudes that convey sentiments of "difference equals deficiency" rather than difference equaling mere difference. Practitioners of the "difference equals deficiency" logic conceptualize the world and its rigid dichotomies of "best–worst, good–bad, and superior–inferior," ascribing the positive descriptions to themselves and relegating others to the position of an inferior status. Intolerance is also practiced in almost every arena of life including personal experiences, education, relationships, race relations, politics, gender relations, the work environment, religion, and yes, psychology and counseling. Sometimes we don't tolerate different opinions; sometimes we don't tolerate different looks; sometimes we don't tolerate different languages or different customs; sometimes we don't tolerate different divisions or dimensions in the same association; sometimes we don't tolerate different cultures, religions, or lifestyle choices; and sometimes we don't tolerate differences in social status or material attainment which we believe separate us from other people. Indeed, intolerance is alive and well in our lives, and we must find a way to confront it.

FACTORS THAT PROMOTE INTOLERANCE

Now, as we turn our attention to examining the factors that promote intolerance, I want to invite you to consider that the substance and foundation for intolerance cannot be revealed through the examination of the subjects of imposition (i.e., those who are imposed upon). Intolerance must be analyzed through the examination of the psyche of the imposer. This means that the pillars that support intolerance and intolerant attitudes, in my opinion, are not composed of the attitudes of the oppressed. Rather, they are reinforced by the hardened steel hearts and concretized attitudes of the oppressor. We can't ask women how they feel about oppression. Sexism isn't a woman's problem, it is a man's problem. Men, we must act ourselves and clean up our own house. We can't ask those who are physically challenged how they feel about oppression. Discrimination is not the problem of the physically challenged, it is a problem of the more able-bodied people among us. We must ask ourselves what the problem is and clean up our own house.

If we delve into the self of ours which is intolerant, that self that is rigid, that self that is inflexible, that self that is unyielding, we may find that intolerance is supported by several character traits. I would like to briefly mention four. The first of these is the *feeling of superiority*, or significance. The extreme of superiority is that feeling which deludes us into believing that we are better than someone else. So invested in this worldview are we that we find ourselves unable to tolerate other people's perceived shortcomings, even when they are represented by members of our own associations. Feelings of superiority give rise to attitudes of racism, sexism, ageism, religionism, ethnocentrism, homophobia, and so forth.

Now my theoretical training and clinical experiences as a practitioner of psychology and of counseling have taught me that excessive feelings of superiority (that some might even call neurotic feelings) are often rooted in the deep-seated feelings of inadequacy and inferiority. As such, my second character trait which supports attitudes of intolerance is the *feeling of inferiority*. Somehow, we may find our own inadequacies too distressing to deal with, so we camouflage our own feeling by denigrating others in order to affirm ourselves. We degrade others as human beings in an attempt to affirm our own humanity. Ladies and gentlemen, my fellow psychologists, please understand that true self-affirmation can never be contingent upon having to denigrate anybody.

The third character trait in us which supports intolerance is the *meshing of ignorance and blindness.* Ignorance in our inability and/or refusal to learn new ideas; blindness in our inability to see beyond our current perspective to a larger view. Unlike physical blindness, which is the result of physiological or environmental factors, intellectual blindness is self-inflicted by one's refusal and failure to use one's mind to the fullest extend or to open one's heart. The fourth character trait in us which supports intolerance is the *fear of loss*—loss of space, loss of privilege, loss of position, or loss of status. That fear centers on the feelings that if we support others, if we accept others, if we help others to actualize their potential and grow as groups or individuals, we will compromise and/or destroy the form and collective existence of our own experience. The assumption here is that the rise of any group is tantamount to the destruction of another. Therefore, I must keep you down at all cost in order to protect myself. How irrational can fear get?

What a shame that a fear of losing ourselves in others compels us to keep other people down, and sadly for all of us, we fail to recognize that allowing other people to be who and what they wish to be helps support and affirm our own humanity. Denial of others' rights or self-affirmation and self-determination robs us of our own comfort in being who we want to be. You see, Maya Angelou (1978) said it best in her poem "Still I Rise." In her first verse she writes,

You may write me down in history
with your bitter twisted lies
you may trod me in the very dirt
but still like dust I'll rise.

She concludes the poem by exclaiming

You may shoot me with your words
you may cut me with your eyes
you may kill me with your hatefulness
but still like air I'll rise.

What does Maya Angelou's "Still I Rise" poem mean for us? We must recognize that the reaction people have to intolerance is not often independently initiated but, instead, is a reaction to being imposed upon. You see, I believe that only if you disrespect my humanity will I rise in anger; only if you disregard my needs will I rise in rebellion; only if you perpetrate your evil and wickedness on me will I rise in retaliation.

THE MULTICULTURAL COMPETENCE MOVEMENT

Take a look around the world in Africa, Armenia, Russia, Central America, Bosnia, China, Korea, right here in the United States, and in our own psychological and counseling associations and understand that only if you degrade my culture and my history will I rise with the resolve and commitment to be myself in spite of you. Therefore, we must find a way to better respect each other's humanity, and we who pride ourselves on being psychologists, counselors, and other educated professionals must lead the charge to regain that spirit which is now lost in the wilderness. And so this focus on multicultural competence brings with it several assumptions.

The first assumption I wish to advance is that *the wave of a movement that is composed of truth and righteousness cannot be shackled by institutional policies and procedures. Movements are bigger than people or institutional barriers.* Fundamentally, I believe that the underground railroads were bigger than the chains of slavery. The civil rights struggle was bigger than the walls of segregation and the laws of Jim Crow. The Black Power Movement and the marvelous militancy of the '70s were bigger than the shackles of self-denigration and institutional racism. Similarly, the movement of multiculturalism is bigger than local, state, or national psychology and counseling associations, and those of us who are committed to this movement are not in need of institutional permission slips in order to assert our right for greater levels of multicultural competence.

The second assumption I would advance centers on the idea that *training for real professional competence cannot occur in a single course or the reading of a single text.* Real challenges in life do not get discussed and solved in 30 minutes or less without commercial interruption. You can't study for a minimum of five years to be a psychologist and then expect to learn everything you wanted to know about multiple cultures in one course in one semester, with no practical experiences to support the didactic learning process.

The third assumption I want to advance is that *the commitment to true multiculturalism cannot be used as a "fashion statement" to dress up or camouflage institutional insincerity.* You can't talk about commitment to diversity and then act in ways which inhibit its progress. You can't express support for diverse ideas in your professional roles and then conduct your personal affairs with scandalous inconsistency. You can't lead departments, agencies, and organizations that preach diversity and a respect for multiculturalism and then make institutional decisions that negatively and disproportionately impact culturally different people.

The fourth assumption I make suggests that *the standards of multicultural competence must move beyond simplistic yardsticks like desegregating professional associations, academic institutions, and institutional boards.* The right to occupy the same geographical space has been fought for and won years ago in the civil rights desegregation struggles. In reality, we no longer just want a seat on the bus; we expect to drive it, make decisions about where it stops, and even determine if the bus will route itself through a particular area. In short, we want and need to share power and not simply share space. Real diversity and multiculturalism is not about counting demographics in a frequency distribution; it's a question of how have the policies and practices of an institution changed as a function of the changes in the demographic makeup.

The fifth assumption I'd like to share with you is that *the gifts of knowledge and skill that we have been blessed to acquire in our professional training are not intended for personal gratification alone.* It is important for us to realize the greatness of our gifts as healers and the proper purpose for which they were intended. It is my opinion that the gifts that we have been blessed to acquire are not intended for our own ego gratification. Our gifts are not intended to increase our ability to live large through managed care or private practice at someone else's expense. Our gifts are not intended to manipulate others in the hopes of easing our own circumstances. Our gifts were certainly not intended to make it easier to acquire material possessions so that we can surround ourselves with the things we believe make us "all that."

You see, the Creator I worship and the African-centered principles I embrace remind us that those who are blessed with talents and degrees will not be judged on how important they seem or the level of prominence they achieve. Rather, they will be judged on how they use their gifts to service our people, our community, and humanity in general. Indeed, you who consider yourselves psychologists, counselors, and educators must also be servants, and to serve the people in our communities properly you cannot do so from elevated positions of arrogance and increased stature, despite what society says about your PhDs.

You see, the higher up we go on the social status ladder, the more potential we have to get cut off from who we really are. Understand, my colleagues and friends, that there is a fundamental difference between what we do for a profession and a living and who we are as people. It is only through our personal struggles and service that we are allowed to experience firsthand our true selves: that self that found the ability to persevere in the face of adversity; that self that found courage in the face of fear; that self that showed hope in the face of despair; that self that showed strength and discipline when the roller-coaster of life seemed out of control; that self that showed compassion in the face of insensitivity; that self that still struggles for self-determination in a world that seeks to control our minds, our bodies, and our spirits. Indeed, we must be careful not to wrap ourselves in the splendor of our degrees and professional attainment; rather, we should use our abilities and gifts to provide assistance and service to the broader community at large.

Now, in refocusing our attention back on the notion of intolerance, the question arises as to how we might become more tolerant and flexible. If intolerance is supported by attitudes of superiority, feelings of inferiority, attitudes of ignorance and blindness, and fear of loss, how do we transform them into more positive attributes? How do we bridge the gap between imposition and acceptance? Ladies and gentlemen, I believe the answer lies in our ability to focus inward in search of self-awareness. Bridging the gap requires that we as psychological, counseling, and educational professionals confront our own values rather than the values of others. Rather than ask "Why don't you change, what is wrong with you?", try turning your sights inward and ask yourself "What is it in me that keeps my attitudes and behaviors more imposing rather than accepting? What is it in me that compels me to rigidity rather than flexibility?" You might find your spirit hounded by the four character traits previously mentioned.

OVERCOMING INTOLERANCE:
BRIDGING THE GAP

Now if we are successful in confronting and removing our feelings of superiority, our feelings of inferiority, our veils of ignorance and blindness, and our fear of loss, what characteristics do we need instead? What should we fill the void with? How do we bridge the gap between imposition and acceptance in multicultural counseling? I would invite you to consider filling that void with some courage—both the courage to confront our own limitations and the courage to risk public condemnation for our stance against intolerance. Try being a nonconformist. In your faculty meetings, you must be a loud and consistent voice for multiculturalism. Those who are licensed and/or otherwise credentialed must question their licensing boards about the ethics of certifying professionals to practice with culturally different people when they have little or no multicultural training and even less competence.

Second, you must become risk takers. You must engage in mental risk (a willingness to stretch your brains and enlighten your minds), you must engage in verbal risk (willingness to say and ask something unusual), and you must engage in behavioral risks (the willingness to do something unconventional). Third, you must supplement and fortify your existing knowledge of "different things" with real experiences. Most of what we know about people who are culturally different we learn through television and the media. Meet somebody different; talk to somebody different. The veils of ignorance and blindness can only be lifted through a conscious effort to expand our mind and expand our vision in order that we might see a greater truth.

We must realize, ladies and gentlemen, that young Black and Latino men who are beaten up on the streets of this country simply for the color of their skin or homosexuals who are assaulted on the streets simply because of their sexual orientation are not just subjected to acts of hatred but also to acts of blindness. Women who are harassed in the workplace or who are battered in the home are not just subjected to acts of abuse but also to acts of blindness. Physically challenged persons in our society who are denied employment in the workplace or are subjected to environments which are insensitive to their needs are not merely subjected to acts of discrimination but also to acts of blindness. Indeed, wisdom born of experience is true enlightenment and through our counseling theories, techniques, and skills we must be able to assist our clients who look to us to help them deal with this social pathology.

Fourth, we must rediscover in ourselves the capacity to trust, and be reminded today, that I believe that real trust is not an external circumstance but an internal virtue. Real acceptance does not require people to jump through hoops so that we can learn to trust them; it requires that we learn to trust ourselves and take a risk with others. And finally, bridging that gap requires that we continually renew our faith in the possibilities of progress and trust in the process. Remember, of course, that renewing our faith requires more than mere acknowledgment. It requires advocacy. In some cases, we are intellectually committed to the ideas and the advancement of multicultural competence. However, intellectual commitment is merely a cognitive activity or state of thinking where one pledges a promise to do something. Intellectual commitment is one thing; however, we must begin to hold ourselves and our professional associations more accountable for better operationalizing the principles and practices of multicultural counseling. We must practice what we preach.

The shape of our world today, our communities, our schools, our families, and even our professional associations, cannot afford passivity on our part. We must become active participants in our own uplifting and the elevation of our own profession and professionalism. We cannot continue to bathe in a pond of annual conference ritual 3 or 4 days a year, and swim in a pool of contradiction the other 360-plus days. Racism is on the rise; what are we doing about it as a profession? Drugs are too prevalent; what are we doing about that as a profession? Homeless people continue to struggle for dignity in the face of very tough times, and rather than being treated with dignity and compassion, they are treated like tokens on a monopoly board, sent directly to jail without passing Go or collecting $200.00. What is our profession doing about that? Women continue to receive less pay for equal work; what is our profession doing about that? Child abuse and neglect are on the rise, transforming childhood dreams into adult nightmares; what is our profession doing about that? And violence is becoming a norm for too many of our nation's families and children; what is our profession doing about that?

Psychological, educational, and counseling professionals, the time for collective action is now! Wake up! Indeed, the courage to be a risk taker, wisdom born from real experience, the capacity to trust, and commitment to social change are all characteristics which facilitate our bridging the gap between imposition and acceptance. We can no longer impose standards of mediocrity when it comes to multiculturalism. We must demand that our students be trained and our professionals be reeducated with the latest knowledge and information that is available.

A CHALLENGE TO YOU

As I close, I am reminded that this time of year in late January has us concluding our Martin Luther King, Jr., celebrations and moving into African American History month. I think it is appropriate that we access some of Dr. King's wisdom for this session. Dr. King's book titled *Strength to Love* (1986) provided us with the formula for bridging the gap. Dr. King, as you remember, was a man whose goal was quite simple. He sought to eradicate injustice, achieve racial harmony, and treat each man and woman, regardless of race, or social economic standards, etcetera, with the dignity and respect which should be afforded to anyone in the human family. King's formula for bridging the gap between imposition and acceptance was to combine a tough mind and a tender heart.

A tough mind is characterized by incisive thinking, realistic appraisals, and decisive judgment. A tough mind sifts through falsehoods to find truth, a serious purpose, and a commitment to a cause. However, a soft mind, among other things, is plagued by irrational fears. A soft mind fears change and believes that security remains in the status quo because change is unsettling. Dr. King also believed that a tough mind should be balanced by a tender heart. Indeed, the African way teaches us that life at its best is a creative synthesis of opposites in fruitful harmony. A tender heart appreciates true love and has compassion for others. A tender heart looks beyond one's own comfort in an attempt to help someone else less fortunate and share that feeling.

Conversely, a hard heart rarely experiences the beauty of inner ethnic friendship because he or she is too cold to feel affection for another and too self-centered to share another's joy and sorrow. A hard heart is unmoved by the pains and afflictions of others. A hard heart is anchored in the past and blinded by the possibilities of the future. But a tender heart knows compassion, knows others' pain, feels others' sorrow, and is compelled to exert some effort in order to make someone else's life better, or in this case, to transform our profession. We must all have a tough mind and tender heart. Ladies and gentlemen, brothers and sisters, members of our profession, there is little hope for us until we become tough-minded enough to break loose of the shackles of oppression, intolerance, discrimination, apathy, prejudice, indignity, and ignorance that are so pervasive in our profession. The shape of our world today does not permit us to be soft-minded. As members of psychology, counseling, and education professions, and members of the human family, we must bring together our tough-mindedness and tender-heartedness if we are to move toward the goal of freedom and justice and eradicating intolerance.

As we prepare to adjourn, I am reminded that in my 44-plus years on the planet and in my years of graduate and undergraduate training, I have learned much. I now know that a psychologist must be sensitive enough to listen, feeling enough to care, secure enough to confront inconsistencies, and experienced enough to empathize.

However, my time on this earth and my nearly 25-year affiliation with professional associations have also taught me that as an African American psychologist committed to the principles and practices of multicultural competence, we must be bold enough to challenge inequality, brave enough to speak out against social injustice, and visionary enough to believe that we can change our condition as a people if we put our collective energies forward. In addition, we must also be respectful enough to know that we stand on the shoulders of our ancestors and elders, principled enough to use our own cultural values as a code of conduct and a standard of aspiration, and humble enough to know that it is not our skill but the Creator's and ancestors' blessings which allow us to do what we do.

As I close, I leave you with two thoughts. An opportunity is a threat to those who predict failure but a challenge to those who think they might win. If you think you might win, if you think we might have the power to promote a greater level of respect for diversity and a greater level of multicultural competence in our profession, within the American Psychological Association, within the American Counseling Association, and in communities across this country, then make a commitment to do something different. And last, we are not asking for a grandiose change. The conveyors of this National Multicultural Conference and Summit and I would like to leave you with an invitation. Rather than attempt to be 100% better on 50 elements of multicultural competence, try being 5% better on 1 element.

Do you think we can win?

Then accept the challenge to help bridge the gap between imposition and acceptance. Remember, an opportunity is a threat if you only predict failure but a challenge to those who believe we can win.

Thank you, and God bless!

REFERENCES

Angelou, M. (1978). *And still I rise.* New York: Bantom Books.

King, M. L., Jr. (1986). *Strength to love.* Atlanta, GA: Fortress Press.

Correspondence regarding this keynote address may be sent to Thomas A. Parham, Assistant Vice Chancellor, Counseling and Health Services, University of California at Irvine, 202 Student Services I, Irvine, CA 92697-2200 (e-mail address: taparham@uci.edu).

NAME INDEX

SUBJECT INDEX

About the Editors

Joseph G. Ponterotto, Ph.D., is Professor of Education and Coordinator of Counseling Programs at Fordham University at Lincoln Center in New York City. Prior to arriving at Fordham in 1987, he was Assistant Professor of Counseling Psychology in the Department of Educational Psychology at the University of Nebraska at Lincoln. He received his Ph.D. in counseling psychology from the University of California at Santa Barbara. His most recent books include coediting the *Handbook of Multicultural Assessment. Clinical, Psychological, and Educational Applications* (2nd ed., 2001), and coauthoring *Multicultural Counseling Competencies* (Sage, 1998). His empirical research program uses both quantitative and qualitative methods to investigate a broad array of topics in multicultural counseling. He has served on the editorial boards of various counseling journals, and is currently International Forum Coeditor for *The Counseling Psychologist.*

J. Manuel Casas, Ph.D., is Professor of Education in the combined Counseling/Clinical/School Psychology Program within the department of Education at the University of California at Santa Barbara. Prior to joining the Santa Barbara program in 1977, he was a staff psychologist in the UCLA Psychological and Counseling Services Center. His Ph.D. in counseling psychology is from Stanford University. He is coauthor (with J. G. Ponterotto) of the *Handbook of Racial/Ethnic Minority Counseling Research.* Much of his present professional activity involves securing and managing grant funding activity designed to improve mental health services and educational access to culturally diverse youths in California. Currently, he is a senior adviser to the Chancellor of the University of California (Santa Barbara), overseeing distributions of research funding for multicultural education initiatives.

Lisa A. Suzuki, Ph.D., is Assistant Professor of Counseling Psychology in the Department of Applied Psychology at New York University. Prior to arriving at NYU, she was a faculty member of both the University of

917

Oregon and Fordham University. Her Ph.D. in counseling psychology is from the University of Nebraska at Lincoln. Her recent books include the second edition of *Handbook of Multicultural Assessment: Clinical, Psychological, and Educational Applications* (2001), *Intelligence Testing and Minority Students: Foundations, Performance Factors, and Assessment Issues* (2000), and *Using Qualitative Methods in Psychology* (1998).

Charlene M. Alexander, Ph.D., is Assistant Professor of Counseling Psychology at Ball State University. Born in Trinidad and educated for some time in England, she received her Ph.D. in counseling psychology from the University of Nebraska at Lincoln. Prior to joining the Ball State faculty, she was on the faculty at Fordham University. Her research specialties are in multicultural counseling training and in creative approaches to the practice of multicultural counseling.

Editors' and Contributors' Affiliations and Addresses

EDITORS

Joseph G. Ponterotto, Ph.D.
Professor
Fordham University at Lincoln Center
PES Room 1008
113 West 60th Street
New York, NY 10023-7478
Jponterott@aol.com

J. Manuel Casas, Ph.D.
Professor
Counseling/Clinical/School
    Psychology Program
Graduate School of Education
University of California, Santa Barbara
Santa Barbara, CA 93106
casas@education.ucsb.edu

Lisa A. Suzuki, Ph.D.
Associate Professor
Department of Applied Psychology
New York University
239 Greene Street, 4th Floor
New York, NY 10003
las1@is.nyu.edu

Charlene M. Alexander, Ph.D.
Assistant Professor
Department of Counseling Psychology
    and Guidance Services
Teachers College 622
Ball State University
Muncie, IN 47306-0585
calexander@bsu.edu

CONTRIBUTORS

José M. Abreu, Ph.D.
Assistant Professor
Waite Phillips Hall 503
Division of Counseling Psychology
University of Southern California
Los Angeles, CA 90089-0031
Abreu@mizar.usc.edu

Patricia Arredondo, Ph.D.
Associate Professor
Division of Psychology in Education
College of Education
Arizona State University
P.O. Box 870611
Tempe, AZ 85287-0611
empower@asu.edu

Donald R. Atkinson, Ph.D.
Professor
Graduate School of Education
University of California, Santa
    Barbara
Santa Barbara, CA 93106
don@education.ucsb.edu

Linda Berg-Cross, Ph.D., A.B.P.P.
Program Coordinator
Howard University
525 Bryant Street
CB Powell
Washington, DC 20059
lberg-cross@howard.edu

Mark A. Bolden
Doctoral Student
College of Education & Human
    Services
Professional Psychology & Family
    Therapy
Seton Hall University
400 South Orange Avenue
South Orange, NJ 07079

Michael A. Boticki
Doctoral Student
Marquette University
School of Education
Schroeder Health Complex
Milwaukie, WI 53201
52A9botickim@marquette.edu

Sharon L. Bowman, Ph.D.
Associate Professor
Department of Counseling Psychology
    and Guidance Services
Teachers College 622
Ball State University
Muncie, IN 47306-0585
Sbowman@gw.bsu.edu

Andrae L. Brown
Doctoral Student
College of Education & Human
    Services
Professional Psychology & Family
    Therapy
Seton Hall University
400 South Orange Avenue
South Orange, NJ 07079

Uyen Bui
Doctoral Student
Counseling/Clinical/School
    Psychology Program
Graduate School of Education
University of California, Santa Barbara
Santa Barbara, CA 93106
ubui@education.ucsb.edu

Alan W. Burkard, Ph.D.
Assistant Professor
Marquette University
Schroeder Health Complex, Room 138

School of Education
Milwaukee, WI 53201
alan.burkard@marquette.edu

Angela M. Byars, Ph.D.
Assistant Professor
University of Wisconsin–Madison
Department of Counseling Psychology
304 Education Building
1000 Bascom Mall
Madison, WI 53706-1398
abyars@mail.soemadison.wisc.edu

Carrie L. Castañeda
Doctoral Student
University of Utah
Department of Educational
    Psychology
1705 E. Campus Center Drive,
    Room 327
Salt Lake City, UH 84112-9255
c.castaneda@m.cc.utah.edu

Eric C. Chen, Ph.D.
Assistant Professor
Fordham University
Division of Psychological and
    Educational Services
Graduate School of Education
113 West 60th Street
New York, NY 10023-7478
echen@fordham.edu

Madonna G. Constantine, Ph.D.
Associate Professor
Department of Counseling and
    Clinical Psychology
Teachers College
Columbia University
525 West 120 Street
Box 102
New York, NY 10027
mc816@columbia.edu

Kellina Craig, Ph.D.
Howard University
525 Bryant Street
CB Powell
Washington, DC 20059

William E. Cross, Jr., Ph.D.
Professor
Department of Psychology: Social-
    Personality Program
The Graduate Center
6th Floor, Office 6301.11
City University of New York
365 Fifth Avenue
New York, NY 10016-4309
Wcross@gc.cuny.edu

Michael D'Andrea, Ph.D.
Professor
Department of Counselor Education
University of Hawaii
1776 University Avenue
Honolulu, HI 96822
Michael@hawaii.edu

Judy Daniels, Ph.D.
Professor
Department of Counselor Education
University of Hawaii
1776 University Avenue
Honolulu, HI 96822
jdaniels@hawaii.edu

Judy Ferris, Ph.D.
Multi-Ethnic Counseling Center
    Alliance
207 Student Services Building
Michigan State University
East Lansing, MI 48824
judyf@secure.couns.msu.edu

Ann R. Fischer, Ph.D.
Associate Professor
Department of Psychology
University of Akron
Akron, OH 44325-4301
ann10@uakron.edu

Nadya A. Fouad, Ph.D.
Professor
Department of Psychology
University of Wisconsin–Milwaukee
P.O. Box 413
Milwaukee, WI 53201
nadya@uwm.edu

Jairo N. Fuertes, Ph.D.
Assistant Professor
Fordham University at Lincoln Center

PES Room 1008
113 West 60th Street
New York, NY 10023-7478
VT320@aol.com

Michael. J. Furlong, Ph.D.
Professor
University of California
Graduate School of Education
Santa Barbara, CA 93106
mfurlong@education.ucsb.edu

Denise Gretchen
Doctoral Candidate
Fordham University, Lincoln Center
PES Room 1008
113 West 60th Street
New York, NY 10023-7478
DeniseGret@aol.com

Ingrid Grieger, Ed.D.
Director, Counseling Center
Iona College
715 North Avenue
New Rochelle, NY 10801
IGrieger@iona.edu

Janet E. Helms, Ph.D.
Professor
Department of Counseling,
    Developmental, and Educational
    Psychology
Boston College
Chestnut Hill, MA 20467
helmsja@bc.edu

Carrie L. Hill
Doctoral Student
Department of Counseling and
    Educational Psychology
Wright Education Building
Indiana University
201 N. Rose Avenue
Bloomington, IN 47405-1006
carhill@indiana.edu

Farah A. Ibrahim, Ph.D.
Professor and Program Director
Counseling Psychology Program
Howard University
2441 Fourth Street, N.W.
Washington, DC 20059
Ffibrahim@aol.com

Mary Bradford Ivey, Ed.D.
NBCC Vice President
Microtraining Associates, Inc.
www.emicrotraining.com

Allen E. Ivey, Ed.D., A.B.P.P.
Distinguished University Professor
    (Emeritus)
University of Massachusetts, Amherst
President, Microtraining Associates,
    Inc.
ivey@srnet.com

Margo A. Jackson, Ph.D.
Assistant Professor
Fordham University at Lincoln Center
PES Room 1008
113 West 60th Street
New York, NY 10023-7478
MJackson@Fordham.edu

Bryan S. K. Kim, Ph.D.
Assistant Professor
Department of Psychology
University of Maryland
College Park, MD 20742
bkim@psyc.umd.edu

Nicholas Ladany, Ph.D.
Associate Professor
111 Research Drive
Counseling Psychology Program
Department of Education and Human
    Services
Lehigh University
Bethlehem, PA 18015
nil3@lehigh.edu

Teresa D. LaFromboise, Ph.D.
Professor
320 School of Education
485 Lausen Mall
Stanford University
Stanford, CA 94305
Lafrom@leland.stanford.edu

Lisa C. Li
Doctoral Student
Department of Counseling Psychology
University of Maryland
College Park, MD 20742
lli@psyc.umd.edu

Monique C. Liddle
Doctoral Student
Department of Counseling and
    Educational Psychology
Wright Education Building
Indiana University
201 N. Rose Avenue
Bloomington, IN 47405-1006
mliddle@indiana.edu

Don C. Locke, Ph.D.
Director, Asheville Graduate Center
123 Karpen Hall, CPO 2140
University of North Carolina at
    Asheville
Asheville, NC 28804
dlocke@unca.edu

Susana M. Lowe, Ph.D.
Asian & Pacific Islander American
    Health Forum
942 Market Street, Suite 200
San Francisco, CA 94102
slowe@apiahf.org

Jackquelyn Mascher
Doctoral Student
Counseling, Developmental, and
    Educational Psychology
School of Education
Boston College
Chestnut Hill, MA 02467

Laurie D. McCubbin, M.A.
Doctoral Student
University of Wisconsin–Madison
Department of Counseling Psychology
304 Education Building
1000 Bascom Hall
Madison, WI 53706-1398
mccubbin@students.wisc.edu

Mary McRae, Ph.D.
Associate Professor
New York University
Department of Applied Psychology
New York University
239 Greene Street, 4th Floor
New York, NY 10003
mm13@is2.nyu.edu

Barbara R. Medler
Doctoral Student
Ball State University
Department of Counseling Psychology
    and Guidance Services
Teachers College 622
Muncie, IN 47306
Bmedler@gw.bsu.edu

Bonnie Moradi, M.A.
Doctoral Student
Department of Psychology
University of Akron
Akron, OH 44325-4301
bmoradi@uakron.edu

Sakurako Mori
Doctoral Student
Counseling/Clinical/School
    Psychology Program
Graduate School of Education
University of California, Santa Barbara
Santa Barbara, CA 93106
smori@cducation.ucsb.cdu

Susan L. Morrow, Ph.D.
Associate Professor and Director of
    Training
Counseling Psychology Program
University of Utah
Department of Educational
    Psychology
1705 E. Campus Center Drive,
    RM 327
Salt Lake City, UT 84112-9255
morrow@gse.utah.edu

Helen A. Neville, Ph.D.
Associate Professor
E&CP/Black Studies
16 Hill Hall
University of Missouri
Columbia, MO 65211
NevilleH@missouri.edu

Christian N. Nutini
Doctoral Student
Fordham University at Lincoln Center
PES Room 1008
113 West 60th Street
New York, NY 10023-7478
nutini@fordham.edu

Beverly O'Bryant, Ph.D.
Director
Community Service and Service
    Learning Programs
District of Columbia Public Schools
Office of the Superintendent
Union Station South
825 North Capitol Street, N. E.,
    Room 8148
Washington, DC 20002
beverly.o'bryant@k12.dc.us

Hifumi Ohnishi
Counseling Psychologist
Counseling Center/MECCA
Michigan State University
207 Student Services
East Lansing, MI 48824-1113
Hifumi@mail.couns.msu.edu

Thomas A. Parham, Ph.D.
Assistant Vice Chancellor
Counseling and Health Services
Director, Counseling Center
University of California, Irvine
202 Student Service I
Irvine, CA 92697-2200
taparham@uci.edu

Renee Pavelski
Doctoral Student
Counseling/Clinical/School
    Psychology Program
University of California, Santa Barbara
Graduate School of Education
Santa Barbara, CA 93106

Paul Bodholdt Pedersen, Ph.D.
1777 Ala Moana Blvd., #726
Honolulu, HI 96815
pedersen_us@yahoo.com

Donald B. Pope-Davis, Ph.D.
Professor
Department of Psychology
118 Haggar Hall
University of Notre Dame
Notre Dame, IN 46556
dpd@nd.edu

Maria Prendes-Lintel, Ph.D.
The Wellness Center
1919 South 40th Street
Suite 111
Lincoln, NE 68506
mlintel@aol.com

Stephen M. Quintana, Ph.D.
Associate Professor and Director of
    Training
Department of Counseling Psychology
Department of Educational
    Psychology
University of Wisconsin–Madison
1000 Bascom Mall
Madison, WI 53706
Quintana@education.wisc.edu

Gita Rakhsha, Ph.D.
Assistant Professor of Psychology
Westminster College
1840 South 1300 East
Salt Lake City, UT 84108
g-rakhsh@wcslc.edu

Saba Rasheed, M.A.
Doctoral Student
Counseling Psychology Program
5251 University of Oregon
Eugene, OR 97403-5251
srasheed@oregon.uoregon.edu

Amy L. Reynolds, Ph.D.
Staff Psychologist
Counseling Center
Buffalo State College of New York
1300 Elmwood Avenue
Buffalo, NY 14222-1095
reynolal@buffalostate.edu

Charles R. Ridley, Ph.D.
Professor
Department of Counseling and
    Educational Psychology
Wright Education Building
Indiana University
201 N. Rose Avenue
Bloomington, IN 47405-1006
cridley@indiana.edu

Lourdes Rivera, Ph.D. Candidate
Fordham University at Lincoln Center
PES Room 1008

113 West 60th Street
New York, NY 10023
Rivera@fordham.edu

Maria P. P. Root, Ph.D.
2457 26th Avenue East
Seattle, WA 98112
Mariaroot@aol.com

Gargi Roysircar-Sodowsky, Ph.D.
Professor, Clinical Psychology and
    Director, Multicultural Center
    for Research and Practice
Antioch New England Graduate
    School
40 Avon Street
Keene, NH 03434-3516
g_roysircar-sodowsky@antiochne.edu

Arthur R. Sanchez, Ph.D.
Professor & Coordinator of Marriage
    & Family Therapy Program
Psychology Department
California State University–Chico
Chico, CA 95929
asanchez@csuchico.edu

Daya Singh Sandhu, Ed.D., NCC,
    NCSC, NCCC
Professor and Chair
Department of Educational and
    Counseling Psychology
320 Education Building
University of Louisville
Louisville, KY 40292
daya.sandhu@louisville.edu

Daniel T. Sciarra, Ph.D.
Associate Professor
Hofstra University
Mason Hall 212
Hempstead, NY 11549
cprdts@hofstra.edu

Lisa B. Spanierman
Doctoral Student
Educational and Counseling
    Psychology
16 Hill Hall
University of Missouri
Columbia, MO 65211
lbs21f@mizzou.edu

Derald Wing Sue, Ph.D.
Professor
California School of Professional
    Psychology
1005 Atlantic Avenue
Alameda, CA 94501
    and Professor
Department of Educational Psychology
Hayward, CA 94542
dwingsue@aol.com

Lina Adachi Sueyoshi
Ph.D. Candidate
Fordham University at Lincoln Center
PES Room 1008
113 West 60th Street
New York, NY 10023
sueyoshi@fordham.edu

Genella Taylor
Doctoral Student
Department of Counseling Psychology
Department of Educational Psychology
University of Wisconsin–Madison
1000 Bascom Mall
Madison, WI 53706

Delores A. Thompson, J.D., Ph.D.
Assistant Professor
College of Education & Human
    Services
Professional Psychology & Family
    Therapy
Seton Hall University
400 South Orange Avenue
South Orange, NJ 07079
Thompsde@shu.edu

Susan Toliver, Ph.D.
Professor
Department of Sociology
Iona College
715 North Avenue
New Rochelle, NY 10801

Joseph E. Trimble, Ph.D.
Fellow
Radcliffe Institute for Advanced Study
Harvard University
10 Garden Street
Cambridge, MA 02138
trimble@radcliffe.edu

Nicolas Troyano
Doctoral Student
Department of Counseling
    Psychology
Department of Educational
    Psychology
University of Wisconsin–Madison
1000 Bascom Mall
Madison, WI 53706

Shawn O. Utsey, Ph.D.
Assistant Professor
College of Education & Human
    Services
Professional Psychology & Family
    Therapy
Seton Hall University
400 South Orange Avenue
South Orange, NJ 07079
Utseysha@shu.edu

Beverly J. Vandiver, Ph.D.
Associate Professor
Pennsylvania State University
Department of Counselor
    Education
Counseling Psychology, &
    Rehabilitation Services
327 Cedar Building
University Park, PA 16802
bjv3@psu.edu

Melba J. T. Vasquez, Ph.D., A.B.P.P.
Anderson House at Heritage Square
2901 Bee Cave Road, Box N
Austin, TX 78746
MelVasquez@aol.com

Lauren Weitzman, Ph.D.
Staff Psychologist
University of Utah
Salt Lake City, UT 84112-9061
Lweitzm@ssb1.saff.utah.edu

Thomas Wessel, Ph.D.
Dean of Counseling
Howard University
525 Bryant Street
CB Powell
Washington, DC 20059

Roger L. Worthington, Ph.D.
Assistant Professor
Educational & Counseling Psychology
16 Hill Hall
University of Missouri
Columbia, MO 65211
WorthingtonR@missouri.edu

Iris Zanglis
Doctoral Student
Counseling/Clinical/School
   Psychology Program
University of California, Santa Barbara
Graduate School of Education
Santa Barbara, CA 93106